Colli

Collins
Rhyming Dictionary

foreword by ANDREW MOTION

Collins

Collins, part of HarperCollinsPublishers
77–85 Fulham Palace Road, London w6 8jb
www.collins.co.uk

First published in Great Britain in 2006 by
HarperCollinsPublishers

10 9 8 7 6 5 4 3 2 1

A catalogue record for this book is available
from the British Library.

ISBN 10: 0 00 720996 7
ISBN 13: 978 0 00 720996 5

Printed and bound in Great Britain by
Clays Ltd, St Ives plc

Contents

Foreword

by Andrew Motion, Poet Laureate

Like a lot of people born shortly after the war, and starting to
read poems in the 1960s, I was brought up to think that rhyming
poetry was done for. My teachers regretted it, but the evidence of
the contemporary they liked best (Ted Hughes), and the rising
chorus of radical poets appearing at the Albert Hall and
elsewhere, told them the great modernist experiment with free
verse during the 1910s and '20s was about to sweep all before it.

In fact things haven't turned out like that. From the vantage
point of a new century, we can see that although the modernist
experiment has flourished and diversified, it has done so
alongside a continuing tradition of poets doing the old things in
new ways. In Great Britain, the rhyming line from Auden and the
poets of the 1930s, through Betjeman and Larkin, has been
extended through most of the major poets of the late c20, and
forward into the best of our contemporaries.

Why is this? Loss of nerve? Another example of local
reactionary instincts? I don't think so. Rhyming poetry – and
rhyme in poems which have no settled formal pattern – has
survived because it is fundamental to our sense of what poetry is,
and what it can achieve. Most of us make our first acquaintance
with it in the playground, chanting and playing word games. We
learn that rhyme brings words to life, gets them to dance, and
makes them memorable. If we forget this later on, when we
develop a more elaborate sense of language and a more
sophisticated idea of composition, we do so at our peril.

But this isn't to say metre has to be tum-ti-tum, and rhyme
has to be obvious and orthodox. One of the best things about
this excellent book is that it encourages us to think broadly

about rhyme – to explore part-rhymes, para-rhymes and half-rhymes as well as full and complete ones. It's easy to use, resourceful in its listing, and ambitious in its reach.

Will people who are already 'professional' writers feel it's somehow beneath them to use it? They shouldn't. One of the greatest pleasures of poetry, for its authors as well as its readers, is the way it combines a sincere exploration of the world and the self with a delight in tricks and playfulness. To varying degrees, poets are able to devise these games in the solitude of their own heads – but as with everything else in life, a little help never comes amiss. This help might clarify an internal process that is already under way. It might equally well lead to something unexpected and unplanned. Byron was not the only poet to admit that 'a rhyme led me to a thought'.

Back at school in the '60s, I mistakenly thought that rhyme was a hindrance: a way of blocking or re-routing what I 'really wanted to say'. I soon saw the error of my ways. Rhyme – in all its delightful diversity of forms – is a reliable way to recognise and release strong feeling, as well as smart thinking, elegant compression and proper concentration. In this respect, the extent to which it appears 'unnatural' (in the sense that we don't usually chat away to one another in rhyme) conceals a vital paradox. The ingenuity of rhyme is in fact a way of proving what is intrinsic to us as human beings.

Using the dictionary

How the words are arranged

The rhymes are arranged in sections according to the main vowel sound of the word. The first half of each section contains words with this sound as their final or only vowel sound (e.g. *cat* and *unpack* in the -a- section); the second half contains words with this sound followed by one or more weaker syllables (e.g. *happy* and *examiner*). The sections are as follows, in this order:

-a- (as in *mat, unpack, happy, examiner*)
-ah- (as in *half, depart, larder, impartially*)
-air- (as in *hair, unfair, scarcely, bearable*)
-ay- (as in *same, display, waiting, Australia*)
-e- (as in *pen, infect, ready, separate*)
-er- (as in *her, return, working, university*)
-eer- (as in *beer, revere, fiercely, endearment*)
-ee- (as in *breed, complete, teacher, meaningless*)
-i- (as in *sit, evict, whistle, revision*)
-ire- (as in *tire, require, admirer, violently*)
-ie- (as in *try, untie, glider, reliable*)
-o- (as in *toss, forgot, copper, historical*)
-or- (as in *ford, implore, daughter, victorious*)
-oor- (as in *cure, endure, purely, maturity*)
-ow- (as in *cow, endow, louder, boundary*)
-ower- (as in *hour, empower, towering, floury*)
-oy- (as in *toy, enjoy, noisy, avoidable*)
-oe- (as in *boat, ago, grocer, totally*)
-u- (as in *run, instruct, double, gluttony*)
-uu- (as in *put, withstood, booking, womanly*)
-oo- (as in *too, rebuke, cruiser, beautiful*)

Within each section, the words are arranged in numbered groups according to the sound that follows this vowel (e.g. *at/bat/ cat, adder/ladder/madder*). Many of these groups contain words that are close but not perfect rhymes (e.g. *hammer/banner*), to give you a fuller range of possibilities.

Within each numbered group, the rhymes are divided by asterisks into sets of words with the same number of syllables (e.g. *hack, jack, pack * aback, attack, repack*) or with the same rhythm (e.g. *aback, attack, repack * hatchback, knapsack, tailback*).

How to find a particular rhyme

If you are looking for a rhyme for a particular word, the easiest way is to use the index at the back of the book, which will guide you to the numbered group in which your word appears. For example, *batter* is in group 2.10. Once you have found this group, cast your eye over all the words – you may find a close rhyme some distance away (e.g. *regatta* and *antimatter*). Some of the longer sets of rhymes, e.g. the *-ation* words, have been divided into several smaller groups, so it is always a good idea to look at the groups above and below the one containing the word you are trying to rhyme.

Words that have more than one sound appear in more than one group. For example, *graph* can rhyme with *naff* or *half*, so both group numbers are given in the index. Similarly, *sow* rhymes with *cow* when it means 'female pig' and with *go* when it means 'put seed in ground'.

If your word is not in the index, does it have an extra ending, such as the *-s* of *stamps* or the *-ed* of *dragged*? If so, remove the ending and look for the main form of the word (i.e. *stamp* or *drag*). You may be able to add the same ending to other words in its group (e.g. *cramps/lamps/ tramps* or *bragged/ lagged/sagged*). Many words with these endings have groups of their own, often with 'etc.' at the end, which means that more rhymes can be made by adding the same ending to other words. For example, group 1.4 contains some of the most common *-acks* words that rhyme with *axe*, but there is not room to include them all – you can make many more by adding *-s* to the other *ack* words in group 1.3.

If you still cannot find a suitable rhyme for your word, you may find a near-rhyme in another group. Words ending in the 'f' sound, for example, are sometimes rhymed with words ending in the 'v' or 'th' sound (e.g. *leaf/weave/teeth/breathe*). Other letter sounds that can be paired in this way are 'b' and 'p' (*crab/tap*), 'k' and 'g' (*rack/stag*), 'd' and 't' (*bed/set*), 'm' and 'n' (*rim/thin*), 's' and 'z' (*miss/fizz*), and 'sh' and 'ch' (*squash/watch*).

Finally, here is a list of words that have no rhyme:

bilge
cusp
damask
depth
eighth
else
gouge
month
ninth
period
scarce
sixth
warmth
wasp
Welsh
width

-a-

The rhymes in this section have the 'a' sound of mat *and* happy *as their main or final vowel sound.*

1.1 blab, cab, crab, Crabbe, dab, drab, fab, flab, gab, grab, jab, lab, Mab, nab, scab, slab, stab, tab, * McNab, Cantab., kebab, vocab, * Ahab, spacelab, prefab, rehab, Skylab, confab, Joab, Moab, * smash-and-grab, hackney cab, taxicab, shish kebab, minicab, baobab

**Mungojerrie and Rumpelteazer had a very unusual gift of the gab,
They were highly efficient cat-burglars as well, and remarkably smart at a smash-and-grab.**
T. S. Eliot

1.2 abs, Babs, cabs, crabs, dabs, grabs, jabs, nabs, scabs, slabs, stabs, * abdabs, prefabs, * dribs and drabs, shish kebabs, minicabs, etc.

1.3 back, black, Black, Braque, clack, claque, crack, flak, hack, jack, Jack, Jacques, knack, lac, lack, mac, Mac, Mach, pack, plaque, quack, rack, sac, sack, shack, slack, smack, snack, stack, tack, thwack, track, vac, wack, whack, WRAC, wrack, yack, yak, Zack, * aback, unpack, macaque, attack, alack, laid-back, repack, Chirac, Dirac, Iraq, * ack-ack, cashback, flashback, splashback, hatchback, backpack, bratpack, ratpack, NASDAQ, lampblack, Shadrach, backtrack, yashmak, knapsack, ransack, Balzac, Anzac, dhansak, flapjack, blackjack, hardback, halfback, hardtack, fast-track, Tarmac®, Carnac, Karnak, bareback, payback, playback, tailback, haystack, hayrack, racetrack, setback, sweptback, shellac, Lurpak®, feedback, greenback, leaseback, Meshach, Taoiseach, cheapjack, kickback, slingback, switchback, ridgeback, six-pack, ticktack, rickrack, gimcrack, knick-knack, skipjack, Dyak, kayak, buy-back, tieback, zwieback, wisecrack, sidetrack, hijack, skyjack, softback, Cognac, Cossack, hopsack, Toshack, clawback, drawback, horseback, Dvořák, outback, soundtrack, blowback, throwback, Kodak, smokestack, Slovak, Prozac®, Kojak, humpback, cutback, comeback, hunchback, mudpack, thumbtack, rucksack, muntjac, fullback, woolpack, bushwhack, woolsack, Blu-Tack®, shoeblack, bootblack, sumac, Cusack, Muzak®, * back-to-back, saddleback, Pasternak, Savernake, almanac, Sassenach, Bacharach, Skagerrak, bladderwrack, anorak, haversack, crackerjack, natterjack, applejack, Cadillac, amphibrach, paddywhack, Dannimac®, heart attack, Armagnac, cardiac, paperback, razorback, maniac, leatherback, Kerouac, Bergerac,

steeplejack, coeliac, stickleback, in the
black, bric-a-brac, hit the sack, iliac,
Syriac, piggyback, ipecac, bivouac,
Pontiac, Mauriac, quarterback, Kodiak,
zodiac, lumberjack, multipack,
multitrack, cul-de-sac, Union Jack,
Cluniac, * celeriac, amnesiac,
insomniac, ammoniac, demoniac,
simoniac, * counterattack, yackety-yak,
* kleptomaniac, egomaniac, nymphomaniac, dipsomaniac, pyromaniac,
monomaniac, necrophiliac,
paedophiliac, haemophiliac, sacroiliac,
paradisiac, aphrodisiac, Dionysiac,
hypochondriac, sal ammoniac,
* megalomaniac

**Then I saw the Congo, creeping
  through the black,
Cutting through the forest with a
  golden track.**
VACHEL LINDSAY

1.4 axe, backs, BACS, Bax, cracks, fax,
flax, jacks, Jack's, lacks, lax, max, Max,
packs, pax, racks, Sachs, Sacks, sax,
shacks, slacks, snacks, stacks, tax,
tracks, wax, whacks, * unpacks, attacks,
repacks, relax, * hatchbacks, Tampax®,
gravlax, backtracks, anthrax, Balzac's,
flapjacks, Fairfax, haystacks, AWACS,
Ajax, Pentax, Ex-Lax®, surtax, earwax,
meataxe, Ceefax®, beeswax, slingbacks,
pickaxe, syntax, hyrax, styrax, kayaks,
climax, sidetracks, hijacks, drawbacks,
borax, storax, thorax, smokestacks,
poleaxe, toadflax, Lomax, * battleaxe,
parallax, gravadlax, almanacs,
Sassenachs, Halifax, paperbacks,
sealing wax, sticklebacks, minimax,
Filofax®, overtax, supertax, Union
Jacks, * anticlimax, * kleptomaniacs,
aphrodisiacs, etc.

1.5 axed, faxed, taxed, waxed,
* untaxed, unwaxed, etc.

1.6 act, backed, bract, cracked, fact,
hacked, lacked, packed, pact, quacked,
smacked, stacked, tact, tracked, tract,
whacked, * compact, unpacked,
attacked, attract, subtract, contract,
jam-packed, abstract, transact, react,
prepacked, detract, retract, refract,
impact, intact, distract, extract,
diffract, enact, exact, entr'acte,
protract, * abstract, backtracked,
ransacked, play-act, extract, impact,
sidetracked, hijacked, compact,
contact, contract, gobsmacked,
humpbacked, hunchbacked, * cataract,
vacuum-packed, artefact, retroact, re-
enact, interact, inexact, Pontefract,
counteract, overact, underact,
subcontract, * counterattacked,
matter-of-fact, overreact, etc.

1.7 batch, catch, hatch, latch, match,
natch, patch, scratch, snatch, thatch,
* attach, unlatch, Brands Hatch, detach,
dispatch, mismatch, * Sandbach,
rematch, mismatch, eyepatch,
crosspatch, crosshatch, nuthatch,
* slanging match, purple patch, reattach

1.8 hatched, latched, matched,
patched, scratched, snatched,
thatched, * attached, unhatched,
unlatched, unscratched, unmatched,
detached, dispatched, mismatched,
* reattached, unattached,
* semidetached

1.9 ad, add, bad, bade, brad, Brad, cad,
chad, Chad, clad, dad, fad, gad, Gad,
glad, grad, had, lad, mad, pad, plaid,
rad, sad, SAD, scad, shad, Strad, tad,

trad, Vlad, * unclad, Baghdad, Riyadh,
egad, begad, jihad, forbad,
* scratchpad, grandad, farad, Amstrad,
Karlsbad, sketchpad, stepdad, keypad,
kneepad, Sinbad, inkpad, dryad, naiad,
triad, cycad, Conrad, monad, launch
pad, small ad, notepad, snowclad,
gonad, nomad, footpad, * Galahad,
Stalingrad, barking mad, helipad,
Leningrad, Petrograd, Gilead, *Iliad*,
Trinidad, ironclad, hopping mad,
Volgograd, * Jalalabad, Islamabad,
bromeliad, Olympiad, Upanishad,
* Faisalabad, Hyderabad

Ask you what provocation I have had?
The strong antipathy of good to bad.
ALEXANDER POPE

1.10 ads, adds, adze, cads, dad's, lads,
pads, scads, * kneepads, Conrad's,
small ads, nomads, gonads, etc.

1.11 caff, chaff, daff, faff, gaff, gaffe,
Graf, graph, naff, RAF, Taff, WAAF,
* carafe, Llandaff, Piaf, giraffe, * decaf,
riffraff, chiffchaff, digraph, Olaf,
* tachograph, barograph, paragraph,
shandygaff, shadowgraph, Cenotaph,
stenograph, epitaph, epigraph,
telegraph, Dictograph®, pictograph,
lithograph, spirograph, micrograph,
seismograph, Chinagraph®,
logograph, holograph, homograph,
chronograph, monograph, polygraph,
autograph, blow the gaff, photograph,
phonograph, * cardiograph,
radiograph, ideograph, Mimeograph®,
choreograph, * encephalograph

1.12 daffs, graphs, Staffs, WAAFs,
* carafes, giraffes, * paragraphs,
photographs, etc.

1.13 bag, blag, brag, Bragg, cag, clag,
crag, dag, drag, fag, flag, gag, hag, jag,
Jag, lag, mag, nag, quag, rag, sag, scrag,
shag, slag, snag, spag, stag, swag, tag,
wag, * debag, reflag, * ragbag,
handbag, sandbag, ratbag, gasbag,
ragtag, stalag, air bag, mailbag, sailbag,
jet lag, greylag, workbag, fleabag,
teabag, feedbag, beanbag, windbag,
kitbag, wigwag, chinwag, zigzag,
dogtag, Sontag, washrag, Morag, Gro-
bag®, postbag, nosebag, toerag,
scumbag, punchbag, Gulag,
* saddlebag, scallywag, carpetbag,
paper bag, Jiffy bag®, Brobdingnag,
tucker-bag

The common cormorant (or shag)
Lays eggs inside a paper bag.
CHRISTOPHER ISHERWOOD

1.14 bags, brags, crags, flags, gags, nags,
rags, wags, * handbags, sandbags, air
bags, mailbags, teabags, beanbags,
* saddlebags, paper bags, moneybags,
etc.

1.15 badge, cadge, hajj, Madge,
* rebadge

1.16 Al, gal, Hal, mall, pal, Sal, shall,
Val, * cabal, Natal, halal, banal, canal,
Pascal, Chagall, Pall Mall, La Salle,
Chantal, mescal, et al., decal, Vidal,
grand mal, low-cal, * caracal, *femme
fatale*, chaparral, falderal, Amytal®,
acetal, barbital, Pentothal®, petit mal,
Nembutal®, L'Oréal, * Guadalcanal

1.17 calque, talc, * catafalque

1.18 Alf, Ralph

1.19 alp, palp, scalp

1.20 shalt, * Gestalt, * asphalt

1.21 salve, valve, * lip salve, bivalve

1.22 am, cam, Cam, clam, cram, Cram, dam, damn, drachm, dram, gam, glam, gram, ham, jam, jamb, lam, lamb, Lamb, ma'am, 'Nam, Pam, pram, ram, RAM, Sam, scam, scram, sham, slam, spam, Spam®, swam, Tam, tram, wham, yam, * madame, Saddam, Pan-Am, Assam, mesdames, Vietnam, exam, Siam, goddamn, cheongsam, pro-am, * CADCAM, pangram, ashram, webcam, Edam, Etam, flimflam, Islam, wigwam, iamb, Priam, NICAM, quondam, Potsdam, Oxfam, logjam, doorjamb, program, programme, * deprogramme, reprogram, * Amsterdam, mammogram, anagram, traffic jam, aerogram, Abraham, cablegram, Babycham®, hectogram, pentagram, tetragram, hexagram, Steadicam®, epigram, telegram, centigram, give a damn, pictogram, histogram, kilogram, kissagram, dithyramb, milligram, diagram, seismogram, diaphragm, Rotterdam, cofferdam, hologram, monogram, oriflamme, Surinam, Uncle Sam, * gorillagram, oscillogram, ad nauseam, temazepam, diazepam, Omar Khayyám, * angiogram, cardiogram, radiogram, stereogram, ideogram, battering ram, * encephalogram, * parallelogram, in memoriam

I had written to Aunt Maud,
Who was on a trip abroad,
When I heard she'd died of cramp
Just too late to save the stamp.
HARRY GRAHAM

1.23 amp, camp, champ, clamp, cramp, damp, gamp, lamp, ramp, scamp, stamp, tamp, tramp, vamp, * decamp, revamp, encamp, * gas lamp, headlamp, wheel clamp, streetlamp, firedamp, oil lamp, blowlamp, chokedamp, * standard lamp, afterdamp, lava lamp, Davy lamp, postage stamp, rubber-stamp

1.24 an, Ann, Anne, ban, bran, can, Cannes, clan, dan, Dan, fan, flan, Fran, gan, gran, Jan, Jeanne, man, Mann, nan, Nan, pan, Pan, plan, ran, scan, scran, span, Stan, tan, than, van, * Strabane, Japan, rattan, pavane, Oran, Moran, unman, Kazan, Tehran, élan, Cézanne, Leanne, trepan, began, sedan, Sedan, divan, Milan, tisane, Cheyenne, Diane, Roxanne, Joanne, Johann, Lausanne, Roseanne, outran, yuan, Sudan, Bhutan, Suzanne, * *kanban*, sampan, cancan, Afghan, gratin, kaftan, banyan, ragman, swagman, adman, badman, sandman, Batman, Salman, gasman, axeman, taxman, claypan, brainpan, brain scan, apeman, caveman, mailman, spaceman, bedpan, deadpan, chessman, pressman, merman, birdman, earthman, pecan, free man, he-man, freedman, liegeman, skidpan, wingspan, hit man, binman, Nissan, fireman, cyan, lifespan, ice man, Chopin, stockman, con man, strongman, saltpan, FORTRAN, doorman, lawman, Outspan®, oilcan, Gauguin, Rodin, snowman, Onan, dustpan, suntan, stuntman, newsman, Poussin, * tragopan, astrakhan, Astrakhan, Aberfan, caravan, Callaghan, Hanrahan, Catalan, rataplan, anchorman, Kazakhstan,

Marianne, Caliban, Taliban, Pakistan, Dagestan, Acrilan®, gamelan, handyman, Bantustan, man-to-man, marzipan, artisan, partisan, Parmesan, dairyman, stableman, ladies' man, weatherman, Telemann, self-made man, jerry can, ferryman, Everyman, exciseman, Turkestan, Kyrgyzstan, Kurdistan, serviceman, turbofan, Peter Pan, spick-and-span, middleman, billycan, minivan, businessman, Hindustan, trimaran, Spiderman, Isle of Man, frying pan, lifeboatman, quarryman, gombeen-man, *coq au vin*, also-ran, slaughterman, courtesan, Moynihan, open-plan, overran, overman, bogeyman, muscleman, Ku Klux Klan, superman, Superman, Houlihan, * extractor fan, Afghanistan, orang-utan, bipartisan, nonpartisan, remainderman, Uzbekistan, Turkmenistan, Tajikistan, committeeman, Baluchistan, * flash in the pan, carry the can, catamaran, cameraman, cavalryman, infantryman, newspaperman, angry young man

Pat-a-cake, pat-a-cake, baker's man,
Bake me a cake as fast as you can.
Nursery rhyme

1.25 ankh, bank, blank, clank, crank, dank, drank, flank, franc, Franck, frank, Frank, hank, Hank, lank, Planck, plank, prank, rank, Rank, sank, shank, shrank, spank, stank, swank, tank, thank, wank, yank, Yank, * embank, outflank, outrank, point-blank, * sandbank, gangplank, redshank, sheepshank, Millbank, think-tank, Clydebank, mudbank, Cruikshank, Ewbank, * antitank, data bank, interbank, riverbank, piggy bank,

Girobank, Jodrell Bank, mountebank, Bundesbank

1.26 banks, Banks, blanks, cranks, flanks, francs, Frank's, Hanks, Lancs, Manx, pranks, ranks, tanks, thanks, Yanks, * sandbanks, phalanx, Fairbanks, * spindleshanks, piggy banks, mountebanks, etc.

1.27 banked, clanked, flanked, ranked, spanked, thanked, yanked, * unfranked, unthanked, outflanked, outranked, * sacrosanct, etc.

1.28 and, band, banned, bland, brand, canned, fanned, gland, grand, hand, land, Land, manned, panned, rand, sand, spanned, stand, strand, Strand, tanned, * unhand, unmanned, unplanned, crash-land, rebrand, disband, expand, withstand, offhand, * hatband, jazz band, bandstand, grandstand, handstand, backhand, Lapland, adland, gangland, armband, chargehand, parkland, heartland, farmland, grassland, waistband, waveband, stagehand, Lakeland, wasteland, neckband, headband, sweatband, headstand, freehand, Queensland, wristband, kickstand, inkstand, inland, quicksand, firebrand, Thailand, Rhineland, watchband, washstand, longhand, dockland, broadband, forehand, shorthand, browband, cowhand, noseband, homeland, own brand, suntanned, clubland, scrubland, newsstand, * behindhand, beforehand, * sarabande, Samarkand, ampersand, Talleyrand, graduand, hand-to-hand, fatherland, Swaziland, fairyland, Maryland, tableland, lend a hand, second-hand, bellyband, Ferdinand, Rio Grande, timberland, hinterland, Kristiansand, Disneyland, Dixieland, Hildebrand, sleight of hand, contraband, borderland, overhand, Oberland, overland, overmanned, no man's land, Togoland, understand, underhand, wonderland, motherland, one-night stand, Krugerrand, Newfoundland, * Somaliland, Sudetenland, Van Diemen's Land, Witwatersrand, misunderstand, cloud-cuckoo-land

The stately homes of England,
How beautiful they stand!
Amidst their tall ancestral trees
O'er all the pleasant land.
FELICIA HEMANS

1.29 bang, Chang, clang, dang, fang, gang, hang, Lang, pang, prang, rang, sang, slang, sprang, tang, Tang, twang, vang, whang, Yang, * harangue, meringue, slap-bang, Shenyang, rehang, shebang, Penang, Pyongyang, * gangbang, headbang, press gang, mustang, Wolfgang, * charabanc, *Sturm und Drang*, overhang, boomerang, * orang-utang

1.30 Ange, flange, * Falange, phalange

1.31 Hans, Hanse, manse, stance, Vance, * askance, Penzance, expanse, finance, romance, * happenstance, Langerhans, circumstance

1.32 Gdansk, Murmansk

1.33 ant, Brandt, cant, Kant, pant, rant, scant, * Brabant, gallant, decant, recant, descant, extant, Levant, Besant,

enceinte, U Thant, * descant, Rembrandt, * gallivant, sycophant, hierophant, commandant, confidant, confidante

1.34 ants, Franz, Hants, Kant's, pants, rants, * decants, recants, Northants, * gallivants, smarty-pants, sycophants, Rosencrantz, underpants, etc.

1.35 tragacanth, amaranth, coelacanth

1.36 Anne's, banns, bans, Cannes, cans, clans, Dan's, fans, glans, Hans, Jan's, pans, plans, Stan's, tans, vans, * kaftans, Ray-Bans®, brain scans, bedpans, oilcans, * caravans, Callaghan's, Marianne's, artisans, Prestonpans, jerry cans, * Lytham Saint Anne's, catamarans, etc.

1.37 bap, cap, chap, clap, crap, dap, flap, gap, Gap, hap, Jap, knap, Knapp, lap, Lapp, map, nap, pap, rap, sap, scrap, slap, snap, strap, tap, trap, WAP, wrap, yap, zap, * uncap, unwrap, unstrap, recap, rewrap, enwrap, entrap, * blackcap, madcap, claptrap, mantrap, catnap, mayhap, redcap, death trap, earflap, kneecap, recap, heeltap, mishap, giftwrap, chinstrap, bitmap, kidnap, wiretap, firetrap, nightcap, whitecap, icecap, flytrap, mobcap, stopgap, jockstrap, watchstrap, mousetrap, snowcap, toecap, hubcap, skullcap, mudflap, suntrap, foolscap, dewlap, bootstrap, * rattletrap, Andy Capp, handicap, take the rap, Tonle Sap, overlap, thunderclap, honeytrap, booby trap

1.38 apse, caps, chaps, claps, craps, daps, flaps, gaps, lapse, maps, raps,

schnapps, scraps, straps, taps, traps,
wraps, yaps, zaps, * perhaps, collapse,
unwraps, elapse, relapse, * earflaps,
kneecaps, toecaps, prolapse, hubcaps,
mudflaps, bootstraps, etc.

1.39 apt, chapped, clapped, flapped,
knapped, rapt, strapped, wrapped,
* adapt, untapped, unwrapped,
unmapped, enwrapped, inapt,
* catnapped, kidnapped, snowcapped,
* handicapped, readapt, overlapped, etc.

1.40 ass, bass, crass, gas, lass, mass,
Mass, sass, strass, TASS, wrasse, vas,
* alas, harass, morass, Madras, Patras,
amass, Laplace, Alsace, degas, kick ass,
crevasse, cuirass, volte-face, en masse,
* jackass, badass, Hamas, landmass,
Sampras, ACAS, Esdras, tear gas,
Mithras, tightass, Ofgas, groundmass,
* Calor gas®, sassafras, Candlemas,
palliasse, Adidas®, Badedas®, gravitas,
Martinmas, Quatermass, demitasse,
Pythias, hippocras, Caiaphas, biogas,
biomass, Fortinbras, Hudibras,
* Tiberias, Leonidas, Herodias,
Asturias, * Ozymandias, Herod
Antipas, * in vino veritas,
materfamilias, paterfamilias

1.41 asp, hasp

1.42 bast, massed, gassed, hast,
* lambast, harassed, amassed,
degassed, * bombast, * pederast,
cineaste, chloroplast, scholiast,
* iconoclast, Elastoplast®, enthusiast

1.43 ash, ASH, Ashe, bash, brash, cache,
cash, clash, crash, dash, flash, gash,
gnash, hash, lash, mash, MASH, Nash,
pash, plash, rash, sash, slash, smash,

splash, stash, tache, thrash, trash,
* abash, unlash, panache, rehash,
encash, * slapdash, backlash, gate-
crash, rehash, whiplash, mishmash,
earbash, eyelash, potash, Saltash,
goulash, newsflash, * have a bash,
calabash, pebbledash, Johnny Cash,
balderdash, water brash, succotash

1.44 bashed, cashed, crashed, flashed,
gashed, mashed, smashed, splashed,
thrashed, trashed, * abashed,
rehashed, * unabashed, etc.

1.45 at, bat, brat, cat, chat, drat, fat, flat,
GATT, gnat, hat, mat, matt, Matt, Nat,
pat, Pat, plait, plat, prat, Pratt, rat, sat,
scat, shat, skat, slat, spat, splat, sprat,
tat, that, twat, vat, VAT, * Sadat, cravat,
fat cat, rat-tat, Passat®, hard hat,
thereat, whereat, expat, Fermat, hereat,
begat, resat, howzat, * backchat,
hellcat, hepcat, Zermatt, meerkat,
brickbat, dingbat, tipcat, Kit Kat®,
diktat, Brinks-Mat, chitchat, whinchat,
wildcat, combat, wombat, bobcat,
tomcat, top hat, doormat, format,
cowpat, Croat, polecat, stonechat,
numbat, mudcat, Muscat, sunhat, mud
flat, muskrat, * concordat, reformat,
* acrobat, rat-a-tat, Ararat, caveat,
Kattegat, habitat, marrow fat, aerostat,
scaredy-cat, baby-sat, Cheshire cat,
democrat, Democrat, technocrat,
thermostat, rheostat, pitapat, tit-for-
tat, ziggurat, Symonds Yat, diplomat,
aegrotat, Montserrat, monocrat,
copycat, autocrat, automat,
Laundromat®, bureaucrat, Eurocrat,
Postman Pat, Photostat®, butterfat,
pussycat, plutocrat, Rubáiyát,
* Jehoshaphat, Magnificat, * aristocrat,
requiescat

But thousands die, without or this or that,
Die, and endow a college, or a cat.
ALEXANDER POPE

1.46 bats, brats, cats, chats, flats, gnats, hats, Katz, mats, Matt's, Pat's, plaits, rats, SATs, * cravats, congrats, fat cats, expats, * ersatz, dingbats, cowpats, mud flats, etc.

1.47 Cath, Gath, hath, lath, Plath, * aftermath, telepath, psychopath, polymath, * naturopath, osteopath, homeopath, sociopath

1.48 Cath's, laths, maths, * telepaths, psychopaths, polymaths, etc.

1.49 chav, have, lav, * satnav, Olav

1.50 as, Baz, Chas, Daz®, Gaz, has, jazz, * La Paz, whereas, Shiraz, pizzazz, * Boaz, topaz, * razzmatazz, Alcatraz

2.1 abbey, Abby, cabbie, crabby, flabby, Gaby, gabby, grabby, Rabbie, scabby, shabby, tabby, yabby, Bambi, can be, Ashby, chappie, crappy, flappy, gappy, happy, nappy, pappy, sappy, scrappy, snappy, strappy, yappy, zappy, scampi, * unhappy, * slaphappy, * Newtownabbey, namby-pamby, happy-clappy

2.2 baccy, Bacchae, Blackie, cacky, Jackie, lackey, Mackie, raki, sake, tacky, wacky, cranky, Frankie, hanky, lanky, manky, Sankey, swanky, Yankee, ASCII, Askey, Laski, Spassky, Aggie, baggy, craggy, daggy, draggy, jaggy, Maggie, quaggy, ragi, saggy, scraggy, shaggy, * Iraqi, Baisakhi, Polanski, * Nagasaki, Kawasaki, Yamasaki, teriyaki, sukiyaki,

catananche, hanky-panky, Killiecrankie, Widow Twankey, Stanislavsky

2.3 Addy, baddie, caddie, caddy, daddy, faddy, gladdie, had he, laddie, Maddy, paddy, Paddy, Andy, bandy, brandy, candy, dandy, *Dandy*, Gandhi, handy, Mandy, randy, sandy, shandy, Tandy, batty, catty, chatty, fatty, flattie, Hattie, natty, Patti, patty, ratty, Satie, scatty, Tati, tattie, tatty, ante, anti, Dante, scanty, shanty, Asti, pasty, * Vivaldi, unhandy, chapati, Hanratty, Scarlatti, Bugatti, bacchante, Ashanti, Ferranti, Chianti, Durante, * grandaddy, * finnan haddie, Fittipaldi, Andy Pandy, Rio Grande, Tonypandy, Kiribati, Cincinnati, Alicante, in flagrante, dilettante, vigilante, rhinoplasty, * Asti spumante, * modus operandi

2.4 café, daffy, NAAFI, Taffy, Malfi, navvy, savvy, Canvey, Cathy, Xanthe, * Gaddafi, Amalfi, * cybercafé, Iolanthe

2.5 Ali, alley, Ally, bally, dally, galley, Halley, pally, Raleigh, rally, sally, Sally, scally, tally, valley, Chablis, brambly, haply, amply, blackly, crackly, frankly, Shankly, straggly, waggly, gangly, badly, Bradley, gladly, Hadleigh, madly, sadly, grandly, Attlee, Batley, flatly, rattly, aptly, Bramley, family, Hanley, Manley, manly, Stanley, Langley, Ashley, rashly, Barrie, Barry, Carrie, carry, Cary, Clarrie, Gary, harry, Harry, Larry, marry, parry, Parry, tarry, blackberry, cranberry, lamprey, angry, Crabtree, gantry, pantry, Langtry, * McNally, Aunt Sally, reveille, O'Malley, doolally, exactly, unmanly, Winstanley, Osmanli, glengarry, remarry, miscarry, du Barry, Deganwy, Myfanwy, * peely-wally, Tin Pan Alley, dilly-dally, shilly-shally, intermarry, etc.

**Of all the girls that are so smart
There's none like pretty Sally,
She is the darling of my heart,
And she lives in our alley.**
HENRY CAREY

2.6 chamois, clammy, gammy, Grammy, hammy, jammy, mammy, ramie, Sammy, shammy, tammy, Tammy, whammy, acme, Lakshmi, Annie, can he, canny, cranny, Danny, fanny, Fanny, granny, nanny, trannie, acne, Hackney, Cagney, Daphne, slangy, tangy, * Miami, uncanny, Giovanni, Evadne, * double whammy, hootenanny, Ariadne, * damn me, sack me, etc.

2.7 Bassey, brassie, Cassie, chassis, gassy, lassie, Lassie, Massey, Plassey, massy, sassy, jacksie, Laxey, maxi, taxi, waxy, Patsy, antsy, Yangtze, Clancy, fancy, Nancy, has he, jazzy, snazzy, Ramsay, Ramsey, pansy, tansy, ashy, flashy, mashie, splashy, trashy, catchy, patchy, scratchy, snatchy, hajji, algae, Algy, Angie, * Manasseh, Apache, Hitachi, Comanche, * Malagasy, Tallahassee, paparazzi, cartomancy, necromancy, * Haile Selassie

2.8 Abba, blabber, crabber, dabber, drabber, grabber, jabber, amber, camber, clamber, mamba, samba, timbre, clapper, crapper, dapper, flapper, grappa, kappa, mapper, nappa, napper, rapper, sapper, scrapper, slapper, snapper, strapper, tapper, trapper, wrapper, yapper, Zappa,

zapper, scalper, camper, clamper, damper, hamper, pamper, scamper, stamper, Tampa, tamper, Caspar, jasper, Jasper, * kidnapper, * liquidambar, handicapper, whippersnapper, * viola da gamba, * grab her, trap her, etc.

2.9 backer, blacker, clacker, cracker, Dakar, Dhaka, hacker, knacker, lacker, lacquer, nutcracker, *Nutcracker*, packer, sacker, slacker, smacker, stacker, tacker, tracker, wacker, Kafka, anchor, banker, canker, chancre, danker, flanker, franker, hanker, rancour, ranker, spanker, tanker, wanker, blagger, bragger, dagger, flagger, gagger, Jagger, lagger, nagger, quagga, ragga, stagger, swagger, alga, anger, Bangor, clangour, kanga, Kanga, languor, manga, * unpacker, attacker, Malacca, maraca, alpaca, Kamchatka, Bianca, Sri Lanka, Alaska, Nebraska, Trafalgar, realgar, Kananga, Northanger, * backpacker, safe-cracker, shelf-stacker, firecracker, hijacker, skyjacker, wisecracker, bushwhacker, Schumacher, * illywhacker, Casablanca, lingua franca, supertanker, Madagascar, Athabaska, carpetbagger, cloak-and-dagger, * thank her, nag her, etc.

**This particularly rapid, unintelligible
    patter
Isn't generally heard, and if it is it
    doesn't matter.**
W. S. GILBERT

2.10 adder, bladder, Claddagh, ladder, madder, sadder, lambda, LAMDA, Banda, blander, candour, dander, gander, grander, panda, pander,

sander, stander, Asda, Mazda, attar,
batter, chatter, clatter, fatter, flatter,
hatter, latter, matter, natter, patter,
platter, ratter, satyr, scatter, shatter,
spatter, splatter, tatter, ABTA, captor,
chapter, raptor, actor, factor, tractor,
BAFTA, Yalta, banter, canter, Fanta®,
Granta, manta, plantar, ranter, Santa,
aster, Astor, pasta, Rasta, raster, Baxter,
hamster, gangsta, gangster, * veranda,
Amanda, germander, pomander,
Menander, backhander, left-hander,
Leander, meander, expander,
philander, Miranda, right-hander,
Lysander, Luanda, Rwanda, Uganda,
Buganda, Luganda, two-hander,
goosander, ciabatta, Al Fatah, Mad
Hatter, Kenyatta, bespatter, regatta,
adaptor, protractor, contractor,
reactor, detractor, retractor, extractor,
refractor, Atlanta, decanter, Vedanta,
infanta, levanter, trochanter, cadaster,
piastre, pilaster, canasta, Jocasta,
* Tadcaster, Lancaster, Doncaster,
* stepladder, Laplander, Queenslander,
bystander, Icelander, * Esmeralda,
jacaranda, salamander, Afrikander,
Netherlander, memoranda, chest-
expander, gerrymander, propaganda,
oleander, coriander, Parramatta,
antimatter, pitter-patter, overmatter,
malefactor, benefactor, chiropractor,
subcontractor, Atalanta, tam-o'-
shanter, alabaster, poetaster, Zoroaster,
* Anaximander, velociraptor,
cotoneaster, * virgo intacta, * forbade
her, sacked her, etc.

2.11 chaffer, gaffer, Jaffa, Shaffer, Staffa,
Agfa, alpha, Balfour, camphor,
chamfer, slaver, salver, salvor, naphtha,
anther, panther, blather, gather, lather,
Mather, * alfalfa, cadaver, Samantha,

ingather, foregather, * Luftwaffe,
quacksalver, * pyracantha, * chaff her,
have her, etc.

2.12 Allah, Bala, Calor®, pallor, valour,
babbler, dabbler, gabbler, ambler,
Ambler, gambler, rambler, scrambler,
trampler, cackler, haggler, straggler,
angler, strangler, wrangler, Adler,
paddler, saddler, Sadler, handler,
battler, prattler, rattler, *Tatler*, tattler,
antler, dazzler, ashlar, Barra, Farrah,
para, Varah, Vanbrugh, chakra,
bhangra, Sandra, Tantra, mantra,
Aphra, camera, CAMRA, Basra, aqua,
stature, Anya, Vanya, * Valhalla,
Alhambra, podagra, pellagra, Niagara,
Viagra®, Cassandra, Biafra, subaqua,
Managua, lasagne, Britannia,
* Alexandra, Cleopatra, * Caracalla,
bobby-dazzler, Nicaragua,
* abracadabra, etc.

2.13 clamour, crammer, gamma,
glamour, grammar, hammer, jammer,
mamma, rammer, scammer, shammer,
slammer, stammer, yammer, drachma,
agma, magma, asthma, Alma, halma,
Palma, palmar, Cranmer, plasma,
Anna, banner, Branagh, canner,
Hanna, Hannah, manna, manner,
manor, nana, planner, scanner,
spanner, tanner, Abner, Wagner,
Radnor, Patna, Ratner, Shatner,
banger, clanger, clangour, ganger,
hangar, hanger, Langer, Sanger,
* enamour, syntagma, Mahatma,
miasma, Havana, Kavanagh, savanna,
Savannah, Alannah, Fermanagh,
bandanna, Diana, Guiana, Guyana,
Montana, goanna, Joanna, hosanna,
Susanna, Stavanger, haranguer,
* sledgehammer, windjammer,

programmer, straphanger, head-banger, cliffhanger, * Alabama, yellowhammer, Santa Ana, caravanner, Indiana, Pollyanna, paperhanger, doppel- gänger, * Louisiana, * ipecacuanha, * damn her, outran her, etc.

It's awf'lly bad luck on Diana,
Her ponies have swallowed their bits;
She fished down their throats with a
    spanner
And frightened them all into fits.
JOHN BETJEMAN

2.14 gasser, NASA, Nasser, Yasser, lapser, Saxa, taxer, waxer, Khalsa, salsa, cancer, Cancer, Hansa, Gazza, Lanza, panzer, stanza, azure, Asher, dasher, flasher, gnasher, Jascha, lasher, masher, pasha, rasher, Sacha, slasher, smasher, thrasher, Hampshire, catcher, dacha, Hatcher, patcher, scratcher, snatcher, stature, thatcher, Thatcher, capture, rapture, fracture, badger, cadger, Alger, ganja, grandeur, * amasser, madrasah, Nyasa, Mombasa, relapser, relaxer, piazza, merganser, romancer, Balthazar, Belshazzar, Braganza, bonanza, organza, Natasha, focaccia, dispatcher, recapture, enrapture, contracture, gastralgia, myalgia, nostalgia, neuralgia, phalanger, * gate-crasher, rat-catcher, backscratcher, flycatcher, spycatcher, cowcatcher, * necromancer, Salmanazar, haberdasher, cradle snatcher, oystercatcher, manufacture, * extravaganza, * antimacassar, * splash her, scratch her, etc.

2.15 Arab, carob, scarab

2.16 Braddock, Craddock, haddock, Madoc, paddock, shaddock, mattock, havoc, arrack, barrack, carrack, hammock, bannock, Cannock, Lanark, Rannoch, Zanuck, cassock, hassock, * Caradoc, Portmadoc

cage me and i d go frantic
my life is so romantic
capricious and corybantic
DON MARQUIS

2.17 aspic, Bacchic, asdic, attic, Attic, batik, static, lactic, tactic, antic, frantic, mantic, drastic, mastic, plastic, spastic, crabstick, chapstick, slapstick, matchstick, * syllabic, iambic, stomachic, sporadic, nomadic, heraldic, Icelandic, aquatic, chromatic, dramatic, fanatic, pragmatic, asthmatic, Carnatic, phlegmatic, spermatic, schematic, thematic, hepatic, ecstatic, emphatic, lymphatic, erratic, stigmatic, prismatic, schismatic, sciatic, climatic, Socratic, quadratic, dogmatic, traumatic, somatic, pneumatic, rheumatic, galactic, syntactic, didactic, climactic, Atlantic, romantic, pedantic, Vedantic, semantic, gigantic, scholastic, monastic, shagtastic, fantastic, sarcastic, aplastic, elastic, dynastic, gymnastic, bombastic, * dissyllabic, trisyllabic, dithyrambic, acrobatic, aromatic, achromatic, pancreatic, Hanseatic, antistatic, astigmatic, charismatic, Adriatic, Asiatic, democratic, emblematic, enigmatic, enzymatic, thermostatic, symptomatic, systematic, cinematic, diplomatic, Hippocratic, hierocratic, operatic, problematic, autocratic, automatic, morganatic, bureaucratic, programmatic, subaquatic, plutocratic, chiropractic, prophylactic, transatlantic, necromantic, sycophantic, Corybantic, unromantic, periphrastic, thermoplastic, inelastic, orgiastic, hudibrastic, * polysyllabic, monosyllabic, aristocratic, meritocratic, undemocratic, semiaquatic, anagrammatic, axiomatic, asymptomatic, melodramatic, telegrammatic, idiomatic, diagrammatic, psychosomatic, undiplomatic, paradigmatic, intergalactic, anaphylactic, anticlimactic, iconoclastic, ecclesiastic, enthusiastic, * semiautomatic, idiosyncratic, unenthusiastic, * overenthusiastic

2.18 graphic, maffick, traffic, Sapphic, * seraphic, empathic, * tachygraphic, calligraphic, cartographic, reprographic, demographic, stenographic, ethnographic, epigraphic, telegraphic, xerographic, geographic, cryptographic, pictographic, lithographic, biographic, typographic, hydrographic, seismographic, topographic, holographic, homographic, polygraphic, autographic, orthographic, pornographic, photographic, phonographic, psychopathic, telepathic, * hagiographic, radiographic, palaeographic, cardiographic, stereographic, lexicographic, bibliographic, choreographic, naturopathic, osteopathic, homeopathic, sociopathic, * cinematographic, photolithographic

2.19 Alec, Gaelic, Gallic, phallic, baric, Garrick, Tariq, fabric, cambric, Patrick,

hat trick, gastric, Chadwick, Gatwick, * smart aleck, italic, metallic, cephalic, oxalic, vocalic, Uralic, Amharic, barbaric, tartaric, Pindaric, Kirkpatrick, theatric, Fitzpatrick, Downpatrick, * bimetallic, nonmetallic, Balearic, geriatric, paediatric, psychiatric, nasogastric

2.20 Alnwick, manic, panic, stannic, tannic, * Islamic, ceramic, dynamic, balsamic, ophthalmic, phantasmic, miasmic, orgasmic, botanic, satanic, tetanic, galvanic, Germanic, tympanic, Hispanic, mechanic, Britannic, titanic, *Titanic*, volcanic, organic, Koranic, * panoramic, dioramic, ectoplasmic, cytoplasmic, protoplasmic, Magellanic, talismanic, messianic, inorganic, oceanic, * aerodynamic, thermodynamic, transoceanic

2.21 classic, Grassic, dabchick, magic, tragic, * boracic, Jurassic, thoracic, Triassic, pelagic, myalgic, nostalgic, neuralgic, * apparatchik, haemorrhagic

2.22 Maddox, paddocks, hallux, barracks, hammocks, bannocks, cassocks, Hassocks, * Appomattox, etc.

2.23 attics, tactics, antics, plastics, matchsticks, affix, graphics, Alec's, Alex, fabrics, Patrick's, classics, * aquatics, dramatics, pneumatics, rheumatics, semantics, gymnastics, theatrics, ceramics, dynamics, mechanics, * acrobatics, aerobatics, mathematics, informatics, numismatics, demographics, geriatrics, paediatrics, * aerodynamics, thermodynamics, etc.

2.24 crabbed, rabid, rapid, vapid, jagged, ragged, caddied, bandied, candid, candied, avid, gravid, dallied, pallid, rallied, tallied, valid, arid, carried, married, tarried, acrid, Astrid, Alfred, languid, hackneyed, acid, flaccid, placid, fancied, rancid, * invalid, unmarried, remarried, miscarried, Mohammed, arachnid, antacid, * caryatid, dilly-dallied, shilly-shallied, semiarid, intermarried, etc.

When the lamp is shattered
The light in the dust lies dead –
When the cloud is scattered
The rainbow's glory is shed.
PERCY BYSSHE SHELLEY

2.25 jabbered, scabbard, tabard, halberd, knackered, lacquered, hankered, tankard, blackguard, haggard, Haggard, laggard, staggered, swaggered, angered, added, laddered, padded, branded, landed, standard, stranded, battered, dratted, fatted, matted, plaited, scattered, shattered, tattered, Apted, acted, bastard, dastard, Stafford, Strafford, Trafford, Bradford, Radford, Blandford, Catford, Ashford, ballad, salad, farad, Garrard, Harrod, backward, landward, galliard, halyard, lanyard, Spaniard, clamoured, Talmud, mannered, hazard, Hazzard, captured, fractured, * substandard, unbranded, backhanded, cack-handed, crash-landed, barehanded, red-handed, left-handed, disbanded, expanded, philandered, high-handed, right-handed, nonstandard, offhanded, forehanded, short-handed, two-handed, adapted, compacted, protracted, abstracted, reacted, impacted, distracted, extracted,

decanted, Angharad, Muhammad, enamoured, unmannered, haphazard, * empty-handed, heavy-handed, even-handed, single-handed, underhanded, unadapted, subcontracted, etc.

2.26 scabbards, tankards, blackguards, bastards, ballads, salads, Harrods, backwards, landwards, Spaniards, hazards, etc.

2.27 Babbage, cabbage, package, baggage, adage, bandage, lavage, ravage, savage, Savage, salvage, carriage, garage, Harwich, marriage, sandwich, Sandwich, language, damage, manage, passage, * repackage, disparage, miscarriage, mismanage, stage-manage, * intermarriage, undercarriage

For you dream you are crossing the
    Channel, and tossing about in a
    steamer from Harwich –
Which is something between a large
    bathing machine and a very small
    second-class carriage.
W. S. GILBERT

2.28 babble, dabble, Drabble, gabble, rabble, scrabble, Scrabble®, amble, bramble, Campbell, gamble, gambol, ramble, scramble, shamble, apple, chapel, Chappell, dapple, grapple, scrapple, scalpel, ample, trample, Aspel, cackle, crackle, grackle, hackle, jackal, mackle, shackle, tackle, ankle, rankle, Wankel, Gaskell, paschal, gaggle, haggle, straggle, waggle, algal, angle, bangle, dangle, jangle, mangel, mangle, spangle, strangle, tangle, wangle, wrangle, addle, paddle, raddle, saddle, staddle, straddle, candle, dandle, Handel, handle, Randall,

sandal, scandal, vandal, battle, Battle,
cattle, chattel, prattle, rattle, tattle,
dactyl, fractal, mantle, pastel, pastille,
baffle, raffle, snaffle, yaffle, thankful,
tactful, manful, bashful, Cavell, gavel,
gravel, ravel, Savile, travel, Athol, Aral,
barrel, carol, Carol, carrel, Carroll,
Darrell, Farrell, gambrel, mackerel,
mandrel, lateral, astral, Avril, tranquil,
Maxwell, Daniel, spaniel, camel,
Hamill, mammal, Tamil, trammel,
annal, channel, Channel, flannel,
panel, grapnel, shrapnel, Bracknell,
cracknel, Bagnell, Cassell, hassle,
tassel, vassal, axle, cancel, Hansel,
Mansell, basil, Basil, dazzle, frazzle,
razzle, damsel, satchel, Tatchell,
* unscramble, preamble, Whitechapel,
pineapple, unshackle, bedraggle,
untangle, entangle, astraddle,
unsaddle, skedaddle, mishandle,
Seattle, embattle, dismantle, unravel,
apparel, collateral, bilateral, trilateral,
Nathaniel, enamel, phantasmal,
empanel, Newcastle, bedazzle,
substantial, financial, Tintagel,
* ramshackle, rectangle, pentangle,
triangle, right angle, quadrangle,
packsaddle, side-saddle, manhandle,
panhandle, Fremantle, * technobabble,
psychobabble, tabernacle, raggle-
taggle, disentangle, fiddle-faddle,
Coromandel, pterodactyl, tittle-tattle,
consonantal, covenantal, equilateral,
quadrilateral, multilateral, unilateral,
multichannel, Newport Pagnell,
razzle-dazzle, antidazzle,
circumstantial, insubstantial,
* Quetzalcoatl

On the coast of Coromandel
Dance they to the tunes of Handel.
OSBERT SITWELL

2.29 dappled, trampled, rankled,
mangled, spangled, tangled, addled,
handled, baffled, travelled, Harold,
Jarrold, panelled, dazzled,
* bedraggled, entangled, embattled,
dismantled, newfangled, unravelled,
untravelled, well-travelled,
untrammelled, etc.

2.30 brambles, shambles, apples,
hackles, shackles, ankles, paddles,
sandals, vandals, baffles, Raffles,
barrels, carols, Darrell's, Daniels,
spaniels, mammals, trammels, annals,
panels, * at right angles, * Feast of
Tabernacles, etc.

2.31 Antrim, passim, maxim, Maxim,
* smacks him, catch him, etc.

2.32 Brabham, album, Clapham,
Rackham, Malcolm, talcum, Adam,
madam, random, tandem, atom,
Chatham, sanctum, bantam, phantom,
anthem, Grantham, fathom, alum,
Balham, Calum, Malham, carom,
marram, antrum, tantrum, angstrom,
ashram, stannum, magnum,
sphagnum, gladsome, handsome,
hansom, ransom, Ransome, transom,
chasm, spasm, Masham, * amalgam,
macadam, McCallum, alarum,
panjandrum, per annum, phantasm,
* sarcasm, orgasm, * memorandum,
cataplasm, ectoplasm, neoplasm,
pleonasm, cytoplasm, protoplasm,
* nil desperandum, iconoclasm,
enthusiasm, * grab 'em, had 'em, etc.

2.33 albums, Adams, Addams, atoms,
fathoms, Calum's, tantrums, spasms, etc.

2.34 cabin, hatpin, backspin, napkin,

Atkin, catkin, Slatkin, lambkin,
Rankin, lambskin, stand-in, Latin,
satin, captain, plantain, Baffin, Gavin,
Alvin, Calvin, chaplain, Chaplin,
Jacklin, Franklin, Shanklin, javelin,
Hamelin, Hamlyn, aspirin, chagrin,
Kathryn, Brangwyn, sanguine,
Chatwin, famine, gamin, admin,
jasmine, Yasmin, tannin, * grimalkin,
Aladdin, Prestatyn, prolactin, examine,
assassin, imagine, * Portakabin®,
alexandrine, re-examine, cross-
examine, * grabbin', slackin', etc.

2.35 cap'n, happen, crampon, dampen,
aspen, blacken, bracken, clachan,
slacken, Strachan, Gascon, dragon,
flagon, wagon, bad 'un, gladden,
madden, sadden, Camden, Hampden,
Brandon, Landon, Ramsden, baton,
batten, fatten, flatten, Grattan, Hatton,
patten, pattern, Patton, platen, Saturn,
slattern, Staten, Tatton, Clapton,
Hampton, Acton, Clacton, plankton,
Lambton, canton, lantern, Langton,
Aston, pastern, capstan, Caxton,
Paxton, Gladstone, Branston, Ashton,
Cavan, cavern, raven, tavern, Alan,
Allen, Callan, Fallon, gallon, talon,
raglan, Raglan, Scanlon, Aran, Arran,
Arun, baron, barren, Darren, Karen,
marron, Sharon, saffron, scallion,
stallion, banyan, canyon, Ammon,
gammon, mammon, salmon, shaman,
cabman, chapman, Chapman,
Hackman, bagman, flagman, ragman,
swagman, adman, Bradman, Caedmon,
madman, batman, hangman, axeman,
cracksman, Flaxman, Paxman,
Manxman, batsman, Tasman,
bandsman, clansman, Flashman,
cannon, canon, Shannon, Casson,
Masson, flaxen, Jackson, klaxon, Saxon,
waxen, Datsun, Samson, Branson,
Jansen, Manson, Nansen, damson,
Kansan, ashen, fashion, passion, ration,
caption, action, faction, fraction,
traction, sanction, mansion, scansion,
stanchion, * Sri Lankan, Alaskan,
Nebraskan, Pendragon, Abaddon,
McFadden, abandon, Rwandan,
Ugandan, Manhattan, harmattan,
Mountbatten, Rockhampton,
Northampton, Southampton,
Okehampton, Hunstanton, Craigavon,
Van Allen, decathlon, heptathlon,
pentathlon, biathlon, triathlon,
McLaren, Biafran, battalion,
rapscallion, medallion, Italian,
companion, d'Artagnan, Cro-Magnon,
colcannon, Dungannon, Clackmannan,
Guianan, Guyanan, Rhiannon,
Montanan, Buchanan, compassion,
refashion, impassion, dispassion,
contraption, compaction, attraction,
protraction, subtraction, contraction,
abstraction, transaction, reaction,
impaction, detraction, retraction,
distraction, extraction, diffraction,
refraction, infraction, inaction,
exaction, olfaction, proaction,
expansion, * snapdragon, bandwagon,
backgammon, * Madagascan,
Littlehampton, Wolverhampton, jack-
o'-lantern, parrot-fashion, abreaction,
satisfaction, rarefaction, petrifaction,
benefaction, retroaction, interaction,
liquefaction, counteraction,
stupefaction, putrefaction,
* self-satisfaction, dissatisfaction,
counterattraction, overreaction,
overexpansion

I can't get no satisfaction
I can't get no girl reaction.
MICK JAGGER & KEITH RICHARDS

2.36 happened, blackened, maddened, saddened, flattened, patterned, Langland, gangland, Hammond, dachshund, rationed, sanctioned, * impassioned, old-fashioned, unsanctioned, etc.

2.37 calends, badlands, dachshunds

2.38 cabins, hatpins, Atkins, catkins, matins, satins, captains, aspirins, Kathryn's, * examines, assassins, etc.

2.39 dragons, flagons, wagons, battens, patterns, lanterns, caverns, taverns, Athens, gallons, talons, barons, Saxons, damsons, fashions, passions, rations, actions, factions, fractions, sanctions, mansions, etc.

2.40 lambent, rampant, bacchant, hadn't, patent, Havant, haven't, savant, advent, Advent, gallant, talent, arrant, Lamont, fragment, catchment, hatchment, stagnant, nascent, passant, absent, accent, hasn't, pageant, plangent, tangent, * attractant, surfactant, reactant, apparent, transparent, entrapment, encampment, embankment, enactment, abashment, encashment, attachment, detachment, renascent, relaxant, cotangent, * re-enactment

2.41 savants, balance, valance, talents, Clarence, fragments, nascence, absence, accents, pageants, * reactance, unbalance, imbalance, off-balance, outbalance, transparence, embankments, renascence, * counterbalance, overbalance, etc.

2.42 grabbing, stabbing, capping, clapping, flapping, mapping, napping, rapping, slapping, strapping, tapping, trapping, wrapping, yapping, scalping, camping, cramping, stamping, tramping, backing, blacking, cracking, hacking, lacking, packing, racking, sacking, slacking, smacking, stacking, tacking, tracking, whacking, banking, clanking, flanking, planking, ranking, spanking, thanking, bragging, dragging, flagging, gagging, lagging, nagging, sagging, wagging, adding, cladding, madding, padding, banding, landing, sanding, standing, batting, chatting, Gatting, matting, plaiting, ratting, tatting, acting, Banting, panting, ranting, chaffing, faffing, having, babbling, dabbling, brambling, gambling, rambling, grappling, sapling, crackling, tackling, angling, gangling, strangling, wrangling, handling, Gatling, rattling, baffling, handspring, hamstring, lapwing, waxwing, batwing, cramming, damming, jamming, lambing, shamming, banning, canning, Canning, Channing, manning, Manning, planning, tanning, banging, clanging, hanging, slanging, gassing, massing, lapsing, taxing, waxing, bashing, crashing, dashing, flashing, gnashing, lashing, mashing, slashing, smashing, thrashing, catching, matching, snatching, scratching, thatching, cadging, * unwrapping, decamping, revamping, unpacking, attacking, outranking, unflagging, debagging, upstanding, freestanding, outstanding, adapting, attracting, contracting, distracting, exacting, decanting, haranguing, relaxing, financing, * handclapping, backslapping, catnapping, kneecapping, kidnapping, phone-

tapping, backpacking, nerve-racking, hijacking, formatting, play-acting, programming, cliffhanging, square-bashing, gate-crashing, tongue-lashing, backscratching,
* understanding, notwithstanding, subcontracting, photographing, undermanning, overhanging,
* misunderstanding, etc.

**While I nodded, nearly napping,
    suddenly there came a tapping,
As of someone gently rapping, rapping
    at my chamber door.**
EDGAR ALLAN POE

2.43 scavenge, challenge

2.44 gallop, Gallup, Salop, scallop

2.45 haggis, caddis, Gladys, brattice, gratis, lattice, practice, practise, mantis, Travis, Alice, chalice, Challis, malice, palace, Sallis, Tallis, Clarice, Harris, Paris, Janice, Daphnis, axis, praxis, taxis, * malpractice, Atlantis, oxalis, Beaumaris, Onassis, * praying mantis, prophylaxis, peristalsis, * anaphylaxis, * *mutatis mutandis*

**They're changing guard at Buckingham
    Palace –
Christopher Robin went down with Alice.**
A. A. MILNE

2.46 Abbas, tapas, Malpas, campus, grampus, pampas, Bacchus, Gracchus, Angus, cactus, Sanctus, cantus, canvas, canvass, aphthous, Callas, callous, callus, Dallas, Pallas, phallus, thallus, hapless, strapless, backless, trackless, thankless, landless, atlas, Atlas, hatless, tactless, cashless, matchless, arras, Arras, harass, mattress, Patras, actress,

Lammas, stannous, drabness, dampness, blackness, slackness, frankness, Agnes, Magnus, badness, gladness, madness, sadness, blandness, grandness, flatness, aptness, rashness, Crassus, Lassus, lapsus, Kansas, captious, factious, fractious, anxious, * Barabbas, Cerne Abbas, Caracas, Damascus, acanthus, dianthus, embarrass, St Pancras, Las Palmas, marasmus, Erasmus, chiasmus, McManus, Manassas, Parnassus, * hippocampus, Diophantus, agapanthus, Rhadamanthus, Erymanthus, helianthus, polyanthus, disembarrass, benefactress, overanxious,
* Grammaticus, * Halicarnassus,
* track us, splash us, etc.

2.47 Trappist, Baptist, practised, backlist, blacklist, fascist,
* unpractised, * Anabaptist

2.48 drabbest, dampest, blackest, slackest, dankest, rankest, maddest, saddest, damnedest, blandest, grandest, fattest, canvassed, ballast, harassed, * embarrassed,
* unembarrassed, etc.

2.49 Lappish, snappish, blackish, brackish, Frankish, waggish, caddish, laddish, radish, Standish, blandish, brandish, flattish, catfish, flatfish, lavish, ravish, parish, vanquish, anguish, languish, Amish, famish, Spanish, banish, clannish, mannish, vanish, hashish, * outlandish, establish, McTavish, * horseradish,
* disestablish

2.50 abbot, Abbott, Cabot, Albert, Lambert, Ascot, mascot, agate, braggart, faggot, maggot, Taggart, Calvert, ballot, palate, Barrett, carat, caret, carrot, claret, garret, Garrett, Jarrett, parrot, gamut, cannot, magnate, * Newton Abbott

2.51 Babbitt, habit, rabbet, rabbit, ambit, gambit, lappet, tappet, sandpit, bracket, jacket, packet, placket, racket, blanket, gasket, bandit, pandit, pamphlet, davit, mallet, palette, pallet, valet, tablet, applet, caplet, chaplet, lamplit, backlit, anklet, flatlet, hamlet, Hamlet, Hazlitt, Sanskrit, banquet, dammit, Hammett, gannet, granite, Janet, planet, Thanet, magnet, asset, basset, facet, tacit, transit, Cratchit, Datchet, hatchet, Pratchett, ratchet, gadget, Paget, * inhabit, cohabit, Hugh Capet, in transit, * pay packet, straitjacket, * leatherjacket, lumberjacket, underblanket, Shepton Mallet, pomegranate, Narragansett, * electromagnet, * had it, catch it, etc.

2.52 sabbath, Lambeth, Gareth, Brandreth, Dankworth, Tamworth, mammoth, Falmouth

2.53 captive, active, massive, passive, * adaptive, attractive, subtractive, reactive, refractive, inactive, proactive, substantive, impassive, * maladaptive, interactive, hyperactive, overactive, underactive, unattractive, unreactive, * radioactive

2.54 abbeys, cabbies, nappies, lackeys, hankies, Yankees, baddies, caddies, Andes, candies, patties, panties, pasties, cafés, navvies, alleys, galleys, rallies, valleys, families, taxis, pansies, Ganges, * Cervantes, * vigilantes, Happy Families, * Ecclesiastes, etc.

2.55 clappers, sappers, champers, Pampers®, crackers, daggers, staggers, tatters, Danvers, ramblers, stragglers, anglers, Stranglers, antlers, Hannah's, manners, planners, lasses, masses, ashes, Ashes, flashes, sashes, patches, scratches, * maracas, molasses, * eyelashes, * carpetbaggers, etc.

Billy, in one of his nice new sashes,
Fell in the fire and was burnt to ashes.
HARRY GRAHAM

2.56 Jacobi, Appleby, canopy, Malachy, anarchy, Saturday, malady, parody, rhapsody, maggoty, Rafferty, carroty, faculty, atrophy, anchovy, apathy, Chatterley, latterly, Natalie, thankfully, tactfully, bashfully, gravelly, mannerly, palpably, affably, damnably, panoply, dastardly, gallantly, valiantly, randomly, handsomely, callously, tactlessly, anxiously, Hattersley, blackberry, Bradbury, Cadbury, Banbury, cranberry, Lansbury, hackery, quackery, Thackeray, Zachary, Calgary, battery, cattery, flattery, Slattery, factory, Calvary, calorie, gallery, Malory, salary, Valerie, saddlery, mammary, cannery, granary, stannary, tannery, brasserie, lingerie, Canterbury, Glastonbury, mandatory, lavatory, amatory, Daventry, gallantry, pageantry, cavalry, cannonry, canonry, alchemy, blasphemy, Laramie, balcony, Gascony, agony, Anthony, Antony, barony, Chamonix, scammony, Tammany, Saxony, calumny, abbacy, Battersea, fallacy, fantasy, bankruptcy, galaxy, Anglesey, allergy, * philanthropy, misanthropy, lycanthropy, O'Flaherty, catastrophe, philately, diastole, unmannerly, substantially, financially, infallibly, haphazardly, apparently, phylactery, refractory, olfactory, menagerie, preparatory, declaratory, retaliatory, defamatory, declamatory, exclamatory, inflammatory, explanatory, reactionary, academy, anatomy, transparency, analogy, metallurgy, tetralogy, * unilaterally, understandably, satisfactory, intercalary, haberdashery, self-explanatory, genealogy, mineralogy, * unsatisfactory, etc.

Oh, dear, what can the matter be?
Three old ladies locked in the lavatory,
They were there from Monday to
Saturday,
Nobody knew they were there.
Children's rhyme

2.57 plasticky, panicky, raggedy, Cassidy, tragedy, sanctity, chastity, cavity, gravity, suavity, charity, clarity, parity, amity, sanity, vanity, laxity, travesty, sacristy, amnesty, majesty, salsify, * rheumaticky, smart-alecky, Macavity, depravity, concavity, fatality, morality, banality, mentality, centrality, reality, legality, vitality, finality, formality, normality, mortality, causality, plurality, locality, modality, sodality, totality, tonality, duality, frugality, brutality, neutrality, vulgarity, polarity, barbarity, disparity, hilarity, alacrity, calamity, profanity, urbanity, inanity, insanity, humanity, capacity, rapacity, sagacity, voracity, pugnacity, mendacity, veracity, edacity, vivacity, tenacity, loquacity, audacity, opacity, fugacity, * nationality, rationality, practicality, abnormality, actuality, partiality, temporality,

generality, bestiality, speciality, technicality, sensuality, sexuality, personality, verticality, geniality, liberality, literality, immorality, triviality, principality, physicality, whimsicality, illegality, criminality, immortality, informality, topicality, logicality, hospitality, cordiality, joviality, functionality, punctuality, mutuality, capillarity, regularity, circularity, similarity, singularity, insularity, solidarity, Solidarity, popularity, jocularity, Christianity, inhumanity, perspicacity, pertinacity, incapacity, * irrationality, impracticality, impartiality, conventionality, potentiality, eventuality, materiality, ethereality, congeniality, conviviality, municipality, originality, illogicality, irregularity, subsidiarity, familiarity, dissimilarity, particularity, unpopularity, peculiarity, overcapacity, undercapacity, * sentimentality, instrumentality, universality, horizontality, spirituality, * confidentiality, homosexuality, artificiality, superficiality, individuality, territoriality, unfamiliarity, perpendicularity, * heterosexuality

O wearisome condition of humanity!
Born under one law, to another bound;
Vainly begot, and yet forbidden vanity;
Created sick, commanded to be sound.
Fulke Greville

2.58 shabbily, happily, scrappily, handily, chattily, nattily, scantily, angrily, family, cannily, flashily, radically, practically, tactically, frantically, drastically, classically, magically, tragically, rapidly, candidly, avidly, languidly, placidly, fancifully, actively, massively, passively, dazzlingly, lavishly, savagely, Valkyrie, category, allegory, banditry, planetary, sanitary, transitory, gadgetry, tapestry, baptistry, ancestry, sanguinary, savagery, sashimi, satiny, captaincy, chaplaincy, cabbagy, strategy, * unhappily, uncannily, sporadically, dramatically, grammatically, fanatically, pragmatically, ecstatically, emphatically, erratically, dogmatically, traumatically, romantically, fantastically, sarcastically, theatrically, nostalgically, attractively, substantively, impassively, outstandingly, subcategory, insanitary, imaginary, * sal volatile, satisfactorily, mathematically, democratically, thermostatically, systematically, diplomatically, automatically, unromantically, geographically, biographically, photographically, telepathically, interplanetary, * enthusiastically, * melodramatically, idiomatically, etc.

2.59 thankfully, tactfully, bashfully, annually, manually, casually, actually, factually, gradually, strangury, January, actuary, sanctuary, statutory, salutary, * contractually, etc.

2.60 galloper, massacre, Málaga, Canada, Agutter, amateur, shamateur, baluster, Pavlova, Agatha, Gallagher, mandala, traveller, caroller, Pamela, bachelor, Angela, Flamborough, Canberra, Ankara, agora, swaggerer, batterer, chatterer, flatterer, amphora, gatherer, camera, hammerer, stammerer, wagoner, flattener,

Kavanagh, Tavener, Taverner, canvasser, balancer, Lancashire, Staffordshire, aperture, tablature, tanager, calibre, calliper, Attica, trafficker, Africa, Anneka, brassica, Candida, lavender, calendar, calender, Lampeter, traditor, taffeta, catheter, janitor, ammeter, character, Alistair, barrister, banister, Bannister, canister, ancestor, Manchester, aquifer, Tabitha, algebra, Fatima, Latimer, maxima, patina, mariner, lamina, stamina, practiser, ravisher, vanquisher, packager, salvager, manager, scavenger, challenger, Salinger, Massinger, passenger, Slazenger, Papua, vacua, jaguar, Mantua, Padua, valuer, tabular, scapula, Dracula, macula, vascular, angular, glandular, spatula, blastula, valvular, annular, granular, * ambassador, parabola, enameller, Diaspora, mandragora, Niagara, philanderer, cataphora, anaphora, in camera, Te Kanawa, Northamptonshire, entablature, Excalibur, sciatica, cohabiter, per capita, parameter, pentameter, hexameter, diameter, voltameter, capacitor, submariner, examiner, Gargantua, coadjutor, oracular, vernacular, spectacular, rectangular, triangular, tarantula, campanula, * Addis Ababa, manufacturer, incunabula, unspectacular, * *deus ex machina*, cardiovascular

2.61 Gambia, Zambia, flabbier, shabbier, happier, scrappier, tackier, wackier, Saskia, baggier, shaggier, faddier, handier, randier, chattier, fattier, nattier, rattier, tattier, scantier, Mafia, raffia, clavier, Xavier, Latvia, salvia, Anthea, dallier, rallier, Anglia,

ganglia, barrier, carrier, farrier,
harrier, Harrier, tarrier, Cambria,
angrier, sangria, Andrea, kalmia,
cannier, pannier, daphnia, cassia,
gassier, glacier, fancier, Lancia,
brassiere, snazzier, catchier,
* unhappier, Slovakia, souvlakia,
Finlandia, agraphia, dysgraphia,
espalier, ophthalmia, Britannia,
Hispania, eclampsia, ataxia, apraxia,
dystaxia, dyspraxia, estancia,
financier, * chocolatier, Alitalia,
Alexandria, pre-eclampsia,
* Czechoslovakia, etc.

2.62 canopied, parodied, atrophied,
galleried, salaried

2.63 balloted, patented, talented,
rabbited, jacketed, blanketed,
faceted, * untalented, inhabited,
cohabited, * uninhabited,
multifaceted

2.64 mappable, palpable, placable,
sackable, stackable, bankable,
tractable, affable, fallible, arable,
parable, sparable, flammable,
scannable, damnable, taxable,
cashable, catchable, matchable,
frangible, tangible, manacle,
Arundel, palatal, mackerel, admiral,
lateral, natural, caramel, bacchanal,
national, rational, factional,
fractional, prandial, axial, mandible,
cannibal, Hannibal, maniple,
manciple, radical, practical, tactical,
canticle, graphical, clavicle, classical,
fascicle, magical, tragical, madrigal,
capital, Capitol, marital, sagittal,
fanciful, lacrimal, animal, maximal,
paginal, Samuel, annual, manual,
casual, actual, factual, tactual,

Rhyme

*The rhymes in this book are based on
the standard pronunciation of British
English, that is, the way words are
spoken in southern England by people
who do not have a regional accent.
Different rhymes are possible in other
parts of the English-speaking world.
In northern Britain, for example,
words such as* class, glass *and* grass
rhyme with gas *and* lass *rather than*
farce. *And in the USA,* missile
rhymes with whistle, *and* fertile *with*
turtle, *as in the following rhyme:*

**The turtle lives 'twixt plated decks
Which practically conceal its sex.
I think it clever of the turtle
In such a fix to be so fertile.**
OGDEN NASH

gradual, valuable, Hasdrubal, chasuble,
* unflappable, impalpable, implacable,
compatible, get-at-able, adaptable,
contactable, intractable, infallible,
inflammable, nonflammable,
programmable, irascible, impassible,
collapsible, nontaxable, unmatchable,
detachable, intangible, collateral,
bilateral, trilateral, Canaveral,
bicameral, unnatural, diaconal,
decagonal, heptagonal, pentagonal,
hexagonal, diagonal, octagonal,
irrational, transactional, preprandial,
postprandial, coaxial, sabbatical,
grammatical, fanatical, piratical,
unpractical, impractical, fantastical,
theatrical, botanical, mechanical,
tyrannical, pyramidal, premarital,
extramarital, Emmanuel, biannual,
contractual, invaluable,
* understandable, incompatible, un-
get-at-able, equilateral, quadrilateral,
multilateral, unilateral, unicameral,
preternatural, supernatural,
international, multinational,
mathematical, ungrammatical,
geographical, biographical,
typographical, puritanical, neoclassical,
* ecclesiastical, * archidiaconal,
lexicographical, * autobiographical

2.65 Absalom, Dagenham, Faversham,
Amersham, cambium, allium, gallium,
thallium, Valium®, capsicum,
maximum, platinum, Sandringham,
alyssum, stratagem, pabulum,
* chrysanthemum, potassium,
* mesembryanthemum

2.66 Aragon, paragon, tarragon,
Flanagan, mastodon, Clarendon,
Sarandon, Chatterton, Atherton,
Allerton, Appleton, Shackleton,

Athelstan, marathon, Marathon,
Callaghan, Hanrahan, Cameron,
Lateran, dragoman, abdomen,
Andaman, Bannerman, cattleman,
Algernon, Andersen, Anderson,
Patterson, Saracen, Mackeson,
Amundsen, Adamson, Amazon,
habergeon, pathogen, allergen,
halogen, androgen, Albion, Gambian,
Zambian, campion, Campion,
champion, Grampian, rampion,
tampion, Andean, Scandian, Dantean,
Kantian, bastion, Latvian, Pantheon,
galleon, scallion, stallion, Anglian,
ganglion, carrion, clarion, Darien,
Marian, Marion, Cambrian, Bactrian,
amnion, halcyon, Vatican, Anglican,
African, Rattigan, harridan, Macedon,
Chalcedon, Abingdon, Farringdon,
Hamilton, badminton, Badminton,
Babington, Addington, Paddington,
Allington, Barrington, Carrington,
Harrington, Accrington, lamington,
Galveston, sacristan, antiphon,
tallyman, Harriman, talisman,
Addison, Madison, Grandison,
Salvesen, Mathieson, Alison, malison,
garrison, Harrison, Acheson, Atkinson,
antigen, Papuan, Paduan, albumen,
acumen, * *Decameron*, Sanatogen®,
Slovakian, Atlantean, Sebastian,
battalion, rapscallion, medallion,
Italian, Heraklion, Calabrian,
Cantabrian, Lancastrian, Parnassian,
Circassian, South African, Penhaligon,
Mohammedan, Samaritan,
Saskatchewan, caparison, comparison,
gargantuan, * Tetragrammaton,
Trinidadian, Alexandrian, Zoroastrian,
* Czechoslovakian

2.67 battalions, Italians, shenanigans,
Samaritans, comparisons, etc.

2.68 arrogant, afferent, adamant, sacrament, battlement, bafflement, harassment, assonant, ambient, sapient, valiant, transient, applicant, accident, habitant, palpitant, aspirant, aliment, blandishment, ravishment, banishment, management, abstinent, adjutant, adjuvant, ambulant, flatulent, * extravagant, entanglement, abandonment, embarrassment, inhabitant, cohabitant, recalcitrant, aggrandizement, enfranchisement, establishment, Establishment, disparagement, mismanagement, contaminant, intransigent, coadjutant, coagulant, * self-aggrandizement, disenfranchisement, * anticoagulant

2.69 arrogance, transference, sacraments, battlements, assonance, ambience, sapience, dalliance, transience, applicants, accidents, appetence, blandishments, abstinence, affluence, ambulance, flatulence, * extravagance, mésalliance, inhabitants, inappetence, capacitance, recalcitrance, intransigence, etc.

2.70 galloping, à la king, barracking, scaffolding, travelling, atheling, jabbering, scampering, tampering, hankering, battering, flattering, nattering, scattering, shattering, smattering, gathering, clamouring, hammering, stammering, Angmering, happening, maddening, fattening, ravening, rationing, canvassing, balancing, Mafeking, trafficking, panicking, practising, brandishing, ravishing, packaging, savaging, managing, scavenging, challenging, * enamelling, meandering, unflattering, embarrassing, etc.

2.71 Antrobus, abacus, hazardous, scandalous, tantalus, Tantalus, talentless, fathomless, cankerous, rancorous, clangorous, languorous, valorous, amorous, clamorous, glamorous, cancerous, Lazarus, rapturous, blasphemous, thalamus, cavernous, ravenous, backwardness, bashfulness, barrenness, callousness, Thaddeus, Marius, pancreas, aqueous, Cassius, gaseous, platypus, varicose, Tacitus, acetous, Angelus, Stanislas, animus, flabbiness, shabbiness, happiness, cattiness, chattiness, tattiness, gangrenous, vacuous, fatuous, garrulous, fabulous, calculus, valueless, annulus, * Caratacus, Galapagos, analogous, asparagus, cantankerous, Pythagoras, Protagoras, unglamorous, ambassadress, diaphanous, left-handedness, right-handedness, Germanicus, Britannicus, calamitous, magnanimous, unanimous, unhappiness, gelatinous, attractiveness, miraculous, * hypothalamus, pusillanimous, Circus Maximus, cartilaginous, oleaginous, Anaxagoras, mucilaginous, ignis fatuus, * Ecclesiasticus, etc.

2.72 flabbiest, shabbiest, happiest, scrappiest, tackiest, wackiest, baggiest, shaggiest, faddiest, handiest, randiest, chattiest, fattiest, nattiest, rattiest, tattiest, scantiest, angriest, canniest, gassiest, fanciest, snazziest, catchiest, * unhappiest, etc.

2.73 anarchist, masochist, dramatist, pragmatist, catalyst, analyst, panellist, Accurist®, mannerist, alchemist, agonist, Jansenist, allergist, pantheist, pacifist, amethyst, activist, satirist,

animist, Calvinist, classicist, strategist,
altruist, * philanthropist, philatelist,
tobacconist, antagonist, protagonist,
metallurgist, evangelist, romanticist,
somnambulist, * sadomasochist,
psychoanalyst, televangelist,
genealogist, mineralogist,
neoclassicist

2.74 parapet, advocate, accurate,
baronet, passionate, chariot, Harriet,
lariat, Marriott, Marryat, patriot,
halibut, aggregate, candidate, aspirate,
adequate, animate, cabinet, laminate,
graduate, Capulet, amulet, * elaborate,
inaccurate, diaconate, permanganate,
compassionate, dispassionate,
Plantagenet, Iscariot, compatriot,
expatriate, inadequate, inanimate,
Palatinate, postgraduate, ejaculate,
immaculate, * undergraduate,
* overelaborate

2.75 Nazareth, azimuth

2.76 palaces, radishes, cabbages,
packages, bandages, savages, carriages,
Claridge's, garages, languages,
challenges, etc.

2.77 faculties, blackberries, cranberries,
calories, Stannaries, lavatories,
fantasies, allergies, cavities, charities,
tapestries, * profanities, * similarities,
* peculiarities, etc.

2.78 admiralty, casualty, naturally,
nationally, rationally, gradually,

actually, factually, annually, manually,
casually, lamentably, fashionably,
amicably, charitably, admirably,
accurately, passionately, adequately,
maddeningly, amorously, glamorously,
ravenously, Canterbury, Glastonbury,
adversary, farriery, January, statuary,
actuary, sanctuary, cabinetry, casuistry,
sanctimony, antimony, alimony,
palimony, acrimony, matrimony,
patrimony, advocacy, accuracy,
magistracy, adequacy, baronetcy,
* unnaturally, diagonally, irrationally,
spectacularly, uncharitably,
inaccurately, compassionately,
dispassionately, inadequately,
contractually, immaculately,
comparatively, embarrassingly,
disparagingly, magnanimously,
unanimously, miraculously,
constabulary, vocabulary, inadequacy,
inaccuracy, * supernaturally,
internationally, unimaginably

2.79 palatable, lamentable, admirable,
fathomable, fashionable, malleable,
fanciable, practicable, amicable,
navigable, habitable, charitable,
salvageable, marriageable, damageable,
manageable, valuable, calculable,
* unpalatable, unfathomable,
companionable, unfashionable,
eradicable, impracticable,
uncharitable, imaginable,
unsalvageable, unmanageable,
invaluable, incalculable,
* ineradicable, indefatigable,
uninhabitable, unimaginable

-ah-

The rhymes in this section have the 'ah' sound of half and larder as their main or final vowel sound

3.1 ah, are, baa, bah, bar, Barr, *barre*, Blois, bra, car, Carr, char, fa, far, Fra, gar, ha, haar, jar, la, lar, Loire, ma, mar, moire, noir, pa, pah, par, parr, Parr, pas, qua, R, Ra, Saar, Sarre, scar, schwa, shah, ska, spa, Spa, spar, star, Starr, ta, tar, tsar, yah, * Dunbar, papa, catarrh, afar, Navarre, galah, hurrah, Accra, mama, hussar, bazaar, ajar, Qatar, ta-ta, Stranraer, aha, ha-ha, tra-la, foie gras, sang-froid, François, Armagh, Lehár, *bête noire*, Del Mar, ER, PR, debar, disbar, cigar, guitar, sitar, film noir, bizarre, OR, faux pas, beaux-arts, * kasbah, grandpa, Caspar, fracas, tramcar, ashlar, fatwa, patois, Valois, chamois, Magyar, grandma, gaga, Dada, ha-ha, La-La, rah-rah, wah-wah, Zsa Zsa, railcar, agar, Degas, radar, daystar, Braemar, Tamar, quasar, feldspar, Redcar, Elgar, Telstar, Kevlar®, memoir, Renoir, earthstar, heel bar, streetcar, dinar, kiblah, Ingmar, sidecar, Weimar, nightjar, crossbar, stock car, boxcar, sol-fa, Colmar, bourgeois, crowbar, towbar, rollbar, co-star, lodestar, Omagh, Omar, sonar, pulsar, toolbar, oompah, nougat, doodah, Utah, Pooh-Bah, hoo-ha, hoopla, boudoir, Dumas, * rum baba, * Calabar, Malabar, handlebar, grandpapa, advocaat, avatar, baklava, samovar, Kandahar, Yamaha, baccarat, abattoir, jacamar, Palomar, grandmama, Panama, Balthazar, caviar, Zanzibar, Hamilcar, iechyd da, Shangri-la, Cantuar., armoured car, R&R, Amen-Ra, langue de chat, entrechat, cha-cha-cha, la-di-da, Mardi Gras, cable car, steak tartare, *aide-mémoire*, APR, megastar, Hezbollah, repertoire, reservoir, SLR, Peckinpah, registrar, petit pois, escritoire, seminar, deodar, Nicobar, cinnabar, millibar, minibar, isobar, Myanmar, Bogotá, waratah, *objet d'art*, Bolivar, Lochinvar, commissar, touring car, Eurostar, motor car, Omaha, *au revoir*, under par, um and ah, cultivar, Buddh Gaya, coolabah, superstar, brouhaha, coup d'état, rouge et noir, Cooch Behar, * conservatoire, * Leamington Spa, kala-azar, *ménage à trois, je ne sais quoi*, budgerigar, avoirdupois

Man's heart expands to tinker with his car
For this is Sunday morning, Fate's great bazaar.
LOUIS MACNEICE

3.2 barb, carb, garb, Saab, sahib, * nawab, Punjab, memsahib, * bicarb, rhubarb

3.3 arc, ark, Bach, bark, Braque, Clark, Clarke, clerk, dark, hark, Jacques, lark, marc, Marc, mark, Mark, marque, narc, nark, park, Park, plaque, quark, Sark, shark, snark, spark, Spark, stark, Stark, * macaque, Kazakh, Lamarck, black mark, debark, embark, Iraq, remark, Remarque, Hyde Park, * bank clerk, landmark, car park, aardvark, waymark, trademark, Petrarch, tetrarch, Denmark, benchmark, birthmark, earmark, skid mark, Widmark, Bismarck, hierarch, tyre mark, skylark, tidemark, Reichsmark, pockmark, ballpark, hallmark, Deutschmark, postmark, loan shark, mudlark, brushmark, woodlark, bookmark, footmark, Plutarch, * matriarch, patriarch, telemark, meadowlark, Regent's Park, re-embark, in the dark, fingermark, disembark, Offenbach, oligarch, watermark, Joan of Arc, double-park, Cutty Sark

3.4 arcs, Bach's, Berks, clerks, larks, Marks, Mark's, Marx, parks, Parkes, sharks, sparks, * landmarks, benchmarks, stretchmarks, pockmarks, brushmarks, footmarks, etc.

3.5 barked, marked, parked, * unmarked, embarked, infarct, remarked, * waymarked, earmarked, pockmarked, hallmarked, postmarked, bookmarked, * disembarked, unremarked, double-parked, etc.

3.6 arch, larch, march, March, parch, starch, * frogmarch, cornstarch, routemarch, * overarch

3.7 arched, marched, parched, starched, * unstarched, * frogmarched, routemarched, * overarched

3.8 baaed, bard, barred, card, chard, charred, Dard, guard, hard, jarred, lard, marred, pard, Sade, sard, shard, scarred, sparred, starred, tarred, yard, Yard, * charade, façade, saccade, estrade, debarred, disbarred, discard, regard, petard, retard, ill-starred, jihad, glissade, bombard, *en garde*, rock-hard, pomade, roulade, * Jacquard, placard, scratchcard, vanguard, Ballard, mallard, Garrard, back yard, canard, Hansard, mansard, smart card, farmyard, barnyard, railcard, racecard, safeguard, graveyard, kaleyard, Maynard, Gerard, churchyard, rearguard, steelyard, Rickard, Liskeard, Fishguard, shipyard, brickyard, vineyard, Izzard, wild card, lifeguard, diehard, spikenard, fireguard, Lombard, Stoppard, Goddard, bollard, Lollard, Pollard, dockyard, stockyard, scorecard, courtyard, postcard, phonecard, Bogarde, coastguard, boatyard, boneyard, mudguard, junkyard, Coulthard, foulard, schoolyard, Cunard, * battle-scarred, Abelard, avant-garde, Savoyard, Everard, esplanade, credit card, self-regard, birthday card, Kierkegaard, greetings card, leotard, zindabad, Isambard, interlard, timberyard, Hilliard, milliard, disregard, Scotland Yard, promenade, bodyguard, Communard, boulevard, * Islamabad, * Allahabad, Faisalabad, Hyderabad, camelopard, fanfaronade, Marquis de Sade, rodomontade

No memory of having starred
Atones for later disregard,
Or keeps the end from being hard.
ROBERT FROST

3.9 barf, calf, chaff, graph, half, laugh, quaff, scarf, Scarfe, staff, strafe, * carafe, behalf, giraffe, Clontarf, * flagstaff, Metcalfe, headscarf, distaff, tipstaff, pikestaff, digraph, Falstaff, mooncalf, * tachograph, Van de Graaff, barograph, paragraph, shadowgraph, Cenotaph, stenograph, epitaph, epigraph, telegraph, Dictograph®, pictograph, lithograph, spirograph, micrograph, seismograph, Chinagraph®, logograph, holograph, homograph, chronograph, monograph, polygraph, quarterstaff, autograph, photograph, phonograph, * cardiograph, radiograph, ideograph, Mimeograph®, choreograph, * encephalograph

3.10 aft, barfed, chaffed, craft, daft, draft, draught, graft, haft, Kraft, laughed, quaffed, raft, shaft, staffed, waft, * abaft, unstaffed, redraft, engraft, * handcraft, crankshaft, camshaft, aircraft, statecraft, spacecraft, stagecraft, fieldcraft, priestcraft, lift shaft, kingcraft, witchcraft, drive shaft, mine shaft, swordcraft, downdraught, updraught, woodcraft, bushcraft, * handicraft, needlecraft, hovercraft, watercraft, overstaffed, photographed, overdraft, understaffed, Wollstonecraft

3.11 blague, Prague, * Camargue, Den Haag, * Reichstag, * Bundestag

3.12 barge, charge, hajj, large, marg, marge, raj, sarge, Taj, targe, * the Raj, recharge, enlarge, in charge, discharge, * surcharge, discharge, * turbocharge, countercharge, overlarge, overcharge, undercharge, supercharge

3.13 plage, raj, * the Raj, ménage, sondage, frottage, potage, montage, collage, corsage, * barrage, garage, massage, dressage, mirage, triage, * badinage, cabotage, sabotage, camouflage, arbitrage, décolletage, decoupage, reportage, persiflage, bricolage, bon voyage, entourage, curettage, fuselage, * espionage, photomontage, * counterespionage

3.14 Arles, Baal, Basle, Carl, Dahl, dhal, gnarl, Karl, kraal, marl, snarl, toile, * Natal, corral, morale, Jamal, Kemal, banal, unsnarl, timbale, halal, Chantal, Vidal, chorale, Bhopal, locale, * Transvaal, Stendahl, mistral, * *femme fatale*, pastorale, Albemarle, rationale, Parsifal, Taj Mahal, Heyerdahl, Emmenthal, Provençal, Provençale, * Neanderthal, Massif Central, Escorial, * Internationale, *succès de scandale*, entente cordiale

3.15 Arles, Charles, Karl's, snarls, etc.

3.16 arm, balm, barm, calm, charm, farm, Guam, harm, ma'am, palm, psalm, qualm, smarm, * madame, alarm, salaam, unarm, rearm, embalm, becalm, imam, disarm, forearm, * yardarm, gendarme, napalm, wind farm, Islam, firearm, forearm, schoolmarm, * Notre Dame, overarm, underarm, * Dar es Salaam, Omar Khayyám

3.17 armed, calmed, charmed, farmed, harmed, * unarmed, unharmed, alarmed, rearmed, embalmed, becalmed, disarmed, forearmed

3.18 alms, arms, Brahms, farms,

Glamis, palms, Psalms, qualms,
* alarms, salaams, rearms, embalms,
becalms, * gendarmes, wind farms,
firearms, etc.

Ben Battle was a soldier bold,
And used to war's alarms:
But a canon-ball took off his legs,
So he laid down his arms!
THOMAS HOOD

3.19 Arne, barn, darn, Hahn, Juan,
khan, Khan, Marne, naan, Sian, tarn,
yarn, * Pathan, pavane, Amman,
McMahon, Hassan, Kazan, Aswan,
Antoine, Tehran, élan, Vientiane,
Tzigane, Iran, Gibran, Sichuan, Dayan,
Taiwan, Koran, Don Juan, Osman,
Oran, Oman, Qumran, Cwmbran,
lucarne, Sudan, Bhutan, * astrakhan,
Astrakhan, Abadan, Ramadan, Karajan,
Kazakhstan, Pakistan, Dagestan,
macedoine, Abidjan, Bantustan, Aga
Khan, Rajasthan, Shah Jahan, Genghis
Khan, Turkestan, Kyrgyzstan,
Kurdistan, Isfahan, Christiaan,
Lindisfarne, Hindustan, t'ai chi
ch'uan, Omdurman, autobahn,
Yucatán, Suleiman, Kublai Khan,
* Afghanistan, Uzbekistan,
Turkmenistan, Tajikistan, Azerbaijan,
Baluchistan

3.20 blanch, Blanche, branch, ranch,
stanch, tranche, * carte blanche,
* avalanche

3.21 darned, * command, demand,
remand, * reprimand, countermand

3.22 chance, dance, France, glance,
lance, prance, stance, trance, Vance,
aunts, chants, grants, plants, * askance,

Provence, advance, perchance,
enhance, entrance, mischance, faïence,
* seance, freelance, off-chance,
mumchance, nuance, * happenstance,
ambience, Afrikaans, renaissance,
Renaissance, circumstance,
contredanse, * par excellence,
* pièce de résistance

O body swayed to music, O brightening
glance,
How can we know the dancer from the
dance?
W. B. YEATS

3.23 aren't, aunt, can't, chant, grant,
Grant, Nantes, plant, shan't, slant,
* supplant, aslant, transplant, détente,
replant, implant, enchant,
* transplant, ashplant, plainchant,
eggplant, implant, house plant,
* debutante, disenchant,
commandant, confidante

3.24 Barnes, barns, darns, naans, Sian's,
tarns, yarns, * Afrikaans, Genghis
Khan's, etc.

3.25 Arp, carp, harp, scarp, sharp,
Sharpe, tarp, * cardsharp, * razor-
sharp, Polycarp

3.26 arse, baas, brass, class, farce, glass,
grass, Mass, pass, sparse, * surpass,
Madras, stained glass, third-class,
first-class, volte-face, outclass,
* impasse, smartarse, bypass, eyeglass,
spyglass, wineglass, Snodgrass,
knotgrass, hourglass, subclass,
bluegrass, goosegrass, * gravitas,
Stallybrass, galloglass, sparrowgrass,
masterclass, second-class, Plexiglas®,
working-class, middle-class, Khyber

Pass, fibreglass, isinglass, overpass, underpass, upper-class, underclass, superclass, supergrass, *coup de grâce*, * snake in the grass

3.27 ask, bask, basque, Basque, cask, casque, flask, mask, masque, task, * unmask, * Monégasque, overtask, multitask

The trivial round, the common task,
Would furnish all we ought to ask.
JOHN KEBLE

3.28 asked, basked, masked,
* unmasked, unasked, etc.

3.29 clasp, gasp, grasp, hasp, rasp,
* unclasp

3.30 arsed, blast, cast, caste, classed, fast, grassed, karst, last, mast, passed, past, vast, * surpassed, aghast, avast, contrast, half-mast, recast, repast, miscast, dismast, outclassed, outlast, * rat-arsed, sandblast, mainmast, webcast, steadfast, Belfast, wormcast, precast, bypassed, flypast, typecast, contrast, topmast, forecast, broadcast, sportscast, foremast, outcast, downcast, stonecast, holdfast, roughcast, Buckfast, newscast, * flabbergast, narrowcast, hard and fast, Prendergast, telecast, simulcast, mizzenmast, Gormenghast, counterblast, overcast, opencast, unsurpassed, colourfast, * Elastoplast®

Love in a palace is perhaps at last
More grievous torment than a hermit's
fast.
JOHN KEATS

3.31 harsh, marsh, * moustache, panache, *démarche*, gouache, * Titchmarsh

3.32 art, Bart, Barthes, cart, chart, dart, fart, hart, Hart, Harte, heart, kart, mart, part, Scart, smart, start, tart, * apart, spare part, Descartes, restart, depart, impart, stop-start, outsmart, * rampart, handcart, Cathcart, Earhart, redstart, Bernhardt, teacart, restart, sweetheart, Britart, kick-start, Reinhardt, op art, dogcart, Lockhart, forepart, mouthpart, Hobart, go-kart, Bogart, Mozart, flow chart, dustcart, upstart, pushcart, Stuttgart, * applecart, à la carte, heart-to-heart, counterpart, D'Oyly Carte, Bonaparte, underpart, Bundesrat, Gujarat, * state-of-the-art

Words may be false and full of art,
Sighs are the natural language of the
heart.
THOMAS SHADWELL

3.33 arts, Bart's, carts, charts, clarts, darts, farts, hearts, Herts, karts, parts, smarts, starts, tarts, * ramparts, handcarts, sweethearts, foreparts, mouthparts, Mozart's, * underparts, etc.

3.34 bath, Bath, Ba'th, garth, Garth, hearth, lath, path, * birdbath, eyebath, warpath, towpath, Hogarth, bloodbath, mudbath, footpath, * aftermath

3.35 calve, carve, grave, Graves, halve, Slav, starve, suave, varve, * Algarve, Gustave, Zouave, * Yugoslav

3.36 calves, halves, scarves,
* headscarves, mooncalves

3.37 bars, cars, jars, Lars, Mars, parse, SARS, scars, stars, vase, * hussars, bazaars, Shiraz, three Rs, cigars, guitars, * memoirs, Renoir's, co-stars, Gauloise, * handlebars, grandpapa's, seminars, vichyssoise, * salade niçoise, etc.

Have you heard it's in the stars,
Next July we collide with Mars?
COLE PORTER

4.1 Barbie®, Darby, Derby, harpy, * kohlrabi, Punjabi, Mugabe, okapi, * Hammurabi, Abu Dhabi

4.2 khaki, larky, narky, parky, sake, Saki, sarky, sparky, Starkey, * malarkey, menarche, Iraqi, * hierarchy, squirearchy, autarky, * Nagasaki, Kawasaki, Yamasaki, teriyaki, matriarchy, patriarchy, oligarchy, sukiyaki

4.3 cardie, hardy, Hardie, Hardy, lardy, Mahdi, mardy, tardy, Yardie, arty, clarty, hearty, party, Smartie, smarty, crafty, draughty, auntie, nasty, * Bacardi®, Lombardi, Coolgardie, chapati, karate, Frascati, Astarte, coati, * foolhardy, * Maserati, charterparty, arty-farty, digerati, glitterati, literati, Moriarty, Gujarati, arty-crafty, * Laurel and Hardy, illuminati

And he chirped and sang, and skipped
about, and laughed with laughter
hearty –
He was wonderfully active for so very
stout a party.
W. S. GILBERT

4.4 ave, Garvey, Harvey, jarvey, larvae,

Ravi, * Gaddafi, agave, peccavi, Mojave, McCarthy, * Rikki-Tikki-Tavi

4.5 Ali, Bali, barley, Carly, charlie, Charlie, Dali, Farley, gnarly, Harley, Kali, Mali, Marley, parley, Raleigh, snarly, sharply, Barclay, Berkeley, clerkly, darkly, sparkly, starkly, hardly, Yardley, Hartley, partly, smartly, ghastly, lastly, vastly, suavely, calmly, Darnley, parsley, sparsely, Barnsley, harshly, archly, largely, Marie, sari, starry, tarry, raspberry, * tamale, Svengali, Diwali, finale, bizarrely, Somali, safari, Polari, Ferrari, Harare, Vasari, Campari®, Qatari, Cagliari, curare, Scutari, Malawi, Mascagni, * Muhammad Ali, Ras Tafari, Kalahari, calamari, Stradivari, Mata Hari, Carbonari, charivari, etc.

4.6 army, balmy, barmy, palmy, smarmy, swami, Arnie, barney, Barney, blarney, Carney, rani, sarnie, Varney, * salami, pastrami, gourami, tsunami, Afghani, Galvani, Armani, Killarney, Giovanni, Omani, McCartney, * origami, Mantovani, maharani, Rafsanjani, frangipani, Pakistani, Mastroianni, biryani, Hindustani, Modigliani, * Azerbaijani, chilli con carne, * debar me, harm me, etc.

4.7 brassy, classy, Darcy, Farsi, glassy, grassy, Nazi, chancy, khazi, quasi, Stasi, Swazi, malmsey, marshy, Archie, starchy, bhaji, * Nastase, Benghazi, Givenchy, Karachi, hibachi, * Ashkenazi, Ashkenazy, kamikaze, Esterházy, mariachi, Liberace, Fibonacci, argy-bargy

4.8 arbour, barber, Barber, Barbour®,

harbour, Saba, carper, Harper, scarper,
sharper, gasper, grasper, * macabre,
Ann Arbor, Pearl Harbor, rum baba,
* Ali Baba, etc.

4.9 Barker, darker, Farquhar, marker,
markka, parka, Parker, starker, Tarka,
asker, masker, Aga®, laager, lager, raga,
saga, * Osaka, moussaka, Lusaka,
* backmarker, waymarker, * Titicaca,
nosy parker, Aga saga, * Hamilcar
Barca, * nark her, ask her, etc.

It is no time for mirth and laughter,
The cold, grey dawn of the morning
**   after.**
GEORGE ADE

4.10 ardour, Bader, cadre, carder,
Garda, harder, Lada®, larder, RADA,
Pravda, slander, barter, charter, carter,
Carter, darter, data, garter, Garter,
martyr, sartor, smarter, Sparta, starter,
strata, tartar, Tartar, after, dafter,
grafter, laughter, rafter, chanter,
Granta, grantor, planter, blaster, caster,
castor, Castor, faster, master, pastor,
plaster, * Haggadah, Granada,
lambada, armada, cicada, retarder,
Nevada, commander, Jakarta, toccata,
sonata, substrata, cassata, passata,
cantata, self-starter, Inkatha,
Siddhartha, frittata, errata, stigmata,
Renata, nonstarter, pro rata, thereafter,
whereafter, hereafter, Vedanta,
headmaster, disaster, old master,
* sought-after, bandmaster,
grandmaster, taskmaster, paymaster,
webmaster, ringmaster, quizmaster,
choirmaster, forecaster, broadcaster,
scoutmaster, housemaster, postmaster,
toastmaster, newscaster, schoolmaster,
* enchilada, Eid-ul-Adha, *intifada*,

promenader, Torquemada, Alexander,
Magna Carta, alma mater, Stabat
Mater, chipolata, protomartyr,
thereinafter, hereinafter, alabaster,
harbour master, stationmaster, ghetto
blaster, burgomaster, concertmaster,
quartermaster, * piña colada,
inamorata, *La Traviata*, desiderata,
persona grata, * *persona non grata*,
* taramasalata, Río de la Plata,
* medulla oblongata, * guard her,
outsmart her, etc.

See-saw, Margery Daw,
Jacky shall have a new master;
Jacky shall have but a penny a day,
Because he can't work any faster.
NURSERY RHYME

4.11 laugher, staffer, carver, Carver,
fava, guava, Java, larva, lava, laver,
Arthur, Martha, farther, father, lather,
rather, * Mustapha, cadaver, palaver,
cassava, MacArthur, * grandfather,
stepfather, godfather, forefather,
* balaclava, Balaklava, Bratislava, Costa
Brava, * bath her, starve her, etc.

4.12 Carla, gala, Mahler, parlour,
snarler, sampler, sparkler, chandler,
Chandler, Clara, Lara, Sara, Tara, Zara,
Barbara, Sandra, Chartres, Sartre,
genre, Farquhar, * cabbala, masala,
Kampala, La Scala, Marsala, impala,
koala, Uppsala, Sahara, Carrara,
Ferrara, Tamara, cascara, mascara,
tiara, O'Hara, O'Mara, macabre,
Cassandra, Sinatra, Montmartre,
Sumatra, Le Havre, Chihuahua,
Campagna, * Guatemala, McNamara,
capybara, carbonara, Che Guevara,
Connemara, candelabra, Alexandra,
Okinawa, Kurosawa, * Guadalajara,

double entendre, * Emilia-Romagna, etc.

4.13 amah, armour, Balmer, Brahma, calmer, charmer, dharma, drama, farmer, Kama, karma, lama, llama, Palmer, Parma, Rama, Schama, bwana, Dana, darner, garner, Garner, Ghana, Lana, Marner, nana, Wagner, gardener, Gardner, Lardner, pardner, partner, * embalmer, Osama, cabana, sultana, banana, *mañana*, Svetlana, nirvana, Tijuana, Guiana, Guyana, liana, gymkhana, piranha, Tirana, iguana, Fontana, Montana, Botswana, * snake charmer, * Atacama, panorama, Dalai Lama, melodrama, Cinerama®, diorama, cyclorama, psychodrama, docudrama, Yokohama, Tatiana, Mariana, Africana, Afrikaner, marijuana, Santayana, Pax Romana, Mahayana, ikebana, Indiana, Lipizzaner, Weimaraner, Silas Marner, Rosh Hashanah, vox humana, Gloriana, rusticana, Juliana, Ljubljana, * Australiana, Americana, Shakespeareana, Louisiana, Victoriana, Edwardiana, * Vasco da Gama, *Fata Morgana*, Bophuthatswana, * Carmina Burana, * ipecacuanha, * harm her, disarm her, etc.

There was a young lady of Parma, Whose conduct grew calmer and calmer.
EDWARD LEAR

4.14 Lhasa, passer, sparser, answer, chancer, dancer, lancer, prancer, Gaza, parser, plaza, harsher, Marsha, pasha, Berkshire, archer, Archer, marcher, starcher, rancher, pasture, charger, larger, rajah, slàinte, * Kinshasa,

advancer, enhancer, departure, recharger, enlarger, discharger, * maharajah, turbocharger, supercharger, * tabula rasa, * entrance her, charge her, etc.

4.15 charlock, Charnock, * Kilmarnock

4.16 Harpic®, bardic, artic, Partick, arctic, Arctic, yardstick, Narvik, Slavic, garlic, Harlech, Hardwick, karmic, arsenic, carsick, heartsick, Tajik, * anarchic, hierarchic, monarchic, Sephardic, cathartic, subarctic, Antarctic, lethargic, * subantarctic

4.17 harboured, larboard, starboard, scarpered, guarded, charted, chartered, martyred, parted, started, drafted, shafted, granted, slanted, bastard, blasted, plastered, Dartford, Hartford, Hertford, Harvard, fathered, armoured, garnered, answered, * unguarded, regarded, retarded, bombarded, uncharted, unchartered, hardhearted, half-hearted, faint-hearted, departed, imparted, big-hearted, kind-hearted, light-hearted, softhearted, warm-hearted, stouthearted, downhearted, wholehearted, enchanted, unanswered, * unregarded, disregarded, tenderhearted, heavy-hearted, brokenhearted, disenchanted, flabbergasted, etc.

4.18 garbage, yardage, vantage, Carthage, carnage, cartridge, partridge, Partridge, * advantage, * disadvantage

4.19 barbel, garble, marble, Schnabel, carpal, carpel, Marple, sample, sparkle, rascal, gargle, startle, stratal, artful, harmful, carvel, larval, Havel, marvel, Marvell, Cherwell, narwhal, Carmel, carnal, charnel, darnel, Parnell, Hartnell, castle, parcel, tarsal, chancel, Basel, marshal, Marshall, martial, Martial, partial, * ensemble, example, debacle, monarchal, catarrhal, impartial, court-martial, * sandcastle, Hardcastle, Newcastle, Boscastle, Oldcastle, * metacarpal, matriarchal, patriarchal, metatarsal

I'm the king of the castle,
Get down, you dirty rascal.
<small>CHILDREN'S RHYME</small>

4.20 garbled, marbled, sampled, startled, Arnold, marshalled, * court-martialled, * unexampled, etc.

4.21 marbles, Sharples, samples, castles, parcels, etc.

4.22 Markham, stardom, datum, stratum, Harlem, slalom, Arnhem, Barnum, Farnham, * substratum, erratum, postpartum, alarum, * superstardom, superstratum, candelabrum, * desideratum, * park 'em, guard 'em, etc.

4.23 Larkin, parkin, sharkskin, calfskin, bargain, marten, martin, Martin, Marvin, marlin, Stalin, Darwen, Darwin, Tarquin, Brahmin, margin, * Gagarin, * markin', starrin', etc.

4.24 carbon, sharpen, Aachen, darken, hearken, kraken, argon, jargon, Arden, Baden, garden, harden, lardon, pardon, Marsden, Aten, Barton, carton, hearten, smarten, Spartan,

tartan, Parton, Grafton, Carlton, Charlton, Marston, Charleston, carven, Javan, Marlon, Amen, barman, Brahman, Carmen, Jarman, Rahman, Scarman, marksman, craftsman, draughtsman, guardsman, arson, Carson, fasten, parson, sarsen, Clarkson, Tarzan, Martian, harshen, stanchion, Farjeon, * Petrarchan, Dumbarton, dishearten, Caernarfon, Carmarthen, Macfarlane, Saharan, Sumatran, unfasten, infarction, * Volkswagen, * hydrocarbon, Interlaken, Copenhagen, Covent Garden, Coloradan, Akhenaten, kindergarten, Sydney Carton, Dolly Parton, Aldermaston, Wilhelmshaven, Guatemalan, Tutankhamen

The kiss of the sun for pardon,
The song of the birds for mirth,
One is nearer God's heart in a garden
Than anywhere else on earth.
<small>DOROTHY FRANCES GURNEY</small>

4.25 sharpened, darkened, hardened, pardoned, garland, Garland, parkland, Cartland, marshland, almond, fastened, * disheartened, unfastened, etc.

4.26 bargains, martins, Darwin's, margins, * Doc Martens®, etc.

4.27 ardent, guardant, garment, parchment, argent, sergeant, Sargent, * retardant, disbarment, escarpment, bombardment, commandment, apartment, compartment, department, enchantment, advancement, enhancement, enlargement, * disenchantment, overgarment, undergarment, self-advancement

4.28 parlance, garments, sergeants, * commandments, apartments, compartments, departments, * overgarments, undergarments, etc.

4.29 carping, harping, grasping, rasping, barking, Barking, larking, marking, parking, asking, basking, masking, guarding, Harding, darting, farting, karting, parting, smarting, starting, drafting, grafting, shafting, chanting, planting, blasting, casting, fasting, lasting, laughing, staffing, calving, carving, starving, farthing, Carling, darling, Darling, marling, snarling, starling, marbling, sampling, darkling, sparkling, starveling, barring, marring, scarring, sparring, starring, arming, calming, charming, farming, harming, darning, classing, passing, parsing, dancing, glancing, lancing, prancing, arching, marching, parching, starching, branching, ranching, barging, charging, * embarking, unmasking, discarding, regarding, bombarding, commanding, demanding, departing, transplanting, enchanting, contrasting, alarming, embalming, disarming, surpassing, advancing, entrancing, recharging, enlarging, discharging, * skylarking, safeguarding, broadcasting, woodcarving, co-starring, bypassing, * multitasking, undemanding, everlasting, photographing, penny-farthing, overarching, overcharging, etc.

4.30 markings, castings, carvings, farthings, starlings, heartstrings, etc.

4.31 Sardis, Tardis, Jarvis, parvis, marquess, marquis, Frances, Francis,

* quo vadis, Polaris, catharsis, * aurora borealis

4.32 carpus, carcass, Marcus, Argus, Cardus, stratus, braless, Carlos, parlous, starless, artless, chartless, heartless, charmless, harmless, classless, grassless, slanderous, harness, sharpness, darkness, Harkness, starkness, hardness, smartness, tartness, fastness, vastness, calmness, harshness, tarsus, Tarsus, * Hipparchus, regardless, enchantress, disastrous, * steadfastness, * metacarpus, streptocarpus, Aristarchus, apparatus, altostratus, nimbostratus, cirrostratus, Nostradamus, *gaudeamus*, metatarsus, * posse comitatus, * coitus reservatus, * mark us, harm us, etc.

4.33 harpist, artist, Chartist, harvest, tsarist, palmist, psalmist, classist, Marxist, * guitarist, alarmist

4.34 sharpest, darkest, starkest, hardest, darnedest, smartest, daftest, fastest, farthest, calmest, harnessed, sparsest, harshest, etc.

4.35 sharpish, smartish, garfish, starfish, garnish, tarnish, varnish, * schoolmarmish

4.36 garnished, tarnished, varnished, * untarnished, unvarnished

4.37 Tarbert, Charlotte, harlot, Margaret, marmot, * incarnate, * reincarnate

4.38 carpet, armpit, market, basket, casket, target, Parfitt, scarlet, starlet, starlit, varlet, Bartlett, martlet, tartlet, halfwit, Barnet, garnet, Garnett, lancet, *Lancet*, * upmarket, Alf Garnett, downmarket, * Haymarket, Newmarket, breadbasket, * hypermarket, Common Market, supermarket, * park it, start it, etc.

An ape's an ape, a varlet's a varlet,
Though they be clad in silk or scarlet.
SAYING

4.39 Yarmouth, Dartmouth, * Great Yarmouth

4.40 darbies, harpies, parties, Smarties®, Barclays, armies, Nazis, * Pilates, Benares, * *primus inter pares*, etc.

4.41 barbers, Flanders, garters, rafters, casters, masters, Masters, Mahler's, Chalmers, farmers, classes, glasses, passes, answers, chances, glances, marshes, arches, archers, Archers, marches, Marches, branches, * Bahamas, pyjamas, sultanas, * forefathers, eyeglasses, sunglasses, * Alexander's, etc.

Men seldom make passes
At girls who wear glasses.
DOROTHY PARKER

4.42 Barnaby, Carnaby, Carnegie, Arcady, bastardy, Flaherty, Tarporley, rascally, masterly, artfully, fatherly, partially, laughably, ardently, guardedly, artlessly, heartlessly, Barbary, raspberry, Shaftesbury, artery, Tartary, mastery, carvery, chandlery, armoury, chancery, archery, Marjorie, harmony, argosy, pharmacy, garlicky,

suavity, sparsity, varsity, heartily, craftily, nastily, farcically, markedly, startlingly, charmingly, marquetry, parquetry, basketry, carpentry, artistry, palmistry, larceny, * grandfatherly, impartially, remarkably, half-heartedly, light-heartedly, wholeheartedly, disastrously, self-mastery, gendarmerie, chinoiserie, disharmony, foolhardily, lethargically, alarmingly, disarmingly, * camaraderie, Devanagari, intervarsity, etc.

4.43 Hanukkah, yarmulke, chancellor, Barbara, Scarborough, yarborough, Marlborough, Farnborough, slanderer, barterer, charterer, plasterer, armourer, Marmara, sharpener, bargainer, gardener, Gardiner, hardener, pardoner, almoner, fastener, Hertfordshire, armature, arbiter, Pargiter, carpenter, harvester, harnesser, Derbyshire, varnisher, harbinger, arguer, * Antarctica

4.44 clarkia, hardier, Nadia, heartier, craftier, draughtier, nastier, Parthia, aria, maria, barmier, Chania, Narnia, classier, Marcia, tarsier, chancier, starchier, * La Guardia, gaillardia, Somalia, Titania, intarsia, bilharzia, Abkhazia, * tachycardia, pericardia, Yugoslavia, passacaglia, Christiania, Kristiania, Oceania, Anastasia, etc.

4.45 Castleford, afterward, carpeted, marketed, targeted, harvested, * uncarpeted

4.46 Castleford's, afterwards

4.47 laughable, farmable, passable, chargeable, Barnstaple, barnacle,

masterful, pastoral, arsenal, Arsenal,
article, particle, farcical, Parsifal,
carnival, cardinal, marginal,
* remarkable, impassable,
rechargeable, anarchical, hierarchical,
* unremarkable, unsurpassable,
pericardial, myocardial

4.48 barnacled, Archibald, articled

4.49 martyrdom, marjoram,
cardamom, * pericardium,
myocardium, * started 'em, answer
'em, etc.

4.50 Harpenden, charlatan,
Palmerston, Parthenon, Farquharson,
Sanderson, guardian, Graafian,
Barthian, Parthian, Charmian,
Marmion, Marylebone, barbican,
Barbican, cardigan, Cardigan,
ptarmigan, Arlington, Darlington,
harvestman, partisan, Parkinson,
* Mozartian, Falstaffian, Hogarthian,
Somalian, Zimbabwean

4.51 parliament, armament, argument,
rearmament, disarmament

4.52 harbouring, scarpering, bartering,

answering, sharpening, darkening,
gardening, hardening, heartening,
fastening, carpeting, marketing,
garnishing, varnishing,
* telemarketing, etc.

4.53 Barnabas, Spartacus, marvellous,
fatherless, partnerless, barbarous,
slanderous, Tartarus, artfulness,
artlessness, heartlessness, arquebus,
Artemas, hardiness, tardiness,
heartiness, craftiness, nastiness,
arduous, * kind-heartedness, light-
heartedness, foolhardiness, etc.

4.54 arsonist, pharmacist, Dadaist,
Stalinist, Darwinist, narcissist,
* Neo-Darwinist

4.55 hardiest, heartiest, craftiest,
draughtiest, nastiest, barmiest,
classiest, chanciest, starchiest, etc.

4.56 marginally, arguably, chancellery,
arbitrary, parsimony

4.57 answerable, pardonable,
marketable, arguable, * unanswerable,
unpardonable, unmarketable,
unarguable

-air-

The rhymes in this section have the 'air' sound of hair and barely
as their main or final vowel sound.

5.1 air, Ayr, bare, bear, Blair, blare, br'er, care, chair, Cher, Claire, Clare, dare, e'er, ere, Eyre, fair, fare, fayre, flair, flare, glair, glare, hair, hare, heir, Herr, Khmer, lair, mare, mayor, ne'er, pair, pare, pear, *père*, prayer, quare, rare, scare, share, snare, spare, square, stair, stare, swear, tare, tear, their, there, they're, ware, wear, where, yeah, * compare, Astaire, affair, unfair, aware, unswear, meunière, Daguerre, Basse-Terre, Sancerre, parterre, éclair, Jane Eyre, elsewhere, whene'er, where'er, Pierre, prepare, repair, impair, despair, midair, Kildare, Hilaire, declare, Sinclair, beware, ensnare, misère, Niger, Voltaire, forbear, forswear, howe'er, coheir, au pair, go spare, O'Hare, Lothair, * ampere, fanfare, flatware, Rambert, hardware, glassware, armchair, haircare, air fare, shareware, daycare, Mayfair, threadbare, hectare, welfare, neckwear, headsquare, set square, menswear, deckchair, Edgware, workfare, workwear, fieldfare, freeware, wheelchair, skincare, slipware, knitwear, swimwear, tinware, childcare, nightwear, nightmare, timeshare, highchair, compère, confrère, software, forebear, warfare, horsehair, foursquare, sportswear, corsair, ploughshare, Flaubert, mohair, nowhere, stoneware, Robespierre, bugbear, funfair, somewhere, footwear, pushchair, groupware, Gruyère, * Camembert, Aberdare, camel hair, cafetiere, savoir-faire, aftercare, jardinière, wear and tear, fair and square, maidenhair, tableware, pied-à-terre, Fred Astaire, Delaware, de la Mare, debonair, questionnaire, laissez faire, derrière, premiere, teddy bear, Medicare, secretaire, everywhere, anywhere, Burke and Hare, earthenware, legionnaire, silverware, kitchenware, billionaire, millionaire, trillionaire, rivière, disrepair, Finisterre, chinaware, ironware, nom de guerre, Molière, solitaire, doctrinaire, commissaire, rocking chair, hollowware, corsetière, overbear, polar bear, Baudelaire, open-air, *au contraire*, thoroughfare, Tupperware®, underwear, unaware, ovenware, * chemin de fer, concessionaire, the worse for wear, commissionaire, Apollinaire, couturière, * chargé d'affaires, devil-may-care, Folies-Bergère, Vanity Fair, surface-to-air, ready-to-wear, * multimillionaire, Weston-super-Mare, son et lumière

What is this life if, full of care,
We have no time to stand and stare.
W. H. Davies

5.2 aired, Baird, bared, cared, dared, fared, flared, glared, laird, paired, pared, scared, shared, snared, squared, stared, * compared, prepared, repaired, impaired, despaired, declared, ensnared, * dark-haired, fair-haired, grey-haired, red-haired, long-haired, short-haired, * unprepared, unrepaired, unimpaired, undeclared

5.3 auberge, * concierge

5.4 bairn, cairn, Nairn, * Auvergne, * Fairbairn, Pitcairn

5.5 airs, Ayers, bears, cares, chairs, Claire's, dares, flares, hairs, pairs, pears, prayers, spares, stairs, theirs, wares, * compares, upstairs, affairs, backstairs, repairs, downstairs, * Carstairs, hectares, deckchairs, nightmares, * legionnaire's, unawares, etc.

Hush! Hush! Whisper who dares!
Christopher Robin is saying his prayers.
A. A. MILNE

6.1 Verdi, barely, Fairlie, fairly, rarely, sparely, squarely, scarcely, airy, Carey, chary, Clary, dairy, fairy, hairy, lairy, Mary, nary, prairie, scary, vary, wary, Airdrie, carefree, * unfairly, contrary, unwary, canary, * Monteverdi, cassowary, Salieri, Alighieri, airy-fairy, Tipperary, Inveraray, Miserere, Nyerere, *condottiere*, * *carabiniere*, *arrivederci*, * Dante Alighieri, etc.

6.2 airer, bearer, carer, Clara, Eire, fairer, parer, rarer, Sarah, scarer, sharer, starer, swearer, tearer, wearer, Ayrshire, * caldera, Sierra, preparer, repairer, declarer, * macebearer, tale-bearer, wayfarer, seafarer, swordbearer, pallbearer, torchbearer, cupbearer, * de Valera, demerara, Riviera, cordillera, * dare her, scare her, etc.

6.3 varied, * unvaried

6.4 careful, prayerful, mayoral

6.5 arum, Fareham, harem, Sarum, Wareham, heirdom, * harum-scarum, * wear 'em, shared 'em, etc.

6.6 hairpin, bearskin, Erin, * carin', wearin', etc.

6.7 Ayrton, Aaron, Charon, airman, chairman

6.8 parent, * transparent, impairment, ensnarement, * grandparent, step-parent, godparent

6.9 parents, * transparence, impairments, forbearance, * grandparents, step-parents, godparents

6.10 airing, baring, bearing, blaring, caring, daring, fairing, glaring, pairing, paring, raring, sharing, sparing, staring, swearing, tearing, Waring, wearing, * comparing, unsparing, hard-wearing, preparing, repairing, despairing, forbearing, ball bearing, * cheeseparing, seafaring, childbearing, time-sharing, * overbearing, etc.

Like whatever they say has no bearing,
It's so scary in a house that allows no
swearing
To see him walking around with his
headphones blaring.
EMINEM

6.11 airless, careless, hairless, bareness, fairness, * Carreras, unfairness, awareness, * self-awareness, * scare us, prepare us, etc.

6.12 bearish, fairish, garish, squarish, * nightmarish

6.13 rarebit, bear pit, * swear it, tear it, etc.

6.14 Aries, dairies, fairies, prairies, varies, * Canaries, etc.

6.15 carefully, carelessly, rarity, scarcity, airily, warily, daringly, glaringly, sparingly, garishly, * unbearably, transparency, overbearingly, etc.

6.16 airier, area, hairier, scarier, warier, * Bulgaria, Bavaria, malaria, aquaria, Samaria, herbaria, filaria, solaria, * Carpentaria, Berengaria, cineraria, Gran Canaria, oceanaria, urticaria, planetaria, araucaria, * calceolaria, etc.

6.17 bearable, tearable, wearable, aerial, Ariel, * unbearable, unwearable, repairable, malarial, bursarial, filarial, * unrepairable, adversarial, secretarial, actuarial, estuarial, * antimalarial

6.18 barium, * aquarium, samarium, herbarium, vivarium, solarium, rosarium, sudarium, * honorarium, oceanarium, planetarium, sanitarium, dolphinarium

6.19 Arian, Arien, Aryan, Darien, dairyman, * Bulgarian, vulgarian, Hungarian, Bavarian, valerian, Valerian, agrarian, Aquarian, grammarian, barbarian, sectarian, Caesarean, Nigerien, riparian, librarian, Voltairean, Ontarian, Rotarian, ovarian, fruitarian, Sumerian, * Sabbatarian, libertarian, Rastafarian, prelapsarian, nonsectarian, Sagittarian, vegetarian, Trinitarian, proletarian, Unitarian, antiquarian, centenarian, seminarian, millenarian, Gibraltarian, * infralapsarian, supralapsarian, parliamentarian, abecedarian, egalitarian, totalitarian, humanitarian, utilitarian, authoritarian, veterinarian, sexagenarian, octogenarian, nonagenarian, premillenarian, disciplinarian, * establishmentarian, * latitudinarian, valetudinarian, septuagenarian

6.20 variant, * invariant

6.21 parenting, dairying, varying, * unvarying, etc.

6.22 parentless, carefulness, carelessness, Arius, carious, Darius, Marius, various, airiness, chariness, wariness, * Aquarius, calcareous, burglarious, precarious, vicarious, gregarious, nefarious, hilarious, denarius, * Sagittarius, multifarious, Stradivarius, etc.

6.23 secretariat, proletariat, commissariat

6.24 variable, * invariable

-ay-

The rhymes in this section have the 'ay' sound of same *and* waiting *as their main or final vowel sound.*

7.1 a, A, ay, bay, brae, bray, cay, Chay, Che, clay, day, dray, eh, fay, Fay, fey, flay, fray, gay, Gay, Gray, grey, hay, hey, J, jay, Jay, K, Kay, Kray, lay, lei, ley, may, May, nay, née, neigh, pay, play, pray, prey, ray, Ray, re, Re, say, slay, sleigh, spay, Spey, splay, spray, stay, stray, sway, Tay, they, trait, tray, trey, vlei, way, weigh, whey, yea

**Beautiful Railway Bridge of the Silv'ry Tay!
Alas, I am very sorry to say
That ninety lives have been taken away
On the last Sabbath day of 1879.**
WILLIAM MCGONAGALL

7.2 today, jeté, convey, allay, Malay, agley, unlay, array, astray, affray, away, aweigh, René, assay, unsay, strathspey, Cathay, pince-nez, dragée, Shar Pei, parfait, halfway, Niamey, Marseilles, daresay, AA, waylay, gainsay, FA, LA, MA, purvey, survey, Earl Grey, per se, BA, PA, prepay, repay, replay, decay, piquet, midday, inveigh, belay, delay, relay, display, misplay, inlay, mislay, betray, distrait, defray, midway, dismay, Taipei, Bombay, Torbay, Corday, portray, outstay, outplay, foul play, downplay, outweigh, obey, okay, Tokay, *au fait*, *au lait*, olé, noway, oyez, O'Shea, José, feng shui, hooray, bouquet, UK, du Pré, Dounreay,

touché, * auto-da-fé, Morgan le Fay, cabriolet, Dorian Gray, out-of-the-way, Appian Way, bioassay, YMCA, Botany Bay, Fotheringay, *café au lait*, ukiyo-e

7.3 frappé, latte, maté, pâté, satay, Dante, backstay, jackstay, café, Pathé, ballet, Calais, chalet, Hallé, palais, valet, barré, laptray, ashtray, tramway, gangway, hatchway, Manet, assay, chassé, glacé, passé, cachet, sachet, sashay, flambé, parquet, *manqué*, margay, ave, Soave, vale, Arblay, Franglais, mare, moiré, soiree, chambré, André, entrée, Yahweh, parkway, partway, pathway, archway, lamé, carnet, blasé, airplay, hairspray, airway, fairway, stairway, heyday, mayday, May Day, payday, mainstay, gameplay, Maigret, gateway, Safeway, railway, épée, reggae, levee, Pelé, melee, endplay, Nestlé, beret, X-ray, segue, headway, Medway, essay, workday, birthday, Thursday, survey, wordplay, ciré, clearway, hearsay, plié, piqué, bidet, vide, weekday, relay, replay, screenplay, respray, Tigré, freeway, leeway, seaway, speedway, lycée, plissé, Bizet, frisé, cliché, guichet, DJ, sickbay, Biscay, risqué, filet, gilet, Millais, Millet, inlay, stingray, in-tray, slipway, ridgeway, Friday, child's play, pipeclay, byway, highway, tideway, driveway, Steinway®, washday, bobsleigh, foray, moray, Conway, Monet, Roget, sorbet, forte, forestay, foreplay, swordplay, horseplay, Fauré, doorway, Norway, walkway, Broadway, Galway, hallway, causeway, gourmet, bourrée, curé, purée, outlay, out-tray, croquet, nosegay, sauté, roadway, rosé, crochet, Loveday, someday, Monday, sundae, Sunday, gunplay, subway, runway, buffet, footway, Douai, roué, coupé, toupee, noonday, Tuesday, doomsday, cuvée, duvet, bouclé, soufflé, outré, soothsay, Suchet, * andante, Le Carré, attaché, écarté, Pasquale, cor anglais, Zimbabwe, Mallarmé, macramé, fiancé, fiancée, vivace, recherché, awayday, *al dente*, expressway, Desirée, appliqué, Enrique, Kol Nidrei, décolleté, consommé, Dubonnet®, cloisonné, de jure, cum laude, *démodé*, Obote, exposé, Le Touquet, *il Duce*, retroussé, * cybercafé, *marron glacé*, papier-mâché, Alicante, diamanté, Tio Pepe®, *nota bene*, action replay, Champs Elysées, bichon frise, superhighway, Don Quixote, paso doble

I've lived a life that's full, I've travelled each and ev'ry highway
And more, much more than this. I did it my way.
PAUL ANKA

7.4 St Tropez, canapé, latter-day, Saturday, Faraday, Santa Fe, Rabelais, Mandalay, Charolais, cabaret, Thackeray, Ballantrae, Hathaway, Galloway, caraway, Massenet, Fabergé, Chabrier, alleyway, Haringey, carriageway, passageway, Poitiers, matinée, San Jose, cassoulet,

Castlereagh, faraway, Chardonnay, castaway, Cartier, tearaway, day-to-day, breakaway, takeaway, straightaway, take-home pay, yesterday, present-day, Wednesday, Chevrolet, getaway, well away, Nescafé®, métier, Perrier®, denier, vérité, Eriskay, everyday, émigré, anyway, Hemingway, negligee, *crème brûlée*, résumé, workaday, steerageway, seize the day, Greenaway, Pinochet, DNA, ETA, PTA, CIA, disobey, interlay, interplay, disarray, giveaway, fricassee, *inter se*, ricochet, virelay, Milky Way, light of day, flyaway, hideaway, bridleway, IRA, Monterey, Holloway, Hogmanay, fromage frais, dossier, holiday, Doris Day, protégé, protégée, popinjay, Stornoway, waterway, Fourier, tourniquet, roundelay, overpay, overstay, overlay, overplay, go away, stowaway, throwaway, soakaway, foldaway, motorway, Beaujolais, Beaumarchais, sobriquet, Hudson Bay, underpay, Muscadet, underlay, underclay, underplay, cutaway, colourway, runaway, sommelier, USA, crudités, * alackaday, companionway, Sabatier, espalier, Chevalier, Lavoisier, Courvoisier®, boulevardier, Grand Marnier®, Prince Rainier, red-letter day, atelier, Montpellier, Tortelier, hotelier, Olivier, habitué, Escoffier, Montgolfier, Du Maurier, couturier, communiqué, * Le Corbusier

7.5 Abe, babe, * McCabe, * astrolabe

'Twas brillig, and the slithy toves
Did gyre and gimble in the wabe;
All mimsy were the borogoves
And the mome raths outgrabe.
LEWIS CARROLL

7.6 ache, bake, Blake, brake, break, cake, crake, drake, Drake, fake, flake, hake, Jake, lake, make, quake, rake, sake, shake, sheikh, slake, snake, spake, stake, steak, strake, take, wake, * opaque, awake, unmake, forsake, partake, retake, remake, betake, mistake, * clambake, backache, pancake, handbrake, mandrake, handshake, heartache, heartbreak, daybreak, jailbreak, namesake, headache, sheldrake, wordbreak, earthquake, earache, teacake, seedcake, beefcake, cream cake, cheesecake, beefsteak, sweepstake, remake, keepsake, fish cake, intake, windbreak, firebreak, rock cake, hot cake, stocktake, shortcake, cornflake, corncrake, outtake, outbreak, Hoylake, oatcake, snowflake, sunbake, cupcake, uptake, grubstake, muckrake, fruitcake, toothache, moonquake, * rattlesnake, bellyache, griddlecake, give-and-take, kittiwake, wide awake, overtake, stomachache, undertake

7.7 baked, braked, caked, faked, flaked, quaked, raked, slaked, staked, * unbaked, unslaked, half-baked, * sunbaked

7.8 aid, aide, bade, bayed, blade, braid, brayed, clade, fade, flayed, frayed, glade, grade, jade, Jade, lade, laid, made, maid, neighed, paid, played, prayed, preyed, raid, shade, Slade, spade, spayed, splayed, staid, stayed, strayed, suede, swayed, they'd, trade, wade, Wade, weighed, * forbade, unpaid, brocade, pervade, surveyed, conveyed, arrayed, parade, abrade, upbraid, upgrade, afraid, unweighed, persuade, pomade, unmade, cascade,

handmade, man-made, arcade, waylaid, well-paid, Belgrade, self-made, well-made, first aid, prepaid, repaid, relaid, replayed, remade, decayed, brigade, evade, invade, delayed, displayed, inlaid, mislaid, degrade, betrayed, dismayed, grenade, Sinead, dissuade, tirade, blockade, cockade, stockade, portrayed, downgrade, obeyed, home-made, new-laid, crusade, * Band Aid, ram raid, lampshade, barmaid, decade, mermaid, nursemaid, Teasmade®, switchblade, milkmaid, Whipsnade, Live Aid, limeade, bridesmaid, eyeshade, nightshade, comrade, Noraid, housemaid, sunshade, * cavalcade, accolade, Adelaide, masquerade, balustrade, cannonade, barricade, marinade, palisade, marmalade, parlourmaid, carbonade, dairymaid, razor blade, make the grade, chambermaid, tailor-made, escapade, escalade, esplanade, serenade, lemonade, Medicaid, renegade, centigrade, ready-made, retrograde, Biggleswade, colonnade, stock-in-trade, orangeade, overpaid, motorcade, overlaid, Rollerblade®, overplayed, underpaid, underlaid, underplayed, unafraid, custom-made, undismayed, Lucozade®, fusillade, * nurserymaid, harlequinade, etc.

A man must serve his time to every trade
Save censure – critics all are ready made.
Lord Byron

7.9 aids, AIDS, blades, grades, maids, raids, shades, spades, trades, * mermaids, nursemaids, bridesmaids, comrades, * accolades, barricades, palisades, escapades, Everglades, etc.

7.10 chafe, safe, strafe, waif, * unsafe, vouchsafe

7.11 Craig, Hague, Haig, plague, vague, * The Hague, Mallaig, renege

Don't be vague, ask for Haig.
ADVERTISING SLOGAN

7.12 age, cage, gage, gauge, mage, page, Paige, phage, rage, sage, stage, swage, wage, * front page, upstage, assuage, rampage, backstage, restage, encage, engage, enrage, presage, offstage, downstage, Osage, * rampage, rain gauge, space age, birdcage, greengage, teenage, ribcage, tyre gauge, Bronze Age, outrage, road rage, Stone Age, school-age, * macrophage, saxifrage, disengage, Iron Age, overage, underage, multistage

7.13 aged, caged, gauged, paged, raged, staged, * uncaged, unwaged, assuaged, engaged, enraged, * teenaged, school-aged, etc.

7.14 beige, greige, * manège, Liège, cortege

7.15 ail, ale, bail, bale, Braille, dale, Dale, fail, flail, frail, Gael, Gail, gale, Grail, hail, hale, Hale, jail, kale, mail, male, nail, pail, pale, quail, Quayle, rail, sail, sale, Sale, scale, shale, snail, stale, Swale, tail, tale, they'll, Thrale, trail, vale, veil, wail, wale, whale, Yale, * percale, McPhail, avail, unveil, assail, exhale, curtail, descale, regale, impale, entail, prevail, inhale, derail, bewail, full-scale, * wagtail, travail, fantail,

rat's-tail, handrail, taffrail, blackmail, hangnail, abseil, gaffsail, Arndale, guardrail, Airedale, airmail, Swaledale, snail mail, facemail, staysail, mainsail, telltale, checkrail, bedrail, headrail, headsail, shirt-tail, sperm whale, seakale, Bleasdale, Ruisdael, detail, e-tail, retail, e-mail, female, treenail, greenmail, resale, Windscale, pigtail, ringtail, fishtail, spritsail, timescale, Drysdale, Clydesdale, hightail, Mondale, Rochdale, Lonsdale, bobtail, cocktail, foxtail, oxtail, hobnail, topsail, horsetail, doornail, foresail, mousetail, toenail, wholesale, dovetail, junk mail, thumbnail, * tattletale, Passchendaele, Abigail, galingale, martingale, farthingale, Armidale, fairy tale, Maida Vale, Skelmersdale, Wensleydale, Ebbw Vale, Richter scale, Chippendale, ginger ale, fingernail, bristletail, disentail, nightingale, Nightingale, cottontail, nonpareil, monorail, swallowtail, Calderdale, countervail, ponytail, Holy Grail, tooth and nail, * Fort Lauderdale

7.16 ailed, bailed, failed, flailed, hailed, jailed, mailed, nailed, quailed, railed, sailed, scaled, tailed, veiled, wailed, * unveiled, assailed, curtailed, entailed, prevailed, derailed, bewailed, * draggletailed, etc.

7.17 ails, ales, Dales, fails, Gaels, Gail's, gales, nails, rails, sails, scales, sales, tales, veils, Wales, * entrails, details, pigtails, cocktails, toenails, * telesales, fingernails, Bloomingdale's, New South Wales, * cat-o'-nine-tails, etc.

7.18 aim, blame, came, claim, dame, Dame, fame, flame, frame, game, hame, lame, maim, name, same, shame, tame, Thame, * acclaim, proclaim, aflame, reframe, rename, became, defame, declaim, reclaim, disclaim, exclaim, inflame, old flame, * mainframe, surname, first name, quitclaim, nickname, endgame, selfsame, filename, doorframe, forename, * maiden name, Christian name, window frame, what's-her-name, what's-his-name, counterclaim, overcame

For when the One Great Scorer comes to mark against your name, He writes – not that you won or lost – but how you played the game.
GRANTLAND RICE.

7.19 aimed, blamed, claimed, framed, maimed, named, shamed, * untamed, acclaimed, proclaimed, unclaimed, unnamed, ashamed, renamed, reclaimed, exclaimed, inflamed, * unashamed, etc.

7.20 aims, claims, flames, games, James, names, * Jesse James, Christian names, * Olympic Games, etc.

7.21 bane, brain, Braine, Cain, cane, chain, crane, Dane, deign, drain, Duane, fain, feign, Frayn, gain, grain, Jain, Jane, lain, lane, main, Maine, mane, pain, Paine, pane, Payne, plain, plane, rain, reign, rein, sane, Seine, Shane, skein, slain, Spain, sprain, stain, strain, swain, ta'en, thane, thegn, train, twain, Twain, vain, vane, vein, wain, wane, Wayne, Zane, * cocaine, McCain, again, mundane, attain, pertain, obtain, contain, sustain, profane, Dunblane, Maclean, complain, arraign, Lorraine, terrain, constrain, domain, Pomagne®,

McShane, unchain, campaign, champagne, abstain, arcane, Bahrain, Mark Twain, Charmaine, Great Dane, maintain, urbane, Germaine, germane, deplane, detrain, retrain, chicane, disdain, regain, detain, retain, Sinn Fein, Elaine, Spillane, emplane, explain, Igraine, ingrain, entrain, distrain, restrain, refrain, demesne, remain, inane, insane, vicereine, Cockaigne, Fonteyn, moraine, Coltrane, John Wayne, ordain, chow mein, Coleraine, romaine, Hussein, Ukraine, humane, * ratsbane, plantain, crackbrain, Gawain, airplane, pearmain, sailplane, tailplane, lamebrain, haywain, henbane, Beltane, membrane, vervain, birdbrain, fleabane, ethane, methane, seaplane, migraine, chilblain, midbrain, biplane, triplane, hindbrain, eyestrain, dogbane, octane, warplane, forebrain, propane, grosgrain, wholegrain, ptomaine, bloodstain, wolfsbane, butane, * appertain, ascertain, halothane, chatelain, chatelaine, Tamerlane, aquaplane, scatterbrain, Alamein, Aquitaine, Charlemagne, aeroplane, entertain, Cellophane®, weather vane, featherbrain, preordain, Cleo Laine, windowpane, inhumane, Michael Caine, gyroplane, hydroplane, right as rain, monoplane, foreordain, urethane, counterpane, counterstain, down the drain, Novocaine®, overlain, underlain, hurricane, Dunsinane, sugar cane, Tubal-cain, suzerain, * Citizen Kane, legerdemain, varicose vein, * polyurethane

The rain in Spain stays mainly in the plain.
ALAN JAY LERNER

7.22 caned, chained, deigned, drained, feigned, gained, pained, rained, reigned, sprained, stained, strained, trained, veined, * obtained, contained, sustained, unstained, complained, untrained, constrained, unstrained, unchained, detained, retained, ingrained, restrained, remained, ordained, close-grained, * crackbrained, harebrained, bird-brained, tear-stained, bloodstained, * ascertained, scatterbrained, entertained, self-contained, preordained, foreordained, unconstrained, unexplained, unrestrained, etc.

7.23 change, grange, mange, range, strange, * arrange, free-range, derange, estrange, exchange, long-range, short-range, short-change, * part exchange, prearrange, rearrange, disarrange, interchange, chop and change, stock exchange

**do you think that i would change
my present freedom to range
for a castle or moated grange**
DON MARQUIS

7.24 changed, ranged, * arranged, unchanged, deranged, estranged, exchanged, * prearranged, rearranged, etc.

7.25 ain't, faint, feint, mayn't, paint, plaint, quaint, saint, taint, * attaint, complaint, constraint, acquaint, repaint, distraint, restraint, * greasepaint, warpaint, * self-restraint, reacquaint, overpaint, unconstraint, unrestraint

7.26 Baines, brains, chains, Danes, drains, gains, Haynes, Jane's, Keynes, mains, pains, plains, rains, reins, Staines, stains, trains, veins, Wayne's, * pertains, obtains, Elaine's, remains, * chilblains, bloodstains, * afterpains, windowpanes, etc.

7.27 ape, cape, Cape, crepe, drape, gape, grape, jape, nape, rape, scrape, shape, tape, * agape, reshape, escape, * landscape, nametape, seascape, shipshape, misshape, moonscape, cloudscape, * masking tape, Sellotape®, ticker tape, out of shape

7.28 apes, drapes, gapes, grapes, scrapes, shapes, traipse, * reshapes, escapes, sour grapes, * jackanapes, etc.

7.29 aped, draped, gaped, raped, scraped, shaped, taped, * pear-shaped, wedge-shaped, V-shaped, U-shaped, etc.

7.30 ace, base, bass, brace, case, chase, dace, face, grace, Grace, lace, mace, Mace®, pace, place, plaice, race, space, Thrace, trace, Wace, * abase, apace, unlace, debase, encase, deface, efface, replace, displace, misplace, enlace, embrace, disgrace, retrace, grimace, outpace, outface, * fanbase, backspace, crankcase, blackface, landrace, airspace, staircase, wheyface, paleface, mainbrace, scapegrace, tailrace, workplace, birthplace, headcase, headrace, wheelbase, seedcase, briefcase, slipcase, millrace, fireplace, typecase, typeface, braaivleis, watchcase, chalkface, showcase, notecase, boldface, coalface, showplace, nutcase, Lovelace, someplace, bookcase, suitcase, shoelace, bootlace, * carapace, Samothrace, marketplace, aerospace, database, waste of space, paper chase, face-to-face, steeplechase, breathing space, interspace, interface, interlace, in-your-face, pillowcase, cyberspace, hyperspace, hiding place, wild-goose chase, contrabass, commonplace, Boniface, lower-case, poker face, outer space, upper-case, pull a face

The rabbit has a charming face
Its private life is a disgrace.
ANONYMOUS

7.31 based, baste, chased, chaste, haste, laced, mayst, paced, paste, placed, raced, spaced, taste, traced, waist, waste, * unlaced, unplaced, lambaste, straight-faced, strait-laced, debased, encased, distaste, defaced, replaced, displaced, misplaced, enlaced, embraced, disgraced, posthaste, * barefaced, shamefaced, shore-based, foretaste, po-faced, toothpaste, * pantywaist, aftertaste, baby-faced, interlaced, poker-faced, cut and paste, etc.

7.32 ate, bait, bate, crate, date, eight, fate, fête, freight, gait, gate, grate, great, hate, Kate, late, mate, pate, plate, prate, rate, sate, skate, slate, spate, state, straight, strait, Tate, Thwaite, trait, wait, Waite, weight

I get too hungry for dinner at eight.
I like the theatre, but never come late.
I never bother with people I hate.
That's why the lady is a tramp.
LORENZ HART

7.33 abate, placate, truncate, update, upstate, collate, conflate, narrate, uprate, frustrate, await, pulsate, palpate, backdate, translate, castrate, stagnate, aerate, vacate, spectate, estate, gestate, fellate, third-rate, first-rate, create, predate, restate, reflate, debate, negate, sedate, dictate, misstate, elate, relate, deflate, inflate, berate, filtrate, equate, cremate, innate, fixate, blind date, dilate, gyrate, irate, vibrate, migrate, hydrate, prostrate, orate, ornate, outdate, locate, postdate, notate, rotate, prorate, donate, pupate, mutate, Kuwait, * alienate, seventy-eight, peregrinate, interrelate, oxygenate, orientate, * deteriorate, ameliorate, deoxygenate, disorientate

7.34 Ramsgate, mandate, flatmate, palmate, magnate, Margate, classmate, tartrate, jailbait, tailgate, nameplate, chainplate, faceplate, makeweight, Braithwaite, playmate, stalemate, dentate, testate, stellate, endplate, breastplate, template, checkmate, helpmate, messmate, sensate, workmate, birth rate, rebate, cheapskate, team-mate, Lydgate, Wingate, lych gate, dictate, ingrate, citrate, filtrate, shipmate, inmate, whitebait, ice-skate, Highgate, Reigate, hydrate, nitrate, titrate, flyweight, lightweight, primate, lock gate, prostate, phosphate, hotplate, prostrate, cognate, chlorate, quorate, portrait, groundbait, housemate, probate, Colgate®, tollgate, ovate, soul mate, floodgate, Vulgate, update, sulphate, substrate, bookplate, footplate, Newgate, sluicegate, schoolmate, roommate, * incarnate, intestate, insensate, apostate, inquorate, self-portrait, inchoate, * carbohydrate

7.35 masturbate, advocate, allocate,

arrogate, Harrogate, abrogate,
annotate, aggravate, flagellate, lacerate,
macerate, saturate, adumbrate,
Bassenthwaite, bantamweight, palliate,
abdicate, masticate, fabricate, castigate,
navigate, aggregate, abnegate,
candidate, antedate, validate, palpitate,
gravitate, acetate, agitate, captivate,
activate, salivate, vacillate, aspirate,
calibrate, magistrate, animate,
Latinate, marinate, laminate, fascinate,
vaccinate, machinate, paginate,
transmigrate, graduate, actuate,
amputate, tabulate, adulate, calculate,
strangulate, granulate, * exacerbate,
extrapolate, collaborate, elaborate,
evaporate, exasperate, exaggerate,
amalgamate, diaconate, permanganate,
Italianate, retaliate, repatriate,
expatriate, substantiate, emancipate,
eradicate, elasticate, prevaricate,
prefabricate, invalidate, decapitate,
capacitate, deactivate, reactivate,
inactivate, reanimate, concatenate,
procrastinate, decaffeinate, desalinate,
contaminate, delaminate, assassinate,
invaginate, evacuate, infatuate,
evaluate, confabulate, perambulate,
somnambulate, ejaculate, recalculate,
miscalculate, emasculate, coagulate,
triangulate, encapsulate, congratulate,
* transubstantiate, consubstantiate,
circumstantiate, circumnavigate,
incapacitate, decontaminate

7.36 carbonate, arbitrate,
* bicarbonate, incarcerate,
* polycarbonate

7.37 paperweight, alienate, tête-à-tête,
radiate, eighty-eight, glaciate, satiate,
caliphate, * irradiate, emaciate,
expatiate, ingratiate

7.38 reprobate, expurgate, derogate,
devastate, excavate, enervate, renovate,
decollate, escalate, tessellate, separate,
decorate, federate, perorate, generate,
venerate, second-rate, demonstrate,
remonstrate, welterweight,
featherweight, detonate, emanate,
resonate, welfare state, extirpate,
expiate, twenty-eight, dedicate,
medicate, predicate, defecate,
replicate, explicate, deprecate,
metricate, extricate, desiccate, vesicate,
delegate, relegate, segregate, meditate,
levitate, hesitate, vegetate, elevate,
depilate, ventilate, legislate, celebrate,
desecrate, execrate, emigrate,
denigrate, penetrate, heavyweight,
estimate, guesstimate, decimate,
designate, sell-by date, Menai Strait,
exculpate, educate, exudate,
menstruate, peculate, speculate,
emulate, regulate, * interrogate, de-
escalate, electroplate, redecorate,
confederate, expectorate, coelenterate,
asseverate, accelerate, decelerate,
commemorate, degenerate, regenerate,
potentiate, authenticate, domesticate,
investigate, desegregate, premeditate,
necessitate, disseminate, inseminate,
attenuate, extenuate, perpetuate,
effectuate, accentuate, eventuate,
deregulate, * supererogate,
differentiate, overestimate,
underestimate

7.39 percolate, perforate, personate,
thirty-eight, permeate, germinate,
terminate, perpetrate, circulate,
* intercalate, interpolate, reverberate,
impersonate, regurgitate, exterminate

7.40 demarcate, mediate, deviate,
re-create, reinstate, dehydrate,

elongate, relocate, neonate,
* ameliorate, alleviate, abbreviate,
inebriate, appreciate, depreciate

7.41 syncopate, dislocate, Bishopsgate,
inundate, interstate, innervate,
innovate, immolate, River Plate,
liberate, iterate, micturate, illustrate,
winterweight, middleweight,
cyclamate, impregnate, fifty-eight,
sixty-eight, vitiate, dissipate, indicate,
syndicate, vindicate, silicate, triplicate,
implicate, litigate, mitigate, instigate,
irrigate, Billingsgate, liquidate,
militate, irritate, imitate, titivate,
titillate, scintillate, integrate,
immigrate, intimate, inculcate, situate,
incubate, stipulate, simulate,
stimulate, insulate, * episcopate,
equivocate, reciprocate, deliberate,
invigorate, alliterate, obliterate,
transliterate, reiterate, proliferate,
vociferate, exhilarate, incinerate,
eviscerate, refrigerate, commiserate,
tergiversate, affiliate, humiliate,
conciliate, delineate, asphyxiate,
officiate, propitiate, initiate, anticipate,
participate, pontificate, intimidate,
precipitate, habilitate, facilitate,
debilitate, felicitate, assimilate,
invigilate, equilibrate, reintegrate,
disintegrate, administrate, legitimate,
eliminate, recriminate, incriminate,
discriminate, originate, habituate,
insinuate, manipulate, articulate,
gesticulate, matriculate, acidulate,
capitulate, dissimulate, * reinvigorate,
disaffiliate, rehabilitate, recapitulate

7.42 bifurcate, divagate, violate, isolate,
hibernate, hyphenate, ideate, ninety-
eight, * annihilate

7.43 altercate, collocate, coruscate,

propagate, corrugate, objurgate,
promulgate, commentate, correlate,
copperplate, contemplate, operate,
moderate, tolerate, concentrate,
Postlethwaite, consummate, alternate,
compensate, obviate, constipate,
complicate, confiscate, obligate,
congregate, cogitate, solid-state,
oscillate, consecrate, pollinate,
dominate, nominate, obfuscate,
conjugate, copulate, populate,
flocculate, osculate, modulate,
postulate, ovulate, * homologate,
accommodate, corroborate, cooperate,
preponderate, agglomerate,
conglomerate, exonerate,
prognosticate, intoxicate, consolidate,
deconsecrate, approximate,
abominate, predominate, denominate,
indoctrinate, hydrogenate, depopulate,
repopulate, inoculate, absquatulate,
expostulate, * overcompensate,
discombobulate

7.44 altercate, Watergate, automate,
alternate, forty-eight, nauseate,
formicate, fornicate, orchestrate,
chlorinate, formulate, * incorporate,
subordinate, coordinate, reformulate,
inaugurate

7.45 fluoridate, fluorinate, urinate,
* infuriate, luxuriate

7.46 out-of-date, counterweight

7.47 roller-skate, potentate, overstate,
overate, overrate, overweight,
procreate, roseate, motivate,
* appropriate, expropriate, negotiate,
associate, dissociate, * misappropriate,
renegotiate, disassociate

7.48 suffocate, surrogate, up-to-date,

understate, numberplate, ulcerate,
underrate, underweight,
summerweight, hundredweight,
sultanate, rusticate, supplicate,
cultivate, sublimate, culminate,
fulminate, fluctuate, punctuate,
subjugate, undulate, pullulate, ululate,
suppurate, * adulterate, calumniate,
denunciate, enunciate, resuscitate

7.49 superstate, cruiserweight,
glutamate, lubricate, duplicate,
fumigate, Unigate, mutilate, ruminate,
use-by date, cumulate, * recuperate,
vituperate, enumerate, remunerate,
rejuvenate, repudiate, excruciate,
adjudicate, centuplicate, reduplicate,
quintuplicate, quadruplicate,
communicate, elucidate, agglutinate,
illuminate, hallucinate, accumulate,
* excommunicate, * intercommunicate

7.50 Bates, crates, dates, Fates, gates,
Greats, Kate's, mates, plates, rates,
skates, States, straits, weights, Yeats,
* flatmates, playmates, inmates, ice
skates, nitrates, phosphates, soul
mates, floodgates, * awaits, pet hates,
Bill Gates, dire straits, vibrates,
mutates, * paperweights, roller skates,
* United States, etc.

7.51 faith, saithe, wraith, * Galbraith

7.52 bathe, lathe, scathe, spathe,
swathe, * enswathe, * sunbathe

7.53 bathed, swathed, * unscathed,
enswathed, * sunbathed

7.54 brave, cave, crave, Dave, fave, gave,
grave, knave, Maeve, nave, pave, rave,
save, shave, slave, stave, they've, waive,
wave, * concave, forgave, behave,

enslave, deprave, engrave, outbrave,
* landgrave, margrave, brainwave,
enclave, exclave, Redgrave, heat wave,
crimewave, conclave, Palgrave,
spokeshave, * rant and rave,
aftershave, architrave, misbehave,
microwave, tidal wave, biconcave,
autoclave

**'Tis the star-spangled banner; O long
     may it wave
O'er the land of the free, and the home
     of the brave.**
FRANCIS SCOTT KEY

7.55 caves, craves, Dave's, graves,
Graves, knaves, raves, saves, shaves,
slaves, staves, waves, * airwaves,
Bygraves, * misbehaves, microwaves,
etc.

7.56 baize, bays, blaze, braise, braze,
chaise, craze, days, daze, faze, frays,
gaze, glaze, graze, Hayes, haze, Jeyes,
Kay's, laze, maize, May's, maze, Naze,
neighs, phase, phrase, praise, raise,
rays, raze, stays, strays, ways,
* Gervaise, allays, malaise, ablaze,
emblaze, appraise, upraise, amaze,
self-praise, liaise, decays, deglaze,
rephrase, erase, dispraise, bouquets,
* ashtrays, catchphrase, stargaze,
pathways, railways, Strangeways,
X-rays, endways, breadthways,
lengthways, edgeways, essays,
weekdays, leastways, clichés,
widthways, byways, highways,
sideways, longways, crossways, mores,
always, Mondays, Sundays, fundraise,
toupees, schooldays, duvets, * canapés,
paraphrase, passageways, castaways,
Marseillaise, waifs and strays,
Béarnaise, mayonnaise, reappraise,

hollandaise, Bolognese, polonaise, holidays, waterways, cornerways, nowadays, overglaze, overgraze, stowaways, underglaze, colourways, multiphase, etc.

Nothing so soon the drooping spirits can raise
As praises from the men, whom all men praise.
ABRAHAM COWLEY

7.57 blazed, braised, crazed, dazed, fazed, gazed, glazed, grazed, lazed, phrased, praised, raised, * unfazed, appraised, amazed, liaised, rephrased, erased, * reappraised, overgrazed, double-glazed, etc.

8.1 baby, maybe, Catesby, Naseby, crepy, grapey, kepi, scrapie, achy, flaky, quaky, reiki, shaky, snaky, Craigie, plaguy, Adie, Brady, lady, Sadie, shady, eighty, Haiti, Katie, matey, slaty, weighty, safety, frailty, dainty, hasty, pasty, tasty, cave, cavy, Davy, gravy, navy, wavy, bailey, Bailey, ceilidh, daily, Daley, gaily, Haley, Hayley, Kayleigh, Rayleigh, scaly, shaly, ably, shapely, vaguely, Madeley, lately, stately, faintly, saintly, bravely, gravely, gamely, lamely, namely, tamely, mainly, plainly, vainly, paisley, Paisley, Ainsley, strangely, debris, Aintree, Braintree, pastry, clayey, Amy, gamey, Jamie, Mamie, pay me, samey, brainy, Cheney, grainy, Janie, rainy, veiny, zany, ha'penny, Basie, Casey, Gracie, lacy, pace, pacey, precis, racy, spacey, Spacey, Stacy, Tracy, crazy, daisy, hazy, lazy, Maisie, mazy, Strachey, cagey, stagey, mangy, rangy, * Carnegie, milady, O'Grady, Kuwaiti, agave,

shillelagh, Disraeli, Israeli, sedately, innately, ungainly, inanely, insanely, humanely, Pompeii, Bahraini, Delaney, Khomeini, Eugénie, shove-ha'penny, O'Casey, Scorsese, * crybaby, bushbaby, headachy, landlady, * wakey-wakey, capercaillie, ukulele, Agnus Dei, cockamamie, Allegheny, Museveni, Sulawesi, calabrese, Bel Paese, upsy-daisy, Buthelezi, prima facie, * Rikki-Tikki-Tavi, etc.

Our honeymoon started so blithely and gaily
But dreams I was dreaming were suddenly wrecked
For she broke my front tooth with her father's shillelagh
Which wasn't what I had been led to expect.
NOËL COWARD

8.2 Bayer, Freya, gayer, Heyer, Mayer, kea, layer, payer, player, prayer, sayer, sprayer, stayer, weigher, * obeyer, conveyor, Malaya, assayer, Marbella, mens rea, purveyor, surveyor, delayer, betrayer, * taxpayer, ratepayer, bricklayer, minelayer, soothsayer, * Eritrea, tennis player, record player, Himalaya, * pay her, betray her, etc.

8.3 caber, labour, neighbour, sabre, tabor, Weber, chamber, caper, draper, Draper, gaper, paper, scraper, shaper, taper, tapir, vapour, * belabour, repaper, escaper, * gas chamber, bedchamber, sandpaper, glasspaper, wastepaper, endpaper, flypaper, skyscraper, wallpaper, notepaper, touchpaper, newspaper, * antechamber, * rape her, shape her, etc.

8.4 acre, baker, Baker, breaker, Dacre,

faker, fakir, Laker, maker, nacre, Quaker, raker, shaker, staker, taker, waker, agar, Hagar, Jaeger, Vega, * Jamaica, partaker, cloaca, Zuleika, bodega, Ortega, * backbreaker, matchmaker, heartbreaker, caretaker, safe-breaker, haymaker, rainmaker, pacemaker, dressmaker, peacemaker, piss-taker, film-maker, kingmaker, tie-breaker, strikebreaker, icebreaker, wiseacre, clockmaker, lossmaker, watchmaker, jawbreaker, lawbreaker, housebreaker, toymaker, homemaker, boneshaker, muckraker, bookmaker, moonraker, shoemaker, toolmaker, * Chandrasekhar, bellyacher, merrymaker, circuit breaker, mischief-maker, wicket-taker, widow-maker, Wanamaker, boilermaker, undertaker, troublemaker, moneymaker, Studebaker, Noriega, rutabaga, * cabinet-maker, holiday-maker, * take her, wake her, etc.

What is a woman that you forsake her,
And the hearth-fire and the home-acre,
To go with the old grey Widow-maker?
RUDYARD KIPLING

8.5 Ada, Adur, aider, grader, Nader, raider, Seder, trader, Veda, wader, cater, Chater, crater, data, freighter, gaiter, grater, greater, hater, later, mater, Mehta, pater, plater, raita, skater, slater, Slater, straighter, tater, traitor, waiter, taster, waster, * parader, upgrader, persuader, Darth Vader, Grenada, first-aider, evader, invader, Criseyde, crusader, attainder, remainder, collator, narrator, peseta, translator, spectator, testator, Mercator, creator, debater, Decatur, dictator, equator, vibrator, curator,

rotator, * tailgater, ice-skater, dumbwaiter, shirtwaister, * masquerader, serenader, travelator, alma mater, gladiator, trafficator, applicator, alligator, navigator, agitator, activator, aspirator, calibrator, animator, valuator, tabulator, calculator, arbitrator, radiator, aviator, excavator, renovator, escalator, separator, decorator, generator, demonstrator, detonator, resonator, elevator, depilator, epilator, ventilator, legislator, respirator, denigrator, estimator, educator, speculator, regulator, percolator, terminator, perpetrator, mediator, innovator, liberator, illustrator, indicator, instigator, liquidator, imitator, infiltrator, imprimatur, incubator, simulator, insulator, biodata, propagator, commentator, operator, moderator, oscillator, nominator, commutator, procurator, alternator, fornicator, orchestrator, formulator, roller-skater, Rotavator®, procreator, cultivator, numerator, lubricator, duplicator, * collaborator, eradicator, prevaricator, deactivator, procrastinator, perambulator, interrogator, accelerator, investigator, impersonator, exterminator, incinerator, refrigerator, initiator, facilitator, defibrillator, invigilator, administrator, originator, articulator, denominator, coordinator, inaugurator, negotiator, resuscitator, adjudicator, communicator, accumulator, * vasodilator, bronchodilator, totalizator, * circumnavigator, * obeyed her, hate her, etc.

8.6 chafer, safer, wafer, Ava, braver,

caver, craver, favour, flavour, graver, haver, Laver, paver, quaver, raver, saver, savour, shaver, slaver, waiver, waver, bather, * UEFA, cadaver, disfavour, engraver, * cockchafer, life-saver, sunbather, * semiquaver, clishmaclaver, * demisemiquaver, * hemidemisemiquaver, * gave her, save her, etc.

Fair Atalanta, as a favour,
Took the boar's head her hero gave her;
JOHN GAY

8.7 bailor, baler, hailer, jailer, Leila, mailer, Mailer, nailer, Naylor, paler, sailor, scalar, scaler, staler, tailor, Taylor, trailer, wailer, whaler, abler, stabler, stapler, Daimler, paviour, saviour, Saviour, dahlia, failure, * Akela, Michaela, inhaler, shillelagh, bewailer, loud-hailer, Kumbh Mela, Chichewa, behaviour, derailleur, * blackmailer, abseiler, retailer, wassailer, boardsailor, wholesaler, * Venezuela, Muzorewa, misbehaviour, * fail her, regale her, etc.

8.8 framer, gamer, Kramer, tamer, Aylmer, Cana, caner, drainer, gainer, Gaynor, plainer, planar, planer, Rayner, scena, stainer, strainer, trainer, vainer, * proclaimer, defamer, reclaimer, disclaimer, container, sustainer, complainer, campaigner, abstainer, arcana, Marlene, maintainer, detainer, retainer, explainer, restrainer, no-brainer, * cordwainer, * lion-tamer, Magdalena, entertainer, * blame her, train her, etc.

8.9 acer, baser, bracer, chaser, facer, lacer, pacer, placer, racer, spacer,

tracer, Ailsa, blazer, Fraser, gazer, Glaser, glazer, grazer, laser, maser, praiser, raiser, razor, Taser®, azure, Asia, Brasher, fascia, geisha, nature, gauger, major, Major, pager, stager, wager, changer, danger, Grainger, manger, ranger, stranger, * defacer, embracer, chalaza, appraiser, eraser, erasure, embrasure, Caucasia, Laurasia, Eurasia, acacia, Galatia, Dalmatia, ex gratia, Hypatia, Croatia, rosacea, denature, Alsager, old stager, arranger, endanger, exchanger, hydrangea, * Spätlese, Auslese, stargazer, trailblazer, hell-raiser, fundraiser, teenager, bushranger, * steeplechaser, Australasia, Appalachia, candidature, legislature, sergeant major, Ursa Major, trumpet major, autochanger, moneychanger, * Maria Theresa, * trace her, enrage her, etc.

Poor World (said I) what wilt thou do
To entertain this starry stranger?
Is this the best thou canst bestow?
A cold, and not too cleanly, manger?
RICHARD CRASHAW

8.10 laic, Gaelic, Salic, hayrick, basic, brainsick, trainsick, * Altaic, archaic, Hebraic, voltaic, mosaic, prosaic, Judaic, nucleic, Arcadic, aphasic, dysphasic, * Aramaic, Ptolemaic, algebraic, Pharisaic, formulaic, * ribonucleic, * deoxyribonucleic

The emmet is an ant (archaic),
The ant is just a pest (prosaic).
OGDEN NASH

8.11 radix, spadix, calyx, matrix, basics, * mosaics, testatrix, creatrix, * generatrix, aviatrix, dominatrix

8.12 naked, tailskid, aphid, David, aged, * Camp David

8.13 laboured, capered, papered, aided, braided, faded, jaded, shaded, catered, dated, fated, gated, mated, plated, rated, sated, stated, waited, fainted, painted, sainted, tainted, tasted, waisted, wasted, favoured, flavoured, savoured, sacred, hatred, Hayward, Haywood, wayward, Aylward, wagered, * upbraided, upgraded, persuaded, unaided, unshaded, invaded, degraded, placated, truncated, updated, undated, unstated, frustrated, translated, serrated, X-rated, created, belated, elated, related, deflated, inflated, cremated, striated, outdated, located, unpainted, untainted, acquainted, hand-painted, untasted, high-waisted, ill-favoured, unflavoured, ill-natured, good-natured, * aggravated, castellated, saturated, antiquated, animated, laminated, vaccinated, calculated, variegated, glaciated, satiated, expurgated, mentholated, separated, decorated, dedicated, desiccated, elevated, celebrated, estimated, decimated, educated, regulated, perforated, herniated, dehydrated, elongated, relocated, syncopated, liberated, illustrated, dissipated, mitigated, irritated, titillated, pixilated, integrated, simulated, stimulated, violated, isolated, hyphenated, corrugated, long-awaited, consummated, constipated, complicated, consecrated, populated, overrated, overstated, unabated, suffocated, understated, untranslated, cultivated, unrelated, unacquainted, lubricated, fumigated,

Limericks

● ● ● ● ● ● ● ● ● ● ● ● ● ● ● ● ● ●

A limerick is a humorous five-line verse with a characteristic rhyming pattern, as shown in these examples:

There was a young lady named
  Bright,
Whose speed was far faster than
  light;
She set out one day
In a relative way
And returned on the previous
  night.
ARTHUR BULLER

An Anglican curate in want
Of a second-hand portable font
Will exchange for the same
A photo (with frame)
Of the Bishop-Elect of Vermont.
RONALD KNOX

It is allegedly so called because the line 'Will you come up to Limerick?' (referring to the place of that name in Ireland) was formerly used as a refrain for similar nonsense verses.

mutilated, * unsaturated, exaggerated, substantiated, emancipated, eradicated, elasticated, dilapidated, decapitated, contaminated, unvaccinated, infatuated, emaciated, unexpurgated, premeditated, uneducated, unregulated, unperforated, exhilarated, refrigerated, opinionated, affiliated, humiliated, sophisticated, unmitigated, corroborated, unconsummated, uncomplicated, unconsecrated, self-pollinated, incorporated, adulterated, uncultivated, communicated, illuminated, accumulated, * unsubstantiated, uncontaminated, superannuated, differentiated, unpremeditated, unappreciated, unaffiliated, unsophisticated, uncorroborated, overpopulated, underpopulated, uncoordinated, unadulterated, * polyunsaturated, monounsaturated, undifferentiated, etc.

8.14 breakage, wastage, weighbridge, Weybridge, Cambridge, Bainbridge, drainage

8.15 Baal, Mayall, Abel, able, Babel, cable, fable, gable, label, Mabel, sable, stable, table, maple, papal, staple, Gaitskell, bagel, Hegel, plagal, Schlegel, cradle, ladle, fatal, natal, ratel, playful, wakeful, fateful, grateful, hateful, tasteful, wasteful, faithful, baleful, shameful, baneful, gainful, painful, graceful, changeful, Flavell, naval, navel, Wavell, April, sacral, wastrel, Bakewell, anal, basal, staysail, mainsail, hazel, Hazel, nasal, phrasal, facial, glacial, racial, spatial, Rachel,

angel, * betrayal, defrayal, portrayal, unable, unstable, Clark Gable, relabel, enable, disable, cloacal, inveigle, finagle, prenatal, hiatal, nonfatal, postnatal, ungrateful, distasteful, unfaithful, disdainful, disgraceful, decanal, appraisal, abbatial, palatial, preglacial, biracial, nonracial, postglacial, archangel, * worktable, turntable, timetable, witch hazel, * antenatal, perinatal, neonatal, reappraisal, interracial, multiracial, * maxillofacial

8.16 abled, cabled, fabled, labelled, stapled, cradled, * unlabelled, enabled, disabled, etc.

8.17 gables, labels, tables, Naples, staples, Rachel's, angels, etc.

8.18 paynim, * verbatim, * restrain him, hate him, etc.

8.19 Graham, Grahame, begum, sheikhdom, saintdom, datum, Tatum, Latham, Nahum, Salem, Abram, sacrum, eightsome, Hailsham, * vade mecum, petrolatum, ultimatum, simulacrum, * pay 'em, fail 'em, etc.

8.20 weigh-in, Sabin, tailspin, Aitken, snakeskin, Fagin, Palin, * Onegin, * riboflavin, * shapin', misbehavin', etc.

8.21 crayon, rayon, capon, bacon, Bacon, shaken, taken, waken, pagan, Reagan, Aden, Aidan, Blaydon, Braden, Gaydon, Haydon, laden, Leyden, maiden, Clayton, Dayton, Deighton, Drayton, greaten, Layton, Paton, Peyton, phaeton, Satan, straighten, straiten, Paignton, Maidstone, Avon, craven, graven, haven, raven, shaven,

Nathan, Galen, apron, matron, patron,
Bremen, cayman, Cayman, Damon,
drayman, Eamon, Hayman, layman,
Lehmann, baseman, statesman,
tradesman, dalesman, salesman,
gamesman, plainsman, Canaan, basin,
caisson, chasten, Grayson, hasten,
Jason, mason, Mason, Jameson,
blazon, brazen, raisin, Asian, suasion,
Cajun, Trajan, * Malayan, Ghanaian,
Linnean, Pompeiian, misshapen,
awaken, Jamaican, forsaken, unshaken,
partaken, mistaken, Nijmegen,
unshaven, O'Faolain, Marquesan,
liaison, emblazon, occasion, pervasion,
abrasion, persuasion, evasion,
invasion, equation, dissuasion,
Caucasian, Eurasian, contagion,
* handmaiden, Newhaven, handbasin,
Freemason, washbasin, stonemason,
* Galilean, Eritrean, Himalayan,
reawaken, godforsaken, overtaken,
unmistaken, Copenhagen, overladen,
Milford Haven, Venezuelan, diapason,
dermabrasion, Australasian, * Kyrie
eleison

8.22 Asian, Haitian, nation, station,
Thracian

8.23 probation, gradation, collation,
Galatian, conflation, Horatian,
narration, serration, natation,
lactation, plantation, salvation,
stagflation, translation, castration,
Dalmatian, stagnation, damnation,
taxation, Alsatian, carnation, tarnation,
starvation, aeration, vacation,
claymation, temptation, gestation,
cessation, vexation, sensation,
purgation, flirtation, creation,
Creation, deflation, reflation,
predation, sedation, cetacean,

dictation, legation, negation, elation,
relation, inflation, filtration,
cremation, fixation, striation, libation,
citation, dilation, gyration, vibration,
migration, titration, privation,
oblation, prostration, oration,
formation, causation, duration,
foundation, Croatian, location,
vocation, rogation, flotation, notation,
potation, quotation, rotation, ovation,
donation, truncation, crustacean,
gustation, slumpflation, frustration,
summation, pulsation, pupation,
mutation, Eustachian

Praise with elation,
Praise every morning,
God's re-creation
Of the new day.
ELEANOR FARJEON

8.24 approbation, masturbation,
avocation, advocation, allocation,
translocation, arrogation, abrogation,
annotation, lamentation,
fragmentation, aggravation,
appellation, Appalachian, cancellation,
flagellation, aberration, adoration,
laceration, maceration, adumbration,
affirmation, acclamation, adaptation,
transplantation, affectation,
attestation, annexation, palliation,
abdication, mastication, application,
fabrication, castigation, navigation,
allegation, aggregation, abnegation,
validation, habitation, capitation,
palpitation, gravitation, sanitation,
agitation, captivation, activation,
salivation, vacillation, aspiration,
transpiration, admiration, calibration,
animation, marination, lamination,
fascination, vaccination, machination,
pagination, assignation, affixation,

transmigration, transportation, malformation, transformation, blaxploitation, graduation, actuation, valuation, amputation, salutation, transmutation, tabulation, calculation, strangulation, adulation, granulation, maturation, saturation, adjuration, accusation, * exacerbation, extrapolation, collaboration, elaboration, evaporation, exasperation, exaggeration, amalgamation, retaliation, repatriation, expatriation, substantiation, emancipation, eradication, elastication, reapplication, prevarication, prefabrication, dilapidation, invalidation, cohabitation, decapitation, deactivation, reactivation, inactivation, concatenation, procrastination, decaffeination, desalination, contamination, examination, assassination, imagination, evacuation, infatuation, devaluation, evaluation, confabulation, perambulation, ejaculation, recalculation, emasculation, coagulation, triangulation, encapsulation, congratulation, * transubstantiation, consubstantiation, astronavigation, circumnavigation, incapacitation, self-examination, decontamination, cross-examination, superannuation, tintinnabulation, self-congratulation

8.25 carbonation, arbitration, * incarceration

8.26 variation, variegation

8.27 radiation, aviation, glaciation, satiation, * irradiation, emaciation, ingratiation, expatiation

8.28 reprobation, extirpation, defecation, evocation, revocation, embrocation, expurgation, derogation, degradation, exultation, presentation, devastation, excavation, enervation, renovation, preservation, reservation, decollation, escalation, revelation, Revelation, crenellation, desolation, tessellation, exhalation, preparation, reparation, separation, desperation, respiration, decoration, federation, restoration, Restoration, exploration, declaration, peroration, generation, veneration, demonstration, remonstration, defamation, deformation, reformation, Reformation, declamation, reclamation, exclamation, detonation, explanation, emanation, expectation, segmentation, expiation, recreation, dedication, medication, replication, explication, deprecation, metrication, extrication, desiccation, delegation, relegation, segregation, trepidation, depredation, meditation, levitation, equitation, recitation, excitation, hesitation, vegetation, elevation, derivation, deprivation, depilation, ventilation, legislation, expiration, celebration, cerebration, desecration, execration, penetration, fenestration, registration, emigration, denigration, estimation, decimation, destination, declination, designation, resignation, exportation, exhortation, exaltation, exploitation, sexploitation, menstruation, education, exudation, deputation, reputation, refutation, peculation, speculation, regulation, emulation, exhumation, mensuration, * interrogation, de-escalation, redecoration, confederation, expectoration, asseveration, acceleration, deceleration, commemoration, degeneration, regeneration, premedication, authentication, domestication, investigation, desegregation, premeditation, necessitation, defenestration, predestination, dissemination, insemination, perpetuation, effectuation, accentuation, attenuation, extenuation, coeducation, deregulation, * supererogation, biodegradation, Counter-Reformation, differentiation, reinvestigation, hyperventilation, overestimation, underestimation, higher education, further education

8.29 perturbation, percolation, perforation, personation, fermentation, permeation, perspiration, perpetration, germination, termination, permutation, sternutation, circulation, * interpolation, intercalation, reverberation, impersonation, interpretation, regurgitation, determination, extermination, * reinterpretation, predetermination

8.30 realization, theorization, * idealization

8.31 relocation, denotation, defalcation, recantation, relaxation, debarkation, demarcation, retardation, emendation, delectation, detestation, sequestration, mediation, deviation, re-creation, dehydration, elongation, deportation, denudation, * remediation, alleviation, abbreviation, inebriation, appreciation, depreciation

8.32 syncopation, invocation,

dislocation, inculcation, inundation, dissertation, innovation, installation, inhalation, immolation, liberation, iteration, illustration, information, disclamation, inflammation, intonation, incantation, mistranslation, implantation, incarnation, indentation, pigmentation, impregnation, indexation, dispensation, dissipation, indication, syndication, vindication, triplication, implication, imprecation, litigation, mitigation, instigation, irrigation, liquidation, invitation, irritation, imitation, limitation, visitation, titivation, distillation, scintillation, titillation, inspiration, integration, immigration, infiltration, ministration, intimation, divination, inclination, indignation, importation, situation, incubation, disputation, tribulation, stipulation, stridulation, simulation, stimulation, insulation, * equivocation, reciprocation, deliberation, invigoration, consideration, alliteration, obliteration, reiteration, proliferation, exhilaration, incineration, evisceration, commiseration, refrigeration, affiliation, humiliation, conciliation, delineation, asphyxiation, propitiation, officiation, initiation, anticipation, participation, sophistication, pontification, intimidation, precipitation, facilitation, debilitation, felicitation, horripilation, defibrillation, assimilation, invigilation, equilibration, reintegration, disintegration, administration, legitimation, elimination, recrimination, incrimination, discrimination, origination,

habituation, continuation,
insinuation, manipulation,
matriculation, articulation,
gesticulation, capitulation,
dissimulation, configuration,
* reinvigoration, nonproliferation,
disaffiliation, reconciliation,
contraindication, self-certification,
rehabilitation, prestidigitation,
individuation, disambiguation, no-win
situation, recapitulation

8.33 bifurcation, divagation, dilatation,
violation, isolation, hibernation,
hyphenation, ideation, * annihilation

8.34 conurbation, altercation,
provocation, convocation, collocation,
obfuscation, coruscation, propagation,
corrugation, promulgation,
connotation, consultation,
confrontation, conservation,
observation, constellation,
consolation, contemplation,
operation, moderation, alteration,
botheration, toleration, conflagration,
concentration, confirmation,
proclamation, consummation,
alternation, consternation,
profanation, coronation, conversation,
commendation, ostentation,
protestation, condemnation,
compensation, condensation,
obviation, constipation, complication,
confiscation, obligation, congregation,
oxidation, cogitation, forestation,
compilation, correlation, oscillation,
consecration, combination,
pollination, domination, nomination,
conformation, occupation,
conjugation, copulation, population,
osculation, modulation, postulation,
ovulation, procuration, conjuration,

confutation, commutation,
computation, * homologation,
accommodation, corroboration,
cooperation, agglomeration,
conglomeration, exoneration,
prognostication, intoxication,
consolidation, afforestation,
deforestation, reforestation,
deconsecration, approximation,
recombination, indoctrination,
abomination, predomination,
denomination, preoccupation,
depopulation, repopulation,
inoculation, demodulation,
expostulation, * noncooperation,
overcompensation, reafforestation,
autocorrelation, overpopulation

8.35 altercation, auscultation,
corporation, alteration, automation,
alternation, augmentation,
claudication, formication, fornication,
orchestration, ordination,
chlorination, Aurignacian,
formulation, * incorporation,
excoriation, subordination,
coordination, amortization,
reformulation, inauguration,
* insubordination

8.36 fluoridation, poor relation,
urination, fluorination, * infuriation

8.37 fomentation, molestation,
procreation, foliation, spoliation,
motivation, prolongation,
* defoliation, despoliation, exfoliation,
appropriation, expropriation,
association, dissociation, negotiation,
* radiolocation, misappropriation,
disassociation, renegotiation

8.38 suffocation, coloration,

ulceration, rustication, publication, supplication, cultivation, sublimation, culmination, fulmination, fluctuation, punctuation, subjugation, undulation, pustulation, suppuration, fulguration, susurration, * adulteration, calumniation, Annunciation, pronunciation, enunciation, denunciation, renunciation, resuscitation, * mispronunciation

8.39 nucleation, duplication, lubrication, fumigation, jubilation, mutilation, ruination, rumination, dubitation, ululation, cumulation, lucubration, * recuperation, vituperation, enumeration, remuneration, rejuvenation, repudiation, adjudication, reduplication, centuplication, communication, elucidation, agglutination, illumination, hallucination, accumulation, * excommunication, * telecommunication, intercommunication

8.40 transfiguration, transliteration, alimentation, manifestation, gratification, ratification, stratification, amplification, clarification, ramification, magnification, classification, standardization, dramatization, glamorization, pasteurization, canonization, magnetization, maximization, anglicization, * syllabification, beatification, declassification, demagnetization, italicization

8.41 aftersensation, argumentation, carbonization, harmonization

8.42 alienation, deification, reification, pale imitation, vaporization, stabilization, * destabilization, containerization

8.43 self-preservation, self-immolation, echolocation, recommendation, sedimentation, regimentation, representation, edification, rectification, verification, gentrification, specification, peregrination, self-pollination, self-mutilation, centralization, generalization, specialization, tenderization, memorization, pressurization, mechanization, westernization, sensitization, sterilization, ghettoization, self-education, centrifugation, * experimentation, misrepresentation, identification, exemplification, electrification, indemnification, intensification, decentralization, extemporization, depressurization, desensitization, collectivization

8.44 tergiversation, certification, versification, verbalization, urbanization, mercerization, fertilization, * desertification, diversification, internalization, externalization, commercialization, suburbanization, self-fertilization, cross-fertilization, deterioration

8.45 reincarnation, prepublication, schematization, legalization, equalization, penalization, etherization, demonization, * amelioration

8.46 disapprobation, disinformation, misinformation, disembarkation, implementation, instrumentation, interrelation, misapplication, prettification, mystification, vilification, simplification, vitrification, signification, Disneyfication, dissimilation, disinclination, improvisation, crystallization, signalization, winterization, Islamization, synchronization, Christianization, digitization, civilization, victimization, minimization, mythicization, visualization, immunization, miscalculation, * solidification, acidification, humidification, demystification, revivification, initialization, familiarization, legitimization, politicization, * dehumidification, oversimplification

8.47 hyperinflation, hydrogenation, nitrification, privatization, idolization, finalization, itemization, ionization, lionization, hybridization, * acclimatization, revitalization, de-ionization

8.48 complementation, documentation, modification, quantification, jollification, mollification, qualification, ossification, falsification, oxygenation, cross-pollination, novelization, moralization, mongrelization, modernization, colonization, solemnization, oxidization, fossilization, optimization, * disqualification, transmogrification, personification, detoxification, democratization, demoralization, prioritization, homogenization

8.49 orientation, fortification,

mortification, glorification, purification, falsification, formalization, normalization, authorization, organization, bowdlerization, * disorientation, immortalization, reorganization, disorganization

8.50 codification, notification, globalization, localization, vocalization, motorization, polarization, mobilization, * deodorization, depolarization, demobilization, immobilization

8.51 yuppification, justification, nullification, uglification, mummification, multiplication, vulgarization, pulverization, customization, vulcanization, * emulsification

8.52 beautification, unification, brutalization, neutralization, unionization, humanization, utilization, unitization, * reunification, dehumanization, computerization

8.53 alphabetization, naturalization, caramelization, nationalization, rationalization, cannibalization, capitalization, categorization, characterization, decimalization, secularization, regularization, personalization, circularization, serialization, regionalization, liberalization, fictionalization, systematization, digitalization, criminalization, militarization, miniaturization, hospitalization, popularization, * denationalization, pedestrianization, Americanization, depersonalization, materialization, demineralization, legitimatization, decriminalization, demilitarization, industrialization, demutualization

8.54 wakened, straightened, straitened, Leyland, Wayland, Lakeland, Maitland, mainland, Raymond, chastened, hastened, stationed, * awakened, emblazoned, etc.

8.55 Asians, Haitians, nations, stations, Thracians, * Galatians, serrations, Dalmatians, damnations, Alsatians, carnations, temptations, relations, cremations, gyrations, vibrations, privations, foundations, quotations, crustaceans, * Lamentations, cancellations, aberrations, lacerations, aspirations, calculations, salutations, conurbations, connotations, operations, alterations, innovations, indentations, indications, implications, invitations, tribulations, stipulations, complications, obligations, oscillations, combinations, nominations, * examinations, congratulations, United Nations, communications, illuminations, hallucinations, * telecommunications, etc.

There's a great text in Galatians
Once you trip on it, entails
Twenty-nine distinct damnations,
One sure, if another fails.
ROBERT BROWNING

8.56 mayn't, vacant, blatant, latent, patent, flagrant, fragrant, vagrant, claimant, payment, raiment, statement, pavement, ailment, bailment, basement, casement,

placement, nascent, patient, ancient, agent, * abeyant, assailant, inhalant, prepayment, repayment, defrayment, nonpayment, escapement, abatement, restatement, misstatement, enslavement, curtailment, derailment, entailment, attainment, containment, arraignment, ordainment, abasement, debasement, encasement, replacement, emplacement, displacement, misplacement, outplacement, amazement, engagement, arrangement, derangement, complainant, complacent, adjacent, renascent, obeisant, complaisant, impatient, reagent, * inpatient, outpatient, newsagent, * overpayment, underpayment, reinstatement, overstatement, understatement, ascertainment, entertainment, edutainment, infotainment, self-abasement, self-effacement, disengagement, prearrangement, rearrangement, liquefacient, stupefacient, * abortifacient

8.57 cadence, patents, valence, fragrance, vagrants, claimants, payments, statements, ailments, nascence, patience, patients, agents, * abeyance, purveyance, conveyance, acquaintance, surveillance, assailants, engagements, arrangements, renaissance, Renaissance, renascence, obeisance, complaisance, impatience, * newsagents, * reacquaintance, entertainments, etc.

8.58 baying, fraying, greying, laying, Maying, neighing, paying, playing, praying, saying, spraying, staying, swaying, weighing, * conveying,

surveying, decaying, delaying,
betraying, nonpaying, nonplaying,
* taxpaying, bricklaying, crocheting, etc.

**Then while time serves, and we are but
decaying;
Come, my Corinna, come, let's go a-
Maying.**
ROBERT HERRICK

8.59 gaping, scraping, shaping, aching,
baking, breaking, faking, making,
quaking, raking, shaking, taking,
waking, plaguing, * escaping,
partaking, mistaking, reneging,
* backbreaking, matchmaking,
heartbreaking, painstaking,
haymaking, lacemaking, breathtaking,
dressmaking, earthshaking,
peacemaking, piss-taking,
strikebreaking, winemaking,
stocktaking, lossmaking,
housebreaking, homemaking,
lovemaking, shoemaking,
* bellyaching, merrymaking,
undertaking, moneymaking, etc.

**And the wheel's kick and the wind's
song and the white sail's shaking,
And a grey mist on the sea's face and a
grey dawn breaking.**
JOHN MASEFIELD

8.60 aiding, fading, grading, lading,
raiding, shading, trading, baiting,
dating, grating, hating, mating,
plating, rating, skating, slating,
waiting, weighting, fainting, painting,
tainting, basting, pasting, tasting,
wasting, * unfading, pervading,
parading, persuading, cascading,
degrading, crusading, updating,
frustrating, pulsating, translating,

spectating, debating, relating,
gyrating, rotating, donating,
repainting, * ice-skating, wine-tasting,
* aggravating, lacerating, captivating,
fascinating, calculating, devastating,
enervating, decorating, resonating,
medicating, hesitating, emigrating,
penetrating, circulating, liberating,
vindicating, irritating, titillating,
scintillating, stimulating, insulating,
isolating, hibernating, operating,
concentrating, cogitating, copulating,
ovulating, alternating, nauseating,
roller-skating, motivating, suffocating,
supplicating, culminating, fluctuating,
undulating, lubricating, duplicating,
* exasperating, self-deprecating,
unhesitating, exhilarating,
participating, debilitating,
incriminating, discriminating,
accommodating, intoxicating,
subordinating, infuriating,
negotiating, excruciating,
communicating, illuminating, etc.

8.61 chafing, caving, craving, paving,
raving, saving, shaving, slaving,
waving, plaything, bathing, scathing,
swathing, * behaving, engraving,
* time-saving, sunbathing, * labour-
saving, misbehaving, etc.

8.62 ailing, failing, grayling, Hayling,
mailing, nailing, paling, railing,
sailing, trailing, veiling, wailing,
whaling, cabling, stabling, stapling,
cradling, ladling, shaveling,
changeling, dayspring, mainspring,
lacewing, * unfailing, availing,
unveiling, prevailing, bewailing,
* blackmailing, abseiling, retailing,
e-mailing, boardsailing, * parasailing,
unavailing, etc.

8.63 aiming, blaming, flaming, framing, gaming, maiming, naming, shaming, taming, caning, draining, feigning, gaining, raining, reigning, staining, training, waning, * defaming, reclaiming, exclaiming, pertaining, complaining, campaigning, abstaining, retraining, explaining, remaining, * entertaining, self-sustaining, uncomplaining, etc.

8.64 bracing, casing, facing, lacing, pacing, placing, racing, spacing, tracing, blazing, gazing, glazing, grazing, phasing, phrasing, praising, raising, ageing, gauging, paging, raging, staging, changing, ranging, * replacing, embracing, amazing, self-raising, rampaging, engaging, arranging, unchanging, * stargazing, trailblazing, hell-raising, * self-effacing, steeplechasing, interfacing, etc.

There on golden sunsets blazing,
Every evening found him gazing,
Singing, 'Orb! you're quite amazing!'
EDWARD LEAR

8.65 sayings, scrapings, makings, ratings, paintings, Hastings, playthings, mailings, railings, * wine-tastings, * undertakings, etc.

8.66 dais, Thaïs, aphis, Avis, Davis, Mavis, Bayliss, Amis, basis, stasis, * clematis, physalis, oasis, Oasis®, * rara avis, digitalis, * *semper fidelis*

8.67 magus, Magus, Tagus, vagus, Vegas, flatus, status, stratus, Dreyfus, rayless, talus, shapeless, dateless, stateless, weightless, tasteless, faithless, nailless, tailless, aimless,

blameless, nameless, shameless, brainless, painless, stainless, baseless, faceless, graceless, placeless, ageless, changeless, glabrous, scabrous, waitress, famous, Seamus, shamus, squamous, anus, greyness, heinous, Janus, vagueness, greatness, lateness, straightness, faintness, quaintness, safeness, braveness, paleness, staleness, lameness, sameness, tameness, strangeness, gracious, spacious, * Andreas, Piraeus, Emmaus, Linnaeus, Priapus, Las Vegas, meatus, hiatus, quietus, Pharsalus, mandamus, Uranus, Marquesas, capacious, rapacious, sagacious, fallacious, salacious, ungracious, pugnacious, mendacious, veracious, vexatious, herbaceous, flirtatious, curvaceous, sebaceous, edacious, predacious, Cretaceous, vivacious, tenacious, Ignatius, voracious, loquacious, audacious, mordacious, bodacious, rosaceous, fugacious, contagious, courageous, rampageous, outrageous, umbrageous, * San Andreas, Menelaus, apparatus, altostratus, nimbostratus, cirrostratus, ignoramus, farinaceous, efficacious, ericaceous, perspicacious, pertinacious, liliaceous, disputatious, ostentatious, contumacious, advantageous, * inefficacious, disadvantageous, * Coriolanus, * plague us, blame us, etc.

8.68 papist, rapist, sadist, playlist, racist, bassist, ageist, * escapist, * landscapist

8.69 gayest, mayest, greatest, latest, straightest, faintest, safest, bravest, gravest, palest, stalest, stablest, tamest, plainest, vainest, basest, strangest, etc.

8.70 greyish, rakish, crayfish, knavish, slavish, palish, Hamish, Danish, * old-maidish

8.71 playlet, platelet, bracelet, * affidavit, * fail it, save it, etc.

8.72 ha'p'orth, Hayworth

8.73 dative, native, plaintive, * creative, pervasive, abrasive, persuasive, evasive, invasive, * innovative, contemplative, noninvasive

8.74 babies, rabies, scabies, Hades, ladies, eighties, frailties, Baileys®, dailies, pastries, Amies, daisies, * Mercedes, Euphrates, Israelis, oases, etc.

**They cannot scare me with their empty spaces
Between stars – on stars where no human race is.**
ROBERT FROST

8.75 players, Sayers, labours, chambers, Chambers, capers, papers, vapours, bakers, breakers, Quakers, shakers, Shakers, takers, traders, waders, taters, flavours, Havers, quavers, sailors, trainers, aces, braces, graces, Graces, laces, places, races, spaces, traces, aitches, ages, pages, stages, wages, dangers, strangers, * spectators, campaigners, * fundraisers, teenagers, * Himalayas, etc.

8.76 Lazenby, neighbourly, fatally, painterly, playfully, gratefully, tastefully, faithfully, gainfully, painfully, gracefully, nasally, facially, racially, favourably, vacantly, blatantly, flagrantly, patiently, matronly,

aimlessly, shamelessly, painlessly, famously, graciously, Avebury, Aylesbury, Sainsbury, apery, creperie, drapery, japery, papery, bakery, fakery, vagary, Avery, knavery, quavery, savory, savoury, slavery, raillery, apiary, aviary, Amory, tracery, masonry, blazonry, stationary, stationery, Naomi, papacy, vacancy, valency, flagrancy, vagrancy, agency, gaiety, laity, deity, shakily, daintily, hastily, crazily, lazily, basically, plaintively, scathingly, papistry, * ungratefully, unfaithfully, disdainfully, disgracefully, unfavourably, insatiably, belatedly, good-naturedly, impatiently, mistakenly, voraciously, audaciously, courageously, outrageously, placatory, gyratory, vibratory, migratory, unsavoury, proslavery, chicanery, Freemasonry, probationary, deflationary, inflationary, complacency, ashamedly, restrainedly, prosaically, persuasively, evasively, amazingly, * unmistakably, ostentatiously, approbatory, ambulatory, adulatory, accusatory, revelatory, dedicatory, deprecatory, celebratory, commendatory, condemnatory, compensatory, antislavery, spontaneity, unashamedly, unrestrainedly, uncomplainingly, * congratulatory, anticipatory, participatory, hallucinatory, * justificatory, improvisatory, simultaneity, etc.

8.77 labeller, labourer, Gainsborough, paperer, caterer, waverer, straightener, stationer, Baedeker, Cambridgeshire, * probationer, vacationer, conveyancer

8.78 labia, Swabia, Napier, rapier,

flakier, shakier, Nadia, shadier, stadia,
weightier, daintier, hastier, tastier,
Flavia, Xavier, dahlia, lamia, brainier,
crania, mania, rainier, zanier, glacier,
racier, brazier, crazier, Frasier, glazier,
grazier, hazier, lazier, fascia, mangier,
* Arabia, Walachia, Arcadia, Batavia,
Belgravia, Moldavia, Octavia, Moravia,
azalea, Westphalia, regalia, Australia,
Albania, Tasmania, Titania, Mount
Rainier, Romania, aphasia, Malaysia,
fantasia, dysphasia, gymnasia,
Caucasia, * Bessarabia, Scandinavia,
Lupercalia, *inter alia*, bacchanalia,
Saturnalia, genitalia, penetralia,
marginalia, kitchenalia, echolalia,
coprolalia, macadamia, miscellanea,
Pomerania, Anglomania, kleptomania,
necromania, egomania,
nymphomania, dipsomania,
hypermania, hypomania, pyromania,
monomania, collectanea, Oceania,
Aquitania, Mauretania, Mauritania,
Ruritania, Lusitania, Transylvania,
Pennsylvania, Lithuania, Anastasia,
Australasia, euthanasia, Appalachia,
* Saudi Arabia, paraphernalia,
Mesopotamia, epithalamia,
megalomania, bibliomania,
balletomania, erotomania, etc.

Oh, life is a glorious cycle of song,
A medley of extemporanea;
And love is a thing that can never go
wrong;
And I am Marie of Roumania.
DOROTHY PARKER

8.79 payable, playable, capable,
breakable, gradable, datable, ratable,
paintable, tastable, mailable, salable,
saleable, scalable, favourable,
blamable, tamable, traceable, satiable,

changeable, flavourful, labial, brachial,
radial, Balliol, Gabriel, atrial, patrial,
cranial, glacial, laical, apical,
* unplayable, incapable, escapable,
unbreakable, unshakable, mistakable,
persuadable, degradable, translatable,
debatable, inflatable, available,
assailable, unsalable, unsaleable,
unfavourable, unnamable, untamable,
reclaimable, attainable, obtainable,
sustainable, maintainable, explainable,
untraceable, replaceable, insatiable,
unchangeable, exchangeable,
behavioural, occasional, sensational,
relational, vocational, bilabial, biradial,
preglacial, postglacial, * inescapable,
unmistakable, untranslatable,
microwavable, unavailable,
unassailable, irreclaimable,
unattainable, unobtainable,
unsustainable, unexplainable,
ineffaceable, irreplaceable,
interchangeable, transformational,
navigational, aspirational, recreational,
educational, inspirational, situational,
confrontational, operational,
conversational, Congregational,
occupational, motivational,
lackadaisical, * denominational,
* biodegradable, representational,
nonoperational, organizational,
co-educational, * nondenominational,
* interdenominational

8.80 Caterham, flavoursome, radium,
stadium, atrium, natrium, cranium,
* palladium, Palladium, vanadium,
geranium, germanium, titanium,
uranium, gymnasium, contagium,
* Verulamium, Herculaneum,
* epithalamium

8.81 Stapleton, Phaethon, Jacobson,

railwayman, Fabian, gabion, Swabian, Hadean, radian, avian, Flavian, Shavian, alien, Adrian, Hadrian, Damian, Samian, Gratian, Haitian, Thracian, Davison, Jamieson, Davidson, * Arabian, Walachian, Palladian, Canadian, Grenadian, Barbadian, Arcadian, circadian, Orcadian, Batavian, Moldavian, Octavian, Moravian, mammalian, Westphalian, Hegelian, Pygmalion, Australian, Deucalion, Bahamian, Albanian, Tasmanian, Iranian, Jordanian, Romanian, Ukrainian, Malaysian, Vespasian, Caucasian, pelagian, Pelagian, * Trinidadian, Scandinavian, bacchanalian, prothalamion, Pomeranian, subterranean, Panamanian, Mauritanian, Ruritanian, Transylvanian, Pennsylvanian, Lithuanian, Rabelaisian, Australasian, Athanasian, Appalachian, * Episcopalian, tatterdemalion, Mesopotamian, Mediterranean

8.82 gradient, radiant, salient, * liquefacient, stupefacient, * abortifacient

8.83 gradients, radiance, salience, maintenance, etc.

8.84 labelling, layering, neighbouring, tapering, catering, favouring, flavouring, Havering, quavering, wavering, crayoning, * unwavering, self-catering, awakening, conveyancing, etc.

8.85 paperless, flavourless, vaporous, traitorous, dangerous, waywardness, playfulness, faithfulness, weightlessness, scabious, radius, Flavius, aqueous, caseous, gaseous, alias, shakiness, weightiness, daintiness, shapeliness, laziness, nakedness, * Sibelius, extraneous, spontaneous, cutaneous, * simultaneous, instantaneous, miscellaneous, subcutaneous, Athanasius, * contemporaneous, extemporaneous, etc.

8.86 flakiest, shakiest, shadiest, weightiest, daintiest, hastiest, tastiest, brainiest, rainiest, zaniest, raciest, craziest, haziest, laziest, mangiest, etc.

8.87 ableist, fatalist, racialist, naturist, plagiarist, Satanist, atheist, * behaviourist, salvationist, * conservationist, isolationist, educationist

8.88 favourable, amiable, * unfavourable, inalienable

-e-

The rhymes in this section have the 'e' sound of pen *and* ready *as their main or final vowel sound.*

9.1 bleb, deb, ebb, neb, pleb, Seb, web, Webb, * celeb, * Maghreb, Zagreb, Caleb, cobweb, * World Wide Web, Aurangzeb

9.2 beck, check, cheque, Czech, Dec, deck, Eck, feck, fleck, heck, Lech, lek, neck, peck, rec, reck, sec, spec, speck, tech, trek, wreck, * V-neck, recheck, Quebec, bedeck, hi-tech, spot-check, crosscheck, low-tech, * Caltech, Aztec, Dalek, fartlek, parsec, háček, breakneck, paycheque, namecheck, henpeck, redneck, Purbeck, Birkbeck, Seebeck, rebec, xebec, pinchbeck, shipwreck, Steinbeck, flyspeck, wryneck, cromlech, Warbeck, foredeck, kopeck, OPEC, codec, rollneck, sun deck, roughneck, Uzbek, Dubček, Lübeck, gooseneck, * Zapotec, Janáček, Chiang Kai-shek, afterdeck, neck-and-neck, leatherneck, demi-sec, turtleneck, nervous wreck, discotheque, Beiderbecke, biotech, bottleneck, bodycheck, quarterdeck, halterneck, Eurocheque, polo neck, rubberneck, double-check, * Melchizedek, Toulouse-Lautrec

The boy stood on the burning deck
Whence all but he had fled;
The flame that lit the battle's wreck
Shone round him o'er the dead.
FELICIA HEMANS

9.3 checks, cheques, decks, ex, Exe, flecks, flex, hex, kecks, lex, necks, pecks, pecs, Rex, sex, specs, specks, Tex, vex, wrecks, X, * convex, perplex, annex, desex, rechecks, bedecks, * Amex, annex, Artex®, Daleks, apex, APEX, latex, Playtex®, Hedex®, Semtex, Tex-Mex, rednecks, Perspex®, vertex, reflex, Kleenex®, Tipp-Ex®, index, triplex, simplex, NIREX, Pyrex®, ibex, ilex, silex, Timex®, complex, Optrex®, cortex, Gore-Tex®, vortex, Durex®, Lurex®, kopecks, Rolex®, duplex, suplex, * retroflex, circumflex, intersex, Middlesex, cybersex, biconvex, Copydex®, pontifex, multiplex, googolplex, Moulinex®, unisex, * traveller's cheques, *Oedipus Rex*, etc.

9.4 flexed, next, sexed, text, vexed, * perplexed, annexed, * pretext, context, subtext, * teletext, hypertext, oversexed, undersexed

9.5 Brecht, checked, decked, flecked, necked, pecked, sect, Sekt, specked, trekked, wrecked, * prospect, suspect, protect, affect, perfect, collect, correct, connect, unchecked, project, object, subject, transect, V-necked, rechecked, respect, expect, inspect, bedecked, detect, defect, effect, infect, elect, select, deflect, reflect, inflect, neglect,

erect, deject, eject, reject, inject, direct,
bisect, dissect, trisect, spot-checked,
crosschecked, * aspect, Albrecht,
abject, henpecked, defect, prefect,
reject, shipwrecked, insect, prospect,
collect, project, suspect, bull-necked,
Utrecht, * architect, retrospect,
resurrect, recollect, self-respect,
genuflect, circumspect, reconnect,
reinfect, reelect, deselect, reselect,
reinspect, redirect, introspect,
disaffect, intellect, incorrect,
disconnect, intersect, interject,
disrespect, disinfect, vivisect, indirect,
misdirect, dialect, side effect,
rubbernecked, double-checked,
* aftereffect, idiolect, interconnect,
hypercorrect, knock-on effect,
overprotect

Never will I give advice
Till you please to ask me thrice;
Which, if you in scorn reject,
'Twill be just as I expect.
JONATHAN SWIFT

9.6 etch, fetch, fletch, ketch, kvetch,
lech, retch, sketch, stretch, vetch,
wretch, * outstretch, * overstretch

9.7 etched, fetched, retched, sketched,
stretched, * unstretched, far-fetched,
outstretched, * overstretched

9.8 bed, bled, bread, bred, cred, dead,
dread, ed, Ed, fed, Fed, fled, Fred,
head, ked, lead, led, Med, Ned, pled,
read, red, said, shed, shred, sled, sped,
spread, stead, ted, Ted, thread, tread,
wed, Z, zed, * abed, ahead, undead,
unread, unthread, unwed, unsaid,
gainsaid, well-fed, well-read, well-
bred, Enzed, embed, reread, see red,

premed, instead, behead, misled,
misread, ill-bred, inbred, sliced bread,
drop dead, force-fed, outspread, co-ed,
stone-dead, lowbred, * Hampstead,
Stansted, slaphead, blackhead,
crackhead, smackhead, fathead,
blacklead, Manfred, packthread,
farmstead, masthead, Ahmed, air bed,
airhead, stairhead, day bed, pay bed,
braindead, Gateshead, deathbed,
bedstead, breast-fed, egghead,
deadhead, redhead, wellhead,
bedspread, spearhead, seabed, reed
bed, seedbed, beachhead, sweetbread,
street cred, retread, sickbed, dickhead,
thickhead, bighead, pithead, Spithead,
pinhead, skinhead, bridgehead,
crispbread, Whitbread, wingspread,
childbed, biped, Minehead,
Brideshead, widespread, hotbed,
Ofsted, blockhead, Godhead, hothead,
pothead, hogshead, bobsled, dogsled,
crossbred, force-fed, forehead,
warhead, shortbread, foresaid,
Muirhead, purebred, Roundhead,
cowshed, flowerbed, Stourhead, Go-
Ped®, moped, roadstead, homestead,
bonehead, sun bed, Plumstead,
bulkhead, drumhead, bloodshed,
woodshed, woolshed, spoonfed,
proofread, toolshed, * aforesaid,
* hammerhead, acidhead, arrowhead,
Samoyed, maidenhead, Maidenhead,
feather bed, letterhead, Leatherhead,
petrolhead, centre spread, Ethelred,
Birkenhead, Peterhead, streets ahead,
sleepyhead, Beachy Head, river bed,
figurehead, in the red, infrared, pitta
bread, interbred, gingerbread, bottle-
fed, Holyhead, Holinshed, quadruped,
watershed, Portishead, fountainhead,
sofa bed, go-ahead, overfed, overhead,
soda bread, slugabed, underfed,

dunderhead, knucklehead, shovelhead, muttonhead, thoroughbred, newlywed

When I am dead, I hope it may be said: 'His sins were scarlet, but his books were read.'
HILAIRE BELLOC

9.9 beds, dreads, Ed's, Fred's, heads, sheds, shreds, spreads, threads, treads, * blackheads, eggheads, skinheads, warheads, flowerbeds, * arrowheads, petrolheads, loggerheads, sofa beds, overheads, newlyweds, etc.

9.10 chef, clef, deaf, def, eff, F, Geoff, Jeff, Neff, ref, * stone-deaf, tone-deaf, * ASLEF, Brezhnev, Kiev, Josef, * RAF, treble clef, VHF, IVF, Nureyev, UNICEF, * Diaghilev, Prokofiev

9.11 cleft, deft, Dreft®, eft, heft, left, theft, weft, * bereft

9.12 beg, Clegg, egg, Eigg, Greg, Greig, keg, leg, Meg, peg, skeg, teg, * unpeg, * blackleg, JPEG, gate-leg, tent peg, nest egg, peg leg, redleg, dogleg, foreleg, clothes peg, nutmeg, bootleg, * Scanderbeg, break a leg, Winnipeg, filibeg

Fain would I kiss my Julia's dainty leg, Which is as white and hairless as an egg.
ROBERT HERRICK

9.13 begs, eggs, dregs, legs, Meg's, * tent pegs, sheerlegs, forelegs, * daddy-long-legs, etc.

9.14 dredge, edge, fledge, hedge, kedge, ledge, pledge, Reg, sedge, sledge, veg, wedge, * allege, on edge

9.15 dredged, edged, fledged, hedged, pledged, wedged, * alleged, unfledged, * gilt-edged, * double-edged, fully fledged

9.16 bel, bell, Bell, belle, Brel, cel, cell, Del, dell, Dell, dwell, ell, fell, gel, hell, jell, knell, L, Mel, Nell, quell, sell, shell, smell, Snell, spell, swell, tell, well, yell, * lapel, propel, compel, Raquel, Adele, Badel, Patel, unwell, Chanel, quenelle, gazelle, rappel, Ravel, Manuel, Danielle, mademoiselle, cartel, Martel, Carmel, Parnell, Marcel, farewell, Snaefell, pell-mell, Dalziel, respell, retell, presell, resell, rebel, repel, impel, dispel, misspell, expel, Miguel, Fidel, Estelle, befell, indwell, excel, Giselle, Michelle, morel, Morrell, Rochelle, Courtelle®, foretell, Scafell, outsell, Noël, Nobel, boatel, hotel, motel, Moselle, Brunel, * handbell, Maxwell, clamshell, barbell, Cherwell, Harwell, Chartwell, harebell, stairwell, Bakewell, Thelwell, Tencel®, eggshell, speedwell, seashell, inkwell, Bridewell, Sizewell, Oftel, Fontwell, Cromwell, Boswell, bombshell, doorbell, Orwell, Caldwell, Cornwell, cowbell, groundswell, dumbbell, nutshell, bluebell, * Annabel, asphodel, bagatelle, caravel, parallel, aquarelle, Camberwell, caramel, carousel, Appenzell, Gabrielle, chanterelle, ne'er-do-well, béchamel, razor shell, Jezebel, Becquerel, demoiselle, decibel, personnel, clientele, Tinkerbell, Christabel, mirabelle, Isabel, citadel, Zinfandel, William Tell, kiss and tell, Philomel, pimpernel, villanelle, infidel, pipistrelle, wishing well, immortelle, fontanelle, tortoiseshell, cockleshell, bodyshell, Duracell®, go to hell, oversell, photocell, muscatel, Motherwell, undersell, * eau de Javelle, crème caramel, crime passionnel, Aix-la-Chapelle, Mont-Saint-Michel, maître d'hôtel, *au naturel*

The danger chiefly lies in acting well;
No crime's so great as daring to excel.
CHARLES CHURCHILL

9.17 elk, whelk

9.18 belch, squelch

9.19 geld, held, meld, quelled, swelled, weld, yelled, * propelled, compelled, upheld, rebelled, repelled, dispelled, expelled, beheld, withheld, excelled, * Danegeld, Ziegfeld, * jet-propelled, single-celled, * unparalleled, etc.

9.20 elf, Guelph, pelf, self, shelf, * herself, themself, oneself, itself, himself, myself, yourself, ourself

Man hands on misery to man.
It deepens like a coastal shelf.
Get out as early as you can,
And don't have any kids yourself.
PHILIP LARKIN

9.21 elm, helm, realm, * Anselm, Wilhelm, * overwhelm, underwhelm

9.22 help, kelp, whelp, yelp

9.23 belt, Celt, dealt, dwelt, felt, gelt, knelt, melt, pelt, Scheldt, smelt, spelt, svelte, veld, welt, * unbelt, misspelt, * fan belt, heartfelt, seat belt, green belt, life belt, Roosevelt, * safety belt, Bible

Belt, Weidenfeld, underfelt, * conveyor belt, Magherafelt

9.24 health, stealth, wealth, twelfth, * Commonwealth

9.25 delve, helve, shelve, twelve

9.26 delves, elves, helves, selves, shelves, twelves, * themselves, yourselves, ourselves

9.27 bells, cells, Del's, dwells, Kwells®, Mel's, sells, shells, smells, tells, Welles, Wells, yells, * lapels, Raquel's, farewells, Seychelles, rebels, excels, hotels, * Dardanelles, infidels, Tunbridge Wells, Book of Kells, etc.

'What is a church?' – Our honest sexton tells,
''Tis a tall building, with a tower and bells.'
GEORGE CRABBE

9.28 Clem, crème, em, *femme*, gem, hem, M, phlegm, REM, Shem, stem, them, * condemn, contemn, ahem, *ad rem*, a.m., FM, GM, p.m., PM, Yquem, Lib Dem, pro tem, suprême, * brainstem, mayhem, xylem, Ofgem, phloem, modem, apophthegm, *La Bohème*, ATM, AGM, requiem, Bethlehem, Eminem, chernozem, diadem, IBM, * *carpe diem*

9.29 hemp, Kemp, temp

9.30 dreamt, kempt, tempt, * unkempt, attempt, contempt, undreamt, pre-empt, exempt

9.31 gems, Ems, hems, stems, Thames, etc.

9.32 Aisne, Ben, Benn, Bren, den, en, Den, fen, gen, glen, Glenn, Gwen, hen, ken, Ken, Len, men, N, pen, Penn, Rennes, Seine, Taine, ten, then, wen, when, wren, Wren, yen, Zen, * again, Loren, Ardennes, amen, cayenne, Chechen, *kaizen*, doyenne, Phnom Penh, UN, Duchenne, * admen, playpen, stamen, apemen, cavemen, spacemen, chessmen, pressmen, peahen, he-men, pigpen, binmen, hymen, dolmen, con men, moorhen, nomen, snowmen, stuntmen, rumen, newsmen, * pathogen, allergen, halogen, Adrienne, antigen, acumen, weathermen, regimen, excisemen, *mise en scène*, histogen, businessmen, Ogaden, born-again, Nurofen®, fountain pen, musclemen, Sun Yat-sen, julienne, * cameramen, newspapermen, angry young men, carcinogen, Valenciennes, equestrienne, comedienne, tragedienne, ibuprofen, *absit omen*, * hallucinogen

Why are the needle and the pen
Thought incompatible by men?
ESTHER LEWIS

9.33 bench, blench, clench, Dench, drench, French, quench, stench, tench, trench, wench, wrench, * retrench, entrench

9.34 blenched, clenched, drenched, quenched, wrenched, * unquenched, retrenched, entrenched, * sun-drenched

9.35 bend, blend, Bridgend, end, fend, friend, lend, mend, penned, rend, send, spend, tend, trend, vend, wend, * unbend, append, upend, suspend, unkenned, attend, subtend, contend, offend, amend, commend, ascend, transcend, tail end, Gravesend, depend, impend, dispend, misspend, expend, pretend, intend, distend, extend, defend, befriend, emend, descend, Ostend, portend, forfend, Southend, * fag end, pen friend, girlfriend, weekend, pitchblende, bin end, stipend, godsend, hornblende, boyfriend, bookend, U-bend, * parascend, apprehend, recommend, reprehend, bitter end, dividend, on the mend, comprehend, condescend, round the bend, overspend, underspend, * superintend, overextend, misapprehend

Hopeless hope hopes on and meets no
end,
Wastes without springs and homes
without a friend.
JOHN CLARE

9.36 ginseng, Kaifeng, Boateng, * Mafikeng, * nasi goreng

9.37 length, strength, * wavelength, calf-length, knee-length

9.38 henge, Penge, * avenge, revenge, Stonehenge

9.39 cense, dense, fence, flense, hence, pence, sense, Spence, tense, thence, whence, cents, dents, gents, scents, tents, vents, * suspense, condense, offence, commence, laments, dispense, expense, pretence, intense, defence, events, ring-fence, immense, incense, Hortense, * frankincense, recompense, recommence, self-defence, common sense

Immodest words admit of no defence,
For want of decency is want of sense.
WENTWORTH DILLON

9.40 fenced, tensed, * against,
condensed, unfenced, commenced,
dispensed, ring-fenced, incensed,
* recompensed, recommenced

9.41 bent, Brent, cent, dent, gent,
Ghent, Gwent, Kent, leant, lent, Lent,
meant, pent, rent, scent, sent, spent,
stent, tent, Trent, vent, went, * unbent,
unspent, content, ferment, lament,
unmeant, ascent, assent, per cent,
consent, Tashkent, fragment, absent,
accent, hellbent, segment, frequent,
repent, misspent, indent, intent,
extent, event, prevent, invent, relent,
cement, descent, dissent, present,
resent, forewent, forwent, torment,
augment, foment, * advent, Advent,
ferment, indent, content, Broadbent,
portent, torment, * malcontent,
Steradent®, heaven-sent, regiment,
represent, circumvent, reinvent, represent, discontent, implement,
nonevent, complement, compliment,
document, ornament, orient,
overspent, Stoke-on-Trent,
underspent, underwent, supplement,
* experiment, misrepresent, reorient,
disorient

And sigh that one thing only has been
lent
To youth and age in common –
discontent.
MATTHEW ARNOLD

9.42 nth, tenth

9.43 Ben's, Benz, cleanse, Fens, gens,

glens, Gwen's, hens, Ken's, lens, pens,
TENS, Wrens, * impatiens, Mercedes-
Benz, vas deferens, * *Homo sapiens*,
* delirium tremens, etc.

9.44 cep, Depp, hep, pep, PEP, prep,
rep, schlep, step, steppe, yep, * unstep,
Dieppe, * quickstep, instep, sidestep,
doorstep, footstep, goosestep, * step-
by-step, overstep

9.45 ceps, crêpes, reps, Schweppes®,
steps, Steppes, * sidesteps, biceps,
triceps, forceps, footsteps,
* quadriceps, etc.

My mother groaned, my father wept.
Into the dangerous world I leapt.
WILLIAM BLAKE

9.46 crept, kept, leapt, sept, slept,
stepped, swept, wept, * adept,
unstepped, unwept, unswept, accept,
backswept, well-kept, yclept, inept,
except, * transept, percept, precept,
windswept, sidestepped, concept,
goosestepped, * intercept, overslept,
overstepped

9.47 Bess, bless, cess, chess, cress,
dress, guess, Hess, Hesse, Jess, less,
mess, ness, press, S, stress, Tess, tress,
yes, * profess, confess, unless, caress,
oppress, suppress, compress, aggress,
progress, address, undress, assess,
process, obsess, success, possess,
chapess, bad press, transgress,
largesse, heiress, mayoress, Caithness,
Skegness, SS, peeress, Sheerness, PS,
priestess, re-dress, depress, repress,
impress, express, regress, distress,
redress, liquesce, finesse, recess,
excess, princess, digress, stop press,

Loch Ness, duress, fluoresce,
Foulness, hostess, noblesse, US,
Jewess, * abbess, abscess, access,
headdress, excess, egress, Negress,
recess, prioress, winepress, tigress,
nightdress, goddess, compress,
congress, Congress, laundress,
prowess, countess, ogress, progress,
process, sundress, * battledress,
baroness, acquiesce, marchioness,
patroness, second-guess, shepherdess,
effervesce, effloresce, letterpress,
retrogress, SAS, NHS, deliquesce, SOS,
murderess, bouillabaisse, decompress,
readdress, deaconess, evanesce,
reassess, prepossess, repossess,
Inverness, dispossess, incandesce,
minidress, intumesce, lioness,
Lyonnesse, pythoness, convalesce,
obsolesce, phosphoresce, prophetess,
politesse, authoress, sorceress,
watercress, trouser press, coalesce,
opalesce, overdress, poetess,
nonetheless, governess, Dungeness,
stewardess, luminesce, * nevertheless,
manageress, couldn't-care-less,
Shoeburyness

9.48 desk, * burlesque, grotesque,
* Kafkaesque, arabesque, statuesque,
picaresque, picturesque, Romanesque,
humoresque, Junoesque, Pythonesque

9.49 best, blessed, blest, breast, Brest,
chest, crest, dressed, fest, guessed,
guest, hest, jest, lest, messed, nest,
pest, pressed, quest, rest, stressed, test,
vest, west, wrest, zest, * attest, protest,
contest, professed, confessed, molest,
unblessed, arrest, caressed, abreast,
oppressed, suppressed, compressed,
progressed, addressed, undressed,
unstressed, unrest, obsessed,

possessed, suggest, congest, NatWest,
hard-pressed, Mae West, well-dressed,
Trieste, retest, prestressed, egest, *id est*,
detest, infest, invest, behest, celeste,
depressed, repressed, impressed,
distressed, bequest, liquesced, request,
Midwest, ingest, divest, digest, George
Best, northwest, southwest, * gabfest,
backrest, armrest, redbreast, headrest,
retest, bitchfest, inquest, incest, digest,
contest, songfest, conquest, house
guest, protest, road test, goldcrest,
processed, love nest, footrest,
* acquiesced, manifest, Sackville-West,
palimpsest, paying guest, second-best,
self-confessed, effervesced, self-
possessed, readdressed, repossessed,
reinvest, rinderpest, interest, disinfest,
disinvest, chimney breast, coalesced,
overdressed, undervest, unaddressed,
underdressed, Sunday best,
unimpressed, unexpressed, Bucharest,
Budapest, * Haverfordwest, *chanson de
geste, Marie Celeste*, etc.

**One flew east and one flew west,
And one flew over the cuckoo's nest.**
NURSERY RHYME

9.50 crèche, flesh, fresh, mesh, nesh,
thresh, * afresh, crème fraîche,
refresh, enmesh, * horseflesh,
gooseflesh, * Marrakech, Bangladesh,
Gilgamesh, synchromesh, * Andhra
Pradesh, Madhya Pradesh

9.51 ate, bet, Brett, debt, fret, get, het,
jet, let, Lett, met, net, pet, Rhett, set,
sett, stet, sweat, threat, vet, wet, whet,
yet, * abet, forget, cadet, Chevette®,
Colette, sublet, arête, barrette, Debrett,
Annette, Jeanette, Nanette, cassette,
upset, gazette, Capet, hackette,

banquette, baguette, ladette, toilette, noisette, aigrette, layette, septet, sextet, curvet, Burnett, revet, preset, reset, Tibet, pipette, briquette, piquet, diskette, beget, quintet, nymphet, Yvette, Gillette, regret, vignette, Lynette, spinet, Wynette, beset, dinette, coquette, croquette, moquette, octet, nonet, offset, brochette, Claudette, quartet, corvette, Paulette, laundrette, lorgnette, courgette, georgette, Georgette, curette, Tourette, Odette, motet, rosette, duet, Phuket, roulette, brunette, Suzette, couchette, * dragnet, handset, Fastnet, hairnet, headset, tea set, inlet, kismet, fishnet, quickset, thickset, film set, inset, twinset, typeset, mind-set, offset, onset, outset, subset, upset, sunset, * alphabet, parapet, baronet, flannelette, avocet, Antoinette, satinet, clarinet, bassinet, statuette, marmoset, martinet, Lafayette, majorette, bayonet, maisonette, crêpe suzette, leatherette, epaulette, Letraset®, etiquette, netiquette, epithet, Exocet®, Bernadette, serviette, turbojet, cigarette, minaret, spinneret, Internet, intranet, winceyette, vinaigrette, kitchenette, silhouette, pirouette, minuet, cyberpet, scilicet, novelette, stockinet, overate, photoset, usherette, Mummerset, Somerset, suffragette, Juliet, oubliette, * marionette, *eau de toilette*

Lord God of Hosts, be with us yet,
Lest we forget – lest we forget!
RUDYARD KIPLING

9.52 bets, Brett's, debts, let's, Metz, pets, sweats, threats, * cadets, Annette's, Donets, cassettes,

courgettes, brunettes, * salopettes, pantalettes, castanets, clarinets, majorettes, serviettes, cigarettes, suffragettes, etc.

9.53 breadth, * handbreadth

9.54 Beth, breath, death, saith, Seth, * Macbeth, * shibboleth

9.55 Beth's, deaths, meths, Seth's, etc.

9.56 Bev, rev, * maglev, Brezhnev, Kiev, * Nureyev, * Diaghilev, Prokofiev

9.57 fez, Kez, Les, says, * des res, Montez, Cortez, oyez, * Baez, Lopez, Gomez, * Fernandez, Rodriguez

10.1 Debbie, plebby, webby, Selby, Denbigh, Denby, Tenby, peppy, preppy, Sheppey, kelpie, tempi, * Giuseppe, Gillespie, Entebbe, * cobwebby, * Tio Pepe®

10.2 Becky, brekky, leccy, recce, techie, Nevski, pesky, eggy, leggy, Peggy, dengue, * kromesky, Radetzky, * Paderewski, Dostoevsky

10.3 eddy, Eddy, Freddy, heady, Neddy, ready, steady, teddy, Teddy, thready, bendy, trendy, Wendy, Bette, Betty, Getty, Hettie, jetty, petty, sweaty, yeti, empty, hefty, lefty, sheltie, Welty, plenty, twenty, chesty, testy, * unsteady, unready, already, Allende, effendi, crescendi, spaghetti, confetti, machete, Andretti, Rossetti, aplenty, * rough-and-ready, oven-ready, amoretti, Serengeti, Olivetti, Donizetti, cognoscenti, * modus vivendi, *Deo volente, festina lente*

10.4 Effie, Delphi, bevvy, bevy, Chevy, heavy, levee, levy, envy, breathy, healthy, stealthy, wealthy, lengthy, * Adelphi, top-heavy, unhealthy, * Abernethy

As o'er my latest book I pored,
Enjoying it immensely,
I suddenly exclaimed 'Good Lord!'
And gripped the volume tensely.
P. G. WODEHOUSE

Drove my Chevy to the levee
But the levee was dry.
DON MCLEAN

10.5 belly, Delhi, deli, Ellie, jelly, Kelly, Melly, Nellie, nelly, Shelley, shelly, smelly, telly, welly, pebbly, trebly, Wembley, freckly, deadly, Hedley, medley, Smedley, friendly, Tetley, wetly, deftly, Bentley, gently, deathly, cleanly, Henley, Bexley, densely, tensely, Lesley, Leslie, Presley, Wesley, fleshly, freshly, Bletchley, Sketchley, beret, berry, Berry, bury, Bury, cherry, Ceri, Derry, ferry, Gerry, jerry, Jerry, Kerry, merry, perry, Perry, sherry, terry, Terry, very, wherry, debris, Hendry, entry, gentry, sentry, vestry, Elstree, Geoffrey, belfry, every, Henry, Dewi, * Grappelli, Clovelly, Corelli, Minnelli, Pwllheli, assembly, grotesquely, unfriendly, correctly, directly, intently, Llanelli, expressly, immensely, intensely, equerry, re-entry, * Leadbelly, potbelly, car ferry, Queensferry, knobkerrie, Horseferry, ancestry, * tagliatelle, Schiaparelli, Gabrieli, self-assembly, Zeffirelli, yellow-belly, vermicelli, incorrectly, indirectly, Botticelli, Torricelli, underbelly, user-friendly, elderberry, beriberi, necessary, whortleberry, serviceberry, Roddenberry, Pondicherry, boysenberry, loganberry, huckleberry, Huckleberry, Londonderry, * unnecessary, * Machiavelli, etc.

10.6 Clemmie, Emmy, jemmy, lemme, phlegmy, semi, Esme, any, Benny, blenny, Denny, Glennie, Jenny, Kenny, Lenny, many, penne, penny, Penny, Rennie, Stepney, Chesney, * antennae, Kilkenny, * spinning jenny, two-a-penny, * Abergavenny, * condemn me, etc.

10.7 Bessie, Crécy, dressy, Jesse, Jessie, messy, Nessie, Plessey, Pepsi®, Dempsey, sexy, Betsy, tsetse, Chelsea, Elsie, Selsey, pressie, frenzy, fleshy, sketchy, stretchy, tetchy, squelchy, Frenchy, edgy, veggie, * in esse, Mackenzie, * catalepsy, narcolepsy, epilepsy, apoplexy, cataplexy, Montmorency, Bangladeshi, Comaneci

10.8 Webber, Elba, Elbe, Melba, ember, member, leper, pepper, stepper, helper, yelper, temper, Vespa®, vesper, * Lloyd Webber, September, remember, dismember, December, November, distemper, * sidestepper, Culpeper, * misremember, * help her, etc.

Thirty days hath September,
April, June, and November.
TRADITIONAL RHYME

10.9 Becker, checker, Decca, decker, Dekker, Mecca, pecker, Secker, trekker, wrecker, Wesker, beggar, Gregor, mega, Edgar, Helga, * Quebecker, Rebecca, exchequer, Francesca, McGregor,

* Baedeker, spellchecker, oxpecker, Voortrekker, woodpecker, Heidegger, bootlegger, * double-decker, * peck her, beg her, etc.

10.10 bedder, Cheddar, Edda, header, Jedda, redder, shedder, shredder, spreader, tedder, threader, treader, elder, welder, Zelda, bender, blender, Brenda, fender, gender, Glenda, lender, mender, render, sender, slender, spender, Spender, splendour, tender, vendor, better, debtor, ETA, feta, fetter, getter, Greta, letter, setter, sweater, wetter, sceptre, tempter, hector, Hector, nectar, rector, sector, Spector, spectre, vector, EFTA, belter, delta, melter, Shelta, shelter, smelter, swelter, welter, centre, enter, renter, tenter, venter, Chester, cresta, ester, Esther, fester, Hester, jester, Leicester, Lester, Nesta, nester, pester, tester, Vesta, wester, zester, Webster, Dempster, Dexter, texter, Leominster, Leinster, * Griselda, suspender, addenda, attender, contender, offender, surrender, ascender, agenda, transgender, weekender, East Ender, pretender, extender, defender, descender, engender, pudenda, Bethesda, abetter, unfetter, Valletta, Loretta, Gambetta, Lambretta®, pancetta, vendetta, begetter, biretta, Rosetta, bruschetta, acceptor, preceptor, receptor, prospector, protector, Protector, convector, collector, connector, projector, objector, respecter, inspector, detector, defector, elector, selector, reflector, erector, ejector, rejector, director, bisector, dissector, lamenter, assentor, placenta, magenta, re-enter, preventer, inventor, frequenter, precentor,

presenter, tormentor, Rowenta, polenta, protester, Avesta, molester, arrester, fiesta, siesta, Sylvester, investor, celesta, sequester, semester, trimester, digester, nor'wester, northwester, sou'wester, southwester, * homesteader, bartender, pacesetter, Leadbetter, trendsetter, typesetter, go-getter, bonesetter, newsletter, daycentre, Jobcentre, ancestor, * van de Velde, parascender, hacienda, referenda, recommender, corrigenda, moneylender, carburettor, Henrietta, operetta, interceptor, helter-skelter, epicentre, empty-nester, Cirencester, polyester, * sinfonietta, impedimenta, experimenter, * send her, let her, etc.

10.11 deafer, heifer, zephyr, clever, ever, never, sever, Trevor, delver, elver, selva, shelver, Denver, Jephthah, blether, feather, heather, Heather, leather, nether, tether, weather, wether, whether, * forever, wherever, whenever, endeavour, whichever, whatever, however, whoever, whomever, together, * Fairweather, bellwether, shoe leather, * wheresoever, never-never, whensoever, Micheldever, whatsoever, howsoever, whosoever, whomsoever, hell for leather, altogether

**The glass is falling hour by hour, the glass will fall for ever,
But if you break the bloody glass you won't hold up the weather.**
Louis MacNeice

10.12 Bella, cellar, Della, dweller, Ella, fella, fellah, feller, Heller, Keller, Mellor, Pella, seller, smeller, speller, Stella, stellar, teller, Weller, Puebla, trembler, Kepler, Templar, heckler, Spengler, meddler, medlar, peddler, pedlar, fettler, settler, gentler, wrestler, error, Ferrar, terror, Deborah, zebra, Petra, plectra, spectra, extra, Defra, Sèvres, Ezra, Quechua, Kenya, Lenya, tenure, * propeller, McKellar, patella, novella, umbrella, lamella, candela, Mandela, Marcella, bestseller, reseller, repeller, impeller, dispeller, expeller, Estella, Fenella, Kinsella, paella, Viyella®, Nigella, foreteller, Floella, Louella, rubella, Prunella, assembler, exemplar, embezzler, þelles-lettres, et cetera, Electra, * tale-teller, cave-dweller, bierkeller, saltcellar, bookseller, knee-trembler, * Arabella, Annabella, a cappella, panatella, tarantella, salmonella, varicella, cerebellar, legionella, Isabella, interstellar, Cinderella, villanella, citronella, Rockefeller, mozzarella, storyteller, *fin de siècle*, cause célèbre, *raison d'être*, Clytemnestra, * Valpolicella, * sell her, tell her, etc.

10.13 Emma, Gemma, hemmer, lemma, stemma, tremor, smegma, Elmer, Selma, Thelma, Mesmer, henna, Jenna, Jenner, penna, senna, Senna, tenner, tenor, Edna, Etna, Gretna, Ventnor, Bremner, Cessna, * ack-emma, pip-emma, dilemma, McKenna, Ravenna, antenna, Siena, sienna, Vienna, Gehenna, Morwenna, duenna, * condemn her, etc.

10.14 dresser, guesser, Hesse, lesser, lessor, stressor, Tessa, TESSA, flexor, sexer, vexer, Elsa, censer, censor, ENSA, fencer, Mensa, sensor, spencer, Spencer, Spenser, tenser, tensor, cleanser, leisure, measure, pleasure,

treasure, Cheshire, Escher, flesher, fresher, pressure, thresher, censure, betcha, etcher, fetcher, fletcher, Fletcher, lecher, sketcher, stretcher, lecture, belcher, squelcher, bencher, denture, quencher, trencher, venture, gesture, texture, dredger, edger, hedger, ledger, pledger, * suppressor, compressor, aggressor, addresser, professor, confessor, Vanessa, assessor, successor, possessor, depressor, repressor, Odessa, Alexa, condenser, Walesa, dispenser, extensor, Demelza, cadenza, credenza, displeasure, refresher, dementia, conjecture, adventure, backbencher, debenture, indenture, frontbencher, St Leger, avenger, * hairdresser, processor, indexer, prefecture, thirst-quencher, * decompressor, repossessor, predecessor, Alka-Seltzer®, influenza, made-to-measure, countermeasure, acupressure, architecture, peradventure, misadventure, Bonaventure, * Nebuchadnezzar, * microprocessor, * assess her, refresh her, etc.

Now hatred is by far the longest pleasure;
Men love in haste, but they detest at leisure.
LORD BYRON

10.15 epic, Vedic, medic, Celtic, peptic, sceptic, septic, hectic, Delphic, Elphick, pelvic, ethic, Smethwick, relic, Berwick, cleric, Derek, derrick, Eric, ferric, Herrick, Merrick, redbrick, Cedric, Ettrick, metric, Prestwick, Sedgewick, Fenwick, Chetnik, ethnic, Selznick, Beswick, Keswick, Belgic, * alembic, prophetic, bathetic, pathetic,

balletic, phonetic, acetic, ascetic,
athletic, magnetic, Helvetic, hermetic,
aesthetic, synthetic, emetic, mimetic,
frenetic, genetic, kinetic, splenetic,
pyretic, prosthetic, cosmetic, poetic,
aseptic, dyspeptic, eupeptic, eclectic,
dyslectic, authentic, domestic,
majestic, malefic, benefic, angelic,
Goidelic, enteric, mesmeric, hysteric,
generic, chimeric, Homeric, numeric,
symmetric, obstetric, electric,
concentric, eccentric, Scalextric®,
polemic, alchemic, pandemic,
endemic, systemic, totemic,
transgenic, Hellenic, irenic, eugenic,
dyslexic, pyrexic, forensic,
* paramedic, alphabetic, apathetic,
parenthetic, Masoretic, anaesthetic,
arithmetic, empathetic, energetic,
theoretic, sympathetic, synergetic,
kinaesthetic, synaesthetic, diabetic,
diuretic, cybernetic, dietetic, copacetic,
cataleptic, analeptic, antiseptic,
narcoleptic, epileptic, neuroleptic,
Euro-sceptic, apoplectic, anorectic,
dialectic, psychedelic, evangelic,
stratospheric, atmospheric, exoteric,
hemispheric, esoteric, climacteric,
isomeric, tachometric, barometric,
parametric, asymmetric, hexametric,
telemetric, thermometric, geometric,
kilometric, biometric, diametric,
psychometric, isometric, dielectric,
bisymmetric, optometric,
chronometric, volumetric,
photometric, ethnocentric, geocentric,
egocentric, Eurocentric, academic,
epidemic, pathogenic, allergenic,
callisthenic, telegenic, oestrogenic,
schizophrenic, cryogenic, psychogenic,
oncogenic, autogenic, neurasthenic,
photogenic, mutagenic, pyrotechnic,
polytechnic, geodesic, anorexic,

* apologetic, * peripatetic,
antipathetic, unsympathetic,
diaphoretic, antimagnetic,
ferromagnetic, photosynthetic,
antiemetic, telekinetic, psychokinetic,
antipyretic, alphanumeric,
anthropometric, trigonometric,
sociometric, hydroelectric,
photoelectric, nonacademic,
radiogenic, carcinogenic, mediagenic,
* electromagnetic, hallucinogenic

10.16 medics, sceptics, ethics, relics,
clerics, Derek's, Eric's, Hendrix, Essex,
Wessex, * appendix, phonetics,
ascetics, athletics, magnetics,
aesthetics, synthetics, emetics,
genetics, kinetics, prosthetics,
cosmetics, poetics, domestics,
hysterics, obstetrics, electrics,
directrix, polemics, eugenics,
* paramedics, anaesthetics, diabetics,
diuretics, Callanetics, cybernetics,
dietetics, homiletics, epileptics, Euro-
sceptics, dialectics, atmospherics,
biometrics, psychometrics, isometrics,
academics, cryogenics, callisthenics,
pyrotechnics, polytechnics, etc.

10.17 tepid, eddied, steadied, splendid,
fetid, emptied, levied, envied, bellied,
gelid, jellied, buried, ferried, serried,
jemmied, blessed, frenzied, wretched,
* intrepid, three-legged, long-legged,
cross-legged, bow-legged, unenvied,
potbellied, unburied, * yellow-bellied,
etc.

10.18 leopard, peppered, shepherd,
Shepard, headed, leaded, shredded,
wedded, blended, ended, mended,
tended, betted, bettered, fretted,
lettered, fettered, sweated, tempted,

sheltered, sweltered, centred, dented, entered, scented, festered, pestered, rested, tested, vested, Bedford, Redford, Deptford, Stretford, Telford, Wexford, Chelmsford, severed, method, tethered, weathered, Herod, Edward, westward, tenured, Leonard, Reynard, censored, leisured, measured, treasured, censured, Trenchard, ventured, * remembered, unleaded, hard-headed, bareheaded, red-headed, clear-headed, three-headed, beheaded, bigheaded, pig-headed, light-headed, hot-headed, baldheaded, two-headed, attended, untended, amended, commended, unmended, ascended, pretended, intended, distended, extended, defended, befriended, descended, unfettered, unlettered, indebted, accepted, excepted, attempted, suspected, protected, affected, collected, corrected, connected, expected, detected, infected, elected, reflected, dejected, directed, dissected, undented, contented, fermented, lamented, consented, unscented, accented, self-centred, repented, invented, demented, augmented, attested, contested, untested, molested, congested, flat-chested, invested, requested, sequestered, digested, eisteddfod, unsevered, untethered, northwestward, southwestward, uncensored, unmeasured, uncensured, * level-headed, empty-headed, muddleheaded, recommended, unattended, unintended, undefended, undescended, apprehended, unaccepted, unattempted, disaffected, disconnected, unsuspected, unprotected, unaffected, uncollected,

uncorrected, unconnected, unexpected, undetected, uninfected, unelected, unreflected, uninflected, undirected, regimented, represented, discontented, documented, ornamented, unfermented, unlamented, unaccented, unfrequented, redigested, single-breasted, unattested, uncontested, unmolested, double-breasted, uncongested, unrequested, undigested, * unprecedented, unrepresented, undocumented, etc.

A little still she strove, and much
    repented,
And whispering 'I will ne'er consent' –
    consented.
LORD BYRON

10.19 leopards, shepherds, Edwards, Leonard's, westwards, * northwest-wards, southwestwards, etc.

10.20 wreckage, tentage, vestige, selvedge, Redbridge, Bembridge, Selfridge, ennage, Greenwich, message, presage, * appendage, curettage, percentage, assemblage

10.21 pebble, rebel, treble, Kemble, tremble, Keppel, sepal, Semple, temple, deckle, freckle, heckle, Jekyll, shekel, speckle, medal, meddle, pedal, peddle, reddle, treadle, Weddell, Grendel, Kendal, Lendl, Mendel, Pendle, Rendell, Wendell, fettle, Gretel, kettle, metal, mettle, nettle, petal, settle, septal, rectal, dental, gentle, lentil, mental, rental, festal, vestal, TEFL, helpful, dreadful, fretful, restful, healthful, Grenfell, stressful, vengeful, bevel, devil, level, Neville,

revel, Bethel, Ethel, ethyl, methyl,
Errol, beryl, Beryl, Cheryl, feral,
ferrule, Meryl, peril, federal, tendril,
petrel, petrol, spectral, central, ventral,
kestrel, dextral, several, general,
fennel, kennel, regnal, Cecil, Chessell,
nestle, pestle, TESL, trestle, vessel,
wrestle, Edsel, pretzel, quetzal, pencil,
stencil, bezel, Denzil, special,
* assemble, dissemble, resemble, back-
pedal, prebendal, pudendal, unsettle,
resettle, parental, placental,
judgmental, unhelpful, forgetful,
regretful, respectful, neglectful,
eventful, resentful, successful,
revengeful, bedevil, split-level,
dishevel, imperil, integral, campestral,
ancestral, sylvestral, orchestral,
commensal, utensil, embezzle,
especial, potential, torrential,
tangential, credential, sequential,
essential, prudential, * gunmetal,
daredevil, she-devil, eyelevel,
* reassemble, disassemble,
sacramental, transcendental,
accidental, temperamental,
sentimental, elemental, detrimental,
regimental, departmental, interdental,
instrumental, incidental, incremental,
compartmental, Oriental, Occidental,
continental, nonjudgmental,
monumental, ornamental,
fundamental, governmental,
supplemental, disrespectful,
uneventful, unsuccessful, deferential,
preferential, referential, reverential,
exponential, evidential, presidential,
residential, penitential, existential,
pestilential, differential, inferential,
quintessential, inessential, influential,
confidential, providential,
consequential, nonessential,
* transcontinental, coincidental,

experimental, environmental,
nonaccidental, nongovernmental,
unsentimental, subcontinental,
nonresidential, experiential,
inconsequential, * Popocatépetl,
interdepartmental, intercontinental,
intergovernmental

Tender-handed stroke a nettle,
And it stings you for your pains;
Grasp it like a man of mettle,
And it soft as silk remains.
AARON HILL

10.22 freckled, heckled, metalled,
nettled, settled, nestled, wrestled,
Gerald, herald, * assembled, unsettled,
bedevilled, Fitzgerald, embezzled, etc.

10.23 pebbles, Eccles, freckles,
speckles, Engels, medals, pedals,
nettles, petals, lentils, kennels, pencils,
* utensils, credentials, essentials, etc.

10.24 Blenheim, denim, * defend him,
lent him, etc.

10.25 Beckham, Peckham, Shechem,
welcome, Wellcome, Egham, seldom,
Streatham, septum, rectum, Eltham,
Feltham, Trentham, Bentham, Pelham,
vellum, emblem, peplum, bedlam,
Meldrum, plectrum, spectrum,
Denham, venom, Epsom, Wrexham,
jetsam, Chesham, Gresham, Belgium,
* unwelcome, addendum, agendum,
pudendum, momentum, flagellum,
post-bellum, exemplum, electrum,
envenom, * referendum, corrigendum,
antebellum, cerebellum, interregnum,
* send 'em, wrecked 'em, etc.

10.26 Pepin, tenpin, Elgin, cretin,

pecten, pectin, Quentin, destine,
elfin, Bevin, Kevin, Previn, Levin,
Kelvin, Melvin, Welwyn, Devlin,
Emlyn, gremlin, Kremlin, Erin,
Perrin, Sherrin, eccrine, penguin,
Edwin, Selwyn, Lenin, rennin, venin,
pepsin, Yeltsin, resin, engine,
* Potemkin, San Quentin, progestin,
clandestine, predestine, intestine,
Helvellyn, Fluellen, Llewellyn,
muezzin, * gibberellin, antivenin,
vasopressin, Taliesin, * settin',
dressin', etc.

10.27 ebon, Melbourne, weapon,
hempen, beckon, Brecon, Deccan,
reckon, Mencken, Megan, deaden,
leaden, redden, Seddon, Sneddon,
Hebdon, Sheldon, Weldon, Brendan,
Hendon, tendon, Dresden, Breton,
jetton, threaten, Repton, lectern,
Elton, Melton, Skelton, Benton,
Denton, Fenton, Kenton, lenten,
Trenton, Preston, western, Weston,
sextan, sexton, deafen, Stéphane,
Bevan, Devon, Evan, heaven, leaven,
seven, Severn, Bethan, lengthen,
strengthen, leathern, Ellen, felon,
Helen, melon, Declan, heron, veteran,
chevron, brethren, Kenyan, Kenyon,
Emmen, Lemmon, lemon, Yemen,
Helpmann, headman, Steadman,
Feldman, bellman, Hellman, penman,
chessman, desman, pressman,
helmsman, freshman, Welshman,
Frenchman, henchman, Brennan,
Lennon, pennon, tenon, * Tibetan,
Avestan, Midwestern, eleven,
McKellen, Magellan, rebellion,
Trevelyan, * muskmelon,
* Armageddon, pademelon,
watermelon, philodendron,
rhododendron, Agamemnon

And bound on that journey you find
your attorney (who started that
morning from Devon);
He's a bit undersized, and you don't
feel surprised when he tells you he's
only eleven.
W. S. GILBERT

10.28 Essen, lessen, lesson, Wesson,
Epson, Texan, Stetson®, Belsen,
Nelson, Benson, ensign, Jensen,
cession, freshen, session, section,
flexion, gentian, mention, pension,
tension, question, Belgian, * half-
nelson, full nelson, profession,
confession, oppression, suppression,
compression, aggression, progression,
procession, obsession, succession,
concession, possession, transgression,
accession, depression, Depression,
repression, impression, expression,
discretion, regression, precession,
recession, secession, digression,
perception, conception, deception,
reception, inception, exception, pre-
emption, redemption, exemption,
protection, affection, perfection,
confection, convection, collection,
complexion, correction, connection,
projection, subsection, objection,
subjection, inspection, detection,
defection, refection, infection,
election, selection, deflection,
reflection, inflection, erection,
resection, dejection, ejection,
rejection, injection, direction,
bisection, dissection, cross-section,
suspension, attention, contention,
subvention, convention, ascension,
Ascension, abstention, detention,
pretension, retention, intention,
distension, extension, prevention,
invention, declension, dissension,

dimension, Laurentian, Lawrentian, suggestion, congestion, ingestion, digestion, * self-possession, self-expression, decompression, prepossession, repossession, intercession, dispossession, indiscretion, nonaggression, apperception, self-deception, preconception, interception, misconception, contraception, retrospection, self-protection, retroflexion, recollection, resurrection, Resurrection, self-selection, genuflection, circumspection, reconnection, reinfection, pre-election, re-election, deselection, reselection, redirection, predilection, introspection, imperfection, disaffection, insurrection, disconnection, intersection, interjection, disinfection, vivisection, by-election, apprehension, reprehension, circumvention, reinvention, inattention, intervention, hypertension, hypotension, contravention, comprehension, condescension, self-suggestion, indigestion, * delicatessen, hypercorrection, misapprehension, incomprehension, nonintervention, autosuggestion, * immunosuppression, antivivisection

10.29 beckoned, fecund, reckoned, second, threatened, deafened, leavened, Cleland, Welland, headland, Shetland, wetland, Westland, errand, gerund, reverend, Reverend, Edmund, Redmond, Esmond, Desmond, lessened, freshened, mentioned, questioned, legend, * split-second, unleavened, unmentioned, unquestioned, * aforementioned,

* nanosecond, millisecond, microsecond, well-intentioned, undermentioned, etc.

George the First was always reckoned Vile, but viler George the Second.
WALTER SAVAGE LANDOR

10.30 seconds, Shetlands, wetlands, errands, Edmonds, legends, * Bury St Edmunds, etc.

10.31 tenpins, Jenkins, Emlyn's, gremlins, penguins, Edwin's, * intestines, etc.

10.32 weapons, reckons, Megan's, tendons, Evans, heavens, sevens, melons, lemons, lessons, sessions, Sessions, sections, pensions, questions, * elevens, good heavens, St Helens, rebellions, professions, processions, concessions, possessions, exceptions, connections, objections, reflections, conventions, abstentions, intentions, suggestions, etc.

10.33 peccant, pedant, pendant, pendent, extant, sextant, errant, gerent, entrant, segment, vestment, clement, Clement, pennant, tenant, Tennant, pregnant, regnant, remnant, Besant, Cheshunt, crescent, peasant, pheasant, pleasant, present, sentient, trenchant, * attendant, ascendant, transcendent, dependant, dependent, defendant, intendant, resplendent, descendant, expectant, repentant, contestant, appellant, propellant, flagellant, repellent, expellent, aberrant, deterrent, inherent, knight-errant, vicegerent, re-entrant, inclement, amendment, abetment,

revetment, curettement, contentment,
resentment, investment, assessment,
commencement, refreshment,
retrenchment, entrenchment,
subtenant, lieutenant, confessant,
suppressant, pearlescent, quiescent,
depressant, excrescent, senescent,
incessant, fluorescent, pubescent,
putrescent, unpleasant, consentient,
presentient, dissentient, insentient,
* independent, disinfectant,
unrepentant, decongestant,
interpellant, reinvestment,
reassessment, sublieutenant,
adolescent, acquiescent, effervescent,
deliquescent, evanescent,
prepubescent, recrudescent,
incandescent, iridescent, convalescent,
obsolescent, phosphorescent,
coalescent, opalescent, juvenescent,
luminescent, omnipresent,
* interdependent, overdependent,
superintendent, antidepressant,
preadolescent, * immunosuppressant

10.34 pedants, pendants, sentence,
semblance, Terence, entrance,
deference, preference, reference,
reverence, Reverence, severance,
vestments, penance, tenants,
remnants, essence, peasants,
pheasants, Pleasence, presence,
presents, sentience, vengeance,
* attendance, attendants, transcendence,
dependants, dependence,
resplendence, acceptance, repentance,
contestants, repellence, resemblance,
aberrance, deterrence, remembrance,
irreverence, amendments, quiescence,
quintessence, excrescence, senescence,
fluorescence, pubescence, putrescence,
insentience, * independence,
nonattendance, adolescence,

adolescents, acquiescence,
effervescence, deliquescence,
evanescence, prepubescence,
recrudescence, inflorescence,
incandescence, iridescence,
convalescence, obsolescence,
phosphorescence, coalescence,
opalescence, juvenescence,
luminescence, omnipresence,
* interdependence, overdependence,
superintendence, antidepressants,
preadolescence, etc.

10.35 seventh, * eleventh

10.36 ebbing, webbing, Epping,
stepping, helping, yelping, checking,
decking, necking, pecking, trekking,
begging, legging, pegging, bedding,
dreading, heading, leading, Reading,
Redding, shredding, spreading,
treading, wedding, gelding, welding,
bending, blending, ending, mending,
pending, spending, tending, letting,
netting, setting, wetting, tempting,
betting, fretting, netting, setting,
sweating, wetting, belting, felting,
melting, pelting, smelting, tenting,
venting, jesting, nesting, resting,
testing, delving, dwelling, felling,
selling, smelling, spelling, swelling,
telling, yelling, trembling, heckling,
meddling, peddling, settling, nestling,
wrestling, fledgling, herring,
headspring, wellspring, redwing,
sweptwing, Fleming, hemming,
lemming, stemming, helming,
Denning, penning, Steyning, blessing,
dressing, guessing, Lessing, pressing,
flexing, vexing, fencing, Tenzing,
threshing, etching, fetching, retching,
sketching, stretching, belching,
squelching, clenching, drenching,

quenching, wrenching, dredging, edging, hedging, pledging, sledging, wedging, * bedecking, spot-checking, beheading, unbending, attending, offending, unending, ascending, transcending, impending, pretending, intending, extending, defending, descending, abetting, forgetting, upsetting, besetting, excepting, prospecting, affecting, collecting, connecting, projecting, respecting, expecting, fermenting, lamenting, consenting, repenting, eventing, relenting, dissenting, presenting, tormenting, protesting, molesting, arresting, suggesting, investing, requesting, compelling, reselling, misspelling, excelling, condemning, confessing, caressing, progressing, undressing, depressing, distressing, digressing, commencing, dispensing, refreshing, alleging, avenging, * doorstepping, bootlegging, deadheading, subheading, heart-rending, mind-bending, trendsetting, filmsetting, typesetting, blood-letting, hairdressing, well-dressing, processing, * double-checking, featherbedding, parascending, condescending, overspending, moneylending, thermosetting, stamp-collecting, self-respecting, intersecting, unsuspecting, unrelenting, unprotesting, storytelling, acquiescing, decompressing, prepossessing, repossessing, * uncomprehending, interconnecting, unprepossessing, etc.

10.37 helpings, leggings, headings, weddings, endings, settings, dwellings, spellings, herrings, lemmings, Jennings, blessings, etchings, etc.

10.38 develop, envelop, * redevelop

10.39 Lesseps, * develops, envelops, * redevelops

10.40 developed, enveloped, * redeveloped, * underdeveloped, undeveloped

10.41 Geddes, Lettice, lettuce, Prentiss, testis, Memphis, crevice, Elvis, pelvis, Ellis, trellis, derris, Ferris, Nerys, Emrys, premise, Dennis, Ennis, Glenys, menace, tennis, Venice, sepsis, lexis, * apprentice, Ben Nevis, Llanberis, Alexis, asepsis, * *compos mentis*, antisepsis, * Thomas à Kempis, *non compos mentis*, amanuensis, * *in loco parentis*

Better mention 'The Merchant of Venice'
When her sweet pound o' flesh you would menace.
COLE PORTER

10.42 trespass, preface, Hellas, jealous, zealous, helpless, feckless, necklace, reckless, legless, headless, endless, friendless, restless, selfless, breathless, deathless, stressless, sexless, senseless, ferrous, terrace, empress, Esdras, temptress, sempstress, dextrous, generous, genus, redness, wetness, deftness, deafness, wellness, freshness, nexus, plexus, Texas, census, precious, * horrendous, tremendous, stupendous, prospectus, conspectus, momentous, portentous, asbestos, Marcellus, relentless, defenceless, Mackerras, nonferrous, ungenerous, rebellious, correctness, directness, consensus, infectious, contentious, tendentious, sententious, pretentious, dissentious, licentious, * overzealous, ambidextrous, overgenerous, solar plexus, Paracelsus, semiprecious, conscientious, unpretentious, * expect us, refresh us, etc.

10.43 tempest, trespassed, reddest, eldest, wettest, deafest, prefaced, breakfast, steadfast, gentlest, terraced, tensest, freshest, etc.

10.44 leftist, dentist, cellist, check list, chemist, menaced, sexist, * librettist, cornettist, apprenticed, * clarinettist, irredentist, biochemist, * heterosexist

10.45 peckish, reddish, Lettish, fetish, pettish, Kentish, wreckfish, elfish, selfish, shellfish, hellish, relish, cherish, perish, blemish, Flemish, Rhenish, * coquettish, unselfish, embellish, replenish

10.46 relished, cherished, perished, blemished, * embellished, unblemished, replenished, * unembellished

10.47 Egbert, Prescot, Prescott, legate, effort, Evert, Helot, prelate, zealot, template, desert

10.48 cesspit, respite, debit, Tebbitt, Nesbit, Becket, Beckett, credit, edit, geddit, velvet, pellet, necklet, ferret, merit, emmet, helmet, pelmet, Bennett, genet, rennet, senate, sennet, tenet, bedsit, exit, Melchett, * decrepit, subedit, accredit, discredit, coedit, demerit, inherit, herb bennet, * disinherit, * check it, said it, etc.

If, with the literate, I am
Impelled to try an epigram,
I never seek to take the credit;
We all assume that Oscar said it.
DOROTHY PARKER

10.49 Elspeth, Hesketh, Knebworth, Hepworth, Petworth, Exmouth, Emsworth, Letchworth, Kenneth

10.50 festive, restive, pensive, * perceptive, deceptive, receptive, pre-emptive, redemptive, perspective, prospective, protective, affective, collective, corrective, connective, objective, subjective, respective, detective, effective, defective, infective, invective, elective, selective, reflective, directive, attentive, retentive, preventive, inventive, incentive, suggestive, digestive, oppressive, aggressive, progressive, obsessive, successive, possessive, depressive, repressive, impressive, expressive, regressive, recessive, excessive, digressive, reflexive, offensive, expensive, intensive, extensive, defensive, * contraceptive, unreceptive, retrospective, irrespective, ineffective, nonselective, unreflective, inattentive, disincentive, unimpressive, apprehensive, inoffensive, inexpensive, comprehensive, coextensive, * overprotective, counteroffensive

10.51 eddies, readies, teddies, Betty's, empties, lefties, twenties, testes, bevvies, heavies, jellies, wellies, berries, cherries, sentries, Jeffreys, Jenny's, pennies, pressies, Menzies, etc.

10.52 members, vespers, checkers,

Chequers, beggars, elders, welders, betters, fetters, feathers, leathers, Bella's, Mellors, Sellers, hecklers, settlers, errors, terrors, tremors, Jenna's, tenors, dresses, guesses, Messrs, tresses, senses, sensors, pleasures, treasures, sketches, wretches, edges, hedges, * Rebecca's, suspenders, offenders, *EastEnders*, directors, investors, expenses, adventures, *Avengers*, etc.

10.53 Enderby, Wetherby, therapy, entropy, jeopardy, yesterday, melody, threnody, Wednesday, Hecate, Hegarty, Peggotty, deputy, penalty, specialty, seventy, beggarly, elderly, slenderly, tenderly, mentally, westerly, helpfully, dreadfully, Beverley, cleverly, Everly, centrally, severally, generally, Thessaly, leisurely, specially, terribly, preferably, memorably, sensibly, legibly, westwardly, secondly, separately, desperately, pleasantly, presently, heavenly, jealously, zealously, recklessly, breathlessly, peppery, peccary, beggary, Gregory, rectory, reverie, feathery, heathery, leathery, celery, Ellery, temporary, equerry, vespiary, bestiary, vestiary, breviary, emery, memory, hennery, venery, pessary, sensory, treasury, lechery, treachery, century, elderberry, heraldry, prebendary, secondary, legendary, repertory, predatory, prefatory, helotry, zealotry, desultory, pedantry, sedentary, errantry, peasantry, pleasantry, devilry, revelry, weaponry, heronry, lectionary, Jeremy, Bellamy, enemy, sesame, ebony, betony, tetany, empathy, Stephanie, Bethany, felony, Melanie, lemony, Yemeni, embassy, legacy, ecstasy,

jealousy, prelacy, heresy, leprosy, Hennessey, tendency, clemency, tenancy, pregnancy, Pevensey, energy, lethargy, * Penelope, synecdoche, telegraphy, telepathy, northwesterly, southwesterly, unhelpfully, regretfully, respectfully, resentfully, successfully, especially, potentially, essentially, impeccably, incredibly, regrettably, perceptibly, respectably, irreparably, ostensibly, illegibly, contentedly, expectantly, unpleasantly, horrendously, tremendously, relentlessly, extempore, *pro tempore*, grotesquery, peremptory, trajectory, refectory, directory, exemplary, contemporary, extemporary, incendiary, stipendiary, millenary, accessory, dispensary, knight-errantry, concessionary, discretionary, confectionery, mastectomy, vasectomy, lumpectomy, McMenemy, arch-enemy, chalcedony, Persephone, telephony, miscellany, anemone, Gethsemane, hegemony, intestacy, supremacy, discrepancy, ascendancy, dependency, expectancy, inclemency, * chemotherapy, hypnotherapy, psychotherapy, hydrotherapy, transcendentally, accidentally, temperamentally, sentimentally, departmentally, incidentally, incrementally, monumentally, fundamentally, disrespectfully, uneventfully, unsuccessfully, preferentially, influentially, confidentially, unforgettably, imperceptibly, unexpectedly, ex-directory, alimentary, parliamentary, testamentary, sedimentary, elementary, complementary, complimentary, documentary, supplementary, rudimentary, extrasensory, penitentiary, appendectomy, hysterectomy, tonsillectomy, open sesame, independency, * electrotherapy, aromatherapy, unsentimentally, experimentally, coincidentally, environmentally, * radiotherapy, physiotherapy, unparliamentary, uncomplimentary, plenipotentiary, etc.

10.54 recipe, remedy, Kennedy, entity, brevity, levity, velvety, verity, equity, Equity, enmity, lenity, density, readily, steadily, heavily, healthily, stealthily, merrily, verily, Emily, Cecily, messily, sketchily, tetchily, medically, sceptically, ethically, chemically, technically, ethnically, splendidly, pensively, temptingly, selfishly, pellitory, territory, secretary, cemetery, presbytery, dentistry, chemistry, registry, veterinary, seminary, destiny, Medici, effigy, elegy, * heredity, identity, nonentity, longevity, fidelity, asperity, dexterity, severity, celerity, temerity, sincerity, prosperity, austerity, posterity, celebrity, integrity, inequity, unsteadily, primarily, prophetically, pathetically, phonetically, magnetically, hermetically, aesthetically, synthetically, frenetically, genetically, poetically, identically, authentically, majestically, angelically, hysterically, generically, numerically, symmetrically, electrically, eccentrically, nonsensically, confessedly, professedly, allegedly, deceptively, protectively, collectively, objectively, subjectively, respectively, effectively, attentively, oppressively, aggressively, progressively,

successively, impressively, excessively, offensively, intensively, extensively, defensively, depressingly, distressingly, refreshingly, unselfishly, hereditary, telemetry, extremity, Yosemite, serenity, obscenity, solemnity, indemnity, necessity, convexity, perplexity, complexity, propensity, intensity, immensity, * infidelity, insincerity, necessarily, voluntarily, ordinarily, momentarily, alphabetically, apathetically, parenthetically, arithmetically, energetically, theoretically, sympathetically, hypothetically, geometrically, diametrically, academically, retrospectively, apprehensively, inoffensively, comprehensively, unsuspectingly, overwhelmingly, undersecretary, biochemistry, * unnecessarily, involuntarily, unsympathetically, apologetically, etc.

10.55 deputy, helpfully, dreadfully, sexually, sensually, February, estuary, penury, * unhelpfully, regretfully, respectfully, resentfully, successfully, perpetually, conceptually, effectually, eventually, * disrespectfully, uneventfully, unsuccessfully, ineffectually, intellectually, etc.

10.56 djellaba, sepulchre, seconder, Shetlander, predator, senator, metaphor, helluva, leveller, reveller, Deborah, emperor, Klemperer, tempera, tempura, plethora, genera, tessera, treasurer, lecturer, reckoner, Smetana, threatener, westerner, Eleanor, Helena, pensioner, questioner, trespasser, Leicestershire, Bedfordshire, premature, sepulture,

replica, erica, Erica, Seneca, Jessica,
Cressida, reseda, presbyter, creditor,
editor, heritor, genitor, Exeter,
register, Pettifer, Jennifer, Hegira,
enema, Bessemer, eczema, retina,
Elinor, perisher, temperature,
messenger, Schlesinger, rescuer,
Hecuba, nebula, fecula, secular,
regular, scheduler, cellular,
* developer, telegrapher, et cetera,
ephemera, confectioner,
remembrancer, nomenclature,
angelica, America, subeditor,
competitor, inheritor, non sequitur,
progenitor, deregister, umbellifer,
expenditure, investiture, divestiture,
progeniture, executor, molecular,
Benbecula, Vulpecula, irregular,
* ready-reckoner, primogenitor,
Quadragesima, Sexagesima,
Quinquagesima, primogeniture,
* Septuagesima,

10.57 peskier, readier, steadier,
trendier, pettier, sweatier, emptier,
heavier, healthier, wealthier, smellier,
deadlier, friendlier, burier, Ferrier,
merrier, terrier, premier, denier,
Chechnya, dressier, messier, sexier,
sketchier, * compendia, Ossetia,
poinsettia, unhealthier, Saint Helier,
sommelier, hotelier, millennia,
dyspepsia, eupepsia, alexia, dyslexia,
pyrexia, Valencia, * in absentia,
Philadelphia, psychedelia, anorexia,
* intelligentsia, etc.

10.58 shepherded, heralded,
heavenward, debited, credited, edited,
merited, exited, registered, Hereford,
Beresford, Hereward, * unheralded,
untenanted, unedited, unmerited,
unregistered

10.59 heavenwards, Hereward's

**It is not that I am not sensible
To merits in themselves ostensible.**
LORD BYRON

10.60 beddable, credible, edible,
spreadable, bendable, mendable,
sendable, spendable, vendible,
gettable, wettable, rentable, vegetable,
effable, sellable, terrible, reparable,
separable, preferable, memorable,
equable, tenable, pregnable, guessable,
flexible, sensible, legible, spectacle,
pentacle, tentacle, temporal, federal,
pectoral, femoral, general, textural,
sectional, bestial, burial, Meriel,
Tenniel, medical, pedicle, sceptical,
testicle, ethical, helical, pellicle,
clerical, spherical, metrical, ventricle,
chemical, technical, vesicle, lexical,
skeletal, genital, vegetal, pedestal,
plentiful, aestival, festival, cerebral,
decimal, retinal, sentinel, seminal,
Lemuel, menstrual, sexual, sensual,
textual, * impeccable, incredible,
inedible, commendable, dependable,
expendable, extendable, defendable,
forgettable, regrettable, perceptible,
susceptible, acceptable, contemptible,
perfectible, collectable, respectable,
detectable, delectable, electable,
injectable, lamentable, preventable,
presentable, contestable, arrestable,
comestible, suggestible, detestable,
digestible, ineffable, unsellable,
indelible, irreparable, inseparable,
unmemorable, inequable, untenable,
impregnable, impressionable,
addressable, accessible, expressible,
inflexible, dispensable, defensible,
insensible, ostensible, unquenchable,
receptacle, electoral, ephemeral,

outgeneral, conjectural, professional,
confessional, congressional,
processional, obsessional, recessional,
exceptional, directional, conventional,
intentional, celestial, terrestrial,
bimestrial, perennial, centennial,
millennial, quinquennial, decennial,
biennial, triennial, quadrennial,
heretical, poetical, conventicle,
identical, unethical, hysterical,
chimerical, numerical, symmetrical,
obstetrical, calendrical, electrical,
polemical, arsenical, nontechnical,
nonsensical, congenital, centesimal,
millesimal, intestinal, trigeminal,
premenstrual, transsexual, asexual,
bisexual, consensual, perpetual,
conceptual, perceptual, aspectual,
effectual, eventual, contextual,
* unforgettable, imperceptible,
unacceptable, undetectable,
unelectable, unpreventable,
incontestable, indigestible,
inaccessible, irrepressible,
inexpressible, reprehensible,
indispensable, indefensible,
comprehensible, architectural,
unprofessional, unexceptional, three-
dimensional, unconventional,
unintentional, two-dimensional,
premillennial, quincentennial,
bicentennial, tricentennial,
postmillennial, alphabetical,
antithetical, arithmetical, theoretical,
hypothetical, evangelical, anticlerical,
hemispherical, asymmetrical,
geometrical, biometrical, diametrical,
academical, agrochemical,
petrochemical, biochemical,
photochemical, ecumenical,
hexadecimal, duodecimal,
homosexual, ineffectual, intellectual,
* incomprehensible, semiprofessional,

omnidirectional, unidirectional,
extraterrestrial, infinitesimal,
gastrointestinal, heterosexual

**So please grip this fact with your
cerebral tentacle**
**The doll and its maker are never
identical.**
ARTHUR CONAN DOYLE

10.61 spectacled, tentacled, emerald,
Reginald, * bespectacled

10.62 Venables, spectacles, tentacles,
chemicals, decimals, etc.

10.63 Debenham, Cheltenham,
venturesome, meddlesome,
mettlesome, speculum, pendulum,
* compendium, millennium

10.64 decagon, heptagon, pentagon,
Pentagon, hexagon, Tenterdon,
Benenden, Pemberton, Chesterton,
Everton, Sheraton, Templeton,
Pendleton, Edmonton, Edgbaston,
Featherstone, veteran, Telamon,
Betjeman, trencherman, gentleman,
Perelman, Lebanon, Henderson,
Jefferson, Emerson, Edmondson,
Mendelssohn, lesbian, Thespian,
Delphian, hessian, Helicon, pelican,
pemmican, lexicon, Mexican, Heligan,
Crediton, skeleton, Benetton,
Ecclestone, Eddington, Teddington,
Hetherington, Ellington, wellington,
Wellington, Remington, Lexington,
Kensington, Eddystone, ferryman,
Edison, medicine, jettison, benison,
venison, Tennyson, Ericsson, netizen,
denizen, Methuen, * dodecagon,
progestogen, Gulbenkian, Ossetian,
rebellion, Cromwellian, Boswellian,

Orwellian, Portmeirion, pedestrian, equestrian, Dickensian, American, pantechnicon, * Christadelphian, Philadelphian, un-American, endoskeleton, exoskeleton, * Machiavellian

Oh, a wondrous bird is the pelican!
His bill will hold more than his belican.
He can take in his beak
Enough food for a week
But I'm damned if I see how the
** helican.**
DIXON LANIER MERRITT

10.65 Westmorland, reverend, Reverend, jettisoned

10.66 Netherlands, Reverend's

10.67 decadent, redolent, prevalent, excellent, deferent, efferent, referent, reverent, eloquent, betterment, testament, temperament, tenement, measurement, settlement, devilment, resonant, sentient, prescient, exeunt, mendicant, desiccant, elegant, evident, precedent, president, resident, penitent, hesitant, elephant, relevant, pestilent, celebrant, emigrant, pediment, sediment, sentiment, element, merriment, decrement, excrement, Egremont, detriment, regiment, revenant, eminent, reticent, negligent, exigent, effluent, petulant, tegument, * malevolent, benevolent, expectorant, irreverent, accelerant, Old Testament, New Testament, development, resettlement, dishevelment, embezzlement, consentient, presentient, dissentient, insentient, inelegant, self-evident, nonresident, impenitent, irrelevant,

impediment, presentiment, experiment, embellishment, replenishment, pre-eminent, maleficent, beneficent, intelligent, integument, * redevelopment, unintelligent

10.68 decadence, redolence, prevalence, excellence, temperance, deference, preference, reference, reverence, Reverence, severance, eloquence, measurements, resonance, sentience, prescience, mendicants, elegance, evidence, precedence, residence, residents, penitence, hesitance, elephants, relevance, pestilence, emigrants, sentiments, elements, eminence, reticence, negligence, effluence, petulance, * malevolence, benevolence, intemperance, irreverence, developments, insentience, inelegance, inheritance, impenitence, irrelevance, impediments, experiments, pre-eminence, maleficence, beneficence, intelligence, * disinheritance, * counterintelligence, etc.

10.69 peppering, rendering, tendering, Kettering, lettering, sheltering, sweltering, mentoring, feathering, weathering, censoring, measuring, welcoming, reckoning, threatening, deafening, lessening, questioning, trespassing, editing, everything, anything, * unquestioning, etc.

10.70 exodus, Exodus, embolus, memberless, measureless, effortless, weaponless, Hesperus, decorous, generous, lecherous, treacherous, venturous, venomous, slenderness, tenderness, tetanus, cleverness, membranous, pleasantness, gentleness, helpfulness, helplessness, fecklessness, recklessness, restlessness, selflessness, breathlessness, Pegasus, Ephesus, plenteous, envious, Celsius, crepitus, perilous, penniless, Wenceslas, Septimus, readiness, steadiness, cretinous, pettiness, sweatiness, emptiness, heaviness, friendliness, cleanliness, dressiness, resinous, edginess, wretchedness, selfishness, strenuous, tenuous, sensuous, nebulous, Regulus, credulous, sedulous, pendulous, querulous, emulous, tremulous, * Telemachus, acephalous, Bucephalus, expressionless, indecorous, ungenerous, adventurous, togetherness, light-headedness, indebtedness, unpleasantness, forgetfulness, pretentiousness, compendious, rebellious, emeritus, necessitous, unfriendliness, effectiveness, inventiveness, unselfishness, impetuous, contemptuous, tempestuous, incestuous, ingenuous, incredulous, * antitetanus, hydrocephalus, overgenerous, unadventurous, disingenuous, etc.

10.71 Everest, peskiest, readiest, steadiest, trendiest, pettiest, sweatiest, emptiest, heaviest, healthiest, wealthiest, smelliest, deadliest, friendliest, merriest, dressiest, messiest, sexiest, sketchiest, * unhealthiest, etc.

10.72 therapist, Methodist, medallist, specialist, terrorist, hedonist, essayist, pessimist, feminist, Leninist, fetishist, exorcist, prejudiced, * nonspecialist, detectorist, adventurist, telephonist, impressionist, expressionist, receptionist, protectionist, perfectionist, projectionist, postfeminist, geneticist, unprejudiced, * hypnotherapist, psychotherapist, instrumentalist, existentialist, sentimentalist, antiterrorist, eco-terrorist, postimpressionist, resurrectionist, vivisectionist, interventionist, * radiotherapist, physiotherapist, * aromatherapist, environmentalist, * antivivisectionist

10.73 desolate, separate, temperate, desperate, Everett, leveret, delegate, sextuplet, * intemperate, confederate, inveterate, protectorate, inspectorate, electorate, directorate, coelenterate, degenerate, regenerate, commensurate, affectionate, Connecticut, indelicate, effeminate, * unregenerate, overestimate, underestimate

10.74 Cheviot, Eliot, Herriot, definite, * licentiate, indefinite

10.75 twentieth, pennyworth, Kenilworth

10.76 trespasses, terraces, lettuces, crevices, premises, blemishes, vestiges, * apprentices, etc.

10.77 melodies, penalties, seventies, memories, pleasantries, enemies, recipes, remedies, * contemporaries, accessories, arch-enemies, discrepancies, elevenses, celebrities, extremities, obscenities, complexities, etc.

For myself, I'm relied on by friends in extremities,
And I don't mind so much if a comfort to them it is.
OLIVER WENDELL HOLMES

10.78 melancholy, sexually, sensually, regularly, temporarily, memorably, pleasurably, questionably, enviably, veritably, negligibly, delicately, definitely, infinitely, eloquently, elegantly, evidently, hesitantly, eminently, petulantly, tentatively, relatively, sensitively, gentlemanly, genuinely, welcomingly, threateningly, deafeningly, questioningly, menacingly, effortlessly, decorously, generously, treacherously, enviously, strenuously, temporary, emissary, necessary, February, estuary, respiratory, testimony, ceremony, celibacy, efficacy, delicacy, Excellency, presidency, residency, hesitancy, * ephemerally, professionally, exceptionally, intentionally, conventionally, congenitally, perpetually, conceptually, effectually, eventually, irregularly, irrevocably, unquestionably, immeasurably, inevitably, intelligibly, affectionately, indefinitely, irreverently,

competitively, insensitively, consecutively, ungentlemanly, adventurously, rebelliously, impetuously, contemptuously, contemporary, extemporary, unnecessary, investigatory, confederacy, degeneracy, inefficacy, indelicacy, effeminacy, * architecturally, unintentionally, ineffectually, intellectually, unintelligibly, * infinitesimally, etc.

10.79 revocable, memorable, venerable, measurable, pleasurable, mentionable, questionable, expiable, enviable, creditable, heritable, veritable, equitable, execrable, penetrable, estimable, perishable, eligible, negligible, educable, reputable, refutable, * irrevocable, unmemorable, inexorable, immeasurable, commensurable, impressionable, exceptionable, objectionable, unmentionable, unquestionable, inexpiable, unenviable, hereditable, discreditable, inevitable, inheritable, inequitable, impenetrable, inestimable, imperishable, intelligible, ineligible, ineducable, disreputable, irrefutable, * unexceptionable, unintelligible

-er-

The rhymes in this section have the 'er' sound of her *and* working *as their main or final vowel sound.*

11.1 blur, br'er, burr, cur, duh, er, err, fir, Fleur, fur, her, Kerr, knur, myrrh, per, purr, shirr, sir, Sir, slur, spur, stir, 'twere, Ur, were, whir, * occur, concur, astir, confer, aver, adieu, monsieur, Pasteur, transfer, chasseur, masseur, coiffeur, voyeur, seigneur, deburr, prie-dieu, milieu, recur, incur, deter, inter, bestir, defer, prefer, refer, infer, demur, longueur, Montreux, auteur, hauteur, chauffeur, poseur, douceur, * transfer, larkspur, cockspur, Hotspur, * saboteur, amateur, shamateur, raconteur, rapporteur, pas de deux, *de rigueur*, Périgueux, reoccur, cri de coeur, Richelieu, disinter, connoisseur, *bon viveur*, force majeure, cordon bleu, butterbur, underfur, * restaurateur, entrepreneur, folie à deux, arbitrageur, droit du seigneur, * *agent provocateur*

11.2 blurb, curb, herb, kerb, Serb, verb, * perturb, disturb, superb, * adverb, EPIRB, proverb, potherb, suburb, * willowherb

The cars and the lorries run over the
  kerb,
And the villagers put up a notice: road
  closed –
So that nothing untoward may chance
  to disturb

Deuteronomy's rest when he feels so
  disposed.

T. S. ELIOT

11.3 curbed, * perturbed, disturbed, * unperturbed, undisturbed

11.4 berk, Burke, Chirk, cirque, dirk, Dirk, erk, irk, jerk, kirk, Kirk, lurk, murk, perk, quirk, Quirke, shirk, smirk, stirk, Turk, work, * Dunkirk, de Klerk, McGurk, berserk, rework, * hackwork, handwork, waxwork, patchwork, artwork, part work, craftwork, glasswork, spadework, paintwork, framework, brainwork, casework, lacework, Selkirk, legwork, headwork, fretwork, network, breastwork, guesswork, earthwork, beadwork, fieldwork, teamwork, piecework, brickwork, shiftwork, bridgework, firework, wirework, brightwork, timework, clockwork, Falkirk, Ormskirk, coursework, groundwork, outwork, housework, coachwork, scrollwork, homework, stonework, brushwork, woodwork, footwork, * Atatürk, handiwork, latticework, masterwork, basketwork, paperwork, metalwork, trelliswork, needlework, timberwork, wickerwork, ironwork, donkey work, bodywork, pokerwork, overwork, openwork, * cabinetwork

11.5 circs, irks, jerks, perks, quirks, works, * gasworks, waxworks, glassworks, steelworks, fireworks, wireworks, saltworks, roadworks, * ironworks, waterworks, etc.

11.6 birch, church, lurch, perch, search, smirch, * besmirch, research, * Fenchurch, wordsearch, research, Whitchurch, Christchurch, * silver birch

11.7 bird, blurred, Byrd, curd, erred, furred, gird, heard, herd, Kurd, nerd, purred, sherd, shirred, slurred, spurred, stirred, surd, third, turd, whirred, word, * occurred, concurred, unstirred, conferred, averred, unheard, absurd, Cape Verde, reword, recurred, begird, deferred, referred, preferred, inferred, misheard, * blackbird, catchword, yardbird, password, swearword, jailbird, game bird, cage bird, headword, f-word, sea bird, keyword, firebird, lyrebird, swineherd, byword, songbird, crossword, watchword, potsherd, shore bird, foreword, cowherd, bowerbird, goatherd, codeword, loan word, lovebird, buzz word, bluebird, * afterword, ladybird, word for word, early bird, whirlybird, weaverbird, reoccurred, dickybird, wattlebird, mockingbird, water bird, overheard, undergird, Douglas Hurd, hummingbird, undeterred, * Richard the Third, four-letter word, etc.

And what mortal ever heard
Any good of George the Third?
WALTER SAVAGE LANDOR

11.8 scurf, serf, Smurf, surf, turf, * windsurf, * AstroTurf®

11.9 berg, Berg, erg, * Hamburg, Hapsburg, Strasbourg, Salzburg, Marburg, Carlsberg, Schoenberg, Sternberg, Lindbergh, Strindberg, Pittsburgh, Spielberg, Freiburg, iceberg, homburg, Coburg, Joburg, Newburg, * Brandenburg, Battenburg, Gettysburg, Württemberg, Königsberg, Hindenburg, Heidelberg, Gothenburg, Nuremberg, Luxembourg, Gutenberg, * Johannesburg, Saint Petersburg

11.10 dirge, merge, purge, scourge, serge, Serge, splurge, spurge, surge, urge, verge, * converge, submerge, demerge, emerge, diverge, * upsurge, * dramaturge, demiurge, thaumaturge

11.11 churl, curl, earl, furl, girl, hurl, knurl, Merle, pearl, Pearl, purl, Searle, skirl, swirl, twirl, whirl, whorl, * uncurl, unfurl, * ball girl, call girl, cowgirl, showgirl, schoolgirl

11.12 curled, furled, hurled, knurled, swirled, twirled, whirled, world, * uncurled, unfurled, * afterworld, underworld

Proud Wellington, with eagle beak so
curled,
That nose, the hook where he suspends
the world!
LORD BYRON

11.13 firm, germ, Herm, perm, sperm, squirm, term, therm, worm, * affirm, confirm, half term, preterm, midterm, infirm, * ragworm, sandworm, flatworm, tapeworm, threadworm, earthworm, wheatgerm, eelworm, mealworm, silkworm, pinworm, ringworm, inchworm, wireworm, blindworm, roundworm, glow-worm, slowworm, lugworm, bookworm, hookworm, woodworm, * pachyderm, endoderm, ectoderm, reaffirm, gymnosperm, isotherm

11.14 permed, squirmed, wormed, * affirmed, confirmed, * unconfirmed, reaffirmed

11.15 Bern, burn, Byrne, CERN, churn, earn, Ern, erne, fern, föhn, girn, kern, Kern, learn, quern, spurn, stern, Sterne, tern, turn, urn, Verne, yearn, * astern, Ahern, Traherne, unlearn, concern, adjourn, relearn, epergne, return, intern, inurn, discern, Sauternes, Auvergne, Jules Verne, lucerne, Lucerne, * Blackburn, pastern, heartburn, Braeburn, Raeburn, Hepburn, lectern, extern, Redfern, windburn, Swinburne, bittern, intern, Tyburn, wyvern, nocturne, sojourn, downturn, Woburn, Cockburn, sunburn, upturn, Crewkerne, U-turn, * Bannockburn, taciturn, three-point turn, Comintern, nonreturn, overturn, unconcern, * pay-as-you-earn

11.16 burned, earned, learned, spurned, turned, yearned, * unburned, upturned, unturned, unlearned, unearned, concerned, adjourned, hard-earned, well-earned, returned, interned, discerned, downturned, * overturned, unconcerned, etc.

11.17 burnt, learnt, weren't, * unburnt, unlearnt, * sunburnt

11.18 Burns, churns, earns, Ern's, ferns, learns, turns, urns, yearns, * concerns, returns, * sideburns, etc.

11.19 burp, chirp, slurp, twerp, * usurp, * Antwerp, * Wyatt Earp

11.20 burps, chirps, SERPS, slurps, stirps, turps, * usurps, * Wyatt Earp's

11.21 burped, chirped, slurped, * usurped, * excerpt

11.22 curse, Erse, hearse, nurse, purse, terse, verse, worse, * asperse, averse, perverse, traverse, adverse, converse, submerse, transverse, disburse, disperse, reverse, inverse, rehearse, immerse, diverse, coerce, * adverse, wet nurse, inverse, obverse, converse, commerce, cutpurse, * reimburse, intersperse, universe

An open foe may prove a curse,
But a pretended friend is worse.
JOHN GAY

11.23 burst, cursed, durst, first, Hearst, Hirst, Hurst, nursed, pursed, thirst, versed, worst, wurst, * accursed, traversed, conversed, submersed, headfirst, well-versed, disbursed, dispersed, reversed, rehearsed, immersed, coerced, * Pankhurst, Sandhurst, knackwurst, bratwurst, starburst, cloudburst, outburst, Dewhurst, * safety first, twenty-first, reimbursed, interspersed, liverwurst, unrehearsed

11.24 Bert, blurt, Burt, cert, curt, dirt, flirt, girt, hurt, Kurt, pert, shirt, skirt, spurt, squirt, wert, wort, * avert,

pervert, subvert, advert, convert,
unhurt, alert, assert, concert, revert,
invert, inert, insert, desert, dessert,
exert, divert, obvert, overt, * Frankfurt,
advert, ragwort, Blackshirt, hair shirt,
expert, sexpert, sweatshirt, pervert,
sneezewort, T-shirt, ribwort, milkwort,
figwort, stitchwort, insert, nightshirt,
convert, outsert, overt, lungwort,
woundwort, * malapert, bladderwort,
Engelbert, Ethelbert, extrovert,
pennywort, reconvert, feverwort,
reassert, reinsert, introvert,
slipperwort, liverwort, disconcert,
inexpert, miniskirt, controvert,
overskirt, underskirt, undershirt,
* overexert

11.25 Bert's, flirts, hertz, Hertz, hurts,
shirts, skirts, squirts, * adverts,
experts, *Weltschmerz*, T-shirts, converts,
outskirts, * extroverts, megahertz,
introverts, gigahertz, kilohertz,
underskirts, just deserts, etc.

11.26 berth, birth, dearth, earth, firth,
girth, mirth, Perth, worth, * unearth,
self-worth, rebirth, * Dankworth,
Tamworth, Hayworth, Knebworth,
Hepworth, Petworth, Emsworth,
Letchworth, Wordsworth, stillbirth,
childbirth, Bosworth, jobsworth,
Wandsworth, Duckworth, Lulworth,
Woolworth, * afterbirth, pennyworth,
Kenilworth, Middle-earth, Illingworth,
Solway Firth, down-to-earth,
Butterworth, Shuttleworth

One for sorrow, two for mirth.
Three for a wedding, four for a birth.
TRADITIONAL RHYME

11.27 curve, derv, Merv, nerve, perv,

serve, swerve, verve, * unnerve,
Deneuve, subserve, conserve, observe,
deserve, preserve, reserve, hors
d'oeuvre

11.28 curved, served, swerved,
* unnerved, conserved, observed,
deserved, preserved, reserved,
* well-preserved, unobserved,
undeserved, unreserved

11.29 blurs, errs, firs, furs, furze, hers,
Meuse, purrs, Sirs, spurs, stirs,
* occurs, masseuse, chanteuse,
coiffeuse, chartreuse, recurs, prefers,
* saboteurs, amateurs, secateurs,
Betelgeuse, connoisseurs, etc.

12.1 Furby®, Herbie, herby, Kirby,
Kirkby, chirpy, jerky, murky, perky,
quirky, turkey, Turkey, Fergie, lurgy,
birdie, nerdy, Purdy, sturdy, wordy,
Thursday, Bertie, dirty, flirty, Gertie,
qwerty, shirty, thirty, Kirsty, thirsty,
furphy, Murphy, scurfy, surfie, turfy,
curvy, nervy, scurvy, Turvey, earthy,
worthy, Berlei, Burghley, burly, curly,
early, girlie, Hurley, pearly, Shirley,
surly, twirly, thirdly, worldly, curtly,
firstly, earthly, firmly, Burnley, sternly,
tersely, blurry, firry, furry, Vyrnwy,
Fermi, wormy, Burney, Ernie, ferny,
Gurney, journey, Kearney, Circe,
mercy, Percy, Chertsey, curtsy, furzy,
jersey, Jersey, kersey, Mersey,
Guernsey, Hershey, clergy, * Euterpe,
unworthy, superbly, absurdly,
unworldly, overtly, unearthly,
perversely, adversely, conversely,
attorney, * bloodthirsty, airworthy,
blameworthy, praiseworthy, seaworthy,
Galsworthy, roadworthy, noteworthy,
trustworthy, newsworthy,

* untrustworthy, * Albuquerque, hurdy-gurdy, vinho verde, olde worlde, topsy-turvy, creditworthy, taxidermy, diathermy, arsy-versy, controversy, dramaturgy, metallurgy, hurly-burly, Curly Wurly, otherworldly, etc.

I'm Burlington Bertie, I rise at ten-thirty.

WILLIAM HARGREAVES

12.2 Berber, Thurber, chirper, Sherpa, burka, circa, Gurkha, lurker, shirker, smirker, worker, burger, burgher, birder, Gerda, girder, herder, murder, purdah, Schroeder, curter, Goethe, perter, squirter, surfer, fervour, server, swerver, Bertha, Eartha, further, murther, curler, pearler, purler, twirler, whirler, burglar, gurgler, hurdler, Koestler, stirrer, oeuvre, verdure, Burma, firmer, Irma, Sturmer, murmur, wormer, burner, earner, learner, Lerner, Myrna, Smyrna, sterner, turner, Turner, Verner, Werner, yearner, bursa, cursor, bursar, mercer, Mercer, purser, Ursa, Persia, lurcher, nurture, percher, searcher, merger, perjure, purger, scourger, urger, verger, * usurper, mazurka, Roberta, perverter, subverter, converter, McWhirter, asserter, Alberta, inverter, deserter, observer, Minerva, deserver, preserver, transferor, *chef-d'oeuvre*, deferrer, referrer, hors d'oeuvre, taverna, returner, precursor, disperser, rehearser, immerser, vice versa, coercer, inertia, researcher, demerger, * networker, tear-jerker, field worker, steelworker, mill worker, outworker, homeworker, woodworker, hamburger, Pressburger, beefburger, cheeseburger, Limburger, frankfurter, windsurfer, timeserver, * metalworker, ironworker, Ethelburga, vegeburger, Luxembourger, terra firma, Annapurna, afterburner, gutta-percha, * hurt her, serve her, etc.

12.3 Turkic, Lerwick, * acerbic, allergic, synergic, lysergic, * hypodermic, taxidermic, metallurgic, * poikilothermic, homoiothermic

12.4 turbid, dirtied, fervid, learned, cursed, curtsied, * perfervid, accursed

12.5 herded, murdered, worded, spurted, squirted, Burford, furthered, earthward, murmured, Bernard, gurnard, nurtured, * averted, perverted, converted, concerted, inverted, inserted, deserted, diverted, * extroverted, introverted, disconcerted, unconverted, etc.

12.6 earthwards, Bernard's

12.7 Burbage, herbage, wordage

12.8 burble, gerbil, Froebel, herbal, verbal, purple, circle, burgle, Fergal, gurgle, curdle, girdle, hurdle, dirndl, hurtle, kirtle, myrtle, Myrtle, turtle, hurtful, chervil, serval, dermal, thermal, colonel, journal, kernel, sternal, vernal, Hirsel, Persil®, Purcell, tercel, kursaal, Herschel, tertial, Virgil, * nonverbal, encircle, transferral, deferral, referral, fraternal, maternal, paternal, eternal, internal, external, infernal, diurnal, hibernal, nocturnal, succursal, transversal, dispersal, reversal, rehearsal, commercial, inertial, * Bracegirdle, * semicircle,

panty girdle, epidermal, geothermal,
sempiternal, coeternal, universal,
mangelwurzel, infomercial,
controversial, noncommercial,
* uncontroversial

12.9 burbles, gerbils, Goebbels, circles,
hurdles, thermals, * rehearsals,
commercials, etc.

12.10 serfdom, earldom, Bertram,
Burnham, sternum, irksome,
* laburnum, viburnum, nasturtium,
* reductio ad absurdum, * heard 'em,
learn 'em, etc.

12.11 Turpin, firkin, gherkin, jerkin,
Perkin, Irvine, Mervyn, Merlin, Irwin,
Gershwin, ermine, Jermyn, vermin,
urchin, virgin, * Dick Turpin,
Dunfermline, determine,
* predetermine, * workin', learnin', etc.

12.12 bourbon, Durban, turban, urban,
Bergen, Jürgen, burden, guerdon,
Burton, certain, curtain, Girton,
Merton, Kirsten, earthen, burthen,
Kirwan, Burman, german, German,
Herman, Hermon, sermon, Sherman,
workman, Bergman, Perlman,
herdsman, churchman, Vernon,
person, worsen, Curzon, Persian,
tertian, version, burgeon, Spurgeon,
sturgeon, surgeon, * suburban,
unburden, disburden, uncertain,
Albertan, Macpherson, aspersion,
aversion, perversion, subversion,
conversion, submersion, assertion,
dispersion, recursion, incursion,
excursion, Cistercian, reversion,
inversion, immersion, insertion,
desertion, exertion, diversion,
coercion, * Spitsbergen, barperson,

chairperson, layperson, salesperson,
sportsperson, spokesperson,
unperson, * Ardnamurchan,
overburden, retroversion,
extroversion, self-assertion,
reconversion, interspersion,
introversion, * animadversion,
overexertion

Like the ancient Medes and Persians,
Always by his own exertions
He subsisted on those hills.
Edward Lear

12.13 burdened, curtained, Bertrand,
* unburdened, * overburdened, etc.

12.14 serpent, verdant, fervent, servant,
Derwent, versant, merchant,
Merchant, urgent, * advertent,
observant, conferment, deferment,
preferment, interment, adjournment,
internment, discernment,
disbursement, conversant, dispersant,
convergent, resurgent, detergent,
emergent, insurgent, divergent,
* maidservant, manservant,
* inadvertent, unobservant,
reimbursement

12.15 serpents, servants, merchants,
* observance, detergents, convergence,
emergence, resurgence, insurgence,
insurgents, divergence, * inadvertence,
re-emergence, etc.

12.16 curbing, burping, chirping,
kerbing, jerking, lurking, shirking,
working, erlking, herding, wording,
flirting, hurting, shirting, skirting,
squirting, bursting, thirsting, surfing,
curving, Irving, serving, swerving,
berthing, birthing, Worthing, curling,

hurling, sterling, Stirling, swirling, whirling, circling, gurgling, hurdling, earthling, nursling, erring, Goering, purring, shirring, stirring, whirring, squirming, Groening, burning, churning, earning, kerning, learning, turning, yearning, cursing, nursing, Pershing, birching, churching, lurching, searching, merging, purging, surging, urging, verging, * perturbing, disturbing, usurping, hard-working, nonworking, converting, deserting, unswerving, unnerving, observing, self-serving, deserving, preserving, unearthing, encircling, occurring, conferring, unerring, recurring, inferring, confirming, concerning, returning, discerning, conversing, dispersing, rehearsing, converging, emerging, * networking, tear-jerking, woodworking, windsurfing, kitesurfing, timeserving, heart-searching, * metalworking, teleworking, disconcerting, undeserving, etc.

Keep the home-fires burning,
While your hearts are yearning.
LENA GUILBERT FORD

12.17 workings, servings, earthlings, purse-strings, earnings, yearnings, etc.

12.18 Curtis, surface, Jervis, Purves, service, surplice, dermis, kermis, furnace, Furness, burgess, Burgess, purchase, * resurface, self-service, disservice, repurchase, * epidermis

12.19 purpose, circus, Fergus, nervous, surplus, workless, wordless, mirthless, worthless, Thermos®, curtness, pertness, firmness, terseness, versus,

Tertius, * Lycurgus, alertness, Propertius, * multipurpose, Carrickfergus, * hurt us, curse us, etc.

12.20 curtest, pertest, furthest, firmest, earnest, Ernest, sternest, etc.

Life is real! Life is earnest!
And the grave is not its goal;
Dust thou art, to dust returnest,
Was not spoken of the soul.
HENRY WADSWORTH LONGFELLOW

12.21 surfaced, serviced, * resurfaced, reservist, repurchased, * taxidermist

12.22 furbish, Kurdish, Turkish, dervish, churlish, girlish, skirmish, burnish, furnish, * refurbish

12.23 burnished, furnished, * refurbished, unfurnished

12.24 burbot, Herbert, sherbet, turbot, Urquhart, ergot, Dermot, * alternate

12.25 turnspit, Burkitt, circuit, surfeit, vervet, circlet, hermit, Kermit, permit, Burnett, * short-circuit, interpret, * reinterpret, misinterpret, * work it, turn it, etc.

12.26 Wordsworth, vermouth

12.27 furtive, cursive, * assertive, subversive, discursive, coercive

12.28 herpes, turkeys, birdies, certes, Surtees, thirties, worthies, Hermes, journeys, mercies, Xerxes, * Laertes, etc.

12.29 Burgundy, certainty, verbally,

personally, fervently, urgently,
earnestly, certainly, purposely,
nervously, Burberry®, servery,
burglary, mercury, Mercury, wormery,
fernery, ternary, turnery, bursary,
cursory, mercery, nursery, tertiary,
perjury, surgery, purgatory, Germany,
fervency, urgency, Bermondsey,
perfidy, furmity, chirpily, sturdily,
dirtily, worthily, vertically, surgically,
perfectly, mercifully, furtively,
churlishly, girlishly, circuitry,
mercenary, courtesy, virtually,
* uncertainty, hyperbole, maternally,
paternally, eternally, internally,
externally, infernally, nocturnally,
impersonally, commercially,
alternately, uncertainly, infirmary,
quaternary, precursory, conservatory,
observatory, confirmatory,
diversionary, conservancy, emergency,
insurgency, acerbity, absurdity,
infirmity, fraternity, maternity,
paternity, eternity, modernity,
perversity, adversity, diversity,
unworthily, deservedly, reservedly,
concernedly, accursedly, unmercifully,
assertively, unnervingly, unerringly,
discourtesy, * universally,
controversially, inadvertently,
anniversary, microsurgery,
neurosurgery, taciturnity, university,
undeservedly, unreservedly,
unconcernedly, disconcertingly,
* counterinsurgency, biodiversity, etc.

12.30 pergola, Berbera, gerbera,
murderer, murmurer, nurturer,
perjurer, surfacer, purchaser,
curvature, nervature, worshipper,
Guernica, Perdita, servitor, vertebra,
Wurlitzer®, furnisher, furniture,
circular, Ursula, * conservator,

hyperbola, interpreter, determiner,
tubercular, * semicircular

12.31 Serbia, chirpier, murkier,
perkier, quirkier, sturdier, dirtier,
thirstier, worthier, curlier, earlier,
surlier, Hermia, hernia, vernier,
Mercia, * suburbia, Calpurnia,
Hibernia, inertia, * hyperthermia,
hypothermia, etc.

12.32 workable, learnable, searchable,
personal, vertical, cervical, versicle,
surgical, merciful, worshipful,
Percival, vertebral, germinal, terminal,
virginal, virtual, * unworkable,
convertible, observable, transferable,
returnable, discernible, submersible,
reversible, puerperal, impersonal,
adverbial, proverbial, liturgical,
unmerciful, * imperturbable,
controvertible, indiscernible,
nonreturnable, irreversible,
intervertebral, interpersonal,
metallurgical, * incontrovertible,
entrepreneurial

12.33 Pergamum, burdensome,
erbium, terbium, Birmingham,
* ytterbium, operculum

12.34 Turkoman, Pergamon, Ferguson,
Serbian, Permian, Surbiton,
Workington, Worthington,
Burlington, journeyman, clergyman,
Murchison, * Gilbertian, quaternion,
Saturnian, Melburnian, Hibernian,
Copernican

12.35 termagant, firmament,
permanent, pertinent, turbulent,
* reverberant, impermanent,
subservient, advertisement,

refurbishment, appurtenant, impertinent, determinant, * antiperspirant

12.36 furtherance, permanence, pertinence, turbulence, * impermanence, subservience, advertisements, appurtenance, impertinence, etc.

12.37 purposeless, Cerberus, murderess, murderous, hurtfulness, nervousness, worthlessness, courteous, pervious, Perseus, merciless, murkiness, sturdiness, dirtiness, worthiness, earliness, terminus, verminous, earnestness, virtuous, * discourteous, impervious, Copernicus, assertiveness, superfluous,

tuberculous, * airworthiness, seaworthiness, roadworthiness, etc.

12.38 herbalist, journalist, * determinist

12.39 chirpiest, murkiest, perkiest, quirkiest, sturdiest, dirtiest, thirstiest, worthiest, curliest, earliest, surliest, etc.

12.40 perforate, vertebrate, * imperforate, invertebrate, determinate, * indeterminate

12.41 merchantable, personable, permeable, terminable, serviceable, * impermeable, determinable, interminable, unserviceable, * semipermeable, indeterminable

-eer-

The rhymes in this section have the 'eer' sound of beer *and* fiercely *as their main or final vowel sound.*

13.1 beer, bier, blear, cere, cheer, clear, dear, deer, drear, ear, fear, gear, Greer, hear, here, jeer, kir, leer, Lear, mere, Mir, near, peer, pier, queer, rear, sear, sere, shear, sheer, smear, sneer, spear, sphere, steer, stere, tear, tier, Trier, veer, Wear, we're, weir, Weir, year, * appear, frontier, De Vere, adhere, unclear, career, uprear, veneer, Kashmir, apnoea, Tangier, cashier, emir, Vermeer, endear, revere, revers, severe, inhere, mishear, King Lear, midyear, besmear, Kinnear, sincere, vizier, Zaïre, idea, austere, chorea, all-clear, cohere, Hosea, * Tranmere, Tangmere, cashmere, Hampshire, Grasmere, Berkshire, Ayrshire, tapir, Shakespeare, fakir, nadir, reindeer, headgear, Ellesmere, Cheshire, wheatear, switchgear, Kingswear, Wiltshire, compeer, Shropshire, Yorkshire, roe deer, Goodyear, * halberdier, Agadir, balladeer, pamphleteer, gazetteer, stratosphere, atmosphere, bandolier, chandelier, cavalier, Cavalier, cameleer, gasolier, Lancashire, Staffordshire, racketeer, gadgeteer, bathysphere, Vladimir, Casimir, Aboukir, Hertfordshire, marketeer, Chanticleer, Derbyshire, Haslemere, Cambridgeshire, belvedere, grenadier, megathere, seborrhoea, yesteryear, Delamere, Benazir, Leicestershire, Bedfordshire, hemisphere, Bedivere, Elzevir, engineer, technofear, persevere, reappear, ecosphere, disappear, ginger beer, brigadier, interfere, lithosphere, crystal-clear, Windermere, cuirassier, Lincolnshire, Guinevere, insincere, privateer, biosphere, diarrhoea, pyorrhoea, Tyne and Wear, pioneer, bombardier, commandeer, volunteer, troposphere, gondolier, logorrhoea, gonorrhoea, Rothermere, Gloucestershire, Oxfordshire, Conybeare, rocketeer, profiteer, sonneteer, domineer, Warwickshire, auctioneer, corsetier, Paul Revere, mountaineer, oversteer, overhear, sloganeer, understeer, Buttermere, buccaneer, puppeteer, musketeer, Worcestershire, souvenir, muleteer, fusilier, mutineer, scrutineer, * titanothere, Northamptonshire, electioneer, ionosphere, ozonosphere, * charioteer, orienteer, amenorrhoea, dysmenorrhoea, adipocere, Nottinghamshire, Buckinghamshire, Golda Meir, Guadalquivir, carabineer

Damn with faint praise, assent with civil leer,
And without sneering, teach the rest to sneer.
ALEXANDER POPE

13.2 beard, cheered, cleared, eared, jeered, leered, peered, reared, smeared, sneered, speared, steered, tiered, veered, weird, * appeared, afeard, adhered, careered, veneered, revered, * Blackbeard, bat-eared, lop-eared, goatsbeard, Bluebeard, * engineered, disappeared, pioneered, domineered, etc.

13.3 real, * surreal, unreal, ideal, * gonorrhoeal

13.4 Bierce, fierce, Pearse, pierce, Pierce, tierce

13.5 beers, cheers, ears, fears, gears, hears, jeers, peers, Piers, Sears, shears, sneers, spears, Spears, Squeers, tears, tiers, years, * appears, arrears, careers, Algiers, Tangiers, in tears, ideas, all ears, * Cavaliers, engineers, etc.

Mademoiselle from Armenteers,

Hasn't been kissed for forty years.

Military song

14.1 realty, Brearley, clearly, dearly, merely, nearly, queerly, really, yearly, weirdly, fiercely, Beardsley, beery, bleary, cheery, Cleary, dearie, dreary, eerie, Erie, eyrie, Leary, leery, Neary, Peary, peri, query, smeary, sneery, teary, theory, weary, Deirdre, Tierney, * unclearly, surreally, severely, sincerely, ideally, Dun Laoghaire, Valkyrie, Kashmiri, O'Leary, * insincerely

14.2 weirder, theatre, era, clearer, dearer, hearer, Hera, lira, nearer, queerer, rearer, sclera, sera, shearer, smearer, sneerer, steerer, Vera, fiercer, piercer, * Madeira, Utsire, Elvira, sincerer, chimera, coherer, * sheepshearer, * amphitheatre, rangatira, lavatera, antisera, aloe vera, D'Oliviera, * reared her, cheer her, etc.

14.3 bearded, rearward

14.4 queried, wearied, * unwearied

14.5 peerage, steerage, * arrearage

14.6 cheerful, fearful, tearful, feral, scleral, spheral, Pearsall, tiercel

14.7 serum, theorem, fearsome, meerschaum, * antiserum, * fear 'em, hear 'em, etc.

14.8 deerskin, Erin, * jeerin', piercin', etc.

14.9 Reardon, Kieran, Viren, spearman, steersman, Pearson, * Madeiran, frontiersman

14.10 cerement, vehement, * adherent, inherent, coherent, endearment, * incoherent

14.11 clearance, vehemence, * appearance, adherence, adherents, coherence, endearments, * perseverance, reappearance, interference, incoherence, nonappearance

14.12 shearling, yearling, cheering, clearing, earring, gearing, hearing, jeering, rearing, searing, shearing, sneering, steering, piercing, * appearing, veneering, endearing, revering, * sheep-shearing, child-rearing, God-fearing, * engineering, persevering, disappearing, interfering, pioneering, profiteering, domineering, auctioneering, mountaineering, scrutineering, * electioneering, * orienteering, * bioengineering, etc.

14.13 peeress, Beatrice

14.14 cheerless, earless, fearless, peerless, beardless, sclerous, serous, clearness, dearness, nearness, weirdness, fierceness, * Severus, * Algeciras, * Ahasuerus, * hear us, feared us, etc.

14.15 realist, theorist, pianist, * surrealist, idealist, careerist

14.16 weirdest, clearest, dearest, nearest, queerest, fiercest, * sincerest, etc.

14.17 Kyrgyz, queries, series, theories, wearies, Deirdre's, * miniseries, etc.

14.18 cheerier, drearier, eerier, wearier, * bacteria, anterior, Algeria, exterior, interior, listeria, wisteria, hysteria, inferior, diphtheria, Iberia, Liberia, Siberia, Nigeria, posterior, ulterior, superior, * cafeteria, sansevieria, Lake Superior, etc.

14.19 hearable, steerable, cereal, ferial, serial, Cheeryble, * material, bacterial, arterial, imperial, Imperial, ethereal, venereal, sidereal, funereal, * immaterial, monasterial, managerial, magisterial, ministerial, * antibacterial

14.20 cerium, * bacterium, imperium, deuterium, * magisterium

14.21 Pierian, * Adlerian, Kashmirian, Cancerian, Algerian, Wagnerian, Shakespearean, Spenserian, Zaïrian, Iberian, Liberian, Siberian, Hyperion, criterion, Nigerian, Chaucerian, Mousterian, Sumerian, * Hanoverian, Presbyterian, trans-Siberian

14.22 experience, * inexperience

14.23 cheerfulness, fearlessness, serious, dreariness, weariness, * imperious, mysterious, Tiberias, Tiberius, * Desiderius, deleterious, etc.

For the writing of verse is a struggle mysterious
And the gayest of rhymes is a matter that's serious.
OLIVER WENDELL HOLMES

-ee-

The rhymes in this section have the 'ee' sound of breed *and* teacher *as their main or final vowel sound. You can also rhyme some of these words with words ending in -y (e.g.* happily, telepathy, capability*), which you will find in other sections.*

15.1 B, be, Bea, bee, Brie, C, Cree, D, Dee, E, fee, flea, flee, free, G, gee, ghee, glee, he, key, knee, lea, lee, Lee, Leigh, me, mi, P, pea, pee, plea, quay, re, sea, scree, see, she, ski, spree, T, te, tea, tee, the, thee, three, tree, Tree, twee, V, we, wee, whee, ye, Z

Stands the church clock at ten to three?
And is there honey still for tea?
RUPERT BROOKE

15.2 McGee, Dundee, suttee, trustee, McPhee, alee, Tralee, Cherie, Marie, sirree, Capri, agree, buckshee, maquis, grandee, standee, tax-free, banshee, marquee, marquis, draftee, grantee, Grand Prix, Parsee, bargee, payee, JP, HP, AD, bailee, trainee, NB, LP, MP, vendee, settee, esprit, rent-free, étui, ME, lessee, MC, PE, CB, GB, TB, GP, CD, three-D, VD, ET, PT, TT, CV, TV, tee-hee, BC, cc, PC, e.g., yippee, decree, degree, jinni, i.e., ID, IT, Tiree, lychee, t'ai chi, off-key, scot-free, Torquay, Pawnee, Shawnee, foresee, low-key, OD, goatee, toll-free, whoopee, cooee, rupee, bootee, tutee, UV, QC, * mother-to-be, Trincomalee, fiddle-de-dee, bouquet garni, GCSE, RSVP, PAYE, interviewee, on the q.t., WC, * Muhammad Ali

15.3 Bacchae, Yankee, latchkey, Atlee, Crabtree, algae, passkey, larvae, carefree, pear tree, Aintree, Braintree, precis, debris, Elstree, turnkey, fir tree, tepee, kiwi, pewee, gee-gee, squeegee, Frisbee®, prithee, Nike, psyche, pine tree, sightsee, spondee, coffee, toffee, crosstree, Rowntree, Toynbee, trochee, ogee, puttee, bungee, look-see, bootee, shoetree, * antennae, Mycenae, committee, banoffee, Milwaukee, alumnae, Grand Coulee, * Tallahassee, prima facie, subcommittee, Murrumbidgee

15.4 manatee, guarantee, absentee, jamboree, transferee, Anne-Marie, *bain-marie*, axletree, ratatouille, apogee, Chatterjee, après-ski, addressee, Galilee, Pharisee, appointee, amputee, jalousie, Sadducee, R&B, R&D, Marshalsea, RAC, RIP, maître d', A&E, HRT, c'est la vie, KGB, ABC, eighty-three, HIV, Cherokee, legatee, devotee, referee, kedgeree, repartee, SAE, escapee, LSD, MSc, MBE, MEP, LED, LCD, Zebedee, Gemini, pedigree, twenty-three, Tennessee, perigee, debauchee, employee, SOB, epopee, MOD, MOT, refugee, fleur-de-lys, verdigris, thirty-three, B&B, Tweedledee, C of E,

Peterlee, vis-à-vis, CJD, PhD, VAT, detainee, ESP, CND, GMT, PMT, TNT, BSE, CFC, plc, TLC, BSc, DVD, BBC, PVC, VIP, CID, deportee, TUC, chickadee, disagree, swingletree, fricassee, Winchelsea, chimpanzee, returnee, internee, filigree, fifty-three, sixty-three, retiree, divorcee, inductee, bride-to-be, licensee, Zuider Zee, ITV, Waikiki, ninety-three, wannabe, warrantee, bonhomie, nominee, monoski, water-ski, forty-three, mortgagee, formulae, bourgeoisie, oversea, oversee, OAP, OBE, OTT, Rosie Lee, bumblebee, dungaree, trouble-free, undersea, honeybee, sugar-free, USP, QED, jubilee, duty-free, * abandonee, examinee, evacuee, chinoiserie, Thermopylae, minutiae

There was an old lady of Winchelsea,
Who said, 'If you needle or pin shall
**   see,**
On the floor of my room,
Sweep it up with the broom!'
That exhaustive old lady of Winchelsea!
EDWARD LEAR

15.5 Beeb, dweeb, glebe, grebe, * Delibes, Antibes

15.6 dweebs, grebes, Thebes

15.7 beak, bleak, cheek, chic, clique, creak, creek, eek, eke, freak, geek, Greek, leak, leek, meek, peak, Peake, peek, peke, pique, reek, seek, shriek, Sikh, sleek, sneak, speak, Speke, squeak, streak, teak, tweak, weak, week, wreak, * unspeak, oblique, batik, pratique, antique, Lalique, Tajik, technique, bespeak, critique, triptyque, mystique, midweek, bezique,

physique, off-peak, boutique, Mustique, unique, * speedfreak, pipsqueak, forepeak, houseleek, newspeak, * Martinique, Chesapeake, fenugreek, stickybeak, hide-and-seek, Dominique, ortanique, Mozambique, tongue-in-cheek, * téléphérique

And I seem to find the happiness I seek
When we're out together dancing
**   cheek-to-cheek.**
IRVING BERLIN

15.8 beaks, breeks, cheeks, freaks, shrieks, speaks, Weekes, weeks, * *idée fixe*, * Macgillicuddy's Reeks, etc.

15.9 beach, beech, bleach, breach, breech, each, leach, Leach, leech, peach, pleach, preach, reach, screech, speech, teach, * unteach, impeach, beseech, * Wisbech, horseleech, outreach, * overreach

Shall I part my hair behind? Do I dare
**   to eat a peach?**
I shall wear white flannel trousers, and
**   walk upon the beach.**
T. S. ELIOT

15.10 beached, bleached, preached, reached, * unbleached, impeached, beseeched, etc.

15.11 bead, Bede, bleed, breed, cede, creed, deed, Eid, feed, freed, Gide, greed, he'd, heed, knead, lead, lied, mead, Meade, Mede, need, plead, read, Reade, reed, Reed, Reid, screed, seed, she'd, skied, speed, steed, swede, Swede, tweed, Tweed, we'd, weed, * agreed, proceed, succeed, concede, stampede, accede, Rashid, Candide,

reread, impede, indeed, misdeed,
mislead, inbreed, misread, precede,
recede, secede, exceed, high-speed,
Godspeed, outbreed, OD'd,
* Flamsteed, handfeed, knapweed,
ragweed, flaxseed, airspeed, fairlead,
hayseed, rapeseed, breast-feed,
birdseed, Siegfried, seaweed, weak-
kneed, drip-feed, lip-read, chickweed,
linseed, mind-read, sight-read,
bindweed, Lockheed, crossbreed,
hogweed, pondweed, knotweed,
knock-kneed, force-feed,
groundspeed, oilseed, nosebleed,
duckweed, spoonfeed, proofread,
* guaranteed, Ganymede, antecede,
aniseed, refereed, centipede, retrocede,
invalid, interbreed, intercede,
millipede, chicken feed, bottle-feed,
cottonseed, waterweed, overfeed,
underfeed, tumbleweed, Runnymede,
bugleweed, supersede, * velocipede

Who to himself is law, no law doth
  need,
Offends no law, and is a king indeed.
GEORGE CHAPMAN

15.12 beads, breeds, deeds, Leeds,
needs, reeds, tweeds, weeds,
* succeeds, misdeeds, * nosebleeds,
proceeds, * centipedes, invalids, etc.

15.13 beef, brief, chief, fief, grief, leaf,
reef, sheaf, thief, * Sharif, massif,
debrief, belief, relief, naïf, corned
beef, roast beef, O'Keeffe, motif,
* kerchief, sneak thief, tea leaf,
wheatsheaf, fig leaf, flyleaf,
* handkerchief, bas-relief, Tenerife,
neckerchief, interleaf, disbelief,
misbelief, leitmotif, overleaf,
cloverleaf, unbelief, * apéritif

15.14 gigue, Grieg, league, * fatigue,
intrigue, renege, * blitzkrieg, sitzkrieg,
colleague

15.15 liege, siege, * besiege

15.16 prestige, * noblesse oblige

15.17 Beale, creel, deal, Deal, eel, feel,
he'll, heal, heel, keel, Keele, Kiel, kneel,
Lille, meal, Neil, peal, peel, Peel, reel,
seal, she'll, spiel, squeal, steal, steel,
Steel, Steele, stele, teal, veal, we'll, weal,
wheal, wheel, zeal, * appeal, allele,
Camille, schlemiel, anneal, chenille,
conceal, unseal, congeal, Bastille,
Castile, square deal, genteel, Emil,
Cecile, reseal, repeal, misdeal, reveal,
ordeal, O'Neill, Lucille, * cartwheel,
selfheal, treadwheel, gearwheel,
freewheel, sweetmeal, wheatmeal,
piecemeal, printwheel, millwheel,
pinwheel, fishmeal, flywheel,
cogwheel, allheal, Mobile, oatmeal,
wholemeal, bonemeal, newsreel,
* blastocoel, deshabille, stainless steel,
daisywheel, rectocele, Ferris wheel,
Estoril, three-course meal, cystocele,
imbecile, glockenspiel, cockatiel,
commonweal, cochineal, Dormobile®,
snowmobile, Popemobile, underseal,
* Achilles heel, * automobile

15.18 field, Field, healed, heeled,
kneeled, pealed, peeled, reeled, sealed,
shield, squealed, Weald, wheeled,
wield, yield, * appealed, afield,
unhealed, annealed, concealed,
unsealed, congealed, well-heeled,
three-wheeled, resealed, repealed,
revealed, high-heeled, four-wheeled,
low-heeled, two-wheeled, * Hatfield,
Anfield, Cranfield, Mansfield, airfield,
hayfield, Wakefield, Masefield,

Sheffield, Enfield, greenfield, midfield, infield, Winfield, Springfield, Lichfield, windshield, minefield, cornfield, outfield, brownfield, oilfield, Schofield, snowfield, Oldfield, coalfield, Nuffield, gumshield, * battlefield, Macclesfield, Dangerfield, chesterfield, Chesterfield, Sellafield, Beaconsfield, Petersfield, ill-concealed, Copperfield, Butterfield, Somerfield, Huddersfield, unconcealed, unrevealed, * Sutton Coldfield

15.19 deals, eels, feels, heels, meals, Neil's, seals, wheels, * appeals, conceals, congeals, reveals, * Galashiels, jellied eels, meals on wheels, imbeciles, etc.

When love congeals
It soon reveals
The faint aroma of performing seals,
The double crossing of a pair of heels.
LORENZ HART

15.20 beam, bream, Bream, Cheam, cream, deem, dream, gleam, Nîmes, ream, scheme, scream, seam, seem, steam, stream, team, teem, theme, * abeam, agleam, Karim, upstream, raceme, blaspheme, regime, redeem, esteem, extreme, midstream, ice cream, onstream, downstream, supreme, * centime, harem, airstream, daydream, mainstream, jetstream, Brylcreem®, slipstream, millstream, whitebeam, bireme, trireme, crossbeam, hornbeam, morpheme, Coldstream, phoneme, sunbeam, bloodstream, Gulf Stream, moonbeam, * academe, self-esteem, Ibrahim, single cream, disesteem,

quinquereme, kibbutzim, clotted cream, monotreme, double cream

But what is man in his own proud
esteem?
Hear him, himself the poet and the
theme.
WILLIAM COWPER

15.21 beamed, dreamed, gleamed, screamed, seemed, steamed, streamed, teemed, * undreamed, unstreamed, blasphemed, redeemed, esteemed, * unredeemed, etc.

15.22 beams, dreams, reams, Rheims, schemes, seams, teams, etc.

15.23 bean, been, clean, dean, Dean, e'en, gean, gene, Gene, glean, green, Greene, Jean, Kean, keen, lean, mean, mien, Nene, peen, preen, queen, Queen, scene, screen, seen, sheen, Sheene, skean, spleen, teen, wean, zine

Pussycat, pussycat, where have you
been?
I've been to London to see the Queen.
NURSERY RHYME

15.24 lateen, umpteen, Devine, Levine, ravine, subvene, convene, baleen, unclean, careen, marine, tureen, latrine, McQueen, Janine, obscene, unseen, machine, Rabin, nankeen, sateen, canteen, shagreen, Racine, Maxine, Harbin, sardine, Martine, Amin, Nadine, James Dean, eighteen, jade green, Céline, French bean, terrine, Benin, thirteen, preteen, shebeen, beguine, fifteen, sixteen, trephine, spring-clean, serene, big screen, between, demean, cuisine,

nineteen, dry-clean, widescreen,
poteen, broad bean, fourteen, small
screen, foreseen, Slovene, Justine,
routine, * mujaheddin, aquamarine,
ultramarine, vending machine,
knitting machine, washing machine,
sewing machine, *nouvelle cuisine*,
Palaeocene, Oligocene

15.25 has-been, caffeine, Kathleen,
gangrene, gamine, vaccine, fanzine,
Charlene, Marlene, guanine, Aileen,
scalene, dentine, Hellene, Essene,
benzene, benzine, theine, Christine,
pristine, Sistine, Springsteen,
Crimplene®, windscreen, quinine,
strychnine, Eileen, Irene, styrene,
flyscreen, glycine, lysine, Nicene,
hygiene, Tolkien, tontine, colleen,
Colleen, morphine, Pauline, chlorine,
Doreen, Maureen, Noreen, fluorine,
purine, soybean, codeine, Roedean,
protein, smokescreen, bromine,
sunscreen, butene, Lutine,
* epinephrine, Benedictine, polystyrene,
diamorphine, * norepinephrine

15.26 atropine, carrageen, Aberdeen,
gabardine, carotene, galantine,
trampoline, Jacqueline, Magdalene,
naphthalene, gasoline, Vaseline®,
tambourine, saccharine, Gadarene,
Nazarene, tangerine, Dramamine®,
anthracene, Damascene, magazine,
Balanchine, aniline, Trasimene,
Plasticine®, Halloween, mangosteen,
Argentine, margarine, tartrazine,
langoustine, crepe de Chine,
grenadine, Geraldine, gelatine,
seventeen, eglantine, clementine,
mescaline, nectarine, pelerine,
evergreen, Gretna Green, Bethnal
Green, melamine, mezzanine,

kerosene, phenazine, fedayeen,
Bellarmine, jellybean, pethidine,
velveteen, ethylene, methylene,
Terylene®, Emmeline, ephedrine,
Benzedrine®, epicene, Bernardine,
Germolene®, creatine, reconvene,
neoprene, Eocene, libertine, nicotine,
guillotine, brigantine, brilliantine,
Byzantine, intervene, Cymbeline,
Windolene®, figurine, Listerine®,
glycerine, Hippocrene, silver screen,
wintergreen, histamine, limousine,
kidney bean, Philippine, Ghibelline,
village green, in-between, indigene,
iodine, thiamine, tyrosine, isoprene,
Miocene, Pliocene, Pleistocene,
Constantine, Florentine, quarantine,
Josephine, contravene, bottle green,
bombazine, olivine, polythene,
propylene, olive green, Holocene,
oncogene, toluene, tourmaline, soya
bean, Ovaltine®, dopamine, overseen,
aubergine, bowling green, go-
between, *haute cuisine*, butter bean,
runner bean, submarine, putting
green, unforeseen, subroutine,
wolverine, fullerene, supervene,
glutamine, * papaverine,
amphetamine, adenosine,
promethazine, acetylene, methionine,
scopolamine, glucosamine,
* betacarotene, polyethylene,
antihistamine, nitroglycerine,
dryopithecine, catecholamine,
polypropylene, antisubmarine,
* benzodiazepine, oxyacetylene,
australopithecine, trinitrotoluene,
buckminsterfullerene,
* polytetrafluoroethylene

15.27 cleaned, fiend, gleaned, preened,
screened, weaned, * unscreened,
unweaned, machined, etc.

15.28 umpteenth, eighteenth, thirteenth, fifteenth, sixteenth, nineteenth, fourteenth, * seventeenth

15.29 beans, Dean's, greens, jeans, Jean's, Keynes, means, queens, Queens, scenes, screens, teens, * latrines, sardines, baked beans, Justine's, * Grenadines, clementines, Milton Keynes, smithereens, limousines, Philippines, aubergines, full of beans, New Orleans, * amphetamines, * antihistamines, etc.

**The woods are lovely, dark and deep.
But I have promises to keep,
And miles to go before I sleep.**
ROBERT FROST

15.30 beep, bleep, cheap, cheep, creep, deep, heap, Jeep®, keep, leap, neap, neep, peep, reap, seep, sheep, sleep, steep, Streep, sweep, veep, weep, * asleep, équipe, knee-deep, bo-peep, * scrapheap, slagheap, upkeep, upsweep, * chimney sweep, oversleep, * Uriah Heep

15.31 beeps, bleeps, creeps, heaps, neaps, neeps, Pepys, sweeps, weeps, etc.

15.32 cease, crease, *fils*, fleece, geese, grease, Greece, lease, Nice, niece, peace, piece, Rees, Rhys, * apiece, Matisse, police, sublease, cerise, caprice, Dumfries, De Vries, Denise, MacNeice, pastis, cassis, pelisse, Bernice, surcease, degrease, release, decrease, increase, decease, obese, Cochise, coulisse, * hairpiece, Makepeace, tailpiece, neckpiece, headpiece, set piece, chesspiece,

workpiece, earpiece, Greenpeace, eyepiece, timepiece, codpiece, crosspiece, showpiece, mouthpiece, * mantelpiece, ambergris, masterpiece, centrepiece, chersonese, verdigris, re-release, predecease, chimneypiece, altarpiece, *War and Peace*, frontispiece, * Peloponnese, archdiocese

**Abou Ben Adhem (may his tribe
increase!)
Awoke one night from a deep dream of
peace.**
LEIGH HUNT

15.33 beast, ceased, creased, east, feast, Geest, greased, least, piste, priest, yeast, * uncreased, batiste, artiste, Far East, archpriest, Near East, released, decreased, increased, deceased, northeast, southeast, modiste, * beanfeast, * arriviste, hartebeest, re-released, wildebeest, unreleased, etc.

15.34 fiche, leash, niche, quiche, * unleash, pastiche, Dalglish, rime riche, schottische, postiche, corniche, * hashish, baksheesh, * microfiche, nouveau riche

15.35 beat, beet, bleat, cheat, cleat, Crete, eat, feat, feet, fleet, Fleet, gîte, gleet, greet, heat, leat, leet, lied, meat, meet, mete, neat, peat, Pete, pleat, seat, sheet, skeet, sleet, street, suite, sweet, teat, treat, tweet, wheat, * compete, petite, complete, accrete, conceit, unseat, flat feet, Magritte, maltreat, *en suite*, dead beat, preheat, reheat, reseat, repeat, defeat, effete, delete, elite, deplete, replete, secrete, discreet, discrete, excrete, retreat, ill-treat, entreat, mistreat, deceit, receipt, gamete, crabmeat, factsheet, heartbeat, mainsheet, deadbeat, Benfleet, helpmeet, spreadsheet, worksheet, aesthete, sweetmeat, freesheet, pigmeat, mincemeat, bystreet, high street, time sheet, offbeat, Longleat, concrete, forefeet, Northfleet, forcemeat, horsemeat, broadsheet, browbeat, downbeat, groundsheet, wholewheat, upbeat, drumbeat, buckwheat, dustsheet, bushmeat, * pentathlete, decathlete, * parakeet, Paraclete, Masorete, marguerite, Marguerite, Harley Street, exegete, meadowsweet, incomplete, bittersweet, indiscreet, indiscrete, trick-or-treat, window seat, spirochaete, driver's seat, obsolete, polychaete, lorikeet, Downing Street, overeat, overheat, sugar beet, superheat, * Carnaby Street, oligochaete

Oh, East is East, and West is West, and never the twain shall meet,
Till Earth and Sky stand presently at God's great Judgement Seat.
RUDYARD KIPLING

15.36 beats, cheats, eats, Keats, Pete's, pleats, seats, sheets, streets, sweets, * athletes, backstreets, heartbeats, sweetmeats, etc.

15.37 heath, Heath, Keith, Leith, Meath, 'neath, Reith, sheath, teeth, wreath, * bequeath, beneath, Monteith, * milk teeth, eyeteeth, buckteeth, * Bexleyheath, Cowdenbeath, underneath, * B'nai B'rith

15.38 breathe, Meath, seethe, sheathe, teethe, wreathe, * unsheathe, enwreath, inbreathe, bequeath, * Pontypridd

15.39 breve, cleave, eve, Eve, greave, grieve, heave, leave, Neave, Niamh, peeve, reeve, reive, sheave, sleeve, Steve, thieve, vive, we've, weave, Yves, * upheave, aggrieve, perceive, conceive, achieve, Rajiv, French leave, qui vive, khedive, believe, relieve, bereave, reprieve, retrieve, inweave, deceive, receive, naive, * wayleave, shirtsleeve, sick leave, Congreve, * apperceive, make-believe, Tel Aviv, Genevieve, semibreve, preconceive, interleave, interweave, misconceive, disbelieve, oversleeve, undeceive, * recitative, overachieve, underachieve

O what a tangled web we weave,
When first we practise to deceive!
SIR WALTER SCOTT

15.40 grieved, heaved, peeved, thieved, * aggrieved, perceived, conceived, achieved, believed, relieved, bereaved, reprieved, deceived, received, long-sleeved, broad-leaved, short-sleeved, * preconceived, interleaved, misconceived, disbelieved, unrelieved, undeceived, etc.

15.41 beeves, eaves, Eve's, Greaves, grieves, heaves, Jeeves, leaves, Reeves, sheaves, sleeves, thieves, * achieves, believes, deceives, receives, * Hargreaves, shirtsleeves, sneak thieves, tea leaves, Greensleeves, wheatsheaves, fig leaves, flyleaves, * Anne of Cleves, Genevieve's, semibreves, etc.

15.42 bees, bise, breeze, cheese, Cleese, ease, fleas, fees, freeze, frieze, he's, keys, knees, lees, peas, please, seas, seize, she's, skis, sleaze, sneeze, squeeze, tease, Tees, these, trees, T's, tweeze, wheeze, etc.

He'd fly through the air with the greatest of ease,
A daring young man on the flying trapeze.
GEORGE LEYBOURNE

15.43 appease, trapeze, trustees, Belize, valise, cerise, Marie's, agrees, unfreeze, chemise, Denise, unease, marquise, trainees, MPs, Kirklees, Burmese, CDs, DTs, degrees, refreeze, deepfreeze, striptease, displease, reprise, disseise, disease, Chinese, Maltese, Louise, rupees, * Senegalese, Peloponnese, Dodecanese, Abdul-Aziz, *éminence grise*, GCSEs, etc.

15.44 Andes, axes, Ganges, heartsease, Ares, Aries, caries, lares, pear trees, rabies, scabies, tabes, stapes, Hades, bases, testes, menses, herpes, stirpes, Surtees, fir trees, Hermes, Xerxes, Ceres, series, faeces, theses, species, gee-gees, pine trees, crises, Pisces, * Cervantes, dolmades, penates, Pilates, Antares, Mercedes, Achates, Euphrates, oases, Orestes, Apelles, Waldenses, Laertes, subspecies, committees, Achilles, Antilles, meninges, pyrites, synopses, litotes, psychoses, prognoses, neuroses, * Ecclesiastes, Mithridates, rarae aves, Albigenses, Holofernes, Artaxerxes, Boanerges, miniseries, Archimedes, diabetes, ecospecies, bona fides, diagnoses, etc.

15.45 Maccabees, absentees, Androcles, Damocles, Anne-Marie's, Gabonese, Japanese, manganese, Cantonese, antifreeze, Rameses, Javanese,

Balinese, Faeroese, sanies, facies, apices, matrices, Cherokees, expertise, Nepalese, Heracles, Vietnamese, Lebanese, Celebes, Hebrides, Pericles, Héloïse, refugees, journalese, vertices, Hercules, legalese, Viennese, Pekinese, helices, Cyclades, Sinhalese, Milanese, Pyrenees, indices, Hyades, Pleiades, Siamese, Guyanese, Taiwanese, Sporades, Socrates, Congolese, novelese, Sophocles, chalk and cheese, cortices, vortices, Portuguese, gourmandise, vocalise, Togolese, overseas, OAPs, codices, dungarees, Sudanese, Ulysses, * cheval-de-frise, cantharides, Los Angeles, analyses, evacuees, Empedocles, Hesperides, appendices, parentheses, antipodes, officialese, Themistocles, Pheidippides, Euripides, Thucydides, Praxiteles, Xenocrates, Hippocrates, anopheles, isosceles, Xenophanes, Demosthenes, Diogenes, hypotheses, computerese, * Alcibiades, Aristophanes, Mephistopheles, Eratosthenes, etc.

16.1 freebie, hebe, Hebe, Phoebe, creepy, sleepy, tepee, weepy, beaky, cheeky, cliquey, creaky, freaky, geeky, Leakey, leaky, peaky, sneaky, squeaky, streaky, beady, Edie, greedy, needy, reedy, seedy, speedy, tweedy, weedy, wieldy, Beattie, Beatty, meaty, peaty, sleety, sweetie, treaty, fealty, beastie, yeasty, beefy, leafy, Revie, Lethe, Leahy, Ely, freely, Greeley, Healey, Keeley, Lely, mealie, mealy, steely, stele, wheelie, feebly, cheaply, deeply, steeply, bleakly, meekly, treacly, weakly, weekly, neatly, sweetly, Wheatley, beastly, Eastleigh, Priestley, priestly, briefly, chiefly, Keighley, seemly, cleanly, keenly, meanly, queenly, measly, Queensberry, Petrie, kiwi, pewee, beamy, creamy, dreamy, Mimi, preemie, REME, seamy, see me, steamy, beanie, Heaney, genie, Jeannie, meanie, Queenie, Rene, Sweeney, teeny, tweeny, weeny, fleecy, greasy, breezy, cheesy, easy, queasy, sleazy, sneezy, wheezy, teensy, specie, Vichy, peachy, preachy, screechy, Fiji, gee-gee, squeegee, * tzatziki, Kon-Tiki, Malpighi, Carnegie, Respighi, Macready, unwieldy, graffiti, Tahiti, entreaty, Haiti, Donleavy, sapele, Swahili, obliquely, uniquely, naively, serenely, obscenely, routinely, completely, discreetly, unseemly, extremely, supremely, tahini, bambini, tankini, Martini®, Bellini, Cellini, Fellini, Bernini, bikini, Selene, linguine, Irene, Mycenae, Rossini, Orsini, zucchini, Houdini, Puccini, Assisi, Tbilisi, uneasy, Zambezi, Medici, Luigi, * speakeasy, * cock-a-leekie, Nefertiti, Matabele, touchy-feely, Lamborghini, Agostini, Pasolini, Paganini, Cherubini, fettucine, teeny-weeny, Rossellini, Boccherini, Borromini, Toscanini, Mussolini, easy-peasy, teensy-weensy, maharishi, etc.

16.2 Gaea, freer, Leah, Mia, ria, Ria, rhea, Rhea, seer, Shiah, skier, Thea, Zia, * trachea, Korea, Maria, sharia, Chaldea, sangria, García, Medea, IKEA, spiraea, Crimea, Nicaea, tortilla, cornea, urea, Sofia, Sophia, Euboea, rupiah, Judaea, Lucía, * Landseer, sightseer, * Galatea, ratafia, Dorothea, mausolea, trattoria, pizzeria, Caesarea, Cytherea, mamma mia, Tanzania, panacea, Nicosia, overseer, Boadicea, Kampuchea, * Cassiopeia,

pharmacopoeia, Arimathea, Tia Maria®, Ave Maria, peripeteia, Laodicea, Andalucía, * onomatopoeia, * free her, see her, etc.

16.3 Sheba, beeper, bleeper, cheaper, creeper, deeper, Dnieper, keeper, leaper, peeper, reaper, sleeper, steeper, sweeper, weeper, * amoeba, Bathsheba, Beersheba, barkeeper, park keeper, gamekeeper, gatekeeper, beekeeper, greenkeeper, peacekeeper, tree creeper, innkeeper, timekeeper, minesweeper, shopkeeper, doorkeeper, scorekeeper, storekeeper, housekeeper, goalkeeper, book-keeper, zoo keeper, * Arequipa, wicketkeeper, * bleep her, keep her, etc.

When we were a soft amoeba, in ages past and gone,
Ere you were the Queen of Sheba, or I King Solomon.
ARTHUR SHIPLEY

16.4 beaker, bleaker, leaker, meeker, seeker, sika, sleeker, sneaker, speaker, Speaker, squeaker, streaker, tikka, tweaker, weaker, eager, leaguer, meagre, Riga, Seeger, Vega, * paprika, self-seeker, Guernica, eureka, loudspeaker, Antigua, beleaguer, intriguer, Swarfega®, * Tanganyika, Frederica, Costa Rica, overeager, * seek her, intrigue her, etc.

16.5 bleeder, Breda, breeder, cedar, Creda, feeder, kneader, leader, Leda, lieder, Ouida, pleader, reader, seeder, speeder, weeder, fielder, Kielder, wielder, yielder, beater, beta, cheater, cheetah, Dieter, eater, fetor, greeter, heater, litre, meeter, meter, metre,

neater, Peta, Peter, pleater, praetor,
Rita, Streeter, sweeter, teeter, theta,
tweeter, Vita, zeta, Dniester, Easter,
keister, quaestor, deemster, teamster,
* succeeder, Aïda, valeta, Anita, granita,
Juanita, raita, partita, repeater, Evita,
excreta, Demeter, Ryvita, pineta, Lolita,
saltpetre, ureter, two-seater,
northeaster, southeaster, * bandleader,
cheerleader, ringleader, mind-reader,
sight-reader, loss leader, stockbreeder,
mouthbreeder, proofreader,
newsreader, midfielder, infielder,
outfielder, anteater, eggbeater,
beefeater, windcheater, tripmeter,
wattmeter, toadeater, voltmeter,
ohmmeter, * al-Qaeda, Etheldreda,
interceder, copyreader, altimeter,
taximeter, nanometre, arboreta,
Margarita, decalitre, decametre,
centilitre, decilitre, centimetre,
decimetre, señorita, hectolitre,
hectometre, Eid-ul-Fitr, kilometre,
millilitre, millimetre, micrometre,
dolce vita, honey-eater, Sandinista,
* follow-my-leader, olla podrida,
Bhagavad-Gita, * feed her, meet her,
etc.

**Here lies that peerless paper peer Lord
Peter,
Who broke the laws of God and man
and metre.**
John Gibson Lockhart

16.6 briefer, reefer, FIFA, Eva, beaver,
Beaver, Cheever, cleaver, diva, fever,
griever, Hever, leaver, lever, reiver,
Siva, viva, weaver, weever, ether,
breather, either, neither, * Recife,
perceiver, achiever, transceiver,
believer, retriever, Geneva, deceiver,
receiver, school-leaver, Aretha, Ibiza,

bequeather, * cantilever, basketweaver,
disbeliever, nonbeliever, unbeliever,
Unilever, * overachiever, underachiever, * debrief her, leave her, etc.

16.7 dealer, feeler, healer, heeler,
Keeler, Keillor, kneeler, Leila, peeler,
sealer, selah, Sheila, squealer, stealer,
vealer, velar, wheeler, Wheeler, feebler,
beagler, Ziegler, Libra, Ypres, Phaedra,
Kenya, senior, * appealer, concealer,
three-wheeler, tequila, revealer,
cathedra, urethra, Monsignor,
* wheeler-dealer, Philomela, * *enfant
terrible*, ex cathedra, tetrahedra,
polyhedra, savoir-vivre, *joie de vivre*,
* heal her, steal her, etc.

16.8 beamer, creamer, dreamer, femur,
lemur, Lima, reamer, schema,
schemer, screamer, seamer, steamer,
streamer, Beena, cleaner, Ena, Gina,
gleaner, greener, keener, leaner, Lena,
meaner, Meena, Nina, screener,
Sheena, Tina, weaner, Wiener, Zena,
* blasphemer, oedema, redeemer,
Redeemer, Robina, subpoena,
convener, Athena, tahina, arena, farina,
marina, Marina, Sabrina, Catriona,
Katrina, pashmina, Martina, tsarina,
Medina, Edwina, Messina, retsina,
verbena, Christina, Melina, Selina,
Serena, demeanour, hyena, Ribena®,
Hygena, Molina, Cortina, Georgina,
Rowena, novena, euglena,
* daydreamer, pipe cleaner,
* emphysema, terza rima, Iwo Jima,
Hiroshima, carabiner, Pasadena,
cavatina, ballerina, Palestrina,
Agrippina, Angelina, Ballymena,
casuarina, scarlatina, Argentina,
St Helena, semolina, Messalina,
intervener, signorina, Philomena,

Wilhelmina, Filipina, misdemeanour, concertina, contravener, ocarina, Thomasina, * ottava rima, Gewürztraminer, * Herzegovina, * esteem her, screen her, etc.

16.9 greaser, Lisa, pizza, Caesar, freezer, geezer, geyser, Pisa, pleaser, seizer, sneezer, squeezer, teaser, visa, freesia, seizure, Esher, Beecher, bleacher, creature, feature, Meacher, Nietzsche, preacher, screecher, teacher, * degreaser, releaser, Teresa, Theresa, El Gîza, Malteser, Louisa, amnesia, nemesia, godetia, Belisha, Phoenicia, magnesia, Helvetia, Venetia, montbretia, Ossetia, Portlaoise, aubrietia, Rhodesia, Lucretia, procedure, besieger, * crowd-pleaser, schoolteacher, * Ebenezer, *Mona Lisa*, Melanesia, Indonesia, Micronesia, Austronesia, Polynesia, alopecia, paraplegia, tetraplegia, aquilegia, hemiplegia, quadriplegia, * Hispano-Suiza, * release her, reach her, etc.

16.10 Greenock, Taoiseach

16.11 greenstick, Friedrich, Dietrich, scenic, beatnik, seasick, peachick, * amoebic, comedic, acetic, anaemic, phonemic, ischaemic, glycaemic, toxaemic, irenic, hygienic, amnesic, strategic, * orthopaedic, unhygienic, geodesic, analgesic, nonstrategic, paraplegic, tetraplegic, hemiplegic, quadriplegic, * encyclopedic, * hyperglycaemic, hypoglycaemic

16.12 prefix, Felix, helix, Friedrich's, remix, phoenix, beatniks, peachicks, etc.

16.13 fetid, Enid, * Aeneid, bikinied

16.14 beaded, heeded, needed, pleaded, seeded, fielded, shielded, wielded, yielded, cheated, heated, metered, treated, feasted, Seaford, levered, leeward, Leeward, seaward, eastward, featured, * beleaguered, unheeded, unneeded, succeeded, conceded, unseeded, impeded, receded, exceeded, unheated, untreated, conceited, reheated, repeated, defeated, depleted, ill-treated, northeastward, southeastward, * unimpeded, overheated, undefeated, etc.

16.15 seawards, eastwards, * northeastwards, southeastwards

16.16 seepage, leakage, leafage, cleavage

16.17 feeble, Keble, peepul, people, sepal, steeple, faecal, Jekyll, treacle, beagle, eagle, legal, regal, Segal, Spiegl, beadle, Cheadle, needle, wheedle, beetle, betel, fetal, gleeful, heedful, needful, peaceful, evil, shrieval, weevil, lethal, equal, prequel, sequel, penal, renal, venal, diesel, easel, teasel, weasel, * tracheal, pineal, corneal, enfeeble, illegal, spread-eagle, viceregal, Threadneedle, deceitful, medieval, retrieval, primeval, coeval, upheaval, cathedral, unequal, adrenal, * tradespeople, townspeople, porbeagle, * perineal, laryngeal, pharyngeal, meningeal, centripetal, Evel Knievel, tetrahedral, hexahedral, octahedral, polyhedral, duodenal, * oesophageal, Till Eulenspiegel

16.18 Peebles, beagles, eagles, needles, Needles, Beatles, beetles, easels, measles, teasels, weasels, * Gleneagles, * pins and needles, etc.

16.19 prelim, Leitrim, * heal him, meet him, etc.

16.20 geum, Liam, sebum, caecum, Secombe, Edom, freedom, Needham, sedum, fiefdom, Cheetham, coelom, velum, Greenham, plenum, threesome, besom, Heysham, Evesham, Beecham, * Lyceum, museum, pinetum, cerebrum, pyrethrum, * mausoleum, Colosseum, Erechtheum, Atheneum, perineum, propylaeum, coliseum, arboretum, equisetum, duodenum, dirigisme, * peritoneum, * see 'em, teach 'em, etc.

You're the top! You're the Coliseum, You're the top! You're the Louvre Museum.
COLE PORTER

16.21 wheelspin, Deakin, Wrekin, sheepskin, sealskin, lead-in, Evelyn, sequin, teach-in, * Kosygin, Dunedin, * seekin', readin', etc.

16.22 Behan, eon, Ian, Leon, lien, paean, peon, Theban, cheapen, deepen, steepen, beacon, deacon, pecan, weaken, Egan, Keegan, Regan, vegan, Bredon, Eden, Sweden, Weedon, wealden, Neasden, beaten, Beaton, Beeton, Cretan, eaten, Eaton, Eton, Keaton, neaten, Seaton, Seton, sweeten, wheaten, chieftain, eastern, Easton, even, Leven, Stephen, Ethan, heathen, Whelan, Libran, daemon, demon, freeman, Freeman, Leman, seaman, semen, Eastman, Cheeseman,

liegeman, Gleason, Nielsen, Nilsson, Pisan, reason, season, treason, Friesian, lesion, Grecian, legion, region, * plebeian, Korean, Chaldean, Andean, Tarpeian, Circean, Aegean, Fijian, Nemean, Linnean, Piscean, Crimean, Nicaean, Strontian, Orphean, Taurean, Augean, protean, Euboean, Judaean, archdeacon, mohican, Mohican, Antiguan, unbeaten, uneaten, Nuneaton, Cleckheaton, Genevan, breakeven, Kesteven, Ibizan, Van Diemen, pentstemon, Philemon, policeman, unreason, adhesion, artesian, Cartesian, Ephesian, inhesion, Rhodesian, cohesion, Tahitian, completion, accretion, concretion, Phoenician, Haitian, Helvetian, deletion, depletion, repletion, secretion, excretion, Venetian, Ossetian, collegian, Galwegian, Glaswegian, Norwegian, * browbeaten, * Jacobean, Maccabean, Aramaean, Tanzanian, Atlantean, Caribbean, Manichaean, Achillean, Galilean, Kampuchean, Erechtheion, Hebridean, Periclean, empyrean, Herculean, Aeschylean, Tyrolean, Pyrenean, Sisyphean, Mycenaean, Sophoclean, Odyssean, European, Puerto Rican, Costa Rican, Mozambican, cotyledon, weather-beaten, overeaten, Tudorbethan, decahedron, tetrahedron, hexahedron, octahedron, polyhedron, cacodemon, Lacedaemon, Melanesian, Indonesian, Micronesian, Austronesian, Polynesian, Diocletian, * antipodean, Archimedean, Laodicean, epicurean, Epicurean, Terpsichorean, Pythagorean, Elizabethan, dodecahedron

Good King Wenceslas looked out,
On the feast of Stephen;
When the snow lay round about,
Deep and crisp and even.
JOHN MASON NEALE

16.23 cheapened, deepened, fecund, weakened, sweetened, eland, Zealand, Zeeland, Priestland, Cleveland, Greenland, Friesland, Queensland, reasoned, seasoned, weasand, * unsweetened, New Zealand, unseasoned, etc.

16.24 eons, Ian's, beacons, deacons, vegans, chieftains, evens, Stephens, heathens, demons, Siemens, reasons, seasons, legions, regions, * plebeians, Koreans, Orleans, Van Diemen's, adhesions, deletions, secretions, * Jacobeans, Europeans, New Orleans, etc.

16.25 piquant, secant, needn't, sealant, frequent, treatment, easement, decent, puissant, recent, regent, * cosecant, infrequent, agreement, maltreatment, ill-treatment, achievement, bereavement, concealment, appeasement, impeachment, indecent, impuissant, malfeasant, allegiant, * antecedent, disagreement, * overachievement, underachievement

16.26 credence, grievance, sequence, * impedance, agreements, achievements, malfeasance, allegiance, * antecedence, etc.

Sure, deck your lower limbs in pants;
Yours are the limbs, my sweeting.
You look divine as you advance –
Have you seen yourself retreating?
OGDEN NASH

16.27 being, fleeing, seeing, skiing, beeping, bleeping, creeping, keeping, leaping, peeping, reaping, sleeping, sweeping, weeping, creaking, leaking, reeking, seeking, shrieking, sneaking, speaking, squeaking, streaking, beading, bleeding, breeding, feeding, kneading, leading, pleading, reading, speeding, weeding, Fielding, wielding, yielding, beating, cheating, eating, fleeting, greeting, heating, Keating, meeting, seating, sheeting, sweeting, bee sting, feasting, briefing, reefing, grieving, heaving, leaving, sleeving, thieving, weaving, breathing, seething, teething, ceiling, dealing, Ealing, feeling, healing, Keeling, kneeling, peeling, sealing, shieling, squealing, stealing, wheeling, weakling, beagling, needling, reedling, seedling, wheedling, Riesling, key ring, G-string, beeswing, beaming, dreaming, gleaming, scheming, screaming, seeming, steaming, streaming, teeming, cleaning, gleaning, keening, leaning, meaning, screening, weaning, evening, ceasing, fleecing, greasing, leasing, freezing, pleasing, seizing, sneezing, squeezing, teasing, wheezing, preaching, reaching, screeching, teaching, * agreeing, unseeing, unsleeping, safekeeping, self-seeking, nonspeaking, fatiguing, intriguing, reneging, unheeding, proceeding, succeeding, rereading, misleading, inbreeding, preceding, receding, exceeding, unyielding, competing, completing, repeating, defeating, retreating, debriefing, perceiving, achieving, believing, deceiving, receiving, bequeathing, appealing, unfeeling, concealing, congealing, Darjeeling, self-sealing, freewheeling, revealing, redeeming, convening, unmeaning, self-cleaning, spring-cleaning, demeaning, policing, unceasing, decreasing, increasing, unleashing, beseeching, far-reaching, nonteaching, besieging, * wellbeing, sightseeing, peacekeeping, timekeeping, shopkeeping, housekeeping, book-keeping, breast-feeding, lip-reading, mind-reading, sight-reading, stockbreeding, force-feeding, spoonfeeding, proofreading, * water-skiing, human being, self-defeating, overeating, overheating, unbelieving, wheeler-dealing, unappealing, unrevealing, intervening, overweening, overreaching, * overachieving, underachieving, etc.

I had a dove and the sweet dove died;
And I have thought it died of grieving:
O, what could it grieve for? Its feet were tied,
With a silken thread of my own hand's weaving.
JOHN KEATS

16.28 beings, sweepings, greetings, meetings, beestings, leavings, dealings, feelings, seedlings, gleanings, leanings, meanings, evenings, * proceedings, etc.

16.29 Leavis, penis, thesis, tmesis, aegis, Regis, * kinesis, mimesis, prosthesis, Lyme Regis, * *in extremis*, exegesis, enuresis, diuresis, Bognor Regis, * diaphoresis, telekinesis, * amniocentesis

16.30 Phoebus, rebus, negus, Negus, foetus, grievous, naevus, Stevas, treeless, sleepless, heedless, needless, seedless, weedless, leafless, sleeveless, heelless, wheelless, dreamless, seamless, ceaseless, speechless, oestrus, seamstress, Remus, genus, heinous, venous, Venus, cheapness, steepness, bleakness, meekness, weakness, neatness, sweetness, keenness, greenness, meanness, Croesus, rhesus, Jesus, specious, * Antaeus, Aeneas, Linnaeus, Piraeus, boletus, quietus, Miletus, Malvinas, Silenus, Maecenas, uniqueness, completeness, discreetness, facetious, Lucretius, egregious, * Maccabaeus, Manichaeus, Nicodemus, Polyphemus, polysemous, intravenous, * see us, believe us, etc.

When I talk, and you are heedless,
I will show no anger needless.
JONATHAN SWIFT

16.31 deist, theist, * defeatist, elitist, extremist, machinist, hygienist, * encyclopedist

16.32 freest, cheapest, deepest, steepest, bleakest, meekest, sleekest, weakest, neatest, sweetest, briefest, feeblest, greenest, leanest, meanest, etc.

16.33 cheapish, sheepish, Swedish, fiendish, cliquish, freakish, peevish, squeamish, cleanish, greenish

16.34 fleapit, eaglet, leaflet, secret, egret, peewit, refit, remit, resit, eejit, * albeit, howbeit, so be it, * keep it, clean it, etc.

16.35 expletive, adhesive, cohesive, * self-adhesive

16.36 freebies, Phoebe's, sweeties, treatise, wheelies, weeklies, faeces, theses, species, gee-gees, * subspecies, * heebie-jeebies, Archimedes, diabetes, ecospecies, etc.

16.37 creepers, jeepers, peepers, sleepers, weepers, beakers, sneakers, speakers, cedars, leaders, fielders, litres, metres, Peters, Rita's, Beavers, cleavers, levers, dealers, peelers, dreamers, cleaners, creases, pieces, tweezers, creatures, features, beaches, peaches, teachers, * loudspeakers, fajitas, repeaters, Evita's, * gamekeepers, goalkeepers, cheerleaders, ringleaders, beefeaters, believers, school-leavers, * nonbelievers, misdemeanours, etc.

Finders keepers, losers weepers.
Saying

16.38 eagerly, legally, meagrely, regally, easterly, gleefully, peacefully, lethally, equally, weaselly, reasonably, peaceably, feasibly, heatedly, eastwardly, frequently, evenly, grievously, heedlessly, needlessly, ceaselessly, Queensberry, eatery, thievery, sealery, Tuileries, breviary, creamery, beanery, deanery, denary, greenery, plenary, scenery, venery, deaconry, peony, frequency, decency, recency, regency, Regency, deity, creepily, sleepily, cheekily, sneakily, greedily, speedily, dreamily, breezily, easily, secretly, fleetingly, seemingly, pleasingly, sheepishly, fiendishly, peevishly, feverishly, secrecy, * illegally, northeasterly, southeasterly, deceitfully, agreeably, conceivably, unreasonably, appreciably, conceitedly,

repeatedly, infrequently, unevenly, facetiously, secretory, excretory, catenary, machinery, centenary, patisserie, rotisserie, archdeaconry, infrequency, indecency, naivety, amenity, hygienically, strategically, misleadingly, exceedingly, appealingly, revealingly, unceasingly, decreasingly, increasingly, obesity, * inconceivably, unbelievably, irretrievably, irredeemably, intermediary, bicentenary, tercentenary, tricentenary, spontaneity, * simultaneity, homogeneity, etc.

I like your moral and machinery;
Your plot, too, has such scope for
scenery.
Lord Byron

16.39 Greenlander, schemata, Queenborough, sweetener, easterner, reasoner, * New Zealander

16.40 sepia, creepier, sleepier, weepier, cheekier, sneakier, squeakier, greedier, media, needier, seedier, speedier, weedier, meatier, meteor, beefier, Celia, Delia, creamier, dreamier, seamier, steamier, senior, taenia, greasier, breezier, easier, freesia, * Karelia, Amelia, camellia, Cecilia, Cordelia, Cornelia, lobelia, Ophelia, anaemia, ischaemia, pyaemia, toxaemia, uraemia, Bohemia, leukaemia, proscenia, asthenia, gardenia, Armenia, Slovenia, trapezia, amnesia, Silesia, * cyclopedia, multimedia, psychedelia, academia, septicaemia, myasthenia, neurasthenia, schizophrenia, * encyclopedia, Melanesia, Indonesia, Micronesia, Austronesia, analgesia, paraesthesia, anaesthesia, kinaesthesia, synaesthesia, hypaesthesia, Polynesia, aqua regia, * hyperglycaemia, hypoglycaemia, hyperaesthesia, etc.

16.41 keepable, readable, eatable, beatable, treatable, breathable, cleanable, reasonable, seasonable, peaceable, feasible, freezable, seizable, squeezable, reachable, teachable, seasonal, regional, medial, genial, menial, venial, Oedipal, vehicle, meaningful, * agreeable, foreseeable, unspeakable, unreadable, unbeatable, untreatable, uneatable, repeatable, unbreathable, perceivable, conceivable, achievable, believable, retrievable, receivable, resealable, redeemable, amenable, unreasonable, unseasonable, appreciable, depreciable, unreachable, unteachable, impeachable, procedural, Ezekiel, remedial, congenial, strategical, * disagreeable, unforeseeable, unrepeatable, inconceivable, irretrievable, unachievable, unbelievable, irredeemable, inappreciable, unimpeachable, endometrial, uncongenial

16.42 medium, tedium, Sealyham, helium, premium, rhenium, caesium, * mycelium, nobelium, proscenium, selenium, ruthenium, trapezium, magnesium, technetium, lutetium, collegium, * endothelium, epithelium, florilegium

16.43 Peterman, Peterson, Stephenson, Stevenson, oestrogen, median, Reithian, Delian, Pelion, Fenian, Friesian, Nietzschean, * comedian, tragedian, Promethean, chameleon,

Hegelian, Mendelian, cornelian, Bohemian, Athenian, Armenian, Tyrrhenian, Slovenian, artesian, Cartesian, Silesian, collegian, * Archimedean, Magdalenian, Melanesian, Indonesian, Micronesian, Austronesian, Polynesian, * Aristotelian, Mephistophelean

16.44 mediant, deviant, lenient, * obedient, submediant, expedient, ingredient, convenient, * disobedient, inexpedient, inconvenient

16.45 deviance, deviants, lenience, * obedience, expedience, ingredients, convenience, * disobedience, inexpedience, inconvenience, etc.

16.46 deepening, weakening, sweetening, reasoning, seasoning, * unreasoning, etc.

16.47 Daedalus, leaderless, featureless, eagerness, meagreness, treasonous, feebleness, evenness, tedious, devious, previous, Delius, Peleus, genius, Theseus, Regius, Oedipus, Aeschylus, meaningless, creepiness, sleepiness, greediness, speediness, dreaminess, greasiness, easiness, seasickness, squeamishness, * unevenness, Asclepius, Prometheus, Boethius, Aurelius, Cornelius, obsequious, abstemious, arsenious, ingenious, egregious, uneasiness, * contumelious, homogeneous, * heterogeneous, etc.

16.48 egotist, legalist, re-enlist, egoist, * anaesthetist, medievalist

16.49 creepiest, sleepiest, weepiest, cheekiest, sneakiest, squeakiest, greediest, neediest, seediest, speediest, weediest, meatiest, beefiest, creamiest, dreamiest, seamiest, steamiest, greasiest, breeziest, easiest, etc.

16.50 Cheviot, * inebriate, collegiate, * intermediate

16.51 Tuileries, frequencies, decencies, * amenities, etc.

16.52 seasonally, regionally, genially, reasonably, leniently, vehemently, previously, deviancy, leniency, * unreasonably, immediately, obediently, conveniently, obsequiously, immediacy, expediency, * disobediently, inconveniently

16.53 reasonable, seasonable, * unreasonable, unseasonable, remediable, * irremediable

The rhymes in this section have the 'i' sound of sit and whistle as their main or final vowel sound. You will find many words ending with a weak 'i' sound in other sections (e.g. – a – for frantic, – e – for resin, – o – for horrid).

17.1 bib, crib, dib, fib, Gibb, glib, jib, lib, nib, rib, sib, snib, squib, * ad-lib, damp squib, sparerib, * Carib, sahib, midrib, * memsahib, * women's lib, * Sennacherib

17.2 bibs, dibs, dribs, fibs, Gibbs, Hibs, nibs, ribs, * ad-libs, spareribs, his nibs, etc.

17.3 Bic®, brick, chick, click, clique, crick, Crick, dick, Dick, flick, hic, hick, kick, lick, Mick, nick, Nick, pic, pick, prick, quick, rick, Rick, shtick, sic, sick, slick, snick, spick, stick, thick, tic, tick, trick, Vic, Wick, wick, wrick, * unpick, matric, unstick, hand-pick, nonstick, Old Vic, * airsick, gearstick, firebrick, cowlick, joystick, oil slick, * Arabic, candlestick, catholic, Catholic, agaric, Catterick, maverick, Alaric, caloric, Scarisbrick, candlewick, Reykjavik, bailiwick, clever Dick, heretic, Menshevik, Metternich, Frederick, rhetoric, turmeric, Leofric, Evo-stik®, fiddlestick, Giggleswick, limerick, Limerick, bishopric, chivalric, biopic, Broderick, Roderick, choleric, politic, Bolshevik, Dominic, Moby Dick, lunatic, Ludovic, * cadaveric, arithmetic, archbishopric, Theodoric

Jack be nimble, Jack be quick,
Jack jump over the candlestick.
Nursery rhyme

17.4 bricks, chicks, clicks, Dick's, fix, flicks, Hicks, kicks, Mick's, Nick's, mix, nix, pix, pricks, Rick's, six, sticks, Styx, ticks, tricks, Wicks, * unpicks, unsticks, affix, commix, admix, hand-picks, transfix, M6, prefix, remix, * cervix, Beatrix, gearsticks, joysticks, oil slicks, * candlesticks, Catholics, apteryx, Asterix, eighty-six, heretics, twenty-six, MI6, thirty-six, Weetabix®, fiddlesticks, limericks, fifty-six, sixty-six, ninety-six, politics, Dominic's, forty-six, lunatics, crucifix, * executrix, * archaeopteryx, etc.

17.5 fixed, mixed, sixte, 'twixt, * affixed, unmixed, transfixed, betwixt, etc.

17.6 clicked, flicked, kicked, licked, nicked, picked, Pict, pricked, strict, ticked, tricked, * unpicked, addict, convict, afflict, conflict, constrict, hand-picked, depict, predict, evict, inflict, restrict, * addict, panicked, Maastricht, relict, verdict, perfect, edict, mimicked, picnicked, district, frolicked, conflict, object, subject, * word-perfect, imperfect, pluperfect,

* Benedict, derelict, derestrict, interdict, contradict, etc.

17.7 bitch, ditch, flitch, glitch, hitch, itch, kitsch, Mitch, niche, pitch, rich, snitch, stitch, switch, titch, twitch, which, witch, * unhitch, unstitch, bewitch, enrich, * Harwich, Magwitch, sandwich, Sandwich, Nantwich, backstitch, Redditch, Prestwich, Greenwich, hemstitch, quidditch, spinach, slipstitch, whipstitch, dip switch, Ipswich, Norwich, Bromwich, topstitch, cross stitch, ostrich, Shoreditch, Aldwych, Northwich, Woolwich, Goodrich, * tsarevitch, Middlewich, * Ivanovich, Milosevic, * Rostropovich, Shostakovich, * son-of-a-bitch

A nasty surprise in a sandwich,
A drawing-pin caught in your sock,
The limpest of shakes from a hand
    which
You'd thought would be firm as a rock.
JAMES FENTON

17.8 bid, chid, did, fid, grid, hid, id, kid, Kidd, lid, mid, quid, rid, Sid, skid, slid, squid, yid, * forbid, undid, amid, Madrid, El Cid, redid, outbid, * canopied, parodied, atrophied, galleried, salaried, katydid, remedied, tertium quid, liveried, pilloried, Winifred, pyramid, propertied, hominid, overbid, overdid, underbid, mutinied, * accompanied, * unaccompanied

17.9 didst, midst

17.10 biff, Cif®, cliff, Cliff, glyph, Griff, if, Jif®, jiff, kif, miff, niff, quiff, riff,

Schiff, skiff, sniff, spliff, stiff, tiff, whiff, * skewwhiff, * Radcliffe, Ratcliffe, tariff, mastiff, plaintiff, bailiff, caliph, Cardiff, serif, sheriff, Pecksniff, Heathcliff, Wycliffe, midriff, pontiff, Joseph, Sutcliffe, * anaglyph, hippogriff, hieroglyph, undercliff

17.11 biffed, drift, gift, GIFT, grift, lift, miffed, niffed, rift, shift, shrift, sift, sniffed, swift, Swift, thrift, whiffed, * adrift, uplift, red shift, * airlift, chairlift, stairlift, facelift, makeshift, spendthrift, festschrift, ski lift, spindrift, shoplift, snowdrift

Time, the avenger! unto thee I lift
My hands, and eyes, and heart, and
    crave of thee a gift.
LORD BYRON

17.12 big, brig, cig, dig, fig, frig, gig, jig, lig, MiG, pig, prig, rig, Rigg, sprig, swig, trig, twig, Whig, wig, * unrig, rejig, * Danzig, Schleswig, earwig, shindig, bigwig, Leipzig, oil rig, Grundig, Ludwig, * periwig, whirligig, infra dig, thimblerig, WYSIWYG, * thingumajig

17.13 Biggs, Briggs, digs, figs, gigs, jigs, pigs, rigs, swigs, twigs, Whigs, wigs, * Bay of Pigs, * syrup of figs, etc.

17.14 bridge, fridge, midge, ridge, smidge, * abridge, * vassalage, anchorage, Anchorage, average, sacrilege, patronage, harbourage, Casterbridge, pasturage, parsonage, Armitage, cartilage, parentage, acreage, beverage, Beveridge, haemorrhage, Breckenridge, heritage, personage, verbiage, hermitage, leverage,

Stevenage, privilege, vicarage, pilferage, pilgrimage, pilotage, lineage, orphanage, Fordingbridge, sortilege, brokerage, Coleridge, foliage, Muggeridge, coverage, sewerage, pupillage, tutelage, mucilage

**He that complies against his will,
Is of his own opinion still.**
SAMUEL BUTLER

17.15 bill, Bill, brill, chill, dill, drill, fill, frill, ghyll, gill, Gill, grill, grille, hill, Hill, ill, Jill, kill, krill, Lil, mill, Mill, nil, Phil, pill, quill, Rhyl, rill, shrill, sill, skill, spill, still, swill, thrill, till, trill, twill, 'twill, will, Will, * McGill, until, Seville, uphill, De Mille, brazil, Brazil, Rainhill, Redhill, Bexhill, Edgehill, deskill, refill, freewill, distil, instil, stock-still, quadrille, downhill, fulfil, goodwill, * handbill, waxbill, Shankill, Catskill, dactyl, pastille, standstill, backfill, landfill, Savile, Sackville, anvil, Granville, Nashville, Ampthill, anthill, Avril, tranquil, Hamill, Tamil, Cahill, Scargill, Cargill, playbill, waybill, cranesbill, ethyl, methyl, Melville, Grenville, treadmill, Denzil, chervil, Churchill, Persil®, Virgil, Jekyll, refill, infill, pistil, pigswill, windmill, windchill, vigil, crossbill, Tocqueville, Knoxville, Bovril®, jonquil, hornbill, sawmill, Cornhill, Orville, Torvill, Bournville, Mobil®, roadkill, Yeovil, Oakville, Tocqueville, molehill, Huntsville, Dullsville, Dunhill, dunghill, foothill, cook-chill, shoebill, spoonbill, * daffodil, Baskerville, Mandeville, Jacksonville, razorbill, Rentokil®, Pentonville, espadrille, peppermill, Selsey Bill, Benny Hill, Clearasil®,

whippoorwill, Yggdrasil, minipill, windowsill, fibrefill, Fothergill, Goneril, chlorophyll, vaudeville, watermill, overspill, overkill, codicil, Somerville, Louisville, * pterodactyl, Invercargill, Merthyr Tydfil, * run-of-the-mill, over the hill, * Cruella De Vil

17.16 bilk, ilk, milk, silk,
* Liebfraumilch, buttermilk

**The cow is of the bovine ilk;
One end is moo, the other, milk.**
OGDEN NASH

17.17 filch, milch, zilch

17.18 billed, build, chilled, drilled, filled, gild, grilled, guild, killed, milled, pilled, sild, skilled, thrilled, willed, * unskilled, unfilled, unwilled, self-willed, weak-willed, rebuild, refilled, distilled, strong-willed, fulfilled, Brunhild, * jerry-build, semiskilled, overbuild, unfulfilled, etc.

17.19 film, * clingfilm, * microfilm

17.20 kiln, Milne, * limekiln

17.21 built, gilt, guilt, hilt, jilt, kilt, lilt, milt, quilt, silt, spilt, stilt, tilt, wilt, * unbuilt, unspilt, well-built, inbuilt, * Vanderbilt, jerry-built, purpose-built, overbuilt, custom-built

17.22 filth, tilth

17.23 bills, Bill's, drills, fills, frills, gills, hills, ills, kills, Lil's, mills, Mills, Phil's, pills, Pils, skills, spills, thrills, wills, Wills, Will's, * no-frills, * pastilles, windmills, molehills, foothills,

* daffodils, espadrilles, * battle of wills, Beverly Hills, etc.

His eye so dim,
So wasted each limb,
That, heedless of grammar, they all
cried, 'That's him!'
R. H. Barham

17.24 brim, dim, grim, Grimm, gym, him, hymn, Jim, Kim, limb, limn, Lymm, prim, Pimm, Pym, quim, rim, scrim, shim, Sim, skim, slim, swim, Tim, trim, vim, whim, * bedim, * antonym, acronym, cherubim, seraphim, eponym, interim, synonym, hypernym, hyponym, toponym, homonym, Joachim, pseudonym, * heteronym

17.25 dimmed, skimmed, slimmed, trimmed, * undimmed, untrimmed, broad-brimmed, loose-limbed, * semi-skimmed, etc.

17.26 lymph, nymph

17.27 blimp, chimp, crimp, gimp, imp, limp, pimp, primp, scrimp, shrimp, skimp, wimp

17.28 chimps, glimpse, imps, limps, pimps, shrimps, wimps, etc.

On a sofa upholstered in panther skin
Mona did researches in original sin.
William Plomer

17.29 bin, Bryn, chin, din, fin, Finn, Flynn, gin, Glyn, grin, Gwyn, in, inn, jinn, kin, Lynn, min, pin, PIN, quin, Quinn, shin, sin, skin, spin, thin, tin, twin, whin, win, Wyn, yin, * unpin,

akin, agin, therein, wherein, Vietminh, Berlin, herein, begin, built-in, within, King's Lynn, Penrhyn, Pinyin, chin-chin, Turin, Boleyn, * Jacobin, atropin, paladin, Saladin, Anadin®, paraffin, trampoline, Jacqueline, Madeleine, Magdalene, mandolin, Carolyn, lanolin, saccharin, mandarin, Catherine, Mazarin, ramekin, mannequin, Sanhedrin, masculine, albumen, albumin, capuchin, Capuchin, harlequin, wafer-thin, kaolin, chamberlain, Chamberlain, terrapin, next-of-kin, gelatin, keratin, zeppelin, mescalin, Gwendolen, heparin, nectarine, Benjamin, melanin, Peregrine, specimen, feminine, medicine, heroin, heroine, endocrine, Bedouin, genuine, Menuhin, eosin, litter bin, whipper-in, Ritalin®, crinoline, Michelin®, glycerine, vitamin, histamine, Mickey Finn, discipline, Silvikrin®, insulin, bitumen, Scriabin, violin, thiamine, niacin, myelin, Borodin, Rosalyn, sovereign, moccasin, origin, globulin, formalin, warfarin, porphyrin, Ho Chi Minh, Lohengrin, underpin, onionskin, muscadine, Gunga Din, rub it in, bulletin, * Led Zeppelin, adrenaline, amphetamine, unfeminine, tuberculin, through thick and thin, self-discipline, indiscipline, * nitroglycerine, antihistamine, * immunoglobulin

17.30 blink, brink, chink, clink, dink, drink, fink, Frink, gink, Inc., ink, jink, kink, link, mink, pink, plink, prink, rink, shrink, sink, skink, slink, stink, sync, think, twink, wink, zinc, * unthink, bethink, rethink, * ratfink, rethink, lip-sync, Haitink, ice rink,

snowblink, cuff link, hoodwink,
* Maeterlinck, skating rink, pen-and-
ink, rinky-dink, tiddlywink, hyperlink,
bobolink, countersink, out of sync,
doublethink

They never taste who always drink;
They always talk, who never think.
MATTHEW PRIOR

17.31 blinks, chinks, clinks, drinks,
jinx, Lincs, links, lynx, minx, shrinks,
sinks, sphinx, stinks, thinks, winks,
* methinks, rethinks, high jinks,
* ratfinks, larynx, pharynx, golf links,
cuff links, * tiddlywinks, forty winks,
etc.

17.32 blinked, clinked, inked, kinked,
linked, pinked, prinked, winked,
* succinct, distinct, extinct, * precinct,
instinct, hoodwinked, * index-linked,
indistinct, etc.

17.33 cinch, clinch, finch, flinch,
grinch, inch, lynch, Lynch, Minch,
pinch, winch, * half-inch, * chaffinch,
greenfinch, goldfinch, bullfinch

17.34 finned, grinned, Lind, pinned,
Sind, sinned, skinned, tinned,
twinned, wind, * unpinned, upwind,
dark-skinned, fair-skinned, rescind,
thick-skinned, thin-skinned,
downwind, * trade wind, tailwind,
headwind, Chetwynd, destined,
whirlwind, sequined, Rifkind,
crosswind, woodwind, ruined,
* examined, predestined, determined,
* Amerind, tamarind, disciplined,
Rosalind, underpinned, wunderkind,
double-chinned, * undisciplined,
* undetermined

17.35 bing, bling, bring, Byng, Ching,
cling, ding, fling, Inge, king, King,
ling, Ming, ping, ring, sing, Singh,
sling, spring, sting, string, swing,
Synge, thing, ting, Ting, Tring, wing,
wring, zing, * unsling, unstring,
Nanking, Ram Singh, Beijing, left-
wing, Peking, I Ching, bling-bling,
Taiping, right-wing

A little learning is a dangerous thing;
Drink deep, or taste not the Pierian
  spring.
ALEXANDER POPE

17.36 brings, clings, kings, Kings,
rings, sings, springs, strings, swings,
things, wings, * Palm Springs, * Alice
Springs, waterwings, underthings, etc.

17.37 binge, cringe, dinge, fringe,
hinge, minge, singe, springe, swinge,
whinge, tinge, twinge, * unhinge,
impinge, syringe, infringe, * scavenge,
challenge, orange, Orange, lozenge

17.38 mince, prince, quince, rinse,
since, Vince, wince, * convince, evince,
* province, * Port-au-Prince

They dined on mince, and slices of
  quince,
Which they ate with a runcible spoon.
EDWARD LEAR

17.39 bint, clint, Clint, dint, flint, Flint,
glint, hint, lint, mint, print, skint,
splint, sprint, squint, stint, tint,
* reprint, imprint, * catmint, varmint,
spearmint, enprint, reprint, skinflint,
imprint, misprint, offprint, voiceprint,
thumbprint, footprint, blueprint,
newsprint, * aquatint, peppermint,

mezzotint, fingerprint, overprint, wunderkind, * Septuagint

17.40 Clint's, flints, glints, hints, chintz, splints, squints, tints, etc.

17.41 plinth, * absinthe, helminth, Corinth, * labyrinth, terebinth, hyacinth

17.42 bins, Binns, chins, fins, Finns, grins, Lynn's, quins, shins, sins, skins, spins, tins, twins, * unpins, begins, * Jacobins, Jacqueline's, Madeleine's, mandolins, Carolyn's, mandarins, Catherine's, ramekins, mannequins, Capuchins, terrapins, nectarines, Benjamin's, medicines, heroines, Bedouins, litter bins, withershins, crinolines, vitamins, violins, moccasins, origins, underpins, bulletins, * amphetamines, etc.

17.43 blip, chip, clip, dip, drip, flip, grip, gyp, hip, kip, lip, nip, pip, Pip, quip, rip, scrip, ship, sip, skip, slip, snip, strip, tip, trip, Tripp, whip, zip, * unhip, unclip, unzip, unship, transship, reship, equip, nonslip, nondrip, round trip, outstrip, * landslip, handgrip, catnip, flagship, parsnip, starship, clerkship, hardship, harelip, hairgrip, airstrip, airship, mayorship, pay slip, day trip, spaceship, felt-tip, headship, friendship, turnip, Worsnip, circlip, worship, sheep-dip, steamship, wing tip, fillip, Philip, gymslip, film strip, kinship, kingship, Ruislip, sideslip, lightship, oxlip, gossip, longship, horsewhip, warship, lordship, wardship, courtship, cowslip, township, rosehip, bunyip, gunship,

judgeship, bullwhip, wood chip, julep, tulip, Q-ship, troopship, * trusteeship, * battleship, captainship, Gaza Strip, partnership, marksmanship, craftsmanship, draughtsmanship, chairmanship, paperclip, statesmanship, salesmanship, gamesmanship, ladyship, sailing ship, membership, censorship, lectureship, penmanship, fellowship, bursarship, workmanship, kirby grip, speakership, leadership, readership, dealership, chieftainship, seamanship, re-equip, fingertip, filter tip, brinkmanship, skinny-dip, pillowslip, fibre-tip, biochip, microchip, scholarship, sponsorship, consulship, comradeship, rocket ship, authorship, horsemanship, sportsmanship, swordsmanship, ownership, showmanship, mother ship, toodle-pip, tutorship, viewership, stewardship, studentship, * companionship, commandership, dictatorship, curatorship, relationship, acquaintanceship, electorship, directorship, professorship, self-censorship, apprenticeship, receivership, musicianship, discipleship, co-ownership, conductorship, instructorship, one-upmanship, * championship, managership, admiralship, magistrateship, landownership, chancellorship, cardinalship, guardianship, partisanship, emperorship, treasurership, generalship, premiership, editorship, presidentship, residentship, deputyship, Möbius strip, ministership, principalship, silicon chip, citizenship, laureateship, Freudian slip, governorship, * ambassadorship, librarianship, executorship, proprietorship, associateship, custodianship, * entrepreneurship, * interrelationship

17.44 chips, clips, Cripps, drips, hips, lips, Phipps, pips, Pip's, quips, ships, sips, snips, strips, thrips, tips, trips, whips, zips, * unclips, unzips, ellipse, eclipse, equips, * Mendips, felt-tips, wing tips, fillips, Philips, Philip's, gymslips, film strips, tin snips, horsewhips, warships, lordships, * amidships, athwartships, * fingertips, filter tips, Mr Chips, fish and chips, pillowslips, scholarships, rocket ships, * relationships, apprenticeships, apocalypse, etc.

17.45 chipped, clipped, crypt, dipped, dripped, flipped, gripped, nipped, ripped, script, shipped, sipped, skipped, slipped, stripped, tipped, whipped, * unclipped, conscript, unzipped, decrypt, encrypt, equipped, outstripped, close-lipped, * transcript, harelipped, prescript, Egypt, typescript, conscript, horsewhipped, cork-tipped, postscript, subscript, * manuscript, well-equipped, filter-tipped, ill-equipped, nondescript, unequipped, eucalypt, superscript, etc.

17.46 bliss, Bliss, Chris, diss, Diss, hiss, kiss, kris, miss, Miss, piss, sis, Swiss, this, * abyss, amiss, near miss, dehisce, remiss, dismiss, * cannabis, avarice, ambergris, Salamis, Charteris, armistice, artifice, Artemis, emphasis, precipice, edifice, benefice, reminisce, emesis, Nemesis, genesis, Genesis, berberis, chrysalis, liquorice, clitoris, hit-and-miss, synthesis, prejudice,

diocese, cockatrice, orifice, cowardice, * Annapolis, metastasis, catalysis, paralysis, analysis, dialysis, Persepolis, ephemeris, mons veneris, parenthesis, diaeresis, antithesis, psoriasis, archdiocese, Acropolis, necropolis, metropolis, hypothesis, hydrolysis, autolysis, * Minneapolis, sui generis, overemphasis, underemphasis, epididymis, photosynthesis, satyriasis, megalopolis, electrolysis, metamorphosis, * Indianapolis, psychoanalysis, microanalysis, haemodialysis, *annus mirabilis*, parthenogenesis, annus horribilis, elephantiasis

You must remember this,
A kiss is still a kiss.
HERMAN HUPFELD

17.47 bisque, brisk, disc, disk, fisc, frisk, risk, whisk, * asterisk, tamarisk, basilisk, obelisk, compact disc, floppy disk

17.48 crisp, lisp, wisp, * will-o'-the-wisp

17.49 cist, cyst, fist, gist, grist, hissed, hist, kissed, list, Liszt, missed, mist, pissed, schist, tryst, twist, whist, wist, wrist, * unkissed, assist, persist, subsist, consist, delist, demist, enlist, dismissed, encyst, insist, desist, resist, exist, * naturalist, nationalist, rationalist, capitalist, separatist, federalist, negativist, relativist, liberalist, minimalist, militarist, spiritualist, Oliver Twist, positivist, structuralist, monetarist, * sensationalist, materialist, imperialist, traditionalist, industrialist,

* conversationalist, Congregationalist, educationalist, individualist, agriculturalist, horticulturalist, etc.

17.50 bish, Bysshe, dish, fish, Frisch, Gish, pish, squish, swish, Trish, wish, * Irish, boyish, * Cavendish, damselfish, angelfish, babyish, jellyfish, feverish, silverfish, gibberish, lickerish, liverish, spinsterish, kittenish, minidish, killifish, tomboyish, butter dish, cuttlefish, womanish, * impoverish

17.51 bit, Brit, chit, fit, flit, git, grit, hit, it, kit, knit, lit, mitt, nit, pit, Pitt, quit, Schmidt, shit, sit, skit, slit, spit, split, Split, squit, tit, twit, whit, Whit, wit, writ, zit, * unfit, alit, unlit, de Witt, acquit, commit, permit, submit, admit, unknit, transmit, refit, keep-fit, relit, resit, befit, mishit, emit, remit, legit, tight-knit, op. cit., outwit, omit, close-knit, * aquavit, candlelit, apposite, manumit, favourite, baby-sit, megabit, preterite, Messerschmitt, benefit, definite, plebiscite, deficit, requisite, Jesuit, perquisite, recommit, resubmit, readmit, retransmit, Hindemith, hypocrite, infinite, Inuit, opposite, composite, *floruit*, conduit, Duraglit®, counterfeit, Photofit®, Chuzzlewit, cuckoo spit, * Plantagenet, banana split, Identikit®, indefinite, prerequisite, * lickety-split, overcommit

Do not adultery commit;
Advantage rarely comes of it.
ARTHUR HUGH CLOUGH

17.52 bits, blitz, Blitz, fits, Fitz, Fritz, glitz, grits, its, it's, mitts, nits, pits, quits, Ritz, Spitz, splits, tits, wits, zits, * St Kitts, submits, admits, Berlitz, Biarritz, befits, emits, * St Moritz, megabits, benefits, Jesuits, slivovitz, hypocrites, Horowitz, opposites, Austerlitz, etc.

17.53 Frith, kith, myth, pith, smith, Smith, with, fifth, * therewith, wherewith, Penrith, herewith, forthwith, outwith, * Asquith, blacksmith, Kenneth, zenith, wordsmith, Edith, Griffith, tinsmith, Gwyneth, Highsmith, Sopwith, locksmith, songsmith, Grossmith, goldsmith, Goldsmith, gunsmith, Judith, tunesmith, * Hammersmith, Arrowsmith, eightieth, Ladysmith, Meredith, megalith, twentieth, thirtieth, Hindemith, silversmith, fiftieth, sixtieth, ninetieth, monolith, coppersmith, fortieth, * Aberystwyth, Merioneth, * seventieth

17.54 div, give, live, sieve, spiv, Viv, * forgive, relive, outlive, * palliative, decorative, meditative, vegetative, legislative, speculative, innovative, figurative, iterative, illustrative, imitative, operative, quantitative, qualitative, nominative, ulcerative, cumulative, * collaborative, imaginative, evaluative, commemorative, degenerative, investigative, deliberative, alliterative, administrative, manipulative, corroborative, inoperative, cooperative, postoperative, authoritative, denominative, vituperative, remunerative, adjudicative, communicative, * unimaginative, uncooperative, unremunerative, uncommunicative

Far and few, far and few,
Are the lands where the Jumblies live;
Their heads are green, and their hands
   are blue,
And they went to sea in a sieve.
EDWARD LEAR

17.55 ablative, narrative, laxative,
additive, transitive, adjective,
calmative, negative, sedative, tentative,
relative, genitive, sensitive, ergative,
purgative, secretive, fricative, privative,
fixative, primitive, combative, locative,
vocative, cognitive, positive, talkative,
formative, normative, causative,
curative, putative, lucrative, nutritive,
punitive, fugitive, * comparative,
declarative, preparative, reparative,
intransitive, rebarbative, preventative,
correlative, contemplative, imperative,
competitive, repetitive, insensitive,
consecutive, executive, conservative,
Conservative, preservative, superlative,
affirmative, alternative, interpretive,
appreciative, predicative, indicative,
explicative, derivative, initiative,
prohibitive, definitive, infinitive,
acquisitive, inquisitive, attributive,
distributive, diminutive, provocative,
evocative, derogative, prerogative,
restorative, pejorative, demonstrative,
remonstrative, appositive,
postpositive, informative, connotative,
denotative, consultative, commutative,
disputative, accusative, intuitive,
* argumentative, representative,
noncompetitive, uncompetitive,
hypersensitive, photosensitive,
nonexecutive, interrogative,
undemonstrative, * unrepresentative,
ultraconservative

17.56 biz, fizz, frizz, his, is, Ms, Liz,

phiz, 'tis, quiz, swizz, tizz, viz, whizz,
wiz, zizz, * Cadiz, buck's fizz, gee-whiz

18.1 Libby, Digby, Rigby, VitBe,
Whitby, Philby, trilby, will be, NIMBY,
Frisbee®, Thisbe, Rigsby, Grimsby,
chippy, clippie, dippy, drippy, gippy,
grippy, hippy, lippy, nippy, slippy,
trippy, zippy, chickpea, impi, skimpy,
Wimpey, Wimpy, crispy, wispy,
* astilbe, Xanthippe, * Mr Whippy,
Mississippi

18.2 bickie, brickie, cliquey, dicky,
Dickie, hickey, icky, Mickey, Nicky,
picky, quickie, Ricky, sickie, sticky,
thickie, tricky, Vicky, milky, silky,
Wilkie, dinky, inky, kinky, minke,
pinkie, slinky, stinky, frisky, risky,
whiskey, whisky, biggie, ciggy, piggy,
twiggy, Twiggy, dinghy, * Helsinki,
Stravinsky, Nijinsky, Miss Piggy,
* doohickey, * take the mickey,
Billericay

18.3 biddy, Biddy, diddy, did he, giddy,
kiddy, midi, bhindi, Cindy, Hindi,
indie, Indy, Lindy, Mindy, shindy,
Sindy, windy, bitty, chitty, city, ditty,
gritty, Intercity, kitty, Kitty, pity, pretty,
shitty, titty, Whitty, witty, fifty, nifty,
shifty, thrifty, guilty, silty, flinty, linty,
minty, shinty, Christie, misty, twisty,
sixty, * McVitie, committee, self-pity,
McGinty, * chickabiddy, Rawalpindi,
intercity, itty-bitty, pretty-pretty, nitty-
gritty, Walter Mitty, Salt Lake City,
subcommittee, fifty-fifty, pepperminty,
Corpus Christi

In Dublin's fair city,
Where the girls are so pretty.
ANONYMOUS

18.4 cliffy, iffy, jiffy, Liffey, miffy, sniffy, squiffy, stiffy, whiffy, chivy, divvy, Livy, privy, skivvy, Sylvie, pithy, filthy, prithee, smithy, withy, * tantivy

18.5 Billy, Chile, chilli, chilly, filly, frilly, gillie, hilly, Jilly, Lillee, lily, Lily, Lyly, Millie, Philly, Scilly, silly, stilly, Tilley, Tilly, will he, Willey, willy, Willy, Dibley, glibly, scribbly, nimbly, Ripley, Shipley, triply, dimply, limply, pimply, simply, crisply, prickly, quickly, sickly, thickly, tickly, crinkly, Hinckley, twinkly, wrinkly, briskly, giggly, niggly, squiggly, wiggly, wriggly, Wrigley, singly, tingly, Zwingli, fiddly, Ridley, Siddeley, tiddly, twiddly, Hindley, spindly, fitly, Whitley, strictly, swiftly, dimly, grimly, primly, Finlay, Linley, thinly, Bingley, kingly, gristly, princely, Bisley, drizzly, grisly, grizzly, Wisley, Tinsley, Kingsley, Critchley, richly, Finchley, Kiri, Pirie, bilberry, indri, wintry, * Chantilly, Caerphilly, Goonhilly, distinctly, McKinley, * hillbilly, * Piccadilly, piccalilli, willy-nilly, willy-willy, indistinctly, rockabilly, Hawker Siddeley, hara-kiri, etc.

But Shakespeare also says, 'tis very silly 'To gild refinèd gold, or paint the lily.'
Lord Byron

18.6 gimme, Jimmy, shimmy, Timmy, pygmy, Pygmy, filmy, blini, cine, Finney, finny, Ginny, guinea, Guinea, jinni, hinny, Linnhe, mini, Minnie, ninny, pinny, Pliny, skinny, spinney, tinny, Trinny, Vinny, whinny, Winnie, Sidney, Sydney, kidney, Britney, Pitney, Whitney, chimney, Disney, isnae, clingy, dinghy, springy, stringy, swingy, thingy, zingy, * borborygmi,

pickaninny, supermini, * give me, kill me, etc.

18.7 Chrissie, Cissie, missy, prissy, sissy, Gypsy, tipsy, Dixie, nixie, pixie, tricksy, Trixie, ditzy, glitzy, Mitzi, ritzy, chintzy, wincey, busy, dizzy, fizzy, frizzy, is he, Izzy, Lizzie, tizzy, whizzy, flimsy, mimsy, whimsy, Kinsey, Lindsay, quinsy, dishy, fishy, squishy, swishy, Vichy, bitchy, itchy, pitchy, Richie, titchy, twitchy, Binchy, ridgy, squidgy, dingy, mingy, stingy, * Uffizi, De Quincey, tin lizzie, da Vinci, * kissy-kissy, itsy-bitsy, busy Lizzie, Mitsubishi, Murrumbidgee

18.8 bibber, Cibber, cribber, fibber, gibber, ribber, Wilbur, limber, Simba, timber, timbre, chipper, clipper, dipper, flipper, gripper, kipper, nipper, Pippa, ripper, shipper, skipper, slipper, snipper, stripper, tipper, tripper, whipper, zipper, crimper, shrimper, simper, whimper, crisper, whisper, * marimba, Agrippa, * winebibber, mudskipper, * women's libber, * rib her, tip her, etc.

18.9 bicker, clicker, dicker, flicker, kicker, licker, liquor, nicker, picker, pricker, quicker, sicker, slicker, snicker, sticker, thicker, ticker, tikka, vicar, Whicker, Wicca, wicker, Sitka, milker, Rilke, Simca, blinker, clinker, drinker, Glinka, Inca, linker, minke, sinker, stinker, thinker, tinker, winker, frisker, risker, whisker, bigger, chigger, digger, figure, Frigga, jigger, ligger, nigger, rigger, rigor, rigour, snigger, swigger, trigger, vigour, finger, linger, * Treblinka, freethinker, stotinka, nondrinker, Soyinka, configure,

transfigure, square-rigger, prefigure,
disfigure, malinger, fishfinger, syringa,
* pigsticker, billsticker, bootlicker,
headshrinker, grave-digger, outrigger,
forefinger, * reconfigure, alcheringa,
ladyfinger, * kick her, sink her, etc.

Candy
Is dandy
But liquor
Is quicker.
OGDEN NASH

18.10 bidder, kidder, whydah, builder,
gilder, guilder, Hilda, Tilda, tilde,
cinder, hinder, Linda, Pindar, tinder,
bitter, critter, fitter, flitter, fritter,
glitter, gritter, hitter, jitter, knitter,
litter, pitta, quitter, Ritter, sitter,
skitter, spitter, titter, twitter, witter,
scripter, dicta, lictor, Richter, victor,
Victor, sphincter, drifter, grifter, lifter,
snifter, swifter, filter, kilter, philtre,
quilter, tilter, Pinter, printer, sinter,
splinter, sprinter, tinter, winter,
Bicester, blister, clyster, glister, lister,
Lister, mister, Mr, sister, twister, vista,
hipster, quipster, tipster, trickster,
minster, spinster, * consider, St Kilda,
Matilda, bewilder, Belinda, Dorinda,
Lucinda, aglitter, committer,
transmitter, bedsitter, Birgitta,
embitter, emitter, remitter, descriptor,
constrictor, predictor, CARIFTA,
gefilte, midwinter, transistor,
demister, enlister, resistor,
* shipbuilder, coach-builder,
Fassbinder, outfitter, bullshitter,
weightlifter, scene-shifter, shoplifter,
half-sister, stepsister, Axminster,
Westminster, * reconsider, overbidder,
underbidder, body-builder, baby-sitter,
counterfeiter, Anaglypta®, Araminta,

teleprinter, overwinter,
Kidderminster, * neurotransmitter,
vasoconstrictor, boa constrictor, * hid
her, missed her, etc.

18.11 differ, sniffer, titfer, pilfer, giver,
liver, quiver, river, shiver, sliver, silver,
sylva, dither, hither, slither, thither,
whither, wither, zither, * forgiver,
deliver, downriver, upriver, Bat
Mitzvah, Bar Mitzvah, * caregiver,
lawgiver, quicksilver, * give her, with
her, etc.

18.12 chiller, Cilla, driller, filler, griller,
Hiller, killer, miller, Miller, pillar,
Schiller, Scylla, shriller, spiller, stiller,
thriller, tiller, villa, Willa, dribbler,
nibbler, quibbler, scribbler, nimbler,
tippler, simpler, pickler, stickler,
tickler, sprinkler, twinkler, giggler,
wriggler, mingler, Swingler, diddler,
fiddler, tiddler, swindler, Hitler, littler,
whittler, riffler, whiffler, sniveller,
Himmler, Simla, whistler, Whistler,
Rizla®, sizzler, mirror, sirrah, Libra,
Libya, * papilla, megillah, Attila,
flotilla, gorilla, guerrilla, zorilla,
Camilla, mamilla, manila, Manila,
vanilla, mantilla, Aquila, Anguilla,
axilla, maxilla, cedilla, scintilla,
distiller, instiller, Priscilla, chinchilla,
Godzilla, fulfiller, Ludmilla, Drusilla,
belittler, * painkiller, weedkiller,
* caterpillar, manzanilla, sarsaparilla,
lady-killer, Polyfilla®, potentilla,
pulsatilla, aspidistra, * kill her, thrill
her, etc.

18.13 dimmer, glimmer, grimmer,
Rimmer, shimmer, simmer, skimmer,
slimmer, Strimmer®, swimmer,
trimmer, Zimmer®, sigma, stigma,

Wilma, Brynner, Cinna, dinner,
grinner, inner, Jinnah, pinna, Pinner,
sinner, skinner, Skinner, spinner,
thinner, tinner, winner, Dymphna,
Kilner, Milner, Pilsner, Krishna,
bringer, clinger, dinger, pinger, ringer,
singer, Singer, springer, stinger,
stringer, swinger, winger, wringer,
* aglimmer, nonswimmer, enigma,
charisma, Berliner, beginner, echidna,
humdinger, * breadwinner,
prizewinner, bell-ringer, Schrödinger,
klipspringer, mudslinger, gunslinger,
* Hare Krishna, mastersinger,
Minnesinger, Meistersinger, * win her,
bring her, etc.

**But, by Jove, your hair is thinner, since
you came to us in Pinner,
And you're fatter now, I'm certain. What
you need is country air.**
JOHN BETJEMAN

18.14 kisser, pisser, fixer, mixer, sixer,
bitser, spritzer, Switzer, mincer,
pincer, fizzer, quizzer, scissor,
Windsor, fisher, Fischer, fissure,
Trisha, Wiltshire, wisher, ditcher,
hitcher, pitcher, richer, stitcher,
twitcher, scripture, picture, stricture,
cincture, tincture, filcher, clincher,
lyncher, pincher, wincher, fixture,
mixture, Bridger, cringer, ginger,
injure, ninja, whinger, * Clarissa,
Larisa, mantissa, abscissa, Melissa,
elixir, Amritsar, Patricia, Phoenicia,
Letitia, militia, admixture, abridger,
infringer, * well-wisher, kingfisher,
* reminiscer, * Doberman pinscher,
* miss her, convince her, etc.

18.15 hillock, pillock, Dimmock,
Dymock, Kinnock

18.16 limbic, nitpick, Indic, syndic,
critic, cryptic, diptych, glyptic, styptic,
triptych, cystic, mystic, dipstick,
lipstick, civic, Britvic®, mythic, Killick,
niblick, skin flick, lyric, Pyrrhic,
pinprick, citric, Cymric, Pickwick,
gimmick, mimic, rhythmic, filmic,
clinic, cynic, picnic, strychnic,
Chiswick, physic, * philippic,
Olympic, acidic, Glenfiddich,
bromidic, Druidic, graphitic, Hamitic,
granitic, arthritic, mephitic, Semitic,
bronchitic, Cushitic, elliptic, ecliptic,
sadistic, statistic, patristic, sophistic,
ballistic, fascistic, logistic, artistic,
realistic, simplistic, linguistic, stylistic,
autistic, heuristic, juristic, puristic,
touristic, holistic, prolific, horrific,
terrific, pacific, Pacific, specific, deific,
pontific, omnific, morbific, Trevithick,
dactylic, acrylic, basilic, exilic, sibyllic,
idyllic, Cyrillic, vampiric, satiric,
satyric, empiric, bulimic, eurhythmic,
rabbinic, actinic, intrinsic, extrinsic,
* genotypic, ecotypic, biotypic,
prototypic, Paralympic, stalactitic,
saprophytic, Glagolitic, catalytic,
paralytic, analytic, stalagmitic,
parasitic, anthracitic, thermolytic,
neophytic, haemolytic, sybaritic,
lymphocytic, syphilitic, dialytic,
diacritic, troglodytic, coprolitic,
dolomitic, oolitic, leucocytic,
masochistic, atavistic, aphoristic,
agonistic, pantheistic, altruistic,
voyeuristic, narcissistic, fatalistic,
plagiaristic, atheistic, mechanistic,
hedonistic, pessimistic, journalistic,
egotistic, legalistic, egoistic, syllogistic,
inartistic, jingoistic, idealistic,
nihilistic, novelistic, moralistic,
modernistic, optimistic, polycystic,
solecistic, formalistic, pluralistic,

socialistic, chauvinistic, surrealistic,
unrealistic, humoristic, futuristic,
humanistic, euphemistic, calorific,
transpacific, beatific, hieroglyphic,
scientific, soporific, honorific,
nonspecific, unspecific, megalithic,
Eolithic, Neolithic, Mesolithic,
microlithic, monolithic, Anglophilic,
carboxylic, necrophilic, haemophilic,
imbecilic, panegyric, pantomimic,
matronymic, patronymic, metonymic,
homonymic, algorithmic, logarithmic,
cataclysmic, nicotinic, * encephalitic,
electrolytic, erythrocytic, apocalyptic,
antagonistic, evangelistic,
behaviouristic, impressionistic,
expressionistic, paternalistic,
neologistic, * naturalistic,
nationalistic, antiballistic,
cannibalistic, minimalistic, ritualistic,
hypocoristic, characteristic,
negativistic, relativistic,
metalinguistic, opportunistic,
nonscientific, unscientific,
Palaeolithic, * semiparasitic,
psychoanalytic, microanalytic,
osteoarthritic, sadomasochistic,
overoptimistic, pseudoscientific,
* uncharacteristic, materialistic,
imperialistic

18.17 critics, mystics, gimmicks,
mimics, clinics, cynics, physics,
* Olympics, cladistics, statistics,
ballistics, logistics, linguistics,
stylistics, heuristics, eurythmics,
* Paralympics, hieroglyphics,
astrophysics, metaphysics, geophysics,
biophysics, * characteristics, etc.

18.18 lipid, limpid, wicked, whizz-kid,
pitied, triffid, divvied, livid, vivid,
skidlid, Ingrid, Wilfred, liquid, timid,
whinnied, winged, viscid, busied,
Brigid, frigid, rigid, * insipid,
* glycolipid, semirigid, etc.

On murder in the first degree
The Law, I knew, is rigid:
Its attitude, if A kills B,
To A is always frigid.
P. G. WODEHOUSE

18.19 tribade, timbered, kippered,
whispered, bickered, figured, jiggered,
niggard, sniggered, lingered, gilded,
hindered, fitted, glittered, knitted,
littered, tittered, scripted, gifted,
lifted, shifted, filtered, stilted, hinted,
minted, printed, tinted, listed, twisted,
Clifford, differed, Pickford, Mitford,
Guildford, Milford, quivered, shivered,
dithered, withered, Mildred, kindred,
inward, windward, vineyard,
glimmered, simmered, synod,
blizzard, gizzard, Izzard, lizard, Lizard,
wizard, Pritchard, Richard, pilchard,
injured, * half-timbered, bewhiskered,
disfigured, considered, unhindered,
unfitted, committed, admitted, half-
witted, quick-witted, unscripted,
addicted, convicted, constricted,
predicted, evicted, restricted,
unprinted, reprinted, imprinted,
unlisted, assisted, enlisted, limp-
wristed, resisted, existed, tightfisted,
delivered, uninjured, * unconsidered,
uncommitted, self-inflicted,
unpredicted, unrestricted, unassisted,
lily-livered, undelivered, etc.

18.20 niggards, Clifford's, inwards,
billiards, innards, blizzards, lizards,
wizards, Richards, pilchards, etc.

18.21 cribbage, slippage, linkage,

shrinkage, sinkage, windage, mintage, vintage, pillage, spillage, tillage, village, image, scrimmage, Greenwich, spinach, visage, * nonvintage, self-image, envisage, * afterimage

18.22 dibble, dribble, fribble, kibble, nibble, quibble, Ribble, scribble, sibyl, Sybil, cymbal, gimbal, nimble, symbol, thimble, timbal, Trimble, wimble, cripple, nipple, ripple, stipple, tipple, triple, dimple, pimple, simple, wimple, chicle, fickle, mickle, nickel, Nicol, pickle, prickle, sickle, tickle, trickle, crinkle, sprinkle, tinkle, twinkle, winkle, wrinkle, Driscoll, fiscal, giggle, jiggle, niggle, squiggle, wiggle, wriggle, cringle, dingle, Fingal, ingle, jingle, mingle, Pringle, shingle, single, tingle, Biddle, diddle, fiddle, griddle, idyll, Liddell, middle, piddle, Riddell, riddle, twiddle, widdle, brindle, dwindle, Hindle, kindle, spindle, swindle, Tyndale, brittle, it'll, little, skittle, Spital, spittle, tittle, victual, whittle, Whittle, lintel, quintal, Bristol, crystal, distal, pistil, pistol, piffle, riffle, skiffle, sniffle, whiffle, fitful, wistful, skilful, wilful, sinful, blissful, wishful, civil, drivel, frivol, shrivel, snivel, swivel, Cyril, squirrel, Tyrol, Tyrrell, Wirral, liberal, Liberal, timbrel, whimbrel, literal, mistral, minstrel, mineral, Chigwell, lingual, Sitwell, dismal, Richmal, signal, hymnal, simnel, Bissell, bristle, Cecil, gristle, missal, mistle, thistle, whistle, pixel, schnitzel, plimsoll, tinsel, chisel, drizzle, fizzle, frizzle, grizzle, mizzle, pizzle, sizzle, swizzle, Mitchell, vigil, brinjal, * Dalrymple, besprinkle, commingle, Kriss Kringle, Christingle, rekindle, acquittal, committal, belittle,

unskilful, uncivil, magistral, bilingual, trilingual, abysmal, baptismal, abyssal, epistle, dismissal, official, initial, solstitial, judicial, provincial, vestigial, * Doolittle, lickspittle, Birtwistle, * Abu Simbel, pumpernickel, cupronickel, periwinkle, Rip Van Winkle, intermingle, paradiddle, tarradiddle, noncommittal, monolingual, multilingual, cacomistle, Oswaldtwistle, paroxysmal, sacrificial, artificial, beneficial, prejudicial, interstitial, unofficial, superficial

Hey diddle diddle,
The cat and the fiddle.
NURSERY RHYME

18.23 dribbled, kibbled, nibbled, ribald, scribbled, gimballed, crippled, rippled, pickled, tickled, sprinkled, wrinkled, mingled, tingled, fiddled, swindled, whittled, shrivelled, swivelled, Tynwald, whistled, chiselled, drizzled, grizzled, sizzled, * rekindled, unmingled, etc.

18.24 cymbals, gimbals, thimbles, nipples, ripples, dimples, pimples, Nichols, Pickles, prickles, tickles, winkles, Biggles, giggles, squiggles, Fingal's, shingles, singles, fiddles, riddles, Tiddles, skittles, victuals, bristols, crystals, pistols, thistles, plimsolls, * epistles, initials, etc.

18.25 Shittim, victim, pilgrim, minim, * hit him, kicked him, etc.

18.26 Shippam, Wickham, Wykeham, dinkum, income, Brigham, Wyndham, kingdom, princedom, wisdom,

symptom, dictum, system, Lytham,
rhythm, Willem, siglum, Whitlam,
Ingram, Tristram, William, Bingham,
gingham, Ingham, jissom, lissom,
gypsum, Brixham, winsome, Grisham,
Mitchum, * High Wycombe,
Fitzwilliam, Fort William,
* Wiveliscombe, ecosystem, solar
system, algorithm, biorhythm,
logarithm, polyrhythm, * pick 'em,
missed 'em, etc.

18.27 Chisholm, chrism, ism, prism,
schism, * abysm, * baptism,
Sapphism, fascism, Chartism,
classism, Marxism, Nazism, papism,
sadism, racism, ageism, sexism,
realism, verism, deism, theism,
Sikhism, Grecism, Jainism, sophism,
autism, dwarfism, purism, tourism,
Maoism, Taoism, tropism, Fauvism,
Gaullism, holism, Buddhism, truism,
cubism, mutism, * alarmism,
escapism, transvestism, voyeurism,
surrealism, idealism, careerism,
defeatism, elitism, extremism,
* vigilantism, ethnocentrism,
egocentrism, Eurocentrism,
photorealism, absenteeism,
metamorphism, geotropism,
opportunism, * heterosexism

18.28 masochism, pragmatism,
atavism, vandalism, cataclysm,
aphorism, aneurysm, mannerism,
Thatcherism, laconism, galvanism,
Rachmanism, Jansenism, paroxysm,
pantheism, catechism, magnetism,
pacifism, activism, animism, albinism,
Latinism, Calvinism, Atticism,
Gallicism, Anglicism, classicism,
vampirism, altruism, barbarism,
Dadaism, archaism, Stalinism,

Darwinism, narcissism, ableism,
fatalism, racialism, naturism,
plagiarism, paganism, Platonism,
Satanism, atheism, Methodism,
nepotism, despotism, embolism,
centralism, specialism, terrorism,
mesmerism, mechanism, hedonism,
westernism, melanism, Pelmanism,
pessimism, cretinism, Hellenism,
feminism, Leninism, scepticism,
Celticism, fetishism, exorcism,
echoism, heroism, ergotism,
verbalism, journalism, egotism,
legalism, veganism, heathenism,
demonism, speciesism, Hebraism,
egoism, sinapism, tribadism,
stigmatism, hypnotism, symbolism,
syllogism, nimbyism, Briticism,
criticism, witticism, mysticism,
lyricism, cynicism, Yiddishism,
jingoism, Hinduism, priapism,
gigantism, tribalism, dynamism,
Zionism, pietism, nihilism, Irishism,
microprism, mongolism, modernism,
ostracism, Trotskyism, cockneyism,
Bolshevism, optimism, Scotticism,
Gnosticism, solecism, occultism,
populism, botulism, communism,
traumatism, formalism, organism,
daltonism, pluralism, bowdlerism,
loyalism, pointillism, localism,
vocalism, socialism, tokenism,
onanism, cronyism, chauvinism,
stoicism, vulgarism, rheumatism,
dualism, feudalism, spoonerism,
futurism, Teutonism, unionism,
humanism, Judaism, pugilism,
euphemism, euphuism, * metabolism,
antagonism, anachronism, Italianism,
expansionism, infantilism,
evangelism, fanaticism, romanticism,
scholasticism, monasticism,
Hispanicism, somnambulism,

McCarthyism, behaviourism,
creationism, adventurism,
impressionism, expressionism,
protectionism, perfectionism,
collectivism, athleticism, asceticism,
eclecticism, Conservatism,
paternalism, commercialism,
determinism, medievalism,
astigmatism, initialism,
provincialism, ventriloquism,
revisionism, recidivism,
descriptivism, prescriptivism,
empiricism, revivalism, automatism,
neologism, eroticism, agnosticism,
Catholicism, Micawberism,
teetotalism, reductionism,
consumerism, Confucianism,
illusionism, * sadomasochism,
televangelism, neoclassicism,
Neo-Darwinism, Neo-Platonism,
isolationism, fundamentalism,
instrumentalism, departmentalism,
transcendentalism, Orientalism,
existentialism, sentimentalism,
eco-terrorism, counterterrorism,
servomechanism, postimpressionism,
resurrectionism, photojournalism,
universalism, abolitionism,
exhibitionism, hypercriticism,
hyperthyroidism, hypothyroidism,
overoptimism, microorganism,
* experimentalism, environmentalism,
homoeroticism, autoeroticism

18.29 naturalism, nationalism,
rationalism, patriotism, cannibalism,
radicalism, capitalism, animalism,
Anglicanism, Africanism, parallelism,
parasitism, malapropism, alcoholism,
absolutism, Parkinsonism, Fabianism,
favouritism, separatism, federalism,
lesbianism, clericalism, secularism,
negativism, relativism, serialism,

Rhymes

∙∙∙∙∙∙∙∙∙∙∙∙∙∙∙∙∙∙∙∙

*Many rhymes have different
spellings (e.g.
mane/reign/vein/plain/ Wayne
or new/through/ blue/coo/do),
and many words with the same
ending do not rhyme (e.g. bear/
fear or mint/pint). When the latter
are used in poetry, the result is
called an eye rhyme or sight rhyme.
Here are some examples:*

**Come live with me, and be my
  love,
And we will all the pleasures
  prove.**
CHRISTOPHER MARLOWE

**You beat your pate, and fancy
  wit will come:
Knock as you please, there's
  nobody at home.**
ALEXANDER POPE

**Goosey goosey gander,
Whither shall I wander?**
NURSERY RHYME

regionalism, liberalism, literalism, idiotism, syndicalism, digitalism, minimalism, militarism, ritualism, nicotinism, primitivism, Philistinism, spiritualism, Protestantism, popularism, Bonapartism, polytheism, monotheism, positivism, structuralism, functionalism, monetarism, hooliganism, mutualism, * Mohammedanism, Tractarianism, sensationalism, Canadianism, Australianism, Pelagianism, professionalism, conventionalism, incendiarism, pedestrianism, equestrianism, Americanism, transsexualism, materialism, imperialism, traditionalism, colloquialism, colonialism, poststructuralism, industrialism, republicanism, * internationalism, Zoroastrianism, Rastafarianism, vegetarianism, Unitarianism, millenarianism, Congregationalism, intellectualism, Presbyterianism, individualism, multiculturalism, institutionalism, * parliamentarianism, egalitarianism, totalitarianism, humanitarianism, utilitarianism, authoritarianism, neocolonialism

18.30 diddums, kingdoms, symptoms, Ingrams, Williams, isms, etc.

18.31 Philbin, sin bin, swing bin, pippin, Gilpin, kingpin, Crispin, linchpin, chicken, pigskin, kidskin, sit-in, Quintin, Tintin, griffin, Griffin, tiffin, Swithin, fibrin, Disprin®, women, linen, trypsin, Hitchin, Itchen, kitchen, lichen, pidgin, * unlived-in, * clanswomen, charwomen, craftswomen,

cavewomen, saleswomen, Welshwomen, churchwomen, kinswomen, Scotswomen, yachtswomen, horsewomen, sportswomen, townswomen, * policewomen, * Rumpelstiltskin, Enniskillen, penicillin, gentlewomen, clergywomen, needlewomen, businesswomen, Englishwomen, Irishwomen, washerwomen, noblewomen, underlinen, Solzhenitsyn, * skippin', knittin', etc.

18.32 gibbon, Gibbon, ribbon, Brisbane, Lisbon, Crippen, Ripon, Rippon, Dickon, quicken, sicken, stricken, thicken, Wiccan, silken, Incan, Lincoln, big 'un, Wigan, bidden, hidden, midden, ridden, stridden, Cliveden, Findon, linden, Swindon, Wisden, bitten, bittern, Britain, Briton, Britten, kitten, Lytton, mitten, smitten, twitten, written, Lipton, Shipton, Skipton, Shrimpton, Clifton, Chiltern, Hilton, Milton, Stilton, Wilton, Clinton, Hinton, Minton, quintan, Tintern, Winton, cistern, piston, Tristan, Whiston, Wystan, Princeton, Winston, Kingston, griffon, gryphon, stiffen, driven, given, Niven, riven, shriven, sylvan, Dillon, Dylan, villain, villein, little 'un, Mirren, Libran, children, Citroën, citron, Libyan, billion, million, pillion, trillion, zillion, Binyon, minion, pinion, Lipman, Shipman, Hickman, milkman, Pitman, Whitman, kinsman, finnan, Bingen, * Fitzgibbon, Franciscan, forbidden, unbidden, unhidden, unridden, unwritten, phlogiston, forgiven, unshriven, Macmillan, pavilion, carillon, vermilion, Brazilian, Castilian,

Quintilian, civilian, Trevelyan, Sicilian, postilion, tourbillion, dominion, opinion, persimmon, McKinnon, Dunsinane, * awestricken, hagridden, bedridden, handwritten, typewritten, frostbitten, festschriften, grandchildren, godchildren, schoolchildren, * San Franciscan, overridden, Hohenlinden, overwritten, underwritten, Bulwer-Lytton, unforgiven, Abbevillian, Maximilian, rack-and-pinion, * Unter den Linden

Nature's decorations glisten
Far above their usual trim;
Birds on box and laurels listen,
As so near the cherubs hymn.
CHRISTOPHER SMART

18.33 christen, glisten, listen, Nissen, Ibsen, Gibson, Simpson, Timpson, Blixen, Dixon, Hickson, Nixon, vixen, Whitsun, Smithson, Stillson, Wilson, Stimson, mizzen, prison, risen, wizen, Pilsen, crimson, Frisian, vision, fission, mission, scission, Titian, diction, fiction, friction, Christian, pigeon, wigeon, smidgen, Injun, St John, * arisen, imprison, provision, collision, concision, division, revision, prevision, envision, elision, derision, decision, precisian, precision, incision, excision, suspicion, addition, perdition, tradition, condition, volition, Mauritian, attrition, patrician, contrition, commission, Domitian, omission, permission, submission, admission, monition, position, logician, magician, tactician, ambition, transmission, transition, partition, rendition, dentition, technician, edition, sedition, petition, detrition, demission, emission,

remission, clinician, ignition, physician, optician, cognition, audition, mortician, coition, fruition, tuition, beautician, nutrition, munition, musician, ascription, subscription, conscription, conniption, transcription, decryption, encryption, description, prescription, inscription, Egyptian, proscription, addiction, conviction, affliction, constriction, depiction, prediction, eviction, infliction, restriction, nonfiction, distinction, extinction, unchristian, religion, * television, circumcision, indecision, imprecision, Eurovision, tunnel vision, subdivision, supervision, abolition, apparition, admonition, apposition, transposition, statistician, acquisition, malnutrition, manumission, ammunition, parturition, extradition, ebullition, demolition, rhetorician, mechanician, premonition, recognition, preposition, exposition, exhibition, expedition, repetition, electrician, definition, requisition, erudition, theoretician, precondition, recondition, decommission, readmission, deposition, reposition, aesthetician, mint condition, micturition, intermission, inanition, imposition, disposition, inhibition, inquisition, Inquisition, disquisition, intuition, dietician, opposition, proposition, composition, obstetrician, competition, politician, cosmetician, coalition, prohibition, Prohibition, phonetician, supposition, superstition, circumscription, superscription, malediction, valediction, dereliction, benediction, derestriction, interdiction, contradiction, jurisdiction,

crucifixion, Crucifixion, irreligion,
* mathematician, academician,
metaphysician, geometrician,
derequisition, paediatrician,
predisposition, decomposition,
presupposition, interposition,
indisposition, diagnostician,
nonrecognition, overambition,
juxtaposition, contradistinction

Thou shalt not covet; but tradition
Approves all forms of competition.
ARTHUR HUGH CLOUGH

18.34 riband, sickened, thickened,
brigand, England, midland, Finland,
inland, Crimond, Grimoned,
Sigmund, Richmond, christened,
glistened, listened, wizened,
* beribboned, conditioned,
commissioned, positioned,
* noncommissioned, etc.

18.35 brigands, Midlands, Symonds,
Sigmund's, etc.

18.36 Crispin's, chickens, dickens,
Dickens, Wilkins, Higgins, Swithin's,
kitchens, etc.

18.37 Gibbons, ribbons, Siddons,
Britons, kittens, mittens, pistons,
Tristan's, villains, millions, minions,
Simmons, glistens, listens, Sissons,
missions, Titian's, Christians, pigeons,
* civilians, Fitzsimmons, provisions,
divisions, decisions, suspicions,
ambitions, editions, beauticians,
munitions, musicians, etc.

Three little kittens they lost their
mittens.
NURSERY RHYME

18.38 flippant, didn't, distant, instant,
infant, brilliant, different, shipment,
figment, pigment, fitment, Vincent,
isn't, stringent, * remittent, assistant,
persistent, subsistent, consistent,
insistent, resistant, existent,
indifferent, delinquent, equipment,
commitment, enlistment, fulfilment,
enrichment, abridgment,
infringement, malignant, indignant,
benignant, dehiscent, proficient,
sufficient, deficient, efficient,
astringent, contingent, refringent,
* intermittent, equidistant,
inconsistent, nonexistent, coexistent,
re-enlistment, non-malignant,
reminiscent, indehiscent, self-
sufficient, insufficient, inefficient,
coefficient

18.39 sixpence, riddance, pittance,
quittance, distance, instance, instants,
infants, hindrance, difference,
brilliance, fitments, * acquittance,
admittance, transmittance, remittance,
assistance, assistants, persistence,
subsistence, insistence, resistance,
Resistance, existence, outdistance,
indifference, deliverance, delinquents,
commitments, dehiscence,
* readmittance, intermittence,
equidistance, nonexistence,
coexistence, reminiscence,
indehiscence, etc.

Friday's child is loving and giving,
Saturday's child works hard for his
living.
TRADITIONAL RHYME

18.40 cribbing, fibbing, ribbing,
chipping, clipping, dipping, dripping,
flipping, gripping, nipping, ripping,

shipping, skipping, slipping, stripping, tipping, whipping, crimping, limping, scrimping, shrimping, lisping, licking, kicking, picking, sticking, ticking, bilking, milking, blinking, chinking, drinking, linking, pinking, shrinking, sinking, stinking, thinking, winking, frisking, risking, whisking, digging, frigging, jigging, rigging, swigging, wigging, bidding, kidding, skidding, building, gilding, wingding, fitting, gritting, hitting, knitting, quitting, sitting, spitting, splitting, witting, kilting, lilting, quilting, tilting, wilting, printing, listing, misting, twisting, biffing, spiffing, giving, living, sieving, billing, chilling, drilling, filling, grilling, killing, milling, pilling, schilling, shilling, spilling, thrilling, willing, dribbling, nibbling, scribbling, sibling, Kipling, crippling, rippling, stripling, pickling, trickling, inkling, sprinkling, tinkling, twinkling, wrinkling, giggling, niggling, wriggling, jingling, tingling, fiddling, middling, piddling, twiddling, kindling, whittling, piffling, brisling, bristling, whistling, quisling, sizzling, brimming, dimming, skimming, slimming, swimming, trimming, grinning, inning, pinning, sinning, skinning, spinning, thinning, twinning, winning, bringing, clinging, ringing, singing, springing, stinging, swinging, wringing, Gissing, hissing, kissing, missing, pissing, glimpsing, fixing, mixing, mincing, fizzing, quizzing, whizzing, bitching, hitching, itching, stitching, twitching, witching, clinching, inching, lynching, pinching, bridging, cringing, hinging, swingeing, whingeing, * unpicking,

unblinking, unthinking, unwinking, right-thinking, forbidding, rebuilding, unwitting, admitting, transmiting, befitting, emitting, afflicting, conflicting, constricting, predicting, restricting, uplifting, unstinting, reprinting, imprinting, assisting, persisting, enlisting, resisting, existing, forgiving, thanksgiving, misgiving, unwilling, deskilling, distilling, fulfilling, beginning, dismissing, convincing, bewitching, enriching, unflinching, abridging, * earwigging, freethinking, shipbuilding, outbuilding, hairsplitting, ear-splitting, side-splitting, shopfitting, weightlifting, shoplifting, downshifting, painkilling, prizewinning, bell-ringing, mudslinging, gunslinging, upbringing, * scavenging, challenging, * bodybuilding, baby-sitting, unbefitting, unremitting, unresisting, forward-thinking, unforgiving, Inniskilling, multiskilling, self-fulfilling, unfulfilling, underpinning, moneyspinning, unconvincing, penny-pinching, etc.

18.41 clippings, pickings, buildings, sittings, fillings, killings, shillings, siblings, trimmings, innings, winnings, * beginnings, * underpinnings, etc.

18.42 chirrup, stirrup, syrup, piss-up, mix-up, bishop, * archbishop

A youth who bore mid snow and ice
A bird that wouldn't chirrup,
And a banner with the strange device –
'Mrs Winslow's soothing syrup.'
A. E. HOUSMAN

18.43 Dilys, Phyllis, Willis, finis,
Glynis, Guinness, Innes, Menzies,
missus, * Charybdis, ex libris,
McGuinness, ellipsis, * Nunc Dimittis,
amaryllis, Amaryllis, Cader Idris

18.44 gibbous, nimbus, incus, discus,
viscous, Findus, Indus, ictus, rictus,
linctus, cistus, Sixtus, villus, Nicklaus,
lidless, windlass, windless, witless,
shiftless, thriftless, guiltless, listless,
limbless, rimless, chinless, sinless,
skinless, stringless, wingless, cirrus,
Pyrrhus, citrus, mistress, grimace,
litmus, Titmus, Christmas, isthmus,
pinnace, glibness, crispness, sickness,
thickness, briskness, Widnes, fitness,
witness, strictness, swiftness, stiffness,
illness, stillness, dimness, grimness,
slimness, business, richness, vicious,
* hibiscus, meniscus, Aer Lingus,
bacillus, headmistress, strabismus,
unfitness, succinctness, forgiveness,
narcissus, Narcissus, propitious,
suspicious, officious, malicious,
Mauritius, capricious, pernicious,
flagitious, ambitious, factitious,
seditious, fictitious, delicious,
auspicious, judicious, lubricious,
nutritious, prodigious, prestigious,
litigious, religious, * housemistress,
postmistress, schoolmistress,
eyewitness, * Aristippus, eohippus,
cunnilingus, eucalyptus, Benedictus,
Trismegistus, avaricious, adventitious,
Aloysius, expeditious, repetitious,
meretricious, inauspicious,
injudicious, surreptitious,
supposititious, unambitious,
unsuspicious, superstitious,
sacrilegious, irreligious, nonreligious,
* cumulonimbus, lactobacillus,
overambitious, * picked us, kill us, etc.

But the apes – though not so vicious
To begin with – were ambitious.
CLARENCE DAY

18.45 wish list, linguist, * violinist

18.46 crispest, quickest, sickest,
slickest, thickest, biggest, fittest,
shrillest, stillest, nimblest, simplest,
littlest, interest, dimmest, grimmest,
slimmest, dynast, thinnest, witnessed,
richest, * self-interest, disinterest, etc.

18.47 impish, wimpish, pinkish,
biggish, priggish, Yiddish, British,
skittish, ticklish, English, Finnish,
finish, * un-British, relinquish,
distinguish, extinguish, diminish

18.48 finished, * relinquished,
distinguished, extinguished,
unfinished, diminished,
* undistinguished, undiminished

18.49 Dilbert, filbert, Gilbert, Didcot,
bigot, frigate, Piggott, spigot, ingot,
divot, pivot, * Don Quixote

18.50 pipit, sippet, snippet, tippet,
Tippett, whippet, limpet, gibbet, titbit,
cricket, picket, snicket, thicket, ticket,
wicket, trinket, biscuit, brisket,
Chindit, ringgit, Tlingit, Kwik-Fit,
misfit, civet, privet, rivet, trivet, with-
it, billet, fillet, millet, skillet, ripplet,
triplet, piglet, singlet, gimlet, kinglet,
ringlet, winglet, spirit, nitwit, dimwit,
limit, innit, linnet, minute, spinet,
cygnet, signet, licit, Tilsit, visit,
Pritchett, Bridget, digit, fidget, midget,
widget, * prohibit, inhibit, exhibit,
Glenlivet, dispirit, delimit, solicit,
elicit, illicit, implicit, explicit, revisit,

exquisite, * flibbertigibbet, * win it, is it, etc.

Off went the cart with the home packed in it,
I walked behind with my old cock linnet.
CHARLES COLLINS

18.51 snippets, whippets, titbits, pickets, rickets, tickets, wickets, biscuits, giblets, triplets, limits, Bridget's, digits, etc.

18.52 Plymouth, Sidmouth, Lynmouth, Teignmouth, bismuth, Gwyneth

18.53 fictive, missive, * addictive, predictive, vindictive, descriptive, prescriptive, restrictive, distinctive, instinctive, assistive, resistive, permissive, submissive, dismissive, * nonaddictive, nonrestrictive

18.54 hippies, kiddies, Indies, Windies, cities, ditties, fifties, Christie's, sixties, civvies, skivvies, Billy's, lilies, Scillies, willies, wrinkles, guineas, kidneys, chimneys, Gypsies, pixies, * West Indies, East Indies, committees, Achilles, Antilles, * hillbillies, etc.

A fine romance, with no kisses!
A fine romance, my friend, this is!
DOROTHY FIELDS

18.55 timbers, clippers, flippers, kippers, nippers, slippers, trippers, whispers, knickers, pickers, Vickers, tinkers, whiskers, Whiskas®, figures, sniggers, fingers, bidders, builders, cinders, Flinders, Linda's, critters, jitters, printers, splinters, winters,

Winters, sisters, Chivers, rivers, Rivers, slivers, Smithers, withers, killers, pillars, slimmers, swimmers, dinners, sinners, winners, kisses, misses, missus, Mrs, pincers, princes, scissors, breeches, riches, stitches, witches, Scriptures, pictures, inches, bridges, Bridges, midges, fringes, * transistors, gorillas, guerrillas, beginners, * caregivers, painkillers, bell-ringers, * camiknickers, butterfingers, caterpillars, lady-killers, rags-to-riches, etc.

18.56 Willoughby, Dimbleby, Nickleby, syncopy, chirrupy, syrupy, schipperke, Picardy, liberty, dynasty, dystrophy, sympathy, Timothy, Kimberley, Tripoli, bitterly, Italy, sisterly, systole, fitfully, wistfully, skilfully, wilfully, sinfully, blissfully, wishfully, Tivoli, liberally, literally, dismally, cicely, Cicely, Wycherley, gingerly, miserably, visibly, niggardly, inwardly, flippantly, distantly, instantly, differently, brilliantly, winsomely, viciously, bilberry, Tilbury, Finsbury, frippery, slippery, chicory, hickory, trickery, Vickery, whiskery, piggery, Whiggery, cindery, tindery, glittery, jittery, twittery, victory, history, mystery, livery, quivery, shivery, silvery, dithery, slithery, Hilary, Hillary, pillory, literary, biliary, ciliary, shimmery, misery, fishery, stitchery, witchery, gingery, injury, wizardry, bigotry, dilatory, minatory, signatory, infantry, inventory, dysentery, industry, chivalry, missionary, visionary, dictionary, bigamy, thingummy, infamy, timpani, Brittany, dittany, litany, Tiffany, symphony, villainy, tyranny, simony, privacy, literacy,

Christmassy, minstrelsy, flippancy,
infancy, stringency, liturgy, trilogy,
synergy, * calligraphy, antipathy,
Gallipoli, abysmally, officially, initially,
judicially, predictably, considerably,
admittedly, deliberately, considerately,
persistently, consistently, indignantly,
proficiently, sufficiently, efficiently,
musicianly, suspiciously, officiously,
maliciously, ambitiously, judiciously,
prodigiously, religiously, Terpsichore,
prehistory, periphery, midwifery,
housewifery, delivery, capillary,
ancillary, artillery, armillary, distillery,
fritillary, antiquary, reliquary,
subsidiary, auxiliary, rotisserie,
justiciary, judiciary, explicatory,
obligatory, depilatory, respiratory,
conciliatory, divinatory, propitiatory,
revisionary, soliloquy, ventriloquy,
polygamy, epitome, Antigone,
antiphony, epiphany, Epiphany,
polyphony, conspiracy, illiteracy,
consistency, delinquency, proficiency,
sufficiency, deficiency, efficiency,
exigency, contingency, * artificially,
unofficially, superficially, inexplicably,
unequivocally, inconsiderately,
intermittently, inconsistently,
insufficiently, inefficiently,
inauspiciously, surreptitiously,
contradictory, valedictory, domiciliary,
disciplinary, beneficiary,
expeditionary, inconsistency, self-
sufficiency, insufficiency, inefficiency,
* higgledy-piggledy, idiosyncrasy,
* interdisciplinary, multidisciplinary,
immunodeficiency, etc.

**There was a young person whose
history,**
Was always considered a mystery.
EDWARD LEAR

18.57 finicky, gimmicky, rickety,
quiddity, dimity, Trinity, dignity, fixity,
witchetty, fidgety, skimpily, trickily,
prettily, wittily, shiftily, thriftily,
guiltily, civilly, simile, Sicily, busily,
principally, typically, critically,
mystically, mythically, biblically,
lyrically, clinically, cynically,
physically, whimsically, wickedly,
vividly, timidly, fixedly, frigidly,
rigidly, pitifully, fittingly, wittingly,
chillingly, willingly, swimmingly,
impishly, gimmickry, mimicry,
military, symmetry, dignitary,
ministry, millinery, imagery, Rimini,
Brindisi, syzygy, * pernickety, rapidity,
avidity, validity, solidity, aridity,
acridity, acidity, liquidity, timidity,
frigidity, rigidity, morbidity, fluidity,
cupidity, stupidity, humidity, lucidity,
Nativity, acclivity, proclivity, captivity,
activity, passivity, festivity, declivity,
sublimity, proximity, affinity, salinity,
virginity, infinity, divinity, felinity,
vicinity, malignity, indignity,
benignity, publicity, complicity,
plasticity, spasticity, ethnicity, felicity,
Felicity, simplicity, toxicity, duplicity,
prolixity, facsimile, politically,
elliptically, sadistically, statistically,
artistically, realistically, prolifically,
horrifically, terrifically, specifically,
idyllically, satirically, empirically,
intrinsically, illicitly, implicitly,
explicitly, exquisitely, distinctively,
instinctively, submissively,
unthinkingly, unwittingly, unwillingly,
convincingly, prohibitory, inhibitory,
asymmetry, preliminary, Eurydice,
Chalcidice, * serendipity, invalidity,
negativity, relativity, sensitivity,
exclusivity, creativity, inactivity,
impassivity, selectivity, objectivity,

positivity, productivity, conductivity, subjectivity, anonymity, magnanimity, equanimity, unanimity, alkalinity, masculinity, femininity, consanguinity, eccentricity, electricity, elasticity, synchronicity, domesticity, authenticity, multiplicity, analytically, hypocritically, altruistically, pessimistically, idealistically, optimistically, euphemistically, scientifically, unconvincingly, paramilitary, alkalimetry, acidimetry, Aborigine, * insensitivity, hyperactivity, overactivity, characteristically, unscientifically, niminy-piminy, * radioactivity, hypersensitivity, hydroelectricity, etc.

Sure there are times when one cries with acidity,
'Where are the limits of human stupidity?'
Arthur Conan Doyle

18.58 ability, stability, scurrility, facility, agility, fragility, tranquillity, gentility, sterility, fertility, servility, debility, civility, virility, senility, hostility, mobility, nobility, motility, docility, utility, futility, humility, obliquity, antiquity, iniquity, ubiquity, propinquity, * fallibility, capability, saleability, changeability, credibility, flexibility, sensibility, legibility, versatility, readability, feasibility, instability, inability, disability, visibility, infertility, incivility, imbecility, immobility, liability, viability, probability, possibility, volatility, solubility, plausibility, durability, notability, culpability, gullibility, suitability, * compatibility, adaptability, infallibility, incapability,

availability, dependability, susceptibility, respectability, accessibility, inflexibility, predictability, divisibility, invisibility, desirability, reliability, excitability, advisability, improbability, impossibility, responsibility, affordability, accountability, unsuitability, * malleability, amicability, variability, amiability, eligibility, permeability, irritability, profitability, vulnerability, * incompatibility, unavailability, inaccessibility, unreliability, irresponsibility, * invariability, impressionability, inevitability, intelligibility, ineligibility, unprofitability, etc.

18.59 fitfully, wistfully, skilfully, wilfully, sinfully, blissfully, wishfully, stimuli, visually, ritually, tributary, * continually, habitually, obituary, contributory, * individually, noncontributory, etc.

18.60 Whitaker, Ithaca, spinnaker, Christopher, Nicola, tricolour, victualler, sniveller, signaller, chiseller, whimperer, whisperer, bickerer, sniggerer, lingerer, titterer, witterer, pilferer, cithera, ditherer, Sisera, viscera, Middlesbrough, thickener, stiffener, scrivener, listener, prisoner, Kitchener, Lincolnshire, ligature, Philippa, silica, mimicker, Lineker, picnicker, vinegar, Phyllida, cylinder, cricketer, limiter, scimitar, visitor, minister, sinister, Chichester, Winchester, Nineveh, miniver, similar, Indira, cinema, minima, milliner, kibitzer, Yiddisher, Britisher, finisher, literature, miniature, signature,

integer, pillager, villager, Kissinger,
issuer, fibula, singular, titular, fistula,
Vistula, primula, insular,
* conspirator, calligrapher, Agricola,
amygdala, malingerer, deliverer,
lonicera, conditioner, parishioner,
commissioner, practitioner, petitioner,
auditioner, basilica, Dominica,
exhibitor, inhibitor, altimeter,
perimeter, solicitor, inquisitor,
administer, dissimilar, artificer,
extinguisher, residua, continua,
contributor, distributor, mandibular,
vestibular, Caligula, particular,
curricula, testicular, ventricular,
vehicular, funicular, peninsula, * Little
Englander, spina bifida, calorimeter,
maladminister, perpendicular,
* extracurricular

18.61 Libya, tibia, grippier, nippier,
slippier, pickier, stickier, trickier,
milkier, silkier, friskier, Ischia, riskier,
Lydia, India, windier, grittier, prettier,
Whittier, wittier, shiftier, thriftier,
mintier, mistier, twistier, clivia, Livia,
Nivea®, trivia, Sylvia, pithier, Cynthia,
chillier, cilia, frillier, hillier, Hillier,
sillier, sicklier, Syria, wintrier, linear,
skinnier, tinea, zinnia, springier,
stringier, tipsier, busier, dizzier,
fizzier, frizzier, flimsier, dishier,
fishier, itchier, Phrygia, dingier,
stingier, * Namibia, Olympia,
chlamydia, Numidia, Bolivia, Olivia,
Carinthia, familiar, Brasília, Assyria,
Illyria, porphyria, bulimia, robinia,
Lavinia, actinia, Sardinia, Virginia,
nonlinear, gloxinia, photinia, insignia,
Alicia, Galicia, asphyxia, Kirghizia,
Tunisia, Letitia, * Escherichia,
Francophilia, Anglophilia, necrophilia,
paedophilia, haemophilia,

coprophilia, Europhilia, bougainvillea,
juvenilia, interlinear, Abyssinia,
* memorabilia, Germanophilia,
overfamiliar, etc.

18.62 pivoted, interested, Hilliard,
Iliad, myriad, picketed, riveted,
filleted, spirited, limited, visited,
Bideford, * uninterested,
disinterested, prohibited, inhibited,
dispirited, unlimited, solicited,
unvisited, * uninhibited, unsolicited,
etc.

18.63 liveried, pilloried, Winifred,
pyramid

18.64 clickable, drinkable, shrinkable,
sinkable, thinkable, biddable, liftable,
printable, Whitstable, livable, syllable,
willable, miserable, winnable, singable,
kissable, miscible, missable, fixable,
mixable, risible, visible, binnacle,
pinnacle, citadel, pivotal, interval,
liberal, Liberal, clitoral, literal, littoral,
mineral, visceral, scriptural, integral,
fictional, frictional, trivial, filial,
vitriol, finial, lineal, pineal, principal,
principle, typical, critical, mystical,
mythical, biblical, cyclical, lyrical,
miracle, rhythmical, clinical, cynical,
finical, physical, quizzical, whimsical,
infidel, digital, pitiful, sinistral,
minimal, criminal, vicinal, spiritual,
visual, ritual, * applicable, despicable,
explicable, undrinkable, unshrinkable,
unsinkable, unthinkable, formidable,
transmittable, hospitable, predictable,
unprintable, forgivable, unkillable,
refillable, considerable, deliverable,
omissible, permissible, admissible,
unmissable, immiscible, invincible,
divisible, invisible, dirigible, episcopal,

equivocal, reciprocal, antipodal, illiberal, peripheral, polygonal, provisional, divisional, additional, traditional, conditional, positional, transitional, nutritional, convivial, Lostwithiel, familial, vestigial, participle, municipal, untypical, atypical, veridical, juridical, Levitical, political, uncritical, elliptical, statistical, logistical, pontifical, umbilical, encyclical, empirical, satirical, cylindrical, inimical, rabbinical, dominical, nonphysical, centripetal, occipital, libidinal, subliminal, medicinal, original, continual, habitual, instinctual, residual, centrifugal, * inapplicable, inexplicable, inextricable, inhospitable, unpredictable, irresistible, unforgivable, monosyllable, unfulfillable, inconsiderable, undeliverable, inadmissible, indivisible, unequivocal, prepositional, compositional, unconditional, suppositional, participial, matrilineal, patrilineal, archetypical, analytical, parasitical, apolitical, hypocritical, diacritical, hypercritical, nonpolitical, egotistical, egoistical, astrophysical, metaphysical, geophysical, Aboriginal, unoriginal, televisual, individual, * archiepiscopal, stereotypical, audiovisual, * psychoanalytical

18.65 principled, * unprincipled, two-syllabled

18.66 Christendom, Chrysostom, Chippenham, tympanum, Twickenham, Hilversum, idiom, tritium, cilium, ileum, ilium, Ilium, Miriam, Librium®, Widdecombe,

minimum, Gillingham, * officialdom, iridium, presidium, rubidium, beryllium, delirium, Elysium, Brundisium, molybdenum, residuum, continuum, curriculum, reticulum, capitulum, * post meridiem, penicillium, equilibrium, neodymium, aluminium, diverticulum, * ante meridiem, disequilibrium

18.67 Wimbledon, Missenden, Pinkerton, Winterton, Tiverton, simpleton, Middleton, Littleton, Lyttelton, Ingleton, singleton, Silverstone, Lindemann, cyclamen, Zimmerman, cinnamon, fisherman, signalman, Richardson, Nicholson, Williamson, histogen, Imogen, Gibeon, Libyan, Crispian, Gideon, Lydian, Midian, Indian, Vivian, Vivien, billion, Chilean, Gillian, Lilian, million, pillion, trillion, zillion, Syrian, Tyrian, Cyprian, Simeon, simian, Guinean, Ninian, Plinian, Trinian, Phrygian, Stygian, silicon, Michigan, Milligan, Finnegan, Hillingdon, Pilkington, Whittington, Withington, Bridlington, Islington, Lymington, Wilmington, Livingston, Livingstone, Vlissingen, Dickinson, Wilkinson, citizen, * militiaman, carcinogen, Namibian, amphibian, Philippian, Olympian, Pickwickian, Malpighian, Dravidian, meridian, viridian, Ovidian, obsidian, quotidian, ophidian, Euclidean, Numidian, Bolivian, oblivion, Maldivian, Corinthian, pavilion, Brazilian, Castilian, reptilian, vermilion, Churchillian, Virgilian, Quintilian, civilian, Sicilian, postilion, Assyrian, Amphitryon, Endymion, prosimian, Justinian, Sardinian, Darwinian,

Arminian, Virginian, Galician,
Parisian, Elysian, Tunisian,
Thuringian, Dominican, McGilligan,
* hallucinogen, Mississippian,
Paralympian, Hesperidian,
postmeridian, Amerindian,
labyrinthian, crocodilian, Abbevillian,
vaudevillian, Maximilian, Argentinian,
Palestinian, Augustinian,
Carthaginian, Abyssinian, Dionysian,
Ordovician, Cantabrigian, callipygian,
Carlovingian, Merovingian,
Carolingian, * antemeridian

18.68 Switzerland, Sigismund

18.69 simpletons, Gillian's, millions,
citizens, * amphibians, Philippians,
St Trinian's, etc.

18.70 impotent, sycophant, indolent,
insolent, different, ignorant, ligament,
filament, instrument, immanent,
dissonant, innocent, brilliant,
miscreant, litigant, diffident,
dissident, incident, militant, irritant,
visitant, sibilant, vigilant, immigrant,
implement, increment, liniment,
imminent, Millicent, indigent,
diligent, impudent, virulent, simulant,
stimulant, * omnipotent, indifferent,
ambivalent, equivalent, itinerant,
belligerent, refrigerant, grandiloquent,
magniloquent, medicament,
predicament, disfigurement,
bewilderment, imprisonment,
percipient, recipient, incipient,
resilient, omniscient, asphyxiant,
officiant, participant, significant,
coincident, precipitant, magnificent,
omnificent, munificent,
relinquishment, mellifluent,
constituent, * hereditament,

microfilament, insignificant,
counterirritant

18.71 impotence, sycophants,
indolence, insolence, difference,
inference, ignorance, ligaments,
filaments, instruments, immanence,
dissonance, innocence, brilliance,
litigants, diffidence, dissidence,
incidence, incidents, militants,
vigilance, immigrants, implements,
increments, imminence, indigence,
diligence, influence, impudence,
virulence, stimulants, * omnipotence,
indifference, deliverance, ambivalence,
equivalence, belligerence,
grandiloquence, magniloquence,
medicaments, percipience, recipients,
incipience, resilience, omniscience,
participants, significance, coincidence,
magnificence, munificence,
mellifluence, constituents,
continuance, * insignificance, etc.

18.72 billionth, millionth, trillionth

18.73 chirruping, interesting,
chitterling, gibbering, whimpering,
whispering, flickering, Pickering,
tinkering, fingering, tittering,
wittering, Wittering, differing,
quivering, shivering, blithering,
dithering, glimmering, simmering,
quickening, sickening, thickening,
stiffening, christening, glistening,
listening, pitying, dizzying, visiting,
* uninteresting, considering,
conditioning, unpitying, politicking,
etc.

18.74 syllabus, Nicholas, fingerless,
sisterless, frivolous, symptomless,
frictionless, Icarus, rigorous, vigorous,

dipterous, timorous, chivalrous, bigamous, infamous, Pyramus, Michaelmas, wilderness, bitterness, villainous, tyrannous, synchronous, nimbleness, fickleness, singleness, listlessness, hideous, piteous, bilious, Sirius, vitreous, Phineas, igneous, ligneous, Vilnius, impetus, Sisyphus, mischievous, pitiless, ticketless, limitless, victimless, stickiness, silkiness, giddiness, prettiness, wittiness, silliness, springiness, dizziness, flimsiness, itchiness, wickedness, vividness, willingness, Britishness, sinuous, incubus, bibulous, mimulus, stimulus, * Callimachus, Lysimachus, viviparous, oviparous, coniferous, vociferous, lactiferous, splendiferous, pestiferous, viniferous, somniferous, cruciferous, granivorous, carnivorous, herbivorous, omnivorous, frugivorous, polygamous, Antigonus, judiciousness, amphibious, fastidious, perfidious, invidious, insidious, oblivious, lascivious, punctilious, Lucilius, delirious, Arminius, Odysseus, Leviticus, umbilicus, precipitous, iniquitous, ubiquitous, solicitous, felicitous, duplicitous, libidinous, indigenous, vertiginous, permissiveness, unwillingness, perspicuous, conspicuous, promiscuous, contiguous, ambiguous, exiguous, assiduous, deciduous, mellifluous, continuous, meticulous, ridiculous, acidulous, * erysipelas, Carboniferous, odoriferous, insectivorous, supercilious, ignominious, Dionysius, serendipitous, infelicitous, inconspicuous, unambiguous, discontinuous, * australopithecus, etc.

18.75 hypnotist, symbolist, bigamist, lyricist, physicist, jingoist, * numismatist, ventriloquist, polygamist, nutritionist, revisionist, recidivist, empiricist, * abolitionist, exhibitionist, prohibitionist, astrophysicist

18.76 grippiest, nippiest, slippiest, pickiest, stickiest, trickiest, milkiest, silkiest, friskiest, riskiest, windiest, grittiest, prettiest, wittiest, shiftiest, thriftiest, mintiest, mistiest, twistiest, pithiest, chilliest, frilliest, hilliest, silliest, sickliest, wintriest, springiest, stringiest, tipsiest, busiest, dizziest, fizziest, frizziest, flimsiest, dishiest, fishiest, itchiest, dingiest, stingiest, etc.

18.77 disparate, literate, idiot, Cypriot, syndicate, silicate, triplicate, intricate, distillate, intimate, infinite, rivulet, quintuplet, * episcopate, deliberate, considerate, preliterate, illiterate, affiliate, novitiate, initiate, sophisticate, certificate, pontificate, precipitate, legitimate, discriminate, articulate, particulate, barbiturate, * inconsiderate, semiliterate, illegitimate, indiscriminate, inarticulate

18.78 shibboleth, fiftieth, sixtieth, Illingworth, * Elizabeth

18.79 abilities, stabilities, hostilities, antiquities, * capabilities, sensibilities, liabilities, possibilities, * responsibilities, etc.

18.80 difficulty, digitally, sinisterly, similarly, minimally, criminally, diligently, ritually, visually, singularly, intricately, intimately, innocently, interestingly, sickeningly, rigorously, vigorously, hideously, mischievously, literary, cinerary, ignominy, literacy, idiocy, intricacy, intimacy, sycophancy, militancy, * sensationally, additionally, traditionally, conditionally, nutritionally, provisionally, familiarly, subliminally, medicinally, originally, continually, habitually, particularly, legitimately, significantly, definitively, inquisitively, bewilderingly, fastidiously, insidiously, conspicuously, ridiculously, meticulously, ambiguously, assiduously, continuously, epistolary, itinerary, obituary, discriminatory, episcopacy, illiteracy, legitimacy, constituency, * unconditionally, individually, indiscriminately, superciliously, inconspicuously, etc.

18.81 miserable, pitiable, irritable, imitable, limitable, spiritual, * deliverable, illimitable, inimitable, distinguishable, attributable, meridional, * undeliverable, indistinguishable

Rhyming slang

●●●●●●●●●●●●●●●●●●●●●

Rhyming slang, traditionally associated with the Cockneys of London's East End, involves substituting rhyming phrases for everyday words. Here are just a few of the best-known examples:

apples and pears = stairs
whistle and flute = suit
syrup of figs = wig
butcher's hook = look
china plate = mate
Adam and Eve = believe
tea leaf = thief
jam jar = car
dog and bone = phone
pork pie = lie
plates of meat = feet
Jimmy Riddle = piddle

Over the course of time, the rhyming part of the phrase is often dropped, with the result that have a butcher's *is now a slang way of saying 'have a look',* china *is a slang word for 'friend', and so on.*

-ire-

The rhymes in this section have the 'ire' sound of tyre *and* admirer *as their main or final vowel sound.*

19.1 [see also **22.2**] briar, brier, byre, choir, dire, Dwyer, fire, friar, gyre, hire, ire, lyre, mire, prior, Prior, pyre, quire, shire, sire, spire, squire, tire, tyre, Tyre, via, wire, * aspire, perspire, conspire, attire, acquire, Maguire, afire, admire, transpire, backfire, barbed wire, spare tyre, rewire, respire, expire, inspire, retire, entire, Kintyre, misfire, require, enquire, esquire, inquire, bemire, desire, Bushire, * vampire, satire, sapphire, campfire, samphire, quagmire, grandsire, haywire, empire, Empire, hellfire, shellfire, cease-fire, sweetbrier, spitfire, Spitfire, tripwire, pismire, wildfire, bonfire, crossfire, saltire, sure-fire, umpire, gunfire, drumfire, bushfire, * lammergeier, McIntyre, retrofire, retrochoir, reacquire

Here lies a poor woman who always was tired,
For she lived in a place where help wasn't hired.
Epitaph

19.2 fired, hired, sired, tired, wired, * aspired, perspired, conspired, attired, acquired, admired, transpired, backfired, rewired, expired, inspired, retired, misfired, required, enquired, desired, * gas-fired, oil-fired, coal-fired, * overtired, underwired, unexpired, uninspired, * semiretired, etc.

19.3 dial, Lyell, Niall, phial, trial, vial, viol, * redial, retrial, espial, misdial, mistrial, denial, * sundial, * self-denial

19.4 Byers, fires, Myers, quires, shires, spires, tyres, wires, * perspires, admires, expires, requires, desires, * vampires, campfires, Blackfriars, Greyfriars, Spitfires, Whitefriars, * Molly Maguires, etc.

Religion blushing veils her sacred fires,
And unawares Morality expires.
Alexander Pope

20.1 direly, Brierley, diary, fiery, friary, miry, priory, wiry, enquiry, inquiry, expiry, * entirely

20.2 dialler, Viola, direr, firer, hirer, Ira, Lyra, Myra, wirer, * aspirer, conspirer, acquirer, admirer, retirer, enquirer, inquirer, * spirogyra, * admire her, inspire her, etc.

20.3 Hiram, tiresome, * fire 'em, wire 'em, etc.

20.4 Ireland, diamond

20.5 violent, tyrant, * nonviolent, acquirement, requirement, retirement

20.6 violence, tyrants, * nonviolence, requirements, etc.

20.7 dialling, hireling, trialling, hiring, firing, tiring, wiring, * aspiring, perspiring, conspiring, untiring, admiring, retiring, inspiring, misfiring, inquiring, desiring, * uninspiring, etc.

20.8 tireless, wireless, Cyrus, virus, tiredness, * papyrus, Epirus, desirous, * parvovirus, retrovirus, herpesvirus, * hire us, fired us, etc.

20.9 triallist, violist, diarist, lyrist

20.10 spirelet, violet, * inviolate, * ultraviolet, * hire it, dial it, etc.

20.11 spirally, violently, tiresomely, tirelessly, * entirety, admiringly, * uninspiringly

20.12 hirable, spiracle, * inviolable, acquirable, desirable, * undesirable

-ie-

The rhymes in this section have the 'ie' sound of try *and* glider *as their main or final vowel sound.*

21.1 ay, aye, bi, Bligh, buy, by, bye, chi, cry, Dai, Di, die, dry, dye, eye, fie, fly, fry, Fry, guy, Guy, hi, hie, high, I, lie, lye, my, nigh, Nye, phi, pi, pie, ply, pry, psi, Pye, rye, Rye, scry, shy, sigh, sky, Skye, sly, spry, spy, sty, stye, Thai, thigh, thy, tie, try, Vi, vie, why, wry, Wye, Y

I must go down to the sea again, to the lonely sea and the sky,
And all I ask is a tall ship and a star to steer her by.
JOHN MASEFIELD

21.2 Mackay, g'day, untie, ally, apply, supply, comply, awry, Transkei, shanghai, Shanghai, banzai, thereby, whereby, Versailles, Desai, hereby, nearby, GI, retie, knee-high, retry, deep-fry, espy, mince pie, defy, belie, rely, reply, imply, decry, descry, drip-dry, spin-dry, deny, bye-bye, I-spy, My Lai, pork pie, bone dry, goodbye, Mumbai, Dubai, July, Brunei

21.3 rabbi, stand-by, magpie, cacti, ally, Adlai, blackfly, gadfly, sandfly, Catseye®, Masai, lay-by, Magi, mayfly, quasi, Jedi, red-eye, necktie, stir-fry, Birds Eye, workshy, Eli, three-ply, greenfly, Levi, pinkeye, nilgai, pigsty, drip-dry, fisheye, firefly, aye-aye, flyby,

tie-dye, hi-fi, sci-fi, whitefly, Sinai, rhombi, thrombi, Popeye, sockeye, bronchi, Bondi, hogtie, botfly, oxeye, bonsai, walleye, sawfly, gallfly, horsefly, housefly, outcry, blowfly, blow-dry, foci, loci, shuteye, fungi, shoofly,
* Iceni, narcissi, thesauri, *E. coli*, alumni,
* decree nisi, * aqua vitae, arbor vitae,
a priori, * modus vivendi, a fortiori,
* modus operandi, a posteriori,
dramatis personae, * curriculum vitae

21.4 apple pie, Malachi, assegai, alkali, damselfly, dragonfly, Paraguay, abaci, Haggai, alibi, dandify, gratify, ratify, stratify, sanctify, amplify, clarify, scarify, ramify, magnify, damnify, classify, gasify, pacify, calcify, satisfy, samurai, passer-by, passers-by, RSI, Nazify, argufy, aerify, rarefy, scarify, radii, deify, reify, ladyfy, FBI, edify, trendify, rectify, testify, jellify, terrify, verify, petrify, specify, Frenchify, Gemini, certify, versify, termini, reapply, resupply, CBI, genii, sweetie-pie, preachify, speechify, DIY, syllabi, bring-and-buy, misapply, high and dry, Philippi, typify, citify, prettify, mystify, vivify, vilify, simplify, vitrify, liquefy, dignify, lignify, signify, Disneyfy, stimuli, by and by, private eye, Private Eye, jai alai, tiger's-eye, Hi-de-Hi, Lorelei, hoverfly, solidi, modify,

quantify, jollify, mollify, qualify,
horrify, torrefy, cockneyfy, ossify,
prophesy, Ross-on-Wye, occupy,
Olduvai, Mordecai, fortify, glorify,
falsify, Uruguay, purify, counterspy,
overbuy, overlie, overfly, goldeneye,
Chou En-lai, codify, notify, Hokusai,
lullaby, hushaby, ultrahigh, underlie,
thunderfly, butterfly, tumble-dry,
yuppify, fructify, stultify, justify,
nullify, uglify, mummify, Russify,
multiply, uteri, hue and cry, UDI,
nuclei, stupefy, beautify, putrefy,
tumefy, unify, crucify, do-or-die,
cumuli, tumuli, * leylandii, syllabify,
beatify, declassify, decalcify, dissatisfy,
denazify, objectify, subjectify, identify,
exemplify, electrify, indemnify,
solemnify, intensify, diversify, Helvetii,
solidify, acidify, rigidify, humidify,
demystify, revivify, sarcophagi,
disqualify, transmogrify, saponify,
personify, detoxify, preoccupy,
reoccupy, vox populi, demulsify,
emulsify, minutiae, reunify,
* caravanserai, lapis lazuli,
dehumidify, oversimplify,
hippopotami, anno Domini

21.5 bribe, gibe, gybe, jibe, kibe, scribe,
tribe, vibe, * ascribe, subscribe,
transcribe, imbibe, describe, prescribe,
inscribe, proscribe, * circumscribe,
diatribe, unsubscribe

21.6 bribed, gibed, gybed, jibed,
* ascribed, subscribed, transcribed,
imbibed, described, prescribed,
inscribed, proscribed,
* circumscribed, unsubscribed,
* oversubscribed, undersubscribed

21.7 bike, like, dyke, grike, hike, Ike,

mike, Mike, pike, psych, Reich, shrike,
Smike, spike, strike, trike, tyke, * alike,
unlike, Van Dyck, van Eyck, dislike,
* catlike, antlike, manlike, garpike,
starlike, glasslike, grasslike, hairlike,
apelike, snakelike, wraithlike,
threadlike, shell-like, turnpike,
wormlike, priestlike, dreamlike,
hitchhike, sylphlike, springlike,
sphinxlike, childlike, Christlike,
lifelike, Klondike, Fosdyke, godlike,
swanlike, Thorndike, warlike,
ghostlike, homelike, Updike, suchlike,
* statesmanlike, ladylike,
workmanlike, seamanlike,
businesslike, sportsmanlike,
soundalike, motorbike, unalike,
lookalike, womanlike, superbike,
* unbusinesslike, unsportsmanlike

21.8 bikes, likes, dykes, hikes, Mike's,
spikes, strikes, Sykes, yikes, * dislikes,
* motorbikes, superbikes, * likes and
dislikes, etc.

**Out flew the web and floated wide;
The mirror cracked from side to side;
'The curse is come upon me,' cried
The Lady of Shalott.**
ALFRED, LORD TENNYSON

21.9 bide, bride, chide, Clyde, cried,
died, dried, dyed, eyed, fried, glide,
guide, Guide, hide, Hyde, I'd, lied,
pied, pride, ride, Ryde, shied, side,
sighed, slide, snide, spied, stride, tide,
tied, tried, vied, wide, etc.

21.10 abide, undyed, untied, confide,
provide, allied, collide, applied,
supplied, McBride, untried, astride,
aside, subside, Strathclyde, worldwide,
retried, deep-fried, misguide, betide,

defied, divide, elide, replied, implied, deride, Kilbride, spin-dried, bestride, beside, decide, inside, preside, reside, offside, Port Said, outride, outside, * nucleotide, Jekyll and Hyde, Bonnie and Clyde, industrywide, etc.

Great wits are sure to madness near allied,
And thin partitions do their bounds divide.
JOHN DRYDEN

21.11 allied, backslide, landslide, pan-fried, backside, carbide, waveguide, Tayside, wayside, lakeside, stateside, graveside, ebb tide, peptide, Twelfthtide, bedside, stir-fried, kerbside, nearside, freeze-dried, quayside, seaside, Cheapside, Teesside, riptide, springtide, hillside, inside, ringside, fireside, pie-eyed, Tyneside, popeyed, cockeyed, Hocktide, phosphide, oxhide, cross-eyed, topside, dockside, oxide, offside, rawhide, horsehide, wall-eyed, chloride, foreside, broadside, fluoride, cowhide, outside, downside, joyride, doe-eyed, sloe-eyed, Shrovetide, blow-dried, bromide, roadside, tongue-tied, sulphide, sun-dried, one-eyed, upside, Brookside, Yuletide, noontide, poolside, * peroxide, monoxide, dioxide, hydroxide, alongside

21.12 Lammastide, paraglide, saccharide, lanthanide, Ambleside, gratified, ratified, stratified, sanctified, amplified, clarified, magnified, classified, pacified, satisfied, aldehyde, parricide, fratricide, matricide, patricide, algicide, park and ride, starry-eyed, rarefied, nationwide,

deicide, set-aside, genocide, edified, rectified, terrified, verified, petrified, specified, pesticide, Heaviside, regicide, certified, herbicide, germicide, spermicide, vermicide, Merseyside, bleary-eyed, reapplied, Eastertide, eventide, eagle-eyed, beady-eyed, feticide, ecocide, Whitsuntide, Christmastide, glyceride, riverside, silverside, citified, prettified, mystified, vilified, simplified, liquefied, dignified, filicide, iodide, cyanide, biocide, glycoside, five-a-side, Ironside, modified, mollified, qualified, horrified, prophesied, homicide, occupied, waterside, fortified, glorified, purified, mountainside, override, codified, notified, coincide, tumble-dried, Humberside, underside, yuppified, justified, mummified, multiplied, subdivide, countrified, undenied, fungicide, countryside, dewy-eyed, beautified, putrefied, unified, crucified, suicide, * disaccharide, unratified, beatified, unsanctified, unamplified, unclassified, declassified, unsatisfied, self-satisfied, dissatisfied, paraldehyde, formaldehyde, infanticide, tyrannicide, unrectified, identified, exemplified, unverified, unspecified, intensified, insecticide, rodenticide, uncertified, bactericide, thalidomide, solidified, unsimplified, undignified, sulphonamide, unmodified, unqualified, disqualified, personified, sororicide, unoccupied, preoccupied, unfortified, unpurified, unjustified, emulsified, * polysaccharide, monosaccharide, unidentified, oversimplified, parasiticide, overqualified, parasuicide, etc.

21.13 brides, Guides, hides, ides, rides, sides, strides, * besides, decides, insides, etc.

21.14 fife, Fife, knife, life, rife, strife, wife, * real life, still life, long-life, pro-life, * jackknife, alewife, shelf life, penknife, midlife, midwife, fishwife, flick knife, highlife, wildlife, nightlife, housewife, lowlife, goodwife, loosestrife, * palette knife, afterlife, paperknife, pocketknife

They all ran after the farmer's wife,
Who cut off their tails with a carving
knife,
Did you ever see such a thing in your
life,
As three blind mice?
NURSERY RHYME

21.15 oblige, * disoblige

21.16 aisle, bile, chyle, file, guile, I'll, isle, Kyle, lisle, Lyle, mile, Nile, pile, rile, smile, stile, style, tile, vile, Weill, while, wile, * compile, awhile, Argyll, argyle, Carlisle, Carlyle, erewhile, ensile, worthwhile, restyle, *Sieg Heil*, meanwhile, beguile, defile, misfile, revile, * tactile, pantile, agile, facile, gracile, fragile, hairstyle, labile, nailfile, reptile, centile, Gentile, sextile, textile, sterile, sessile, exile, tensile, fertile, turnstile, servile, erstwhile, aedile, freestyle, ethyl, methyl, febrile, penile, phenyl, senile, virile, fissile, missile, scissile, lifestyle, stockpile, condyle, hostile, quartile, puerile, mobile, motile, profile, docile, ductile, woodpile, nubile, butyl, futile, * contractile, retractile, projectile, trajectile, erectile, percentile, prehensile, infertile, presenile,

immobile, immotile, high-profile, * Francophile, Anglophile, rank and file, camomile, acetyl, arctophile, carbonyl, necrophile, xenophile, technophile, reconcile, peristyle, thermopile, versatile, mercantile, paedophile, oenophile, infantile, cyclostyle, crocodile, volatile, domicile, Europhile, Russophile, juvenile, * ailurophile, bibliophile, audiophile

21.17 child, filed, Fylde, mild, riled, smiled, styled, tiled, wild, Wilde, * compiled, self-styled, restyled, beguiled, defiled, reviled, * grandchild, Fairchild, exiled, stepchild, brainchild, godchild, Rothschild, love child, schoolchild, * reconciled, Oscar Wilde, domiciled, etc.

I call that parent rash and wild
Who'd reason with a six-year child.
PHYLLIS MCGINLEY

21.18 aisles, files, Giles, miles, Miles, piles, smiles, tiles, wiles, * compiles, defiles, reviles, betweenwhiles, * pantiles, reptiles, textiles, missiles, * paedophiles, Western Isles, Scilly Isles, British Isles, crocodiles, Northern Isles, etc.

21.19 Chaim, chime, chyme, climb, clime, crime, dime, grime, I'm, lime, Lyme, mime, prime, rhyme, rime, slime, thyme, time, * sublime, part-time, half-time, spare time, mistime, begrime, all-time, old-time, full-time, two-time, * ragtime, Mannheim, pastime, airtime, daytime, playtime, bedtime, enzyme, birdlime, teatime, mealtime, Dreamtime, meantime,

peacetime, springtime, quicklime,
night-time, lifetime, longtime,
Sondheim, Trondheim, wartime,
downtime, Stroheim, uptime,
sometime, one-time, lunchtime,
noontime, * paradigm, Anaheim,
pantomime, maritime, Father Time,
extra time, anytime, flexitime,
wintertime, dinner time,
Christmastime, cybercrime, ribozyme,
Oppenheim, overtime, closing time,
supper time, summertime,
Guggenheim

**I'm tired of Love: I'm still more tired of
Rhyme.**
**But Money gives me pleasure all the
time.**
<small>HILAIRE BELLOC</small>

21.20 chimed, climbed, limed, mimed,
rhymed, timed, * unclimbed,
unrhymed, well-timed, ill-timed,
begrimed

21.21 chimes, climbs, climes, crimes,
dimes, Grimes, rhymes, times,
* The Times, betimes, begrimes,
* pastimes, enzymes, mealtimes,
ofttimes, sometimes, * betweentimes,
* pantomimes, Maritimes, oftentimes,
etc.

21.22 bine, brine, chine, cline, dine,
dyne, fine, Fyne, Jain, kine, Klein,
Kline, line, mine, nine, pine, Rhine,
shine, shrine, sign, sine, spine, spline,
stein, Stein, Strine, swine, thine, tine,
twine, Tyne, vine, whine, wine,
* combine, condign, confine, align,
malign, front line, assign, consign,
re-sign, repine, define, refine, divine,
decline, recline, incline, enshrine,

entwine, benign, design, resign,
offline, online, cloud nine, outshine,
opine, * Sabine, rapine, alpine, Alpine,
strapline, land line, chatline, tramline,
land mine, carbine, carmine, airline,
hairline, grapevine, A-line, ley line,
saline, dateline, waistline, mainline,
baseline, canine, Epstein, Bechstein,
helpline, neckline, breadline, deadline,
headline, hemline, eccrine, equine,
Pennine, ensign, turbine, Bernstein,
Irvine, ursine, earthshine, beeline,
feline, tree line, streamline, V-sign,
incline, syncline, slimline, Einstein,
by-line, skyline, pipeline, guideline,
sideline, sightline, lifeline, timeline,
Holbein, combine, Holstein, hotline,
Fräulein, jawline, shoreline, taurine,
porcine, outline, Goldstein, bovine,
ovine, snow line, towline, coastline,
clothesline, gold mine, coal mine,
cosine, road sign, bloodline, plumb
line, rhumb line, touchline, punch
line, sunshine, woodbine, lupine,
supine, shoeshine, moonshine,
* McAlpine, Byzantine, * anodyne,
Palatine, Ballantyne, valentine,
Valentine, Hammerstein, alkaline,
Caroline, saccharine, passerine,
calamine, saturnine, Palestine,
Frankenstein, aquiline, anticline,
asinine, Argentine, party line, table
wine, eighty-nine, twenty-nine,
Sensodyne®, celandine, Heseltine,
Levantine, eglantine, Clementine,
endocrine, serpentine, Serpentine,
turpentine, thirty-nine, Ursuline,
recombine, realign, leonine, reassign,
redefine, redesign, Wittgenstein,
Liechtenstein, Ghibelline, zibeline,
interline, crystalline, riverine,
intertwine, Philistine, sibylline,
disincline, picket line, disentwine,

fifty-nine, sixty-nine, firing line,
Eisenstein, ninety-nine, columbine,
Columbine, Constantine, Florentine,
concubine, borderline, water line,
auld lang syne, story line, forty-nine,
porcupine, countersign, opaline,
underline, undermine, superfine,
uterine, Rubinstein, * Capitoline,
estuarine, seventy-nine, overrefine,
* diamantine, elephantine,
alexandrine, internecine, labyrinthine,
Schleswig-Holstein

And Noah he often said to his wife
when he sat down to dine,
'I don't care where the water goes if it
doesn't get into the wine.'
G. K. CHESTERTON

21.23 bind, blind, dined, find, grind,
hind, kind, lined, mind, mined,
pined, rind, signed, whined, wind,
* combined, unbind, unkind, confined,
aligned, maligned, unlined, unwind,
unsigned, mankind, rewind, defined,
refined, behind, inclined, entwined,
remind, designed, resigned,
* Gradgrind, spellbind, purblind,
streamlined, snow-blind,
* mastermind, misaligned,
intertwined, disinclined, wined and
dined, nonaligned, womankind,
Golden Hind, overwind, unconfined,
underlined, colour-blind,
undermined, undersigned, undefined,
unrefined, undesigned, humankind,
* overrefined, etc.

For Justice, though she's painted blind,
Is to the weaker side inclined.
SAMUEL BUTLER

21.24 pint, * Geraint, * cuckoopint

21.25 Fiennes, Heinz, Hines, lines,
mines, pines, signs, tines, vines,
* hard lines, designs, * Sabines,
tramlines, land mines, airlines,
headlines, Pennines, guidelines,
sidelines, confines, outlines, road
signs, * Apennines, etc.

21.26 gripe, hype, pipe, ripe, snipe,
stripe, swipe, tripe, type, wipe,
* unripe, retype, mistype, * standpipe,
tailpipe, drainpipe, windpipe,
pinstripe, sideswipe, hornpipe,
downpipe, blowpipe, stovepipe,
hosepipe, subtype, * archetype,
Teletype®, genotype, serotype, ecotype,
phenotype, biotype, logotype,
Monotype®, prototype, overripe,
guttersnipe, underripe,
* daguerreotype, electrotype,
* stereotype

21.27 cripes, gripes, pipes, stripes,
types, wipes, * bagpipes, panpipes,
drainpipes, pinstripes, stovepipes,
* Stars and Stripes, etc.

21.28 griped, hyped, piped, striped,
swiped, typed, wiped, * unstriped,
unwiped, retyped, mistyped,
* stereotyped, etc.

21.29 Brice, dice, gneiss, ice, lice, mice,
nice, price, Price, rice, slice, spice,
splice, thrice, trice, twice, vice, Zeiss,
* suffice, advice, concise, half-price,
de-ice, entice, device, precise, * pack
ice, Jarndyce, fieldmice, titmice,
choc-ice, allspice, dormice, woodlice,
* paradise, sacrifice, edelweiss,
merchandise, imprecise, cockatrice,
overnice, * self-sacrifice

It was a miracle of rare device,
A sunny pleasure-dome with caves of
   ice.
SAMUEL TAYLOR COLERIDGE

21.30 Christ, diced, heist, iced, priced,
sliced, spiced, spliced, * sufficed,
unsliced, unpriced, de-iced, enticed,
* *Zeitgeist*, * sacrificed, Antichrist,
poltergeist, overpriced, underpriced

21.31 bight, bite, blight, bright, Bright,
byte, cite, Dwight, fight, flight, fright,
height, kite, knight, Knight, krait,
light, lite, might, mite, night, plight,
quite, right, rite, shite, sight, site, skite,
sleight, slight, smite, spite, sprite,
tight, trite, twite, white, White, wight,
wright, Wright, write

Biting my truant pen, beating myself
   for spite,
'Fool,' said my Muse to me; 'look in thy
   heart and write.'
PHILIP SIDNEY

21.32 alight, polite, uptight, aright,
contrite, affright, tonight, Twelfth
Night, relight, preflight, rewrite,
despite, indict, skintight, invite,
delight, in-flight, requite, ignite,
recite, excite, incite, off-white, all
right, outright, Snow White,
goodnight, unite, * Gileadite,
Ishmaelite, Israelite, meteorite,
spermatocyte

21.33 graphite, catfight, lamplight,
fanlight, gaslight, flashlight, samite,
campsite, starlight, Arkwright,
cartwright, Cartwright, Marmite®,
airtight, Blairite, snakebite, daylight,
space flight, tail-light, playwright,

wainwright, Wainwright, respite,
headlight, Enright, website, perlite,
earthlight, searchlight, birthright,
termite, Shiite, fleabite, Levite,
streetlight, wheelwright, Semite,
weeknight, Hittite, shipwright,
millwright, midnight, insight,
firefight, prizefight, highlight,
skylight, stylite, twilight, sidelight,
night-light, limelight, typewrite, finite,
eyesight, hindsight, frostbite,
cockfight, dogfight, stoplight,
spotlight, bomb site, gobshite, cordite,
torchlight, Albright, forthright,
fortnight, foresight, Forsyte,
Plowright, downright, lowlight,
ghostwrite, lovebite, Luddite, bunfight,
gunfight, floodlight, sunlight, upright,
bullfight, moonlight, * apartheid,
bipartite, tripartite, transvestite,
gesundheit

21.34 Jacobite, blatherskite, Araldite®,
stalactite, halophyte, saprophyte,
Fahrenheit, acolyte, satellite,
candlelight, anchorite, Nazarite,
Thatcherite, black-and-white,
catamite, stalagmite, aconite,
ammonite, phagocyte, parasite,
anthracite, appetite, Hashemite,
landfill site, Carmelite, marcasite,
Bakelite®, Labourite, Canaanite,
Rechabite, megabyte, extradite,
recondite, Hepplewhite, belemnite,
expedite, epiphyte, eremite,
Vegemite®, gelignite, plebiscite,
erudite, cellulite, urbanite, coenobite,
steatite, haematite, neophyte, Edomite,
reignite, reunite, gigabyte, kilobyte,
impolite, sybarite, lymphocyte, lily-
white, disunite, trilobite, bryophyte,
microlight, Isle of Wight, dynamite,
fly-by-night, troglodyte, coprolite,

dolerite, sodomite, dolomite, Trotskyite, proselyte, copyright, Bonfire Night, watertight, quarterlight, outasight, Moabite, overbite, oolite, socialite, overflight, overwrite, overnight, oocyte, oversight, Muscovite, underwrite, leucocyte, * hermaphrodite, Pre-Raphaelite, McCarthyite, electrolyte, suburbanite, erythrocyte, theodolite, toxophilite, * Areopagite

21.35 bites, fights, kites, knights, lights, nights, rights, sights, tights, whites, * delights, excites, * campsites, daylights, tail-lights, headlights, searchlights, termites, streetlights, weeknights, highlights, sidelights, pyrites, floodlights, footlights, * Jacobites, satellites, ammonites, Carmelites, Canaanites, megabytes, see the sights, gigabytes, kilobytes, civil rights, troglodytes, Dolomites, socialites, Golan Heights, human rights, * Wuthering Heights, etc.

**And the milkmaid singeth blithe,
And the mower whets his scythe.**
JOHN MILTON

21.36 blithe, Blyth, Hythe, lithe, scythe, Smythe, tithe, withe, writhe, * Rotherhithe

21.37 chive, Clive, dive, drive, five, gyve, hive, I've, jive, live, rive, shrive, skive, strive, thrive, wive, * survive, alive, arrive, contrive, connive, derive, deprive, revive, * archive, endive, beehive, skydive, nose dive, ogive, * eighty-five, twenty-five, MI5, thirty-five, fifty-five, sixty-five, ninety-five, four-wheel drive, forty-five, overdrive

**This is the law of the Yukon, that only
the Strong shall thrive;
That surely the Weak shall perish, and
only the Fit survive.**
ROBERT W. SERVICE

21.38 chives, Clive's, dives, drives, fives, gyves, hives, Ives, knives, lives, wives, * St Ives, * archives, endives, penknives, midwives, fishwives, flick knives, housewives, * paperknives, under-fives, etc.

21.39 buys, cries, dies, Di's, dries, dyes, eyes, flies, fries, guise, guys, Guy's, highs, lies, lyse, pies, prise, prize, rise, sighs, size, skies, spies, thighs, tries, wise, etc.

**Early to bed and early to rise,
Makes a man healthy, wealthy, and
wise.**
SAYING

21.40 advise, applies, supplies, arise, apprise, surprise, uprise, comprise, unwise, assize, baptize, chastise, capsize, surmise, despise, mince pies, disguise, defies, devise, revise, demise, denies, disprize, misprize, excise, incise, outsize, downsize, goodbyes, etc.

21.41 rabbis, magpies, allies, Allies, crabwise, franchise, slantwise, neckties, stepwise, endwise, breadthwise, lengthwise, edgewise, excise, realize, Levi's®, streetwise, leastwise, widthwise, king-size, fireflies, stylize, high-rise, likewise, Popeye's, clockwise, longwise, crosswise, low-rise, nowise, somewise, sunrise, moonrise, * aggrandize, enfranchise, idealize, synopsize, amortize, * disenfranchise, anticlockwise, counterclockwise, etc.

21.42 standardize, anodize, rhapsodize, advertise, dramatize, alkalize, scandalize, vandalize, catalyse, chaptalize, tantalize, paralyse, analyse, dragonflies, factorize, pasteurize, valorize, glamorize, randomize, atomize, agonize, fraternize, galvanize, patronize, canonize, fantasize, catechize, sanitize, magnetize, gratifies, amplifies, tranquillize, maximize, Latinize, satirize, plasticize, Gallicize, anglicize, bastardize, marmalize, carbonize, jargonize, harmonize, barbarize, nasalize, racialize, vaporize, plagiarize, paganize, stabilize, laicize, * readvertise, metabolize, anatomize, antagonize, metastasize, analogize, demagnetize, beatifies, dissatisfies, evangelize, romanticize, elasticize, italicize, contrariwise, containerize, destabilize, * psychoanalyse, etc.

21.43 jeopardize, methodize, empathize, metallize, breathalyse, centralize, specialize, temporize, slenderize, tenderize, terrorize, memorize, mesmerize, pressurize, enterprise, ebonize, mechanize, westernize, recognize, emphasize, exercise, energize, sensitize, terrifies, specifies, televise, sterilize, anywise, feminize, elegize, exorcize, ghettoize, deputize, merchandise, verbalize, burglarize, mercerize, urbanize, sermonize, circumcise, fertilize, worldly-wise, schematize, legalize, equalize, penalize, theorize, etherize, demonize, * electrolyse, decentralize, extemporize, accessorize, depressurize,

derecognize, desensitize, identifies, collectivize, incentivize, poeticize, parenthesize, eternalize, internalize, externalize, commercialize, diversifies, anaesthetize, * departmentalize, compartmentalize, Orientalize, Occidentalize, sentimentalize, overemphasize, universalize, Europeanize, etc.

21.44 stigmatize, hypnotize, sympathize, improvise, symbolize, crystallize, signalize, winterize, tyrannize, synchronize, liquidize, digitize, typifies, mystifies, civilize, victimize, minimize, criticize, mythicize, synthesize, immunize, iodize, privatize, dialyse, idolize, vitalize, hydrolyse, finalize, itemize, ionize, lionize, hybridize, * initialize, transistorize, familiarize, soliloquize, epitomize, solidifies, legitimize, politicize, acclimatize, devitalize, revitalize, de-ionize, * oversimplifies, depoliticize, photosynthesize, etc.

21.45 dogmatize, moralize, novelize, hoverflies, sodomize, compromise, modernize, colonize, solemnize, ostracize, oxidize, modifies, qualifies, fossilize, optimize, occupies, communize, gormandize, traumatize, formalize, normalize, pauperize, cauterize, authorize, cornerwise, organize, pluralize, ruralize, bowdlerize, moisturize, robotize, globalize, localize, vocalize, totalize, socialize, motorize, polarize, Romanize, oversize, Nobel prize, mobilize, * apostatize, democratize, bureaucratize, apostrophize, philosophize, monopolize, demoralize, dichotomize, economize, apologize, anthologize, homologize, prioritize, personifies, homogenize, eroticize, hypothesize, catholicize, immortalize, reorganize, disorganize, deodorize, depolarize, demobilize, immobilize, * demythologize, etc.

21.46 lullabies, mongrelize, butterflies, rubberize, vulgarize, pulverize, summarize, otherwise, customize, vulcanize, subsidize, monetize, mummifies, multiplies, publicize, womanize, supervise, brutalize, neutralize, unionize, humanize, eulogize, putrefies, utilize, booby prize, euphemize, scrutinize, * computerize, dehumanize, * revolutionize, attitudinize, platitudinize, etc.

21.47 alphabetize, naturalize, caramelize, nationalize, rationalize, emblematize, federalize, generalize, personalize, liberalize, mineralize, fictionalize, Lord of the Flies, Morecambe and Wise, bestialize, serialize, trivialize, cannibalize, capitalize, catheterize, characterize, categorize, allegorize, marginalize, lexicalize, decimalize, skeletonize, systematize, digitalize, criminalize, militarize, miniaturize, proselytize, hospitalize, polymerize, annualize, actualize, sexualize, ritualize, visualize, mutualize, communalize, tabularize, secularize, regularize, circularize, popularize, formularize, masculinize, * denaturalize, denationalize, renationalize, sensationalize, professionalize, conventionalize, depersonalize, impersonalize, demineralize, Australianize, pedestrianize, materialize,

memorialize, industrialize, Americanize, decriminalize, demilitarize, republicanize, desexualize, conceptualize, contextualize, demutualize, particularize, * internationalize, institutionalize, dematerialize, editorialize, territorialize, overcapitalize, undercapitalize, individualize

21.48 prized, sized, * advised, surprised, unsized, baptized, chastised, despised, disguised, revised, excised, incised, * franchised, pearlized, realized, stylized, * enfranchised, unrealized, idealized, * standardized, anodized, advertised, dramatized, vandalized, paralysed, Sanforized®, pasteurized, agonized, galvanized, sanitized, magnetized, anglicized, stabilized, well-advised, centralized, specialized, tenderized, terrorized, mesmerized, pressurized, mechanized, westernized, recognized, sensitized, televised, sterilized, mercerized, circumcised, fertilized, creolized, legalized, hypnotized, improvised, ill-advised, crystallized, synchronized, middle-sized, civilized, immunized, privatized, finalized, itemized, modernized, ostracized, fossilized, formalized, authorized, organized, localized, motorized, polarized, oversized, mobilized, unadvised, rubberized, summarized, unsurprised, undersized, undisguised, subsidized, publicized, supervised, neutralized, unionized, * readvertised, unpasteurized, demagnetized, romanticized, elasticized, unplasticized, italicized, depressurized, unrecognized,

commercialized, uncircumcised,
unfertilized, anaesthetized,
uncivilized, politicized, de-ionized,
demoralized, prioritized,
immortalized, unauthorized,
disorganized, unorganized,
demobilized, unpublicized,
unsupervised, computerized,
* naturalized, nationalized,
personalized, serialized, characterized,
decimalized, miniaturized,
hospitalized, annualized, ritualized,
popularized, * denationalized,
renationalized, sensationalized,
demineralized, pedestrianized,
industrialized, decriminalized,
demilitarized, * institutionalized,
dematerialized, individualized, etc.

22.1 stripy, crikey, Nike, psyche, spiky,
Tyche, Bridie, Friday, Heidi, tidy,
Blighty, flighty, Haiti, mighty, nightie,
ninety, feisty, ivy, Ivy, dryly, Filey, Haile,
highly, Kylie, Riley, shyly, slyly, smiley,
Wiley, wily, likely, idly, widely, mildly,
wildly, blindly, kindly, brightly,
knightly, lightly, nightly, rightly,
sightly, slightly, sprightly, tightly,
Whiteley, lively, blithely, timely, finely,
nicely, wisely, blimey, limey, limy, rimy,
slimy, stymie, briny, gynae, Heiney,
piny, shiny, spiny, tiny, whiny, winey,
dicey, icy, pricey, spicy, * untidy,
almighty, Almighty, O'Reilly, unlikely,
unkindly, Golightly, politely, unsightly,
untimely, sublimely, divinely,
concisely, precisely, unwisely, Hawaii,
cor blimey, * forthrightly, fortnightly,
sunshiny, * Ciba-Geigy, bona fide,
Aphrodite, Amphitrite, high-and-
mighty, impolitely, Berenice, etc.

22.2 [see also 19.1] ayah, buyer, crier,

drier, dryer, dyer, flyer, fryer, Gaia,
higher, liar, Maia, Maya, Meyer, pryer,
shyer, slyer, stria, trier, vier, wryer,
* papaya, Achaia, supplier, Aglaia,
Maria, pariah, defier, spin-dryer,
denier, Messiah, high-flyer, Isaiah,
town crier, Sophia, Josiah, Uriah,
* hairdryer, Niemeyer, housebuyer,
outlier, * Obadiah, jambalaya,
Zachariah, Black Maria, Zechariah,
tumble-dryer, Zephaniah, deep-fat
fryer, Zedekiah, Hezekiah, amplifier,
magnifier, classifier, pacifier, rectifier,
testifier, verifier, versifier, simplifier,
signifier, modifier, quantifier,
qualifier, fortifier, purifier, *Billy Liar*,
multiplier, Jeremiah, Nehemiah,
prophesier, first-time buyer, occupier,
* preamplifier, identifier, intensifier,
humidifier, emulsifier, * Iphigenia,
* dehumidifier, owner-occupier, * buy
her, untie her, etc.

22.3 briber, fibre, Khyber, Schreiber,
Tiber, diaper, griper, hyper, piper,
sniper, swiper, viper, wiper,
* subscriber, transcriber, imbiber,
prescriber, inscriber, * bagpiper,
sandpiper, Pied Piper, * microfibre,
windscreen wiper, * bribe her,
describe her, etc.

22.4 biker, hiker, liker, mica, Micah,
pica, striker, Eiger, Geiger, liger,
Steiger, tiger, * Formica®,
* hitchhiker, * balalaika, * like her,
strike her, etc.

There came a big spider,
Who sat down beside her.
Nursery rhyme

22.5 cider, eider, glider, Guider, Ida,

rider, Ryder, Schneider, slider, spider, strider, Wilder, binder, blinder, finder, grinder, hinder, kinda, kinder, minder, winder, biter, blighter, fighter, lighter, mitre, nitre, righter, sighter, slighter, tighter, titre, whiter, writer, shyster, rhymester, * provider, al-Qaeda, divider, decider, insider, outsider, Oneida, rewinder, reminder, politer, igniter, all-nighter, * hang-glider, backslider, nightrider, Tynesider, outrider, joyrider, pathfinder, rangefinder, spellbinder, ring binder, sidewinder, child minder, fault-finder, bookbinder, viewfinder, backbiter, lamplighter, nailbiter, screenwriter, scriptwriter, firefighter, firelighter, prizefighter, highlighter, typewriter, songwriter, Gauleiter, ghostwriter, uplighter, bullfighter, * paraglider, overrider, organ-grinder, autowinder, copywriter, underwriter, capellmeister, * guide her, fight her, etc.

22.6 cipher, Haifa, knifer, lifer, diver, driver, fiver, Ivor, jiver, Liver, skiver, striver, viva, either, neither, * decipher, encipher, Godiva, survivor, saliva, conniver, reviver, co-driver, * slave-driver, skin-diver, skydiver, pile-driver, screwdriver, * conjunctiva, * knife her, deprive her, etc.

22.7 filer, Isla, Islay, miler, phyla, smiler, styler, tiler, Tyler, idler, trifler, Chrysler, Lycra®, Hydra, ayah, * compiler, beguiler, defiler, Delilah, recycler, De Falla, * stockpiler, Rottweiler, * beguile her, revile her, etc.

22.8 climber, mimer, primer, rhymer, timer, china, China, Dinah, diner,

finer, Heine, liner, miner, minor, mynah, shiner, signer, Steiner, Viner, whiner, * part-timer, Jemima, full-timer, two-timer, assignor, consignor, vagina, angina, hardliner, definer, refiner, diviner, recliner, designer, Regina, * Hochheimer, airliner, jetliner, Niersteiner, eyeliner, coal miner, moonshiner, * Maritimer, Oppenheimer, autotimer, Carolina, Ursa Minor, Liechtensteiner, Indochina, forty-niner, * two-time her, malign her, etc.

Dinner in the diner, nothing could be finer,
Than to have your ham'n eggs in Carolina.
MACK GORDON

22.9 dicer, ISA, Neisse, nicer, pricer, ricer, slicer, splicer, Schweitzer, Dreiser, guiser, Kaiser, Liza, miser, Pfizer, riser, sizer, Tizer®, visor, Niger, * conciser, de-icer, enticer, adviser, chastiser, despiser, devisor, divisor, reviser, Eliza, incisor, Elisha, obliger, Elijah, * Budweiser®, * advertiser, atomizer, appetizer, tranquillizer, vaporizer, stabilizer, Breathalyser®, tenderizer, exerciser, sterilizer, fertilizer, nebulizer, equalizer, sympathizer, improviser, liquidizer, synthesizer, dialyser, ionizer, moralizer, modernizer, organizer, bowdlerizer, moisturizer, womanizer, supervisor, neutralizer, * economizer, deodorizer, immobilizer, * entice her, advise her, etc.

22.10 lilac, Isaac, Izaak, * elegiac

22.11 psychic, sidekick, cyclic, hydric,

Heinrich, nitric, thymic, seismic,
* enzymic

22.12 tidied, bifid, trifid, ivied, eyelid,
hybrid, stymied

22.13 dryad, triad, guided, blighted,
lighted, mitred, sighted, slighted,
whited, Twyford, skyward, sideward,
* provided, collided, misguided,
divided, derided, decided, presided,
resided, lopsided, unguided, one-
sided, reminded, high-minded, like-
minded, broad-minded, small-
minded, alighted, unsighted, far-
sighted, clear-sighted, near-sighted,
invited, delighted, requited,
benighted, excited, long-sighted,
short-sighted, united, deciphered,
* jeremiad, undivided, undecided,
absent-minded, narrow-minded,
simple-minded, single-minded, open-
minded, uninvited, unrequited,
unexcited, undeciphered,
* overexcited, etc.

22.14 dryads, triads, skywards,
sidewards

22.15 triage, mileage, silage,
Knightsbridge, linage, signage

22.16 Bible, libel, scribal, tribal, typal,
cycle, Michael, bridal, bridle, idle, idol,
Rydal, sidle, tidal, title, vital, Eiffel,
rifle, stifle, trifle, mindful, frightful,
rightful, spiteful, rival, spiral, viral,
fibril, mitral, Sizewell, primal, final,
spinal, vinyl, Faisal, IJssel, sisal, trysail,
Nigel, * disciple, Carmichael, cervical,
recycle, unbridle, entitle, retitle,
requital, recital, unmindful, delightful,
arrival, survival, arch-rival, aestival,

revival, retiral, postviral, vaginal,
doctrinal, urinal, reprisal, * surtitle,
subtitle, * kilocycle, motorcycle,
umbilical, unicycle, herbicidal,
germicidal, spermicidal, intertidal,
homicidal, fungicidal, suicidal,
adjectival, antiviral, semifinal,
intestinal, polyvinyl, quarterfinal,
paradisal, * cerebrospinal,
* gastrointestinal

22.17 libelled, idled, titled, rifled,
stifled, trifled, rivalled, * recycled,
unbridled, untitled, entitled,
unrivalled, * subtitled, etc.

22.18 Higham, Priam, item, phylum,
whilom, xylem, Lynam, * asylum,
* sempervivum, antirrhinum,
botulinum, * ad infinitum, * buy 'em,
fight 'em, etc.

**Big fleas have little fleas upon their
    backs to bite 'em,
And little fleas have lesser fleas, and so
    ad infinitum.**
Saying

22.19 lie-in, tiepin, ninepin, wineskin,
chitin, ricin, * Aneurin,
* streptomycin, * fightin', jivin', etc.

22.20 Brian, cyan, ion, iron, lion, Lyon,
Mayan, prion, Ryan, scion, Zion, ripen,
lichen, liken, tigon, Dryden, Haydn,
Leiden, Leyden, Phaidon, Sidon,
widen, Blyton, brighten, Brighton,
Crichton, frighten, heighten, Huyton,
lighten, tighten, Titan, Triton, whiten,
hyphen, siphon, Ivan, liven, wyvern,
python, Python, pylon, Byron, Chiron,
siren, Siren, Nyman, pieman, Simon,
Timon, Wyman, lineman, Weizmann,

Wiseman, tribesman, linesman,
Tynan, bison, Bryson, Dyson, Fison,
grison, Meissen, Tyson, * Orion,
Hawaiian, cast iron, noniron, wrought
iron, O'Brien, * sadiron, andiron,
cation, flatiron, antlion, anion,
gridiron, Poseidon, enlighten, enliven,
upsilon, epsilon, environ, horizon,
bedizen, * Paraguayan, dandelion,
Geminian, zwitterion, Uruguayan,
Monty Python

Simple Simon met a pieman,
Going to the fair.
NURSERY RHYME

22.21 ironed, viand, ripened, widened,
brightened, frightened, lightened,
whitened, highland, Highland, island,
Thailand, Rhineland, Iceland,
Streisand, * unironed, enlightened,
enlivened, * unenlightened, etc.

22.22 viands, Highlands, islands

22.23 Brian's, irons, lions, Lyons,
Huygens, Titans, Byron's, sirens,
Sirens, * environs, horizons, etc.

22.24 Bryant, client, giant, pliant,
strident, trident, Trident, mightn't,
silent, tyrant, vibrant, migrant,
hydrant, * compliant, defiant, reliant,
excitant, indictment, incitement,
excitement, beguilement, defilement,
revilement, confinement, alignment,
assignment, consignment, refinement,
enshrinement, enticement,
advisement, chastisement, * self-
reliant, supergiant, realignment,
reassignment, misalignment

22.25 clients, giants, science, guidance,

silence, tyrants, migrants, licence,
license, * affiance, alliance, appliance,
compliance, defiance, reliance,
subsidence, contrivance, connivance,
refinements, * misalliance,
noncompliance, self-reliance,
parascience, social science,
neuroscience, pseudoscience,
* overreliance, etc.

22.26 crying, drying, dyeing, dying,
flying, lying, trying, bribing, griping,
piping, sniping, typing, wiping,
biking, hiking, liking, striking, Viking,
chiding, gliding, Guiding, hiding,
riding, siding, sliding, striding,
binding, finding, grinding, minding,
winding, biting, fighting, lighting,
righting, sighting, slighting, whiting,
writing, knifing, diving, driving,
jiving, skiving, striving, thriving,
tithing, scything, writhing, filing,
piling, smiling, styling, tiling, cycling,
idling, sidling, rifling, stifling, trifling,
hindwing, chiming, climbing,
miming, rhyming, timing, dining,
lining, mining, pining, shining,
signing, twining, Twining, whining,
frightening, lightning, icing, pricing,
slicing, splicing, rising, * undying,
untying, transcribing, imbibing,
describing, disliking, abiding,
confiding, providing, subsiding,
dividing, deciding, presiding, residing,
self-winding, inviting, exciting,
surviving, arriving, conniving,
reviving, compiling, unsmiling,
restyling, beguiling, defiling, two-
timing, combining, confining,
defining, refining, divining, declining,
reclining, designing, resigning,
enticing, surprising, chastising,
revising, downsizing, obliging,

* outlying, fact-finding, bookbinding, fault-finding, backlighting, handwriting, playwriting, Speedwriting®, screenwriting, infighting, scriptwriting, firefighting, bullfighting, skywriting, typewriting, signwriting, songwriting, moonlighting, skydiving, realizing, stylizing, uprising, * underlying, gratifying, edifying, terrifying, horrifying, paragliding, overriding, uninviting, unexciting, copywriting, motorcycling, interlining, intertwining, underlining, undermining, undesigning, appetizing, advertising, tantalizing, agonizing, patronizing, mesmerizing, enterprising, energizing, merchandising, fertilizing, sympathizing, improvising, civilizing, moralizing, compromising, authorizing, organizing, moisturizing, * unsatisfying, unedifying, self-sacrificing, unappetizing, uncompromising, etc.

He cursed him in sitting, in standing, in lying;
He cursed him in walking, in riding, in flying,
He cursed him in living, he cursed him in dying!
R. H. BARHAM

22.27 Vikings, sidings, tidings, sightings, filings, etc.

22.28 ibis, iris, Iris, tigress, Tigris, crisis, Isis, lysis, phthisis, * colitis, mastitis, gastritis, arthritis, bursitis, phlebitis, cystitis, rhinitis, bronchitis, neuritis, Osiris, * hepatitis, dermatitis, enteritis, fibrositis, myelitis, tonsillitis, laryngitis, pharyngitis, sinusitis, meningitis, * encephalitis, peritonitis, conjunctivitis, appendicitis, * gastroenteritis, osteoarthritis, diverticulitis, * poliomyelitis

22.29 bias, Caius, Gaius, pious, Pius, Midas, Titus, Vitus, typhus, eyeless, Silas, stylus, tieless, childless, mindless, flightless, sightless, lifeless, guileless, rhymeless, timeless, spineless, priceless, Cyrus, virus, fibrous, cypress, Cyprus, hydrous, Hydrus, nitrous, Primus®, thymus, dryness, Highness, Linus, minus, shyness, sinus, slyness, spinous, vinous, ripeness, likeness, mildness, wildness, blindness, kindness, brightness, lightness, rightness, tightness, triteness, whiteness, fineness, niceness, righteous, * Matthias, Darius, impious, Elias, Tobias, Josias, St Vitus, detritus, tinnitus, pruritus, papyrus, Epirus, anhydrous, Aquinas, Plotinus, Longinus, Paulinus, unkindness, politeness, conciseness, unrighteous, * Zacharias, Ananias, callipygous, Heraclitus, parvovirus, retrovirus, herpesvirus, Antoninus, Severinus, Dionysus, * defy us, fine us, etc.

22.30 typist, stylist, cyclist, * motorcyclist, * audiotypist

22.31 biased, driest, highest, shyest, slyest, wryest, lightest, slightest, tightest, whitest, idlest, finest, nicest, * unbiased, politest, divinest, concisest, etc.

22.32 dryish, side dish, childish, whitish, whitefish, stylish, swinish

22.33 eyelet, islet, twilit, pikelet, spikelet, * file it, buy it, etc.

22.34 Byatt, diet, fiat, quiet, riot, Wyatt, private, Pilate, pilot, pirate, climate, * disquiet, * copilot, * Pontius Pilate, autopilot, macroclimate, microclimate

22.35 eyelets, islets, pikelets, spikelets, Leibnitz

22.36 Tynemouth, * Goliath

22.37 decisive, divisive, derisive, incisive, * indecisive

22.38 nineties, Kylie's, limeys, crises, Pisces, * bona fides, etc.

22.39 buyers, liars, pliers, fibres, snipers, wipers, bikers, strikers, spiders, minders, writers, divers, drivers, fivers, climbers, diners, miners, ices, prices, slices, vices, misers, prizes, * suppliers, high-flyers, subscribers, dividers, insiders, outsiders, survivors, part-timers, devices, advisers, surprises, Devizes, * housebuyers, hitchhikers, joyriders, firefighters, Alzheimer's, * first-time buyers, windscreen wipers, sympathizers, etc.

22.40 Niobe, tribally, vitally, writerly, frightfully, rightfully, spitefully, finally, miserly, quietly, privately, silently, piously, bribery, spidery, bindery, grindery, ivory, library, primary, binary, finery, pinery, vinery, winery, spicery, ribaldry, dietary, rivalry, bryony, Bryony, irony, privacy, piracy, vibrancy, primacy, piety, nicety, tidily, mightily, icily, strikingly, blindingly, bitingly, frighteningly, childishly,

stylishly, daiquiri, * delightfully, reliably, misguidedly, decidedly, defiantly, self-righteously, salivary, refinery, advisory, derisory, proprietary, psychiatry, podiatry, Alcyone, Hermione, satiety, variety, sobriety, propriety, society, anxiety, impiety, dubiety, untidily, designedly, resignedly, advisedly, disguisedly, derisively, decisively, invitingly, surprisingly, obligingly, * suicidally, adjectivally, justifiably, undeniably, indefinably, single-mindedly, interlibrary, supervisory, insobriety, impropriety, inebriety, contrariety, notoriety, etc.

A person of sobriety
Who cherishes propriety
Feels conscious of satiety
When in a clown's society.
CLARENCE DAY

22.41 Highlander, islander, Icelander, Viola, libeller, Iowa, isomer, frightener, tightener, whitener, silencer, licensor, Heidegger, dieter, rioter, * proprietor, variola, * Bandaranaike

22.42 tidier, flightier, mightier, feistier, wilier, shinier, tinier, icier, spicier, * untidier, * forsythia, etc.

22.43 buyable, dyeable, flyable, friable, pliable, liable, triable, viable, bribable, likable, ridable, findable, rightable, writable, drivable, climbable, finable, sliceable, sizable, Lionel, psychical, cyclical, bicycle, icicle, tricycle, * reliable, deniable, describable, unridable, unwritable, indictable, excitable, undrivable, recyclable,

unclimbable, definable, reclinable,
advisable, realizable, maniacal,
zodiacal, varietal, societal,
* classifiable, rectifiable, verifiable,
specifiable, certifiable, quantifiable,
qualifiable, notifiable, justifiable,
unreliable, undeniable, indescribable,
extraditable, reconcilable,
indecipherable, indefinable,
magnetizable, memorizable,
recognizable, hypnotizable,
inadvisable, ammoniacal, demoniacal,
* unclassifiable, identifiable,
unverifiable, unquantifiable,
unjustifiable, irreconcilable,
unrecognizable, paradisiacal,
* unidentifiable

22.44 quieten, Iowan, Chinaman,
Heinemann, rifleman, glycogen,
hydrogen, nitrogen, highwayman,
Heineken®, Irishman, * Goliathan,
leviathan

22.45 Stuyvesant, * entitlement,
enlightenment, environment

22.46 riotous, libellous, riderless,
driverless, quietness, idleness,
childlessness, righteousness, tidiness,
flightiness, kindliness, sprightliness,
liveliness, childishness, * proprietress,
short-sightedness, self-righteousness,
untidiness, * absent-mindedness, etc.

22.47 scientist, finalist, Zionist,
nihilist, * revivalist, psychiatrist,
* semifinalist

22.48 tidiest, flightiest, mightiest,
feistiest, wiliest, shiniest, tiniest, iciest,
spiciest, * untidiest, etc.

22.49 inviolable, decipherable,
* indecipherable

-O-

The rhymes in this section have the 'o' sound of toss and copper as their main or final vowel sound.

23.1 bob, Bob, blob, cob, dob, fob, glob, gob, hob, job, knob, lob, mob, nob, rob, Rob, slob, snob, sob, squab, swab, throb, yob, * McJob, demob, * heart-throb, hobnob, corncob, doorknob, * rent-a-mob, * thingumabob, corn on the cob

**I could not dig: I dared not rob:
Therefore I lied to please the mob.**
RUDYARD KIPLING

23.2 Bob's, blobs, Hobbes, Hobbs, knobs, mobs, nobs, snobs, yobs, etc.

23.3 bloc, Bloch, block, bock, brock, choc, chock, clock, cock, croc, crock, doc, dock, flock, frock, hock, jock, Jock, knock, loch, lock, Locke, lough, mock, pock, roc, rock, schlock, shock, smock, sock, Spock, stock, wok, * unlock, unblock, o'clock, baroque, unfrock, amok, Bangkok, ad hoc, half-cock, *en bloc*, Médoc, defrock, restock, post hoc, * Hancock, spatchcock, daglock, padlock, Matlock, Havelock, shamrock, matchlock, charlock, Bartók, airlock, kapok, haycock, gamecock, gemsbok, Belloc, deadlock, headlock, wedlock, fetlock, elflock, hemlock, bedrock, bed sock, shell shock, burdock, Murdoch, Sherlock, Reebok®, rhebok, epoch, Leacock, peacock, seacock, breeze block, pibroch, Enoch, springbok, Springbok, Hitchcock, ticktock, whipstock, drillstock, picklock, gridlock, flintlock, wristlock, windsock, livestock, Shylock, stopcock, Quantock, Bostock, Rostock, Vostok, Alcock, ball cock, Baldock, forelock, oarlock, Porlock, warlock, Warnock, moorcock, moloch, Moloch, roadblock, sun block, gunlock, bloodstock, gunstock, woodcock, Woodstock, rootstock, Prufrock, * alpenstock, Abersoch, Antioch, manioc, Tavistock, carriage clock, antiknock, Ragnarök, aftershock, laughing stock, weathercock, *belle époque*, speaking clock, interlock, monocoque, chock-a-block, poppycock, hollyhock, overstock, postman's knock, shuttlecock, double-lock, culture shock, stumbling block, * Vladivostok

**Your Chablis is acid, away with the Hock,
Give me the pure juice of the purple Médoc.**
ARTHUR HUGH CLOUGH

23.4 Bloch, Koch, loch, lough, och, * Van Gogh, * pibroch

23.5 blocks, box, chocs, clocks, cox, Cox,

docks, flocks, fox, Fox, Jock's, knocks, Knox, locks, lox, MOX, Nox, ox, phlox, pox, rocks, socks, stocks, vox, * Fort Knox, outfox, * bandbox, sandbox, hatbox, cashbox, matchbox, mailbox, paintbox, brainbox, Radox®, dreadlocks, bed socks, gearbox, Xerox®, detox, Reeboks®, squeezebox, peacocks, breeze blocks, pillbox, Springboks, Wilcox, Simcox, firebox, icebox, Ibrox, strongbox, saltbox, Quantocks, horsebox, smallpox, oarlocks, aurochs, soapbox, postbox, Botox®, soundbox, cowpox, tuck box, snuffbox, lunchbox, shoebox, jukebox, toolbox, loosebox, boondocks, * chatterbox, paradox, equinox, tinderbox, pillar box, chickenpox, building blocks, gogglebox, on the rocks, orthodox, Orthodox, Goldilocks, thunderbox, moneybox, * nonorthodox, unorthodox, * jack-in-the-box, heterodox, school of hard knocks, etc.

23.6 blocked, cocked, docked, knocked, locked, mocked, rocked, shocked, stocked, * concoct, unlocked, unblocked, unfrocked, half-cocked, defrocked, restocked, decoct, * padlocked, landlocked, deadlocked, dreadlocked, shell-shocked, gridlocked, etc.

23.7 blotch, botch, crotch, notch, scotch, Scotch, splotch, swatch, watch, * top-notch, * deathwatch, wristwatch, hotchpotch, hopscotch, stopwatch, dogwatch, doomwatch, * butterscotch

I am a sundial, and I make a botch Of what is done much better by a watch.
HILAIRE BELLOC

23.8 bod, clod, cod, god, Dodd, God, hod, mod, nod, odd, plod, pod, prod, quad, quod, rod, Rod, shod, sod, squad, tod, Todd, trod, wad, * ramrod, Nimrod, slipshod, bipod, iPod®, tripod, tightwad, odd bod, hot rod, godsquad, sun god, roughshod, pushrod, * gastropod, cattle prod, arthropod, decapod, tetrapod, hexapod, Hesiod, demigod, Sweeney Todd, Ichabod, flying squad, octopod, monopod, Ormerod, goldenrod, * cephalopod

23.9 cough, doff, Gough, off, prof, quaff, scoff, toff, trough, * Van Gogh, well-off, browned-off, * Cracow, standoff, Markov, blastoff, castoff, Karloff, payoff, play-off, takeoff, Chekhov, Geldof, sendoff, rip-off, kickoff, liftoff, spin-off, show-off, cutoff, Khrushchev, * Nabokov, Sakharov, Asimov, Glazunov, telling-off, whooping cough, Molotov, stroganoff, Godunov, Gorbachov, Romanov, Ustinov, * Kalashnikov, Rachmaninoff, * Poliakoff, Baader-Meinhof, * Rimsky-Korsakov

23.10 coughed, croft, doffed, loft, oft, quaffed, scoffed, soft, waft, * aloft, * Bancroft, Ashcroft, hayloft, cockloft, Cockcroft, Moorcroft, * Microsoft®, Lowestoft

23.11 blog, bog, clog, cog, dog, flog, fog, frog, glogg, Gog, grog, hog, Hogg, jog, log, nog, prog, quag, slog, smog, snog, sprog, tog, trog, wog, Zog, * agog, unclog, befog, * lapdog, hangdog, backlog, quahog, Magog, hedgehog, Kellogg, weblog, eclogue, eggnog, Herzog, seadog, sheepdog, leapfrog, phizog, firedog, hot dog, watchdog, warthog, groundhog, road hog, prologue, gundog, bulldog, footslog, bullfrog, goosegog, * apologue, Tagalog, catalogue, travelogue, analogue, antilog, pedagogue, demagogue, Decalogue, pettifog, epilogue, synagogue, dialogue, homologue, monologue, golliwog, polliwog, underdog, duologue, * Ffestiniog, * Phileas Fogg, ideologue

23.12 clogged, flogged, fogged, hogged, jogged, logged, snogged, * unclogged, befogged, waterlogged, etc.

23.13 Bloggs, cogs, dogs, frogs, logs, togs, * hedgehogs, Kellogg's, etc.

23.14 bodge, dodge, Hodge, lodge, Lodge, podge, splodge, stodge, wodge, * dislodge, * hodgepodge

23.15 col, doll, loll, moll, Moll, Scholl, skol, sol, Sol, troll, * Algol, atoll, Castrol®, AWOL, Dettol®, menthol, VTOL, obol, podzol, COBOL, Gogol, googol, * Panadol®, alcohol, parasol, barcarole, aerosol, ethanol, methanol, Interpol, glycerol, Ingersoll, Limassol, vitriol, falderol, protocol, Cuprinol®, * Sebastopol, cholesterol, * Costa del Sol, * paracetamol

23.16 golf, Rolf, * Adolf, Randolph, Botolph, Rudolph

23.17 false, waltz

23.18 fault, Galt, halt, malt, salt, SALT, vault, Walt, * assault, default, exalt, * Hainault, basalt, cobalt, pole vault, * somersault

23.19 salts, schmaltz, vaults, etc.

23.20 solve, * absolve, devolve, evolve, revolve, involve, dissolve, resolve

23.21 solved, * unsolved, absolved, devolved, evolved, revolved, involved, dissolved, resolved, * uninvolved, undissolved, unresolved

23.22 dolls, hols, Moll's, trolls, * atolls, obols, consols, etc.

23.23 bomb, dom, from, mom, pom, prom, rhomb, ROM, Somme, tom, Tom, * aplomb, shalom, therefrom, wherefrom, * maelstrom, stink bomb, sitcom, firebomb, pompom, condom, tom-tom, coulomb, Coulomb, * atom bomb, CARICOM, telecom, CD-ROM, Peeping Tom, intercom, minicom, diatom, Uncle Tom

23.24 chomp, clomp, comp, pomp, romp, stomp, swamp, yomp

23.25 chomped, clomped, prompt, romped, stomped, swamped, yomped

23.26 Omsk, Tomsk

Diddle diddle dumpling, my son John, Went to bed with his trousers on.
NURSERY RHYME

23.27 Bonn, con, don, Don, gone, Hon., john, John, on, phon, Ron, scone, shone, swan, Swann, wan, yon, * Gabon, upon, Perón, Sharon, anon, hands-on, head-on, thereon, whereon, cretonne, hereon, Dion, Dionne, begone, Yvonne, Ceylon, Saigon, spot-on, won ton, odds-on, Sorbonne, foregone, outshone, Luzon,

* crampon, tampon, baton, Anton, canton, Canton, Danton, salon, Fablon®, Savlon®, Dacron®, macron, axon, taxon, argon, Sargon, air-con, crayon, kaon, rayon, radon, Avon, Dralon®, Teflon®, Revlon, bouillon, eon, Leon, neon, prion, piton, chignon, xenon, Nippon, Nikon, stick-on, krypton, chiffon, ion, icon, bygone, triton, nylon, pylon, Heilbronn, micron, bonbon, doggone, Oxon., walk-on, boron, moron, fleuron, Huron, neuron, zoon, photon, proton, colon, roll-on, gnomon, boson, coupon, Yukon, crouton, futon, neutron, Tucson, *soupçon*, * decathlon, heptathlon, pentathlon, biathlon, triathlon, Cro-Magnon, liaison, electron, court-bouillon, * mastodon, Avalon, Al-Anon, Algernon, hanger-on, cabochon, Papillon, baryon, carry-on, Macedon, antiphon, Babylon, magnetron, Parthenon, Barbizon, thereupon, whereupon, aileron, decagon, heptagon, pentagon, Pentagon, hexagon, echelon, Lebanon, Elton John, Benetton, telethon, epsilon, etymon, demijohn, Percheron, fermion, Myrmidon, hereupon, Simenon, sit-upon, synchrotron, cyclotron, dynatron, octagon, nonagon, Mogadon®, colophon, Comecon, polygon, positron, Audubon, Bourguignonne, Oberon, woebegone, goings-on, undergone, nucleon, Rubicon, * iguanodon, dodecagon, Bellerophon, encephalon, automaton, Laocoon, emoticon, * Agamemnon, interferon, filet mignon, oxymoron, protozoon, antiproton, semicolon, antineutron, * sine qua non, * spermatozoon

23.28 bonk, clonk, conch, conk, gonk, honk, plonk, zonk, * honky-tonk

23.29 bonks, Bronx, gonks, honks, yonks, etc.

23.30 blond, blonde, bond, Bond, conned, donned, fond, frond, Fronde, pond, sonde, wand, * abscond, James Bond, despond, respond, second, Gironde, beyond, beau monde, * keeshond, millpond, * vagabond, demimonde, Trebizond, correspond, overfond, Eurobond

23.31 bong, Caen, dong, gong, long, pong, prong, song, strong, thong, throng, Wong, wrong, * along, prolong, sarong, mah jong, erelong, chaise longue, Vietcong, Mekong, qigong, King Kong, belong, Geelong, Hong Kong, foo yong, * Armstrong, daylong, plainsong, headlong, restaurant, headstrong, furlong, birdsong, yearlong, Ping-Pong®, ding-dong, biltong, diphthong, livelong, singsong, sidelong, nightlong, lifelong, oblong, swan song, hourlong, folk song, dugong, bouffant, oolong, * aide-de-camp, cradlesong, restaurant, evensong, billabong, Chittagong, sing-along, wobbegong, *bon vivant*, vol-au-vent, overlong, Wollongong, Goolagong, * Lapsang Souchong

Be the day weary or be the day long,
At last it ringeth to evensong.
Saying

23.32 gongs, longs, prongs, songs, throngs, tongs, wrongs, etc.

23.33 bonce, nonce, ponce, sconce, fonts, wants, * response, ensconce

23.34 font, Quant, want, * Lamont, Vermont, Dupont, * Chalfont, Egmont, Belmont, restaurant, Piedmont, Stormont, Beaumont, * restaurant, Hellespont, symbiont

23.35 bronze, dons, Don's, Johns, John's, pons, Ron's, scones, swans, * St John's, Yvonne's, mod cons, * crayons, icons, croutons, goujons, etc.

23.36 bop, chop, clop, cop, crop, drop, flop, fop, hop, kop, lop, mop, op, plop, pop, prop, shop, slop, sop, stop, strop, swap, top, wop, * the Kop, atop, unstop, vox pop, nonstop, * laptop, tank top, backstop, backdrop, hard top, palmtop, sharecrop, airdrop, raindrop, desktop, bellhop, hedgehop, sweatshop, worktop, Worksop, workshop, teardrop, treetop, eavesdrop, Aesop, sweetsop, teashop, sweetshop, Britpop, tiptop, clifftop, hilltop, hip-hop, clip-clop, flip-flop, Hislop, Winthrop, milksop, soft top, doorstop, Allsop, pawnshop, outcrop, soursop, coin-op, toyshop, Co-op, stonecrop, snowdrop, rollmop, Dunlop, gumdrop, tuck shop, junk shop, bookshop, screw top, rooftop, dewdrop, * Malaprop, paradrop, drag-and-drop, agitprop, alcopop, barbershop, escalope, megaflop, belly flop, Blenkinsop, turboprop, Ethiop, gigaflop, intercrop, Ribbentrop, whistle-stop, window-shop, lollipop, mountaintop, overtop, * over the top

Don't you wish you'd go on forever and you'd never stop?
In that shiny little surrey with the fringe on the top.
RICHARD RODGERS

23.37 chops, cops, copse, crops, drops, hops, ops, props, shops, stops, tops, * raindrops, worktops, eardrops, teardrops, treetops, flip-flops, Cyclops, eyedrops, snowdrops, rooftops, * Keystone Kops, lollipops, muttonchops, Woodentops, * triceratops, etc.

23.38 chopped, Copt, cropped, dropped, flopped, hopped, mopped, popped, opt, stopped, swapped, topped, * adopt, unstopped, uncropped, co-opt, close-cropped, etc.

23.39 boss, Bros, cos, cross, crosse, DOS, doss, dross, floss, Gosse, gloss, goss, Jos, joss, Kos, loss, moss, Moss, os, Ross, toss, * across, lacrosse, uncross, recross, emboss, Kinross, * Athos, Patmos, Naxos, Marcos, Argos, Carlos, Lagos, bathos, pathos, weight loss, Amos, Samos, chaos, Lesbos, Eros, reredos, Chios, Eos, EPOS, ethos, Delos, Melos, crisscross, tripos, mythos, cosmos, Knossos, Phobos, Cronos, kudos, bugloss, * Dos Passos, Niarchos, Barbados, extrados, intrados, Domestos®, asbestos, * Calvados, Thanatos, albatross, adios, candyfloss, rallycross, dental floss, MS-DOS®, Míkonos, autocross, motocross, double-cross, * Los Alamos, Makarios, * Ballesteros, Villa-Lobos, * Torremolinos

23.40 bosk, mosque, * kiosk

23.41 bossed, cost, crossed, dossed, flossed, frost, Frost, glossed, lost, Prost, tossed, wast, * accost, uncrossed, Jack Frost, recrossed, defrost, embossed, riposte, * *glasnost*, star-crossed, compost, provost, storm-tossed, hoarfrost, * Van der Post, Pentecost, teleost, permafrost, double-crossed

23.42 Boche, Bosch, bosh, cloche, cosh, dosh, gosh, josh, nosh, posh, quash, Roche, slosh, splosh, squash, swash, tosh, wash, Wash, * awash, prewash, brioche, * backwash, car wash, brainwash, prewash, kibosh, eyewash, whitewash, hogwash, mouthwash, musquash, Pugwash, * Mackintosh, mackintosh, colourwash

23.43 coshed, doshed, joshed, noshed, quashed, sloshed, squashed, washed, * unwashed, prewashed, * brainwashed, whitewashed, stonewashed

23.44 blot, bot, clot, cot, dot, Dot, got, grot, hot, jot, knot, lot, Lot, mot, not, motte, plot, pot, rot, Scot, Scott, shot, slot, snot, sot, spot, squat, swat, swot, tot, trot, twat, Wat, watt, Watt, what, wot, yacht, * cocotte, forgot, gavotte, allot, shallot, garrotte, red-hot, repot, begot, Pol Pot, * crackpot, jackpot, black spot, mascot, backlot, sandlot, cannot, have-not, snapshot, Bagshot, wainscot, grapeshot, mailshot, space shot, despot, sexpot, earshot, teapot, tinpot, Phillpott, Didcot, inkblot, Wilmot, slipknot, slingshot, nightspot, eyeshot, stockpot, hotpot, tosspot, hot spot, Oflot, godslot, dogtrot, jog trot, foxtrot, Ofwat, topknot, whatnot, hotshot, pot shot, Alcott, flowerpot, boycott, Boycott, robot, bowshot, fusspot, sunspot, dovecot, subplot, kumquat, somewhat, upshot, buckshot, mug shot, bloodshot, gunshot, woodlot, moonshot, * Camelot, cachalot, Paraquat®,

carrycot, aliquot, sans-culotte, Lancelot, parking lot, parting shot, chamber pot, apricot, pepper pot, megawatt, melting pot, Bernadotte, Winalot®, bergamot, kilowatt, chimneypot, misbegot, diddly-squat, guillemot, Wyandotte, microdot, lobster pot, on the spot, polka dot, Hottentot, monoglot, coffeepot, ocelot, polyglot, tommyrot, Aldershot, Turandot, counterplot, go to pot, overshot, trouble spot, undershot, honeypot, you-know-what, * forget-me-not

**Ere Time and Place were, Time and
    Place were not,
When primitive Nothing Something
    straight begot,
Then all proceeded from the great
    united – What?**
JOHN WILMOT, EARL OF ROCHESTER

23.45 blots, clots, dots, Dot's, hots, knots, lots, Notts, pots, plots, Potts, Scots, spots, trots, Watts, * shallots, the trots, culottes, * crackpots, mascots, snapshots, sexpots, fleshpots, teapots, robots, * chimneypots, call the shots, * forget-me-nots, etc.

23.46 broth, cloth, froth, Goth, moth, Roth, swath, troth, wrath, wroth, * backcloth, sackcloth, haircloth, J-cloth®, sailcloth, facecloth, cerecloth, cheesecloth, dishcloth, washcloth, floorcloth, broadcloth, hawk moth, oilcloth, loincloth, * behemoth, * tablecloth, Visigoth, tiger moth, Ostrogoth

23.47 of, * thereof, whereof, * Cracow, Pavlov, Chekhov, Kirov, * unheard-of, undreamt-of, * Asimov, Ustinov

23.48 Boz, cos, Oz, Ros, 'twas, was,
* because, * tiz-woz

24.1 bobby, Bobby, Gobbi, gobby,
hobby, knobby, lobby, Robbie, snobby,
Colby, Dolby®, combi, Dombey,
zombie, Crosby, choppy, copy, floppy,
kopje, poppy, sloppy, soppy, stroppy,
Pompey, swampy, * jalopy, * Mr
Blobby, Abercrombie, photocopy

24.2 choccy, cocky, gnocchi, hockey,
jockey, rocky, Rocky, stocky, bronchi,
donkey, wonky, Trotsky, Chomsky,
boggy, doggy, foggy, groggy, moggy,
quaggy, soggy, * outjockey, Stokowski,
Tchaikovsky, * disc jockey,
* jabberwocky, pedagogy, demagogy

24.3 body, cloddy, Noddy, Oddie,
Roddy, shoddy, squaddie, toddy, wadi,
Aldi, Caldy, Blondie, spondee, dotty,
grotty, knotty, Lottie, potty, Scottie,
snotty, spotty, swotty, totty, yachtie,
zloty, lofty, softie, balti, faulty, malty,
salty, Solti, Brontë, Conteh, Monte,
Monty, frosty, * Kirkcaldy, embody,
Grimaldi, Menotti, Del Monte, full
monty, * Peabody, dogsbody,
homebody, * antibody, anybody,
everybody, Irrawaddy, busybody,
disembody, underbody, Pavarotti,
Lanzarote, Megawati, Belafonte

24.4 coffee, toffee, bothy, frothy,
mothy, * banoffee

24.5 Bolly, brolly, Colley, collie, dolly,
Dolly, folly, golly, Holi, holly, Holly,
jolly, lolly, Molly, Ollie, Polly, poly,
Solly, Tolley, trolley, volley, wally,
Wally, Whalley, wolly, knobbly, wobbly,
Bodley, godly, oddly, fondly, hotly,

motley, Otley, promptly, softly, costly,
Bromley, Swanley, wanly, strongly,
wrongly, crossly, Locksley, falsely,
corrie, Corrie, Florrie, Laurie, lorry,
MORI, quarry, Snorri, sorry, Daltrey,
paltry, palfrey, Godfrey, Conwy,
* ungodly, Macquarie, Pitlochry,
* Barbirolli, melancholy, *fait accompli*,
softly-softly, Buddy Holly, etc.

Sweet bird that shunn'st the noise of folly,
Most musical, most melancholy!
JOHN MILTON

24.6 commie, commis, mommy,
pommy, Tommy, bonny, Bonny,
Connie, Donny, Johnny, Lonnie,
Ronnie, Swanee, cockney, Hockney,
Rodney, Watney, Romney, pongy,
* bomb me, etc.

24.7 bossy, Flossie, flossy, glossy,
mossy, posse, Rossi, dropsy, popsy,
Topsy, boxy, doxy, foxy, poxy, proxy,
Roxy, schmaltzy, Rothesay, poncy,
Aussie, cossie, mossie, Ozzy, was he,
palsy, Romsey, Swansea, sloshy,
squashy, washy, bolshie, blotchy,
botchy, notchy, splotchy, conchie,
dodgy, podgy, stodgy, splodgy,
* biopsy, epoxy, * autopsy,
* orthodoxy, Pestalozzi, wishy-washy,
pedagogy, demagogy, * heterodoxy

24.8 clobber, cobber, jobber, robber,
slobber, swabber, ombre, sombre,
bopper, chopper, copper, cropper,
dropper, hopper, Hopper, Joppa,
poppa, popper, Popper, proper,
shopper, stopper, swapper, topper,
whopper, comper, romper, stomper,
RoSPA, prosper, * improper,

* stockjobber, grasshopper, sharecropper, name-dropper, wife-swapper, gobstopper, froghopper, clodhopper, show stopper, * teenybopper, window-shopper, * rob her, swap her, etc.

Pull out the stopper;
Let's have a whopper;
But get me to the church on time!
ALAN JAY LERNER

24.9 blocker, chocker, cocker, Cocker, Fokker, docker, knocker, locker, mocha, mocker, ocker, quokka, rocker, shocker, soccer, stocker, vodka, polka, conker, conquer, honker, plonker, stonker, Oscar, Tosca, Dogger, flogger, hogger, jogger, logger, slogger, brolga, Olga, Volga, conga, conger, donga, longer, stronger, Tonga, * Rioja, * doorknocker, * saltimbocca, beta-blocker, Willy Wonka, cataloguer, pettifogger, Wagga Wagga, Alba Longa, Rarotonga, * mock her, shock her, etc.

24.10 dodder, fodder, Hodder, plodder, prodder, alder, Balder, Calder, solder, blonder, Fonda, fonder, Honda, ponder, Rhondda, squander, Wanda, wander, yonder, blotter, cotter, gotta, hotter, jotter, knotter, lotta, otter, plotter, potter, Potter, rotter, spotter, squatter, swatter, swotter, totter, trotter, 'copter, prompter, doctor, proctor, crofter, softer, altar, alter, falter, halter, Malta, palter, Psalter, salter, vaulter, Volta, Walter, Costa, foster, Foster, Gloucester, hosta, roster, lobster, mobster, monster, songster, * Isolde, Deronda, transponder, pelota, ricotta, adopter, dioptre, assaulter, Gibraltar, defaulter, Minolta,

defroster, impostor, * plane spotter, train spotter, fly swatter, bogtrotter, globetrotter, witch doctor, pole-vaulter, * anaconda, *La Gioconda*, terracotta, helicopter, Teleprompter®, paternoster, herpes zoster, * shot her, lost her, etc.

Doctor Foster went to Gloucester.
NURSERY RHYME

24.11 coffer, cougher, Offa, offer, proffer, quaffer, scoffer, golfer, phosphor, bovver, hover, solver, bother, pother, Rhondda, * absolver, resolver, revolver, * windhover, * counteroffer, Hiawatha, * off her, involve her, etc.

24.12 choler, collar, dollar, holler, loller, scholar, squalor, wallah, Waller, cobbler, gobbler, hobbler, nobbler, squabbler, wobbler, Doppler, poplar, toddler, waddler, bottler, ostler, horror, cobra, copra, opera, okra, contra, rostra, Lockyer, Sonia, * corolla, Gomorrah, begorra, Bologna, * white-collar, blue-collar, * ayatollah, eurodollar, *amour-propre*, Cosa Nostra, etc.

24.13 bomber, comma, momma, dogma, dolma, Bonar, Bonner, Connor, doner, Donna, goner, gonna, honour, wanna, Bognor, Costner, * Madonna, dishonour, O'Connor, * Maradona, belladonna, prima donna, * from her, con her, etc.

24.14 crosser, dosser, fossa, Ossa, Prosser, tosser, boxer, Boxer, balsa, falser, waltzer, sponsor, rozzer, bonzer, Monza, cosher, posher, quassia, washer, Shropshire, tonsure, botcher,

gotcha, watcher, wotcher, posture,
bodger, codger, dodger, lodger, loggia,
roger, Roger, todger, * imposture,
* kick-boxer, dishwasher, bird-watcher,
* Saragossa, Barbarossa, bobbysoxer,
bottle-washer, * fox her, watch her, etc.

24.15 pollack, Pollock, rowlock,
monarch

24.16 topic, tropic, dropkick, Roddick,
Coptic, optic, Bostik®, Gnostic,
knobstick, chopstick, * Canopic,
atopic, ectopic, myopic, parodic,
anodic, cathodic, spasmodic,
rhapsodic, psalmodic, melodic,
threnodic, prosodic, aquatic, narcotic,
chaotic, nepotic, despotic, sclerotic,
erotic, necrotic, demotic, hypnotic,
exotic, quixotic, biotic, psychotic,
thrombotic, osmotic, robotic,
neurotic, synoptic, orthoptic, acrostic,
agnostic, prognostic, * macroscopic,
endoscopic, spectroscopic,
stethoscopic, presbyopic, telescopic,
periscopic, Ethiopic, thixotropic,
philanthropic, misanthropic,
gyroscopic, microscopic, isotopic,
psychotropic, lycanthropic,
horoscopic, stroboscopic, episodic,
periodic, amniotic, asymptotic,
patriotic, semiotic, idiotic, diagnostic,
orthodontic, probiotic, posthypnotic,
subaquatic, * stereoscopic,
antispasmodic, antibiotic,
antipsychotic, macrobiotic,
homoerotic, autoerotic, autohypnotic,
unpatriotic, * kaleidoscopic

24.17 strophic, trophic, Gothic,
* atrophic, dystrophic, eutrophic,
* apostrophic, catastrophic,
philosophic, Ostrogothic, Visigothic

24.18 colic, folic, frolic, rollick, choric,
Doric, Warwick, Yorick, con trick,
* shambolic, carbolic, embolic,
symbolic, systolic, hydraulic, bucolic,
amphoric, camphoric, caloric, historic,
dysphoric, pyloric, phosphoric,
euphoric, dioptric, * catabolic,
parabolic, anabolic, apostolic,
alcoholic, metabolic, melancholic,
workaholic, vitriolic, diabolic,
hyperbolic, diastolic, shopaholic,
chocoholic, cataphoric, anaphoric,
categoric, allegoric, paregoric,
metaphoric, semaphoric, meteoric,
prehistoric, hydrochloric, unhistoric,
* nonalcoholic, phantasmagoric

> **Yes it's ironic –**
> **I used to think all poets were Byronic.**
> **They're mostly as wicked as a ginless**
> **   tonic.**
> WENDY COPE

24.19 comic, cosmic, chronic, clonic,
conic, phonic, sonic, tonic, * atomic,
syndromic, Draconic, laconic, agonic,
Platonic, subtonic, sulphonic,
Slavonic, colonic, moronic, ammonic,
canonic, masonic, subsonic,
planktonic, carbonic, sardonic,
harmonic, tectonic, sermonic,
Miltonic, symphonic, synchronic,
demonic, mnemonic, bionic, ionic,
Ionic, iconic, cyclonic, Byronic, ironic,
Brythonic, pythonic, ozonic, bubonic,
Teutonic, euphonic, pneumonic,
Dubrovnik, * anatomic, agronomic,
astronomic, gastronomic, taxonomic,
macrocosmic, tragicomic,
palindromic, economic, metronomic,
ergonomic, microcosmic, autonomic,
subatomic, catatonic, gramophonic,
saxophonic, macaronic, Panasonic,

halcyonic, pandemonic, avionic,
pentatonic, megaphonic, embryonic,
telephonic, electronic, thermionic,
Freemasonic, Philharmonic,
infrasonic, histrionic, diatonic,
myotonic, isotonic, xylophonic,
microphonic, hypersonic, monotonic,
quadraphonic, homophonic,
polyphonic, ultrasonic, supertonic,
supersonic, * seriocomic,
physiognomic, uneconomic,
radiophonic, stereophonic,
animatronic, architectonic,
anticyclonic, * electrophonic,
chameleonic, Napoleonic,
* socioeconomic

24.20 fossick, coccic, toxic, logic,
* nontoxic, illogic, * virtuosic,
* pathologic, astrologic, analogic,
pedagogic, demagogic, ethnologic,
geologic, hypnagogic, mythologic,
philologic, hydrologic, horologic,
chronologic, tautologic,
* archaeologic, radiologic, embryologic,
etymologic, immunologic,
gynaecologic, climatologic

24.21 bollocks, Pollux, rowlocks,
monarchs, Trossachs

24.22 tropics, optics, chopsticks,
frolics, oryx, comics, onyx, phonics,
coccyx, * aquatics, narcotics, exotics,
robotics, neurotics, orthoptics,
agnostics, hydraulics, sardonyx,
harmonics, tectonics, mnemonics,
bionics, cryonics, * semiotics,
orthodontics, diagnostics, alcoholics,
workaholics, shopaholics, chocoholics,
agronomics, economics, ergonomics,
hydroponics, quadraphonics,
ultrasonics, supersonics, avionics,

thermionics, histrionics, electronics,
* macrobiotics, antibiotics,
animatronics, architectonics,
* macroeconomics, microeconomics,
microelectronics, etc.

24.23 lobbied, copied, dogged, Ovid,
solid, squalid, stolid, florid, forehead,
horrid, quarried, torrid, palsied,
* embodied, carotid, * photocopied,
able-bodied, disembodied, semisolid,
etc.

There was a little girl
Who had a little curl
Right in the middle of her forehead,
When she was good
She was very, very good
But when she was bad she was horrid.
HENRY WADSWORTH LONGFELLOW

24.24 clobbered, slobbered, prospered,
conquered, Goddard, nodded,
plodded, Stoddard, bonded, pondered,
squandered, wandered, blotted,
dotted, knotted, potted, pottered,
rotted, spotted, opted, prompted,
doctored, altered, faltered, halted,
malted, salted, wanted, fostered,
frosted, offered, Crockford, Rockford,
Watford, Salford, Walford, Longford,
Oxford, bothered, bollard, collared,
hollered, Lollard, pollard, onward,
honoured, * unconquered, responded,
unspotted, allotted, St Gotthard,
besotted, adopted, unprompted,
unaltered, assaulted, unsalted, exalted,
unwanted, accosted, defrosted, * time-
honoured, * unadopted, etc.

24.25 bollards, Lollards, onwards, etc.

24.26 stoppage, blockage, dockage,

lockage, socage, bondage, cottage,
pottage, wattage, Wantage, hostage,
college, knowledge, borage, forage,
Norwich, porridge, Stockbridge,
Oxbridge, Longbridge, Bromwich,
homage, Swanage, sausage,
* acknowledge, self-knowledge,
West Bromwich, * vagabondage,
telecottage

I am Master of this college:
What I don't know isn't knowledge.
H. C. BEECHING

24.27 bobble, cobble, gobble, hobble,
nobble, squabble, wobble, topple,
gospel, cockle, grockle, boggle, goggle,
joggle, toggle, woggle, dongle, Mongol,
coddle, doddle, Hoddle, model,
noddle, swaddle, toddle, twaddle,
waddle, fondle, bottle, Cottle, glottal,
mottle, throttle, wattle, costal, hostel,
offal, waffle, wrongful, watchful,
grovel, hovel, novel, brothel, coral,
laurel, Laurel, moral, Orrell, quarrel,
sorrel, Worrall, cockerel, jonquil,
doggerel, mongrel, Cottrell, dotterel,
rostral, Bovril®, Cromwell, pommel,
Rommel, Connell, Donnell, fossil,
jostle, throstle, wassail, topsail, consul,
tonsil, nozzle, schnozzle, * Chernobyl,
diphthongal, remodel, St Austell,
Balmoral, amoral, immoral,
McConnell, McDonnell, O'Connell,
O'Donnell, apostle, colossal, fore-
topsail, vice-consul, proconsul,
shemozzle, * epochal, corncockle,
hornswoggle, bluebottle,
* streptococcal, synagogal,
mollycoddle, supermodel, axolotl,
Aristotle, epiglottal, horizontal,
Pentecostal, antinovel, equinoctial,
* staphylococcal, periodontal

For I've read in many a novel that,
  unless they've souls that grovel,
Folks prefer in fact a hovel to your
  dreary marble halls.
C. S. CALVERLEY

24.28 cobbled, hobbled, nobbled,
boggled, coddled, modelled, waddled,
bottled, throttled, quarrelled, Oswald,
Donald, Ronald, jostled, sozzled,
* remodelled, Macdonald, etc.

24.29 cobbles, wobbles, cockles,
grockles, bottles, wattles, morals,
quarrels, fossils, tonsils, * apostles,
* collywobbles, supermodels,
Aristotle's, etc.

24.30 Cobham, wampum, Ockham,
Sodom, Wadham, bottom, quantum,
Swaffham, Gotham, Waltham, Colum,
column, Gollum, solemn, problem,
grogram, pogrom, Mottram, nostrum,
rostrum, Bonham, blossom, possum,
flotsam, balsam, Frodsham, dodgem,
* rock-bottom, colostrum, opossum,
* Ramsbottom, * Higginbottom,
macrocosm, microcosm, * knock 'em,
got 'em, etc.

24.31 columns, problems, doldrums,
Bonhams, dodgems, etc.

24.32 bobbin, dobbin, robin, Robin,
topspin, bodkin, Hopkin, Hodgkin,
noggin, Austen, Austin, Mostyn,
boffin, coffin, dolphin, Colin, goblin,
Joplin, poplin, Jocelyn, Corin, florin,
foreign, doctrine, sovereign, Blodwen,
Godwin, Colwyn, Olwen, Bronwen,
tocsin, toxin, rosin, * round robin,
Algonquin, Kropotkin, Godolphin,
hobgoblin, dioxin, Wisconsin,
* antitoxin, * hobblin', boxin', etc.

24.33 Alban, Balkan, falcon, Tongan,
Flodden, modern, sodden, trodden,
Cobden, Ogden, Alden, Malden,
Longden, cotton, Cotton, gotten,
rotten, Wotton, Brompton, Compton,
Crompton, Stockton, Crofton, often,
Alton, Dalton, Galton, Halton, saltern,
Walton, wanton, Boston, postern,
Oxton, Johnston, soften, Malvern,
pollen, stollen, Lachlan, Coren, Lauren,
Moran, sporran, warren, Warren,
Cochrane, squadron, cauldron,
roentgen, Roentgen, common,
stockman, frogman, Hoffman,
Hoffmann, Rothman, dolman,
Longman, Scotsman, yachtsman,
Osman, bondsman, Scotchman,
watchman, wrong 'un, Dobson,
Hobson, Robson, Thompson,
coxswain, oxen, Oxon., Dodson,
Hodson, Watson, Thomson, Johnson,
Jonson, Ronson, Swanson, Dodgson,
Hodgson, option, auction, sojourn,
* Moroccan, gyrfalcon, toboggan,
Culloden, untrodden, postmodern,
forgotten, begotten, ill-gotten,
Carshalton, autochthon, McLachlan,
uncommon, Roscommon, adoption,
concoction, decoction, * downtrodden,
guncotton, * ultramodern, Saffron
Walden, misbegotten, polycotton,
Hohenzollern, Eilean Donan, Hobson-
Jobson, readoption

**And time remembered is grief
 forgotten,
And frosts are slain and flowers
 begotten.**
ALGERNON CHARLES SWINBURNE

24.34 jocund, softened, Dollond,
Holland, dockland, Gotland, Scotland,
Osmond, auctioned, etc.

24.35 Hollands, docklands, Osmonds

24.36 Balkans, falcons, squadrons,
commons, options, * St Albans,
Moroccans, House of Commons, etc.

24.37 bobbins, robins, Robbins,
Hopkins, Watkins, Pontin's, boffins,
coffins, Collins, goblins, florins, etc.

24.38 fondant, constant, solvent,
convent, torrent, warrant, quadrant,
oddment, lodgment, wasn't,
* despondent, respondent, inconstant,
insolvent, abhorrent, remonstrant,
secondment, allotment, ballottement,
involvement, dislodgment,
* correspondent, co-respondent

24.39 Constance, solvents, Florence,
Laurence, Torrance, torrents,
monstrance, conference, oddments,
nonsense, conscience, * abhorrence, St
Lawrence, remonstrance, allotments,
no-nonsense, * correspondence,
correspondents, guilty conscience, etc.

24.40 bobbing, robbing, sobbing,
throbbing, bopping, chopping,
dropping, hopping, mopping,
popping, shopping, sopping,
swapping, topping, Wapping,
whopping, chomping, stomping,
blocking, docking, knocking, locking,
mocking, rocking, shocking,
smocking, stocking, twoccing,
bonking, honking, stonking, flogging,
hogging, jogging, logging, slogging,
snogging, nodding, plodding,
prodding, sodding, wadding, bonding,
blotting, dotting, jotting, knotting,
plotting, potting, rotting, spotting,
squatting, swotting, trotting, yachting,

opting, prompting, lofting, wafting, halting, malting, salting, vaulting, costing, frosting, coughing, offing, quaffing, scoffing, golfing, solving, frothing, lolling, hobbling, squabbling, toppling, codling, toddling, gosling, offspring, bombing, conning, donning, longing, thronging, crossing, flossing, tossing, boxing, foxing, waltzing, joshing, squashing, washing, botching, watching, bodging, dodging, lodging, * unlocking, self-locking, defrocking, responding, adopting, concocting, defrosting, evolving, revolving, involving, dissolving, prolonging, belonging, embossing, dislodging, * hobnobbing, wife-swapping, clodhopping, showstopping, bluestocking, leapfrogging, plane spotting, train spotting, globetrotting, mind-boggling, kick-boxing, brainwashing, bird-watching, * teleshopping, interlocking, pettifogging, corresponding, cybersquatting, double-crossing, etc.

In olden days a glimpse of stocking Was looked on as something shocking.
COLE PORTER

24.41 collop, dollop, lollop, scallop, trollop, Trollope, wallop, * codswallop

24.42 coppice, hospice, bodice, goddess, glottis, solstice, office, novice, Hollis, polis, solace, Wallace, Wallis, Boris, Doris, Horace, Maurice, Morris, Norris, orris, commis, promise, Dolcis, * Cornwallis, proboscis, synopsis, * epiglottis, torticollis, deoch-an-doruis

24.43 rhombus, thrombus, pompous,

coccus, locus, bronchus, Aldous, Loftus, Pontus, Qantas, jobless, topless, Toklas, godless, spotless, faultless, coxless, monstrous, songstress, Thomas, oddness, fondness, hotness, Totnes, promptness, softness, Knossos, noxious, conscious, Pontius, * Duns Scotus, Patroclus, colossus, obnoxious, subconscious, unconscious, self-conscious, * streptococcus, Pocahontas, semiconscious, unselfconscious, * staphylococcus, * swamped us, watch us, etc.

24.44 longest, strongest, blondest, promptest, provost, topmast, crossest, falsest, poshest, etc.

24.45 coppiced, stockist, modest, sophist, solaced, florist, forest, Forrest, promised, honest, * immodest, deforest, reforest, dishonest, * rainforest, * orthodontist

24.46 foppish, snobbish, yobbish, blockish, doggish, hoggish, Scottish, hottish, offish, toffish, rockfish, stockfish, dogfish, codfish, polish, donnish, * standoffish, abolish, demolish, astonish, admonish, * spit and polish

24.47 polished, * abolished, unpolished, demolished, astonished, admonished

24.48 Robert, nobbut, Talbot, Osbert, boggart, yogurt, Stoddart, Moffatt, Montfort, chocolate, stalwart, concert, * Port Talbot, de Montfort

24.49 Cobbett, gobbet, hobbit, obit, moppet, poppet, cockpit, Crockett,

docket, locket, pocket, rocket, socket,
sprocket, tomtit, profit, prophet, soffit,
Colet, Smollett, wallet, goblet, droplet,
omelette, floret, godwit, comet,
Gromit, grommet, vomit, bonnet,
sonnet, cosset, posset, whatsit,
Consett, closet, posit, crotchet,
* Mahomet, deposit, * pickpocket,
skyrocket, sunbonnet, * retrorocket,
* drop it, knock it, etc.

All these are vile. But viler
Wordsworth's sonnet
On Dover. Dover! Who could write
upon it?
JOHN KEATS

24.50 Toxteth, Bosworth, Wandsworth,
Monmouth, * Merioneth

24.51 octave, costive, olive, * adoptive,
Palmolive®, responsive,
* unresponsive

24.52 Bobby's, hobbies, zombies,
copies, poppies, choccies, jockeys,
Rockies, donkeys, bodies, squaddies,
Frosties, toffees, follies, Molly's,
trolleys, lorries, commies, cockneys,
Aussies, falsies, * synopses, etc.

24.53 robbers, poppers, shoppers,
jodhpurs, rompers, knockers,
mockers, rockers, bonkers, conkers,
Yonkers, joggers, plodders, squatters,
trotters, Walters, Foster's, offers,
dollars, scholars, horrors, bombers,
commas, Connors, honours, bosses,
crosses, boxes, foxes, washers,
blotches, notches, watches, Hodges,
lodgers, Rodgers, Rogers, splodges,
* galoshes, * wife-swappers,
gobstoppers, plane spotters, train

spotters, Cockfosters,
Weightwatchers®, bird-watchers,
* teenyboppers, knickerbockers, beta-
blockers, helicopters, etc.

24.54 Lockerbie, wallaby, Ponsonby,
monarchy, Lombardy, property,
Docherty, Fogarty, poverty, Cromarty,
novelty, warranty, Dorothy, Mobberley,
sombrely, Stromboli, properly,
broccoli, Offaly, wrongfully, scholarly,
morally, Connolly, Donnelly, probably,
horribly, honourably, possibly,
moderately, constantly, Bottomley,
solemnly, rottenly, commonly,
faultlessly, consciously, jobbery,
robbery, snobbery, yobbery, Dogberry,
Fosbury, coppery, foppery, crockery,
mockery, rockery, doddery, quandary,
lottery, Ottery, pottery, tottery,
psaltery, contrary, colliery, Connery,
swannery, glossary, Roddenberry,
Conakry, offertory, oratory, Coventry,
voluntary, commentary, promontory,
Oswestry, monastery, hostelry,
falconry, coronary, colloquy, obloquy,
sodomy, Ptolemy, Albany, Alderney,
botany, cottony, Zoffany, colony,
Wallasey, constancy, solvency,
* endoscopy, spectroscopy,
microscopy, horoscopy, Andromache,
chiropody, topography, photography,
stenography, mammography,
cartography, ethnography, geography,
discography, cryptography,
demography, filmography, biography,
typography, holography, orthography,
pornography, apostrophe, theosophy,
philosophy, allopathy, hydropathy,
monopoly, Monopoly®, Thermopylae,
improperly, duopoly, immorally,
anomaly, colossally, improbably,
demonstrably, impossibly, responsibly,

immoderately, despondently,
uncommonly, subconsciously,
unconsciously, self-consciously,
corollary, Montgomery, derogatory,
bardolatry, idolatry, laboratory,
exploratory, involuntary, monogamy,
phlebotomy, dichotomy, lobotomy,
colostomy, agronomy, astronomy,
gastronomy, taxonomy, economy,
autonomy, mahogany, cosmogony,
monotony, cacophony, theophany,
quadraphony, homophony,
controversy, hypocrisy, democracy,
autocracy, bureaucracy, plutocracy,
apostasy, despondency, inconstancy,
insolvency, * laparoscopy,
hagiography, radiography,
lexicography, crystallography,
bibliography, iconography,
choreography, chromatography,
oceanography, naturopathy,
osteopathy, homeopathy, horizontally,
irresponsibly, demagoguery,
pettifoggery, interrogatory, hagiolatry,
Mariolatry, demonolatry, tracheotomy,
physiognomy, Deuteronomy,
stereophony, aristocracy, meritocracy,
anthropophagy, * encephalopathy,
* cinematography, etc.

virology, seismology, oncology,
ontology, horology, cosmology,
doxology, tautology, morphology,
neurology, urology, zoology, ufology,
* anthropology, campanology,
pharmacology, archaeology,
cardiology, Mariology, radiology,
phraseology, escapology,
methodology, eschatology,
entomology, embryology, etymology,
gerontology, dermatology,
herpetology, terminology,
haematology, demonology,
reflexology, aetiology, speleology,
semiology, Egyptology, ichthyology,
physiology, criminology,
immunology, climatology,
Scientology, ideology, gynaecology,
ophthalmology, volcanology,
toxicology, ornithology, sociology,
numerology, musicology,
* bacteriology, epistemology,
phenomenology, * meteorology,
dendrochronology, dialectology,
nanotechnology, biotechnology,
parasitology, endocrinology,
microbiology, parapsychology,
palaeontology, * epidemiology,
anaesthesiology

**There was an old man of Thermopylae,
Who never did anything properly.**
Edward Lear

**And therefore it chimes with the
word's etymology
That the sons of Apollo are great on
apology.**
Oliver Wendell Holmes

24.55 ology, * apology, pathology,
astrology, chronology, phonology,
scatology, graphology, anthology,
psephology, necrology, technology,
ethnology, sexology, geology, theology,
ecology, kidology, histology,
mythology, philology, phrenology,
hymnology, biology, bryology,
mycology, psychology, cytology,

24.56 gossipy, colicky, holiday,
comedy, oddity, quantity, jollity,
polity, quality, comity, falsity,
crotchety, modesty, honesty, sloppily,
stockily, foggily, groggily, bodily,
shoddily, frostily, homily, bossily,
topically, optically, comically,

logically, prodigally, doggedly, solidly, modestly, honestly, shockingly, longingly, snobbishly, dromedary, coquetry, rocketry, solitary, sophistry, forestry, orangery, dominie, hominy, progeny, Odyssey, prophecy, policy, Morrissey, porridgy, prodigy, * commodity, equality, frivolity, sonority, sorority, majority, priority, minority, authority, ferocity, atrocity, verbosity, precocity, viscosity, velocity, pomposity, monstrosity, porosity, dishonesty, immodesty, toxophily, spasmodically, methodically, chaotically, erotically, hypnotically, symbolically, hydraulically, rhetorically, historically, laconically, sardonically, ironically, illogically, dishonestly, apothecary, chronometry, geometry, optometry, admonitory, premonitory, suppository, depository, repository, expository, synonymy, metonymy, Mnemosyne, misogyny, geodesy, theodicy, * tragicomedy, inequality, seniority, mediocrity, grandiosity, animosity, generosity, preciosity, reciprocity, virtuosity, sinuosity, curiosity, luminosity, microscopically, periodically, patriotically, idiotically, catastrophically, philosophically, diabolically, categorically, metaphorically, anatomically, astronomically, ergonomically, economically, histrionically, pathologically, technologically, geologically, theologically, ecologically, biologically, psychologically, chronologically, correspondingly, trigonometry, * inferiority, superiority, impetuosity, voluminosity, * archaeologically, etymologically, physiologically, ideologically, etc.

24.57 walloper, onager, colander, Hollander, orator, Golgotha, Coppola, gospeller, modeller, gondola, hosteller, groveller, quarreller, opera, conqueror, dodderer, squanderer, wanderer, cholera, posturer, Ottawa, gossamer, monomer, softener, coroner, commoner, Gloucestershire, Oxfordshire, onager, swastika, frolicker, Honecker, Monica, moniker, Honegger, Florida, provender, monitor, Rossiter, chorister, forester, Forester, Rochester, Potiphar, conifer, Oliver, chronicler, polymer, Modena, foreigner, officer, promiser, polisher, Warwickshire, cottager, forager, Bollinger, porringer, Joshua, Yoruba, globular, lobular, copula, popular, ocular, jocular, modular, nodular, scrofula, consular, * Cadwallader, idolater, automata, photographer, stenographer, cartographer, geographer, cryptographer, biographer, typographer, pornographer, phylloxera, astronomer, gastronomer, horologer, astrologer, sockdologer, erotica, exotica, majolica, nux vomica, japonica, Salonika, Veronica, harmonica, Andromeda, Hippolyta, barometer, thermometer, chronometer, manometer, clapometer, tachometer, planometer, gasometer, spectrometer, geometer, speedometer, pedometer, kilometre, clinometer, swingometer, pyrometer, mileometer, cyclometer, micrometer, micrometre, hygrometer, hydrometer, odometer, optometer, Comptometer®, photometer, Uttoxeter, compositor, depositor, expositor, Apocrypha, gypsophila, Hiroshima, phenomena, abolisher, demolisher, unpopular, binocular, monocular, * Hagiographa,

hagiographer, radiographer,
lexicographer, bibliographer,
choreographer, oceanographer,
Thessalonica, tacheometer,
anemometer, pluviometer, ovipositor,
Herzegovina, interlocutor,
* cinematographer, historiographer

24.58 choppier, copier, floppier,
sloppier, soppier, cockier, rockier,
stockier, boggier, foggier, groggier,
shoddier, dottier, grottier, pottier,
spottier, loftier, saltier, frostier, Ostia,
frothier, collier, jollier, volleyer,
cochlea, cochlear, costlier, quarrier,
sorrier, warrior, Austria, bonnier,
Bothnia, Bosnia, dossier, bossier,
glossier, squashier, blotchier, dodgier,
podgier, stodgier, * crocosmia,
anosmia, insomnia, anoxia, hypoxia,
* photocopier, hypochondria,
mitochondria, etc.

24.59 warranted, pocketed, rocketed,
profited, forested, vomited, cosseted,
closeted, * unwarranted, deposited,
deforested, reforested

24.60 propertied, hominid

24.61 probable, stoppable, lockable,
solvable, horrible, operable,
comparable, honourable, possible,
squashable, washable, watchable,
obstacle, coracle, oracle, monocle,
cockerel, doggerel, doctoral, postural,
coronal, optional, bronchial, topical,
tropical, optical, follicle, comical,
chronicle, conical, ossicle, dropsical,
Popsicle®, logical, prodigal, hospital,
optimal, proximal, nominal, soluble,
voluble, conjugal, communal,
* improbable, unstoppable,

unshockable, unsolvable, resolvable,
inoperable, incomparable,
demonstrable, dishonourable,
impossible, responsible, unwatchable,
McGonagall, hebdomadal,
postdoctoral, orthogonal, subtropical,
methodical, symbolical, rhetorical,
historical, canonical, ironical, illogical,
apocryphal, abdominal, prenominal,
phenomenal, binominal, pronominal,
dissoluble, insoluble, * unresolvable,
irresponsible, microscopical,
semitropical, periodical,
philosophical, theosophical,
diabolical, categorical, allegorical,
metaphorical, oratorical, anatomical,
astronomical, gastronomical,
economical, paradoxical, pedagogical,
demagogical, scatological,
pathological, analogical, astrological,
gastrological, technological,
ethnological, geological, theological,
ecological, histological, mythological,
philological, biological, psychological,
seismological, topological,
homological, cosmological,
chronological, oncological,
horological, tautological,
morphological, zoological,
phonological, neurological, urological,
* uneconomical, anthropological,
pharmacological, archaeological,
phraseological, methodological,
entomological, embryological,
etymological, dermatological,
terminological, aetiological,
genealogical, mineralogical,
physiological, criminological,
immunological, ideological,
gynaecological, climatological,
ophthalmological, toxicological,
nonbiological, ornithological,
sociological, numerological,

* bacteriological, * meteorological, microbiological

I know the kings of England, and I
   quote the fights historical,
From Marathon to Waterloo, in order
   categorical.
W. S. GILBERT

24.62 obstacles, follicles, Chronicles, hospitals, * canonicals, etc.

24.63 poppadom, Rotherham, Tottenham, bothersome, quarrelsome, modicum, optimum, Nottingham, Altrincham, Walsingham, frolicsome

24.64 octagon, nonagon, Todmorden, Alderton, Salterton, Gordonstoun, colophon, Donovan, Jonathan, alderman, ottoman, Ottoman, Solomon, Alderson, Donaldson, Robertson, collagen, congressman, Bodleian, Austrian, Bosnian, Ossian, Corrigan, Oregon, oppidan, Honiton, Boddington, Waddington, Donington, Norrington, Warrington, Washington, Coniston, quarryman, Orangeman, Groningen, Morrison, Robinson, Collinson, Tomlinson, orison, oxygen, * automaton, Algonquian, Colossian, phenomenon, diocesan, * metropolitan, Neapolitan, cosmopolitan

24.65 Rosamund, moribund, orotund

24.66 Jonathan's, Austrians, Bosnians, orisons, * Colossians, etc.

24.67 combatant, somnolent, nonchalant, tolerant, operant, consonant, toxicant, congregant, confident, provident, Occident, oxidant, competent, Protestant, Oliphant, consequent, condiment, complement, compliment, continent, Continent, dominant, prominent, cognizant, congruent, occupant, opulent, flocculent, postulant, document, monument, * preponderant, intolerant, emollient, intoxicant, self-confident, improvident, incompetent, concomitant, inconsequent, embodiment, impoverishment, astonishment, admonishment, acknowledgment, subcontinent, incontinent, subdominant, predominant, incognizant, emolument, * overconfident, antioxidant, disembodiment

24.68 somnolence, nonchalance, conference, tolerance, consonants, confidence, providence, competence, Protestants, consequence, compliments, continence, provenance, dominance, prominence, cognizance, confluence, congruence, opulence, documents, * preponderance, intolerance, self-confidence, improvidence, incompetence, inconsequence, acknowledgments, incontinence, predominance, reconnaissance, incognizance, * teleconference, overconfidence, etc.

24.69 lolloping, walloping, bollocking, fosterling, hostelling, clobbering, conquering, doddering, pondering, wandering, offering, bothering, posturing, Godalming, frolicking, rollicking, coppicing, promising, cottaging, * unpromising

24.70 octopus, obolus, collarless,

bottomless, Bosporus, prosperous, ponderous, Bosphorus, phosphorous, phosphorus, dolorous, onerous, sonorous, commonness, consciousness, obvious, osseous, Roscius, omnibus, solidus, obelus, choppiness, sloppiness, cockiness, ominous, doggedness, snobbishness, yobbishness, nocuous, congruous, populace, populous, modulus, scrofulous, Romulus, posthumous, * diplodocus, sarcophagus, oesophagus, homologous, tautologous, Herodotus, discobolus, anomalous, preposterous, rhinoceros, idolatrous, monogamous, dichotomous, autonomous, monotonous, cacophonous, homophonous, autochthonous, homogenous, subconsciousness, unconsciousness, self-consciousness, Autolycus, Hippolytus, Theocritus, Democritus, Herophilus, Theophilus, anonymous, antonymous, eponymous, synonymous, Hieronymus, euonymus, pseudonymous, androgynous, endogenous, exogenous, erogenous, misogynous, hydrogenous, nitrogenous, innocuous, incongruous, convolvulus, * Areopagus, adipocerous, hippopotamus, acidophilus, etc.

Hogamus, higamous
Man is polygamous
Higamus, hogamous
Woman monogamous.
WILLIAM JAMES

24.71 choppiest, floppiest, sloppiest, soppiest, cockiest, rockiest, stockiest, boggiest, foggiest, groggiest, shoddiest, dottiest, grottiest, pottiest, spottiest, loftiest, saltiest, frostiest, frothiest, jolliest, costliest, sorriest, bonniest, bossiest, glossiest, squashiest, blotchiest, dodgiest, podgiest, stodgiest, etc.

24.72 monarchist, novelist, moralist, modernist, botanist, colonist, columnist, copyist, lobbyist, Trotskyist, optimist, populist, oculist, communist, * chiropodist, economist, *Economist*, saxophonist, xylophonist, apologist, pathologist, graphologist, technologist, ethnologist, sexologist, geologist, ecologist, philologist, biologist, psychologist, horologist, neurologist, zoologist, ufologist, optometrist, Soroptimist, misogynist, * lepidopterist, anthropologist, campanologist, pharmacologist, archaeologist, cardiologist, radiologist, escapologist, entomologist, etymologist, dermatologist, reflexologist, Egyptologist, physiologist, Scientologist, gynaecologist, ophthalmologist, ornithologist, sociologist, musicologist, * bacteriologist, * endocrinologist, microbiologist, palaeontologist

24.73 collocate, chocolate, moderate, doctorate, obdurate, consummate, coronet, laureate, proximate, obstinate, postulate, consulate, quadruplet, * immoderate, conglomerate, approximate, innominate, * Poet Laureate

24.74 wanderers, choristers, foreigners, Joshua's, * photographers, astrologers, binoculars, etc.

24.75 wallabies, properties, novelties,

robberies, Potteries, colonies, oddities, qualities, obsequies, prophecies, policies, * apostrophes, apologies, anthologies, commodities, minorities, authorities, etc.

24.76 optionally, optimally, nominally, popularly, contumely, communally, tolerably, honourably, profitably, knowledgeably, obstinately, competently, consequently, prominently, positively, promisingly, prosperously, ponderously, obviously, ominously, posthumously, honorary, commissary, promissory, ossuary, obduracy, profligacy, obstinacy, occupancy, * abdominally, phenomenally, intolerably,

abominably, incorrigibly, disconsolately, approximately, predominantly, provocatively, pejoratively, astonishingly, monotonously, preposterously, anonymously, incongruously, etc.

24.77 warrantable, comparable, conquerable, alterable, tolerable, honourable, conscionable, hospitable, profitable, knowledgeable, * unwarrantable, incomparable, unconquerable, imponderable, unalterable, intolerable, dishonourable, unconscionable, inhospitable, unprofitable, indomitable, abominable, incorrigible

-or-

The rhymes in this section have the 'or' sound of ford *and* daughter *as their main or final vowel sound.*

25.1 aw, awe, boar, Boer, Bohr, bore, braw, caw, chore, claw, cor, core, corps, craw, door, draw, drawer, faugh, flaw, floor, for, fore, four, gnaw, gore, Gore, haw, hoar, jaw, law, lor', lore, maw, moor, Moor, Moore, more, nor, o'er, oar, or, ore, paw, poor, pore, pour, pshaw, raw, roar, saw, score, Shaw, shore, slaw, snore, soar, sore, spoor, spore, squaw, store, straw, sure, swore, tau, taw, thaw, Thor, tor, tore, war, Waugh, whore, wore, yaw, yore, your, you're

Stately as a galleon, I sail across the floor,
Doing the Military Two-step, as in the days of yore.
JOYCE GRENFELL

25.2 Gabor, rapport, macaw, Tagore, adore, afore, guffaw, Lahore, abhor, galore, unmoor, tussore, ashore, assure, next door, señor, Dior, rebore, heehaw, redraw, prewar, before, restore, deplore, implore, explore, withdraw, signor, ignore, ensure, inshore, insure, Mysore, offshore, onshore, forbore, foreswore, foresaw, outpour, prowar, postwar, unsure, *du jour,* * esprit de corps, toreador, plesiosaur, ichthyosaur, George Bernard Shaw, father-in-law, daughter-in-law, brother-in-law, mother-in-law, sister-in-law, Ollerenshaw, underinsure

25.3 trapdoor, jackdaw, Blackmore, Nassau, hacksaw, Bradshaw, handsaw, Fanshawe, hardcore, Dartmoor, therefore, wherefore, décor, claymore, chain saw, emptor, centaur, mentor, stentor, Mentmore, Exmoor, Sedgemoor, bedstraw, bedsore, fret saw, Eeyore, Dior, threescore, fetor, Seymour, Timor, Esau, seesaw, seashore, indoor, ripsaw, whipsaw, jigsaw, rickshaw, scrimshaw, bylaw, Whitelaw, eyesore, condor, Choctaw, Roquefort, cocksure, lockjaw, Haw-Haw, forepaw, pawpaw, Cawnpore, fourscore, Broadmoor, Hawksmoor, foreshore, downpour, southpaw, outdoor, outlaw, ground floor, folklore, coleslaw, Cold War, cold sore, drugstore, uproar, bookstore, footsore, smoothbore, dewclaw

25.4 matador, Salvador, Labrador, battledore, guarantor, Bangalore, antiwar, Aviemore, Barrymore, Arkansas, carnivore, theretofore, eighty-four, Ecuador, metaphor, semaphore, evermore, nevermore, stegosaur, pterosaur, Melchior, hellebore, petit four, twenty-four,

anymore, Elsinore, furthermore,
thermidor, thirty-four, herbivore,
heretofore, Theodore, stevedore,
reassure, Singapore, picador, pinafore,
interwar, sycamore, Michelmore,
Chickasaw, Wichita, fifty-four, sixty-
four, Minotaur, either-or, cyberwar,
dinosaur, ninety-four, commodore,
warrantor, common-law, sophomore,
brontosaur, corridor, omnivore, door-
to-door, mortgagor, forty-four,
Baltimore, overawe, overdraw, oversaw,
underscore, underfloor, tug-of-war,
usquebaugh, *Ruddigore*, son-in-law,
superstore, louis d'or, humidor, * San
Salvador, El Salvador, tyrannosaur,
forevermore, excelsior, insectivore,
conquistador, hereinbefore,
Securicor®

**Take thy beak from out my heart, and
    take thy form from off my door!
Quoth the Raven, 'Nevermore'.**
EDGAR ALLAN POE

25.5 daub, orb, * absorb, adsorb,
bedaub, * reabsorb

25.6 auk, balk, baulk, caulk, chalk,
cork, Cork, dork, fork, gawk, hawk,
Hawke, nork, orc, pork, squawk, stalk,
stork, talk, torc, torque, walk, York,
* uncork, Dundalk, New York,
* catwalk, hayfork, jaywalk, spacewalk,
pep talk, sweet-talk, beanstalk,
sleepwalk, pitchfork, nighthawk,
sidewalk, shoptalk, crosstalk, goshawk,
small talk, boardwalk, Mohawk,
ropewalk, uptalk, newshawk,
* tomahawk, sparrowhawk, tuning fork

25.7 Fawkes, forks, hawks, Hawks,
lawks, squawks, talks, etc.

25.8 porch, scorch, torch, * debauch,
* blowtorch

25.9 baud, bawd, board, bored, broad,
cawed, chord, Claude, clawed, cord,
fjord, flawed, floored, ford, Ford,
fraud, Gawd, gnawed, gored, hoard,
horde, laud, lord, Lord, Maud,
moored, oared, pawed, poured, roared,
scored, snored, soared, stored, sward,
sword, thawed, ward, * aboard, accord,
adored, afford, guffawed, abhorred,
applaud, abroad, maraud, award,
toward, assured, record, restored,
defraud, milord, deplored, implored,
explored, reward, ignored, ensured,
insured, * blackboard, dashboard,
splashboard, landlord, starboard,
cardboard, hardboard, dartboard,
draughtboard, bargeboard, skateboard,
pasteboard, sailboard, tailboard,
pegboard, breadboard, headboard,
chessboard, record, surfboard,
freeboard, keyboard, leeboard,
seaboard, cheeseboard, greensward,
chipboard, clipboard, shipboard,
billboard, inboard, springboard,
switchboard, ripcord, whipcord,
discord, sideboard, whiteboard,
signboard, blockboard, washboard,
concord, Concorde, floorboard,
scoreboard, warlord, broadsword,
outboard, outlawed, snowboard,
duckboard, footboard, * clapperboard,
clavichord, plasterboard, harpsichord,
scraperboard, tape-record,
chequerboard, centreboard,
weatherboard, skirting board,
leaderboard, Ouija board®,
needlecord, reassured, fingerboard,
disaccord, spinal cord, diving board,
bodyboard, mortarboard,
smorgasbord, storyboard, overawed,

overboard, overlord, notice board, motherboard, underscored, untoward, unexplored, uninsured, * ironing board, underinsured

Mine eyes have seen the glory of the coming of the Lord:
He is trampling out the vintage where the grapes of wrath are stored;
H hath loosed the fateful lightning of his terrible swift sword:
His truth is marching on.
JULIA WARD HOWE

25.10 boards, Claude's, cords, hordes, Lord's, wards, * towards, defrauds, * keyboards, sideboards, floorboards, * Norfolk Broads, House of Lords, vocal cords, * Madame Tussauds, etc.

25.11 Corfe, dwarf, morph, orfe, Orff, swarf, wharf, * Waldorf, * endomorph, ectomorph, mesomorph, polymorph, Düsseldorf

25.12 Borg, morgue, * Cherbourg, cyborg, * Helsingborg, Swedenborg

25.13 forge, George, gorge, * St George, engorge, disgorge

25.14 all, awl, ball, bawl, brawl, call, caul, crawl, drawl, fall, gall, Gaul, hall, haul, mall, maul, pall, Paul, Saul, scrawl, shawl, small, sprawl, squall, stall, tall, thrall, trawl, wall, waul, yawl, * appal, Bacall, Bengal, Nepal, recall, de Gaulle, install, befall, withal, enthral, Porthcawl, forestall, town hall, * blackball, handball, catcall, bradawl, landfall, pratfall, Blackwall, catch-all, fastball, dancehall, hairball, paintball, baseball, rainfall, netball, Threlfall,

meatball, sleazeball, keelhaul, pinball, windfall, pitfall, guildhall, Milwall, fireball, firewall, eyeball, highball, Naipaul, nightfall, Whitehall, sidewall, oddball, softball, mothball, Rockall, long-haul, Vauxhall, shortfall, short-haul, Cornwall, Walsall, outfall, Southall, downfall, outhaul, downhaul, no-ball, snowball, holdall, snowfall, stonewall, Rosewall, puffball, punchball, Nuttall, thumbstall, pub crawl, football, Goodall, bookstall, footfall, screwball, goofball, * trackerball, cannonball, caterwaul, Tattersall, carryall, basketball, Aspinwall, Charles de Gaulle, Senegal, market stall, wherewithal, evenfall, free-for-all, reinstall, fingerstall, disenthral, off-the-wall, Montreal, volleyball, Donegal, waterfall, wall-to-wall, warts and all, all in all, rollerball, overhaul, overall, know-it-all, butterball, coverall, * belle of the ball, Vincent de Paul

Mirror, mirror on the wall,
Who is the fairest of them all?
JACOB & WILHELM GRIMM

25.15 auld, bald, called, scald, sprawled, stalled, walled, * appalled, recalled, installed, enthralled, forestalled, * blackballed, keelhauled, piebald, snowballed, so-called, close-hauled, skewbald, * caterwauled, Archibald, Theobald, reinstalled, disenthralled, overhauled, Cumbernauld, etc.

25.16 false, waltz

25.17 fault, Galt, halt, malt, salt, SALT, vault, Walt, * assault, default, exalt,

* asphalt, Hainault, basalt, cobalt, pole vault, * somersault

25.18 salts, schmaltz, vaults, etc.

25.19 balls, calls, crawls, falls, mauls, smalls, stalls, walls, Walls, etc.

25.20 Baum, corm, dorm, form, haulm, Maugham, norm, Norm, Orme, shawm, storm, swarm, warm, * perform, conform, aswarm, transform, re-form, deform, reform, inform, * sandstorm, landform, platform, barnstorm, Cairngorm, hailstorm, brainstorm, rainstorm, waveform, windstorm, firestorm, snowstorm, lukewarm, * gasiform, Benidorm, misinform, chloroform, Cominform, outperform, oviform, thunderstorm, multiform, spongiform, uniform, cuneiform, cruciform

25.21 formed, stormed, swarmed, warmed, * unformed, unwarmed, malformed, transformed, deformed, reformed, informed, * well-informed, ill-informed, uninformed, uniformed, etc.

25.22 awn, Bjorn, born, borne, bourn, Braun, brawn, corn, dawn, Dawn, drawn, faun, fawn, horn, Horne, lawn, lorn, morn, mourn, Mourne, pawn, porn, prawn, Quorn®, sawn, scorn, Sean, shorn, SORN, spawn, sworn, thorn, torn, Vaughan, warn, Warne, worn, yawn, * suborn, unborn, adorn, Siobhan, forlorn, unworn, Cape Horn, well-worn, reborn, dehorn, redrawn, inborn, withdrawn, indrawn, forborne, forewarn, forsworn, outworn, * blackthorn, alphorn, Langhorne,

saxhorn, ramshorn, airborne, chairborne, careworn, Ayckbourn, baseborn, acorn, Melbourne, Leghorn, firstborn, earthborn, freeborn, seaborne, Eastbourne, sweetcorn, greenhorn, stillborn, inkhorn, stinkhorn, Bighorn, highborn, Glyndebourne, tricorn, timeworn, Osborne, Osbourne, frogspawn, popcorn, foghorn, longhorn, shopworn, war-torn, hawthorn, Hawthorne, Rawsthorne, shorthorn, lowborn, Runcorn, buckthorn, crumhorn, lovelorn, newborn, shoehorn, * Matterhorn, alpenhorn, Capricorn, barleycorn, weatherworn, peppercorn, leprechaun, winterbourne, Sittingbourne, waterborne, overdrawn, flugelhorn, unicorn

This is the farmer sowing his corn,
That kept the cock that crowed in the
**   morn,**
That waked the priest all shaven and
**   shorn,**
That married the man all tattered and
**   torn,**
That kissed the maiden all forlorn,
That milked the cow with the crumpled
**   horn.**
NURSERY RHYME

25.23 graunch, haunch, launch, paunch, staunch, * relaunch

25.24 dawned, horned, mourned, pawned, scorned, * suborned, adorned, dehorned, forewarned, * unadorned, etc.

25.25 chaunt, daunt, flaunt, gaunt, haunt, jaunt, taunt, vaunt, * avaunt

25.26 Corp., gawp, Thorpe, warp,
* Scunthorpe

25.27 corpse, gawps, warps,
* Cleethorpes

25.28 coarse, course, force, gorse,
hoarse, horse, Morse, Norse, sauce,
source, * perforce, unhorse, recourse,
endorse, enforce, divorce, remorse,
resource, outsource, * dampcourse,
packhorse, carthorse, racecourse, gale
force, drayhorse, racehorse, workforce,
workhorse, seahorse, discourse,
concourse, forecourse, sawhorse,
warhorse, clotheshorse, downforce,
* Ladislaus, Stanislaus, reinforce,
intercourse, Wilberforce, hobbyhorse,
rocking horse, watercourse, *tour de
force*, vaulting horse, Trojan horse

**I know two things about the horse
And one of them is rather coarse.**
NAOMI ROYDE-SMITH

25.29 coursed, forced, horst, sourced,
* unforced, unhorsed, endorsed,
enforced, divorced, exhaust,
outsourced, * holocaust, reinforced,
hypocaust, unenforced

25.30 borsch, Porsche

25.31 aught, bought, brought, caught,
court, fort, fought, fraught, Mort,
naught, nought, ought, port, quart,
short, snort, sort, sought, sport,
taught, taut, thought, thwart, tort,
torte, wart, wrought, * abort, support,
comport, contort, untaught, cavort,
athwart, assort, consort, unsought,
transport, hard-fought, self-taught,
purport, rethought, re-sort, deport,

report, import, disport, export, escort,
retort, distort, extort, methought,
distraught, besought, resort, exhort,
* transport, carport, airport, Fairport,
spaceport, export, escort,.
dreadnought, seaport, import,
Bridgeport, hillfort, Stockport,
Gosport, onslaught, Connaught,
consort, forecourt, lawcourt,
forethought, Southport, spoilsport,
Coalport, Beaufort, cohort, Newport,
* aforethought, * Davenport,
Hampton Court, astronaut, alphasort,
Agincourt, afterthought, Argonaut,
aeronaut, Devonport, heliport,
teleport, reimport, re-export, Inns of
Court, misreport, life-support,
hoverport, cosmonaut, overwrought,
juggernaut, worrywart

25.32 courts, forts, noughts, orts, ports,
quartz, Schwartz, shorts, sorts, sports,
thoughts, warts, * aborts, supports,
cavorts, Cinque Ports, imports,
exports, retorts, distorts, * astronauts,
Argonauts, second thoughts, winter
sports, water sports, juggernauts,
undershorts, etc.

25.33 forth, Forth, fourth, north, swath,
* henceforth, thenceforth,
* Carnforth, Seaforth, Bridgnorth,
* back and forth, Ampleforth,
Perranporth

25.34 dwarves, wharves

25.35 cause, chores, clause, claws,
doors, Dors, drawers, floors, gauze,
hawse, jaws, *Jaws*, laws, moors, oars,
pause, paws, shores, stores, tawse,
wars, Waugh's, whores, yaws, yours,
* adores, applause, Azores, indoors,

implores, ignores, outdoors, outpours, plus-fours, * trapdoors, jackdaws, jackstraws, hacksaws, * matadors, Santa Claus, metaphors, menopause, out of doors, * Louis Quatorze

With first-rate sherry flowing into
   second-rate whores,
And third-rate conversation without
   one single pause:
Just like a young couple
Between the wars.
WILLIAM PLOMER

26.1 corbie, Corby, dauby, Formby, Hornby, Moresby, chalky, corky, gawky, Gorky, pawky, porky, stalky, talkie, Yorkie, corgi, porgy, bawdy, gaudy, Geordie, lordy, Saudi, Aldi, baldy, Caldy, Maundy, Corti, forty, haughty, naughty, shorty, sortie, sporty, warty, balti, faulty, Fawlty, malty, salty, flaunty, jaunty, Morphy, wharfie, swarthy, Haughey, Cawley, Chorley, Crawley, Fawley, Morley, Pauli, poorly, Raleigh, scrawly, squally, sorely, surely, Audley, broadly, lordly, baldly, courtly, portly, shortly, tautly, fourthly, Gormley, warmly, Thornley, coarsely, hoarsely, falsely, Maudsley, staunchly, Corey, dory, Florey, fury, glory, gory, hoary, lory, MORI, Rory, storey, story, Tory, Aubrey, strawberry, Audrey, Cawdrey, bawdry, tawdry, Baldry, laundry, Hawtrey, Daltrey, paltry, palfrey, dormie, stormy, brawny, corny, horny, scrawny, tawny, thorny, tourney, Orkney, Courtney, Dorsey, Glauce, gorsy, horsey, saucy, torsi, Orczy, schmaltzy, gauzy, ballsy, palsy, paunchy, raunchy, orgy, Georgie, * Treorchy, Milwaukee, Sikorsky, Mussorgsky, cum laude, Kirkcaldy,

Grimaldi, Macaulay, Bengali, Nepali, unsurely, forlornly, Maggiore, satori, vainglory, tandoori, John Dory, furore, Trelawney, * centaury, clerestory, blindstorey, outlawry, * walkie-talkie, garibaldi, Garibaldi, pianoforte, creepy-crawly, uniformly, cacciatore, yakitori, a priori, *West Side Story*, con amore, Montessori, Tobermory, hunky-dory, multistorey, * memento mori, a fortiori, * Alpha Centauri, mulligatawny, etc.

26.2 dauber, Zorba, gawper, pauper, torpor, * absorber, Micawber, * shock absorber, * daub her, absorb her, etc.

26.3 Chalker, corker, hawker, Lorca, orca, porker, squawker, stalker, talker, walker, Walker, auger, augur, * Majorca, Minorca, New Yorker, * jaywalker, deerstalker, sleepwalker, streetwalker, * kwashiorkor, baby-walker, * stalk her, sweet-talk her, etc.

26.4 boarder, border, broader, hoarder, Korda, Lauder, order, warder, alder, balder, Balder, Calder, launder, maunder, daughter, mortar, oughta, porter, Porter, quarter, shorter, slaughter, snorter, sorter, tauter, torte, water, altar, alter, falter, halter, Malta, palter, Psalter, salter, vaulter, Walter, flaunter, gaunter, saunter, taunter, vaunter, Forster, fraudster, * marauder, reorder, defrauder, recorder, disorder, tall order, suborder, supporter, transporter, aorta, three-quarter, reporter, importer, exporter, extorter, hot water, assaulter, Gibraltar, defaulter, * camcorder, mail order, sailboarder, skateboarder, keyboarder, backwater,

granddaughter, manslaughter,
breakwater, rainwater, meltwater,
stepdaughter, freshwater, shearwater,
sea water, Piesporter, Drinkwater,
ripsnorter, dishwater, ditchwater,
Bridgwater, firewater, tidewater,
hindquarter, goddaughter, colporteur,
forequarter, saltwater, Bowater,
Ullswater, * una corda, tape recorder,
postal order, teleporter, Derwentwater,
underwater, * ignored her, caught her

**This is the Night Mail crossing the
    Border,**
**Bringing the cheque and the postal
    order.**
W. H. AUDEN

26.5 Forfar, author

26.6 bawler, brawler, caller, crawler,
drawler, faller, hauler, mauler, Paula,
scrawler, smaller, sprawler, taller,
trawler, warbler, dawdler, aura, borer,
Cora, corer, Dora, flora, Flora, Laura,
Norah, Morar, poorer, pourer, roarer,
scorer, snorer, sorer, surer, Thora,
Torah, * mandorla, installer, adorer,
Atora®, Andorra, Pandora, angora,
fedora, menorah, restorer, explorer,
señora, signora, insurer, aurora, * kerb
crawler, footballer, * kia ora, Leonora,
Theodora, Isadora, Bora Bora,
Tuscarora, * call her, ignore her, etc.

26.7 dormer, former, Norma, korma,
ormer, stormer, trauma, warmer,
corner, fauna, fawner, Horner, Lorna,
Morna, mourner, sauna, scorner,
Warner, yawner, Faulkner,
* performer, conformer, transformer,
reformer, informer, pro forma,
* barnstormer, legwarmer, bedwarmer,

sixth-former, * inform her, forewarn
her, etc.

Little Jack Horner
Sat in the corner,
Eating a Christmas pie.
NURSERY RHYME

26.8 coarser, courser, Chaucer, dorsa,
forcer, hoarser, saucer, balsa, falser,
waltzer, causer, hawser, Porsche,
Portia, Yorkshire, scorcher, torture,
launcher, stauncher, Borgia, forger,
Georgia, gorger, * endorser, enforcer,
debaucher, * reinforcer, flying saucer,
* force her, adores her, etc.

26.9 Nordic, Baltic, caustic,
swordstick, Orphic, Jorvik, Norvic, salt
lick, boric, chloric, baldric, Baldrick,
formic, georgic, * aortic, hydraulic,
McCormick, * metamorphic,
endomorphic, ectomorphic,
mesomorphic, polymorphic,
hydrochloric

26.10 swordsticks, salt licks,
Horlicks®, Baldrick's, * hydraulics, etc.

26.11 morbid, torpid, orchid, sordid,
gloried, lurid, storied, palsied, * three-
storeyed, two-storeyed

26.12 halberd, boarded, bordered,
corded, hoarded, ordered, laundered,
courted, quartered, sorted, thwarted,
watered, altered, faltered, halted,
malted, salted, daunted, haunted,
taunted, sauntered, vaunted, Orford,
Salford, Walford, Crawford, Mordred,
forward, shoreward, awkward,
northward, orchard, tortured,
* applauded, reordered, defrauded,

recorded, rewarded, disordered, supported, assorted, contorted, deported, reported, distorted, unaltered, assaulted, unsalted, exalted, undaunted, exhausted, straightforward, henceforward, thenceforward, three-cornered, * prerecorded, unrecorded, unrewarded, unsupported, unreported, unescorted, etc.

26.13 halberds, forwards, shorewards, northwards, orchards, etc.

26.14 corkage, mortgage, cordage, shortage, wharfage, haulage, moorage, storage, drawbridge, Aldridge, * remortgage

26.15 bauble, corbel, warble, snorkel, caudal, dawdle, Wardle, chortle, mortal, portal, Borstal, awful, lawful, thoughtful, mournful, scornful, forceful, formal, normal, aural, choral, floral, oral, corporal, rorqual, dorsal, foresail, morsel, causal, * withdrawal, aortal, immortal, St Austell, unlawful, remorseful, resourceful, abnormal, informal, subnormal, * paranormal, menopausal

Guns aren't lawful;
Nooses give;
Gas smells awful;
You might as well live.
DOROTHY PARKER

26.16 baubles, Gorbals, mortals, portals, morsels, etc.

26.17 boredom, Fordham, whoredom, autumn, Waltham, Fortnum, sorghum, forum, quorum, Shoreham, awesome,

foursome, balsam, * postmortem, decorum, * Karakoram, ad valorem, variorum, indecorum, * sanctum sanctorum, * brought 'em, wore 'em, etc.

26.18 Corbin, Dworkin, walk-in, foreskin, Aldrin, Austen, Austin, dauphin, Magdalen, Magdalene, maudlin, porcelain, Baldwin, * endorphin, tarpaulin, * talkin', fallin', etc.

26.19 auburn, Bourbon, Alban, saucepan, Lorcan, Balkan, falcon, Gorgon, Morgan, organ, Auden, Borden, bourdon, broaden, cordon, Gordon, Hordern, Jordan, Norden, warden, Alden, Malden, Bourton, Broughton, Houghton, Laughton, Moreton, Morton, Naughton, Norton, Orton, quartan, quartern, shorten, Stoughton, tauten, Wharton, Alton, Chorlton, Dalton, Galton, Halton, saltern, Walton, Taunton, Thornton, Launceston, orphan, Malvern, northern, fallen, Coren, Lauren, Moran, cauldron, doorman, foreman, Gorman, lawman, Mormon, Norman, storeman, Walkman®, Kaufman, horseman, Norseman, sportsman, oarsman, swordsman, coarsen, Dawson, hoarsen, Lawson, Orson, Porson, whoreson, caution, portion, torsion, auction, fortune, Georgian, * Majorcan, Minorcan, gyrfalcon, Glamorgan, Brize Norton, Throgmorton, foreshorten, Carshalton, Andorran, abortion, apportion, proportion, contortion, precaution, distortion, extortion, absorption, misfortune, exhaustion, * churchwarden, firewarden, crestfallen, * traffic warden, Saffron Walden, Salvadoran, Ecuadoran, disproportion, proabortion, malabsorption, self-absorption

26.20 broadened, cordoned, shortened, orphaned, foreland, moorland, Auckland, Falkland, Portland, Ormond, gourmand, Dortmund, coarsened, cautioned, auctioned, * North Foreland, South Foreland, apportioned, proportioned, etc.

26.21 saucepans, Balkans, falcons, Gorgons, wardens, orphans, Mormons, Normans, portions, * St Albans, abortions, proportions, precautions, etc.

26.22 Dawkins, Hawkins, foreskins, Baldwin's, * endorphins, tarpaulins, etc.

26.23 mordant, mordent, oughtn't, portent, dormant, Stormont, * absorbent, accordant, concordant, discordant, important, informant, comportment, assortment, deportment, instalment, enthralment, adornment, endorsement, enforcement, divorcement, engorgement, disgorgement, * self-important, all-important, unimportant, reinforcement

26.24 portents, ordnance, * accordance, concordance, discordance, importance, performance, conformance, informants, instalments, adornments, assurance, insurance, * self-importance, unimportance, reassurance, * underperformance, etc.

26.25 drawing, gnawing, sawing, thawing, corking, Dorking, Hawking, squawking, stalking, talking, walking, boarding, hoarding, balding, scalding, Spalding, courting, sorting, sporting, halting, malting, salting, vaulting, daunting, haunting, taunting, bawling, brawling, calling, crawling, falling, galling, hauling, mauling, Pauling, scrawling, sprawling, stalling, trawling, dawdling, lordling, Maudling, chortling, boring, flooring, Goring, mooring, pouring, roaring, scoring, snoring, soaring, storing, warring, drawstring, forewing, forming, storming, swarming, warming, awning, dawning, fawning, morning, mourning, warning, yawning, coursing, forcing, waltzing, causing, pausing, scorching, torching, forging, gorging, * guffawing, withdrawing, absorbing, uncorking, according, applauding, marauding, recording, rewarding, supporting, cavorting, transporting, reporting, importing, exporting, escorting, ripsnorting, distorting, unsporting, assaulting, exalting, exhausting, appalling, enthralling, adoring, assuring, skijoring, imploring, exploring, rip-roaring, outpouring, performing, conforming, transforming, reforming, informing, adorning, forewarning, endorsing, enforcing, divorcing, outsourcing, debauching, disgorging, * jaywalking, sleepwalking, sweet-talking, hillwalking, bushwalking, sailboarding, skateboarding, keyboarding, snowboarding, blackballing, name-calling, paintballing, kerb crawling, keelhauling, snowballing, stonewalling, footballing, barnstorming, heart-warming, brainstorming, housewarming, * tape-recording, weatherboarding, bodyboarding, unrewarding, self-supporting, caterwauling, overhauling, reassuring, underflooring, underscoring, reinforcing, etc.

Come in the evening, or come in the morning,
Come when you're looked for, or come without warning.
THOMAS DAVIS

26.26 auspice, Aldis, jaundice, mortise, loris, cornice, * aqua fortis, rigor mortis

26.27 corpus, porpoise, Malpas, Aldous, Plautus, tortoise, caucus, Dorcas, glaucous, raucous, clawless, flawless, lawless, scoreless, stalkless, cordless, thoughtless, faultless, dauntless, formless, gormless, hornless, thornless, horseless, causeless, chorus, porous, Taurus, torus, wardress, laundress, fortress, walrus, poorness, rawness, soreness, sureness, baldness, shortness, tautness, smallness, tallness, coarseness, hoarseness, cautious, tortious, gorgeous, * amorphous, remorseless, Dolores, sonorous, Centaurus, thesaurus, nonporous, enormous, ginormous, incautious, * polymorphous, stegosaurus, Epidaurus, brontosaurus, * tyrannosaurus, * habeas corpus, ichthyosaurus, * fought us, bore us, etc.

26.28 Yorkist, jaundiced, flautist,

shortlist, * conformist, * nonconformist

26.29 August, shortest, tautest, smallest, tallest, chorused, warmest, coarsest, hoarsest, falsest, etc.

26.30 hawkish, mawkish, shortish, crawfish, dwarfish, swordfish, warmish, Cornish, Dawlish, Gaulish, smallish, tallish, Moorish, moreish

26.31 Korbut, Norbert, Talbot, Alcott, curate, stalwart, * Port Talbot

26.32 Corbett, orbit, chalkpit, audit, plaudit, forfeit, gauntlet, torchlit, floret, cornet, hornet, corset, Dorset, faucet, Fawcett, * what-do-you-call-it, * hoard it, worn it, etc.

26.33 Morpeth, Bournemouth, Portsmouth

26.34 sportive, * abortive, supportive, exhaustive

26.35 talkies, walkies, corgis, Geordies, forties, Furies, glories, storeys, stories, Tories, strawberries, Audrey's, Orkneys, falsies, orgies, * creepy-crawlies

26.36 stalkers, walkers, boarders, orders, Saunders, daughters, porters, quarters, waters, Waters, Walters, authors, callers, Paula's, corners, mourners, courses, forces, horses, saucers, causes, clauses, pauses, torches, * marauders, recorders, three-quarters, reporters, supporters, headquarters, performers, armed forces, St George's, * sleepwalkers, stepdaughters, headwaters, hindquarters, forequarters, footballers, legwarmers, sixth-formers, * tape recorders, flying saucers, etc.

26.37 organdie, Normandy, orderly, daughterly, mortally, quarterly, awfully, lawfully, thoughtfully, mournfully, scornfully, forcefully, northerly, orally, formally, formerly, normally, audibly, forcibly, awkwardly, awesomely, faultlessly, cautiously, strawberry, Salisbury, cautery, watery, psaltery, augury, sorcery, mortuary, forgery, laudatory, falconry, cautionary, Albany, Alderney, Shaughnessy, normalcy, dormancy, paucity, falsity, gaudily, haughtily, naughtily, jauntily, stormily, saucily, morbidly, sportingly, porphyry, auditory, dormitory, corsetry, ordinary, * disorderly, immortally, unlawfully, resourcefully, abnormally, informally, deplorably, reportedly, remorselessly, debauchery, reformatory, precautionary, O'Shaughnessy, absorbency, conformity, deformity, enormity, hydraulically, assuredly, exhaustively, accordingly, rewardingly, unsportingly, appallingly, extraordinary, * nonconformity, uniformity, reassuringly, etc.

**There's an Irishman, Arthur O'Shaughnessy –
On the chessboard of poets a pawn is he.**
DANTE GABRIEL ROSSETTI

26.38 Córdoba, forwarder, Cordova, snorkeller, Aldeburgh, Marlborough, corpora, orderer, launderer, slaughterer, sorcerer, torturer, northerner, Corsica, orbiter, auditor, Dorchester, orchestra, Gordimer, Mortimer, forfeiture, mortgagor, wharfinger, formula

26.39 chalkier, bawdier, Claudia, gaudier, courtier, haughtier, naughtier, sportier, saltier, jauntier, morphia, swarthier, haulier, gloria, Gloria, gorier, scoria, stormier, brawnier, cornea, cornier, hornier, scrawnier, thornier, saucier, nausea, raunchier, * euphorbia, primordia, consortia, saintpaulia, Astoria, emporia, Pretoria, Victoria, dysphoria, euphoria, * sanatoria, crematoria, moratoria, auditoria, California, * phantasmagoria, etc.

26.40 Waterford, orbited, audited, * unaudited

26.41 audible, fordable, laudable, portable, sortable, forcible, plausible, corporal, cordial, corneal, boreal, oriel, cortical, nautical, vortical, ordinal, orbital, Portugal, * affordable, recordable, inaudible, supportable, transportable, exhaustible, adorable, restorable, deplorable, implausible, inaugural, proportional, primordial, manorial, factorial, arboreal, armorial, marmoreal, sartorial, Escorial, memorial, pictorial, corporeal, authorial, uxorial, tutorial, * unaffordable, insupportable, inexhaustible, unenforceable, lavatorial, janitorial, senatorial, equatorial, editorial, territorial, dictatorial, immemorial, incorporeal, professorial, aeronautical, astronautical, * ambassadorial, subequatorial, conspiratorial, inquisitorial

26.42 laudanum, organum, Altrincham, Walsingham, * exordium, consortium, emporium, scriptorium, * californium, sanatorium, crematorium, in memoriam, moratorium, auditorium

26.43 Worplesdon, Warburton, Alderton, Salterton, Auberon, alderman, Yorkshireman, Cornishman, Alderson, Sorbian, Scorpian, scorpion, Claudian, Gordian, Orphean, chorion, Dorian, saurian, Taurean, Corsican, Orpington, Mornington, Rawlinson, * accordion, Edwardian, stentorian, Gregorian, Victorian, historian, praetorian, Ivorian, * Perigordian, Capricornean, Californian, Salvadorian, Ecuadorean, Terpsichorean, Singaporean

26.44 scorpions, * Edwardians, Victorians, New Orleans, * Californians, etc.

26.45 cormorant, ornament, tournament, orient, Orient, corpulent, fraudulent, * apportionment, reorient, disorient, euphoriant, exorbitant

26.46 ornaments, tournaments, audience, ordinance, corpulence, fraudulence, etc.

26.47 daughterless, waterless, slaughterous, sorceress, sorcerous, torturous, Uranus, forwardness, awkwardness, thoughtfulness,

mournfulness, lawlessness, thoughtlessness, cautiousness, Caucasus, Claudius, Morpheus, Orpheus, glorious, nauseous, nautilus, haughtiness, naughtiness, jauntiness, tawdriness, sauciness, tortuous, * straightforwardness, laborious, notorious, vainglorious, censorious, Nestorius, inglorious, Pretorius, victorious, uproarious, uxorious, * meritorious, etc.

Send her victorious,
Happy, and glorious,
Long to reign over us:
God save the queen!
NATIONAL ANTHEM

26.48 formalist, organist, pluralist, * abortionist, contortionist, extortionist

26.49 chalkiest, bawdiest, gaudiest, haughtiest, naughtiest, sportiest, saltiest, jauntiest, swarthiest, goriest, stormiest, brawniest, corniest, horniest, scrawniest, thorniest, sauciest, raunchiest, etc.

26.50 corporate, fortunate, aureate, laureate, ordinate, * proportionate, extortionate, unfortunate, subordinate, inordinate, coordinate, * disproportionate, baccalaureate, Poet Laureate, professoriate, insubordinate, superordinate

26.51 alterable, formidable, * unalterable

-oor-

The rhymes in this section have the 'oor' sound of cure *and*
purely *as their main or final vowel sound. Many of these words
can also be rhymed with words in the – or – section.*

27.1 Boer, boor, cure, dour, lure,
moor, Moor, Moore, Muir, poor, pure,
Ruhr, spoor, sure, tour, Tours, Ure,
your, you're, * velour, McClure,
procure, gravure, allure, manure,
amour, unmoor, assure, unsure,
mature, adjure, abjure, conjure,
tandoor, Latour, Cavour, coiffure,
Namur, hachure, Kanpur, Darfur,
guipure, impure, liqueur, secure,
endure, immure, demure, inure,
ensure, insure, obscure, couture, du
jour, * tambour, grandeur, Dartmoor,
tenure, Exmoor, Sedgemoor, detour,
Tweedsmuir, concours, Goncourt,
contour, cocksure, tonsure, ordure,
Broadmoor, Hawksmoor, brochure,
* Aznavour, amateur, aperture,
Lammermuir, paramour,
Jamshedpur, manicure, plat du jour,
armature, Réaumur, premature,
epicure, pedicure, sepulture,
curvature, reassure, prefecture,
reinsure, ligature, immature,
sinecure, insecure, cynosure,
Pompadour, Yom Kippur, confiture,
commissure, embouchure, *hors
concours*, overture, Côte d'Azur,
Kohinoor, *haute couture*, troubadour,
* caricature, magistrature,
photogravure, musculature,
underinsure

How small, of all that human hearts
   endure,
That part which laws or kings can cause
   or cure!
OLIVER GOLDSMITH

27.2 cured, gourd, Lourdes, lured,
moored, * procured, manured,
unmoored, assured, matured,
coiffured, secured, immured, inured,
insured, obscured, * manicured, self-
assured, reassured, reinsured,
unsecured, uninsured, * caricatured,
underinsured, etc.

27.3 Boers, boors, cures, lures, moors,
tours, yours, * matures, allures,
amours, Elburz, liqueurs, endures, etc.

28.1 dourly, Gourlay, poorly, purely,
surely, curie, Curie, Drury, fury, houri,
Jewry, jury, Lurie, Newry, Uri,
* Kalgoorlie, securely, demurely,
obscurely, tandoori, Venturi, Mercouri,
Missouri, potpourri, * prematurely,
Dioscuri, etc.

28.2 curer, Dürer, *Führer*, Jura, juror,
lurer, pleura, poorer, purer, surer,
tourer, * assurer, procurer, bravura,
insurer, securer, caesura, nonjuror,
* Angostura, El Mansûra, tessitura,

* acciaccatura, appoggiatura,
* coloratura, Bonaventura, * camera
obscura, * cure her, lure her, etc.

28.3 uric, Zürich, * telluric, mercuric,
sulphuric

28.4 mural, neural, pleural, plural,
rural, Ural, * extramural, epidural

28.5 Purim, Urim

28.6 Van Buren, Honduran

28.7 burin, urine, * moorin', allurin',
etc.

28.8 moorland, gourmand

28.9 procurement, allurement

28.10 durance, * assurance, insurance,
endurance, * self-assurance,
reassurance

28.11 curing, during, luring, mooring,
touring, Turing, * procuring, alluring,
assuring, maturing, securing,
enduring, ensuring, insuring,
obscuring, * manicuring, reassuring,
* caricaturing, underinsuring, etc.

28.12 poorness, sureness, Arcturus,
mercurous, Honduras, sulphurous,
* Epicurus, * lure us, assure us, etc.

28.13 poorest, purest, surest,
* securest, etc.

28.14 jurist, purist, tourist,
* manicurist, pedicurist, * caricaturist

28.15 boorish, Moorish, * amateurish

28.16 Curies, Furies, juries

28.17 gourami, curacy, purity, surety,
touristy, urinary, pleurisy, * incurably,
maturity, impurity, security, obscurity,
futurity, assuredly, * immaturity,
insecurity, reassuringly, etc.

28.18 curia, * Manchuria, Etruria,
Liguria, dysuria, * haematuria,
glycosuria, etc.

28.19 curable, durable, thurible,
Muriel, * procurable, insurable,
incurable, endurable, Escurial,
centurial, tenurial, mercurial,
* uninsurable, unendurable

28.20 curium, * tellurium

28.21 puritan, juryman, * Manchurian,
Arthurian, Ben-Gurion, tellurian,
centurion, Etrurian, Ligurian,
Missourian, Silurian, * Khachaturian,
holothurian

28.22 prurient, * parturient, esurient,
luxuriant

28.23 prurience, * luxuriance

28.24 curious, furious, spurious,
* penurious, perjurious, incurious,
injurious, sulphureous, luxurious,
usurious

-OW-

The rhymes in this section have the 'ow' sound of cow *and* louder
as their main or final vowel sound.

29.1 bough, bow, brow, chow, *ciao*, cow,
Dão, dhow, Dow, Frau, how, Howe,
Lao, Mao, now, ow, plough, Plough,
prow, row, scow, slough, Slough,
sough, sow, Tao, tau, thou, vow, wow,
* cacao, Macao, avow, allow, meow,
Bilbao, endow, enow, kowtow,
* Cracow, Spandau, Nassau, pilau,
eyebrow, highbrow, Moldau, hausfrau,
bow-wow, powwow, Mau Mau, know-
how, nohow, snowplough, lowbrow,
somehow, Lucknow, Jungfrau, moo-
cow, * anyhow, disavow, disallow,
middlebrow, Mindanao, Löwenbräu,
Curaçao, * Concertgebouw, Guinea-
Bissau, * Oberammergau

**Come, friendly bombs, and fall on
Slough**
It isn't fit for humans now,
There isn't grass to graze a cow.
Swarm over, Death!
JOHN BETJEMAN

29.2 couch, crouch, grouch, ouch,
pouch, slouch, vouch

29.3 bowed, cloud, cowed, crowd, loud,
Oudh, ploughed, proud, rowed, Saud,
shroud, Stroud, vowed, * unbowed,
avowed, aloud, Macleod, unploughed,
endowed, becloud, enshroud, O'Dowd,
kowtowed, * in-crowd, * beetle-
browed, ibn-Saud, overcloud,
overcrowd, thundercloud

29.4 [see also 31.3] cowl, foul, fowl,
growl, howl, jowl, owl, prowl, Raoul,
scowl, yowl, * afoul, befoul, * peafowl,
wildfowl, moorfowl, * waterfowl,
cheek by jowl

29.5 Braun, brown, Brown, Browne,
clown, crown, Crown, down, Down,
drown, frown, gown, noun, town,
* run-down, uptown, sit-down,
renown, lie-down, von Braun,
downtown, * clampdown, crackdown,
Sandown, Lansdowne, Ashdown,
splashdown, markdown, breakdown,
shakedown, Cape Town, Jamestown,
letdown, meltdown, Freetown,
Queenstown, Piltdown, Kingstown,
Bridgetown, climb-down, nightgown,
swan's-down, Yorktown, Georgetown,
countdown, Southdown, toytown,
hoedown, lowdown, showdown,
slowdown, close-down, Motown,
pronoun, rubdown, shutdown,
comedown, rundown, sundown,
thumbs-down, touchdown, nutbrown,
put-down, Cookstown, Newtown,
boom town, * Campbeltown, Camden
Town, hand-me-down, shantytown,
dressing-down, dressing gown,
thistledown, Tinseltown, eiderdown,

Chinatown, Portadown, broken-down, tumbledown, dumbing down, upside down, one-horse town

Wee Willie Winkie runs through the town,
Upstairs and downstairs in his nightgown.
NURSERY RHYME

29.6 bound, found, ground, hound, mound, pound, Pound, round, sound, Sound, wound, * abound, unbound, propound, compound, astound, profound, dumbfound, confound, around, surround, uncrowned, aground, unwound, unsound, rewound, re-sound, rebound, impound, expound, redound, renowned, resound, * wrapround, background, hardbound, brassbound, chairbound, fairground, casebound, greyhound, playground, changeround, westbound, spellbound, elkhound, hellhound, earthbound, turnround, deerhound, rebound, eastbound, windbound, inbound, whip-round, milk round, strikebound, hidebound, ice-bound, fogbound, pot-bound, softbound, frostbound, clothbound, compound, foxhound, northbound, stormbound, horehound, foreground, all-round, outbound, southbound, housebound, showground, snowbound, homebound, stoneground, bloodhound, wolfhound, sleuthhound, newshound, * wraparound, battleground, Afghan hound, stamping ground, Sensurround®, turnaround, infrasound, ironbound, Outward Bound®, overground, overwound, run-around, underground,

ultrasound, * superabound, merry-go-round, * theatre-in-the-round, happy hunting ground

Come, knit hands, and beat the ground,
In a light fantastic round.
JOHN MILTON

29.7 bounds, grounds, hounds, pounds, sounds, zounds, * abounds, surrounds, resounds, etc.

29.8 lounge, scrounge

29.9 bounce, flounce, jounce, ounce, pounce, trounce, counts, founts, mounts, * accounts, amounts, announce, pronounce, denounce, enounce, renounce, * mispronounce

29.10 bounced, flounced, jounced, pounced, trounced, * announced, pronounced, denounced, enounced, renounced, * unannounced, mispronounced

29.11 Blount, count, fount, mount, * account, amount, surmount, re-count, remount, recount, discount, miscount, dismount, * head count, re-count, discount, viscount, * bank account, catamount, tantamount, paramount

We all know a kitten, but come to a catamount
The beast is a stranger when grown up to that amount.
OLIVER WENDELL HOLMES

29.12 douse, gauss, Gauss, grouse, house, Klaus, Laos, louse, mouse, nous, Rowse, scouse, Scouse, souse, spouse, Strauss, * degauss, delouse, in-house, * taphouse, madhouse, sandgrouse, guardhouse, bathhouse, farmhouse, glasshouse, almshouse, warehouse, playhouse, bakehouse, steakhouse, gatehouse, alehouse, jailhouse, deckhouse, penthouse, guesthouse, henhouse, workhouse, birdhouse, teahouse, treehouse, wheelhouse, greenhouse, fieldmouse, Brighouse, titmouse, lighthouse, White House, ice house, lobscouse, chophouse, flophouse, doghouse, hothouse, dosshouse, doll's house, wash house, Moorhouse, poorhouse, storehouse, whorehouse, courthouse, dormouse, Bauhaus, roundhouse, outhouse, town house, powerhouse, smokehouse, roadhouse, boathouse, oast house, tollhouse, coach house, clubhouse, bunkhouse, Monkhouse, roughhouse, cookhouse, Wodehouse, Woodhouse, woodlouse, woodgrouse, schoolhouse, * chapterhouse, manor house, Ladislaus, Charterhouse, Lévi-Strauss, clearing house, Peterhouse, meeting house, flittermouse, Mickey Mouse, porterhouse, slaughterhouse, Waterhouse, bawdyhouse, boarding house, house-to-house, summerhouse, custom house, * *Die Fledermaus*, * Holyroodhouse

29.13 doused, Faust, frowst, groused, joust, oust, roust, soused, * degaussed, deloused, etc.

29.14 bout, clout, doubt, drought, flout, gout, grout, lout, nowt, out, owt, pout, Prout, rout, scout, Scout, shout, snout, spout, sprout, stout, tout, trout, * about, mahout, clapped out, way-out, spaced out, self-doubt, redoubt, devout, without, washed out, all-out, throughout, * blackout, hand-out, hang-out, payout, break-out, stakeout, checkout, sellout, workout, turnout, clear-out, eelpout, readout, bean sprout, printout, buyout, hide-out, whiteout, time-out, cop-out, dropout, knockout, lockout, opt-out, walkout, fallout, sauerkraut, blowout, foldout, dugout, cutout, lookout, umlaut, shoot-out, * gadabout, carry-out, lager lout, layabout, turnabout, litter lout, ticket tout, knockabout, walkabout, waterspout, well-thought-out, inside out, long-drawn-out, roundabout, roustabout, out-and-out, down-and-out, runabout, Brussels sprout

**Ne'er cast a clout till May be out.
Saying**

29.15 doubts, grouts, louts, Scouts, shouts, sprouts, touts, * blackouts, bean sprouts, dropouts, * lager louts, layabouts, thereabouts, whereabouts, hereabouts, Brussels sprouts, etc.

29.16 Louth, mouth, Routh, south, * bad-mouth, Grangemouth, bigmouth, Tynemouth, loudmouth, goalmouth, * blabbermouth, hand-to-mouth, Avonmouth, Lossiemouth, mouth-to-mouth

29.17 blouse, boughs, bows, brows, browse, Cowes, cows, dowse, drowse, house, Mao's, ploughs, rouse, rows, spouse, vows, * allows, arouse, carouse, meows, rehouse, espouse, endows, * eyebrows, * disavows, disallows, overblouse, etc.

30.1 Audi, cloudy, dowdy, howdy, rowdy, Saudi, doughty, gouty, bounty,

Bounty, county, Mountie, frowsty, mouthy, Southey, Cowley, foulie, Pauli, loudly, proudly, roundly, soundly, stoutly, cowrie, dowry, floury, Gowrie, Lowry, Maori, Cowdrey, foundry, Rowntree, Bowie, Cowie, Howie, brownie, Brownie, downy, townie, mousy, bouncy, blowsy, drowsy, frowzy, lousy, grouchy, slouchy, * profoundly, devoutly, Blairgowrie, Dalhousie, * housey-housey

30.2 Glauber, Cowper, chowder, Gouda, howdah, powder, Lauda, louder, prouder, bounder, flounder, founder, pounder, rounder, sounder, doubter, grouter, outer, pouter, router, Scouter, shouter, spouter, stouter, touter, counter, mounter, ouster, jouster, Crowther, mouther, fouler, Fowler, growler, howler, prowler, scowler, Bowdler, browner, crowner, downer, frowner, grouser, Hausa, mouser, Scouser, schnauzer, bouncer, browser, dowser, Mauser, rouser, trouser, voucher, gouger, lounger, scrounger, * profounder, encounter, announcer, denouncer, arouser, carouser, * gunpowder, rev counter, wildfowler, sundowner, sun-lounger, * Geiger counter, rabble-rouser, * found her, rouse her, etc.

We two should be like clams in a dish of chowder,
But we just fizz like parts of a Seidlitz powder.
DOROTHY FIELDS

30.3 clouded, crowded, powdered, shrouded, bounded, founded, grounded, pounded, rounded, sounded, doubted, flouted, grouted,

outed, routed, shouted, spouted, sprouted, counted, mounted, jousted, ousted, outward, southward, downward, * unclouded, uncrowded, enshrouded, unbounded, compounded, astounded, confounded, unfounded, surrounded, unsounded, impounded, resounded, undoubted, uncounted, unmounted, re-counted, recounted, dismounted, * overcrowded, unaccounted, etc.

30.4 outwards, southwards, downwards

30.5 groundage, poundage, Routledge

30.6 Oundle, poundal, roundel, doubtful, scoundrel, council, counsel, groundsel, Mousehole, spousal, tousle, * arousal, carousal, espousal

30.7 fountain, mountain, * shoutin', countin', etc.

30.8 Cowan, Gowan, rowan, louden, Plowden, bounden, Broughton, Houghton, Rowton, Stoughton, cowman, ploughman, Hauptmann, Kaufman, houseman, Housman, groundsman, roundsman, townsman, * McCowan, McGowan, * Stockhausen, Munchausen

30.9 Dowland, thousand, * Newfoundland

30.10 couchant, * accountant, endowment, impoundment, announcement, pronouncement

30.11 accountants, allowance, endowments, announcements, pronouncements

30.12 bowing, ploughing, vowing, clouding, crowding, Dowding, shrouding, bounding, grounding, hounding, pounding, sounding, doubting, flouting, grouting, outing, pouting, Scouting, shouting, spouting, sprouting, touting, counting, mounting, jousting, ousting, cowling, Dowling, fouling, growling, howling, prowling, scowling, foundling, groundling, downswing, browning, Browning, clowning, crowning, Downing, drowning, frowning, bouncing, flouncing, trouncing, browsing, dowsing, housing, rousing, crouching, grouching, slouching, lounging, scrounging, * allowing, endowing, kowtowing, enshrouding, abounding, astounding, surrounding, resounding, accounting, amounting, discounting, announcing, pronouncing, befouling, arousing, carousing, * wildfowling, * disavowing, overcrowding, antifouling, etc.

30.13 Powys, prowess, countess

30.14 cloudless, boundless, groundless, soundless, doubtless, countless, foundress, loudness, roundness, soundness, stoutness, * bound us, count us, etc.

30.15 Maoist, Taoist

30.16 loudest, proudest, stoutest, foulest, brownest, * profoundest, etc.

30.17 roundish, loutish, owlish, brownish, clownish

30.18 Jowett, outfit, Howlett, owlet, * found it, drown it, etc.

30.19 outfits, Auschwitz, owlets, etc.

30.20 counties, Mounties, Maoris, Brownies, townies, etc.

30.21 powders, rounders, prowlers, browsers, trousers, vouchers, scroungers, etc.

30.22 doubtfully, scoundrelly, outwardly, downwardly, Chaudhury, powdery, boundary, drowsily, * undoubtedly, accountancy, avowedly, astoundingly, * unaccountably, etc.

30.23 counsellor, flounderer, Gautama, dowager, councillor, howitzer, * Newfoundlander

30.24 countable, bountiful, * allowable, redoubtable, accountable, uncountable, surmountable, pronounceable, * unaccountable, insurmountable, unputdownable, unpronounceable

30.25 countenance, * discountenance

30.26 trouserless, bounteous, cloudiness, mountainous, drowsiness, etc.

-ower-

The rhymes in this section have the 'ower' sound of hour *and* towering *as their main or final vowel sound.*

31.1 bower, cower, dour, dower, flour, flower, glower, Gower, hour, lour, our, power, scour, shower, sour, Stour, tower, * half-hour, Glendower, deflower, empower, devour, * man-hour, manpower, brainpower, mayflower, Mayflower, plain flour, watchtower, bell tower, willpower, windflower, fire power, horsepower, wallflower, cornflour, cornflower, sunflower, rush-hour, moonflower, * candlepower, passionflower, Adenauer, staying power, Beckenbauer, elderflower, Penmaenmawr, sweet-and-sour, disempower, gillyflower, Eisenhower, Schopenhauer, cauliflower, overpower, superpower, * ivory tower, self-raising flour, kilowatt-hour

Not Heaven itself upon the past has power;
But what has been, has been, and I have had my hour.
JOHN DRYDEN

31.2 coward, Coward, cowered, flowered, glowered, Howard, loured, powered, scoured, showered, soured, towered, * deflowered, empowered, devoured, * Frankie Howerd, Castle Howard, overpowered, solar-powered, Noël Coward, underpowered

31.3 [see also 29.4] bowel, Cowal, Cowell, dowel, Dowell, Howell, Hywel, Powell, rowel, towel, trowel, vowel, * McDowell, avowal, * Baden-Powell, semivowel, Enoch Powell, disavowal, disembowel

31.4 bowels, Howells, towels, vowels, etc.

31.5 flowers, hours, ours, Powers, showers, towers, * Alton Towers, *Fawlty Towers*, superpowers, etc.

Here the youthful Giorgione gazed
upon the domes and towers,
And interpreted his era in a way which
pleases ours.
JOHN BETJEMAN

32.1 dourly, hourly, sourly, cowardly, bowery, Bowery, dowry, floury, flowery, showery

32.2 flowerer, scourer, * devourer, * shower her, empower her, etc.

32.3 cowering, flowering, glowering, louring, powering, scouring, showering, towering, dowelling, towelling, * deflowering, empowering, devouring, * overpowering, etc.

-oy-

The rhymes in this section have the 'oy' sound of toy *and* noisy *as their main or final vowel sound.*

33.1 boy, buoy, cloy, coy, Fowey, goy, joy, Joy, koi, oi, ploy, Roy, soy, toy, Troy, * McCoy, Savoy, ahoy, alloy, Molloy, Amoy, annoy, Hanoi, deploy, employ, destroy, enjoy, Rob Roy, * sandboy, alloy, Tannoy®, dayboy, playboy, pageboy, rent boy, envoy, bellboy, sepoy, decoy, Leroy, Kilroy, killjoy, choirboy, life buoy, viceroy, tomboy, Tolstoy, Conroy, Bolshoi, ball boy, tallboy, Korchnoi, borzoi, cowboy, houseboy, toy boy, Khoikhoi, doughboy, lowboy, homeboy, Lovejoy, schoolboy, newsboy, * attaboy, saveloy, paperboy, stableboy, ladyboy, real McCoy, redeploy, Iroquois, didicoy, Illinois, pride and joy, altar boy, Fauntleroy, corduroy, hoi polloi, bullyboy, blue-eyed boy, * hobbledehoy, Old Man of Hoy

The Harbour of Fowey
Is a beautiful spot,
And it's there I enjowey
To sail in a yot;
Or to race in a yacht
Round a mark or a buoy –
Such a beautiful spacht
Is the Harbour of Fuoy!
SIR ARTHUR QUILLER-COUCH

33.2 Hawick, hoick, oik

33.3 hoicks, oiks, yoicks

33.4 Boyd, buoyed, cloyed, Floyd, Freud, Lloyd, toyed, void, * avoid, annoyed, devoid, deployed, employed, Pink Floyd, destroyed, enjoyed, * tabloid, Ackroyd, android, steroid, Negroid, typhoid, thyroid, colloid, Holroyd, ovoid, cuboid, Boothroyd, * anthropoid, alkaloid, aneroid, asteroid, paranoid, planetoid, amyloid, adenoid, metalloid, haemorrhoid, Betws-y-Coed, self-employed, celluloid, dermatoid, Murgatroyd, redeployed, crystalloid, myeloid, Mongoloid, Australoid, hominoid, Caucasoid, Polaroid®, overjoyed, solenoid, unalloyed, unemployed, rheumatoid, humanoid, * meteoroid, underemployed

33.5 Lloyd's, * tabloids, steroids, * adenoids, haemorrhoids, etc.

33.6 boil, Boyle, broil, coil, Doyle, foil, Foyle, Hoyle, moil, Moyle, noil, oil, roil, Royle, soil, spoil, toil, voile, * uncoil, despoil, recoil, embroil, * parboil, gargoyle, trefoil, jetfoil, turmoil, tinfoil, topsoil, gumboil, subsoil, * castor oil, aerofoil, disembroil, hydrofoil, olive oil,

counterfoil, Conan Doyle, undersoil,
* cod liver oil

**Whence is thy learning? Hath thy toil
O'er books consumed the midnight oil?**
JOHN GAY

33.7 boiled, oiled, soiled, spoiled,
toiled, * unspoiled, uncoiled,
despoiled, recoiled, embroiled,
* parboiled, hard-boiled, soft-boiled,
shopsoiled, etc.

33.8 Boyne, coin, groin, groyne, join,
loin, quoin, * Des Moines, adjoin,
conjoin, Ardoyne, Burgoyne, purloin,
rejoin, enjoin, disjoin, Dordogne,
Boulogne, * Gascoigne, sirloin,
* tenderloin

33.9 boink, oink

33.10 joint, point, * appoint, anoint,
conjoint, repoint, disjoint,
* standpoint, cashpoint, flash point,
waypoint, breakpoint, checkpoint,
endpoint, clip joint, strip joint,
midpoint, pinpoint, knifepoint, strong
point, sore point, ballpoint, power
point, gunpoint, dew point, viewpoint,
* vantage point, reappoint,
needlepoint, freezing point,
silverpoint, disappoint, boiling point,
counterpoint

33.11 Boyce, choice, Joyce, Royce, voice,
* rejoice, Rolls-Royce, pro-choice,
* invoice

33.12 foist, hoist, joist, moist, voiced,
* unvoiced, rejoiced

33.13 quoit, * dacoit, adroit, exploit,
Detroit, Bayreuth, * maladroit

33.14 quoits, * dacoits, exploits,
* *Hakenkreuz*

33.15 boys, buoys, Joy's, noise, poise,
Roy's, toys, * annoys, employs,
destroys, enjoys, * pageboys, turquoise,
decoys, choirboys, cowboys,
schoolboys, * paperboys, stableboys,
equipoise, redeploys, altar boys,
corduroys, counterpoise, bullyboys,
etc.

**Secrets with girls, like loaded guns with
boys,
Are never valued till they make a noise.**
GEORGE CRABBE

34.1 Toynbee, pointy, coyly, doily, oily,
jointly, noisy, * dacoity, adroitly,
* hoity-toity

34.2 Boyer, coyer, foyer, Goya, lawyer,
sawyer, Sawyer, soya, Toyah, troika,
broider, moider, joinder, goitre,
loiter, Reuter, jointer, pointer,
cloister, moister, oyster, roister,
boiler, broiler, Euler, oiler, spoiler,
toiler, Moira, coiner, joiner, choicer,
moisture, * employer, sequoia,
destroyer, Tom Sawyer, embroider,
avoider, rejoinder, exploiter,
appointer, anointer, despoiler,
purloiner, rejoicer, * potboiler,
Tannhäuser, * paranoia, *perestroika*,
Schadenfreude, reconnoitre, * employ
her, avoid her, etc.

34.3 jointed, pointed, foisted, hoisted,
* avoided, embroidered, exploited,
appointed, anointed, disjointed,
* unexploited, well-appointed, self-
appointed, reappointed, disappointed,
etc.

34.4 buoyage, voyage, soilage, spoilage, coinage

34.5 loyal, royal, foible, Brueghel, joyful, * disloyal, * adenoidal, haemorrhoidal

34.6 noisome, toilsome, * destroys 'em, spoils 'em, etc.

34.7 oilskin, hoisin, * boilin', pointin', etc.

34.8 doyen, Croydon, hoyden, Royston, Boyson, moisten, foison, poison, * Iroquoian, Illinoisan

34.9 buoyant, poignant, ointment, * flamboyant, clairvoyant, deployment, employment, enjoyment, appointment, * self-employment, redeployment, unemployment, disappointment

34.10 annoyance, flamboyance, clairvoyance, clairvoyants, avoidance, appointments, etc.

34.11 cloying, toying, pointing, foisting, hoisting, boiling, broiling, oiling, soiling, spoiling, toiling, coining, joining, voicing, * annoying, destroying, enjoying, avoiding, appointing, anointing, recoiling, adjoining, purloining, rejoicing, * soul-destroying, disappointing, etc.

34.12 joyous, joyless, Troilus, pointless, voiceless, noiseless, boisterous, coyness, * adroitness, * annoy us, spoil us, etc.

34.13 toilet, * oil it, spoil it, etc.

34.14 loyalty, royalty, royally, loyally, joyfully, pointedly, poignantly, joyously, pointlessly, boisterously, joinery, buoyancy, poignancy, moiety, noisily, boyishly, toiletry, * disloyalty, viceroyalty, flamboyantly, embroidery, flamboyancy, annoyingly, * disappointingly, etc.

34.15 loiterer, roisterer, poisoner, Drogheda, voyager, * embroiderer

34.16 boilable, joinable, coital, * employable, destroyable, enjoyable, avoidable, exploitable, * unemployable, unavoidable

34.17 Freudian, Moynihan, Joycean

34.18 boisterous, roisterous, poisonous, joyfulness, coitus, etc.

34.19 loyalist, royalist, pointillist

34.20 pointiest, oiliest, noisiest, etc.

-oe-

The rhymes in this section have the 'oe' sound of boat *and*
grocer *as their main or final vowel sound.*

35.1 beau, blow, bow, bro, Co., Coe,
crow, Crowe, doe, doh, dough, Flo,
floe, flow, foe, fro, glow, go, grow, ho,
hoe, Jo, Joe, know, lo, low, Mo, mo',
mow, no, O, oh, owe, po, Po, Poe, pro,
roe, row, Rowe, sew, show, sloe, slow,
snow, so, soh, sow, stow, Stowe,
though, throe, throw, toe, tow, woe, yo

Let your little verses flow
Gently, sweetly, row by row.
HENRY CAREY

35.2 ago, gung-ho, hullo, aglow,
Moreau, Thoreau, *de trop*, Monroe,
Munro, dunno, just so, Lascaux,
Margaux, Bardot, bravo, heigh-ho,
Glencoe, hello, per pro, BO, CO,
regrow, bestow, Defoe, below, skid row,
righto, John Doe, forego, forgo,
Bordeaux, although, foreknow,
foreshow, go-slow, outgrow, good-oh

35.3 Abo, jabot, sabot, flambeau,
mambo, Rambo, Rimbaud, Tambo,
ASBO, capo, cachepot, Franco, NALGO,
Django, mango, quango, tango,
Tango®, saddo, shadow, bandeau,
Brando, chateau, gateau, plateau, alto,
canto, panto, Padstow, salvo, aloe,
Boileau, callow, fallow, hallow, mallow,
sallow, shallow, tallow, Pablo, tableau,
cash flow, arrow, barrow, farrow,

harrow, Harrow, Jarrow, marrow,
narrow, sparrow, tarot, yarrow, macro,
aggro, Afro, ammo, piano, fatso, matzo,
chat show, macho, banjo,
* wheelbarrow, * foreshadow, glissando,
Orlando, annatto, mulatto, de facto,
contralto, Rialto, Taranto, bel canto,
portmanteau, impasto, tobacco,
Tabasco, fiasco, hidalgo, fandango,
marshmallow, piano, sargasso, El Paso,
Picasso, gazpacho, * overshadow,
rallentando, San Fernando, Palo Alto,
Esperanto, antipasto, paparazzo

I, said the Sparrow,
With my bow and arrow,
I killed Cock Robin.
NURSERY RHYME

35.4 Garbo, Marco, taco, Argo, argot,
cargo, Fargo, largo, Margot, Glasgow,
Prado, arvo, bravo, Barlow, Carlo,
Carlow, Harlow, Marlow, Marlowe,
Arnaud, Arno, Carnot, guano, Kano,
* Gestapo, farrago, embargo, Chicago,
Zhivago, virago, bravado, Barnardo,
Bernardo, Mikado, Ricardo,
commando, staccato, tomato, castrato,
legato, vibrato, St Malo, Pissarro,
soprano, Meccano®, Cinzano®,
Locarno, * Santiago, Pago Pago,
avocado, muscovado, desperado,
El Dorado, Colorado, Leonardo,

bastinado, moderato, pizzicato,
obbligato, Monte Carlo, Marciano,
oregano, * aficionado, amontillado,
inamorato, Kilimanjaro,
* incommunicado

35.5 scarecrow, airflow, Aero®, faro,
Pharaoh, airshow, * caballero

35.6 Mayo, rainbow, sago, credo, dado,
Cato, NATO, Plato, halo, Day-Glo®,
peso, * Tobago, lumbago, Diego,
Toledo, Laredo, tornado, potato,
Soweto, Delano, volcano, * Bulawayo,
Galileo, San Diego, Winnebago,
Valparaiso, * Alfa Romeo, Montevideo,
* Tierra del Fuego

35.7 elbow, depot, tempo, dekko, echo,
Eco, gecko, fresco, Tesco, Lego®,
meadow, kendo, ghetto, Steptoe, recto,
lento, pesto, presto, Chepstow, bellow,
cello, fellow, Jell-o®, mellow, yellow,
Pueblo, deathblow, Velcro®, escrow,
metro, retro, Jethro, hedgerow, demo,
memo, Renault, Esso, gesso, Enzo,
* bedfellow, Oddfellow, Longfellow,
schoolfellow, * Aleppo, Art Deco, El
Greco, re-echo, flamenco, Lysenko,
alfresco, UNESCO, Marengo,
Nintendo®, crescendo, Soweto, stiletto,
libretto, falsetto, Sorrento, trecento,
memento, pimento, Novello, Othello,
morello, Martello, Marcello, Costello,
bordello, Uccello, allegro, espresso,
Lorenzo, Vincenzo, * Timoshenko,
Yevtushenko, Ionesco, innuendo,
Canaletto, vaporetto, amaretto,
amoretto, Tintoretto, allegretto,
Sacramento, quattrocento,
pentimento, cinquecento, manifesto,
Portobello, Pirandello, Donatello,
Punchinello, intermezzo,

* diminuendo, divertimento,
Risorgimento, violoncello

35.8 turbo, ergo, Virgo, Merlot,
furlough, Pernod®, verso, Peugeot,
* Umberto, concerto, Alberto, Palermo,
Salerno, inferno, bolero, sombrero

35.9 weirdo, hero, Nero, Pierrot, Spiro,
zero, * Shapiro, subzero, De Niro,
Pinero, * antihero, superhero, * Rio de
Janeiro

35.10 brio, Cleo, Clio, Leo, Rio, trio,
cheapo, repo, Biko, Chico, pekoe, picot,
ego, credo, lido, speedo, Tito, veto, filo,
kilo, Negro, bistro, chemo, beano,
Beano, chino, fino, Gino, Reno, vino,
peepshow, * con brio, Trujillo, placebo,
gazebo, Enrico, amigo, Rodrigo,
tuxedo, libido, torpedo, graffito,
Benito, magneto, mosquito, yo-heave-
ho, El Niño, supremo, Aquino, Latino,
Trevino, merino, amino, casino,
Pacino, albino, bambino, neutrino,
* Puerto Rico, alter ego, superego,
Hirohito, incognito, Borodino,
Tarantino, Valentino, Bardolino, San
Marino, palomino, maraschino,
Filipino, cappuccino

35.11 bimbo, Chrimbo, limbo, gyppo,
hippo, sicko, thicko, wilco, gingko,
pinko, disco, bingo, dingo, gringo,
jingo, lingo, Ringo, widow, dildo,
window, ditto, tiptoe, pinto, Shinto,
Bisto®, Bristow, nympho, info, billow,
pillow, willow, Wicklow, whitlow,
inflow, limo, gizmo, minnow, winnow,
dipso, schizo, * akimbo, Francisco,
flamingo, Murillo, machismo, calypso,
* San Francisco, Monte Cristo,
armadillo, peccadillo, Amarillo,

cigarillo, * Santo Domingo, * in flagrante delicto

35.12 hypo, typo, psycho, Tycho, Sligo, Dido, Fido, litho, Lilo®, Milo, Shiloh, silo, Biro®, Cairo, giro, tyro, maestro, lino, rhino, wino, sideshow, * Ohio, Hokkaido, * impetigo

35.13 yobbo, fogbow, combo, longbow, crossbow, oxbow, oppo, bronco, Moscow, doggo, bongo, Congo, drongo, Pongo, condo, rondeau, rondo, blotto, Giotto, grotto, lotto, motto, Otto, potto, Watteau, pronto, Volvo, follow, hollow, Rollo, swallow, wallow, Oslo, borrow, Corot, morrow, sorrow, cockcrow, Cointreau®, mono, tonneau, Oxo®, honcho, poncho, * Morocco, sirocco, Belmondo, risotto, Toronto, Apollo, tomorrow, Alfonso, * Mato Grosso

**Eagerly I wished the morrow, – vainly
   had I sought to borrow
From my books surcease of sorrow –
   sorrow for the lost Lenore.**
EDGAR ALLAN POE

35.14 Waldo, auto, quarto, porno, torso, also, * Oporto, Livorno

35.15 bureau, Douro, euro, Truro, * Politburo, chiaroscuro

35.16 hobo, oboe, Coco, cocoa, loco, logo, Togo, dodo, Frodo, photo, Toto, Soho, polo, Polo, Rolo®, solo, yo-yo, Tokyo, Como, homo, promo, slo-mo, no-no, so-so, bozo, * Limpopo, rococo, iroko, *ex voto*, Kyoto, *in toto*, con moto, Barolo, kimono, * Orinoco, Quasimodo, telephoto, Marco Polo,

major-domo, Ecce Homo, Perry Como, amoroso, doloroso, oloroso, mafioso, virtuoso

35.17 dumbo, Dumbo, gumbo, jumbo, stucco, Mungo, gusto, Ludlow, burrow, furrow, * Colombo, Columbo, * mumbo jumbo

35.18 duo, Hugo, Cluedo®, judo, ludo, pseudo, Trudeau, Bhutto, Pluto, rouleau, sumo, Bruno, Gounod, Juno, Clouseau, Crusoe, Rousseau, trousseau, whoso, ouzo, * escudo, testudo, prosciutto, Profumo

35.19 apropos, hammertoe, Navaho, Scapa Flow, Alamo, aquashow, patio, cameo, Anzio, tally-ho, calico, haricot, aristo, McEnroe, Maginot, afterglow, Martineau, Art Nouveau, status quo, Status Quo, radio, ratio, pedalo, tremolo, ebb and flow, Blériot, stereo, embryo, NCO, medico, Jellicoe, Jericho, Mexico, Bendigo, Eskimo, Herstmonceux, vertigo, furbelow, cheerio, PLO, VSO, PTO, Felixstowe, mistletoe, piccolo, gigolo, Figaro, Cicero, tick-tack-toe, Scipio, video, billyo, indigo, quid pro quo, Idaho, dynamo, tae kwon do, Monaco, Kosovo, contraflow, Prospero, comme il faut, Fontainebleau, domino, Scorpio, audio, Claudio, Borneo, Curaçao, curio, tournedos, overflow, overthrow, oversew, so-and-so, Tokyo, rodeo, folio, polio, Romeo, do-si-do, blow-by-blow, undergo, touch and go, undertow, bungalow, buffalo, bummalo, underflow, nuncio, to and fro, Huguenot, UFO, studio, Boucicault, subito, * malapropos, Arapaho, diabolo, Ajaccio, DiMaggio, simpatico, seraglio, intaglio, scenario, Lothario, mustachio, pistachio, Boccaccio, adagio, Correggio, arpeggio, solfeggio, Abednego, presidio, punctilio, capriccio, politico, magnifico, fortissimo, continuo, Geronimo, Pinocchio, imbroglio, portfolio, Antonio, * Michelangelo, impresario, archipelago, ex officio, pianissimo, oratorio, San Antonio, braggadocio, * generalissimo

35.20 daube, globe, Job, lobe, probe, robe, strobe, * enrobe, disrobe, * bathrobe, aerobe, ear lobe, microbe, wardrobe, * Francophobe, Anglophobe, xenophobe, technophobe, homophobe, claustrophobe, Europhobe, Russophobe, * agoraphobe

35.21 bloke, broke, choke, cloak, coke, Coke®, croak, folk, joke, moke, oak, poke, smoke, soak, spoke, stoke, stroke, woke, yoke, yolk, * provoke, convoke, baroque, awoke, unyoke, decoke, bespoke, evoke, revoke, invoke, * backstroke, Greystoke, menfolk, Pembroke, breaststroke, keystroke, heatstroke, kinfolk, kinsfolk, in-joke, cowpoke, townsfolk, downstroke, slowpoke, upstroke, sunstroke, * masterstroke, artichoke, Basingstoke, gentlefolk, womenfolk, counterstroke, Roanoke, Holyoake, stony-broke, okey-doke

35.22 coax, chokes, cloaks, folks, hoax, Noakes, oaks, Oakes, stokes, yolks, * artichokes, Sevenoaks, etc.

35.23 choked, cloaked, croaked, smoked, stoked, stroked, * provoked,

unyoked, unsoaked, unsmoked, evoked, revoked, * unprovoked, unrevoked, etc.

35.24 broach, brooch, coach, Loach, poach, roach, Roach, * approach, reproach, encroach, * stagecoach, mailcoach, cockroach, slowcoach, * motorcoach, self-reproach

35.25 blowed, bode, bowed, code, crowed, flowed, glowed, goad, load, lode, mode, mowed, node, ode, owed, road, rode, rowed, snowed, Spode, strode, toad, towed, woad, * abode, unload, upload, corrode, commode, decode, reload, encode, bestowed, explode, implode, erode, off-load, forebode, Morse code, download, * cathode, hallowed, vanload, arrowed, narrowed, bar code, cartload, payload, railroad, echoed, mellowed, yellowed, shedload, freeload, workload, zip code, widowed, tiptoed, shipload, diode, triode, byroad, highroad, sideroad, followed, swallowed, borrowed, sorrowed, download, postcode, boatload, coachload, toll road, truckload, burrowed, furrowed, * foreshadowed, unhallowed, re-echoed, electrode, * wagonload, à la mode, nematode, anyroad, episode, pigeon-toed, incommode, discommode, lorryload, overload, overflowed, overrode, * mustachioed, etc.

Before the Roman came to Rye or out to Severn strode,
The rolling English drunkard made the rolling English road.
G. K. CHESTERTON

35.26 codes, goads, loads, Rhodes,

toads, * cartloads, inroads, byroads, highroads, crossroads, truckloads, etc.

35.27 loaf, oaf

35.28 brogue, drogue, Pogue, rogue, vogue, *Vogue*, * Minogue, prorogue, * disembogue

35.29 doge, loge, Vosges, * Limoges

35.30 bole, boll, bowl, coal, Cole, dole, droll, foal, goal, hole, Knole, knoll, Knowle, kohl, Kohl, mole, pole, Pole, poll, prole, role, roll, Scholl, scroll, Seoul, shoal, skol, sole, soul, stole, stroll, toll, troll, vole, whole, * condole, parole, patrol, control, unroll, console, cajole, Nicole, de Gaulle, pistole, extol, Tyrol, enrol, North Pole, South Pole, * flagpole, tadpole, manhole, asshole, bankroll, bargepole, charcoal, armhole, arsehole, air hole, maypole, payroll, hellhole, bedroll, wormhole, earhole, Creole, Sheol, beanpole, keyhole, kneehole, peephole, fishbowl, Wimpole, ridgepole, pinhole, sinkhole, rissole, insole, dipole, eyehole, spyhole, foxhole, knothole, pothole, logroll, console, straw poll, Walpole, borehole, porthole, mousehole, rose bowl, blowhole, dust bowl, punchbowl, Rumpole, lughole, plughole, loophole, * Gallup poll, caracole, farandole, banderole, casserole, cabriole, dariole, Nat King Cole, camisole, vacuole, barcarole, Charles de Gaulle, self-control, Seminole, pigeonhole, rigmarole, hidy-hole, rock'n'roll, bronchiole, MORI poll, sausage roll, water hole, aureole, gloriole, oriole, glory hole, totem pole, buttonhole, cubbyhole, multirole, * arteriole, profiterole

Old King Cole was a merry old soul.
Nursery rhyme

35.31 bold, bowled, cold, fold, gold, hold, mould, old, polled, rolled, scold, sold, soled, strolled, told, wold, * unpolled, untold, unfold, uphold, paroled, patrolled, controlled, unrolled, unsold, consoled, cajoled, retold, remould, extolled, enfold, behold, withhold, enrolled, ice-cold, foretold, stone-cold, * mangold, scaffold, handhold, bankrolled, eightfold, gatefold, Penfold, tenfold, threshold, threefold, sheepfold, freehold, leasehold, remould, sixfold, billfold, blindfold, fivefold, ninefold, Reinhold, potholed, stronghold, Cotswold, Courtauld, fourfold, household, toehold, Rumbold, foothold, twofold, * stranglehold, casseroled, marigold, manifold, centrefold, sevenfold, self-controlled, semibold, Leopold, pigeonholed, hundredfold, buttonholed, uncontrolled, multifold, * remote-controlled, * lo and behold, Stow-on-the-Wold, etc.

The Assyrian came down like the wolf on the fold,
And his cohorts were gleaming in purple and gold.
Lord Byron

35.32 bolt, Bolt, Boult, colt, Colt, dolt, holt, jolt, moult, poult, smolt, volt, * unbolt, revolt, * eyebolt, ringbolt, Northolt, Humboldt, U-bolt, * megavolt, kilovolt, thunderbolt, * electronvolt

35.33 Bowles, bowls, coals, holes,

Knowles, poles, rolls, Rolls, Scholes, voles, etc.

35.34 chrome, comb, dome, foam, Frome, gnome, holm, home, loam, ohm, Ohm, Om, pome, roam, Rome, tome, * Jerome, backcomb, rehome, * maelstrom, Beerbohm, genome, syndrome, biome, rhizome, cockscomb, coxcomb, Stockholm, Bornholm, prodrome, * astrodome, gastronome, palindrome, aerodrome, velodrome, metronome, hippodrome, liposome, Styrofoam®, ribosome, fine-tooth comb, monochrome, polychrome, Kodachrome®, chromosome, tumblehome, currycomb, honeycomb, Wolstenholme

Mid pleasures and palaces though we may roam,
Be it ever so humble, there's no place like home.
J. H. Payne

35.35 combs, gnomes, Holmes, Soames, tomes, etc.

35.36 Beaune, blown, bone, clone, cone, crone, drone, flown, groan, grown, hone, Joan, known, loan, lone, moan, mown, none, own, phone, pone, prone, Rhône, roan, scone, sewn, shown, Sloane, sown, stone, throne, thrown, tone, zone, * Capone, condone, atone, alone, cologne, Cologne, Malone, Stallone, unknown, unsewn, well-known, dethrone, intone, ingrown, enthrone, bemoan, Simone, disown, Tyrone, trombone, outgrown, postpone, home-grown, full-blown, * backbone, Rathbone, capstone, Blackstone, flagstone, sandstone, halftone, cardphone, whalebone, aitchbone, Maidstone, gravestone, hailstone, payphone, breastbone, headstone, whetstone, gemstone, cellphone, kerbstone, birthstone, turnstone, earphone, cheekbone, keystone, freephone, hipbone, shinbone, fishbone, wishbone, millstone, brimstone, clingstone, windblown, firestone, thighbone, pine cone, grindstone, milestone, limestone, rhinestone, flyblown, cyclone, jawbone, gallstone, hormone, warzone, neurone, nose cone, copestone, soapstone, lodestone, ozone, bloodstone, touchstone, two-tone, tombstone, moonstone, * anklebone, Al Capone, staddlestone, Francophone, Anglophone, gramophone, saxophone, stand-alone, chaperone, baritone, acetone, marrowbone, answerphone, barbitone, methadone, megaphone, pheromone, herringbone, semitone, stepping-stone, entryphone, telephone, Yellowstone, skin and bone, Silverstone, Dictaphone®, Linguaphone®, pick-your-own, silicone, bridging loan, ironstone, xylophone, vibraphone, microphone, collarbone, monotone, cobblestone, homophone, cornerstone, cortisone, eurozone, overtone, home-alone, overblown, Toblerone®, overgrown, overthrown, holystone, mobile phone, knucklebone, cuttlebone, undertone, undergrown, unbeknown, fully grown, sousaphone, Movietone®, * Rosetta Stone, progesterone, testosterone, * eau de Cologne, accident-prone, Marylebone, anticyclone, radiophone, videophone, * Sierra Leone, * hydrocortisone

There may be times when couples need
   a chaperone,
But mothers ought to learn to leave a
   chap alone.
DION TITHERAGE

35.37 boned, cloned, groaned, moaned,
owned, phoned, stoned, * unboned,
condoned, atoned, unstoned,
dethroned, intoned, enthroned,
bemoaned, disowned, postponed,
* state-owned, rawboned, * chaperoned,
telephoned, * unchaperoned, etc.

35.38 don't, wont, won't

35.39 bones, clones, Joan's, Jones,
nones, phones, stones, Stones, zones,
* condones, atones, Simone's,
trombones, Tom Jones, postpones,
Dow-Jones, * flagstones, hailstones,
headphones, gemstones, fishbones,
Flintstones, pine cones, rhinestones,
crossbones, sawbones, hormones,
* lazybones, Davy Jones, pheromones,
cobblestones, Rolling Stones,
knucklebones, * skull and crossbones,
etc.

35.40 cope, dope, grope, hope, lope,
mope, nope, pope, rope, scope, slope,
soap, taupe, tope, trope, * aslope,
elope, Bob Hope, soft-soap,
* tightrope, towrope, * gastroscope,
allotrope, antipope, antelope,
endoscope, stethoscope, spectroscope,
envelope, telescope, periscope,
philanthrope, misanthrope, skipping
rope, gyroscope, microscope, isotope,
lycanthrope, horoscope, docu-soap,
stroboscope, zoetrope,
* ophthalmoscope, electroscope,
oscilloscope, * laparoscope,

stereoscope, CinemaScope®,
heliotrope

35.41 hopes, mopes, ropes, Stopes, etc.

And scribbled lines like fallen hopes
On backs of tattered envelopes.
FRANCIS HOPE

35.42 close, dose, gross, * jocose,
morose, verbose, engross, * lactose,
dextrose, viscose, ribose, fructose,
glucose, sucrose, * grandiose, adipose,
varicose, lachrymose, bellicose,
cellulose, overdose, comatose, otiose

35.43 boast, coast, dosed, ghost, host,
most, oast, post, roast, toast, * riposte,
engrossed, * lamppost, backmost,
gatepost, bedpost, endmost,
sternmost, rearmost, Freepost®,
seacoast, midmost, inmost, guidepost,
milepost, signpost, hindmost,
topmost, doorpost, foremost, almost,
soundpost, outpost, outmost, goalpost,
upmost, utmost, * lattermost,
aftermost, farthermost, nethermost,
westernmost, furthermost,
easternmost, innermost, middlemost,
bottommost, northernmost,
outermost, overdosed, lowermost,
uppermost, undermost, uttermost,
southernmost, newel post

35.44 gauche, Roche

35.45 bloat, boat, coat, dote, float, gloat,
goat, groat, moat, mote, note, oat,
quote, rote, smote, stoat, throat, tote,
vote, wrote, * afloat, promote, connote,
unquote, refloat, rewrote, devote,
misquote, demote, emote, remote,
denote, outvote, * catboat, flatboat,

banknote, sailboat, whaleboat, greatcoat, waistcoat, tailcoat, raincoat, scapegoat, redcoat, endnote, turncoat, speedboat, keelboat, dreamboat, steamboat, sheepcote, keynote, swingboat, lifeboat, zygote, whitethroat, longboat, topcoat, sauce boat, houseboat, housecoat, powerboat, rowboat, showboat, tugboat, gunboat, dovecote, cut-throat, footnote, U-boat, Bluecoat, * nanny goat, antidote, anecdote, asymptote, narrow boat, table d'hôte, gravy boat, sailing boat, ferry boat, petticoat, redingote, creosote, billy goat, entrecôte, motorboat, overcoat, overwrote, rowing boat, undercoat, underwrote

The llama is a woolly sort of fleecy hairy goat,
With an indolent expression and an undulating throat.
HILAIRE BELLOC

35.46 Coates, coats, floats, goats, groats, notes, Oates, oats, votes, * banknotes, redcoats, speedboats, lifeboats, footnotes, * anecdotes, ferry boats, John o'Groats, motorboats, etc.

35.47 both, growth, loath, oath, quoth, sloth, troth, * Arbroath, regrowth, ingrowth, outgrowth, * overgrowth, undergrowth

35.48 clothe, loathe, * unclothe, reclothe, betroth

35.49 clothes, loathes, * unclothes, plain clothes, reclothes, betroths, * bedclothes, nightclothes, * underclothes

35.50 clove, cove, drove, grove, hove, Hove, Jove, mauve, rove, shrove, stove, strove, throve, trove, wove, * behove, * alcove, mangrove, Bromsgrove, Musgrove, * treasure trove, interwove, Primus stove®, olive grove

35.51 cloves, droves, groves, Groves, loaves, stoves, etc.

35.52 blows, chose, close, crows, doze, flows, foes, froze, gloze, goes, hose, Joe's, Mo's, nose, pose, prose, rose, Rose, shows, snows, those, throes, toes, woes, * oppose, propose, suppose, compose, arose, transpose, depose, refroze, repose, impose, dispose, expose, bestows, enclose, disclose, Montrose, foreclose, outgrows, * lactose, aloes, gallows, arrows, narrows, sparrows, Ambrose, cargoes, Margot's, Faeroes, scarecrows, rainbows, Plato's, Waitrose, elbows, echoes, bellows, Fellowes, mellows, Melrose, windows, pillows, primrose, minnows, crossbows, bongos, follows, swallows, sorrows, rockrose, hobos, photos, bulldoze, hooknose, glucose, mucose, Hugo's, * foreshadows, marshmallows, Allhallows, Picasso's, * adipose, pantihose, lachrymose, granulose, guelder-rose, quelquechose, bellicose, pettitoes, cellulose, Berlioz, furbelows, presuppose, decompose, recompose, reimpose, predispose, interpose, discompose, indispose, diagnose, Comoros, bottlenose, dominoes, curios, comatose, stone the crows, otiose, juxtapose, bungalows, come to blows, shovelnose, superpose, tuberose, studios, * arpeggios, misdiagnose, portfolios, * photocompose, superimpose,

overexpose, underexpose,
* metamorphose, etc.

**Whilst Adam slept, Eve from his side
  arose:**
**Strange his first sleep should be his
  last repose.**
ANONYMOUS

35.53 closed, dozed, hosed, nosed,
posed, * opposed, proposed,
supposed, composed, unposed,
deposed, imposed, disposed, exposed,
enclosed, disclosed, * well-disposed,
decomposed, predisposed,
discomposed, ill-disposed, indisposed,
snotty-nosed, toffee-nosed,
unopposed, unexposed, undisclosed,
superposed, * undiagnosed,
misdiagnosed, * superimposed,
overexposed, underexposed, etc.

36.1 Chloe, doughy, joey, Joey, showy,
snowy, Zoe, dhobi, Gobi, goby, obi,
Robey, Roby, Scobie, Toby, dopey,
Hopi, mopy, Opie, ropey, soapy, topee,
blokey, chokey, croaky, jokey, Loki,
oaky, poky, smoky, trochee, bogey,
Bogie, dogie, fogey, Logie, yogi, Yogi,
Brodie, Cody, Jodie, roadie, toady,
Goldie, mouldy, oldie, dhoti, floaty,
goaty, oaty, throaty, postie, toasty,
Brophy, Kofi, Sophie, strophe, trophy,
Povey, Tovey, coaly, coley, Foley, goalie,
holey, holy, lowly, Rowley, slowly,
nobly, Oakley, Mowgli, boldly, coldly,
ghostly, mostly, solely, wholly, homely,
lonely, only, Stoneleigh, closely,
grossly, Knowsley, Mosley, snowberry,
poultry, blowy, Bowie, foamy, homey,
know me, loamy, bony, coney, crony,
phony, pony, stony, Toni, Tony, Josie,
folksy, cosy, dozy, Losey, mosey, nosy,

posy, prosy, Rosie, rosy, ogee, * adobe,
Nairobi, Capote, coyote, unholy, aïoli,
ignobly, remotely, jocosely, morosely,
Dahomey, Salome, Naomi, Bodoni,
Mahoney, baloney, Maloney,
Mulroney, Marconi, Leonie, Oenone,
Giorgione, * shadowy, willowy,
shallowly, narrowly, sorrowfully,
* kalanchoe, karaoke, hokey-cokey,
okey-dokey, golden oldie, Don
Quixote, guacamole, ravioli, roly-poly,
Gaborone, mascarpone, panettone,
abalone, cannelloni, zabaglione,
macaroni, Annigoni, Castiglione,
Albinoni, pepperoni, Berlusconi,
cicerone, minestrone, virtuosi,
* Antonioni, * Sierra Leone,
* Obi-Wan Kenobi, *conversazione*, etc.

36.2 blower, boa, Boer, Goa, goer,
grower, lower, moa, mower, Noah, o'er,
rower, sewer, slower, sower, stoa,
thrower, zoa, * aloha, Samoa, Balboa,
jerboa, * racegoer, flamethrower,
churchgoer, winegrower, Hornblower,
lawn mower, snowblower, woolgrower,
* Alloa, shallower, narrower, mellower,
genoa, Genoa, widower, follower,
borrower, * Shenandoah, Krakatoa,
theatregoer, partygoer, concertgoer,
protozoa, * cinemagoer, Mies van der
Rohe, spermatozoa, * know her, throw
her, etc.

A million million spermatozoa,
All of them alive:
**Out of their cataclysm but one poor
  Noah**
Dare hope to survive.
ALDOUS HUXLEY

36.3 lobar, sober, dopa, groper, hoper,
moper, Roper, Soper, toper, * October,

jojoba, eloper, Europa, no-hoper,
* Manitoba, interloper, * probe her,
dope her, etc.

36.4 broker, choker, coca, croaker,
joker, ochre, poker, smoker, stoker,
Stoker, ogre, toga, yoga, * provoker,
invoker, nonsmoker, * shipbroker,
stockbroker, pawnbroker, * tapioca,
mediocre, Saratoga, hatha yoga,
* Ticonderoga, * woke her, provoke
her, etc.

36.5 Clodagh, coda, coder, loader,
Oder, odour, Rhoda, Skoda, soda,
bolder, boulder, colder, folder, Golda,
holder, moulder, older, polder,
shoulder, smoulder, solder, bloater,
boater, floater, gloater, motor, quota,
rota, rotor, scoter, scrota, voter,
moulter, Poulter, boaster, coaster,
poster, roaster, toaster, Towcester,
bolster, holster, pollster, * pagoda,
decoder, encoder, beholder, cold-
shoulder, Dakota, promoter, iota,
nonvoter, Toyota, four-poster,
upholster, * freeloader, gasholder,
cardholder, shareholder, stakeholder,
freeholder, keyholder, leaseholder,
stockholder, bondholder, smallholder,
stallholder, householder, fundholder,
billposter, * candleholder, titleholder,
record-holder, Minnesota, roller-
coaster, * policyholder, * told her,
promote her, etc.

36.6 chauffeur, gofer, goffer, gopher,
loafer, sofa, clover, Dover, drover,
Grover, nova, ova, over, rover, Rover,
loather, * Pavlova, Markova, ars nova,
Jehovah, Moldova, moreover,
* Hanover, handover, hangover, Land
Rover, flashover, Passover, makeover,

takeover, changeover, Range Rover,
Wendover, leftover, turnover,
sleepover, slipover, tick-over, flyover,
stopover, crossover, Bolsover,
walkover, voice-over, rollover, once-
over, pullover, pushover, * Casanova,
bossa nova, supernova, going-over,
* Navratilova, * drove her, loathe her,
etc.

There'll be bluebirds over
The white cliffs of Dover.
NAT BURTON

36.7 bola, bowler, coaler, cola, droller,
Lola, molar, polar, roller, solar,
stroller, Zola, nobler, ogler, cobra,
Oprah, Bowyer, * aloha, patroller,
controller, Angola, payola, premolar,
viola, bipolar, tombola, Loyola,
* steamroller, potholer, roadroller,
* alveolar, Pepsi-Cola®, Pianola®,
minneola, rock'n'roller, bronchiolar,
Gorgonzola, Coca-Cola®, Motorola,
Moviola®, unipolar, * Hispaniola,
* stole her, console her, etc.

36.8 coma, comber, Cromer, Gomer,
homer, Homer, Omagh, omer, roamer,
Roma, soma, stoma, boner, donor,
groaner, Jonah, krona, krone, loner,
moaner, Mona, owner, Rhona, Shona,
stoner, toner, Grosvenor, * Tacoma,
aroma, sarcoma, diploma, lymphoma,
misnomer, fibroma, glaucoma,
neuroma, corona, Verona, Pomona,
Ramona, Ancona, Pamplona, Daytona,
persona, Fiona, cinchona, Cremona,
Winona, Iona, co-owner,
* beachcomber, landowner, shipowner,
homeowner, * papilloma, adenoma,
carcinoma, melanoma, haematoma,
Oklahoma, Arizona, Barcelona,

Desdemona, * phone her, disown her, etc.

36.9 closer, grocer, grosser, hoaxer, dozer, poser, Rosa, closure, brochure, kosher, poacher, loggia, soldier, * samosa, mimosa, Formosa, mucosa, opposer, proposer, composer, sub rosa, Mendoza, Spinoza, composure, exposure, disclosure, enclosure, foreclosure, * greengrocer, bulldozer, * Nova Scotia, apologia, * underexposure, overexposure, * anorexia nervosa, * knows her, reproach her, etc.

36.10 stoic, Stoic, phobic, strobic, * echoic, heroic, aerobic, * Mesozoic, Cenozoic, unheroic, acrophobic, aquaphobic, anaerobic, aquaerobic, xenophobic, technophobic, necrophobic, hydrophobic, photophobic, homophobic, claustrophobic, Europhobic, yogic, strophic, folic, bromic, chromic, gnomic, homesick, * achromic, dichromic, * polychromic, photochromic, * arachnophobic, * agoraphobic, Islamophobic

36.11 prolix, * heroics, aerobics, * aquaerobics

36.12 froward, brokered, boded, coded, goaded, loaded, folded, mouldered, smouldered, soldered, bloated, coated, dotard, doted, floated, gloated, noted, quoted, voted, wonted, posted, toasted, roasted, bolstered, chauffeured, homeward, soldiered, * uncoded, unloaded, uploaded, corroded, decoded, reloaded, exploded, encoded, spring-loaded, eroded, downloaded,

outmoded, unfolded, round-shouldered, promoted, demoted, denoted, devoted, misquoted, outvoted, unwonted, * railroaded, freeloaded, steamrollered, * overloaded, colour-coded, unexploded, creosoted, sugar-coated, etc.

36.13 dotards, homewards

36.14 flowage, stowage, towage, soakage, dotage, flotage, voltage, postage, dosage, Trowbridge, tollbridge, * anecdotage, overdosage

36.15 Joel, Lowell, Noel, Powell, Froebel, global, Mobil®, noble, opal, focal, local, socle, vocal, yokel, bogle, mogul, ogle, modal, nodal, yodel, scrotal, total, coastal, postal, woeful, hopeful, boastful, slothful, doleful, soulful, oval, Oval, Yeovil, tonal, zonal, fo'c's'le, social, * bestowal, Chernobyl, ennoble, Grenoble, ignoble, bifocal, nonlocal, subtotal, teetotal, reproachful, betrothal, coronal, atonal, hormonal, proposal, deposal, disposal, unsocial, asocial, * Adrianople, Constantinople, varifocal, sacerdotal, anecdotal, chromosomal, monoclonal, antisocial, * counterproposal

36.16 Roald, ogled, yodelled, * ennobled, etc.

36.17 Joel's, nobles, locals, yokels, * bifocals, * varifocals, etc.

36.18 Noam, poem, phloem, hokum, locum, Oakham, oakum, Slocombe, Oldham, popedom, scrotum, totem, ovum, Botham, Bolam, Mowlem,

loathsome, wholesome, lonesome,
* Siloam, factotum, unwholesome,
* Jeroboam, Rehoboam, * grow 'em,
wrote 'em, etc.

36.19 Bowen, Cohen, Owen, throw-in,
Tobin, goatskin, moleskin, Odin,
bowline, Goldwyn, Cronin, phone-in,
* pangolin, * haemoglobin, melatonin,
serotonin, * rollin', moanin', etc.

36.20 rowan, Oban, Woburn, open,
broken, oaken, spoken, token, woken,
brogan, Cogan, Grogan, Hogan,
Logan, shogun, slogan, Wogan, loden,
Snowdon, Woden, golden, Holden,
olden, oaten, Stoughton, Bolton,
Boulton, Doulton, molten, Poulton,
Folkestone, cloven, proven, woven,
colon, Nolan, Solon, stolen, stollen,
swollen, bowman, foeman, omen,
Roman, showman, yeoman, Goldman,
boatman, postman, coalman,
Coleman, Colman, coachman, Conan,
Onan, Ronan, bosun, Robeson, Jolson,
chosen, frozen, Rosen, plosion, lotion,
motion, notion, ocean, potion, Trojan,
* Samoan, Virgoan, Minoan, Iowan,
reopen, unspoken, unbroken, awoken,
plain-spoken, well-spoken, betoken,
foretoken, outspoken, beholden,
embolden, Dakotan, unproven,
Moldovan, Angolan, abdomen,
patrolman, unfrozen, well-chosen,
refrozen, corrosion, explosion,
implosion, erosion, commotion,
promotion, demotion, emotion,
devotion, * heartbroken, Hoboken,
Beethoven, Eindhoven, * protozoan,
Manitoban, Minnesotan, ibuprofen,
interwoven, semicolon, Oklahoman,
Arizonan, lederhosen, locomotion,
Nova Scotian, theologian

And many a word, at random spoken,
May soothe or wound a heart that's
broken.
Sir Walter Scott

36.21 opened, jocund, lowland, Poland,
Roland, Copeland, Copland,
* unopened, betokened, emboldened,
ill-omened, Loch Lomond, etc.

36.22 rodent, potent, Solent, moment,
quotient, cogent, * elopement,
cajolement, enrolment, atonement,
enthronement, postponement,
encroachment, opponent, proponent,
component, exponent

36.23 rodents, moments, * condolence,
opponents, components, etc.

36.24 Boeing, bowing, flowing,
glowing, going, growing, knowing,
owing, rowing, sewing, snowing,
probing, robing, coping, groping,
hoping, moping, sloping, choking,
croaking, joking, smoking, soaking,
Woking, boding, coding, goading,
loading, folding, Golding, holding,
moulding, scolding, boating, coating,
doting, floating, gloating, quoting,
voting, jolting, moulting, boasting,
coasting, ghosting, hosting, posting,
roasting, toasting, bowstring, loafing,
coving, roving, clothing, loathing,
bowling, polling, rolling, Rowling,
scrolling, strolling, tolling, ogling,
O-ring, nose ring, coaming, combing,
foaming, gloaming, homing, roaming,
boning, cloning, droning, groaning,
moaning, owning, phoning, stoning,
closing, dozing, hosing, posing,
broaching, coaching, poaching,
* unknowing, bestowing, foregoing,

enrobing, disrobing, eloping,
provoking, no-smoking, unloading,
uploading, corroding, decoding,
reloading, exploding, encoding,
eroding, foreboding, downloading,
unfolding, upholding, enfolding,
beholding, promoting, denoting,
misquoting, nonvoting, revolting,
patrolling, controlling, unrolling,
consoling, cajoling, extolling,
enrolling, condoning, intoning,
bemoaning, disowning, postponing,
opposing, proposing, supposing,
composing, reposing, imposing,
enclosing, disclosing, foreclosing,
approaching, reproaching,
encroaching, * glass-blowing, ingoing,
ingrowing, mind-blowing, ongoing,
foregoing, outgoing, stockbroking,
pawnbroking, railroading, freeloading,
breech-loading, shareholding,
smallholding, roadholding,
fundholding, billposting, flyposting,
potholing, logrolling, backcombing,
Wyoming, landowning, homeowning,
bulldozing, * shadowing, harrowing,
echoing, bellowing, seagoing,
billowing, winnowing, following,
borrowing, sorrowing, burrowing,
* easy-going, ocean-going, overflowing,
thoroughgoing, undergoing, thought-
provoking, autoloading, overloading,
underclothing, casseroling, tenpin
bowling, pigeonholing, buttonholing,
chaperoning, telephoning,
presupposing, decomposing,
diagnosing, juxtaposing, etc.

**He that goes a-borrowing, goes a-
   sorrowing.**
SAYING

36.25 loess, Lois, Powys, notice, Otis,

poultice, Bovis, Hovis®, Clovis, gnosis,
ptosis, * Adonis, sclerosis, narcosis,
necrosis, cirrhosis, stenosis, hypnosis,
fibrosis, meiosis, psychosis, mitosis,
thrombosis, osmosis, prognosis,
lordosis, neurosis, * allantois,
stephanotis, myosotis, Issigonis,
anthracosis, psittacosis, cyanosis,
diagnosis, asbestosis, silicosis,
toxicosis, acidosis, halitosis,
brucellosis, scoliosis, symbiosis,
* myxomatosis, anastomosis,
misdiagnosis, autohypnosis,
psychoneurosis, apotheosis,
tuberculosis, * osteoporosis,
endometriosis, pneumoconiosis,
mononucleosis, * arteriosclerosis

36.26 globus, opus, crocus, focus,
hocus, locus, bogus, lotus, Scotus,
bolus, solus, toeless, hopeless,
smokeless, goalless, soulless,
homeless, boneless, stoneless, bonus,
Cronus, Jonas, lowness, slowness,
onus, tonus, boldness, coldness,
wholeness, closeness, * Canopus,
refocus, Duns Scotus, Aeolus,
remoteness, atrocious, ferocious,
precocious, * shadowless, shallowness,
narrowness, mellowness, yellowness,
windowless, hollowness, * magnum
opus, diplodocus, autofocus, hocus-
pocus, ceanothus, gladiolus,
* pithecanthropus, * know us, told us,
etc.

**Supercalifragilisticexpialidocious
Even though the sound of it is
   something quite atrocious
If you say it loud enough, you'll always
   sound precocious.
Supercalifragilisticexpialidocious!**
RICHARD & ROBERT SHERMAN

36.27 noticed, Fauvist, Gaullist,
* unnoticed, trombonist

36.28 goest, knowest, slowest, focused,
locust, boldest, coldest, oldest,
drollest, noblest, closest, grossest,
* unfocused, refocused, * narrowest,
shallowest, mellowest, etc.

36.29 slowish, modish, soapdish,
oldish, roguish, voguish, oafish,
toadfish, goldfish, stonefish, Polish

36.30 poet, obit, Tobit, notelet,
bowsprit, * inchoate, * know it, hold
it, etc.

Sir, I admit your gen'ral rule
That every poet is a fool:
But you yourself may serve to show it,
That every fool is not a poet.
ALEXANDER POPE

36.31 poets, obits, Colditz, notelets,
bowsprits

36.32 motive, votive, plosive,
* emotive, corrosive, explosive,
implosive, * locomotive, automotive

36.33 Toby's, showbiz, fogeys, oldies,
trophies, Chloe's, cronies, ponies,
posies, * litotes, psychoses, prognoses,
neuroses, * golden oldies, diagnoses,
* holy of holies, etc.

36.34 mowers, rowers, Sobers, brokers,
jokers, smokers, boulders, shoulders,
voters, coasters, Klosters, molars,
rollers, owners, Rhona's, doses,
grocers, closes, dozes, Moses, noses,
posers, roses, Joneses, coaches,
poachers, soldiers, * no-hopers,

nonsmokers, opposes, proposes,
* churchgoers, stockbroker,
shareholders, householders, leftovers,
homeowners, greengrocers,
cockroaches, * theatregoers,
interlopers, etc.

36.35 nobody, prosody, Ogilvy,
globally, Moberly, soberly, locally,
vocally, totally, woefully, hopefully,
boastfully, dolefully, overly, Rosalie,
socially, soldierly, notably, openly,
hopelessly, snowberry, Shrewsbury,
popery, roguery, coterie, notary, rotary,
votary, Bovary, ovary, drollery, topiary,
hosiery, rosemary, Rosemary, grocery,
causerie, rosary, gaucherie, soldiery,
loganberry, momentary, yeomanry,
Romany, potency, cogency, probity,
showily, croakily, throatily, stonily,
cosily, stoically, knowingly, jokingly,
roguishly, poetry, poesy, * devotedly,
ferociously, atrociously, upholstery,
cajolery, diplomacy, improbity,
heroically, supposedly, unknowingly,
* uncontrollably, inconsolably,
* jiggery-pokery, etc.

36.36 lowlander, yodeller,
Crowborough, poulterer, opener,
focuser, overture, omega, Colchester,
Frobisher, * teetotaller, upholsterer,
Eroica, * can-opener, tin-opener

36.37 obeah, phobia, dopier, ropier,
soapier, croakier, pokier, smokier,
podia, mouldier, fovea, clothier,
Grolier, holier, lowlier, ghostlier,
lonelier, showier, bonier, phonier,
stonier, cosier, crosier, dozier, hosier,
osier, nosier, rosier, * Zenobia,
dystopia, myopia, Utopia, Cambodia,
Segovia, Fitzrovia, synovia, Monrovia,

magnolia, Mongolia, mahonia, ammonia, Antonia, Estonia, dystonia, sinfonia, dysphonia, Livonia, begonia, Ionia, Snowdonia, pneumonia, ambrosia, symposia, * acrophobia, aquaphobia, aerophobia, xenophobia, technophobia, necrophobia, neophobia, hydrophobia, zoophobia, photophobia, homophobia, nosophobia, claustrophobia, Europhobia, presbyopia, Ethiopia, cornucopia, pseudopodia, Anatolia, melancholia, Patagonia, catatonia, Catalonia, escallonia, Cephalonia, Amazonia, Caledonia, Macedonia, wellingtonia, Babylonia, Cappadocia, apologia, * arachnophobia, * agoraphobia, Islamophobia, bronchopneumonia, etc.

36.38 growable, knowable, mowable, throwable, towable, foldable, mouldable, notable, potable, quotable, sociable, notional, jovial, stoical, coital, * unknowable, revokable, controllable, opposable, disposable, unsociable, negotiable, approachable, reproachable, promotional, emotional, devotional, microbial, parochial, custodial, synovial, colloquial, binomial, colonial, baronial, * uncontrollable, inconsolable, non-negotiable, unapproachable, irreproachable, unemotional, polynomial, matrimonial, patrimonial, testimonial, ceremonial

Ev'ry corner that you turn you meet a notable
With a statement that is eminently quotable!
IRA GERSHWIN

36.39 opium, odium, podium, rhodium, sodium, chromium, Wokingham, * petroleum, linoleum, opprobrium, encomium, polonium, ammonium, harmonium, zirconium, meconium, plutonium, euphonium, * monosodium, pseudopodium, pelargonium, pandemonium

36.40 Auberon, Doberman, nobleman, Odeon, Rhodian, Jovian, Lothian, Groningen, * Fallopian, Salopian, Cyclopean, Utopian, custodian, Cambodian, melodeon, Pavlovian, Harrovian, Chekhovian, Midlothian, Napoleon, Ashmolean, aeolian, Mongolian, Draconian, Dundonian, Estonian, Devonian, Etonian, Miltonian, Livonian, Smithsonian, Ionian, Oxonian, Johnsonian, Newtonian, * Ethiopian, nickelodeon, Nabokovian, Anatolian, Patagonian, Aberdonian, Thessalonian, Ciceronian, Amazonian, Caledonian, Macedonian, Washingtonian, Babylonian, Tennysonian, Cappadocian, theologian

36.41 deodorant, ennoblement, defoliant

36.42 odourless, ownerless, motionless, odorous, onerous, hopefulness, boastfulness, openness, hopelessness, homelessness, copious, Gropius, odious, Grotius, Proteus, coitus, showiness, soapiness, holiness, Holiness, lowliness, loneliness, cosiness, doziness, nosiness, homesickness, * malodorous, precociousness, melodious, commodious, Antonius, harmonious, felonious, Polonius, Thelonious,

erroneous, Petronius, euphonious,
* unmelodious, incommodious,
Apollonius, inharmonious,
disharmonious, Suetonius,
sanctimonious, acrimonious,
parsimonious, ceremonious,
* unceremonious, etc.

36.43 vocalist, socialist, motorist,
chauvinist, coexist, oboist, soloist

36.44 dopiest, ropiest, soapiest,
croakiest, pokiest, smokiest,
mouldiest, holiest, lowliest, ghostliest,
loneliest, showiest, boniest, phoniest,
stoniest, cosiest, doziest, nosiest,
rosiest, etc.

36.45 opiate, foliate, Soviet, roseate,
* appropriate, associate, * inappropriate

36.46 focusable, noticeable

-u-

The rhymes in this section have the 'u' sound of run *and* double *as their main or final vowel sound. You can also rhyme some of these words with words ending in a weak 'u' sound (e.g.* maximum, exodus*), which you will find in other sections.*

37.1 blub, bub, chub, Chubb®, club, cub, Cub, drub, dub, grub, hub, nub, pub, rub, scrub, shrub, slub, snub, stub, sub, tub, * bathtub, Jacob, cherub, nightclub, washtub, hubbub, * syllabub, overdub, * Beelzebub

Rub-a-dub-dub,
Three men in a tub.
NURSERY RHYME

37.2 clubs, cubs, Cubs, grubs, pubs, shrubs, stubs, Stubbs, subs, * mulligrubs, etc.

37.3 buck, Buck, chuck, Chuck, cluck, cruck, duck, fuck, guck, Huck, luck, muck, pluck, puck, Puck, ruck, schmuck, shuck, snuck, struck, stuck, suck, truck, tuck, yuck, * untuck, unstuck, amok, Canuck, lame duck, Friar Tuck, pot luck, * Kalmuck, Tarbuck, stage-struck, shelduck, sawbuck, Norfolk, awestruck, roebuck, jumbuck, mukluk, dumbstruck, bullock, Bullock, bulwark, woodchuck, nubuck, moonstruck, * liposuck, waterbuck, fork-lift truck, thunderstruck, * high-muck-a-muck

37.4 bucks, Bucks, Chuck's, crux, ducks, dux, flux, shucks, sucks, trucks, tux, * de luxe, * reflux, influx, conflux, Dulux®, * megabucks, Benelux, fork-lift trucks, etc.

37.5 chucked, clucked, ducked, duct, plucked, sucked, tucked, * product, conduct, untucked, unplucked, obstruct, construct, abduct, deduct, induct, instruct, * conduct, construct, * misconduct, * aqueduct, self-destruct, deconstruct, reconstruct, viaduct, oviduct, usufruct, * autodestruct, etc.

37.6 clutch, crutch, Dutch, hutch, Kutch, much, such, touch, * retouch, declutch, * nonesuch, * forasmuch, inasmuch, insomuch, overmuch, such-and-such

37.7 clutched, touched, * untouched, retouched, declutched

37.8 blood, bud, crud, cud, dud, flood, Judd, mud, rudd, scud, spud, stud, thud, * m'lud, debud, disbud, * taste bud, lifeblood, oxblood, rosebud, * chew the cud, * stick-in-the-mud

Mud, mud, glorious mud
Nothing quite like it for cooling the
   blood.
MICHAEL FLANDERS & DONALD SWANN

37.9 buds, duds, floods, spuds, studs, suds, * taste buds, rosebuds, soapsuds, etc.

37.10 bluff, Brough, buff, chough, chuff, Clough, cuff, duff, fluff, gruff, guff, huff, luff, muff, puff, rough, ruff, scruff, scuff, slough, snuff, stuff, tough, * McDuff, rebuff, enough, * handcuff, dandruff, Fairclough, seraph, earmuff, feedstuff, greenstuff, dyestuff, bumfluff, woodruff, Woodruff, foodstuff, * off-the-cuff, powder puff, overstuff

37.11 cuffs, muffs, puffs, * handcuffs, earmuffs, * fisticuffs, powder puffs, etc.

37.12 bluffed, chuffed, puffed, scuffed, stuffed, tuft, * unstuffed, rebuffed, * candytuft, overstuffed, etc.

37.13 Crufts, tufts

37.14 bug, chug, Doug, drug, dug, fug, glug, hug, jug, lug, mug, plug, pug, rug, shrug, slug, smug, snug, thug, trug, tug, * unplug, debug, * hearth rug, bedbug, earplug, firebug, Rawlplug®, humbug, * jitterbug, litterbug, superbug, doodlebug

37.15 bludge, budge, drudge, fudge, grudge, judge, nudge, pudge, Rudge, sludge, smudge, trudge, * adjudge, prejudge, begrudge, misjudge

**There comes Poe with his raven, like Barnaby Rudge,
Three-fifths of him genius, and two-fifths sheer fudge.**
JAMES RUSSELL LOWELL

37.16 cull, dull, gull, hull, Hull, lull, mull, Mull, null, scull, skull, * annul, * seagull, mogul, Mogul, numbskull, * Jethro Tull, disannul, monohull, Solihull, multihull

37.17 bulb, * flashbulb

37.18 bulk, hulk, skulk, sulk

37.19 bulked, hulked, skulked, sulked, mulct

37.20 gulch, mulch

37.21 gulf, Gulf, * engulf, * Ranulph, Biddulph

37.22 bulge, * indulge, divulge, * overindulge

37.23 gulp, pulp

37.24 gulped, pulped, sculpt

37.25 dulse, Hulse, pulse, * convulse, repulse, * impulse

37.26 cult, * adult, consult, insult, result, exult, occult, * adult, insult, occult, tumult, * catapult, difficult, * jurisconsult

37.27 Brum, bum, chum, come, crumb, drum, dumb, glum, gum, hum, mum, numb, plum, plumb, Rum, rhumb, rum, scrum, scum, slum, some, strum, sum, swum, thrum, thumb, tum, um, * succumb, become, benumb, dim sum, Tom Thumb, ho-hum, yum-yum, * breadcrumb, eardrum, outcome, dumdum, humdrum, * kettledrum, wearisome, Tweedledum, overcome, bubble gum, sugarplum, chewing gum

Silence the pianos and with muffled
  drum
Bring out the coffin, let the mourners
  come.
W. H. AUDEN

O Captain! my Captain! our fearful trip
  is done,
The ship has weathered every rack, the
  prize we sought is won.
WALT WHITMAN

37.28 bumf, humph, * galumph,
harrumph, * triumph

37.29 bump, chump, clump, dump,
frump, grump, hump, jump, lump,
plump, pump, rump, scrump, slump,
stump, sump, thump, trump, tump,
* gazump, * ski jump, bilge pump,
high jump, long jump, mugwump,
* Forrest Gump, overtrump,
undertrump, sugar lump

37.30 bumps, dumps, humps, lumps,
mumps, pumps, trumps,
* goosebumps, * sugar lumps, etc.

37.31 bun, done, Donne, dun, Dunn,
fun, gun, Gunn, Hun, Lunn, none,
nun, Nunn, one, pun, run, shun, son,
spun, stun, sun, Sun, ton, tonne, tun,
won, * undone, hard-won, A1, Verdun,
redone, rerun, begun, forerun, outgun,
outdone, outrun, close-run,
* handgun, grandson, air gun, Bren
gun, Sten gun, stepson, rerun,
finespun, popgun, shotgun, godson,
homespun, blowgun, shogun, no-one,
someone, * great-grandson, machine
gun, * Gatling gun, Sally Lunn,
aftersun, eighty-one, megaton, Trevor
Nunn, twenty-one, everyone, anyone,
thirty-one, kiloton, hit-and-run, fifty-
one, sixty-one, ninety-one, Tommy
gun, forty-one, overdone, overrun,
underdone, one-to-one, honeybun,
dummy run, * seventy-one, son-of-a-
gun

37.32 bunk, chunk, clunk, drunk,
dunk, flunk, funk, gunk, hunk, junk,
monk, Monk, plunk, punk, shrunk,
skunk, slunk, spunk, stunk, sunk,
thunk, trunk, * preshrunk, debunk,
* chipmunk, quidnunc, punch-drunk,
* cyberpunk, countersunk

37.33 bunks, chunks, hunks, monks,
punks, trunks, * quincunx,
chipmunks, etc.

37.34 clunked, dunked, flunked,
* debunked, defunct, * adjunct,
conjunct, disjunct

37.35 brunch, bunch, crunch, hunch,
lunch, munch, punch, Punch, scrunch,
* honeybunch

37.36 fund, gunned, punned,
shunned, stunned, * refund, rotund,
outgunned, * gerund, fecund, refund,
jocund, * Sigismund, Rosamund,
moribund, orotund, cummerbund,
rubicund

37.37 bung, clung, dung, flung, hung,
lung, rung, slung, sprung, strung,
stung, sung, swung, tongue, wrung,
young, Yonge, Young, * unhung,
unsprung, unstrung, among, unsung,
Shantung, far-flung, rehung, restrung,
* hamstrung, Samsung, oxtongue,
Hoffnung, * aqualung, iron lung,
highly strung, overhung, overstrung,
underhung, underslung

To the vile dust, from whence he
sprung,
Unwept, unhonoured, and unsung.
SIR WALTER SCOTT

37.38 grunge, gunge, lunge, plunge,
sponge, * expunge, * muskellunge

37.39 dunce, once, grunts, hunts,
punts, shunts, * witch-hunts, Y-fronts®,
etc.

37.40 blunt, brunt, Blunt, bunt, cunt,
front, grunt, hunt, Hunt, Lunt, punt,
runt, shunt, stunt, * affront, upfront,
confront, * manhunt, head-hunt,
seafront, witch-hunt, fox hunt, shop
front, forefront, * exeunt, waterfront

37.41 cup, pup, sup, tup, up, yup,
* made-up, fed up, het up, pent up,
World Cup, built-up, mixed-up,
grown-up, stuck-up, jumped-up,
trumped-up, thumbs-up, souped-up,
* backup, hang-up, mark-up, snarl-up,
break-up, make-up, shake-up, paste-
up, rave-up, lace-up, step-up, checkup,
egg cup, send-up, get-up, let-up, setup,
press-up, ketchup, turn-up, teacup,
knees-up, slip-up, hiccup, pick-up,
stick-up, Sidcup, kingcup, linkup,
build-up, sit-up, split-up, pin-up, piss-
up, mix-up, fry-up, eyecup, wind-up,
write-up, pile-up, line-up, pop-up,
top-up, cockup, lockup, mock-up, toss-
up, nosh-up, call-up, warm-up,
roundup, hold-up, grown-up, close-up,
run-up, sunup, punch-up, * Davis
Cup, FA Cup, giddy-up, pick-me-up,
Ryder Cup, coffee cup, washing-up,
follow-up, buttercup, cover-up,
runner-up, up-and-up, summing-up

37.42 cupped, supped, tupped,

* corrupt, abrupt, erupt, irrupt, disrupt,
* bankrupt, hiccuped, * interrupt

37.43 bus, buss, cuss, fuss, Gus, huss,
Huss, muss, plus, pus, Russ, suss,
thus, truss, us, * percuss, concuss,
untruss, debus, embus, discuss,
nonplus, * Airbus®, walrus, postbus,
* battlebus, Belarus, minibus,
trolleybus, omnibus, motorbus,
overplus, blunderbuss

37.44 brusque, busk, dusk, husk, musk,
rusk, tusk, Usk, * mollusc, subfusc

37.45 bust, crust, dost, dust, fussed,
gust, just, lust, mussed, must, rust,
sussed, thrust, trussed, trust,
* combust, concussed, untrussed,
adjust, unjust, discussed, disgust,
encrust, entrust, distrust, mistrust,
nonplussed, august, robust, * stardust,
piecrust, sawdust, shortcrust,
bloodlust, upthrust, * antirust, angel
dust, readjust, bite the dust,
wanderlust, upper crust, unit trust,
etc.

Love in a hut, with water and a crust,
Is – Love forgive us! – cinders, ashes,
dust.
JOHN KEATS

37.46 blush, brush, crush, flush, gush,
hush, lush, mush, plush, rush, slush,
thrush, tush, * hush-hush, * airbrush,
hairbrush, paintbrush, nailbrush,
sagebrush, Windrush, inrush, onrush,
songthrush, outrush, clothes brush,
uprush, bulrush, toothbrush, * mistle
thrush, bottlebrush, underbrush,
scrubbing brush

37.47 but, butt, cut, glut, gut, hut, jut,

mutt, nut, phut, putt, rut, scut, shut, slut, smut, strut, tut, ut, * abut, uncut, clear-cut, clean-cut, rebut, low-cut, tut-tut, * sackbut, catgut, haircut, chestnut, offcut, cobnut, peanut, beechnut, crosscut, rotgut, short cut, walnut, groundnut, doughnut, woodcut, crew cut, * horse chestnut, brazil nut, * halibut, hazelnut, Lilliput, linocut, occiput, coconut, scuttlebutt, uppercut, undercut, butternut, monkey nut

37.48 cuts, guts, huts, klutz, nuts, smuts, Smuts, struts, * chestnuts, peanuts, * hazelnuts, greedy guts, worryguts, monkey nuts, etc.

37.49 dove, glove, love, guv, shove, * above, * foxglove, ringdove, truelove, * ladylove, turtledove, cupboard love, tug-of-love

In the spring a livelier iris changes on the burnished dove;
In the spring a young man's fancy lightly turns to thoughts of love.
ALFRED, LORD TENNYSON

37.50 gloved, loved, shoved, * unloved, beloved, * Wellbeloved

37.51 buzz, coz, does, fuzz, muzz, * abuzz, redoes, outdoes, * overdoes

38.1 chubby, clubby, cubby, grubby, hubby, nubby, scrubby, shrubby, stubby, tubby, brumby, busby, guppy, puppy, yuppie, pulpy, bumpy, dumpy, frumpy, grumpy, humpy, jumpy, lumpy, scrumpy, stumpy, * rumpy-pumpy

38.2 clucky, ducky, lucky, mucky, plucky, truckie, yucky, bulky, sulky, chunky, clunky, flunky, funky, hunky, junkie, monkey, spunky, dusky, husky, musky, buggy, Dougie, druggie, fuggy, muggy, * unlucky, Kentucky, * happy-go-lucky

38.3 bloody, buddy, cruddy, muddy, ruddy, study, Grundy, Lundy, Monday, Sunday, butty, nutty, puttee, putty, rutty, smutty, mufti, shufty, tufty, Bunty, runty, busty, crusty, dusty, fusty, gusty, lusty, musty, rusty, trusty, * McNulty, * in the nuddy, understudy, fuddy-duddy, salmagundi, barramundi, Humpty Dumpty

38.4 Duffy, fluffy, huffy, puffy, roughie, scruffy, stuffy, toughie, comfy, covey, Dovey, lovey, luvvie, Southey, * Aberdovey, lovey-dovey

38.5 gully, Lully, Scully, sully, Sully, Tully, bubbly, doubly, stubbly, crumbly, humbly, Buckley, smugly, snuggly, UGLI®, ugly, Budleigh, cuddly, Dudley, subtly, Uttley, bluntly, Huntley, justly, snuffly, lovely, monthly, dully, Cholmondeley, comely, glumly, Lumley, Plomley, muscly, Huxley, curry, Curry, flurry, hurry, Murray, scurry, slurry, surrey, Surrey, worry, mulberry, hungry, sundry, sultry, country, comfrey, Humphrey, Guthrie, * abruptly, unjustly, robustly, unlovely, upcountry, * *fait accompli*, etc.

38.6 Brummie, chummy, crumby, crummy, dummy, gummy, lumme, mummy, plummy, rummy, scrummy, scummy, slummy, tummy, yummy, bunny, dunny, funny, honey, money, runny, sonny, Sunni, sunny, tunny, chutney, Putney, * unfunny, alumnae, * Ballymoney, loadsamoney, * overcome me, etc.

**Isn't it funny
How a bear likes honey?**
A. A. MILNE

38.7 fussy, Hussey, hussy, mussy, pussy, gutsy, Dulcie, Runcie, does he, fuzzy, muzzy, SCSI, scuzzy, Pudsey, sudsy, clumsy, mumsy, brushy, gushy, mushy, rushy, slushy, duchy, touchy, bunchy, Crunchie, crunchy, punchy, scrunchie, budgie, pudgy, sludgy, smudgy, bungee, gungy, grungy, scungy, spongy, * unfussy, archduchy

38.8 blubber, clubber, grubber, lubber, rubber, scrubber, bulbar, clumber, cumber, Humber, lumbar, lumber, number, rumba, slumber, umber, crupper, cuppa, scupper, supper, upper, gulper, pulper, bumper, jumper, plumper, * Columba, renumber, encumber, outnumber, gazumper, * landlubber, cucumber, showjumper, queue-jumper, * disencumber, * snub her, dump her, etc.

38.9 chucker, chukker, ducker, fucker, mucker, plucker, pucker, pukka, succour, sucker, trucker, tucker, UCCA, yucca, skulker, sulker, bunker, clunker, hunker, punkah, busker, tusker, bugger, hugger, lugger, mugger, plugger, rugger, slugger, smugger, snugger, tugger, bulgur, vulgar, hunger, monger, younger, Younger, * debunker, spelunker, debugger, Srinagar, * sapsucker, seersucker, goatsucker, bloodsucker,

scaremonger, cheesemonger, fishmonger, warmonger, whoremonger, newsmonger, * motherfucker, hugger-mugger, scandalmonger, ironmonger, costermonger, gossipmonger, * struck her, hug her, etc.

38.10 chador, judder, rudder, shudder, udder, blunder, chunder, plunder, Sunda, sunder, thunder, under, wonder, butter, clutter, cutter, flutter, gutter, mutter, nutter, putter, scutter, shutter, splutter, sputter, stutter, utter, Gupta, sculptor, blunter, Bunter, chunter, grunter, Gunter, hunter, Hunter, junta, punter, shunter, bluster, buster, cluster, Custer, duster, fluster, lustre, muster, thruster, ulster, Ulster, Munster, punster, youngster, * asunder, gazunder, thereunder, hereunder, rotunda, aflutter, Calcutta, rebutter, corrupter, disrupter, conductor, abductor, destructor, inductor, instructor, Fort Sumter, combustor, adjuster, lacklustre, Augusta, * stonecutter, woodcutter, head-hunter, pothunter, fox-hunter, Dambuster, stressbuster, blockbuster, bonkbuster, ghostbuster, * floribunda, up-and-under, interrupter, nonconductor, filibuster, loss adjuster, broncobuster, * semiconductor, * stunned her, confront her, etc.

**When I read Shakespeare I am struck
    with wonder
That such trivial people should muse
    and thunder
In such lovely language.**
D. H. LAWRENCE

38.11 bluffer, buffer, duffer, gruffer,

puffer, rougher, snuffer, stuffer, suffer, tougher, sulphur, cover, glover, Glover, lover, plover, Culver, vulva, brother, mother, other, smother, t'other, * uncover, re-cover, recover, discover, triumvir, another, * hardcover, slipcover, softcover, fun-lover, Anstruther, grandmother, half-brother, Fairbrother, stepbrother, stepmother, godmother, housemother, * rediscover, undercover, * rebuff her, love her, etc.

38.12 colour, culler, duller, Muller, sculler, Sulla, bubbler, troubler, bumbler, fumbler, grumbler, mumbler, tumbler, suppler, buckler, chuckler, suckler, juggler, smuggler, struggler, bungler, muddler, butler, Butler, cutler, subtler, sutler, muffler, ruffler, shuffler, hustler, rustler, guzzler, puzzler, borough, Currer, thorough, umbra, tundra, ultra, * Abdullah, discolour, medulla, demurrer, penumbra, * Weissmuller, swashbuckler, gas-guzzler, * Technicolor®, technicolour, watercolour, multicolour, Attenborough, Edinburgh, Peterborough, kookaburra, * lull her, etc.

38.13 bummer, comer, drummer, dumber, glummer, Gummer, hummer, Hummer®, mummer, number, plumber, rummer, strummer, summer, gunner, runner, stunner, Sunna, Bugner, guv'nor, ulna, Cumnor, Sumner, * midsummer, Corunna, alumna, columnar, * latecomer, incomer, newcomer, forerunner, roadrunner, frontrunner, gunrunner, * shun her, stun her, etc.

38.14 fusser, Tulsa, ulcer, oncer, buzzer, blusher, crusher, flusher, gusher, lusher, plusher, Prussia, rusher, Russia, usher, toucher, rupture, sculpture, structure, juncture, puncture, culture, vulture, cruncher, luncher, puncher, bludger, grudger, nudger, trudger, conjure, plunger, sponger, * discusser, Tecumseh, retoucher, conjuncture, * substructure, subculture, * infrastructure, superstructure, acupuncture, agriculture, viticulture, silviculture, horticulture, number-cruncher, * rush her, punch her, etc.

38.15 cultic, fustic, rustic, drumstick, public, Brunswick, Sputnik, prussic, lovesick, * republic

38.16 Ruddock, buttock, Suffolk, Southwark, Tulloch, Thurrock, hummock, stomach, dunnock, tussock, * McCullough

38.17 buttocks, flummox, lummox, hummocks, stomachs, dunnocks, tussocks, * McCullough's, etc.

38.18 rustics, drumsticks, suffix, Sputniks, Sussex, * republics

38.19 cuspid, rugged, bloodied, muddied, studied, Dyfed, sullied, curried, hurried, scurried, worried, honeyed, moneyed, cussed, * bicuspid, unstudied, beloved, unsullied, unhurried, unworried, etc.

Old Mother Hubbard
Went to the cupboard
To fetch her poor dog a bone.
NURSERY RHYME

38.20 blubbered, cupboard, Hubbard, numbered, slumbered, scuppered, drunkard, buggered, sluggard, flooded, shuddered, studded, blundered, funded, plundered, thundered, wondered, buttered, fluttered, gutted, jutted, muttered, strutted, uttered, tufted, blunted, fronted, grunted, hunted, stunted, bustard, busted, custard, dusted, flustered, mustard, trusted, Knutsford, covered, mothered, smothered, coloured, dullard, hundred, upward, Rudyard, buzzard, ruptured, structured, cultured, punctured, * unnumbered, encumbered, outnumbered, red-blooded, hot-blooded, warm-blooded, cold-blooded, unfunded, abutted, tut-tutted, corrupted, erupted, disrupted, conducted, obstructed, constructed, abducted, deducted, instructed, insulted, resulted, affronted, confronted, unflustered, adjusted, disgusted, entrusted, distrusted, uncovered, recovered, discovered, self-coloured, discoloured, unstructured, uncultured, * head-hunted, * Mother Hubbard, unencumbered, underfunded, interrupted, uncorrupted, deconstructed, reconstructed, unobstructed, maladjusted, well-adjusted, unrecovered, undiscovered, multicoloured, * uninterrupted, unreconstructed, etc.

38.21 cupboards, drunkards, sluggards, upwards, etc.

38.22 luggage, frontage, roughage, lovage, Dulwich, sullage, ullage, courage, Uxbridge, umbrage, Tonbridge, suffrage, Gummidge, rummage, scrummage, tonnage, * encourage, discourage, demurrage

38.23 bubble, double, Hubble, nubble, rubble, stubble, trouble, bumble, crumble, fumble, grumble, humble, jumble, mumble, rumble, scumble, stumble, tumble, umbel, couple, supple, crumple, rumple, buccal, buckle, chuckle, knuckle, muckle, suckle, truckle, nuncle, uncle, juggle, smuggle, snuggle, struggle, bungle, fungal, jungle, cuddle, fuddle, huddle, muddle, puddle, ruddle, Blundell, bundle, trundle, cuttle, scuttle, shuttle, subtle, frontal, duffel, muffle, ruffle, scuffle, shuffle, snuffle, truffle, lustful, trustful, Lovell, shovel, vulval, Burrell, Durrell, tumbrel, umbral, guttural, Brummell, Hummel, pummel, Chunnel, funnel, Gunnell, gunwale, runnel, tunnel, bustle, hustle, muscle, mussel, Russell, rustle, tussle, guzzle, muzzle, nuzzle, puzzle, nuptial, cudgel, * redouble, uncouple, unbuckle, peduncle, befuddle, unbundle, rebuttal, unsubtle, disgruntle, kerfuffle, reshuffle, distrustful, triumphal, demurral, penumbral, sepulchral, Beau Brummell, autumnal, Jack Russell, unmuzzle, Rapunzel, prenuptial, * pinochle, turnbuckle, carbuncle, Garfunkel, Tolpuddle, corpuscle, * rough-and-tumble, thermocouple, honeysuckle, antifungal, contrapuntal, Eurotunnel, antenuptial

Double, double toil and trouble;
Fire burn and cauldron bubble.
WILLIAM SHAKESPEARE

38.24 doubled, troubled, grumbled, jumbled, stumbled, crumpled, chuckled, cuckold, smuggled, struggled, bungled, muddled, gruntled, muffled, ruffled, puzzled, * untroubled, befuddled, disgruntled, unruffled, reshuffled, etc.

38.25 bubbles, doubles, troubles, grumbles, Mumbles, rumbles, cuddles, puddles, bundles, snuffles, truffles, Brussels, muscles, mussels, Russell's, puzzles, etc.

38.26 plumbum, Duckham, bunkum, custom, frustum, Durham, buckram, Puttnam, buxom, * corundum, Saxmundham, accustom, conundrum, * Carborundum®, * stunned 'em, trust 'em, etc.

38.27 dubbin, dustbin, bumpkin, pumpkin, Ruskin, buckskin, Dustin, Justin, muffin, puffin, Dublin, drumlin, dunlin, muslin, murrain, Unwin, cumin, run-in, * Augustine, MacGuffin, * ragamuffin, * trustin', bubblin', etc.

38.28 stubborn, lumpen, Buchan, Vulcan, drunken, Duncan, shrunken, sunken, Tuscan, Duggan, sudden, Blunden, London, Lumsden, button, Dutton, glutton, Hutton, mutton, Sutton, Upton, sultan, Buxton, Dunstan, tungsten, Rushton, roughen, toughen, coven, Govan, govern, oven, sloven, southern, Cullen, Mullen, sullen, Curran, bunion, Bunyan, onion, Runyon, summon, clubman, dustman, gunman, busman, huntsman, Dutchman, Hudson, Bunsen, cousin, cozen, dozen,

Prussian, Russian, gumption, fluxion, ruction, suction, function, junction, unction, scutcheon, luncheon, truncheon, bludgeon, dudgeon, gudgeon, dungeon, * Etruscan, unbutton, Augustan, McGovern, misgovern, Catullan, Lucullan, percussion, concussion, discussion, corruption, eruption, irruption, disruption, assumption, consumption, presumption, resumption, production, conduction, obstruction, construction, abduction, deduction, reduction, seduction, induction, destruction, instruction, compunction, conjunction, malfunction, dysfunction, injunction, disjunction, propulsion, compulsion, convulsion, repulsion, impulsion, expulsion, revulsion, emulsion, escutcheon, combustion, curmudgeon, high dudgeon, * Newcomen, * bellybutton, Flying Dutchman, Belarussian, repercussion, interruption, self-destruction, preproduction, reproduction, deconstruction, reconstruction, introduction, misconstruction, liposuction, postproduction, multifunction, * overconsumption, underconsumption, reintroduction, overproduction, underproduction

38.29 husband, buttoned, roughened, toughened, governed, upland, Studland, Jutland, Rutland, Drummond, summoned, functioned, * unbuttoned, ungoverned, * househusband, etc.

38.30 gubbins, dustbins, pumpkins, Buggins, muggins, muffins, puffins, Butlins, etc.

38.31 buttons, Lutyens, bunions, onions, summons, cousins, Cousins, dozens, functions, junctions, dungeons, * repercussions, interruptions, introductions, etc.

**There were noblemen in coronets, and
   military cousins,
There were captains by the hundred,
   there were baronets by dozens.**
W. S. GILBERT

38.32 currant, current, judgment, mustn't, doesn't, Ushant, fulgent, pungent, * recumbent, incumbent, abundant, redundant, reluctant, consultant, resultant, exultant, triumphant, concurrent, recurrent, abutment, adjustment, engulfment, annulment, prejudgment, misjudgment, repugnant, convulsant, demulcent, indulgent, effulgent, refulgent, * blackcurrant, redcurrant, crosscurrent, * undercurrent, maladjustment, readjustment, self-indulgent, * superabundant, anticonvulsant, overindulgent

38.33 tuppence, substance, currants, cumbrance, sufferance, * comeuppance, abundance, conductance, inductance, reluctance, consultants, occurrence, concurrence, recurrence, incurrence, encumbrance, adjustments, repugnance, indulgence, effulgence, refulgence, * reoccurrence, self-indulgence, * superabundance, overindulgence, etc.

38.34 blubbing, clubbing, drubbing, dubbing, rubbing, scrubbing, cupping, supping, gulping, pulping, jumping, thumping, clucking, ducking, fucking, plucking, sucking, trucking, bulking, hulking, skulking, sulking, clunking, dunking, trunking, busking, bugging, chugging, hugging, mugging, shrugging, budding, flooding, scudding, studding, thudding, funding, cutting, jutting, nutting, putting, shutting, strutting, bunting, grunting, hunting, punting, shunting, dusting, gusting, lusting, rusting, thrusting, trusting, bluffing, chuffing, huffing, puffing, scuffing, snuffing, stuffing, loving, shoving, nothing, something, culling, lulling, sculling, bubbling, troubling, bumbling, crumbling, grumbling, mumbling, rumbling, coupling, dumpling, buckling, duckling, suckling, Suckling, bungling, shuffling, bustling, rustling, puzzling, upspring, gull-wing, upswing, bumming, coming, Cumming, drumming, humming, mumming, plumbing, slumming, strumming, cunning, gunning, punning, running, shunning, stunning, cussing, fussing, buzzing, blushing, crushing, flushing, Flushing, gushing, rushing, clutching, touching, crunching, munching, punching, budging, grudging, judging, smudging, trudging, bulging, * debugging, debunking, abutting, corrupting, erupting, disrupting, conducting, instructing, consulting, insulting, resulting, adjusting, disgusting, distrusting, rebuffing, engulfing, unloving, annulling, becoming, benumbing, forthcoming, discussing, unblushing, retouching, ungrudging, begrudging, * swan-upping, showjumping, bloodsucking, blockbusting, fun-loving, swashbuckling, incoming, mind-numbing, oncoming, shortcoming, homecoming, upcoming, frontrunning, gunrunning, * underfunding, interrupting, self-adjusting, up-and-coming, unbecoming, unforthcoming, up and running, etc.

Bye, baby bunting,
Daddy's gone a hunting.
NURSERY RHYME

38.35 muggings, cuttings, hustings, dumplings, ducklings, sucklings, Cummings, * shortcomings, etc.

38.36 orange, lozenge

38.37 justice, Dulles, pumice, duchess, * injustice, portcullis, accomplice

38.38 bulbous, plumbous, compass, rumpus, ruckus, fungous, fungus, cultus, troublous, luckless, Douglas, bloodless, cutlass, gutless, loveless, sonless, sunless, cumbrous, slumberous, thunderous, wondrous, buttress, sculptress, huntress, lustrous, plumpness, smugness, bluntness, roughness, toughness, numbness, luscious, bumptious, scrumptious, * Columbus, encompass, humongous, singultus, Augustus, Catullus, Lucullus, conductress, seductress, instructress, abruptness, robustness, alumnus, rambunctious, * gyrocompass, * coitus interruptus, * thump us, struck us, etc.

38.39 druggist, smuggest, snuggest, youngest, bluntest, gruffest, roughest, toughest, supplest, subtlest, dumbest, glummest, numbest, lushest, plushest, * encompassed, etc.

38.40 dumpish, frumpish, lumpish, rubbish, monkish, sluggish, thuggish, sluttish, lumpfish, monkfish, mudfish, drumfish, sunfish, lungfish, publish, flourish, nourish, Hunnish, punish, youngish, * accomplish, * undernourish

38.41 published, flourished, nourished, punished, * unpublished, accomplished, malnourished, unpunished , * unaccomplished, undernourished

38.42 Cuthbert, Humbert, ducat, comfort, covert, lovat, culvert, * discomfort

38.43 muppet, puppet, crumpet, strumpet, trumpet, bucket, Blunkett, junket, Plunket, musket, nougat, nugget, pundit, buffet, tuffet, comfit, covet, gullet, mullet, doublet, couplet, floodlit, cutlet, sunlit, turret, worrit, culprit, plummet, summit, punnet, gusset, russet, dulcet, budget, * Nantucket, discomfit, whodunnit, * gutbucket, rust bucket, * love it, run it, etc.

Little Miss Muffet
Sat on a tuffet.
NURSERY RHYME

38.44 gerundive, eruptive, disruptive, consumptive, presumptive, productive, conductive, obstructive, constructive, deductive, seductive, inductive, destructive, instructive, conjunctive, subjunctive, percussive, propulsive, compulsive, repulsive, impulsive, * reproductive, nonproductive, unproductive,

antitussive, * counterproductive,
* electroconvulsive

38.45 rubbers, numbers, slumbers,
uppers, puckers, truckers, shudders,
udders, cutters, hunters, punters,
buffers, covers, lovers, brothers,
colours, tumblers, smugglers,
drummers, mummers, summers,
Summers, gunners, runners, buses,
ulcers, blushes, rushes, ushers,
clutches, crutches, vultures, bunches,
punches, judges, Judges, smudges,
bulges, spongers, * instructors,
Carruthers, McCullers, * bloodsuckers,
fishmongers, head-hunters,
latecomers, all-comers, newcomers,
bulrushes, * ironmongers,
watercolours, etc.

Tell me not, in mournful numbers,
Life is but an empty dream!
For the soul is dead that slumbers,
And things are not what they seem.
HENRY WADSWORTH LONGFELLOW

38.46 puppies, monkeys, buddies,
studies, undies, butties, worries,
sundries, countries, Humphries,
funnies, monies, munchies

38.47 Sotheby, tussocky, somebody,
custody, subtlety, Muscovy, lubberly,
utterly, brotherly, motherly, Coverley,
southerly, thoroughly, comfortably,
upwardly, currently, wonderfully,
stubbornly, drunkenly, suddenly,
slovenly, sullenly, blubbery, rubbery,
shrubbery, mulberry, Bunbury,
trumpery, succory, buggery, snuggery,
thuggery, Hungary, thundery, buttery,
fluttery, blustery, scullery, jugglery,
butlery, cutlery, flummery, mummery,

summary, summery, gunnery,
nunnery, luxury, drudgery,
huckleberry, Huckleberry, cuckoldry,
husbandry, customary, pulmonary,
functionary, tuppenny, company,
Tuscany, gluttony, oniony, currency,
pungency, subsidy, uppity, grubbily,
luckily, pluckily, sulkily, huskily,
grumpily, lustily, huffily, scruffily,
hungrily, funnily, clumsily, publicly,
hurriedly, worriedly, cuttingly,
lovingly, puzzlingly, cunningly,
stunningly, touchingly, grudgingly,
sluggishly, puppetry, summitry,
monetary, budgetary, culinary,
rubbishy, punctually, * grandmotherly,
uncomfortably, cold-bloodedly,
abundantly, reluctantly, triumphantly,
concurrently, skulduggery,
perfunctory, adultery, effrontery,
recovery, discovery, Montgomery,
compulsory, uncustomary, accompany,
redundancy, consultancy, profundity,
fecundity, jocundity, unluckily,
unhurriedly, constructively,
seductively, compulsively, impulsively,
disgustingly, * ironmongery,
introductory, rediscovery, etc.

38.48 stomacher, colander, comforter,
Mustapha, shoveller, tunneller,
Loughborough, slumberer, blunderer,
plunderer, thunderer, wonderer,
mutterer, stutterer, sufferer, conjuror,
customer, Londoner, governor,
southerner, summoner, trumpeter,
Gulliver, dulcimer, Dubliner,
publisher, muscular, jugular, pustular,
* adulterer, discoverer, discomfiture,
avuncular, corpuscular, crepuscular

38.49 chubbier, grubbier, stubbier,
tubbier, bumpier, frumpier, grumpier,

lumpier, luckier, muckier, pluckier, bulkier, sulkier, chunkier, funkier, hunkier, spunkier, muggier, bloodier, muddier, nuttier, smuttier, crustier, dustier, lustier, rustier, fluffier, scruffier, stuffier, comfier, bubblier, crumblier, uglier, buddleia, cuddlier, lovelier, courier, currier, furrier, worrier, Cumbria, Umbria, hungrier, sultrier, crummier, yummier, funnier, runnier, sunnier, fussier, gutsier, fuzzier, clumsier, mushier, slushier, crunchier, spongier, * Colombia, Columbia, unluckier, Northumbria, etc.

38.50 husbanded, comforted, Hungerford, Rutherford, trumpeted, bucketed, buffeted, coveted, turreted, plummeted, budgeted, Hunniford, * uncomforted, discomfited, etc.

38.51 underbid, * accompanied, * unaccompanied

38.52 clubbable, culpable, jumpable, huggable, comfortable, Huxtable, constable, Constable, Dunstable, lovable, gullible, sufferable, vulnerable, hummable, crushable, spongeable, wonderful, colourful, guttural, sculptural, structural, cultural, functional, uncial, runcible, multiple, curricle, punctual, * refundable, corruptible, deductible, destructible, uncomfortable, combustible, adjustable, unlovable, unutterable, insufferable, recoverable, invulnerable, uncrushable, untouchable, instructional, dysfunctional, industrial, unpunctual, * tax-deductible, ineluctable, incorruptible, indestructible, incombustible,

agricultural, horticultural, multicultural, multifunctional, preindustrial, postindustrial

38.53 cumbersome, troublesome, cuddlesome, Brummagem, yuppiedom, Buckingham, Cunningham, worrisome

38.54 suffragan, doubleton, subaltern, Huddleston, Ulsterman, husbandman, Cuthbertson, fustian, ruffian, mullion, scullion, Cumbrian, Umbrian, publican, hurricane, Mulligan, Huntingdon, Sullivan, countryman, Runciman, Huskisson, Hutchinson, * Colombian, Columbian, Kentuckian, Burgundian, Procrustean, Tertullian, Northumbrian, republican, Republican, O'Sullivan, * Liverpudlian, * slubberdegullion

38.55 cummerbund, Cumberland, Sunderland, Sutherland, * Northumberland

38.56 colorant, fundament, wonderment, puzzlement, government, covenant, supplicant, subsequent, worriment, nourishment, punishment, unguent, succulent, truculent, undulant, * adulterant, befuddlement, self-government, ebullient, accompaniment, accomplishment, malnourishment, encouragement, discouragement

**I test my bath before I sit,
And I'm always moved to wonderment
That what chills the finger not a bit
Is so frigid upon the fundament.**
Ogden Nash

38.56

38.57 utterance, sufferance, governance, supplicants, subsidence, subsequence, punishments, sustenance, succulence, truculence, * circumference, ebullience, accomplishments, etc.

38.58 underling, blubbering, slumbering, shuddering, plundering, thundering, wondering, guttering, muttering, shuttering, stuttering, suffering, covering, mothering, smothering, wuthering, colouring, underwing, trumpeting, buffeting, publishing, flourishing, nourishing, rummaging, * scaremongering, self-governing, encouraging, discouraging

38.59 covetous, numberless, supperless, rudderless, brotherless, motherless, colourless, slumberous, thunderous, sulphurous, gluttonous, otherness, thoroughness, suppleness, stubbornness, drunkenness, suddenness, scurrilous, chubbiness, grubbiness, grumpiness, sulkiness, smuttiness, scruffiness, stuffiness, ugliness, loveliness, sultriness, fussiness, clumsiness, nothingness, sluggishness, sumptuous, unctuous, succubus, pustulous, * adulteress, adulterous, rumbustious, industrious, illustrious, destructiveness, voluptuous, presumptuous, tumultuous, homunculus, etc.

38.60 publicist, * accompanist, percussionist, obstructionist, destructionist, * agriculturist, horticulturist

38.61 chubbiest, grubbiest, stubbiest, tubbiest, bumpiest, frumpiest, grumpiest, lumpiest, luckiest, muckiest, pluckiest, bulkiest, sulkiest, chunkiest, funkiest, hunkiest, spunkiest, muggiest, bloodiest, muddiest, nuttiest, smuttiest, crustiest, dustiest, lustiest, rustiest, fluffiest, scruffiest, stuffiest, comfiest, bubbliest, crumbliest, ugliest, cuddliest, loveliest, hungriest, sultriest, crummiest, yummiest, funniest, runniest, sunniest, fussiest, gutsiest, fuzziest, clumsiest, mushiest, slushiest, crunchiest, spongiest, * unluckiest, etc.

38.62 surrogate, coverlet, sultanate, ultimate, ungulate, * triumvirate, penultimate, * antepenultimate

38.63 Sotheby's, luxuries, companies, * discoveries, redundancies, etc.

38.64 structurally, culturally, functionally, punctually, summarily, comfortably, ultimately, subsequently, worryingly, surrogacy, * uncomfortably, encouragingly, discouragingly, voluptuary

38.65 sufferable, vulnerable, cultivable, publishable, punishable, * unutterable, insufferable, recoverable, invulnerable, ungovernable, unpublishable, unpunishable

-uu-

The rhymes in this section have the 'uu' sound of put *and* booking *as their main or final vowel sound.*

39.1 book, brook, Brooke, Bruch, chook, cook, Cook, crook, Gluck, hook, Hooke, look, nook, rook, shook, shtuck, took, * unhook, Tobruk, forsook, partook, precook, retook, betook, mistook, Chinook, * chapbook, scrapbook, bankbook, handbook, cash book, Ladbroke, passbook, prayer book, daybook, casebook, phrase book, chequebook, textbook, sketchbook, workbook, wordbook, yearbook, e-book, hymn book, billhook, fish-hook, Innsbruck, guidebook, stylebook, logbook, pothook, hornbook, outlook, notebook, boathook, phone book, studbook, cookbook, rule book, school book, * Alanbrooke, Captain Cook, Carisbrooke, tenterhook, Beaverbrook, picture book, inglenook, Osnabrück, copybook, pocketbook, donnybrook, Bolingbroke, storybook, overcook, overlook, undercook, undertook, Domesday Book, * cookery book

His wife learns astrology out of a book,
Says: 'Your horoscope's queer and I
**   don't like its look.**
With the Moon against Virgo you might
**   be a crook.'**
W. H. AUDEN

39.2 booked, cooked, hooked, looked, * uncooked, unhooked, precooked, * overbooked, overcooked, overlooked, double-booked, undercooked, etc.

39.3 butch, putsch

39.4 could, good, hood, Hood, pud, should, stood, 'twould, wood, Wood, would, * Likud, withstood, touch wood, * manhood, Blackwood, Atwood, matchwood, Yarwood, hardwood, heartwood, sainthood, Heywood, Halewood, deadwood, redwood, bentwood, Brentwood, Westwood, Kenwood, Wedgwood, girlhood, Sherwood, wormwood, Gielgud, Fleetwood, priesthood, greenwood, driftwood, Ringwood, firewood, childhood, knighthood, plywood, wildwood, whitewood, godhood, Lockwood, dogwood, softwood, falsehood, Smallwood, boyhood, rosewood, monkshood, brushwood, Goodwood, * sandalwood, adulthood, fatherhood, hardihood, parenthood, neighbourhood, maidenhood, babyhood, Burtonwood, sisterhood, spinsterhood, Isherwood, Littlewood, likelihood, livelihood, widowhood, Robin Hood, Bollywood, Hollywood, balsawood, understood,

brotherhood, motherhood,
Underwood, womanhood,
* unlikelihood, misunderstood

**The stubborn spear-men still made
good
Their dark impenetrable wood,
Each stepping where his comrade
stood,
The instant that he fell.**
SIR WALTER SCOTT

39.5 couldst, shouldst, wouldst

39.6 poof, woof

39.7 bull, full, pull, wool, * Kabul,
brimful, John Bull, * Abdul, capful,
sackful, tankful, thankful, bagful,
handful, tactful, manful, bashful,
lambswool, carful, jarful, artful,
armful, harmful, careful, prayerful,
playful, wakeful, spadeful, fateful,
grateful, hateful, plateful, tasteful,
wasteful, faithful, baleful, shameful,
baneful, gainful, painful, graceful,
changeful, helpful, dreadful, fretful,
restful, healthful, stressful, vengeful,
Turnbull, hurtful, cheerful, earful,
fearful, tearful, gleeful, heedful,
needful, peaceful, ringpull, fitful,
fistful, wistful, skilful, wilful, skinful,
sinful, blissful, dishful, wishful, eyeful,
mindful, frightful, rightful, spiteful,
wrongful, watchful, awful, drawerful,
lawful, forkful, thoughtful, mournful,
scornful, forceful, doubtful, mouthful,
powerful, joyful, woeful, hopeful,
boatful, boastful, slothful, bowlful,
doleful, soulful, cupful, jugful, mugful,
lustful, trustful, bulbul, rueful,
fruitful, truthful, youthful, roomful,
spoonful, tuneful, useful, * ungrateful,

distasteful, unfaithful, disdainful,
disgraceful, unhelpful, forgetful,
regretful, respectful, neglectful,
eventful, resentful, successful,
revengeful, deceitful, unskilful,
unmindful, delightful, unlawful,
remorseful, resourceful, all-powerful,
reproachful, distrustful, unfruitful,
untruthful, * barrelful, fanciful,
masterful, basketful, flavourful,
plentiful, bellyful, merciful,
worshipful, meaningful, teaspoonful,
thimbleful, Istanbul, Sitting Bull,
pitiful, cock-and-bull, bottleful,
pocketful, sorrowful, saucerful,
bountiful, overfull, wonderful,
colourful, shovelful, bucketful,
beautiful, dutiful, * unmerciful,
* disrespectful, uneventful, unsuccessful

**Baa, baa, black sheep, have you any
wool?
Yes sir, yes sir, three bags full.**
NURSERY RHYME

39.8 wolf, Wolfe, Woolf, * aardwolf,
werewolf, she-wolf, * Beowulf

39.9 broom, cwm, groom, room,
shtoom, vroom, * taproom, chatroom,
vacuum, barroom, darkroom,
guardroom, staff room, bathroom,
classroom, dayroom, playroom,
stateroom, saleroom, salesroom,
legroom, bedroom, headroom, guest
room, rest room, pressroom,
workroom, tearoom, greenroom,
sickroom, grillroom, bridegroom,
stockroom, strongroom, boxroom,
washroom, volume, storeroom,
boardroom, wardroom, courtroom,
ballroom, houseroom, showroom,
cloakroom, post room, clubroom,

sunroom, mushroom, lunchroom,
poolroom, schoolroom, newsroom,
* anteroom, waiting room, changing
room, dressing room, engine room,
elbowroom, sitting room, living room,
dining room, common room, drawing
room, powder room, boiler room,
* *cogito ergo sum*

**Think then, my soul, that death is but a
    groom,**
**Which brings a taper to the outward
    room.**
JOHN DONNE

39.10 Jung, * Samsung, Hoffnung,
* Nibelung, Mao Tse-tung,
* Götterdämmerung

39.11 oops, whoops

39.12 puss, schuss, wuss, * Anschluss,
sourpuss, * Belarus

39.13 bush, Bush, mush, push, shush,
swoosh, tush, whoosh, * ambush, bell
push, rose bush, * Hindu Kush

39.14 foot, put, soot, * kaput, afoot,
barefoot, hotfoot, wrong-foot,
* flatfoot, input, forefoot, output,
coltsfoot, club foot, throughput,
* tenderfoot, Lilliput, underfoot,
pussyfoot, * Inuktitut

39.15 puts, * kibbutz

40.1 would-be, bookie, cookie, hooky,
nooky, rookie, Wookey, could he,
goody, hoodie, should he, woody,
would he, Rushdie, footy, sooty, tutti,
bully, fully, puli, pulley, Woolley,
woolly, goodly, Wolseley, gooseberry,

Clerihews
• •

*A clerihew is a humorous four-line
verse about a famous person, made
up of two pairs of rhyming lines of
uneven length. It is named after the
English writer Edmund Clerihew
Bentley (1875–1956), who invented it.
Here are some of Bentley's own
contributions to the genre:*

Sir Christopher Wren
**Said, 'I am going to dine with
    some men.**
If anybody calls
Say I am designing St Paul's.'

What I like about Clive
Is that he is no longer alive.
There is a great deal to be said
For being dead.

pussy, wussy, footsie, Footsie, tootsy, Tutsi, Wolsey, Bushey, bushy, cushy, pushy, * Dunwoody, Burundi, Abruzzi, * fortune cookie, Mappa Mundi, fancifully, mercifully, pitifully, sorrowfully, wonderfully, colourfully, beautifully, dutifully, linsey-woolsey, * unmercifully, etc.

40.2 chutzpah, booker, Booker, cooker, hookah, hooker, looker, Junker, sugar, Buddha, footer, putter, poofter, woofter, Gunther, junta, Wooster, Worcester, Münster, bulla, fuller, Fuller, mullah, Müller, puller, Bulmer, fulmar, Brookner, Bruckner, pusher, butcher, * Zeebrugge, do-gooder, Kaunda, ampulla, Abdullah, * onlooker, shot-putter, Weissmuller, penpusher, * *mea culpa*, Famagusta, * took her, push her, etc.

40.3 crooked, bullied

40.4 sugared, hooded, wooded, worsted, Woodward, butchered, * unsugared, barefooted, web-footed, light-footed, wrong-footed, etc.

40.5 footage, Woolwich, Woodbridge, footbridge

40.6 Hummel, kümmel, Bushnell, bushel

40.7 Muslim, * pull him, push him, etc.

40.8 Cookham, Fulham, fulcrum, wolfram, fulsome, bosom, * unbosom, * took 'em, put 'em, etc.

40.9 Pushkin, Brooklyn, Goodwin, * cookin', puttin', etc.

40.10 good 'un, wooden, Wootton, Fulton, Bullen, Pullen, woollen, Gudrun, woman, bookman, goodman, Goodman, woodman, footman, Pullman, Ullman, woodsman, bushman, Bushman, Cookson, cushion, * Saarbrücken, madwoman, Manxwoman, batswoman, clanswoman, charwoman, markswoman, craftswoman, draughtswoman, airwoman, chairwoman, laywoman, cavewoman, spacewoman, stateswoman, saleswoman, Frenchwoman, Welshwoman, churchwoman, kinswoman, Scotswoman, yachtswoman, Scotchwoman, horsewoman, sportswoman, oarswoman, townswoman, postwoman, spokeswoman, stuntwoman, Dutchwoman, newswoman, * backwoodsman, ombudsman, pincushion, * policewoman, * dairywoman, weatherwoman, gentlewoman, clergywoman, servicewoman, needlewoman, businesswoman, Englishwoman, Irishwoman, washerwoman, congresswoman, jurywoman, countrywoman, superwoman

40.11 Brooklands, woodlands

40.12 couldn't, shouldn't, wouldn't

40.13 hoodless, hummus, goodness, fullness, * stood us, pull us, etc.

40.14 Buddhist, fullest

40.15 booking, Brooking, cooking, hooking, looking, hooding, pudding, footing, putting, pulling, bullring, Cushing, pushing, whooshing, * off-putting, wrong-footing, * overlooking, pussyfooting, etc.

40.16 bookish, wolfish, bullish

40.17 pulpit, bullet, pullet, booklet, bullshit, * cook it, pull it, etc.

40.18 could've, should've, would've

40.19 bookies, cookies, goodies, bullies, Woollies, tootsies, etc.

40.20 woodenly, womanly, gooseberry, cookery, rookery, sugary, butchery, pulmonary, crookedly, * off-puttingly

40.21 woodlander, Pulborough, Woomera, Worcestershire, Pulitzer

40.22 bookable, cookable

40.23 Wolfenden, Zuckerman, Jungian, bullion, Goodison, * Burundian

-oo-

The rhymes in this section have the 'oo' sound of too *and* cruiser *as their main or final vowel sound.*

41.1 blew, blue, boo, brew, chew, choux, clew, clue, coo, coup, crew, Crewe, cru, cue, dew, do, drew, Drew, due, ewe, few, flew, flu, flue, glue, gnu, goo, grew, hew, Hoo, hue, Hugh, Jew, jus, Kew, knew, lieu, loo, Looe, Lou, mew, moo, mu, new, nu, ooh, pew, phew, poo, pooh, Pooh, Pru, Pugh, Q, queue, roo, Roo, roux, rue, screw, shoe, shoo, shrew, Sioux, skew, slew, smew, sou, spew, sprue, stew, strew, sue, Sue, thew, threw, through, to, too, true, two, U, view, who, Who, woo, yew, you, zoo

'Tis distance lends enchantment to the view,
And robes the mountain in its azure hue.
THOMAS CAMPBELL

41.2 taboo, Magoo, ado, to-do, undo, tattoo, kung fu, yahoo, halloo, Carew, Peru, Theroux, accrue, unscrew, untrue, construe, askew, adieu, subdue, undue, anew, pursue, canoe, kazoo, bamboo, shampoo, ragout, snafu, brand-new, Camus, lasso, cachou, cashew, Manchu, Barcoo, mangetout, thereto, whereto, K2, HQ, *chez nous*, hereto, redo, redrew, EU, shih-tzu, in lieu, withdrew, bestrew, imbue, miscue, bedew, endue, review, revue, renew, ensue, eschew, Typhoo®, sky blue, IQ, non-U, Corfu, outdo,

outgrew, Lao-tzu, pooh-pooh, boohoo, yoo-hoo, *Who's Who*, true-blue, * Winnie the Pooh, how-do-you-do, hullabaloo, Brian Boru, Kalamazoo, tickety-boo, didgeridoo, seventy-two, Catch-22, tiramisu

41.3 Bantu, Andrew, thank you, Askew, statue, Matthew, value, Agnew, sandshoe, ZAPU, Yahoo, argue, Cardew, KANU, ZANU, Anjou, hairdo, Nehru, aircrew, breakthrough, debut, ague, set-to, ecru, ECU, fescue, rescue, nephew, menu, venue, virtue, curfew, world-view, curlew, purlieu, lean-to, Hebrew, see-through, read-through, preview, emu, Jesu, bijou, Hindu, into, igloo, mildew, sinew, Vishnu, issue, tissue, haiku, onto, fondue, Honshu, corkscrew, walk-through, horseshoe, Urdu, coypu, tofu, snowshoe, unto, thumbscrew, run-through, sundew, gumshoe, cuckoo, guru, woodscrew, boo-boo, hoopoe, doo-doo, hoodoo, kudu, voodoo, Hutu, tutu, Tutu, froufrou, Lulu, Zulu, choo-choo, juju, * devalue, revalue, shiatsu, Daihatsu, hereinto, thereinto, *in situ*, continue, jujitsu, atishoo, reissue, impromptu, sudoku, hereunto, thereunto, Mobutu, KwaZulu, * Vanuatu, undervalue, Tamil Nadu, Nosferatu, Netanyahu, Papandreou, R2-D2, Machu Picchu, discontinue, Mogadishu, Ouagadougou, Desmond Tutu, Honolulu

41.4 marabou, marabout, Xanadu, black and blue, jackeroo, kangaroo, acajou, Katmandu, passe-partout, ingénue, Malibu, Cariboo, caribou, ballyhoo, avenue, parvenu, parvenue, carcajou, barbecue, Martinu, Bakerloo, pay-per-view, *déjà vu*, eighty-two, navy blue, well-to-do, FAQ, Dien Bien Phu, derring-do, twenty-two, Pettigrew, residue, clerihew, retinue, revenue, Herstmonceux, thirty-two, curlicue, bird's-eye view, peekaboo, sgian-dhu, Peterloo, feverfew, VDU, bill and coo, hitherto, thitherto, vindaloo, jillaroo, misconstrue, interview, kinkajou, billet-doux, fifty-two, sixty-two, Timbuktu, ninety-two, IOU, cockatoo, wallaroo, Montague, rendezvous, Montesquieu, Molyneux, follow-through, Waterloo, ormolu, Port-Salut, Pompidou, forty-two, talking-to, Fortescue, Autocue®, royal blue, overdo, overdrew, overthrew, overdue, overview, overshoe, Sutton Hoo, buckaroo, W, honeydew, Luton Hoo, superloo, toodle-oo, Tuvalu, superglue, Subaru, Uluru, Scooby Doo, you-know-who, * tu-whit tu-whoo, Bartholomew, * cock-a-doodle-doo

41.5 boob, cube, pube, rube, tube, * flashcube, Danube, boob tube, jujube

41.6 duke, fluke, kook, Luke, nuke, puke, souk, spook, stook, * Farouk, peruque, archduke, Chinook, rebuke, * Mameluke, Marmaduke, Heptateuch, Pentateuch, Hexateuch, Volapük, * gobbledegook

41.7 dukes, Fuchs, Luke's, pukes, spooks, * gadzooks, rebukes, etc.

41.8 Gooch, hooch, mooch, pooch, smooch, * Scaramouch, Quiller-Couch

Would you adopt a strong logical
   attitude,
Bear this in mind, and, whatever you
   do,
Always allow your opponent full
   latitude,
Whether or not his assumption be true.
Then, when he manifests feelings of
   gratitude
Merely because you've not shut him up
   flat,
Turn his pet paradox into a platitude,
With the remark, 'Why, of course, we
   know that!'
GODFREY TURNER

41.9 booed, brewed, brood, Bude, chewed, crewed, crude, dude, feud, food, glued, Jude, lewd, mewed, mood, mooed, nude, prude, pseud, queued, rood, rude, screwed, shrewd, slewed, snood, spewed, stewed, Strood, sued, viewed, who'd, wooed, you'd, * tattooed, allude, collude, occlude, conclude, unglued, accrued, unscrewed, protrude, obtrude, subdued, pursued, shampooed, lassoed, delude, elude, preclude, seclude, include, exclude, intrude, extrude, denude, exude, reviewed, renewed, ensued, pooh-poohed, * catfood, valued, argued, étude, rescued, prelude, Gertrude, seafood, issued, dogfood, wholefood, * devalued, revalued, continued, * habitude, attitude, gratitude, latitude, platitude, aptitude, altitude, amplitude, magnitude, lassitude, barbecued, hebetude, rectitude, plenitude, Ermintrude, turpitude, certitude, servitude, interlude, misconstrued, interviewed, quietude, Holyrood, longitude, promptitude, solitude, fortitude, multitude, pulchritude, * beatitude, ingratitude, exactitude, decrepitude, correctitude, ineptitude, incertitude, similitude, solicitude, vicissitude, inquietude, disquietude, desuetude, * verisimilitude, etc.

41.10 goof, hoof, pouffe, proof, roof, spoof, woof, * shadoof, aloof, Tartuffe, re-roof, behoof, reproof, disproof, * flameproof, rainproof, shellproof, heatproof, greaseproof, windproof, fireproof, childproof, lightproof, shockproof, mothproof, bombproof, stormproof, soundproof, showerproof, rustproof, sunroof, foolproof, * shatterproof, weatherproof, waterproof, ovenproof, underproof, bulletproof, * opéra bouffe

41.11 fugue, Moog®

41.12 Goodge, huge, Scrooge, smoodge, stooge, * refuge, deluge, * centrifuge, vermifuge, subterfuge

41.13 Bruges, luge, rouge, * Khmer Rouge, * Baton Rouge, Moulin Rouge

41.14 Boole, boule, cool, drool, fool, ghoul, Goole, joule, mewl, mule, pool, Poole, rule, school, shul, spool, stool, Thule, tool, tulle, who'll, you'll, Yule, * uncool, cagoule, self-rule, deschool, retool, misrule, tomfool, O'Toole, home rule, * Blackpool, ampoule,

capsule, playschool, cesspool, Welshpool, ferrule, schedule, cellule, whirlpool, virgule, preschool, globule, module, nodule, toadstool, pustule, footstool, tubule, * reschedule, * majuscule, paddling pool, graticule, fascicule, gallinule, Hartlepool, vestibule, reticule, work-to-rule, Liverpool, minuscule, swimming pool, ridicule, Pontypool, molecule, overrule, Ullapool, Sunday school, ubercool, supercool

Prove to me that you're no fool
Walk across my swimming pool.
TIM RICE

41.15 cooled, fooled, Gould, pooled, ruled, schooled, * unschooled, retooled, * air-cooled, scheduled, * unscheduled, rescheduled, nonscheduled, * ridiculed, water-cooled, overruled, supercooled, etc.

41.16 fools, gules, Jools, Jules, mules, pools, rules, schools, spools, stools, tools, * capsules, globules, modules, nodules, pustules, etc.

41.17 bloom, boom, broom, coomb, cwm, doom, flume, Frome, fume, gloom, groom, Hume, loom, plume, rheum, room, spume, tomb, vroom, whom, womb, zoom, * abloom, perfume, assume, subsume, consume, Khartoum, exhume, entomb, simoom, presume, resume, foredoom, * taproom, chatroom, vacuum, barroom, darkroom, guardroom, staff room, bathroom, classroom, heirloom, dayroom, playroom, stateroom, saleroom, salesroom, legroom, bedroom, headroom, guest room,

rest room, pressroom, legume,
workroom, perfume, tearoom,
greenroom, sickroom, grillroom,
bridegroom, stockroom, strongroom,
boxroom, washroom, costume, volume,
broadloom, storeroom, boardroom,
wardroom, courtroom, ballroom,
houseroom, showroom, cloakroom,
post room, clubroom, sunroom,
mushroom, lunchroom, poolroom,
schoolroom, newsroom, * catacomb,
va-va-voom, anteroom, waiting room,
changing room, hecatomb, dressing
room, engine room, elbowroom,
Leverhulme, disentomb, sitting room,
living room, dining room, nom de
plume, common room, drawing room,
powder room, boiler room

**The proper way to leave a room
Is not to plunge it into gloom.**
GELETT BURGESS

41.18 bloomed, doomed, fumed,
groomed, loomed, zoomed,
* perfumed, assumed, consumed,
exhumed, entombed, presumed,
resumed, * unperfumed,
unconsumed, etc.

41.19 boon, Boone, coon, croon, dune,
goon, hewn, June, loon, moon, Moon,
noon, prune, rune, Scone, shoon,
soon, spoon, strewn, swoon, toon,
Troon, tune, * baboon, cocoon,
raccoon, dragoon, lagoon, Muldoon,
platoon, buffoon, Colquhoun, balloon,
saloon, doubloon, maroon, oppugn,
attune, commune, Dunoon, bassoon,
lampoon, Rangoon, Sassoon, harpoon,
lardoon, cartoon, festoon, retune,
spittoon, impugn, immune, jejune,
tycoon, typhoon, *High Noon*, pontoon,

Walloon, quadroon, poltroon,
monsoon, Kowloon, * sand dune,
Neptune, teaspoon, tribune,
commune, forenoon, fortune, soup
spoon, * dessertspoon, importune,
misfortune, * Saskatoon, Pantaloon,
macaroon, Cameroon, afternoon,
tablespoon, *Brigadoon*, rigadoon,
picayune, octoroon, opportune, coffee
spoon, Lorna Doone, honeymoon,
* inopportune, Tutankhamun,
autoimmune

**Slowly, silently, now the moon
Walks the night in her silver shoon.**
WALTER DE LA MARE

41.20 crooned, mooned, pruned,
spooned, swooned, tuned, wound,
* dragooned, marooned, unpruned,
attuned, untuned, lampooned,
festooned, etc.

41.21 dunes, loons, prunes, runes,
spoons, tunes, * balloons, doubloons,
cartoons, eftsoons, * pantaloons,
afternoons, tablespoons, etc.

41.22 coop, coupe, croup, droop,
drupe, dupe, group, hoop, loop, poop,
scoop, sloop, snoop, soup, stoop,
swoop, troop, troupe, whoop,
* regroup, recoup, Ind Coope,
* playgroup, hencoop, peer group,
subgroup, Woop Woop, newsgroup,
* cantaloupe, Guadeloupe,
nincompoop, cock-a-hoop, Hula
Hoop®, supergroup

41.23 groups, hoops, loops, oops,
troops, * Kamloops, subgroups,
* paratroops, Hula Hoops®, etc.

41.24 Bruce, deuce, goose, juice, loose,

moose, mousse, noose, puce, schuss, sluice, spruce, truce, use, Zeus, * caboose, papoose, unloose, Larousse, abstruse, obtuse, abuse, adduce, produce, traduce, conduce, vamoose, profuse, burnous, reuse, recluse, excuse, deduce, reduce, seduce, induce, diffuse, effuse, ill-use, disuse, misuse, * wayzgoose, refuse, verjuice, prepuce, lime juice, mongoose, produce, footloose, couscous, * calaboose, Antabuse®, mass-produce, Ballets Russes, charlotte russe, self-abuse, lemon juice, reproduce, Beetlejuice, Betelgeuse, introduce, orange juice, over-use, under-use, * reintroduce, overproduce

**O sweet Fancy! let her loose;
Summer's joys are spoilt by use.**
JOHN KEATS

41.25 boost, deuced, Proust, roost, sluiced, used, * produced, unused, deduced, reduced, induced, *mot juste*, * langouste, * mass-produced, self-induced, introduced, * reintroduced, overproduced, etc.

41.26 douche, louche, ruche, * *farouche*, cartouche, * Scaramouche, * Ashby-de-la-Zouch

41.27 beaut, Bute, boot, brut, brute, butte, chute, coot, cute, flute, fruit, hoot, jute, Jute, loot, lute, moot, mute, newt, root, route, scoot, shoot, Shute, snoot, suit, toot, ut, ute, * pollute, salute, cheroot, uproot, compute, acute, astute, confute, commute, permute, Canute, pursuit, Salyut, transmute, square root, Beirut, reboot, re-route, recruit, depute, repute, impute, dispute, refute, dilute, minute,

en route, solute, * jackboot, taproot, statute, tracksuit, catsuit, pantsuit, grapefruit, playsuit, spacesuit, breadfruit, wetsuit, sweat suit, shell suit, freeboot, beetroot, bean shoot, tribute, swimsuit, Paiute, drysuit, offshoot, lawsuit, lounge suit, gumboot, club root, sunsuit, choucroute, droop-snoot, zoot suit, * attribute, contribute, distribute, * absolute, passion fruit, parachute, bandicoot, attribute, arrowroot, resolute, execute, destitute, birthday suit, persecute, kiwi fruit, dissolute, disrepute, institute, convolute, prosecute, prostitute, constitute, comminute, bodysuit, autoroute, overboot, overshoot, undershoot, troubleshoot, substitute, * irresolute, electrocute, reconstitute, * redistribute

41.28 boots, Boots, brutes, flutes, fruits, hoots, Jutes, Rootes, roots, shoots, suits, * cahoots, salutes, commutes, recruits, * jackboots, statutes, bean shoots, tributes, slyboots, gumboots, * attributes, institutes, prostitutes, etc.

41.29 couth, Ruth, sleuth, sooth, strewth, tooth, truth, youth, * uncouth, untruth, vermouth, forsooth, half-truth, * Redruth, milk tooth, eyetooth, sawtooth, dogtooth, hound's-tooth, bucktooth, * snaggletooth, sabretooth

**Habit with him was all the test of truth,
'It must be right: I've done it from my
   youth.'**
GEORGE CRABBE

41.30 booth, Booth, smooth, soothe, * tollbooth

41.31 groove, move, prove, who've, you've, * approve, behoove, reprove, improve, disprove, remove, * disapprove, microgroove, countermove, tongue-and-groove

41.32 grooved, moved, proved, * approved, unproved, unmoved, reproved, improved, disproved, removed, * disapproved, unapproved, unimproved

41.33 Bewes, blues, booze, bruise, chews, choose, clues, cruise, cruse, Cruz, do's, dues, Druze, fuse, Hughes, Jews, lose, Lou's, mews, muse, Muse, news, ooze, Ouse, pews, queues, ruse, schmooze, screws, shoes, snooze, Sue's, thews, trews, use, views, who's, whose, zoos, * tattoos, peruse, canoes, abuse, accuse, contuse, perfuse, suffuse, confuse, amuse, transfuse, reuse, defuse, excuse, diffuse, effuse, refuse, infuse, enthuse, reviews, ill-use, bemuse, misuse, Hormuz, Toulouse, * Andrews, statues, Matthews, values, nephews, virtues, Hebrews, Jesu's, Hindus, sinews, issues, tissues, horseshoes, Lulu's, Zulus, booze cruise, * St Andrews, * kangaroos, Santa Cruz, avenues, barbecues, Veracruz, disabuse, interviews, Syracuse, IOUs, over-use, under-use, * Bartholomew's, hypotenuse, * rhythm and blues, etc.

About binomial theorem I'm teeming
with a lot of news,
With many cheerful facts about the
square on the hypotenuse.
W. S. GILBERT

41.34 boozed, bruised, cruised, fused, mused, oozed, snoozed, used, * perused, abused, accused, confused, amused, unused, reused, defused, excused, refused, enthused, ill-used, bemused, disused, misused, * over-used, under-used, unamused, etc.

42.1 bluey, chewy, Dewey, dewy, fluey, gluey, gooey, hooey, Hughie, Louis, phooey, screwy, booby, looby, newbie, Newby, ruby, Boothby, droopy, gloopy, groupie, loopy, NUPE, Snoopy, soupy, fluky, kooky, Newquay, spooky, Sukie, boogie, Googie, broody, foodie, Judy, moody, Moody, Rudi, Trudi, Tuesday, beauty, bootee, booty, cootie, cutie, duty, fruity, snooty, goofy, Sufi, groovy, movie, toothy, smoothie, Beaulieu, coolie, coulis, Dooley, duly, goolie, hooley, Julie, mooli, newly, puli, Thule, truly, googly, brusquely, crudely, rudely, shrewdly, smoothly, coolly, loosely, muesli, hugely, Jewry, blueberry, gloomy, knew me, plumy, rheumy, roomy, Clooney, Cluny, loony, moony, Moonie, puny, Rooney, spoony, uni, goosy, juicy, Lucy, cutesy, tootsy, Tutsi, bluesy, Boosey, boozy, choosy, floozy, newsy, oozy, Pusey, snoozy, Susie, woozy, sushi, Gucci, smoochy, Fuji, * Drambuie®, St Louis, chop suey, Saluki, kabuki, adzuki, bouzouki, Suzuki, Yehudi, agouti, Djibouti, Carnoustie, unruly, unduly, patchouli, Grand Coulee, Friuli, acutely, astutely, minutely, profusely, halloumi, excuse-me, Debussy, Zanussi, Jacuzzi®, Brancusi, Baluchi, Vespucci, * mildewy, sinewy, * Rapa Nui, boogie-woogie, Punch and Judy, tutti-frutti, Bertolucci, absolutely, resolutely, * ultima Thule, etc.

I slept, and dreamed that life was beauty;
I woke, and found that life was duty.
ELLEN STURGIS HOOPER

42.2 brewer, chewer, doer, Dewar, ewer, fewer, hewer, newer, sewer, skewer, skua, viewer, wooer, * tattooer, pursuer, reviewer, * wrongdoer, * revenuer, evildoer, interviewer, Rotorua, * Nicaragua, * knew her, pursue her, etc.

42.3 Cuba, goober, scuba, tuba, tuber, uber, blooper, BUPA, cooper, Cooper, Cowper, grouper, Hooper, looper, pupa, scooper, snooper, stupa, stupor, super, trooper, trouper, whooper, * peasouper, * mosstrooper, storm trooper, * paratrooper, party pooper, pooper-scooper, super-duper, * dupe her, etc.

42.4 euchre, Luca, lucre, snooker, cougar, Kruger, Luger, * verruca, bazooka, babushka, beluga, * Chattanooga, * Juan de Fuca, * spook her, rebuke her, etc.

42.5 brooder, Cooder, cruder, Judah, lewder, ruder, shrewder, Tudor, cuter, fluter, fruiter, hooter, looter, neuter, pewter, Pooter, rooter, router, scooter, shooter, suitor, tutor, Brewster, booster, rooster, * Barbuda, Bermuda, excluder, intruder, Laputa, accoutre, polluter, computer, acuter, astuter, commuter, recruiter, disputer, refuter, * mouthbrooder, sharpshooter, freebooter, peashooter, * barracuda, draught-excluder, Buxtehude, persecutor, prosecutor, troubleshooter, * supercomputer,

telecommuter, * booed her, shoot her, etc.

42.6 hoofer, loofah, roofer, woofer, groover, Hoover®, louvre, mover, Luther, Uther, smoother, soother, * manoeuvre, Vancouver, improver, remover, * outmanoeuvre, * opera buffa, * move her, soothe her, etc.

42.7 Beulah, cooler, hula, moolah, ruler, tooler, bugler, doodler, Louvre, thuja, junior, * Tallulah, pre-schooler, Petula, vicuña, * water cooler, hula-hula, Brahmaputra, *Kama Sutra*, Zarathustra, hallelujah, * cool her, fool her, etc.

42.8 bloomer, boomer, *duma*, humour, puma, rumour, Sumer, tumour, crooner, lunar, Oonagh, Poona, pruner, schooner, sooner, spooner, Spooner, tuna, tuner, Una, * Nkrumah, perfumer, consumer, mazuma, satsuma, costumer, lacuna, lampooner, vicuna, Futuna, * baby-boomer, Montezuma, honeymooner, * Tristan da Cunha, * groom her, festoon her, etc.

42.9 juicer, looser, sprucer, Susa, boozer, bruiser, chooser, cruiser, loser, snoozer, Sousa, user, fuchsia, future, moocher, smoocher, suture, * producer, transducer, reducer, seducer, inducer, abuser, accuser, Medusa, diffuser, refuser, infuser, misuser, St Lucia, Perugia, * Appaloosa, babirusa, reproducer, introducer, Lampedusa, Arethusa, * lollapalooza, * seduce her, excuse her, etc.

42.10 Newark, eunuch

42.11 Bewick, Buick, cubic, pubic, Rubik, toothpick, broomstick, bootlick, Kubrick, rubric, Ugric, Munich, Punic, runic, tunic, music, muzhik, * cherubic, scorbutic, acoustic, refusenik, * therapeutic, hermeneutic, Finno-Ugric

42.12 Rubik's, toothpicks, broomsticks, tunics, * acoustics, spondulix, refuseniks, * therapeutics, hermeneutics

42.13 Clwyd, druid, fluid, Cupid, stupid, schoolkid, boogied, Euclid, putrid, humid, tumid, deuced, lucid, * pellucid, Seleucid, * semifluid, superfluid

42.14 leeward, skewered, steward, snookered, wounded, booted, fluted, hooted, muted, neutered, rooted, suited, tutored, boosted, roosted, louvred, rumoured, * alluded, concluded, protruded, deluded, secluded, included, excluded, untutored, polluted, saluted, uprooted, unsuited, reputed, disputed, refuted, diluted, ill-humoured, good-humoured, * attributed, contributed, distributed, * unpolluted, convoluted, undisputed, persecuted, prosecuted, constituted, undiluted, etc.

42.15 brewage, sewage, Coolidge, plumage, usage

42.16 crewel, cruel, dual, duel, Ewell, gruel, jewel, newel, Newell, Sewell, rouble, tubal, cupel, duple, pupal, pupil, scruple, ducal, bugle, Dougal, frugal, fugal, Google, googol, boodle, doodle, feudal, noodle, poodle, strudel, Bootle, brutal, footle, pootle, rootle, Tootal®, tootle, rueful, fruitful, truthful, youthful, tuneful, useful, neutral, ouzel, crucial, Trucial, * accrual, refuel, renewal, eschewal, bejewel, septuple, centuple, sextuple, quintuple, octuple, quadruple, archducal, McDougall, caboodle, canoodle, flapdoodle, refutal, unfruitful, untruthful, approval, removal, communal, tribunal, perusal, bamboozle, refusal, preputial, * Pantagruel, biofuel, febrifugal, centrifugal, vermifugal, apple strudel, Yankee Doodle, disapproval

42.17 jewels, pupils, scruples, doodles, noodles, oodles, poodles, etc.

42.18 brougham, Newham, Newcombe, dukedom, scutum, sputum, hoodlum, Newnham, Woosnam, gruesome, twosome, toothsome, * jejunum, * grew 'em, shoot 'em, etc.

42.19 bruin, ruin, shoo-in, lupin, Tutin, moulin, Newlyn, lumen, * Rasputin, illumine, * bilirubin, highfalutin, * doin', foolin', etc.

Fire, water, women, are man's ruin,
Says wise Professor Vander Bruin.
MATTHEW PRIOR

42.20 Ewan, Siouan, Cuban, Reuben, Lucan, toucan, Luton, gluten, Newton, Teuton, Euston, Houston, Huston, proven, Doolan, union, crewman, human, Newman, Schumann, Trueman, Truman, schoolman, Jewson, loosen, Susan, fusion, * McGoohan, McLuhan, McEwan, Don Juan, Barbudan,

Bermudan, Laputan, unproven, communion, reunion, nonunion, prounion, subhuman, inhuman, ichneumon, contusion, perfusion, profusion, suffusion, confusion, allusion, collusion, occlusion, conclusion, protrusion, obtrusion, transfusion, diffusion, effusion, infusion, delusion, illusion, preclusion, reclusion, seclusion, inclusion, exclusion, intrusion, extrusion, pollution, solution, ablution, locution, Confucian, Aleutian, dilution, * superhuman, malocclusion, Rediffusion®, disillusion, absolution, allocution, attribution, elocution, revolution, resolution, retribution, execution, destitution, restitution, persecution, devolution, evolution, dissolution, distribution, Lilliputian, institution, diminution, convolution, contribution, prosecution, prostitution, constitution, Rosicrucian, substitution, * electrocution, irresolution, * intercommunion, antipollution, redistribution, reconstitution, circumlocution, interlocution, high-resolution, * counter-revolution

42.21 Cubans, Reuben's, Rubens, humans, Goossens, Susan's, etc.

42.22 fluent, truant, prudent, student, mutant, coolant, movement, lucent, usedn't, Nugent, * pursuant, imprudent, pollutant, disputant, recruitment, improvement, entombment, inducement, amusement, translucent, recusant, * jurisprudent, self-improvement, disentombment

42.23 truants, prudence, Prudence, students, movements, nuisance, usance, * pursuance, imprudence, pollutants, disputants, inducements, amusements, translucence, * jurisprudence, etc.

42.24 brewing, chewing, doing, Ewing, gluing, hewing, mewing, mooing, queuing, screwing, spewing, stewing, viewing, wooing, tubing, drooping, grouping, looping, snooping, swooping, trooping, whooping, puking, brooding, feuding, wounding, booting, fluting, hooting, looting, rooting, scooting, shooting, suiting, tooting, Tooting, boosting, roosting, proofing, roofing, moving, proving, sleuthing, smoothing, soothing, cooling, drooling, fooling, mewling, ruling, schooling, tooling, doodling, shoestring, blooming, booming, fuming, grooming, looming, zooming, crooning, Kooning, mooning, pruning, spooning, swooning, tuning, loosing, sluicing, bruising, choosing, cruising, losing, musing, oozing, snoozing, using, mooching, smooching, * undoing, accruing, pursuing, canoeing, shampooing, reviewing, ensuing, regrouping, rebuking, alluding, concluding, protruding, including, excluding, polluting, saluting, computing, commuting, recruiting, disputing, refuting, approving, unmoving, reproving, improving, removing, assuming, consuming, presuming, resuming, communing, reducing, seducing, abusing, accusing, confusing, amusing, excusing, refusing, bemusing, * wrongdoing, trapshooting, sharpshooting,

* valuing, rescuing, issuing, scheduling, vacuuming, * continuing, rescheduling, * parachuting, persecuting, highfaluting, nonpolluting, prosecuting, troubleshooting, disapproving, ridiculing, unassuming, reproducing, * telecommuting, etc.

42.25 Lewes, Lewis, Louis, pubis, hubris, kumiss, Eunice, Souness, Tunis, * Day-Lewis, Anubis, * anacrusis

42.26 lupus, Lucas, mucous, mucus, Judas, Brutus, Eustace, Rufus, clueless, shoeless, viewless, tubeless, bootless, fruitless, rootless, ruthless, toothless, moonless, tuneless, useless, cuprous, humus, newness, crudeness, rudeness, shrewdness, cuteness, smoothness, coolness, * arbutus, astuteness, Confucius, * elude us, rule us, etc.

42.27 doest, newest, crudest, lewdest, rudest, shrewdest, cutest, smoothest, coolest, soonest, loosest, sprucest, * acutest, astutest, etc.

42.28 Uist, cubist, nudist, UWIST, UMIST, * tattooist, canoeist, balloonist, bassoonist, cartoonist, * absolutist, parachutist, opportunist

42.29 Hewish, Jewish, bluish, newish, shrewish, prudish, soup dish, Jutish, brutish, moonfish, coolish, foolish, ghoulish, mulish, * Ballachulish

42.30 Blewitt, cruet, Hewitt, suet, cubit, toolkit, Newgate, bluetit, moonlit, unit, Puget, * intuit, septuplet, sextuplet, quintuplet, quadruplet, * subunit, * *tempus fugit*, * do it, lose it, etc.

42.31 Ewart, Stewart, Stuart, Hubert, Schubert, Rupert

42.32 cubits, bluetits, units, * septuplets, sextuplets, quintuplets, quadruplets, * Massachusetts, etc.

42.33 allusive, conclusive, obtrusive, abusive, conducive, elusive, inclusive, exclusive, intrusive, effusive, * inconclusive, unobtrusive

42.34 brewers, viewers, Tudors, juniors, bloomers, rumours, tumours, Bruce's, uses, bruises, cruises, losers, * reviewers, Bermudas, intruders, computers, commuters, consumers, accusers, * paratroopers, baby-boomers, honeymooners, etc.

42.35 Suez, groupies, bootees, duties, movies, goolies, Julie's, tootsies

42.36 puberty, cruelty, cruelly, frugally, brutally, neutrally, crucially, suitably, fluently, prudently, humanly, fruitlessly, ruthlessly, brewery, blueberry, Newbury, Tewkesbury, Dewsbury, Shrewsbury, Bloomsbury, dupery, brusquerie, foolery, usury, jewellery, euphony, numeracy, lunacy, fluency, truancy, eulogy, crudity, nudity, unity, moodily, snootily, gloomily, musically, stupidly, lucidly, beautifully, dutifully, foolishly, unitary, luminary, mutiny, scrutiny, ruefully, fruitfully, truthfully, usefully, usually, mutually, * unsuitably, presumably, reputedly, inhumanly, tomfoolery, pecuniary, perfumery, buffoonery,

festoonery, delusory, illusory,
fiduciary, salutatory, accusatory,
innumeracy, acuity, vacuity, fatuity,
gratuity, annuity, congruity, fortuity,
credulity, salubrity, community,
impunity, immunity, disunity,
cherubically, confusedly, bemusedly,
conclusively, obtrusively, abusively,
inclusively, exclusively, approvingly,
accusingly, confusingly, amusingly,
pituitary, untruthfully, unusually,
* centrifugally, indisputably,
microbrewery, persecutory,
revolutionary, ambiguity, assiduity,
perspicuity, perpetuity, ingenuity,
incongruity, promiscuity, contiguity,
continuity, superfluity, incredulity,
insalubrity, opportunity, importunity,
unobtrusively, disapprovingly,
unassumingly, * circumlocutory,
discontinuity, * counter-revolutionary,
etc.

42.37 dueller, jeweller, cupola,
fruiterer, usurer, juniper, Boudicca,
Jupiter, crucifer, Lucifer, tubular,
uvula, * Methusaleh, * executioner

42.38 Nubia, croupier, droopier,
loopier, spookier, moodier, fruitier,
snootier, groovier, uvea, Julia, nuclear,
chewier, screwier, gloomier, roomier,
junior, punier, juicier, choosier,
* alluvia, effluvia, abulia, peculiar,
perfumier, costumier, petunia,
Seleucia, minutia, * dyscalculia,
antinuclear, thermonuclear,
Andalusia, etc.

42.39 doable, chewable, viewable,
mutable, scrutable, suitable, movable,
provable, superable, tunable, crucible,
Crucible, usable, fusible, tubercle,

pubertal, humeral, numeral, funeral,
Juvenal, gluteal, fluvial, pluvial,
cubicle, cuticle, utricle, musical,
beautiful, dutiful, usual, mutual,
* renewable, computable,
commutable, unsuitable, imputable,
disputable, refutable, inscrutable,
unprovable, improvable, disprovable,
immovable, removable, insuperable,
manoeuvrable, innumerable,
consumable, presumable, deducible,
reducible, unusable, confusable,
reusable, excusable, delusional,
connubial, marsupial, alluvial, diluvial,
unmusical, unusual, * unrenewable,
nonrenewable, executable,
indisputable, irrefutable, substitutable,
reproducible, irreducible, inexcusable,
institutional, constitutional,
pharmaceutical, attitudinal,
latitudinal, longitudinal, pari-mutuel,
* unconstitutional

42.40 Houyhnhnm, Lewisham,
* Jerusalem, alluvium, effluvium

42.41 Hughenden, Lutheran, mutagen,
Nubian, Boolean, Julian, union,
Lucian, Rubicon, hooligan,
Newington, Houlihan, unison,
UNISON, * Danubian, trade union,
alluvion, Peruvian, Vesuvian,
Acheulian, cerulean, communion,
Mancunian, Réunion, Neptunian,
reunion, nonunion, prounion,
Malthusian, Carthusian, Venusian,
* postdiluvian, Zarathustrian,
Andalusian, * antediluvian, Soviet
Union, intercommunion

42.42 Newfoundland, rubicund

42.43 nutrient, lubricant, fumigant,

jubilant, rudiment, supplement,
nutriment, muniment, ruminant,
* exuberant, protuberant,
accoutrement, insouciant,
communicant, concupiscent,
* disillusionment

42.44 nutrients, jubilance, rudiments,
ruminants, * exuberance,
protuberance, insouciance,
concupiscence, etc.

42.45 duelling, gruelling, ruining,
skewering, neutering, tutoring, etc.

42.46 humourless, tuberous, uterus,
humerus, humorous, numerous,
usefulness, ruthlessness, dubious,
studious, beauteous, duteous, gluteus,
Julius, nucleus, Junius, Lucius,
ludicrous, ruinous, moodiness,
glutinous, mutinous, snootiness,
luminous, numinous, juiciness,
scrupulous, cumulus, tumulus,
* Vesuvius, salubrious, lugubrious,
caduceus, Manutius, gratuitous,
circuitous, fortuitous, aluminous,
voluminous, leguminous, bituminous,
unscrupulous, * insalubrious,
impecunious, platitudinous,
multitudinous, pulchritudinous,
altocumulus, stratocumulus,
cirrocumulus, etc.

42.47 droopiest, loopiest, spookiest,
moodiest, fruitiest, snootiest,
grooviest, chewiest, screwiest,
gloomiest, roomiest, puniest, juiciest,
choosiest, etc.

42.48 duellist, feudalist, Eucharist,
humorist, futurist, lutenist, unionist,
Unionist, humanist, pugilist,

Rhymes in sayings

*The use of rhyme is not restricted to
poems and songs. Many sayings and
slogans are made memorable in this
way, e.g. 'Red sky at night,
shepherd's delight', 'No pain, no
gain', 'A Mars a day helps you work,
rest, and play', 'Coughs and sneezes
spread diseases'. Rhyme is also
found in many everyday words and
phrases. Some of these are well-
established compounds made up of
two parts that are now meaningless
on their own, e.g.* fuddy-duddy,
hanky-panky, helter-skelter,
mumbo-jumbo, namby-pamby,
nitty-gritty. *Others are newer
coinages in which both parts have
meaning and are chosen because
they rhyme. Here are some examples:*

blast from the past
booze cruise
chalk and talk
chick flick
culture vulture
doom and gloom
fair and square
fat cat
gender bender
highways and byways
hire and fire
horses for courses
latest and greatest
make or break
meals on wheels
name and shame
nearest and dearest
pooper-scooper
pub grub
snail mail
surf and turf
thrills and spills
wear and tear
wheel and deal

* consumerist, phillumenist, illusionist, * revolutionist, evolutionist

42.49 numerate, duplicate, * quintuplicate, quadruplicate

42.50 mutually, usually, tutelary, funerary, numeracy, * exuberantly, peculiarly, indubitably, unusually, innumeracy, * institutionally, constitutionally, supernumerary

42.51 insuperable, innumerable, dutiable, communicable, indubitable, * incommunicable

Index

abulia 42.38
abundance 38.33
abundant 38.32
abundantly 38.47
abuse 41.24; 41.33
abused 41.34
abuser 42.9
Abu Simbel 18.22
abusing 42.24
abusive 42.33
abusively 42.36
abut 37.47
abutment 38.32
abutted 38.20
abutting 38.34
abuzz 37.51
abysm 18.27
abysmal 18.22
abysmally 18.56
abyss 17.46
abyssal 18.22
Abyssinia 18.61
Abyssinian 18.67
acacia 8.9
academe 15.20
academia 16.40
academic 10.15
academical 10.60
academically 10.54
academician 18.33
academics 10.16
academy 2.56
acajou 41.4
acanthus 2.46
a cappella 10.12
ACAS 1.40
accede 15.11
accelerant 10.67
accelerate 7.38
acceleration 8.28
accelerator 8.5
accent 2.40; 9.41
accented 10.18
accents 2.41
accentuate 7.38
accentuation 8.28
accept 9.46
acceptable 10.60
acceptance 10.34
accepted 10.18
acceptor 10.10
access 9.47
accessibility 18.58
accessible 10.60
accession 10.28
accessories 10.77
accessorize 21.43
accessory 10.53

acciaccatura 28.2
accident 2.68
accidental 10.21
accidentally 10.53
accident-prone 35.36
accidents 2.69
acclaim 7.18
acclaimed 7.19
acclamation 8.24
acclimatization 8.47
acclimatize 21.44
acclivity 18.57
accolade 7.8
accolades 7.9
accommodate 7.43
accommodating 8.60
accommodation 8.34
accompanied 17.8; 38.51
accompaniment 38.56
accompanist 38.60
accompany 38.47
accomplice 38.37
accomplish 38.40
accomplished 38.41
accomplishment 38.56
accomplishments 38.57
accord 25.9
accordance 26.24
accordant 26.23
according 26.25
accordingly 26.37
accordion 26.43
accost 23.41
accosted 24.24
account 29.11
accountability 18.58
accountable 30.24
accountancy 30.22
accountant 30.10
accountants 30.11
accounting 30.12
accounts 29.9
accoutre 42.5
accoutrement 42.43
Accra 3.1
accredit 10.48
accrete 15.35
accretion 16.22
Accrington 2.66
accrual 42.16
accrue 41.2
accrued 41.9
accruing 42.24
accumulate 7.49
accumulated 8.13

accumulation 8.39
accumulator 8.5
accuracy 2.78
accurate 2.74
accurately 2.78
Accurist® 2.73
accursed 11.23; 12.4
accursedly 12.29
accusation 8.24
accusative 17.55
accusatory 42.36
accusatory 8.76
accuse 41.33
accused 41.34
accuser 42.9
accusers 42.34
accusing 42.24
accusingly 42.36
accustom 38.26
ace 7.30
acephalous 10.70
acer 8.9
acerbic 12.3
acerbity 12.29
aces 8.75
acetal 1.16
acetate 7.35
acetic 10.15; 16.11
acetone 35.36
acetous 2.71
acetyl 21.16
acetylene 15.26
Achaia 22.2
Achates 15.44
ache 7.6
Acheson 2.66
Acheulian 42.41
achievable 16.41
achieve 15.39
achieved 15.40
achievement 16.25
achievements 16.26
achiever 16.6
achieves 15.41
achieving 16.27
Achillean 16.22
Achilles 15.44; 18.54
Achilles heel 15.17
aching 8.59
achromatic 2.17
achromic 36.10
achy 8.1
acid 2.24
acidhead 9.8
acidic 18.16
acidification 8.46
acidify 21.4
acidimetry 18.57

acidity 18.57
acidophilus 24.70
acidosis 36.25
acidulate 7.41
acidulous 18.74
ack-ack 1.3
ack-emma 10.13
acknowledge 24.26
acknowledgment 24.67
acknowledgments 24.68
Ackroyd 33.4
acme 2.6
acne 2.6
acolyte 21.34
aconite 21.34
acorn 25.22
acoustic 42.11
acoustics 42.12
acquaint 7.25
acquaintance 8.57
acquaintanceship 17.43
acquainted 8.13
acquiesce 9.47
acquiesced 9.49
acquiescence 10.34
acquiescent 10.33
acquiescing 10.36
acquirable 20.12
acquire 19.1
acquired 19.2
acquirement 20.5
acquirer 20.2
acquisition 18.33
acquisitive 17.55
acquit 17.51
acquittal 18.22
acquittance 18.39
acre 8.4
acreage 17.14
acrid 2.24
acridity 18.57
Acrilan® 1.24
acrimonious 36.42
acrimony 2.78
acrobat 1.45
acrobatic 2.17
acrobatics 2.23
acronym 17.24
acrophobia 36.37
acrophobic 36.10
Acropolis 17.46
across 23.39
acrostic 24.16
acrylic 18.16
act 1.6

acted 2.25
acting 2.42
actinia 18.61
actinic 18.16
action 2.35
action replay 7.3
actions 2.39
activate 7.35
activation 8.24
activator 8.5
active 2.53
actively 2.58
activism 18.28
activist 2.73
activity 18.57
Acton 2.35
actor 2.10
actress 2.46
actual 2.64
actuality 2.57
actualize 21.47
actually 2.59; 2.78
actuarial 6.17
actuary 2.59; 2.78
actuate 7.35
actuation 8.24
acuity 42.36
acumen 2.66; 9.32
acupressure 10.14
acupuncture 38.14
acute 41.27
acutely 42.1
acuter 42.5
acutest 42.27
ad 1.9
AD 15.2
Ada 8.5
adage 2.27
adagio 35.19
Adam 2.32
adamant 2.68
Adams 2.33
Adamson 2.66
adapt 1.39
adaptability 18.58
adaptable 2.64
adaptation 8.24
adapted 2.25
adapting 2.42
adaptive 2.53
adaptor 2.10
add 1.9
Addams 2.33
added 2.25
addenda 10.10
addendum 10.25
adder 2.10
addict 17.6

addicted 18.19
addiction 18.33
addictive 18.53
adding 2.42
Addington 2.66
Addis Ababa 2.60
Addison 2.66
addition 18.33
additional 18.64
additionally 18.80
additive 17.55
addle 2.28
addled 2.29
address 9.47
addressable 10.60
addressed 9.49
addressee 15.4
addresser 10.14
adds 1.10
adduce 41.24
Addy 2.3
Adelaide 7.8
Adele 9.16
Adelphi 10.4
Aden 8.21
Adenauer 31.1
adenoid 33.4
adenoidal 34.5
adenoids 33.5
adenoma 36.8
adenosine 15.26
adept 9.46
adequacy 2.78
adequate 2.74
adequately 2.78
adhere 13.1
adhered 13.2
adherence 14.11
adherent 14.10
adherents 14.11
adhesion 16.22
adhesions 16.24
adhesive 16.35
ad hoc 23.3
Adidas® 1.40
Adie 8.1
adieu 11.1; 41.2
ad infinitum 22.18
adios 23.39
adipocere 13.1
adipocerous 24.70
adipose 35.42; 35.52
adjacent 8.56
adjectival 22.16
adjectivally 22.40
adjective 17.55
adjoin 33.8
adjoining 34.11

adjourn 11.15
adjourned 11.16
adjournment 12.14
adjudge 37.15
adjudicate 7.49
adjudication 8.39
adjudicative 17.54
adjudicator 8.5
adjunct 37.34
adjuration 8.24
adjure 27.1
adjust 37.45
adjustable 38.52
adjusted 38.20
adjuster 38.10
adjusting 38.34
adjustment 38.32
adjustments 38.33
adjutant 2.68
adjuvant 2.68
Adlai 21.3
adland 1.28
Adler 2.12
Adlerian 14.21
ad-lib 17.1
ad-libs 17.2
adman 1.24; 2.35
admen 9.32
admin 2.34
administer 18.60
administrate 7.41
administration 8.32
administrative 17.54
administrator 8.5
admirable 2.79
admirably 2.78
admiral 2.64
admiralship 17.43
admiralty 2.78
admiration 8.24
admire 19.1
admired 19.2
admirer 20.2
admires 19.4
admiring 20.7
admiringly 20.11
admissible 18.64
admission 18.33
admit 17.51
admits 17.52
admittance 18.39
admitted 18.19
admittedly 18.56
admitting 18.40
admix 17.4
admixture 18.14
admonish 24.46
admonished 24.47

admonishment 24.67
admonition 18.33
admonitory 24.56
ad nauseam 1.22
ado 41.2
adobe 36.1
adolescence 10.34
adolescent 10.33
adolescents 10.34
Adolf 23.16
Adonis 36.25
adopt 23.38
adopted 24.24
adopter 24.10
adopting 24.40
adoption 24.33
adoptive 24.51
adorable 26.41
adoration 8.24
adore 25.2
adored 25.9
adorer 26.6
adores 25.35
adoring 26.25
adorn 25.22
adorned 25.24
adorning 26.25
adornment 26.23
adornments 26.24
ad rem 9.28
adrenal 16.17
adrenaline 17.29
Adrian 8.81
Adrianople 36.15
Adriatic 2.17
Adrienne 9.32
adrift 17.11
adroit 33.13
adroitly 34.1
adroitness 34.12
ads 1.10
adsorb 25.5
adulate 7.35
adulation 8.24
adulatory 8.76
adult 37.26
adulterant 38.56
adulterate 7.48
adulterated 8.13
adulteration 8.38
adulterer 38.48
adulteress 38.59
adulterous 38.59
adultery 38.47
adulthood 39.4
adumbrate 7.35
adumbration 8.24
Adur 8.5

ad valorem 26.17
advance 3.22
advancement 4.27
advancer 4.14
advancing 4.29
advantage 4.18
advantageous 8.67
advent 2.40; 9.41
Advent 2.40; 9.41
adventitious 18.44
adventure 10.14
adventures 10.52
adventurism 18.28
adventurist 10.72
adventurous 10.70
adventurously 10.78
adverb 11.2
adverbial 12.32
adversarial 6.17
adversary 2.78
adverse 11.22
adversely 12.1
adversity 12.29
advert 11.24
advertent 12.14
advertise 21.42
advertised 21.48
advertisement 12.35
advertisements 12.36
advertiser 22.9
advertising 22.26
adverts 11.25
advice 21.29
advisability 18.58
advisable 22.43
advise 21.40
advised 21.48
advisedly 22.40
advisement 22.24
adviser 22.9
advisers 22.39
advisory 22.40
advocaat 3.1
advocacy 2.78
advocate 2.74; 7.35
advocation 8.24
adze 1.10
adzuki 42.1
aedile 21.16
Aegean 16.22
aegis 16.29
aegrotat 1.45
Aeneas 16.30
Aeneid 16.13
aeolian 36.40
Aeolus 36.26
aerate 7.33
aeration 8.23

aerial 6.17
aerify 21.4
Aer Lingus 18.44
Aero® 35.5
aerobatics 2.23
aerobe 35.20
aerobic 36.10
aerobics 36.11
aerodrome 35.34
aerodynamic 2.20
aerodynamics 2.23
aerofoil 33.6
aerogram 1.22
aeronaut 25.31
aeronautical 26.41
aerophobia 36.37
aeroplane 7.21
aerosol 23.15
aerospace 7.30
aerostat 1.45
Aeschylean 16.22
Aeschylus 16.47
Aesop 23.36
aesthete 15.35
aesthetic 10.15
aesthetically 10.54
aesthetician 18.33
aesthetics 10.16
aestival 10.60
aestival 22.16
aetiological 24.61
aetiology 24.55
afar 3.1
afeard 13.2
affable 2.64
affably 2.56
affair 5.1
affairs 5.5
affect 9.5
affectation 8.24
affected 10.18
affecting 10.36
affection 10.28
affectionate 10.73
affectionately 10.78
affective 10.50
afferent 2.68
affiance 22.25
affidavit 8.71
affiliate 7.41; 18.77
affiliated 8.13
affiliation 8.32
affinity 18.57
affirm 11.13
affirmation 8.24
affirmative 17.55
affirmed 11.14
affix 2.23; 17.4

affixation 8.24
affixed 17.5
afflict 17.6
afflicting 18.40
affliction 18.33
affluence 2.69
afford 25.9
affordability 18.58
affordable 26.41
afforestation 8.34
affray 7.2
affright 21.32
affront 37.40
affronted 38.20
Afghan 1.24
Afghan hound 29.6
Afghani 4.6
Afghanistan 1.24; 3.19
aficionado 35.4
afield 15.18
afire 19.1
aflame 7.18
afloat 35.45
aflutter 38.10
afoot 39.14
afore 25.2
aforementioned 10.29
aforesaid 9.8
aforethought 25.31
a fortiori 21.3; 26.1
afoul 29.4
afraid 7.8
afresh 9.50
Africa 2.60
African 2.66
Africana 4.13
Africanism 18.29
Afrikaans 3.22; 3.24
Afrikander 2.10
Afrikaner 4.13
Afro 35.3
aft 3.10
after 4.10
afterbirth 11.26
afterburner 12.2
aftercare 5.1
afterdamp 1.23
afterdeck 9.2
aftereffect 9.5
afterglow 35.19
afterimage 18.21
afterlife 21.14
aftermath 1.47; 3.34
aftermost 35.43
afternoon 41.19
afternoons 41.21
afterpains 7.26

aftersensation 8.41
aftershave 7.54
aftershock 23.3
aftersun 37.31
aftertaste 7.31
afterthought 25.31
afterward 4.45
afterwards 4.46
afterword 11.7
afterworld 11.12
Aga® 4.9
Agadir 13.1
again 7.21; 9.32
against 9.40
Aga Khan 3.19
Agamemnon 10.27; 23.27
agapanthus 2.46
agape 7.27
agar 3.1; 8.4
agaric 17.3
Aga saga 4.9
agate 2.50
Agatha 2.60
agave 4.4; 8.1
age 7.12
aged 7.13; 8.12
ageing 8.64
ageism 18.27
ageist 8.68
ageless 8.67
agency 8.76
agenda 10.10
agendum 10.25
agent 8.56
agent provocateur 11.1
agents 8.57
ages 8.75
Agfa 2.11
Aggie 2.2
agglomerate 7.43
agglomeration 8.34
agglutinate 7.49
agglutination 8.39
aggrandize 21.41
aggrandizement 2.68
aggravate 7.35
aggravated 8.13
aggravating 8.60
aggravation 8.24
aggregate 2.74; 7.35
aggregation 8.24
aggress 9.47
aggression 10.28
aggressive 10.50
aggressively 10.54
aggressor 10.14
aggrieve 15.39

aggrieved 15.40
aggro 35.3
aghast 3.30
agile 21.16
agility 18.58
agin 17.29
Agincourt 25.31
agitate 7.35
agitation 8.24
agitator 8.5
agitprop 23.36
Aglaia 22.2
agleam 15.20
agley 7.2
aglimmer 18.13
aglitter 18.10
aglow 35.2
AGM 9.28
agma 2.13
Agnes 2.46
Agnew 41.3
agnostic 24.16
agnosticism 18.28
agnostics 24.22
Agnus Dei 8.1
ago 35.2
agog 23.11
agonic 24.19
agonist 2.73
agonistic 18.16
agonize 21.42
agonized 21.48
agonizing 22.26
agony 2.56
agora 2.60
agoraphobe 35.20
agoraphobia 36.37
agoraphobic 36.10
Agostini 16.1
agouti 42.1
agraphia 2.61
agrarian 6.19
agree 15.2
agreeable 16.41
agreeably 16.38
agreed 15.11
agreeing 16.27
agreement 16.25
agreements 16.26
agrees 15.43
Agricola 18.60
agricultural 38.52
agriculturalist 17.49
agriculture 38.14
agriculturist 38.60
Agrippa 18.8
Agrippina 16.8
agrochemical 10.60

agronomic 24.19
agronomics 24.22
agronomy 24.54
aground 29.6
ague 41.3
Agutter 2.60
ah 3.1
aha 3.1
Ahab 1.1
Ahasuerus 14.14
ahead 9.8
ahem 9.28
Ahern 11.15
Ahmed 9.8
ahoy 33.1
aid 7.8
Aïda 16.5
Aidan 8.21
aide 7.8
aided 8.13
aide-de-camp 23.31
aide-mémoire 3.1
aider 8.5
aiding 8.60
aids 7.9
AIDS 7.9
aigrette 9.51
ail 7.15
ailed 7.16
Aileen 15.25
aileron 23.27
ailing 8.62
ailment 8.56
ailments 8.57
ails 7.17
Ailsa 8.9
ailurophile 21.16
aim 7.18
aimed 7.19
aiming 8.63
aimless 8.67
aimlessly 8.76
aims 7.20
Ainsley 8.1
ain't 7.25
Aintree 8.1; 15.3
aïoli 36.1
air 5.1
air bag 1.13
air bags 1.14
air bed 9.8
airborne 25.22
airbrush 37.46
Airbus® 37.43
air-con 23.27
air-cooled 41.15
aircraft 3.10
aircrew 41.3

Airdrie 6.1
airdrop 23.36
aired 5.2
Airedale 7.15
airer 6.2
air fare 5.1
airfield 15.18
airflow 35.5
air gun 37.31
airhead 9.8
air hole 35.30
airier 6.16
airily 6.15
airiness 6.22
airing 6.10
airless 6.11
airlift 17.11
airline 21.22
airliner 22.8
airlines 21.25
airlock 23.3
airmail 7.15
airman 6.7
airplane 7.21
airplay 7.3
airport 25.31
airs 5.5
airship 17.43
airshow 35.5
airsick 17.3
airspace 7.30
airspeed 15.11
airstream 15.20
airstrip 17.43
airtight 21.33
airtime 21.19
airwaves 7.55
airway 7.3
airwoman 40.10
airworthiness 12.37
airworthy 12.1
airy 6.1
airy-fairy 6.1
aisle 21.16
aisles 21.18
Aisne 9.32
aitchbone 35.36
aitches 8.75
Aitken 8.20
Aix-la-Chapelle 9.16
Ajaccio 35.19
ajar 3.1
Ajax 1.4
Akela 8.7
Akhenaten 4.24
akimbo 35.11
akin 17.29
Al 1.16

Alabama 2.13
alabaster 2.10; 4.10
à la carte 3.32
alack 1.3
alackaday 7.4
alacrity 2.57
Aladdin 2.34
à la king 2.70
Alamein 7.21
Alamo 35.19
à la mode 35.25
Alan 2.35
Alanbrooke 39.1
Alannah 2.13
Al-Anon 23.27
Alaric 17.3
alarm 3.16
alarmed 3.17
alarming 4.29
alarmingly 4.42
alarmism 18.27
alarmist 4.33
alarms 3.18
alarum 2.32; 4.22
alas 1.40
Alaska 2.9
Alaskan 2.35
Alba Longa 24.9
Alban 24.33; 26.19
Albania 8.78
Albanian 8.81
Albany 24.54; 26.37
albatross 23.39
albeit 16.34
Albemarle 3.14
Albert 2.50
Alberta 12.2
Albertan 12.12
Alberto 35.8
Albigenses 15.44
albinism 18.28
albino 35.10
Albinoni 36.1
Albion 2.66
Albrecht 9.5
Albright 21.33
album 2.32
albumen 2.66; 17.29
albumin 17.29
albums 2.33
Albuquerque 12.1
Al Capone 35.36
Alcatraz 1.50
alchemic 10.15
alchemist 2.73
alchemy 2.56
alcheringa 18.9
Alcibiades 15.45

alpha 2.11
alphabet 9.51
alphabetic 10.15
alphabetical 10.60
alphabetically 10.54
alphabetization 8.53
alphabetize 21.47
Alpha Centauri 26.1
alphanumeric 10.15
alphasort 25.31
alphorn 25.22
alpine 21.22
Alpine 21.22
al-Qaeda 16.5; 22.5
already 10.3
Alsace 1.40
Alsager 8.9
Alsatian 8.23
Alsatians 8.55
also 35.14
also-ran 1.24
Altaic 8.10
altar 24.10; 26.4
altar boy 33.1
altar boys 33.15
altarpiece 15.32
alter 24.10; 26.4
alterable 24.77; 26.51
alteration 8.34; 8.35
alterations 8.55
altercate 7.43; 7.44
altercation 8.34; 8.35
altered 24.24; 26.12
alter ego 35.10
alternate 7.43; 7.44;
  12.24
alternately 12.29
alternating 8.60
alternation 8.34; 8.35
alternative 17.55
alternator 8.5
although 35.2
altimeter 16.5; 18.60
altitude 41.9
alto 35.3
altocumulus 42.46
altogether 10.11
Alton 24.33; 26.19
Alton Towers 31.5
altostratus 4.32; 8.67
Altrincham 24.63;
  26.42
altruism 18.28
altruist 2.73
altruistic 18.16
altruistically 18.57
alum 2.32
aluminium 18.66

aluminous 42.46
alumna 38.13
alumnae 15.3; 38.6
alumni 21.3
alumnus 38.38
alveolar 36.7
Alvin 2.34
always 7.56
alyssum 2.65
Alzheimer's 22.39
am 1.22
a.m. 9.28
amah 4.13
Amalfi 2.4
amalgam 2.32
amalgamate 7.35
amalgamation 8.24
Amanda 2.10
amanuensis 10.41
amaranth 1.35
amaretto 35.7
Amarillo 35.11
amaryllis 18.43
Amaryllis 18.43
amass 1.40
amassed 1.42
amasser 2.14
amateur 2.60; 11.1;
  27.1
amateurish 28.15
amateurs 11.29
amatory 2.56
amaze 7.56
amazed 7.57
amazement 8.56
amazing 8.64
amazingly 8.76
Amazon 2.66
Amazonia 36.37
Amazonian 36.40
ambassador 2.60
ambassadorial 26.41
ambassadorship 17.43
ambassadress 2.71
amber 2.8
ambergris 15.32; 17.46
ambidextrous 10.42
ambience 2.69; 3.22
ambient 2.68
ambiguity 42.36
ambiguous 18.74
ambiguously 18.80
ambit 2.51
ambition 18.33
ambitions 18.37
ambitious 18.44
ambitiously 18.56
ambivalence 18.71

ambivalent 18.70
amble 2.28
ambler 2.12
Ambler 2.12
Ambleside 21.12
Ambrose 35.52
ambrosia 36.37
ambulance 2.69
ambulant 2.68
ambulatory 8.76
ambush 39.13
Amelia 16.40
ameliorate 7.33; 7.40
amelioration 8.45
amen 9.32
Amen 4.24
amenable 16.41
amend 9.35
amended 10.18
amendment 10.33
amendments 10.34
amenities 16.51
amenity 16.38
amenorrhoea 13.1
Amen-Ra 3.1
America 10.56
American 10.64
Americana 4.13
Americanism 18.29
Americanization 8.53
Americanize 21.47
Amerind 17.34
Amerindian 18.67
Amersham 2.65
amethyst 2.73
Amex 9.3
Amharic 2.19
amiability 18.58
amiable 8.88
amicability 18.58
amicable 2.79
amicably 2.78
amid 17.8
amidships 17.44
amigo 35.10
Amin 15.24
amino 35.10
Amis 8.66
Amish 2.49
amiss 17.46
amity 2.57
Amman 3.19
ammeter 2.60
ammo 35.3
Ammon 2.35
ammonia 36.37
ammoniac 1.3

ammoniacal 22.43
ammonic 24.19
ammonite 21.34
ammonites 21.35
ammonium 36.39
ammunition 18.33
amnesia 16.9; 16.40
amnesiac 1.3
amnesic 16.11
amnesty 2.57
amniocentesis 16.29
amnion 2.66
amniotic 24.16
amoeba 16.3
amoebic 16.11
amok 23.3; 37.3
among 37.37
amontillado 35.4
amoral 24.27
amoretti 10.3
amoretto 35.7
amoroso 35.16
amorous 2.71
amorously 2.78
amorphous 26.27
amortization 8.35
amortize 21.41
Amory 8.76
Amos 23.39
amount 29.11
amounting 30.12
amounts 29.9
amour 27.1
amour-propre 24.12
amours 27.3
Amoy 33.1
amp 1.23
ampere 5.1
ampersand 1.28
amphetamine 15.26;
  17.29
amphetamines 15.29;
  17.42
amphibian 18.67
amphibians 18.69
amphibious 18.74
amphibrach 1.3
amphitheatre 14.2
Amphitrite 22.1
Amphitryon 18.67
amphora 2.60
amphoric 24.18
ample 2.28
Ampleforth 25.33
amplification 8.40
amplified 21.12
amplifier 22.2
amplifies 21.42

amplify 21.4
amplitude 41.9
amply 2.5
ampoule 41.14
Ampthill 17.15
ampulla 40.2
amputate 7.35
amputation 8.24
amputee 15.4
Amritsar 18.14
Amsterdam 1.22
Amstrad 1.9
amulet 2.74
Amundsen 2.66
amuse 41.33
amused 41.34
amusement 42.22
amusements 42.23
amusing 42.24
amusingly 42.36
Amy 8.1
amygdala 18.60
amyloid 33.4
Amytal® 1.16
an 1.24
Anabaptist 2.47
anabolic 24.18
anachronism 18.28
anaconda 24.10
anacrusis 42.25
Anadin® 17.29
anaemia 16.40
anaemic 16.11
anaerobic 36.10
anaesthesia 16.40
anaesthesiology 24.55
anaesthetic 10.15
anaesthetics 10.16
anaesthetist 16.48
anaesthetize 21.43
anaesthetized 21.48
anaglyph 17.10
Anaglypta® 18.10
anagram 1.22
anagrammatic 2.17
Anaheim 21.19
anal 8.15
analeptic 10.15
analgesia 16.40
analgesic 16.11
analogic 24.20
analogical 24.61
analogize 21.42
analogous 2.71
analogue 23.11
analogy 2.56
analyse 21.42
analyses 15.45

analysis 17.46
analyst 2.73
analytic 18.16
analytical 18.64
analytically 18.57
Ananias 22.29
anaphora 2.60
anaphoric 24.18
anaphylactic 2.17
anaphylaxis 2.45
anarchic 4.16
anarchical 4.47
anarchist 2.73
anarchy 2.56
Anastasia 4.44; 8.78
anastomosis 36.25
Anatolia 36.37
Anatolian 36.40
anatomic 24.19
anatomical 24.61
anatomically 24.56
anatomize 21.42
anatomy 2.56
Anaxagoras 2.71
Anaximander 2.10
ancestor 2.60; 10.10
ancestral 10.21
ancestry 2.58; 10.5
anchor 2.9
anchorage 17.14
Anchorage 17.14
anchorite 21.34
anchorman 1.24
anchovy 2.56
ancient 8.56
ancillary 18.56
Ancona 36.8
and 1.28
Andalucía 16.2
Andalusia 42.38
Andalusian 42.41
Andaman 2.66
andante 7.3
Andean 2.66; 16.22
Andersen 2.66
Anderson 2.66
Andes 2.54; 15.44
Andhra Pradesh 9.50
andiron 22.20
Andorra 26.6
Andorran 26.19
André 7.3
Andrea 2.61
Andreas 8.67
Andretti 10.3
Andrew 41.3
Andrews 41.33
Androcles 15.45

androgen 2.66
androgynous 24.70
android 33.4
Andromache 24.54
Andromeda 24.57
Andy 2.3
Andy Capp 1.37
Andy Pandy 2.3
anecdotage 36.14
anecdotal 36.15
anecdote 35.45
anecdotes 35.46
anemometer 24.57
anemone 10.53
aneroid 33.4
Aneurin 22.19
aneurysm 18.28
anew 41.2
Anfield 15.18
Ange 1.30
angel 8.15
Angela 2.60
angel dust 37.45
angelfish 17.50
angelic 10.15
angelica 10.56
angelically 10.54
Angelina 16.8
angels 8.17
Angelus 2.71
anger 2.9
angered 2.25
Angharad 2.25
Angie 2.7
angina 22.8
angiogram 1.22
angle 2.28
angler 2.12
anglers 2.55
Anglesey 2.56
Anglia 2.61
Anglian 2.66
Anglican 2.66
Anglicanism 18.29
Anglicism 18.28
anglicization 8.40
anglicize 21.42
anglicized 21.48
angling 2.42
Anglomania 8.78
Anglophile 21.16
Anglophilia 18.61
Anglophilic 18.16
Anglophobe 35.20
Anglophone 35.36
Angmering 2.70
Angola 36.7
Angolan 36.20

angora 26.6
Angostura 28.2
angrier 2.61
angriest 2.72
angrily 2.58
angry 2.5
angry young man
1.24
angry young men
9.32
angstrom 2.32
Anguilla 18.12
anguish 2.49
angular 2.60
Angus 2.46
anhydrous 22.29
aniline 15.26
animadversion 12.12
animal 2.64
animalism 18.29
animate 2.74; 7.35
animated 8.13
animation 8.24
animator 8.5
animatronic 24.19
animatronics 24.22
animism 18.28
animist 2.73
animosity 24.56
animus 2.71
anion 22.20
aniseed 15.11
Anita 16.5
Anjou 41.3
Ankara 2.60
ankh 1.25
ankle 2.28
anklebone 35.36
ankles 2.30
anklet 2.51
Ann 1.24
Anna 2.13
Annabel 9.16
Annabella 10.12
annal 2.28
annals 2.30
Annapolis 17.46
Annapurna 12.2
Ann Arbor 4.8
annatto 35.3
Anne 1.24
Anne of Cleves 15.41
anneal 15.17
annealed 15.18
Anneka 2.60
Anne-Marie 15.4
Anne-Marie's 15.45
Anne's 1.36

Annette 9.51
Annette's 9.52
annex 9.3
annexation 8.24
annexed 9.4
Annie 2.6
Annigoni 36.1
annihilate 7.42
annihilation 8.33
anniversary 12.29
anno Domini 21.4
annotate 7.35
annotation 8.24
announce 29.9
announced 29.10
announcement 30.10
announcements 30.11
announcer 30.2
announcing 30.12
annoy 33.1
annoyance 34.10
annoyed 33.4
annoying 34.11
annoyingly 34.14
annoys 33.15
annual 2.64
annualize 21.47
annualized 21.48
annually 2.59; 2.78
annuity 42.36
annul 37.16
annular 2.60
annulling 38.34
annulment 38.32
annulus 2.71
Annunciation 8.38
annus horribilis 17.46
annus mirabilis 17.46
anodic 24.16
anodize 21.42
anodized 21.48
anodyne 21.22
anoint 33.10
anointed 34.3
anointer 34.2
anointing 34.11
anomalous 24.70
anomaly 24.54
anon 23.27
anonymity 18.57
anonymous 24.70
anonymously 24.76
anopheles 15.45
anorak 1.3
anorectic 10.15
anorexia 10.57
anorexia nervosa 36.9
anorexic 10.15

anosmia 24.58
another 38.11
anoxia 24.58
Anschluss 39.12
Anselm 9.21
Anstruther 38.11
answer 4.14
answerable 4.57
answered 4.17
answering 4.52
answerphone 35.36
answers 4.41
ant 1.33
Antabuse® 41.24
antacid 2.24
Antaeus 16.30
antagonism 18.28
antagonist 2.73
antagonistic 18.16
antagonize 21.42
Antarctic 4.16
Antarctica 4.43
Antares 15.44
ante 2.3
anteater 16.5
antebellum 10.25
antecede 15.11
antecedence 16.26
antecedent 16.25
antechamber 8.3
antedate 7.35
antediluvian 42.41
antelope 35.40
antemeridian 18.67
ante meridiem 18.66
antenatal 8.15
antenna 10.13
antennae 10.6; 15.3
antenuptial 38.23
antepenultimate
38.62
anterior 14.18
anteroom 39.9; 41.17
Anthea 2.61
anthem 2.32
anther 2.11
anthill 17.15
anthologies 24.75
anthologize 21.45
anthology 24.55
Anthony 2.56
anthracene 15.26
anthracite 21.34
anthracitic 18.16
anthracosis 36.25
anthrax 1.4
anthropoid 33.4
anthropological 24.61

anthropologist 24.72
anthropology 24.55
anthropometric 10.15
anthropophagy 24.54
anti 2.3
antibacterial 14.19
antiballistic 18.16
Antibes 15.5
antibiotic 24.16
antibiotics 24.22
antibody 24.3
antic 2.17
Antichrist 21.30
anticipate 7.41
anticipation 8.32
anticipatory 8.76
anticlerical 10.60
anticlimactic 2.17
anticlimax 1.4
anticline 21.22
anticlockwise 21.41
anticoagulant 2.68
anticonvulsant 38.32
antics 2.23
anticyclone 35.36
anticyclonic 24.19
antidazzle 2.28
antidepressant 10.33
antidepressants 10.34
antidote 35.45
antiemetic 10.15
antifouling 30.12
antifreeze 15.45
antifungal 38.23
antigen 2.66; 9.32
Antigone 18.56
Antigonus 18.74
Antigua 16.4
Antiguan 16.22
antihero 35.9
antihistamine 15.26;
17.29
antihistamines 15.29
antiknock 23.3
Antilles 15.44; 18.54
antilog 23.11
antimacassar 2.14
antimagnetic 10.15
antimalarial 6.17
antimatter 2.10
antimony 2.78
antineutron 23.27
antinovel 24.27
antinuclear 42.38
Antioch 23.3
antioxidant 24.67
antipasto 35.3
antipathetic 10.15

antipathy 18.56
antiperspirant 12.35
antiphon 2.66; 23.27
antiphony 18.56
antipodal 18.64
antipodean 16.22
antipodes 15.45
antipollution 42.20
antipope 35.40
antiproton 23.27
antipsychotic 24.16
antipyretic 10.15
antiquarian 6.19
antiquary 18.56
antiquated 8.13
antique 15.7
antiquities 18.79
antiquity 18.58
antirrhinum 22.18
antirust 37.45
antisepsis 10.41
antiseptic 10.15
antisera 14.2
antiserum 14.7
antislavery 8.76
antisocial 36.15
antispasmodic 24.16
antistatic 2.17
antisubmarine 15.26
antitank 1.25
antiterrorist 10.72
antitetanus 10.70
antithesis 17.46
antithetical 10.60
antitoxin 24.32
antitussive 38.44
antivenin 10.26
antiviral 22.16
antivivisection 10.28
antivivisectionist
10.72
antiwar 25.4
antler 2.12
antlers 2.55
antlike 21.7
antlion 22.20
Antoine 3.19
Antoinette 9.51
Anton 23.27
Antonia 36.37
Antoninus 22.29
Antonio 35.19
Antonioni 36.1
Antonius 36.42
Antony 2.56
antonym 17.24
antonymous 24.70
Antrim 2.31

Antrobus 2.71
antrum 2.32
ants 1.34
antsy 2.7
Antwerp 11.19
Anubis 42.25
anus 8.67
anvil 17.15
anxiety 22.40
anxious 2.46
anxiously 2.56
any 10.6
Anya 2.12
anybody 24.3
anyhow 29.1
anymore 25.4
anyone 37.31
anyroad 35.25
anything 10.69
anytime 21.19
anyway 7.4
anywhere 5.1
anywise 21.43
Anzac 1.3
Anzio 35.19
aorta 26.4
aortal 26.15
aortic 26.9
apace 7.30
Apache 2.7
apart 3.32
apartheid 21.33
apartment 4.27
apartments 4.28
apathetic 10.15
apathetically 10.54
apathy 2.56
ape 7.27
aped 7.29
apelike 21.7
Apelles 15.44
apeman 1.24
apemen 9.32
Apennines 21.25
apéritif 15.13
aperture 2.60
aperture 27.1
apery 8.76
apes 7.28
apex 9.3
APEX 9.3
aphasia 8.78
aphasic 8.10
aphid 8.12
aphis 8.66
aphorism 18.28
aphoristic 18.16
Aphra 2.12

aphrodisiac 1.3
aphrodisiacs 1.4
Aphrodite 22.1
aphthous 2.46
apiary 8.76
apical 8.79
apices 15.45
apiece 15.32
aplastic 2.17
aplenty 10.3
aplomb 23.23
apnoea 13.1
apocalypse 17.44
apocalyptic 18.16
Apocrypha 24.57
apocryphal 24.61
apogee 15.4
apolitical 18.64
Apollinaire 5.1
Apollo 35.13
Apollonius 36.42
apologetic 10.15
apologetically 10.54
apologia 36.9; 36.37
apologies 24.75
apologist 24.72
apologize 21.45
apologue 23.11
apology 24.55
apophthegm 9.28
apoplectic 10.15
apoplexy 10.7
apostasy 24.54
apostate 7.34
apostatize 21.45
a posteriori 21.3
apostle 24.27
apostles 24.29
apostolic 24.18
apostrophe 24.54
apostrophes 24.75
apostrophic 24.17
apostrophize 21.45
apothecary 24.56
apotheosis 36.25
appal 25.14
Appalachia 8.9; 8.78
Appalachian 8.24;
8.81
appalled 25.15
appalling 26.25
appallingly 26.37
Appaloosa 42.9
apparatchik 2.21
apparatus 4.32; 8.67
apparel 2.28
apparent 2.40
apparently 2.56

apparition 18.33
appeal 15.17
appealed 15.18
appealer 16.7
appealing 16.27
appealingly 16.38
appeals 15.19
appear 13.1
appearance 14.11
appeared 13.2
appearing 14.12
appears 13.5
appease 15.43
appeasement 16.25
appellant 10.33
appellation 8.24
append 9.35
appendage 10.20
appendectomy 10.53
appendices 15.45
appendicitis 22.28
appendix 10.16
Appenzell 9.16
apperceive 15.39
apperception 10.28
appertain 7.21
appetence 2.69
appetite 21.34
appetizer 22.9
appetizing 22.26
Appian Way 7.2
applaud 25.9
applauded 26.12
applauding 26.25
applause 25.35
apple 2.28
Appleby 2.56
applecart 3.32
applejack 1.3
apple pie 21.4
apples 2.30
apple strudel 42.16
applet 2.51
Appleton 2.66
appliance 22.25
applicable 18.64
applicant 2.68
applicants 2.69
application 8.24
applicator 8.5
applied 21.10
applies 21.40
appliqué 7.3
apply 21.2
appoggiatura 28.2
appoint 33.10
appointed 34.3
appointee 15.4

appointer 34.2
appointing 34.11
appointment 34.9
appointments 34.10
Appomattox 2.22
apportion 26.19
apportioned 26.20
apportionment 26.45
apposite 17.51
apposition 18.33
appositive 17.55
appraisal 8.15
appraise 7.56
appraised 7.57
appraiser 8.9
appreciable 16.41
appreciably 16.38
appreciate 7.40
appreciation 8.31
appreciative 17.55
apprehend 9.35
apprehended 10.18
apprehension 10.28
apprehensive 10.50
apprehensively 10.54
apprentice 10.41
apprenticed 10.44
apprentices 10.76
apprenticeship 17.43
apprenticeships 17.44
apprise 21.40
approach 35.24
approachable 36.38
approaching 36.24
approbation 8.24
approbatory 8.76
appropriate 7.47;
36.45
appropriation 8.37
approval 42.16
approve 41.31
approved 41.32
approving 42.24
approvingly 42.36
approximate 7.43;
24.73
approximately 24.76
approximation 8.34
appurtenance 12.36
appurtenant 12.35
APR 3.1
apraxia 2.61
après-ski 15.4
apricot 23.44
April 8.15
a priori 21.3; 26.1
apron 8.21
apropos 35.19

apse 1.38
apt 1.39
Apted 2.25
apteryx 17.4
aptitude 41.9
aptly 2.5
aptness 2.46
aqua 2.12
aquaerobic 36.10
aquaerobics 36.11
aqua fortis 26.26
aqualung 37.37
aquamarine 15.24
aquaphobia 36.37
aquaphobic 36.10
aquaplane 7.21
aqua regia 16.40
aquarelle 9.16
aquaria 6.16
Aquarian 6.19
aquarium 6.18
Aquarius 6.22
aquashow 35.19
aquatic 2.17; 24.16
aquatics 2.23
aquatics 24.22
aquatint 17.39
aquavit 17.51
aqua vitae 21.3
aqueduct 37.5
aqueous 2.71; 8.85
aquifer 2.60
Aquila 18.12
aquilegia 16.9
aquiline 21.22
Aquinas 22.29
Aquino 35.10
Aquitaine 7.21
Aquitania 8.78
Arab 2.15
Arabella 10.12
arabesque 9.48
Arabia 8.78
Arabian 8.81
Arabic 17.3
arable 2.64
arachnid 2.24
arachnophobia 36.37
arachnophobic 36.10
Aragon 2.66
Aral 2.28
Araldite® 21.34
Aramaean 16.22
Aramaic 8.10
Araminta 18.10
Aran 2.35
Arapaho 35.19
Ararat 1.45

araucaria 6.16
arbiter 4.43
arbitrage 3.13
arbitrageur 11.1
arbitrary 4.56
arbitrate 7.36
arbitration 8.25
arbitrator 8.5
Arblay 7.3
arboreal 26.41
arboreta 16.5
arboretum 16.20
arbor vitae 21.3
arbour 4.8
Arbroath 35.47
arbutus 42.26
arc 3.3
arcade 7.8
Arcadia 8.78
Arcadian 8.81
Arcadic 8.10
Arcady 4.42
arcana 8.8
arcane 7.21
arch 3.6
archaeologic 24.20
archaeological 24.61
archaeologically 24.56
archaeologist 24.72
archaeology 24.55
archaeopteryx 17.4
archaic 8.10
archaism 18.28
archangel 8.15
archbishop 18.42
archbishopric 17.3
archdeacon 16.22
archdeaconry 16.38
archdiocese 15.32;
   17.46
archducal 42.16
archduchy 38.7
archduke 41.6
arched 3.7
arch-enemies 10.77
arch-enemy 10.53
archer 4.14
Archer 4.14
archers 4.41
Archers 4.41
archery 4.42
arches 4.41
archetype 21.26
archetypical 18.64
Archibald 4.48; 25.15
archidiaconal 2.64
Archie 4.7
archiepiscopal 18.64

Archimedean 16.22;
   16.43
Archimedes 15.44;
   16.36
arching 4.29
archipelago 35.19
architect 9.5
architectonic 24.19
architectonics 24.22
architectural 10.60
architecturally 10.78
architecture 10.14
architrave 7.54
archive 21.37
archives 21.38
archly 4.5
archpriest 15.33
arch-rival 22.16
archway 7.3
arcs 3.4
arctic 4.16
Arctic 4.16
arctophile 21.16
Arcturus 28.12
Arden 4.24
Ardennes 9.32
ardent 4.27
ardently 4.42
Ardnamurchan 12.12
ardour 4.10
Ardoyne 33.8
arduous 4.53
are 3.1
area 6.16
arena 16.8
aren't 3.23
Areopagite 21.34
Areopagus 24.70
Arequipa 16.3
Ares 15.44
arête 9.51
Aretha 16.6
Arethusa 42.9
argent 4.27
Argentina 16.8
Argentine 15.26
Argentine 21.22
Argentinian 18.67
Argo 35.4
argon 4.24; 23.27
Argonaut 25.31
Argonauts 25.32
Argos 23.39
argosy 4.42
argot 35.4
arguable 4.57
arguably 4.56
argue 41.3

argued 41.9
arguer 4.43
argufy 21.4
argument 4.51
argumentation 8.41
argumentative 17.55
Argus 4.32
argy-bargy 4.7
argyle 21.16
Argyll 21.16
aria 4.44
Ariadne 2.6
Arian 6.19
arid 2.24
aridity 18.57
Ariel 6.17
Arien 6.19
Aries 6.14; 15.44
aright 21.32
Arimathea 16.2
arise 21.40
arisen 18.33
Aristarchus 4.32
Aristippus 18.44
aristo 35.19
aristocracy 24.54
aristocrat 1.45
aristocratic 2.17
Aristophanes 15.45
Aristotelian 16.43
Aristotle 24.27
Aristotle's 24.29
arithmetic 10.15; 17.3
arithmetical 10.60
arithmetically 10.54
Arius 6.22
Arizona 36.8
Arizonan 36.20
ark 3.3
Arkansas 25.4
Arkwright 21.33
Arles 3.14; 3.15
Arlington 4.50
arm 3.16
armada 4.10
armadillo 35.11
Armageddon 10.27
Armagh 3.1
Armagnac 1.3
armament 4.51
Armani 4.6
armature 4.43; 27.1
armband 1.28
armchair 5.1
armed 3.17
armed forces 26.36
Armenia 16.40
Armenian 16.43

armful 39.7
armhole 35.30
Armidale 7.15
armies 4.40
armillary 18.56
arming 4.29
Arminian 18.67
Arminius 18.74
armistice 17.46
Armitage 17.14
armorial 26.41
armour 4.13
armoured 4.17
armoured car 3.1
armourer 4.43
armoury 4.42
armpit 4.38
armrest 9.49
arms 3.18
Armstrong 23.31
army 4.6
Arnaud 35.4
Arndale 7.15
Arne 3.19
Arnhem 4.22
Arnie 4.6
Arno 35.4
Arnold 4.20
aroma 36.8
aromatherapist 10.72
aromatherapy 10.53
aromatic 2.17
arose 35.52
around 29.6
arousal 30.6
arouse 29.17
arouser 30.2
arousing 30.12
Arp 3.25
arpeggio 35.19
arpeggios 35.52
arquebus 4.53
arrack 2.16
arraign 7.21
arraignment 8.56
Arran 2.35
arrange 7.23
arranged 7.24
arrangement 8.56
arrangements 8.57
arranger 8.9
arranging 8.64
arrant 2.40
arras 2.46
Arras 2.46
array 7.2
arrayed 7.8
arrearage 14.5

arrears 13.5
arrest 9.49
arrestable 10.60
arrester 10.10
arresting 10.36
arrival 22.16
arrive 21.37
arrivederci 6.1
arriving 22.26
arriviste 15.33
arrogance 2.69
arrogant 2.68
arrogate 7.35
arrogation 8.24
arrow 35.3
arrowed 35.25
arrowhead 9.8
arrowheads 9.9
arrowroot 41.27
arrows 35.52
Arrowsmith 17.53
arse 3.26
arsed 3.30
arsehole 35.30
arsenal 4.47
Arsenal 4.47
arsenic 4.16
arsenical 10.60
arsenious 16.47
ars nova 36.6
arson 4.24
arsonist 4.54
arsy-versy 12.1
art 3.32
Artaxerxes 15.44
Art Deco 35.7
artefact 1.6
Artemas 4.53
Artemis 17.46
arterial 14.19
arteriole 35.30
arteriosclerosis 36.25
artery 4.42
artesian 16.22; 16.43
Artex® 9.3
artful 4.19; 39.7
artfully 4.42
artfulness 4.53
arthritic 18.16
arthritis 22.28
arthropod 23.8
Arthur 4.11
Arthurian 28.21
artic 4.16
artichoke 35.21
artichokes 35.22
article 4.47
articled 4.48

articulate 7.41; 18.77
articulation 8.32
articulator 8.5
artifice 17.46
artificer 18.60
artificial 18.22
artificiality 2.57
artificially 18.56
artillery 18.56
artisan 1.24
artisans 1.36
artist 4.33
artiste 15.33
artistic 18.16
artistically 18.57
artistry 4.42
artless 4.32
artlessly 4.42
artlessness 4.53
Art Nouveau 35.19
arts 3.33
artwork 11.4
arty 4.3
arty-crafty 4.3
arty-farty 4.3
arum 6.5
Arun 2.35
Arundel 2.64
arvo 35.4
Aryan 6.19
as 1.50
asbestos 10.42; 23.39
asbestosis 36.25
ASBO 35.3
ascend 9.35
ascendancy 10.53
ascendant 10.33
ascended 10.18
ascender 10.10
ascending 10.36
ascension 10.28
Ascension 10.28
ascent 9.41
ascertain 7.21
ascertained 7.22
ascertainment 8.56
ascetic 10.15
asceticism 18.28
ascetics 10.16
ASCII 2.2
Asclepius 16.47
Ascot 2.50
ascribe 21.5
ascribed 21.6
ascription 18.33
Asda 2.10
asdic 2.17
asepsis 10.41

aseptic 10.15
asexual 10.60
ash 1.43
ASH 1.43
ashamed 7.19
ashamedly 8.76
Ashanti 2.3
Ashby 2.1
Ashby-de-la-Zouch
41.26
Ashcroft 23.10
Ashdown 29.5
Ashe 1.43
ashen 2.35
Asher 2.14
ashes 2.55
Ashes 2.55
Ashford 2.25
Ashkenazi 4.7
Ashkenazy 4.7
ashlar 2.12; 3.1
Ashley 2.5
Ashmolean 36.40
ashore 25.2
ashplant 3.23
ashram 1.22; 2.32
Ashton 2.35
ashtray 7.3
ashtrays 7.56
ashy 2.7
Asia 8.9
Asian 8.21; 8.22
Asians 8.55
Asiatic 2.17
aside 21.10
Asimov 23.47
Asimov 23.9
asinine 21.22
ask 3.27
askance 1.31; 3.22
asked 3.28
asker 4.9
askew 41.2
Askew 41.3
Askey 2.2
asking 4.29
aslant 3.23
asleep 15.30
ASLEF 9.10
aslope 35.40
asocial 36.15
asp 1.41
asparagus 2.71
aspect 9.5
aspectual 10.60
Aspel 2.28
aspen 2.35
asperity 10.54

asperse 11.22
aspersion 12.12
asphalt 1.20; 25.17
asphodel 9.16
asphyxia 18.61
asphyxiant 18.70
asphyxiate 7.41
asphyxiation 8.32
aspic 2.17
aspidistra 18.12
Aspinwall 25.14
aspirant 2.68
aspirate 2.74; 7.35
aspiration 8.24
aspirational 8.79
aspirations 8.55
aspirator 8.5
aspire 19.1
aspired 19.2
aspirer 20.2
aspirin 2.34
aspiring 20.7
aspirins 2.38
Asquith 17.53
ass 1.40
assail 7.15
assailable 8.79
assailant 8.56
assailants 8.57
assailed 7.16
Assam 1.22
assassin 2.34
assassinate 7.35
assassination 8.24
assassins 2.38
assault 23.18; 25.17
assaulted 24.24; 26.12
assaulter 24.10; 26.4
assaulting 26.25
assay 7.2; 7.3
assayer 8.2
assegai 21.4
assemblage 10.20
assemble 10.21
assembled 10.22
assembler 10.12
assembly 10.5
assent 9.41
assentor 10.10
assert 11.24
asserter 12.2
assertion 12.12
assertive 12.27
assertively 12.29
assertiveness 12.37
assess 9.47
assessment 10.33
assessor 10.14

asset 2.51
asseverate 7.38
asseveration 8.28
asshole 35.30
assiduity 42.36
assiduous 18.74
assiduously 18.80
assign 21.22
assignation 8.24
assignment 22.24
assignor 22.8
assimilate 7.41
assimilation 8.32
Assisi 16.1
assist 17.49
assistance 18.39
assistant 18.38
assistants 18.39
assisted 18.19
assisting 18.40
assistive 18.53
assize 21.40
associate 7.47; 36.45
associateship 17.43
association 8.37
assonance 2.69
assonant 2.68
assort 25.31
assorted 26.12
assortment 26.23
assuage 7.12
assuaged 7.13
assume 41.17
assumed 41.18
assuming 42.24
assumption 38.28
assurance 26.24;
   28.10
assure 25.2; 27.1
assured 25.9; 27.2
assuredly 26.37; 28.17
assurer 28.2
assuring 26.25; 28.11
Assyria 18.61
Assyrian 18.67
Astaire 5.1
Astarte 4.3
aster 2.10
asterisk 17.47
Asterix 17.4
astern 11.15
asteroid 33.4
asthenia 16.40
asthma 2.13
asthmatic 2.17
Asti 2.3
astigmatic 2.17
astigmatism 18.28

astilbe 18.1
astir 11.1
Asti spumante 2.3
Aston 2.35
astonish 24.46
astonished 24.47
astonishingly 24.76
astonishment 24.67
Astor 2.10
Astoria 26.39
astound 29.6
astounded 30.3
astounding 30.12
astoundingly 30.22
astraddle 2.28
astrakhan 1.24; 3.19
Astrakhan 1.24; 3.19
astral 2.28
astray 7.2
Astrid 2.24
astride 21.10
astringent 18.38
astrodome 35.34
astrolabe 7.5
astrologer 24.57
astrologers 24.74
astrologic 24.20
astrological 24.61
astrology 24.55
astronaut 25.31
astronautical 26.41
astronauts 25.32
astronavigation 8.24
astronomer 24.57
astronomic 24.19
astronomical 24.61
astronomically 24.56
astronomy 24.54
astrophysical 18.64
astrophysicist 18.75
astrophysics 18.17
AstroTurf® 11.8
Asturias 1.40
astute 41.27
astutely 42.1
astuteness 42.26
astuter 42.5
astutest 42.27
asunder 38.10
Aswan 3.19
aswarm 25.20
asylum 22.18
asymmetric 10.15
asymmetrical 10.60
asymmetry 18.57
asymptomatic 2.17
asymptote 35.45
asymptotic 24.16

at 1.45
Atacama 4.13
Atalanta 2.10
Atatürk 11.4
atavism 18.28
atavistic 18.16
ataxia 2.61
ate 7.32; 9.51
atelier 7.4
Aten 4.24
Athabaska 2.9
Athanasian 8.81
Athanasius 8.85
atheism 18.28
atheist 8.87
atheistic 18.16
atheling 2.70
Athelstan 2.66
Athena 16.8
Atheneum 16.20
Athenian 16.43
Athens 2.39
Atherton 2.66
athlete 15.35
athletes 15.36
athletic 10.15
athleticism 18.28
athletics 10.16
Athol 2.28
Athos 23.39
athwart 25.31
athwartships 17.44
atishoo 41.3
Atkin 2.34
Atkins 2.38
Atkinson 2.66
Atlanta 2.10
Atlantean 2.66; 16.22
Atlantic 2.17
Atlantis 2.45
atlas 2.46
Atlas 2.46
Atlee 15.3
ATM 9.28
atmosphere 13.1
atmospheric 10.15
atmospherics 10.16
atoll 23.15
atolls 23.22
atom 2.32
atom bomb 23.23
atomic 24.19
atomize 21.42
atomizer 22.9
atoms 2.33
atonal 36.15
atone 35.36
atoned 35.37

atonement 36.22
atones 35.39
atop 23.36
atopic 24.16
Atora® 26.6
atrial 8.79
atrium 8.80
atrocious 36.26
atrociously 36.35
atrocity 24.56
atrophic 24.17
atrophied 2.62; 17.8
atrophy 2.56
atropin 17.29
atropine 15.26
attaboy 33.1
attach 1.7
attaché 7.3
attached 1.8
attachment 2.40
attack 1.3
attacked 1.6
attacker 2.9
attacking 2.42
attacks 1.4
attain 7.21
attainable 8.79
attainder 8.5
attainment 8.56
attaint 7.25
attar 2.10
attempt 9.30
attempted 10.18
Attenborough 38.12
attend 9.35
attendance 10.34
attendant 10.33
attendants 10.34
attended 10.18
attender 10.10
attending 10.36
attention 10.28
attentive 10.50
attentively 10.54
attenuate 7.38
attenuation 8.28
attest 9.49
attestation 8.24
attested 10.18
attic 2.17
Attic 2.17
Attica 2.60
Atticism 18.28
attics 2.23
Attila 18.12
attire 19.1
attired 19.2
attitude 41.9

attitudinal 42.39
attitudinize 21.46
Attlee 2.5
attorney 12.1
attract 1.6
attractant 2.40
attracting 2.42
attraction 2.35
attractive 2.53
attractively 2.58
attractiveness 2.71
attributable 18.81
attribute 41.27
attributed 42.14
attributes 41.28
attribution 42.20
attributive 17.55
attrition 18.33
attune 41.19
attuned 41.20
Atwood 39.4
atypical 18.64
auberge 5.3
aubergine 15.26
aubergines 15.29
Auberon 26.43; 36.40
Aubrey 26.1
aubrietia 16.9
auburn 26.19
Auckland 26.20
au contraire 5.1
auction 24.33; 26.19
auctioned 24.34;
26.20
auctioneer 13.1
auctioneering 14.12
audacious 8.67
audaciously 8.76
audacity 2.57
Auden 26.19
Audi 30.1
audible 26.41
audibly 26.37
audience 26.46
audio 35.19
audiophile 21.16
audiotypist 22.30
audiovisual 18.64
audit 26.32
audited 26.40
audition 18.33
auditioner 18.60
auditor 26.38
auditoria 26.39
auditorium 26.42
auditory 26.37
Audley 26.1
Audrey 26.1

Audrey's 26.35
Audubon 23.27
au fait 7.2
Augean 16.22
auger 26.3
aught 25.31
augment 9.41
augmentation 8.35
augmented 10.18
augur 26.3
augury 26.37
august 37.45
August 26.29
Augusta 38.10
Augustan 38.28
Augustine 38.27
Augustinian 18.67
Augustus 38.38
auk 25.6
au lait 7.2
auld 25.15
auld lang syne 21.22
au naturel 9.16
aunt 3.23
auntie 4.3
aunts 3.22
Aunt Sally 2.5
au pair 5.1
aura 26.6
aural 26.15
Aurangzeb 9.1
aureate 26.50
Aurelius 16.47
aureole 35.30
au revoir 3.1
Aurignacian 8.35
aurochs 23.5
aurora 26.6
aurora borealis 4.31
Auschwitz 30.19
auscultation 8.35
Auslese 8.9
auspice 26.26
auspicious 18.44
Aussie 24.7
Aussies 24.52
Austen 24.32; 26.18
austere 13.1
austerity 10.54
Austerlitz 17.52
Austin 24.32; 26.18
Australasia 8.9; 8.78
Australasian 8.21;
8.81
Australia 8.78
Australian 8.81
Australiana 4.13
Australianism 18.29

Australianize 21.47
Australoid 33.4
australopithecine
15.26
australopithecus
18.74
Austria 24.58
Austrian 24.64
Austrians 24.66
Austronesia 16.9;
16.40
Austronesian 16.22;
16.43
autarky 4.2
auteur 11.1
authentic 10.15
authentically 10.54
authenticate 7.38
authentication 8.28
authenticity 18.57
author 26.5
authoress 9.47
authorial 26.41
authoritarian 6.19
authoritarianism
18.29
authoritative 17.54
authorities 24.75
authority 24.56
authorization 8.49
authorize 21.45
authorized 21.48
authorizing 22.26
authors 26.36
authorship 17.43
autism 18.27
autistic 18.16
auto 35.14
autobahn 3.19
autobiographical 2.64
autochanger 8.9
autochthon 24.33
autochthonous 24.70
autoclave 7.54
autocorrelation 8.34
autocracy 24.54
autocrat 1.45
autocratic 2.17
autocross 23.39
Autocue® 41.4
auto-da-fé 7.2
autodestruct 37.5
autoerotic 24.16
autoeroticism 18.28
autofocus 36.26
autogenic 10.15
autograph 1.11; 3.9
autographic 2.18

autohypnosis 36.25
autohypnotic 24.16
autoimmune 41.19
autoloading 36.24
Autolycus 24.70
autolysis 17.46
automat 1.45
automata 24.57
automate 7.44
automatic 2.17
automatically 2.58
automation 8.35
automatism 18.28
automaton 23.27;
    24.64
automobile 15.17
automotive 36.32
autonomic 24.19
autonomous 24.70
autonomy 24.54
autopilot 22.34
autopsy 24.7
autoroute 41.27
autosuggestion 10.28
autotimer 22.8
autowinder 22.5
autumn 26.17
autumnal 38.23
Auvergne 5.4; 11.15
auxiliary 18.56
Ava 8.6
avail 7.15
availability 18.58
available 8.79
availing 8.62
avalanche 3.20
Avalon 23.27
avant-garde 3.8
avarice 17.46
avaricious 18.44
avast 3.30
avatar 3.1
avaunt 25.25
ave 4.4; 7.3
Avebury 8.76
Ave Maria 16.2
avenge 9.38
avenger 10.14
Avengers 10.52
avenging 10.36
avenue 41.4
avenues 41.33
aver 11.1
average 17.14
averred 11.7
averse 11.22
aversion 12.12
avert 11.24

averted 12.5
Avery 8.76
Avesta 10.10
Avestan 10.27
avian 8.81
aviary 8.76
aviation 8.27
aviator 8.5
aviatrix 8.11
avid 2.24
avidity 18.57
avidly 2.58
Aviemore 25.4
avionic 24.19
avionics 24.22
Avis 8.66
avocado 35.4
avocation 8.24
avocet 9.51
avoid 33.4
avoidable 34.16
avoidance 34.10
avoided 34.3
avoider 34.2
avoiding 34.11
avoirdupois 3.1
Avon 8.21; 23.27
Avonmouth 29.16
avow 29.1
avowal 31.3
avowed 29.3
avowedly 30.22
Avril 2.28; 17.15
avuncular 38.48
aw 25.1
AWACS 1.4
await 7.33
awaits 7.50
awake 7.6
awaken 8.21
awakened 8.54
awakening 8.84
award 25.9
aware 5.1
awareness 6.11
awash 23.42
away 7.2
awayday 7.3
awe 25.1
aweigh 7.2
awesome 26.17
awesomely 26.37
awestricken 18.32
awestruck 37.3
awful 26.15; 39.7
awfully 26.37
awhile 21.16
awkward 26.12

awkwardly 26.37
awkwardness 26.47
awl 25.14
awn 25.22
awning 26.25
awoke 35.21
awoken 36.20
AWOL 23.15
awry 21.2
axe 1.4
axed 1.5
axeman 1.24; 2.35
axes 15.44
axial 2.64
axilla 18.12
axiomatic 2.17
axis 2.45
axle 2.28
axletree 15.4
Axminster 18.10
axolotl 24.27
axon 23.27
ay 7.1; 21.1
ayah 22.2; 22.7
ayatollah 24.12
Ayckbourn 25.22
aye 21.1
aye-aye 21.3
Ayers 5.5
Aylesbury 8.76
Aylmer 8.8
Aylward 8.13
Ayr 5.1
Ayrshire 6.2; 13.1
Ayrton 6.7
azalea 8.78
Azerbaijan 3.19
Azerbaijani 4.6
azimuth 2.75
Aznavour 27.1
Azores 25.35
Aztec 9.2
azure 2.14; 8.9
B 15.1
BA 7.2
baa 3.1
Baader-Meinhof 23.9
baaed 3.8
Baal 3.14; 8.15
baas 3.26
Babbage 2.27
Babbitt 2.51
babble 2.28
babbler 2.12
babbling 2.42
babe 7.5
Babel 8.15
babies 8.74

Babington 2.66
babirusa 42.9
baboon 41.19
Babs 1.2
babushka 42.4
baby 8.1
baby-boomer 42.8
baby-boomers 42.34
Babycham® 1.22
baby-faced 7.31
babyhood 39.4
babyish 17.50
Babylon 23.27
Babylonia 36.37
Babylonian 36.40
baby-sat 1.45
baby-sit 17.51
baby-sitter 18.10
baby-sitting 18.40
baby-walker 26.3
Bacall 25.14
Bacardi® 4.3
baccalaureate 26.50
baccarat 3.1
Bacchae 2.2; 15.3
bacchanal 2.64
bacchanalia 8.78
bacchanalian 8.81
bacchant 2.40
bacchante 2.3
Bacchic 2.17
Bacchus 2.46
baccy 2.2
Bach 3.3
Bacharach 1.3
bachelor 2.60
Bach's 3.4
bacillus 18.44
back 1.3
backache 7.6
back and forth 25.33
backbencher 10.14
backbiter 22.5
backbone 35.36
backbreaker 8.4
backbreaking 8.59
backchat 1.45
backcloth 23.46
backcomb 35.34
backcombing 36.24
backdate 7.33
backdrop 23.36
backed 1.6
backer 2.9
backfill 17.15
backfire 19.1
backfired 19.2
backgammon 2.35

background 29.6
backhand 1.28
backhanded 2.25
backhander 2.10
backing 2.42
backlash 1.43
backless 2.46
backlighting 22.26
backlist 2.47
backlit 2.51
backlog 23.11
backlot 23.44
backmarker 4.9
backmost 35.43
backpack 1.3
backpacker 2.9
backpacking 2.42
back-pedal 10.21
backrest 9.49
backs 1.4
backscratcher 2.14
backscratching 2.42
backside 21.11
backslapping 2.42
backslide 21.11
backslider 22.5
backspace 7.30
backspin 2.34
backstage 7.12
backstairs 5.5
backstay 7.3
backstitch 17.7
backstop 23.36
backstreet 15.35
backstreets 15.36
backstroke 35.21
backswept 9.46
back-to-back 1.3
backtrack 1.3
backtracked 1.6
backtracks 1.4
backup 37.41
backward 2.25
backwardness 2.71
backwards 2.26
backwash 23.42
backwater 26.4
backwoodsman 40.10
back yard 3.8
bacon 8.21
Bacon 8.21
BACS 1.4
bacteria 14.18
bacterial 14.19
bactericide 21.12
bacteriological 24.61
bacteriologist 24.72
bacteriology 24.55

bacterium 14.20
Bactrian 2.66
bad 1.9
badass 1.40
baddie 2.3
baddies 2.54
bade 1.9; 7.8
Badedas® 1.40
Badel 9.16
Baden 4.24
Baden-Powell 31.3
Bader 4.10
badge 1.15
badger 2.14
badinage 3.13
badlands 2.37
badly 2.5
badman 1.24
badminton 2.66
Badminton 2.66
bad-mouth 29.16
badness 2.46
bad press 9.47
bad 'un 2.35
Baedeker 8.77; 10.9
Baez 9.57
Baffin 2.34
baffle 2.28
baffled 2.29
bafflement 2.68
baffles 2.30
baffling 2.42
BAFTA 2.10
bag 1.13
bagatelle 9.16
bagel 8.15
bagful 39.7
baggage 2.27
baggier 2.61
baggiest 2.72
baggy 2.2
Baghdad 1.9
bagman 2.35
Bagnell 2.28
bagpiper 22.3
bagpipes 21.27
bags 1.14
Bagshot 23.44
baguette 9.51
bah 3.1
Bahamas 4.41
Bahamian 8.81
Bahrain 7.21
Bahraini 8.1
bail 7.15
bailed 7.16
bailee 15.2
bailey 8.1

Bailey 8.1
Baileys® 8.74
bailiff 17.10
bailiwick 17.3
bailment 8.56
bailor 8.7
Bainbridge 8.14
Baines 7.26
bain-marie 15.4
Baird 5.2
bairn 5.4
Baisakhi 2.2
bait 7.32
baiting 8.60
baize 7.56
bake 7.6
baked 7.7
baked beans 15.29
bakehouse 29.12
Bakelite® 21.34
baker 8.4
Baker 8.4
Bakerloo 41.4
bakers 8.75
bakery 8.76
Bakewell 8.15; 9.16
baking 8.59
baklava 3.1
baksheesh 15.34
Bala 2.12
balaclava 4.11
Balaklava 4.11
balalaika 22.4
balance 2.41
balancer 2.60
Balanchine 15.26
balancing 2.70
Balboa 36.2
balcony 2.56
bald 25.15
balder 26.4
Balder 24.10; 726.4
balderdash 1.43
baldheaded 10.18
balding 26.25
baldly 26.1
baldness 26.27
Baldock 23.3
baldric 26.9
Baldrick 26.9
Baldrick's 26.10
Baldry 26.1
Baldwin 26.18
Baldwin's 26.22
baldy 26.1
bale 7.15
Balearic 2.19
baleen 15.24

baleful 8.15; 39.7
baler 8.7
Balfour 2.11
Balham 2.32
Bali 4.5
Balinese 15.45
balk 25.6
Balkan 24.33; 26.19
Balkans 24.36; 26.21
ball 25.14
Ballachulish 42.29
ballad 2.25
balladeer 13.1
ballads 2.26
Ballantrae 7.4
Ballantyne 21.22
Ballard 3.8
ballast 2.48
ball bearing 6.10
ball boy 33.1
ball cock 23.3
ballerina 16.8
Ballesteros 23.39
ballet 7.3
balletic 10.15
balletomania 8.78
Ballets Russes 41.24
ball girl 11.11
Balliol 8.79
ballistic 18.16
ballistics 18.17
balloon 41.19
balloonist 42.28
balloons 41.21
ballot 2.50
balloted 2.63
ballottement 24.38
ballpark 3.3
ballpoint 33.10
ballroom 39.9; 41.17
balls 25.19
ballsy 26.1
bally 2.5
ballyhoo 41.4
Ballymena 16.8
Ballymoney 38.6
balm 3.16
Balmer 4.13
Balmoral 24.27
balmy 4.6
baloney 36.1
balsa 24.14; 26.8
balsam 24.30; 26.17
balsamic 2.20
balsawood 39.4
Balthazar 2.14; 3.1
balti 24.3; 26.1
Baltic 26.9

Baltimore 25.4
Baluchi 42.1
Baluchistan 1.24; 3.19
baluster 2.60
balustrade 7.8
Balzac 1.3
Balzac's 1.4
Bambi 2.1
bambini 16.1
bambino 35.10
bamboo 41.2
bamboozle 42.16
ban 1.24
banal 1.16; 3.14
banality 2.57
banana 4.13
banana split 17.51
Banbury 2.56
Bancroft 23.10
band 1.28
Banda 2.10
bandage 2.27
bandages 2.76
Band Aid 7.8
bandanna 2.13
Bandaranaike 22.41
B&B 15.4
bandbox 23.5
bandeau 35.3
banderole 35.30
bandicoot 41.27
bandied 2.24
banding 2.42
bandit 2.51
banditry 2.58
bandleader 16.5
bandmaster 4.10
bandolier 13.1
bandsman 2.35
bandstand 1.28
bandwagon 2.35
bandy 2.3
bane 7.21
baneful 8.15; 39.7
bang 1.29
Bangalore 25.4
banger 2.13
banging 2.42
Bangkok 23.3
Bangladesh 9.50
Bangladeshi 10.7
bangle 2.28
Bangor 2.9
banish 2.49
banishment 2.68
banister 2.60
banjo 35.3
bank 1.25

bankable 2.64
bank account 29.11
bankbook 39.1
bank clerk 3.3
banked 1.27
banker 2.9
banking 2.42
banknote 35.45
banknotes 35.46
bankroll 35.30
bankrolled 35.31
bankrupt 37.42
bankruptcy 2.56
banks 1.26
Banks 1.26
banned 1.28
banner 2.13
Bannerman 2.66
banning 2.42
Bannister 2.60
bannock 2.16
Bannockburn 11.15
bannocks 2.22
banns 1.36
banoffee 15.3; 24.4
banquet 2.51
banquette 9.51
bans 1.36
banshee 15.2
bantam 2.32
bantamweight 7.35
banter 2.10
Banting 2.42
Bantu 41.3
Bantustan 1.24; 3.19
banyan 1.24; 2.35
banzai 21.2
baobab 1.1
bap 1.37
baptism 18.27
baptismal 18.22
Baptist 2.47
baptistry 2.58
baptize 21.40
baptized 21.48
bar 3.1
Barabbas 2.46
barb 3.2
Barbadian 8.81
Barbados 23.39
Barbara 4.12; 4.43
barbarian 6.19
barbaric 2.19
barbarism 18.28
barbarity 2.57
Barbarossa 24.14
barbarous 4.53

Barbary 4.42
barbecue 41.4
barbecued 41.9
barbecues 41.33
barbed wire 19.1
barbel 4.19
barbell 9.16
barber 4.8
Barber 4.8
barbers 4.41
barbershop 23.36
barbican 4.50
Barbican 4.50
Barbie® 4.1
Barbirolli 24.5
barbital 1.16
barbitone 35.36
barbiturate 18.77
Barbizon 23.27
Barbour® 4.8
Barbuda 42.5
Barbudan 42.20
barcarole 23.15; 35.30
Barcelona 36.8
Barclay 4.5
Barclays 4.40
bar code 35.25
Barcoo 41.2
bard 3.8
bardic 4.16
bardolatry 24.54
Bardolino 35.10
Bardot 35.2
bare 5.1
bareback 1.3
bared 5.2
barefaced 7.31
barefoot 39.14
barefooted 40.4
barehanded 2.25
bareheaded 10.18
barely 6.1
bareness 6.11
barf 3.9
barfed 3.10
bargain 4.23
bargainer 4.43
bargains 4.26
barge 3.12
bargeboard 25.9
bargee 15.2
bargepole 35.30
barging 4.29
baric 2.19
baring 6.10
baritone 35.36
barium 6.18
bark 3.3

barked 3.5
barkeeper 16.3
Barker 4.9
barking 4.29
Barking 4.29
barking mad 1.9
barley 4.5
barleycorn 25.22
Barlow 35.4
barm 3.16
barmaid 7.8
barman 4.24
barmier 4.44
barmiest 4.55
Bar Mitzvah 18.11
barmy 4.6
barn 3.19
Barnabas 4.53
Barnaby 4.42
barnacle 4.47
barnacled 4.48
Barnardo 35.4
Barnes 3.24
Barnet 4.38
barney 4.6
Barney 4.6
barns 3.24
Barnsley 4.5
Barnstaple 4.47
barnstorm 25.20
barnstormer 26.7
barnstorming 26.25
Barnum 4.22
barnyard 3.8
barograph 1.11; 3.9
Barolo 35.16
barometer 24.57
barometric 10.15
baron 2.35
baroness 9.47
baronet 2.74; 9.51
baronetcy 2.78
baronial 36.38
barons 2.39
barony 2.56
baroque 23.3; 35.21
barperson 12.12
Barr 3.1
Barra 2.12
barrack 2.16
barracking 2.70
barracks 2.22
barracuda 42.5
barrage 3.13
barramundi 38.3
barre 3.1
barré 7.3
barred 3.8

begs 9.13
beguile 21.16
beguiled 21.17
beguilement 22.24
beguiler 22.7
beguiling 22.26
beguine 15.24
begum 8.19
begun 37.31
behalf 3.9
Behan 16.22
behave 7.54
behaving 8.61
behaviour 8.7
behavioural 8.79
behaviourism 18.28
behaviourist 8.87
behaviouristic 18.16
behead 9.8
beheaded 10.18
beheading 10.36
beheld 9.19
behemoth 23.46
behest 9.49
behind 21.23
behindhand 1.28
behold 35.31
beholden 36.20
beholder 36.5
beholding 36.24
behoof 41.10
behoove 41.31
behove 35.50
Beiderbecke 9.2
beige 7.14
Beijing 17.35
being 16.27
beings 16.28
Beirut 41.27
bejewel 42.16
bel 9.16
belabour 8.3
Belafonte 24.3
Belarus 37.43; 39.12
Belarussian 38.28
belated 8.13
belatedly 8.76
belay 7.2
bel canto 35.3
belch 9.18
belcher 10.14
belching 10.36
beleaguer 16.4
beleaguered 16.14
belemnite 21.34
Belfast 3.30
belfry 10.5
Belgian 10.28

Belgic 10.15
Belgium 10.25
Belgrade 7.8
Belgravia 8.78
belie 21.2
belief 15.13
believable 16.41
believe 15.39
believed 15.40
believer 16.6
believers 16.37
believes 15.41
believing 16.27
Belinda 18.10
Belisha 16.9
belittle 18.22
belittler 18.12
Belize 15.43
bell 9.16
Bell 9.16
Bella 10.12
belladonna 24.13
Bellamy 10.53
Bellarmine 15.26
Bella's 10.52
bellboy 33.1
belle 9.16
belle époque 23.3
belle of the ball 25.14
Bellerophon 23.27
belles-lettres 10.12
bellhop 23.36
bellicose 35.42; 35.52
bellied 10.17
belligerence 18.71
belligerent 18.70
Bellini 16.1
bellman 10.27
Belloc 23.3
bellow 35.7
bellowing 36.24
bellows 35.52
bell push 39.13
bell-ringer 18.13
bell-ringers 18.55
bell-ringing 18.40
bells 9.27
bell tower 31.1
bellwether 10.11
belly 10.5
bellyache 7.6
bellyacher 8.4
bellyaching 8.59
bellyband 1.28
bellybutton 38.28
belly flop 23.36
bellyful 39.7
Belmondo 35.13

Belmont 23.34
belong 23.31
belonging 24.40
beloved 37.50; 38.19
below 35.2
Bel Paese 8.1
Belsen 10.28
Belshazzar 2.14
belt 9.23
Beltane 7.21
belter 10.10
belting 10.36
beluga 42.4
belvedere 13.1
Bembridge 10.20
bemire 19.1
bemoan 35.36
bemoaned 35.37
bemoaning 36.24
bemuse 41.33
bemused 41.34
bemusedly 42.36
bemusing 42.24
Ben 9.32
Benares 4.40
Benazir 13.1
Benbecula 10.56
bench 9.33
bencher 10.14
benchmark 3.3
benchmarks 3.4
bend 9.35
bendable 10.60
bender 10.10
Bendigo 35.19
bending 10.36
bendy 10.3
beneath 15.37
Benedict 17.6
Benedictine 15.25
benediction 18.33
Benedictus 18.44
benefaction 2.35
benefactor 2.10
benefactress 2.46
benefic 10.15
benefice 17.46
beneficence 10.68
beneficent 10.67
beneficial 18.22
beneficiary 18.56
benefit 17.51
benefits 17.52
Benelux 37.4
Benenden 10.64
Benetton 10.64; 23.27
benevolence 10.68
benevolent 10.67

Benfleet 15.35
Bengal 25.14
Bengali 26.1
Benghazi 4.7
Ben-Gurion 28.21
Benidorm 25.20
benighted 22.13
benign 21.22
benignant 18.38
benignity 18.57
Benin 15.24
benison 10.64
Benito 35.10
Benjamin 17.20
Benjamin's 17.42
Benn 9.32
Bennett 10.48
Ben Nevis 10.41
Benny 10.6
Benny Hill 17.15
Ben's 9.43
Benson 10.28
bent 9.41
Bentham 10.25
Bentley 10.5
Benton 10.27
bentwood 39.4
benumb 37.27
benumbing 38.34
Benz 9.43
Benzedrine® 15.26
benzene 15.25
benzine 15.25
benzodiazepine 15.26
Beowulf 39.8
bequeath 15.37; 15.38
bequeather 16.6
bequeathing 16.27
bequest 9.49
berate 7.33
Berber 12.2
Berbera 12.30
berberis 17.46
bereave 15.39
bereaved 15.40
bereavement 16.25
bereft 9.11
Berengaria 6.16
Berenice 22.1
Beresford 10.58
beret 7.3; 10.5
berg 11.9
Berg 11.9
bergamot 23.44
Bergen 12.12
Bergerac 1.3
Bergman 12.12
beribboned 18.34

beriberi 10.5
berk 11.4
Berkeley 4.5
Berks 3.4
Berkshire 13.1; 4.14
Berlei 12.1
Berlin 17.29
Berliner 18.13
Berlioz 35.52
Berlitz 17.52
Berlusconi 36.1
Bermondsey 12.29
Bermuda 42.5
Bermudan 42.20
Bermudas 42.34
Bern 11.15
Bernadette 9.51
Bernadotte 23.44
Bernard 12.5
Bernardine 15.26
Bernardo 35.4
Bernard's 12.6
Bernhardt 3.32
Bernice 15.32
Bernini 16.1
Bernstein 21.22
berries 10.51
berry 10.5
Berry 10.5
berserk 11.4
Bert 11.24
berth 11.26
Bertha 12.2
berthing 12.16
Bertie 12.1
Bertolucci 42.1
Bertram 12.10
Bertrand 12.13
Bert's 11.25
Berwick 10.15
beryl 10.21
Beryl 10.21
beryllium 18.66
Besant 1.33; 10.33
beseech 15.9
beseeched 15.10
beseeching 16.27
beset 9.51
besetting 10.36
beside 21.10
besides 21.13
besiege 15.15
besieger 16.9
besieging 16.27
besmear 13.1
besmirch 11.6
besom 16.20
besotted 24.24

besought 25.31
bespatter 2.10
bespeak 15.7
bespectacled 10.61
bespoke 35.21
besprinkle 18.22
Bess 9.47
Bessarabia 8.78
Bessemer 10.56
Bessie 10.7
best 9.49
bestial 10.60
bestiality 2.57
bestialize 21.47
bestiary 10.53
bestir 11.1
bestow 35.2
bestowal 36.15
bestowed 35.25
bestowing 36.24
bestows 35.52
bestrew 41.2
bestride 21.10
bestseller 10.12
Beswick 10.15
bet 9.51
beta 16.5
beta-blocker 24.9
beta-blockers 24.53
betacarotene 15.26
betake 7.6
betcha 10.14
betel 16.17
Betelgeuse 11.29;
    41.24
bête noire 3.1
Beth 9.54
Bethan 10.27
Bethany 10.53
Bethel 10.21
Bethesda 10.10
Beth's 9.55
bethink 17.30
Bethlehem 9.28
Bethnal Green 15.26
betide 21.10
betimes 21.21
Betjeman 10.64
betoken 36.20
betokened 36.21
betony 10.53
betook 39.1
betray 7.2
betrayal 8.15
betrayed 7.8
betrayer 8.2
betraying 8.58
betroth 35.48

betrothal 36.15
betroths 35.49
bets 9.52
Betsy 10.7
Bette 10.3
betted 10.18
better 10.10
bettered 10.18
betterment 10.67
betters 10.52
betting 10.36
Betty 10.3
Betty's 10.51
between 15.24
betweentimes 21.21
betweenwhiles 21.18
betwixt 17.5
Betws-y-Coed 33.4
Beulah 42.7
Bev 9.56
Bevan 10.27
bevel 10.21
beverage 17.14
Beveridge 17.14
Beverley 10.53
Beverly Hills 17.23
Bevin 10.26
bevvies 10.51
bevvy 10.4
bevy 10.4
bewail 7.15
bewailed 7.16
bewailer 8.7
bewailing 8.62
beware 5.1
Bewes 41.33
bewhiskered 18.19
Bewick 42.11
bewilder 18.10
bewilderingly 18.80
bewilderment 18.70
bewitch 17.7
bewitching 18.40
Bexhill 17.15
Bexley 10.5
Bexleyheath 15.37
beyond 23.30
bezel 10.21
bezique 15.7
Bhagavad-Gita 16.5
bhaji 4.7
bhangra 2.12
bhindi 18.3
Bhopal 3.14
Bhutan 1.24; 3.19
Bhutto 35.18
bi 21.1
Biafra 2.12

Biafran 2.35
Bianca 2.9
biannual 2.64
Biarritz 17.52
bias 22.29
biased 22.31
biathlon 2.35; 23.27
bib 17.1
bibber 18.8
Bible 22.16
Bible Belt 9.23
biblical 18.64
biblically 18.57
bibliographer 24.57
bibliographic 2.18
bibliography 24.54
bibliomania 8.78
bibliophile 21.16
bibs 17.2
bibulous 18.74
Bic® 17.3
bicameral 2.64
bicarb 3.2
bicarbonate 7.36
bicentenary 16.38
bicentennial 10.60
biceps 9.45
Bicester 18.10
bichon frise 7.3
bicker 18.9
bickered 18.19
bickerer 18.60
bickie 18.2
biconcave 7.54
biconvex 9.3
bicuspid 38.19
bicycle 22.43
bid 17.8
biddable 18.64
bidden 18.32
bidder 18.10
bidders 18.55
bidding 18.40
Biddle 18.22
Biddulph 37.21
biddy 18.3
Biddy 18.3
bide 21.9
Bideford 18.62
bidet 7.3
biennial 10.60
bier 13.1
Bierce 13.4
bierkeller 10.12
biff 17.10
biffed 17.11
biffing 18.40
bifid 22.12

bifocal 36.15
bifocals 36.17
bifurcate 7.42
bifurcation 8.33
big 17.12
bigamist 18.75
bigamous 18.74
bigamy 18.56
bigger 18.9
biggest 18.46
biggie 18.2
biggish 18.47
Biggles 18.24
Biggleswade 7.8
Biggs 17.13
bighead 9.8
bigheaded 10.18
big-hearted 4.17
Bighorn 25.22
bight 21.31
bigmouth 29.16
bigot 18.49
bigotry 18.56
big screen 15.24
big 'un 18.32
bigwig 17.12
bijou 41.3
bike 21.7
biker 22.4
bikers 22.39
bikes 21.8
biking 22.26
bikini 16.1
bikinied 16.13
Biko 35.10
bilabial 8.79
bilateral 2.28; 2.64
Bilbao 29.1
bilberry 18.5; 18.56
bile 21.16
bilge pump 37.29
bilharzia 4.44
biliary 18.56
bilingual 18.22
bilious 18.74
bilirubin 42.19
bilk 17.16
bilking 18.40
bill 17.15
Bill 17.15
billabong 23.31
billboard 25.9
billed 17.18
Billericay 18.2
billet 18.50
billet-doux 41.4
billfold 35.31

Bill Gates 7.50
billhook 39.1
billiards 18.20
billing 18.40
Billingsgate 7.41
billion 18.32; 18.67
billionaire 5.1
billionth 18.72
billow 35.11
billowing 36.24
billposter 36.5
billposting 36.24
bills 17.23
Bill's 17.23
billsticker 18.9
Billy 18.5
Billy's 18.54
billycan 1.24
billy goat 35.45
Billy Liar 22.2
billyo 35.19
biltong 23.31
bimbo 35.11
bimestrial 10.60
bimetallic 2.19
bin 17.29
binary 22.40
Binchy 18.7
bind 21.23
binder 22.5
bindery 22.40
binding 22.26
bindweed 15.11
bine 21.22
bin end 9.35
bing 17.35
binge 17.37
Bingen 18.32
Bingham 18.26
Bingley 18.5
bingo 35.11
binman 1.24
binmen 9.32
binnacle 18.64
Binns 17.42
binocular 24.57
binoculars 24.74
binomial 36.38
binominal 24.61
bins 17.42
bint 17.39
Binyon 18.32
bioassay 7.2
biochemical 10.60
biochemist 10.44
biochemistry 10.54
biochip 17.43
biocide 21.12

biodata 8.5
biodegradable 8.79
biodegradation 8.28
biodiversity 12.29
bioengineering 14.12
biofuel 42.16
biogas 1.40
biographer 24.57
biographic 2.18
biographical 2.64
biographically 2.58
biography 24.54
biological 24.61
biologically 24.56
biologist 24.72
biology 24.55
biomass 1.40
biome 35.34
biometric 10.15
biometrical 10.60
biometrics 10.16
bionic 24.19
bionics 24.22
biophysics 18.17
biopic 17.3
biopsy 24.7
biorhythm 18.26
biosphere 13.1
biotech 9.2
biotechnology 24.55
biotic 24.16
biotype 21.26
biotypic 18.16
bipartisan 1.24
bipartite 21.33
biped 9.8
biplane 7.21
bipod 23.8
bipolar 36.7
biracial 8.15
biradial 8.79
birch 11.6
birching 12.16
bird 11.7
birdbath 3.34
birdbrain 7.21
bird-brained 7.22
birdcage 7.12
birder 12.2
birdhouse 29.12
birdie 12.1
birdies 12.28
birdlime 21.19
birdman 1.24
birdseed 15.11
Birds Eye 21.3
bird's-eye view 41.4
birdsong 23.31

bird-watcher 24.14
bird-watchers 24.53
bird-watching 24.40
bireme 15.20
biretta 10.10
Birgitta 18.10
Birkbeck 9.2
Birkenhead 9.8
Birmingham 12.33
Biro® 35.12
birth 11.26
birthday 7.3
birthday card 3.8
birthday suit 41.27
birthing 12.16
birthmark 3.3
birthplace 7.30
birth rate 7.34
birthright 21.33
birthstone 35.36
Birtwistle 18.22
biryani 4.6
Biscay 7.3
biscuit 18.50
biscuits 18.51
bise 15.42
bisect 9.5
bisection 10.28
bisector 10.10
bisexual 10.60
bish 17.50
bishop 18.42
bishopric 17.3
Bishopsgate 7.41
Bisley 18.5
Bismarck 3.3
bismuth 18.52
bison 22.20
bisque 17.47
Bissell 18.22
Bisto® 35.11
bistro 35.10
bisymmetric 10.15
bit 17.51
bitch 17.7
bitchfest 9.49
bitching 18.40
bitchy 18.7
bite 21.31
biter 22.5
bites 21.35
bite the dust 37.45
biting 22.26
bitingly 22.40
bitmap 1.37
bits 17.52
bitser 18.14
bitten 18.32

bitter 18.10
bitter end 9.35
bitterly 18.56
bittern 11.15
bittern 18.32
bitterness 18.74
bittersweet 15.35
bitty 18.3
bitumen 17.29
bituminous 42.46
bivalve 1.21
bivouac 1.3
biz 17.56
bizarre 3.1
bizarrely 4.5
Bizet 7.3
Bjorn 25.22
blab 1.1
blabber 2.8
blabbermouth 29.16
black 1.3
Black 1.3
black and blue 41.4
black-and-white 21.34
blackball 25.14
blackballed 25.15
blackballing 26.25
Blackbeard 13.2
blackberries 2.77
blackberry 2.5; 2.56
blackbird 11.7
blackboard 25.9
Blackburn 11.15
blackcap 1.37
blackcurrant 38.32
blacken 2.35
blackened 2.36
blacker 2.9
blackest 2.48
blackface 7.30
blackfly 21.3
Blackfriars 19.4
blackguard 2.25
blackguards 2.26
blackhead 9.8
blackheads 9.9
Blackie 2.2
blacking 2.42
blackish 2.49
blackjack 1.3
blacklead 9.8
blackleg 9.12
blacklist 2.47
blackly 2.5
blackmail 7.15
blackmailer 8.7
blackmailing 8.62
Black Maria 22.2

black mark 3.3
Blackmore 25.3
blackness 2.46
blackout 29.14
blackouts 29.15
Blackpool 41.14
Blackshirt 11.24
blacksmith 17.53
black spot 23.44
Blackstone 35.36
blackthorn 25.22
Blackwall 25.14
Blackwood 39.4
bladder 2.10
bladderwort 11.24
bladderwrack 1.3
blade 7.8
blades 7.9
blag 1.13
blagger 2.9
blague 3.11
Blair 5.1
Blairgowrie 30.1
Blairite 21.33
Blake 7.6
blamable 8.79
blame 7.18
blamed 7.19
blameless 8.67
blameworthy 12.1
blaming 8.63
blanch 3.20
Blanche 3.20
bland 1.28
blander 2.10
blandest 2.48
Blandford 2.25
blandish 2.49
blandishment 2.68
blandishments 2.69
blandness 2.46
blank 1.25
blanket 2.51
blanketed 2.63
blanks 1.26
blare 5.1
blaring 6.10
blarney 4.6
blasé 7.3
blaspheme 15.20
blasphemed 15.21
blasphemer 16.8
blasphemous 2.71
blasphemy 2.56
blast 3.30
blasted 4.17
blaster 4.10
blasting 4.29

blastocoel 15.17
blastoff 23.9
blastula 2.60
blatant 8.56
blatantly 8.76
blather 2.11
blatherskite 21.34
blaxploitation 8.24
Blaydon 8.21
blaze 7.56
blazed 7.57
blazer 8.9
blazing 8.64
blazon 8.21
blazonry 8.76
bleach 15.9
bleached 15.10
bleacher 16.9
bleak 15.7
bleaker 16.4
bleakest 16.32
bleakly 16.1
bleakness 16.30
blear 13.1
bleary 14.1
bleary-eyed 21.12
Bleasdale 7.15
bleat 15.35
bleb 9.1
bled 9.8
bleed 15.11
bleeder 16.5
bleeding 16.27
bleep 15.30
bleeper 16.3
bleeping 16.27
bleeps 15.31
blemish 10.45
blemished 10.46
blemishes 10.76
blench 9.33
blenched 9.34
blend 9.35
blended 10.18
blender 10.10
blending 10.36
Blenheim 10.24
Blenkinsop 23.36
blenny 10.6
Blériot 35.19
bless 9.47
blessed 9.49; 10.17
blessing 10.36
blessings 10.37
blest 9.49
Bletchley 10.5
blether 10.11
blew 41.1

Blewitt 42.30
Bligh 21.1
blight 21.31
blighted 22.13
blighter 22.5
Blighty 22.1
blimey 22.1
blimp 17.27
blind 21.23
blind date 7.33
blinder 22.5
blindfold 35.31
blindingly 22.40
blindly 22.1
blindness 22.29
blindstorey 26.1
blindworm 11.13
bling 17.35
bling-bling 17.35
blini 18.6
blink 17.30
blinked 17.32
blinker 18.9
blinking 18.40
blinks 17.31
blip 17.43
bliss 17.46
Bliss 17.46
blissful 18.22; 39.7
blissfully 18.56; 18.59
blister 18.10
blithe 21.36
blithely 22.1
blithering 18.73
blitz 17.52
Blitz 17.52
blitzkrieg 15.14
Blixen 18.33
blizzard 18.19
blizzards 18.20
bloat 35.45
bloated 36.12
bloater 36.5
blob 23.1
blobs 23.2
bloc 23.3
Bloch 23.3; 23.4
block 23.3
blockade 7.8
blockage 24.26
blockboard 25.9
blockbuster 38.10
blockbusting 38.34
blocked 23.6
blocker 24.9
blockhead 9.8
blocking 24.40
blockish 24.46

blocks 23.5
Blodwen 24.32
blog 23.11
Bloggs 23.13
Blois 3.1
bloke 35.21
blokey 36.1
blond 23.30
blonde 23.30
blonder 24.10
blondest 24.44
Blondie 24.3
blood 37.8
bloodbath 3.34
bloodhound 29.6
bloodied 38.19
bloodier 38.49
bloodiest 38.61
bloodless 38.38
blood-letting 10.36
bloodline 21.22
bloodlust 37.45
bloodshed 9.8
bloodshot 23.44
bloodstain 7.21
bloodstained 7.22
bloodstains 7.26
bloodstock 23.3
bloodstone 35.36
bloodstream 15.20
bloodsucker 38.9
bloodsuckers 38.45
bloodsucking 38.34
bloodthirsty 12.1
bloody 38.3
bloom 41.17
bloomed 41.18
bloomer 42.8
bloomers 42.34
blooming 42.24
Bloomingdale's 7.17
Bloomsbury 42.36
blooper 42.3
blossom 24.30
blot 23.44
blotch 23.7
blotches 24.53
blotchier 24.58
blotchiest 24.71
blotchy 24.7
blots 23.45
blotted 24.24
blotter 24.10
blotting 24.40
blotto 35.13
Blount 29.11
blouse 29.17
blow 35.1

blowback 1.3
blow-by-blow 35.19
blow-dried 21.11
blow-dry 21.3
blowed 35.25
blower 36.2
blowfly 21.3
blowgun 37.31
blowhole 35.30
blowlamp 1.23
blown 35.36
blowout 29.14
blowpipe 21.26
blows 35.52
blowsy 30.1
blow the gaff 1.11
blowtorch 25.8
blowy 36.1
blub 37.1
blubber 38.8
blubbered 38.20
blubbering 38.58
blubbery 38.47
blubbing 38.34
bludge 37.15
bludgeon 38.28
bludger 38.14
blue 41.1
Bluebeard 13.2
bluebell 9.16
blueberry 42.1; 42.36
bluebird 11.7
bluebottle 24.27
Bluecoat 35.45
blue-collar 24.12
blue-eyed boy 33.1
bluegrass 3.26
blueprint 17.39
blues 41.33
bluestocking 24.40
bluesy 42.1
bluetit 42.30
bluetits 42.32
bluey 42.1
bluff 37.10
bluffed 37.12
bluffer 38.11
bluffing 38.34
bluish 42.29
Blundell 38.23
Blunden 38.28
blunder 38.10
blunderbuss 37.43
blundered 38.20
blunderer 38.48
blunt 37.40
Blunt 37.40

blunted 38.20
blunter 38.10
bluntest 38.39
bluntly 38.5
bluntness 38.38
blur 11.1
blurb 11.2
blurred 11.7
blurry 12.1
blurs 11.29
blurt 11.24
blush 37.46
blusher 38.14
blushes 38.45
blushing 38.34
bluster 38.10
blustery 38.47
Blu-Tack® 1.3
Blyth 21.36
Blyton 22.20
B'nai B'rith 15.37
BO 35.2
boa 36.2
boa constrictor 18.10
Boadicea 16.2
Boanerges 15.44
boar 25.1
board 25.9
boarded 26.12
boarder 26.4
boarders 26.36
boarding 26.25
boarding house 29.12
boardroom 39.9; 41.17
boards 25.10
boardsailing 8.62
boardsailor 8.7
boardwalk 25.6
boast 35.43
boaster 36.5
boastful 36.15; 39.7
boastfully 36.35
boastfulness 36.42
boasting 36.24
boat 35.45
boatel 9.16
Boateng 9.36
boater 36.5
boatful 39.7
boathook 39.1
boathouse 29.12
boating 36.24
boatload 35.25
boatman 36.20
boatyard 3.8
Boaz 1.50
bob 23.1
Bob 23.1

bobbin 24.32
bobbing 24.40
bobbins 24.37
bobble 24.27
bobby 24.1
Bobby 24.1
Bobby's 24.52
bobby-dazzler 2.12
bobbysoxer 24.14
bobcat 1.45
Bob Hope 35.40
bobolink 17.30
Bob's 23.2
bobsled 9.8
bobsleigh 7.3
bobtail 7.15
Boccaccio 35.19
Boccherini 16.1
Boche 23.42
bock 23.3
bod 23.8
bodacious 8.67
Boddington 24.64
bode 35.25
boded 36.12
bodega 8.4
bodge 23.14
bodger 24.14
bodger 24.14
bodging 24.40
bodice 24.42
bodies 24.52
bodily 24.56
boding 36.24
bodkin 24.32
Bodleian 24.64
Bodley 24.5
Bodoni 36.1
body 24.3
bodyboard 25.9
bodyboarding 26.25
body-builder 18.10
bodybuilding 18.40
bodycheck 9.2
bodyguard 3.8
bodyshell 9.16
bodysuit 41.27
bodywork 11.4
Boeing 36.24
Boer 25.1; 27.1; 36.2
Boers 27.3
Boethius 16.47
boffin 24.32
boffins 24.37
bog 23.11
Bogarde 3.8
Bogart 3.32
bogey 36.1
bogeyman 1.24

boggart 24.48
boggier 24.58
boggiest 24.71
boggle 24.27
boggled 24.28
boggy 24.2
Bogie 36.1
bogle 36.15
Bognor 24.13
Bognor Regis 16.29
Bogotá 3.1
bogtrotter 24.10
bogus 36.26
Bohemia 16.40
Bohemian 16.43
Bohr 25.1
boil 33.6
boilable 34.16
Boileau 35.3
boiled 33.7
boiler 34.2
boilermaker 8.4
boiler room 39.9;
  41.17
boiling 34.11
boiling point 33.10
boink 33.9
boisterous 34.12
boisterous 34.18
boisterously 34.14
bola 36.7
Bolam 36.18
bold 35.31
bolder 36.5
boldest 36.28
boldface 7.30
boldly 36.1
boldness 36.26
bole 35.30
bolero 35.8
boletus 16.30
Boleyn 17.29
Bolingbroke 39.1
Bolivar 3.1
Bolivia 18.61
Bolivian 18.67
boll 35.30
bollard 3.8; 24.24
bollards 24.25
Bollinger 24.57
bollocking 24.69
bollocks 24.21
Bolly 24.5
Bollywood 39.4
Bologna 24.12
Bolognese 7.56
Bolshevik 17.3
Bolshevism 18.28

bolshie 24.7
Bolshoi 33.1
Bolsover 36.6
bolster 36.5
bolstered 36.12
bolt 35.32
Bolt 35.32
Bolton 36.20
bolus 36.26
bomb 23.23
bombard 3.8
bombarded 4.17
bombardier 13.1
bombarding 4.29
bombardment 4.27
bombast 1.42
bombastic 2.17
Bombay 7.2
bombazine 15.26
bomber 24.13
bombers 24.53
bombing 24.40
bombproof 41.10
bombshell 9.16
bomb site 21.33
bona fide 22.1
bona fides 15.44; 22.38
bonanza 2.14
Bonaparte 3.32
Bonapartism 18.29
Bonar 24.13
Bonaventura 28.2
Bonaventure 10.14
bonbon 23.27
bonce 23.33
bond 23.30
Bond 23.30
bondage 24.26
bonded 24.24
bondholder 36.5
Bondi 21.3
bonding 24.40
bondsman 24.33
bone 35.36
boned 35.37
bone dry 21.2
bonehead 9.8
boneless 36.26
bonemeal 15.17
boner 36.8
bones 35.39
bonesetter 10.10
boneshaker 8.4
boneyard 3.8
bonfire 19.1
Bonfire Night 21.34
bong 23.31
bongo 35.13

bongos 35.52
Bonham 24.30
Bonhams 24.31
bonhomie 15.4
bonier 36.37
boniest 36.44
Boniface 7.30
boning 36.24
bonk 23.28
bonkbuster 38.10
bonkers 24.53
bonking 24.40
bonks 23.29
Bonn 23.27
Bonner 24.13
bonnet 24.49
Bonnie and Clyde
  21.10
bonnier 24.58
bonniest 24.71
bonny 24.6
Bonny 24.6
bonsai 21.3
bonus 36.26
bon vivant 23.31
bon viveur 11.1
bon voyage 3.13
bony 36.1
bonzer 24.14
boo 41.1
boob 41.5
boo-boo 41.3
boob tube 41.5
booby 42.1
booby prize 21.46
booby trap 1.37
boodle 42.16
booed 41.9
boogie 42.1
boogied 42.13
boogie-woogie 42.1
boohoo 41.2
book 39.1
bookable 40.22
bookbinder 25.5
bookbinding 22.26
bookcase 7.30
booked 39.2
bookend 9.35
booker 40.2
Booker 40.2
bookie 40.1
bookies 40.19
booking 40.15
bookish 40.16
book-keeper 16.3
book-keeping 16.27
booklet 40.17

bookmaker 8.4
bookman 40.10
bookmark 3.3
bookmarked 3.5
Book of Kells 9.27
bookplate 7.34
bookseller 10.12
bookshop 23.36
bookstall 25.14
bookstore 25.3
bookworm 11.13
Boole 41.14
Boolean 42.41
boom 41.17
boomer 42.8
boomerang 1.29
booming 42.24
boom town 29.5
boon 41.19
boondocks 23.5
Boone 41.19
boor 27.1
boorish 28.15
boors 27.3
Boosey 42.1
boost 41.25
boosted 42.14
booster 42.5
boosting 42.24
boot 41.27
bootblack 1.3
booted 42.14
bootee 15.2; 15.3; 42.1
bootees 42.35
booth 41.30
Booth 41.30
Boothby 42.1
Boothroyd 33.4
booting 42.24
bootlace 7.30
Bootle 42.16
bootleg 9.12
bootlegger 10.9
bootlegging 10.36
bootless 42.26
bootlick 42.11
bootlicker 18.9
boots 41.28
Boots 41.28
bootstrap 1.37
bootstraps 1.38
booty 42.1
booze 41.33
booze cruise 41.33
boozed 41.34
boozer 42.9
boozy 42.1
bop 23.36

bo-peep 15.30
Bophuthatswana 4.13
bopper 24.8
bopping 24.40
Bora Bora 26.6
boracic 2.21
borage 24.26
borax 1.4
borborygmi 18.6
Bordeaux 35.2
bordello 35.7
Borden 26.19
border 26.4
bordered 26.12
borderland 1.28
borderline 21.22
bore 25.1
boreal 26.41
bored 25.9
boredom 26.17
borehole 35.30
borer 26.6
Borg 25.12
Borgia 26.8
boric 26.9
boring 26.25
Boris 24.42
born 25.22
born-again 9.32
borne 25.22
Borneo 35.19
Bornholm 35.34
Borodin 17.29
Borodino 35.10
boron 23.27
borough 38.12
Borromini 16.1
borrow 35.13
borrowed 35.25
borrower 36.2
borrowing 36.24
borsch 25.30
Borstal 26.15
borzoi 33.1
Boscastle 4.19
Bosch 23.42
bosh 23.42
bosk 23.40
Bosnia 24.58
Bosnian 24.64
Bosnians 24.66
bosom 40.8
boson 23.27
Bosphorus 24.70
Bosporus 24.70
boss 23.39
bossa nova 36.6
bossed 23.41

bosses 24.53
bossier 24.58
bossiest 24.71
bossily 24.56
bossy 24.7
Bostik® 24.16
Bostock 23.3
Boston 24.33
bosun 36.20
Boswell 9.16
Boswellian 10.64
Bosworth 11.26; 24.50
bot 23.44
botanic 2.20
botanical 2.64
botanist 24.72
botany 24.54
Botany Bay 7.2
botch 23.7
botcher 24.14
botching 24.40
botchy 24.7
botfly 21.3
both 35.47
Botham 36.18
bother 24.11
botheration 8.34
bothered 24.24
bothering 24.69
bothersome 24.63
Bothnia 24.58
bothy 24.4
Botolph 23.16
Botox® 23.5
Botswana 4.13
Botticelli 10.5
bottle 24.27
bottlebrush 37.46
bottled 24.28
bottle-fed 9.8
bottle-feed 15.11
bottleful 39.7
bottle green 15.26
bottleneck 9.2
bottlenose 35.52
bottler 24.12
bottles 24.29
bottle-washer 24.14
bottom 24.30
bottomless 24.70
Bottomley 24.54
bottommost 35.43
botulinum 22.18
botulism 18.28
Boucicault 35.19
bouclé 7.3
Boudicca 42.37
boudoir 3.1

bouffant 23.31
bougainvillea 18.61
bough 29.1
boughs 29.17
bought 25.31
bouillabaisse 9.47
bouillon 23.27
boulder 36.5
boulders 36.34
boule 41.14
boulevard 3.8
boulevardier 7.4
Boulogne 33.8
Boult 35.32
Boulton 36.20
bounce 29.9
bounced 29.10
bouncer 30.2
bouncing 30.12
bouncy 30.1
bound 29.6
boundary 30.22
bounded 30.3
bounden 30.8
bounder 30.2
bounding 30.12
boundless 30.14
bounds 29.7
bounteous 30.26
bountiful 30.24; 39.7
bounty 30.1
Bounty 30.1
bouquet 7.2
bouquet garni 15.2
bouquets 7.56
bourbon 12.12
Bourbon 26.19
bourdon 26.19
bourgeois 3.1
bourgeoisie 15.4
Bourguignonne 23.27
bourn 25.22
Bournemouth 26.33
Bournville 17.15
bourrée 7.2
Bourton 26.19
bout 29.14
boutique 15.7
bouzouki 42.1
Bovary 36.35
bovine 21.22
Bovis 36.25
Bovril® 17.15; 24.27
bovver 24.11
bow 29.1; 35.1
Bowater 26.4
Bowdler 30.2
bowdlerism 18.28

bowdlerization 8.49
bowdlerize 21.45
bowdlerizer 22.9
bowed 29.3; 35.25
bowel 31.3
bowels 31.4
Bowen 36.19
bower 31.1
bowerbird 11.7
bowery 32.1
Bowery 32.1
Bowie 30.1; 36.1
bowing 30.12; 36.24
bowl 35.30
bowled 35.31
bow-legged 10.17
bowler 36.7
Bowles 35.33
bowlful 39.7
bowline 36.19
bowling 36.24
bowling green 15.26
bowls 35.33
bowman 36.20
bows 29.17
bowshot 23.44
bowsprit 36.30
bowsprits 36.31
bowstring 36.24
bow-wow 29.1
Bowyer 36.7
box 23.5
boxcar 3.1
boxer 24.14
Boxer 24.14
boxes 24.53
boxing 24.40
boxroom 39.9; 41.17
boxy 24.7
boy 33.1
Boyce 33.11
boycott 23.44
Boycott 23.44
Boyd 33.4
Boyer 34.2
boyfriend 9.35
boyhood 39.4
boyish 17.50
boyishly 34.14
Boyle 33.6
Boyne 33.8
boys 33.15
boysenberry 10.5
Boyson 34.8
Boz 23.48
bozo 35.16
bra 3.1
braaivleis 7.30

Brabant 1.33
Brabham 2.32
brace 7.30
Bracegirdle 12.8
bracelet 8.71
bracer 8.9
braces 8.75
brachial 8.79
bracing 8.64
bracken 2.35
bracket 2.51
brackish 2.49
Bracknell 2.28
bract 1.6
brad 1.9
Brad 1.9
bradawl 25.14
Bradbury 2.56
Braddock 2.16
Braden 8.21
Bradford 2.25
Bradley 2.5
Bradman 2.35
Bradshaw 25.3
Bradstreet 15.35
Brady 8.1
brae 7.1
Braeburn 11.15
Braemar 3.1
brag 1.13
Braganza 2.14
Bragg 1.13
braggadocio 35.19
braggart 2.50
bragger 2.9
bragging 2.42
brags 1.14
Brahma 4.13
Brahman 4.24
Brahmaputra 42.7
Brahmin 4.23
Brahms 3.18
braid 7.8
braided 8.13
Braille 7.15
brain 7.21
brainbox 23.5
brainchild 21.17
braindead 9.8
Braine 7.21
brainier 8.78
brainiest 8.86
brainless 8.67
brainpan 1.24
brainpower 31.1
brains 7.26
brain scan 1.24
brain scans 1.36

brainsick 8.10
brainstem 9.28
brainstorm 25.20
brainstorming 26.25
Braintree 8.1; 15.3
brainwash 23.42
brainwashed 23.43
brainwashing 24.40
brainwave 7.54
brainwork 11.4
brainy 8.1
braise 7.56
braised 7.57
Braithwaite 7.34
brake 7.6
braked 7.7
braless 4.32
bramble 2.28
brambles 2.30
brambling 2.42
brambly 2.5
Bramley 2.5
bran 1.24
Branagh 2.13
branch 3.20
branches 4.41
branching 4.29
Brancusi 42.1
brand 1.28
branded 2.25
Brandenburg 11.9
brandish 2.49
brandishing 2.70
brand-new 41.2
Brando 35.3
Brandon 2.35
Brandreth 2.52
Brands Hatch 1.7
Brandt 1.33
brandy 2.3
Brangwyn 2.34
Branson 2.35
Branston 2.35
Braque 1.3, 3.3
brash 1.43
Brasher 8.9
Brasília 18.61
brass 3.26
brassbound 29.6
brasserie 2.56
brassica 2.60
brassie 2.7
brassiere 2.61
brassy 4.7
brat 1.45
Bratislava 4.11
bratpack 1.3
brats 1.46

brattice 2.45
bratwurst 11.23
Braun 25.22; 29.5
bravado 35.4
brave 7.54
bravely 8.1
braveness 8.67
braver 8.6
bravest 8.69
bravo 35.2
bravo 35.4
bravura 28.2
braw 25.1
brawl 25.14
brawler 26.6
brawling 26.25
brawn 25.22
brawnier 26.39
brawniest 26.49
brawny 26.1
bray 7.1
brayed 7.8
braze 7.56
brazen 8.21
brazier 8.78
brazil 17.15
Brazil 17.15
Brazilian 18.32; 18.67
brazil nut 37.47
breach 15.9
bread 9.8
breadbasket 4.38
breadboard 25.9
breadcrumb 37.27
breadfruit 41.27
breadline 21.22
breadth 9.53
breadthways 7.56
breadthwise 21.41
breadwinner 18.13
break 7.6
breakable 8.79
breakage 8.14
break a leg 9.12
breakaway 7.4
breakdown 29.5
breaker 8.4
breakers 8.75
breakeven 16.22
breakfast 10.43
breaking 8.59
breakneck 9.2
break-out 29.14
breakpoint 33.10
breakthrough 41.3
break-up 37.41
breakwater 26.4
bream 15.20

Bream 15.20
Brearley 14.1
breast 9.49
breastbone 35.36
breast-fed 9.8
breast-feed 15.11
breast-feeding 16.27
breastplate 7.34
breaststroke 35.21
breastwork 11.4
breath 9.54
breathable 16.41
breathalyse 21.43
Breathalyser® 22.9
breathe 15.38
breather 16.6
breathing 16.27
breathing space 7.30
breathless 10.42
breathlessly 10.53
breathlessness 10.70
breathtaking 8.59
breathy 10.4
Brecht 9.5
Breckenridge 17.14
Brecon 10.27
bred 9.8
Breda 16.5
Bredon 16.22
breech 15.9
breeches 18.55
breech-loading 36.24
breed 15.11
breeder 16.5
breeding 16.27
breeds 15.12
breeks 15.8
breeze 15.42
breeze block 23.3
breeze blocks 23.5
breezier 16.40
breeziest 16.49
breezily 16.38
breezy 16.1
brekky 10.2
Brel 9.16
Bremen 8.21
Bremner 10.13
Bren 9.32
Brenda 10.10
Brendan 10.27
Bren gun 37.31
Brennan 10.27
Brent 9.41
Brentwood 39.4
br'er 5.1; 11.1
Brest 9.49
brethren 10.27

Breton 10.27
Brett 9.51
Brett's 9.52
breve 15.39
breviary 10.53; 16.38
brevity 10.54
brew 41.1
brewage 42.15
brewed 41.9
brewer 42.2
brewers 42.34
brewery 42.36
brewing 42.24
Brewster 42.5
Brezhnev 9.10; 9.56
Brian 22.20
Brian Boru 41.2
Brian's 22.23
briar 19.1
bribable 22.43
bribe 21.5
bribed 21.6
briber 22.3
bribery 22.40
bribing 22.26
bric-a-brac 1.3
Brice 21.29
brick 17.3
brickbat 1.45
brickie 18.2
bricklayer 8.2
bricklaying 8.58
bricks 17.4
brickwork 11.4
brickyard 3.8
bricolage 3.13
bridal 22.16
bride 21.9
bridegroom 39.9; 41.17
brides 21.13
Brideshead 9.8
bridesmaid 7.8
bridesmaids 7.9
bride-to-be 15.4
Bridewell 9.16
bridge 17.14
bridgehead 9.8
Bridgend 9.35
Bridgeport 25.31
Bridger 18.14
bridges 18.55
Bridges 18.55
Bridget 18.50
Bridgetown 29.5
Bridget's 18.51
bridgework 11.4
bridging 18.40

bridging loan 35.36
Bridgnorth 25.33
Bridgwater 26.4
Bridie 22.1
bridle 22.16
bridleway 7.4
Bridlington 18.67
Brie 15.1
brief 15.13
briefcase 7.30
briefer 16.6
briefest 16.32
briefing 16.27
briefly 16.1
brier 19.1
Brierley 20.1
brig 17.12
brigade 7.8
brigadier 13.1
Brigadoon 41.19
brigand 18.34
brigands 18.35
brigantine 15.26
Briggs 17.13
Brigham 18.26
Brighouse 29.12
bright 21.31
Bright 21.31
brighten 22.20
brightened 22.21
brightly 22.1
brightness 22.29
Brighton 22.20
brightwork 11.4
Brigid 18.18
Brigitte 15.35
brill 17.15
brilliance 18.39; 18.71
brilliant 18.38; 18.70
brilliantine 15.26
brilliantly 18.56
brim 17.24
brimful 39.7
brimming 18.40
brimstone 35.36
Brindisi 18.57
brindle 18.22
brine 21.22
bring 17.35
bring-and-buy 21.4
bringer 18.13
bringing 18.40
brings 17.36
brinjal 18.22
brink 17.30
brinkmanship 17.43
Brinks-Mat 1.45
briny 22.1

brio 35.10
brioche 23.42
briquette 9.51
Brisbane 18.32
brisk 17.47
brisket 18.50
briskly 18.5
briskness 18.44
brisling 18.40
bristle 18.22
bristletail 7.15
bristling 18.40
Bristol 18.22
bristols 18.24
Bristow 35.11
Brit 17.51
Britain 18.32
Britannia 2.12; 2.61
Britannic 2.20
Britannicus 2.71
Britart 3.52
Briticism 18.28
British 18.47
Britisher 18.60
British Isles 21.18
Britishness 18.74
Britney 18.6
Briton 18.32
Britons 18.37
Britpop 23.36
Brittany 18.56
Britten 18.32
brittle 18.22
Britvic® 18.16
Brixham 18.26
Brize Norton 26.19
bro 35.1
broach 35.24
broaching 36.24
broad 25.9
broadband 1.28
broad bean 15.24
Broadbent 9.41
broad-brimmed 17.25
broadcast 3.30
broadcaster 4.10
broadcasting 4.29
broadcloth 23.46
broaden 26.19
broadened 26.20
broader 26.4
broad-leaved 15.40
broadloom 41.17
broadly 26.1
broad-minded 22.13
Broadmoor 25.3; 27.1
broadsheet 15.35
broadside 21.11

broadsword 25.9
Broadway 7.3
Brobdingnag 1.13
brocade 7.8
broccoli 24.54
brochette 9.51
brochure 27.1; 36.9
brock 23.3
Broderick 17.3
Brodie 36.1
brogan 36.20
brogue 35.28
broider 34.2
broil 33.6
broiler 34.2
broiling 34.11
broke 35.21
broken 36.20
broken-down 29.5
brokenhearted 4.17
broker 36.4
brokerage 17.14
brokered 36.12
brokers 36.34
brolga 24.9
brolly 24.5
bromeliad 1.9
bromic 36.10
bromide 21.11
bromidic 18.16
bromine 15.25
Bromley 24.5
Brompton 24.33
Bromsgrove 35.50
Bromwich 17.7; 24.26
bronchi 21.3; 24.2
bronchial 24.61
bronchiolar 36.7
bronchiole 35.30
bronchitic 18.16
bronchitis 22.28
bronchodilator 8.5
bronchopneumonia 36.37
bronchus 24.43
bronco 35.13
broncobuster 38.10
Brontë 24.3
brontosaur 25.4
brontosaurus 26.27
Bronwen 24.32
Bronx 23.29
bronze 23.35
Bronze Age 7.12
brooch 35.24
brood 41.9
brooder 42.5
brooding 42.24

broody 42.1
brook 39.1
Brooke 39.1
Brooking 40.15
Brooklands 40.11
Brooklyn 40.9
Brookner 40.2
Brookside 21.11
broom 39.9; 41.17
broomstick 42.11
broomsticks 42.12
Brophy 36.1
Bros 23.39
broth 23.46
brothel 24.27
brother 38.11
brotherhood 39.4
brother-in-law 25.2
brotherless 38.59
brotherly 38.47
brothers 38.45
Brough 37.10
brougham 42.18
brought 25.31
Broughton 26.19;
30.8
brouhaha 3.1
brow 29.1
browband 1.28
browbeat 15.35
browbeaten 16.22
brown 29.5
Brown 29.5
Browne 29.5
browned-off 23.9
browner 30.2
brownest 30.16
brownfield 15.18
brownie 30.1
Brownie 30.1
Brownies 30.20
browning 30.12
Browning 30.12
brownish 30.17
brows 29.17
browse 29.17
browser 30.2
browsers 30.21
browsing 30.12
Bruce 41.24
brucellosis 36.25
Bruce's 42.34
Bruch 39.1
Bruckner 40.2
Brueghel 34.5
Bruges 41.13
bruin 42.19
bruise 41.33

bruised 41.34
bruiser 42.9
bruises 42.34
bruising 42.24
Brum 37.27
brumby 38.1
Brummagem 38.53
Brummell 38.23
Brummie 38.6
brunch 37.35
Brundisium 18.66
Brunei 21.2
Brunel 9.16
brunette 9.51
brunettes 9.52
Brunhild 17.18
Bruno 35.18
Brunswick 38.15
brunt 37.40
bruschetta 10.10
brush 37.46
brushmark 3.3
brushmarks 3.4
brushwood 39.4
brushwork 11.4
brushy 38.7
brusque 37.44
brusquely 42.1
brusquerie 42.36
Brussels 38.25
Brussels sprout 29.14
Brussels sprouts
29.15
brut 41.27
brutal 42.16
brutality 2.57
brutalization 8.52
brutalize 21.46
brutally 42.36
brute 41.27
brutes 41.28
brutish 42.29
Brutus 42.26
Bryant 22.24
Brylcreem® 15.20
Bryn 17.29
Brynner 18.13
bryology 24.55
bryony 22.40
Bryony 22.40
bryophyte 21.34
Bryson 22.20
Brythonic 24.19
BSc 15.4
BSE 15.4
bub 37.1
bubble 38.23
bubble gum 37.27

bubbler 38.12
bubbles 38.25
bubblier 38.49
bubbliest 38.61
bubbling 38.34
bubbly 38.5
bubonic 24.19
buccal 38.23
buccaneer 13.1
Bucephalus 10.70
Buchan 38.28
Buchanan 2.35
Bucharest 9.49
buck 37.3
Buck 37.3
buckaroo 41.4
bucket 38.43
bucketed 38.50
bucketful 39.7
Buckfast 3.30
Buckingham 38.53
Buckinghamshire
13.1
buckle 38.23
buckler 38.12
Buckley 38.5
buckling 38.34
buckminsterfullerene
15.26
buckram 38.26
bucks 37.4
Bucks 37.4
buck's fizz 17.56
buckshee 15.2
buckshot 23.44
buckskin 38.27
buckteeth 15.37
buckthorn 25.22
bucktooth 41.29
buckwheat 15.35
bucolic 24.18
bud 37.8
Budapest 9.49
Buddha 40.2
Buddh Gaya 3.1
Buddhism 18.27
Buddhist 40.14
buddies 38.46
budding 38.34
buddleia 38.49
buddy 38.3
Buddy Holly 24.5
Bude 41.9
budge 37.15
budgerigar 3.1
budget 38.43
budgetary 38.47
budgeted 38.50

budgie 38.7
budging 38.34
Budleigh 38.5
buds 37.9
Budweiser® 22.9
buff 37.10
buffalo 35.19
buffer 38.11
buffers 38.45
buffet 38.43
buffet 7.3
buffeted 38.50
buffeting 38.58
buffoon 41.19
buffoonery 42.36
bug 37.14
Buganda 2.10
Bugatti 2.3
bugbear 5.1
bugger 38.9
buggered 38.20
buggery 38.47
bugging 38.34
Buggins 38.30
buggy 38.2
bugle 42.16
bugler 42.7
bugleweed 15.11
bugloss 23.39
Bugner 38.13
Buick 42.11
build 17.18
builder 18.10
builders 18.55
building 18.40
building blocks 23.5
buildings 18.41
build-up 37.41
built 17.21
built-in 17.29
built-up 37.41
Bulawayo 35.6
bulb 37.17
bulbar 38.8
bulbous 38.38
bulbul 39.7
Bulgaria 6.16
Bulgarian 6.19
bulge 37.22
bulges 38.45
bulging 38.34
bulgur 38.9
bulimia 18.61
bulimic 18.16
bulk 37.18
bulked 37.19
bulkhead 9.8
bulkier 38.49

bulkiest 38.61
bulking 38.34
bulky 38.2
bull 39.7
bulla 40.2
bulldog 23.11
bulldoze 35.52
bulldozer 36.9
bulldozing 36.24
Bullen 40.10
bullet 40.17
bulletin 17.29
bulletins 17.42
bulletproof 41.10
bullfight 21.33
bullfighter 22.5
bullfighting 22.26
bullfinch 17.33
bullfrog 23.11
bullied 40.3
bullies 40.19
bullion 40.23
bullish 40.16
bull-necked 9.5
bullock 37.3
Bullock 37.3
bullring 40.15
bullshit 40.17
bullshitter 18.10
bullwhip 17.43
bully 40.1
bullyboy 33.1
bullyboys 33.15
Bulmer 40.2
bulrush 37.46
bulrushes 38.45
bulwark 37.3
Bulwer-Lytton 18.32
bum 37.27
bumble 38.23
bumblebee 15.4
bumbler 38.12
bumbling 38.34
bumf 37.28
bumfluff 37.10
bummalo 35.19
bummer 38.13
bumming 38.34
bump 37.29
bumper 38.8
bumpier 38.49
bumpiest 38.61
bumpkin 38.27
bumps 37.30
bumptious 38.38
bumpy 38.1
bun 37.31
Bunbury 38.47

bunch 37.35
bunches 38.45
bunchy 38.7
Bundesbank 1.25
Bundesrat 3.32
Bundestag 3.11
bundle 38.23
bundles 38.25
bunfight 21.33
bung 37.37
bungalow 35.19
bungalows 35.52
bungee 15.3; 38.7
bungle 38.23
bungled 38.24
bungler 38.12
bungling 38.34
bunion 38.28
bunions 38.31
bunk 37.32
bunker 38.9
bunkhouse 29.12
bunks 37.33
bunkum 38.26
bunny 38.6
Bunsen 38.28
bunt 37.40
Bunter 38.10
bunting 38.34
Bunty 38.3
Bunyan 38.28
bunyip 17.43
buoy 33.1
buoyage 34.4
buoyancy 34.14
buoyant 34.9
buoyed 33.4
buoys 33.15
BUPA 42.3
Burbage 12.7
Burberry® 12.29
burble 12.8
burbles 12.9
burbot 12.24
burden 12.12
burdened 12.13
burdensome 12.33
burdock 23.3
bureau 35.15
bureaucracy 24.54
bureaucrat 1.45
bureaucratic 2.17
bureaucratize 21.45
Burford 12.5
burgeon 12.12
burger 12.2
burgess 12.18
Burgess 12.18

burgher 12.2
Burghley 12.1
burglar 12.2
burglarious 6.22
burglarize 21.43
burglary 12.29
burgle 12.8
burgomaster 4.10
Burgoyne 33.8
Burgundian 38.54
Burgundy 12.29
burial 10.60
buried 10.17
burier 10.57
burin 28.7
burka 12.2
Burke 11.4
Burke and Hare 5.1
Burkitt 12.25
burlesque 9.48
Burlington 12.34
burly 12.1
Burma 12.2
Burman 12.12
Burmese 15.43
burn 11.15
burned 11.16
burner 12.2
Burnett 9.51; 12.25
Burney 12.1
Burnham 12.10
burning 12.16
burnish 12.22
burnished 12.23
Burnley 12.1
burnous 41.24
Burns 11.18
burnt 11.17
burp 11.19
burped 11.21
burping 12.16
burps 11.20
burr 11.1
Burrell 38.23
burrow 35.17
burrowed 35.25
burrowing 36.24
bursa 12.2
bursar 12.2
bursarial 6.17
bursarship 17.43
bursary 12.29
bursitis 22.28
burst 11.23
bursting 12.16
Burt 11.24
burthen 12.12
Burton 12.12

Burtonwood 39.4
Burundi 40.1
Burundian 40.23
bury 10.5
Bury 10.5
Bury St Edmunds
 10.30
bus 37.43
busby 38.1
buses 38.45
bush 39.13
Bush 39.13
bushbaby 8.1
bushcraft 3.10
bushel 40.6
Bushey 40.1
bushfire 19.1
Bushire 19.1
bushman 40.10
Bushman 40.10
bushmeat 15.35
Bushnell 40.6
bushranger 8.9
bushwalking 26.25
bushwhack 1.3
bushwhacker 2.9
bushy 40.1
busied 18.18
busier 18.61
busiest 18.76
busily 18.57
business 18.44
businesslike 21.7
businessman 1.24
businessmen 9.32
businesswoman
 40.10
businesswomen 18.31
busk 37.44
busker 38.9
busking 38.34
busman 38.28
buss 37.43
bust 37.45
bustard 38.20
busted 38.20
buster 38.10
bustle 38.23
bustling 38.34
busty 38.3
busy 18.7
busybody 24.3
busy Lizzie 18.7
but 37.47
butane 7.21
butch 39.3
butcher 40.2
butchered 40.4

butchery 40.20
Bute 41.27
butene 15.25
Buthelezi 8.1
butler 38.12
Butler 38.12
butlery 38.47
Butlins 38.30
butt 37.47
butte 41.27
butter 38.10
butterball 25.14
butter bean 15.26
butterbur 11.1
buttercup 37.41
butter dish 17.50
buttered 38.20
butterfat 1.45
Butterfield 15.18
butterfingers 18.55
butterflies 21.46
butterfly 21.4
Buttermere 13.1
buttermilk 17.16
butternut 37.47
butterscotch 23.7
Butterworth 11.26
buttery 38.47
butties 38.46
buttock 38.16
buttocks 38.17
button 38.28
buttoned 38.29
buttonhole 35.30
buttonholed 35.31
buttonholing 36.24
buttons 38.31
buttress 38.38
butty 38.3
butyl 21.16
buxom 38.26
Buxtehude 42.5
Buxton 38.28
buy 21.1
buyable 22.43
buy-back 1.3
buyer 22.2
buyers 22.39
buyout 29.14
buys 21.39
buzz 37.51
buzzard 38.20
buzzer 38.14
buzzing 38.34
buzz word 11.7
bwana 4.13
by 21.1
by and by 21.4

Byatt 22.34
bye 21.1
bye-bye 21.2
by-election 10.28
Byers 19.4
bygone 23.27
Bygraves 7.55
bylaw 25.3
by-line 21.22
Byng 17.35
bypass 3.26
bypassed 3.30
bypassing 4.29
Byrd 11.7
byre 19.1
Byrne 11.15
byroad 35.25
byroads 35.26
Byron 22.20
Byronic 24.19
Byron's 22.23
Bysshe 17.50
bystander 2.10
bystreet 15.35
byte 21.31
byway 7.3
byways 7.56
byword 11.7
Byzantine 15.26; 21.22
C 15.1
cab 1.1
cabal 1.16
caballero 35.5
cabana 4.13
cabaret 7.4
cabbage 2.27
cabbages 2.76
cabbagy 2.58
cabbala 4.12
cabbie 2.1
cabbies 2.54
caber 8.3
cabin 2.34
cabinet 2.74
cabinet-maker 8.4
cabinetry 2.78
cabinetwork 11.4
cabins 2.38
cable 8.15
cable car 3.1
cabled 8.16
cablegram 1.22
cabling 8.62
cabman 2.35
cabochon 23.27
caboodle 42.16
caboose 41.24
Cabot 2.50

cabotage 3.13
cabriole 35.30
cabriolet 7.2
cabs 1.2
cacao 29.1
cacciatore 26.1
cachalot 23.44
cache 1.43
cachepot 35.3
cachet 7.3
cachou 41.2
cack-handed 2.25
cackle 2.28
cackler 2.12
cacky 2.2
cacodemon 16.22
cacomistle 18.22
cacophonous 24.70
cacophony 24.54
cacti 21.3
cactus 2.46
cad 1.9
cadaster 2.10
cadaver 2.11; 4.11; 8.6
cadaveric 17.3
Cadbury 2.56
CADCAM 1.22
caddie 2.3
caddied 2.24
caddies 2.54
caddis 2.45
caddish 2.49
caddy 2.3
cadence 8.57
cadenza 10.14
Cader Idris 18.43
cadet 9.51
cadets 9.52
cadge 1.15
cadger 2.14
cadging 2.42
Cadillac 1.3
Cadiz 17.56
cadre 4.10
cads 1.10
caduceus 42.46
Cadwallader 24.57
caecum 16.20
Caedmon 2.35
Caen 23.31
Caernarfon 4.24
Caerphilly 18.5
Caesar 16.9
Caesarea 16.2
Caesarean 6.19
caesium 16.42
caesura 28.2
café 2.4; 7.3

café au lait 7.2
cafés 2.54
cafeteria 14.18
cafetiere 5.1
caff 1.11
caffeine 15.25
cag 1.13
cage 7.12
cage bird 11.7
caged 7.13
cagey 8.1
Cagliari 4.5
Cagney 2.6
cagoule 41.14
Cahill 17.15
cahoots 41.28
Caiaphas 1.40
Cain 7.21
cairn 5.4
Cairngorm 25.20
Cairo 35.12
caisson 8.21
Caithness 9.47
Caius 22.29
cajole 35.30
cajoled 35.31
cajolement 36.22
cajolery 36.35
cajoling 36.24
Cajun 8.21
cake 7.6
caked 7.7
Calabar 3.1
calabash 1.43
calaboose 41.24
calabrese 8.1
Calabrian 2.66
Calais 7.3
calamari 4.5
calamine 21.22
calamitous 2.71
calamity 2.57
calcareous 6.22
calceolaria 6.16
calcify 21.4
calculable 2.79
calculate 7.35
calculated 8.13
calculating 8.60
calculation 8.24
calculations 8.55
calculator 8.5
calculus 2.71
Calcutta 38.10
Calder 24.10; 26.4
caldera 6.2
Calderdale 7.15
Caldwell 9.16

Caldy 24.3; 26.1
Caleb 9.1
Caledonia 36.37
Caledonian 36.40
calendar 2.60
calender 2.60
calendrical 10.60
calends 2.37
calf 3.9
calf-length 9.37
calfskin 4.23
Calgary 2.56
Caliban 1.24
calibrate 7.35
calibration 8.24
calibrator 8.5
calibre 2.60
calico 35.19
California 26.39
Californian 26.43
Californians 26.44
californium 26.42
Caligula 18.60
caliph 17.10
caliphate 7.37
call 25.14
Callaghan 1.24; 2.66
Callaghan's 1.36
Callan 2.35
Callanetics 10.16
Callas 2.46
called 25.15
caller 26.6
callers 26.36
call girl 11.11
calligrapher 18.60
calligraphic 2.18
calligraphy 18.56
Callimachus 18.74
calling 26.25
calliper 2.60
callipygian 18.67
callipygous 22.29
callisthenic 10.15
callisthenics 10.16
callous 2.46
callously 2.56
callousness 2.71
callow 35.3
calls 25.19
call the shots 23.45
call-up 37.41
callus 2.46
calm 3.16
calmative 17.55
calmed 3.17
calmer 4.13
calmest 4.34

calming 4.29
calmly 4.5
calmness 4.32
Calor® 2.12
Calor gas® 1.40
caloric 17.3; 24.18
calorie 2.56
calories 2.77
calorific 18.16
calorimeter 18.60
Calpurnia 12.31
calque 1.17
Caltech 9.2
Calum 2.32
calumniate 7.48
calumniation 8.38
calumny 2.56
Calum's 2.33
Calvados 23.39
Calvary 2.56
calve 3.35
Calvert 2.50
calves 3.36
Calvin 2.34
calving 4.29
Calvinism 18.28
Calvinist 2.73
calypso 35.11
calyx 8.11
cam 1.22
Cam 1.22
camaraderie 4.42
Camargue 3.11
camber 2.8
Camberwell 9.16
cambium 2.65
Cambodia 36.37
Cambodian 36.40
Cambria 2.61
Cambrian 2.66
cambric 2.19
Cambridge 8.14
Cambridgeshire 8.77;
13.1
camcorder 26.4
Camden 2.35
Camden Town 29.5
came 7.18
camel 2.28
cameleer 13.1
camel hair 5.1
camellia 16.40
camelopard 3.8
Camelot 23.44
Camembert 5.1
cameo 35.19
camera 2.12; 2.60
cameraman 1.24

cameramen 9.32
camera obscura 28.2
Cameron 2.66
Cameroon 41.19
camiknickers 18.55
Camilla 18.12
Camille 15.17
camisole 35.30
camomile 21.16
camouflage 3.13
camp 1.23
Campagna 4.12
campaign 7.21
campaigner 8.8
campaigners 8.75
campaigning 8.63
campanologist 24.72
campanology 24.55
campanula 2.60
Campari® 4.5
Campbell 2.28
Campbeltown 29.5
Camp David 8.12
camper 2.8
campestral 10.21
campfire 19.1
campfires 19.4
camphor 2.11
camphoric 24.18
camping 2.42
campion 2.66
Campion 2.66
campsite 21.33
campsites 21.35
campus 2.46
CAMRA 2.12
camshaft 3.10
Camus 41.2
can 1.24
Cana 8.8
Canaan 8.21
Canaanite 21.34
Canaanites 21.35
Canada 2.60
Canadian 8.81
Canadianism 18.29
canal 1.16
Canaletto 35.7
canapé 7.4
canapés 7.56
canard 3.8
Canaries 6.14
canary 6.1
canasta 2.10
Canaveral 2.64
Canberra 2.60
cancan 1.24
cancel 2.28

cancellation 8.24
cancellations 8.55
cancer 2.14
Cancer 2.14
Cancerian 14.21
cancerous 2.71
candela 10.12
candelabra 4.12
candelabrum 4.22
candid 2.24
Candida 2.60
candidate 2.74; 7.35
candidature 8.9
Candide 15.11
candidly 2.58
candied 2.24
candies 2.54
candle 2.28
candleholder 36.5
candlelight 21.34
candlelit 17.51
Candlemas 1.40
candlepower 31.1
candlestick 17.3
candlesticks 17.4
candlewick 17.3
candour 2.10
candy 2.3
candyfloss 23.39
candytuft 37.12
cane 7.21
caned 7.22
caner 8.8
canine 21.22
caning 8.63
canister 2.60
canker 2.9
cankerous 2.71
cannabis 17.46
canned 1.28
cannelloni 36.1
canner 2.13
cannery 2.56
Cannes 1.24; 1.36
cannibal 2.64
cannibalism 18.29
cannibalistic 18.16
cannibalization 8.53
cannibalize 21.47
cannier 2.61
canniest 2.72
cannily 2.58
canning 2.42
Canning 2.42
Cannock 2.16
cannon 2.35
cannonade 7.8
cannonball 25.14

cannonry 2.56
cannot 2.50; 23.44
canny 2.6
canoe 41.2
canoeing 42.24
canoeist 42.28
canoes 41.33
canon 2.35
canonic 24.19
canonical 24.61
canonicals 24.62
canonization 8.40
canonize 21.42
canonry 2.56
canoodle 42.16
can-opener 36.36
Canopic 24.16
canopied 2.62; 17.8
Canopus 36.26
canopy 2.56
cans 1.36
cant 1.33
can't 3.23
Cantab. 1.1
Cantabrian 2.66
Cantabrigian 18.67
cantaloupe 41.22
cantankerous 2.71
cantata 4.10
canteen 15.24
canter 2.10
Canterbury 2.56; 2.78
cantharides 15.45
canticle 2.64
cantilever 16.6
canto 35.3
canton 2.35; 23.27
Canton 23.27
Cantonese 15.45
Cantuar. 3.1
cantus 2.46
Canuck 37.3
Canute 41.27
canvas 2.46
canvass 2.46
canvassed 2.48
canvasser 2.60
canvassing 2.70
Canvey 2.4
canyon 2.35
cap 1.37
capabilities 18.79
capability 18.58
capable 8.79
capacious 8.67
capacitance 2.69
capacitate 7.35
capacitor 2.60

capacity 2.57
caparison 2.66
cape 7.27
Cape 7.27
Cape Horn 25.22
capellmeister 22.5
caper 8.3
capercaillie 8.1
capered 8.13
capers 8.75
Capet 9.51
Cape Town 29.5
Cape Verde 11.7
capful 39.7
capillarity 2.57
capillary 18.56
capital 2.64
capitalism 18.29
capitalist 17.49
capitalization 8.53
capitalize 21.47
capitation 8.24
Capitol 2.64
Capitoline 21.22
capitulate 7.41
capitulation 8.32
capitulum 18.66
caplet 2.51
cap'n 2.35
capo 35.3
capon 8.21
Capone 35.36
Capote 36.1
Cappadocia 36.37
Cappadocian 36.40
capping 2.42
cappuccino 35.10
Capri 15.2
capriccio 35.19
caprice 15.32
capricious 18.44
Capricorn 25.22
Capricornean 26.43
caps 1.38
capsicum 2.65
capsize 21.40
capstan 2.35
capstone 35.36
capsule 41.14
capsules 41.16
captain 2.34
Captain Cook 39.1
captaincy 2.58
captains 2.38
captainship 17.43
caption 2.35
captious 2.46
captivate 7.35

captivating 8.60
captivation 8.24
captive 2.53
captivity 18.57
captor 2.10
capture 2.14
captured 2.25
capuchin 17.29
Capuchin 17.29
Capuchins 17.42
Capulet 2.74
capybara 4.12
car 3.1
carabineer 13.1
carabiner 16.8
carabiniere 6.1
caracal 1.16
Caracalla 2.12
Caracas 2.46
caracole 35.30
Caradoc 2.16
carafe 1.11
carafe 3.9
carafes 1.12
caramel 2.64
caramel 9.16
caramelization 8.53
caramelize 21.47
carapace 7.30
carat 2.50
Caratacus 2.71
caravan 1.24
caravanner 2.13
caravans 1.36
caravanserai 21.4
caravel 9.16
caraway 7.4
carb 3.2
carbide 21.11
carbine 21.22
carbohydrate 7.34
carbolic 24.18
carbon 4.24
carbonade 7.8
carbonara 4.12
Carbonari 4.5
carbonate 7.36
carbonation 8.25
carbonic 24.19
Carboniferous 18.74
carbonization 8.41
carbonize 21.42
carbonyl 21.16
Carborundum® 38.26
carboxylic 18.16
carbuncle 38.23
carburettor 10.10
carcajou 41.4

carcass 4.32
carcinogen 18.67
carcinogen 9.32
carcinogenic 10.15
carcinoma 36.8
card 3.8
cardamom 4.49
cardboard 25.9
carder 4.10
Cardew 41.3
cardholder 36.5
cardiac 1.3
cardie 4.3
Cardiff 17.10
cardigan 4.50
Cardigan 4.50
cardinal 4.47
cardinalship 17.43
cardiogram 1.22
cardiograph 1.11; 3.9
cardiographic 2.18
cardiologist 24.72
cardiology 24.55
cardiovascular 2.60
cardphone 35.36
cardsharp 3.25
Cardus 4.32
care 5.1
cared 5.2
careen 15.24
career 13.1
careered 13.2
careerism 18.27
careerist 14.15
careers 13.5
carefree 6.1; 15.3
careful 6.4; 39.7
carefully 6.15
carefulness 6.22
caregiver 18.11
caregivers 18.55
careless 6.11
carelessly 6.15
carelessness 6.22
carer 6.2
cares 5.5
caress 9.47
caressed 9.49
caressing 10.36
caret 2.50
caretaker 8.4
Carew 41.2
careworn 25.22
Carey 6.1
car ferry 10.5
carful 39.7
Cargill 17.15
cargo 35.4

cargoes 35.52
Carib 17.1
Caribbean 16.22
Cariboo 41.4
caribou 41.4
caricature 27.1
caricatured 27.2
caricaturing 28.11
caricaturist 28.14
CARICOM 23.23
caries 15.44
CARIFTA 18.10
carillon 18.32
caring 6.10
Carinthia 18.61
carious 6.22
Carisbrooke 39.1
Carl 3.14
Carla 4.12
Carling 4.29
Carlisle 21.16
Carlo 35.4
Carlos 4.32; 23.39
Carlovingian 18.67
Carlow 35.4
Carlsberg 11.9
Carlton 4.24
Carly 4.5
Carlyle 21.16
Carmarthen 4.24
Carmel 4.19; 9.16
Carmelite 21.34
Carmelites 21.35
Carmen 4.24
Carmichael 22.16
Carmina Burana 4.13
carmine 21.22
Carnaby 4.42
Carnaby Street 15.35
Carnac 1.3
carnage 4.18
carnal 4.19
Carnatic 2.17
carnation 8.23
carnations 8.55
Carnegie 4.42; 8.1;
  16.1
carnet 7.3
Carney 4.6
Carnforth 25.33
carnival 4.47
carnivore 25.4
carnivorous 18.74
Carnot 35.4
Carnoustie 42.1
carob 2.15
carol 2.28
Carol 2.28

Carolina 22.8
Caroline 21.22
Carolingian 18.67
caroller 2.60
carols 2.30
Carolyn 17.29
Carolyn's 17.42
carom 2.32
carotene 15.26
carotid 24.23
carousal 30.6
carouse 29.17
carousel 9.16
carouser 30.2
carousing 30.12
carp 3.25
carpal 4.19
car park 3.3
carpe diem 9.28
carpel 4.19
Carpentaria 6.16
carpenter 4.43
carpentry 4.42
carper 4.8
carpet 4.38
carpetbag 1.13
carpetbagger 2.9
carpetbaggers 2.55
carpeted 4.45
carpeting 4.52
carping 4.29
carport 25.31
carpus 4.32
Carr 3.1
carrack 2.16
carrageen 15.26
Carrara 4.12
carrel 2.28
Carreras 6.11
carriage 2.27
carriage clock 23.3
carriages 2.76
carriageway 7.4
Carrickfergus 12.19
Carrie 2.5
carried 2.24
carrier 2.61
Carrington 2.66
carrion 2.66
Carroll 2.28
carrot 2.50
carroty 2.56
Carruthers 38.45
carry 2.5
carryall 25.14
carrycot 23.44
carry-on 23.27
carry-out 29.14

carry the can 1.24
cars 3.37
Carshalton 24.33
Carshalton 26.19
carsick 4.16
Carson 4.24
Carstairs 5.5
cart 3.32
carte blanche 3.20
cartel 9.16
carter 4.10
Carter 4.10
Cartesian 16.22
Cartesian 16.43
Carthage 4.18
Carthaginian 18.67
carthorse 25.28
Carthusian 42.41
Cartier 7.4
cartilage 17.14
cartilaginous 2.71
Cartland 4.25
cartload 35.25
cartloads 35.26
cartographer 24.57
cartographic 2.18
cartography 24.54
cartomancy 2.7
carton 4.24
cartoon 41.19
cartoonist 42.28
cartoons 41.21
cartouche 41.26
cartridge 4.18
carts 3.33
cartwheel 15.17
cartwright 21.33
Cartwright 21.33
carve 3.35
carvel 4.19
carven 4.24
carver 4.11
Carver 4.11
carvery 4.42
carving 4.29
carvings 4.30
car wash 23.42
Cary 2.5
caryatid 2.24
Casablanca 2.9
Casanova 36.6
cascade 7.8
cascading 8.60
cascara 4.12
case 7.30
casebook 39.1
casebound 29.6
casement 8.56

caseous 8.85
casework 11.4
Casey 8.1
cash 1.43
cashable 2.64
cashback 1.3
cash book 39.1
cashbox 23.5
cashed 1.44
cashew 41.2
cash flow 35.3
cashier 13.1
cashless 2.46
cashmere 13.1
cashpoint 33.10
Casimir 13.1
casing 8.64
casino 35.10
cask 3.27
casket 4.38
Caspar 2.8; 3.1
casque 3.27
Cassandra 2.12; 4.12
cassata 4.10
cassava 4.11
Cassell 2.28
casserole 35.30
casseroled 35.31
casseroling 36.24
cassette 9.51
cassettes 9.52
cassia 2.61
Cassidy 2.57
Cassie 2.7
Cassiopeia 16.2
cassis 15.32
Cassius 2.71
cassock 2.16
cassocks 2.22
Casson 2.35
cassoulet 7.4
cassowary 6.1
cast 3.30
castanets 9.52
castaway 7.4
castaways 7.56
caste 3.30
castellated 8.13
caster 4.10
Casterbridge 17.14
casters 4.41
castigate 7.35
castigation 8.24
Castiglione 36.1
Castile 15.17
Castilian 18.32; 18.67
casting 4.29
castings 4.30

cast iron 22.20
castle 4.19
Castleford 4.45
Castleford's 4.46
Castle Howard 31.2
Castlereagh 7.4
castles 4.21
castoff 23.9
castor 4.10
Castor 4.10
castor oil 33.6
castrate 7.33
castration 8.23
castrato 35.4
Castrol® 23.15
casual 2.64
casually 2.59; 2.78
casualty 2.78
casuarina 16.8
casuistry 2.78
cat 1.45
catabolic 24.18
cataclysm 18.28
cataclysmic 18.16
catacomb 41.17
catafalque 1.17
Catalan 1.24
catalepsy 10.7
cataleptic 10.15
catalogue 23.11
cataloguer 24.9
Catalonia 36.37
catalyse 21.42
catalysis 17.46
catalyst 2.73
catalytic 18.16
catamaran 1.24
catamarans 1.36
catamite 21.34
catamount 29.11
catananche 2.2
cataphora 2.60
cataphoric 24.18
cataplasm 2.32
cataplexy 10.7
catapult 37.26
cataract 1.6
catarrh 3.1
catarrhal 4.19
catastrophe 2.56
catastrophic 24.17
catastrophically 24.56
catatonia 36.37
catatonic 24.19
catboat 35.45
catcall 25.14
catch 1.7
Catch-22 41.2

catchable 2.64
catch-all 25.14
catcher 2.14
catchier 2.61
catchiest 2.72
catching 2.42
catchment 2.40
catchphrase 7.56
catchword 11.7
catchy 2.7
catechism 18.28
catechize 21.42
catecholamine 15.26
categoric 24.18
categorical 24.61
categorically 24.56
categorization 8.53
categorize 21.47
category 2.58
catenary 16.38
cater 8.5
catered 8.13
caterer 8.77
Caterham 8.80
catering 8.84
caterpillar 18.12
caterpillars 18.55
caterwaul 25.14
caterwauled 25.15
caterwauling 26.25
Catesby 8.1
catfight 21.33
catfish 2.49
catfood 41.9
Catford 2.25
catgut 37.47
Cath 1.47
catharsis 4.31
cathartic 4.16
Cathay 7.2
Cathcart 3.32
cathedra 16.7
cathedral 16.17
Catherine 17.29
Catherine's 17.42
catheter 2.60
catheterize 21.47
cathode 35.25
cathodic 24.16
catholic 17.3
Catholic 17.3
Catholicism 18.28
catholicize 21.45
Catholics 17.4
Cath's 1.48
Cathy 2.4
cation 22.20
catkin 2.34

catkins 2.38
catlike 21.7
catmint 17.39
catnap 1.37
catnapped 1.39
catnapping 2.42
catnip 17.43
Cato 35.6
cat-o'-nine-tails 7.17
Catriona 16.8
cats 1.46
Catseye® 21.3
Catskill 17.15
catsuit 41.27
Catterick 17.3
cattery 2.56
cattiness 2.71
cattle 2.28
cattleman 2.66
cattle prod 23.8
catty 2.3
Catullan 38.28
Catullus 38.38
catwalk 25.6
Caucasia 8.78
Caucasia 8.9
Caucasian 8.21; 8.81
Caucasoid 33.4
Caucasus 26.47
caucus 26.27
caudal 26.15
caught 25.31
caul 25.14
cauldron 24.33; 26.19
cauliflower 31.1
caulk 25.6
causal 26.15
causality 2.57
causation 8.23
causative 17.55
cause 25.35
cause célèbre 10.12
causeless 26.27
causer 26.8
causerie 36.35
causes 26.36
causeway 7.3
causing 26.25
caustic 26.9
cauterize 21.45
cautery 26.37
caution 26.19
cautionary 26.37
cautioned 26.20
cautious 26.27
cautiously 26.37
cautiousness 26.47
cavalcade 7.8

cavalier 13.1
Cavalier 13.1
Cavaliers 13.5
cavalry 2.56
cavalryman 1.24
Cavan 2.35
cavatina 16.8
cave 8.1
caveat 1.45
cave-dweller 10.12
Cavell 2.28
caveman 1.24
cavemen 9.32
Cavendish 17.50
caver 8.6
cavern 2.35
cavernous 2.71
caverns 2.39
caves 7.55
cavewoman 40.10
cavewomen 18.31
caviar 3.1
caving 8.61
cavities 2.77
cavity 2.57
cavort 25.31
cavorting 26.25
cavorts 25.32
Cavour 27.1
cavy 8.1
caw 25.1
Cawdrey 26.1
cawed 25.9
Cawley 26.1
Cawnpore 25.3
Caxton 2.35
cay 7.1
cayenne 9.32
cayman 8.21
Cayman 8.21
CB 15.2
CBI 21.4
cc 15.2
CD 15.2
CD-ROM 23.23
CDs 15.43
ceanothus 36.26
cease 15.32
ceased 15.33
cease-fire 19.1
ceaseless 16.30
ceaselessly 16.38
ceasing 16.27
Cecil 10.21; 18.22
Cecile 15.17
Cecilia 16.40
Cecily 10.54

cedar 16.5
cedars 16.37
cede 15.11
cedilla 18.12
Cedric 10.15
Ceefax® 1.4
ceilidh 8.1
ceiling 16.27
cel 9.16
celandine 21.22
celeb 9.1
Celebes 15.45
celebrant 10.67
celebrate 7.38
celebrated 8.13
celebration 8.28
celebratory 8.76
celebrities 10.77
celebrity 10.54
celeriac 1.3
celerity 10.54
celery 10.53
celesta 10.10
celeste 9.49
celestial 10.60
Celia 16.40
celibacy 10.78
Céline 15.24
cell 9.16
cellar 10.12
Cellini 16.1
cellist 10.44
cello 35.7
Cellophane® 7.21
cellphone 35.36
cells 9.27
cellular 10.56
cellule 41.14
cellulite 21.34
celluloid 33.4
cellulose 35.42; 35.52
Celsius 10.70
Celt 9.23
Celtic 10.15
Celticism 18.28
cement 9.41
cemetery 10.54
Cenotaph 1.11; 3.9
Cenozoic 36.10
cense 9.39
censer 10.14
censor 10.14
censored 10.18
censoring 10.69
censorious 26.47
censorship 17.43
censure 10.14
censured 10.18

census 10.42
cent 9.41
centaur 25.3
Centaurus 26.27
centaury 26.1
centenarian 6.19
centenary 16.38
centennial 10.60
centesimal 10.60
centigrade 7.8
centigram 1.22
centile 21.16
centilitre 16.5
centime 15.20
centimetre 16.5
centipede 15.11
centipedes 15.12
central 10.21
centralism 18.28
centrality 2.57
centralization 8.43
centralize 21.43
centralized 21.48
centrally 10.53
centre 10.10
centreboard 25.9
centred 10.18
centrefold 35.31
centrepiece 15.32
centre spread 9.8
centrifugal 18.64;
  42.16
centrifugally 42.36
centrifugation 8.43
centrifuge 41.12
centripetal 16.17;
  18.64
cents 9.39
centuple 42.16
centuplicate 7.49
centuplication 8.39
centurial 28.19
centurion 28.21
century 10.53
cep 9.44
cephalic 2.19
Cephalonia 36.37
cephalopod 23.8
ceps 9.45
ceramic 2.20
ceramics 2.23
Cerberus 12.37
cere 13.1
cereal 14.19
cerebellar 10.12
cerebellum 10.25
cerebral 10.60
cerebration 8.28

cerebrospinal 22.16
cerebrum 16.20
cerecloth 23.46
cerement 14.10
ceremonial 36.38
ceremonious 36.42
ceremony 10.78
Ceres 15.44
Ceri 10.5
cerise 15.32
cerise 15.43
cerium 14.20
CERN 11.15
Cerne Abbas 2.46
cert 11.24
certain 12.12
certainly 12.29
certainty 12.29
certes 12.28
certifiable 22.43
certificate 18.77
certification 8.44
certified 21.12
certify 21.4
certitude 41.9
cerulean 42.41
Cervantes 2.54; 15.44
cervical 12.32; 22.16
cervix 17.4
cess 9.47
cessation 8.23
cession 10.28
Cessna 10.13
cesspit 10.48
cesspool 14.14
c'est la vie 15.4
cetacean 8.23
Ceylon 23.27
Cézanne 1.24
CFC 15.4
Chablis 2.5
Chabrier 7.4
cha-cha-cha 3.1
chad 1.9
Chad 1.9
chador 38.10
Chadwick 2.19
chafe 7.10
chafer 8.6
chaff 1.11
chaff 3.9
chaffed 3.10
chaffer 2.11
chaffinch 17.33
chaffing 2.42
chafing 8.61
Chagall 1.16
chagrin 2.34

Chaim 21.19
chain 7.21
chained 7.22
chainplate 7.34
chains 7.26
chain saw 25.3
chair 5.1
chairborne 25.22
chairbound 29.6
chairlift 17.11
chairman 6.7
chairmanship 17.43
chairperson 12.12
chairs 5.5
chairwoman 40.10
chaise 7.56
chaise longue 23.31
chakra 2.12
chalaza 8.9
Chalcedon 2.66
chalcedony 10.53
Chalcidice 18.57
Chaldea 16.2
Chaldean 16.22
chalet 7.3
Chalfont 23.34
chalice 2.45
chalk 25.6
chalk and cheese
  15.45
Chalker 26.3
chalkface 7.30
chalkier 26.39
chalkiest 26.49
chalkpit 26.32
chalky 26.1
challenge 2.43; 17.37
challenger 2.60
challenges 2.76
challenging 2.70;
  18.40
Challis 2.45
Chalmers 4.41
chamber 8.3
chamberlain 17.29
Chamberlain 17.29
chambermaid 7.8
chamber pot 23.44
chambers 8.75
Chambers 8.75
chambré 7.3
chameleon 16.43
chameleonic 24.19
chamfer 2.11
chamois 2.6; 3.1
Chamonix 2.56
champ 1.23
champagne 7.21

checkers 10.52
checking 10.36
check list 10.44
checkmate 7.34
checkout 29.14
checkpoint 33.10
checkrail 7.15
checks 9.3
checkup 37.41
Cheddar 10.10
cheek 15.7
cheekbone 35.36
cheek by jowl 29.4
cheekier 16.40
cheekiest 16.49
cheekily 16.38
cheeks 15.8
cheeky 16.1
cheep 15.30
cheer 13.1
cheered 13.2
cheerful 14.6; 39.7
cheerfulness 14.23
cheerier 14.18
cheering 14.12
cheerio 35.19
cheerleader 16.5
cheerleaders 16.37
cheerless 14.14
cheers 13.5
cheery 14.1
Cheeryble 14.19
cheese 15.42
cheeseboard 25.9
cheeseburger 12.2
cheesecake 7.6
cheesecloth 23.46
Cheeseman 16.22
cheesemonger 38.9
cheeseparing 6.10
cheesy 16.1
cheetah 16.5
Cheetham 16.20
Cheever 16.6
chef 9.10
chef-d'oeuvre 12.2
Che Guevara 4.12
Chekhov 23.47
Chekhov 23.9
Chekhovian 36.40
Chelmsford 10.18
Chelsea 10.7
Cheltenham 10.63
chemical 10.60
chemically 10.54
chemicals 10.62
chemin de fer 5.1
chemise 15.43

chemist 10.44
chemistry 10.54
chemo 35.10
chemotherapy 10.53
Cheney 8.1
chenille 15.17
cheongsam 1.22
Chepstow 35.7
cheque 9.2
chequebook 39.1
chequerboard 25.9
Chequers 10.52
cheques 9.3
Cher 5.1
Cherbourg 25.12
Cherie 15.2
cherish 10.45
cherished 10.46
Chernobyl 24.27
Chernobyl 36.15
chernozem 9.28
Cherokee 15.4
Cherokees 15.45
cheroot 41.27
cherries 10.51
cherry 10.5
chersonese 15.32
Chertsey 12.1
cherub 37.1
cherubic 42.11
cherubically 42.36
cherubim 17.24
Cherubini 16.1
chervil 12.8
chervil 17.15
Cherwell 4.19; 9.16
Cheryl 10.21
Chesapeake 15.7
Chesham 10.25
Cheshire 10.14; 13.1
Cheshire cat 1.45
Cheshunt 10.33
Chesney 10.6
chess 9.47
chessboard 25.9
Chessell 10.21
chessman 1.24
chessman 10.27
chessmen 9.32
chesspiece 15.32
chest 9.49
Chester 10.10
chesterfield 15.18
Chesterfield 15.18
Chesterton 10.64
chest-expander 2.10
chestnut 37.47
chestnuts 37.48

chesty 10.3
Chetnik 10.15
Chetwynd 17.34
cheval-de-frise 15.45
Chevalier 7.4
Chevette® 9.51
Cheviot 10.74; 16.50
Chevrolet 7.4
chevron 10.27
Chevy 10.4
chew 41.1
chewable 42.39
chewed 41.9
chewer 42.2
chewier 42.38
chewiest 42.47
chewing 42.24
chewing gum 37.27
chews 41.33
chew the cud 37.8
chewy 42.1
Cheyenne 1.24
chez nous 41.2
chi 21.1
Chiang Kai-shek 9.2
Chianti 2.3
chiaroscuro 35.15
chiasmus 2.46
chic 15.7
Chicago 35.4
chicane 7.21
chicanery 8.76
Chichester 18.60
Chichewa 8.7
chick 17.3
chickabiddy 18.3
chickadee 15.4
Chickasaw 25.4
chicken 18.31
chicken feed 15.11
chickenpox 23.5
chickens 18.36
chickpea 18.1
chicks 17.4
chickweed 15.11
chicle 18.22
Chico 35.10
chicory 18.56
chid 17.8
chide 21.9
chiding 22.26
chief 15.13
chiefly 16.1
chieftain 16.22
chieftains 16.24
chieftainship 17.43
chiffchaff 1.11
chiffon 23.27

chigger 18.9
chignon 23.27
Chigwell 18.22
Chihuahua 4.12
chilblain 7.21
chilblains 7.26
child 21.17
childbearing 6.10
childbed 9.8
childbirth 11.26
childcare 5.1
childhood 39.4
childish 22.32
childishly 22.40
childishness 22.46
childless 22.29
childlessness 22.46
childlike 21.7
child minder 22.5
childproof 41.10
child-rearing 14.12
children 18.32
child's play 7.3
Chile 18.5
Chilean 18.67
chill 17.15
chilled 17.18
chiller 18.12
chilli 18.5
chilli con carne 4.6
chillier 18.61
chilliest 18.76
chilling 18.40
chillingly 18.57
chilly 18.5
Chiltern 18.32
chime 21.19
chimed 21.20
chimera 14.2
chimeric 10.15
chimerical 10.60
chimes 21.21
chiming 22.26
chimney 18.6
chimney breast 9.49
chimneypiece 15.32
chimneypot 23.44
chimneypots 23.45
chimneys 18.54
chimney sweep 15.30
chimp 17.27
chimpanzee 15.4
chimps 17.28
chin 17.29
china 22.8
China 22.8
Chinagraph® 1.11; 3.9
Chinaman 22.44

Chinatown 29.5
chinaware 5.1
chinchilla 18.12
chin-chin 17.29
Chindit 18.50
chine 21.22
Chinese 15.43
Ching 17.35
chink 17.30
chinking 18.40
chinks 17.31
chinless 18.44
chino 35.10
chinoiserie 15.4
chinoiserie 4.42
Chinook 39.1; 41.6
chins 17.42
chinstrap 1.37
chintz 17.40
chintzy 18.7
chinwag 1.13
Chios 23.39
chip 17.43
chipboard 25.9
chipmunk 37.32
chipmunks 37.33
chipolata 4.10
chipped 17.45
Chippendale 7.15
Chippenham 18.66
chipper 18.8
chipping 18.40
chippy 18.1
chips 17.44
Chirac 1.3
Chirk 11.4
Chiron 22.20
chiropodist 24.72
chiropody 24.54
chiropractic 2.17
chiropractor 2.10
chirp 11.19
chirped 11.21
chirper 12.2
chirpier 12.31
chirpiest 12.39
chirpily 12.29
chirping 12.16
chirps 11.20
chirpy 12.1
chirrup 18.42
chirruping 18.73
chirrupy 18.56
chisel 18.22
chiselled 18.23
chiseller 18.60
Chisholm 18.27
Chiswick 18.16

chit 17.51
chitchat 1.45
chitin 22.19
Chittagong 23.31
chitterling 18.73
chitty 18.3
chivalric 17.3
chivalrous 18.74
chivalry 18.56
chive 21.37
Chivers 18.55
chives 21.38
chivy 18.4
chlamydia 18.61
Chloe 36.1
Chloe's 36.33
chlorate 7.34
chloric 26.9
chloride 21.11
chlorinate 7.44
chlorination 8.35
chlorine 15.25
chloroform 25.20
chlorophyll 17.15
chloroplast 1.42
choc 23.3
choccies 24.52
choccy 24.2
choc-ice 21.29
chock 23.3
chock-a-block 23.3
chocker 24.9
chocoholic 24.18
chocoholics 24.22
chocolate 24.48
chocolate 24.73
chocolatier 2.61
chocs 23.5
Choctaw 25.3
choice 33.11
choicer 34.2
choir 19.1
choirboy 33.1
choirboys 33.15
choirmaster 4.10
choke 35.21
choked 35.23
chokedamp 1.23
choker 36.4
chokes 35.22
chokey 36.1
choking 36.24
choler 24.12
cholera 24.57
choleric 17.3
cholesterol 23.15
Cholmondeley 38.5
chomp 23.24

chomped 23.25
chomping 24.40
Chomsky 24.2
choo-choo 41.3
chook 39.1
choose 41.33
chooser 42.9
choosier 42.38
choosiest 42.47
choosing 42.24
choosy 42.1
chop 23.36
chop and change 7.23
chophouse 29.12
Chopin 1.24
chopped 23.38
chopper 24.8
choppier 24.58
choppiest 24.71
choppiness 24.70
chopping 24.40
choppy 24.1
chops 23.37
chopstick 24.16
chopsticks 24.22
chop suey 42.1
choral 26.15
chorale 3.14
chord 25.9
chore 25.1
chorea 13.1
choreograph 1.11; 3.9
choreographer 24.57
choreographic 2.18
choreography 24.54
chores 25.35
choric 24.18
chorion 26.43
chorister 24.57
choristers 24.74
Chorley 26.1
Chorlton 26.19
chortle 26.15
chortling 26.25
chorus 26.27
chorused 26.29
chose 35.52
chosen 36.20
choucroute 41.27
Chou En-lai 21.4
chough 37.10
choux 41.1
chow 29.1
chowder 30.2
chow mein 7.21
Chrimbo 35.11
Chris 17.46
chrism 18.27

Chrissie 18.7
Christ 21.30
Christabel 9.16
Christadelphian
  10.64
Christchurch 11.6
christen 18.33
Christendom 18.66
christened 18.34
christening 18.73
Christiaan 3.19
Christian 18.33
Christiania 4.44
Christianity 2.57
Christianization 8.46
Christian name 7.18
Christian names 7.20
Christians 18.37
Christie 18.3
Christie's 18.54
Christina 16.8
Christine 15.25
Christingle 18.22
Christlike 21.7
Christmas 18.44
Christmassy 18.56
Christmastide 21.12
Christmastime 21.19
Christopher 18.60
chromatic 2.17
chromatography
  24.54
chrome 35.34
chromic 36.10
chromium 36.39
chromosomal 36.15
chromosome 35.34
chronic 24.19
chronicle 24.61
chronicler 24.57
Chronicles 24.62
chronograph 1.11; 3.9
chronologic 24.20
chronological 24.61
chronologically 24.56
chronology 24.55
chronometer 24.57
chronometric 10.15
chronometry 24.56
chrysalis 17.46
chrysanthemum 2.65
Chrysler 22.7
Chrysostom 18.66
chub 37.1
Chubb® 37.1
chubbier 38.49
chubbiest 38.61
chubbiness 38.59

chubby 38.1
chuck 37.3
Chuck 37.3
chucked 37.5
chucker 38.9
chuckle 38.23
chuckled 38.24
chuckler 38.12
Chuck's 37.4
chuff 37.10
chuffed 37.12
chuffing 38.34
chug 37.14
chugging 38.34
chukker 38.9
chum 37.27
chummy 38.6
chump 37.29
chunder 38.10
chunk 37.32
chunkier 38.49
chunkiest 38.61
chunks 37.33
chunky 38.2
Chunnel 38.23
chunter 38.10
church 11.6
churchgoer 36.2
churchgoers 36.34
Churchill 17.15
Churchillian 18.67
churching 12.16
churchman 12.12
churchwarden 26.19
churchwoman 40.10
churchwomen 18.31
churchyard 3.8
churl 11.11
churlish 12.22
churlishly 12.29
churn 11.15
churning 12.16
churns 11.18
chute 41.27
chutney 38.6
chutzpah 40.2
Chuzzlewit 17.51
chyle 21.16
chyme 21.19
CIA 7.4
ciabatta 2.10
ciao 29.1
Ciba-Geigy 22.1
Cibber 18.8
cicada 4.10
cicely 18.56
Cicely 18.56
Cicero 35.19

cicerone 36.1
Ciceronian 36.40
CID 15.4
cider 22.5
Cif® 17.10
cig 17.12
cigar 3.1
cigarette 9.51
cigarettes 9.52
cigarillo 35.11
cigars 3.37
ciggy 18.2
cilia 18.61
ciliary 18.56
cilium 18.66
Cilla 18.12
cinch 17.33
cinchona 36.8
Cincinnati 2.3
cincture 18.14
cinder 18.10
Cinderella 10.12
cinders 18.55
cindery 18.56
Cindy 18.3
cine 18.6
cineaste 1.42
cinema 18.60
cinemagoer 36.2
CinemaScope® 35.40
cinematic 2.17
cinematographer
   24.57
cinematographic 2.18
cinematography 24.54
Cinerama® 4.13
cineraria 6.16
cinerary 18.80
Cinna 18.13
cinnabar 3.1
cinnamon 18.67
cinquecento 35.7
Cinque Ports 25.32
Cinzano® 35.4
cipher 22.6
circa 12.2
circadian 8.81
Circassian 2.66
Circe 12.1
Circean 16.22
circle 12.8
circles 12.9
circlet 12.25
circling 12.16
circlip 17.43
circs 11.5
circuit 12.25
circuit breaker 8.4

circuitous 42.46
circuitry 12.29
circular 12.30
circularity 2.57
circularization 8.53
circularize 21.47
circulate 7.39
circulating 8.60
circulation 8.29
circumcise 21.43
circumcised 21.48
circumcision 18.33
circumference 38.57
circumflex 9.3
circumlocution 42.20
circumlocutory 42.36
circumnavigate 7.35
circumnavigation
   8.24
circumnavigator 8.5
circumscribe 21.5
circumscribed 21.6
circumscription 18.33
circumspect 9.5
circumspection 10.28
circumstance 1.31
circumstance 3.22
circumstantial 2.28
circumstantiate 7.35
circumvent 9.41
circumvention 10.28
circus 12.19
Circus Maximus 2.71
ciré 7.3
Cirencester 10.10
cirque 11.4
cirrhosis 36.25
cirrocumulus 42.46
cirrostratus 4.32; 8.67
cirrus 18.44
Cissie 18.7
cist 17.49
Cistercian 12.12
cistern 18.32
cistus 18.44
citadel 9.16; 18.64
citation 8.23
cite 21.31
cithera 18.60
cities 18.54
citified 21.12
citify 21.4
citizen 18.67
Citizen Kane 7.21
citizens 18.69
citizenship 17.43
citrate 7.34
citric 18.16

Citroën 18.32
citron 18.32
citronella 10.12
citrus 18.44
city 18.3
civet 18.50
civic 18.16
civil 18.22
civilian 18.32; 18.67
civilians 18.37
civility 18.58
civilization 18.46
civilize 21.44
civilized 21.48
civilizing 22.26
civilly 18.57
civil rights 21.35
civvies 18.54
CJD 15.4
clachan 2.35
clack 1.3
clacker 2.9
Clackmannan 2.35
Clacton 2.35
clad 1.9
Claddagh 2.10
cladding 2.42
clade 7.8
cladistics 18.17
clag 1.13
claim 7.18
claimant 8.56
claimants 8.57
claimed 7.19
claims 7.20
Claire 5.1
Claire's 5.5
clairvoyance 34.10
clairvoyant 34.9
clairvoyants 34.10
clam 1.22
clambake 7.6
clamber 2.8
clammy 2.6
clamorous 2.71
clamour 2.13
clamoured 2.25
clamouring 2.70
clamp 1.23
clampdown 29.5
clamper 2.8
clamshell 9.16
clan 1.24
Clancy 2.7
clandestine 10.26
clang 1.29
clanger 2.13
clanging 2.42

clangorous 2.71
clangour 2.13
clangour 2.9
clank 1.25
clanked 1.27
clanking 2.42
clannish 2.49
clans 1.36
clansman 2.35
clanswoman 40.10
clanswomen 18.31
clap 1.37
Clapham 2.32
clapometer 24.57
clapped 1.39
clapped out 29.14
clapper 2.8
clapperboard 25.9
clappers 2.55
clapping 2.42
claps 1.38
Clapton 2.35
claptrap 1.37
claque 1.3
Clara 4.12; 6.2
Clare 5.1
Clarence 2.41
Clarendon 2.66
claret 2.50
Clarice 2.45
Claridge's 2.76
clarification 8.40
clarified 21.12
clarify 21.4
clarinet 9.51
clarinets 9.52
clarinettist 10.44
clarion 2.66
Clarissa 18.14
clarity 2.57
Clark 3.3
Clarke 3.3
Clark Gable 8.15
clarkia 4.44
Clarkson 4.24
Clarrie 2.5
clarts 3.33
clarty 4.3
Clary 6.1
clash 1.43
clasp 3.29
class 3.26
classed 3.30
classes 4.41
classic 2.21
classical 2.64
classically 2.58
classicism 18.28

classicist 2.73
classics 2.23
classier 4.44
classiest 4.55
classifiable 22.43
classification 8.40
classified 21.12
classifier 22.2
classify 21.4
classing 4.29
classism 18.27
classist 4.33
classless 4.32
classmate 7.34
classroom 39.9; 41.17
classy 4.7
clatter 2.10
Claude 25.9
Claude's 25.10
Claudette 9.51
Claudia 26.39
Claudian 26.43
claudication 8.35
Claudio 35.19
Claudius 26.47
clause 25.35
clauses 26.36
claustrophobe 35.20
claustrophobia 36.37
claustrophobic 36.10
clavichord 25.9
clavicle 2.64
clavier 2.61
claw 25.1
clawback 1.3
clawed 25.9
clawless 26.27
claws 25.35
clay 7.1
clayey 8.1
claymation 8.23
claymore 25.3
claypan 1.24
Clayton 8.21
clean 15.23
cleanable 16.41
clean-cut 37.47
cleaned 15.27
cleaner 16.8
cleaners 16.37
cleaning 16.27
cleanish 16.33
cleanliness 10.70
cleanly 10.5; 16.1
cleanse 9.43
cleanser 10.14
clear 13.1
clearance 14.11

Clearasil® 17.15
clear-cut 37.47
cleared 13.2
clearer 14.2
clearest 14.16
clear-headed 10.18
clearing 14.12
clearing house 29.12
clearly 14.1
clearness 14.14
clear-out 29.14
clear-sighted 22.13
clearway 7.3
Cleary 14.1
cleat 15.35
cleavage 16.16
cleave 15.39
cleaver 16.6
cleavers 16.37
Cleckheaton 16.22
Cleese 15.42
Cleethorpes 25.27
clef 9.10
cleft 9.11
Clegg 9.12
Cleland 10.29
Clem 9.28
clematis 8.66
clemency 10.53
clement 10.33
Clement 10.33
clementine 15.26
Clementine 21.22
clementines 15.29
Clemmie 10.6
clench 9.33
clenched 9.34
clenching 10.36
Cleo 35.10
Cleo Laine 7.21
Cleopatra 2.12
clerestory 26.1
clergy 12.1
clergyman 12.34
clergywoman 40.10
clergywomen 18.31
cleric 10.15
clerical 10.60
clericalism 18.29
clerics 10.16
clerihew 41.4
clerk 3.3
clerkly 4.5
clerks 3.4
clerkship 17.43
Cleveland 16.23
clever 10.11
clever Dick 17.3

cleverly 10.53
cleverness 10.70
clew 41.1
cliché 7.3
clichés 7.56
click 17.3
clickable 18.64
clicked 17.6
clicker 18.9
clicks 17.4
client 22.24
clientele 9.16
clients 22.25
cliff 17.10
Cliff 17.10
cliffhanger 2.13
cliffhanging 2.42
Clifford 18.19
Clifford's 18.20
clifftop 23.36
cliffy 18.4
Clifton 18.32
climacteric 10.15
climactic 2.17
climate 22.34
climatic 2.17
climatologic 24.20
climatological 24.61
climatology 24.55
climax 1.4
climb 21.19
climbable 22.43
climb-down 29.5
climbed 21.20
climber 22.8
climbers 22.39
climbing 22.26
climbs 21.21
clime 21.19
climes 21.21
clinch 17.33
clincher 18.14
clinching 18.40
cline 21.22
cling 17.35
clinger 18.13
clingfilm 17.19
clinging 18.40
clings 17.36
clingstone 35.36
clingy 18.6
clinic 18.16
clinical 18.64
clinically 18.57
clinician 18.33
clinics 18.17
clink 17.30
clinked 17.32

clinker 18.9
clinks 17.31
clinometer 24.57
clint 17.39
Clint 17.39
Clinton 18.32
Clint's 17.40
Clio 35.10
clip 17.43
clipboard 25.9
clip-clop 23.36
clip joint 33.10
clipped 17.45
clipper 18.8
clippers 18.55
clippie 18.1
clipping 18.40
clippings 18.41
clips 17.44
clique 15.7; 17.3
cliquey 16.1; 18.2
cliquish 16.33
clishmaclaver 8.6
clitoral 18.64
clitoris 17.46
Clive 21.37
Cliveden 18.32
Clive's 21.38
clivia 18.61
cloaca 8.4
cloacal 8.15
cloak 35.21
cloak-and-dagger 2.9
cloaked 35.23
cloakroom 39.9; 41.17
cloaks 35.22
clobber 24.8
clobbered 24.24
clobbering 24.69
cloche 23.42
clock 23.3
clockmaker 8.4
clocks 23.5
clockwise 21.41
clockwork 11.4
clod 23.8
Clodagh 36.5
cloddy 24.3
clodhopper 24.8
clodhopping 24.40
clog 23.11
clogged 23.12
cloisonné 7.3
cloister 34.2
clomp 23.24
clomped 23.25
clone 35.36
cloned 35.37

clones 35.39
clonic 24.19
cloning 36.24
clonk 23.28
Clontarf 3.9
Clooney 42.1
clop 23.36
close 35.42
close 35.52
close-cropped 23.38
closed 35.53
close-down 29.5
close-grained 7.22
close-hauled 25.15
close-knit 17.51
close-lipped 17.45
closely 36.1
closeness 36.26
closer 36.9
close-run 37.31
closes 36.34
closest 36.28
closet 24.49
closeted 24.59
close-up 37.41
closing 36.24
closing time 21.19
closure 36.9
clot 23.44
cloth 23.46
clothbound 29.6
clothe 35.48
clothes 35.49
clothes brush 37.46
clotheshorse 25.28
clothesline 21.22
clothes peg 9.12
clothier 36.37
clothing 36.24
clots 23.45
clotted cream 15.20
cloud 29.3
cloudburst 11.23
cloud-cuckoo-land 1.28
clouded 30.3
cloudiness 30.26
clouding 30.12
cloudless 30.14
cloud nine 21.22
cloudscape 7.27
cloudy 30.1
Clough 37.10
Clouseau 35.18
clout 29.14
clove 35.50
Clovelly 10.5
cloven 36.20

clover 36.6
cloverleaf 15.13
cloves 35.51
Clovis 36.25
clown 29.5
clowning 30.12
clownish 30.17
cloy 33.1
cloyed 33.4
cloying 34.11
club 37.1
clubbable 38.52
clubber 38.8
clubbing 38.34
clubby 38.1
club foot 39.14
clubhouse 29.12
clubland 1.28
clubman 38.28
clubroom 39.9; 41.17
clubroot 41.27
clubs 37.2
cluck 37.3
clucked 37.5
clucking 38.34
clucky 38.2
clue 41.1
Cluedo® 35.18
clueless 42.26
clues 41.33
clumber 38.8
clump 37.29
clumsier 38.49
clumsiest 38.61
clumsily 38.47
clumsiness 38.59
clumsy 38.7
clung 37.37
Cluniac 1.3
clunk 37.32
clunked 37.34
clunker 38.9
clunking 38.34
clunky 38.2
Cluny 42.1
cluster 38.10
clutch 37.6
clutched 37.7
clutches 38.45
clutching 38.34
clutter 38.10
Clwyd 42.13
Clyde 21.9
Clydebank 1.25
Clydesdale 7.15
clyster 18.10
Clytemnestra 10.12
CND 15.4

CO 35.2
Co. 35.1
coach 35.24
coach-builder 18.10
coaches 36.34
coach house 29.12
coaching 36.24
coachload 35.25
coachman 36.20
coachwork 11.4
coadjutant 2.68
coadjutor 2.60
coagulant 2.68
coagulate 7.35
coagulation 8.24
coal 35.30
coaler 36.7
coalesce 9.47
coalesced 9.49
coalescence 10.34
coalescent 10.33
coalface 7.30
coalfield 15.18
coal-fired 19.2
coalition 18.33
coalman 36.20
coal mine 21.22
coal miner 22.8
Coalport 25.31
coals 35.33
coaly 36.1
coaming 36.24
coarse 25.28
coarsely 26.1
coarsen 26.19
coarsened 26.20
coarseness 26.27
coarser 26.8
coarsest 26.29
coast 35.43
coastal 36.15
coaster 36.5
coasters 36.34
coastguard 3.8
coasting 36.24
coastline 21.22
coat 35.45
coated 36.12
Coates 35.46
coati 4.3
coating 36.24
coats 35.46
coax 35.22
coaxial 2.64
cob 23.1
cobalt 23.18
cobalt 25.17
cobber 24.8

Cobbett 24.49
cobble 24.27
cobbled 24.28
cobbler 24.12
cobbles 24.29
cobblestone 35.36
cobblestones 35.39
Cobden 24.33
Cobham 24.30
cobnut 37.47
COBOL 23.15
cobra 24.12
cobra 36.7
Coburg 11.9
cobweb 9.1
cobwebby 10.1
coca 36.4
Coca-Cola® 36.7
cocaine 7.21
coccic 24.20
coccus 24.43
coccyx 24.22
cochineal 15.17
Cochise 15.32
cochlea 24.58
cochlear 24.58
Cochrane 24.33
cock 23.3
cockade 7.8
cock-a-doodle-doo 41.4
cock-a-hoop 41.22
Cockaigne 7.21
cock-a-leekie 16.1
cockamamie 8.1
cock-and-bull 39.7
cockatiel 15.17
cockatoo 41.4
cockatrice 17.46
cockatrice 21.29
Cockburn 11.15
cockchafer 8.6
Cockcroft 23.10
cockcrow 35.13
cocked 23.6
cocker 24.9
Cocker 24.9
cockerel 24.27
cockerel 24.61
cockeyed 21.11
cockfight 21.33
Cockfosters 24.53
cockier 24.58
cockiest 24.71
cockiness 24.70
cockle 24.27
cockles 24.29
cockleshell 9.16

cockloft 23.10
cockney 24.6
cockneyfy 21.4
cockneyism 18.28
cockneys 24.52
cockpit 24.49
cockroach 35.24
cockroaches 36.34
cockscomb 35.34
cockspur 11.1
cocksure 25.3
cocksure 27.1
cocktail 7.15
cocktails 7.17
cockup 37.41
cocky 24.2
Coco 35.16
cocoa 35.16
coconut 37.47
cocoon 41.19
cocotte 23.44
cod 23.8
coda 36.5
coddle 24.27
coddled 24.28
code 35.25
codec 9.2
coded 36.12
codeine 15.25
codes 35.26
codeword 11.7
codfish 24.46
codger 24.14
codices 15.45
codicil 17.15
codification 8.50
codified 21.12
codify 21.4
coding 36.24
codling 24.40
cod liver oil 33.6
codpiece 15.32
co-driver 22.6
codswallop 24.41
Cody 36.1
Coe 35.1
co-ed 9.8
coedit 10.48
coeducation 8.28
co-educational 8.79
coefficient 18.38
coelacanth 1.35
coelenterate 10.73
coelenterate 7.38
coeliac 1.3
coelom 16.20
coenobite 21.34

coerce 11.22
coerced 11.23
coercer 12.2
coercion 12.12
coercive 12.27
coeternal 12.8
coeval 16.17
coexist 36.43
coexistence 18.39
coexistent 18.38
coextensive 10.50
C of E 15.4
coffee 15.3
coffee 24.4
coffee cup 37.41
coffeepot 23.44
coffee spoon 41.19
coffer 24.11
cofferdam 1.22
coffin 24.32
coffins 24.37
cog 23.11
Cogan 36.20
cogency 36.35
cogent 36.22
cogitate 7.43
cogitating 8.60
cogitation 8.34
cogito ergo sum 39.9
Cognac 1.3
cognate 7.34
cognition 18.33
cognitive 17.55
cognizance 24.68
cognizant 24.67
cognoscenti 10.3
cogs 23.13
cogwheel 15.17
cohabit 2.51
cohabitant 2.68
cohabitation 8.24
cohabited 2.63
cohabiter 2.60
coheir 5.1
Cohen 36.19
cohere 13.1
coherence 14.11
coherent 14.10
coherer 14.2
cohesion 16.22
cohesive 16.35
cohort 25.31
coiffeur 11.1
coiffeuse 11.29
coiffure 27.1
coiffured 27.2
coil 33.6
coin 33.8

coinage 34.4
coincide 21.12
coincidence 18.71
coincident 18.70
coincidental 10.21
coincidentally 10.53
coiner 34.2
coining 34.11
coin-op 23.36
Cointreau® 35.13
coital 34.16
coital 36.38
coition 18.33
coitus 34.18
coitus 36.42
coitus interruptus 38.38
coitus reservatus 4.32
coke 35.21
Coke® 35.21
col 23.15
cola 36.7
colander 24.57; 38.48
Colby 24.1
colcannon 2.35
Colchester 36.36
cold 35.31
cold-blooded 38.20
cold-bloodedly 38.47
colder 36.5
coldest 36.28
Colditz 36.31
coldly 36.1
coldness 36.26
cold-shoulder 36.5
cold sore 25.3
Coldstream 15.20
Cold War 25.3
Cole 35.30
Coleman 36.20
Coleraine 7.21
Coleridge 17.14
coleslaw 25.3
Colet 24.49
Colette 9.51
coley 36.1
Colgate® 7.34
colic 24.18
colicky 24.56
Colin 24.32
coliseum 16.20
colitis 22.28
collaborate 7.35
collaboration 8.24
collaborative 17.54
collaborator 8.5
collage 3.13
collagen 24.64

collapse

collapse 1.38
collapsible 2.64
collar 24.12
collarbone 35.36
collared 24.24
collarless 24.70
collate 7.33
collateral 2.28; 2.64
collation 8.23
collator 8.5
colleague 15.14
collect 9.5
collectable 10.60
collectanea 8.78
collected 10.18
collecting 10.36
collection 10.28
collective 10.50
collectively 10.54
collectivism 18.28
collectivization 8.43
collectivize 21.43
collector 10.10
colleen 15.25
Colleen 15.25
college 24.26
collegian 16.22
collegian 16.43
collegiate 16.50
collegium 16.42
Colley 24.5
collide 21.10
collided 22.13
collie 24.5
collier 24.58
colliery 24.54
Collins 24.37
Collinson 24.64
collision 18.33
collocate 24.73
collocate 7.43
collocation 8.34
colloid 33.4
collop 24.41
colloquial 36.38
colloquialism 18.29
colloquy 24.54
collude 41.9
collusion 42.20
collywobbles 24.29
Colman 36.20
Colmar 3.1
cologne 35.36
Cologne 35.36
Colombia 38.49
Colombian 38.54
Colombo 35.17
colon 23.27; 36.20

colonel 12.8
colonial 36.38
colonialism 18.29
colonic 24.19
colonies 24.75
colonist 24.72
colonization 8.48
colonize 21.45
colonnade 7.8
colony 24.54
colophon 23.27; 24.64
Coloradan 4.24
Colorado 35.4
colorant 38.56
coloration 8.38
coloratura 28.2
colossal 24.27
colossally 24.54
Colosseum 16.20
Colossian 24.64
Colossians 24.66
colossus 24.43
colostomy 24.54
colostrum 24.30
colour 38.12
colour-blind 21.23
colour-coded 36.12
coloured 38.20
colourfast 3.30
colourful 38.52; 39.7
colourfully 40.1
colouring 38.58
colourless 38.59
colours 38.45
colourwash 23.42
colourway 7.4
colourways 7.56
colporteur 26.4
Colquhoun 41.19
colt 35.32
Colt 35.32
Coltrane 7.21
coltsfoot 39.14
Colum 24.30
Columba 38.8
Columbia 38.49
Columbian 38.54
columbine 21.22
Columbine 21.22
Columbo 35.17
Columbus 38.38
column 24.30
columnar 38.13
columnist 24.72
columns 24.31
Colwyn 24.32
coma 36.8
Comanche 2.7

Comaneci 10.7
comatose 35.42
comatose 35.52
comb 35.34
combat 1.45
combatant 24.67
combative 17.55
comber 36.8
combi 24.1
combination 8.34
combinations 8.55
combine 21.22
combined 21.23
combing 36.24
combining 22.26
combo 35.13
combs 35.35
combust 37.45
combustible 38.52
combustion 38.28
combustor 38.10
come 37.27
comeback 1.3
Comecon 23.27
comedian 16.43
comedic 16.11
comedienne 9.32
comedown 29.5
comedy 24.56
comely 38.5
comer 38.13
comestible 10.60
comet 24.49
come to blows 35.52
comeuppance 38.33
comfier 38.49
comfiest 38.61
comfit 38.43
comfort 38.42
comfortable 38.52
comfortably 38.47; 38.64
comforted 38.50
comforter 38.48
comfrey 38.5
comfy 38.4
comic 24.19
comical 24.61
comically 24.56
comics 24.22
Cominform 25.20
coming 38.34
Comintern 11.15
comity 24.56
comma 24.13
command 3.21
commandant 1.33; 3.23

commandeer 13.1
commander 4.10
commandership 17.43
commanding 4.29
commandment 4.27
commandments 4.28
commando 35.4
commas 24.53
comme il faut 35.19
commemorate 7.38
commemoration 8.28
commemorative 17.54
commence 9.39
commenced 9.40
commencement 10.33
commencing 10.36
commend 9.35
commendable 10.60
commendation 8.34
commendatory 8.76
commended 10.18
commensal 10.21
commensurable 10.79
commensurate 10.73
commentary 24.54
commentate 7.43
commentator 8.5
commerce 11.22
commercial 12.8
commercialism 18.28
commercialization 8.44
commercialize 21.43
commercialized 21.48
commercially 12.29
commercials 12.9
commie 24.6
commies 24.52
commingle 18.22
comminute 41.27
commis 24.6; 24.42
commiserate 7.41
commiseration 8.32
commissaire 5.1
commissar 3.1
commissariat 6.23
commissary 24.76
commission 18.33
commissionaire 5.1
commissioned 18.34
commissioner 18.60
commissure 27.1
commit 17.51
commitment 18.38
commitments 18.39
committal 18.22
committed 18.19

committee 15.3; 18.3
committeeman 1.24
committees 15.44; 18.54
committer 18.10
commix 17.4
commode 35.25
commodious 36.42
commodities 24.75
commodity 24.56
commodore 25.4
common 24.33
commoner 24.57
common-law 25.4
commonly 24.54
Common Market 4.38
commonness 24.70
commonplace 7.30
common room 39.9; 41.17
commons 24.36
common sense 9.39
commonweal 15.17
Commonwealth 9.24
commotion 36.20
communal 24.61; 42.16
communalize 21.47
communally 24.76
Communard 3.8
commune 41.19
communicable 42.51
communicant 42.43
communicate 7.49
communicated 8.13
communicating 8.60
communication 8.39
communications 8.55
communicative 17.54
communicator 8.5
communing 42.24
communion 42.20
communion 42.41
communiqué 7.4
communism 18.28
communist 24.72
community 42.36
communize 21.45
commutable 42.39
commutation 8.34
commutative 17.55
commutator 8.5
commute 41.27
commuter 42.5
commuters 42.34
commutes 41.28
commuting 42.24

Como 35.16
Comoros 35.52
comp 23.24
compact 1.6
compact 1.6
compact disc 17.47
compacted 2.25
compaction 2.35
companies 38.63
companion 2.35
companionable 2.79
companionship 17.43
companionway 7.4
company 38.47
comparable 24.61
comparable 24.77
comparative 17.55
comparatively 2.78
compare 5.1
compared 5.2
compares 5.5
comparing 6.10
comparison 2.66
comparisons 2.67
compartment 4.27
compartmental 10.21
compartmentalize 21.43
compartments 4.28
compass 38.38
compassion 2.35
compassionate 2.74
compassionately 2.78
compatibility 18.58
compatible 2.64
compatriot 2.74
compeer 13.1
compel 9.16
compelled 9.19
compelling 10.36
compendia 10.57
compendious 10.70
compendium 10.63
compensate 7.43
compensation 8.34
compensatory 8.76
comper 24.8
compère 5.1
compete 15.35
competence 24.68
competent 24.67
competently 24.76
competing 16.27
competition 18.33
competitive 17.55
competitively 10.78
competitor 10.56
compilation 8.34

compile 21.16
compiled 21.17
compiler 22.7
compiles 21.18
compiling 22.26
complacency 8.76
complacent 8.56
complain 7.21
complainant 8.56
complained 7.22
complainer 8.8
complaining 8.63
complaint 7.25
complaisance 8.57
complaisant 8.56
complement 9.41; 24.67
complementary 10.53
complementation 8.48
complete 15.35
completely 16.1
completeness 16.30
completing 16.27
completion 16.22
complex 9.3
complexion 10.28
complexities 10.77
complexity 10.54
compliance 22.25
compliant 22.24
complicate 7.43
complicated 8.13
complication 8.34
complications 8.55
complicity 18.57
compliment 9.41; 24.67
complimentary 10.53
compliments 24.68
comply 21.2
component 36.22
components 36.23
comport 25.31
comportment 26.23
compose 35.52
composed 35.53
composer 36.9
composing 36.24
composite 17.51
composition 18.33
compositional 18.64
compositor 24.57
compos mentis 10.41
compost 23.41
composure 36.9
compound 29.6
compound 29.6

compounded 30.3
comprehend 9.35
comprehensible 10.60
comprehension 10.28
comprehensive 10.50
comprehensively 10.54
compress 9.47
compressed 9.49
compression 10.28
compressor 10.14
comprise 21.40
compromise 21.45
compromising 22.26
Comptometer® 24.57
Compton 24.33
compulsion 38.28
compulsive 38.44
compulsively 38.47
compulsory 38.47
compunction 38.28
computable 42.39
computation 8.34
compute 41.27
computer 42.5
computerese 15.45
computerization 8.52
computerize 21.46
computerized 21.48
computers 42.34
computing 42.24
comrade 7.8
comrades 7.9
comradeship 17.43
con 23.27
Conakry 24.54
cona more 26.1
Conan 36.20
Conan Doyle 33.6
con brio 35.10
concatenate 7.35
concatenation 8.24
concave 7.54
concavity 2.57
conceal 15.17
concealed 15.18
concealer 16.7
concealing 16.27
concealment 16.25
conceals 15.19
concede 15.11
conceded 16.14
conceit 15.35
conceited 16.14
conceitedly 16.38
conceivable 16.41
conceivably 16.38

conceive 15.39
conceived 15.40
concentrate 7.43
concentrating 8.60
concentration 8.34
concentric 10.15
concept 9.46
conception 10.28
conceptual 10.60
conceptualize 21.47
conceptually 10.55; 10.78
concern 11.15
concerned 11.16
concernedly 12.29
concerning 12.16
concerns 11.18
concert 11.24
concert 24.48
concerted 12.5
Concertgebouw 29.1
concertgoer 36.2
concertina 16.8
concertmaster 4.10
concerto 35.8
concession 10.28
concessionaire 5.1
concessionary 10.53
concessions 10.32
conch 23.28
conchie 24.7
concierge 5.3
conciliate 7.41
conciliation 8.32
conciliatory 18.56
concise 21.29
concisely 22.1
conciseness 22.29
conciser 22.9
concisest 22.31
concision 18.33
conclave 7.54
conclude 41.9
concluded 42.14
concluding 42.24
conclusion 42.20
conclusive 42.33
conclusively 42.36
concoct 23.6
concocting 24.40
concoction 24.33
concomitant 24.67
concord 25.9
concordance 26.24
concordant 26.23
concordat 1.45
Concorde 25.9
concours 27.1

concourse 25.28
concrete 15.35
concretion 16.22
concubine 21.22
concupiscence 42.44
concupiscent 42.43
concur 11.1
concurred 11.7
concurrence 38.33
concurrent 38.32
concurrently 38.47
concuss 37.43
concussed 37.45
concussion 38.28
condemn 9.28
condemnation 8.34
condemnatory 8.76
condemning 10.36
condensation 8.34
condense 9.39
condensed 9.40
condenser 10.14
condescend 9.35
condescending 10.36
condescension 10.28
condign 21.22
condiment 24.67
condition 18.33
conditional 18.64
conditionally 18.80
conditioned 18.34
conditioner 18.60
conditioning 18.73
condo 35.13
condole 35.30
condolence 36.23
condom 23.23
condone 35.36
condoned 35.37
condones 35.39
condoning 36.24
condor 25.3
condottiere 6.1
conduce 41.24
conducive 42.33
conduct 37.5
conductance 38.33
conducted 38.20
conducting 38.34
conduction 38.28
conductive 38.44
conductivity 18.57
conductor 38.10
conductorship 17.43
conductress 38.38
conduit 17.51
condyle 21.16
cone 35.36

coney 36.1
confab 1.1
confabulate 7.35
confabulation 8.24
confection 10.28
confectioner 10.56
confectionery 10.53
confederacy 10.78
confederate 7.38; 10.73
confederation 8.28
confer 11.1
conference 24.39; 24.68
conferment 12.14
conferred 11.7
conferring 12.16
confess 9.47
confessant 10.33
confessed 9.49
confessedly 10.54
confessing 10.36
confession 10.28
confessional 10.60
confessor 10.14
confetti 10.3
confidant 1.33
confidante 1.33; 3.23
confide 21.10
confidence 24.68
confident 24.67
confidential 10.21
confidentiality 2.57
confidentially 10.53
confiding 22.26
configuration 8.32
configure 18.9
confine 21.22
confined 21.23
confinement 22.24
confines 21.25
confining 22.26
confirm 11.13
confirmation 8.34
confirmatory 12.29
confirmed 11.14
confirming 12.16
confiscate 7.43
confiscation 8.34
confiture 27.1
conflagration 8.34
conflate 7.33
conflation 8.23
conflict 17.6
conflict 17.6
conflicting 18.40
confluence 24.68
conflux 37.4

conform 25.20
conformance 26.24
conformation 8.34
conformer 26.7
conforming 26.25
conformist 26.28
conformity 26.37
confound 29.6
confounded 30.3
confrère 5.1
confront 37.40
confrontation 8.34
confrontational 8.79
confronted 38.20
Confucian 42.20
Confucianism 18.28
Confucius 42.26
confusable 42.39
confuse 41.33
confused 41.34
confusedly 42.36
confusing 42.24
confusingly 42.36
confusion 42.20
confutation 8.34
confute 41.27
conga 24.9
congeal 15.17
congealed 15.18
congealing 16.27
congeals 15.19
congenial 16.41
congeniality 2.57
congenital 10.60
congenitally 10.78
conger 24.9
congest 9.49
congested 10.18
congestion 10.28
conglomerate 7.43
conglomerate 24.73
conglomeration 8.34
Congo 35.13
Congolese 15.45
congrats 1.46
congratulate 7.35
congratulation 8.24
congratulations 8.55
congratulatory 8.76
congregant 24.67
congregate 7.43
congregation 8.34
Congregational 8.79
Congregationalism 18.29
Congregationalist 17.49
congress 9.47

coon 41.19
Co-op 23.36
coop 41.22
cooper 42.3
Cooper 42.3
cooperate 7.43
cooperation 8.34
cooperative 17.54
co-opt 23.38
coordinate 7.44; 26.50
coordination 8.35
coordinator 8.5
coot 41.27
cootie 42.1
co-owner 36.8
co-ownership 17.43
cop 23.36
copacetic 10.15
cope 35.40
Copeland 36.21
Copenhagen 4.24; 8.21
Copernican 12.34
Copernicus 12.37
copestone 35.36
copied 24.23
copier 24.58
copies 24.52
copilot 22.34
coping 36.24
copious 36.42
Copland 36.21
cop-out 29.14
copper 24.8
Copperfield 15.18
copperplate 7.43
coppersmith 17.53
coppery 24.54
coppice 24.42
coppiced 24.45
coppicing 24.69
Coppola 24.57
copra 24.12
coprolalia 8.78
coprolite 21.34
coprolitic 18.16
coprophilia 18.61
cops 23.37
copse 23.37
Copt 23.38
'copter 24.10
Coptic 24.16
copula 24.57
copulate 7.43
copulating 8.60
copulation 8.34
copy 24.1
copybook 39.1

copycat 1.45
Copydex® 9.3
copyist 24.72
copyreader 16.5
copyright 21.34
copywriter 22.5
copywriting 22.26
coq au vin 1.24
coquetry 24.56
coquette 9.51
coquettish 10.45
cor 25.1
Cora 26.6
coracle 24.61
coral 24.27
cor anglais 7.3
corbel 26.15
Corbett 26.32
corbie 26.1
Corbin 26.18
cor blimey 22.1
Corby 26.1
cord 25.9
cordage 26.14
Corday 7.2
corded 26.12
Cordelia 16.40
cordial 26.41
cordiality 2.57
cordillera 6.2
cordite 21.33
cordless 26.27
Córdoba 26.38
cordon 26.19
cordon bleu 11.1
cordoned 26.20
Cordova 26.38
cords 25.10
corduroy 33.1
corduroys 33.15
cordwainer 8.8
core 25.1
Corelli 10.5
Coren 24.33; 26.19
corer 26.6
co-respondent 24.38
Corey 26.1
Corfe 25.11
Corfu 41.2
corgi 26.1
corgis 26.35
coriander 2.10
Corin 24.32
Corinth 17.41
Corinthian 18.67
Coriolanus 8.67
cork 25.6
Cork 25.6

corkage 26.14
corker 26.3
corking 26.25
corkscrew 41.3
cork-tipped 17.45
corky 26.1
corm 25.20
cormorant 26.45
corn 25.22
corncob 23.1
corncockle 24.27
corncrake 7.6
cornea 16.2; 26.39
corneal 16.17; 26.41
corned beef 15.13
Cornelia 16.40
cornelian 16.43
Cornelius 16.47
corner 26.7
corners 26.36
cornerstone 35.36
cornerways 7.56
cornerwise 21.45
cornet 26.32
cornettist 10.44
cornfield 15.18
cornflake 7.6
cornflour 31.1
cornflower 31.1
Cornhill 17.15
cornice 26.26
corniche 15.34
cornier 26.39
corniest 26.49
Cornish 26.30
Cornishman 26.43
corn on the cob 23.1
cornstarch 3.6
cornucopia 36.37
Cornwall 25.14
Cornwallis 24.42
Cornwell 9.16
corny 26.1
corolla 24.12
corollary 24.54
Coromandel 2.28
corona 36.8
coronal 24.61; 36.15
coronary 24.54
coronation 8.34
coroner 24.57
coronet 24.73
Corot 35.13
Corp. 25.26
corpora 26.38
corporal 26.15; 26.41
corporate 26.50
corporation 8.35

corporeal 26.41
corps 25.1
corpse 25.27
corpulence 26.46
corpulent 26.45
corpus 26.27
Corpus Christi 18.3
corpuscle 38.23
corpuscular 38.48
corral 3.14
correct 9.5
corrected 10.18
correction 10.28
correctitude 41.9
corrective 10.50
correctly 10.5
correctness 10.42
Correggio 35.19
correlate 7.43
correlation 8.34
correlative 17.55
correspond 23.30
correspondence 24.39
correspondent 24.38
correspondents 24.39
corresponding 24.40
correspondingly 24.56
corridor 25.4
corrie 24.5
Corrie 24.5
Corrigan 24.64
corrigenda 10.10
corrigendum 10.25
corroborate 7.43
corroborated 8.13
corroboration 8.34
corroborative 17.54
corrode 35.25
corroded 36.12
corroding 36.24
corrosion 36.20
corrosive 36.32
corrugate 7.43
corrugated 8.13
corrugation 8.34
corrupt 37.42
corrupted 38.20
corrupter 38.10
corruptible 38.52
corrupting 38.34
corruption 38.28
corsage 3.13
corsair 5.1
corset 26.32
corsetier 13.1
corsetière 5.1
corsetry 26.37

Corsica 26.38
Corsican 26.43
cortege 7.14
cortex 9.3
Cortez 9.57
Corti 26.1
cortical 26.41
cortices 15.45
Cortina 16.8
cortisone 35.36
corundum 38.26
Corunna 38.13
coruscate 7.43
coruscation 8.34
corvette 9.51
Corybantic 2.17
cos 23.39; 23.48
Cosa Nostra 24.12
cosecant 16.25
cosh 23.42
coshed 23.43
cosher 24.14
cosier 36.37
cosiest 36.44
cosily 36.35
cosine 21.22
cosiness 36.42
cosmetic 10.15
cosmetician 18.33
cosmetics 10.16
cosmic 24.19
cosmogony 24.54
cosmological 24.61
cosmology 24.55
cosmonaut 25.31
cosmopolitan 24.64
cosmos 23.39
Cossack 1.3
cosset 24.49
cosseted 24.59
cossie 24.7
cost 23.41
Costa 24.10
Costa Brava 4.11
Costa del Sol 23.15
costal 24.27
co-star 3.1
Costa Rica 16.4
Costa Rican 16.22
co-starring 4.29
co-stars 3.37
Costello 35.7
costermonger 38.9
costing 24.40
costive 24.51
costlier 24.58
costliest 24.71
costly 24.5

Costner 24.13
costume 41.17
costumer 42.8
costumier 42.38
cosy 36.1
cot 23.44
cotangent 2.40
Côte d'Azur 27.1
coterie 36.35
cotoneaster 2.10
Cotswold 35.31
cottage 24.26
cottager 24.57
cottaging 24.69
cotter 24.10
Cottle 24.27
cotton 24.33
Cotton 24.33
cottonseed 15.11
cottontail 7.15
cottony 24.54
Cottrell 24.27
cotyledon 16.22
couch 29.2
couchant 30.10
couchette 9.51
cougar 42.4
cough 23.9
coughed 23.10
cougher 24.11
coughing 24.40
could 39.4
couldn't 40.12
couldn't-care-less
9.47
couldst 39.5
could've 40.18
coulis 42.1
coulisse 15.32
coulomb 23.23
Coulomb 23.23
Coulthard 3.8
council 30.6
councillor 30.23
counsel 30.6
counsellor 30.23
count 29.11
countable 30.24
countdown 29.5
counted 30.3
countenance 30.25
counter 30.2
counteract 1.6
counteraction 2.35
counterattack 1.3
counterattacked 1.6
counterattraction
2.35

counterbalance 2.41
counterblast 3.30
countercharge 3.12
counterclaim 7.18
counterclockwise
21.41
counterespionage
3.13
counterfeit 17.51
counterfeiter 18.10
counterfoil 33.6
counterinsurgency
12.29
counterintelligence
10.68
counterirritant 18.70
countermand 3.21
countermeasure
10.14
countermove 41.31
counteroffensive
10.50
counteroffer 24.11
counterpane 7.21
counterpart 3.32
counterplot 23.44
counterpoint 33.10
counterpoise 33.15
counterproductive
38.44
counterproposal
36.15
Counter-Reformation
8.28
counter-revolution
42.20
counter-revolutionary
42.36
countersign 21.22
countersink 17.30
counterspy 21.4
counterstain 7.21
counterstroke 35.21
countersunk 37.32
counterterrorism
18.28
countervail 7.15
counterweight 7.46
countess 9.47; 30.13
counties 30.20
counting 30.12
countless 30.14
countries 38.46
countrified 21.12
country 38.5
countryman 38.54
countryside 21.12
countrywoman 40.10

counts 29.9
county 30.1
coup 41.1
coup de grâce 3.26
coup d'état 3.1
coupe 41.22
coupé 7.3
couple 38.23
couplet 38.43
coupling 38.34
coupon 23.27
courage 38.22
courageous 8.67
courageously 8.76
courgette 9.51
courgettes 9.52
courier 38.49
course 25.28
coursed 25.29
courser 26.8
courses 26.36
coursework 11.4
coursing 26.25
court 25.31
Courtauld 35.31
court-bouillon 23.27
courted 26.12
Courtelle® 9.16
courteous 12.37
courtesan 1.24
courtesy 12.29
courthouse 29.12
courtier 26.39
courting 26.25
courtly 26.1
court-martial 4.19
court-martialled 4.20
Courtney 26.1
courtroom 39.9; 41.17
courts 25.32
courtship 17.43
courtyard 3.8
Courvoisier® 7.4
couscous 41.24
cousin 38.28
cousins 38.31
Cousins 38.31
couth 41.29
couture 27.1
couturier 7.4
couturière 5.1
cove 35.50
coven 38.28
covenant 38.56
covenantal 2.28
Covent Garden 4.24
Coventry 24.54
cover 38.11

coverage 17.14
coverall 25.14
covered 38.20
covering 38.58
coverlet 38.62
Coverley 38.47
covers 38.45
covert 38.42
cover-up 37.41
covet 38.43
coveted 38.50
covetous 38.59
covey 38.4
coving 36.24
cow 29.1
Cowal 31.3
Cowan 30.8
coward 31.2
Coward 31.2
cowardice 17.46
cowardly 32.1
cowbell 9.16
cowboy 33.1
cowboys 33.15
cowcatcher 2.14
Cowdenbeath 15.37
Cowdrey 30.1
cowed 29.3
Cowell 31.3
cower 31.1
cowered 31.2
cowering 32.3
Cowes 29.17
cowgirl 11.11
cowhand 1.28
cowherd 11.7
cowhide 21.11
Cowie 30.1
cowl 29.4
Cowley 30.1
cowlick 17.3
cowling 30.12
cowman 30.8
cowpat 1.45
cowpats 1.46
Cowper 30.2; 42.3
cowpoke 35.21
cowpox 23.5
cowrie 30.1
cows 29.17
cowshed 9.8
cowslip 17.43
cox 23.5
Cox 23.5
coxcomb 35.34
coxless 24.43
coxswain 24.33
coy 33.1

coyer 34.2
coyly 34.1
coyness 34.12
coyote 36.1
coypu 41.3
coz 37.51
cozen 38.28
crab 1.1
Crabbe 1.1
crabbed 2.24
crabber 2.8
crabby 2.1
crabmeat 15.35
crabs 1.2
crabstick 2.17
Crabtree 2.5; 15.3
crabwise 21.41
crack 1.3
crackbrain 7.21
crackbrained 7.22
crackdown 29.5
cracked 1.6
cracker 2.9
crackerjack 1.3
crackers 2.55
crackhead 9.8
cracking 2.42
crackle 2.28
crackling 2.42
crackly 2.5
cracknel 2.28
crackpot 23.44
crackpots 23.45
cracks 1.4
cracksman 2.35
Cracow 23.9; 23.47;
  29.1
Craddock 2.16
cradle 8.15
cradled 8.16
cradle snatcher 2.14
cradlesong 23.31
cradling 8.62
craft 3.10
craftier 4.44
craftiest 4.55
craftily 4.42
craftiness 4.53
craftsman 4.24
craftsmanship 17.43
craftswoman 40.10
craftswomen 18.31
craftwork 11.4
crafty 4.3
crag 1.13
craggy 2.2
crags 1.14
Craig 7.11

Craigavon 2.35
Craigie 8.1
crake 7.6
cram 1.22
Cram 1.22
crammer 2.13
cramming 2.42
cramp 1.23
cramping 2.42
crampon 2.35; 23.27
cranberries 2.77
cranberry 2.5; 2.56
crane 7.21
cranesbill 17.15
Cranfield 15.18
crania 8.78
cranial 8.79
cranium 8.80
crank 1.25
crankcase 7.30
cranks 1.26
crankshaft 3.10
cranky 2.2
Cranmer 2.13
cranny 2.6
crap 1.37
crapper 2.8
crappy 2.1
craps 1.38
crash 1.43
crashed 1.44
crashing 2.42
crash-land 1.28
crash-landed 2.25
crass 1.40
Crassus 2.46
Cratchit 2.51
crate 7.32
crater 8.5
crates 7.50
cravat 1.45
cravats 1.46
crave 7.54
craven 8.21
craver 8.6
craves 7.55
craving 8.61
craw 25.1
crawfish 26.30
Crawford 26.12
crawl 25.14
crawler 26.6
Crawley 26.1
crawling 26.25
crawls 25.19
crayfish 8.70
crayon 8.21; 23.27
crayoning 8.84

crayons 23.35
craze 7.56
crazed 7.57
crazier 8.78
craziest 8.86
crazily 8.76
crazy 8.1
creak 15.7
creaking 16.27
creaky 16.1
cream 15.20
cream cake 7.6
creamer 16.8
creamery 16.38
creamier 16.40
creamiest 16.49
creamy 16.1
crease 15.32
creased 15.33
creases 16.37
create 7.33
created 8.13
creatine 15.26
creation 8.23
Creation 8.23
creationism 18.28
creative 8.73
creativity 18.57
creator 8.5
creatrix 8.11
creature 16.9
creatures 16.37
crèche 9.50
Crécy 10.7
cred 9.8
Creda 16.5
credence 16.26
credential 10.21
credentials 10.23
credenza 10.14
credibility 18.58
credible 10.60
credit 10.48
creditable 10.79
credit card 3.8
credited 10.58
Crediton 10.64
creditor 10.56
creditworthy 12.1
credo 35.6; 35.10
credulity 42.36
credulous 10.70
Cree 15.1
creed 15.11
creek 15.7
creel 15.17
creep 15.30
creeper 16.3

creepers 16.37
creepier 16.40
creepiest 16.49
creepily 16.38
creepiness 16.47
creeping 16.27
creeps 15.31
creepy 16.1
creepy-crawlies 26.35
creepy-crawly 26.1
cremate 7.33
cremated 8.13
cremation 8.23
cremations 8.55
crematoria 26.39
crematorium 26.42
crème 9.28
crème brûlée 7.4
crème caramel 9.16
crème fraîche 9.50
Cremona 36.8
crenellation 8.28
Creole 35.30
creolized 21.48
creosote 35.45
creosoted 36.12
crepe 7.27
crepe de Chine 15.26
creperie 8.76
crêpes 9.45
crêpe suzette 9.51
crepitus 10.70
crept 9.46
crepuscular 38.48
crepy 8.1
crescendi 10.3
crescendo 35.7
crescent 10.33
cress 9.47
Cressida 10.56
crest 9.49
cresta 10.10
crestfallen 26.19
Cretaceous 8.67
Cretan 16.22
Crete 15.35
cretin 10.26
cretinism 18.28
cretinous 10.70
cretonne 23.27
crevasse 1.40
crevice 10.41
crevices 10.76
crew 41.1
crew cut 37.47
Crewe 41.1
crewed 41.9
crewel 42.16

Crewkerne 11.15
crewman 42.20
crib 17.1
cribbage 18.21
cribber 18.8
cribbing 18.40
Crichton 22.20
crick 17.3
Crick 17.3
cricket 18.50
cricketer 18.60
cri de coeur 11.1
cried 21.9
crier 22.2
cries 21.39
crikey 22.1
crime 21.19
Crimea 16.2
Crimean 16.22
crime passionnel 9.16
crimes 21.21
crimewave 7.54
criminal 18.64
criminality 2.57
criminalization 8.53
criminalize 21.47
criminally 18.80
criminological 24.61
criminology 24.55
Crimond 18.34
crimp 17.27
crimper 18.8
crimping 18.40
Crimplene® 15.25
crimson 18.33
cringe 17.37
cringer 18.14
cringing 18.40
cringle 18.22
crinkle 18.22
crinkly 18.5
crinoline 17.29
crinolines 17.42
cripes 21.27
Crippen 18.32
cripple 18.22
crippled 18.23
crippling 18.40
Cripps 17.44
crises 15.44; 22.38
Criseyde 8.5
crisis 22.28
crisp 17.48
crispbread 9.8
crisper 18.8
crispest 18.46
Crispian 18.67

Crispin 18.31
Crispin's 18.36
crisply 18.5
crispness 18.44
crispy 18.1
crisscross 23.39
Critchley 18.5
criterion 14.21
critic 18.16
critical 18.64
critically 18.57
criticism 18.28
criticize 21.44
critics 18.17
critique 15.7
critter 18.10
critters 18.55
croak 35.21
croaked 35.23
croaker 36.4
croakier 36.37
croakiest 36.44
croakily 36.35
croaking 36.24
croaky 36.1
Croat 1.45
Croatia 8.9
Croatian 8.23
croc 23.3
crochet 7.3
crocheting 8.58
crock 23.3
crockery 24.54
Crockett 24.49
Crockford 24.24
crocodile 21.16
crocodiles 21.18
crocodilian 18.67
crocosmia 24.58
crocus 36.26
Croesus 16.30
croft 23.10
crofter 24.10
Crofton 24.33
Cro-Magnon 2.35; 23.27
Cromarty 24.54
Cromer 36.8
cromlech 9.2
Crompton 24.33
Cromwell 9.16; 24.27
Cromwellian 10.64
crone 35.36
cronies 36.33
Cronin 36.19
Cronos 23.39
Cronus 36.26
crony 36.1

cronyism 18.28
crook 39.1
crooked 40.3
crookedly 40.20
croon 41.19
crooned 41.20
crooner 42.8
crooning 42.24
crop 23.36
cropped 23.38
cropper 24.8
crops 23.37
croquet 7.3
croquette 9.51
Crosby 24.1
crosier 36.37
cross 23.39
crossbar 3.1
crossbeam 15.20
crossbill 17.15
crossbones 35.39
crossbow 35.13
crossbows 35.52
crossbred 9.8
crossbreed 15.11
crosscheck 9.2
crosschecked 9.5
crosscurrent 38.32
crosscut 37.47
crosse 23.39
crossed 23.41
crosser 24.14
crosses 24.53
crossest 24.44
cross-examination 8.24
cross-examine 2.34
cross-eyed 21.11
cross-fertilization 8.44
crossfire 19.1
crosshatch 1.7
crossing 24.40
cross-legged 10.17
crossly 24.5
crossover 36.6
crosspatch 1.7
crosspiece 15.32
cross-pollination 8.48
crossroads 35.26
cross-section 10.28
cross stitch 17.7
crosstalk 25.6
crosstree 15.3
crossways 7.56
crosswind 17.34
crosswise 21.41

crossword 11.7
crotch 23.7
crotchet 24.49
crotchety 24.56
crouch 29.2
crouching 30.12
croup 41.22
croupier 42.38
crouton 23.27
croutons 23.35
crow 35.1
crowbar 3.1
Crowborough 36.36
crowd 29.3
crowded 30.3
crowding 30.12
crowd-pleaser 16.9
Crowe 35.1
crowed 35.25
crown 29.5
Crown 29.5
crowner 30.2
crowning 30.12
crows 35.52
Crowther 30.2
Croydon 34.8
cru 41.1
crucial 42.16
crucially 42.36
crucible 42.39
Crucible 42.39
crucifer 42.37
cruciferous 18.74
crucified 21.12
crucifix 17.4
crucifixion 18.33
Crucifixion 18.33
cruciform 25.20
crucify 21.4
cruck 37.3
crud 37.8
cruddy 38.3
crude 41.9
crudely 42.1
crudeness 42.26
cruder 42.5
crudest 42.27
crudités 7.4
crudity 42.36
cruel 42.16
Cruella De Vil 17.15
cruelly 42.36
cruelty 42.36
cruet 42.30
Crufts 37.13
Cruikshank 1.25
cruise 41.33
cruised 41.34

cruiser 42.9
cruiserweight 7.49
cruises 42.34
cruising 42.24
crumb 37.27
crumble 38.23
crumblier 38.49
crumbliest 38.61
crumbling 38.34
crumbly 38.5
crumby 38.6
crumhorn 25.22
crummier 38.49
crummiest 38.61
crummy 38.6
crumpet 38.43
crumple 38.23
crumpled 38.24
crunch 37.35
cruncher 38.14
Crunchie 38.7
crunchier 38.49
crunchiest 38.61
crunching 38.34
crunchy 38.7
crupper 38.8
crusade 7.8
crusader 8.5
crusading 8.60
cruse 41.33
crush 37.46
crushable 38.52
crusher 38.14
crushing 38.34
Crusoe 35.18
crust 37.45
crustacean 8.23
crustaceans 8.55
crustier 38.49
crustiest 38.61
crusty 38.3
crutch 37.6
crutches 38.45
crux 37.4
Cruz 41.33
cry 21.1
crybaby 8.1
crying 22.26
cryogenic 10.15
cryogenics 10.16
cryonics 24.22
crypt 17.45
cryptic 18.16
cryptographer 24.57
cryptographic 2.18
cryptography 24.54
crystal 18.22
crystal-clear 13.1

crystalline 21.22
crystallization 8.46
crystallize 21.44
crystallized 21.48
crystallography 24.54
crystalloid 33.4
crystals 18.24
cub 37.1
Cub 37.1
Cuba 42.3
Cuban 42.20
Cubans 42.21
cubby 38.1
cubbyhole 35.30
cube 41.5
cubic 42.11
cubicle 42.39
cubism 18.27
cubist 42.28
cubit 42.30
cubits 42.32
cuboid 33.4
cubs 37.2
Cubs 37.2
cuckold 38.24
cuckoldry 38.47
cuckoo 41.3
cuckoopint 21.24
cuckoo spit 17.51
cucumber 38.8
cud 37.8
cuddle 38.23
cuddles 38.25
cuddlesome 38.53
cuddlier 38.49
cuddliest 38.61
cuddly 38.5
cudgel 38.23
cue 41.1
cuff 37.10
cuff link 17.30
cuff links 17.31
cuffs 37.11
cuirass 1.40
cuirassier 13.1
cuisine 15.24
cul-de-sac 1.3
culinary 38.47
cull 37.16
Cullen 38.28
culler 38.12
culling 38.34
Culloden 24.33
culminate 7.48
culminating 8.60
culmination 8.38
culottes 23.45
culpability 18.58

culpable 38.52
Culpeper 10.8
culprit 38.43
cult 37.26
cultic 38.15
cultivable 38.65
cultivar 3.1
cultivate 7.48
cultivated 8.13
cultivation 8.38
cultivator 8.5
cultural 38.52
culturally 38.64
culture 38.14
culture shock 23.3
cultured 38.20
cultus 38.38
Culver 38.11
culvert 38.42
cumber 38.8
Cumberland 38.55
Cumbernauld 25.15
cumbersome 38.53
cumbrance 38.33
Cumbria 38.49
Cumbrian 38.54
cumbrous 38.38
cumin 38.27
cum laude 7.3; 26.1
cummerbund 37.36;
38.55
Cumming 38.34
Cummings 38.35
Cumnor 38.13
cumulate 7.49
cumulation 8.39
cumulative 17.54
cumuli 21.4
cumulonimbus 18.44
cumulus 42.46
Cunard 3.8
cuneiform 25.20
cunnilingus 18.44
cunning 38.34
Cunningham 38.53
cunningly 38.47
cunt 37.40
cup 37.41
cupbearer 6.2
cupboard 38.20
cupboard love 37.49
cupboards 38.21
cupcake 7.6
cupel 42.16
cupful 39.7
Cupid 42.13
cupidity 18.57
cupola 42.37

cuppa 38.8
cupped 37.42
cupping 38.34
Cuprinol® 23.15
cupronickel 18.22
cuprous 42.26
cur 11.1
curable 28.19
Curaçao 29.1; 35.19
curacy 28.17
curare 4.5
curate 26.31
curative 17.55
curator 8.5
curatorship 17.43
curb 11.2
curbed 11.3
curbing 12.16
curd 11.7
curdle 12.8
cure 27.1
curé 7.3
cured 27.2
curer 28.2
cures 27.3
curettage 3.13; 10.20
curette 9.51
curettement 10.33
curfew 41.3
curia 28.18
curie 28.1
Curie 28.1
Curies 28.16
curing 28.11
curio 35.19
curios 35.52
curiosity 24.56
curious 28.24
curium 28.20
curl 11.11
curled 11.12
curler 12.2
curlew 41.3
curlicue 41.4
curlier 12.31
curliest 12.39
curling 12.16
curly 12.1
Curly Wurly 12.1
curmudgeon 38.28
Curran 38.28
currant 38.32
currants 38.33
currency 38.47
current 38.32
currently 38.47
Currer 38.12
curricle 38.52

curricula 18.60
curriculum 18.66
curriculum vitae 21.3
curried 38.19
currier 38.49
curry 38.5
Curry 38.5
currycomb 35.34
curse 11.22
cursed 11.23; 12.4
cursing 12.16
cursive 12.27
cursor 12.2
cursory 12.29
curt 11.24
curtail 7.15
curtailed 7.16
curtailment 8.56
curtain 12.12
curtained 12.13
curter 12.2
curtest 12.20
Curtis 12.18
curtly 12.1
curtness 12.19
curtsied 12.4
curtsy 12.1
curvaceous 8.67
curvature 12.30; 27.1
curve 11.27
curved 11.28
curvet 9.51
curving 12.16
curvy 12.1
Curzon 12.12
Cusack 1.3
Cushing 40.15
cushion 40.10
Cushitic 18.16
cushy 40.1
cuspid 38.19
cuss 37.43
cussed 38.19
cussing 38.34
custard 38.20
Custer 38.10
custodial 36.38
custodian 36.40
custodianship 17.43
custody 38.47
custom 38.26
customary 38.47
custom-built 17.21
customer 38.48
custom house 29.12
customization 8.51
customize 21.46
custom-made 7.8

cut 37.47
cut and paste 7.31
cutaneous 8.85
cutaway 7.4
cutback 1.3
cute 41.27
cuteness 42.26
cuter 42.5
cutest 42.27
cutesy 42.1
Cuthbert 38.42
Cuthbertson 38.54
cuticle 42.39
cutie 42.1
cutlass 38.38
cutler 38.12
cutlery 38.47
cutlet 38.43
cutoff 23.9
cutout 29.14
cutpurse 11.22
cuts 37.48
cutter 38.10
cutters 38.45
cut-throat 35.45
cutting 38.34
cuttingly 38.47
cuttings 38.35
cuttle 38.23
cuttlebone 35.36
cuttlefish 17.50
Cutty Sark 3.3
cuvée 7.3
CV 15.2
cwm 39.9; 41.17
Cwmbran 3.19
cyan 1.24; 22.20
cyanide 21.12
cyanosis 36.25
cybercafé 2.4; 7.3
cybercrime 21.19
cybernetic 10.15
cybernetics 10.16
cyberpet 9.51
cyberpunk 37.32
cybersex 9.3
cyberspace 7.30
cybersquatting 24.40
cyberwar 25.4
cyborg 25.12
cycad 1.9
Cyclades 15.45
cyclamate 7.41
cyclamen 18.67
cycle 22.16
cyclic 22.11
cyclical 18.64; 22.43
cycling 22.26

cyclist 22.30
cyclometer 24.57
cyclone 35.36
cyclonic 24.19
Cyclopean 36.40
cyclopedia 16.40
Cyclops 23.37
cyclorama 4.13
cyclostyle 21.16
cyclotron 23.27
cygnet 18.50
cylinder 18.60
cylindrical 18.64
cymbal 18.22
cymbals 18.24
Cymbeline 15.26
Cymric 18.16
cynic 18.16
cynical 18.64
cynically 18.57
cynicism 18.28
cynics 18.17
cynosure 27.1
Cynthia 18.61
cypress 22.29
Cyprian 18.67
Cypriot 18.77
Cyprus 22.29
Cyril 18.22
Cyrillic 18.16
Cyrus 20.8; 22.29
cyst 17.49
cystic 18.16
cystitis 22.28
cystocele 15.17
Cytherea 16.2
cytology 24.55
cytoplasm 2.32
cytoplasmic 2.20
Czech 9.2
Czechoslovakia 2.61
Czechoslovakian 2.66
D 15.1
dab 1.1
dabber 2.8
dabble 2.28
dabbler 2.12
dabbling 2.42
dabchick 2.21
dabs 1.2
dace 7.30
dacha 2.14
dachshund 2.36
dachshunds 2.37
dacoit 33.13
dacoits 33.14
dacoity 34.1
Dacre 8.4

Dacron® 23.27
dactyl 2.28; 17.15
dactylic 18.16
dad 1.9
Dada 3.1
Dadaism 18.28
Dadaist 4.54
daddy 2.3
daddy-long-legs 9.13
dado 35.6
dad's 1.10
Daedalus 16.47
daemon 16.22
daff 1.11
daffodil 17.15
daffodils 17.23
daffs 1.12
daffy 2.4
daft 3.10
dafter 4.10
daftest 4.34
dag 1.13
Dagenham 2.65
Dagestan 1.24; 3.19
dagger 2.9
daggers 2.55
daggy 2.2
daglock 23.3
Daguerre 5.1
daguerreotype 21.26
Dahl 3.14
dahlia 8.7; 8.78
Dahomey 36.1
Dai 21.1
Daihatsu 41.3
dailies 8.74
daily 8.1
Daimler 8.7
daintier 8.78
daintiest 8.86
daintily 8.76
daintiness 8.85
dainty 8.1
daiquiri 22.40
dairies 6.14
dairy 6.1
dairying 6.21
dairymaid 7.8
dairyman 1.24
dairyman 6.19
dairywoman 40.10
dais 8.66
daisies 8.74
daisy 8.1
daisywheel 15.17
Dakar 2.9
Dakota 36.5
Dakotan 36.20

Dalai Lama 4.13
dale 7.15
Dale 7.15
Dalek 9.2
Daleks 9.3
Dales 7.17
dalesman 8.21
Daley 8.1
Dalglish 15.34
Dalhousie 30.1
Dali 4.5
Dallas 2.46
dalliance 2.69
dallied 2.24
dallier 2.61
dally 2.5
Dalmatia 8.9
Dalmatian 8.23
Dalmatians 8.55
Dalrymple 18.22
Dalton 24.33; 26.19
daltonism 18.28
Dalziel 9.16
dam 1.22
damage 2.27
damageable 2.79
Damascene 15.26
Damascus 2.46
Dambuster 38.10
dame 7.18
Dame 7.18
Damian 8.81
damming 2.42
dammit 2.51
damn 1.22
damnable 2.64
damnably 2.56
damnation 8.23
damnations 8.55
damnedest 2.48
damnify 21.4
Damocles 15.45
Damon 8.21
damp 1.23
dampcourse 25.28
dampen 2.35
damper 2.8
dampest 2.48
dampness 2.46
damp squib 17.1
damsel 2.28
damselfish 17.50
damselfly 21.4
damson 2.35
damsons 2.39
dan 1.24
Dan 1.24

Dana 4.13
dance 3.22
dancehall 25.14
dancer 4.14
dancing 4.29
dandelion 22.20
dander 2.10
dandify 21.4
dandle 2.28
dandruff 37.10
dandy 2.3
Dandy 2.3
Dane 7.21
Danegeld 9.19
Danes 7.26
dang 1.29
danger 8.9
Dangerfield 15.18
dangerous 8.85
dangers 8.75
dangle 2.28
Daniel 2.28
Danielle 9.16
Daniels 2.30
Danish 8.70
dank 1.25
danker 2.9
dankest 2.48
Dankworth 2.52; 11.26
Dannimac® 1.3
Danny 2.6
Dan's 1.36
Dante 2.3; 7.3
Dante Alighieri 6.1
Dantean 2.66
Danton 23.27
Danube 41.5
Danubian 42.41
Danvers 2.55
Danzig 17.12
Dão 29.1
dap 1.37
Daphne 2.6
daphnia 2.61
Daphnis 2.45
dapper 2.8
dapple 2.28
dappled 2.29
daps 1.38
darbies 4.40
Darby 4.1
Darcy 4.7
Dard 3.8
Dardanelles 9.27
dare 5.1
dared 5.2
daredevil 10.21
dares 5.5

daresay 7.2
Dar es Salaam 3.16
Darfur 27.1
Darien 2.66; 6.19
daring 6.10
daringly 6.15
dariole 35.30
Darius 6.22; 22.29
Darjeeling 16.27
dark 3.3
darken 4.24
darkened 4.25
darkening 4.52
darker 4.9
darkest 4.34
dark-haired 5.2
darkling 4.29
darkly 4.5
darkness 4.32
darkroom 39.9; 41.17
dark-skinned 17.34
darling 4.29
Darling 4.29
Darlington 4.50
darn 3.19
darned 3.21
darnedest 4.34
darnel 4.19
darner 4.13
darning 4.29
Darnley 4.5
darns 3.24
Darrell 2.28
Darrell's 2.30
Darren 2.35
dart 3.32
d'Artagnan 2.35
dartboard 25.9
darter 4.10
Dartford 4.17
Darth Vader 8.5
darting 4.29
Dartmoor 25.3; 27.1
Dartmouth 4.39
darts 3.33
Darwen 4.23
Darwin 4.23
Darwinian 18.67
Darwinism 18.28
Darwinist 4.54
Darwin's 4.26
dash 1.43
dashboard 25.9
dasher 2.14
dashing 2.42
dastard 2.25
dastardly 2.56
data 4.10; 8.5

data bank 1.25
database 7.30
datable 8.79
Datchet 2.51
date 7.32
dated 8.13
dateless 8.67
dateline 21.22
dates 7.50
dating 8.60
dative 8.73
Datsun 2.35
datum 4.22; 8.19
daub 25.5
daube 35.20
dauber 26.2
dauby 26.1
daughter 26.4
daughter-in-law 25.2
daughterless 26.47
daughterly 26.37
daughters 26.36
daunt 25.25
daunted 26.12
daunting 26.25
dauntless 26.27
dauphin 26.18
Dave 7.54
Davenport 25.31
Daventry 2.56
Dave's 7.55
David 8.12
Davidson 8.81
da Vinci 18.7
Davis 8.66
Davis Cup 37.41
Davison 8.81
davit 2.51
Davy 8.1
Davy Jones 35.39
Davy lamp 1.23
dawdle 26.15
dawdler 26.6
dawdling 26.25
Dawkins 26.22
Dawlish 26.30
dawn 25.22
Dawn 25.22
dawned 25.24
dawning 26.25
Dawson 26.19
day 7.1
Dayan 3.19
day bed 9.8
daybook 39.1
dayboy 33.1
daybreak 7.6
daycare 5.1

daycentre 10.10
daydream 15.20
daydreamer 16.8
Day-Glo® 35.6
Day-Lewis 42.25
daylight 21.33
daylights 21.35
daylong 23.31
dayroom 39.9; 41.17
days 7.56
dayspring 8.62
daystar 3.1
daytime 21.19
day-to-day 7.4
Dayton 8.21
Daytona 36.8
day trip 17.43
Daz® 1.50
daze 7.56
dazed 7.57
dazzle 2.28
dazzled 2.29
dazzler 2.12
dazzlingly 2.58
deacon 16.22
deaconess 9.47
deaconry 16.38
deacons 16.24
deactivate 7.35
deactivation 8.24
deactivator 8.5
dead 9.8
deadbeat 15.35
dead beat 15.35
deaden 10.27
deadhead 9.8
deadheading 10.36
deadlier 10.57
deadliest 10.71
deadline 21.22
deadlock 23.3
deadlocked 23.6
deadly 10.5
deadpan 1.24
deadwood 39.4
deaf 9.10
deafen 10.27
deafened 10.29
deafening 10.69
deafeningly 10.78
deafer 10.11
deafest 10.43
deafness 10.42
Deakin 16.21
deal 15.17
Deal 15.17
dealer 16.7
dealers 16.37

dealership 17.43
dealing 16.27
dealings 16.28
deals 15.19
dealt 9.23
dean 15.23
Dean 15.23
deanery 16.38
Dean's 15.29
dear 13.1
dearer 14.2
dearest 14.16
dearie 14.1
dearly 14.1
dearness 14.14
dearth 11.26
death 9.54
deathbed 9.8
deathblow 35.7
deathless 10.42
deathly 10.5
deaths 9.55
death trap 1.37
deathwatch 23.7
deb 9.1
debacle 4.19
debag 1.13
debagging 2.42
debar 3.1
debark 3.3
debarkation 8.31
debarred 3.8
debase 7.30
debased 7.31
debasement 8.56
debatable 8.79
debate 7.33
debater 8.5
debating 8.60
debauch 25.8
debauchee 15.4
debaucher 26.8
debauchery 26.37
debauching 26.25
Debbie 10.1
Debenham 10.63
debenture 10.14
debilitate 7.41
debilitating 8.60
debilitation 8.32
debility 18.58
debit 10.48
debited 10.58
debonair 5.1
Deborah 10.12; 10.56
Debrett 9.51
debrief 15.13
debriefing 16.27

debris 8.1; 10.5; 15.3
debt 9.51
debtor 10.10
debts 9.52
debud 37.8
debug 37.14
debugger 38.9
debugging 38.34
debunk 37.32
debunked 37.34
debunker 38.9
debunking 38.34
deburr 11.1
debus 37.43
Debussy 42.1
debut 41.3
debutante 3.23
Dec 9.2
decade 7.8
decadence 10.68
decadent 10.67
decaf 1.11
decaffeinate 7.35
decaffeination 8.24
decagon 10.64; 23.27
decagonal 2.64
decahedron 16.22
decal 1.16
decalcify 21.4
decalitre 16.5
Decalogue 23.11
Decameron 2.66
decametre 16.5
decamp 1.23
decamping 2.42
decanal 8.15
decant 1.33
decanted 2.25
decanter 2.10
decanting 2.42
decants 1.34
decapitate 7.35
decapitated 8.13
decapitation 8.24
decapod 23.8
decathlete 15.35
decathlon 2.35; 23.27
Decatur 8.5
decay 7.2
decayed 7.8
decaying 8.58
decays 7.56
Decca 10.9
Deccan 10.27
decease 15.32
deceased 15.33
deceit 15.35
deceitful 16.17; 39.7

definitely 10.78
definition 18.33
definitive 17.55
definitively 18.80
deflate 7.33
deflated 8.13
deflation 8.23
deflationary 8.76
deflect 9.5
deflection 10.28
deflower 31.1
deflowered 31.2
deflowering 32.3
Defoe 35.2
defoliant 36.41
defoliation 8.37
deforest 24.45
deforestation 8.34
deforested 24.59
deform 25.20
deformation 8.28
deformed 25.21
deformity 26.37
Defra 10.12
defraud 25.9
defrauded 26.12
defrauder 26.4
defrauds 25.10
defray 7.2
defrayal 8.15
defrayment 8.56
defrock 23.3
defrocked 23.6
defrocking 24.40
defrost 23.41
defrosted 24.24
defroster 24.10
defrosting 24.40
deft 9.11
deftly 10.5
deftness 10.42
defunct 37.34
defuse 41.33
defused 41.34
defy 21.2
Deganwy 2.5
degas 1.40
Degas 3.1
degassed 1.42
de Gaulle 25.14; 35.30
degauss 29.12
degaussed 29.13
degeneracy 10.78
degenerate 7.38; 10.73
degeneration 8.28
degenerative 17.54
deglaze 7.56
degradable 8.79

degradation 8.28
degrade 7.8
degraded 8.13
degrading 8.60
degrease 15.32
degreaser 16.9
degree 15.2
degrees 15.43
dehisce 17.46
dehiscence 18.39
dehiscent 18.38
dehorn 25.22
dehorned 25.24
dehumanization 8.52
dehumanize 21.46
dehumidification
  8.46
dehumidifier 22.2
dehumidify 21.4
dehydrate 7.40
dehydrated 8.13
dehydration 8.31
de-ice 21.29
de-iced 21.30
de-icer 22.9
deicide 21.12
deific 18.16
deification 8.42
deify 21.4
Deighton 8.21
deign 7.21
deigned 7.22
de-ionization 8.47
de-ionize 21.44
de-ionized 21.48
Deirdre 14.1
Deirdre's 14.17
deism 18.27
deist 16.31
deity 8.76; 16.38
déjà vu 41.4
deject 9.5
dejected 10.18
dejection 10.28
de jure 7.3
Dekker 10.9
dekko 35.7
de Klerk 11.4
Del 9.16
de la Mare 5.1
Delamere 13.1
delaminate 7.35
Delaney 8.1
Delano 35.6
Delaware 5.1
delay 7.2
delayed 7.8
delayer 8.2

delaying 8.58
delectable 10.60
delectation 8.31
delegate 7.38; 10.73
delegation 8.28
delete 15.35
deleterious 14.23
deletion 16.22
deletions 16.24
Delhi 10.5
deli 10.5
Delia 16.40
Delian 16.43
deliberate 7.41
deliberate 18.77
deliberately 18.56
deliberation 8.32
deliberative 17.54
Delibes 15.5
delicacy 10.78
delicately 10.78
delicatessen 10.28
delicious 18.44
delight 21.32
delighted 22.13
delightful 22.16; 39.7
delightfully 22.40
delights 21.35
Delilah 22.7
delimit 18.50
delineate 7.41
delineation 8.32
delinquency 18.56
delinquent 18.38
delinquents 18.39
deliquesce 9.47
deliquescence 10.34
deliquescent 10.33
delirious 18.74
delirium 18.66
delirium tremens
  9.43
delist 17.49
Delius 16.47
deliver 18.11
deliverable 18.64;
  18.81
deliverance 18.39;
  18.71
delivered 18.19
deliverer 18.60
delivery 18.56
dell 9.16
Dell 9.16
Della 10.12
Del Mar 3.1
Del Monte 24.3
Delos 23.39

delouse 29.12
deloused 29.13
Delphi 10.4
Delphian 10.64
Delphic 10.15
Del's 9.27
delta 10.10
delude 41.9
deluded 42.14
deluge 41.12
delusion 42.20
delusional 42.39
delusory 42.36
de luxe 37.4
delve 9.25
delver 10.11
delves 9.26
delving 10.36
demagnetization 8.40
demagnetize 21.42
demagnetized 21.48
demagogic 24.20
demagogical 24.61
demagogue 23.11
demagoguery 24.54
demagogy 24.2; 24.7
demand 3.21
demanding 4.29
demarcate 7.40
demarcation 8.31
démarche 3.31
dematerialize 21.47
dematerialized 21.48
demean 15.24
demeaning 16.27
demeanour 16.8
Demelza 10.14
demented 10.18
dementia 10.14
demerara 6.2
demerge 11.10
demerger 12.2
demerit 10.48
demesne 7.21
Demeter 16.5
demigod 23.8
demijohn 23.27
demilitarization 8.53
demilitarize 21.47
demilitarized 21.48
De Mille 17.15
demimonde 23.30
demineralization 8.53
demineralize 21.47
demineralized 21.48
demise 21.40
demi-sec 9.2
demisemiquaver 8.6

demission 18.33
demist 17.49
demister 18.10
demitasse 1.40
demiurge 11.10
demo 35.7
demob 23.1
demobilization 8.50
demobilize 21.45
demobilized 21.48
democracy 24.54
democrat 1.45
Democrat 1.45
democratic 2.17
democratically 2.58
democratization 8.48
democratize 21.45
Democritus 24.70
démodé 7.3
demodulation 8.34
demographic 2.18
demographics 2.23
demography 24.54
demoiselle 9.16
demolish 24.46
demolished 24.47
demolisher 24.57
demolition 18.33
demon 16.22
demoniac 1.3
demoniacal 22.43
demonic 24.19
demonism 18.28
demonization 8.45
demonize 21.43
demonolatry 24.54
demonology 24.55
demons 16.24
demonstrable 24.61
demonstrably 24.54
demonstrate 7.38
demonstration 8.28
demonstrative 17.55
demonstrator 8.5
de Montfort 24.48
demoralization 8.48
demoralize 21.45
demoralized 21.48
Demosthenes 15.45
demote 35.45
demoted 36.12
demotic 24.16
demotion 36.20
Dempsey 10.7
Dempster 10.10
demulcent 38.32
demulsify 21.4
demur 11.1

demure 27.1
demurely 28.1
demurrage 38.22
demurral 38.23
demurrer 38.12
demutualization 8.53
demutualize 21.47
demystification 8.46
demystify 21.4
demythologize 21.45
den 9.32
Den 9.32
denarius 6.22
denary 16.38
denationalization
8.53
denationalize 21.47
denationalized 21.48
denaturalize 21.47
denature 8.9
denazify 21.4
Denbigh 10.1
Denby 10.1
Dench 9.33
dendrochronology
24.55
Deneuve 11.27
dengue 10.2
Den Haag 3.11
Denham 10.25
deniable 22.43
denial 19.3
denier 7.4; 10.57
denier 22.2
denies 21.40
denigrate 7.38
denigration 8.28
denigrator 8.5
denim 10.24
De Niro 35.9
Denise 15.32; 15.43
denizen 10.64
Denmark 3.3
Denning 10.36
Dennis 10.41
Denny 10.6
denominate 7.43
denomination 8.34
denominational 8.79
denominative 17.54
denominator 8.5
denotation 8.31
denotative 17.55
denote 35.45
denoted 36.12
denoting 36.24
denounce 29.9
denounced 29.10

denouncer 30.2
dense 9.39
densely 10.5
density 10.54
dent 9.41
dental 10.21
dental floss 23.39
dentate 7.34
dented 10.18
dentine 15.25
dentist 10.44
dentistry 10.54
dentition 18.33
Denton 10.27
dents 9.39
denture 10.14
denudation 8.31
denude 41.9
denunciate 7.48
denunciation 8.38
Denver 10.11
deny 21.2
Denzil 10.21; 17.15
deoch-an-doruis
24.42
deodar 3.1
deodorant 36.41
deodorization 8.50
deodorize 21.45
deodorizer 22.9
Deo volente 10.3
deoxygenate 7.33
deoxyribonucleic
8.10
depart 3.32
departed 4.17
departing 4.29
department 4.27
departmental 10.21
departmentalism
18.28
departmentalize 21.43
departmentally 10.53
departments 4.28
departure 4.14
depend 9.35
dependability 18.58
dependable 10.60
dependant 10.33
dependants 10.34
dependence 10.34
dependency 10.53
dependent 10.33
depersonalization 8.53
depersonalize 21.47
depict 17.6
depiction 18.33
depilate 7.38

depilation 8.28
depilator 8.5
depilatory 18.56
deplane 7.21
deplete 15.35
depleted 16.14
depletion 16.22
deplorable 26.41
deplorably 26.37
deplore 25.2
deplored 25.9
deploy 33.1
deployed 33.4
deployment 34.9
depolarization 8.50
depolarize 21.45
depoliticize 21.44
depopulate 7.43
depopulation 8.34
deport 25.31
deportation 8.31
deported 26.12
deportee 15.4
deportment 26.23
deposal 36.15
depose 35.52
deposed 35.53
deposit 24.49
deposited 24.59
deposition 18.33
depositor 24.57
depository 24.56
depot 35.7
Depp 9.44
deprave 7.54
depravity 2.57
deprecate 7.38
deprecation 8.28
deprecatory 8.76
depreciable 16.41
depreciate 7.40
depreciation 8.31
depredation 8.28
depress 9.47
depressant 10.33
depressed 9.49
depressing 10.36
depressingly 10.54
depression 10.28
Depression 10.28
depressive 10.50
depressor 10.14
depressurization 8.43
depressurize 21.43
depressurized 21.48
deprivation 8.28
deprive 21.37
deprogramme 1.22

Deptford 10.18
deputation 8.28
depute 41.27
deputize 21.43
deputy 10.53; 10.55
deputyship 17.43
De Quincey 18.7
derail 7.15
derailed 7.16
derailleur 8.7
derailment 8.56
derange 7.23
deranged 7.24
derangement 8.56
Derby 4.1
Derbyshire 4.43; 13.1
derecognize 21.43
deregister 10.56
deregulate 7.38
deregulation 8.28
Derek 10.15
Derek's 10.16
derelict 17.6
dereliction 18.33
derequisition 18.33
derestrict 17.6
derestriction 18.33
deride 21.10
derided 22.13
de rigueur 11.1
derision 18.33
derisive 22.37
derisively 22.40
derisory 22.40
derivation 8.28
derivative 17.55
derive 21.37
dermabrasion 8.21
dermal 12.8
dermatitis 22.28
dermatoid 33.4
dermatological 24.61
dermatologist 24.72
dermatology 24.55
dermis 12.18
Dermot 12.24
derogate 7.38
derogation 8.28
derogative 17.55
derogatory 24.54
Deronda 24.10
derrick 10.15
derrière 5.1
derring-do 41.4
derris 10.41
Derry 10.5
derv 11.27
dervish 12.22

Derwent 12.14
Derwentwater 26.4
Desai 21.2
desalinate 7.35
desalination 8.24
descale 7.15
descant 1.33
Descartes 3.32
descend 9.35
descendant 10.33
descended 10.18
descender 10.10
descending 10.36
descent 9.41
deschool 41.14
describable 22.43
describe 21.5
described 21.6
describing 22.26
description 18.33
descriptive 18.53
descriptivism 18.28
descriptor 18.10
descry 21.2
Desdemona 36.8
desecrate 7.38
desecration 8.28
desegregate 7.38
desegregation 8.28
deselect 9.5
deselection 10.28
desensitization 8.43
desensitize 21.43
desert 10.47; 11.24
deserted 12.5
deserter 12.2
desertification 8.44
deserting 12.16
desertion 12.12
deserve 11.27
deserved 11.28
deservedly 12.29
deserver 12.2
deserving 12.16
desex 9.3
desexualize 21.47
deshabille 15.17
desiccant 10.67
desiccate 7.38
desiccated 8.13
desiccation 8.28
desiderata 4.10
desideratum 4.22
Desiderius 14.23
design 21.22
designate 7.38
designation 8.28
designed 21.23

designedly 22.40
designer 22.8
designing 22.26
designs 21.25
desirability 18.58
desirable 20.12
desire 19.1
desired 19.2
Desirée 7.3
desires 19.4
desiring 20.7
desirous 20.8
desist 17.49
desk 9.48
deskill 17.15
deskilling 18.40
desktop 23.36
desman 10.27
Des Moines 33.8
Desmond 10.29
Desmond Tutu 41.3
desolate 10.73
desolation 8.28
despair 5.1
despaired 5.2
despairing 6.10
desperado 35.4
desperate 10.73
desperately 10.53
desperation 8.28
despicable 18.64
despise 21.40
despised 21.48
despiser 22.9
despite 21.32
despoil 33.6
despoiled 33.7
despoiler 34.2
despoliation 8.37
despond 23.30
despondency 24.54
despondent 24.38
despondently 24.54
despot 23.44
despotic 24.16
despotism 18.28
des res 9.57
dessert 11.24
dessertspoon 41.19
destabilization 8.42
destabilize 21.42
destination 8.28
destine 10.26
destined 17.34
destiny 10.54
destitute 41.27
destitution 42.20
destroy 33.1

destroyable 34.16
destroyed 33.4
destroyer 34.2
destroying 34.11
destroys 33.15
destructible 38.52
destruction 38.28
destructionist 38.60
destructive 38.44
destructiveness 38.59
destructor 38.10
desuetude 41.9
desultory 10.53
detach 1.7
detachable 2.64
detached 1.8
detachment 2.40
detail 7.15
details 7.17
detain 7.21
detained 7.22
detainee 15.4
detainer 8.8
detect 9.5
detectable 10.60
detected 10.18
detection 10.28
detective 10.50
detector 10.10
detectorist 10.72
détente 3.23
detention 10.28
deter 11.1
detergent 12.14
detergents 12.15
deteriorate 7.33
deterioration 8.44
determinable 12.41
determinant 12.35
determinate 12.40
determination 8.29
determine 12.11
determined 17.34
determiner 12.30
determinism 18.28
determinist 12.38
deterrence 10.34
deterrent 10.33
detest 9.49
detestable 10.60
detestation 8.31
dethrone 35.36
dethroned 35.37
detonate 7.38
detonation 8.28
detonator 8.5
detour 27.1
detox 23.5

detoxification 8.48
detoxify 21.4
detract 1.6
detraction 2.35
detractor 2.10
detrain 7.21
detriment 10.67
detrimental 10.21
detrition 18.33
detritus 22.29
Detroit 33.13
de trop 35.2
Dettol® 23.15
Deucalion 8.81
deuce 41.24
deuced 41.25
deuced 42.13
deus ex machina 2.60
deuterium 14.20
Deuteronomy 24.54
Deutschmark 3.3
de Valera 6.2
devaluation 8.24
devalue 41.3
devalued 41.9
Devanagari 4.42
devastate 7.38
devastating 8.60
devastation 8.28
develop 10.38
developed 10.40
developer 10.56
development 10.67
developments 10.68
develops 10.39
De Vere 13.1
deviance 16.45
deviancy 16.52
deviant 16.44
deviants 16.45
deviate 7.40
deviation 8.31
device 21.29
devices 22.39
devil 10.21
devil-may-care 5.1
devilment 10.67
devilry 10.53
Devine 15.24
devious 16.47
devise 21.40
devisor 22.9
devitalize 21.44
Devizes 22.39
Devlin 10.26
devoid 33.4
devolution 42.20
devolve 23.20

devolved 23.21
Devon 10.27
Devonian 36.40
Devonport 25.31
devote 35.45
devoted 36.12
devotedly 36.35
devotee 15.4
devotion 36.20
devotional 36.38
devour 31.1
devoured 31.2
devourer 32.2
devouring 32.3
devout 29.14
devoutly 30.1
De Vries 15.32
dew 41.1
Dewar 42.2
dewclaw 25.3
dewdrop 23.36
Dewey 42.1
Dewhurst 11.23
Dewi 10.5
de Witt 17.51
dewlap 1.37
dew point 33.10
Dewsbury 42.36
dewy 42.1
dewy-eyed 21.12
Dexter 10.10
dexterity 10.54
dextral 10.21
dextrose 35.42
dextrous 10.42
Dhaka 2.9
dhal 3.14
dhansak 1.3
dharma 4.13
dhobi 36.1
dhoti 36.1
dhow 29.1
Di 21.1
diabetes 15.44; 16.36
diabetic 10.15
diabetics 10.16
diabolic 24.18
diabolical 24.61
diabolically 24.56
diabolo 35.19
diaconal 2.64
diaconate 2.74; 7.35
diacritic 18.16
diacritical 18.64
diadem 9.28
diaeresis 17.46
Diaghilev 9.10; 9.56
diagnose 35.52

diagnoses 15.44; 36.33
diagnosing 36.24
diagnosis 36.25
diagnostic 24.16
diagnostician 18.33
diagnostics 24.22
diagonal 2.64
diagonally 2.78
diagram 1.22
diagrammatic 2.17
dial 19.3
dialect 9.5
dialectic 10.15
dialectics 10.16
dialectology 24.55
dialler 20.2
dialling 20.7
dialogue 23.11
dialyse 21.44
dialyser 22.9
dialysis 17.46
dialytic 18.16
diamanté 7.3
diamantine 21.22
diameter 2.60
diametric 10.15
diametrical 10.60
diametrically 10.54
diamond 20.4
diamorphine 15.25
Diana 2.13
Diane 1.24
dianthus 2.46
diapason 8.21
diaper 22.3
diaphanous 2.71
diaphoresis 16.29
diaphoretic 10.15
diaphragm 1.22
diarist 20.9
diarrhoea 13.1
diary 20.1
Diaspora 2.60
diastole 2.56
diastolic 24.18
diathermy 12.1
diatom 23.23
diatonic 24.19
diatribe 21.5
diazepam 1.22
dib 17.1
dibble 18.22
Dibley 18.5
dibs 17.2
dice 21.29
diced 21.30
dicer 22.9
dicey 22.1

dichotomize 21.45
dichotomous 24.70
dichotomy 24.54
dichromic 36.10
dick 17.3
Dick 17.3
dickens 18.36
Dickens 18.36
Dickensian 10.64
dicker 18.9
dickhead 9.8
Dickie 18.2
Dickinson 18.67
Dickon 18.32
Dick's 17.4
Dick Turpin 12.11
dicky 18.2
dickybird 11.7
dicta 18.10
Dictaphone® 35.36
dictate 7.33
dictate 7.34
dictation 8.23
dictator 8.5
dictatorial 26.41
dictatorship 17.43
diction 18.33
dictionary 18.56
Dictograph® 1.11; 3.9
dictum 18.26
did 17.8
didactic 2.17
Didcot 18.49; 23.44
diddle 18.22
diddler 18.12
diddly-squat 23.44
diddums 18.30
diddy 18.3
didgeridoo 41.2
didicoy 33.1
didn't 18.38
Dido 35.12
didst 17.9
die 21.1
died 21.9
Die Fledermaus 29.12
Diego 35.6
diehard 3.8
dielectric 10.15
Dien Bien Phu 41.4
Dieppe 9.44
dies 21.39
diesel 16.17
diet 22.34
dietary 22.40
Dieter 16.5
dieter 22.41
dietetic 10.15

dietetics 10.16
dietician 18.33
Dietrich 16.11
differ 18.11
differed 18.19
difference 18.39; 18.71
different 18.38; 18.70
differential 10.21
differentiate 7.38
differentiated 8.13
differentiation 8.28
differently 18.56
differing 18.73
difficult 37.26
difficulty 18.80
diffidence 18.71
diffident 18.70
diffract 1.6
diffraction 2.35
diffuse 41.24; 41.33
diffuser 42.9
diffusion 42.20
dig 17.12
Digby 18.1
digerati 4.3
digest 9.49
digested 10.18
digester 10.10
digestible 10.60
digestion 10.28
digestive 10.50
digger 18.9
digging 18.40
digit 18.50
digital 18.64
digitalis 8.66
digitalism 18.29
digitalization 8.53
digitalize 21.47
digitally 18.80
digitization 8.46
digitize 21.44
digits 18.51
dignified 21.12
dignify 21.4
dignitary 18.57
dignity 18.57
digraph 1.11; 3.9
digress 9.47
digressing 10.36
digression 10.28
digressive 10.50
digs 17.13
diktat 1.45
dilapidated 8.13
dilapidation 8.24
dilate 7.33

dilation 8.23
dilatory 18.56
Dilbert 18.49
dildo 35.11
dilemma 10.13
dilettante 2.3
diligence 18.71
diligent 18.70
diligently 18.80
dill 17.15
Dillon 18.32
dilly-dallied 2.24
dilly-dally 2.5
dilute 41.27
diluted 42.14
dilution 42.20
diluvial 42.39
Dilys 18.43
dim 17.24
DiMaggio 35.19
Dimbleby 18.56
dime 21.19
dimension 10.28
dimes 21.21
diminish 18.47
diminished 18.48
diminuendo 35.7
diminution 42.20
diminutive 17.55
dimity 18.57
dimly 18.5
dimmed 17.25
dimmer 18.13
dimmest 18.46
dimming 18.40
Dimmock 18.15
dimness 18.44
dimple 18.22
dimples 18.24
dimply 18.5
dim sum 37.27
dimwit 18.50
din 17.29
Dinah 22.8
dinar 3.1
dine 21.22
dined 21.23
diner 22.8
diners 22.39
dinette 9.51
ding 17.35
dingbat 1.45
dingbats 1.46
ding-dong 23.31
dinge 17.37
dinger 18.13
dinghy 18.2; 18.6
dingier 18.61

dingiest 18.76
dingle 18.22
dingo 35.11
dingy 18.7
dining 22.26
dining room 39.9; 41.17
dink 17.30
dinkum 18.26
dinky 18.2
dinner 18.13
dinners 18.55
dinner time 21.19
dinosaur 25.4
dint 17.39
diocesan 24.64
diocese 17.46
Diocletian 16.22
diode 35.25
Diogenes 15.45
Dion 23.27
Dionne 23.27
Dionysiac 1.3
Dionysian 18.67
Dionysius 18.74
Dionysus 22.29
Diophantus 2.46
dioptre 24.10
dioptric 24.18
Dior 25.2; 25.3
diorama 4.13
dioramic 2.20
Dioscuri 28.1
dioxide 21.11
dioxin 24.32
dip 17.43
diphtheria 14.18
diphthong 23.31
diphthongal 24.27
diplodocus 24.70; 36.26
diploma 36.8
diplomacy 36.35
diplomat 1.45
diplomatic 2.17
diplomatically 2.58
dipole 35.30
dipped 17.45
dipper 18.8
dipping 18.40
dippy 18.1
dipso 35.11
dipsomania 8.78
dipsomaniac 1.3
dipstick 18.16
dip switch 17.7
dipterous 18.74
diptych 18.16

Dirac 1.3
dire 19.1
direct 9.5
directed 10.18
direction 10.28
directional 10.60
directive 10.50
directly 10.5
directness 10.42
director 10.10
directorate 10.73
directors 10.52
directorship 17.43
directory 10.53
directrix 10.16
direly 20.1
direr 20.2
dire straits 7.50
dirge 11.10
dirigible 18.64
dirigisme 16.20
dirk 11.4
Dirk 11.4
dirndl 12.8
dirt 11.24
dirtied 12.4
dirtier 12.31
dirtiest 12.39
dirtily 12.29
dirtiness 12.37
dirty 12.1
Di's 21.39
disability 18.58
disable 8.15
disabled 8.16
disabuse 41.33
disaccharide 21.12
disaccord 25.9
disadvantage 4.18
disadvantageous 8.67
disaffect 9.5
disaffected 10.18
disaffection 10.28
disaffiliate 7.41
disaffiliation 8.32
disagree 15.4
disagreeable 16.41
disagreement 16.25
disallow 29.1
disallows 29.17
disambiguation 8.32
disannul 37.16
disappear 13.1
disappeared 13.2
disappearing 14.12
disappoint 33.10
disappointed 34.3
disappointing 34.11

disk 17.47
diskette 9.51
dislike 21.7
dislikes 21.8
disliking 22.26
dislocate 7.41
dislocation 8.32
dislodge 23.14
dislodging 24.40
dislodgment 24.38
disloyal 34.5
disloyalty 34.14
dismal 18.22
dismally 18.56
dismantle 2.28
dismantled 2.29
dismast 3.30
dismay 7.2
dismayed 7.8
dismember 10.8
dismiss 17.46
dismissal 18.22
dismissed 17.49
dismissing 18.40
dismissive 18.53
dismount 29.11
dismounted 30.3
Disney 18.6
Disneyfication 8.46
Disneyfy 21.4
Disneyland 1.28
disobedience 16.45
disobedient 16.44
disobediently 16.52
disobey 7.4
disoblige 21.15
disorder 26.4
disordered 26.12
disorderly 26.37
disorganization 8.49
disorganize 21.45
disorganized 21.48
disorient 9.41; 26.45
disorientate 7.33
disorientation 8.49
disown 35.36
disowned 35.37
disowning 36.24
disparage 2.27
disparagement 2.68
disparagingly 2.78
disparate 18.77
disparity 2.57
dispassion 2.35
dispassionate 2.74
dispassionately 2.78
dispatch 1.7
dispatched 1.8

dispatcher 2.14
dispel 9.16
dispelled 9.19
dispeller 10.12
dispend 9.35
dispensable 10.60
dispensary 10.53
dispensation 8.32
dispense 9.39
dispensed 9.40
dispenser 10.14
dispensing 10.36
dispersal 12.8
dispersant 12.14
disperse 11.22
dispersed 11.23
disperser 12.2
dispersing 12.16
dispersion 12.12
dispirit 18.50
dispirited 18.62
displace 7.30
displaced 7.31
displacement 8.56
display 7.2
displayed 7.8
displease 15.43
displeasure 10.14
disport 25.31
disposable 36.38
disposal 36.15
dispose 35.52
disposed 35.53
disposition 18.33
dispossess 9.47
dispossession 10.28
dispraise 7.56
Disprin® 18.31
disprize 21.40
disproof 41.10
disproportion 26.19
disproportionate
  26.50
disprovable 42.39
disprove 41.31
disproved 41.32
disputable 42.39
disputant 42.22
disputants 42.23
disputation 8.32
disputatious 8.67
disputative 17.55
dispute 41.27
disputed 42.14
disputer 42.5
disputing 42.24
disqualification 8.48
disqualified 21.12

disqualify 21.4
disquiet 22.34
disquietude 41.9
disquisition 18.33
Disraeli 8.1
disregard 3.8
disregarded 4.17
disrepair 5.1
disreputable 10.79
disrepute 41.27
disrespect 9.5
disrespectful 10.21;
  39.7
disrespectfully 10.53;
  10.55
disrobe 35.20
disrobing 36.24
disrupt 37.42
disrupted 38.20
disrupter 38.10
disrupting 38.34
disruption 38.28
disruptive 38.44
diss 17.46
Diss 17.46
dissatisfaction 2.35
dissatisfied 21.12
dissatisfies 21.42
dissatisfy 21.4
dissect 9.5
dissected 10.18
dissection 10.28
dissector 10.10
disseise 15.43
dissemble 10.21
disseminate 7.38
dissemination 8.28
dissension 10.28
dissent 9.41
dissentient 10.33;
  10.67
dissenting 10.36
dissentious 10.42
dissertation 8.32
disservice 12.18
dissidence 18.71
dissident 18.70
dissimilar 18.60
dissimilarity 2.57
dissimilation 8.46
dissimulate 7.41
dissimulation 8.32
dissipate 7.41
dissipated 8.13
dissipation 8.32
dissociate 7.47
dissociation 8.37
dissoluble 24.61

dissolute 41.27
dissolution 42.20
dissolve 23.20
dissolved 23.21
dissolving 24.40
dissonance 18.71
dissonant 18.70
dissuade 7.8
dissuasion 8.21
dissyllabic 2.17
distaff 3.9
distal 18.22
distance 18.39
distant 18.38
distantly 18.56
distaste 7.31
distasteful 8.15; 39.7
distemper 10.8
distend 9.35
distended 10.18
distension 10.28
distil 17.15
distillate 18.77
distillation 8.32
distilled 17.18
distiller 18.12
distillery 18.56
distilling 18.40
distinct 17.32
distinction 18.33
distinctive 18.53
distinctively 18.57
distinctly 18.5
distinguish 18.47
distinguishable 18.81
distinguished 18.48
distort 25.31
distorted 26.12
distorting 26.25
distortion 26.19
distorts 25.32
distract 1.6
distracted 2.25
distracting 2.42
distraction 2.35
distrain 7.21
distraint 7.25
distrait 7.2
distraught 25.31
distress 9.47
distressed 9.49
distressing 10.36
distressingly 10.54
distribute 41.27
distributed 42.14
distribution 42.20
distributive 17.55
distributor 18.60

district 17.6
distrust 37.45
distrusted 38.20
distrustful 38.23; 39.7
distrusting 38.34
disturb 11.2
disturbed 11.3
disturbing 12.16
disunite 21.34
disunity 42.36
disuse 41.24
disused 41.34
ditch 17.7
ditcher 18.14
ditchwater 26.4
dither 18.11
dithered 18.19
ditherer 18.60
dithering 18.73
dithery 18.56
dithyramb 1.22
dithyrambic 2.17
dittany 18.56
ditties 18.54
ditto 35.11
ditty 18.3
ditzy 18.7
diuresis 16.29
diuretic 10.15
diuretics 10.16
diurnal 12.8
div 17.54
diva 16.6
divagate 7.42
divagation 8.33
divan 1.24
dive 21.37
diver 22.6
diverge 11.10
divergence 12.15
divergent 12.14
divers 22.39
diverse 11.22
diversification 8.44
diversifies 21.43
diversify 21.4
diversion 12.12
diversionary 12.29
diversity 12.29
divert 11.24
diverted 12.5
diverticulitis 22.28
diverticulum 18.66
divertimento 35.7
dives 21.38
divest 9.49
divestiture 10.56
divide 21.10

divided 22.13
dividend 9.35
divider 22.5
dividers 22.39
dividing 22.26
divination 8.32
divinatory 18.56
divine 21.22
divinely 22.1
diviner 22.8
divinest 22.31
diving 22.26
diving board 25.9
divining 22.26
divinity 18.57
divisibility 18.58
divisible 18.64
division 18.33
divisional 18.64
divisions 18.37
divisive 22.37
divisor 22.9
divorce 25.28
divorced 25.29
divorcee 15.4
divorcement 26.23
divorcing 26.25
divot 18.49
divulge 37.22
divvied 18.18
divvy 18.4
Diwali 4.5
Dixie 18.7
Dixieland 1.28
Dixon 18.33
DIY 21.4
dizzier 18.61
dizziest 18.76
dizziness 18.74
dizzy 18.7
dizzying 18.73
DJ 7.3
Django 35.3
djellaba 10.56
Djibouti 42.1
DNA 7.4
Dnieper 16.3
Dniester 16.5
do 41.1
doable 42.39
dob 23.1
dobbin 24.32
Doberman 36.40
Doberman pinscher
18.14
Dobson 24.33
doc 23.3
Docherty 24.54

docile 21.16
docility 18.58
dock 23.3
dockage 24.26
docked 23.6
docker 24.9
docket 24.49
docking 24.40
dockland 1.28; 24.34
docklands 24.35
docks 23.5
dockside 21.11
dockyard 3.8
Doc Martens® 4.26
doctor 24.10
doctoral 24.61
doctorate 24.73
doctored 24.24
doctrinaire 5.1
doctrinal 22.16
doctrine 24.32
docudrama 4.13
document 9.41; 24.67
documentary 10.53
documentation 8.48
documented 10.18
documents 24.68
docu-soap 35.40
Dodd 23.8
dodder 24.10
dodderer 24.57
doddering 24.69
doddery 24.54
doddle 24.27
dodecagon 10.64;
23.27
dodecahedron 16.22
Dodecanese 15.43
dodge 23.14
dodgem 24.30
dodgems 24.31
dodger 24.14
dodgier 24.58
dodgiest 24.71
dodging 24.40
Dodgson 24.33
dodgy 24.7
dodo 35.16
Dodson 24.33
doe 35.1
doe-eyed 21.11
doer 42.2
does 37.51
doesn't 38.32
doest 42.27
doff 23.9
doffed 23.10
dog 23.11

dogbane 7.21
Dogberry 24.54
dogcart 3.32
doge 35.29
dogfight 21.33
dogfish 24.46
dogfood 41.9
dogged 24.23
doggedly 24.56
doggedness 24.70
Dogger 24.9
doggerel 24.27; 24.61
doggish 24.46
doggo 35.13
doggone 23.27
doggy 24.2
doghouse 29.12
dogie 36.1
dogleg 9.12
dogma 24.13
dogmatic 2.17
dogmatically 2.58
dogmatize 21.45
do-gooder 40.2
dogs 23.13
dogsbody 24.3
dogsled 9.8
dogtag 1.13
dogtooth 41.29
dogtrot 23.44
dogwatch 23.7
dogwood 39.4
doh 35.1
doily 34.1
doing 42.24
Dolby® 24.1
dolce vita 16.5
Dolcis 24.42
doldrums 24.31
dole 35.30
doleful 36.15; 39.7
dolefully 36.35
dolerite 21.34
D'Oliviera 14.2
doll 23.15
dollar 24.12
dollars 24.53
Dollond 24.34
dollop 24.41
dolls 23.22
doll's house 29.12
dolly 24.5
Dolly 24.5
Dolly Parton 4.24
dolma 24.13
dolmades 15.44
dolman 24.33
dolmen 9.32

dolomite 21.34
Dolomites 21.35
dolomitic 18.16
Dolores 26.27
doloroso 35.16
dolorous 24.70
dolphin 24.32
dolphinarium 6.18
dolt 35.32
dom 23.23
domain 7.21
Dombey 24.1
dome 35.34
Domesday Book 39.1
domestic 10.15
domesticate 7.38
domestication 8.28
domesticity 18.57
domestics 10.16
Domestos® 23.39
domicile 21.16
domiciled 21.17
domiciliary 18.56
dominance 24.68
dominant 24.67
dominate 7.43
domination 8.34
dominatrix 8.11
domineer 13.1
domineered 13.2
domineering 14.12
Dominic 17.3
Dominica 18.60
dominical 18.64
Dominican 18.67
Dominic's 17.4
dominie 24.56
dominion 18.32
Dominique 15.7
domino 35.19
dominoes 35.52
Domitian 18.33
don 23.27
Don 23.27
Donald 24.28
Donaldson 24.64
donate 7.33
Donatello 35.7
donating 8.60
donation 8.23
Doncaster 2.10
done 37.31
Donegal 25.14
doner 24.13
Donets 9.52
dong 23.31
donga 24.9
dongle 24.27

Donington 24.64
Donizetti 10.3
Don Juan 3.19; 42.20
donkey 24.2
donkeys 24.52
donkey work 11.4
Donleavy 16.1
Donna 24.13
Donne 37.31
donned 23.30
Donnell 24.27
Donnelly 24.54
donning 24.40
donnish 24.46
Donny 24.6
donnybrook 39.1
donor 36.8
Donovan 24.64
Don Quixote 7.3;
    18.49; 36.1
dons 23.35
Don's 23.35
don't 35.38
doodah 3.1
doodle 42.16
doodlebug 37.14
doodler 42.7
doodles 42.17
doodling 42.24
doo-doo 41.3
doohickey 18.2
doolally 2.5
Doolan 42.20
Dooley 42.1
Doolittle 18.22
doom 41.17
doomed 41.18
doomsday 7.3
doomwatch 23.7
door 25.1
doorbell 9.16
do-or-die 21.4
doorframe 7.18
doorjamb 1.22
doorkeeper 16.3
doorknob 23.1
doorknocker 24.9
doorman 1.24
doorman 26.19
doormat 1.45
doornail 7.15
doorpost 35.43
doors 25.35
doorstep 9.44
doorstepping 10.36
doorstop 23.36
door-to-door 25.4
doorway 7.3

dopa 36.3
dopamine 15.26
dope 35.40
dopey 36.1
dopier 36.37
dopiest 36.44
doppelgänger 2.13
Doppler 24.12
Dora 26.6
Dorcas 26.27
Dorchester 26.38
Dordogne 33.8
Doreen 15.25
Dorian 26.43
Dorian Gray 7.2
Doric 24.18
Dorinda 18.10
Doris 24.42
Doris Day 7.4
dork 25.6
Dorking 26.25
dorm 25.20
dormancy 26.37
dormant 26.23
dormer 26.7
dormice 21.29
dormie 26.1
dormitory 26.37
Dormobile® 15.17
dormouse 29.12
Dorothea 16.2
Dorothy 24.54
Dors 25.35
dorsa 26.8
dorsal 26.15
Dorset 26.32
Dorsey 26.1
Dortmund 26.20
dory 26.1
DOS 23.39
do's 41.33
dosage 36.14
dose 35.42
dosed 35.43
doses 36.34
dosh 23.42
doshed 23.43
do-si-do 35.19
Dos Passos 23.39
doss 23.39
dossed 23.41
dosser 24.14
dosshouse 29.12
dossier 7.4; 24.58
dost 37.45
Dostoevsky 10.2
dot 23.44
Dot 23.44

dotage 36.14
dotard 36.12
dotards 36.13
dote 35.45
doted 36.12
doting 36.24
dots 23.45
Dot's 23.45
dotted 24.24
dotterel 24.27
dottier 24.58
dottiest 24.71
dotting 24.40
dotty 24.3
Douai 7.3
double 38.23
double-booked 39.2
double-breasted
    10.18
double-check 9.2
double-checked 9.5
double-checking
    10.36
double-chinned 17.34
double cream 15.20
double-cross 23.39
double-crossed 23.41
double-crossing 24.40
doubled 38.24
double-decker 10.9
double-edged 9.15
double entendre 4.12
double-glazed 7.57
double-lock 23.3
double-park 3.3
double-parked 3.5
doubles 38.25
doublet 38.43
doublethink 17.30
doubleton 38.54
double whammy 2.6
doubloon 41.19
doubloons 41.21
doubly 38.5
doubt 29.14
doubted 30.3
doubter 30.2
doubtful 30.6; 39.7
doubtfully 30.22
doubting 30.12
doubtless 30.14
doubts 29.15
douceur 11.1
douche 41.26
Doug 37.14
Dougal 42.16
dough 35.1
doughboy 33.1

doughnut 37.47
doughty 30.1
doughy 36.1
Dougie 38.2
Douglas 38.38
Douglas Hurd 11.7
Doulton 36.20
Dounreay 7.2
dour 27.1; 31.1
dourly 28.1; 32.1
Douro 35.15
douse 29.12
doused 29.13
dove 37.49
dovecot 23.44
dovecote 35.45
Dover 36.6
dovetail 7.15
Dovey 38.4
Dow 29.1
dowager 30.23
Dowding 30.12
dowdy 30.1
dowel 31.3
Dowell 31.3
dowelling 32.3
dower 31.1
Dow-Jones 35.39
Dowland 30.9
Dowling 30.12
down 29.5
Down 29.5
down-and-out 29.14
downbeat 15.35
downcast 3.30
downdraught 3.10
downer 30.2
downfall 25.14
downforce 25.28
downgrade 7.8
downhaul 25.14
downhearted 4.17
downhill 17.15
Downing 30.12
Downing Street 15.35
download 35.25
downloaded 36.12
downloading 36.24
downmarket 4.38
Downpatrick 2.19
downpipe 21.26
downplay 7.2
downpour 25.3
downright 21.33
downriver 18.11
downshifting 18.40
downside 21.11
downsize 21.40

downsizing 22.26
downstage 7.12
downstairs 5.5
downstream 15.20
downstroke 35.21
downswing 30.12
down the drain 7.21
downtime 21.19
down-to-earth 11.26
downtown 29.5
downtrodden 24.33
downturn 11.15
downturned 11.16
downward 30.3
downwardly 30.22
downwards 30.4
downwind 17.34
downy 30.1
dowry 30.1; 32.1
dowse 29.17
dowser 30.2
dowsing 30.12
doxology 24.55
doxy 24.7
doyen 34.8
doyenne 9.32
Doyle 33.6
D'Oyly Carte 3.32
doze 35.52
dozed 35.53
dozen 38.28
dozens 38.31
dozer 36.9
dozes 36.34
dozier 36.37
doziest 36.44
doziness 36.42
dozing 36.24
dozy 36.1
drab 1.1
drabber 2.8
drabbest 2.48
Drabble 2.28
drabness 2.46
drachm 1.22
drachma 2.13
Draconian 36.40
Draconic 24.19
Dracula 2.60
draft 3.10
drafted 4.17
draftee 15.2
drafting 4.29
drag 1.13
drag-and-drop 23.36
dragée 7.2
dragging 2.42
draggletailed 7.16

draggy 2.2
dragnet 9.51
dragoman 2.66
dragon 2.35
dragonflies 21.42
dragonfly 21.4
dragons 2.39
dragoon 41.19
dragooned 41.20
drain 7.21
drainage 8.14
drained 7.22
drainer 8.8
draining 8.63
drainpipe 21.26
drainpipes 21.27
drains 7.26
drake 7.6
Drake 7.6
Dralon® 23.27
dram 1.22
drama 4.13
Dramamine® 15.26
dramatic 2.17
dramatically 2.58
dramatics 2.23
dramatis personae
   21.3
dramatist 2.73
dramatization 8.40
dramatize 21.42
dramatized 21.48
dramaturge 11.10
dramaturgy 12.1
Drambuie® 42.1
drank 1.25
drape 7.27
draped 7.29
draper 8.3
Draper 8.3
drapery 8.76
drapes 7.28
drastic 2.17
drastically 2.58
drat 1.45
dratted 2.25
draught 3.10
draughtboard 25.9
draught-excluder
   42.5
draughtier 4.44
draughtiest 4.55
draughtsman 4.24
draughtsmanship
   17.43
draughtswoman
   40.10
draughty 4.3

Dravidian 18.67
draw 25.1
drawback 1.3
drawbacks 1.4
drawbridge 26.14
drawer 25.1
drawerful 39.7
drawers 25.35
drawing 26.25
drawing room 39.9;
   41.17
drawl 25.14
drawler 26.6
drawn 25.22
drawstring 26.25
dray 7.1
drayhorse 25.28
drayman 8.21
Drayton 8.21
dread 9.8
dreadful 10.21; 39.7
dreadfully 10.53; 10.55
dreading 10.36
dreadlocked 23.6
dreadlocks 23.5
dreadnought 25.31
dreads 9.9
dream 15.20
dreamboat 35.45
dreamed 15.21
dreamer 16.8
dreamers 16.37
dreamier 16.40
dreamiest 16.49
dreamily 16.38
dreaminess 16.47
dreaming 16.27
dreamless 16.30
dreamlike 21.7
dreams 15.22
dreamt 9.30
Dreamtime 21.19
dreamy 16.1
drear 13.1
drearier 14.18
dreariness 14.23
dreary 14.1
dredge 9.14
dredged 9.15
dredger 10.14
dredging 10.36
Dreft® 9.11
dregs 9.13
Dreiser 22.9
drench 9.33
drenched 9.34
drenching 10.36
Dresden 10.27

dress 9.47
dressage 3.13
dressed 9.49
dresser 10.14
dresses 10.52
dressier 10.57
dressiest 10.71
dressiness 10.70
dressing 10.36
dressing-down 29.5
dressing gown 29.5
dressing room 39.9;
41.17
dressmaker 8.4
dressmaking 8.59
dressy 10.7
drew 41.1
Drew 41.1
Dreyfus 8.67
dribble 18.22
dribbled 18.23
dribbler 18.12
dribbling 18.40
dribs 17.2
dribs and drabs 1.2
dried 21.9
drier 22.2
dries 21.39
driest 22.31
drift 17.11
drifter 18.10
driftwood 39.4
drill 17.15
drilled 17.18
driller 18.12
drilling 18.40
drills 17.23
drillstock 23.3
drink 17.30
drinkable 18.64
drinker 18.9
drinking 18.40
drinks 17.31
Drinkwater 26.4
drip 17.43
drip-dry 21.2
drip-dry 21.3
drip-feed 15.11
dripped 17.45
dripping 18.40
drippy 18.1
drips 17.44
Driscoll 18.22
drivable 22.43
drive 21.37
drivel 18.22
driven 18.32
driver 22.6

driverless 22.46
drivers 22.39
driver's seat 15.35
drives 21.38
drive shaft 3.10
driveway 7.3
driving 22.26
drizzle 18.22
drizzled 18.23
drizzly 18.5
Drogheda 34.15
drogue 35.28
droit du seigneur
11.1
droll 35.30
droller 36.7
drollery 36.35
drollest 36.28
dromedary 24.56
drone 35.36
drongo 35.13
droning 36.24
drool 41.14
drooling 42.24
droop 41.22
droopier 42.38
droopiest 42.47
drooping 42.24
droop-snoot 41.27
droopy 42.1
drop 23.36
drop dead 9.8
dropkick 24.16
droplet 24.49
dropout 29.14
dropouts 29.15
dropped 23.38
dropper 24.8
dropping 24.40
drops 23.37
dropsical 24.61
dropsy 24.7
dross 23.39
drought 29.14
drove 35.50
drover 36.6
droves 35.51
drown 29.5
drowning 30.12
drowse 29.17
drowsily 30.22
drowsiness 30.26
drowsy 30.1
drub 37.1
drubbing 38.34
drudge 37.15
drudgery 38.47
drug 37.14

druggie 38.2
druggist 38.39
drugstore 25.3
druid 42.13
Druidic 18.16
drum 37.27
drumbeat 15.35
drumfire 19.1
drumfish 38.40
drumhead 9.8
drumlin 38.27
drummer 38.13
drummers 38.45
drumming 38.34
Drummond 38.29
drumstick 38.15
drumsticks 38.18
drunk 37.32
drunkard 38.20
drunkards 38.21
drunken 38.28
drunkenly 38.47
drunkenness 38.59
drupe 41.22
Drury 28.1
Drusilla 18.12
Druze 41.33
dry 21.1
dryad 1.9; 22.13
dryads 22.14
dry-clean 15.24
Dryden 22.20
dryer 22.2
drying 22.26
dryish 22.32
dryly 22.1
dryness 22.29
dryopithecine 15.26
Drysdale 7.15
drysuit 41.27
DTs 15.43
dual 42.16
dualism 18.28
duality 2.57
Duane 7.21
dub 37.1
Dubai 21.2
du Barry 2.5
dubbin 38.27
dubbing 38.34
Dubček 9.2
dubiety 22.40
dubious 42.46
dubitation 8.39
Dublin 38.27
Dubliner 38.48
Dubonnet® 7.3
Dubrovnik 24.19

ducal 42.16
ducat 38.42
Duchenne 9.32
duchess 38.37
duchy 38.7
duck 37.3
duckboard 25.9
ducked 37.5
ducker 38.9
Duckham 38.26
ducking 38.34
duckling 38.34
ducklings 38.35
ducks 37.4
duckweed 15.11
Duckworth 11.26
ducky 38.2
duct 37.5
ductile 21.16
dud 37.8
dude 41.9
dudgeon 38.28
Dudley 38.5
duds 37.9
due 41.1
duel 42.16
dueller 42.37
duelling 42.45
duellist 42.48
duenna 10.13
dues 41.33
duet 9.51
duff 37.10
duffel 38.23
duffer 38.11
Duffy 38.4
dug 37.14
Duggan 38.28
dugong 23.31
dugout 29.14
duh 11.1
du jour 25.2; 27.1
duke 41.6
dukedom 42.18
dukes 41.7
dulcet 38.43
Dulcie 38.7
dulcimer 38.48
dull 37.16
dullard 38.20
duller 38.12
Dulles 38.37
Dullsville 17.15
dully 38.5
dulse 37.25
Dulux® 37.4
Dulwich 38.22
duly 42.1

duma 42.8
Dumas 3.1
Du Maurier 7.4
dumb 37.27
Dumbarton 4.24
dumbbell 9.16
dumber 38.13
dumbest 38.39
dumbfound 29.6
dumbing down 29.5
dumbo 35.17
Dumbo 35.17
dumbstruck 37.3
dumbwaiter 8.5
dumdum 37.27
Dumfries 15.32
dummy 38.6
dummy run 37.31
dump 37.29
dumpish 38.40
dumpling 38.34
dumplings 38.35
dumps 37.30
dumpy 38.1
dun 37.31
Dunbar 3.1
Dunblane 7.21
Duncan 38.28
dunce 37.39
Dundalk 25.6
Dundee 15.2
dunderhead 9.8
Dundonian 36.40
dune 41.19
Dunedin 16.21
dunes 41.21
Dunfermline 12.11
dung 37.37
Dungannon 2.35
dungaree 15.4
dungarees 15.45
Dungeness 9.47
dungeon 38.28
dungeons 38.31
dunghill 17.15
Dunhill 17.15
dunk 37.32
dunked 37.34
dunking 38.34
Dunkirk 11.4
Dun Laoghaire 14.1
dunlin 38.27
Dunlop 23.36
Dunn 37.31
dunno 35.2
dunnock 38.16
dunnocks 38.17
dunny 38.6

Dunoon 41.19
Dunsinane 7.21; 18.32
Duns Scotus 24.43; 36.26
Dunstable 38.52
Dunstan 38.28
Dunwoody 40.1
duo 35.18
duodecimal 10.60
duodenal 16.17
duodenum 16.20
duologue 23.11
duopoly 24.54
dupe 41.22
dupery 42.36
duple 42.16
duplex 9.3
duplicate 7.49
duplicate 42.49
duplicating 8.60
duplication 8.39
duplicator 8.5
duplicitous 18.74
duplicity 18.57
Dupont 23.34
du Pré 7.2
durability 18.58
durable 28.19
Duracell® 9.16
Duraglit® 17.51
durance 28.10
Durante 2.3
duration 8.23
Durban 12.12
Dürer 28.2
duress 9.47
Durex® 9.3
Durham 38.26
during 28.11
Durrell 38.23
durst 11.23
dusk 37.44
dusky 38.2
Düsseldorf 25.11
dust 37.45
dustbin 38.27
dustbins 38.30
dust bowl 35.30
dustcart 3.32
dusted 38.20
duster 38.10
dustier 38.49
dustiest 38.61
Dustin 38.27
dusting 38.34
dustman 38.28
dustpan 1.24
dustsheet 15.35

dusty 38.3
Dutch 37.6
Dutchman 38.28
Dutchwoman 40.10
duteous 42.46
dutiable 42.51
duties 42.35
dutiful 39.7; 42.39
dutifully 41.7; 42.36
Dutton 38.28
duty 42.1
duty-free 15.4
duvet 7.3
duvets 7.56
dux 37.4
DVD 15.4
Dvořák 1.3
dwarf 25.11
dwarfish 26.30
dwarfism 18.27
dwarves 25.34
dweeb 15.5
dweebs 15.6
dwell 9.16
dweller 10.12
dwelling 10.36
dwellings 10.37
dwells 9.27
dwelt 9.23
Dwight 21.31
dwindle 18.22
Dworkin 26.18
Dwyer 19.1
Dyak 1.3
dye 21.1
dyeable 22.43
dyed 21.9
dyeing 22.26
dyer 22.2
dyes 21.39
dyestuff 37.10
Dyfed 38.19
dying 22.26
dyke 21.7
dykes 21.8
Dylan 18.32
Dymock 18.15
Dymphna 18.13
dynamic 2.20
dynamics 2.23
dynamism 18.28
dynamite 21.34
dynamo 35.19
dynast 18.46
dynastic 2.17
dynasty 18.56
dynatron 23.27
dyne 21.22

dyscalculia 42.38
dysentery 18.56
dysfunction 38.28
dysfunctional 38.52
dysgraphia 2.61
dyslectic 10.15
dyslexia 10.57
dyslexic 10.15
dysmenorrhoea 13.1
Dyson 22.20
dyspepsia 10.57
dyspeptic 10.15
dysphasia 8.78
dysphasic 8.10
dysphonia 36.37
dysphoria 26.39
dysphoric 24.18
dyspraxia 2.61
dystaxia 2.61
dystonia 36.37
dystopia 36.37
dystrophic 24.17
dystrophy 18.56
dysuria 28.18
E 15.1
each 15.9
eager 16.4
eagerly 16.38
eagerness 16.47
eagle 16.17
eagle-eyed 21.12
eagles 16.18
eaglet 16.34
Ealing 16.27
Eamon 8.21
ear 13.1
earache 7.6
earbash 1.43
eardrops 23.37
eardrum 37.27
eared 13.2
earflap 1.37
earflaps 1.38
earful 39.7
Earhart 3.32
earhole 35.30
earl 11.11
earldom 12.10
earless 14.14
Earl Grey 7.2
earlier 12.31
earliest 12.39
earliness 12.37
ear lobe 35.20
early 12.1
early bird 11.7
earmark 3.3
earmarked 3.5

earmuff 37.10
earmuffs 37.11
earn 11.15
earned 11.16
earner 12.2
earnest 12.20
earnestly 12.29
earnestness 12.37
earning 12.16
earnings 12.17
earns 11.18
earphone 35.36
earpiece 15.32
earplug 37.14
earring 14.12
ears 13.5
earshot 23.44
ear-splitting 18.40
earth 11.26
Eartha 12.2
earthborn 25.22
earthbound 29.6
earthen 12.12
earthenware 5.1
earthlight 21.33
earthling 12.16
earthlings 12.17
earthly 12.1
earthman 1.24
earthquake 7.6
earthshaking 8.59
earthshine 21.22
earthstar 3.1
earthward 12.5
earthwards 12.6
earthwork 11.4
earthworm 11.13
earthy 12.1
earwax 1.4
earwig 17.12
earwigging 18.40
ease 15.42
easel 16.17
easels 16.18
easement 16.25
easier 16.40
easiest 16.49
easily 16.38
easiness 16.47
east 15.33
eastbound 29.6
Eastbourne 25.22
East Ender 10.10
EastEnders 10.52
Easter 16.5
easterly 16.38
eastern 16.22
easterner 16.39

easternmost 35.43
Eastertide 21.12
East Indies 18.54
Eastleigh 16.1
Eastman 16.22
Easton 16.22
eastward 16.14
eastwardly 16.38
eastwards 16.15
easy 16.1
easy-going 36.24
easy-peasy 16.1
eat 15.35
eatable 16.41
eaten 16.22
eater 16.5
eatery 16.38
eating 16.27
Eaton 16.22
eats 15.36
eau de Cologne 35.36
eau de Javelle 9.16
eau de toilette 9.51
eaves 15.41
eavesdrop 23.36
ebb 9.1
ebb and flow 35.19
ebbing 10.36
ebb tide 21.11
Ebbw Vale 7.15
Ebenezer 16.9
ebon 10.27
ebonize 21.43
ebony 10.53
e-book 39.1
ebullience 38.57
ebullient 38.56
ebullition 18.33
écarté 7.3
Ecce Homo 35.16
eccentric 10.15
eccentrically 10.54
eccentricity 18.57
Eccles 10.23
Ecclesiastes 2.54;
  15.44
ecclesiastic 2.17
ecclesiastical 2.64
Ecclesiasticus 2.71
Ecclestone 10.64
eccrine 10.26; 21.22
echelon 23.27
echidna 18.13
echo 35.7
echoed 35.25
echoes 35.52
echoic 36.10
echoing 36.24

echoism 18.28
echolalia 8.78
echolocation 8.43
Eck 9.2
éclair 5.1
eclampsia 2.61
eclectic 10.15
eclecticism 18.28
eclipse 17.44
ecliptic 18.16
eclogue 23.11
Eco 35.7
ecocide 21.12
E. coli 21.3
ecological 24.61
ecologically 24.56
ecologist 24.72
ecology 24.55
economic 24.19
economical 24.61
economically 24.56
economics 24.22
economist 24.72
Economist 24.72
economize 21.45
economizer 22.9
economy 24.54
ecospecies 15.44;
  16.36
ecosphere 13.1
ecosystem 18.26
eco-terrorism 18.28
eco-terrorist 10.72
ecotype 21.26
ecotypic 18.16
ectopic 24.16
ectoplasm 2.32
ectoplasmic 2.20
ECU 41.3
Ecuador 25.4
Ecuadoran 26.19
Ecuadorean 26.43
ecumenical 10.60
eczema 10.56
ed 9.8
Ed 9.8
edacious 8.67
edacity 2.57
Edam 1.22
Edda 10.10
eddied 10.17

eddies 10.51
Eddington 10.64
eddy 10.3
Eddy 10.3
Eddystone 10.64
edelweiss 21.29
Eden 16.22
Edgar 10.9
Edgbaston 10.64
edge 9.14
edged 9.15
Edgehill 17.15
edger 10.14
edges 10.52
edgeways 7.56
edgewise 21.41
edginess 10.70
edging 10.36
Edgware 5.1
edgy 10.7
edible 10.60
edict 17.6
Edie 16.1
edification 8.43
edifice 17.46
edified 21.12
edify 21.4
edifying 22.26
Edinburgh 38.12
Edison 10.64
edit 10.48
edited 10.58
Edith 17.53
editing 10.69
edition 18.33
editions 18.37
editor 10.56
editorial 26.41
editorialize 21.47
editorship 17.43
Edmonds 10.30
Edmondson 10.64
Edmonton 10.64
Edmund 10.29
Edna 10.13
Edom 16.20
Edomite 21.34
Ed's 9.9
Edsel 10.21
educable 10.79
educate 7.38
educated 8.13
education 8.28
educational 8.79
educationalist 17.49
educationist 8.87
educator 8.5
edutainment 8.56

Edward 10.18
Edwardian 26.43
Edwardiana 4.13
Edwardians 26.44
Edwards 10.19
Edwin 10.26
Edwina 16.8
Edwin's 10.31
eejit 16.34
eek 15.7
eel 15.17
eelpout 29.14
eels 15.19
eelworm 11.13
e'en 15.23
e'er 5.1
eerie 14.1
eerier 14.18
Eeyore 25.3
eff 9.10
effable 10.60
efface 7.30
effect 9.5
effective 10.50
effectively 10.54
effectiveness 10.70
effectual 10.60
effectually 10.55; 10.78
effectuate 7.38
effectuation 8.28
effeminacy 10.78
effeminate 10.73
effendi 10.3
efferent 10.67
effervesce 9.47
effervesced 9.49
effervescence 10.34
effervescent 10.33
effete 15.35
efficacious 8.67
efficacy 10.78
efficiency 18.56
efficient 18.38
efficiently 18.56
Effie 10.4
effigy 10.54
effloresce 9.47
effluence 10.68
effluent 10.67
effluvia 42.38
effluvium 42.40
effort 10.47
effortless 10.70
effortlessly 10.78
effrontery 38.47
effulgence 38.33
effulgent 38.32
effuse 41.24

effuse 41.33
effusion 42.20
effusive 42.33
eft 9.11
EFTA 10.10
eftsoons 41.21
e.g. 15.2
egad 1.9
egalitarian 6.19
egalitarianism 18.29
Egan 16.22
Egbert 10.47
egest 9.49
egg 9.12
eggbeater 16.5
egg cup 37.41
egghead 9.8
eggheads 9.9
eggnog 23.11
eggplant 3.23
eggs 9.13
eggshell 9.16
eggy 10.2
Egham 10.25
eglantine 15.26; 21.22
Egmont 23.34
ego 35.10
egocentric 10.15
egocentrism 18.27
egoism 18.28
egoist 16.48
egoistic 18.16
egoistical 18.64
egomania 8.78
egomaniac 1.3
egotism 18.28
egotist 16.48
egotistic 18.16
egotistical 18.64
egregious 16.30; 16.47
Egremont 10.67
egress 9.47
egret 16.34
Egypt 17.45
Egyptian 18.33
Egyptologist 24.72
Egyptology 24.55
eh 7.1
Eid 15.11
eider 22.5
eiderdown 29.5
Eid-ul-Adha 4.10
Eid-ul-Fitr 16.5
Eiffel 22.16
Eiger 22.4
Eigg 9.12
eight 7.32
eighteen 15.24

eighteenth 15.28
eightfold 35.31
eighties 8.74
eightieth 17.53
eightsome 8.19
eighty 8.1
eighty-eight 7.37
eighty-five 21.37
eighty-four 25.4
eighty-nine 21.22
eighty-one 37.31
eighty-six 17.4
eighty-three 15.4
eighty-two 41.4
Eilean Donan 24.33
Eileen 15.25
Eindhoven 36.20
Einstein 21.22
Eire 6.2
Eisenhower 31.1
Eisenstein 21.22
eisteddfod 10.18
either 16.6; 22.6
either-or 25.4
ejaculate 2.74
ejaculate 7.35
ejaculation 8.24
eject 9.5
ejection 10.28
ejector 10.10
eke 15.7
elaborate 2.74; 7.35
elaboration 8.24
Elaine 7.21
Elaine's 7.26
élan 1.24; 3.19
eland 16.23
elapse 1.38
elastic 2.17
elasticate 7.35
elasticated 8.13
elastication 8.24
elasticity 18.57
elasticize 21.42
elasticized 21.48
Elastoplast® 1.42; 3.30
elate 7.33
elated 8.13
elation 8.23
Elba 10.8
Elbe 10.8
elbow 35.7
elbowroom 39.9; 41.17
elbows 35.52
Elburz 27.3
El Cid 17.8
elder 10.10
elderberry 10.5; 10.53

elderflower 31.1
elderly 10.53
elders 10.52
eldest 10.43
El Dorado 35.4
Eleanor 10.56
elect 9.5
electable 10.60
elected 10.18
election 10.28
electioneer 13.1
electioneering 14.12
elective 10.50
elector 10.10
electoral 10.60
electorate 10.73
electorship 17.43
Electra 10.12
electric 10.15
electrical 10.60
electrically 10.54
electrician 18.33
electricity 18.57
electrics 10.16
electrification 8.43
electrify 21.4
electroconvulsive 38.44
electrocute 41.27
electrocution 42.20
electrode 35.25
electrolyse 21.43
electrolysis 17.46
electrolyte 21.34
electrolytic 18.16
electromagnet 2.51
electromagnetic 10.15
electron 23.27
electronic 24.19
electronics 24.22
electronvolt 35.32
electrophonic 24.19
electroplate 7.38
electroscope 35.40
electrotherapy 10.53
electrotype 21.26
electrum 10.25
elegance 10.68
elegant 10.67
elegantly 10.78
elegiac 22.10
elegize 21.43
elegy 10.54
element 10.67
elemental 10.21
elementary 10.53
elements 10.68
elephant 10.67

elephantiasis 17.46
elephantine 21.22
elephants 10.68
elevate 7.38
elevated 8.13
elevation 8.28
elevator 8.5
eleven 10.27
elevens 10.32
elevenses 10.77
eleventh 10.35
elf 9.20
elfin 10.26
elfish 10.45
elflock 23.3
Elgar 3.1
Elgin 10.26
El Gîza 16.9
El Greco 35.7
Eli 21.3
Elias 22.29
elicit 18.50
elide 21.10
eligibility 18.58
eligible 10.79
Elijah 22.9
eliminate 7.41
elimination 8.32
Elinor 10.56
Eliot 10.74
Elisha 22.9
elision 18.33
elite 15.35
elitism 18.27
elitist 16.31
elixir 18.14
Eliza 22.9
Elizabeth 18.78
Elizabethan 16.22
elk 9.17
elkhound 29.6
ell 9.16
Ella 10.12
Ellen 10.27
Ellery 10.53
Ellesmere 13.1
Ellie 10.5
Ellington 10.64
ellipse 17.44
ellipsis 18.43
elliptic 18.16
elliptical 18.64
elliptically 18.57
Ellis 10.41
elm 9.21
El Mansûra 28.2
Elmer 10.13
El Niño 35.10

elocution 42.20
elongate 7.40
elongated 8.13
elongation 8.31
elope 35.40
elopement 36.22
eloper 36.3
eloping 36.24
eloquence 10.68
eloquent 10.67
eloquently 10.78
El Paso 35.3
Elphick 10.15
Elsa 10.14
El Salvador 25.4
elsewhere 5.1
Elsie 10.7
Elsinore 25.4
Elspeth 10.49
Elstree 10.5; 15.3
Eltham 10.25
Elton 10.27
Elton John 23.27
elucidate 7.49
elucidation 8.39
elude 41.9
elusive 42.33
elver 10.11
elves 9.26
Elvira 14.2
Elvis 10.41
Ely 16.1
Elysian 18.67
Elysium 18.66
Elzevir 13.1
em 9.28
emaciate 7.37
emaciated 8.13
emaciation 8.27
e-mail 7.15
e-mailing 8.62
emanate 7.38
emanation 8.28
emancipate 7.35
emancipated 8.13
emancipation 8.24
emasculate 7.35
emasculation 8.24
embalm 3.16
embalmed 3.17
embalmer 4.13
embalming 4.29
embalms 3.18
embank 1.25
embankment 2.40
embankments 2.41
embargo 35.4
embark 3.3

embarked 3.5
embarking 4.29
embarrass 2.46
embarrassed 2.48
embarrassing 2.70
embarrassingly 2.78
embarrassment 2.68
embassy 10.53
embattle 2.28
embattled 2.29
embed 9.8
embellish 10.45
embellished 10.46
embellishment 10.67
ember 10.8
embezzle 10.21
embezzled 10.22
embezzlement 10.67
embezzler 10.12
embitter 18.10
emblaze 7.56
emblazon 8.21
emblazoned 8.54
emblem 10.25
emblematic 2.17
emblematize 21.47
embodied 24.23
embodiment 24.67
embody 24.3
embolden 36.20
emboldened 36.21
embolic 24.18
embolism 18.28
embolus 10.70
emboss 23.39
embossed 23.41
embossing 24.40
embouchure 27.1
embrace 7.30
embraced 7.31
embracer 8.9
embracing 8.64
embrasure 8.9
embrocation 8.28
embroider 34.2
embroidered 34.3
embroiderer 34.15
embroidery 34.14
embroil 33.6
embroiled 33.7
embryo 35.19
embryologic 24.20
embryological 24.61
embryology 24.55
embryonic 24.19
embus 37.43
emend 9.35
emendation 8.31

emerald 10.61
emerge 11.10
emergence 12.15
emergency 12.29
emergent 12.14
emerging 12.16
emeritus 10.70
Emerson 10.64
emery 10.53
emesis 17.46
emetic 10.15
emetics 10.16
emigrant 10.67
emigrants 10.68
emigrate 7.38
emigrating 8.60
emigration 8.28
émigré 7.4
Emil 15.17
Emilia-Romagna 4.12
Emily 10.54
Eminem 9.28
eminence 10.68
éminence grise 15.43
eminent 10.67
eminently 10.78
emir 13.1
emissary 10.78
emission 18.33
emit 17.51
emits 17.52
emitter 18.10
emitting 18.40
Emlyn 10.26
Emlyn's 10.31
Emma 10.13
Emmanuel 2.64
Emmaus 8.67
Emmeline 15.26
Emmen 10.27
Emmenthal 3.14
emmet 10.48
Emmy 10.6
emollient 24.67
emolument 24.67
emote 35.45
emoticon 23.27
emotion 36.20
emotional 36.38
emotive 36.32
empanel 2.28
empathetic 10.15
empathic 2.18
empathize 21.43
empathy 10.53
Empedocles 15.45
emperor 10.56
emperorship 17.43

engulf 37.21
engulfing 38.34
engulfment 38.32
enhance 3.22
enhancement 4.27
enhancer 4.14
Enid 16.13
enigma 18.13
enigmatic 2.17
enjoin 33.8
enjoy 33.1
enjoyable 34.16
enjoyed 33.4
enjoying 34.11
enjoyment 34.9
enjoys 33.15
enlace 7.30
enlaced 7.31
enlarge 3.12
enlargement 4.27
enlarger 4.14
enlarging 4.29
enlighten 22.20
enlightened 22.21
enlightenment 22.45
enlist 17.49
enlisted 18.19
enlister 18.10
enlisting 18.40
enlistment 18.38
enliven 22.20
enlivened 22.21
en masse 1.40
enmesh 9.50
enmity 10.54
ennage 10.20
Ennis 10.41
Enniskillen 18.31
ennoble 36.15
ennobled 36.16
ennoblement 36.41
Enoch 23.3
Enoch Powell 31.3
enormity 26.37
enormous 26.27
enough 37.10
enounce 29.9
enounced 29.10
enow 29.1
enprint 17.39
enquire 19.1
enquired 19.2
enquirer 20.2
enquiry 20.1
enrage 7.12
enraged 7.13
enrapture 2.14
enrich 17.7

enriching 18.40
enrichment 18.38
Enrico 35.10
Enright 21.33
Enrique 7.3
enrobe 35.20
enrobing 36.24
enrol 35.30
enrolled 35.31
enrolling 36.24
enrolment 36.22
en route 41.27
ENSA 10.14
ensconce 23.33
ensemble 4.19
enshrine 21.22
enshrinement 22.24
enshroud 29.3
enshrouded 30.3
enshrouding 30.12
ensign 10.28; 21.22
ensile 21.16
enslave 7.54
enslavement 8.56
ensnare 5.1
ensnared 5.2
ensnarement 6.8
ensue 41.2
ensued 41.9
ensuing 42.24
en suite 15.35
ensure 25.2; 27.1
ensured 25.9
ensuring 28.11
enswathe 7.52
enswathed 7.53
entablature 2.60
entail 7.15
entailed 7.16
entailment 8.56
entangle 2.28
entangled 2.29
entanglement 2.68
Entebbe 10.1
entente cordiale 3.14
enter 10.10
entered 10.18
enteric 10.15
enteritis 22.28
enterprise 21.43
enterprising 22.26
entertain 7.21
entertained 7.22
entertainer 8.8
entertaining 8.63
entertainment 8.56
entertainments 8.57
enthral 25.14

enthralled 25.15
enthralling 26.25
enthralment 26.23
enthrone 35.36
enthroned 35.37
enthronement 36.22
enthuse 41.33
enthused 41.34
enthusiasm 2.32
enthusiast 1.42
enthusiastic 2.17
enthusiastically 2.58
entice 21.29
enticed 21.30
enticement 22.24
enticer 22.9
enticing 22.26
entire 19.1
entirely 20.1
entirety 20.11
entitle 22.16
entitled 22.17
entitlement 22.45
entity 10.54
entomb 41.17
entombed 41.18
entombment 42.22
entomological 24.61
entomologist 24.72
entomology 24.55
entourage 3.13
entr'acte 1.6
entrails 7.17
entrain 7.21
entrance 3.22
entrance 10.34
entrancing 4.29
entrant 10.33
entrap 1.37
entrapment 2.40
entreat 15.35
entreaty 16.1
entrechat 3.1
entrecôte 35.45
entrée 7.3
entrench 9.33
entrenched 9.34
entrenchment 10.33
entrepreneur 11.1
entrepreneurial 12.32
entrepreneurship 17.43
entropy 10.53
entrust 37.45
entrusted 38.20
entry 10.5
entryphone 35.36
entwine 21.22

entwined 21.23
enumerate 7.49
enumeration 8.39
enunciate 7.48
enunciation 8.38
enuresis 16.29
envelop 10.38
envelope 35.40
enveloped 10.40
envelops 10.39
envenom 10.25
enviable 10.79
enviably 10.78
envied 10.17
envious 10.70
enviously 10.78
environ 22.20
environment 22.45
environmental 10.21
environmentalism 18.28
environmentalist 10.72
environmentally 10.53
environs 22.23
envisage 18.21
envision 18.33
envoy 33.1
envy 10.4
enwrap 1.37
enwrapped 1.39
enwreath 15.38
Enzed 9.8
Enzo 35.7
enzymatic 2.17
enzyme 21.19
enzymes 21.21
enzymic 22.11
Eocene 15.26
eohippus 18.44
Eolithic 18.16
eon 16.22; 23.27
eons 16.24
Eos 23.39
eosin 17.29
epaulette 9.51
épée 7.3
epergne 11.15
ephedrine 15.26
ephemera 10.56
ephemeral 10.60
ephemerally 10.78
ephemeris 17.46
Ephesian 16.22
Ephesus 10.70
epic 10.15
epicene 15.26

epicentre 10.10
epicure 27.1
epicurean 16.22
Epicurean 16.22
Epicurus 28.12
Epidaurus 26.27
epidemic 10.15
epidemiology 24.55
epidermal 12.8
epidermis 12.18
epididymis 17.46
epidural 28.4
epiglottal 24.27
epiglottis 24.42
epigram 1.22
epigraph 1.11; 3.9
epigraphic 2.18
epilator 8.5
epilepsy 10.7
epileptic 10.15
epileptics 10.16
epilogue 23.11
epinephrine 15.25
epiphany 18.56
Epiphany 18.56
epiphyte 21.34
EPIRB 11.2
Epirus 20.8; 22.29
episcopacy 18.80
episcopal 18.64
Episcopalian 8.81
episcopate 7.41; 18.77
episode 35.25
episodic 24.16
epistemology 24.55
epistle 18.22
epistles 18.24
epistolary 18.80
epitaph 1.11; 3.9
epithalamia 8.78
epithalamium 8.80
epithelium 16.42
epithet 9.51
epitome 18.56
epitomize 21.44
epoch 23.3
epochal 24.27
eponym 17.24
eponymous 24.70
epopee 15.4
EPOS 23.39
epoxy 24.7
Epping 10.36
epsilon 22.20; 23.27
Epsom 10.25
Epson 10.28
Epstein 21.22
equable 10.60

equal 16.17
equality 24.56
equalization 8.45
equalize 21.43
equalizer 22.9
equally 16.38
equanimity 18.57
equate 7.33
equation 8.21
equator 8.5
equatorial 26.41
equerry 10.5; 10.53
equestrian 10.64
equestrianism 18.29
equestrienne 9.32
equidistance 18.39
equidistant 18.38
equilateral 2.28; 2.64
equilibrate 7.41
equilibration 8.32
equilibrium 18.66
equine 21.22
equinoctial 24.27
equinox 23.5
equip 17.43
équipe 15.30
equipment 18.38
equipoise 33.15
equipped 17.45
equips 17.44
equisetum 16.20
equitable 10.79
equitation 8.28
equity 10.54
Equity 10.54
equivalence 18.71
equivalent 18.70
equivocal 18.64
equivocate 7.41
equivocation 8.32
er 11.1
ER 3.1
era 14.2
eradicable 2.79
eradicate 7.35
eradicated 8.13
eradication 8.24
eradicator 8.5
erase 7.56
erased 7.57
eraser 8.9
Erasmus 2.46
erasure 8.9
Eratosthenes 15.45
erbium 12.33
ere 5.1
Erechtheion 16.22
Erechtheum 16.20

erect 9.5
erectile 21.16
erection 10.28
erector 10.10
erelong 23.31
eremite 21.34
erewhile 21.16
erg 11.9
ergative 17.55
ergo 35.8
ergonomic 24.19
ergonomically 24.56
ergonomics 24.22
ergot 12.24
ergotism 18.28
Eric 10.15
erica 10.56
Erica 10.56
ericaceous 8.67
Eric's 10.16
Ericsson 10.64
Erie 14.1
Erin 6.6; 10.26; 14.8
Eriskay 7.4
Eritrea 8.2
Eritrean 8.21
erk 11.4
erlking 12.16
ermine 12.11
Ermintrude 41.9
Ern 11.15
erne 11.15
Ernest 12.20
Ernie 12.1
Ern's 11.18
erode 35.25
eroded 36.12
eroding 36.24
erogenous 24.70
Eroica 36.36
Eros 23.39
erosion 36.20
erotic 24.16
erotica 24.57
erotically 24.56
eroticism 18.28
eroticize 21.45
erotomania 8.78
err 11.1
errand 10.29
errands 10.30
errant 10.33
errantry 10.53
errata 4.10
erratic 2.17
erratically 2.58
erratum 4.22
erred 11.7

erring 12.16
Errol 10.21
erroneous 36.42
error 10.12
errors 10.52
errs 11.29
ersatz 1.46
Erse 11.22
erstwhile 21.16
erudite 21.34
erudition 18.33
erupt 37.42
erupted 38.20
erupting 38.34
eruption 38.28
eruptive 38.44
Erymanthus 2.46
erysipelas 18.74
erythrocyte 21.34
erythrocytic 18.16
Esau 25.3
escalade 7.8
escalate 7.38
escalation 8.28
escalator 8.5
escallonia 36.37
escalope 23.36
escapable 8.79
escapade 7.8
escapades 7.9
escape 7.27
escapee 15.4
escapement 8.56
escaper 8.3
escapes 7.28
escaping 8.59
escapism 18.27
escapist 8.68
escapologist 24.72
escapology 24.55
escarpment 4.27
eschatology 24.55
Escher 10.14
Escherichia 18.61
eschew 41.2
eschewal 42.16
Escoffier 7.4
Escorial 3.14; 26.41
escort 25.31
escorting 26.25
escritoire 3.1
escrow 35.7
escudo 35.18
Escurial 28.19
escutcheon 38.28
Esdras 1.40; 10.42
Esher 16.9
Eskimo 35.19

Esme 10.6
Esmeralda 2.10
Esmond 10.29
esoteric 10.15
ESP 15.4
espadrille 17.15
espadrilles 17.23
espalier 7.4; 2.61
especial 10.21
especially 10.53
Esperanto 35.3
espial 19.3
espionage 3.13
esplanade 3.8; 7.8
espousal 30.6
espouse 29.17
espresso 35.7
esprit 15.2
esprit de corps 25.2
espy 21.2
esquire 19.1
essay 7.3
essayist 10.72
essays 7.56
Essen 10.28
essence 10.34
Essene 15.25
essential 10.21
essentially 10.53
essentials 10.23
Essex 10.16
Esso 35.7
establish 2.49
establishment 2.68
Establishment 2.68
establishmentarian 6.19
estancia 2.61
estate 7.33
esteem 15.20
esteemed 15.21
Estella 10.12
Estelle 9.16
ester 10.10
Esterházy 4.7
Esther 10.10
estimable 10.79
estimate 7.38
estimated 8.13
estimation 8.28
estimator 8.5
Estonia 36.37
Estonian 36.40
Estoril 15.17
estrade 3.8
estrange 7.23
estranged 7.24
estuarial 6.17

estuarine 21.22
estuary 10.55; 10.78
esurient 28.22
ET 15.2
ETA 7.4; 10.10
e-tail 7.15
et al. 1.16
Etam 1.22
et cetera 10.12; 10.56
etch 9.6
etched 9.7
etcher 10.14
etching 10.36
etchings 10.37
eternal 12.8
eternalize 21.43
eternally 12.29
eternity 12.29
Ethan 16.22
ethane 7.21
ethanol 23.15
Ethel 10.21
Ethelbert 11.24
Ethelburga 12.2
Etheldreda 16.5
Ethelred 9.8
ether 16.6
ethereal 14.19
ethereality 2.57
etherization 8.45
etherize 21.43
ethic 10.15
ethical 10.60
ethically 10.54
ethics 10.16
Ethiop 23.36
Ethiopia 36.37
Ethiopian 36.40
Ethiopic 24.16
ethnic 10.15
ethnically 10.54
ethnicity 18.57
ethnocentric 10.15
ethnocentrism 18.27
ethnographic 2.18
ethnography 24.54
ethnologic 24.20
ethnological 24.61
ethnologist 24.72
ethnology 24.55
ethos 23.39
ethyl 10.21; 17.15; 21.16
ethylene 15.26
etiquette 9.51
Etna 10.13
Eton 16.22
Etonian 36.40

Etruria 28.18
Etrurian 28.21
Etruscan 38.28
Ettrick 10.15
étude 41.9
étui 15.2
etymologic 24.20
etymological 24.61
etymologically 24.56
etymologist 24.72
etymology 24.55
etymon 23.27
EU 41.2
Euboea 16.2
Euboean 16.22
eucalypt 17.45
eucalyptus 18.44
Eucharist 42.48
euchre 42.4
Euclid 42.13
Euclidean 18.67
eugenic 10.15
eugenics 10.16
Eugénie 8.1
euglena 16.8
Euler 34.2
eulogize 21.46
eulogy 42.36
Eunice 42.25
eunuch 42.10
euonymus 24.70
eupepsia 10.57
eupeptic 10.15
euphemism 18.28
euphemistic 18.16
euphemistically 18.57
euphemize 21.46
euphonic 24.19
euphonious 36.42
euphonium 36.39
euphony 42.36
euphorbia 26.39
euphoria 26.39
euphoriant 26.45
euphoric 24.18
Euphrates 8.74; 15.44
euphuism 18.28
Eurasia 8.9
Eurasian 8.21
eureka 16.4
eurhythmic 18.16
Euripides 15.45
euro 35.15
Eurobond 23.30
Eurocentric 10.15
Eurocentrism 18.27
Eurocheque 9.2
Eurocrat 1.45

eurodollar 24.12
Europa 36.3
European 16.22
Europeanize 21.43
Europeans 16.24
Europhile 21.16
Europhilia 18.61
Europhobe 35.20
Europhobia 36.37
Europhobic 36.10
Euro-sceptic 10.15
Euro-sceptics 10.16
Eurostar 3.1
Eurotunnel 38.23
Eurovision 18.33
eurozone 35.36
Eurydice 18.57
eurythmics 18.17
Eustace 42.26
Eustachian 8.23
Euston 42.20
Euterpe 12.1
euthanasia 8.78
eutrophic 24.17
Eva 16.6
evacuate 7.35
evacuation 8.24
evacuee 15.4
evacuees 15.45
evade 7.8
evader 8.5
Evadne 2.6
evaluate 7.35
evaluation 8.24
evaluative 17.54
Evan 10.27
evanesce 9.47
evanescence 10.34
evanescent 10.33
evangelic 10.15
evangelical 10.60
evangelism 18.28
evangelist 2.73
evangelistic 18.16
evangelize 21.42
Evans 10.32
evaporate 7.35
evaporation 8.24
evasion 8.21
evasive 8.73
evasively 8.76
eve 15.39
Eve 15.39
Evel Knievel 16.17
Evelyn 16.21
even 16.22
evenfall 25.14
even-handed 2.25

exile 21.16
exiled 21.17
exilic 18.16
exist 17.49
existed 18.19
existence 18.39
existent 18.38
existential 10.21
existentialism 18.28
existentialist 10.72
existing 18.40
exit 10.48
exited 10.58
Ex-Lax® 1.4
ex libris 18.43
Exmoor 25.3; 27.1
Exmouth 10.49
Exocet® 9.51
exodus 10.70
Exodus 10.70
ex officio 35.19
exogenous 24.70
exonerate 7.43
exoneration 8.34
exorbitant 26.45
exorcism 18.28
exorcist 10.72
exorcize 21.43
exordium 26.42
exoskeleton 10.64
exoteric 10.15
exotic 24.16
exotica 24.57
exotics 24.22
expand 1.28
expanded 2.25
expander 2.10
expanse 1.31
expansion 2.35
expansionism 18.28
expat 1.45
expatiate 7.37
expatiation 8.27
expatriate 2.74
expatriate 7.35
expatriation 8.24
expats 1.46
expect 9.5
expectancy 10.53
expectant 10.33
expectantly 10.53
expectation 8.28
expected 10.18
expecting 10.36
expectorant 10.67
expectorate 7.38
expectoration 8.28
expedience 16.45

expediency 16.52
expedient 16.44
expedite 21.34
expedition 18.33
expeditionary 18.56
expeditious 18.44
expel 9.16
expellant 10.33
expelled 9.19
expeller 10.12
expend 9.35
expendable 10.60
expenditure 10.56
expense 9.39
expenses 10.52
expensive 10.50
experience 14.22
experiential 10.21
experiment 10.67
experiment 9.41
experimental 10.21
experimentalism
  18.28
experimentally 10.53
experimentation 8.43
experimenter 10.10
experiments 10.68
expert 11.24
expertise 15.45
experts 11.25
expiable 10.79
expiate 7.38
expiation 8.28
expiration 8.28
expire 19.1
expired 19.2
expires 19.4
expiry 20.1
explain 7.21
explainable 8.79
explainer 8.8
explaining 8.63
explanation 8.28
explanatory 2.56
expletive 16.35
explicable 18.64
explicate 7.38
explication 8.28
explicative 17.55
explicatory 18.56
explicit 18.50
explicitly 18.57
explode 35.25
exploded 36.12
exploding 36.24
exploit 33.13
exploitable 34.16
exploitation 8.28

exploited 34.3
exploiter 34.2
exploits 33.14
exploration 8.28
exploratory 24.54
explore 25.2
explored 25.9
explorer 26.6
exploring 26.25
explosion 36.20
explosive 36.32
exponent 36.22
exponential 10.21
export 25.31
exportation 8.28
exporter 26.4
exporting 26.25
exports 25.32
expose 35.52
exposé 7.3
exposed 35.53
exposition 18.33
expositor 24.57
expository 24.56
expostulate 7.43
expostulation 8.34
exposure 36.9
expound 29.6
express 9.47
expressible 10.60
expression 10.28
expressionism 18.28
expressionist 10.72
expressionistic 18.16
expressionless 10.70
expressive 10.50
expressly 10.5
expressway 7.3
expropriate 7.47
expropriation 8.37
expulsion 38.28
expunge 37.38
expurgate 7.38
expurgated 8.13
expurgation 8.28
exquisite 18.50
exquisitely 18.57
extant 1.33; 10.33
extemporaneous 8.85
extemporary 10.53;
  10.78
extempore 10.53
extemporization 8.43
extemporize 21.43
extend 9.35
extendable 10.60
extended 10.18
extender 10.10

extending 10.36
extension 10.28
extensive 10.50
extensively 10.54
extensor 10.14
extent 9.41
extenuate 7.38
extenuation 8.28
exterior 14.18
exterminate 7.39
extermination 8.29
exterminator 8.5
extern 11.15
external 12.8
externalization 8.44
externalize 21.43
externally 12.29
extinct 17.32
extinction 18.33
extinguish 18.47
extinguished 18.48
extinguisher 18.60
extirpate 7.38
extirpation 8.28
extol 35.30
extolled 35.31
extolling 36.24
extort 25.31
extorter 26.4
extortion 26.19
extortionate 26.50
extortionist 26.48
extra 10.12
extract 1.6
extracted 2.25
extraction 2.35
extractor 2.10
extractor fan 1.24
extracurricular 18.60
extraditable 22.43
extradite 21.34
extradition 18.33
extrados 23.39
extramarital 2.64
extramural 28.4
extraneous 8.85
extraordinary 26.37
extrapolate 7.35
extrapolation 8.24
extrasensory 10.53
extraterrestrial 10.60
extra time 21.19
extravagance 2.69
extravagant 2.68
extravaganza 2.14
extreme 15.20
extremely 16.1
extremism 18.27

enact 1.6
enactment 2.40
enamel 2.28
enameller 2.60
enamelling 2.70
enamour 2.13
enamoured 2.25
en bloc 23.3
encage 7.12
encamp 1.23
encampment 2.40
encapsulate 7.35
encapsulation 8.24
encase 7.30
encased 7.31
encasement 8.56
encash 1.43
encashment 2.40
enceinte 1.33
encephalitic 18.16
encephalitis 22.28
encephalogram 1.22
encephalograph 1.11; 3.9
encephalon 23.27
encephalopathy 24.54
enchant 3.23
enchanted 4.17
enchanting 4.29
enchantment 4.27
enchantress 4.32
enchilada 4.10
encipher 22.6
encircle 12.8
encircling 12.16
enclave 7.54
enclose 35.52
enclosed 35.53
enclosing 36.24
enclosure 36.9
encode 35.25
encoded 36.12
encoder 36.5
encoding 36.24
encomium 36.39
encompass 38.38
encompassed 38.39
encounter 30.2
encourage 38.22
encouragement 38.56
encouraging 38.58
encouragingly 38.64
encroach 35.24
encroaching 36.24
encroachment 36.22
encrust 37.45
encrypt 17.45
encryption 18.33

encumber 38.8
encumbered 38.20
encumbrance 38.33
encyclical 18.64
encyclopedia 16.40
encyclopedic 16.11
encyclopedist 16.31
encyst 17.49
end 9.35
endanger 8.9
endear 13.1
endearing 14.12
endearment 14.10
endearments 14.11
endeavour 10.11
ended 10.18
endemic 10.15
Enderby 10.53
endgame 7.18
ending 10.36
endings 10.37
endive 21.37
endives 21.38
endless 10.42
endmost 35.43
endnote 35.45
endocrine 17.29
endocrine 21.22
endocrinologist 24.72
endocrinology 24.55
endoderm 11.13
endogenous 24.70
endometrial 16.41
endometriosis 36.25
endomorph 25.11
endomorphic 26.9
endorphin 26.18
endorphins 26.22
endorse 25.28
endorsed 25.29
endorsement 26.23
endorser 26.8
endorsing 26.25
endoscope 35.40
endoscopic 24.16
endoscopy 24.54
endoskeleton 10.64
endothelium 16.42
endow 29.1
endowed 29.3
endowing 30.12
endowment 30.10
endowments 30.11
endows 29.17
endpaper 8.3
endplate 7.34
endplay 7.3
endpoint 33.10

endue 41.2
endurable 28.19
endurance 28.10
endure 27.1
endures 27.3
enduring 28.11
endways 7.56
endwise 21.41
Endymion 18.67
enema 10.56
enemies 10.77
enemy 10.53
energetic 10.15
energetically 10.54
energize 21.43
energizing 22.26
energy 10.53
enervate 7.38
enervating 8.60
enervation 8.28
enfant terrible 16.7
enfeeble 16.17
Enfield 15.18
enfold 35.31
enfolding 36.24
enforce 25.28
enforced 25.29
enforcement 26.23
enforcer 26.8
enforcing 26.25
enfranchise 21.41
enfranchised 21.48
enfranchisement 2.68
engage 7.12
engaged 7.13
engagement 8.56
engagements 8.57
engaging 8.64
en garde 3.8
Engelbert 11.24
Engels 10.23
engender 10.10
engine 10.26
engineer 13.1
engineered 13.2
engineering 14.12
engineers 13.5
engine room 39.9; 41.17
England 18.34
English 18.47
Englishwoman 40.10
Englishwomen 18.31
engorge 25.13
engorgement 26.23
engraft 3.10
engrave 7.54
engraver 8.6

engraving 8.61
engross 35.42
engrossed 35.43
engulf 37.21
engulfing 38.34
engulfment 38.32
enhance 3.22
enhancement 4.27
enhancer 4.14
Enid 16.13
enigma 18.13
enigmatic 2.17
enjoin 33.8
enjoy 33.1
enjoyable 34.16
enjoyed 33.4
enjoying 34.11
enjoyment 34.9
enjoys 33.15
enlace 7.30
enlaced 7.31
enlarge 3.12
enlargement 4.27
enlarger 4.14
enlarging 4.29
enlighten 22.20
enlightened 22.21
enlightenment 22.45
enlist 17.49
enlisted 18.19
enlister 18.10
enlisting 18.40
enlistment 18.38
enliven 22.20
enlivened 22.21
en masse 1.40
enmesh 9.50
enmity 10.54
ennage 10.20
Ennis 10.41
Enniskillen 18.31
ennoble 36.15
ennobled 36.16
ennoblement 36.41
Enoch 23.3
Enoch Powell 31.3
enormity 26.37
enormous 26.27
enough 37.10
enounce 29.9
enounced 29.10
enow 29.1
enprint 17.39
enquire 19.1
enquired 19.2
enquirer 20.2
enquiry 20.1
enrage 7.12

family 2.5; 2.58
famine 2.34
famish 2.49
famous 8.67
famously 8.76
fan 1.24
fanatic 2.17
fanatical 2.64
fanatically 2.58
fanaticism 18.28
fanbase 7.30
fan belt 9.23
fanciable 2.79
fancied 2.24
fancier 2.61
fanciest 2.72
fanciful 2.64; 39.7
fancifully 2.58; 40.1
fancy 2.7
fandango 35.3
fanfare 5.1
fanfaronade 3.8
fang 1.29
fanlight 21.33
fanned 1.28
fanny 2.6
Fanny 2.6
fans 1.36
Fanshawe 25.3
Fanta® 2.10
fantail 7.15
fantasia 8.78
fantasies 2.77
fantasize 21.42
fantastic 2.17
fantastical 2.64
fantastically 2.58
fantasy 2.56
fanzine 15.25
FAQ 41.4
far 3.1
farad 1.9; 2.25
Faraday 7.4
farandole 35.30
faraway 7.4
farce 3.26
farcical 4.47
farcically 4.42
fare 5.1
Far East 15.33
fared 5.2
Fareham 6.5
farewell 9.16
farewells 9.27
far-fetched 9.7
far-flung 37.37
Fargo 35.4
farina 16.8

farinaceous 8.67
Farjeon 4.24
Farley 4.5
farm 3.16
farmable 4.47
farmed 3.17
farmer 4.13
farmers 4.41
farmhouse 29.12
farming 4.29
farmland 1.28
farms 3.18
farmstead 9.8
farmyard 3.8
Farnborough 4.43
Farnham 4.22
faro 35.5
farouche 41.26
Farouk 41.6
Farquhar 4.9; 4.12
Farquharson 4.50
farrago 35.4
Farrah 2.12
far-reaching 16.27
Farrell 2.28
farrier 2.61
farriery 2.78
Farringdon 2.66
farrow 35.3
Farsi 4.7
far-sighted 22.13
fart 3.32
farther 4.11
farthermost 35.43
farthest 4.34
farthing 4.29
farthingale 7.15
farthings 4.30
farting 4.29
fartlek 9.2
farts 3.33
fascia 8.9; 8.78
fascicle 2.64
fascicule 41.14
fascinate 7.35
fascinating 8.60
fascination 8.24
fascism 18.27
fascist 2.47
fascistic 18.16
fashion 2.35
fashionable 2.79
fashionably 2.78
fashions 2.39
Fassbinder 18.10
fast 3.30
fastball 25.14
fasten 4.24

fastened 4.25
fastener 4.43
fastening 4.52
faster 4.10
fastest 4.34
fastidious 18.74
fastidiously 18.80
fasting 4.29
fastness 4.32
Fastnet 9.51
fast-track 1.3
fat 1.45
fatal 8.15
fatalism 18.28
fatalist 8.87
fatalistic 18.16
fatality 2.57
fatally 8.76
Fata Morgana 4.13
fat cat 1.45
fat cats 1.46
fate 7.32
fated 8.13
fateful 8.15; 39.7
Fates 7.50
fathead 9.8
father 4.11
fathered 4.17
fatherhood 39.4
father-in-law 25.2
fatherland 1.28
fatherless 4.53
fatherly 4.42
Father Time 21.19
fathom 2.32
fathomable 2.79
fathomless 2.71
fathoms 2.33
fatigue 15.14
fatiguing 16.27
Fatima 2.60
fatso 35.3
fatted 2.25
fatten 2.35
fattening 2.70
fatter 2.10
fattest 2.48
fattier 2.61
fattiest 2.72
fatty 2.3
fatuity 42.36
fatuous 2.71
fatwa 3.1
faucet 26.32
faugh 25.1
Faulkner 26.7
fault 23.18; 25.17
fault-finder 22.5

fault-finding 22.26
faultless 24.43; 26.27
faultlessly 24.54; 26.37
faulty 24.3; 26.1
faun 25.22
fauna 26.7
Fauntleroy 33.1
Fauré 7.3
Faust 29.13
Fauvism 18.27
Fauvist 36.27
faux pas 3.1
fava 4.11
fave 7.54
Faversham 2.65
favour 8.6
favourable 8.79; 8.88
favourably 8.76
favoured 8.13
favouring 8.84
favourite 17.51
favouritism 18.29
Fawcett 26.32
Fawkes 25.7
Fawley 26.1
Fawlty 26.1
Fawlty Towers 31.5
fawn 25.22
fawner 26.7
fawning 26.25
fax 1.4
faxed 1.5
fay 7.1
Fay 7.1
fayre 5.1
faze 7.56
fazed 7.57
FBI 21.4
fealty 16.1
fear 13.1
fearful 14.6; 39.7
fearless 14.14
fearlessness 14.23
fears 13.5
fearsome 14.7
feasibility 18.58
feasible 16.41
feasibly 16.38
feast 15.33
feasted 16.14
feasting 16.27
Feast of Tabernacles
  2.30
feat 15.35
feather 10.11
feather bed 9.8
featherbedding 10.36
featherbrain 7.21

feathering 10.69
feathers 10.52
Featherstone 10.64
featherweight 7.38
feathery 10.53
feature 16.9
featured 16.14
featureless 16.47
features 16.37
febrifugal 42.16
febrile 21.16
February 10.55; 10.78
feck 9.2
feckless 10.42
fecklessness 10.70
fecula 10.56
fecund 10.29; 16.23; 37.36
fecundity 38.47
fed 9.8
Fed 9.8
fedayeen 15.26
federal 10.21; 10.60
federalism 18.29
federalist 17.49
federalize 21.47
federate 7.38
federation 8.28
fedora 26.6
fed up 37.41
fee 15.1
feeble 16.17
feebleness 16.47
feebler 16.7
feeblest 16.32
feebly 16.1
feed 15.11
feedback 1.3
feedbag 1.13
feeder 16.5
feeding 16.27
feedstuff 37.10
feel 15.17
feeler 16.7
feeling 16.27
feelings 16.28
feels 15.19
fees 15.42
feet 15.35
feign 7.21
feigned 7.22
feigning 8.63
feint 7.25
feistier 22.42
feistiest 22.48
feisty 22.1
Feldman 10.27
feldspar 3.1

felicitate 7.41
felicitation 8.32
felicitous 18.74
felicity 18.57
Felicity 18.57
feline 21.22
felinity 18.57
Felix 16.12
Felixstowe 35.19
fell 9.16
fella 10.12
fellah 10.12
fellate 7.33
feller 10.12
felling 10.36
Fellini 16.1
fellow 35.7
Fellowes 35.52
fellowship 17.43
felon 10.27
felonious 36.42
felony 10.53
felt 9.23
Feltham 10.25
felting 10.36
felt-tip 17.43
felt-tips 17.44
female 7.15
feminine 17.29
femininity 18.57
feminism 18.28
feminist 10.72
feminize 21.43
femme 9.28
femme fatale 1.16; 3.14
femoral 10.60
femur 16.8
fen 9.32
fence 9.39
fenced 9.40
fencer 10.14
Fenchurch 11.6
fencing 10.36
fend 9.35
fender 10.10
Fenella 10.12
fenestration 8.28
feng shui 7.2
Fenian 16.43
fennel 10.21
Fens 9.43
Fenton 10.27
fenugreek 15.7
Fenwick 10.15
feral 10.21
feral 14.6
Ferdinand 1.28
Fergal 12.8

Fergie 12.1
Fergus 12.19
Ferguson 12.34
ferial 14.19
Fermanagh 2.13
Fermat 1.45
ferment 9.41
fermentation 8.29
fermented 10.18
fermenting 10.36
Fermi 12.1
fermion 23.27
fern 11.15
Fernandez 9.57
fernery 12.29
ferns 11.18
ferny 12.1
ferocious 36.26
ferociously 36.35
ferocity 24.56
Ferranti 2.3
Ferrar 10.12
Ferrara 4.12
Ferrari 4.5
ferret 10.48
ferric 10.15
ferried 10.17
Ferrier 10.57
Ferris 10.41
Ferris wheel 15.17
ferromagnetic 10.15
ferrous 10.42
ferrule 10.21; 41.14
ferry 10.5
ferry boat 35.45
ferry boats 35.46
ferryman 1.24; 10.64
fertile 21.16
fertility 18.58
fertilization 8.44
fertilize 21.43
fertilized 21.48
fertilizer 22.9
fertilizing 22.26
fervency 12.29
fervent 12.14
fervently 12.29
fervid 12.4
fervour 12.2
fescue 41.3
fest 9.49
festal 10.21
fester 10.10
festered 10.18
festina lente 10.3
festival 10.60
festive 10.50
festivity 18.57

festoon 41.19
festooned 41.20
festoonery 42.36
festschrift 17.11
festschriften 18.32
feta 10.10
fetal 16.17
fetch 9.6
fetched 9.7
fetcher 10.14
fetching 10.36
fête 7.32
feticide 21.12
fetid 10.17; 16.13
fetish 10.45
fetishism 18.28
fetishist 10.72
fetlock 23.3
fetor 16.5; 25.3
fetter 10.10
fettered 10.18
fetters 10.52
fettle 10.21
fettler 10.12
fettucine 16.1
feud 41.9
feudal 42.16
feudalism 18.28
feudalist 42.48
feuding 42.24
fever 16.6
feverfew 41.4
feverish 17.50
feverishly 16.38
feverwort 11.24
few 41.1
fewer 42.2
fey 7.1
fez 9.57
Ffestiniog 23.11
fiancé 7.3
fiancée 7.3
fiasco 35.3
fiat 22.34
fib 17.1
fibber 18.8
fibbing 18.40
Fibonacci 4.7
fibre 22.3
fibrefill 17.15
fibreglass 3.26
fibres 22.39
fibre-tip 17.43
fibril 22.16
fibrin 18.31
fibroma 36.8
fibrosis 36.25
fibrositis 22.28

firebrand 1.28
firebreak 7.6
firebrick 17.3
firebug 37.14
firecracker 2.9
fired 19.2
firedamp 1.23
firedog 23.11
firefight 21.33
firefighter 22.5
firefighters 22.39
firefighting 22.26
fireflies 21.41
firefly 21.3
fireguard 3.8
firelighter 22.5
fireman 1.24
fireplace 7.30
fire power 31.1
fireproof 41.10
firer 20.2
fires 19.4
fireside 21.11
firestone 35.36
firestorm 25.20
firetrap 1.37
firewall 25.14
firewarden 26.19
firewater 26.4
firewood 39.4
firework 11.4
fireworks 11.5
firing 20.7
firing line 21.22
firkin 12.11
firm 11.13
firmament 12.35
firmer 12.2
firmest 12.20
firmly 12.1
firmness 12.19
firry 12.1
firs 11.29
first 11.23
first aid 7.8
first-aider 8.5
firstborn 25.22
first-class 3.26
firstly 12.1
first name 7.18
first-rate 7.33
first-time buyer 22.2
first-time buyers 22.39
firth 11.26
fir tree 15.3
fir trees 15.44
fisc 17.47

fiscal 18.22
Fischer 18.14
fish 17.50
fish and chips 17.44
fishbone 35.36
fishbones 35.39
fishbowl 35.30
fish cake 7.6
fisher 18.14
fisherman 18.67
fishery 18.56
fisheye 21.3
fishfinger 18.9
Fishguard 3.8
fish-hook 39.1
fishier 18.61
fishiest 18.76
fishmeal 15.17
fishmonger 38.9
fishmongers 38.45
fishnet 9.51
fishtail 7.15
fishwife 21.14
fishwives 21.38
fishy 18.7
Fison 22.20
fissile 21.16
fission 18.33
fissure 18.14
fist 17.49
fistful 39.7
fisticuffs 37.11
fistula 18.60
fit 17.51
fitful 18.22; 39.7
fitfully 18.56; 18.59
fitly 18.5
fitment 18.38
fitments 18.39
fitness 18.44
fits 17.52
fitted 18.19
fitter 18.10
fittest 18.46
fitting 18.40
fittingly 18.57
Fittipaldi 2.3
Fitz 17.52
Fitzgerald 10.22
Fitzgibbon 18.32
Fitzpatrick 2.19
Fitzrovia 36.37
first-time buyers
  22.39
Fitzsimmons 18.37
Fitzwilliam 18.26
five 21.37
five-a-side 21.12
fivefold 35.31
fiver 22.6

fivers 22.39
fives 21.38
fix 17.4
fixable 18.64
fixate 7.33
fixation 8.23
fixative 17.55
fixed 17.5
fixedly 18.57
fixer 18.14
fixing 18.40
fixity 18.57
fixture 18.14
fizz 17.56
fizzer 18.14
fizzier 18.61
fizziest 18.76
fizzing 18.40
fizzle 18.22
fizzy 18.7
fjord 25.9
flab 1.1
flabbergast 3.30
flabbergasted 4.17
flabbier 2.61
flabbiest 2.72
flabbiness 2.71
flabby 2.1
flaccid 2.24
flag 1.13
flagellant 10.33
flagellate 7.35
flagellation 8.24
flagellum 10.25
flagger 2.9
flagging 2.42
flagitious 18.44
flagman 2.35
flagon 2.35
flagons 2.39
flagpole 35.30
flagrancy 8.76
flagrant 8.56
flagrantly 8.76
flags 1.14
flagship 17.43
flagstaff 3.9
flagstone 35.36
flagstones 35.39
Flaherty 4.42
flail 7.15
flailed 7.16
flair 5.1
flak 1.3
flake 7.6
flaked 7.7
flakier 8.78
flakiest 8.86

flaky 8.1
flambé 7.3
flambeau 35.3
Flamborough 2.60
flamboyance 34.10
flamboyancy 34.14
flamboyant 34.9
flamboyantly 34.14
flame 7.18
flamenco 35.7
flameproof 41.10
flames 7.20
flamethrower 36.2
flaming 8.63
flamingo 35.11
flammable 2.64
Flamsteed 15.11
flan 1.24
Flanagan 2.66
Flanders 4.41
flange 1.30
flank 1.25
flanked 1.27
flanker 2.9
flanking 2.42
flanks 1.26
flannel 2.28
flannelette 9.51
flap 1.37
flapdoodle 42.16
flapjack 1.3
flapjacks 1.4
flapped 1.39
flapper 2.8
flapping 2.42
flappy 2.1
flaps 1.38
flare 5.1
flared 5.2
flares 5.5
flash 1.43
flashback 1.3
flashbulb 37.17
flashcube 41.5
flashed 1.44
flasher 2.14
flashes 2.55
flashily 2.58
flashing 2.42
flash in the pan 1.24
flashlight 21.33
Flashman 2.35
flashover 36.6
flash point 33.10
flashy 2.7
flask 3.27
flat 1.45
flatboat 35.45

flat-chested 10.18
flat feet 15.35
flatfish 2.49
flatfoot 39.14
flatiron 22.20
flatlet 2.51
flatly 2.5
flatmate 7.34
flatmates 7.50
flatness 2.46
flats 1.46
flatten 2.35
flattened 2.36
flattener 2.60
flatter 2.10
flatterer 2.60
flattering 2.70
flattery 2.56
flattie 2.3
flattish 2.49
flatulence 2.69
flatulent 2.68
flatus 8.67
flatware 5.1
flatworm 11.13
Flaubert 5.1
flaunt 25.25
flaunter 26.4
flaunty 26.1
flautist 26.28
Flavell 8.15
Flavia 8.78
Flavian 8.81
Flavius 8.85
flavour 8.6
flavoured 8.13
flavourful 8.79; 39.7
flavouring 8.84
flavourless 8.85
flavours 8.75
flavoursome 8.80
flaw 25.1
flawed 25.9
flawless 26.27
flax 1.4
flaxen 2.35
Flaxman 2.35
flaxseed 15.11
flay 7.1
flayed 7.8
flea 15.1
fleabag 1.13
fleabane 7.21
fleabite 21.33
fleapit 16.34
fleas 15.42
fleck 9.2
flecked 9.5

flecks 9.3
fled 9.8
fledge 9.14
fledged 9.15
fledgling 10.36
flee 15.1
fleece 15.32
fleecing 16.27
fleecy 16.1
fleeing 16.27
fleet 15.35
Fleet 15.35
fleeting 16.27
fleetingly 16.38
Fleetwood 39.4
Fleming 10.36
Flemish 10.45
flense 9.39
flesh 9.50
flesher 10.14
fleshly 10.5
fleshpots 23.45
fleshy 10.7
fletch 9.6
fletcher 10.14
Fletcher 10.14
Fleur 11.1
fleur-de-lys 15.4
fleuron 23.27
flew 41.1
flex 9.3
flexed 9.4
flexibility 18.58
flexible 10.60
flexing 10.36
flexion 10.28
flexitime 21.19
flexor 10.14
flibbertigibbet 18.50
flick 17.3
flicked 17.6
flicker 18.9
flickering 18.73
flick knife 21.14
flick knives 21.38
flicks 17.4
flies 21.39
flight 21.31
flightier 22.42
flightiest 22.48
flightiness 22.46
flightless 22.29
flighty 22.1
flimflam 1.22
flimsier 18.61
flimsiest 18.76
flimsiness 18.74
flimsy 18.7

flinch 17.33
Flinders 18.55
fling 17.35
flint 17.39
Flint 17.39
flintlock 23.3
flints 17.40
Flintstones 35.39
flinty 18.3
flip 17.43
flip-flop 23.36
flip-flops 23.37
flippancy 18.56
flippant 18.38
flippantly 18.56
flipped 17.45
flipper 18.8
flippers 18.55
flipping 18.40
flirt 11.24
flirtation 8.23
flirtatious 8.67
flirting 12.16
flirts 11.25
flirty 12.1
flit 17.51
flitch 17.7
flitter 18.10
flittermouse 29.12
Flo 35.1
float 35.45
floated 36.12
floater 36.5
floating 36.24
floats 35.46
floaty 36.1
flocculate 7.43
flocculent 24.67
flock 23.3
flocks 23.5
Flodden 24.33
floe 35.1
Floella 10.12
flog 23.11
flogged 23.12
flogger 24.9
flogging 24.40
flood 37.8
flooded 38.20
floodgate 7.34
floodgates 7.50
flooding 38.34
floodlight 21.33
floodlights 21.35
floodlit 38.43
floods 37.9
floor 25.1
floorboard 25.9

floorboards 25.10
floorcloth 23.46
floored 25.9
flooring 26.25
floors 25.35
floozy 42.1
flop 23.36
flophouse 29.12
flopped 23.38
floppier 24.58
floppiest 24.71
floppy 24.1
floppy disk 17.47
flora 26.6
Flora 26.6
floral 26.15
Florence 24.39
Florentine 15.26
Florentine 21.22
floret 24.49; 26.32
Florey 26.1
floribunda 38.10
florid 24.23
Florida 24.57
florilegium 16.42
florin 24.32
florins 24.37
florist 24.45
Florrie 24.5
floruit 17.51
floss 23.39
flossed 23.41
Flossie 24.7
flossing 24.40
flossy 24.7
flotage 36.14
flotation 8.23
flotilla 18.12
flotsam 24.30
flounce 29.9
flounced 29.10
flouncing 30.12
flounder 30.2
flounderer 30.23
flour 31.1
flourish 38.40
flourished 38.41
flourishing 38.58
floury 30.1; 32.1
flout 29.14
flouted 30.3
flouting 30.12
flow 35.1
flowage 36.14
flow chart 3.32
flowed 35.25
flower 31.1
flowerbed 9.8

flowerbeds 9.9
flowered 31.2
flowerer 32.2
flowering 32.3
flowerpot 23.44
flowers 31.5
flowery 32.1
flowing 36.24
flown 35.36
flows 35.52
Floyd 33.4
flu 41.1
fluctuate 7.48
fluctuating 8.60
fluctuation 8.38
flue 41.1
Fluellen 10.26
fluency 42.36
fluent 42.22
fluently 42.36
fluey 42.1
fluff 37.10
fluffier 38.49
fluffiest 38.61
fluffy 38.4
flugelhorn 25.22
fluid 42.13
fluidity 18.57
fluke 41.6
fluky 42.1
flume 41.17
flummery 38.47
flummox 38.17
flung 37.37
flunk 37.32
flunked 37.34
flunky 38.2
fluoresce 9.47
fluorescence 10.34
fluorescent 10.33
fluoridate 7.45
fluoridation 8.36
fluoride 21.11
fluorinate 7.45
fluorination 8.36
fluorine 15.25
flurry 38.5
flush 37.46
flusher 38.14
flushing 38.34
Flushing 38.34
fluster 38.10
flustered 38.20
flute 41.27
fluted 42.14
fluter 42.5
flutes 41.28
fluting 42.24

flutter 38.10
fluttered 38.20
fluttery 38.47
fluvial 42.39
flux 37.4
fluxion 38.28
fly 21.1
flyable 22.43
flyaway 7.4
flyblown 35.36
flyby 21.3
fly-by-night 21.34
flycatcher 2.14
flyer 22.2
flying 22.26
Flying Dutchman 38.28
flying saucer 26.8
flying saucers 26.36
flying squad 23.8
flyleaf 15.13
flyleaves 15.41
Flynn 17.29
flyover 36.6
flypaper 8.3
flypast 3.30
flyposting 36.24
flyscreen 15.25
flyspeck 9.2
fly swatter 24.10
flytrap 1.37
flyweight 7.34
flywheel 15.17
FM 9.28
foal 35.30
foam 35.34
foaming 36.24
foamy 36.1
fob 23.1
focaccia 2.14
focal 36.15
foci 21.3
fo'c's'le 36.15
focus 36.26
focusable 36.46
focused 36.28
focuser 36.36
fodder 24.10
foe 35.1
foeman 36.20
foes 35.52
foetus 16.30
fog 23.11
Fogarty 24.54
fogbound 29.6
fogbow 35.13
fogey 36.1
fogeys 36.33

fogged 23.12
foggier 24.58
foggiest 24.71
foggily 24.56
foggy 24.2
foghorn 25.22
föhn 11.15
foible 34.5
foie gras 3.1
foil 33.6
foison 34.8
foist 33.12
foisted 34.3
foisting 34.11
Fokker 24.9
fold 35.31
foldable 36.38
foldaway 7.4
folded 36.12
folder 36.5
folding 36.24
foldout 29.14
Foley 36.1
foliage 17.14
foliate 36.45
foliation 8.37
folic 24.18; 36.10
folie à deux 11.1
Folies-Bergère 5.1
folio 35.19
folk 35.21
Folkestone 36.20
folklore 25.3
folks 35.22
folk song 23.31
folksy 36.1
follicle 24.61
follicles 24.62
follies 24.52
follow 35.13
followed 35.25
follower 36.2
following 36.24
follow-my-leader 16.5
follows 35.52
follow-through 41.4
follow-up 37.41
folly 24.5
foment 9.41
fomentation 8.37
fond 23.30
Fonda 24.10
fondant 24.38
fonder 24.10
fondle 24.27
fondly 24.5
fondness 24.43
fondue 41.3

font 23.34
Fontainebleau 35.19
Fontana 4.13
fontanelle 9.16
Fonteyn 7.21
fonts 23.33
Fontwell 9.16
food 41.9
foodie 42.1
foodstuff 37.10
fool 41.14
fooled 41.15
foolery 42.36
foolhardily 4.42
foolhardiness 4.53
foolhardy 4.3
fooling 42.24
foolish 42.29
foolishly 42.36
foolproof 41.10
fools 41.16
foolscap 1.37
foot 39.14
footage 40.5
football 25.14
footballer 26.6
footballers 26.36
footballing 26.25
footboard 25.9
footbridge 40.5
footer 40.2
footfall 25.14
foothill 17.15
foothills 17.23
foothold 35.31
footing 40.15
footle 42.16
footlights 21.35
footloose 41.24
footman 40.10
footmark 3.3
footmarks 3.4
footnote 35.45
footnotes 35.46
footpad 1.9
footpath 3.34
footplate 7.34
footprint 17.39
footrest 9.49
footsie 40.1
Footsie 40.1
footslog 23.11
footsore 25.3
footstep 9.44
footsteps 9.45
footstool 41.14
footway 7.3
footwear 5.1

footwork 11.4
footy 40.1
foo yong 23.31
fop 23.36
foppery 24.54
foppish 24.46
for 25.1
forage 24.26
forager 24.57
forasmuch 37.6
foray 7.3
forbad 1.9
forbade 7.8
forbear 5.1
forbearance 6.9
forbearing 6.10
forbid 17.8
forbidden 18.32
forbidding 18.40
forbore 25.2
forborne 25.22
force 25.28
forced 25.29
force-fed 9.8
force-fed 9.8
force-feed 15.11
force-feeding 16.27
forceful 26.15; 39.7
forcefully 26.37
force majeure 11.1
forcemeat 15.35
forceps 9.45
forcer 26.8
forces 26.36
forcible 26.41
forcibly 26.37
forcing 26.25
ford 25.9
Ford 25.9
fordable 26.41
Fordham 26.17
Fordingbridge 17.14
fore 25.1
forearm 3.16
forearm 3.16
forearmed 3.17
forebear 5.1
forebode 35.25
foreboding 36.24
forebrain 7.21
forecast 3.30
forecaster 4.10
foreclose 35.52
foreclosing 36.24
foreclosure 36.9
forecourse 25.28
forecourt 25.31
foredeck 9.2

foredoom 41.17
forefather 4.11
forefathers 4.41
forefeet 15.35
forefinger 18.9
forefoot 39.14
forefront 37.40
foregather 2.11
forego 35.2
foregoing 36.24
foregoing 36.24
foregone 23.27
foreground 29.6
forehand 1.28
forehanded 2.25
forehead 9.8; 24.23
foreign 24.32
foreigner 24.57
foreigners 24.74
foreknow 35.2
foreland 26.20
foreleg 9.12
forelegs 9.13
forelock 23.3
foreman 26.19
foremast 3.30
foremost 35.43
forename 7.18
forenoon 41.19
forensic 10.15
foreordain 7.21
foreordained 7.22
forepart 3.32
foreparts 3.33
forepaw 25.3
forepeak 15.7
foreplay 7.3
forequarter 26.4
forequarters 26.36
forerun 37.31
forerunner 38.13
foresaid 9.8
foresail 7.15; 26.15
foresaw 25.2
foresee 15.2
foreseeable 16.41
foreseen 15.24
foreshadow 35.3
foreshadowed 35.25
foreshadows 35.52
foreshore 25.3
foreshorten 26.19
foreshow 35.2
foreside 21.11
foresight 21.33
foreskin 26.18
foreskins 26.22
forest 24.45

forestall 25.14
forestalled 25.15
forestation 8.34
forestay 7.3
forested 24.59
forester 24.57
Forester 24.57
forestry 24.56
foreswore 25.2
foretaste 7.31
foretell 9.16
foreteller 10.12
forethought 25.31
foretoken 36.20
foretold 35.31
fore-topsail 24.27
forever 10.11
forevermore 25.4
forewarn 25.22
forewarned 25.24
forewarning 26.25
forewent 9.41
forewing 26.25
foreword 11.7
Forfar 26.5
forfeit 26.32
forfeiture 26.38
forfend 9.35
forgave 7.54
forge 25.13
forger 26.8
forgery 26.37
forget 9.51
forgetful 10.21; 39.7
forgetfulness 10.70
forget-me-not 23.44
forget-me-nots 23.45
forgettable 10.60
forgetting 10.36
forging 26.25
forgivable 18.64
forgive 17.54
forgiven 18.32
forgiveness 18.44
forgiver 18.11
forgiving 18.40
forgo 35.2
forgot 23.44
forgotten 24.33
fork 25.6
forkful 39.7
fork-lift truck 37.3
fork-lift trucks 37.4
forks 25.7
forlorn 25.22
forlornly 26.1
form 25.20
formal 26.15

formaldehyde 21.12
formalin 17.29
formalism 18.28
formalist 26.48
formalistic 18.16
formality 2.57
formalization 8.49
formalize 21.45
formalized 21.48
formally 26.37
format 1.45
formation 8.23
formative 17.55
formatting 2.42
Formby 26.1
formed 25.21
former 26.7
formerly 26.37
formic 26.9
Formica® 22.4
formicate 7.44
formication 8.35
formidable 18.64;
  26.51
forming 26.25
formless 26.27
Formosa 36.9
formula 26.38
formulae 15.4
formulaic 8.10
formularize 21.47
formulate 7.44
formulation 8.35
formulator 8.5
fornicate 7.44
fornication 8.35
fornicator 8.5
Forrest 24.45
Forrest Gump 37.29
forsake 7.6
forsaken 8.21
forsook 39.1
forsooth 41.29
Forster 26.4
forswear 5.1
forsworn 25.22
Forsyte 21.33
forsythia 22.42
fort 25.31
forte 7.3
Fortescue 41.4
forth 25.33
Forth 25.33
forthcoming 38.34
forthright 21.33
forthrightly 22.1
forthwith 17.53
forties 26.35

fortieth 17.53
fortification 8.49
fortified 21.12
fortifier 22.2
fortify 21.4
Fortinbras 1.40
fortissimo 35.19
fortitude 41.19
Fort Knox 23.5
Fort Lauderdale 7.15
fortnight 21.33
fortnightly 22.1
Fortnum 26.17
FORTRAN 1.24
fortress 26.27
forts 25.32
Fort Sumter 38.10
fortuitous 42.46
fortuity 42.36
fortunate 26.50
fortune 26.19; 41.19
fortune cookie 40.1
Fort William 18.26
forty 26.1
forty-eight 7.44
forty-five 21.37
forty-four 25.4
forty-nine 21.22
forty-niner 22.8
forty-one 37.31
forty-six 17.4
forty-three 15.4
forty-two 41.4
forty winks 17.31
forum 26.17
forward 26.12
forwarder 26.38
forwardness 26.47
forwards 26.13
forward-thinking 18.40
forwent 9.41
Fosbury 24.54
Fosdyke 21.7
fossa 24.14
fossick 24.20
fossil 24.27
fossilization 8.48
fossilize 21.45
fossilized 21.48
fossils 24.29
foster 24.10
Foster 24.10
fostered 24.24
fosterling 24.69
Foster's 24.53
Fothergill 17.15
Fotheringay 7.2

fought 25.31
foul 29.4
foulard 3.8
fouler 30.2
foulest 30.16
foulie 30.1
fouling 30.12
Foulness 9.47
foul play 7.2
found 29.6
foundation 8.23
foundations 8.55
founded 30.3
founder 30.2
foundling 30.12
foundress 30.14
foundry 30.1
fount 29.11
fountain 30.7
fountainhead 9.8
fountain pen 9.32
founts 29.9
four 25.1
fourfold 35.31
Fourier 7.4
four-letter word 11.7
four-poster 36.5
fourscore 25.3
foursome 26.17
foursquare 5.1
fourteen 15.24
fourteenth 15.28
fourth 25.33
fourthly 26.1
four-wheel drive 21.37
four-wheeled 15.18
fovea 36.37
Fowey 33.1
fowl 29.4
Fowler 30.2
fox 23.5
Fox 23.5
foxes 24.53
foxglove 37.49
foxhole 35.30
foxhound 29.6
fox hunt 37.40
fox-hunter 38.10
foxing 24.40
foxtail 7.15
foxtrot 23.44
foxy 24.7
foyer 34.2
Foyle 33.6
Fra 3.1
fracas 3.1
fractal 2.28

fraction 2.35
fractional 2.64
fractions 2.39
fractious 2.46
fracture 2.14
fractured 2.25
fragile 21.16
fragility 18.58
fragment 2.40; 9.41
fragmentation 8.24
fragments 2.41
fragrance 8.57
fragrant 8.56
frail 7.15
frailties 8.74
frailty 8.1
frame 7.18
framed 7.19
framer 8.8
framework 11.4
framing 8.63
Fran 1.24
franc 1.25
France 3.22
Frances 4.31
Francesca 10.9
franchise 21.41
franchised 21.48
Francis 4.31
Franciscan 18.32
Francisco 35.11
Franck 1.25
Franco 35.3
François 3.1
Francophile 21.16
Francophilia 18.61
Francophobe 35.20
Francophone 35.36
francs 1.26
frangible 2.64
frangipani 4.6
Franglais 7.3
frank 1.25
Frank 1.25
Frankenstein 21.22
franker 2.9
Frankfurt 11.24
frankfurter 12.2
Frankie 2.2
Frankie Howerd 31.2
frankincense 9.39
Frankish 2.49
Franklin 2.34
frankly 2.5
frankness 2.46
Frank's 1.26
frantic 2.17
frantically 2.58

Franz 1.34
frappé 7.3
Frascati 4.3
Fraser 8.9
Frasier 8.78
fraternal 12.8
fraternity 12.29
fraternize 21.42
fratricide 21.12
Frau 29.1
fraud 25.9
fraudster 26.4
fraudulence 26.46
fraudulent 26.45
fraught 25.31
Fräulein 21.22
fray 7.1
frayed 7.8
fraying 8.58
Frayn 7.21
frays 7.56
frazzle 2.28
freak 15.7
freakish 16.33
freaks 15.8
freaky 16.1
freckle 10.21
freckled 10.22
freckles 10.23
freckly 10.5
Fred 9.8
Fred Astaire 5.1
Freddy 10.3
Frederica 16.4
Frederick 17.3
Fred's 9.9
free 15.1
freebie 16.1
freebies 16.36
freeboard 25.9
freeboot 41.27
freebooter 42.5
freeborn 25.22
freed 15.11
freedman 1.24
freedom 16.20
free-for-all 25.14
freehand 1.28
freehold 35.31
freeholder 36.5
freelance 3.22
freeload 35.25
freeloaded 36.12
freeloader 36.5
freeloading 36.24
freely 16.1
free man 1.24
freeman 16.22

Freeman 16.22
Freemason 8.21
Freemasonic 24.19
Freemasonry 8.76
freephone 35.36
Freepost® 35.43
freer 16.2
free-range 7.23
freesheet 15.35
freesia 16.9; 16.40
freest 16.32
freestanding 2.42
freestyle 21.16
freethinker 18.9
freethinking 18.40
Freetown 29.5
freeware 5.1
freeway 7.3
freewheel 15.17
freewheeling 16.27
freewill 17.15
freezable 16.41
freeze 15.42
freeze-dried 21.11
freezer 16.9
freezing 16.27
freezing point 33.10
Freiburg 11.9
freight 7.32
freighter 8.5
Fremantle 2.28
French 9.33
French bean 15.24
Frenchify 21.4
French leave 15.39
Frenchman 10.27
Frenchwoman 40.10
Frenchy 10.7
frenetic 10.15
frenetically 10.54
frenzied 10.17
frenzy 10.7
frequencies 16.51
frequency 16.38
frequent 9.41; 16.25
frequenter 10.10
frequently 16.38
fresco 35.7
fresh 9.50
freshen 10.28
freshened 10.29
fresher 10.14
freshest 10.43
freshly 10.5
freshman 10.27
freshness 10.42
freshwater 26.4
fret 9.51

fretful 10.21; 39.7
fret saw 25.3
fretted 10.18
fretting 10.36
fretwork 11.4
Freud 33.4
Freudian 34.17
Freudian slip 17.43
Freya 8.2
friable 22.43
friar 19.1
Friar Tuck 37.3
friary 20.1
fribble 18.22
fricassee 7.4; 15.4
fricative 17.55
friction 18.33
frictional 18.64
frictionless 18.74
Friday 7.3; 22.1
fridge 17.14
fried 21.9
Friedrich 16.11
Friedrich's 16.12
friend 9.35
friendless 10.42
friendlier 10.57
friendliest 10.71
friendliness 10.70
friendly 10.5
friendship 17.43
fries 21.39
Friesian 16.22; 16.43
Friesland 16.23
frieze 15.42
frig 17.12
frigate 18.49
Frigga 18.9
frigging 18.40
fright 21.31
frighten 22.20
frightened 22.21
frightener 22.41
frightening 22.26
frighteningly 22.40
frightful 22.16; 39.7
frightfully 22.40
frigid 18.18
frigidity 18.57
frigidly 18.57
frill 17.15
frillier 18.61
frilliest 18.76
frills 17.23
frilly 18.5
fringe 17.37
fringes 18.55
Frink 17.30

frippery 18.56
Frisbee® 15.3; 18.1
Frisch 17.50
frisé 7.3
Frisian 18.33
frisk 17.47
frisker 18.9
friskier 18.61
friskiest 18.76
frisking 18.40
frisky 18.2
Frith 17.53
fritillary 18.56
frittata 4.10
fritter 18.10
Fritz 17.52
Friuli 42.1
frivol 18.22
frivolity 24.56
frivolous 18.74
frizz 17.56
frizzier 18.61
frizziest 18.76
frizzle 18.22
frizzy 18.7
fro 35.1
Frobisher 36.36
frock 23.3
Frodo 35.16
Frodsham 24.30
Froebel 12.8; 36.15
frog 23.11
froghopper 24.8
frogman 24.33
frogmarch 3.6
frogmarched 3.7
frogs 23.13
frogspawn 25.22
frolic 24.18
frolicked 17.6
frolicker 24.57
frolicking 24.69
frolics 24.22
frolicsome 24.63
from 23.23
fromage frais 7.4
Frome 35.34; 41.17
frond 23.30
Fronde 23.30
front 37.40
frontage 38.22
frontal 38.23
frontbencher 10.14
fronted 38.20
frontier 13.1
frontiersman 14.9
frontispiece 15.32
front line 21.22

front page 7.12
frontrunner 38.13
frontrunning 38.34
frost 23.41
Frost 23.41
frostbite 21.33
frostbitten 18.32
frostbound 29.6
frosted 24.24
frostier 24.58
Frosties 24.52
frostiest 24.71
frostily 24.56
frosting 24.40
frosty 24.3
froth 23.46
frothier 24.58
frothiest 24.71
frothing 24.40
frothy 24.4
frottage 3.13
froufrou 41.3
froward 36.12
frown 29.5
frowner 30.2
frowning 30.12
frowst 29.13
frowsty 30.1
frowzy 30.1
froze 35.52
frozen 36.20
fructify 21.4
fructose 35.42
frugal 42.16
frugality 2.57
frugally 42.36
frugivorous 18.74
fruit 41.27
fruitarian 6.19
fruitcake 7.6
fruiter 42.5
fruiterer 42.37
fruitful 39.7; 42.16
fruitfully 42.36
fruitier 42.38
fruitiest 42.47
fruition 18.33
fruitless 42.26
fruitlessly 42.36
fruits 41.28
fruity 42.1
frump 37.29
frumpier 38.49
frumpiest 38.61
frumpish 38.40
frumpy 38.1
frustrate 7.33
frustrated 8.13

frustrating 8.60
frustration 8.23
frustum 38.26
fry 21.1
Fry 21.1
fryer 22.2
frying pan 1.24
fry-up 37.41
Fuchs 41.7
fuchsia 42.9
fuck 37.3
fucker 38.9
fucking 38.34
fuddle 38.23
fuddy-duddy 38.3
fudge 37.15
fug 37.14
fugacious 8.67
fugacity 2.57
fugal 42.16
fuggy 38.2
fugitive 17.55
fugue 41.11
Führer 28.2
Fuji 42.1
fulcrum 40.8
fulfil 17.15
fulfilled 17.18
fulfiller 18.12
fulfilling 18.40
fulfilment 18.38
fulgent 38.32
fulguration 8.38
Fulham 40.8
full 39.7
fullback 1.3
full-blown 35.36
fuller 40.2
Fuller 40.2
fullerene 15.26
fullest 40.14
full monty 24.3
full nelson 10.28
fullness 40.13
full of beans 15.29
full-scale 7.15
full-time 21.19
full-timer 22.8
fully 40.1
fully fledged 9.15
fully grown 35.36
fulmar 40.2
fulminate 7.48
fulmination 8.38
fulsome 40.8
Fulton 40.10
fumble 38.23
fumbler 38.12

fume 41.17
fumed 41.18
fumigant 42.43
fumigate 7.49
fumigated 8.13
fumigation 8.39
fuming 42.24
fun 37.31
function 38.28
functional 38.52
functionalism 18.29
functionality 2.57
functionally 38.64
functionary 38.47
functioned 38.29
functions 38.31
fund 37.36
fundament 38.56
fundamental 10.21
fundamentalism 18.28
fundamentally 10.53
funded 38.20
fundholder 36.5
fundholding 36.24
funding 38.34
fundraise 7.56
fundraiser 8.9
fundraisers 8.75
funeral 42.39
funerary 42.50
funereal 14.19
funfair 5.1
fungal 38.23
fungi 21.3
fungicidal 22.16
fungicide 21.12
fungous 38.38
fungus 38.38
funicular 18.60
funk 37.32
funkier 38.49
funkiest 38.61
funky 38.2
fun-lover 38.11
fun-loving 38.34
funnel 38.23
funnier 38.49
funnies 38.46
funniest 38.61
funnily 38.47
funny 38.6
fur 11.1
furbelow 35.19
furbelows 35.52
furbish 12.22
Furby® 12.1
Furies 26.35; 28.16

furious 28.24
furl 11.11
furled 11.12
furlong 23.31
furlough 35.8
furmity 12.29
furnace 12.18
Furness 12.18
furnish 12.22
furnished 12.23
furnisher 12.30
furniture 12.30
furore 26.1
furphy 12.1
furred 11.7
furrier 38.49
furrow 35.17
furrowed 35.25
furry 12.1
furs 11.29
further 12.2
furtherance 12.36
furthered 12.5
further education 8.28
furthermore 25.4
furthermost 35.43
furthest 12.20
furtive 12.27
furtively 12.29
fury 26.1; 28.1
furze 11.29
furzy 12.1
fuse 41.33
fused 41.34
fuselage 3.13
fusible 42.39
fusilier 13.1
fusillade 7.8
fusion 42.20
fuss 37.43
fussed 37.45
fusser 38.14
fussier 38.49
fussiest 38.61
fussiness 38.59
fussing 38.34
fusspot 23.44
fussy 38.7
fustian 38.54
fustic 38.15
fusty 38.3
futile 21.16
futility 18.58
futon 23.27
Futuna 42.8
future 42.9
futurism 18.28

futurist 42.48
futuristic 18.16
futurity 28.17
fuzz 37.51
fuzzier 38.49
fuzziest 38.61
fuzzy 38.7
f-word 11.7
Fylde 21.17
Fyne 21.22
G 15.1
gab 1.1
gabardine 15.26
gabble 2.28
gabbler 2.12
gabby 2.1
gabfest 9.49
gabion 8.81
gable 8.15
gables 8.17
Gabon 23.27
Gabonese 15.45
Gabor 25.2
Gaborone 36.1
Gabriel 8.79
Gabrieli 10.5
Gabrielle 9.16
Gaby 2.1
gad 1.9
Gad 1.9
gadabout 29.14
Gadarene 15.26
Gaddafi 2.4; 4.4
gadfly 21.3
gadget 2.51
gadgeteer 13.1
gadgetry 2.58
gadzooks 41.7
Gaea 16.2
Gael 7.15
Gaelic 2.19; 8.10
Gaels 7.17
gaff 1.11
gaffe 1.11
gaffer 2.11
gaffsail 7.15
gag 1.13
gaga 3.1
Gagarin 4.23
gage 7.12
gagger 2.9
gagging 2.42
gaggle 2.28
gags 1.14
Gaia 22.2
gaiety 8.76
Gail 7.15
gaillardia 4.44

Gail's 7.17
gaily 8.1
gain 7.21
gained 7.22
gainer 8.8
gainful 8.15; 39.7
gainfully 8.76
gaining 8.63
gains 7.26
gainsaid 9.8
gainsay 7.2
Gainsborough 8.77
gait 7.32
gaiter 8.5
Gaitskell 8.15
Gaius 22.29
gal 1.16
gala 4.12
galactic 2.17
galah 3.1
Galahad 1.9
galantine 15.26
Galapagos 2.71
Galashiels 15.19
Galatea 16.2
Galatia 8.9
Galatian 8.23
Galatians 8.55
galaxy 2.56
Galbraith 7.51
gale 7.15
gale force 25.28
Galen 8.21
gales 7.17
Galicia 18.61
Galician 18.67
Galilean 8.21; 16.22
Galilee 15.4
Galileo 35.6
galingale 7.15
gall 25.14
Gallagher 2.60
gallant 1.33; 2.40
gallantly 2.56
gallantry 2.56
galleon 2.66
galleried 2.62; 17.8
gallery 2.56
galley 2.5
galleys 2.54
gallfly 21.3
galliard 2.25
Gallic 2.19
Gallicism 18.28
Gallicize 21.42
galling 26.25
gallinule 41.14
Gallipoli 18.56

gallium 2.65
gallivant 1.33
gallivants 1.34
galloglass 3.26
gallon 2.35
gallons 2.39
gallop 2.44
galloper 2.60
galloping 2.70
Galloway 7.4
gallows 35.52
gallstone 35.36
Gallup 2.44
Gallup poll 35.30
galore 25.2
galoshes 24.53
Galsworthy 12.1
Galt 23.18; 25.17
Galton 24.33; 26.19
galumph 37.28
Galvani 4.6
galvanic 2.20
galvanism 18.28
galvanize 21.42
galvanized 21.48
Galveston 2.66
Galway 7.3
Galwegian 16.22
gam 1.22
Gambetta 10.10
Gambia 2.61
Gambian 2.66
gambit 2.51
gamble 2.28
gambler 2.12
gambling 2.42
gambol 2.28
gambrel 2.28
game 7.18
game bird 11.7
gamecock 23.3
gamekeeper 16.3
gamekeepers 16.37
gamelan 1.24
gamely 8.1
gameplay 7.3
gamer 8.8
games 7.20
gamesman 8.21
gamesmanship 17.43
gamete 15.35
gamey 8.1
gamin 2.34
gamine 15.25
gaming 8.63
gamma 2.13
gammon 2.35
gammy 2.6

gamp 1.23
gamut 2.50
gan 1.24
gander 2.10
Gandhi 2.3
gang 1.29
gangbang 1.29
ganger 2.13
Ganges 2.54; 15.44
gangland 1.28; 2.36
ganglia 2.61
gangling 2.42
ganglion 2.66
gangly 2.5
gangplank 1.25
gangrene 15.25
gangrenous 2.71
gangsta 2.10
gangster 2.10
gangway 7.3
ganja 2.14
gannet 2.51
gantry 2.5
Ganymede 15.11
gap 1.37
Gap 1.37
gape 7.27
gaped 7.29
gaper 8.3
gapes 7.28
gaping 8.59
gappy 2.1
gaps 1.38
gar 3.1
garage 2.27; 3.13
garages 2.76
garb 3.2
garbage 4.18
garble 4.19
garbled 4.20
Garbo 35.4
García 16.2
Garda 4.10
garden 4.24
gardener 4.13
gardener 4.43
gardenia 16.40
gardening 4.52
Gardiner 4.43
Gardner 4.13
Gareth 2.52
garfish 4.35
Garfunkel 38.23
Gargantua 2.60
gargantuan 2.66
gargle 4.19
gargoyle 33.6
garibaldi 26.1

Garibaldi 26.1
garish 6.12
garishly 6.15
garland 4.25
Garland 4.25
garlic 4.16
garlicky 4.42
garment 4.27
garments 4.28
garner 4.13
Garner 4.13
garnered 4.17
garnet 4.38
Garnett 4.38
garnish 4.35
garnished 4.36
garnishing 4.52
garpike 21.7
Garrard 2.25; 3.8
garret 2.50
Garrett 2.50
Garrick 2.19
garrison 2.66
garrotte 23.44
garrulous 2.71
garter 4.10
Garter 4.10
garters 4.41
garth 3.34
Garth 3.34
Garvey 4.4
Gary 2.5
gas 1.40
gasbag 1.13
gas chamber 8.3
Gascoigne 33.8
Gascon 2.35
Gascony 2.56
gaseous 2.71
gaseous 8.85
gas-fired 19.2
gas-guzzler 38.12
gash 1.43
gashed 1.44
gasholder 36.5
gasiform 25.20
gasify 21.4
Gaskell 2.28
gasket 2.51
gas lamp 1.23
gaslight 21.33
gasman 1.24
gasolier 13.1
gasoline 15.26
gasometer 24.57
gasp 3.29
gasper 4.8
gassed 1.42

gasser 2.14
gassier 2.61
gassiest 2.72
gassing 2.42
gassy 2.7
gastralgia 2.14
gastric 2.19
gastritis 22.28
gastroenteritis 22.28
gastrointestinal
   10.60; 22.16
gastrological 24.61
gastronome 35.34
gastronomer 24.57
gastronomic 24.19
gastronomical 24.61
gastronomy 24.54
gastropod 23.8
gastroscope 35.40
gasworks 11.5
gate 7.32
gateau 35.3
gate-crash 1.43
gate-crasher 2.14
gate-crashing 2.42
gated 8.13
gatefold 35.31
gatehouse 29.12
gatekeeper 16.3
gate-leg 9.12
gatepost 35.43
gates 7.50
Gateshead 9.8
gateway 7.3
Gath 1.47
gather 2.11
gatherer 2.60
gathering 2.70
Gatling 2.42
Gatling gun 37.31
GATT 1.45
Gatting 2.42
Gatwick 2.19
gauche 35.44
gaucherie 36.35
gaudeamus 4.32
gaudier 26.39
gaudiest 26.49
gaudily 26.37
gaudy 26.1
gauge 7.12
gauged 7.13
gauger 8.9
gauging 8.64
Gauguin 1.24
Gaul 25.14
Gauleiter 22.5
Gaulish 26.30

Gaullism 18.27
Gaullist 36.27
Gauloise 3.37
gaunt 25.25
gaunter 26.4
gauntlet 26.32
gauss 29.12
Gauss 29.12
Gautama 30.23
gauze 25.35
gauzy 26.1
gave 7.54
gavel 2.28
Gavin 2.34
gavotte 23.44
Gawain 7.21
Gawd 25.9
gawk 25.6
gawky 26.1
gawp 25.26
gawper 26.2
gawps 25.27
gay 7.1
Gay 7.1
Gaydon 8.21
gayer 8.2
gayest 8.69
Gaynor 8.8
Gaz 1.50
Gaza 4.14
Gaza Strip 17.43
gaze 7.56
gazebo 35.10
gazed 7.57
gazelle 9.16
gazer 8.9
gazette 9.51
gazetteer 13.1
gazing 8.64
gazpacho 35.3
gazump 37.29
gazumper 38.8
gazunder 38.10
Gazza 2.14
GB 15.2
GCSE 15.2
GCSEs 15.43
Gdansk 1.32
g'day 21.2
gean 15.23
gear 13.1
gearbox 23.5
gearing 14.12
gears 13.5
gearstick 17.3
gearsticks 17.4
gearwheel 15.17
gecko 35.7

Geddes 10.41
geddit 10.48
gee 15.1
gee-gee 15.3; 16.1
gee-gees 15.44; 16.36
geek 15.7
geeky 16.1
Geelong 23.31
geese 15.32
Geest 15.33
gee-whiz 17.56
geezer 16.9
gefilte 18.10
Gehenna 10.13
Geiger 22.4
Geiger counter 30.2
geisha 8.9
gel 9.16
gelatin 17.29
gelatine 15.26
gelatinous 2.71
geld 9.19
gelding 10.36
Geldof 23.9
gelid 10.17
gelignite 21.34
gelt 9.23
gem 9.28
Gemini 15.4; 21.4
Geminian 22.20
Gemma 10.13
gems 9.31
gemsbok 23.3
gemstone 35.36
gemstones 35.39
gen 9.32
gendarme 3.16
gendarmerie 4.42
gendarmes 3.18
gender 10.10
gene 15.23
Gene 15.23
genealogical 24.61
genealogist 2.73
genealogy 2.56
genera 10.56
general 10.21; 10.60
generalissimo 35.19
generality 2.57
generalization 8.43
generalize 21.47
generally 10.53
generalship 17.43
generate 7.38
generation 8.28
generator 8.5
generatrix 8.11
generic 10.15

generically 10.54
generosity 24.56
generous 10.42; 10.70
generously 10.78
genesis 17.46
Genesis 17.46
genet 10.48
genetic 10.15
genetically 10.54
geneticist 10.72
genetics 10.16
Geneva 16.6
Genevan 16.22
Genevieve 15.39
Genevieve's 15.41
Genghis Khan 3.19
Genghis Khan's 3.24
genial 16.41
geniality 2.57
genially 16.52
genie 16.1
genii 21.4
genital 10.60
genitalia 8.78
genitive 17.55
genitor 10.56
genius 16.47
genoa 36.2
Genoa 36.2
genocide 21.12
genome 35.34
genotype 21.26
genotypic 18.16
genre 4.12
gens 9.43
gent 9.41
genteel 15.17
gentian 10.28
Gentile 21.16
gentility 18.58
gentle 10.21
gentlefolk 35.21
gentleman 10.64
gentlemanly 10.78
gentleness 10.70
gentler 10.12
gentlest 10.43
gentlewoman 40.10
gentlewomen 18.31
gently 10.5
gentrification 8.43
gentry 10.5
gents 9.39
genuflect 9.5
genuflection 10.28
genuine 17.29
genuinely 10.78
genus 10.42; 16.30

geocentric 10.15
geodesic 10.15; 16.11
geodesy 24.56
Geoff 9.10
Geoffrey 10.5
geographer 24.57
geographic 2.18
geographical 2.64
geographically 2.58
geography 24.54
geologic 24.20
geological 24.61
geologically 24.56
geologist 24.72
geology 24.55
geometer 24.57
geometric 10.15
geometrical 10.60
geometrically 10.54
geometrician 18.33
geometry 24.56
geophysical 18.64
geophysics 18.17
Geordie 26.1
Geordies 26.35
George 25.13
George Bernard Shaw 25.2
George Best 9.49
Georgetown 29.5
georgette 9.51
Georgette 9.51
Georgia 26.8
Georgian 26.19
georgic 26.9
Georgie 26.1
Georgina 16.8
geothermal 12.8
geotropism 18.27
Geraint 21.24
Gerald 10.22
Geraldine 15.26
geranium 8.80
Gerard 3.8
gerbera 12.30
gerbil 12.8
gerbils 12.9
Gerda 12.2
gerent 10.33
geriatric 2.19
geriatrics 2.23
germ 11.13
Germaine 7.21
german 12.12
German 12.12
germander 2.10
germane 7.21
Germanic 2.20

Germanicus 2.71
germanium 8.80
Germanophilia 18.61
Germany 12.29
germicidal 22.16
germicide 21.12
germinal 12.32
germinate 7.39
germination 8.29
Germolene® 15.26
Geronimo 35.19
gerontology 24.55
Gerry 10.5
gerrymander 2.10
Gershwin 12.11
Gertie 12.1
Gertrude 41.9
gerund 10.29; 37.36
gerundive 38.44
Gervaise 7.56
gesso 35.7
Gestalt 1.20
Gestapo 35.4
gestate 7.33
gestation 8.23
gesticulate 7.41
gesticulation 8.32
gesture 10.14
gesundheit 21.33
get 9.51
get-at-able 2.64
getaway 7.4
Gethsemane 10.53
gettable 10.60
getter 10.10
Getty 10.3
Gettysburg 11.9
get-up 37.41
geum 16.20
Gewürztraminer 16.8
geyser 16.9
Ghana 4.13
Ghanaian 8.21
ghastly 4.5
ghee 15.1
Ghent 9.41
gherkin 12.11
ghetto 35.7
ghetto blaster 4.10
ghettoization 8.43
ghettoize 21.43
Ghibelline 15.26; 21.22
ghost 35.43
ghostbuster 38.10
ghosting 36.24
ghostlier 36.37
ghostliest 36.44

ghostlike 21.7
ghostly 36.1
ghostwrite 21.33
ghostwriter 22.5
ghoul 41.14
ghoulish 42.29
ghyll 17.15
GI 21.2
giant 22.24
giants 22.25
Gibb 17.1
gibber 18.8
gibberellin 10.26
gibbering 18.73
gibberish 17.50
gibbet 18.50
gibbon 18.32
Gibbon 18.32
Gibbons 18.37
gibbous 18.44
Gibbs 17.2
gibe 21.5
gibed 21.6
Gibeon 18.67
giblets 18.51
Gibraltar 24.10; 26.4
Gibraltarian 6.19
Gibran 3.19
Gibson 18.33
giddiness 18.74
giddy 18.3
giddy-up 37.41
Gide 15.11
Gideon 18.67
Gielgud 39.4
gift 17.11
GIFT 17.11
gifted 18.19
giftwrap 1.37
gig 17.12
gigabyte 21.34
gigabytes 21.35
gigaflop 23.36
gigahertz 11.25
gigantic 2.17
gigantism 18.28
giggle 18.22
giggler 18.12
giggles 18.24
Giggleswick 17.3
giggling 18.40
giggly 18.5
gigolo 35.19
gigs 17.13
gigue 15.14
Gilbert 18.49
Gilbertian 12.34
gild 17.18

gilded 18.19
gilder 18.10
gilding 18.40
Gilead 1.9
Gileadite 21.32
Giles 21.18
gilet 7.3
Gilgamesh 9.50
gill 17.15
Gill 17.15
Gillespie 10.1
Gillette 9.51
Gillian 18.67
Gillian's 18.69
gillie 18.5
Gillingham 18.66
gills 17.23
gillyflower 31.1
Gilpin 18.31
gilt 17.21
gilt-edged 9.15
gimbal 18.22
gimballed 18.23
gimbals 18.24
gimcrack 1.3
gimlet 18.50
gimme 18.6
gimmick 18.16
gimmickry 18.57
gimmicks 18.17
gimmicky 18.57
gimp 17.27
gin 17.29
Gina 16.8
ginger 18.14
ginger ale 7.15
ginger beer 13.1
gingerbread 9.8
gingerly 18.56
gingery 18.56
gingham 18.26
gingko 35.11
gink 17.30
Ginny 18.6
Gino 35.10
ginormous 26.27
ginseng 9.36
Giorgione 36.1
Giotto 35.13
Giovanni 2.6; 4.6
gippy 18.1
giraffe 1.11; 3.9
giraffes 1.12
gird 11.7
girder 12.2
girdle 12.8
girl 11.11
girlfriend 9.35

girlhood 39.4
girlie 12.1
girlish 12.22
girlishly 12.29
girn 11.15
giro 35.12
Girobank 1.25
Gironde 23.30
girt 11.24
girth 11.26
Girton 12.12
Giselle 9.16
Gish 17.50
Gissing 18.40
gist 17.49
git 17.51
gîte 15.35
Giuseppe 10.1
give 17.54
give a damn 1.22
give-and-take 7.6
giveaway 7.4
given 18.32
Givenchy 4.7
giver 18.11
giving 18.40
gizmo 35.11
gizzard 18.19
glabrous 8.67
glacé 7.3
glacial 8.15; 8.79
glaciate 7.37
glaciated 8.13
glaciation 8.27
glacier 2.61; 8.78
glad 1.9
gladden 2.35
gladdie 2.3
glade 7.8
gladiator 8.5
gladiolus 36.26
gladly 2.5
gladness 2.46
gladsome 2.32
Gladstone 2.35
Gladys 2.45
Glagolitic 18.16
glair 5.1
glam 1.22
Glamis 3.18
Glamorgan 26.19
glamorization 8.40
glamorize 21.42
glamorous 2.71
glamorously 2.78
glamour 2.13
glance 3.22
glances 4.41

glancing 4.29
gland 1.28
glandular 2.60
glans 1.36
glare 5.1
glared 5.2
glaring 6.10
glaringly 6.15
Glaser 8.9
Glasgow 35.4
glasnost 23.41
glass 3.26
glass-blowing 36.24
glasses 4.41
glasshouse 29.12
glasslike 21.7
glasspaper 8.3
glassware 5.1
glasswork 11.4
glassworks 11.5
glassy 4.7
Glastonbury 2.56;
2.78
Glaswegian 16.22
Glauber 30.2
Glauce 26.1
glaucoma 36.8
glaucous 26.27
glaze 7.56
glazed 7.57
glazer 8.9
glazier 8.78
glazing 8.64
Glazunov 23.9
gleam 15.20
gleamed 15.21
gleaming 16.27
glean 15.23
gleaned 15.27
gleaner 16.8
gleaning 16.27
gleanings 16.28
Gleason 16.22
glebe 15.5
glee 15.1
gleeful 16.17; 39.7
gleefully 16.38
gleet 15.35
glen 9.32
Glencoe 35.2
Glenda 10.10
Glendower 31.1
Gleneagles 16.18
Glenfiddich 18.16
glengarry 2.5
Glenlivet 18.50
Glenn 9.32
Glennie 10.6

glens 9.43
Glenys 10.41
glib 17.1
glibly 18.5
glibness 18.44
glide 21.9
glider 22.5
gliding 22.26
glimmer 18.13
glimmered 18.19
glimmering 18.73
glimpse 17.28
glimpsing 18.40
Glinka 18.9
glint 17.39
glints 17.40
glissade 3.8
glissando 35.3
glisten 18.33
glistened 18.34
glistening 18.73
glistens 18.37
glister 18.10
glitch 17.7
glitter 18.10
glitterati 4.3
glittered 18.19
glittery 18.56
glitz 17.52
glitzy 18.7
gloaming 36.24
gloat 35.45
gloated 36.12
gloater 36.5
gloating 36.24
glob 23.1
global 36.15
globalization 8.50
globalize 21.45
globally 36.35
globe 35.20
globetrotter 24.10
globetrotting 24.40
globular 24.57
globule 41.14
globules 41.16
globulin 17.29
globus 36.26
glockenspiel 15.17
glogg 23.11
gloom 41.17
gloomier 42.38
gloomiest 42.47
gloomily 42.36
gloomy 42.1
gloopy 42.1
gloria 26.39
Gloria 26.39

Gloriana 4.13
gloried 26.11
glories 26.35
glorification 8.49
glorified 21.12
glorify 21.4
gloriole 35.30
glorious 26.47
glory 26.1
glory hole 35.30
gloss 23.39
glossary 24.54
glossed 23.41
glossier 24.58
glossiest 24.71
glossy 24.7
glottal 24.27
glottis 24.42
Gloucester 24.10
Gloucestershire 13.1;
24.57
glove 37.49
gloved 37.50
glover 38.11
Glover 38.11
glow 35.1
glowed 35.25
glower 31.1
glowered 31.2
glowering 32.3
glowing 36.24
glow-worm 11.13
gloxinia 18.61
gloze 35.52
Gluck 39.1
glucosamine 15.26
glucose 35.42; 35.52
glue 41.1
glued 41.9
gluey 42.1
glug 37.14
gluing 42.24
glum 37.27
glumly 38.5
glummer 38.13
glummest 38.39
glut 37.47
glutamate 7.49
glutamine 15.26
gluteal 42.39
gluten 42.20
gluteus 42.46
glutinous 42.46
glutton 38.28
gluttonous 38.59
gluttony 38.47
glycaemic 16.11
glyceride 21.12

glycerine 15.26
glycerine 17.29
glycerol 23.15
glycine 15.25
glycogen 22.44
glycolipid 18.18
glycoside 21.12
glycosuria 28.18
Glyn 17.29
Glyndebourne 25.22
Glynis 18.43
glyph 17.10
glyptic 18.16
GM 9.28
GMT 15.4
gnarl 3.14
gnarly 4.5
gnash 1.43
gnasher 2.14
gnashing 2.42
gnat 1.45
gnats 1.46
gnaw 25.1
gnawed 25.9
gnawing 26.25
gneiss 21.29
gnocchi 24.2
gnome 35.34
gnomes 35.35
gnomic 36.10
gnomon 23.27
gnosis 36.25
Gnostic 24.16
Gnosticism 18.28
gnu 41.1
go 35.1
Goa 36.2
goad 35.25
goaded 36.12
goading 36.24
goads 35.26
go-ahead 9.8
goal 35.30
goalie 36.1
goalkeeper 16.3
goalkeepers 16.37
goalless 36.26
goalmouth 29.16
goalpost 35.43
goanna 2.13
goat 35.45
goatee 15.2
goatherd 11.7
goats 35.46
goatsbeard 13.2
goatskin 36.19
goatsucker 38.9
goaty 36.1

go away 7.4
gob 23.1
gobbet 24.49
Gobbi 24.1
gobble 24.27
gobbledegook 41.6
gobbler 24.12
gobby 24.1
go-between 15.26
Gobi 36.1
goblet 24.49
goblin 24.32
goblins 24.37
goby 36.1
god 23.8
God 23.8
Godalming 24.69
godchild 21.17
godchildren 18.32
goddamn 1.22
Goddard 3.8; 24.24
goddaughter 26.4
goddess 9.47; 24.42
godetia 16.9
godfather 4.11
God-fearing 14.12
godforsaken 8.21
Godfrey 24.5
Godhead 9.8
Godiva 22.6
godless 24.43
godlike 21.7
godly 24.5
godmother 38.11
Godolphin 24.32
godparent 6.8
godparents 6.9
godsend 9.35
godslot 23.44
godson 37.31
Godspeed 15.11
godsquad 23.8
Godunov 23.9
Godwin 24.32
godwit 24.49
Godzilla 18.12
Goebbels 12.9
goer 36.2
Goering 12.16
goes 35.52
goest 36.28
Goethe 12.2
gofer 36.6

goffer 36.6
Gog 23.11
go-getter 10.10
goggle 24.27
gogglebox 23.5
Gogol 23.15
Goidelic 10.15
going 36.24
going-over 36.6
goings-on 23.27
goitre 34.2
go-kart 3.32
Golan Heights 21.35
gold 35.31
Golda 36.5
Golda Meir 13.1
goldcrest 9.49
golden 36.20
goldeneye 21.4
Golden Hind 21.23
golden oldie 36.1
golden oldies 36.33
goldenrod 23.8
goldfinch 17.33
goldfish 36.29
Goldie 36.1
Goldilocks 23.5
Golding 36.24
Goldman 36.20
gold mine 21.22
goldsmith 17.53
Goldsmith 17.53
Goldstein 21.22
Goldwyn 36.19
golf 23.16
golfer 24.11
golfing 24.40
golf links 17.31
Golgotha 24.57
Goliath 22.36
Goliathan 22.44
Golightly 22.1
golliwog 23.11
Gollum 24.30
golly 24.5
gombeen-man 1.24
Gomer 36.8
Gomez 9.57
Gomorrah 24.12
gonad 1.9
gonads 1.10
gondola 24.57
gondolier 13.1
gone 23.27
goner 24.13
Goneril 17.15
gong 23.31

gongs 23.32
gonk 23.28
gonks 23.29
gonna 24.13
gonorrhoea 13.1
gonorrhoeal 13.3
goo 41.1
goober 42.3
Gooch 41.8
good 39.4
Goodall 25.14
goodbye 21.2
goodbyes 21.40
Goodge 41.12
good heavens 10.32
good-humoured
    42.14
goodies 40.19
Goodison 40.23
goodly 40.1
goodman 40.10
Goodman 40.10
good-natured 8.13
good-naturedly 8.76
goodness 40.13
goodnight 21.32
good-oh 35.2
Goodrich 17.7
good 'un 40.10
goodwife 21.14
goodwill 17.15
Goodwin 40.9
Goodwood 39.4
goody 40.1
Goodyear 13.1
gooey 42.1
goof 41.10
goofball 25.14
goofy 42.1
Googie 42.1
Google 42.16
googly 42.1
googol 23.15; 42.16
googolplex 9.3
Goolagong 23.31
Goole 41.14
goolie 42.1
goolies 42.35
goon 41.19
Goonhilly 18.5
goosander 2.10
goose 41.24
gooseberry 40.1;
    40.20
goosebumps 37.30
gooseflesh 9.50
goosegog 23.11
goosegrass 3.26

gooseneck 9.2
goosestep 9.44
goosestepped 9.46
Goossens 42.21
goosy 42.1
Go-Ped® 9.8
gopher 36.6
Gorbachov 23.9
Gorbals 26.16
Gordian 26.43
Gordimer 26.38
Gordon 26.19
Gordonstoun 24.64
gore 25.1
Gore 25.1
gored 25.9
Gore-Tex® 9.3
gorge 25.13
gorgeous 26.27
gorger 26.8
gorging 26.25
Gorgon 26.19
Gorgons 26.21
Gorgonzola 36.7
gorier 26.39
goriest 26.49
gorilla 18.12
gorillagram 1.22
gorillas 18.55
Goring 26.25
Gorky 26.1
Gorman 26.19
gormandize 21.45
Gormenghast 3.30
gormless 26.27
Gormley 26.1
gorse 25.28
gorsy 26.1
gory 26.1
gosh 23.42
goshawk 25.6
gosling 24.40
go-slow 35.2
go spare 5.1
gospel 24.27
gospeller 24.57
Gosport 25.31
goss 23.39
gossamer 24.57
Gosse 23.39
gossip 17.43
gossipmonger 38.9
gossipy 24.56
got 23.44
gotcha 24.14
Goth 23.46
Gotham 24.30
Gothenburg 11.9

Gothic 24.17
Gotland 24.34
go to hell 9.16
go to pot 23.44
gotta 24.10
gotten 24.33
Götterdämmerung 39.10
gouache 3.31
Gouda 30.2
gouger 30.2
Gough 23.9
goujons 23.35
goulash 1.43
Gould 41.15
Gounod 35.18
gourami 4.6; 28.17
gourd 27.2
Gourlay 28.1
gourmand 26.20; 28.8
gourmandise 15.45
gourmet 7.3
gout 29.14
gouty 30.1
Govan 38.28
govern 38.28
governance 38.57
governed 38.29
governess 9.47
government 38.56
governmental 10.21
governor 38.48
governorship 17.43
Gowan 30.8
Gower 31.1
gown 29.5
Gowrie 30.1
goy 33.1
Goya 34.2
GP 15.2
Graafian 4.50
grab 1.1
grabber 2.8
grabbing 2.42
grabby 2.1
grabs 1.2
Gracchus 2.46
grace 7.30
Grace 7.30
graceful 8.15; 39.7
gracefully 8.76
graceless 8.67
graces 8.75
Graces 8.75
Gracie 8.1
gracile 21.16
gracious 8.67
graciously 8.76

grackle 2.28
grad 1.9
gradable 8.79
gradation 8.23
grade 7.8
grader 8.5
grades 7.9
Gradgrind 21.23
gradient 8.82
gradients 8.83
grading 8.60
gradual 2.64
gradually 2.59; 2.78
graduand 1.28
graduate 2.74; 7.35
graduation 8.24
Graf 1.11
graffiti 16.1
graffito 35.10
graft 3.10
grafter 4.10
grafting 4.29
Grafton 4.24
Graham 8.19
Grahame 8.19
Grail 7.15
grain 7.21
Grainger 8.9
grainy 8.1
gram 1.22
grammar 2.13
grammarian 6.19
grammatical 2.64
grammatically 2.58
Grammaticus 2.46
Grammy 2.6
gramophone 35.36
gramophonic 24.19
Grampian 2.66
grampus 2.46
gran 1.24
Granada 4.10
granary 2.56
Gran Canaria 6.16
grand 1.28
grandad 1.9
grandaddy 2.3
grandchild 21.17
grandchildren 18.32
Grand Coulee 15.3; 42.1
granddaughter 26.4
grandee 15.2
grander 2.10
grandest 2.48
grandeur 2.14; 27.1
grandfather 4.11
grandfatherly 4.42

grandiloquence 18.71
grandiloquent 18.70
grandiose 35.42
grandiosity 24.56
Grandison 2.66
grandly 2.5
grandma 3.1
grand mal 1.16
grandmama 3.1
Grand Marnier® 7.4
grandmaster 4.10
grandmother 38.11
grandmotherly 38.47
grandness 2.46
grandpa 3.1
grandpapa 3.1
grandpapa's 3.37
grandparent 6.8
grandparents 6.9
Grand Prix 15.2
grandsire 19.1
grandson 37.31
grandstand 1.28
grange 7.23
Grangemouth 29.16
granita 16.5
granite 2.51
granitic 18.16
granivorous 18.74
granny 2.6
grant 3.23
Grant 3.23
Granta 2.10; 4.10
granted 4.17
grantee 15.2
Grantham 2.32
grantor 4.10
grants 3.22
granular 2.60
granulate 7.35
granulation 8.24
granulose 35.52
Granville 17.15
grape 7.27
grapefruit 41.27
grapes 7.28
grapeshot 23.44
grapevine 21.22
grapey 8.1
graph 1.11; 3.9
graphic 2.18
graphical 2.64
graphics 2.23
graphite 21.33
graphitic 18.16
graphologist 24.72
graphology 24.55
graphs 1.12

grapnel 2.28
grappa 2.8
Grappelli 10.5
grapple 2.28
grappling 2.42
Grasmere 13.1
grasp 3.29
grasper 4.8
grasping 4.29
grass 3.26
grassed 3.30
grasshopper 24.8
Grassic 2.21
grassland 1.28
grassless 4.32
grasslike 21.7
grassy 4.7
grate 7.32
grateful 8.15; 39.7
gratefully 8.76
grater 8.5
Gratian 8.81
graticule 41.14
gratification 8.40
gratified 21.12
gratifies 21.42
gratify 21.4
gratifying 22.26
gratin 1.24
grating 8.60
gratis 2.45
gratitude 41.9
Grattan 2.35
gratuitous 42.46
gratuity 42.36
graunch 25.23
gravadlax 1.4
grave 3.35
grave 7.54
grave-digger 18.9
gravel 2.28
gravelly 2.56
gravely 8.1
graven 8.21
graver 8.6
graves 7.55
Graves 3.35; 7.55
Gravesend 9.35
graveside 21.11
gravest 8.69
gravestone 35.36
graveyard 3.8
gravid 2.24
gravitas 1.40; 3.26
gravitate 7.35
gravitation 8.24
gravity 2.57
gravlax 1.4

gravure 27.1
gravy 8.1
gravy boat 35.45
Gray 7.1
grayling 8.62
Grayson 8.21
graze 7.56
grazed 7.57
grazer 8.9
grazier 8.78
grazing 8.64
grease 15.32
greased 15.33
greasepaint 7.25
greaseproof 41.10
greaser 16.9
greasier 16.40
greasiest 16.49
greasiness 16.47
greasing 16.27
greasy 16.1
great 7.32
greatcoat 35.45
Great Dane 7.21
greaten 8.21
greater 8.5
greatest 8.69
great-grandson 37.31
greatness 8.67
Greats 7.50
Great Yarmouth 4.39
greave 15.39
Greaves 15.41
grebe 15.5
grebes 15.6
Grecian 16.22
Grecism 18.27
Greece 15.32
greed 15.11
greedier 16.40
greediest 16.49
greedily 16.38
greediness 16.47
greedy 16.1
greedy guts 37.48
Greek 15.7
Greeley 16.1
green 15.23
Greenaway 7.4
greenback 1.3
green belt 9.23
Greene 15.23
greener 16.8
greenery 16.38
greenest 16.32
greenfield 15.18
greenfinch 17.33
greenfly 21.3

greengage 7.12
greengrocer 36.9
greengrocers 36.34
Greenham 16.20
greenhorn 25.22
greenhouse 29.12
greenish 16.33
greenkeeper 16.3
Greenland 16.23
Greenlander 16.39
greenmail 7.15
greenness 16.30
Greenock 16.10
Greenpeace 15.32
greenroom 39.9; 41.17
greens 15.29
Greensleeves 15.41
greenstick 16.11
greenstuff 37.10
greensward 25.9
Greenwich 10.20;
   17.7; 18.21
greenwood 39.4
Greer 13.1
greet 15.35
greeter 16.5
greeting 16.27
greetings 16.28
greetings card 3.8
Greg 9.12
gregarious 6.22
Gregor 10.9
Gregorian 26.43
Gregory 10.53
Greig 9.12
greige 7.14
gremlin 10.26
gremlins 10.31
Grenada 8.5
grenade 7.8
Grenadian 8.81
grenadier 13.1
grenadine 15.26
Grenadines 15.29
Grendel 10.21
Grenfell 10.21
Grenoble 36.15
Grenville 17.15
Gresham 10.25
Greta 10.10
Gretel 10.21
Gretna 10.13
Gretna Green 15.26
grew 41.1
grey 7.1
Greyfriars 19.4
grey-haired 5.2
greyhound 29.6

greying 8.58
greyish 8.70
greylag 1.13
greyness 8.67
Greystoke 35.21
grid 17.8
griddle 18.22
griddlecake 7.6
gridiron 22.20
gridlock 23.3
gridlocked 23.6
grief 15.13
Grieg 15.14
grievance 16.26
grieve 15.39
grieved 15.40
griever 16.6
grieves 15.41
grieving 16.27
grievous 16.30
grievously 16.38
Griff 17.10
griffin 18.31
Griffin 18.31
Griffith 17.53
griffon 18.32
grift 17.11
grifter 18.10
grike 21.7
grill 17.15
grille 17.15
grilled 17.18
griller 18.12
grilling 18.40
grillroom 39.9; 41.17
grim 17.24
grimace 7.30; 18.44
Grimaldi 24.3; 26.1
grimalkin 2.34
grime 21.19
Grimes 21.21
grimly 18.5
Grimm 17.24
grimmer 18.13
grimmest 18.46
grimness 18.44
Grimoned 18.34
Grimsby 18.1
grin 17.29
grinch 17.33
grind 21.23
grinder 22.5
grindery 22.40
grinding 22.26
grindstone 35.36
gringo 35.11
grinned 17.34
grinner 18.13

grinning 18.40
grins 17.42
grip 17.43
gripe 21.26
griped 21.28
griper 22.3
gripes 21.27
griping 22.26
gripped 17.45
gripper 18.8
grippier 18.61
grippiest 18.76
gripping 18.40
grippy 18.1
Griselda 10.10
Grisham 18.26
grisly 18.5
grison 22.20
grist 17.49
gristle 18.22
gristly 18.5
grit 17.51
grits 17.52
gritter 18.10
grittier 18.61
grittiest 18.76
gritting 18.40
gritty 18.3
grizzle 18.22
grizzled 18.23
grizzly 18.5
groan 35.36
groaned 35.37
groaner 36.8
groaning 36.24
groat 35.45
groats 35.46
Gro-bag® 1.13
grocer 36.9
grocers 36.34
grocery 36.35
grockle 24.27
grockles 24.29
Groening 12.16
grog 23.11
Grogan 36.20
groggier 24.58
groggiest 24.71
groggily 24.56
groggy 24.2
grogram 24.30
groin 33.8
Grolier 36.37
Gromit 24.49
grommet 24.49
Groningen 24.64;
  36.40
groom 39.9; 41.17

groomed 41.18
grooming 42.24
groove 41.31
grooved 41.32
groover 42.6
groovier 42.38
grooviest 42.47
groovy 42.1
grope 35.40
groper 36.3
groping 36.24
Gropius 36.42
grosgrain 7.21
gross 35.42
grosser 36.9
grossest 36.28
grossly 36.1
Grossmith 17.53
Grosvenor 36.8
grot 23.44
grotesque 9.48
grotesquely 10.5
grotesquery 10.53
Grotius 36.42
grottier 24.58
grottiest 24.71
grotto 35.13
grotty 24.3
grouch 29.2
grouching 30.12
grouchy 30.1
ground 29.6
groundage 30.5
groundbait 7.34
grounded 30.3
ground floor 25.3
groundhog 23.11
grounding 30.12
groundless 30.14
groundling 30.12
groundmass 1.40
groundnut 37.47
grounds 29.7
groundsel 30.6
groundsheet 15.35
groundsman 30.8
groundspeed 15.11
groundswell 9.16
groundwork 11.4
group 41.22
grouper 42.3
groupie 42.1
groupies 42.35
grouping 42.24
groups 41.23
groupware 5.1
grouse 29.12
groused 29.13

grouser 30.2
grout 29.14
grouted 30.3
grouter 30.2
grouting 30.12
grouts 29.15
grove 35.50
grovel 24.27
groveller 24.57
Grover 36.6
groves 35.51
Groves 35.51
grow 35.1
growable 36.38
grower 36.2
growing 36.24
growl 29.4
growler 30.2
growling 30.12
grown 35.36
grown-up 37.41
growth 35.47
groyne 33.8
grub 37.1
grubber 38.8
grubbier 38.49
grubbiest 38.61
grubbily 38.47
grubbiness 38.59
grubby 38.1
grubs 37.2
grubstake 7.6
grudge 37.15
grudger 38.14
grudging 38.34
grudgingly 38.47
gruel 42.16
gruelling 42.45
gruesome 42.18
gruff 37.10
gruffer 38.11
gruffest 38.39
grumble 38.23
grumbled 38.24
grumbler 38.12
grumbles 38.25
grumbling 38.34
grump 37.29
grumpier 38.49
grumpiest 38.61
grumpily 38.47
grumpiness 38.59
grumpy 38.1
Grundig 17.12
Grundy 38.3
grunge 37.38
grungy 38.7
grunt 37.40

grunted 38.20
grunter 38.10
grunting 38.34
gruntled 38.24
grunts 37.39
Gruyère 5.1
gryphon 18.32
G-string 16.27
guacamole 36.1
Guadalajara 4.12
Guadalcanal 1.16
Guadalquivir 13.1
Guadeloupe 41.22
Guam 3.16
guanine 15.25
guano 35.4
guarantee 15.4
guaranteed 15.11
guarantor 25.4
guard 3.8
guardant 4.27
guarded 4.17
guardedly 4.42
guardhouse 29.12
guardian 4.50
guardianship 17.43
guarding 4.29
guardrail 7.15
guardroom 39.9; 41.17
guardsman 4.24
Guatemala 4.12
Guatemalan 4.24
guava 4.11
gubbins 38.30
Gucci 42.1
guck 37.3
gudgeon 38.28
Gudrun 40.10
guelder-rose 35.52
Guelph 9.20
guerdon 12.12
Guernica 12.30; 16.4
Guernsey 12.1
guerrilla 18.12
guerrillas 18.55
guess 9.47
guessable 10.60
guessed 9.49
guesser 10.14
guesses 10.52
guessing 10.36
guesstimate 7.38
guesswork 11.4
guest 9.49
guesthouse 29.12
guest room 39.9;
  41.17
guff 37.10

guffaw 25.2
guffawed 25.9
guffawing 26.25
Guggenheim 21.19
Guiana 2.13; 4.13
Guianan 2.35
guichet 7.3
guidance 22.25
guide 21.9
Guide 21.9
guidebook 39.1
guided 22.13
guideline 21.22
guidelines 21.25
guidepost 35.43
Guider 22.5
Guides 21.13
Guiding 22.26
guild 17.18
guilder 18.10
Guildford 18.19
guildhall 25.14
guile 21.16
guileless 22.29
guillemot 23.44
guillotine 15.26
guilt 17.21
guiltily 18.57
guiltless 18.44
guilty 18.3
guilty conscience 24.39
guinea 18.6
Guinea 18.6
Guinea-Bissau 29.1
Guinean 18.67
guineas 18.54
Guinevere 13.1
Guinness 18.43
guipure 27.1
guise 21.39
guiser 22.9
guitar 3.1
guitarist 4.33
guitars 3.37
Gujarat 3.32
Gujarati 4.3
Gulag 1.13
Gulbenkian 10.64
gulch 37.20
gules 41.16
gulf 37.21
Gulf 37.21
Gulf Stream 15.20
gull 37.16
gullet 38.43
gullibility 18.58
gullible 38.52

Gulliver 38.48
gull-wing 38.34
gully 38.5
gulp 37.23
gulped 37.24
gulper 38.8
gulping 38.34
gum 37.27
gumbo 35.17
gumboil 33.6
gumboot 41.27
gumboots 41.28
gumdrop 23.36
Gummer 38.13
Gummidge 38.22
gummy 38.6
gumption 38.28
gumshield 15.18
gumshoe 41.3
gun 37.31
gunboat 35.45
guncotton 24.33
gundog 23.11
gunfight 21.33
gunfire 19.1
Gunga Din 17.29
gunge 37.38
gung-ho 35.2
gungy 38.7
gunk 37.32
gunlock 23.3
gunman 38.28
gunmetal 10.21
Gunn 37.31
gunned 37.36
Gunnell 38.23
gunner 38.13
gunners 38.45
gunnery 38.47
gunning 38.34
gunplay 7.3
gunpoint 33.10
gunpowder 30.2
gunrunner 38.13
gunrunning 38.34
gunship 17.43
gunshot 23.44
gunslinger 18.13
gunslinging 18.40
gunsmith 17.53
gunstock 23.3
Gunter 38.10
Gunther 40.2
gunwale 38.23
guppy 38.1
Gupta 38.10
gurgle 12.8
gurgler 12.2

gurgling 12.16
Gurkha 12.2
gurnard 12.5
Gurney 12.1
guru 41.3
Gus 37.43
gush 37.46
gusher 38.14
gushing 38.34
gushy 38.7
gusset 38.43
gust 37.45
gustation 8.23
Gustave 3.35
gusting 38.34
gusto 35.17
gusty 38.3
gut 37.47
gutbucket 38.43
Gutenberg 11.9
Guthrie 38.5
gutless 38.38
guts 37.48
gutsier 38.49
gutsiest 38.61
gutsy 38.7
gutta-percha 12.2
gutted 38.20
gutter 38.10
guttering 38.58
guttersnipe 21.26
guttural 38.23; 38.52
guv 37.49
guv'nor 38.13
guy 21.1
Guy 21.1
Guyana 2.13; 4.13
Guyanan 2.35
Guyanese 15.45
Guy's 21.39
guys 21.39
guzzle 38.23
guzzler 38.12
Gwen 9.32
Gwendolen 17.29
Gwen's 9.43
Gwent 9.41
Gwyn 17.29
Gwyneth 17.53; 18.52
gybe 21.5
gybed 21.6
gym 17.24
gymkhana 4.13
gymnasia 8.78
gymnasium 8.80
gymnastic 2.17
gymnastics 2.23
gymnosperm 11.13

gymslip 17.43
gymslips 17.44
gynae 22.1
gynaecologic 24.20
gynaecological 24.61
gynaecologist 24.72
gynaecology 24.55
gyp 17.43
gyppo 35.11
Gypsies 18.54
gypsophila 24.57
gypsum 18.26
Gypsy 18.7
gyrate 7.33
gyrating 8.60
gyration 8.23
gyrations 8.55
gyratory 8.76
gyre 19.1
gyrfalcon 24.33; 26.19
gyrocompass 38.38
gyroplane 7.21
gyroscope 35.40
gyroscopic 24.16
gyve 21.37
gyves 21.38
ha 3.1
haar 3.1
habeas corpus 26.27
haberdasher 2.14
haberdashery 2.56
habergeon 2.6
habilitate 7.41
habit 2.51
habitable 2.79
habitant 2.68
habitat 1.45
habitation 8.24
habitual 18.64
habitually 18.59; 18.80
habituate 7.41
habituation 8.32
habitude 41.9
habitué 7.4
háček 9.2
hachure 27.1
hacienda 10.10
hack 1.3
hacked 1.6
hacker 2.9
hackery 2.56
hackette 9.51
hacking 2.42
hackle 2.28
hackles 2.30
Hackman 2.35
Hackney 2.6
hackney cab 1.1

hackneyed 2.24
hacksaw 25.3
hacksaws 25.35
hackwork 11.4
had 1.9
haddock 2.16
Hadean 8.81
Hades 8.74; 15.44
Hadleigh 2.5
hadn't 2.40
Hadrian 8.81
haematite 21.34
haematology 24.55
haematoma 36.8
haematuria 28.18
haemodialysis 17.46
haemoglobin 18.19
haemolytic 18.16
haemophilia 18.61
haemophiliac 1.3
haemophilic 18.16
haemorrhage 17.14
haemorrhagic 2.21
haemorrhoid 33.4
haemorrhoidal 34.5
haemorrhoids 33.5
haft 3.10
hag 1.13
Hagar 8.4
Haggadah 4.10
Haggai 21.4
haggard 2.25
Haggard 2.25
haggis 2.45
haggle 2.28
haggler 2.12
Hagiographa 24.57
hagiographer 24.57
hagiographic 2.18
hagiography 24.54
hagiolatry 24.54
hagridden 18.32
Hague 7.11
ha-ha 3.1
Hahn 3.19
Haifa 22.6
Haig 7.11
haiku 41.3
hail 7.15
Haile 22.1
hailed 7.16
hailer 8.7
Haile Selassie 2.7
Hailsham 8.19
hailstone 35.36
hailstones 35.39
hailstorm 25.20
Hainault 23.18; 25.17

hair 5.1
hairball 25.14
hairbrush 37.46
haircare 5.1
haircloth 23.46
haircut 37.47
hairdo 41.3
hairdresser 10.14
hairdressing 10.36
hairdryer 22.2
hairgrip 17.43
hairier 6.16
hairless 6.11
hairlike 21.7
hairline 21.22
hairnet 9.51
hairpiece 15.32
hairpin 6.6
hairs 5.5
hair shirt 11.24
hairsplitting 18.40
hairspray 7.3
hairstyle 21.16
hairy 6.1
Haiti 8.1; 16.1; 22.1
Haitian 8.22; 8.81;
  16.22
Haitians 8.55
Haitink 17.30
hajj 1.15; 3.12
hajji 2.7
hake 7.6
Hakenkreuz 33.14
Hal 1.16
halal 1.16; 3.14
halberd 2.25; 26.12
halberdier 13.1
halberds 26.13
halcyon 2.66
halcyonic 24.19
hale 7.15
Hale 7.15
Halewood 39.4
Haley 8.1
half 3.9
halfback 1.3
half-baked 7.7
half-brother 38.11
half-cock 23.3
half-cocked 23.6
half-hearted 4.17
half-heartedly 4.42
half-hour 31.1
half-inch 17.33
half-mast 3.30
half-nelson 10.28
half-price 21.29
half-sister 18.10

half term 11.13
half-timbered 18.19
half-time 21.19
halftone 35.36
half-truth 41.29
halfway 7.2
halfwit 4.38
half-witted 18.19
halibut 2.74; 37.47
Halicarnassus 2.46
Halifax 1.4
halitosis 36.25
hall 25.14
Hallé 7.3
hallelujah 42.7
Halley 2.5
hallmark 3.3
hallmarked 3.5
halloo 41.2
halloumi 42.1
hallow 35.3
hallowed 35.25
Halloween 15.26
hallucinate 7.49
hallucination 8.39
hallucinations 8.55
hallucinatory 8.76
hallucinogen 9.32;
  18.67
hallucinogenic 10.15
hallux 2.22
hallway 7.3
halma 2.13
halo 35.6
halogen 2.66; 9.32
halophyte 21.34
halothane 7.21
halt 23.18; 25.17
halted 24.24; 26.12
halter 24.10; 26.4
halterneck 9.2
halting 24.40; 26.25
Halton 24.33; 26.19
halve 3.35
halves 3.36
halyard 2.25
ham 1.22
Hamas 1.40
Hamburg 11.9
hamburger 12.2
hame 7.18
Hamelin 2.34
Hamilcar 3.1
Hamilcar Barca 4.9
Hamill 2.28; 17.15
Hamilton 2.66
Hamish 8.70
Hamitic 18.16

hamlet 2.51
Hamlet 2.51
Hamlyn 2.34
hammer 2.13
hammerer 2.60
hammerhead 9.8
hammering 2.70
Hammersmith 17.53
Hammerstein 21.22
hammertoe 35.19
Hammett 2.51
hammock 2.16
hammocks 2.22
Hammond 2.36
Hammurabi 4.1
hammy 2.6
Hampden 2.35
hamper 2.8
Hampshire 2.14; 13.1
Hampstead 9.8
Hampton 2.35
Hampton Court 25.31
hamster 2.10
hamstring 2.42
hamstrung 37.37
Hancock 23.3
hand 1.28
handbag 1.13
handbags 1.14
handball 25.14
handbasin 8.21
handbell 9.16
handbill 17.15
handbook 39.1
handbrake 7.6
handbreadth 9.53
handcart 3.32
handcarts 3.33
handclapping 2.42
handcraft 3.10
handcuff 37.10
handcuffs 37.11
Handel 2.28
handfeed 15.11
handful 39.7
handgrip 17.43
handgun 37.31
handhold 35.31
handicap 1.37
handicapped 1.39
handicapper 2.8
handicraft 3.10
handier 2.61
handiest 2.72
handily 2.58
handiwork 11.4
handkerchief 15.13
handle 2.28

hearer 14.2
hearing 14.12
hearken 4.24
hears 13.5
hearsay 7.3
hearse 11.22
Hearst 11.23
heart 3.32
heartache 7.6
heart attack 1.3
heartbeat 15.35
heartbeats 15.36
heartbreak 7.6
heartbreaker 8.4
heartbreaking 8.59
heartbroken 36.20
heartburn 11.15
hearten 4.24
heartening 4.52
heartfelt 9.23
hearth 3.34
hearth rug 37.14
heartier 4.44
heartiest 4.55
heartily 4.42
heartiness 4.53
heartland 1.28
heartless 4.32
heartlessly 4.42
heartlessness 4.53
heart-rending 10.36
hearts 3.33
heart-searching 12.16
heartsease 15.44
heartsick 4.16
heartstrings 4.30
heart-throb 23.1
heart-to-heart 3.32
heart-warming 26.25
heartwood 39.4
hearty 4.3
heat 15.35
heated 16.14
heatedly 16.38
heater 16.5
heath 15.37
Heath 15.37
Heathcliff 17.10
heathen 16.22
heathenism 18.28
heathens 16.24
heather 10.11
Heather 10.11
heathery 10.53
heating 16.27
heatproof 41.10
heatstroke 35.21
heat wave 7.54

heave 15.39
heaved 15.40
heaven 10.27
heavenly 10.53
heavens 10.32
heaven-sent 9.41
heavenward 10.58
heavenwards 10.59
heaves 15.41
heavier 10.57
heavies 10.51
heaviest 10.71
heavily 10.54
heaviness 10.70
heaving 16.27
Heaviside 21.12
heavy 10.4
heavy-handed 2.25
heavy-hearted 4.17
heavyweight 7.38
hebdomadal 24.61
Hebdon 10.27
hebe 16.1
Hebe 16.1
hebetude 41.9
Hebraic 8.10
Hebraism 18.28
Hebrew 41.3
Hebrews 41.33
Hebridean 16.22
Hebrides 15.45
Hecate 10.53
hecatomb 41.17
heck 9.2
heckle 10.21
heckled 10.22
heckler 10.12
hecklers 10.52
heckling 10.36
hectare 5.1
hectares 5.5
hectic 10.15
hectogram 1.22
hectolitre 16.5
hectometre 16.5
hector 10.10
Hector 10.10
Hecuba 10.56
he'd 15.11
Hedex® 9.3
hedge 9.14
hedged 9.15
hedgehog 23.11
hedgehogs 23.13
hedgehop 23.36
hedger 10.14
hedgerow 35.7
hedges 10.52

hedging 10.36
Hedley 10.5
hedonism 18.28
hedonist 10.72
hedonistic 18.16
heebie-jeebies 16.36
heed 15.11
heeded 16.14
heedful 16.17; 39.7
heedless 16.30
heedlessly 16.38
heehaw 25.2
heel 15.17
heel bar 3.1
heeled 15.18
heeler 16.7
heelless 16.30
heels 15.19
heeltap 1.37
heft 9.11
hefty 10.3
Hegarty 10.53
Hegel 8.15
Hegelian 8.81; 16.43
hegemony 10.53
Hegira 10.56
Heidegger 10.9; 22.41
Heidelberg 11.9
Heidi 22.1
heifer 10.11
heigh-ho 35.2
height 21.31
heighten 22.20
Heilbronn 23.27
Heine 22.8
Heineken® 22.44
Heinemann 22.44
Heiney 22.1
heinous 8.67; 16.30
Heinrich 22.11
Heinz 21.25
heir 5.1
heirdom 6.5
heiress 9.47
heirloom 41.17
heist 21.30
held 9.19
Helen 10.27
Helena 10.56
Helga 10.9
helianthus 2.46
helical 10.60
helices 15.45
Helicon 10.64
helicopter 24.10
helicopters 24.53
Heligan 10.64
heliotrope 35.40

helipad 1.9
heliport 25.31
helium 16.42
helix 16.12
hell 9.16
he'll 15.17
Hellas 10.42
hellbent 9.41
hellcat 1.45
hellebore 25.4
Hellene 15.25
Hellenic 10.15
Hellenism 18.28
Heller 10.12
Hellespont 23.34
hellfire 19.1
hell for leather 10.11
hellhole 35.30
hellhound 29.6
hellish 10.45
Hellman 10.27
hello 35.2
hell-raiser 8.9
hell-raising 8.64
helluva 10.56
helm 9.21
helmet 10.48
helming 10.36
helminth 17.41
helmsman 10.27
Héloïse 15.45
Helot 10.47
helotry 10.53
help 9.22
helper 10.8
helpful 10.21; 39.7
helpfully 10.53; 10.55
helpfulness 10.70
helping 10.36
helpings 10.37
helpless 10.42
helplessness 10.70
helpline 21.22
Helpmann 10.27
helpmate 7.34
helpmeet 15.35
Helsingborg 25.12
Helsinki 18.2
helter-skelter 10.10
helve 9.25
Helvellyn 10.26
helves 9.26
Helvetia 16.9
Helvetian 16.22
Helvetic 10.15
Helvetii 21.4
hem 9.28
he-man 1.24

he-men 9.32
hemidemisemiquaver 8.6
Hemingway 7.4
hemiplegia 16.9
hemiplegic 16.11
hemisphere 13.1
hemispheric 10.15
hemispherical 10.60
hemline 21.22
hemlock 23.3
hemmer 10.13
hemming 10.36
hemp 9.29
hempen 10.27
hems 9.31
hemstitch 17.7
hen 9.32
henbane 7.21
hence 9.39
henceforth 25.33
henceforward 26.12
henchman 10.27
hencoop 41.22
Henderson 10.64
Hendon 10.27
Hendrix 10.16
Hendry 10.5
henge 9.38
henhouse 29.12
Henley 10.5
henna 10.13
hennery 10.53
Hennessey 10.53
henpeck 9.2
henpecked 9.5
Henrietta 10.10
Henry 10.5
hens 9.43
hep 9.44
heparin 17.29
hepatic 2.17
hepatitis 22.28
Hepburn 11.15
hepcat 1.45
Hepplewhite 21.34
heptagon 10.64; 23.27
heptagonal 2.64
Heptateuch 41.6
heptathlon 2.35; 23.27
Hepworth 10.49; 11.26
her 11.1
Hera 14.2
Heracles 15.45
Heraclitus 22.29
Heraklion 2.66
herald 10.22

heralded 10.58
heraldic 2.17
heraldry 10.53
herb 11.2
herbaceous 8.67
herbage 12.7
herbal 12.8
herbalist 12.38
herbaria 6.16
herbarium 6.18
herb bennet 10.48
Herbert 12.24
herbicidal 22.16
herbicide 21.12
Herbie 12.1
herbivore 25.4
herbivorous 18.74
herby 12.1
Herculaneum 8.80
Herculean 16.22
Hercules 15.45
herd 11.7
herded 12.5
herder 12.2
herding 12.16
herdsman 12.12
here 13.1
hereabouts 29.15
hereafter 4.10
hereat 1.45
hereby 21.2
hereditable 10.79
hereditament 18.70
hereditary 10.54
heredity 10.54
Hereford 10.58
herein 17.29
hereinafter 4.10
hereinbefore 25.4
hereinto 41.3
hereon 23.27
heresy 10.53
heretic 17.3
heretical 10.60
heretics 17.4
hereto 41.2
heretofore 25.4
hereunder 38.10
hereunto 41.3
hereupon 23.27
Hereward 10.58
Hereward's 10.59
herewith 17.53
heritable 10.79
heritage 17.14
heritor 10.56
Herm 11.13
Herman 12.12

hermaphrodite 21.34
hermeneutic 42.11
hermeneutics 42.12
Hermes 12.28; 15.44
hermetic 10.15
hermetically 10.54
Hermia 12.31
Hermione 22.40
hermit 12.25
hermitage 17.14
Hermon 12.12
hernia 12.31
herniated 8.13
hero 35.9
Herod 10.18
Herod Antipas 1.40
Herodias 1.40
Herodotus 24.70
heroic 36.10
heroically 36.35
heroics 36.11
heroin 17.29
heroine 17.29
heroines 17.42
heroism 18.28
heron 10.27
heronry 10.53
Herophilus 24.70
herpes 12.28; 15.44
herpesvirus 20.8; 22.29
herpes zoster 24.10
herpetology 24.55
Herr 5.1
Herrick 10.15
herring 10.36
herringbone 35.36
herrings 10.37
Herriot 10.74
hers 11.29
Herschel 12.8
herself 9.20
Hershey 12.1
Herstmonceux 35.19; 41.4
Hertford 4.17
Hertfordshire 4.43; 13.1
Herts 3.33
hertz 11.25
Hertz 11.25
Herzegovina 16.8; 24.57
Herzog 23.11
he's 15.42
Heseltine 21.22
Hesiod 23.8
hesitance 10.68

hesitancy 10.78
hesitant 10.67
hesitantly 10.78
hesitate 7.38
hesitating 8.60
hesitation 8.28
Hesketh 10.49
Hesperides 15.45
Hesperidian 18.67
Hesperus 10.70
Hess 9.47
Hesse 9.47; 10.14
hessian 10.64
hest 9.49
Hester 10.10
het 9.51
heterodox 23.5
heterodoxy 24.7
heterogeneous 16.47
heteronym 17.24
heterosexism 18.27
heterosexist 18.27
heterosexual 10.60
heterosexuality 2.57
Hetherington 10.64
Hettie 10.3
het up 37.41
heuristic 18.16
heuristics 18.17
Hever 16.6
hew 41.1
hewer 42.2
hewing 42.24
Hewish 42.29
Hewitt 42.30
hewn 41.19
hex 9.3
hexadecimal 10.60
hexagon 10.64; 23.27
hexagonal 2.64
hexagram 1.22
hexahedral 16.17
hexahedron 16.22
hexameter 2.60
hexametric 10.15
hexapod 23.8
Hexateuch 41.6
hey 7.1
heyday 7.3
Heyer 8.2
Heyerdahl 3.14
Heysham 16.20
Heywood 39.4
Hezbollah 3.1
Hezekiah 22.2
hi 21.1
hiatal 8.15
hiatus 8.67

Hiawatha 24.11
hibachi 4.7
hibernal 12.8
hibernate 7.42
hibernating 8.60
hibernation 8.33
Hibernia 12.31
Hibernian 12.34
hibiscus 18.44
Hibs 17.2
hic 17.3
hiccup 37.41
hiccuped 37.42
hick 17.3
hickey 18.2
Hickman 18.32
hickory 18.56
Hicks 17.4
Hickson 18.33
hid 17.8
hidalgo 35.3
hidden 18.32
hide 21.9
hide-and-seek 15.7
hideaway 7.4
hidebound 29.6
Hi-de-Hi 21.4
hideous 18.74
hideously 18.80
hide-out 29.14
hides 21.13
hiding 22.26
hiding place 7.30
hidy-hole 35.30
hie 21.1
hierarch 3.3
hierarchic 4.16
hierarchical 4.47
hierarchy 4.2
hierocratic 2.17
hieroglyph 17.10
hieroglyphic 18.16
hieroglyphics 18.17
Hieronymus 24.70
hierophant 1.33
hi-fi 21.3
Higginbottom 24.30
Higgins 18.36
higgledy-piggledy 18.56
high 21.1
Higham 22.18
high and dry 21.4
high-and-mighty 22.1
highball 25.14
highborn 25.22
highbrow 29.1
highchair 5.1

high dudgeon 38.28
higher 22.2
higher education 8.28
highest 22.31
highfalutin 42.19
highfaluting 42.24
high-flyer 22.2
high-flyers 22.39
Highgate 7.34
high-handed 2.25
high-heeled 15.18
high jinks 17.31
high jump 37.29
highland 22.21
Highland 22.21
Highlander 22.41
Highlands 22.22
highlife 21.14
highlight 21.33
highlighter 22.5
highlights 21.35
highly 22.1
highly strung 37.37
high-minded 22.13
high-muck-a-muck 37.3
Highness 22.29
High Noon 41.19
high-profile 21.16
high-resolution 42.20
high-rise 21.41
highroad 35.25
highroads 35.26
highs 21.39
Highsmith 17.53
high-speed 15.11
high street 15.35
hightail 7.15
high-waisted 8.13
highway 7.3
highwayman 22.44
highways 7.56
High Wycombe 18.26
hijack 1.3
hijacked 1.6
hijacker 2.9
hijacking 2.42
hijacks 1.4
hike 21.7
hiker 22.4
hikes 21.8
hiking 22.26
Hilaire 5.1
hilarious 6.22
hilarity 2.57
Hilary 18.56
Hilda 18.10

Hildebrand 1.28
hill 17.15
Hill 17.15
Hillary 18.56
hillbillies 18.54
hillbilly 18.5
Hiller 18.12
hillfort 25.31
Hilliard 3.8; 18.62
hillier 18.61
Hillier 18.61
hilliest 18.76
Hillingdon 18.67
hillock 18.15
hills 17.23
hillside 21.11
hilltop 23.36
hillwalking 26.25
hilly 18.5
hilt 17.21
Hilton 18.32
Hilversum 18.66
him 17.24
Himalaya 8.2
Himalayan 8.21
Himalayas 8.75
Himmler 18.12
himself 9.20
Hinckley 18.5
hind 21.23
hindbrain 7.21
Hindemith 17.51; 17.53
Hindenburg 11.9
hinder 18.10; 22.5
hindered 18.19
Hindi 18.3
Hindle 18.22
Hindley 18.5
hindmost 35.43
hindquarter 26.4
hindquarters 26.36
hindrance 18.39
hindsight 21.33
Hindu 41.3
Hinduism 18.28
Hindu Kush 39.13
Hindus 41.33
Hindustan 1.24; 3.19
Hindustani 4.6
hindwing 22.26
Hines 21.25
hinge 17.37
hinging 18.40
hinny 18.6
hint 17.39
hinted 18.19
hinterland 1.28
Hinton 18.32

hints 17.40
hip 17.43
hipbone 35.36
hip-hop 23.36
Hipparchus 4.32
hippies 18.54
hippo 35.11
hippocampus 2.46
hippocras 1.40
Hippocrates 15.45
Hippocratic 2.17
Hippocrene 15.26
hippodrome 35.34
hippogriff 17.10
Hippolyta 24.57
Hippolytus 24.70
hippopotami 21.4
hippopotamus 24.70
hippy 18.1
hips 17.44
hipster 18.10
hirable 20.12
Hiram 20.3
hire 19.1
hired 19.2
hireling 20.7
hirer 20.2
hiring 20.7
Hirohito 35.10
Hiroshima 16.8; 24.57
Hirsel 12.8
Hirst 11.23
his 17.56
Hislop 23.36
his nibs 17.2
Hispania 2.61
Hispanic 2.20
Hispanicism 18.28
Hispaniola 36.7
Hispano-Suiza 16.9
hiss 17.46
hissed 17.49
hissing 18.40
hist 17.49
histamine 15.26; 17.29
histogen 9.32; 18.67
histogram 1.22
histological 24.61
histology 24.55
historian 26.43
historic 24.18
historical 24.61
historically 24.56
historiographer 24.57
history 18.56
histrionic 24.19
histrionically 24.56
histrionics 24.22

hit 17.51
Hitachi 2.7
hit-and-miss 17.46
hit-and-run 37.31
hitch 17.7
Hitchcock 23.3
hitcher 18.14
hitchhike 21.7
hitchhiker 22.4
hitchhikers 22.39
Hitchin 18.31
hitching 18.40
hi-tech 9.2
hither 18.11
hitherto 41.4
Hitler 18.12
hit man 1.24
hitter 18.10
hit the sack 1.3
hitting 18.40
Hittite 21.33
HIV 15.4
hive 21.37
hives 21.38
ho 35.1
hoar 25.1
hoard 25.9
hoarded 26.12
hoarder 26.4
hoarding 26.25
hoarfrost 23.41
hoarse 25.28
hoarsely 26.1
hoarsen 26.19
hoarseness 26.27
hoarser 26.8
hoarsest 26.29
hoary 26.1
hoax 35.22
hoaxer 36.9
hob 23.1
Hobart 3.32
Hobbes 23.2
hobbies 24.52
hobbit 24.49
hobble 24.27
hobbled 24.28
hobbledehoy 33.1
hobbler 24.12
hobbling 24.40
Hobbs 23.2
hobby 24.1
hobbyhorse 25.28
hobgoblin 24.32
hobnail 7.15
hobnob 23.1
hobnobbing 24.40
hobo 35.16

Hoboken 36.20
hobos 35.52
Hobson 24.33
Hobson-Jobson 24.33
Hochheimer 22.8
Ho Chi Minh 17.29
hock 23.3
hockey 24.2
Hockney 24.6
Hocktide 21.11
hocus 36.26
hocus-pocus 36.26
hod 23.8
Hodder 24.10
Hoddle 24.27
Hodge 23.14
hodgepodge 23.14
Hodges 24.53
Hodgkin 24.32
Hodgson 24.33
Hodson 24.33
hoe 35.1
hoedown 29.5
Hoffman 24.33
Hoffmann 24.33
Hoffnung 37.37; 39.10
hog 23.11
Hogan 36.20
Hogarth 3.34
Hogarthian 4.50
Hogg 23.11
hogged 23.12
hogger 24.9
hogging 24.40
hoggish 24.46
hogshead 9.8
hogtie 21.3
hogwash 23.42
hogweed 15.11
Hohenlinden 18.32
Hohenzollern 24.33
ho-hum 37.27
hoick 33.2
hoicks 33.3
hoi polloi 33.1
hoisin 34.7
hoist 33.12
hoisted 34.3
hoisting 34.11
hoity-toity 34.1
hokey-cokey 36.1
Hokkaido 35.12
hokum 36.18
Hokusai 21.4
Holbein 21.22
hold 35.31
holdall 25.14

Holden 36.20
holder 36.5
holdfast 3.30
holding 36.24
hold-up 37.41
hole 35.30
holes 35.33
holey 36.1
Holi 24.5
holiday 7.4; 24.56
holiday-maker 8.4
holidays 7.56
holier 36.37
holiest 36.44
holiness 36.42
Holiness 36.42
Holinshed 9.8
holism 18.27
holistic 18.16
Holland 24.34
hollandaise 7.56
Hollander 24.57
Hollands 24.35
holler 24.12
hollered 24.24
Hollis 24.42
hollow 35.13
Holloway 7.4
hollowness 36.26
hollowware 5.1
holly 24.5
Holly 24.5
hollyhock 23.3
Hollywood 39.4
holm 35.34
Holmes 35.35
holocaust 25.29
Holocene 15.26
Holofernes 15.44
hologram 1.22
holograph 1.11; 3.9
holographic 2.18
holography 24.54
holothurian 28.21
Holroyd 33.4
hols 23.22
Holstein 21.22
holster 36.5
holt 35.32
holy 36.1
Holy Grail 7.15
Holyhead 9.8
Holyoake 35.21
holy of holies 36.33
Holyrood 41.9
Holyroodhouse 29.12
holystone 35.36
homage 24.26

homburg 11.9
home 35.34
home-alone 35.36
homebody 24.3
homebound 29.6
homeboy 33.1
homecoming 38.34
home-grown 35.36
homeland 1.28
homeless 36.26
homelessness 36.42
homelike 21.7
homely 36.1
home-made 7.8
homemaker 8.4
homemaking 8.59
homeopath 1.47
homeopathic 2.18
homeopathy 24.54
homeowner 36.8
homeowners 36.34
homeowning 36.24
homer 36.8
Homer 36.8
Homeric 10.15
home rule 41.14
homesick 36.10
homesickness 36.42
homespun 37.31
homestead 9.8
homesteader 10.10
homeward 36.12
homewards 36.13
homework 11.4
homeworker 12.2
homey 36.1
homicidal 22.16
homicide 21.12
homiletics 10.16
homily 24.56
homing 36.24
hominid 17.8; 24.60
hominoid 33.4
hominy 24.56
homo 35.16
homoerotic 24.16
homoeroticism 18.28
homogeneity 16.38
homogeneous 16.47
homogenization 8.48
homogenize 21.45
homogenous 24.70
homograph 1.11; 3.9
homographic 2.18
homoiothermic 12.3
homologate 7.43
homologation 8.34
homological 24.61

homologize 21.45
homologous 24.70
homologue 23.11
homonym 17.24
homonymic 18.16
homophobe 35.20
homophobia 36.37
homophobic 36.10
homophone 35.36
homophonic 24.19
homophonous 24.70
homophony 24.54
Homo sapiens 9.43
homosexual 10.60
homosexuality 2.57
homunculus 38.59
Hon. 23.27
honcho 35.13
Honda 24.10
Honduran 28.6
Honduras 28.12
hone 35.36
Honecker 24.57
Honegger 24.57
honest 24.45
honestly 24.56
honesty 24.56
honey 38.6
honeybee 15.4
honeybun 37.31
honeybunch 37.35
honeycomb 35.34
honeydew 41.4
honey-eater 16.5
honeyed 38.19
honeymoon 41.19
honeymooner 42.8
honeymooners 42.34
honeypot 23.44
honeysuckle 38.23
honeytrap 1.37
Hong Kong 23.31
Honiton 24.64
honk 23.28
honker 24.9
honking 24.40
honks 23.29
honky-tonk 23.28
Honolulu 41.3
honorarium 6.18
honorary 24.76
honorific 18.16
honour 24.13
honourable 24.61;
  24.77
honourably 24.54;
  24.76
honoured 24.24

honours 24.53
Honshu 41.3
Hoo 41.1
hooch 41.8
hood 39.4
Hood 39.4
hooded 40.4
hoodie 40.1
hooding 40.15
hoodless 40.13
hoodlum 42.18
hoodoo 41.3
hoodwink 17.30
hoodwinked 17.32
hooey 42.1
hoof 41.10
hoofer 42.6
hoo-ha 3.1
hook 39.1
hookah 40.2
Hooke 39.1
hooked 39.2
hooker 40.2
hooking 40.15
hooknose 35.52
hookworm 11.13
hooky 40.1
hooley 42.1
hooligan 42.41
hooliganism 18.29
hoop 41.22
Hooper 42.3
hoopla 3.1
hoopoe 41.3
hoops 41.23
hooray 7.2
hoot 41.27
hooted 42.14
hootenanny 2.6
hooter 42.5
hooting 42.24
hoots 41.28
Hoover® 42.6
hop 23.36
hope 35.40
hopeful 36.15; 39.7
hopefully 36.35
hopefulness 36.42
hopeless 36.26
hopelessly 36.35
hopelessness 36.42
hoper 36.3
hopes 35.41
Hopi 36.1
hoping 36.24
Hopkin 24.32
Hopkins 24.37
hopped 23.38

hopper 24.8
Hopper 24.8
hopping 24.40
hopping mad 1.9
hops 23.37
hopsack 1.3
hopscotch 23.7
Horace 24.42
Horatian 8.23
horde 25.9
Hordern 26.19
hordes 25.10
horehound 29.6
horizon 22.20
horizons 22.23
horizontal 24.27
horizontality 2.57
horizontally 24.54
Horlicks® 26.10
hormonal 36.15
hormone 35.36
hormones 35.39
Hormuz 41.33
horn 25.22
hornbeam 15.20
hornbill 17.15
hornblende 9.35
Hornblower 36.2
hornbook 39.1
Hornby 26.1
Horne 25.22
horned 25.24
Horner 26.7
hornet 26.32
hornier 26.39
horniest 26.49
hornless 26.27
hornpipe 21.26
hornswoggle 24.27
horny 26.1
horologer 24.57
horologic 24.20
horological 24.61
horologist 24.72
horology 24.55
horoscope 35.40
horoscopic 24.16
horoscopy 24.54
Horowitz 17.52
horrendous 10.42
horrendously 10.53
horrible 24.61
horribly 24.54
horrid 24.23
horrific 18.16
horrifically 18.57
horrified 21.12
horrify 21.4

horrifying 22.26
horripilation 8.32
horror 24.12
horrors 24.53
hors concours 27.1
hors d'oeuvre 11.27;
  12.2
horse 25.28
horseback 1.3
horsebox 23.5
horse chestnut 37.47
Horseferry 10.5
horseflesh 9.50
horsefly 21.3
horsehair 5.1
horsehide 21.11
horseleech 15.9
horseless 26.27
horseman 26.19
horsemanship 17.43
horsemeat 15.35
horseplay 7.3
horsepower 31.1
horseradish 2.49
horses 26.36
horseshoe 41.3
horseshoes 41.33
horsetail 7.15
horsewhip 17.43
horsewhipped 17.45
horsewhips 17.44
horsewoman 40.10
horsewomen 18.31
horsey 26.1
horst 25.29
Hortense 9.39
horticultural 38.52
horticulturalist 17.49
horticulture 38.14
horticulturist 38.60
hosanna 2.13
hose 35.52
Hosea 13.1
hosed 35.53
hosepipe 21.26
hosier 36.37
hosiery 36.35
hosing 36.24
hospice 24.42
hospitable 18.64;
  24.77
hospital 24.61
hospitality 2.57
hospitalization 8.53
hospitalize 21.47
hospitalized 21.48
hospitals 24.62
host 35.43

humoristic 18.16
humorous 42.46
humour 42.8
humourless 42.46
hump 37.29
humpback 1.3
humpbacked 1.6
humph 37.28
Humphrey 38.5
Humphries 38.46
humps 37.30
Humpty Dumpty 38.3
humpy 38.1
humus 42.26
Hun 37.31
hunch 37.35
hunchback 1.3
hunchbacked 1.6
hundred 38.20
hundredfold 35.31
hundredweight 7.48
hung 37.37
Hungarian 6.19
Hungary 38.47
hunger 38.9
Hungerford 38.50
hungrier 38.49
hungriest 38.61
hungrily 38.47
hungry 38.5
hunk 37.32
hunker 38.9
hunkier 38.49
hunkiest 38.61
hunks 37.33
hunky 38.2
hunky-dory 26.1
Hunniford 38.50
Hunnish 38.40
Hunstanton 2.35
hunt 37.40
Hunt 37.40
hunted 38.20
hunter 38.10
Hunter 38.10
hunters 38.45
hunting 38.34
Huntingdon 38.54
Huntley 38.5
huntress 38.38
hunts 37.39
huntsman 38.28
Huntsville 17.15
hurdle 12.8
hurdler 12.2
hurdles 12.9
hurdling 12.16
hurdy-gurdy 12.1

hurl 11.11
hurled 11.12
Hurley 12.1
hurling 12.16
hurly-burly 12.1
Huron 23.27
hurrah 3.1
hurricane 7.21; 38.54
hurried 38.19
hurriedly 38.47
hurry 38.5
Hurst 11.23
hurt 11.24
hurtful 12.8; 39.7
hurtfulness 12.37
hurting 12.16
hurtle 12.8
hurts 11.25
husband 38.29
husbanded 38.50
husbandman 38.54
husbandry 38.47
hush 37.46
hushaby 21.4
hush-hush 37.46
husk 37.44
huskily 38.47
Huskisson 38.54
husky 38.2
huss 37.43
Huss 37.43
hussar 3.1
hussars 3.37
Hussein 7.21
Hussey 38.7
hussy 38.7
hustings 38.35
hustle 38.23
hustler 38.12
Huston 42.20
hut 37.47
hutch 37.6
Hutchinson 38.54
huts 37.48
Hutton 38.28
Hutu 41.3
Huxley 38.5
Huxtable 38.52
Huygens 22.23
Huyton 22.20
hyacinth 17.41
Hyades 15.45
hybrid 22.12
hybridization 8.47
hybridize 21.44
Hyde 21.9
Hyde Park 3.3
Hyderabad 1.9; 3.8

Hydra 22.7
hydrangea 8.9
hydrant 22.24
hydrate 7.33; 7.34
hydraulic 24.18; 26.9
hydraulically 24.56;
  26.37
hydraulics 24.22;
  26.10
hydric 22.11
hydrocarbon 4.24
hydrocephalus 10.70
hydrochloric 24.18;
  26.9
hydrocortisone 35.36
hydroelectric 10.15
hydroelectricity 18.57
hydrofoil 33.6
hydrogen 22.44
hydrogenate 7.43
hydrogenation 8.47
hydrogenous 24.70
hydrographic 2.18
hydrologic 24.20
hydrolyse 21.44
hydrolysis 17.46
hydrometer 24.57
hydropathy 24.54
hydrophobia 36.37
hydrophobic 36.10
hydroplane 7.21
hydroponics 24.22
hydrotherapy 10.53
hydrous 22.29
hydroxide 21.11
Hydrus 22.29
hyena 16.8
Hygena 16.8
hygiene 15.25
hygienic 16.11
hygienically 16.38
hygienist 16.31
hygrometer 24.57
hymen 9.32
hymn 17.24
hymnal 18.22
hymn book 39.1
hymnology 24.55
hypaesthesia 16.40
Hypatia 8.9
hype 21.26
hyped 21.28
hyper 22.3
hyperactive 2.53
hyperactivity 18.57
hyperaesthesia 16.40
hyperbola 12.30
hyperbole 12.29

hyperbolic 24.18
hypercorrect 9.5
hypercorrection
  10.28
hypercritical 18.64
hypercriticism 18.28
hyperglycaemia 16.40
hyperglycaemic 16.11
hyperinflation 8.47
Hyperion 14.21
hyperlink 17.30
hypermania 8.78
hypermarket 4.38
hypernym 17.24
hypersensitive 17.55
hypersensitivity 18.57
hypersonic 24.19
hyperspace 7.30
hypertension 10.28
hypertext 9.4
hyperthermia 12.31
hyperthyroidism
  18.28
hyperventilation 8.28
hyphen 22.20
hyphenate 7.42
hyphenated 8.13
hyphenation 8.33
hypnagogic 24.20
hypnosis 36.25
hypnotherapist 10.72
hypnotherapy 10.53
hypnotic 24.16
hypnotically 24.56
hypnotism 18.28
hypnotist 18.75
hypnotizable 22.43
hypnotize 21.44
hypnotized 21.48
hypo 35.12
hypocaust 25.29
hypochondria 24.58
hypochondriac 1.3
hypocoristic 18.16
hypocrisy 24.54
hypocrite 17.51
hypocrites 17.52
hypocritical 18.64
hypocritically 18.57
hypodermic 12.3
hypoglycaemia 16.40
hypoglycaemic 16.11
hypomania 8.78
hyponym 17.24
hypotension 10.28
hypotenuse 41.33
hypothalamus 2.71
hypothermia 12.31

hypotheses 15.45
hypothesis 17.46
hypothesize 21.45
hypothetical 10.60
hypothetically 10.54
hypothyroidism 18.28
hypoxia 24.58
hyrax 1.4
hysterectomy 10.53
hysteria 14.18
hysteric 10.15
hysterical 10.60
hysterically 10.54
hysterics 10.16
Hythe 21.36
Hywel 31.3
I 21.1
iamb 1.22
iambic 2.17
Ian 16.22
Ian's 16.24
Iberia 14.18
Iberian 14.21
ibex 9.3
ibis 22.28
Ibiza 16.6
Ibizan 16.22
IBM 9.28
ibn-Saud 29.3
Ibrahim 15.20
Ibrox 23.5
Ibsen 18.33
ibuprofen 9.32; 36.20
Icarus 18.74
ice 21.29
iceberg 11.9
icebound 29.6
icebox 23.5
icebreaker 8.4
icecap 1.37
ice-cold 35.31
ice cream 15.20
iced 21.30
ice house 29.12
Iceland 22.21
Icelander 2.10; 22.41
Icelandic 2.17
ice man 1.24
Iceni 21.3
ice rink 17.30
ices 22.39
ice-skate 7.34
ice-skater 8.5
ice skates 7.50
ice-skating 8.60
Ichabod 23.8
I Ching 17.35

ichneumon 42.20
ichthyology 24.55
ichthyosaur 25.2
ichthyosaurus 26.27
icicle 22.43
icier 22.42
iciest 22.48
icily 22.40
icing 22.26
icky 18.2
icon 23.27
iconic 24.19
iconoclasm 2.32
iconoclast 1.42
iconoclastic 2.17
iconography 24.54
icons 23.35
ictus 18.44
icy 22.1
ID 15.2
id 17.8
I'd 21.9
Ida 22.5
Idaho 35.19
idea 13.1
ideal 13.3
idealism 18.27
idealist 14.15
idealistic 18.16
idealistically 18.57
idealization 8.30
idealize 21.41
idealized 21.48
ideally 14.1
ideas 13.5
ideate 7.42
ideation 8.33
idée fixe 15.8
identical 10.60
identically 10.54
identifiable 22.43
identification 8.43
identified 21.12
identifier 22.2
identifies 21.43
identify 21.4
Identikit® 17.51
identity 10.54
ideogram 1.22
ideograph 1.11; 3.9
ideological 24.61
ideologically 24.56
ideologue 23.11
ideology 24.55
ides 21.13
id est 9.49
idiocy 18.80
idiolect 9.5

idiom 18.66
idiomatic 2.17
idiomatically 2.58
idiosyncrasy 18.56
idiosyncratic 2.17
idiot 18.77
idiotic 24.16
idiotically 24.56
idiotism 18.29
idle 22.16
idled 22.17
idleness 22.46
idler 22.7
idlest 22.31
idling 22.26
idly 22.1
idol 22.16
idolater 24.57
idolatrous 24.70
idolatry 24.54
idolization 8.47
idolize 21.44
idyll 18.22
idyllic 18.16
idyllically 18.57
i.e. 15.2
iechyd da 3.1
if 17.10
iffy 18.4
igloo 41.3
Ignatius 8.67
igneous 18.74
ignis fatuus 2.71
ignite 21.32
igniter 22.5
ignition 18.33
ignoble 36.15
ignobly 36.1
ignominious 18.74
ignominy 18.80
ignoramus 8.67
ignorance 18.71
ignorant 18.70
ignore 25.2
ignored 25.9
ignores 25.35
Igraine 7.21
iguana 4.13
iguanodon 23.27
IJssel 22.16
Ike 21.7
IKEA 16.2
ikebana 4.13
il Duce 9.1
ileum 18.66
ilex 9.3
iliac 1.3
Iliad 1.9; 18.62

ilium 18.66
Ilium 18.66
ilk 17.16
ill 17.15
I'll 21.16
ill-advised 21.48
ill-bred 9.8
ill-concealed 15.18
ill-disposed 35.53
illegal 16.17
illegality 2.57
illegally 16.38
illegibly 10.53
illegitimate 18.77
ill-equipped 17.45
ill-favoured 8.13
ill-gotten 24.33
ill-humoured 42.14
illiberal 18.64
illicit 18.50
illicitly 18.57
illimitable 18.81
ill-informed 25.21
Illingworth 11.26; 18.78
Illinois 33.1
Illinoisan 34.8
illiteracy 18.56; 18.80
illiterate 18.77
ill-natured 8.13
illness 18.44
illogic 24.20
illogical 24.61
illogicality 2.57
illogically 24.56
ill-omened 36.21
ills 17.23
ill-starred 3.8
ill-timed 21.20
ill-treat 15.35
ill-treated 16.14
ill-treatment 16.25
illuminate 7.49
illuminated 8.13
illuminati 4.3
illuminating 8.60
illumination 8.39
illuminations 8.55
illumine 42.19
ill-use 41.24; 41.33
ill-used 41.34
illusion 42.20
illusionism 18.28
illusionist 42.48
illusory 42.36
illustrate 7.41
illustrated 8.13
illustration 8.32

inertial 12.8
inescapable 8.79
in esse 10.7
inessential 10.21
inestimable 10.79
inevitability 18.58
inevitable 10.79
inevitably 10.78
inexact 1.6
inexcusable 42.39
inexhaustible 26.41
inexorable 10.79
inexpedience 16.45
inexpedient 16.44
inexpensive 10.50
inexperience 14.22
inexpert 11.24
inexpiable 10.79
inexplicable 18.64
inexplicably 18.56
inexpressible 10.60
in extremis 16.29
inextricable 18.64
infallibility 18.58
infallible 2.64
infallibly 2.56
infamous 18.74
infamy 18.56
infancy 18.56
infant 18.38
infanta 2.10
infanticide 21.12
infantile 21.16
infantilism 18.28
infantry 18.56
infantryman 1.24
infants 18.39
infarct 3.5
infarction 4.24
infatuate 7.35
infatuated 8.13
infatuation 8.24
infect 9.5
infected 10.18
infection 10.28
infectious 10.42
infective 10.50
infelicitous 18.74
infer 11.1
inference 18.71
inferential 10.21
inferior 14.18
inferiority 24.56
infernal 12.8
infernally 12.29
inferno 35.8
inferred 11.7
inferring 12.16

infertile 21.16
infertility 18.58
infest 9.49
infidel 9.16; 18.64
infidelity 10.54
infidels 9.27
infield 15.18
infielder 16.5
infighting 22.26
infill 17.15
infiltration 8.32
infiltrator 8.5
infinite 17.51
infinite 18.77
infinitely 10.78
infinitesimal 10.60
infinitesimally 10.78
infinitive 17.55
infinity 18.57
infirm 11.13
infirmary 12.29
infirmity 12.29
in flagrante 2.3
in flagrante delicto
  35.11
inflame 7.18
inflamed 7.19
inflammable 2.64
inflammation 8.32
inflammatory 2.56
inflatable 8.79
inflate 7.33
inflated 8.13
inflation 8.23
inflationary 8.76
inflect 9.5
inflection 10.28
inflexibility 18.58
inflexible 10.60
inflict 17.6
infliction 18.33
in-flight 21.32
inflorescence 10.34
inflow 35.11
influence 18.71
influential 10.21
influentially 10.53
influenza 10.14
influx 37.4
info 35.11
infomercial 12.8
inform 25.20
informal 26.15
informality 2.57
informally 26.37
informant 26.23
informants 26.24
informatics 2.23

information 8.32
informative 17.55
informed 25.21
informer 26.7
informing 26.25
infotainment 8.56
infraction 2.35
infra dig 17.12
infralapsarian 6.19
infrared 9.8
infrasonic 24.19
infrasound 29.6
infrastructure 38.14
infrequency 16.38
infrequent 16.25
infrequently 16.38
infringe 17.37
infringement 18.38
infringer 18.14
infuriate 7.45
infuriating 8.60
infuriation 8.36
infuse 41.33
infuser 42.9
infusion 42.20
ingather 2.11
Inge 17.35
ingenious 16.47
ingénue 41.4
ingenuity 42.36
ingenuous 10.70
Ingersoll 23.15
ingest 9.49
ingestion 10.28
Ingham 18.26
ingle 18.22
inglenook 39.1
Ingleton 18.67
inglorious 26.47
Ingmar 3.1
ingoing 36.24
ingot 18.49
ingrain 7.21
ingrained 7.22
Ingram 18.26
Ingrams 18.30
ingrate 7.34
ingratiate 7.37
ingratiation 8.27
ingratitude 41.9
ingredient 16.44
ingredients 16.45
Ingrid 18.18
ingrowing 36.24
ingrown 35.36
ingrowth 35.47
inhabit 2.51
inhabitant 2.68

inhabitants 2.69
inhabited 2.63
inhalant 8.56
inhalation 8.32
inhale 7.15
inhaler 8.7
inharmonious 36.42
inhere 13.1
inherent 10.33; 14.10
inherit 10.48
inheritable 10.79
inheritance 10.68
inheritor 10.56
inhesion 16.22
inhibit 18.50
inhibited 18.62
inhibition 18.33
inhibitor 18.60
inhibitory 18.57
inhospitable 18.64;
  24.77
in-house 29.12
inhuman 42.20
inhumane 7.21
inhumanity 2.57
inhumanly 42.36
inimical 18.64
inimitable 18.81
iniquitous 18.74
iniquity 18.58
initial 18.22
initialism 18.28
initialization 8.46
initialize 21.44
initially 18.56
initials 18.24
initiate 7.41; 18.77
initiation 8.32
initiative 17.55
initiator 8.5
inject 9.5
injectable 10.60
injection 10.28
in-joke 35.21
injudicious 18.44
Injun 18.33
injunction 38.28
injure 18.14
injured 18.19
injurious 28.24
injury 18.56
injustice 38.37
ink 17.30
Inkatha 4.10
inkblot 23.44
inked 17.32
inkhorn 25.22
inkling 18.40

inkpad 1.9
inkstand 1.28
inkwell 9.16
inky 18.2
inlaid 7.8
inland 1.28; 18.34
inlay 7.2
inlay 7.3
inlet 9.51
in lieu 41.2
in loco parentis 10.41
inmate 7.34
inmates 7.50
in memoriam 1.22; 26.42
inmost 35.43
inn 17.29
innards 18.20
innate 7.33
innately 8.1
inner 18.13
innermost 35.43
innervate 7.41
Innes 18.43
inning 18.40
innings 18.41
Inniskilling 18.40
innit 18.50
innkeeper 16.3
innocence 18.71
innocent 18.70
innocently 18.80
innocuous 24.70
innominate 24.73
innovate 7.41
innovation 8.32
innovations 8.55
innovative 8.73; 17.54
innovator 8.5
Innsbruck 39.1
Inns of Court 25.31
innuendo 35.7
innumerable 42.39; 42.51
innumeracy 42.36
innumeracy 42.50
inoculate 7.43
inoculation 8.34
inoffensive 10.50
inoffensively 10.54
inoperable 24.61
inoperative 17.54
inopportune 41.19
inordinate 26.50
inorganic 2.20
inpatient 8.56
input 39.14
inquest 9.49

inquietude 41.9
inquire 19.1
inquirer 20.2
inquiring 20.7
inquiry 20.1
inquisition 18.33
Inquisition 18.33
inquisitive 17.55
inquisitively 18.80
inquisitor 18.60
inquisitorial 26.41
inquorate 7.34
inroads 35.26
inrush 37.46
insalubrious 42.46
insalubrity 42.36
insane 7.21
insanely 8.1
insanitary 2.58
insanity 2.57
insatiable 8.79
insatiably 8.76
inscribe 21.5
inscribed 21.6
inscriber 22.3
inscription 18.33
inscrutable 42.39
insect 9.5
insecticide 21.12
insectivore 25.4
insectivorous 18.74
insecure 27.1
insecurity 28.17
inseminate 7.38
insemination 8.28
insensate 7.34
insensible 10.60
insensitive 17.55
insensitively 10.78
insensitivity 18.57
insentience 10.34; 10.68
insentient 10.33; 10.67
inseparable 10.60
insert 11.24
inserted 12.5
insertion 12.12
inset 9.51
inshore 25.2
inside 21.10; 21.11
inside out 29.14
insider 22.5
insiders 22.39
insides 21.13
insidious 18.74
insidiously 18.80
insight 21.33
insignia 18.61

insignificance 18.71
insignificant 18.70
insincere 13.1
insincerely 14.1
insincerity 10.54
insinuate 7.41
insinuation 8.32
insipid 18.18
insist 17.49
insistence 18.39
insistent 18.38
in situ 41.3
insobriety 22.40
insole 35.30
insolence 18.71
insolent 18.70
insoluble 24.61
insolvency 24.54
insolvent 24.38
insomnia 24.58
insomniac 1.3
insomuch 37.6
insouciance 42.44
insouciant 42.43
inspect 9.5
inspection 10.28
inspector 10.10
inspectorate 10.73
inspiration 8.32
inspirational 8.79
inspire 19.1
inspired 19.2
inspiring 20.7
instability 18.58
install 25.14
installation 8.32
installed 25.15
installer 26.6
instalment 26.23
instalments 26.24
instance 18.39
instant 18.38
instantaneous 8.85
instantly 18.56
instants 18.39
instead 9.8
instep 9.44
instigate 7.41
instigation 8.32
instigator 8.5
instil 17.15
instiller 18.12
instinct 17.32
instinctive 18.53
instinctively 18.57
instinctual 18.64
institute 41.27
institutes 41.28

institution 42.20
institutional 42.39
institutionalism 18.29
institutionalize 21.47
institutionalized 21.48
institutionally 42.50
instruct 37.5
instructed 38.20
instructing 38.34
instruction 38.28
instructional 38.52
instructive 38.44
instructor 38.10
instructors 38.45
instructorship 17.43
instructress 38.38
instrument 18.70
instrumental 10.21
instrumentalism 18.28
instrumentalist 10.72
instrumentality 2.57
instrumentation 8.46
instruments 18.71
insubordinate 26.50
insubordination 8.35
insubstantial 2.28
insufferable 38.52; 38.65
insufficiency 18.56
insufficient 18.38
insufficiently 18.56
insular 18.60
insularity 2.57
insulate 7.41
insulating 8.60
insulation 8.32
insulator 8.5
insulin 17.29
insult 37.26
insult 37.26
insulted 38.20
insulting 38.34
insuperable 42.39; 42.51
insupportable 26.41
insurable 28.19
insurance 26.24; 28.10
insure 25.2; 27.1
insured 25.9; 27.2
insurer 26.6; 28.2
insurgence 12.15
insurgency 12.29
insurgent 12.14
insurgents 12.15

insuring 28.11
insurmountable 30.24
insurrection 10.28
intact 1.6
intaglio 35.19
intake 7.6
intangible 2.64
intarsia 4.44
in tears 13.5
integer 18.60
integral 10.21
integral 18.64
integrate 7.41
integrated 8.13
integration 8.32
integrity 10.54
integument 10.67
intellect 9.5
intellectual 10.60
intellectualism 18.29
intellectually 10.55; 10.78
intelligence 10.68
intelligent 10.67
intelligentsia 10.57
intelligibility 18.58
intelligible 10.79
intelligibly 10.78
intemperance 10.68
intemperate 10.73
intend 9.35
intendant 10.33
intended 10.18
intending 10.36
intense 9.39
intensely 10.5
intensification 8.43
intensified 21.12
intensifier 22.2
intensify 21.4
intensity 10.54
intensive 10.50
intensively 10.54
intent 9.41
intention 10.28
intentional 10.60
intentionally 10.78
intentions 10.32
intently 10.5
inter 11.1
interact 1.6
interaction 2.35
interactive 2.53
inter alia 8.78
interbank 1.25
interbred 9.8
interbreed 15.11

intercalary 2.56
intercalate 7.39
intercalation 8.29
intercede 15.11
interceder 16.5
intercept 9.46
interception 10.28
interceptor 10.10
intercession 10.28
interchange 7.23
interchangeable 8.79
intercity 18.3
Intercity 18.3
intercom 23.23
intercommunicate 7.49
intercommunication 8.39
intercommunion 42.20; 42.41
interconnect 9.5
interconnecting 10.36
intercontinental 10.21
intercourse 25.28
intercrop 23.36
interdenominational 8.79
interdental 10.21
interdepartmental 10.21
interdependence 10.34
interdependent 10.33
interdict 17.6
interdiction 18.33
interdisciplinary 18.56
interest 9.49; 18.46
interested 18.62
interesting 18.73
interestingly 18.80
interface 7.30
interfacing 8.64
interfere 13.1
interference 14.11
interfering 14.12
interferon 23.27
intergalactic 2.17
intergovernmental 10.21
interim 17.24
interior 14.18
interject 9.5
interjection 10.28
interlace 7.30
interlaced 7.31

Interlaken 4.24
interlard 3.8
interlay 7.4
interleaf 15.13
interleave 15.39
interleaved 15.40
interlibrary 22.40
interline 21.22
interlinear 18.61
interlining 22.26
interlock 23.3
interlocking 24.40
interlocution 42.20
interlocutor 24.57
interloper 36.3
interlopers 36.34
interlude 41.9
intermarriage 2.27
intermarried 2.24
intermarry 2.5
intermediary 16.38
intermediate 16.50
interment 12.14
intermezzo 35.7
interminable 12.41
intermingle 18.22
intermission 18.33
intermittence 18.39
intermittent 18.38
intermittently 18.56
intern 11.15
internal 12.8
internalization 8.44
internalize 21.43
internally 12.29
international 2.64
Internationale 3.14
internationalism 18.29
internationalize 21.47
internationally 2.78
internecine 21.22
interned 11.16
internee 15.4
Internet 9.51
internment 12.14
interpellant 10.33
interpersonal 12.32
interplanetary 2.58
interplay 7.4
Interpol 23.15
interpolate 7.39
interpolation 8.29
interpose 35.52
interposition 18.33
interpret 12.25
interpretation 8.29
interpreter 12.30

interpretive 17.55
interracial 8.15
interregnum 10.25
interrelate 7.33
interrelation 8.46
interrelationship 17.43
interrogate 7.38
interrogation 8.28
interrogative 17.55
interrogator 8.5
interrogatory 24.54
interrupt 37.42
interrupted 38.20
interrupter 38.10
interrupting 38.34
interruption 38.28
interruptions 38.31
inter se 7.4
intersect 9.5
intersecting 10.36
intersection 10.28
intersex 9.3
interspace 7.30
intersperse 11.22
interspersed 11.23
interspersion 12.12
interstate 7.41
interstellar 10.12
interstitial 18.22
intertidal 22.16
intertwine 21.22
intertwined 21.23
intertwining 22.26
interval 18.64
intervarsity 4.42
intervene 15.26
intervener 16.8
intervening 16.27
intervention 10.28
interventionist 10.72
intervertebral 12.32
interview 41.4
interviewed 41.9
interviewee 15.2
interviewer 42.2
interviews 41.33
interwar 25.4
interweave 15.39
interwove 35.50
interwoven 36.20
intestacy 10.53
intestate 7.34
intestinal 10.60; 22.16
intestine 10.26
intestines 10.31
in the black 1.3
in the dark 3.3

jagged 2.24
Jagger 2.9
jaggy 2.2
jaguar 2.60
jai alai 21.4
jail 7.15
jailbait 7.34
jailbird 11.7
jailbreak 7.6
jailed 7.16
jailer 8.7
jailhouse 29.12
Jain 7.21; 21.22
Jainism 18.27
Jakarta 4.10
Jake 7.6
Jalalabad 1.9
jalopy 24.1
jalousie 15.4
jam 1.22
Jamaica 8.4
Jamaican 8.21
Jamal 3.14
jamb 1.22
jambalaya 22.2
jamboree 15.4
James 7.20
James Bond 23.30
James Dean 15.24
Jameson 8.21
Jamestown 29.5
Jamie 8.1
Jamieson 8.81
jammer 2.13
jamming 2.42
jammy 2.6
jam-packed 1.6
Jamshedpur 27.1
Jan 1.24
Janáček 9.2
Jane 7.21
Jane Eyre 5.1
Jane's 7.26
Janet 2.51
jangle 2.28
Janice 2.45
Janie 8.1
Janine 15.24
janitor 2.60
janitorial 26.41
Jan's 1.36
Jansen 2.35
Jansenism 18.28
Jansenist 2.73
January 2.59; 2.78
Janus 8.67
Jap 1.37
Japan 1.24

Japanese 15.45
jape 7.27
japery 8.76
japonica 24.57
jar 3.1
jardinière 5.1
jarful 39.7
jargon 4.24
jargonize 21.42
Jarman 4.24
Jarndyce 21.29
jarred 3.8
Jarrett 2.50
Jarrold 2.29
Jarrow 35.3
jars 3.37
jarvey 4.4
Jarvis 4.31
Jascha 2.14
jasmine 2.34
Jason 8.21
jasper 2.8
Jasper 2.8
jaundice 26.26
jaundiced 26.28
jaunt 25.25
jauntier 26.39
jauntiest 26.49
jauntily 26.37
jauntiness 26.47
jaunty 26.1
Java 4.11
Javan 4.24
Javanese 15.45
javelin 2.34
jaw 25.1
jawbone 35.36
jawbreaker 8.4
jawline 21.22
jaws 25.35
Jaws 25.35
jay 7.1
Jay 7.1
jaywalk 25.6
jaywalker 26.3
jaywalking 26.25
jazz 1.50
jazz band 1.28
jazzy 2.7
J-cloth® 23.46
jealous 10.42
jealously 10.53
jealousy 10.53
Jean 15.23
Jeanette 9.51
Jeanne 1.24
Jeannie 16.1
jeans 15.29

Jean's 15.29
Jedda 10.10
Jedi 21.3
Jeep® 15.30
jeepers 16.37
jeer 13.1
jeered 13.2
jeering 14.12
jeers 13.5
Jeeves 15.41
Jeff 9.10
Jefferson 10.64
Jeffreys 10.51
Jehoshaphat 1.45
Jehovah 36.6
jejune 41.19
jejunum 42.18
Jekyll 10.21; 16.17;
    17.15
Jekyll and Hyde 21.10
jell 9.16
Jellicoe 35.19
jellied 10.17
jellied eels 15.19
jellies 10.51
jellify 21.4
Jell-o® 35.7
jelly 10.5
jellybean 15.26
jellyfish 17.50
Jemima 22.8
jemmied 10.17
jemmy 10.6
je ne sais quoi 3.1
Jenkins 10.31
Jenna 10.13
Jenna's 10.52
Jenner 10.13
Jennifer 10.56
Jennings 10.37
Jenny 10.6
Jenny's 10.51
Jensen 10.28
jeopardize 21.43
jeopardy 10.53
Jephthah 10.11
jerboa 36.2
jeremiad 22.13
Jeremiah 22.2
Jeremy 10.53
Jericho 35.19
jerk 11.4
jerkin 12.11
jerking 12.16
jerks 11.5
jerky 12.1
Jermyn 12.11
Jeroboam 36.18

Jerome 35.34
jerry 10.5
Jerry 10.5
jerry-build 17.18
jerry-built 17.21
jerry can 1.24
jerry cans 1.36
jersey 12.1
Jersey 12.1
Jerusalem 42.40
Jervis 12.18
Jess 9.47
Jesse 10.7
Jesse James 7.20
Jessica 10.56
Jessie 10.7
jest 9.49
jester 10.10
jesting 10.36
Jesu 41.3
Jesuit 17.51
Jesuits 17.52
Jesus 16.30
Jesu's 41.33
jet 9.51
jeté 7.2
jetfoil 33.6
Jethro 35.7
Jethro Tull 37.16
jet lag 1.13
jetliner 22.8
jet-propelled 9.19
jetsam 10.25
jetstream 15.20
jettison 10.64
jettisoned 10.65
jetton 10.27
jetty 10.3
Jew 41.1
jewel 42.16
jeweller 42.37
jewellery 42.36
jewels 42.17
Jewess 9.47
Jewish 42.29
Jewry 28.1; 42.1
Jews 41.33
Jewson 42.20
Jeyes 7.56
Jezebel 9.16
jib 17.1
jibe 21.5
jibed 21.6
Jif® 17.10
jiff 17.10
jiffy 18.4
Jiffy bag® 1.13
jig 17.12

jigger 18.9
jiggered 18.19
jiggery-pokery 36.35
jigging 18.40
jiggle 18.22
jigs 17.13
jigsaw 25.3
jihad 1.9; 3.8
Jill 17.15
jillaroo 41.4
Jilly 18.5
jilt 17.21
Jim 17.24
Jimmy 18.6
jingle 18.22
jingling 18.40
jingo 35.11
jingoism 18.28
jingoist 18.75
jingoistic 18.16
jink 17.30
jinn 17.29
Jinnah 18.13
jinni 15.2; 18.6
jinx 17.31
jissom 18.26
jitter 18.10
jitterbug 37.14
jitters 18.55
jittery 18.56
jive 21.37
jiver 22.6
jiving 22.26
Jo 35.1
Joab 1.1
Joachim 17.24
Joan 35.36
Joanna 2.13
Joanne 1.24
Joan of Arc 3.3
Joan's 35.39
job 23.1
Job 35.20
jobber 24.8
jobbery 24.54
Jobcentre 10.10
jobless 24.43
jobsworth 11.26
Joburg 11.9
Jocasta 2.10
Jocelyn 24.32
jock 23.3
Jock 23.3
jockey 24.2
jockeys 24.52
Jock's 23.5
jockstrap 1.37
jocose 35.42

jocosely 36.1
jocular 24.57
jocularity 2.57
jocund 24.34; 36.21; 37.36
jocundity 38.47
jodhpurs 24.53
Jodie 36.1
Jodrell Bank 1.25
Joe 35.1
Joel 36.15
Joel's 36.17
Joe's 35.52
joey 36.1
Joey 36.1
jog 23.11
jogged 23.12
jogger 24.9
joggers 24.53
jogging 24.40
joggle 24.27
jog trot 23.44
Johann 1.24
Johannesburg 11.9
john 23.27
John 23.27
John Bull 39.7
John Doe 35.2
John Dory 26.1
Johnny 24.6
Johnny Cash 1.43
John o'Groats 35.46
Johns 23.35
John's 23.35
Johnson 24.33
Johnsonian 36.40
Johnston 24.33
John Wayne 7.21
joie de vivre 16.7
join 33.8
joinable 34.16
joinder 34.2
joiner 34.2
joinery 34.14
joining 34.11
joint 33.10
jointed 34.3
jointer 34.2
jointly 34.1
joist 33.12
jojoba 36.3
joke 35.21
joker 36.4
jokers 36.34
jokey 36.1
joking 36.24
jokingly 36.35
jollier 24.58

jolliest 24.71
jollification 8.48
jollify 21.4
jollity 24.56
jolly 24.5
Jolson 36.20
jolt 35.32
jolting 36.24
Jonah 36.8
Jonas 36.26
Jonathan 24.64
Jonathan's 24.66
Jones 35.39
Joneses 36.34
jonquil 17.15; 24.27
Jonson 24.33
Jools 41.16
Joplin 24.32
Joppa 24.8
Jordan 26.19
Jordanian 8.81
Jorvik 26.9
Jos 23.39
José 7.2
Josef 9.10
Joseph 17.10
Josephine 15.26
josh 23.42
joshed 23.43
joshing 24.40
Joshua 24.57
Joshua's 24.74
Josiah 22.2
Josias 22.29
Josie 36.1
joss 23.39
jostle 24.27
jostled 24.28
jot 23.44
jotter 24.10
jotting 24.40
joule 41.14
jounce 29.9
jounced 29.10
journal 12.8
journalese 15.45
journalism 18.28
journalist 12.38
journalistic 18.16
journey 12.1
journeyman 12.34
journeys 12.28
joust 29.13
jousted 30.3
jouster 30.2
jousting 30.12
Jove 35.50
jovial 36.38

joviality 2.57
Jovian 36.40
Jowett 30.18
jowl 29.4
joy 33.1
Joy 33.1
Joyce 33.11
Joycean 34.17
joyful 34.5; 39.7
joyfully 34.14
joyfulness 34.18
joyless 34.12
joyous 34.12
joyously 34.14
joyride 21.11
joyrider 22.5
joyriders 22.39
Joy's 33.15
joystick 17.3
joysticks 17.4
JP 15.2
JPEG 9.12
Juan 3.19
Juan de Fuca 42.4
Juanita 16.5
jubilance 42.44
jubilant 42.43
jubilation 8.39
jubilee 15.4
Judaea 16.2
Judaean 16.22
Judah 42.5
Judaic 8.10
Judaism 18.28
Judas 42.26
Judd 37.8
judder 38.10
Jude 41.9
judge 37.15
judges 38.45
Judges 38.45
judgeship 17.43
judging 38.34
judgment 38.32
judgmental 10.21
judicial 18.22
judicially 18.56
judiciary 18.56
judicious 18.44
judiciously 18.56
judiciousness 18.74
Judith 17.53
judo 35.18
Judy 42.1
jug 37.14
jugful 39.7
juggernaut 25.31
juggernauts 25.32

juggle 38.23
juggler 38.12
jugglery 38.47
jugular 38.48
juice 41.24
juicer 42.9
juicier 42.38
juiciest 42.47
juiciness 42.46
juicy 42.1
jujitsu 41.3
juju 41.3
jujube 41.5
jukebox 23.5
julep 17.43
Jules 41.16
Jules Verne 11.15
Julia 42.38
Julian 42.41
Juliana 4.13
Julie 42.1
julienne 9.32
Julie's 42.35
Juliet 9.51
Julius 42.46
July 21.2
jumble 38.23
jumbled 38.24
jumbo 35.17
jumbuck 37.3
jump 37.29
jumpable 38.52
jumped-up 37.41
jumper 38.8
jumping 38.34
jumpy 38.1
junction 38.28
junctions 38.31
juncture 38.14
June 41.19
Jung 39.10
Jungfrau 29.1
Jungian 40.23
jungle 38.23
junior 42.7; 42.38
juniors 42.34
juniper 42.37
Junius 42.46
junk 37.32
Junker 40.2
junket 38.43
junkie 38.2
junk mail 7.15
junk shop 23.36
junkyard 3.8
Juno 35.18
Junoesque 9.48
junta 38.10; 40.2

Jupiter 42.37
Jura 28.2
Jurassic 2.21
Jürgen 12.12
juridical 18.64
juries 28.16
jurisconsult 37.26
jurisdiction 18.33
jurisprudence 42.23
jurisprudent 42.22
jurist 28.14
juristic 18.16
juror 28.2
jury 28.1
juryman 28.21
jurywoman 40.10
jus 41.1
just 37.45
just deserts 11.25
justice 38.37
justiciary 18.56
justifiable 22.43
justifiably 22.40
justification 8.51
justificatory 8.76
justified 21.12
justify 21.4
Justin 38.27
Justine 15.24
Justine's 15.29
Justinian 18.67
justly 38.5
just so 35.2
jut 37.47
jute 41.27
Jute 41.27
Jutes 41.28
Jutish 42.29
Jutland 38.29
jutted 38.20
jutting 38.34
Juvenal 42.39
juvenescence 10.34
juvenescent 10.33
juvenile 21.16
juvenilia 18.61
juxtapose 35.52
juxtaposing 36.24
juxtaposition 18.33
K 7.1
K2 41.2
kabuki 42.1
Kabul 39.7
Kafka 2.9
Kafkaesque 9.48
kaftan 1.24
kaftans 1.36
Kaifeng 9.36

Kaiser 22.9
kaizen 9.32
kala-azar 3.1
Kalahari 4.5
Kalamazoo 41.2
kalanchoe 36.1
Kalashnikov 23.9
kale 7.15
kaleidoscopic 24.16
kaleyard 3.8
Kalgoorlie 28.1
Kali 4.5
kalmia 2.61
Kalmuck 37.3
Kama 4.13
Kama Sutra 42.7
Kamchatka 2.9
kamikaze 4.7
Kamloops 41.23
Kampala 4.12
Kampuchea 16.2
Kampuchean 16.22
Kananga 2.9
kanban 1.24
Kandahar 3.1
kanga 2.9
Kanga 2.9
kangaroo 41.4
kangaroos 41.33
Kano 35.4
Kanpur 27.1
Kansan 2.35
Kansas 2.46
Kant 1.33
Kantian 2.66
Kant's 1.34
KANU 41.3
kaolin 17.29
kaon 23.27
kapok 23.3
kappa 2.8
kaput 39.14
Karachi 4.7
Karajan 3.19
Karakoram 26.17
karaoke 36.1
karate 4.3
Karelia 16.40
Karen 2.35
Karim 15.20
Karl 3.14
Karloff 23.9
Karl's 3.15
Karlsbad 1.9
karma 4.13
karmic 4.16
Karnak 1.3
karst 3.30

kart 3.32
karting 4.29
karts 3.33
kasbah 3.1
Kashmir 13.1
Kashmiri 14.1
Kashmirian 14.21
Kate 7.32
Kate's 7.50
Kathleen 15.25
Kathryn 2.34
Kathryn's 2.38
Katie 8.1
Katmandu 41.4
Katrina 16.8
Kattegat 1.45
katydid 17.8
Katz 1.46
Kaufman 26.19; 30.8
Kaunda 40.2
Kavanagh 2.13; 2.60
Kawasaki 2.2
Kawasaki 4.2
Kay 7.1
kayak 1.3
kayaks 1.4
Kayleigh 8.1
Kay's 7.56
Kazakh 3.3
Kazakhstan 1.24; 3.19
Kazan 1.24; 3.19
kazoo 41.2
kea 8.2
Kean 15.23
Kearney 12.1
Keating 16.22
Keaton 16.22
Keats 15.36
Keble 16.17
kecks 9.3
ked 9.8
kedge 9.14
kedgeree 15.4
Keegan 16.22
keel 15.17
keelboat 35.45
Keele 15.17
Keeler 16.7
Keeley 16.1
keelhaul 25.14
keelhauled 25.15
keelhauling 26.25
Keeling 16.22
keen 15.23
keener 16.8
keening 16.27
keenly 16.1

keenness 16.30
keep 15.30
keepable 16.41
keeper 16.3
keep-fit 17.51
keeping 16.27
keepsake 7.6
keeshond 23.30
keg 9.12
Keighley 16.1
Keillor 16.7
keister 16.5
Keith 15.37
Keller 10.12
Kellogg 23.11
Kellogg's 23.13
Kelly 10.5
kelp 9.22
kelpie 10.1
Kelvin 10.26
Kemal 3.14
Kemble 10.21
Kemp 9.29
kempt 9.30
ken 9.32
Ken 9.32
Kendal 10.21
kendo 35.7
Kenilworth 10.75;
    11.26
Kennedy 10.54
kennel 10.21
kennels 10.23
Kenneth 10.49; 17.53
Kenny 10.6
Ken's 9.43
Kensington 10.64
Kent 9.41
Kentish 10.45
Kenton 10.27
Kentuckian 38.54
Kentucky 38.2
Kenwood 39.4
Kenya 10.12; 16.7
Kenyan 10.27
Kenyatta 2.10
Kenyon 10.27
kepi 8.1
Kepler 10.12
Keppel 10.21
kept 9.46
keratin 17.29
kerb 11.2
kerb crawler 26.6
kerb crawling 26.25
kerbing 12.16
kerbside 21.11
kerbstone 35.36

kerchief 15.13
kerfuffle 38.23
kermis 12.18
Kermit 12.25
kern 11.15
Kern 11.15
kernel 12.8
kerning 12.16
kerosene 15.26
Kerouac 1.3
Kerr 11.1
Kerry 10.5
kersey 12.1
Kesteven 16.22
kestrel 10.21
Keswick 10.15
ketch 9.6
ketchup 37.41
Kettering 10.69
kettle 10.21
kettledrum 37.27
Kevin 10.26
Kevlar® 3.1
Kew 41.1
key 15.1
keyboard 25.9
keyboarder 26.4
keyboarding 26.25
keyboards 25.10
keyholder 36.5
keyhole 35.30
Keynes 7.26; 15.29
keynote 35.45
keypad 1.9
key ring 16.27
keys 15.42
keystone 35.36
Keystone Kops 23.37
keystroke 35.21
keyword 11.7
Kez 9.57
KGB 15.4
Khachaturian 28.21
khaki 4.2
Khalsa 2.14
khan 3.19
Khan 3.19
Khartoum 41.17
khazi 4.7
khedive 15.39
Khmer 5.1
Khmer Rouge 41.13
Khoikhoi 33.1
Khomeini 8.1
Khrushchev 23.9
Khyber 22.3
Khyber Pass 3.26
kia ora 26.6

kibble 18.22
kibbled 18.23
kibbutz 39.15
kibbutzim 15.20
kibe 21.5
kibitzer 18.60
kiblah 3.1
kibosh 23.42
kick 17.3
kick ass 1.40
kickback 1.3
kick-boxer 24.14
kick-boxing 24.40
kicked 17.6
kicker 18.9
kicking 18.40
kickoff 23.9
kicks 17.4
kickstand 1.28
kick-start 3.32
kid 17.8
Kidd 17.8
kidder 18.10
Kidderminster 18.10
kiddies 18.54
kidding 18.40
kiddy 18.3
kidnap 1.37
kidnapped 1.39
kidnapper 2.8
kidnapping 2.42
kidney 18.6
kidney bean 15.26
kidneys 18.54
kidology 24.55
kidskin 18.31
Kiel 15.17
Kielder 16.5
Kieran 14.9
Kierkegaard 3.8
Kiev 9.10; 9.56
kif 17.10
Kilbride 21.10
Kildare 5.1
Kilimanjaro 35.4
Kilkenny 10.6
kill 17.15
Killarney 4.6
killed 17.18
killer 18.12
killers 18.55
Killick 18.16
Killiecrankie 2.2
killifish 17.50
killing 18.40
killings 18.41
killjoy 33.1
kills 17.23

Kilmarnock 4.15
kiln 17.20
Kilner 18.13
kilo 35.10
kilobyte 21.34
kilobytes 21.35
kilocycle 22.16
kilogram 1.22
kilohertz 11.25
kilometre 16.5; 24.57
kilometric 10.15
kiloton 37.31
kilovolt 35.32
kilowatt 23.44
kilowatt-hour 31.1
Kilroy 33.1
kilt 17.21
kilter 18.10
kilting 18.40
Kim 17.24
Kimberley 18.56
kimono 35.16
kin 17.29
kinaesthesia 16.40
kinaesthetic 10.15
kind 21.23
kinda 22.5
kinder 22.5
kindergarten 4.24
kind-hearted 4.17
kind-heartedness 4.53
kindle 18.22
kindliness 22.46
kindling 18.40
kindly 22.1
kindness 22.29
kindred 18.19
kine 21.22
kinesis 16.29
kinetic 10.15
kinetics 10.16
kinfolk 35.21
king 17.35
King 17.35
kingcraft 3.10
kingcup 37.41
kingdom 18.26
kingdoms 18.30
kingfisher 18.14
King Kong 23.31
King Lear 13.1
kinglet 18.50
kingly 18.5
kingmaker 8.4
kingpin 18.31
kings 17.36
Kings 17.36
kingship 17.43

king-size 21.41
Kingsley 18.5
King's Lynn 17.29
Kingston 18.32
Kingstown 29.5
Kingswear 13.1
kink 17.30
kinkajou 41.4
kinked 17.32
kinky 18.2
Kinnear 13.1
Kinnock 18.15
Kinross 23.39
Kinsella 10.12
Kinsey 18.7
kinsfolk 35.21
Kinshasa 4.14
kinship 17.43
kinsman 18.32
kinswoman 40.10
kinswomen 18.31
Kintyre 19.1
kiosk 23.40
kip 17.43
Kipling 18.40
kipper 18.8
kippered 18.19
kippers 18.55
kir 13.1
Kirby 12.1
kirby grip 17.43
Kirghizia 18.61
Kiri 18.5
Kiribati 2.3
kirk 11.4
Kirk 11.4
Kirkby 12.1
Kirkcaldy 24.3; 26.1
Kirklees 15.43
Kirkpatrick 2.19
Kirov 23.47
Kirsten 12.12
Kirsty 12.1
kirtle 12.8
Kirwan 12.12
kismet 9.51
kiss 17.46
kissable 18.64
kissagram 1.22
kiss and tell 9.16
kissed 17.49
kisser 18.14
kisses 18.55
kissing 18.40
Kissinger 18.60
kissy-kissy 18.7
kit 17.51
kitbag 1.13

kitchen 18.31
kitchenalia 8.78
Kitchener 18.60
kitchenette 9.51
kitchens 18.36
kitchenware 5.1
kite 21.31
kites 21.35
kitesurfing 12.16
kith 17.53
Kit Kat® 1.45
kitsch 17.7
kitten 18.32
kittenish 17.50
kittens 18.37
kittiwake 7.6
kitty 18.3
Kitty 18.3
kiwi 15.3; 16.1
kiwi fruit 41.27
Klaus 29.12
klaxon 2.35
Kleenex® 9.3
Klein 21.22
Klemperer 10.56
kleptomania 8.78
kleptomaniac 1.3
kleptomaniacs 1.4
Kline 21.22
klipspringer 18.13
Klondike 21.7
Klosters 36.34
klutz 37.48
knack 1.3
knacker 2.9
knackered 2.25
knackwurst 11.23
knap 1.37
Knapp 1.37
knapped 1.39
knapsack 1.3
knapweed 15.11
knave 7.54
knavery 8.76
knaves 7.55
knavish 8.70
knead 15.11
kneader 16.5
kneading 16.27
Knebworth 10.49;
11.26
knee 15.1
kneecap 1.37
kneecapping 2.42
kneecaps 1.38
knee-deep 15.30
knee-high 21.2
kneehole 35.30

kneel 15.17
kneeled 15.18
knee-length 9.37
kneeler 16.7
kneeling 16.27
kneepad 1.9
kneepads 1.10
knees 15.42
knees-up 37.41
knee-trembler 10.12
knell 9.16
knelt 9.23
knew 41.1
knickerbockers 24.53
knickers 18.55
knick-knack 1.3
knife 21.14
knifepoint 33.10
knifer 22.6
knifing 22.26
knight 21.31
Knight 21.31
knight-errant 10.33
knight-errantry 10.53
knighthood 39.4
knightly 22.1
knights 21.35
Knightsbridge 22.15
knit 17.51
knitted 18.19
knitter 18.10
knitting 18.40
knitting machine
15.24
knitwear 5.1
knives 21.38
knob 23.1
knobbly 24.5
knobby 24.1
knobkerrie 10.5
knobs 23.2
knobstick 24.16
knock 23.3
knockabout 29.14
knocked 23.6
knocker 24.9
knockers 24.53
knocking 24.40
knock-kneed 15.11
knock-on effect 9.5
knockout 29.14
knocks 23.5
Knole 35.30
knoll 35.30
Knossos 23.39; 24.43
knot 23.44
knotgrass 3.26
knothole 35.30

knots 23.45
knotted 24.24
knotter 24.10
knotting 24.40
knotty 24.3
knotweed 15.11
know 35.1
knowable 36.38
knowest 36.28
know-how 29.1
knowing 36.24
knowingly 36.35
know-it-all 25.14
Knowle 35.30
knowledge 24.26
knowledgeable 24.77
knowledgeably 24.76
Knowles 35.33
known 35.36
Knowsley 36.1
Knox 23.5
Knoxville 17.15
knuckle 38.23
knucklebone 35.36
knucklebones 35.39
knucklehead 9.8
knur 11.1
knurl 11.11
knurled 11.12
Knutsford 38.20
koala 4.12
Koch 23.4
Kodachrome® 35.34
Kodak 1.3
Kodiak 1.3
Koestler 12.2
Kofi 36.1
Kohinoor 27.1
kohl 35.30
Kohl 35.30
kohlrabi 4.1
koi 33.1
Kojak 1.3
Kol Nidrei 7.3
Königsberg 11.9
Kon-Tiki 16.1
kook 41.6
kookaburra 38.12
kooky 42.1
Kooning 42.24
kop 23.36
kopeck 9.2
kopecks 9.3
kopje 24.1
Koran 3.19
Koranic 2.20
Korbut 26.31
Korchnoi 33.1

Latvian

lob 23.1
lobar 36.3
lobbied 24.23
lobby 24.1
lobbyist 24.72
lobe 35.20
lobelia 16.40
lobotomy 24.54
lobscouse 29.12
lobster 24.10
lobster pot 23.44
lobular 24.57
local 36.15
locale 3.14
localism 18.28
locality 2.57
localization 8.50
localize 21.45
localized 21.48
locally 36.35
locals 36.17
Locarno 35.4
locate 7.33
located 8.13
location 8.23
locative 17.55
loch 23.3; 23.4
Lochinvar 3.1
Loch Lomond 36.21
Loch Ness 9.47
loci 21.3
lock 23.3
lockable 24.61
lockage 24.26
Locke 23.3
locked 23.6
locker 24.9
Lockerbie 24.54
locket 24.49
lock gate 7.34
Lockhart 3.32
Lockheed 15.11
locking 24.40
lockjaw 25.3
lockout 29.14
locks 23.5
Locksley 24.5
locksmith 17.53
lockup 37.41
Lockwood 39.4
Lockyer 24.12
loco 35.16
locomotion 36.20
locomotive 36.32
locum 36.18
locus 24.43; 36.26
locust 36.28
locution 42.20

lode 35.25
loden 36.20
lodestar 3.1
lodestone 35.36
lodge 23.14
Lodge 23.14
lodger 24.14
lodgers 24.53
lodging 24.40
lodgment 24.38
loess 36.25
loft 23.10
loftier 24.58
loftiest 24.71
lofting 24.40
Loftus 24.43
lofty 24.3
log 23.11
Logan 36.20
loganberry 10.5; 36.35
logarithm 18.26
logarithmic 18.16
logbook 39.1
loge 35.29
logged 23.12
logger 24.9
loggerheads 9.9
loggia 24.14; 36.9
logging 24.40
logic 24.20
logical 24.61
logicality 2.57
logically 24.56
logician 18.33
Logie 36.1
logistic 18.16
logistical 18.64
logistics 18.17
logjam 1.22
logo 35.16
logograph 1.11; 3.9
logorrhoea 13.1
logotype 21.26
logroll 35.30
logrolling 36.24
logs 23.13
Lohengrin 17.29
loin 33.8
loincloth 23.46
Loire 3.1
Lois 36.25
loiter 34.2
loiterer 34.15
Loki 36.1
Lola 36.7
Lolita 16.5
loll 23.15
lollapalooza 42.9

Lollard 3.8; 24.24
Lollards 24.25
loller 24.12
lolling 24.40
lollipop 23.36
lollipops 23.37
lollop 24.41
lolloping 24.69
lolly 24.5
Lomax 1.4
Lombard 3.8
Lombardi 4.3
Lombardy 24.54
London 38.28
Londonderry 10.5
Londoner 38.48
lone 35.36
lonelier 36.37
loneliest 36.44
loneliness 36.42
lonely 36.1
loner 36.8
lonesome 36.18
long 23.31
long-awaited 8.13
longboat 35.45
longbow 35.13
Longbridge 24.26
Longden 24.33
long-drawn-out 29.14
longer 24.9
longest 24.44
longevity 10.54
Longfellow 35.7
Longford 24.24
long-haired 5.2
longhand 1.28
long-haul 25.14
longhorn 25.22
longing 24.40
longingly 24.56
Longinus 22.29
longitude 41.9
longitudinal 42.39
long jump 37.29
Longleat 15.35
long-legged 10.17
long-life 21.14
Longman 24.33
long-range 7.23
longs 23.32
longship 17.43
long-sighted 22.13
long-sleeved 15.40
longtime 21.19
longueur 11.1
longways 7.56
longwise 21.41

lonicera 18.60
Lonnie 24.6
Lonsdale 7.15
loo 41.1
looby 42.1
Looe 41.1
loofah 42.6
look 39.1
lookalike 21.7
looked 39.2
looker 40.2
looking 40.15
lookout 29.14
look-see 15.3
loom 41.17
loomed 41.18
looming 42.24
loon 41.19
loons 41.21
loony 42.1
loop 41.22
looper 42.3
loophole 35.30
loopier 42.38
loopiest 42.47
looping 42.24
loops 41.23
loopy 42.1
loose 41.24
loosebox 23.5
loose-limbed 17.25
loosely 42.1
loosen 42.20
looser 42.9
loosest 42.27
loosestrife 21.14
loosing 42.24
loot 41.27
looter 42.5
looting 42.24
lop 23.36
lope 35.40
lop-eared 13.2
Lopez 9.57
lopsided 22.13
loquacious 8.67
loquacity 2.57
lor' 25.1
Lorca 26.3
Lorcan 26.19
lord 25.9
Lord 25.9
lordling 26.25
lordly 26.1
Lord of the Flies
  21.47
lordosis 36.25
Lord's 25.10

luminary 42.36
luminesce 9.47
luminescence 10.34
luminescent 10.33
luminosity 24.56
luminous 42.46
Lumley 38.5
lumme 38.6
lummox 38.17
lump 37.29
lumpectomy 10.53
lumpen 38.28
lumpfish 38.40
lumpier 38.49
lumpiest 38.61
lumpish 38.40
lumps 37.30
lumpy 38.1
Lumsden 38.28
lunacy 42.36
lunar 42.8
lunatic 17.3
lunatics 17.4
lunch 37.35
lunchbox 23.5
luncheon 38.28
luncher 38.14
lunchroom 39.9; 41.17
lunchtime 21.19
Lundy 38.3
lung 37.37
lunge 37.38
lungfish 38.40
lungwort 11.24
Lunn 37.31
Lunt 37.40
Lupercalia 8.78
lupin 42.19
lupine 21.22
lupus 42.26
lurch 11.6
lurcher 12.2
lurching 12.16
lure 27.1
lured 27.2
lurer 28.2
lures 27.3
Lurex® 9.3
lurgy 12.1
lurid 26.11
Lurie 28.1
luring 28.11
lurk 11.4
lurker 12.2
lurking 12.16
Lurpak® 1.3
Lusaka 4.9
luscious 38.38

lush 37.46
lusher 38.14
lushest 38.39
Lusitania 8.78
lust 37.45
lustful 38.23; 39.7
lustier 38.49
lustiest 38.61
lustily 38.47
lusting 38.34
lustre 38.10
lustrous 38.38
lusty 38.3
lute 41.27
lutenist 42.48
lutetium 16.42
Luther 42.6
Lutheran 42.41
Lutine 15.25
Luton 42.20
Luton Hoo 41.4
Lutyens 38.31
luvvie 38.4
Luxembourg 11.9
Luxembourger 12.2
luxuriance 28.23
luxuriant 28.22
luxuriate 7.45
luxuries 38.63
luxurious 28.24
luxury 38.47
Luzon 23.27
lycanthrope 35.40
lycanthropic 24.16
lycanthropy 2.56
lycée 7.3
Lyceum 16.20
lychee 15.2
lych gate 7.34
Lycra® 22.7
Lycurgus 12.19
Lydgate 7.34
Lydia 18.61
Lydian 18.67
lye 21.1
Lyell 19.3
lying 22.26
Lyle 21.16
Lyly 18.5
Lyme 21.19
Lyme Regis 16.29
Lymington 18.67
Lymm 17.24
lymph 17.26
lymphatic 2.17
lymphocyte 21.34
lymphocytic 18.16
lymphoma 36.8

Lynam 22.18
lynch 17.33
Lynch 17.33
lyncher 18.14
lynching 18.40
Lynette 9.51
Lynmouth 18.52
Lynn 17.29
Lynn's 17.42
lynx 17.31
Lyon 22.20
Lyonnesse 9.47
Lyons 22.23
Lyra 20.2
lyre 19.1
lyrebird 11.7
lyric 18.16
lyrical 18.64
lyrically 18.57
lyricism 18.28
lyricist 18.75
lyrist 20.9
Lysander 2.10
lyse 21.39
Lysenko 35.7
lysergic 12.3
Lysimachus 18.74
lysine 15.25
lysis 22.28
Lytham 18.26
Lytham Saint Anne's
  1.36
Lyttelton 18.67
Lytton 18.32
M 9.28
M6 17.4
ma 3.1
MA 7.2
ma'am 1.22; 3.16
Maastricht 17.6
Mab 1.1
Mabel 8.15
mac 1.3
Mac 1.3
macabre 4.8; 4.12
macadam 2.32
macadamia 8.78
Macao 29.1
macaque 1.3; 3.3
macaroni 36.1
macaronic 24.19
macaroon 41.19
MacArthur 4.11
Macaulay 26.1
Macavity 2.57
macaw 25.2
Macbeth 9.54
Maccabaeus 16.30

Maccabean 16.22
Maccabees 15.45
Macclesfield 15.18
Macdonald 24.28
mace 7.30
Mace® 7.30
macebearer 6.2
macedoine 3.19
Macedon 2.66; 23.27
Macedonia 36.37
Macedonian 36.40
macerate 7.35
maceration 8.24
Macfarlane 4.24
Macgillicuddy's Reeks
  15.8
MacGuffin 38.27
Mach 1.3
machete 10.3
Machiavelli 10.5
Machiavellian 10.64
machinate 7.35
machination 8.24
machine 15.24
machined 15.27
machine gun 37.31
machinery 16.38
machinist 16.31
machismo 35.11
macho 35.3
Machu Picchu 41.3
Mackay 21.2
Mackenzie 10.7
mackerel 2.28; 2.64
Mackerras 10.42
Mackeson 2.66
Mackie 2.2
mackintosh 23.42
Mackintosh 23.42
mackle 2.28
Maclean 7.21
Macleod 29.3
Macmillan 18.32
MacNeice 15.32
Macpherson 12.12
Macquarie 24.5
macramé 7.3
Macready 16.1
macro 35.3
macrobiotic 24.16
macrobiotics 24.22
macroclimate 22.34
macrocosm 24.30
macrocosmic 24.19
macroeconomics
  24.22
macron 23.27
macrophage 7.12

macroscopic 24.16
macula 2.60
mad 1.9
Madagascan 2.35
Madagascar 2.9
madam 2.32
madame 1.22; 3.16
Madame Tussauds 25.10
madcap 1.37
madden 2.35
maddened 2.36
maddening 2.70
maddeningly 2.78
madder 2.10
maddest 2.48
madding 2.42
Maddox 2.22
Maddy 2.3
made 7.8
Madeira 14.2
Madeiran 14.9
Madeleine 17.29
Madeleine's 17.42
Madeley 8.1
mademoiselle 9.16
made-to-measure 10.14
made-up 37.41
Madge 1.15
Mad Hatter 2.10
madhouse 29.12
Madhya Pradesh 9.50
Madison 2.66
madly 2.5
madman 2.35
madness 2.46
Madoc 2.16
Madonna 24.13
Madras 1.40; 3.26
madrasah 2.14
Madrid 17.8
madrigal 2.64
madwoman 40.10
Maecenas 16.30
maelstrom 23.23; 35.34
maestro 35.12
Maeterlinck 17.30
Maeve 7.54
Mae West 9.49
Mafeking 2.70
maffick 2.18
Mafia 2.61
Mafikeng 9.36
mafioso 35.16
mag 1.13
magazine 15.26
Magdalen 26.18

Magdalena 8.8
Magdalene 15.26; 17.29; 26.18
Magdalenian 16.43
mage 7.12
Magellan 10.27
Magellanic 2.20
magenta 10.10
Maggie 2.2
Maggiore 26.1
maggot 2.50
maggoty 2.56
Magherafelt 9.23
Maghreb 9.1
Magi 21.3
magic 2.21
magical 2.64
magically 2.58
magician 18.33
Maginot 35.19
magisterial 14.19
magisterium 14.20
magistracy 2.78
magistral 18.22
magistrate 7.35
magistrateship 17.43
magistrature 27.1
maglev 9.56
magma 2.13
Magna Carta 4.10
magnanimity 18.57
magnanimous 2.71
magnanimously 2.78
magnate 2.50; 7.34
magnesia 16.9
magnesium 16.42
magnet 2.51
magnetic 10.15
magnetically 10.54
magnetics 10.16
magnetism 18.28
magnetizable 22.43
magnetization 8.40
magnetize 21.42
magnetized 21.48
magneto 35.10
magnetron 23.27
Magnificat 1.45
magnification 8.40
magnificence 18.71
magnificent 18.70
magnifico 35.19
magnified 21.12
magnifier 22.2
magnify 21.4
magniloquence 18.71
magniloquent 18.70
magnitude 41.9

magnolia 36.37
magnum 2.32
magnum opus 36.26
Magnus 2.46
Magog 23.11
Magoo 41.2
magpie 21.3
magpies 21.41
Magritte 15.35
Maguire 19.1
magus 8.67
Magus 8.67
Magwitch 17.7
Magyar 3.1
maharajah 4.14
maharani 4.6
maharishi 16.1
Mahatma 2.13
Mahayana 4.13
Mahdi 4.3
mah jong 23.31
Mahler 4.12
Mahler's 4.41
mahogany 24.54
Mahomet 24.49
Mahoney 36.1
mahonia 36.37
mahout 29.14
Maia 22.2
maid 7.8
Maida Vale 7.15
maiden 8.21
maidenhair 5.1
maidenhead 9.8
Maidenhead 9.8
maidenhood 39.4
maiden name 7.18
maids 7.9
maidservant 12.14
Maidstone 8.21; 35.36
Maigret 7.3
mail 7.15
mailable 8.79
mailbag 1.13
mailbags 1.14
mailbox 23.5
mailcoach 35.24
mailed 7.16
mailer 8.7
Mailer 8.7
mailing 8.62
mailings 8.65
mailman 1.24
mail order 26.4
mailshot 23.44
maim 7.18
maimed 7.19
maiming 8.63

main 7.21
mainbrace 7.30
Maine 7.21
mainframe 7.18
mainland 8.54
mainline 21.22
mainly 8.1
mainmast 3.30
mains 7.26
mainsail 7.15; 8.15
mainsheet 15.35
mainspring 8.62
mainstay 7.3
mainstream 15.20
maintain 7.21
maintainable 8.79
maintainer 8.8
maintenance 8.83
Maisie 8.1
maisonette 9.51
Maitland 8.54
maître d' 15.4
maître d'hôtel 9.16
maize 7.56
majestic 10.15
majestically 10.54
majesty 2.57
majolica 24.57
major 8.9
Major 8.9
Majorca 26.3
Majorcan 26.19
major-domo 35.16
majorette 9.51
majorettes 9.52
majority 24.56
majuscule 41.14
Makarios 23.39
make 7.6
make-believe 15.39
makeover 36.6
Makepeace 15.32
maker 8.4
makeshift 17.11
make the grade 7.8
make-up 37.41
makeweight 7.34
making 8.59
makings 8.65
Malabar 3.1
malabsorption 26.19
Malacca 2.9
Malachi 21.4
Malachy 2.56
maladaptive 2.53
maladjusted 38.20
maladjustment 38.32
maladminister 18.60

maladroit 33.13
malady 2.56
Málaga 2.60
Malagasy 2.7
malaise 7.56
malapert 11.24
Malaprop 23.36
malapropism 18.29
malapropos 35.19
malaria 6.16
malarial 6.17
malarkey 4.2
Malawi 4.5
Malay 7.2
Malaya 8.2
Malayan 8.21
Malaysia 8.78
Malaysian 8.81
Malcolm 2.32
malcontent 9.41
Malden 24.33; 26.19
Maldivian 18.67
male 7.15
malediction 18.33
malefactor 2.10
malefic 10.15
maleficence 10.68
maleficent 10.67
malevolence 10.68
malevolent 10.67
malfeasance 16.26
malfeasant 16.25
Malfi 2.4
malformation 8.24
malformed 25.21
malfunction 38.28
Malham 2.32
Mali 4.5
Malibu 41.4
malice 2.45
malicious 18.44
maliciously 18.56
malign 21.22
malignant 18.38
maligned 21.23
malignity 18.57
malinger 18.9
malingerer 18.60
malison 2.66
mall 1.16; 25.14
Mallaig 7.11
mallard 3.8
Mallarmé 7.3
malleability 18.58
malleable 2.79
mallet 2.51
mallow 35.3
malmsey 4.7

malnourished 38.41
malnourishment
  38.56
malnutrition 18.33
malocclusion 42.20
malodorous 36.42
Malone 35.36
Maloney 36.1
Malory 2.56
Malpas 2.46; 26.27
Malpighi 16.1
Malpighian 18.67
malpractice 2.45
malt 23.18; 25.17
Malta 24.10; 26.4
malted 24.24; 26.12
Maltese 15.43
Malteser 16.9
Malthusian 42.41
malting 24.40; 26.25
maltreat 15.35
maltreatment 16.25
malty 24.3; 26.1
Malvern 24.33; 26.19
Malvinas 16.30
mama 3.1
mamba 2.8
mambo 35.3
Mameluke 41.6
Mamie 8.1
mamilla 18.12
mamma 2.13
mammal 2.28
mammalian 8.81
mammals 2.30
mamma mia 16.2
mammary 2.56
mammogram 1.22
mammography 24.54
mammon 2.35
mammoth 2.52
mammy 2.6
man 1.24
manacle 2.64
manage 2.27
manageable 2.79
management 2.68
manager 2.60
manageress 9.47
managerial 14.19
managership 17.43
managing 2.70
Managua 2.12
mañana 4.13
Manassas 2.46
Manasseh 2.7
manatee 15.4
Manchester 2.60

Manchu 41.2
Manchuria 28.18
Manchurian 28.21
manciple 2.64
Mancunian 42.41
mandala 2.60
Mandalay 7.4
mandamus 8.67
mandarin 17.29
mandarins 17.42
mandate 7.34
mandatory 2.56
Mandela 10.12
Mandeville 17.15
mandible 2.64
mandibular 18.60
mandolin 17.29
mandolins 17.42
mandorla 26.6
mandragora 2.60
mandrake 7.6
mandrel 2.28
Mandy 2.3
mane 7.21
manège 7.14
Manet 7.3
Manfred 9.8
manful 2.28; 39.7
manga 2.9
manganese 15.45
mange 7.23
mangel 2.28
mangelwurzel 12.8
manger 8.9
mangetout 41.2
mangier 8.78
mangiest 8.86
mangle 2.28
mangled 2.29
mango 35.3
mangold 35.31
mangosteen 15.26
mangrove 35.50
mangy 8.1
manhandle 2.28
Manhattan 2.35
manhole 35.30
manhood 39.4
man-hour 31.1
manhunt 37.40
mania 8.78
maniac 1.3
maniacal 22.43
manic 2.20
Manichaean 16.22
Manichaeus 16.30
manicure 27.1
manicured 27.2

manicuring 28.11
manicurist 28.14
manifest 9.49
manifestation 8.40
manifesto 35.7
manifold 35.31
manila 18.12
Manila 18.12
manioc 23.3
maniple 2.64
manipulate 7.41
manipulation 8.32
manipulative 17.54
Manitoba 36.3
Manitoban 36.20
mankind 21.23
manky 2.2
Manley 2.5
manlike 21.7
manly 2.5
man-made 7.8
Mann 1.24
manna 2.13
manned 1.28
mannequin 17.29
mannequins 17.42
manner 2.13
mannered 2.25
mannerism 18.28
mannerist 2.73
mannerly 2.56
manners 2.55
Mannheim 21.19
manning 2.42
Manning 2.42
mannish 2.49
manoeuvrable 42.39
manoeuvre 42.6
manometer 24.57
manor 2.13
manor house 29.12
manorial 26.41
manpower 31.1
manqué 7.3
mansard 3.8
manse 1.31
Mansell 2.28
manservant 12.14
Mansfield 15.18
mansion 2.35
mansions 2.39
manslaughter 26.4
Manson 2.35
manta 2.10
mantelpiece 15.32
mantic 2.17
mantilla 18.12
mantis 2.45

mantissa 18.14
mantle 2.28
man-to-man 1.24
Mantovani 4.6
mantra 2.12
mantrap 1.37
Mantua 2.60
manual 2.64
manually 2.59; 2.78
Manuel 9.16
manufacture 2.14
manufacturer 2.60
manumission 18.33
manumit 17.51
manure 27.1
manured 27.2
manuscript 17.45
Manutius 42.46
Manx 1.26
Manxman 2.35
Manxwoman 40.10
many 10.6
manzanilla 18.12
Mao 29.1
Maoism 18.27
Maoist 30.15
Maori 30.1
Maoris 30.20
Mao's 29.17
Mao Tse-tung 39.10
map 1.37
maple 8.15
mappable 2.64
Mappa Mundi 40.1
mapper 2.8
mapping 2.42
maps 1.38
maquis 15.2
mar 3.1
marabou 41.4
marabout 41.4
maraca 2.9
maracas 2.55
Maradona 24.13
maraschino 35.10
marasmus 2.46
marathon 2.66
Marathon 2.66
maraud 25.9
marauder 26.4
marauders 26.36
marauding 26.25
Marbella 8.2
marble 4.19
marbled 4.20
marbles 4.21
marbling 4.29
Marburg 11.9

marc 3.3
Marc 3.3
marcasite 21.34
Marcel 9.16
Marcella 10.12
Marcello 35.7
Marcellus 10.42
march 3.6
March 3.6
marched 3.7
marcher 4.14
marches 4.41
Marches 4.41
marching 4.29
marchioness 9.47
Marcia 4.44
Marciano 35.4
Marco 35.4
Marconi 36.1
Marco Polo 35.16
Marcos 23.39
Marcus 4.32
Mardi Gras 3.1
mardy 4.3
mare 5.1
mare 7.3
Marengo 35.7
marg 3.12
Margaret 4.37
margarine 15.26
Margarita 16.5
Margate 7.34
Margaux 35.2
margay 7.3
marge 3.12
margin 4.23
marginal 4.47
marginalia 8.78
marginalize 21.47
marginally 4.56
margins 4.26
Margot 35.4
Margot's 35.52
margrave 7.54
marguerite 15.35
Marguerite 15.35
maria 4.44
Maria 16.2; 22.2
mariachi 4.7
Marian 2.66
Mariana 4.13
Marianne 1.24
Marianne's 1.36
Maria Theresa 8.9
Marie 4.5; 15.2
Marie Celeste 9.49
Marie's 15.43
marigold 35.31

marijuana 4.13
marimba 18.8
marina 16.8
Marina 16.8
marinade 7.8
marinate 7.35
marination 8.24
marine 15.24
mariner 2.60
Mariolatry 24.54
Mariology 24.55
Marion 2.66
marionette 9.51
marital 2.64
maritime 21.19
Maritimer 22.8
Maritimes 21.21
Marius 2.71; 6.22
marjoram 4.49
Marjorie 4.42
mark 3.3
Mark 3.3
markdown 29.5
marked 3.5
markedly 4.42
marker 4.9
market 4.38
marketable 4.57
marketed 4.45
marketeer 13.1
marketing 4.52
marketplace 7.30
market stall 25.14
Markham 4.22
marking 4.29
markings 4.30
markka 4.9
Markov 23.9
Markova 36.6
Marks 3.4
Mark's 3.4
marksman 4.24
marksmanship 17.43
markswoman 40.10
Mark Twain 7.21
mark-up 37.41
marl 3.14
Marlborough 4.43; 26.38
Marlene 8.8; 15.25
Marley 4.5
marlin 4.23
marling 4.29
Marlon 4.24
Marlow 35.4
Marlowe 35.4
Marmaduke 41.6
marmalade 7.8

marmalize 21.42
Marmara 4.43
Marmion 4.50
Marmite® 21.33
marmoreal 26.41
marmoset 9.51
marmot 4.37
Marne 3.19
Marner 4.13
maroon 41.19
marooned 41.20
Marple 4.19
marque 3.3
marquee 15.2
Marquesan 8.21
Marquesas 8.67
marquess 4.31
marquetry 4.42
marquis 4.31; 15.2
Marquis de Sade 3.8
marquise 15.43
Marrakech 9.50
marram 2.32
marred 3.8
marriage 2.27
marriageable 2.79
married 2.24
marring 4.29
Marriott 2.74
marron 2.35
marron glacé 7.3
marrow 35.3
marrowbone 35.36
marrow fat 1.45
marry 2.5
Marryat 2.74
Mars 3.37
Marsala 4.12
Marsden 4.24
Marseillaise 7.56
Marseilles 7.2
marsh 3.31
Marsha 4.14
marshal 4.19
Marshall 4.19
marshalled 4.20
Marshalsea 15.4
marshes 4.41
marshland 4.25
marshmallow 35.3
marshmallows 35.52
marshy 4.7
Marston 4.24
marsupial 42.39
mart 3.32
Martel 9.16
Martello 35.7
marten 4.23

Martha 4.11
martial 4.19
Martial 4.19
Martian 4.24
martin 4.23
Martin 4.23
Martina 16.8
Martine 15.24
Martineau 35.19
martinet 9.51
martingale 7.15
Martini® 16.1
Martinique 15.7
Martinmas 1.40
martins 4.26
Martinu 41.4
martlet 4.38
martyr 4.10
martyrdom 4.49
martyred 4.17
marvel 4.19
Marvell 4.19
marvellous 4.53
Marvin 4.23
Marx 3.4
Marxism 18.27
Marxist 4.33
Mary 6.1
Maryland 1.28
Marylebone 4.50; 35.36
marzipan 1.24
Masai 21.3
masala 4.12
Mascagni 4.5
mascara 4.12
mascarpone 36.1
mascot 2.50; 23.44
mascots 23.45
masculine 17.29
masculinity 18.57
masculinize 21.47
Masefield 15.18
maser 8.9
Maserati 4.3
mash 1.43
MASH 1.43
Masham 2.32
mashed 1.44
masher 2.14
mashie 2.7
mashing 2.42
mask 3.27
masked 3.28
masker 4.9
masking 4.29
masking tape 7.27
masochism 18.28

masochist 2.73
masochistic 18.16
mason 8.21
Mason 8.21
masonic 24.19
masonry 8.76
Masorete 15.35
Masoretic 10.15
masque 3.27
masquerade 7.8
masquerader 8.5
mass 1.40
Mass 1.40; 3.26
Massachusetts 42.32
massacre 2.60
massage 3.13
massed 1.42
Massenet 7.4
masses 2.55
masseur 11.1
masseuse 11.29
Massey 2.7
massif 15.13
Massif Central 3.14
massing 2.42
Massinger 2.60
massive 2.53
massively 2.58
Masson 2.35
mass-produce 41.24
mass-produced 41.25
massy 2.7
mast 3.30
mastectomy 10.53
master 4.10
masterclass 3.26
masterful 4.47; 39.7
masterly 4.42
mastermind 21.23
masterpiece 15.32
masters 4.41
Masters 4.41
mastersinger 18.13
masterstroke 35.21
masterwork 11.4
mastery 4.42
masthead 9.8
mastic 2.17
masticate 7.35
mastication 8.24
mastiff 17.10
mastitis 22.28
mastodon 2.66; 23.27
Mastroianni 4.6
masturbate 7.35
masturbation 8.24
mat 1.45
Matabele 16.1

matador 25.4
matadors 25.35
Mata Hari 4.5
match 1.7
matchable 2.64
matchbox 23.5
matched 1.8
matching 2.42
matchless 2.46
matchlock 23.3
matchmaker 8.4
matchmaking 8.59
matchstick 2.17
matchsticks 2.23
matchwood 39.4
mate 7.32
maté 7.3
mated 8.13
mater 8.5
materfamilias 1.40
material 14.19
materialism 18.29
materialist 17.49
materialistic 18.16
materiality 2.57
materialization 8.53
materialize 21.47
maternal 12.8
maternally 12.29
maternity 12.29
mates 7.50
matey 8.1
mathematical 2.64
mathematically 2.58
mathematician 18.33
mathematics 2.23
Mather 2.11
Mathieson 2.66
maths 1.48
Matilda 18.10
matinée 7.4
mating 8.60
matins 2.38
Matisse 15.32
Matlock 23.3
Mato Grosso 35.13
matriarch 3.3
matriarchal 4.19
matriarchy 4.2
matric 17.3
matrices 15.45
matricide 21.12
matriculate 7.41
matriculation 8.32
matrilineal 18.64
matrimonial 36.38
matrimony 2.78
matrix 8.11

matron 8.21
matronly 8.76
matronymic 18.16
mats 1.46
matt 1.45
Matt 1.45
matted 2.25
matter 2.10
Matterhorn 25.22
matter-of-fact 1.6
Matthew 41.3
Matthews 41.33
Matthias 22.29
matting 2.42
mattock 2.16
mattress 2.46
Matt's 1.46
maturation 8.24
mature 27.1
matured 27.2
matures 27.3
maturing 28.11
maturity 28.17
matzo 35.3
Maud 25.9
maudlin 26.18
Maudling 26.25
Maudsley 26.1
Maugham 25.20
maul 25.14
mauler 26.6
mauling 26.25
mauls 25.19
Mau Mau 29.1
maunder 26.4
Maundy 26.1
Maureen 15.25
Mauretania 8.78
Mauriac 1.3
Maurice 24.42
Mauritania 8.78
Mauritanian 8.81
Mauritian 18.33
Mauritius 18.44
Mauser 30.2
mausolea 16.2
mausoleum 16.20
mauve 35.50
maverick 17.3
Mavis 8.66
maw 25.1
mawkish 26.30
max 1.4
Max 1.4
maxi 2.7
maxilla 18.12
maxillofacial 8.15
maxim 2.31

Meena 16.8
meerkat 1.45
meerschaum 14.7
meet 15.35
meeter 16.5
meeting 16.27
meeting house 29.12
meetings 16.28
Meg 9.12
mega 10.9
megabit 17.51
megabits 17.52
megabucks 37.4
megabyte 21.34
megabytes 21.35
megaflop 23.36
megahertz 11.25
megalith 17.53
megalithic 18.16
megalomania 8.78
megalomaniac 1.3
megalopolis 17.46
Megan 10.27
Megan's 10.32
megaphone 35.36
megaphonic 24.19
megastar 3.1
megathere 13.1
megaton 37.31
megavolt 35.32
Megawati 24.3
megawatt 23.44
megillah 18.12
Meg's 9.13
Mehta 8.5
meiosis 36.25
Meissen 22.20
Meistersinger 18.13
Mekong 23.31
Mel 9.16
melamine 15.26
melancholia 36.37
melancholic 24.18
melancholy 10.78;
24.5
Melanesia 16.9; 16.40
Melanesian 16.22;
16.43
Melanie 10.53
melanin 17.29
melanism 18.28
melanoma 36.8
melatonin 36.19
Melba 10.8
Melbourne 10.27;
25.22
Melburnian 12.34
Melchett 10.48

Melchior 25.4
Melchizedek 9.2
meld 9.19
Meldrum 10.25
melee 7.3
Melina 16.8
Melissa 18.14
mellifluence 18.71
mellifluent 18.70
mellifluous 18.74
Mellor 10.12
Mellors 10.52
mellow 35.7
mellowed 35.25
mellower 36.2
mellowest 36.28
mellowness 36.26
mellows 35.52
Melly 10.5
melodeon 36.40
melodic 24.16
melodies 10.77
melodious 36.42
melodrama 4.13
melodramatic 2.17
melodramatically
2.58
melody 10.53
melon 10.27
melons 10.32
Melos 23.39
Melrose 35.52
Mel's 9.27
melt 9.23
meltdown 29.5
melter 10.10
melting 10.36
melting pot 23.44
Melton 10.27
meltwater 26.4
Melville 17.15
Melvin 10.26
member 10.8
memberless 10.70
members 10.52
membership 17.43
membrane 7.21
membranous 10.70
memento 35.7
memento mori 26.1
memo 35.7
memoir 3.1
memoirs 3.37
memorabilia 18.61
memorable 10.60;
10.79
memorably 10.53;
10.78

memoranda 2.10
memorandum 2.32
memorial 26.41
memorialize 21.47
memories 10.77
memorizable 22.43
memorization 8.43
memorize 21.43
memory 10.53
Memphis 10.41
memsahib 3.2; 17.1
men 9.32
menace 10.41
menaced 10.44
menacingly 10.78
ménage 3.13
ménage à trois 3.1
menagerie 2.56
Menai Strait 7.38
Menander 2.10
menarche 4.2
Mencken 10.27
mend 9.35
mendable 10.60
mendacious 8.67
mendacity 2.57
mended 10.18
Mendel 10.21
Mendelian 16.43
Mendelssohn 10.64
mender 10.10
mendicant 10.67
mendicants 10.68
mending 10.36
Mendips 17.44
Mendoza 36.9
Menelaus 8.67
menfolk 35.21
menial 16.41
meningeal 16.17
meninges 15.44
meningitis 22.28
meniscus 18.44
menopausal 26.15
menopause 25.35
menorah 26.6
Menotti 24.3
Mensa 10.14
menses 15.44
Menshevik 17.3
mens rea 8.2
menstrual 10.60
menstruate 7.38
menstruation 8.28
mensuration 8.28
menswear 5.1
mental 10.21
mentality 2.57

mentally 10.53
menthol 23.15
mentholated 8.13
mention 10.28
mentionable 10.79
mentioned 10.29
Mentmore 25.3
mentor 25.3
mentoring 10.69
menu 41.3
Menuhin 17.29
Menzies 10.51; 18.43
meow 29.1
meows 29.17
MEP 15.4
Mephistophelean
16.43
Mephistopheles 15.45
mephitic 18.16
mercantile 21.16
Mercator 8.5
Mercedes 8.74; 15.44
Mercedes-Benz 9.43
mercenary 12.29
mercer 12.2
Mercer 12.2
mercerization 8.44
mercerize 21.43
mercerized 21.48
mercery 12.29
merchandise 21.29;
21.43
merchandising 22.26
merchant 12.14
Merchant 12.14
merchantable 12.41
merchants 12.15
Mercia 12.31
mercies 12.28
merciful 12.32; 39.7
mercifully 12.29; 40.1
merciless 12.37
Mercouri 28.1
mercurial 28.19
mercuric 28.3
mercurous 28.12
mercury 12.29
Mercury 12.29
mercy 12.1
mere 13.1
Meredith 17.53
merely 14.1
meretricious 18.44
merganser 2.14
merge 11.10
merger 12.2
merging 12.16
meridian 18.67

microprocessor 10.14
microscope 35.40
microscopic 24.16
microscopical 24.61
microscopically 24.56
microscopy 24.54
microsecond 10.29
Microsoft® 23.10
microsurgery 12.29
microwavable 8.79
microwave 7.54
microwaves 7.55
micturate 7.41
micturition 18.33
mid 17.8
midair 5.1
Midas 22.29
midbrain 7.21
midday 7.2
midden 18.32
middle 18.22
middlebrow 29.1
middle-class 3.26
Middle-earth 11.26
middleman 1.24
middlemost 35.43
Middlesbrough 18.60
Middlesex 9.3
middle-sized 21.48
Middleton 18.67
middleweight 7.41
Middlewich 17.7
middling 18.40
midfield 15.18
midfielder 16.5
midge 17.14
midges 18.55
midget 18.50
midi 18.3
Midian 18.67
midland 18.34
Midlands 18.35
midlife 21.14
Midlothian 36.40
midmost 35.43
midnight 21.33
midpoint 33.10
midrib 17.1
midriff 17.10
midst 17.9
midstream 15.20
midsummer 38.13
midterm 11.13
midway 7.2
midweek 15.7
Midwest 9.49
Midwestern 10.27
midwife 21.14

midwifery 18.56
midwinter 18.10
midwives 21.38
midyear 13.1
mien 15.23
Mies van der Rohe 36.2
miff 17.10
miffed 17.11
miffy 18.4
MiG 17.12
might 21.31
mightier 22.42
mightiest 22.48
mightily 22.40
mightn't 22.24
mighty 22.1
migraine 7.21
migrant 22.24
migrants 22.25
migrate 7.33
migration 8.23
migratory 8.76
Miguel 9.16
Mikado 35.4
mike 21.7
Mike 21.7
Mike's 21.8
Míkonos 23.39
milady 8.1
Milan 1.24
Milanese 15.45
milch 17.17
mild 21.17
mildew 41.3
mildewy 42.1
mildly 22.1
mildness 22.29
Mildred 18.19
mile 21.16
mileage 22.15
mileometer 24.57
milepost 35.43
miler 22.7
miles 21.18
Miles 21.18
milestone 35.36
Miletus 16.30
Milford 18.19
Milford Haven 8.21
milieu 11.1
militancy 18.80
militant 18.70
militants 18.71
militarism 18.29
militarist 17.49
militarization 8.53
militarize 21.47

military 18.57
militate 7.41
militia 18.14
militiaman 18.67
milk 17.16
milker 18.9
milkier 18.61
milkiest 18.76
milking 18.40
milkmaid 7.8
milkman 18.32
milk round 29.6
milksop 23.36
milk teeth 15.37
milk tooth 41.29
milkwort 11.24
milky 18.2
Milky Way 7.4
mill 17.15
Mill 17.15
Millais 7.3
Millbank 1.25
milled 17.18
millenarian 6.19
millenarianism 18.29
millenary 10.53
millennia 10.57
millennial 10.60
millennium 10.63
miller 18.12
Miller 18.12
millesimal 10.60
millet 18.50
Millet 7.3
milliard 3.8
millibar 3.1
Millicent 18.70
Millie 18.5
Milligan 18.67
milligram 1.22
millilitre 16.5
millimetre 16.5
milliner 18.60
millinery 18.57
milling 18.40
million 18.32; 18.67
millionaire 5.1
millions 18.37; 18.69
millionth 18.72
millipede 15.11
millisecond 10.29
millpond 23.30
millrace 7.30
mills 17.23
Mills 17.23
millstone 35.36
millstream 15.20
millwheel 15.17

mill worker 12.2
millwright 21.33
Milne 17.20
Milner 18.13
Milo 35.12
milord 25.9
Milosevic 17.7
milt 17.21
Milton 18.32
Miltonian 36.40
Miltonic 24.19
Milton Keynes 15.29
Milwall 25.14
Milwaukee 15.3; 26.1
mime 21.19
mimed 21.20
Mimeograph® 1.11; 3.9
mimer 22.8
mimesis 16.29
mimetic 10.15
Mimi 16.1
mimic 18.16
mimicked 17.6
mimicker 18.60
mimicry 18.57
mimics 18.17
miming 22.26
mimosa 36.9
mimsy 18.7
mimulus 18.74
min 17.29
minaret 9.51
minatory 18.56
mince 17.38
mincemeat 15.35
mince pie 21.2
mince pies 21.40
mincer 18.14
Minch 17.33
mincing 18.40
mind 21.23
Mindanao 29.1
mind-bending 10.36
mind-blowing 36.24
mind-boggling 24.40
minder 22.5
minders 22.39
mindful 22.16; 39.7
minding 22.26
mindless 22.29
mind-numbing 38.34
mind-read 15.11
mind-reader 16.5
mind-reading 16.27
mind-set 9.51
Mindy 18.3
mine 21.22

mined 21.23
minefield 15.18
Minehead 9.8
minelayer 8.2
miner 22.8
mineral 18.22; 18.64
mineralize 21.47
mineralogical 24.61
mineralogist 2.73
mineralogy 2.56
miners 22.39
Minerva 12.2
mines 21.25
mine shaft 3.10
minestrone 36.1
minesweeper 16.3
Ming 17.35
minge 17.37
mingle 18.22
mingled 18.23
mingler 18.12
mingy 18.7
mini 18.6
miniature 18.60
miniaturization 8.53
miniaturize 21.47
miniaturized 21.48
minibar 3.1
minibus 37.43
minicab 1.1
minicabs 1.2
minicom 23.23
minidish 17.50
minidress 9.47
minim 18.25
minima 18.60
minimal 18.64
minimalism 18.29
minimalist 17.49
minimalistic 18.16
minimally 18.80
minimax 1.4
minimization 8.46
minimize 21.44
minimum 18.66
mining 22.26
minion 18.32
minions 18.37
minipill 17.15
miniseries 14.17; 15.44
miniskirt 11.24
minister 18.60
ministerial 14.19
ministership 17.43
ministration 8.32
ministry 18.57
minivan 1.24
miniver 18.60

mink 17.30
minke 18.2; 18.9
Minneapolis 17.46
Minnelli 10.5
minneola 36.7
Minnesinger 18.13
Minnesota 36.5
Minnesotan 36.20
Minnie 18.6
minnow 35.11
minnows 35.52
Minoan 36.20
Minogue 35.28
Minolta 24.10
minor 22.8
Minorca 26.3
Minorcan 26.19
minorities 24.75
minority 24.56
Minotaur 25.4
minster 18.10
minstrel 18.22
minstrelsy 18.56
mint 17.39
mintage 18.21
mint condition 18.33
minted 18.19
mintier 18.61
mintiest 18.76
Minton 18.32
minty 18.3
minuet 9.51
minus 22.29
minuscule 41.14
minute 18.50
minute 41.27
minutely 42.1
minutia 42.38
minutiae 15.4; 21.4
minx 17.31
Miocene 15.26
Mir 13.1
mirabelle 9.16
miracle 18.64
miraculous 2.71
miraculously 2.78
mirage 3.13
Miranda 2.10
mire 19.1
Miriam 18.66
Mirren 18.32
mirror 18.12
mirth 11.26
mirthless 12.19
miry 20.1
misadventure 10.14
misaligned 21.23
misalignment 22.24

misalliance 22.25
misanthrope 35.40
misanthropic 24.16
misanthropy 2.56
misapplication 8.46
misapply 21.4
misapprehend 9.35
misapprehension
10.28
misappropriate 7.47
misappropriation
8.37
misbegot 23.44
misbegotten 24.33
misbehave 7.54
misbehaves 7.55
misbehaving 8.61
misbehaviour 8.7
misbelief 15.13
miscalculate 7.35
miscalculation 8.46
miscarriage 2.27
miscarried 2.24
miscarry 2.5
miscast 3.30
miscellanea 8.78
miscellaneous 8.85
miscellany 10.53
mischance 3.22
mischief-maker 8.4
mischievous 18.74
mischievously 18.80
miscible 18.64
misconceive 15.39
misconceived 15.40
misconception 10.28
misconduct 37.5
misconstruction
38.28
misconstrue 41.4
misconstrued 41.9
miscount 29.11
miscreant 18.70
miscue 41.2
misdeal 15.17
misdeed 15.11
misdeeds 15.12
misdemeanour 16.8
misdemeanours 16.37
misdiagnose 35.52
misdiagnosed 35.53
misdiagnosis 36.25
misdial 19.3
misdirect 9.5
mise en scène 9.32
miser 22.9
miserable 18.64; 18.81
miserably 18.56

misère 5.1
Miserere 6.1
miserly 22.40
misers 22.39
misery 18.56
misfile 21.16
misfire 19.1
misfired 19.2
misfiring 20.7
misfit 18.50
misfortune 26.19;
41.19
misgiving 18.40
misgovern 38.28
misguide 21.10
misguided 22.13
misguidedly 22.40
mishandle 2.28
mishap 1.37
mishear 13.1
misheard 11.7
mishit 17.51
mishmash 1.43
misinform 25.20
misinformation 8.46
misinterpret 12.25
misjudge 37.15
misjudgment 38.32
mislaid 7.8
mislay 7.2
mislead 15.11
misleading 16.27
misleadingly 16.38
misled 9.8
mismanage 2.27
mismanagement 2.68
mismatch 1.7
mismatch 1.7
mismatched 1.8
misnomer 36.8
misogynist 24.72
misogynous 24.70
misogyny 24.56
misplace 7.30
misplaced 7.31
misplacement 8.56
misplay 7.2
misprint 17.39
misprize 21.40
mispronounce 29.9
mispronounced 29.10
mispronunciation
8.38
misquote 35.45
misquoted 36.12
misquoting 36.24
misread 9.8
misread 15.11

misremember 10.8
misreport 25.31
misrepresent 9.41
misrepresentation 8.43
misrule 41.14
miss 17.46
Miss 17.46
missable 18.64
missal 18.22
missed 17.49
Missenden 18.67
misses 18.55
misshape 7.27
misshapen 8.21
missile 21.16
missiles 21.18
missing 18.40
mission 18.33
missionary 18.56
missions 18.37
Mississippi 18.1
Mississippian 18.67
missive 18.53
Missouri 28.1
Missourian 28.21
misspell 9.16
misspelling 10.36
misspelt 9.23
misspend 9.35
misspent 9.41
Miss Piggy 18.2
misstate 7.33
misstatement 8.56
missus 18.43; 18.55
missy 18.7
mist 17.49
mistakable 8.79
mistake 7.6
mistaken 8.21
mistakenly 8.76
mistaking 8.59
mister 18.10
mistier 18.61
mistiest 18.76
mistime 21.19
misting 18.40
mistle 18.22
mistle thrush 37.46
mistletoe 35.19
mistook 39.1
mistral 3.14; 18.22
mistranslation 8.32
mistreat 15.35
mistress 18.44
mistrial 19.3
mistrust 37.45
misty 18.3

mistype 21.26
mistyped 21.28
misunderstand 1.28
misunderstanding 2.42
misunderstood 39.4
misuse 41.24
misuse 41.33
misused 41.34
misuser 42.9
Mitch 17.7
Mitchell 18.22
Mitchum 18.26
mite 21.31
Mitford 18.19
Mithras 1.40
Mithridates 15.44
mitigate 7.41
mitigated 8.13
mitigation 8.32
mitochondria 24.58
mitosis 36.25
mitral 22.16
mitre 22.5
mitred 22.13
Mitsubishi 18.7
mitt 17.51
mitten 18.32
mittens 18.37
mitts 17.52
Mitzi 18.7
mix 17.4
mixable 18.64
mixed 17.5
mixed-up 37.41
mixer 18.14
mixing 18.40
mixture 18.14
mix-up 18.42; 37.41
mizzen 18.33
mizzenmast 3.30
mizzle 18.22
m'lud 37.8
mnemonic 24.19
mnemonics 24.22
Mnemosyne 24.56
Mo 35.1
mo' 35.1
moa 36.2
Moab 1.1
Moabite 21.34
moan 35.36
moaned 35.37
moaner 36.8
moaning 36.24
moat 35.45
mob 23.1
Mobberley 24.54

mobcap 1.37
Moberly 36.35
Mobil® 17.15; 36.15
mobile 21.16
Mobile 15.17
mobile phone 35.36
mobility 18.58
mobilization 8.50
mobilize 21.45
mobilized 21.48
Möbius strip 17.43
mobs 23.2
mobster 24.10
Mobutu 41.3
Moby Dick 17.3
moccasin 17.29
moccasins 17.42
mocha 24.9
mock 23.3
mocked 23.6
mocker 24.9
mockers 24.53
mockery 24.54
mocking 24.40
mockingbird 11.7
mock-up 37.41
mod 23.8
MOD 15.4
modal 36.15
modality 2.57
mod cons 23.35
mode 35.25
model 24.27
modelled 24.28
modeller 24.57
modem 9.28
Modena 24.57
moderate 7.43
moderate 24.73
moderately 24.54
moderation 8.34
moderato 35.4
moderator 8.5
modern 24.33
modernism 18.28
modernist 24.72
modernistic 18.16
modernity 12.29
modernization 8.48
modernize 21.45
modernized 21.48
modernizer 22.9
modest 24.45
modestly 24.56
modesty 24.56
modicum 24.63
modification 8.48
modified 21.12

modifier 22.2
modifies 21.45
modify 21.4
Modigliani 4.6
modish 36.29
modiste 15.33
modular 24.57
modulate 7.43
modulation 8.34
module 41.14
modules 41.16
modulus 24.70
modus operandi 2.3; 21.3
modus vivendi 10.3; 21.3
Moffatt 24.48
Mogadishu 41.3
Mogadon® 23.27
moggy 24.2
mogul 36.15; 37.16
Mogul 37.16
mohair 5.1
Mohammed 2.24
Mohammedan 2.66
Mohammedanism 18.29
Mohawk 25.6
mohican 16.22
Mohican 16.22
moider 34.2
moiety 34.14
moil 33.6
Moira 34.2
moire 3.1
moiré 7.3
moist 33.12
moisten 34.8
moister 34.2
moisture 34.2
moisturize 21.45
moisturizer 22.9
moisturizing 22.26
Mojave 4.4
moke 35.21
molar 36.7
molars 36.34
molasses 2.55
Moldau 29.1
Moldavia 8.78
Moldavian 8.81
Moldova 36.6
Moldovan 36.20
mole 35.30
molecular 10.56
molecule 41.14
molehill 17.15
molehills 17.23

mounts 29.9
mourn 25.22
Mourne 25.22
mourned 25.24
mourner 26.7
mourners 26.36
mournful 26.15; 39.7
mournfully 26.37
mournfulness 26.47
mourning 26.25
mouse 29.12
mousehole 35.30
Mousehole 30.6
mouser 30.2
mousetail 7.15
mousetrap 1.37
moussaka 4.9
mousse 41.24
moustache 3.31
Mousterian 14.21
mousy 30.1
mouth 29.16
mouthbreeder 16.5
mouthbrooder 42.5
mouther 30.2
mouthful 39.7
mouthpart 3.32
mouthparts 3.33
mouthpiece 15.32
mouth-to-mouth 29.16
mouthwash 23.42
mouthy 30.1
movable 42.39
move 41.31
moved 41.32
movement 42.22
movements 42.23
mover 42.6
movie 42.1
movies 42.35
Movietone® 35.36
moving 42.24
Moviola® 36.7
mow 35.1
mowable 36.38
mowed 35.25
mower 36.2
mowers 36.34
Mowgli 36.1
Mowlem 36.18
mown 35.36
MOX 23.5
Moyle 33.6
Moynihan 1.24; 34.17
Mozambican 16.22
Mozambique 15.7
Mozart 3.32

Mozartian 4.50
Mozart's 3.33
mozzarella 10.12
MP 15.2
MPs 15.43
Mr 18.10
Mr Blobby 24.1
Mr Chips 17.44
Mrs 18.55
Mr Whippy 18.1
Ms 17.56
MSc 15.4
MS-DOS® 23.39
mu 41.1
much 37.6
mucilage 17.14
mucilaginous 2.71
muck 37.3
mucker 38.9
muckier 38.49
muckiest 38.61
muckle 38.23
muckrake 7.6
muckraker 8.4
mucky 38.2
mucosa 36.9
mucose 35.52
mucous 42.26
mucus 42.26
mud 37.8
mudbank 1.25
mudbath 3.34
mudcat 1.45
muddied 38.19
muddier 38.49
muddiest 38.61
muddle 38.23
muddled 38.24
muddleheaded 10.18
muddler 38.12
muddy 38.3
mudfish 38.40
mudflap 1.37
mudflaps 1.38
mud flat 1.45
mud flats 1.46
mudguard 3.8
mudlark 3.3
mudpack 1.3
mudskipper 18.8
mudslinger 18.13
mudslinging 18.40
muesli 42.1
muezzin 10.26
muff 37.10
muffin 38.27
muffins 38.30
muffle 38.23

muffled 38.24
muffler 38.12
muffs 37.11
mufti 38.3
mug 37.14
Mugabe 4.1
mugful 39.7
mugger 38.9
Muggeridge 17.14
muggier 38.49
muggiest 38.61
mugging 38.34
muggins 38.35
muggins 38.30
muggy 38.2
mug shot 23.44
mugwump 37.29
Muhammad 2.25
Muhammad Ali 4.5; 15.2
Muir 27.1
Muirhead 9.8
mujaheddin 15.24
mukluk 37.3
mulatto 35.3
mulberry 38.5; 38.47
mulch 37.20
mulct 37.19
Muldoon 41.19
mule 41.14
mules 41.16
muleteer 13.1
mulish 42.29
mull 37.16
Mull 37.16
mullah 40.2
Mullen 38.28
Muller 38.12
Müller 40.2
mullet 38.43
Mulligan 38.54
mulligatawny 26.1
mulligrubs 37.2
mullion 38.54
Mulroney 36.1
multichannel 2.28
multicolour 38.12
multicoloured 38.20
multicultural 38.52
multiculturalism 18.29
multidisciplinary 18.56
multifaceted 2.63
multifarious 6.22
multifold 35.31
multiform 25.20
multifunction 38.28

multifunctional 38.52
multihull 37.16
multilateral 2.28; 2.64
multilingual 18.22
multimedia 16.40
multimillionaire 5.1
multinational 2.64
multipack 1.3
multiphase 7.56
multiple 38.52
multiplex 9.3
multiplication 8.51
multiplicity 18.57
multiplied 21.12
multiplier 22.2
multiplies 21.46
multiply 21.4
multipurpose 12.19
multiracial 8.15
multirole 35.30
multiskilling 18.40
multistage 7.12
multistorey 26.1
multitask 3.27
multitasking 4.29
multitrack 1.3
multitude 41.9
multitudinous 42.46
mum 37.27
Mumbai 21.2
mumble 38.23
mumbler 38.12
Mumbles 38.25
mumbling 38.34
mumbo jumbo 35.17
mumchance 3.22
mummer 38.13
mummers 38.45
Mummerset 9.51
mummery 38.47
mummification 8.51
mummified 21.12
mummifies 21.46
mummify 21.4
mumming 38.34
mummy 38.6
mumps 37.30
mumsy 38.7
munch 37.35
Munchausen 30.8
munchies 38.46
munching 38.34
mundane 7.21
Mungo 35.17
Munich 42.11
municipal 18.64
municipality 2.57
munificence 18.71

munificent 18.70
muniment 42.43
munition 18.33
munitions 18.37
Munro 35.2
Munster 38.10
Münster 40.2
muntjac 1.3
muppet 38.43
mural 28.4
Murchison 12.34
murder 12.2
murdered 12.5
murderer 12.30
murderess 9.47; 12.37
murderous 12.37
Murdoch 23.3
Murgatroyd 33.4
Muriel 28.19
Murillo 35.11
murk 11.4
murkier 12.31
murkiest 12.39
murkiness 12.37
murky 12.1
Murmansk 1.32
murmur 12.2
murmured 12.5
murmurer 12.30
Murphy 12.1
murrain 38.27
Murray 38.5
Murrumbidgee 15.3;
  18.7
murther 12.2
Muscadet 7.4
muscadine 17.29
Muscat 1.45
muscatel 9.16
muscle 38.23
muscleman 1.24
musclemen 9.32
muscles 38.25
muscly 38.5
muscovado 35.4
Muscovite 21.34
Muscovy 38.47
muscular 38.48
musculature 27.1
muse 41.33
Muse 41.33
mused 41.34
museum 16.20
Museveni 8.1
Musgrove 35.50
mush 37.46; 39.13
mushier 38.49
mushiest 38.61

mushroom 39.9; 41.17
mushy 38.7
music 42.11
musical 42.39
musically 42.36
musician 18.33
musicianly 18.56
musicians 18.37
musicianship 17.43
musicologist 24.72
musicology 24.55
musing 42.24
musk 37.44
muskellunge 37.38
musket 38.43
musketeer 13.1
muskmelon 10.27
muskrat 1.45
musky 38.2
Muslim 40.7
muslin 38.27
musquash 23.42
muss 37.43
mussed 37.45
mussel 38.23
mussels 38.25
Mussolini 16.1
Mussorgsky 26.1
mussy 38.7
must 37.45
mustachio 35.19
mustachioed 35.25
mustang 1.29
Mustapha 4.11; 38.48
mustard 38.20
muster 38.10
Mustique 15.7
mustn't 38.32
musty 38.3
mutable 42.39
mutagen 42.41
mutagenic 10.15
mutant 42.22
mutate 7.33
mutates 7.50
mutation 8.23
mutatis mutandis 2.45
mute 41.27
muted 42.14
mutilate 7.49
mutilated 8.13
mutilation 8.39
mutineer 13.1
mutinied 17.8
mutinous 42.46
mutiny 42.36
mutism 18.27
mutt 37.47

mutter 38.10
muttered 38.20
mutterer 38.48
muttering 38.58
mutton 38.28
muttonchops 23.37
muttonhead 9.8
mutual 42.39
mutualism 18.29
mutuality 2.57
mutualize 21.47
mutually 42.36; 42.50
Muzak® 1.3
muzhik 42.11
Muzorewa 8.7
muzz 37.51
muzzle 38.23
muzzy 38.7
my 21.11
myalgia 2.14
myalgic 2.21
Myanmar 3.1
myasthenia 16.40
mycelium 16.42
Mycenae 15.3; 16.1
Mycenaean 16.22
mycology 24.55
myelin 17.29
myelitis 22.28
myeloid 33.4
Myers 19.4
Myfanwy 2.5
My Lai 21.2
mynah 22.8
myocardial 4.47
myocardium 4.49
myopia 36.37
myopic 24.16
myosotis 36.25
myotonic 24.19
Myra 20.2
myriad 18.62
Myrmidon 23.27
Myrna 12.2
myrrh 11.1
myrtle 12.8
Myrtle 12.8
myself 9.20
Mysore 25.2
mysterious 14.23
mystery 18.56
mystic 18.16
mystical 18.64
mystically 18.57
mysticism 18.28
mystics 18.17
mystification 8.46
mystified 21.12

mystifies 21.44
mystify 21.4
mystique 15.7
myth 17.53
mythic 18.16
mythical 18.64
mythically 18.57
mythicization 8.46
mythicize 21.44
mythologic 24.20
mythological 24.61
mythology 24.55
mythos 23.39
myxomatosis 36.25
N 9.32
NAAFI 2.4
naan 3.19
naans 3.24
nab 1.1
Nabokov 23.9
Nabokovian 36.40
nabs 1.2
nacre 8.4
Nader 8.5
Nadia 4.44; 8.78
Nadine 15.24
nadir 13.1
naevus 16.30
naff 1.11
nag 1.13
Nagasaki 2.2; 4.2
nagger 2.9
nagging 2.42
nags 1.14
Nahum 8.19
naiad 1.9
naïf 15.13
nail 7.15
nailbiter 22.5
nailbrush 37.46
nailed 7.16
nailer 8.7
nailfile 21.16
nailing 8.62
nailless 8.67
nails 7.17
Naipaul 25.14
Nairn 5.4
Nairobi 36.1
naive 15.39
naively 16.1
naivety 16.38
naked 8.12
nakedness 8.85
NALGO 35.3
'Nam 1.22
namby-pamby 2.1
name 7.18

name-calling 26.25
namecheck 9.2
named 7.19
name-dropper 24.8
nameless 8.67
namely 8.1
nameplate 7.34
names 7.20
namesake 7.6
nametape 7.27
Namibia 18.61
Namibian 18.67
naming 8.63
Namur 27.1
nan 1.24
Nan 1.24
nana 2.13; 4.13
Nancy 2.7
Nanette 9.51
nankeen 15.24
Nanking 17.35
nanny 2.6
nanny goat 35.45
nanometre 16.5
nanosecond 10.29
nanotechnology 24.55
Nansen 2.35
Nantes 3.23
Nantucket 38.43
Nantwich 17.7
Naomi 8.76; 36.1
nap 1.37
napalm 3.16
nape 7.27
naphtha 2.11
naphthalene 15.26
Napier 8.78
napkin 2.34
Naples 8.17
Napoleon 36.40
Napoleonic 24.19
nappa 2.8
napper 2.8
nappies 2.54
napping 2.42
nappy 2.1
narc 3.3
narcissi 21.3
narcissism 18.28
narcissist 4.54
narcissistic 18.16
Narcissus 18.44
narcissus 18.44
narcolepsy 10.7
narcoleptic 10.15
narcosis 36.25
narcotic 24.16
narcotics 24.22

nark 3.3
narky 4.2
Narnia 4.44
Narragansett 2.51
narrate 7.33
narration 8.23
narrative 17.55
narrator 8.5
narrow 35.3
narrow boat 35.45
narrowcast 3.30
narrowed 35.25
narrower 36.2
narrowest 36.28
narrowly 36.1
narrow-minded 22.13
narrowness 36.26
narrows 35.52
Narvik 4.16
narwhal 4.19
nary 6.1
NASA 2.14
nasal 8.15
nasalize 21.42
nasally 8.76
nascence 2.41; 8.57
nascent 2.40; 8.56
NASDAQ 1.3
Naseby 8.1
Nash 1.43
Nashville 17.15
nasi goreng 9.36
nasogastric 2.19
Nassau 25.3; 29.1
Nasser 2.14
Nastase 4.7
nastier 4.44
nastiest 4.55
nastily 4.42
nastiness 4.53
nasturtium 12.10
nasty 4.3
Nat 1.45
natal 8.15
Natal 1.16; 3.14
Natalie 2.56
Natasha 2.14
natation 8.23
natch 1.7
Nathan 8.21
Nathaniel 2.28
nation 8.22
national 2.64
nationalism 18.29
nationalist 17.49
nationalistic 18.16
nationality 2.57
nationalization 8.53

nationalize 21.47
nationalized 21.48
nationally 2.78
nations 8.55
nationwide 21.12
native 8.73
Nativity 18.57
Nat King Cole 35.30
NATO 35.6
natrium 8.80
natter 2.10
nattering 2.70
natterjack 1.3
nattier 2.61
nattiest 2.72
nattily 2.58
natty 2.3
natural 2.64
naturalism 18.29
naturalist 17.49
naturalistic 18.16
naturalization 8.53
naturalize 21.47
naturalized 21.48
naturally 2.78
nature 8.9
naturism 18.28
naturist 8.87
naturopath 1.47
naturopathic 2.18
naturopathy 24.54
NatWest 9.49
naught 25.31
naughtier 26.39
naughtiest 26.49
naughtily 26.37
naughtiness 26.47
Naughton 26.19
naughty 26.1
nausea 26.39
nauseate 7.44
nauseating 8.60
nauseous 26.47
nautical 26.41
nautilus 26.47
Navaho 35.19
naval 8.15
Navarre 3.1
nave 7.54
navel 8.15
navigable 2.79
navigate 7.35
navigation 8.24
navigational 8.79
navigator 8.5
Navratilova 36.6
navvies 2.54
navvy 2.4

navy 8.1
navy blue 41.4
nawab 3.2
Naxos 23.39
nay 7.1
Naylor 8.7
Nazarene 15.26
Nazareth 2.75
Nazarite 21.34
Naze 7.56
Nazi 4.7
Nazify 21.4
Nazis 4.40
Nazism 18.27
NB 15.2
NCO 35.19
Neanderthal 3.14
neap 15.30
Neapolitan 24.64
neaps 15.31
near 13.1
nearby 21.2
Near East 15.33
nearer 14.2
nearest 14.16
nearly 14.1
nearmiss 17.46
nearness 14.14
nearside 21.11
near-sighted 22.13
Neary 14.1
Neasden 16.22
neat 15.35
neaten 16.22
neater 16.5
neatest 16.32
'neath 15.37
neatly 16.1
neatness 16.30
Neave 15.39
neb 9.1
Nebraska 2.9
Nebraskan 2.35
Nebuchadnezzar
10.14
nebula 10.56
nebulizer 22.9
nebulous 10.70
necessarily 10.54
necessary 10.5; 10.78
necessitate 7.38
necessitation 8.28
necessitous 10.70
necessity 10.54
neck 9.2
neck-and-neck 9.2
neckband 1.28
necked 9.5

neckerchief 15.13
necking 10.36
necklace 10.42
necklet 10.48
neckline 21.22
neckpiece 15.32
necks 9.3
necktie 21.3
neckties 21.41
neckwear 5.1
necrology 24.55
necromancer 2.14
necromancy 2.7
necromania 8.78
necromantic 2.17
necrophile 21.16
necrophilia 18.61
necrophiliac 1.3
necrophilic 18.16
necrophobia 36.37
necrophobic 36.10
necropolis 17.46
necrosis 36.25
necrotic 24.16
nectar 10.10
nectarine 15.26; 17.29
nectarines 17.42
Ned 9.8
Neddy 10.3
née 7.1
need 15.11
needed 16.14
needful 16.17; 39.7
Needham 16.20
needier 16.40
neediest 16.49
needle 16.17
needlecord 25.9
needlecraft 3.10
needlepoint 33.10
needles 16.18
Needles 16.18
needless 16.30
needlessly 16.38
needlewoman 40.10
needlewomen 18.31
needlework 11.4
needling 16.27
needn't 16.25
needs 15.12
needy 16.1
neep 15.30
neeps 15.31
ne'er 5.1
ne'er-do-well 9.16
nefarious 6.22
Nefertiti 16.1
Neff 9.10

negate 7.33
negation 8.23
negative 17.55
negativism 18.29
negativist 17.49
negativistic 18.16
negativity 18.57
neglect 9.5
neglectful 10.21; 39.7
negligee 7.4
negligence 10.68
negligent 10.67
negligible 10.79
negligibly 10.78
negotiable 36.38
negotiate 7.47
negotiating 8.60
negotiation 8.37
negotiator 8.5
Negress 9.47
Negro 35.10
Negroid 33.4
negus 16.30
Negus 16.30
Nehemiah 22.2
Nehru 41.3
neigh 7.1
neighbour 8.3
neighbourhood 39.4
neighbouring 8.84
neighbourly 8.76
neighed 7.8
neighing 8.58
neighs 7.56
Neil 15.17
Neil's 15.19
Neisse 22.9
neither 16.6; 22.6
Nell 9.16
Nellie 10.5
nelly 10.5
Nelson 10.28
nematode 35.25
Nembutal® 1.16
Nemean 16.22
nemesia 16.9
Nemesis 17.46
Nene 15.23
neoclassical 2.64
neoclassicism 18.28
neoclassicist 2.73
neocolonialism 18.29
Neo-Darwinism
18.28
Neo-Darwinist 4.54
neodymium 18.66
Neolithic 18.16
neologism 18.28

neologistic 18.16
neon 23.27
neonatal 8.15
neonate 7.40
neophobia 36.37
neophyte 21.34
neophytic 18.16
neoplasm 2.32
Neo-Platonism 18.28
neoprene 15.26
Nepal 25.14
Nepalese 15.45
Nepali 26.1
nephew 41.3
nephews 41.33
nepotic 24.16
nepotism 18.28
Neptune 41.19
Neptunian 42.41
nerd 11.7
nerdy 12.1
Nero 35.9
nervature 12.30
nerve 11.27
nerve-racking 2.42
nervous 12.19
nervously 12.29
nervousness 12.37
nervous wreck 9.2
nervy 12.1
Nerys 10.41
Nesbit 10.48
Nescafé® 7.4
nesh 9.50
ness 9.47
Nessie 10.7
nest 9.49
Nesta 10.10
nest egg 9.12
nester 10.10
nesting 10.36
nestle 10.21
Nestlé 7.3
nestled 10.22
nestling 10.36
Nestorius 26.47
net 9.51
Netanyahu 41.3
netball 25.14
nether 10.11
Netherlander 2.10
Netherlands 10.66
nethermost 35.43
netiquette 9.51
netizen 10.64
netting 10.36
netting 10.36
nettle 10.21

nettled 10.22
nettles 10.23
network 11.4
networker 12.2
networking 12.16
neural 28.4
neuralgia 2.14
neuralgic 2.21
neurasthenia 16.40
neurasthenic 10.15
neuritis 22.28
neuroleptic 10.15
neurological 24.61
neurologist 24.72
neurology 24.55
neuroma 36.8
neuron 23.27
neurone 35.36
neuroscience 22.25
neuroses 15.44; 36.33
neurosis 36.25
neurosurgery 12.29
neurotic 24.16
neurotics 24.22
neurotransmitter
18.10
neuter 42.5
neutered 42.14
neutering 42.45
neutral 42.16
neutrality 2.57
neutralization 8.52
neutralize 21.46
neutralized 21.48
neutralizer 22.9
neutrally 42.36
neutrino 35.10
neutron 23.27
Nevada 4.10
never 10.11
nevermore 25.4
never-never 10.11
nevertheless 9.47
Neville 10.21
Nevski 10.2
new 41.1
Newark 42.10
newbie 42.1
newborn 25.22
Newburg 11.9
Newbury 42.36
Newby 42.1
Newcastle 2.28; 4.19
Newcombe 42.18
Newcomen 38.28
newcomer 38.13
newcomers 38.45
newel 42.16

Newell 42.16
newel post 35.43
newer 42.2
newest 42.27
newfangled 2.29
Newfoundland 1.28;
30.9; 42.42
Newfoundlander
30.23
Newgate 7.34; 42.30
Newham 42.18
Newhaven 8.21
Newington 42.41
newish 42.29
new-laid 7.8
newly 42.1
Newlyn 42.19
newlywed 9.8
newlyweds 9.9
Newman 42.20
Newmarket 4.38
newness 42.26
Newnham 42.18
New Orleans 15.29;
16.24; 26.44
Newport 25.31
Newport Pagnell 2.28
Newquay 42.1
Newry 28.1
news 41.33
newsagent 8.56
newsagents 8.57
newsboy 33.1
newscast 3.30
newscaster 4.10
newsflash 1.43
newsgroup 41.22
newshawk 25.6
newshound 29.6
newsletter 10.10
newsman 1.24
newsmen 9.32
newsmonger 38.9
New South Wales 7.17
newspaper 8.3
newspaperman 1.24
newspapermen 9.32
newspeak 15.7
newsprint 17.39
newsreader 16.5
newsreel 15.17
newsroom 39.9; 41.17
newsstand 1.28
newswoman 40.10
newsworthy 12.1
newsy 42.1
newt 41.27
New Testament 10.67

Newton 42.20
Newton Abbott 2.50
Newtonian 36.40
Newtown 29.5
Newtownabbey 2.1
New York 25.6
New Yorker 26.3
New Zealand 16.23
New Zealander 16.39
next 9.4
next door 25.2
next-of-kin 17.29
nexus 10.42
NHS 9.47
niacin 17.29
Niagara 2.12; 2.60
Niall 19.3
Niamey 7.2
Niamh 15.39
Niarchos 23.39
nib 17.1
nibble 18.22
nibbled 18.23
nibbler 18.12
nibbling 18.40
Nibelung 39.10
niblick 18.16
nibs 17.2
Nicaea 16.2
Nicaean 16.22
NICAM 1.22
Nicaragua 2.12; 42.2
nice 21.29
Nice 15.32
nicely 22.1
Nicene 15.25
niceness 22.29
nicer 22.9
nicest 22.31
nicety 22.40
niche 15.34; 17.7
Nicholas 18.74
Nichols 18.24
Nicholson 18.67
nick 17.3
Nick 17.3
nicked 17.6
nickel 18.22
nickelodeon 36.40
nicker 18.9
Nicklaus 18.44
Nickleby 18.56
nickname 7.18
Nick's 17.4
Nicky 18.2
Nicobar 3.1
Nicodemus 16.30
Nicol 18.22

Nicola 18.60
Nicole 35.30
Nicosia 16.2
nicotine 15.26
nicotinic 18.16
nicotinism 18.29
niece 15.32
Nielsen 16.22
Niemeyer 22.2
Niersteiner 22.8
Nietzsche 16.9
Nietzschean 16.43
niff 17.10
niffed 17.11
nifty 18.3
Nigel 22.16
Nigella 10.12
Niger 5.1; 22.9
Nigeria 14.18
Nigerian 14.21
Nigerien 6.19
niggard 18.19
niggardly 18.56
niggards 18.20
nigger 18.9
niggle 18.22
niggling 18.40
niggly 18.5
nigh 21.1
night 21.31
nightcap 1.37
nightclothes 35.49
nightclub 37.1
nightdress 9.47
nightfall 25.14
nightgown 29.5
nighthawk 25.6
nightie 22.1
nightingale 7.15
Nightingale 7.15
nightjar 3.1
nightlife 21.14
night-light 21.33
nightlong 23.31
nightly 22.1
nightmare 5.1
nightmares 5.5
nightmarish 6.12
nightrider 22.5
nights 21.35
nightshade 7.8
nightshirt 11.24
nightspot 23.44
night-time 21.19
nightwear 5.1
nihilism 18.28
nihilist 22.47
nihilistic 18.16

Nijinsky 18.2
Nijmegen 8.21
Nike 15.3; 22.1
Nikon 23.27
nil 17.15
nil desperandum
2.32
Nile 21.16
nilgai 21.3
Nilsson 16.22
nimble 18.22
nimbleness 18.74
nimbler 18.12
nimblest 18.46
nimbly 18.5
nimbostratus 4.32;
8.67
nimbus 18.44
NIMBY 18.1
nimbyism 18.28
Nîmes 15.20
niminy-piminy 18.57
Nimrod 23.8
Nina 16.8
nincompoop 41.22
nine 21.22
ninefold 35.31
ninepin 22.19
nineteen 15.24
nineteenth 15.28
nineties 22.38
ninetieth 17.53
ninety 22.1
ninety-eight 7.42
ninety-five 21.37
ninety-four 25.4
ninety-nine 21.22
ninety-one 37.31
ninety-six 17.4
ninety-three 15.4
ninety-two 41.4
Nineveh 18.60
Ninian 18.67
ninja 18.14
ninny 18.5
Nintendo® 35.7
Niobe 22.40
nip 17.43
nipped 17.45
nipper 18.8
nippers 18.55
nippier 18.61
nippiest 18.76
nipping 18.40
nipple 18.22
nipples 18.24
Nippon 23.27
nippy 18.1

NIREX 9.3
nirvana 4.13
Nissan 1.24
Nissen 18.33
nit 17.51
nitpick 18.16
nitrate 7.34
nitrates 7.50
nitre 22.5
nitric 22.11
nitrification 8.47
nitrogen 22.44
nitrogenous 24.70
nitroglycerine 15.26; 17.29
nitrous 22.29
nits 17.52
nitty-gritty 18.3
nitwit 18.50
Nivea® 18.61
Niven 18.32
nix 17.4
nixie 18.7
Nixon 18.33
Nkrumah 42.8
no 35.1
Noah 36.2
Noakes 35.22
Noam 36.18
nob 23.1
no-ball 25.14
nobble 24.27
nobbled 24.28
nobbler 24.12
nobbut 24.48
Nobel 9.16
nobelium 16.42
Nobel prize 21.45
nobility 18.58
noble 36.15
nobleman 36.40
nobler 36.7
nobles 36.17
noblesse 9.47
noblesse oblige 15.16
noblest 36.28
noblewomen 18.31
nobly 36.1
nobody 36.35
no-brainer 8.8
nobs 23.2
nocturnal 12.8
nocturnally 12.29
nocturne 11.15
nocuous 24.70
nod 23.8
nodal 36.15
nodded 24.24

nodding 24.40
noddle 24.27
Noddy 24.3
node 35.25
nodular 24.57
nodule 41.14
nodules 41.16
Noel 36.15
Noël 9.16
Noël Coward 31.2
no-frills 17.23
nog 23.11
noggin 24.32
no-hoper 36.3
no-hopers 36.34
nohow 29.1
noil 33.6
noir 3.1
noise 33.15
noiseless 34.12
noisette 9.51
noisiest 34.20
noisily 34.14
noisome 34.6
noisy 34.1
Nolan 36.20
nomad 1.9
nomadic 2.17
nomads 1.10
no man's land 1.28
nom de guerre 5.1
nom de plume 41.17
nomen 9.32
nomenclature 10.56
nominal 24.61
nominally 24.76
nominate 7.43
nomination 8.34
nominations 8.55
nominative 17.54
nominator 8.5
nominee 15.4
nonacademic 10.15
nonaccidental 10.21
nonaddictive 18.53
nonagenarian 6.19
nonaggression 10.28
nonagon 23.27; 24.64
nonalcoholic 24.18
nonaligned 21.23
nonappearance 14.11
nonattendance 10.34
nonbeliever 16.6
nonbelievers 16.37
nonbiological 24.61
nonce 23.33
nonchalance 24.68
nonchalant 24.67

noncommercial 12.8
noncommissioned 18.34
noncommittal 18.22
noncompetitive 17.55
noncompliance 22.25
non compos mentis 10.41
nonconductor 38.10
nonconformist 26.28
nonconformity 26.37
noncontributory 18.59
noncooperation 8.34
nondenominational 8.79
nondescript 17.45
nondrinker 18.9
nondrip 17.43
none 35.36
none 37.31
nonentity 10.54
nones 35.39
nonessential 10.21
nonesuch 37.6
nonet 9.51
nonetheless 9.47
nonevent 9.41
nonexecutive 17.55
nonexistence 18.39
nonexistent 18.38
nonfatal 8.15
nonferrous 10.42
nonfiction 18.33
nonflammable 2.64
nongovernmental 10.21
nonintervention 10.28
noninvasive 8.73
noniron 22.20
nonjudgmental 10.21
nonjuror 28.2
nonlinear 18.61
nonlocal 36.15
non-malignant 18.38
nonmetallic 2.19
non-negotiable 36.38
no-no 35.16
no-nonsense 24.39
nonoperational 8.79
nonorthodox 23.5
nonpareil 7.15
nonpartisan 1.24
nonpaying 8.58
nonpayment 8.56
nonphysical 18.64
nonplaying 8.58

nonplus 37.43
nonplussed 37.45
nonpolitical 18.64
nonpolluting 42.24
nonporous 26.27
nonproductive 38.44
nonproliferation 8.32
nonracial 8.15
nonrecognition 18.33
nonreligious 18.44
nonrenewable 42.39
nonresident 10.67
nonresidential 10.21
nonrestrictive 18.53
nonreturn 11.15
nonreturnable 12.32
nonscheduled 41.15
nonscientific 18.16
nonsectarian 6.19
nonselective 10.50
nonsense 24.39
nonsensical 10.60
nonsensically 10.54
non sequitur 10.56
nonslip 17.43
nonsmoker 36.4
nonsmokers 36.34
nonspeaking 16.27
nonspecialist 10.72
nonspecific 18.16
nonstandard 2.25
nonstarter 4.10
nonstick 17.3
nonstop 23.36
nonstrategic 16.11
nonswimmer 18.13
nontaxable 2.64
nonteaching 16.27
nontechnical 10.60
nontoxic 24.20
non-U 41.2
nonverbal 12.8
nonvintage 18.21
nonviolence 20.6
nonviolent 20.5
nonvoter 36.5
nonvoting 36.24
nonworking 12.16
noodle 42.16
noodles 42.17
nook 39.1
nooky 40.1
noon 41.19
noonday 7.3
no-one 37.31
noontide 21.11

noontime 21.19
noose 41.24
nope 35.40
nor 25.1
Norah 26.6
Noraid 7.8
Norbert 26.31
Norden 26.19
Nordic 26.9
Noreen 15.25
norepinephrine 15.25
Norfolk 37.3
Norfolk Broads 25.10
Noriega 8.4
nork 25.6
norm 25.20
Norm 25.20
Norma 26.7
normal 26.15
normalcy 26.37
normality 2.57
normalization 8.49
normalize 21.45
normally 26.37
Norman 26.19
Normandy 26.37
Norman's 26.21
normative 17.55
Norrington 24.64
Norris 24.42
Norse 25.28
Norseman 26.19
north 25.33
Northampton 2.35
Northamptonshire 13.1; 2.60
Northanger 2.9
Northants 1.34
northbound 29.6
northeast 15.33
northeaster 16.5
northeasterly 16.38
northeastward 16.14
northeastwards 16.15
northerly 26.37
northern 26.19
northerner 26.38
Northern Isles 21.18
northernmost 35.43
Northfleet 15.35
North Foreland 26.20
Northolt 35.32
North Pole 35.30
Northumberland 38.55
Northumbria 38.49
Northumbrian 38.54
northward 26.12

northwards 26.13
northwest 9.49
northwester 10.10
northwesterly 10.53
northwestward 10.18
northwestwards 10.19
Northwich 17.7
Norton 26.19
Norvic 26.9
Norway 7.3
Norwegian 16.22
nor'wester 10.10
Norwich 17.7; 24.26
nose 35.52
nosebag 1.13
noseband 1.28
nosebleed 15.11
nosebleeds 15.12
nose cone 35.36
nosed 35.53
nose dive 21.37
nosegay 7.3
nose ring 36.24
noses 36.34
Nosferatu 41.3
nosh 23.42
noshed 23.43
nosh-up 37.41
nosier 36.37
nosiest 36.44
nosiness 36.42
no-smoking 36.24
nosophobia 36.37
nostalgia 2.14
nostalgic 2.21
nostalgically 2.58
Nostradamus 4.32
nostrum 24.30
nosy 36.1
nosy parker 4.9
not 23.44
nota bene 7.3
notability 18.58
notable 36.38
notably 36.35
notary 36.35
notate 7.33
notation 8.23
notch 23.7
notches 24.53
notchy 24.7
note 35.45
notebook 39.1
notecase 7.30
noted 36.12
notelet 36.30
notelets 36.31
notepad 1.9

notepaper 8.3
notes 35.46
noteworthy 12.1
nothing 38.34
nothingness 38.59
notice 36.25
noticeable 36.46
notice board 25.9
noticed 36.27
notifiable 22.43
notification 8.50
notified 21.12
notify 21.4
notion 36.20
notional 36.38
notoriety 22.40
notorious 26.47
Notre Dame 3.16
Nottingham 24.63
Nottinghamshire 13.1
Notts 23.45
notwithstanding 2.42
nougat 3.1; 38.43
nought 25.31
noughts 25.32
noun 29.5
nourish 38.40
nourished 38.41
nourishing 38.58
nourishment 38.56
nous 29.12
nouveau riche 15.34
nouvelle cuisine 15.24
nova 36.6
Nova Scotia 36.9
Nova Scotian 36.20
novel 24.27
novelese 15.45
novelette 9.51
novelist 24.72
novelistic 18.16
novelization 8.48
novelize 21.45
novella 10.12
Novello 35.7
novelties 24.75
novelty 24.54
November 10.8
novena 16.8
novice 24.42
novitiate 18.77
Novocaine® 7.21
now 29.1
nowadays 7.56
noway 7.2
nowhere 5.1
no-win situation 8.32
nowise 21.41

nowt 29.14
Nox 23.5
noxious 24.43
nozzle 24.27
nth 9.42
nu 41.1
nuance 3.22
nub 37.1
nubble 38.23
nubby 38.1
Nubia 42.38
Nubian 42.41
nubile 21.16
nubuck 37.3
nuclear 42.38
nucleation 8.39
nuclei 21.4
nucleic 8.10
nucleon 23.27
nucleotide 21.10
nucleus 42.46
nude 41.9
nudge 37.15
nudger 38.14
nudist 42.28
nudity 42.36
Nuffield 15.18
Nugent 42.22
nugget 38.43
nuisance 42.23
nuke 41.6
null 37.16
nullification 8.51
nullify 21.4
numb 37.27
numbat 1.45
number 38.8
number 38.13
number-cruncher 38.14
numbered 38.20
numberless 38.59
numberplate 7.48
numbers 38.45
numbest 38.39
numbness 38.38
numbskull 37.16
numeracy 42.36; 42.50
numeral 42.39
numerate 42.49
numerator 8.5
numeric 10.15
numerical 10.60
numerically 10.54
numerological 24.61
numerology 24.55
numerous 42.46
Numidia 18.61

Numidian 18.67
numinous 42.46
numismatics 2.23
numismatist 18.75
nun 37.31
Nunc Dimittis 18.43
nuncio 35.19
nuncle 38.23
Nuneaton 16.22
Nunn 37.31
nunnery 38.47
NUPE 42.1
nuptial 38.23
Nuremberg 11.9
Nureyev 9.10; 9.56
Nurofen® 9.32
nurse 11.22
nursed 11.23
nursemaid 7.8
nursemaids 7.9
nursery 12.29
nurserymaid 7.8
nursing 12.16
nursling 12.16
nurture 12.2
nurtured 12.5
nurturer 12.30
nut 37.47
nutbrown 29.5
nutcase 7.30
nutcracker 2.9
Nutcracker 2.9
nuthatch 1.7
nutmeg 9.12
nutrient 42.43
nutrients 42.44
nutriment 42.43
nutrition 18.33
nutritional 18.64
nutritionally 18.80
nutritionist 18.75
nutritious 18.44
nutritive 17.55
nuts 37.48
nutshell 9.16
Nuttall 25.14
nutter 38.10
nuttier 38.49
nuttiest 38.61
nutting 38.34
nutty 38.3
nux vomica 24.57
nuzzle 38.23
Nyasa 2.14
Nye 21.1
Nyerere 6.1
nylon 23.27
Nyman 22.20

nymph 17.26
nymphet 9.51
nympho 35.11
nymphomania 8.78
nymphomaniac 1.3
O 35.1
oaf 35.27
oafish 36.29
oak 35.21
oaken 36.20
Oakes 35.22
Oakham 36.18
Oakley 36.1
oaks 35.22
oakum 36.18
Oakville 17.15
oaky 36.1
OAP 15.4
OAPs 15.45
oar 25.1
oared 25.9
oarlock 23.3
oarlocks 23.5
oars 25.35
oarsman 26.19
oarswoman 40.10
oases 8.74; 15.44
oasis 8.66
Oasis® 8.66
oast 35.43
oast house 29.12
oat 35.45
oatcake 7.6
oaten 36.20
Oates 35.46
oath 35.47
oatmeal 15.17
oats 35.46
oaty 36.1
Obadiah 22.2
Oban 36.20
obbligato 35.4
obduracy 24.76
obdurate 24.73
OBE 15.4
obeah 36.37
obedience 16.45
obedient 16.44
obediently 16.52
obeisance 8.57
obeisant 8.56
obelisk 17.47
obelus 24.70
Oberammergau 29.1
Oberland 1.28
Oberon 23.27
obese 15.32
obesity 16.38

obey 7.2
obeyed 7.8
obeyer 8.2
obfuscate 7.43
obfuscation 8.34
obi 36.1
obit 24.49; 36.30
obits 36.31
obituary 18.59; 18.80
Obi-Wan Kenobi 36.1
object 9.5; 17.6
objectify 21.4
objection 10.28
objectionable 10.79
objections 10.32
objective 10.50
objectively 10.54
objectivity 18.57
objector 10.10
objet d'art 3.1
objurgate 7.43
oblation 8.23
obligate 7.43
obligation 8.34
obligations 8.55
obligatory 18.56
oblige 21.15
obliger 22.9
obliging 22.26
obligingly 22.40
oblique 15.7
obliquely 16.1
obliquity 18.58
obliterate 7.41
obliteration 8.32
oblivion 18.67
oblivious 18.74
oblong 23.31
obloquy 24.54
obnoxious 24.43
oboe 35.16
oboist 36.43
obol 23.15
obols 23.22
obolus 24.70
Obote 7.3
O'Brien 22.20
obscene 15.24
obscenely 16.1
obscenities 10.77
obscenity 10.54
obscure 27.1
obscured 27.2
obscurely 28.1
obscuring 28.11
obscurity 28.17
obsequies 24.75
obsequious 16.47

obsequiously 16.52
observable 12.32
observance 12.15
observant 12.14
observation 8.34
observatory 12.29
observe 11.27
observed 11.28
observer 12.2
observing 12.16
obsess 9.47
obsessed 9.49
obsession 10.28
obsessional 10.60
obsessive 10.50
obsidian 18.67
obsolesce 9.47
obsolescence 10.34
obsolescent 10.33
obsolete 15.35
obstacle 24.61
obstacles 24.62
obstetric 10.15
obstetrical 10.60
obstetrician 18.33
obstetrics 10.16
obstinacy 24.76
obstinate 24.73
obstinately 24.76
obstruct 37.5
obstructed 38.20
obstruction 38.28
obstructionist 38.60
obstructive 38.44
obtain 7.21
obtainable 8.79
obtained 7.22
obtains 7.26
obtrude 41.9
obtrusion 42.20
obtrusive 42.33
obtrusively 42.36
obtuse 41.24
obverse 11.22
obvert 11.24
obviate 7.43
obviation 8.34
obvious 24.70
obviously 24.76
ocarina 16.8
O'Casey 8.1
occasion 8.21
occasional 8.79
Occident 24.67
Occidental 10.21
Occidentalize 21.43
occipital 18.64
occiput 37.47

occlude 41.9
occlusion 42.20
occult 37.26
occult 37.26
occultism 18.28
occupancy 24.76
occupant 24.67
occupation 8.34
occupational 8.79
occupied 21.12
occupier 22.2
occupies 21.45
occupy 21.4
occur 11.1
occurred 11.7
occurrence 38.33
occurring 12.16
occurs 11.29
ocean 36.20
oceanaria 6.16
oceanarium 6.18
ocean-going 36.24
Oceania 4.44
Oceania 8.78
oceanic 2.20
oceanographer 24.57
oceanography 24.54
ocelot 23.44
och 23.4
ochre 36.4
ocker 24.9
Ockham 24.30
o'clock 23.3
O'Connell 24.27
O'Connor 24.13
octagon 23.27; 24.64
octagonal 2.64
octahedral 16.17
octahedron 16.22
octane 7.21
octave 24.51
Octavia 8.78
Octavian 8.81
octet 9.51
October 36.3
octogenarian 6.19
octopod 23.8
octopus 24.70
octoroon 41.19
octuple 42.16
ocular 24.57
oculist 24.72
OD 15.2
OD'd 15.11
odd 23.8
oddball 25.14
odd bod 23.8
Oddfellow 35.7

Oddie 24.3
oddities 24.75
oddity 24.56
oddly 24.5
oddment 24.38
oddments 24.39
oddness 24.43
odds-on 23.27
ode 35.25
Odeon 36.40
Oder 36.5
Odessa 10.14
Odette 9.51
Odin 36.19
odious 36.42
odium 36.39
odometer 24.57
O'Donnell 24.27
odoriferous 18.74
odorous 36.42
odour 36.5
odourless 36.42
O'Dowd 29.3
Odyssean 16.22
Odysseus 18.74
Odyssey 24.56
oedema 16.8
Oedipal 16.41
Oedipus 16.47
Oedipus Rex 9.3
Oenone 36.1
oenophile 21.16
o'er 25.1; 36.2
oesophageal 16.17
oesophagus 24.70
oestrogen 16.43
oestrogenic 10.15
oestrus 16.30
oeuvre 12.2
of 23.47
O'Faolain 8.21
off 23.9
Offa 24.11
offal 24.27
Offaly 24.54
off-balance 2.41
offbeat 15.35
off-chance 3.22
offcut 37.47
Offenbach 3.3
offence 9.39
offend 9.35
offender 10.10
offenders 10.52
offending 10.36
offensive 10.50
offensively 10.54
offer 24.11

offered 24.24
offering 24.69
offers 24.53
offertory 24.54
offhand 1.28
offhanded 2.25
office 24.42
officer 24.57
official 18.22
officialdom 18.66
officialese 15.45
officially 18.56
officiant 18.70
officiate 7.41
officiation 8.32
officious 18.44
officiously 18.56
offing 24.40
offish 24.46
off-key 15.2
offline 21.22
off-load 35.25
off-peak 15.7
offprint 17.39
off-putting 40.15
off-puttingly 40.20
offset 9.51
offset 9.51
offshoot 41.27
offshore 25.2
offside 21.10; 21.11
offspring 24.40
offstage 7.12
off-the-cuff 37.10
off-the-wall 25.14
off-white 21.32
Ofgas 1.40
Ofgem 9.28
O'Flaherty 2.56
Oflot 23.44
Ofsted 9.8
oft 23.10
Oftel 9.16
often 24.33
oftentimes 21.21
ofttimes 21.21
Ofwat 23.44
Ogaden 9.32
Ogden 24.33
ogee 15.3; 36.1
Ogilvy 36.35
ogive 21.37
ogle 36.15
ogled 36.16
ogler 36.7
ogling 36.24
O'Grady 8.1
ogre 36.4

ogress 9.47
oh 35.1
O'Hara 4.12
O'Hare 5.1
Ohio 35.12
ohm 35.34
Ohm 35.34
ohmmeter 16.5
oi 33.1
oik 33.2
oiks 33.3
oil 33.6
oilcan 1.24
oilcans 1.36
oilcloth 23.46
oiled 33.7
oiler 34.2
oilfield 15.18
oil-fired 19.2
oiliest 34.20
oiling 34.11
oil lamp 1.23
oil rig 17.12
oilseed 15.11
oilskin 34.7
oil slick 17.3
oil slicks 17.4
oily 34.1
oink 33.9
ointment 34.9
okapi 4.1
okay 7.2
O'Keeffe 15.13
Okehampton 2.35
okey-doke 35.21
okey-dokey 36.1
Okinawa 4.12
Oklahoma 36.8
Oklahoman 36.20
okra 24.12
Olaf 1.11
Olav 1.49
old 35.31
Oldcastle 4.19
olden 36.20
older 36.5
oldest 36.28
olde worlde 12.1
old-fashioned 2.36
Oldfield 15.18
old flame 7.18
Oldham 36.18
oldie 36.1
oldies 36.33
oldish 36.29
old-maidish 8.70
Old Man of Hoy 33.1
old master 4.10

old stager 8.9
Old Testament 10.67
old-time 21.19
Olduvai 21.4
Old Vic 17.3
olé 7.2
oleaginous 2.71
oleander 2.10
O'Leary 14.1
olfaction 2.35
olfactory 2.56
Olga 24.9
oligarch 3.3
oligarchy 4.2
Oligocene 15.24
oligochaete 15.35
Oliphant 24.67
olive 24.51
olive green 15.26
olive grove 35.50
olive oil 33.6
Oliver 24.57
Oliver Twist 17.49
Olivetti 10.3
Olivia 18.61
Olivier 7.4
olivine 15.26
olla podrida 16.5
Ollerenshaw 25.2
Ollie 24.5
ology 24.55
oloroso 35.16
Olwen 24.32
Olympia 18.61
Olympiad 1.9
Olympian 18.67
Olympic 18.16
Olympic Games 7.20
Olympics 18.17
Om 35.34
Omagh 3.1; 36.8
Omaha 3.1
O'Malley 2.5
Oman 3.19
Omani 4.6
Omar 3.1
O'Mara 4.12
Omar Khayyám 1.22;
   3.16
ombre 24.8
ombudsman 40.10
Omdurman 3.19
omega 36.36
omelette 24.49
omen 36.20
omer 36.8
ominous 24.70
ominously 24.76

omissible 18.64
omission 18.33
omit 17.51
omnibus 24.70; 37.43
omnidirectional
   10.60
omnific 18.16
omnificent 18.70
omnipotence 18.71
omnipotent 18.70
omnipresence 10.34
omnipresent 10.33
omniscience 18.71
omniscient 18.70
omnivore 25.4
omnivorous 18.74
Omsk 23.26
on 23.27
onager 24.57; 24.57
Onan 1.24; 36.20
onanism 18.28
Onassis 2.45
once 37.39
once-over 36.6
oncer 38.14
oncogene 15.26
oncogenic 10.15
oncological 24.61
oncology 24.55
oncoming 38.34
one 37.31
on edge 9.14
one-eyed 21.11
Onegin 8.20
one-horse town 29.5
Oneida 22.5
O'Neill 15.17
one-night stand 1.28
onerous 24.70; 36.42
oneself 9.20
one-sided 22.13
one-time 21.19
one-to-one 37.31
one-upmanship 17.43
ongoing 36.24
onion 38.28
onions 38.31
onionskin 17.29
oniony 38.47
online 21.22
onlooker 40.2
only 36.1
onomatopoeia 16.2
onrush 37.46
onset 9.51
onshore 25.2
onslaught 25.31
onstream 15.20

Ontarian 6.19
on the mend 9.35
on the q.t. 15.2
on the rocks 23.5
on the spot 23.44
onto 41.3
ontology 24.55
onus 36.26
onward 24.24
onwards 24.25
onyx 24.22
oocyte 21.34
oodles 42.17
ooh 41.1
oolite 21.34
oolitic 18.16
oolong 23.31
Oonagh 42.8
oops 39.11; 41.23
ooze 41.33
oozed 41.34
oozing 42.24
oozy 42.1
op 23.36
opacity 2.57
opal 36.15
opalesce 9.47
opalescence 10.34
opalescent 10.33
opaline 21.22
opaque 7.6
op art 3.32
op. cit. 17.51
OPEC 9.2
open 36.20
open-air 5.1
opencast 3.30
opened 36.21
opener 36.36
openly 36.35
open-minded 22.13
openness 36.42
open-plan 1.24
open sesame 10.53
openwork 11.4
opera 24.12; 24.57
operable 24.61
opéra bouffe 41.10
opera buffa 42.6
operant 24.67
operate 7.43
operatic 2.17
operating 8.60
operation 8.34
operational 8.79
operations 8.55
operative 17.54

operator 8.5
operculum 12.33
operetta 10.10
Ophelia 16.40
ophidian 18.67
ophthalmia 2.61
ophthalmic 2.20
ophthalmological
   24.61
ophthalmologist
   24.72
ophthalmology 24.55
ophthalmoscope
   35.40
opiate 36.45
Opie 36.1
opine 21.22
opinion 18.32
opinionated 8.13
opium 36.39
Oporto 35.14
opossum 24.30
Oppenheim 21.19
Oppenheimer 22.8
oppidan 24.64
oppo 35.13
opponent 36.22
opponents 36.23
opportune 41.19
opportunism 18.27
opportunist 42.28
opportunistic 18.16
opportunity 42.36
opposable 36.38
oppose 35.52
opposed 35.53
opposer 36.9
opposes 36.34
opposing 36.24
opposite 17.51
opposites 17.52
opposition 18.33
oppress 9.47
oppressed 9.49
oppression 10.28
oppressive 10.50
oppressively 10.54
opprobrium 36.39
oppugn 41.19
Oprah 36.7
ops 23.37
opt 23.38
opted 24.24
optic 24.16
optical 24.61
optically 24.56
optician 18.33
optics 24.22

optimal 24.61
optimally 24.76
optimism 18.28
optimist 24.72
optimistic 18.16
optimistically 18.57
optimization 8.48
optimize 21.45
optimum 24.63
opting 24.40
option 24.33
optional 24.61
optionally 24.76
options 24.36
optometer 24.57
optometric 10.15
optometrist 24.72
optometry 24.56
opt-out 29.14
Optrex® 9.3
opulence 24.68
opulent 24.67
opus 36.26
or 25.1
OR 3.1
oracle 24.61
oracular 2.60
oral 26.15
orally 26.37
Oran 1.24; 3.19
orange 17.37; 38.36
Orange 17.37
orangeade 7.8
orange juice 41.24
Orangeman 24.64
orangery 24.56
orang-utan 1.24
orang-utang 1.29
orate 7.33
oration 8.23
orator 24.57
oratorical 24.61
oratorio 35.19
oratory 24.54
orb 25.5
orbit 26.32
orbital 26.41
orbited 26.40
orbiter 26.38
orc 25.6
orca 26.3
Orcadian 8.81
orchard 26.12
orchards 26.13
orchestra 26.38
orchestral 10.21
orchestrate 7.44
orchestration 8.35

orchestrator 8.5
orchid 26.11
Orczy 26.1
ordain 7.21
ordained 7.22
ordainment 8.56
ordeal 15.17
order 26.4
ordered 26.12
orderer 26.38
orderly 26.37
orders 26.36
ordinal 26.41
ordinance 26.46
ordinarily 10.54
ordinary 26.37
ordinate 26.50
ordination 8.35
ordnance 26.24
Ordovician 18.67
ordure 27.1
ore 25.1
oregano 35.4
Oregon 24.64
O'Reilly 22.1
Orestes 15.44
orfe 25.11
Orff 25.11
Orford 26.12
organ 26.19
organdie 26.37
organ-grinder 22.5
organic 2.20
organism 18.28
organist 26.48
organization 8.49
organizational 8.79
organize 21.45
organized 21.48
organizer 22.9
organizing 22.26
organum 26.42
organza 2.14
orgasm 2.32
orgasmic 2.20
orgiastic 2.17
orgies 26.35
orgy 26.1
oriel 26.41
orient 26.45
orient 9.41
Orient 26.45
Oriental 10.21
Orientalism 18.28
Orientalize 21.43
orientate 7.33
orientation 8.49
orienteer 13.1

orienteering 14.12
orifice 17.46
oriflamme 1.22
origami 4.6
origin 17.29
original 18.64
originality 2.57
originally 18.80
originate 7.41
origination 8.32
originator 8.5
origins 17.42
O-ring 36.24
Orinoco 35.16
oriole 35.30
Orion 22.20
orison 24.64
orisons 24.66
Orkney 26.1
Orkneys 26.35
Orlando 35.3
Orleans 16.24
Orme 25.20
ormer 26.7
Ormerod 23.8
ormolu 41.4
Ormond 26.20
Ormskirk 11.4
ornament 9.41; 26.45
ornamental 10.21
ornamented 10.18
ornaments 26.46
ornate 7.33
ornithological 24.61
ornithologist 24.72
ornithology 24.55
orotund 24.65; 37.36
orphan 26.19
orphanage 17.14
orphaned 26.20
orphans 26.21
Orphean 16.22; 26.43
Orpheus 26.47
Orphic 26.9
Orpington 26.43
Orrell 24.27
orris 24.42
Orsini 16.1
Orson 26.19
ortanique 15.7
Ortega 8.4
orthodontic 24.16
orthodontics 24.22
orthodontist 24.45
orthodox 23.5
Orthodox 23.5
orthodoxy 24.7
orthogonal 24.61

orthographic 2.18
orthography 24.54
orthopaedic 16.11
orthoptic 24.16
orthoptics 24.22
Orton 26.19
orts 25.32
Orville 17.15
Orwell 9.16
Orwellian 10.64
oryx 24.22
os 23.39
Osage 7.12
Osaka 4.9
Osama 4.13
Osbert 24.48
Osborne 25.22
Osbourne 25.22
Oscar 24.9
Oscar Wilde 21.17
oscillate 7.43
oscillation 8.34
oscillations 8.55
oscillator 8.5
oscillogram 1.22
oscilloscope 35.40
osculate 7.43
osculation 8.34
O'Shaughnessy 26.37
O'Shea 7.2
osier 36.37
Osiris 22.28
Oslo 35.13
Osman 3.19; 24.33
Osmanli 2.5
Osmond 24.34
Osmonds 24.35
osmosis 36.25
osmotic 24.16
Osnabrück 39.1
Ossa 24.14
osseous 24.70
Ossetia 10.57; 16.9
Ossetian 10.64; 16.22
Ossian 24.64
ossicle 24.61
ossification 8.48
ossify 21.4
ossuary 24.76
Ostend 9.35
ostensible 10.60
ostensibly 10.53
ostentation 8.34
ostentatious 8.67
ostentatiously 8.76
osteoarthritic 18.16
osteoarthritis 22.28
osteopath 1.47

overthrow 35.19
overthrown 35.36
overtime 21.19
overtired 19.2
overtly 12.1
overtone 35.36
overtop 23.36
overtrump 37.29
overture 27.1; 36.36
overturn 11.15
overturned 11.16
over-use 41.24
over-use 41.33
over-used 41.34
overview 41.4
overweening 16.27
overweight 7.47
overwhelm 9.21
overwhelmingly 10.54
overwind 21.23
overwinter 18.10
overwork 11.4
overwound 29.6
overwrite 21.34
overwritten 18.32
overwrote 35.45
overwrought 25.31
overzealous 10.42
Ovid 24.23
Ovidian 18.67
oviduct 37.5
oviform 25.20
ovine 21.22
oviparous 18.74
ovipositor 24.57
ovoid 33.4
ovulate 7.43
ovulating 8.60
ovulation 8.34
ovum 36.18
ow 29.1
owe 35.1
owed 35.25
Owen 36.19
owing 36.24
owl 29.4
owlet 30.18
owlets 30.19
owlish 30.17
own 35.36
own brand 1.28
owned 35.37
owner 36.8
ownerless 36.42
owner-occupier 22.2
owners 36.34
ownership 17.43
owning 36.24

owt 29.14
ox 23.5
oxalic 2.19
oxalis 2.45
oxblood 37.8
oxbow 35.13
Oxbridge 24.26
oxen 8.24
oxeye 21.3
Oxfam 1.22
Oxford 24.24
Oxfordshire 13.1; 24.57
oxhide 21.11
oxidant 24.67
oxidation 8.34
oxide 21.11
oxidization 8.48
oxidize 21.45
oxlip 17.43
Oxo® 35.13
Oxon. 23.27; 24.33
Oxonian 36.40
oxpecker 10.9
oxtail 7.15
Oxton 24.33
oxtongue 37.37
oxyacetylene 15.26
oxygen 24.64
oxygenate 7.33
oxygenation 8.48
oxymoron 23.27
oyez 7.2; 9.57
oyster 34.2
oystercatcher 2.14
Oz 23.48
ozone 35.36
ozonic 24.19
ozonosphere 13.1
Ozymandias 1.40
Ozzy 24.7
P 15.1
pa 3.1
PA 7.2
Pablo 35.3
pabulum 2.65
pace 7.30; 8.1
paced 7.31
pacemaker 8.4
pacer 8.9
pacesetter 10.10
pacey 8.1
pachyderm 11.13
pacific 18.16
Pacific 18.16
pacified 21.12
pacifier 22.2
pacifism 18.28

pacifist 2.73
pacify 21.4
pacing 8.64
Pacino 35.10
pack 1.3
package 2.27
packager 2.60
packages 2.76
packaging 2.70
packed 1.6
packer 2.9
packet 2.51
packhorse 25.28
pack ice 21.29
packing 2.42
packs 1.4
packsaddle 2.28
packthread 9.8
pact 1.6
pad 1.9
padded 2.25
padding 2.42
Paddington 2.66
paddle 2.28
paddler 2.12
paddles 2.30
paddling pool 41.14
paddock 2.16
paddocks 2.22
paddy 2.3
Paddy 2.3
paddywhack 1.3
pademelon 10.27
Paderewski 10.2
padlock 23.3
padlocked 23.6
pads 1.10
Padstow 35.3
Padua 2.60
Paduan 2.66
paean 16.22
paediatric 2.19
paediatrician 18.33
paediatrics 2.23
paedophile 21.16
paedophiles 21.18
paedophilia 18.61
paedophiliac 1.3
paella 10.12
pagan 8.21
Paganini 16.1
paganism 18.28
paganize 21.42
page 7.12
pageant 2.40
pageantry 2.56
pageants 2.41
pageboy 33.1

pageboys 33.15
paged 7.13
pager 8.9
pages 8.75
Paget 2.51
paginal 2.64
paginate 7.35
pagination 8.24
paging 8.64
pagoda 36.5
Pago Pago 35.4
pah 3.1
paid 7.8
Paige 7.12
pail 7.15
pain 7.21
Paine 7.21
pained 7.22
painful 8.15; 39.7
painfully 8.76
painkiller 18.12
painkillers 18.55
painkilling 18.40
painless 8.67
painlessly 8.76
pains 7.26
painstaking 8.59
paint 7.25
paintable 8.79
paintball 25.14
paintballing 26.25
paintbox 23.5
paintbrush 37.46
painted 8.13
painterly 8.76
painting 8.60
paintings 8.65
paintwork 11.4
pair 5.1
paired 5.2
pairing 6.10
pairs 5.5
paisley 8.1
Paisley 8.1
Paiute 41.27
Pakistan 1.24; 3.19
Pakistani 4.6
pal 1.16
palace 2.45
palaces 2.76
paladin 17.29
Palaeocene 15.24
palaeographic 2.18
Palaeolithic 18.16
palaeontologist 24.72
palaeontology 24.55
palais 7.3

palatable 2.79
palatal 2.64
palate 2.50
palatial 8.15
Palatinate 2.74
Palatine 21.22
palaver 4.11
pale 7.15
paleface 7.30
pale imitation 8.42
paleness 8.67
paler 8.7
Palermo 35.8
palest 8.69
Palestine 21.22
Palestinian 18.67
Palestrina 16.8
palette 2.51
palette knife 21.14
palfrey 24.5; 26.1
Palgrave 7.54
palimony 2.78
palimpsest 9.49
Palin 8.20
palindrome 35.34
palindromic 24.19
paling 8.62
palisade 7.8
palisades 7.9
palish 8.70
pall 25.14
Palladian 8.81
palladium 8.80
Palladium 8.80
Pallas 2.46
pallbearer 6.2
pallet 2.51
palliasse 1.40
palliate 7.35
palliation 8.24
palliative 17.54
pallid 2.24
Pall Mall 1.16
pallor 2.12
pally 2.5
palm 3.16
Palma 2.13
palmar 2.13
palmate 7.34
Palmer 4.13
Palmerston 4.50
palmist 4.33
palmistry 4.42
Palmolive® 24.51
palms 3.18
Palm Springs 17.36
palmtop 23.36
palmy 4.6

Palo Alto 35.3
Palomar 3.1
palomino 35.10
palp 1.19
palpable 2.64
palpably 2.56
palpate 7.33
palpitant 2.68
palpitate 7.35
palpitation 8.24
palsied 24.23; 26.11
palsy 24.7; 26.1
palter 24.10; 26.4
paltry 24.5; 26.1
Pam 1.22
Pamela 2.60
pampas 2.46
pamper 2.8
Pampers® 2.55
pamphlet 2.51
pamphleteer 13.1
Pamplona 36.8
pan 1.24
Pan 1.24
panacea 16.2
panache 1.43; 3.31
Panadol® 23.15
Pan-Am 1.22
Panama 3.1
Panamanian 8.81
Panasonic 24.19
panatella 10.12
pancake 7.6
pancetta 10.10
pancreas 2.71
pancreatic 2.17
panda 2.10
pandemic 10.15
pandemonic 24.19
pandemonium 36.39
pander 2.10
pandit 2.51
Pandora 26.6
pane 7.21
panegyric 18.16
panel 2.28
panelled 2.29
panellist 2.73
panels 2.30
panettone 36.1
pan-fried 21.11
pang 1.29
pangolin 36.19
pangram 1.22
panhandle 2.28
panic 2.20
panicked 17.6
panicking 2.70

panicky 2.57
panjandrum 2.32
Pankhurst 11.23
panned 1.28
pannier 2.61
panoply 2.56
panorama 4.13
panoramic 2.20
panpipes 21.27
pans 1.36
pansies 2.54
pansy 2.7
pant 1.33
Pantagruel 42.16
pantalettes 9.52
Pantaloon 41.19
pantaloons 41.21
pantechnicon 10.64
pantheism 18.28
pantheist 2.73
pantheistic 18.16
Pantheon 2.66
panther 2.11
panties 2.54
pantihose 35.52
pantile 21.16
pantiles 21.18
panting 2.42
panto 35.3
pantomime 21.19
pantomimes 21.21
pantomimic 18.16
pantry 2.5
pants 1.34
pantsuit 41.27
panty girdle 12.8
pantywaist 7.31
panzer 2.14
pap 1.37
papa 3.1
papacy 8.76
papal 8.15
Papandreou 41.3
paparazzi 2.7
paparazzo 35.3
papaverine 15.26
papaya 22.2
paper 8.3
paperback 1.3
paperbacks 1.4
paper bag 1.13
paper bags 1.14
paperboy 33.1
paperboys 33.15
paper chase 7.30
paperclip 17.43
papered 8.13
paperer 8.77

paperhanger 2.13
paperknife 21.14
paperknives 21.38
paperless 8.85
papers 8.75
paperweight 7.37
paperweights 7.50
paperwork 11.4
papery 8.76
papier-mâché 7.3
papilla 18.12
papilloma 36.8
Papillon 23.27
papism 18.27
papist 8.68
papistry 8.76
papoose 41.24
pappy 2.1
paprika 16.4
Papua 2.60
Papuan 2.66
papyrus 20.8; 22.29
par 3.1
para 2.12
parable 2.64
parabola 2.60
parabolic 24.18
Paracelsus 10.42
paracetamol 23.15
parachute 41.27
parachuting 42.24
parachutist 42.28
Paraclete 15.35
parade 7.8
parader 8.5
paradiddle 18.22
paradigm 21.19
paradigmatic 2.17
parading 8.60
paradisal 22.16
paradise 21.29
paradisiac 1.3
paradisiacal 22.43
paradox 23.5
paradoxical 24.61
paradrop 23.36
paraesthesia 16.40
paraffin 17.29
paraglide 21.12
paraglider 22.5
paragliding 22.26
paragon 2.66
paragraph 1.11; 3.9
paragraphs 1.12
Paraguay 21.4
Paraguayan 22.20
parakeet 15.35
paraldehyde 21.12

parallax 1.4
parallel 9.16
parallelism 18.29
parallelogram 1.22
Paralympian 18.67
Paralympic 18.16
Paralympics 18.17
paralyse 21.42
paralysed 21.48
paralysis 17.46
paralytic 18.16
paramedic 10.15
paramedics 10.16
parameter 2.60
parametric 10.15
paramilitary 18.57
paramount 29.11
paramour 27.1
paranoia 34.2
paranoid 33.4
paranormal 26.15
parapet 2.74; 9.51
paraphernalia 8.78
paraphrase 7.56
paraplegia 16.9
paraplegic 16.11
parapsychology 24.55
Paraquat® 23.44
parasailing 8.62
parascend 9.35
parascender 10.10
parascending 10.36
parascience 22.25
parasite 21.34
parasitic 18.16
parasitical 18.64
parasiticide 21.12
parasitism 18.29
parasitology 24.55
parasol 23.15
parasuicide 21.12
paratrooper 42.3
paratroopers 42.34
paratroops 41.23
parboil 33.6
parboiled 33.7
parcel 4.19
parcels 4.21
parch 3.6
parched 3.7
parching 4.29
parchment 4.27
pard 3.8
pardner 4.13
pardon 4.24
pardonable 4.57
pardoned 4.25
pardoner 4.43

pare 5.1
pared 5.2
paregoric 24.18
parent 6.8
parentage 17.14
parental 10.21
parentheses 15.45
parenthesis 17.46
parenthesize 21.43
parenthetic 10.15
parenthetically 10.54
parenthood 39.4
parenting 6.21
parentless 6.22
parents 6.9
parer 6.2
par excellence 3.22
parfait 7.2
Parfitt 4.38
Pargiter 4.43
pariah 22.2
pari-mutuel 42.39
paring 6.10
Paris 2.45
parish 2.49
parishioner 18.60
Parisian 18.67
parity 2.57
park 3.3
Park 3.3
parka 4.9
park and ride 21.12
parked 3.5
Parker 4.9
Parkes 3.4
parkin 4.23
parking 4.29
parking lot 23.44
Parkinson 4.50
Parkinsonism 18.29
park keeper 16.3
parkland 1.28; 4.25
parks 3.4
parkway 7.3
parky 4.2
parlance 4.28
parley 4.5
parliament 4.51
parliamentarian 6.19
parliamentarianism
  18.29
parliamentary 10.53
parlour 4.12
parlourmaid 7.8
parlous 4.32
Parma 4.13
Parmesan 1.24
Parnassian 2.66

Parnassus 2.46
Parnell 4.19; 9.16
parochial 36.38
parodic 24.16
parodied 17.8; 2.62
parody 2.56
parole 35.30
paroled 35.31
paroxysm 18.28
paroxysmal 18.22
parquet 7.3
parquetry 4.42
parr 3.1
Parr 3.1
Parramatta 2.10
parricide 21.12
parrot 2.50
parrot-fashion 2.35
parry 2.5
Parry 2.5
parse 3.37
parsec 9.2
Parsee 15.2
parser 4.14
Parsifal 3.14; 4.47
parsimonious 36.42
parsimony 4.56
parsing 4.29
parsley 4.5
parsnip 17.43
parson 4.24
parsonage 17.14
part 3.32
partake 7.6
partaken 8.21
partaker 8.4
partaking 8.59
parted 4.17
parterre 5.1
part exchange 7.23
parthenogenesis
  17.46
Parthenon 4.50; 23.27
Parthia 4.44
Parthian 4.50
partial 4.19
partiality 2.57
partially 4.42
participant 18.70
participants 18.71
participate 7.41
participating 8.60
participation 8.32
participatory 8.76
participial 18.64
participle 18.64
Partick 4.16
particle 4.47

particular 18.60
particularity 2.57
particularize 21.47
particularly 18.80
particulate 18.77
parties 4.40
parting 4.29
parting shot 23.44
partisan 1.24; 4.50
partisanship 17.43
partita 16.5
partition 18.33
partly 4.5
partner 4.13
partnerless 4.53
partnership 17.43
Parton 4.24
partook 39.1
partridge 4.18
Partridge 4.18
parts 3.33
part-time 21.19
part-timer 22.8
part-timers 22.39
parturient 28.22
parturition 18.33
partway 7.3
part work 11.4
party 4.3
partygoer 36.2
party line 21.22
party pooper 42.3
parvenu 41.4
parvenue 41.4
parvis 4.31
parvovirus 20.8
parvovirus 22.29
pas 3.1
Pasadena 16.8
Pascal 1.16
paschal 2.28
pas de deux 11.1
pash 1.43
pasha 2.14; 4.14
pashmina 16.8
paso doble 7.3
Pasolini 16.1
Pasquale 7.3
pass 3.26
passable 4.47
passacaglia 4.44
passage 2.27
passageway 7.4
passageways 7.56
passant 2.40
Passat® 1.45
passata 4.10
passbook 39.1

Passchendaele 7.15
passé 7.3
passed 3.30
passenger 2.60
passe-partout 41.4
passer 4.14
passer-by 21.4
passerine 21.22
passers-by 21.4
passes 4.41
passim 2.31
passing 4.29
passion 2.35
passionate 2.74
passionately 2.78
passionflower 31.1
passion fruit 41.27
passions 2.39
passive 2.53
passively 2.58
passivity 18.57
passkey 15.3
Passover 36.6
password 11.7
past 3.30
pasta 2.10
paste 7.31
pasteboard 25.9
pastel 2.28
pastern 2.35; 11.15
Pasternak 1.3
paste-up 37.41
Pasteur 11.1
pasteurization 8.40
pasteurize 21.42
pasteurized 21.48
pastiche 15.34
pasties 2.54
pastille 2.28; 17.15
pastilles 17.23
pastime 21.19
pastimes 21.21
pasting 8.60
pastis 15.32
pastor 4.10
pastoral 4.47
pastorale 3.14
pastrami 4.6
pastries 8.74
pastry 8.1
pasturage 17.14
pasture 4.14
pasty 2.3; 8.1
pat 1.45
Pat 1.45
Patagonia 36.37
Patagonian 36.40
patch 1.7

patched 1.8
patcher 2.14
patches 2.55
patchouli 42.1
patchwork 11.4
patchy 2.7
pate 7.32
pâté 7.3
Patel 9.16
patella 10.12
patent 2.40
patent 8.56
patented 2.63
patents 8.57
pater 8.5
paterfamilias 1.40
paternal 12.8
paternalism 18.28
paternalistic 18.16
paternally 12.29
paternity 12.29
paternoster 24.10
path 3.34
Pathan 3.19
Pathé 7.3
pathetic 10.15
pathetically 10.54
pathfinder 22.5
pathogen 2.66
pathogen 9.32
pathogenic 10.15
pathologic 24.20
pathological 24.61
pathologically 24.56
pathologist 24.72
pathology 24.55
pathos 23.39
pathway 7.3
pathways 7.56
patience 8.57
patient 8.56
patiently 8.76
patients 8.57
patina 2.60
patio 35.19
patisserie 16.38
Patmos 23.39
Patna 2.13
patois 3.1
Paton 8.21
Patras 1.40; 2.46
patrial 8.79
patriarch 3.3
patriarchal 4.19
patriarchy 4.2
Patricia 18.14
patrician 18.33
patricide 21.12

Patrick 2.19
Patrick's 2.23
patrilineal 18.64
patrimonial 36.38
patrimony 2.78
patriot 2.74
patriotic 24.16
patriotically 24.56
patriotism 18.29
patristic 18.16
Patroclus 24.43
patrol 35.30
patrolled 35.31
patroller 36.7
patrolling 36.24
patrolman 36.20
patron 8.21
patronage 17.14
patroness 9.47
patronize 21.42
patronizing 22.26
patronymic 18.16
Pat's 1.46
Patsy 2.7
patten 2.35
patter 2.10
pattern 2.35
patterned 2.36
patterns 2.39
Patterson 2.66
Patti 2.3
patties 2.54
Patton 2.35
patty 2.3
paucity 26.37
Paul 25.14
Paula 26.6
Paula's 26.36
Paulette 9.51
Pauli 26.1; 30.1
Pauline 15.25
Pauling 26.25
Paulinus 22.29
Paul Revere 13.1
paunch 25.23
paunchy 26.1
pauper 26.2
pauperize 21.45
pause 25.35
pauses 26.36
pausing 26.25
pavane 1.24; 3.19
Pavarotti 24.3
pave 7.54
pavement 8.56
paver 8.6
pavilion 18.32; 18.67
paving 8.61

paviour 8.7
Pavlov 23.47
Pavlova 2.60; 36.6
Pavlovian 36.40
paw 25.1
pawed 25.9
pawky 26.1
pawn 25.22
pawnbroker 36.4
pawnbroking 36.24
pawned 25.24
Pawnee 15.2
pawnshop 23.36
pawpaw 25.3
paws 25.35
pax 1.4
Paxman 2.35
Pax Romana 4.13
Paxton 2.35
pay 7.1
payable 8.79
pay-as-you-earn 11.15
payback 1.3
pay bed 9.8
paycheque 9.2
payday 7.3
PAYE 15.2
payee 15.2
payer 8.2
paying 8.58
paying guest 9.49
payload 35.25
paymaster 4.10
payment 8.56
payments 8.57
Payne 7.21
paynim 8.18
payoff 23.9
payola 36.7
payout 29.14
pay packet 2.51
pay-per-view 41.4
payphone 35.36
payroll 35.30
pay slip 17.43
PC 15.2
PE 15.2
pea 15.1
Peabody 24.3
peace 15.32
peaceable 16.41
peaceably 16.38
peaceful 16.17; 39.7
peacefully 16.38
peacekeeper 16.3
peacekeeping 16.27
peacemaker 8.4
peacemaking 8.59

pennies 10.51
penniless 10.70
Pennine 21.22
Pennines 21.25
penning 10.36
pennon 10.27
Pennsylvania 8.78
Pennsylvanian 8.81
penny 10.6
Penny 10.6
penny-farthing 4.29
penny-pinching 18.40
pennywort 11.24
pennyworth 10.75; 11.26
penpusher 40.2
Penrhyn 17.29
Penrith 17.53
pens 9.43
pension 10.28
pensioner 10.56
pensions 10.32
pensive 10.50
pensively 10.54
pent 9.41
pentacle 10.60
pentagon 10.64; 23.27
Pentagon 10.64; 23.27
pentagonal 2.64
pentagram 1.22
pentameter 2.60
pentangle 2.28
Pentateuch 41.6
pentathlete 15.35
pentathlon 2.35; 23.27
pentatonic 24.19
Pentax 1.4
Pentecost 23.41
Pentecostal 24.27
penthouse 29.12
pentimento 35.7
Pentonville 17.15
Pentothal® 1.16
pentstemon 16.22
pent up 37.41
penultimate 38.62
penumbra 38.12
penumbral 38.23
penurious 28.24
penury 10.55
Penzance 1.31
peon 16.22
peony 16.38
people 16.17
pep 9.44
PEP 9.44
Pepin 10.26

peplum 10.25
pepper 10.8
peppercorn 25.22
peppered 10.18
peppering 10.69
peppermill 17.15
peppermint 17.39
pepperminty 18.3
pepperoni 36.1
pepper pot 23.44
peppery 10.53
peppy 10.1
Pepsi® 10.7
Pepsi-Cola® 36.7
pepsin 10.26
pep talk 25.6
peptic 10.15
peptide 21.11
Pepys 15.31
per 11.1
peradventure 10.14
perambulate 7.35
perambulation 8.24
perambulator 8.5
per annum 2.32
percale 7.15
per capita 2.60
perceivable 16.41
perceive 15.39
perceived 15.40
perceiver 16.6
perceiving 16.27
per cent 9.41
percentage 10.20
percentile 21.16
percept 9.46
perceptible 10.60
perceptibly 10.53
perception 10.28
perceptive 10.50
perceptual 10.60
perch 11.6
perchance 3.22
percher 12.2
Percheron 23.27
percipience 18.71
percipient 18.70
Percival 12.32
percolate 7.39
percolation 8.29
percolator 8.5
percuss 37.43
percussion 38.28
percussionist 38.60
percussive 38.44
Percy 12.1
Perdita 12.30
perdition 18.33

père 5.1
peregrinate 7.33
peregrination 8.43
Peregrine 17.29
Perelman 10.64
peremptory 10.53
perennial 10.60
perestroika 34.2
perfect 9.5
perfect 17.6
perfectible 10.60
perfection 10.28
perfectionism 18.28
perfectionist 10.72
perfectly 12.29
perfervid 12.4
perfidious 18.74
perfidy 12.29
perforate 7.39
perforate 12.40
perforated 8.13
perforation 8.29
perforce 25.28
perform 25.20
performance 26.24
performer 26.7
performers 26.36
performing 26.25
perfume 41.17
perfumed 41.18
perfumer 42.8
perfumery 42.36
perfumier 42.38
perfunctory 38.47
perfuse 41.33
perfusion 42.20
Pergamon 12.34
Pergamum 12.33
pergola 12.30
perhaps 1.38
peri 14.1
pericardia 4.44
pericardial 4.47
pericardium 4.49
Periclean 16.22
Pericles 15.45
perigee 15.4
Perigordian 26.43
Périgueux 11.1
peril 10.21
perilous 10.70
perimeter 18.60
perinatal 8.15
perineal 16.17
perineum 16.20
periodic 24.16
periodical 24.61
periodically 24.56

periodontal 24.27
peripatetic 10.15
peripeteia 16.2
peripheral 18.64
periphery 18.56
periphrastic 2.17
periscope 35.40
periscopic 24.16
perish 10.45
perishable 10.79
perished 10.46
perisher 10.56
peristalsis 2.45
peristyle 21.16
peritoneum 16.20
peritonitis 22.28
periwig 17.12
periwinkle 18.22
perjure 12.2
perjurer 12.30
perjurious 28.24
perjury 12.29
perk 11.4
perkier 12.31
perkiest 12.39
Perkin 12.11
perks 11.5
perky 12.1
perlite 21.33
Perlman 12.12
perm 11.13
permafrost 23.41
permanence 12.36
permanent 12.35
permanganate 2.74; 7.35
permeability 18.58
permeable 12.41
permeate 7.39
permeation 8.29
permed 11.14
Permian 12.34
permissible 18.64
permission 18.33
permissive 18.53
permissiveness 18.74
permit 12.25
permit 17.51
permutation 8.29
permute 12.29
pernicious 18.44
pernickety 18.57
Pernod® 35.8
Perón 23.27
perorate 7.38
peroration 8.28
peroxide 21.11
perpendicular 18.60

pipeclay 7.3
pipe cleaner 16.8
piped 21.28
pipeline 21.22
pip-emma 10.13
piper 22.3
pipes 21.27
pipette 9.51
piping 22.26
pipistrelle 9.16
pipit 18.50
Pippa 18.8
pippin 18.31
pips 17.44
Pip's 17.44
pipsqueak 15.7
piquant 16.25
pique 15.7
piqué 7.3
piquet 7.2; 9.51
piracy 22.40
Piraeus 8.67; 16.30
Pirandello 35.7
piranha 4.13
pirate 22.34
piratical 2.64
Pirie 18.5
pirouette 9.51
Pisa 16.9
Pisan 16.22
Piscean 16.22
Pisces 15.44; 22.38
pish 17.50
pismire 19.1
piss 17.46
Pissarro 35.4
pissed 17.49
pisser 18.14
pissing 18.40
piss-taker 8.4
piss-taking 8.59
piss-up 18.42; 37.41
pistachio 35.19
piste 15.33
pistil 17.15; 18.22
pistol 18.22
pistole 35.30
pistols 18.24
piston 18.32
pistons 18.37
pit 17.51
pitapat 1.45
Pitcairn 5.4
pitch 17.7
pitchblende 9.35
pitcher 18.14
pitchfork 25.6
pitchy 18.7

piteous 18.74
pitfall 25.14
pith 17.53
pithead 9.8
pithecanthropus
36.26
pithier 18.61
pithiest 18.76
pithy 18.4
pitiable 18.81
pitied 18.18
pitiful 18.64; 39.7
pitifully 18.57; 40.1
pitiless 18.74
Pitlochry 24.5
Pitman 18.32
Pitney 18.6
piton 23.27
pits 17.52
Pitt 17.51
pitta 18.10
pitta bread 9.8
pittance 18.39
pitter-patter 2.10
Pittsburgh 11.9
pituitary 42.36
pity 18.3
pitying 18.73
Pius 22.29
pivot 18.49
pivotal 18.64
pivoted 18.62
pix 17.4
pixel 18.22
pixie 18.7
pixies 18.54
pixilated 8.13
pizza 16.9
pizzazz 1.50
pizzeria 16.2
pizzicato 35.4
pizzle 18.22
placable 2.64
placard 3.8
placate 7.33
placated 8.13
placatory 8.76
place 7.30
placebo 35.10
placed 7.31
placeless 8.67
placement 8.56
placenta 10.10
placental 10.21
placer 8.9
places 8.75
placid 2.24
placidly 2.58

placing 8.64
placket 2.51
plagal 8.15
plage 3.13
plagiarism 18.28
plagiarist 8.87
plagiaristic 18.16
plagiarize 21.42
plague 7.11
plaguing 8.59
plaguy 8.1
plaice 7.30
plaid 1.9
plain 7.21
plainchant 3.23
plain clothes 35.49
plainer 8.8
plainest 8.69
plain flour 31.1
plainly 8.1
plains 7.26
plainsman 8.21
plainsong 23.31
plain-spoken 36.20
plaint 7.25
plaintiff 17.10
plaintive 8.73
plaintively 8.76
plait 1.45
plaited 2.25
plaiting 2.42
plaits 1.46
plan 1.24
planar 8.8
Planck 1.25
plane 7.21
planer 8.8
plane spotter 24.10
plane spotters 24.53
plane spotting 24.40
planet 2.51
planetaria 6.16
planetarium 6.18
planetary 2.58
planetoid 33.4
plangent 2.40
plank 1.25
planking 2.42
plankton 2.35
planktonic 24.19
planner 2.13
planners 2.55
planning 2.42
planometer 24.57
plans 1.36
plant 3.23
Plantagenet 17.51; 2.74
plantain 2.34; 7.21

plantar 2.10
plantation 8.23
planter 4.10
planting 4.29
plants 3.22
plaque 1.3; 3.3
plash 1.43
plasma 2.13
Plassey 2.7
plaster 4.10
plasterboard 25.9
plastered 4.17
plasterer 4.43
plastic 2.17
Plasticine® 15.26
plasticity 18.57
plasticize 21.42
plasticky 2.57
plastics 2.23
plat 1.45
plat du jour 27.1
plate 7.32
plateau 35.3
plated 8.13
plateful 39.7
platelet 8.71
platen 2.35
plater 8.5
plates 7.50
platform 25.20
Plath 1.47
plating 8.60
platinum 2.65
platitude 41.9
platitudinize 21.46
platitudinous 42.46
Plato 35.6
Platonic 24.19
Platonism 18.28
platoon 41.19
Plato's 35.52
platter 2.10
platypus 2.71
plaudit 26.32
plausibility 18.58
plausible 26.41
Plautus 26.27
play 7.1
playable 8.79
play-act 1.6
play-acting 2.42
playback 1.3
playbill 17.15
playboy 33.1
played 7.8
player 8.2
players 8.75
playful 8.15; 39.7

playfully 8.76
playfulness 8.85
playground 29.6
playgroup 41.22
playhouse 29.12
playing 8.58
playlet 8.71
playlist 8.68
playmate 7.34
playmates 7.50
play-off 23.9
playpen 9.32
playroom 39.9; 41.17
playschool 41.14
playsuit 41.27
Playtex® 9.3
plaything 8.61
playthings 8.65
playtime 21.19
playwright 21.33
playwriting 22.26
plaza 4.14
plc 15.4
plea 15.1
pleach 15.9
plead 15.11
pleaded 16.14
pleader 16.5
pleading 16.27
pleasant 10.33
pleasantly 10.53
pleasantness 10.70
pleasantries 10.77
pleasantry 10.53
please 15.42
Pleasence 10.34
pleaser 16.9
pleasing 16.27
pleasingly 16.38
pleasurable 10.79
pleasurably 10.78
pleasure 10.14
pleasures 10.52
pleat 15.35
pleater 16.5
pleats 15.36
pleb 9.1
plebby 10.1
plebeian 16.22
plebeians 16.24
plebiscite 17.51; 21.34
plectra 10.12
plectrum 10.25
pled 9.8
pledge 9.14
pledged 9.15
pledger 10.14
pledging 10.36

Pleiades 15.45
Pleistocene 15.26
plenary 16.38
plenipotentiary 10.53
plenitude 41.9
plenteous 10.70
plentiful 10.60; 39.7
plenty 10.3
plenum 16.20
pleonasm 2.32
plesiosaur 25.2
Plessey 10.7
plethora 10.56
pleura 28.2
pleural 28.4
pleurisy 28.17
Plexiglas® 3.26
plexus 10.42
pliable 22.43
pliant 22.24
plié 7.3
pliers 22.39
plight 21.31
plimsoll 18.22
plimsolls 18.24
Plinian 18.67
plink 17.30
plinth 17.41
Pliny 18.6
Pliocene 15.26
plissé 7.3
PLO 35.19
plod 23.8
plodded 24.24
plodder 24.10
plodders 24.53
plodding 24.40
Plomley 38.5
plonk 23.28
plonker 24.9
plop 23.36
plosion 36.20
plosive 36.32
plot 23.44
Plotinus 22.29
plots 23.45
plotter 24.10
plotting 24.40
plough 29.1
Plough 29.1
ploughed 29.3
ploughing 30.12
ploughman 30.8
ploughs 29.17
ploughshare 5.1
plover 38.11
Plowden 30.8
Plowright 21.33

ploy 33.1
pluck 37.3
plucked 37.5
plucker 38.9
pluckier 38.49
pluckiest 38.61
pluckily 38.47
plucking 38.34
plucky 38.2
plug 37.14
plugger 38.9
plughole 35.30
plum 37.27
plumage 42.15
plumb 37.27
plumber 38.13
plumbing 38.34
plumb line 21.22
plumbous 38.38
plumbum 38.26
plume 41.17
plummet 38.43
plummeted 38.50
plummy 38.6
plump 37.29
plumper 38.8
plumpness 38.38
Plumstead 9.8
plumy 42.1
plunder 38.10
plundered 38.20
plunderer 38.48
plundering 38.58
plunge 37.38
plunger 38.14
plunk 37.32
Plunket 38.43
pluperfect 17.6
plural 28.4
pluralism 18.28
pluralist 26.48
pluralistic 18.16
plurality 2.57
pluralize 21.45
plus 37.43
plus-fours 25.35
plush 37.46
plusher 38.14
plushest 38.39
Plutarch 3.3
Pluto 35.18
plutocracy 24.54
plutocrat 1.45
plutocratic 2.17
plutonium 36.39
pluvial 42.39
pluviometer 24.57
ply 21.1

Plymouth 18.52
plywood 39.4
PM 9.28
p.m. 9.28
PMT 15.4
pneumatic 2.17
pneumatics 2.23
pneumoconiosis
  36.25
pneumonia 36.37
pneumonic 24.19
po 35.1
Po 35.1
poach 35.24
poacher 36.9
poachers 36.34
poaching 36.24
Pocahontas 24.43
pock 23.3
pocket 24.49
pocketbook 39.1
pocketed 24.59
pocketful 39.7
pocketknife 21.14
pockmark 3.3
pockmarked 3.5
pockmarks 3.4
pod 23.8
podagra 2.12
podge 23.14
podgier 24.58
podgiest 24.71
podgy 24.7
podia 36.37
podiatry 22.40
podium 36.39
podzol 23.15
Poe 35.1
poem 36.18
poesy 36.35
poet 36.30
poetaster 2.10
poetess 9.47
poetic 10.15
poetical 10.60
poetically 10.54
poeticize 21.43
poetics 10.16
Poet Laureate 24.73;
  26.50
poetry 36.35
poets 36.31
po-faced 7.31
pogrom 24.30
Pogue 35.28
poignancy 34.14
poignant 34.9
poignantly 34.14

poikilothermic 12.3
poinsettia 10.57
point 33.10
point-blank 1.25
pointed 34.3
pointedly 34.14
pointer 34.2
pointiest 34.20
pointillism 18.28
pointillist 34.19
pointing 34.11
pointless 34.12
pointlessly 34.14
pointy 34.1
poise 33.15
poison 34.8
poisoner 34.15
poisonous 34.18
Poitiers 7.4
poke 35.21
poker 36.4
poker face 7.30
poker-faced 7.31
pokerwork 11.4
pokier 36.37
pokiest 36.44
poky 36.1
Poland 36.21
Polanski 2.2
polar 36.7
polar bear 5.1
Polari 4.5
Polaris 4.31
polarity 2.57
polarization 8.50
polarize 21.45
polarized 21.48
Polaroid® 33.4
polder 36.5
pole 35.30
Pole 35.30
poleaxe 1.4
polecat 1.45
polemic 10.15
polemical 10.60
polemics 10.16
polenta 10.10
poles 35.33
pole vault 23.18; 25.17
pole-vaulter 24.10
Poliakoff 23.9
police 15.32
policeman 16.22
policewoman 40.10
policewomen 18.31
policies 24.75
policing 16.27
policy 24.56

policyholder 36.5
polio 35.19
poliomyelitis 22.28
polis 24.42
polish 24.46
Polish 36.29
polished 24.47
polisher 24.57
Politburo 35.15
polite 21.32
politely 22.1
politeness 22.29
politer 22.5
politesse 9.47
politest 22.31
politic 17.3
political 18.64
politically 18.57
politician 18.33
politicization 8.46
politicize 21.44
politicized 21.48
politicking 18.73
politico 35.19
politics 17.4
polity 24.56
polka 24.9
polka dot 23.44
poll 35.30
pollack 24.15
pollard 24.24
Pollard 3.8
polled 35.31
pollen 24.33
pollinate 7.43
pollination 8.34
polling 36.24
polliwog 23.11
Pollock 24.15
pollster 36.5
pollutant 42.22
pollutants 42.23
pollute 41.27
polluted 42.14
polluter 42.5
polluting 42.24
pollution 42.20
Pollux 24.21
Polly 24.5
Pollyanna 2.13
polo 35.16
Polo 35.16
polonaise 7.56
polo neck 9.2
polonium 36.39
Polonius 36.42
Pol Pot 23.44
poltergeist 21.30

poltroon 41.19
poly 24.5
polyanthus 2.46
polycarbonate 7.36
Polycarp 3.25
polychaete 15.35
polychrome 35.34
polychromic 36.10
polycotton 24.33
polycystic 18.16
polyester 10.10
polyethylene 15.26
Polyfilla® 18.12
polygamist 18.75
polygamous 18.74
polygamy 18.56
polyglot 23.44
polygon 23.27
polygonal 18.64
polygraph 1.11; 3.9
polygraphic 2.18
polyhedra 16.7
polyhedral 16.17
polyhedron 16.22
polymath 1.47
polymaths 1.48
polymer 24.57
polymerize 21.47
polymorph 25.11
polymorphic 26.9
polymorphous 26.27
Polynesia 16.9; 16.40
Polynesian 16.22;
    16.43
polynomial 36.38
Polyphemus 16.30
polyphonic 24.19
polyphony 18.56
polypropylene 15.26
polyrhythm 18.26
polysaccharide 21.12
polysemous 16.30
polystyrene 15.25
polysyllabic 2.17
polytechnic 10.15
polytechnics 10.16
polytetrafluoroethyle
    ne 15.26
polytheism 18.29
polythene 15.26
polyunsaturated 8.13
polyurethane 7.21
polyvinyl 22.16
pom 23.23
pomade 3.8; 7.8
pomander 2.10
pome 35.34

pomegranate 2.51
Pomerania 8.78
Pomeranian 8.81
pommel 24.27
pommy 24.6
Pomona 36.8
pomp 23.24
Pompadour 27.1
Pompeii 8.1
Pompeiian 8.21
Pompey 24.1
Pompidou 41.4
pompom 23.23
pomposity 24.56
pompous 24.43
ponce 23.33
poncho 35.13
poncy 24.7
pond 23.30
ponder 24.10
pondered 24.24
pondering 24.69
ponderous 24.70
ponderously 24.76
Pondicherry 10.5
pondweed 15.11
pone 35.36
pong 23.31
Pongo 35.13
pongy 24.6
ponies 36.33
pons 23.35
Ponsonby 24.54
Pontefract 1.6
Pontiac 1.3
pontifex 9.3
pontiff 17.10
pontific 18.16
pontifical 18.64
pontificate 7.41; 18.77
pontification 8.32
Pontin's 24.37
Pontius 24.43
Pontius Pilate 22.34
pontoon 41.19
Pontus 24.43
Pontypool 41.14
Pontypridd 15.38
pony 36.1
ponytail 7.15
poo 41.1
pooch 41.8
poodle 42.16
poodles 42.17
poof 39.6
poofter 40.2
pooh 41.1
Pooh 41.1

presumptuous 38.59
presuppose 35.52
presupposing 36.24
presupposition 18.33
preteen 15.24
pretence 9.39
pretend 9.35
pretended 10.18
pretender 10.10
pretending 10.36
pretension 10.28
pretentious 10.42
pretentiousness 10.70
preterite 17.51
preterm 11.13
preternatural 2.64
pretext 9.4
Pretoria 26.39
Pretorius 26.47
prettier 18.61
prettiest 18.76
prettification 8.46
prettified 21.12
prettify 21.4
prettily 18.57
prettiness 18.74
pretty 18.3
pretty-pretty 18.3
pretzel 10.21
prevail 7.15
prevailed 7.16
prevailing 8.62
prevalence 10.68
prevalent 10.67
prevaricate 7.35
prevarication 8.24
prevaricator 8.5
prevent 9.41
preventable 10.60
preventative 17.55
preventer 10.10
prevention 10.28
preventive 10.50
preview 41.3
Previn 10.26
previous 16.47
previously 16.52
prevision 18.33
prewar 25.2
prewash 23.42
prewashed 23.43
prey 7.1
preyed 7.8
Priam 1.22; 22.18
priapism 18.28
Priapus 8.67
price 21.29

Price 21.29
priced 21.30
priceless 22.29
pricer 22.9
prices 22.39
pricey 22.1
pricing 22.26
prick 17.3
pricked 17.6
pricker 18.9
prickle 18.22
prickles 18.24
prickly 18.5
pricks 17.4
pride 21.9
pride and joy 33.1
prie-dieu 11.1
priest 15.33
priestcraft 3.10
priestess 9.47
priesthood 39.4
Priestland 16.23
Priestley 16.1
priestlike 21.7
priestly 16.1
prig 17.12
priggish 18.47
prim 17.24
primacy 22.40
prima donna 24.13
prima facie 8.1; 15.3
primal 22.16
primarily 10.54
primary 22.40
primate 7.34
prime 21.19
primer 22.8
primeval 16.17
primitive 17.55
primitivism 18.29
primly 18.5
primogenitor 10.56
primogeniture 10.56
primordia 26.39
primordial 26.41
primp 17.27
primrose 35.52
primula 18.60
Primus® 22.29
primus inter pares 4.40
Primus stove® 35.50
prince 17.38
princedom 18.26
princely 18.5
Prince Rainier 7.4
princes 18.55
princess 9.47
Princeton 18.32

principal 18.64
principality 2.57
principally 18.57
principalship 17.43
principle 18.64
principled 18.65
Pringle 18.22
prink 17.30
prinked 17.32
print 17.39
printable 18.64
printed 18.19
printer 18.10
printers 18.55
printing 18.40
printout 29.14
printwheel 15.17
prion 22.20; 23.27
prior 19.1
Prior 19.1
prioress 9.47
prioritization 8.48
prioritize 21.45
prioritized 21.48
priority 24.56
priory 20.1
Priscilla 18.12
prise 21.39
prism 18.27
prismatic 2.17
prison 18.33
prisoner 18.60
prissy 18.7
pristine 15.25
Pritchard 18.19
Pritchett 18.50
prithee 15.3; 18.4
privacy 18.56; 22.40
private 22.34
privateer 13.1
private eye 21.4
Private Eye 21.4
privately 22.40
privation 8.23
privations 8.55
privative 17.55
privatization 8.47
privatize 21.44
privatized 21.48
privet 18.50
privilege 17.14
privy 18.4
prize 21.39
prized 21.48
prizefight 21.33
prizefighter 22.5
prizes 22.39
prizewinner 18.13

prizewinning 18.40
pro 35.1
proabortion 26.19
proaction 2.35
proactive 2.53
pro-am 1.22
probability 18.58
probable 24.61
probably 24.54
probate 7.34
probation 8.23
probationary 8.76
probationer 8.77
probe 35.20
probing 36.24
probiotic 24.16
probity 36.35
problem 24.30
problematic 2.17
problems 24.31
proboscis 24.42
procedural 16.41
procedure 16.9
proceed 15.11
proceeding 16.27
proceedings 16.28
proceeds 15.12
process 9.47
processed 9.49
processing 10.36
procession 10.28
processional 10.60
processions 10.32
processor 10.14
pro-choice 33.11
proclaim 7.18
proclaimed 7.19
proclaimer 8.8
proclamation 8.34
proclivity 18.57
proconsul 24.27
procrastinate 7.35
procrastination 8.24
procrastinator 8.5
procreate 7.47
procreation 8.37
procreator 8.5
Procrustean 38.54
proctor 24.10
procurable 28.19
procuration 8.34
procurator 8.5
procure 27.1
procured 27.2
procurement 28.9
procurer 28.2
procuring 28.11
prod 23.8

prodder 24.10
prodding 24.40
prodigal 24.61
prodigally 24.56
prodigious 18.44
prodigiously 18.56
prodigy 24.56
prodrome 35.34
produce 41.24
produced 41.25
producer 42.9
product 37.5
production 38.28
productive 38.44
productivity 18.57
prof 23.9
profanation 8.34
profane 7.21
profanities 2.77
profanity 2.57
profess 9.47
professed 9.49
professedly 10.54
profession 10.28
professional 10.60
professionalism 18.29
professionalize 21.47
professionally 10.78
professions 10.32
professor 10.14
professorial 26.41
professoriate 26.50
professorship 17.43
proffer 24.11
proficiency 18.56
proficient 18.38
proficiently 18.56
profile 21.16
profit 24.49
profitability 18.58
profitable 24.77
profitably 24.76
profited 24.59
profiteer 13.1
profiteering 14.12
profiterole 35.30
profligacy 24.76
pro forma 26.7
profound 29.6
profounder 30.2
profoundest 30.16
profoundly 30.1
Profumo 35.18
profundity 38.47
profuse 41.24
profusely 42.1
profusion 42.20

prog 23.11
progenitor 10.56
progeniture 10.56
progeny 24.56
progesterone 35.36
progestin 10.26
progestogen 10.64
prognoses 15.44; 36.33
prognosis 36.25
prognostic 24.16
prognosticate 7.43
prognostication 8.34
program 1.22
programmable 2.64
programmatic 2.17
programme 1.22
programmer 2.13
programming 2.42
progress 9.47
progressed 9.49
progressing 10.36
progression 10.28
progressive 10.50
progressively 10.54
prohibit 18.50
prohibited 18.62
prohibition 18.33
Prohibition 18.33
prohibitionist 18.75
prohibitive 17.55
prohibitory 18.57
project 9.5
project 9.5
projectile 21.16
projecting 10.36
projection 10.28
projectionist 10.72
projector 10.10
Prokofiev 9.10; 9.56
prolactin 2.34
prolapse 1.38
prole 35.30
proletarian 6.19
proletariat 6.23
pro-life 21.14
proliferate 7.41
proliferation 8.32
prolific 18.16
prolifically 18.57
prolix 36.11
prolixity 18.57
prologue 23.11
prolong 23.31
prolongation 8.37
prolonging 24.40
prom 23.23
promenade 3.8
promenader 4.10

promethazine 15.26
Promethean 16.43
Prometheus 16.47
prominence 24.68
prominent 24.67
prominently 24.76
promiscuity 42.36
promiscuous 18.74
promise 24.42
promised 24.45
promiser 24.57
promising 24.69
promisingly 24.76
promissory 24.76
promo 35.16
promontory 24.54
promote 35.45
promoted 36.12
promoter 36.5
promoting 36.24
promotion 36.20
promotional 36.38
prompt 23.25
prompted 24.24
prompter 24.10
promptest 24.44
prompting 24.40
promptitude 41.9
promptly 24.5
promptness 24.43
promulgate 7.43
promulgation 8.34
prone 35.36
prong 23.31
prongs 23.32
pronominal 24.61
pronoun 29.5
pronounce 29.9
pronounceable 30.24
pronounced 29.10
pronouncement 30.10
pronouncements 30.11
pronouncing 30.12
pronto 35.13
pronunciation 8.38
proof 41.10
proofing 42.24
proofread 9.8; 15.11
proofreader 16.5
proofreading 16.27
prop 23.36
propaganda 2.10
propagate 7.43
propagation 8.34
propagator 8.5
propane 7.21

propel 9.16
propellant 10.33
propelled 9.19
propeller 10.12
propensity 10.54
proper 24.8
properly 24.54
propertied 17.8; 24.60
properties 24.75
Propertius 12.19
property 24.54
prophecies 24.75
prophecy 24.56
prophesied 21.12
prophesier 22.2
prophesy 21.4
prophet 24.49
prophetess 9.47
prophetic 10.15
prophetically 10.54
prophylactic 2.17
prophylaxis 2.45
propinquity 18.58
propitiate 7.41
propitiation 8.32
propitiatory 18.56
propitious 18.44
proponent 36.22
proportion 26.19
proportional 26.41
proportionate 26.50
proportioned 26.20
proportions 26.21
proposal 36.15
propose 35.52
proposed 35.53
proposer 36.9
proposes 36.34
proposing 36.24
proposition 18.33
propound 29.6
proprietary 22.40
proprietor 22.41
proprietorship 17.43
proprietress 22.46
propriety 22.40
props 23.37
propulsion 38.28
propulsive 38.44
propylaeum 16.20
propylene 15.26
pro rata 4.10
prorate 7.33
prorogue 35.28
prosaic 8.10
prosaically 8.76
proscenia 16.40
proscenium 16.42

prosciutto 35.18
proscribe 21.5
proscribed 21.6
proscription 18.33
prose 35.52
prosecute 41.27
prosecuted 42.14
prosecuting 42.24
prosecution 42.20
prosecutor 42.5
proselyte 21.34
proselytize 21.47
prosimian 18.67
proslavery 8.76
prosodic 24.16
prosody 36.35
prospect 9.5
prospect 9.5
prospecting 10.36
prospective 10.50
prospector 10.10
prospectus 10.42
prosper 24.8
prospered 24.24
prosperity 10.54
Prospero 35.19
prosperous 24.70
prosperously 24.76
Prosser 24.14
Prost 23.41
prostate 7.34
prosthesis 16.29
prosthetic 10.15
prosthetics 10.16
prostitute 41.27
prostitutes 41.28
prostitution 42.20
prostrate 7.33
prostrate 7.34
prostration 8.23
prosy 36.1
protagonist 2.73
Protagoras 2.71
protean 16.22
protect 9.5
protected 10.18
protection 10.28
protectionism 18.28
protectionist 10.72
protective 10.50
protectively 10.54
protector 10.10
Protector 10.10
protectorate 10.73
protégé 7.4
protégée 7.4
protein 15.25
pro tem 9.28

pro tempore 10.53
protest 9.49
protest 9.49
Protestant 24.67
Protestantism 18.29
Protestants 24.68
protestation 8.34
protester 10.10
protesting 10.36
Proteus 36.42
prothalamion 8.81
protocol 23.15
protomartyr 4.10
proton 23.27
protoplasm 2.32
protoplasmic 2.20
prototype 21.26
prototypic 18.16
protozoa 36.2
protozoan 36.20
protozoon 23.27
protract 1.6
protracted 2.25
protraction 2.35
protractor 2.10
protrude 41.9
protruded 42.14
protruding 42.24
protrusion 42.20
protuberance 42.44
protuberant 42.43
proud 29.3
prouder 30.2
proudest 30.16
proudly 30.1
prounion 42.20; 42.41
Proust 41.25
Prout 29.14
provable 42.39
prove 41.31
proved 41.32
proven 36.20; 42.20
provenance 24.68
Provençal 3.14
Provençale 3.14
Provence 3.22
provender 24.57
proverb 11.2
proverbial 12.32
provide 21.10
provided 22.13
providence 24.68
provident 24.67
providential 10.21
provider 22.5
providing 22.26
province 17.38
provincial 18.22

provincialism 18.28
proving 42.24
provision 18.33
provisional 18.64
provisionally 18.80
provisions 18.37
provocation 8.34
provocative 17.55
provocatively 24.76
provoke 35.21
provoked 35.23
provoker 36.4
provoking 36.24
provost 23.41
provost 24.44
prow 29.1
prowar 25.2
prowess 9.47; 30.13
prowl 29.4
prowler 30.2
prowlers 30.21
prowling 30.12
proximal 24.61
proximate 24.73
proximity 18.57
proxy 24.7
Prozac® 1.3
Pru 41.1
prude 41.9
prudence 42.23
Prudence 42.23
prudent 42.22
prudential 10.21
prudently 42.36
prudish 42.29
prudishness 18.57
Prufrock 23.3
prune 41.19
pruned 41.20
Prunella 10.12
pruner 42.8
prunes 41.21
pruning 42.24
prurience 28.23
prurient 28.22
pruritus 22.29
Prussia 38.14
Prussian 38.28
prussic 38.15
pry 21.1
pryer 22.2
PS 9.47
psalm 3.16
psalmist 4.33
psalmodic 24.16
Psalms 3.18
Psalter 24.10; 26.4
psaltery 24.54; 26.37
psephology 24.55

pseud 41.9
pseudo 35.18
pseudonym 17.24
pseudonymous 24.70
pseudopodia 36.37
pseudopodium 36.39
pseudoscience 22.25
pseudoscientific
18.16
pshaw 25.1
psi 21.1
psittacosis 36.25
psoriasis 17.46
psych 21.7
psyche 15.3; 22.1
psychedelia 10.57;
16.40
psychedelic 10.15
psychiatric 2.19
psychiatrist 22.47
psychiatry 22.40
psychic 22.11
psychical 22.43
psycho 35.12
psychoanalyse 21.42
psychoanalysis 17.46
psychoanalyst 2.73
psychoanalytic 18.16
psychoanalytical
18.64
psychobabble 2.28
psychodrama 4.13
psychogenic 10.15
psychokinetic 10.15
psychological 24.61
psychologically 24.56
psychologist 24.72
psychology 24.55
psychometric 10.15
psychometrics 10.16
psychoneurosis 36.25
psychopath 1.47
psychopathic 2.18
psychopaths 1.48
psychoses 15.44
psychoses 36.33
psychosis 36.25
psychosomatic 2.17
psychotherapist 10.72
psychotherapy 10.53
psychotic 24.16
psychotropic 24.16
PT 15.2
PTA 7.4
ptarmigan 4.50
pterodactyl 2.28; 17.15
pterosaur 25.4
PTO 35.19

Ptolemaic 8.10
Ptolemy 24.54
ptomaine 7.21
ptosis 36.25
pub 37.1
pub crawl 25.14
pube 41.5
pubertal 42.39
puberty 42.36
pubescence 10.34
pubescent 10.33
pubic 42.11
pubis 42.25
public 38.15
publican 38.54
publication 8.38
publicist 38.60
publicity 18.57
publicize 21.46
publicized 21.48
publicly 38.47
publish 38.40
publishable 38.65
published 38.41
publisher 38.48
publishing 38.58
pubs 37.2
Puccini 16.1
puce 41.24
puck 37.3
Puck 37.3
pucker 38.9
puckers 38.45
pud 39.4
pudding 40.15
puddle 38.23
puddles 38.25
pudenda 10.10
pudendal 10.21
pudendum 10.25
pudge 37.15
pudgy 38.7
Pudsey 38.7
Puebla 10.12
Pueblo 35.7
puerile 21.16
puerperal 12.32
Puerto Rican 16.22
Puerto Rico 35.10
puff 37.10
puffball 25.14
puffed 37.12
puffer 38.11
puffin 38.27
puffing 38.34
puffins 38.30
puffs 37.11
puffy 38.4

pug 37.14
Puget 42.30
Pugh 41.1
pugilism 18.28
pugilist 42.48
pugnacious 8.67
pugnacity 2.57
Pugwash 23.42
puissant 16.25
puke 41.6
pukes 41.7
puking 42.24
pukka 38.9
Pulborough 40.21
pulchritude 41.9
pulchritudinous
    42.46
puli 40.1; 42.1
Pulitzer 40.21
pull 39.7
Pullen 40.10
puller 40.2
pullet 40.17
pulley 40.1
pulling 40.15
Pullman 40.10
pullover 36.6
pullulate 7.48
pulmonary 38.47;
    40.20
pulp 37.23
pulped 37.24
pulper 38.8
pulping 38.34
pulpit 40.17
pulpy 38.1
pulsar 3.1
pulsate 7.33
pulsatilla 18.12
pulsating 8.60
pulsation 8.23
pulse 37.25
pulverization 8.51
pulverize 21.46
puma 42.8
pumice 38.37
pummel 38.23
pump 37.29
pumpernickel 18.22
pumpkin 38.27
pumpkins 38.30
pumps 37.30
pun 37.31
punch 37.35
Punch 37.35
Punch and Judy 42.1
punchbag 1.13
punchball 25.14

punchbowl 35.30
punch-drunk 37.32
puncher 38.14
punches 38.45
Punchinello 35.7
punching 38.34
punch line 21.22
punch-up 37.41
punchy 38.7
punctilio 35.19
punctilious 18.74
punctual 38.52
punctuality 2.57
punctually 38.47;
    38.64
punctuate 7.48
punctuation 8.38
puncture 38.14
punctured 38.20
pundit 38.43
pungency 38.47
pungent 38.32
Punic 42.11
punier 42.38
puniest 42.47
punish 38.40
punishable 38.65
punished 38.41
punishment 38.56
punishments 38.57
punitive 17.55
Punjab 3.2
Punjabi 4.1
punk 37.32
punkah 38.9
punks 37.33
punned 37.36
punnet 38.43
punning 38.34
punster 38.10
punt 37.40
punter 38.10
punters 38.45
punting 38.34
punts 37.39
puny 42.1
pup 37.41
pupa 42.3
pupal 42.16
pupate 7.33
pupation 8.23
pupil 42.16
pupillage 17.14
pupils 42.17
puppet 38.43
puppeteer 13.1
puppetry 38.47
puppies 38.46

puppy 38.1
Purbeck 9.2
purblind 21.23
Purcell 12.8
purchase 12.18
purchaser 12.30
purdah 12.2
Purdy 12.1
pure 27.1
purebred 9.8
purée 7.3
purely 28.1
purer 28.2
purest 28.13
purgation 8.23
purgative 17.55
purgatory 12.29
purge 11.10
purger 12.2
purging 12.16
purification 8.49
purified 21.12
purifier 22.2
purify 21.4
Purim 28.5
purine 15.25
purism 18.27
purist 28.14
puristic 18.16
puritan 28.21
puritanical 2.64
purity 28.17
purl 11.11
purler 12.2
purlieu 41.3
purloin 33.8
purloiner 34.2
purloining 34.11
purple 12.8
purple patch 1.7
purport 25.31
purpose 12.19
purpose-built 17.21
purposeless 12.37
purposely 12.29
purr 11.1
purred 11.7
purring 12.16
purrs 11.29
purse 11.22
pursed 11.23
purser 12.2
purse-strings 12.17
pursuance 42.23
pursuant 42.22
pursue 41.2
pursued 41.9
pursuer 42.2

queenly 16.1
queens 15.29
Queens 15.29
Queensberry 16.1; 16.38
Queensferry 10.5
Queensland 1.28; 16.23
Queenslander 2.10
Queenstown 29.5
queer 13.1
queerer 14.2
queerest 14.16
queerly 14.1
quell 9.16
quelled 9.19
quelquechose 35.52
quench 9.33
quenched 9.34
quencher 10.14
quenching 10.36
quenelle 9.16
Quentin 10.26
queried 14.4
queries 14.17
quern 11.15
querulous 10.70
query 14.1
quest 9.49
question 10.28
questionable 10.79
questionably 10.78
questioned 10.29
questioner 10.56
questioning 10.69
questioningly 10.78
questionnaire 5.1
questions 10.32
quetzal 10.21
Quetzalcoatl 2.28
queue 41.1
queued 41.9
queue-jumper 38.8
queues 41.33
queuing 42.24
quibble 18.22
quibbler 18.12
quiche 15.34
quick 17.3
quicken 18.32
quickening 18.73
quicker 18.9
quickest 18.46
quickie 18.2
quicklime 21.19
quickly 18.5
quicksand 1.28
quickset 9.51

quicksilver 18.11
quickstep 9.44
quick-witted 18.19
quid 17.8
quidditch 17.7
quiddity 18.57
quidnunc 37.32
quid pro quo 35.19
quiescence 10.34
quiescent 10.33
quiet 22.34
quieten 22.44
quietly 22.40
quietness 22.46
quietude 41.9
quietus 8.67; 16.30
quiff 17.10
quill 17.15
Quiller-Couch 41.8
quilt 17.21
quilter 18.10
quilting 18.40
quim 17.24
quin 17.29
quince 17.38
quincentennial 10.60
quincunx 37.33
quinine 15.25
Quinn 17.29
Quinquagesima 10.56
quinquennial 10.60
quinquereme 15.20
quins 17.42
quinsy 18.7
quintal 18.22
quintan 18.32
quintessence 10.34
quintessential 10.21
quintet 9.51
Quintilian 18.32; 18.67
Quintin 18.31
quintuple 42.16
quintuplet 18.77; 42.30
quintuplets 42.32
quintuplicate 7.49; 42.49
quip 17.43
quips 17.44
quipster 18.10
quire 19.1
quires 19.4
quirk 11.4
Quirke 11.4
quirkier 12.31
quirkiest 12.39
quirks 11.5

quirky 12.1
quisling 18.40
quit 17.51
quitclaim 7.18
quite 21.31
quits 17.52
quittance 18.39
quitter 18.10
quitting 18.40
quiver 18.11
quivered 18.19
quivering 18.73
quivery 18.56
qui vive 15.39
quixotic 24.16
quiz 17.56
quizmaster 4.10
quizzer 18.14
quizzical 18.64
quizzing 18.40
Qumran 3.19
quod 23.8
quoin 33.8
quoit 33.13
quoits 33.14
quokka 24.9
quondam 1.22
quorate 7.34
Quorn® 25.22
quorum 26.17
quota 36.5
quotable 36.38
quotation 8.23
quotations 8.55
quote 35.45
quoted 36.12
quoth 35.47
quotidian 18.67
quotient 36.22
quoting 36.24
quo vadis 4.31
qwerty 12.1
R 3.1
R2-D2 41.3
Ra 3.1
rabbet 2.51
rabbi 21.3
Rabbie 2.1
rabbinic 18.16
rabbinical 18.64
rabbis 21.41
rabbit 2.51
rabbited 2.63
rabble 2.28
rabble-rouser 30.2
Rabelais 7.4
Rabelaisian 8.81
rabid 2.24

rabies 8.74; 15.44
Rabin 15.24
RAC 15.4
raccoon 41.19
race 7.30
racecard 3.8
racecourse 25.28
raced 7.31
racegoer 36.2
racehorse 25.28
raceme 15.20
racer 8.9
races 8.75
racetrack 1.3
Rachel's 8.15
Rachel's 8.17
Rachmaninoff 23.9
Rachmanism 18.28
racial 8.15
racialism 18.28
racialist 8.87
racialize 21.42
racially 8.76
racier 8.78
raciest 8.86
Racine 15.24
racing 8.64
racism 18.27
racist 8.68
rack 1.3
rack-and-pinion 18.32
racket 2.51
racketeer 13.1
Rackham 2.32
racking 2.42
racks 1.4
raconteur 11.1
racy 8.1
rad 1.9
RADA 4.10
radar 3.1
Radcliffe 17.10
raddle 2.28
Radetzky 10.2
Radford 2.25
radial 8.79
radian 8.81
radiance 8.83
radiant 8.82
radiate 7.37
radiation 8.27
radiator 8.5
radical 2.64
radicalism 18.29
radically 2.58
radii 21.4
radio 35.19

radioactive 2.53
radioactivity 18.57
radiogenic 10.15
radiogram 1.22
radiograph 1.11; 3.9
radiographer 24.57
radiographic 2.18
radiography 24.54
radiolocation 8.37
radiologic 24.20
radiologist 24.72
radiology 24.55
radiophone 35.36
radiophonic 24.19
radiotherapist 10.72
radiotherapy 10.53
radish 2.49
radishes 2.76
radium 8.80
radius 8.85
radix 8.11
Radnor 2.13
radon 23.27
Radox® 23.5
Raeburn 11.15
RAF 1.11; 9.10
Rafferty 2.56
raffia 2.61
raffle 2.28
Raffles 2.30
Rafsanjani 4.6
raft 3.10
rafter 4.10
rafters 4.41
rag 1.13
raga 4.9
ragamuffin 38.27
ragbag 1.13
rage 7.12
raged 7.13
ragga 2.9
ragged 2.24
raggedy 2.57
raggle-taggle 2.28
ragi 2.2
raging 8.64
raglan 2.35
Raglan 2.35
ragman 1.24; 2.35
Ragnarök 23.3
ragout 41.2
rags 1.14
rags-to-riches 18.55
ragtag 1.13
ragtime 21.19
ragweed 15.11
ragworm 11.13
ragwort 11.24

Rahman 4.24
rah-rah 3.1
raid 7.8
raider 8.5
raiding 8.60
raids 7.9
rail 7.15
railcar 3.1
railcard 3.8
railed 7.16
railing 8.62
railings 8.65
raillery 8.76
railroad 35.25
railroaded 36.12
railroading 36.24
rails 7.17
railway 7.3
railwayman 8.81
railways 7.56
raiment 8.56
rain 7.21
rainbow 35.6
rainbows 35.52
raincoat 35.45
raindrop 23.36
raindrops 23.37
rained 7.22
rainfall 25.14
rainforest 24.45
rain gauge 7.12
Rainhill 17.15
rainier 8.78
rainiest 8.86
raining 8.63
rainmaker 8.4
rainproof 41.10
rains 7.26
rainstorm 25.20
rainwater 26.4
rainy 8.1
raise 7.56
raised 7.57
raiser 8.9
raisin 8.21
raising 8.64
raison d'être 10.12
raita 8.5; 16.5
raj 3.12; 3.13
rajah 4.14
Rajasthan 3.19
Rajiv 15.39
rake 7.6
raked 7.7
raker 8.4
raki 2.2
raking 8.59
rakish 8.70

Raleigh 2.5; 4.5; 26.1
rallentando 35.3
rallied 2.24
rallier 2.61
rallies 2.54
rally 2.5
rallycross 23.39
Ralph 1.18
ram 1.22
RAM 1.22
Rama 4.13
Ramadan 3.19
Rambert 5.1
ramble 2.28
rambler 2.12
ramblers 2.55
rambling 2.42
Rambo 35.3
rambunctious 38.38
ramekin 17.29
ramekins 17.42
Rameses 15.45
ramie 2.6
ramification 8.40
ramify 21.4
rammer 2.13
Ramona 36.8
ramp 1.23
rampage 7.12
rampage 7.12
rampageous 8.67
rampaging 8.64
rampant 2.40
rampart 3.32
ramparts 3.33
rampion 2.66
ram raid 7.8
ramrod 23.8
Ramsay 2.7
Ramsbottom 24.30
Ramsden 2.35
Ramsey 2.7
Ramsgate 7.34
ramshackle 2.28
ramshorn 25.22
Ram Singh 17.35
ran 1.24
ranch 3.20
rancher 4.14
ranching 4.29
rancid 2.24
rancorous 2.71
rancour 2.9
rand 1.28
Randall 2.28
R&B 15.4
R&D 15.4
randier 2.61

randiest 2.72
Randolph 23.16
random 2.32
randomize 21.42
randomly 2.56
R&R 3.1
randy 2.3
rang 1.29
rangatira 14.2
range 7.23
ranged 7.24
rangefinder 22.5
ranger 8.9
Range Rover 36.6
ranging 8.64
Rangoon 41.19
rangy 8.1
rani 4.6
rank 1.25
Rank 1.25
rank and file 21.16
ranked 1.27
ranker 2.9
rankest 2.48
Rankin 2.34
ranking 2.42
rankle 2.28
rankled 2.29
ranks 1.26
Rannoch 2.16
ransack 1.3
ransacked 1.6
ransom 2.32
Ransome 2.32
rant 1.33
rant and rave 7.54
ranter 2.10
ranting 2.42
rants 1.34
Ranulph 37.21
Raoul 29.4
rap 1.37
rapacious 8.67
rapacity 2.57
Rapa Nui 42.1
rape 7.27
raped 7.29
rapeseed 15.11
rapid 2.24
rapidity 18.57
rapidly 2.58
rapier 8.78
rapine 21.22
rapist 8.68
rappel 9.16
rapper 2.8
rapping 2.42
rapport 25.2

rapporteur 11.1
raps 1.38
rapscallion 2.35; 2.66
rapt 1.39
raptor 2.10
rapture 2.14
rapturous 2.71
Rapunzel 38.23
Raquel 9.16
Raquel's 9.27
rara avis 8.66
rarae aves 15.44
rare 5.1
rarebit 6.13
rarefaction 2.35
rarefied 21.12
rarefy 21.4
rarely 6.1
rarer 6.2
raring 6.10
rarity 6.15
Rarotonga 24.9
rascal 4.19
rascally 4.42
rash 1.43
rasher 2.14
Rashid 15.11
rashly 2.5
rashness 2.46
rasp 3.29
raspberry 4.5; 4.42
rasping 4.29
Rasputin 42.19
Rasta 2.10
Ras Tafari 4.5
Rastafarian 6.19
Rastafarianism 18.29
raster 2.10
rat 1.45
ratable 8.79
ratafia 16.2
rataplan 1.24
rat-arsed 3.30
rat-a-tat 1.45
ratatouille 15.4
ratbag 1.13
rat-catcher 2.14
ratchet 2.51
Ratcliffe 17.10
rate 7.32
rated 8.13
ratel 8.15
ratepayer 8.2
rates 7.50
ratfink 17.30
ratfinks 17.31
Rathbone 35.36
rather 4.11

ratification 8.40
ratified 21.12
ratify 21.4
rating 8.60
ratings 8.65
ratio 35.19
ration 2.35
rational 2.64
rationale 3.14
rationalism 18.29
rationalist 17.49
rationality 2.57
rationalization 8.53
rationalize 21.47
rationally 2.78
rationed 2.36
rationing 2.70
rations 2.39
Ratner 2.13
ratpack 1.3
rats 1.46
ratsbane 7.21
rat's-tail 7.15
rattan 1.24
rat-tat 1.45
ratter 2.10
rattier 2.61
rattiest 2.72
Rattigan 2.66
ratting 2.42
rattle 2.28
rattler 2.12
rattlesnake 7.6
rattletrap 1.37
rattling 2.42
rattly 2.5
ratty 2.3
raucous 26.27
raunchier 26.39
raunchiest 26.49
raunchy 26.1
ravage 2.27
rave 7.54
ravel 2.28
Ravel 9.16
raven 2.35; 8.21
ravening 2.70
Ravenna 10.13
ravenous 2.71
ravenously 2.78
raver 8.6
raves 7.55
rave-up 37.41
Ravi 4.4
ravine 15.24
raving 8.61
ravioli 36.1
ravish 2.49

ravisher 2.60
ravishing 2.70
ravishment 2.68
raw 25.1
Rawalpindi 18.3
rawboned 35.37
rawhide 21.11
Rawlinson 26.43
Rawlplug® 37.14
rawness 26.27
Rawsthorne 25.22
ray 7.1
Ray 7.1
Ray-Bans® 1.36
Rayleigh 8.1
rayless 8.67
Raymond 8.54
Rayner 8.8
rayon 23.27
rayon 8.21
rays 7.56
raze 7.56
razor 8.9
razorback 1.3
razorbill 17.15
razor blade 7.8
razor-sharp 3.25
razor shell 9.16
razzle 2.28
razzle-dazzle 2.28
razzmatazz 1.50
re 7.1; 15.1
Re 7.1
reabsorb 25.5
reach 15.9
reachable 16.41
reached 15.10
reaching 16.27
reacquaint 7.25
reacquaintance 8.57
reacquire 19.1
react 1.6
reactance 2.41
reactant 2.40
reacted 2.25
reaction 2.35
reactionary 2.56
reactivate 7.35
reactivation 8.24
reactive 2.53
reactor 2.10
read 9.8; 15.11
readability 18.58
readable 16.41
readapt 1.39
readdress 9.47
readdressed 9.49
Reade 15.11

reader 16.5
readership 17.43
readier 10.57
readies 10.51
readiest 10.71
readily 10.54
readiness 10.70
Reading 10.36
reading 16.27
readjust 37.45
readjustment 38.32
readmission 18.33
readmit 17.51
readmittance 18.39
readoption 24.33
readout 29.14
read-through 41.3
readvertise 21.42
readvertised 21.48
ready 10.3
ready-made 7.8
ready-reckoner 10.56
ready-to-wear 5.1
reaffirm 11.13
reaffirmed 11.14
reafforestation 8.34
Reagan 8.21
reagent 8.56
real 13.3
realgar 2.9
realign 21.22
realignment 22.24
realism 18.27
realist 14.15
realistic 18.16
realistically 18.57
reality 2.57
realizable 22.43
realization 8.30
realize 21.41
realized 21.48
realizing 22.26
real life 21.14
really 14.1
realm 9.21
real McCoy 33.1
realty 14.1
ream 15.20
reamer 16.8
reams 15.22
reanimate 7.35
reap 15.30
reaper 16.3
reaping 16.27
reappear 13.1
reappearance 14.11
reapplication 8.24
reapplied 21.12

recriminate 7.41
recrimination 8.32
recross 23.39
recrossed 23.41
recrudescence 10.34
recrudescent 10.33
recruit 41.27
recruiter 42.5
recruiting 42.24
recruitment 42.22
recruits 41.28
rectal 10.21
rectangle 2.28
rectangular 2.60
rectifiable 22.43
rectification 8.43
rectified 21.12
rectifier 22.2
rectify 21.4
rectitude 41.9
recto 35.7
rectocele 15.17
rector 10.10
rectory 10.53
rectum 10.25
recumbent 38.32
recuperate 7.49
recuperation 8.39
recur 11.1
recurred 11.7
recurrence 38.33
recurrent 38.32
recurring 12.16
recurs 11.29
recursion 12.12
recusant 42.22
recyclable 22.43
recycle 22.16
recycled 22.17
recycler 22.7
red 9.8
red-blooded 38.20
redbreast 9.49
redbrick 10.15
Redbridge 10.20
redcap 1.37
Redcar 3.1
redcoat 35.45
redcoats 35.46
redcurrant 38.32
redden 10.27
redder 10.10
reddest 10.43
Redding 10.36
reddish 10.45
Redditch 17.7
reddle 10.21
redecorate 7.38

redecoration 8.28
redeem 15.20
redeemable 16.41
redeemed 15.21
redeemer 16.8
Redeemer 16.8
redeeming 16.27
redefine 21.22
redemption 10.28
redemptive 10.50
redeploy 33.1
redeployed 33.4
redeployment 34.9
redeploys 33.15
redesign 21.22
redevelop 10.38
redeveloped 10.40
redevelopment 10.67
redevelops 10.39
red-eye 21.3
Redfern 11.15
Redford 10.18
Redgrave 7.54
red-haired 5.2
red-handed 2.25
redhead 9.8
red-headed 10.18
Redhill 17.15
red-hot 23.44
redial 19.3
redid 17.8
Rediffusion® 42.20
redigested 10.18
redirect 9.5
redirection 10.28
rediscover 38.11
rediscovery 38.47
redistribute 41.27
redistribution 42.20
redleg 9.12
red-letter day 7.4
Redmond 10.29
redneck 9.2
rednecks 9.3
redness 10.42
redo 41.2
redoes 37.51
redolence 10.68
redolent 10.67
redone 37.31
redouble 38.23
redoubt 29.14
redoubtable 30.24
redound 29.6
redraft 3.10
redraw 25.2
redrawn 25.22

redress 9.47
re-dress 9.47
redrew 41.2
Redruth 41.29
redshank 1.25
red shift 17.11
redstart 3.32
reduce 41.24
reduced 41.25
reducer 42.9
reducible 42.39
reducing 42.24
reductio ad
    absurdum 12.10
reduction 38.28
reductionism 18.28
redundancies 38.63
redundancy 38.47
redundant 38.32
reduplicate 7.49
reduplication 8.39
redwing 10.36
redwood 39.4
Reebok® 23.3
Reeboks® 23.5
re-echo 35.7
re-echoed 35.25
reed 15.11
Reed 15.11
reed bed 9.8
reedling 16.27
reeds 15.12
reedy 16.1
reef 15.13
reefer 16.6
reefing 16.27
reek 15.7
reeking 16.27
reel 15.17
reelect 9.5
re-election 10.28
reeled 15.18
re-embark 3.3
re-emergence 12.15
re-enact 1.6
re-enactment 2.40
re-enlist 16.48
re-enlistment 18.38
re-enter 10.10
re-entrant 10.33
re-entry 10.5
re-equip 17.43
Rees 15.32
reeve 15.39
Reeves 15.41
re-examine 2.34
re-export 25.31
ref 9.10

refashion 2.35
refection 10.28
refectory 10.53
refer 11.1
referee 15.4
refereed 15.11
reference 10.34; 10.68
referenda 10.10
referendum 10.25
referent 10.67
referential 10.21
referral 12.8
referred 11.7
referrer 12.2
refill 17.15
refillable 18.64
refilled 17.18
refine 21.22
refined 21.23
refinement 22.24
refinements 22.25
refiner 22.8
refinery 22.40
refining 22.26
refit 16.34; 17.51
reflag 1.13
reflate 7.33
reflation 8.23
reflect 9.5
reflected 10.18
reflection 10.28
reflections 10.32
reflective 10.50
reflector 10.10
reflex 9.3
reflexive 10.50
reflexologist 24.72
reflexology 24.55
refloat 35.45
reflux 37.4
refocus 36.26
refocused 36.28
reforest 24.45
reforestation 8.34
reforested 24.59
reform 25.20
re-form 25.20
reformat 1.45
reformation 8.28
Reformation 8.28
reformatory 26.37
reformed 25.21
reformer 26.7
reforming 26.25
reformulate 7.44
reformulation 8.35
refract 1.6
refraction 2.35

refractive 2.53
refractor 2.10
refractory 2.56
refrain 7.21
reframe 7.18
refreeze 15.43
refresh 9.50
refresher 10.14
refreshing 10.36
refreshingly 10.54
refreshment 10.33
refrigerant 18.70
refrigerate 7.41
refrigerated 8.13
refrigeration 8.32
refrigerator 8.5
refringent 18.38
refroze 35.52
refrozen 36.20
refuel 42.16
refuge 41.12
refugee 15.4
refugees 15.45
refulgence 38.33
refulgent 38.32
refund 37.36
refund 37.36
refundable 38.52
refurbish 12.22
refurbished 12.23
refurbishment 12.35
refusal 42.16
refuse 41.24; 41.33
refused 41.34
refusenik 42.11
refuseniks 42.12
refuser 42.9
refusing 42.24
refutable 10.79; 42.39
refutal 42.16
refutation 8.28
refute 41.27
refuted 42.14
refuter 42.5
refuting 42.24
Reg 9.14
regain 7.21
regal 16.17
regale 7.15
regalia 8.78
regally 16.38
Regan 16.22
regard 3.8
regarded 4.17
regarding 4.29
regardless 4.32
regatta 2.10
regency 16.38

Regency 16.38
regenerate 10.73
regenerate 7.38
regeneration 8.28
regent 16.25
Regent's Park 3.3
reggae 7.3
regicide 21.12
regime 15.20
regimen 9.32
regiment 10.67
regiment 9.41
regimental 10.21
regimentation 8.43
regimented 10.18
Regina 22.8
Reginald 10.61
region 16.22
regional 16.41
regionalism 18.29
regionalization 8.53
regionally 16.52
regions 16.24
Regis 16.29
register 10.56
registered 10.58
registrar 3.1
registration 8.28
registry 10.54
Regius 16.47
regnal 10.21
regnant 10.33
regress 9.47
regression 10.28
regressive 10.50
regret 9.51
regretful 10.21; 39.7
regretfully 10.53; 10.55
regrettable 10.60
regrettably 10.53
regroup 41.22
regrouping 42.24
regrow 35.2
regrowth 35.47
regular 10.56
regularity 2.57
regularization 8.53
regularize 21.47
regularly 10.78
regulate 7.38
regulated 8.13
regulation 8.28
regulator 8.5
Regulus 10.70
regurgitate 7.39
regurgitation 8.29
rehab 1.1
rehabilitate 7.41

rehabilitation 8.32
rehang 1.29
rehash 1.43
rehashed 1.44
rehearsal 12.8
rehearsals 12.9
rehearse 11.22
rehearsed 11.23
rehearser 12.2
rehearsing 12.16
reheat 15.35
reheated 16.14
Rehoboam 36.18
rehome 35.34
rehouse 29.17
rehung 37.37
Reich 21.7
Reichsmark 3.3
Reichstag 3.11
Reid 15.11
reification 8.42
reify 21.4
Reigate 7.34
reign 7.21
reigned 7.22
reigning 8.63
reignite 21.34
reiki 8.1
reimburse 11.22
reimbursed 11.23
reimbursement 12.14
reimport 25.31
reimpose 35.52
rein 7.21
reincarnate 4.37
reincarnation 8.45
reindeer 13.1
reinfect 9.5
reinfection 10.28
reinforce 25.28
reinforced 25.29
reinforcement 26.23
reinforcer 26.8
reinforcing 26.25
Reinhardt 3.32
Reinhold 35.31
reins 7.26
reinsert 11.24
reinspect 9.5
reinstall 25.14
reinstalled 25.15
reinstate 7.40
reinstatement 8.56
reinsure 27.1
reinsured 27.2
reintegrate 7.41
reintegration 8.32
reinterpret 12.25

reinterpretation 8.29
reintroduce 41.24
reintroduced 41.25
reintroduction 38.28
reinvent 9.41
reinvention 10.28
reinvest 9.49
reinvestigation 8.28
reinvestment 10.33
reinvigorate 7.41
reinvigoration 8.32
reissue 41.3
reiterate 7.41
reiteration 8.32
Reith 15.37
Reithian 16.43
reive 15.39
reiver 16.6
reject 9.5
rejection 10.28
rejector 10.10
rejig 17.12
rejoice 33.11
rejoiced 33.12
rejoicer 34.2
rejoicing 34.11
rejoin 33.8
rejoinder 34.2
rejuvenate 7.49
rejuvenation 8.39
rekindle 18.22
rekindled 18.23
relabel 8.15
relaid 7.8
relapse 1.38
relapser 2.14
relate 7.33
related 8.13
relating 8.60
relation 8.23
relational 8.79
relations 8.55
relationship 17.43
relationships 17.44
relative 17.55
relatively 10.78
relativism 18.29
relativist 17.49
relativistic 18.16
relativity 18.57
relaunch 25.23
relax 1.4
relaxant 2.40
relaxation 8.31
relaxer 2.14
relaxing 2.42
relay 7.2; 7.3
relearn 11.15

release 15.32
released 15.33
releaser 16.9
relegate 7.38
relegation 8.28
relent 9.41
relenting 10.36
relentless 10.42
relentlessly 10.53
relevance 10.68
relevant 10.67
reliability 18.58
reliable 22.43
reliably 22.40
reliance 22.25
reliant 22.24
relic 10.15
relics 10.16
relict 17.6
relief 15.13
relieve 15.39
relieved 15.40
relight 21.32
religion 18.33
religious 18.44
religiously 18.56
relinquish 18.47
relinquished 18.48
relinquishment 18.70
reliquary 18.56
relish 10.45
relished 10.46
relit 17.51
relive 17.54
reload 35.25
reloaded 36.12
reloading 36.24
relocate 7.40
relocated 8.13
relocation 8.31
reluctance 38.33
reluctant 38.32
reluctantly 38.47
rely 21.2
REM 9.28
remade 7.8
remain 7.21
remainder 8.5
remainderman 1.24
remained 7.22
remaining 8.63
remains 7.26
remake 7.6
remake 7.6
remand 3.21
remark 3.3
remarkable 4.47
remarkably 4.42

remarked 3.5
Remarque 3.3
remarried 2.24
remarry 2.5
rematch 1.7
Rembrandt 1.33
REME 16.1
remediable 16.53
remedial 16.41
remediation 8.31
remedied 17.8
remedies 10.77
remedy 10.54
remember 10.8
remembered 10.18
remembrance 10.34
remembrancer 10.56
remind 21.23
reminded 22.13
reminder 22.5
Remington 10.64
reminisce 17.46
reminiscence 18.39
reminiscent 18.38
reminiscer 18.14
remiss 17.46
remission 18.33
remit 16.34; 17.51
remittance 18.39
remittent 18.38
remitter 18.10
remix 16.12
remix 17.4
remnant 10.33
remnants 10.34
remodel 24.27
remodelled 24.28
remonstrance 24.39
remonstrant 24.38
remonstrate 7.38
remonstration 8.28
remonstrative 17.55
remorse 25.28
remorseful 26.15; 39.7
remorseless 26.27
remorselessly 26.37
remortgage 26.14
remote 35.45
remote-controlled 35.31
remotely 36.1
remoteness 36.26
remould 35.31
remount 29.11
removable 42.39
removal 42.16
remove 41.31
removed 41.32

remover 42.6
removing 42.24
remunerate 7.49
remuneration 8.39
remunerative 17.54
Remus 16.30
renaissance 3.22
Renaissance 3.22
renaissance 8.57
Renaissance 8.57
renal 16.17
rename 7.18
renamed 7.19
renascence 2.41; 8.57
renascent 2.40; 8.56
Renata 4.10
renationalize 21.47
renationalized 21.48
Renault 35.7
rend 9.35
Rendell 10.21
render 10.10
rendering 10.69
rendezvous 41.4
rendition 18.33
Rene 16.1
René 7.2
renegade 7.8
renege 7.11; 15.14
reneging 16.27
reneging 8.59
renegotiate 7.47
renegotiation 8.37
renew 41.2
renewable 42.39
renewal 42.16
renewed 41.9
Rennes 9.32
rennet 10.48
Rennie 10.6
rennin 10.26
Reno 35.10
Renoir 3.1
Renoir's 3.37
renounce 29.9
renounced 29.10
renovate 7.38
renovation 8.28
renovator 8.5
renown 29.5
renowned 29.6
rent 9.41
rentable 10.60
rental 10.21
rent-a-mob 23.1
rent boy 33.1
renter 10.10
rent-free 15.2

Rentokil® 17.15
renumber 38.8
renunciation 8.38
reoccupy 21.4
reoccur 11.1
reoccurred 11.7
reoccurrence 38.33
reopen 36.20
reorder 26.4
reordered 26.12
reorganization 8.49
reorganize 21.45
reorient 9.41; 26.45
rep 9.44
repack 1.3
repackage 2.27
repacks 1.4
repaid 7.8
repaint 7.25
repainting 8.60
repair 5.1
repairable 6.17
repaired 5.2
repairer 6.2
repairing 6.10
repairs 5.5
repaper 8.3
reparable 10.60
reparation 8.28
reparative 17.55
repartee 15.4
repast 3.30
repatriate 7.35
repatriation 8.24
repay 7.2
repayment 8.56
repeal 15.17
repealed 15.18
repeat 15.35
repeatable 16.41
repeated 16.14
repeatedly 16.38
repeater 16.5
repeaters 16.37
repeating 16.27
repel 9.16
repelled 9.19
repellence 10.34
repellent 10.33
repeller 10.12
repent 9.41
repentance 10.34
repentant 10.33
repented 10.18
repenting 10.36
repercussion 38.28
repercussions 38.31
repertoire 3.1

resourceful 26.15; 39.7
resourcefully 26.37
respect 9.5
respectability 18.58
respectable 10.60
respectably 10.53
respecter 10.10
respectful 10.21; 39.7
respectfully 10.53;
   10.55
respecting 10.36
respective 10.50
respectively 10.54
respell 9.16
Respighi 16.1
respiration 8.28
respirator 8.5
respiratory 10.78;
   18.56
respire 19.1
respite 10.48; 21.33
resplendence 10.34
resplendent 10.33
respond 23.30
responded 24.24
respondent 24.38
responding 24.40
response 23.33
responsibilities 18.79
responsibility 18.58
responsible 24.61
responsibly 24.54
responsive 24.51
respray 7.3
rest 9.49
restage 7.12
restart 3.32
restate 7.33
restatement 8.56
restaurant 23.31; 23.34
restaurateur 11.1
rested 10.18
restful 10.21; 39.7
resting 10.36
restitution 42.20
restive 10.50
restless 10.42
restlessness 10.70
restock 23.3
restocked 23.6
restorable 26.41
restoration 8.28
Restoration 8.28
restorative 17.55
restore 25.2
restored 25.9
restorer 26.6
restrain 7.21

restrained 7.22
restrainedly 8.76
restrainer 8.8
restraint 7.25
restrict 17.6
restricted 18.19
restricting 18.40
restriction 18.33
restrictive 18.53
rest room 39.9; 41.17
restrung 37.37
restyle 21.16
restyled 21.17
restyling 22.26
resubmit 17.51
result 37.26
resultant 38.32
resulted 38.20
resulting 38.34
resume 41.17
résumé 7.4
resumed 41.18
resuming 42.24
resumption 38.28
resupply 21.4
resurface 12.18
resurfaced 12.21
resurgence 12.15
resurgent 12.14
resurrect 9.5
resurrection 10.28
Resurrection 10.28
resurrectionism
   18.28
resurrectionist 10.72
resuscitate 7.48
resuscitation 8.38
resuscitator 8.5
retail 7.15
retailer 8.7
retailing 8.62
retain 7.21
retained 7.22
retainer 8.8
retake 7.6
retaliate 7.35
retaliation 8.24
retaliatory 2.56
retard 3.8
retardant 4.27
retardation 8.31
retarded 4.17
retarder 4.10
retch 9.6
retched 9.7
retching 10.36
retell 9.16
retention 10.28

retentive 10.50
retest 9.49
rethink 17.30
rethinks 17.31
rethought 25.31
reticence 10.68
reticent 10.67
reticule 41.14
reticulum 18.66
retie 21.2
retina 10.56
retinal 10.60
retinue 41.4
retiral 22.16
retire 19.1
retired 19.2
retiree 15.4
retirement 20.5
retirer 20.2
retiring 20.7
retitle 22.16
retold 35.31
retook 39.1
retool 41.14
retooled 41.15
retort 25.31
retorts 25.32
retouch 37.6
retouched 37.7
retoucher 38.14
retouching 38.34
retrace 7.30
retract 1.6
retractile 21.16
retraction 2.35
retractor 2.10
retrain 7.21
retraining 8.63
retransmit 17.51
retread 9.8
retreat 15.35
retreating 16.27
retrench 9.33
retrenched 9.34
retrenchment 10.33
retrial 19.3
retribution 42.20
retried 21.10
retrievable 16.41
retrieval 16.17
retrieve 15.39
retriever 16.6
retro 35.7
retroact 1.6
retroaction 2.35
retrocede 15.11
retrochoir 19.1
retrofire 19.1

retroflex 9.3
retroflexion 10.28
retrograde 7.8
retrogress 9.47
retrorocket 24.49
retrospect 9.5
retrospection 10.28
retrospective 10.50
retrospectively 10.54
retroussé 7.3
retroversion 12.12
retrovirus 20.8; 22.29
retry 21.2
retsina 16.8
retune 41.19
return 11.15
returnable 12.32
returned 11.16
returnee 15.4
returner 12.2
returning 12.16
returns 11.18
retype 21.26
retyped 21.28
Reuben 42.20
Reuben's 42.21
reunification 8.52
reunify 21.4
reunion 42.20; 42.41
Réunion 42.41
reunite 21.34
reusable 42.39
reuse 41.24; 41.33
reused 41.34
Reuter 34.2
rev 9.56
revalue 41.3
revalued 41.9
revamp 1.23
revamping 2.42
rev counter 30.2
reveal 15.17
revealed 15.18
revealer 16.7
revealing 16.27
revealingly 16.38
reveals 15.19
reveille 2.5
revel 10.21
revelation 8.28
Revelation 8.28
revelatory 8.76
reveller 10.56
revelry 10.53
revenant 10.67
revenge 9.38
revengeful 10.21; 39.7
revenue 41.4

Ridley 18.5
Riesling 16.27
rife 21.14
riff 17.10
riffle 18.22
riffler 18.12
riffraff 1.11
Rifkind 17.34
rifle 22.16
rifled 22.17
rifleman 22.44
rifling 22.26
rift 17.11
rig 17.12
Riga 16.4
rigadoon 41.19
Rigby 18.1
Rigg 17.12
rigger 18.9
rigging 18.40
right 21.31
rightable 22.43
right angle 2.28
right as rain 7.21
righteous 22.29
righteousness 22.46
righter 22.5
rightful 22.16; 39.7
rightfully 22.40
right-handed 2.25
right-handedness 2.71
right-hander 2.10
righting 22.26
rightly 22.1
rightness 22.29
righto 35.2
rights 21.35
right-thinking 18.40
right-wing 17.35
rigid 18.18
rigidify 21.4
rigidity 18.57
rigidly 18.57
rigmarole 35.30
rigor 18.9
rigor mortis 26.26
rigorous 18.74
rigorously 18.80
rigour 18.9
rigs 17.13
Rigsby 18.1
Rikki-Tikki-Tavi 4.4; 8.1
rile 21.16
riled 21.17
Riley 22.1
Rilke 18.9

rill 17.15
rim 17.24
Rimbaud 35.3
rime 21.19
rime riche 15.34
Rimini 18.57
rimless 18.44
Rimmer 18.13
Rimsky-Korsakov 23.9
rimy 22.1
rind 21.23
rinderpest 9.49
ring 17.35
ring binder 22.5
ringbolt 35.32
ringdove 37.49
ringer 18.13
ring-fence 9.39
ring-fenced 9.40
ringgit 18.50
ringing 18.40
ringleader 16.5
ringleaders 16.37
ringlet 18.50
ringmaster 4.10
Ringo 35.11
ringpull 39.7
rings 17.36
ringside 21.11
ringtail 7.15
Ringwood 39.4
ringworm 11.13
rink 17.30
rinky-dink 17.30
rinse 17.38
Rio 35.10
Rio de Janeiro 35.9
Río de la Plata 4.10
Rio Grande 1.28; 2.3
Rioja 24.9
riot 22.34
rioter 22.41
riotous 22.46
RIP 15.4
rip 17.43
riparian 6.19
ripcord 25.9
ripe 21.26
ripen 22.20
ripened 22.21
ripeness 22.29
Ripley 18.5
rip-off 23.9
Ripon 18.32
riposte 23.41; 35.43
ripped 17.45
ripper 18.8

ripping 18.40
ripple 18.22
rippled 18.23
ripples 18.24
ripplet 18.50
rippling 18.40
Rippon 18.32
rip-roaring 26.25
ripsaw 25.3
ripsnorter 26.4
ripsnorting 26.25
riptide 21.11
Rip Van Winkle 18.22
rise 21.39
risen 18.33
riser 22.9
risible 18.64
rising 22.26
risk 17.47
risker 18.9
riskier 18.61
riskiest 18.76
risking 18.40
risky 18.2
Risorgimento 35.7
risotto 35.13
risqué 7.3
rissole 35.30
Rita 16.5
Ritalin® 17.29
Rita's 16.37
rite 21.31
Ritter 18.10
ritual 18.64
ritualism 18.29
ritualistic 18.16
ritualize 21.47
ritualized 21.48
ritually 18.59; 18.80
Ritz 17.52
ritzy 18.7
rival 22.16
rivalled 22.17
rivalry 22.40
rive 21.37
riven 18.32
river 18.11
riverbank 1.25
river bed 9.8
riverine 21.22
River Plate 7.41
rivers 18.55
Rivers 18.55
riverside 21.12
rivet 18.50
riveted 18.62
Riviera 6.2
rivière 5.1

rivulet 18.77
Riyadh 1.9
Rizla® 18.12
roach 35.24
Roach 35.24
road 35.25
roadblock 23.3
road hog 23.11
roadholding 36.24
roadhouse 29.12
roadie 36.1
roadkill 17.15
road rage 7.12
roadroller 36.7
roadrunner 38.13
roadside 21.11
road sign 21.22
road signs 21.25
roadstead 9.8
road test 9.49
roadway 7.3
roadworks 11.5
roadworthiness 12.37
roadworthy 12.1
Roald 36.16
roam 35.34
roamer 36.8
roaming 36.24
roan 35.36
Roanoke 35.21
roar 25.1
roared 25.9
roarer 26.6
roaring 26.25
roast 35.43
roast beef 15.13
roasted 36.12
roaster 36.5
roasting 36.24
rob 23.1
Rob 23.1
robber 24.8
robberies 24.75
robbers 24.53
robbery 24.54
Robbie 24.1
robbing 24.40
Robbins 24.37
robe 35.20
Robert 24.48
Roberta 12.2
Robertson 24.64
Robeson 36.20
Robespierre 5.1
Robey 36.1
robin 24.32
Robin 24.32
Robina 16.8

robing 36.24
Robin Hood 39.4
robinia 18.61
robins 24.37
Robinson 24.64
robot 23.44
robotic 24.16
robotics 24.22
robotize 21.45
robots 23.45
Rob Roy 33.1
Robson 24.33
robust 37.45
robustly 38.5
robustness 38.38
Roby 36.1
roc 23.3
Rochdale 7.15
Roche 23.42; 35.44
Rochelle 9.16
Rochester 24.57
rock 23.3
rockabilly 18.5
Rockall 25.14
rock-bottom 24.30
rock cake 7.6
rocked 23.6
Rockefeller 10.12
rocker 24.9
rockers 24.53
rockery 24.54
rocket 24.49
rocketed 24.59
rocketeer 13.1
rocketry 24.56
rocket ship 17.43
rocket ships 17.44
rockfish 24.46
Rockford 24.24
Rockhampton 2.35
rock-hard 3.8
rockier 24.58
Rockies 24.52
rockiest 24.71
rocking 24.40
rocking chair 5.1
rocking horse 25.28
rock'n'roll 35.30
rock'n'roller 36.7
rockrose 35.52
rocks 23.5
rocky 24.2
Rocky 24.2
rococo 35.16
rod 23.8
Rod 23.8
Roddenberry 10.5;
    24.54

Roddick 24.16
Roddy 24.3
rode 35.25
rodent 36.22
rodenticide 21.12
rodents 36.23
rodeo 35.19
Roderick 17.3
Rodgers 24.53
Rodin 1.24
Rodney 24.6
rodomontade 3.8
Rodrigo 35.10
Rodriguez 9.57
roe 35.1
roebuck 37.3
Roedean 15.25
roe deer 13.1
roentgen 24.33
Roentgen 24.33
rogation 8.23
roger 24.14
Roger 24.14
Rogers 24.53
Roget 7.3
rogue 35.28
roguery 36.35
roguish 36.29
roguishly 36.35
roil 33.6
roister 34.2
roisterer 34.15
roisterous 34.18
Roland 36.21
role 35.30
Rolex® 9.3
Rolf 23.16
roll 35.30
rollbar 3.1
rolled 35.31
roller 36.7
rollerball 25.14
Rollerblade® 7.8
roller-coaster 36.5
rollers 36.34
roller-skate 7.47
roller-skater 8.5
roller skates 7.50
roller-skating 8.60
rollick 24.18
rollicking 24.69
rolling 36.24
Rolling Stones 35.39
rollmop 23.36
rollneck 9.2
Rollo 35.13
roll-on 23.27
rollover 36.6

rolls 35.33
Rolls 35.33
Rolls-Royce 33.11
Rolo® 35.16
roly-poly 36.1
ROM 23.23
Roma 36.8
romaine 7.21
Roman 36.20
romance 1.31
romancer 2.14
Romanesque 9.48
Romania 8.78
Romanian 8.81
Romanize 21.45
Romanov 23.9
romantic 2.17
romantically 2.58
romanticism 18.28
romanticist 2.73
romanticize 21.42
romanticized 21.48
Romany 36.35
Rome 35.34
Romeo 35.19
Rommel 24.27
Romney 24.6
romp 23.24
romped 23.25
romper 24.8
rompers 24.53
Romsey 24.7
Romulus 24.70
Ron 23.27
Ronald 24.28
Ronan 36.20
rondeau 35.13
rondo 35.13
Ronnie 24.6
Ron's 23.35
Ronson 24.33
roo 41.1
Roo 41.1
rood 41.9
roof 41.10
roofer 42.6
roofing 42.24
rooftop 23.36
rooftops 23.37
rook 39.1
rookery 40.20
rookie 40.1
room 39.9; 41.17
roomful 39.7
roomier 42.38
roomiest 42.47
roommate 7.34
roomy 42.1

Rooney 42.1
Roosevelt 9.23
roost 41.25
roosted 42.14
rooster 42.5
roosting 42.24
root 41.27
rooted 42.14
rooter 42.5
Rootes 41.28
rooting 42.24
rootle 42.16
rootless 42.26
roots 41.28
rootstock 23.3
rope 35.40
Roper 36.3
ropes 35.41
ropewalk 25.6
ropey 36.1
ropier 36.37
ropiest 36.44
Roquefort 25.3
rorqual 26.15
Rory 26.1
Ros 23.48
Rosa 36.9
rosacea 8.9
rosaceous 8.67
Rosalie 36.35
Rosalind 17.34
Rosalyn 17.29
Rosamund 24.65;
    37.36
rosarium 6.18
rosary 36.35
Roscius 24.70
Roscommon 24.33
rose 35.52
Rose 35.52
rosé 7.3
Roseanne 1.24
roseate 7.47; 36.45
rose bowl 35.30
rosebud 37.8
rosebuds 37.9
rose bush 39.13
rosehip 17.43
rosemary 36.35
Rosemary 36.35
Rosen 36.20
Rosencrantz 1.34
roses 36.34
Rosetta 10.10
Rosetta Stone 35.36
rosette 9.51
Rosewall 25.14
rosewood 39.4

Rum 37.27
rumba 38.8
rum baba 3.1; 4.8
rumble 38.23
rumbles 38.25
rumbling 38.34
Rumbold 35.31
rumbustious 38.59
rumen 9.32
ruminant 42.43
ruminants 42.44
ruminate 7.49
rumination 8.39
rummage 38.22
rummaging 38.58
rummer 38.13
rummy 38.6
rumour 42.8
rumoured 42.14
rumours 42.34
rump 37.29
Rumpelstiltskin 18.31
rumple 38.23
Rumpole 35.30
rumpus 38.38
rumpy-pumpy 38.1
run 37.31
runabout 29.14
run-around 29.6
runaway 7.4
runcible 38.52
Runcie 38.7
Runciman 38.54
Runcorn 25.22
rundown 29.5
run-down 29.5
rune 41.19
runes 41.21
rung 37.37
runic 42.11
run-in 38.27
runnel 38.23
runner 38.13
runner bean 15.26
runners 38.45
runner-up 37.41
runnier 38.49
runniest 38.61
running 38.34
runny 38.6
Runnymede 15.11
run-of-the-mill 17.15
runt 37.40
run-through 41.3
runty 38.3
run-up 37.41
runway 7.3
Runyon 38.28

rupee 15.2
rupees 15.43
Rupert 42.31
rupiah 16.2
rupture 38.14
ruptured 38.20
rural 28.4
ruralize 21.45
Ruritania 8.78
Ruritanian 8.81
ruse 41.33
rush 37.46
Rushdie 40.1
rusher 38.14
rushes 38.45
rush-hour 31.1
rushing 38.34
Rushton 38.28
rushy 38.7
rusk 37.44
Ruskin 38.27
Russ 37.43
Russell 38.23
Russell's 38.25
russet 38.43
Russia 38.14
Russian 38.28
Russify 21.4
Russophile 21.16
Russophobe 35.20
rust 37.45
rust bucket 38.43
rustic 38.15
rusticana 4.13
rusticate 7.48
rustication 8.38
rustics 38.18
rustier 38.49
rustiest 38.61
rusting 38.34
rustle 38.23
rustler 38.12
rustling 38.34
rustproof 41.10
rusty 38.3
rut 37.47
rutabaga 8.4
Ruth 41.29
ruthenium 16.42
Rutherford 38.50
ruthless 42.26
ruthlessly 42.36
ruthlessness 42.46
Rutland 38.29
rutty 38.3
Rwanda 2.10
Rwandan 2.35
Ryan 22.20

Rydal 22.16
Ryde 21.9
Ryder 22.5
Ryder Cup 37.41
rye 21.1
Rye 21.1
Ryvita 16.5
S 9.47
Saab 3.2
Saar 3.1
Saarbrücken 40.10
Saba 4.8
Sabatier 7.4
Sabbatarian 6.19
sabbath 2.52
sabbatical 2.64
Sabin 8.20
Sabine 21.22
Sabines 21.25
sable 8.15
sabot 35.3
sabotage 3.13
saboteur 11.1
saboteurs 11.29
sabre 8.3
sabretooth 41.29
Sabrina 16.8
sac 1.3
saccade 3.8
saccharide 21.12
saccharin 17.29
saccharine 15.26;
   21.22
sacerdotal 36.15
Sacha 2.14
sachet 7.3
Sachs 1.4
sack 1.3
sackable 2.64
sackbut 37.47
sackcloth 23.46
sacker 2.9
sackful 39.7
sacking 2.42
Sacks 1.4
Sackville 17.15
Sackville-West 9.49
sacral 8.15
sacrament 2.68
sacramental 10.21
Sacramento 35.7
sacraments 2.69
sacred 8.13
sacrifice 21.29
sacrificed 21.30
sacrificial 18.22
sacrilege 17.14
sacrilegious 18.44

sacristan 2.66
sacristy 2.57
sacroiliac 1.3
sacrosanct 1.27
sacrum 8.19
sad 1.9
SAD 1.9
Sadat 1.45
Saddam 1.22
sadden 2.35
saddened 2.36
sadder 2.10
saddest 2.48
saddle 2.28
saddleback 1.3
saddlebag 1.13
saddlebags 1.14
saddler 2.12
saddlery 2.56
saddo 35.3
Sadducee 15.4
Sade 3.8
Sadie 8.1
sadiron 22.20
sadism 18.27
sadist 8.68
sadistic 18.16
sadistically 18.57
Sadler 2.12
sadly 2.5
sadness 2.46
sadomasochism
   18.28
sadomasochist 2.73
sadomasochistic
   18.16
SAE 15.4
safari 4.5
safe 7.10
safe-breaker 8.4
safe-cracker 2.9
safeguard 3.8
safeguarding 4.29
safekeeping 16.27
safeness 8.67
safer 8.6
safest 8.69
safety 8.1
safety belt 9.23
safety first 11.23
Safeway 7.3
saffron 2.35
Saffron Walden 24.33;
   26.19
sag 1.13
saga 4.9
sagacious 8.67
sagacity 2.57

sage 7.12
sagebrush 37.46
sagging 2.42
saggy 2.2
sagittal 2.64
Sagittarian 6.19
Sagittarius 6.22
sago 35.6
Sahara 4.12
Saharan 4.24
sahib 3.2; 17.1
said 9.8
Saigon 23.27
sail 7.15
sailbag 1.13
sailboard 25.9
sailboarder 26.4
sailboarding 26.25
sailboat 35.45
sailcloth 23.46
sailed 7.16
sailing 8.62
sailing boat 35.45
sailing ship 17.43
sailor 8.7
sailors 8.75
sailplane 7.21
sails 7.17
Sainsbury 8.76
saint 7.25
saintdom 8.19
sainted 8.13
Saint Helier 10.57
sainthood 39.4
saintly 8.1
saintpaulia 26.39
Saint Petersburg 11.9
saith 9.54
saithe 7.51
sake 2.2; 4.2
sake 7.6
Sakharov 23.9
Saki 4.2
Sal 1.16
salaam 3.16
salaams 3.18
salable 8.79
salacious 8.67
salad 2.25
salade niçoise 3.37
Saladin 17.29
salads 2.26
salamander 2.10
salami 4.6
Salamis 17.46
sal ammoniac 1.3
salaried 2.62; 17.8
salary 2.56

sale 7.15
Sale 7.15
saleability 18.58
saleable 8.79
Salem 8.19
Salerno 35.8
saleroom 39.9; 41.17
sales 7.17
salesman 8.21
salesmanship 17.43
salesperson 12.12
salesroom 39.9; 41.17
saleswoman 40.10
saleswomen 18.31
Salford 24.24; 26.12
Salic 8.10
salience 8.83
salient 8.82
Salieri 6.1
saline 21.22
Salinger 2.60
salinity 18.57
Salisbury 26.37
saliva 22.6
salivary 22.40
salivate 7.35
salivation 8.24
Sallis 2.45
sallow 35.3
sally 2.5
Sally 2.5
Sally Lunn 37.31
salmagundi 38.3
Salman 1.24
Salmanazar 2.14
salmon 2.35
salmonella 10.12
Salome 36.1
salon 23.27
Salonika 24.57
saloon 41.19
Salop 2.44
salopettes 9.52
Salopian 36.40
salsa 2.14
salsify 2.57
salt 23.18; 25.17
SALT 23.18; 25.17
Saltash 1.43
saltbox 23.5
saltcellar 10.12
salted 24.24; 26.12
salter 24.10; 26.4
saltern 24.33; 26.19
Salterton 24.64; 26.43
saltier 24.58; 26.39
saltiest 24.71; 26.49
saltimbocca 24.9

salting 24.40; 26.25
saltire 19.1
Salt Lake City 18.3
salt lick 26.9
salt licks 26.10
saltpan 1.24
saltpetre 16.5
salts 23.19; 25.18
saltwater 26.4
saltworks 11.5
salty 24.3; 26.1
salubrious 42.46
salubrity 42.36
Saluki 42.1
salutary 2.59
salutation 8.24
salutations 8.55
salutatory 42.36
salute 41.27
saluted 42.14
salutes 41.28
saluting 42.24
Salvador 25.4
Salvadoran 26.19
Salvadorian 26.43
salvage 2.27
salvageable 2.79
salvager 2.60
salvation 8.23
salvationist 8.87
salve 1.21
salver 2.11
Salvesen 2.66
salvia 2.61
salvo 35.3
sal volatile 2.58
salvor 2.11
Salyut 41.27
Salzburg 11.9
Sam 1.22
Samantha 2.11
Samaria 6.16
Samaritan 2.66
Samaritans 2.67
samarium 6.18
Samarkand 1.28
samba 2.8
same 7.18
sameness 8.67
samey 8.1
Samian 8.81
samite 21.33
Sammy 2.6
Samoa 36.2
Samoan 36.20
Samos 23.39
samosa 36.9
Samothrace 7.30

samovar 3.1
Samoyed 9.8
sampan 1.24
samphire 19.1
sample 4.19
sampled 4.20
sampler 4.12
samples 4.21
sampling 4.29
Sampras 1.40
Samson 2.35
Samsung 37.37; 39.10
Samuel 2.64
samurai 21.4
San Andreas 8.67
San Antonio 35.19
Sanatogen® 2.66
sanatoria 26.39
sanatorium 26.42
Sancerre 5.1
sanctified 21.12
sanctify 21.4
sanctimonious 36.42
sanctimony 2.78
sanction 2.35
sanctioned 2.36
sanctions 2.39
sanctity 2.57
sanctuary 2.59; 2.78
sanctum 2.32
sanctum sanctorum
  26.17
Sanctus 2.46
sand 1.28
sandal 2.28
sandals 2.30
sandalwood 39.4
Sandbach 1.7
sandbag 1.13
sandbags 1.14
sandbank 1.25
sandbanks 1.26
sandblast 3.30
sandbox 23.5
sandboy 33.1
sandcastle 4.19
sand dune 41.19
sander 2.10
Sanderson 4.50
sandfly 21.3
sandgrouse 29.12
Sandhurst 11.23
San Diego 35.6
sanding 2.42
Sandinista 16.5
sandlot 23.44
sandman 1.24
Sandown 29.5

sandpaper 8.3
sandpiper 22.3
sandpit 2.51
Sandra 2.12; 4.12
Sandringham 2.65
sandshoe 41.3
sandstone 35.36
sandstorm 25.20
sandwich 17.7; 2.27
Sandwich 17.7; 2.27
sandworm 11.13
sandy 2.3
sane 7.21
San Fernando 35.3
Sanforized® 21.48
San Franciscan 18.32
San Francisco 35.11
sang 1.29
Sanger 2.13
sang-froid 3.1
sangria 2.61; 16.2
sanguinary 2.58
sanguine 2.34
Sanhedrin 17.29
sanies 15.45
sanitarium 6.18
sanitary 2.58
sanitation 8.24
sanitize 21.42
sanitized 21.48
sanity 2.57
San Jose 7.4
sank 1.25
Sankey 2.2
San Marino 35.10
San Quentin 10.26
San Salvador 25.4
sans-culotte 23.44
sansevieria 14.18
Sanskrit 2.51
Santa 2.10
Santa Ana 2.13
Santa Claus 25.35
Santa Cruz 41.33
Santa Fe 7.4
Santayana 4.13
Santiago 35.4
Santo Domingo 35.11
sap 1.37
sapele 16.1
sapience 2.69
sapient 2.68
sapling 2.42
saponify 21.4
sapper 2.8
sappers 2.55
Sapphic 2.18
sapphire 19.1

Sapphism 18.27
sappy 2.1
saprophyte 21.34
saprophytic 18.16
sapsucker 38.9
Sara 4.12
sarabande 1.28
Saracen 2.66
Saragossa 24.14
Sarah 6.2
Sarandon 2.66
Saratoga 36.4
sarcasm 2.32
sarcastic 2.17
sarcastically 2.58
sarcoma 36.8
sarcophagi 21.4
sarcophagus 24.70
sard 3.8
sardine 15.24
sardines 15.29
Sardinia 18.61
Sardinian 18.67
Sardis 4.31
sardonic 24.19
sardonically 24.56
sardonyx 24.22
sargasso 35.3
sarge 3.12
Sargent 4.27
Sargon 23.27
sari 4.5
Sark 3.3
sarky 4.2
sarnie 4.6
sarong 23.31
Sarre 3.1
SARS 3.37
sarsaparilla 18.12
sarsen 4.24
sartor 4.10
sartorial 26.41
Sartre 4.12
Sarum 6.5
SAS 9.47
sash 1.43
sashay 7.3
sashes 2.55
sashimi 2.58
Saskatchewan 2.66
Saskatoon 41.19
Saskia 2.61
sass 1.40
sassafras 1.40
Sassenach 1.3
Sassenachs 1.4
Sassoon 41.19
sassy 2.7

sat 1.45
Satan 8.21
satanic 2.20
Satanism 18.28
Satanist 8.87
satay 7.3
satchel 2.28
sate 7.32
sated 8.13
sateen 15.24
satellite 21.34
satellites 21.35
satiable 8.79
satiate 7.37
satiated 8.13 .
satiation 8.27
Satie 2.3
satiety 22.40
satin 2.34
satinet 9.51
satins 2.38
satiny 2.58
satire 19.1
satiric 18.16
satirical 18.64
satirically 18.57
satirist 2.73
satirize 21.42
satisfaction 2.35
satisfactorily 2.58
satisfactory 2.56
satisfied 21.12
satisfy 21.4
satnav 1.49
satori 26.1
SATs 1.46
satsuma 42.8
saturate 7.35
saturated 8.13
saturation 8.24
Saturday 2.56; 7.4
Saturn 2.35
Saturnalia 8.78
Saturnian 12.34
saturnine 21.22
satyr 2.10
satyriasis 17.46
satyric 18.16
sauce 25.28
sauce boat 35.45
saucepan 26.19
saucepans 26.21
saucer 26.8
saucerful 39.7
saucers 26.36
saucier 26.39
sauciest 26.49
saucily 26.37

sauciness 26.47
saucy 26.1
Saud 29.3
Saudi 26.1; 30.1
Saudi Arabia 8.78
sauerkraut 29.14
Saul 25.14
sauna 26.7
Saunders 26.36
saunter 26.4
sauntered 26.12
saurian 26.43
sausage 24.26
sausage roll 35.30
sauté 7.3
Sauternes 11.15
savage 2.27
Savage 2.27
savagely 2.58
savagery 2.58
savages 2.76
savaging 2.70
savanna 2.13
Savannah 2.13
savant 2.40
savants 2.41
save 7.54
saveloy 33.1
saver 8.6
Savernake 1.3
saves 7.55
Savile 2.28; 17.15
saving 8.61
saviour 8.7
Saviour 8.7
Savlon® 23.27
savoir-faire 5.1
savoir-vivre 16.7
savory 8.76
savour 8.6
savoured 8.13
savoury 8.76
Savoy 33.1
Savoyard 3.8
savvy 2.4
saw 25.1
sawbones 35.39
sawbuck 37.3
sawdust 37.45
sawfly 21.3
sawhorse 25.28
sawing 26.25
sawmill 17.15
sawn 25.22
sawtooth 41.29
sawyer 34.2
Sawyer 34.2
sax 1.4

schools 41.16
schoolteacher 16.9
schoolyard 3.8
schooner 42.8
Schopenhauer 31.1
schottische 15.34
Schreiber 22.3
Schrödinger 18.13
Schroeder 12.2
Schubert 42.31
Schumacher 2.9
Schumann 42.20
schuss 39.12; 41.24
schwa 3.1
Schwartz 25.32
Schweitzer 22.9
Schweppes® 9.45
sciatic 2.17
sciatica 2.60
science 22.25
scientific 18.16
scientifically 18.57
scientist 22.47
Scientologist 24.72
Scientology 24.55
sci-fi 21.3
scilicet 9.51
Scillies 18.54
Scilly 18.5
Scilly Isles 21.18
scimitar 18.60
scintilla 18.12
scintillate 7.41
scintillating 8.60
scintillation 8.32
scion 22.20
Scipio 35.19
scissile 21.16
scission 18.33
scissor 18.14
scissors 18.55
sclera 14.2
scleral 14.6
sclerosis 36.25
sclerotic 24.16
sclerous 14.14
Scobie 36.1
scoff 23.9
scoffed 23.10
scoffer 24.11
scoffing 24.40
scold 35.31
scolding 36.24
scoliosis 36.25
sconce 23.33
scone 23.27; 35.36
Scone 41.19
scones 23.35

Scooby Doo 41.4
scoop 41.22
scooper 42.3
scoot 41.27
scooter 42.5
scooting 42.24
scope 35.40
scopolamine 15.26
scorbutic 42.11
scorch 25.8
scorcher 26.8
scorching 26.25
score 25.1
scoreboard 25.9
scorecard 3.8
scored 25.9
scorekeeper 16.3
scoreless 26.27
scorer 26.6
scoria 26.39
scoring 26.25
scorn 25.22
scorned 25.24
scorner 26.7
scornful 26.15; 39.7
scornfully 26.37
Scorpian 26.43
Scorpio 35.19
scorpion 26.43
scorpions 26.44
Scorsese 8.1
Scot 23.44
scotch 23.7
Scotch 23.7
Scotchman 24.33
Scotchwoman 40.10
scoter 36.5
scot-free 15.2
Scotland 24.34
Scotland Yard 3.8
Scots 23.45
Scotsman 24.33
Scotswoman 40.10
Scotswomen 18.31
Scott 23.44
Scotticism 18.28
Scottie 24.3
Scottish 24.46
Scotus 36.26
scoundrel 30.6
scoundrelly 30.22
scour 31.1
scoured 31.2
scourer 32.2
scourge 11.10
scourger 12.2
scouring 32.3
scouse 29.12

Scouse 29.12
Scouser 30.2
scout 29.14
Scout 29.14
Scouter 30.2
Scouting 30.12
scoutmaster 4.10
Scouts 29.15
scow 29.1
scowl 29.4
scowler 30.2
scowling 30.12
scrabble 2.28
Scrabble® 2.28
scrag 1.13
scraggy 2.2
scram 1.22
scramble 2.28
scrambler 2.12
scran 1.24
scrap 1.37
scrapbook 39.1
scrape 7.27
scraped 7.29
scraper 8.3
scraperboard 25.9
scrapes 7.28
scrapheap 15.30
scrapie 8.1
scraping 8.59
scrapings 8.65
scrapper 2.8
scrappier 2.61
scrappiest 2.72
scrappily 2.58
scrapple 2.28
scrappy 2.1
scraps 1.38
scratch 1.7
scratchcard 3.8
scratched 1.8
scratcher 2.14
scratches 2.55
scratching 2.42
scratchpad 1.9
scratchy 2.7
scrawl 25.14
scrawler 26.6
scrawling 26.25
scrawly 26.1
scrawnier 26.39
scrawniest 26.49
scrawny 26.1
scream 15.20
screamed 15.21
screamer 16.8
screaming 16.27
scree 15.1

screech 15.9
screecher 16.9
screeching 16.27
screechy 16.1
screed 15.11
screen 15.23
screened 15.27
screener 16.8
screening 16.27
screenplay 7.3
screens 15.29
screenwriter 22.5
screenwriting 22.26
screw 41.1
screwball 25.14
screwdriver 22.6
screwed 41.9
screwier 42.38
screwiest 42.47
screwing 42.24
screws 41.33
screw top 23.36
screwy 42.1
Scriabin 17.29
scribal 22.16
scribble 18.22
scribbled 18.23
scribbler 18.12
scribbling 18.40
scribbly 18.5
scribe 21.5
scrim 17.24
scrimmage 18.21
scrimp 17.27
scrimping 18.40
scrimshaw 25.3
scrip 17.43
script 17.45
scripted 18.19
scripter 18.10
scriptorium 26.42
scriptural 18.64
scripture 18.14
Scriptures 18.55
scriptwriter 22.5
scriptwriting 22.26
scrivener 18.60
scrofula 24.57
scrofulous 24.70
scroll 35.30
scrolling 36.24
scrollwork 11.4
Scrooge 41.12
scrota 36.5
scrotal 36.15
scrotum 36.18
scrounge 29.8
scrounger 30.2

scroungers 30.21
scrounging 30.12
scrub 37.1
scrubber 38.8
scrubbing 38.34
scrubbing brush
37.46
scrubby 38.1
scrubland 1.28
scruff 37.10
scruffier 38.49
scruffiest 38.61
scruffily 38.47
scruffiness 38.59
scruffy 38.4
scrum 37.27
scrummage 38.22
scrummy 38.6
scrump 37.29
scrumptious 38.38
scrumpy 38.1
scrunch 37.35
scrunchie 38.7
scruple 42.16
scruples 42.17
scrupulous 42.46
scrutable 42.39
scrutineer 13.1
scrutineering 14.12
scrutinize 21.46
scrutiny 42.36
scry 21.1
SCSI 38.7
scuba 42.3
scud 37.8
scudding 38.34
scuff 37.10
scuffed 37.12
scuffing 38.34
scuffle 38.23
scull 37.16
sculler 38.12
scullery 38.47
sculling 38.34
scullion 38.54
Scully 38.5
sculpt 37.24
sculptor 38.10
sculptress 38.38
sculptural 38.52
sculpture 38.14
scum 37.27
scumbag 1.13
scumble 38.23
scummy 38.6
scungy 38.7
Scunthorpe 25.26
scupper 38.8

scuppered 38.20
scurf 11.8
scurfy 12.1
scurried 38.19
scurrility 18.58
scurrilous 38.59
scurry 38.5
scurvy 12.1
scut 37.47
Scutari 4.5
scutcheon 38.28
scutter 38.10
scuttle 38.23
scuttlebutt 37.47
scutum 42.18
scuzzy 38.7
Scylla 18.12
scythe 21.36
scything 22.26
sea 15.1
seabed 9.8
sea bird 11.7
seaboard 25.9
seaborne 25.22
seacoast 35.43
seacock 23.3
seadog 23.11
seafarer 6.2
seafaring 6.10
seafood 41.9
Seaford 16.14
Seaforth 25.33
seafront 37.40
seagoing 36.24
seagull 37.16
seahorse 25.28
seakale 7.15
seal 15.17
sealant 16.25
sealed 15.18
sealer 16.7
sealery 16.38
sealing 16.27
sealing wax 1.4
seals 15.19
sealskin 16.21
Sealyham 16.42
seam 15.20
seaman 16.22
seamanlike 21.7
seamanship 17.43
seamer 16.8
seamier 16.40
seamiest 16.49
seamless 16.30
seams 15.22
seamstress 16.30
Seamus 8.67

seamy 16.1
Sean 25.22
seance 3.22
seaplane 7.21
seaport 25.31
sear 13.1
search 11.6
searchable 12.32
searcher 12.2
searching 12.16
searchlight 21.33
searchlights 21.35
searing 14.12
Searle 11.11
Sears 13.5
seas 15.42
seascape 7.27
seashell 9.16
seashore 25.3
seasick 16.11
seasickness 16.47
seaside 21.11
season 16.22
seasonable 16.41;
16.53
seasonal 16.41
seasonally 16.52
seasoned 16.23
seasoning 16.46
seasons 16.24
seat 15.35
seat belt 9.23
seating 16.27
Seaton 16.22
seats 15.36
Seattle 2.28
seaward 16.14
seawards 16.15
sea water 26.4
seaway 7.3
seaweed 15.11
seaworthiness 12.37
seaworthy 12.1
Seb 9.1
sebaceous 8.67
Sebastian 2.66
Sebastopol 23.15
seborrhoea 13.1
sebum 16.20
sec 9.2
secant 16.25
secateurs 11.29
secede 15.11
secession 10.28
Secker 10.9
seclude 41.9
secluded 42.14
seclusion 42.20

Secombe 16.20
second 10.29
second 23.30
secondary 10.53
second-best 9.49
second-class 3.26
seconder 10.56
second-guess 9.47
second-hand 1.28
secondly 10.53
secondment 24.38
second-rate 7.38
seconds 10.30
second thoughts
25.32
secrecy 16.38
secret 16.34
secretaire 5.1
secretarial 6.17
secretariat 6.23
secretary 10.54
secrete 15.35
secretion 16.22
secretions 16.24
secretive 17.55
secretly 16.38
secretory 16.38
sect 9.5
sectarian 6.19
section 10.28
sectional 10.60
sections 10.32
sector 10.10
secular 10.56
secularism 18.29
secularization 8.53
secularize 21.47
secure 27.1
secured 27.2
securely 28.1
securer 28.2
securest 28.13
Securicor® 25.4
securing 28.11
security 28.17
sedan 1.24
Sedan 1.24
sedate 7.33
sedately 8.1
sedation 8.23
sedative 17.55
Seddon 10.27
sedentary 10.53
Seder 8.5
sedge 9.14
Sedgemoor 25.3; 27.1
Sedgewick 10.15
sediment 10.67

semblance 10.34
semen 16.22
semester 10.10
semi 10.6
semiaquatic 2.17
semiarid 2.24
semiautomatic 2.17
semibold 35.31
semibreve 15.39
semibreves 15.41
semicircle 12.8
semicircular 12.30
semicolon 23.27; 36.20
semiconductor 38.10
semiconscious 24.43
semidetached 1.8
semifinal 22.16
semifinalist 22.47
semifluid 42.13
semiliterate 18.77
seminal 10.60
seminar 3.1
seminarian 6.19
seminars 3.37
seminary 10.54
Seminole 35.30
semiology 24.55
semiotic 24.16
semiotics 24.22
semiparasitic 18.16
semipermeable 12.41
semiprecious 10.42
semiprofessional 10.60
semiquaver 8.6
semiretired 19.2
semirigid 18.18
semiskilled 17.18
semi-skimmed 17.25
semisolid 24.23
Semite 21.33
Semitic 18.16
semitone 35.36
semitropical 24.61
semivowel 31.3
semolina 16.8
semper fidelis 8.66
sempervivum 22.18
sempiternal 22.8
Semple 10.21
sempstress 10.42
Semtex 9.3
senate 10.48
senator 10.56
senatorial 26.41
send 9.35
sendable 10.60

sender 10.10
sendoff 23.9
send-up 37.41
Seneca 10.56
Senegal 25.14
Senegalese 15.43
senescence 10.34
senescent 10.33
senile 21.16
senility 18.58
senior 16.7; 16.40
seniority 24.56
senna 10.13
Senna 10.13
Sennacherib 17.1
sennet 10.48
señor 25.2
señora 26.6
señorita 16.5
sensate 7.34
sensation 8.23
sensational 8.79
sensationalism 18.29
sensationalist 17.49
sensationalize 21.47
sensationalized 21.48
sensationally 18.80
sense 9.39
senseless 10.42
senses 10.52
sensibilities 18.79
sensibility 18.58
sensible 10.60
sensibly 10.53
sensitive 17.55
sensitively 10.78
sensitivity 18.57
sensitization 8.43
sensitize 21.43
sensitized 21.48
Sensodyne® 21.22
sensor 10.14
sensors 10.52
sensory 10.53
sensual 10.60
sensuality 2.57
sensually 10.55; 10.78
sensuous 10.70
Sensurround® 29.6
sent 9.41
sentence 10.34
sententious 10.42
sentience 10.34; 10.68
sentient 10.33; 10.67
sentiment 10.67
sentimental 10.21
sentimentalism 18.28
sentimentalist 10.72

sentimentality 2.57
sentimentalize 21.43
sentimentally 10.53
sentiments 10.68
sentinel 10.60
sentries 10.51
sentry 10.5
Seoul 35.30
sepal 10.21; 16.17
separable 10.60
separate 7.38; 10.73
separated 8.13
separately 10.53
separation 8.28
separatism 18.29
separatist 17.49
separator 8.5
Sephardic 4.16
sepia 16.40
sepoy 33.1
sepsis 10.41
sept 9.46
septal 10.21
September 10.8
septet 9.51
septic 10.15
septicaemia 16.40
Septimus 10.70
septuagenarian 6.19
Septuagesima, 10.56
Septuagint 17.39
septum 10.25
septuple 42.16
septuplet 42.30
septuplets 42.32
sepulchral 38.23
sepulchre 10.56
sepulture 10.56; 27.1
sequel 16.17
sequence 16.26
sequential 10.21
sequester 10.10
sequestered 10.18
sequestration 8.31
sequin 16.21
sequined 17.34
sequoia 34.2
sera 14.2
seraglio 35.19
seraph 37.10
seraphic 2.18
seraphim 17.24
Serb 11.2
Serbia 12.31
Serbian 12.34
sere 13.1
Serena 16.8
serenade 7.8

serenader 8.5
serendipitous 18.74
serendipity 18.57
serene 15.24
serenely 16.1
Serengeti 10.3
serenity 10.54
serf 11.8
serfdom 12.10
serge 11.10
Serge 11.10
sergeant 4.27
sergeant major 8.9
sergeants 4.28
serial 14.19
serialism 18.29
serialization 8.53
serialize 21.47
serialized 21.48
series 14.17
series 15.44
serif 17.10
seriocomic 24.19
serious 14.23
sermon 12.12
sermonic 24.19
sermonize 21.43
serotonin 36.19
serotype 21.26
serous 14.14
serpent 12.14
serpentine 21.22
Serpentine 21.22
serpents 12.15
SERPS 11.20
serrated 8.13
serration 8.23
serrations 8.55
serried 10.17
serum 14.7
serval 12.8
servant 12.14
servants 12.15
serve 11.27
served 11.28
server 12.2
servery 12.29
service 12.18
serviceable 12.41
serviceberry 10.5
serviced 12.21
serviceman 1.24
servicewoman 40.10
serviette 9.51
serviettes 9.52
servile 21.16
servility 18.58
serving 12.16

shockproof 41.10
shod 23.8
shoddier 24.58
shoddiest 24.71
shoddily 24.56
shoddy 24.3
shoe 41.1
shoebill 17.15
shoeblack 1.3
shoebox 23.5
Shoeburyness 9.47
shoehorn 25.22
shoelace 7.30
shoe leather 10.11
shoeless 42.26
shoemaker 8.4
shoemaking 8.59
shoes 41.33
shoeshine 21.22
shoestring 42.24
shoetree 15.3
shogun 36.20; 37.31
Shona 36.8
shone 23.27
shoo 41.1
shoofly 21.3
shoo-in 42.19
shook 39.1
shoon 41.19
shoot 41.27
shooter 42.5
shooting 42.24
shoot-out 29.14
shoots 41.28
shop 23.36
shopaholic 24.18
shopaholics 24.22
shopfitting 18.40
shop front 37.40
shopkeeper 16.3
shopkeeping 16.27
shoplift 17.11
shoplifter 18.10
shoplifting 18.40
shopper 24.8
shoppers 24.53
shopping 24.40
shops 23.37
shopsoiled 33.7
shoptalk 25.6
shopworn 25.22
shore 25.1
shore-based 7.31
shore bird 11.7
Shoreditch 17.7
Shoreham 26.17
shoreline 21.22
shores 25.35

shoreward 26.12
shorewards 26.13
shorn 25.22
short 25.31
shortage 26.14
shortbread 9.8
shortcake 7.6
short-change 7.23
short-circuit 12.25
shortcoming 38.34
shortcomings 38.35
shortcrust 37.45
short cut 37.47
shorten 26.19
shortened 26.20
shorter 26.4
shortest 26.29
shortfall 25.14
short-haired 5.2
shorthand 1.28
short-handed 2.25
short-haul 25.14
shorthorn 25.22
shortish 26.30
shortlist 26.28
shortly 26.1
shortness 26.27
short-range 7.23
shorts 25.32
short-sighted 22.13
short-sightedness 22.46
short-sleeved 15.40
shorty 26.1
Shostakovich 17.7
shot 23.44
shotgun 37.31
shot-putter 40.2
should 39.4
shoulder 36.5
shoulders 36.34
shouldn't 40.12
shouldst 39.5
should've 40.18
shout 29.14
shouted 30.3
shouter 30.2
shouting 30.12
shouts 29.15
shove 37.49
shoved 37.50
shove-ha'penny 8.1
shovel 38.23
shovelful 39.7
shovelhead 9.8
shoveller 38.48
shovelnose 35.52
shoving 38.34

show 35.1
showbiz 36.33
showboat 35.45
showcase 7.30
showdown 29.5
shower 31.1
showered 31.2
showering 32.3
showerproof 41.10
showers 31.5
showery 32.1
showgirl 11.11
showground 29.6
showier 36.37
showiest 36.44
showily 36.35
showiness 36.42
showjumper 38.8
showjumping 38.34
showman 36.20
showmanship 17.43
shown 35.36
show-off 23.9
showpiece 15.32
showplace 7.30
showroom 39.9; 41.17
shows 35.52
show stopper 24.8
showstopping 24.40
showy 36.1
shrank 1.25
shrapnel 2.28
shred 9.8
shredded 10.18
shredder 10.10
shredding 10.36
shreds 9.9
shrew 41.1
shrewd 41.9
shrewder 42.5
shrewdest 42.27
shrewdly 42.1
shrewdness 42.26
shrewish 42.29
Shrewsbury 36.35; 42.36
shriek 15.7
shrieking 16.27
shrieks 15.8
shrieval 16.17
shrift 17.11
shrike 21.7
shrill 17.15
shriller 18.12
shrillest 18.46
shrimp 17.27
shrimper 18.8
shrimping 18.40

shrimps 17.28
Shrimpton 18.32
shrine 21.22
shrink 17.30
shrinkable 18.64
shrinkage 18.21
shrinking 18.40
shrinks 17.31
shrive 21.37
shrivel 18.22
shrivelled 18.23
shriven 18.32
Shropshire 13.1; 24.14
shroud 29.3
shrouded 30.3
shrouding 30.12
shrove 35.50
Shrovetide 21.11
shrub 37.1
shrubbery 38.47
shrubby 38.1
shrubs 37.2
shrug 37.14
shrugging 38.34
shrunk 37.32
shrunken 38.28
shtick 17.3
shtoom 39.9
shtuck 39.1
shuck 37.3
shucks 37.4
shudder 38.10
shuddered 38.20
shuddering 38.58
shudders 38.45
shuffle 38.23
shuffler 38.12
shuffling 38.34
shufty 38.3
shul 41.14
shun 37.31
shunned 37.36
shunning 38.34
shunt 37.40
shunter 38.10
shunting 38.34
shunts 37.39
shush 39.13
shut 37.47
shutdown 29.5
Shute 41.27
shuteye 21.3
shutter 38.10
shuttering 38.58
shutting 38.34
shuttle 38.23
shuttlecock 23.3
Shuttleworth 11.26

shy 21.1
shyer 22.2
shyest 22.31
Shylock 23.3
shyly 22.1
shyness 22.29
shyster 22.5
Siam 1.22
Siamese 15.45
Sian 3.19
Sian's 3.24
sib 17.1
Sibelius 8.85
Siberia 14.18
Siberian 14.21
sibilant 18.70
sibling 18.40
siblings 18.41
sibyl 18.22
sibyllic 18.16
sibylline 21.22
sic 17.3
Sichuan 3.19
Sicilian 18.32
Sicilian 18.67
Sicily 18.57
sick 17.3
sickbay 7.3
sickbed 9.8
sicken 18.32
sickened 18.34
sickening 18.73
sickeningly 18.80
sicker 18.9
sickest 18.46
sickie 18.2
sickle 18.22
sick leave 15.39
sicklier 18.61
sickliest 18.76
sickly 18.5
sickness 18.44
sicko 35.11
sickroom 39.9; 41.17
Sid 17.8
Sidcup 37.41
Siddeley 18.5
Siddhartha 4.10
Siddons 18.37
side 21.9
sideboard 25.9
sideboards 25.10
sideburns 11.18
sidecar 3.1
side dish 22.32
side effect 9.5
sidekick 22.11
sidelight 21.33

sidelights 21.35
sideline 21.22
sidelines 21.25
sidelong 23.31
sidereal 14.19
sideroad 35.25
sides 21.13
side-saddle 2.28
sideshow 35.12
sideslip 17.43
side-splitting 18.40
sidestep 9.44
sidestepped 9.46
sidestepper 10.8
sidesteps 9.45
sideswipe 21.26
sidetrack 1.3
sidetracked 1.6
sidetracks 1.4
sidewalk 25.6
sidewall 25.14
sideward 22.13
sidewards 22.14
sideways 7.56
sidewinder 22.5
siding 22.26
sidings 22.27
sidle 22.16
sidling 22.26
Sidmouth 18.52
Sidney 18.6
Sidon 22.20
siege 15.15
Siegfried 15.11
Sieg Heil 21.16
Siemens 16.24
Siena 10.13
sienna 10.13
Sierra 6.2
Sierra Leone 35.36;
   36.1
siesta 10.10
sieve 17.54
sieving 18.40
sift 17.11
sigh 21.1
sighed 21.9
sighs 21.39
sight 21.31
sighted 22.13
sighter 22.5
sighting 22.26
sightings 22.27
sightless 22.29
sightline 21.22
sightly 22.1
sight-read 15.11
sight-reader 16.5

sight-reading 16.27
sights 21.35
sightsee 15.3
sightseeing 16.27
sightseer 16.2
Sigismund 18.68;
   37.36
siglum 18.26
sigma 18.13
Sigmund 18.34
Sigmund's 18.35
sign 21.22
signage 22.15
signal 18.22
signalization 8.46
signalize 21.44
signaller 18.60
signalman 18.67
signatory 18.56
signature 18.60
signboard 25.9
signed 21.23
signer 22.8
signet 18.50
significance 18.71
significant 18.70
significantly 18.80
signification 8.46
signifier 22.2
signify 21.4
signing 22.26
signor 25.2
signora 26.6
signorina 16.8
signpost 35.43
signs 21.25
signwriting 22.26
sika 16.4
Sikh 15.7
Sikhism 18.27
Sikorsky 26.1
silage 22.15
Silas 22.29
Silas Marner 4.13
sild 17.18
silence 22.25
silencer 22.41
silent 22.24
silently 22.40
Silenus 16.30
Silesia 16.40
Silesian 16.43
silex 9.3
silhouette 9.51
silica 18.60
silicate 7.41; 18.77
silicon 18.67
silicon chip 17.43

silicone 35.36
silicosis 36.25
silk 17.16
silken 18.32
silkier 18.61
silkiest 18.76
silkiness 18.74
silkworm 11.13
silky 18.2
sill 17.15
sillier 18.61
silliest 18.76
silliness 18.74
silly 18.5
silo 35.12
Siloam 36.18
silt 17.21
silty 18.3
Silurian 28.21
silver 18.11
silver birch 11.6
silverfish 17.50
silverpoint 33.10
silver screen 15.26
silverside 21.12
silversmith 17.53
Silverstone 18.67;
   35.36
silverware 5.1
silvery 18.56
silviculture 38.14
Silvikrin® 17.29
Sim 17.24
Simba 18.8
Simca 18.9
Simcox 23.5
Simenon 23.27
Simeon 18.67
simian 18.67
similar 18.60
similarities 2.77
similarity 2.57
similarly 18.80
simile 18.57
similitude 41.9
Simla 18.12
simmer 18.13
simmered 18.19
simmering 18.73
Simmons 18.37
simnel 18.22
Simon 22.20
Simone 35.36
Simone's 35.39
simoniac 1.3
simony 18.56
simoom 41.17
simpatico 35.19

simper 18.8
simple 18.22
simple-minded 22.13
simpler 18.12
simplest 18.46
simpleton 18.67
simpletons 18.69
simplex 9.3
simplicity 18.57
simplification 8.46
simplified 21.12
simplifier 22.2
simplify 21.4
simplistic 18.16
simply 18.5
Simpson 18.33
simulacrum 8.19
simulant 18.70
simulate 7.41
simulated 8.13
simulation 8.32
simulator 8.5
simulcast 3.30
simultaneity 16.38
simultaneity 8.76
simultaneous 8.85
sin 17.29
Sinai 21.3
sinapism 18.28
Sinatra 4.12
Sinbad 1.9
sin bin 18.31
since 17.38
sincere 13.1
sincerely 14.1
sincerer 14.2
sincerest 14.16
sincerity 10.54
Sinclair 5.1
Sind 17.34
Sindy 18.3
sine 21.22
Sinead 7.8
sinecure 27.1
sine qua non 23.27
sinew 41.3
sinews 41.33
sinewy 42.1
sinfonia 36.37
sinfonietta 10.10
sinful 18.22; 39.7
sinfully 18.56; 18.59
sing 17.35
singable 18.64
sing-along 23.31
Singapore 25.4
Singaporean 26.43
singe 17.37

singer 18.13
Singer 18.13
Singh 17.35
singing 18.40
single 18.22
single-breasted 10.18
single-celled 9.19
single cream 15.20
single-handed 2.25
single-minded 22.13
single-mindedly 22.40
singleness 18.74
singles 18.24
singlet 18.50
singleton 18.67
singly 18.5
sings 17.36
singsong 23.31
singular 18.60
singularity 2.57
singularly 18.80
singultus 38.38
Sinhalese 15.45
sinister 18.60
sinisterly 18.80
sinistral 18.64
sink 17.30
sinkable 18.64
sinkage 18.21
sinker 18.9
sinkhole 35.30
sinking 18.40
sinks 17.31
sinless 18.44
sinned 17.34
sinner 18.13
sinners 18.55
Sinn Fein 7.21
sinning 18.40
sins 17.42
sinter 18.10
sinuosity 24.56
sinuous 18.74
sinus 22.29
sinusitis 22.28
Siobhan 25.22
Siouan 42.20
Sioux 41.1
sip 17.43
siphon 22.20
sipped 17.45
sippet 18.50
sips 17.44
sir 11.1
Sir 11.1
sire 19.1
sired 19.2

siren 22.20
Siren 22.20
sirens 22.23
Sirens 22.23
Sirius 18.74
sirloin 33.8
sirocco 35.13
sirrah 18.12
sirree 15.2
Sirs 11.29
sis 17.46
sisal 22.16
Sisera 18.60
Sissons 18.37
sissy 18.7
sister 18.10
sisterhood 39.4
sister-in-law 25.2
sisterless 18.74
sisterly 18.56
sisters 18.55
Sistine 15.25
Sisyphean 16.22
Sisyphus 18.74
sit 17.51
sitar 3.1
sitcom 23.23
sit-down 29.5
site 21.31
sit-in 18.31
Sitka 18.9
sitter 18.10
sitting 18.40
Sittingbourne 25.22
Sitting Bull 39.7
sitting room 39.9; 41.17
sittings 18.41
situate 7.41
situation 8.32
situational 8.79
sit-up 37.41
sit-upon 23.27
Sitwell 18.22
sitzkrieg 15.14
Siva 16.6
six 17.4
sixer 18.14
sixfold 35.31
six-pack 1.3
sixpence 18.39
sixte 17.5
sixteen 15.24
sixteenth 15.28
sixth-former 26.7
sixth-formers 26.36
sixties 18.54
sixtieth 17.53; 18.78

Sixtus 18.44
sixty 18.3
sixty-eight 7.41
sixty-five 21.37
sixty-four 25.4
sixty-nine 21.22
sixty-one 37.31
sixty-six 17.4
sixty-three 15.4
sixty-two 41.4
sizable 22.43
size 21.39
sized 21.48
sizer 22.9
Sizewell 9.16; 22.16
sizzle 18.22
sizzled 18.23
sizzler 18.12
sizzling 18.40
ska 3.1
Skagerrak 1.3
skat 1.45
skate 7.32
skateboard 25.9
skateboarder 26.4
skateboarding 26.25
skater 8.5
skates 7.50
skating 8.60
skating rink 17.30
skean 15.23
skedaddle 2.28
skeet 15.35
skeg 9.12
Skegness 9.47
skein 7.21
skeletal 10.60
skeleton 10.64
skeletonize 21.47
Skelmersdale 7.15
Skelton 10.27
sketch 9.6
sketchbook 39.1
sketched 9.7
sketcher 10.14
sketches 10.52
sketchier 10.57
sketchiest 10.71
sketchily 10.54
sketching 10.36
Sketchley 10.5
sketchpad 1.9
sketchy 10.7
skew 41.1
skewbald 25.15
skewer 42.2
skewered 42.14
skewering 42.45

skewwhiff 17.10
ski 15.1
skid 17.8
skidding 18.40
skidlid 18.18
skid mark 3.3
skidpan 1.24
skid row 35.2
skied 15.11
skier 16.2
skies 21.39
skiff 17.10
skiffle 18.22
skiing 16.27
skijoring 26.25
ski jump 37.29
skilful 18.22; 39.7
skilfully 18.56; 18.59
ski lift 17.11
skill 17.15
skilled 17.18
skillet 18.50
skills 17.23
skim 17.24
skimmed 17.25
skimmer 18.13
skimming 18.40
skimp 17.27
skimpily 18.57
skimpy 18.1
skin 17.29
skin and bone 35.36
skincare 5.1
skin-diver 22.6
skin flick 18.16
skinflint 17.39
skinful 39.7
skinhead 9.8
skinheads 9.9
skink 17.30
skinless 18.44
skinned 17.34
skinner 18.13
Skinner 18.13
skinnier 18.61
skinning 18.40
skinny 18.6
skinny-dip 17.43
skins 17.42
skint 17.39
skintight 21.32
skip 17.43
skipjack 1.3
skipped 17.45
skipper 18.8
skipping 18.40
skipping rope 35.40
Skipton 18.32

skirl 11.11
skirmish 12.22
skirt 11.24
skirting 12.16
skirting board 25.9
skirts 11.25
skis 15.42
skit 17.51
skite 21.31
skitter 18.10
skittish 18.47
skittle 18.22
skittles 18.24
skive 21.37
skiver 22.6
skiving 22.26
skivvies 18.54
skivvy 18.4
Skoda 36.5
skol 23.15
skol 35.30
skua 42.2
skulduggery 38.47
skulk 37.18
skulked 37.19
skulker 38.9
skulking 38.34
skull 37.16
skull and crossbones 35.39
skullcap 1.37
skunk 37.32
sky 21.1
sky blue 41.2
skydive 21.37
skydiver 22.6
skydiving 22.26
Skye 21.1
skyjack 1.3
skyjacker 2.9
Skylab 1.1
skylark 3.3
skylarking 4.29
skylight 21.33
skyline 21.22
skyrocket 24.49
skyscraper 8.3
skyward 22.13
skywards 22.14
skywriting 22.26
slab 1.1
slabs 1.2
slack 1.3
slacken 2.35
slacker 2.9
slackest 2.48
slacking 2.42
slackness 2.46

slacks 1.4
Slade 7.8
slag 1.13
slagheap 15.30
slain 7.21
slàinte 4.14
slake 7.6
slaked 7.7
slalom 4.22
slam 1.22
slammer 2.13
slander 4.10
slanderer 4.43
slanderous 4.32
slanderous 4.53
slang 1.29
slanging 2.42
slanging match 1.7
slangy 2.6
slant 3.23
slanted 4.17
slantwise 21.41
slap 1.37
slap-bang 1.29
slapdash 1.43
slaphappy 2.1
slaphead 9.8
slapper 2.8
slapping 2.42
slapstick 2.17
slash 1.43
slasher 2.14
slashing 2.42
slat 1.45
slate 7.32
slater 8.5
Slater 8.5
slating 8.60
Slatkin 2.34
slattern 2.35
Slattery 2.56
slaty 8.1
slaughter 26.4
slaughterer 26.38
slaughterhouse 29.12
slaughterman 1.24
slaughterous 26.47
Slav 3.35
slave 7.54
slave-driver 22.6
slaver 2.11
slaver 8.6
slavery 8.76
slaves 7.55
Slavic 4.16
slaving 8.61
slavish 8.70
Slavonic 24.19

slaw 25.1
slay 7.1
Slazenger 2.60
sleaze 15.42
sleazeball 25.14
sleazy 16.1
sled 9.8
sledge 9.14
sledgehammer 2.13
sledging 10.36
sleek 15.7
sleeker 16.4
sleekest 16.32
sleep 15.30
sleeper 16.3
sleepers 16.37
sleepier 16.40
sleepiest 16.49
sleepily 16.38
sleepiness 16.47
sleeping 16.27
sleepless 16.30
sleepover 36.6
sleepwalk 25.6
sleepwalker 26.3
sleepwalkers 26.36
sleepwalking 26.25
sleepy 16.1
sleepyhead 9.8
sleet 15.35
sleety 16.1
sleeve 15.39
sleeveless 16.30
sleeves 15.41
sleeving 16.27
sleigh 7.1
sleight 21.31
sleight of hand 1.28
slender 10.10
slenderize 21.43
slenderly 10.53
slenderness 10.70
slept 9.46
sleuth 41.29
sleuthhound 29.6
sleuthing 42.24
slew 41.1
slewed 41.9
slice 21.29
sliceable 22.43
sliced 21.30
sliced bread 9.8
slicer 22.9
slices 22.39
slicing 22.26
slick 17.3
slicker 18.9
slickest 18.46

slid 17.8
slide 21.9
slider 22.5
sliding 22.26
slight 21.31
slighted 22.13
slighter 22.5
slightest 22.31
slighting 22.26
slightly 22.1
Sligo 35.12
slim 17.24
slime 21.19
slimline 21.22
slimmed 17.25
slimmer 18.13
slimmers 18.55
slimmest 18.46
slimming 18.40
slimness 18.44
slimy 22.1
sling 17.35
slingback 1.3
slingbacks 1.4
slingshot 23.44
slink 17.30
slinky 18.2
slip 17.43
slipcase 7.30
slipcover 38.11
slipknot 23.44
slipover 36.6
slippage 18.21
slipped 17.45
slipper 18.8
slippers 18.55
slipperwort 11.24
slippery 18.56
slippier 18.61
slippiest 18.76
slipping 18.40
slippy 18.1
slipshod 23.8
slipstitch 17.7
slipstream 15.20
slip-up 37.41
slipware 5.1
slipway 7.3
slit 17.51
slither 18.11
slithery 18.56
sliver 18.11
slivers 18.55
slivovitz 17.52
Sloane 35.36
slob 23.1
slobber 24.8
slobbered 24.24

Slocombe 36.18
sloe 35.1
sloe-eyed 21.11
slog 23.11
slogan 36.20
sloganeer 13.1
slogger 24.9
slogging 24.40
slo-mo 35.16
sloop 41.22
slop 23.36
slope 35.40
sloping 36.24
sloppier 24.58
sloppiest 24.71
sloppily 24.56
sloppiness 24.70
sloppy 24.1
slosh 23.42
sloshed 23.43
sloshy 24.7
slot 23.44
sloth 35.47
slothful 36.15; 39.7
slouch 29.2
slouching 30.12
slouchy 30.1
slough 29.1; 37.10
Slough 29.1
Slovak 1.3
Slovakia 2.61
Slovakian 2.66
sloven 38.28
Slovene 15.24
Slovenia 16.40
Slovenian 16.43
slovenly 38.47
slow 35.1
slowcoach 35.24
slowdown 29.5
slower 36.2
slowest 36.28
slowish 36.29
slowly 36.1
slowness 36.26
slowpoke 35.21
slowworm 11.13
SLR 3.1
slub 37.1
slubberdegullion
    38.54
sludge 37.15
sludgy 38.7
slug 37.14
slugabed 9.8
sluggard 38.20
sluggards 38.21
slugger 38.9

sluggish 38.40
sluggishly 38.47
sluggishness 38.59
sluice 41.24
sluiced 41.25
sluicegate 7.34
sluicing 42.24
slum 37.27
slumber 38.8
slumbered 38.20
slumberer 38.48
slumbering 38.58
slumberous 38.38;
    38.59
slumbers 38.45
slumming 38.34
slummy 38.6
slump 37.29
slumpflation 8.23
slung 37.37
slunk 37.32
slur 11.1
slurp 11.19
slurped 11.21
slurps 11.20
slurred 11.7
slurry 38.5
slush 37.46
slushier 38.49
slushiest 38.61
slushy 38.7
slut 37.47
sluttish 38.40
sly 21.1
slyboots 41.28
slyer 22.2
slyest 22.31
slyly 22.1
slyness 22.29
smack 1.3
smacked 1.6
smacker 2.9
smackhead 9.8
smacking 2.42
small 25.14
small ad 1.9
small ads 1.10
smaller 26.6
smallest 26.29
smallholder 36.5
smallholding 36.24
smallish 26.30
small-minded 22.13
smallness 26.27
smallpox 23.5
smalls 25.19
small screen 15.24
small talk 25.6

Smallwood 39.4
smarm 3.16
smarmy 4.6
smart 3.32
smart aleck 2.19
smart-alecky 2.57
smartarse 3.26
smart card 3.8
smarten 4.24
smarter 4.10
smartest 4.34
Smartie 4.3
Smarties® 4.40
smarting 4.29
smartish 4.35
smartly 4.5
smartness 4.32
smarts 3.33
smarty 4.3
smarty-pants 1.34
smash 1.43
smash-and-grab 1.1
smashed 1.44
smasher 2.14
smashing 2.42
smattering 2.70
smear 13.1
smeared 13.2
smearer 14.2
smeary 14.1
Smedley 10.5
smegma 10.13
smell 9.16
smeller 10.12
smellier 10.57
smelliest 10.71
smelling 10.36
smells 9.27
smelly 10.5
smelt 9.23
smelter 10.10
smelting 10.36
Smetana 10.56
Smethwick 10.15
smew 41.1
smidge 17.14
smidgen 18.33
Smike 21.7
smile 21.16
smiled 21.17
smiler 22.7
smiles 21.18
smiley 22.1
smiling 22.26
smirch 11.6
smirk 11.4
smirker 12.2
smite 21.31

smith 17.53
Smith 17.53
smithereens 15.29
Smithers 18.55
Smithson 18.33
Smithsonian 36.40
smithy 18.4
smitten 18.32
smock 23.3
smocking 24.40
smog 23.11
smoke 35.21
smoked 35.23
smokehouse 29.12
smokeless 36.26
smoker 36.4
smokers 36.34
smokescreen 15.25
smokestack 1.3
smokestacks 1.4
smokier 36.37
smokiest 36.44
smoking 36.24
smoky 36.1
Smollett 24.49
smolt 35.32
smooch 41.8
smoocher 42.9
smooching 42.24
smoochy 42.1
smoodge 41.12
smooth 41.30
smoothbore 25.3
smoother 42.6
smoothest 42.27
smoothie 42.1
smoothing 42.24
smoothly 42.1
smoothness 42.26
smorgasbord 25.9
smote 35.45
smother 38.11
smothered 38.20
smothering 38.58
smoulder 36.5
smouldered 36.12
smudge 37.15
smudges 38.45
smudging 38.34
smudgy 38.7
smug 37.14
smugger 38.9
smuggest 38.39
smuggle 38.23
smuggled 38.24
smuggler 38.12
smugglers 38.45
smugly 38.5

smugness 38.38
Smurf 11.8
smut 37.47
smuts 37.48
Smuts 37.48
smuttier 38.49
smuttiest 38.61
smuttiness 38.59
smutty 38.3
Smyrna 12.2
Smythe 21.36
snack 1.3
snacks 1.4
Snaefell 9.16
snaffle 2.28
snafu 41.2
snag 1.13
snaggletooth 41.29
snail 7.15
snail mail 7.15
snake 7.6
snakebite 21.33
snake charmer 4.13
snake in the grass
  3.26
snakelike 21.7
snakeskin 8.20
snaky 8.1
snap 1.37
snapdragon 2.35
snapper 2.8
snappish 2.49
snappy 2.1
snapshot 23.44
snapshots 23.45
snare 5.1
snared 5.2
snark 3.3
snarl 3.14
snarler 4.12
snarling 4.29
snarls 3.15
snarl-up 37.41
snarly 4.5
snatch 1.7
snatched 1.8
snatcher 2.14
snatching 2.42
snatchy 2.7
snazzier 2.61
snazziest 2.72
snazzy 2.7
sneak 15.7
sneaker 16.4
sneakers 16.37
sneakier 16.40
sneakiest 16.49
sneakily 16.38

sneaking 16.27
sneak thief 15.13
sneak thieves 15.41
sneaky 16.1
Sneddon 10.27
sneer 13.1
sneered 13.2
sneerer 14.2
sneering 14.12
sneers 13.5
sneeze 15.42
sneezer 16.9
sneezewort 11.24
sneezing 16.27
sneezy 16.1
Snell 9.16
snib 17.1
snick 17.3
snicker 18.9
snicket 18.50
snide 21.9
sniff 17.10
sniffed 17.11
sniffer 18.11
sniffle 18.22
sniffy 18.4
snifter 18.10
snigger 18.9
sniggered 18.19
sniggerer 18.60
sniggers 18.55
snip 17.43
snipe 21.26
sniper 22.3
snipers 22.39
sniping 22.26
snipper 18.8
snippet 18.50
snippets 18.51
snips 17.44
snitch 17.7
snivel 18.22
sniveller 18.12; 18.60
snob 23.1
snobbery 24.54
snobbish 24.46
snobbishly 24.56
snobbishness 24.70
snobby 24.1
snobs 23.2
Snodgrass 3.26
snog 23.11
snogged 23.12
snogging 24.40
snood 41.9
snooker 42.4
snookered 42.14

snoop 41.22
snooper 42.3
snooping 42.24
Snoopy 42.1
snoot 41.27
snootier 42.38
snootiest 42.47
snootily 42.36
snootiness 42.46
snooty 42.1
snooze 41.33
snoozed 41.34
snoozer 42.9
snoozing 42.24
snoozy 42.1
snore 25.1
snored 25.9
snorer 26.6
snoring 26.25
snorkel 26.15
snorkeller 26.38
Snorri 24.5
snort 25.31
snorter 26.4
snot 23.44
snotty 24.3
snotty-nosed 35.53
snout 29.14
snow 35.1
snowball 25.14
snowballed 25.15
snowballing 26.25
snowberry 36.1; 36.35
snow-blind 21.23
snowblink 17.30
snowblower 36.2
snowboard 25.9
snowboarding 26.25
snowbound 29.6
snowcap 1.37
snowcapped 1.39
snowclad 1.9
Snowdon 36.20
Snowdonia 36.37
snowdrift 17.11
snowdrop 23.36
snowdrops 23.37
snowed 35.25
snowfall 25.14
snowfield 15.18
snowflake 7.6
snowing 36.24
snow line 21.22
snowman 1.24
snowmen 9.32
snowmobile 15.17
snowplough 29.1
snows 35.52

somnambulist 2.73
somniferous 18.74
somnolence 24.68
somnolent 24.67
son 37.31
sonar 3.1
sonata 4.10
sondage 3.13
sonde 23.30
Sondheim 21.19
son et lumière 5.1
song 23.31
songbird 11.7
songfest 9.49
songs 23.32
songsmith 17.53
songster 24.10
songstress 24.43
songthrush 37.46
songwriter 22.5
songwriting 22.26
Sonia 24.12
sonic 24.19
son-in-law 25.4
sonless 38.38
sonnet 24.49
sonneteer 13.1
sonny 38.6
son-of-a-bitch 17.7
son-of-a-gun 37.31
sonority 24.56
sonorous 24.70; 26.27
Sontag 1.13
soon 41.19
sooner 42.8
soonest 42.27
soot 39.14
sooth 41.29
soothe 41.30
soother 42.6
soothing 42.24
soothsay 7.3
soothsayer 8.2
sooty 40.1
sop 23.36
Soper 36.3
Sophia 16.2; 22.2
Sophie 36.1
sophism 18.27
sophist 24.45
sophistic 18.16
sophisticate 18.77
sophisticated 8.13
sophistication 8.32
sophistry 24.56
Sophoclean 16.22
Sophocles 15.45
sophomore 25.4

soporific 18.16
soppier 24.58
soppiest 24.71
sopping 24.40
soppy 24.1
soprano 35.4
Sopwith 17.53
sorbet 7.3
Sorbian 26.43
Sorbonne 23.27
sorcerer 26.38
sorceress 26.47
sorceress 9.47
sorcerous 26.47
sorcery 26.37
sordid 26.11
sore 25.1
sorely 26.1
soreness 26.27
sore point 33.10
sorer 26.6
sorghum 26.17
SORN 25.22
Soroptimist 24.72
sororicide 21.12
sorority 24.56
sorrel 24.27
Sorrento 35.7
sorrier 24.58
sorriest 24.71
sorrow 35.13
sorrowed 35.25
sorrowful 39.7
sorrowfully 36.1; 40.1
sorrowing 36.24
sorrows 35.52
sorry 24.5
sort 25.31
sortable 26.41
sorted 26.12
sorter 26.4
sortie 26.1
sortilege 17.14
sorting 26.25
sorts 25.32
SOS 9.47
so-so 35.16
sot 23.44
Sotheby 38.47
Sotheby's 38.63
sou 41.1
soufflé 7.3
sough 29.1
sought 25.31
sought-after 4.10
souk 41.6
soul 35.30
soul-destroying 34.11

soulful 36.15; 39.7
soulless 36.26
soul mate 7.34
soul mates 7.50
sound 29.6
Sound 29.6
soundalike 21.7
soundbox 23.5
sounded 30.3
sounder 30.2
sounding 30.12
soundless 30.14
soundly 30.1
soundness 30.14
soundpost 35.43
soundproof 41.10
sounds 29.7
soundtrack 1.3
Souness 42.25
soup 41.22
soupçon 23.27
soup dish 42.29
souped-up 37.41
soup spoon 41.19
soupy 42.1
sour 31.1
source 25.28
sourced 25.29
soured 31.2
sour grapes 7.28
sourly 32.1
sourpuss 39.12
soursop 23.36
Sousa 42.9
sousaphone 35.36
souse 29.12
soused 29.13
south 29.16
South African 2.66
Southall 25.14
Southampton 2.35
southbound 29.6
Southdown 29.5
southeast 15.33
southeaster 16.5
southeasterly 16.38
southeastward 16.14
southeastwards 16.15
Southend 9.35
southerly 38.47
southern 38.28
southerner 38.48
southernmost 35.43
Southey 30.1
Southey 38.4
South Foreland 26.20
southpaw 25.3
South Pole 35.30

Southport 25.31
southward 30.3
southwards 30.4
Southwark 38.16
southwest 9.49
southwester 10.10
southwesterly 10.53
southwestward 10.18
southwestwards 10.19
souvenir 13.1
souvlakia 2.61
sou'wester 10.10
sovereign 17.29; 24.32
Soviet 36.45
Soviet Union 42.41
sow 29.1; 35.1
sower 36.2
Soweto 35.6; 35.7
sown 35.36
soy 33.1
soya 34.2
soya bean 15.26
soybean 15.25
Soyinka 18.9
sozzled 24.28
spa 3.1
Spa 3.1
space 7.30
space age 7.12
spacecraft 3.10
spaced 7.31
spaced out 29.14
space flight 21.33
spacelab 1.1
spaceman 1.24
spacemen 9.32
spaceport 25.31
spacer 8.9
spaces 8.75
spaceship 17.43
space shot 23.44
spacesuit 41.27
spacewalk 25.6
spacewoman 40.10
spacey 8.1
Spacey 8.1
spacing 8.64
spacious 8.67
spade 7.8
spadeful 39.7
spades 7.9
spadework 11.4
spadix 8.11
spag 1.13
spaghetti 10.3
Spain 7.21
spake 7.6
Spalding 26.25

spam 1.22
Spam® 1.22
span 1.24
Spandau 29.1
spangle 2.28
spangled 2.29
Spaniard 2.25
Spaniards 2.26
spaniel 2.28
spaniels 2.30
Spanish 2.49
spank 1.25
spanked 1.27
spanker 2.9
spanking 2.42
spanned 1.28
spanner 2.13
spar 3.1
sparable 2.64
spare 5.1
sparely 6.1
spare part 3.32
sparerib 17.1
spareribs 17.2
spares 5.5
spare time 21.19
spare tyre 19.1
sparing 6.10
sparingly 6.15
spark 3.3
Spark 3.3
sparkle 4.19
sparkler 4.12
sparkling 4.29
sparkly 4.5
sparks 3.4
sparky 4.2
sparred 3.8
sparring 4.29
sparrow 35.3
sparrowgrass 3.26
sparrowhawk 25.6
sparrows 35.52
sparse 3.26
sparsely 4.5
sparser 4.14
sparsest 4.34
sparsity 4.42
Sparta 4.10
Spartacus 4.53
Spartan 4.24
spasm 2.32
spasmodic 24.16
spasmodically 24.56
spasms 2.33
Spassky 2.2
spastic 2.17
spasticity 18.57

spat 1.45
spatchcock 23.3
spate 7.32
spathe 7.52
spatial 8.15
Spätlese 8.9
spatter 2.10
spatula 2.60
spawn 25.22
spay 7.1
spayed 7.8
speak 15.7
speakeasy 16.1
speaker 16.4
Speaker 16.4
speakers 16.37
speakership 17.43
speaking 16.27
speaking clock 23.3
speaks 15.8
spear 13.1
speared 13.2
spearhead 9.8
spearman 14.9
spearmint 17.39
spears 13.5
Spears 13.5
spec 9.2
special 10.21
specialism 18.28
specialist 10.72
speciality 2.57
specialization 8.43
specialize 21.43
specialized 21.48
specially 10.53
specialty 10.53
specie 16.1
species 15.44; 16.36
speciesism 18.28
specifiable 22.43
specific 18.16
specifically 18.57
specification 8.43
specified 21.12
specifies 21.43
specify 21.4
specimen 17.29
specious 16.30
speck 9.2
specked 9.5
speckle 10.21
speckles 10.23
specks 9.3
specs 9.3
spectacle 10.60
spectacled 10.61
spectacles 10.62

spectacular 2.60
spectacularly 2.78
spectate 7.33
spectating 8.60
spectator 8.5
spectators 8.75
Spector 10.10
spectra 10.12
spectral 10.21
spectre 10.10
spectrometer 24.57
spectroscope 35.40
spectroscopic 24.16
spectroscopy 24.54
spectrum 10.25
speculate 7.38
speculation 8.28
speculative 17.54
speculator 8.5
speculum 10.63
sped 9.8
speech 15.9
speechify 21.4
speechless 16.30
speed 15.11
speedboat 35.45
speedboats 35.46
speeder 16.5
speedfreak 15.7
speedier 16.40
speediest 16.49
speedily 16.38
speediness 16.47
speeding 16.27
speedo 35.10
speedometer 24.57
speedway 7.3
speedwell 9.16
Speedwriting® 22.26
speedy 16.1
Speke 15.7
speleology 24.55
spell 9.16
spellbind 21.23
spellbinder 22.5
spellbound 29.6
spellchecker 10.9
speller 10.12
spelling 10.36
spellings 10.37
spelt 9.23
spelunker 38.9
Spence 9.39
spencer 10.14
Spencer 10.14
spend 9.35
spendable 10.60
spender 10.10

Spender 10.10
spending 10.36
spendthrift 17.11
Spengler 10.12
Spenser 10.14
Spenserian 14.21
spent 9.41
sperm 11.13
spermatic 2.17
spermatocyte 21.32
spermatozoa 36.2
spermatozoon 23.27
spermicidal 22.16
spermicide 21.12
sperm whale 7.15
spew 41.1
spewed 41.9
spewing 42.24
Spey 7.1
sphagnum 2.32
spheral 14.6
sphere 13.1
spherical 10.60
sphincter 18.10
sphinx 17.31
sphinxlike 21.7
spice 21.29
spiced 21.30
spicery 22.40
spicier 22.42
spiciest 22.48
spick 17.3
spick-and-span 1.24
spicy 22.1
spider 22.5
Spiderman 1.24
spiders 22.39
spidery 22.40
spied 21.9
Spiegl 16.17
spiel 15.17
Spielberg 11.9
spies 21.39
spiffing 18.40
spigot 18.49
spike 21.7
spikelet 22.33
spikelets 22.35
spikenard 3.8
spikes 21.8
spiky 22.1
spill 17.15
spillage 18.21
Spillane 7.21
spiller 18.12
spilling 18.40
spills 17.23
spilt 17.21

stale 7.15
stalemate 7.34
staleness 8.67
staler 8.7
stalest 8.69
Stalin 4.23
Stalingrad 1.9
Stalinism 18.28
Stalinist 4.54
stalk 25.6
stalker 26.3
stalkers 26.36
stalking 26.25
stalkless 26.27
stalky 26.1
stall 25.14
stalled 25.15
stallholder 36.5
stalling 26.25
stallion 2.35; 2.66
Stallone 35.36
stalls 25.19
Stallybrass 3.26
stalwart 24.48; 26.31
stamen 9.32
stamina 2.60
stammer 2.13
stammerer 2.60
stammering 2.70
stamp 1.23
stamp-collecting 10.36
stampede 15.11
stamper 2.8
stamping 2.42
stamping ground 29.6
Stan 1.24
stance 1.31; 3.22
stanch 3.20
stanchion 2.35; 4.24
stand 1.28
stand-alone 35.36
standard 2.25
standardization 8.40
standardize 21.42
standardized 21.48
standard lamp 1.23
stand-by 21.3
standee 15.2
stander 2.10
stand-in 2.34
standing 2.42
Standish 2.49
standoff 23.9
standoffish 24.46
standpipe 21.26
standpoint 33.10

St Andrews 41.33
standstill 17.15
Stanislas 2.71
Stanislaus 25.28
Stanislavsky 2.2
stank 1.25
Stanley 2.5
Stannaries 2.77
stannary 2.56
stannic 2.20
stannous 2.46
stannum 2.32
Stan's 1.36
Stansted 9.8
stanza 2.14
stapes 15.44
staphylococcal 24.27
staphylococcus 24.43
staple 8.15
stapled 8.16
stapler 8.7
staples 8.17
Stapleton 8.81
stapling 8.62
star 3.1
starboard 4.17; 25.9
starburst 11.23
starch 3.6
starched 3.7
starcher 4.14
starchier 4.44
starchiest 4.55
starching 4.29
starchy 4.7
star-crossed 23.41
stardom 4.22
stardust 37.45
stare 5.1
stared 5.2
starer 6.2
starfish 4.35
stargaze 7.56
stargazer 8.9
stargazing 8.64
staring 6.10
stark 3.3
Stark 3.3
starker 4.9
starkest 4.34
Starkey 4.2
starkly 4.5
starkness 4.32
starless 4.32
starlet 4.38
starlight 21.33
starlike 21.7
starling 4.29
starlings 4.30

starlit 4.38
Starr 3.1
starred 3.8
starring 4.29
starry 4.5
starry-eyed 21.12
stars 3.37
Stars and Stripes 21.27
starship 17.43
start 3.32
started 4.17
starter 4.10
starting 4.29
startle 4.19
startled 4.20
startlingly 4.42
starts 3.33
starvation 8.23
starve 3.35
starveling 4.29
starving 4.29
stash 1.43
Stasi 4.7
stasis 8.66
state 7.32
statecraft 3.10
stated 8.13
stateless 8.67
stately 8.1
statement 8.56
statements 8.57
Staten 2.35
state-of-the-art 3.32
state-owned 35.37
stateroom 39.9; 41.17
States 7.50
stateside 21.11
statesman 8.21
statesmanlike 21.7
statesmanship 17.43
stateswoman 40.10
static 2.17
station 8.22
stationary 8.76
stationed 8.54
stationer 8.77
stationery 8.76
stationmaster 4.10
stations 8.55
statistic 18.16
statistical 18.64
statistically 18.57
statistician 18.33
statistics 18.17
statuary 2.78
statue 41.3
statues 41.33

statuesque 9.48
statuette 9.51
stature 2.12
stature 2.14
status 8.67
status quo 35.19
Status Quo 35.19
statute 41.27
statutes 41.28
statutory 2.59
staunch 25.23
stauncher 26.8
staunchly 26.1
St Austell 24.27; 26.15
Stavanger 2.13
stave 7.54
staves 7.55
stay 7.1
stayed 7.8
stayer 8.2
staying 8.58
staying power 31.1
stays 7.56
staysail 7.15; 8.15
stead 9.8
steadfast 10.43
steadfast 3.30
steadfastness 4.32
Steadicam® 1.22
steadied 10.17
steadier 10.57
steadiest 10.71
steadily 10.54
steadiness 10.70
Steadman 10.27
steady 10.3
steak 7.6
steakhouse 29.12
steak tartare 3.1
steal 15.17
stealer 16.7
stealing 16.27
stealth 9.24
stealthily 10.54
stealthy 10.4
steam 15.20
steamboat 35.45
steamed 15.21
steamer 16.8
steamier 16.40
steamiest 16.49
steaming 16.27
steamroller 36.7
steamrollered 36.12
steamship 17.43
steamy 16.1
steatite 21.34
steed 15.11

studding

subtle 38.23
subtler 38.12
subtlest 38.39
subtlety 38.47
subtly 38.5
subtonic 24.19
subtotal 36.15
subtract 1.6
subtraction 2.35
subtractive 2.53
subtropical 24.61
subtype 21.26
subunit 42.30
suburb 11.2
suburban 12.12
suburbanite 21.34
suburbanization 8.44
suburbia 12.31
subvene 15.24
subvention 10.28
subversion 12.12
subversive 12.27
subvert 11.24
subverter 12.2
subway 7.3
subzero 35.9
succeed 15.11
succeeded 16.14
succeeder 16.5
succeeding 16.27
succeeds 15.12
succès de scandale 3.14
success 9.47
successful 10.21; 39.7
successfully 10.53; 10.55
succession 10.28
successive 10.50
successively 10.54
successor 10.14
succinct 17.32
succinctness 18.44
succory 38.47
succotash 1.43
succour 38.9
succubus 38.59
succulence 38.57
succulent 38.56
succumb 37.27
succursal 12.8
such 37.6
such-and-such 37.6
Suchet 7.3
suchlike 21.7
suck 37.3
sucked 37.5
sucker 38.9
sucking 38.34

suckle 38.23
suckler 38.12
suckling 38.34
Suckling 38.34
sucklings 38.35
sucks 37.4
sucrose 35.42
suction 38.28
Sudan 1.24
Sudan 3.19
Sudanese 15.45
sudarium 6.18
sudden 38.28
suddenly 38.47
suddenness 38.59
Sudetenland 1.28
sudoku 41.3
suds 37.9
sudsy 38.7
sue 41.1
Sue 41.1
sued 41.9
suede 7.8
Sue's 41.33
suet 42.30
Suetonius 36.42
Suez 42.35
suffer 38.11
sufferable 38.52; 38.65
sufferance 38.33; 38.57
sufferer 38.48
suffering 38.58
suffice 21.29
sufficed 21.30
sufficiency 18.56
sufficient 18.38
sufficiently 18.56
suffix 38.18
suffocate 7.48
suffocated 8.13
suffocating 8.60
suffocation 8.38
Suffolk 38.16
suffragan 38.54
suffrage 38.22
suffragette 9.51
suffragettes 9.52
suffuse 41.33
suffusion 42.20
Sufi 42.1
sugar 40.2
sugar beet 15.35
sugar cane 7.21
sugar-coated 36.12
sugared 40.4
sugar lump 37.29
sugar lumps 37.30

sugarplum 37.27
sugary 40.20
suggest 9.49
suggestible 10.60
suggesting 10.36
suggestion 10.28
suggestions 10.32
suggestive 10.50
suicidal 22.16
suicidally 22.40
suicide 21.12
sui generis 17.46
suit 41.27
suitability 18.58
suitable 42.39
suitably 42.36
suitcase 7.30
suite 15.35
suited 42.14
suiting 42.24
suitor 42.5
suits 41.28
Sukie 42.1
sukiyaki 2.2; 4.2
Sulawesi 8.1
Suleiman 3.19
sulk 37.18
sulked 37.19
sulker 38.9
sulkier 38.49
sulkiest 38.61
sulkily 38.47
sulkiness 38.59
sulking 38.34
sulky 38.2
Sulla 38.12
sullage 38.22
sullen 38.28
sullenly 38.47
sullied 38.19
Sullivan 38.54
sully 38.5
Sully 38.5
sulphate 7.34
sulphide 21.11
sulphonamide 21.12
sulphonic 24.19
sulphur 38.11
sulphureous 28.24
sulphuric 28.3
sulphurous 28.12; 38.59
sultan 38.28
sultana 4.13
sultanas 4.41
sultanate 7.48; 38.62
sultrier 38.49
sultriest 38.61

sultriness 38.59
sultry 38.5
sum 37.27
sumac 1.3
Sumatra 4.12
Sumatran 4.24
Sumer 42.8
Sumerian 14.21
Sumerian 6.19
summarily 38.64
summarize 21.46
summarized 21.48
summary 38.47
summation 8.23
summer 38.13
summerhouse 29.12
summers 38.45
Summers 38.45
summertime 21.19
summerweight 7.48
summery 38.47
summing-up 37.41
summit 38.43
summitry 38.47
summon 38.28
summoned 38.29
summoner 38.48
summons 38.31
Sumner 38.13
sumo 35.18
sump 37.29
sumptuous 38.59
sun 37.31
Sun 37.31
sunbake 7.6
sunbaked 7.7
sunbathe 7.52
sunbathed 7.53
sunbather 8.6
sunbathing 8.61
sunbeam 15.20
sun bed 9.8
sun block 23.3
sunbonnet 24.49
sunburn 11.15
sunburnt 11.17
Sunda 38.10
sundae 7.3
Sunday 7.3; 38.3
Sunday best 9.49
Sundays 7.56
Sunday school 41.14
sun deck 9.2
sunder 38.10
Sunderland 38.55
sundew 41.3
sundial 19.3
sundown 29.5

sundowner 30.2
sun-drenched 9.34
sundress 9.47
sun-dried 21.11
sundries 38.46
sundry 38.5
sunfish 38.40
sunflower 31.1
sung 37.37
sunglasses 4.41
sun god 23.8
sunhat 1.45
sunk 37.32
sunken 38.28
sunless 38.38
sunlight 21.33
sunlit 38.43
sun-lounger 30.2
Sunna 38.13
Sunni 38.6
sunnier 38.49
sunniest 38.61
sunny 38.6
sunrise 21.41
sunroof 41.10
sunroom 39.9; 41.17
sunscreen 15.25
sunset 9.51
sunshade 7.8
sunshine 21.22
sunshiny 22.1
sunspot 23.44
sunstroke 35.21
sunsuit 41.27
suntan 1.24
suntanned 1.28
suntrap 1.37
sunup 37.41
Sun Yat-sen 9.32
sup 37.41
super 42.3
superable 42.39
superabound 29.6
superabundance 38.33
superabundant 38.32
superannuated 8.13
superannuation 8.24
superb 11.2
superbike 21.7
superbikes 21.8
superbly 12.1
superbug 37.14
supercharge 3.12
supercharger 4.14
supercilious 18.74
superciliously 18.80
superclass 3.26

supercomputer 42.5
supercool 41.14
supercooled 41.15
super-duper 42.3
superego 35.10
supererogate 7.38
supererogation 8.28
superficial 18.22
superficiality 2.57
superficially 18.56
superfine 21.22
superfluid 42.13
superfluity 42.36
superfluous 12.37
supergiant 22.24
superglue 41.4
supergrass 3.26
supergroup 41.22
superheat 15.35
superhero 35.9
superhighway 7.3
superhuman 42.20
superimpose 35.52
superimposed 35.53
superintend 9.35
superintendence 10.34
superintendent 10.33
superior 14.18
superiority 24.56
superlative 17.55
superloo 41.4
superman 1.24
Superman 1.24
supermarket 4.38
supermini 18.6
supermodel 24.27
supermodels 24.29
supernatural 2.64
supernaturally 2.78
supernova 36.6
supernumerary 42.50
superordinate 26.50
superpose 35.52
superposed 35.53
superpower 31.1
superpowers 31.5
superscript 17.45
superscription 18.33
supersede 15.11
supersonic 24.19
supersonics 24.22
superstar 3.1
superstardom 4.22
superstate 7.49
superstition 18.33
superstitious 18.44
superstore 25.4

superstratum 4.22
superstructure 38.14
supertanker 2.9
supertax 1.4
supertonic 24.19
supervene 15.26
supervise 21.46
supervised 21.48
supervision 18.33
supervisor 22.9
supervisory 22.40
superwoman 40.10
supine 21.22
suplex 9.3
supped 37.42
supper 38.8
supperless 38.59
supper time 21.19
supping 38.34
supplant 3.23
supple 38.23
supplement 9.41; 42.43
supplemental 10.21
supplementary 10.53
suppleness 38.59
suppler 38.12
supplest 38.39
supplicant 38.56
supplicants 38.57
supplicate 7.48
supplicating 8.60
supplication 8.38
supplied 21.10
supplier 22.2
suppliers 22.39
supplies 21.40
supply 21.2
support 25.31
supportable 26.41
supported 26.12
supporter 26.4
supporters 26.36
supporting 26.25
supportive 26.34
supports 25.32
suppose 35.52
supposed 35.53
supposedly 36.35
supposing 36.24
supposition 18.33
suppositional 18.64
suppositious 18.44
suppository 24.56
suppress 9.47
suppressant 10.33
suppressed 9.49
suppression 10.28

suppressor 10.14
suppurate 7.48
suppuration 8.38
supralapsarian 6.19
supremacy 10.53
supreme 15.20
suprême 9.28
supremely 16.1
supremo 35.10
Surbiton 12.34
surcease 15.32
surcharge 3.12
surd 11.7
sure 25.1; 27.1
sure-fire 19.1
surely 26.1; 28.1
sureness 26.27; 28.12
surer 26.6; 28.2
surest 28.13; 28.17
surf 11.8
surface 12.18
surfaced 12.21
surfacer 12.30
surface-to-air 5.1
surfactant 2.40
surfboard 25.9
surfeit 12.25
surfer 12.2
surfie 12.1
surfing 12.16
surge 11.10
surgeon 12.12
surgery 12.29
surgical 12.32
surgically 12.29
surging 12.16
Surinam 1.22
surlier 12.31
surliest 12.39
surly 12.1
surmise 21.40
surmount 29.11
surmountable 30.24
surname 7.18
surpass 3.26
surpassed 3.30
surpassing 4.29
surplice 12.18
surplus 12.19
surprise 21.40
surprised 21.48
surprises 22.39
surprising 22.26
surprisingly 22.40
surreal 13.3
surrealism 18.27
surrealist 14.15
surrealistic 18.16

swineherd 11.7
swing 17.35
swing bin 18.31
swingboat 35.45
swinge 17.37
swingeing 18.40
swinger 18.13
swinging 18.40
Swingler 18.12
swingletree 15.4
swingometer 24.57
swings 17.36
swingy 18.6
swinish 22.32
swipe 21.26
swiped 21.28
swiper 22.3
swirl 11.11
swirled 11.12
swirling 12.16
swish 17.50
swishy 18.7
Swiss 17.46
switch 17.7
switchback 1.3
switchblade 7.8
switchboard 25.9
switchgear 13.1
Swithin 18.31
Swithin's 18.36
Switzer 18.14
Switzerland 18.68
swivel 18.22
swivelled 18.23
swizz 17.56
swizzle 18.22
swollen 36.20
swoon 41.19
swooned 41.20
swooning 42.24
swoop 41.22
swooping 42.24
swoosh 39.13
sword 25.9
swordbearer 6.2
swordcraft 3.10
swordfish 26.30
swordplay 7.3
swordsman 26.19
swordsmanship 17.43
swordstick 26.9
swordsticks 26.10
swore 25.1
sworn 25.22
swot 23.44
swotter 24.10
swotting 24.40
swotty 24.3

swum 37.27
swung 37.37
sybarite 21.34
sybaritic 18.16
Sybil 18.22
sycamore 25.4
sycophancy 18.80
sycophant 1.33; 18.70
sycophantic 2.17
sycophants 1.34; 18.71
Sydney 18.6
Sydney Carton 4.24
Sykes 21.8
syllabi 21.4
syllabic 2.17
syllabification 8.40
syllabify 21.4
syllable 18.64
syllabub 37.1
syllabus 18.74
syllogism 18.28
syllogistic 18.16
sylphlike 21.7
sylva 18.11
sylvan 18.32
Sylvester 10.10
sylvestral 10.21
Sylvia 18.61
Sylvie 18.4
symbiont 23.34
symbiosis 36.25
symbol 18.22
symbolic 24.18
symbolical 24.61
symbolically 24.56
symbolism 18.28
symbolist 18.75
symbolize 21.44
symmetric 10.15
symmetrical 10.60
symmetrically 10.54
symmetry 18.57
Symonds 18.35
Symonds Yat 1.45
sympathetic 10.15
sympathetically 10.54
sympathize 21.44
sympathizer 22.9
sympathizers 22.39
sympathizing 22.26
sympathy 18.56
symphonic 24.19
symphony 18.56
symposia 36.37
symptom 18.26
symptomatic 2.17
symptomless 18.74
symptoms 18.30

synaesthesia 16.40
synaesthetic 10.15
synagogal 24.27
synagogue 23.11
sync 17.30
synchromesh 9.50
synchronic 24.19
synchronicity 18.57
synchronization 8.46
synchronize 21.44
synchronized 21.48
synchronous 18.74
synchrotron 23.27
syncline 21.22
syncopate 7.41
syncopated 8.13
syncopation 8.32
syncopy 18.56
syndic 18.16
syndicalism 18.29
syndicate 7.41; 18.77
syndication 8.32
syndrome 35.34
syndromic 24.19
synecdoche 10.53
synergetic 10.15
synergic 12.3
synergy 18.56
Synge 17.35
synod 18.19
synonym 17.24
synonymous 24.70
synonymy 24.56
synopses 15.44
synopses 24.52
synopsis 24.42
synopsize 21.41
synoptic 24.16
synovia 36.37
synovial 36.38
syntactic 2.17
syntagma 2.13
syntax 1.4
synthesis 17.46
synthesize 21.44
synthesizer 22.9
synthetic 10.15
synthetically 10.54
synthetics 10.16
syphilitic 18.16
Syracuse 41.33
Syria 18.61
Syriac 1.3
Syrian 18.67
syringa 18.9
syringe 17.37
syrup 18.42
syrup of figs 17.13

syrupy 18.56
system 18.26
systematic 2.17
systematically 2.58
systematization 8.53
systematize 21.47
systemic 10.15
systole 18.56
systolic 24.18
syzygy 18.57
T 15.1
ta 3.1
tab 1.1
tabard 2.25
Tabasco 35.3
tabby 2.1
tabernacle 2.28
tabes 15.44
Tabitha 2.60
tablature 2.60
table 8.15
tableau 35.3
tablecloth 23.46
table d'hôte 35.45
tableland 1.28
tables 8.17
tablespoon 41.19
tablespoons 41.21
tablet 2.51
tableware 5.1
table wine 21.22
tabloid 33.4
tabloids 33.5
taboo 41.2
tabor 8.3
tabular 2.60
tabula rasa 4.14
tabularize 21.47
tabulate 7.35
tabulation 8.24
tabulator 8.5
tache 1.43
tacheometer 24.57
tachograph 1.11; 3.9
tachometer 24.57
tachometric 10.15
tachycardia 4.44
tachygraphic 2.18
tacit 2.51
taciturn 11.15
taciturnity 12.29
Tacitus 2.71
tack 1.3
tacker 2.9
tackier 2.61
tackiest 2.72
tacking 2.42
tackle 2.28

Tara

Tara 4.12
taramasalata 4.10
tarantella 10.12
Tarantino 35.10
Taranto 35.3
tarantula 2.60
Tarbert 4.37
Tarbuck 37.3
tardiness 4.53
Tardis 4.31
tardy 4.3
tare 5.1
targe 3.12
target 4.38
targeted 4.45
tariff 17.10
Tariq 2.19
Tarka 4.9
Tarmac® 1.3
tarn 3.19
tarnation 8.23
tarnish 4.35
tarnished 4.36
tarns 3.24
tarot 35.3
tarp 3.25
tarpaulin 26.18
tarpaulins 26.22
Tarpeian 16.22
Tarporley 4.42
Tarquin 4.23
tarradiddle 18.22
tarragon 2.66
tarred 3.8
tarried 2.24
tarrier 2.61
tarry 2.5; 4.5
tarsal 4.19
tarsier 4.44
tarsus 4.32
Tarsus 4.32
tart 3.32
tartan 4.24
tartar 4.10
Tartar 4.10
tartaric 2.19
Tartarus 4.53
Tartary 4.42
tartlet 4.38
tartness 4.32
tartrate 7.34
tartrazine 15.26
tarts 3.33
Tartuffe 41.10
Tarzan 4.24
Taser® 8.9
Tashkent 9.41
task 3.27

taskmaster 4.10
Tasman 2.35
Tasmania 8.78
Tasmanian 8.81
TASS 1.40
tassel 2.28
tastable 8.79
taste 7.31
taste bud 37.8
taste buds 37.9
tasted 8.13
tasteful 39.7; 8.15
tastefully 8.76
tasteless 8.67
taster 8.5
tastier 8.78
tastiest 8.86
tasting 8.60
tasty 8.1
tat 1.45
ta-ta 3.1
Tatchell 2.28
Tate 7.32
tater 8.5
taters 8.75
Tati 2.3
Tatiana 4.13
Tatler 2.12
tatter 2.10
tatterdemalion 8.81
tattered 2.25
tatters 2.55
Tattersall 25.14
tattie 2.3
tattier 2.61
tattiest 2.72
tattiness 2.71
tatting 2.42
tattle 2.28
tattler 2.12
tattletale 7.15
Tatton 2.35
tattoo 41.2
tattooed 41.9
tattooer 42.2
tattooist 42.28
tattoos 41.33
tatty 2.3
Tatum 8.19
tau 25.1; 29.1
taught 25.31
taunt 25.25
taunted 26.12
taunter 26.4
taunting 26.25
Taunton 26.19
taupe 35.40
Taurean 16.22; 26.43

taurine 21.22
Taurus 26.27
taut 25.31
tauten 26.19
tauter 26.4
tautest 26.29
tautly 26.1
tautness 26.27
tautologic 24.20
tautological 24.61
tautologous 24.70
tautology 24.55
Tavener 2.60
tavern 2.35
taverna 12.2
Taverner 2.60
taverns 2.39
Tavistock 23.3
taw 25.1
tawdriness 26.47
tawdry 26.1
tawny 26.1
tawse 25.35
tax 1.4
taxable 2.64
taxation 8.23
tax-deductible 38.52
taxed 1.5
taxer 2.14
tax-free 15.2
taxi 2.7
taxicab 1.1
taxidermic 12.3
taxidermist 12.21
taxidermy 12.1
taximeter 16.5
taxing 2.42
taxis 2.45; 2.54
taxman 1.24
taxon 23.27
taxonomic 24.19
taxonomy 24.54
taxpayer 8.2
taxpaying 8.58
Tay 7.1
Taylor 8.7
Tayside 21.11
TB 15.2
Tbilisi 16.1
Tchaikovsky 24.2
te 15.1
tea 15.1
teabag 1.13
teabags 1.14
teacake 7.6
teacart 3.32
teach 15.9
teachable 16.41

teacher 16.9
teachers 16.37
teach-in 16.21
teaching 16.27
teacup 37.41
teahouse 29.12
teak 15.7
teal 15.17
tea leaf 15.13
tea leaves 15.41
team 15.20
team-mate 7.34
teams 15.22
teamster 16.5
teamwork 11.4
teapot 23.44
teapots 23.45
tear 5.1; 13.1
tearable 6.17
tearaway 7.4
teardrop 23.36
teardrops 23.37
tearer 6.2
tearful 14.6; 39.7
tear gas 1.40
tearing 6.10
tear-jerker 12.2
tear-jerking 12.16
tearoom 39.9; 41.17
tears 13.5
tear-stained 7.22
teary 14.1
tease 15.42
teasel 16.17
teasels 16.18
teaser 16.9
tea set 9.51
teashop 23.36
teasing 16.27
Teasmade® 7.8
teaspoon 41.19
teaspoonful 39.7
teat 15.35
teatime 21.19
Tebbitt 10.48
tech 9.2
techie 10.2
technetium 16.42
technical 10.60
technicality 2.57
technically 10.54
technician 18.33
Technicolor® 38.12
technicolour 38.12
technique 15.7
technobabble 2.28
technocrat 1.45
technofear 13.1

technological 24.61
technologically 24.56
technologist 24.72
technology 24.55
technophile 21.16
technophobe 35.20
technophobia 36.37
technophobic 36.10
tectonic 24.19
tectonics 24.22
Tecumseh 38.14
ted 9.8
Ted 9.8
tedder 10.10
teddies 10.51
Teddington 10.64
teddy 10.3
Teddy 10.3
teddy bear 5.1
tedious 16.47
tedium 16.42
tee 15.1
tee-hee 15.2
teem 15.20
teemed 15.21
teeming 16.27
teen 15.23
teenage 7.12
teenaged 7.13
teenager 8.9
teenagers 8.75
teens 15.29
teensy 16.1
teensy-weensy 16.1
teeny 16.1
teenybopper 24.8
teenyboppers 24.53
teeny-weeny 16.1
Tees 15.42
Teesside 21.11
teeter 16.5
teeth 15.37
teethe 15.38
teething 16.27
teetotal 36.15
teetotalism 18.28
teetotaller 36.36
TEFL 10.21
Teflon® 23.27
teg 9.12
tegument 10.67
Tehran 1.24
Tehran 3.19
Teignmouth 18.52
Te Kanawa 2.60
Telamon 10.64
Tel Aviv 15.39
telecast 3.30

telecom 23.23
telecommunication
  8.39
telecommunications
  8.55
telecommuter 42.5
telecommuting 42.24
teleconference 24.68
telecottage 24.26
telegenic 10.15
telegram 1.22
telegrammatic 2.17
telegraph 1.11; 3.9
telegrapher 10.56
telegraphic 2.18
telegraphy 10.53
telekinesis 16.29
telekinetic 10.15
Telemachus 10.70
Telemann 1.24
telemark 3.3
telemarketing 4.52
telemetric 10.15
telemetry 10.54
teleost 23.41
telepath 1.47
telepathic 2.18
telepathically 2.58
telepaths 1.48
telepathy 10.53
téléphérique 15.7
telephone 35.36
telephoned 35.37
telephonic 24.19
telephoning 36.24
telephonist 10.72
telephony 10.53
telephoto 35.16
teleport 25.31
teleporter 26.4
teleprinter 18.10
Teleprompter® 24.10
telesales 7.17
telescope 35.40
telescopic 24.16
teleshopping 24.40
teletext 9.4
telethon 23.27
Teletype® 21.26
televangelism 18.28
televangelist 2.73
televise 21.43
televised 21.48
television 18.33
televisual 18.64
teleworking 12.16
Telford 10.18
tell 9.16

teller 10.12
telling 10.36
telling-off 23.9
tells 9.27
telltale 7.15
tellurian 28.21
telluric 28.3
tellurium 28.20
telly 10.5
Telstar 3.1
temazepam 1.22
temerity 10.54
temp 9.29
temper 10.8
tempera 10.56
temperament 10.67
temperamental 10.21
temperamentally
  10.53
temperance 10.68
temperate 10.73
temperature 10.56
tempest 10.43
tempestuous 10.70
tempi 10.1
Templar 10.12
template 7.34; 10.47
temple 10.21
Templeton 10.64
tempo 35.7
temporal 10.60
temporality 2.57
temporarily 10.78
temporary 10.53;
  10.78
temporize 21.43
tempt 9.30
temptation 8.23
temptations 8.55
tempted 10.18
tempter 10.10
tempting 10.36
temptingly 10.54
temptress 10.42
tempura 10.56
tempus fugit 42.30
ten 9.32
tenable 10.60
tenacious 8.67
tenacity 2.57
tenancy 10.53
tenant 10.33
tenants 10.34
Tenby 10.1
Tencel® 9.16
tench 9.33
tend 9.35
tended 10.18

tendency 10.53
tendentious 10.42
tender 10.10
tenderfoot 39.14
tenderhearted 4.17
tendering 10.69
tenderization 8.43
tenderize 21.43
tenderized 21.48
tenderizer 22.9
tenderloin 33.8
tenderly 10.53
tenderness 10.70
tending 10.36
tendon 10.27
tendons 10.32
tendril 10.21
tenement 10.67
Tenerife 15.13
tenet 10.48
tenfold 35.31
Tennant 10.33
tenner 10.13
Tennessee 15.4
Tenniel 10.60
tennis 10.41
tennis player 8.2
Tennyson 10.64
Tennysonian 36.40
tenon 10.27
tenor 10.13
tenors 10.52
tenpin 10.26
tenpin bowling 36.24
tenpins 10.31
TENS 9.43
tense 9.39
tensed 9.40
tensely 10.5
tenser 10.14
tensest 10.43
tensile 21.16
tension 10.28
tensor 10.14
tent 9.41
tentacle 10.60
tentacled 10.61
tentacles 10.62
tentage 10.20
tentative 17.55
tentatively 10.78
tenter 10.10
Tenterdon 10.64
tenterhook 39.1
tenth 9.42
tenting 10.36
tent peg 9.12
tent pegs 9.13

theoretician 18.33
theories 14.17
theorist 14.15
theorization 8.30
theorize 21.43
theory 14.1
theosophical 24.61
theosophy 24.54
therapeutic 42.11
therapeutics 42.12
therapist 10.72
therapy 10.53
there 5.1
thereabouts 29.15
thereafter 4.10
thereat 1.45
thereby 21.2
therefore 25.3
therefrom 23.23
therein 17.29
thereinafter 4.10
thereinto 41.3
thereof 23.47
thereon 23.27
Theresa 16.9
thereto 41.2
theretofore 25.4
thereunder 38.10
thereunto 41.3
thereupon 23.27
therewith 17.53
therm 11.13
thermal 12.8
thermals 12.9
thermidor 25.4
thermionic 24.19
thermionics 24.22
thermocouple 38.23
thermodynamic 2.20
thermodynamics 2.23
thermolytic 18.16
thermometer 24.57
thermometric 10.15
thermonuclear 42.38
thermopile 21.16
thermoplastic 2.17
Thermopylae 15.4
Thermos® 12.19
thermosetting 10.36
thermostat 1.45
thermostatic 2.17
thermostatically 2.58
Theroux 41.2
thesauri 21.3
thesaurus 26.27
these 15.42
theses 15.44; 16.36
Theseus 16.47

thesis 16.29
Thespian 10.64
Thessalonian 36.40
Thessalonica 24.57
Thessaly 10.53
theta 16.5
thew 41.1
thews 41.33
they 7.1
they'd 7.8
they'll 7.15
they're 5.1
they've 7.54
thiamine 15.26; 17.29
thick 17.3
thicken 18.32
thickened 18.34
thickener 18.60
thickening 18.73
thicker 18.9
thickest 18.46
thicket 18.50
thickhead 9.8
thickie 18.2
thickly 18.5
thickness 18.44
thicko 35.11
thickset 9.51
thick-skinned 17.34
thief 15.13
thieve 15.39
thieved 15.40
thievery 16.38
thieves 15.41
thieving 16.27
thigh 21.1
thighbone 35.36
thighs 21.39
thimble 18.22
thimbleful 39.7
thimblerig 17.12
thimbles 18.24
thin 17.29
thine 21.22
thing 17.35
things 17.36
thingumabob 23.1
thingumajig 17.12
thingummy 18.56
thingy 18.6
think 17.30
thinkable 18.64
thinker 18.9
thinking 18.40
thinks 17.31
think-tank 1.25
thinly 18.5
thinner 18.13

thinnest 18.46
thinning 18.40
thin-skinned 17.34
third 11.7
third-class 3.26
thirdly 12.1
third-rate 7.33
thirst 11.23
thirstier 12.31
thirstiest 12.39
thirsting 12.16
thirst-quencher 10.14
thirsty 12.1
thirteen 15.24
thirteenth 15.28
thirties 12.28
thirtieth 17.53
thirty 12.1
thirty-eight 7.39
thirty-five 21.37
thirty-four 25.4
thirty-nine 21.22
thirty-one 37.31
thirty-six 17.4
thirty-three 15.4
thirty-two 41.4
this 17.46
Thisbe 18.1
thistle 18.22
thistledown 29.5
thistles 18.24
thither 18.11
thitherto 41.4
thixotropic 24.16
Thomas 24.43
Thomas à Kempis
  10.41
Thomasina 16.8
Thompson 24.33
Thomson 24.33
thong 23.31
Thor 25.1
Thora 26.6
thoracic 2.21
thorax 1.4
Thoreau 35.2
thorn 25.22
Thorndike 21.7
thornier 26.39
thorniest 26.49
thornless 26.27
Thornley 26.1
Thornton 26.19
thorny 26.1
thorough 38.12
thoroughbred 9.8
thoroughfare 5.1
thoroughgoing 36.24

thoroughly 38.47
thoroughness 38.59
Thorpe 25.26
those 35.52
thou 29.1
though 35.1
thought 25.31
thoughtful 26.15; 39.7
thoughtfully 26.37
thoughtfulness 26.47
thoughtless 26.27
thoughtlessness
  26.47
thought-provoking
  36.24
thoughts 25.32
thousand 30.9
Thrace 7.30
Thracian 8.22; 8.81
Thracians 8.55
Thrale 7.15
thrall 25.14
thrash 1.43
thrashed 1.44
thrasher 2.14
thrashing 2.42
thread 9.8
threadbare 5.1
threader 10.10
threadlike 21.7
Threadneedle 16.17
threads 9.9
threadworm 11.13
thready 10.3
threat 9.51
threaten 10.27
threatened 10.29
threatener 10.56
threatening 10.69
threateningly 10.78
threats 9.52
three 15.1
three-cornered 26.12
three-course meal
  15.17
three-D 15.2
three-dimensional
  10.60
threefold 35.31
three-headed 10.18
three-legged 10.17
three-ply 21.3
three-point turn 11.15
three-quarter 26.4
three-quarters 26.36
three Rs 3.37
threesome 16.20

three-storeyed 26.11
three-wheeled 15.18
three-wheeler 16.7
Threlfall 25.14
threnodic 24.16
threnody 10.53
thresh 9.50
thresher 10.14
threshing 10.36
threshold 35.31
threw 41.1
thrice 21.29
thrift 17.11
thriftier 18.61
thriftiest 18.76
thriftily 18.57
thriftless 18.44
thrifty 18.3
thrill 17.15
thrilled 17.18
thriller 18.12
thrilling 18.40
thrills 17.23
thrips 17.44
thrive 21.37
thriving 22.26
throat 35.45
throatily 36.35
throaty 36.1
throb 23.1
throbbing 24.40
throe 35.1
throes 35.52
Throgmorton 26.19
thrombi 21.3
thrombosis 36.25
thrombotic 24.16
thrombus 24.43
throne 35.36
throng 23.31
thronging 24.40
throngs 23.32
throstle 24.27
throttle 24.27
throttled 24.28
through 41.1
throughout 29.14
throughput 39.14
throve 35.50
throw 35.1
throwable 36.38
throwaway 7.4
throwback 1.3
thrower 36.2
throw-in 36.19
thrown 35.36
thrum 37.27
thrush 37.46

thrust 37.45
thruster 38.10
thrusting 38.34
Thucydides 15.45
thud 37.8
thudding 38.34
thug 37.14
thuggery 38.47
thuggish 38.40
thuja 42.7
Thule 41.14; 42.1
thumb 37.27
thumbnail 7.15
thumbprint 17.39
thumbscrew 41.3
thumbs-down 29.5
thumbstall 25.14
thumbs-up 37.41
thumbtack 1.3
thump 37.29
thumping 38.34
thunder 38.10
thunderbolt 35.32
thunderbox 23.5
thunderclap 1.37
thundercloud 29.3
thundered 38.20
thunderer 38.48
thunderfly 21.4
thundering 38.58
thunderous 38.38;
   38.59
thunderstorm 25.20
thunderstruck 37.3
thundery 38.47
thunk 37.32
Thurber 12.2
thurible 28.19
Thuringian 18.67
Thurrock 38.16
Thursday 7.3; 12.1
thus 37.43
thwack 1.3
Thwaite 7.32
thwart 25.31
thwarted 26.12
thy 21.1
thyme 21.19
thymic 22.11
thymus 22.29
thyroid 33.4
Tia Maria® 16.2
tiara 4.12
Tiber 22.3
Tiberias 1.40; 14.23
Tiberius 14.23
Tibet 9.51
Tibetan 10.27

tibia 18.61
tic 17.3
tick 17.3
ticked 17.6
ticker 18.9
ticker tape 7.27
ticket 18.50
ticketless 18.74
tickets 18.51
ticket tout 29.14
tickety-boo 41.2
ticking 18.40
tickle 18.22
tickled 18.23
tickler 18.12
tickles 18.24
ticklish 18.47
tickly 18.5
tick-over 36.6
ticks 17.4
ticktack 1.3
tick-tack-toe 35.19
ticktock 23.3
Ticonderoga 36.4
tidal 22.16
tidal wave 7.54
tiddler 18.12
Tiddles 18.24
tiddly 18.5
tiddlywink 17.30
tiddlywinks 17.31
tide 21.9
tidemark 3.3
tidewater 26.4
tideway 7.3
tidied 22.12
tidier 22.42
tidiest 22.48
tidily 22.40
tidiness 22.46
tidings 22.27
tidy 22.1
tie 21.1
tieback 1.3
tie-breaker 8.4
tied 21.9
tie-dye 21.3
tieless 22.29
tiepin 22.19
tier 13.1
tierce 13.4
tiercel 14.6
tiered 13.2
Tierney 14.1
Tierra del Fuego 35.6
tiers 13.5
tiff 17.10
Tiffany 18.56

tiffin 18.31
tiger 22.4
tiger moth 23.46
tiger's-eye 21.4
tight 21.31
tightass 1.40
tighten 22.20
tightener 22.41
tighter 22.5
tightest 22.31
tightfisted 18.19
tight-knit 17.51
tightly 22.1
tightness 22.29
tightrope 35.40
tights 21.35
tightwad 23.8
tigon 22.20
Tigré 7.3
tigress 9.47; 22.28
Tigris 22.28
Tijuana 4.13
tikka 16.4; 18.9
Tilbury 18.56
Tilda 18.10
tilde 18.10
tile 21.16
tiled 21.17
tiler 22.7
tiles 21.18
tiling 22.26
till 17.15
tillage 18.21
tiller 18.12
Till Eulenspiegel
   16.17
Tilley 18.5
Tilly 18.5
Tilsit 18.50
tilt 17.21
tilter 18.10
tilth 17.22
tilting 18.40
Tim 17.24
timbal 18.22
timbale 3.14
timber 18.8
timbered 18.19
timberland 1.28
timbers 18.55
timberwork 11.4
timberyard 3.8
timbre 18.8
timbre 2.8
timbrel 18.22
Timbuktu 41.4
time 21.19
timed 21.20

time-honoured 24.24
timekeeper 16.3
timekeeping 16.27
timeless 22.29
timeline 21.22
timely 22.1
time-out 29.14
timepiece 15.32
timer 22.8
times 21.21
time-saving 8.61
timescale 7.15
timeserver 12.2
timeserving 12.16
timeshare 5.1
time-sharing 6.10
time sheet 15.35
timetable 8.15
timework 11.4
timeworn 25.22
Timex® 9.3
timid 18.18
timidity 18.57
timidly 18.57
timing 22.26
Timmy 18.6
Timon 22.20
Timor 25.3
timorous 18.74
Timoshenko 35.7
Timothy 18.56
timpani 18.56
Timpson 18.33
tin 17.29
Tina 16.8
tincture 18.14
tinder 18.10
tinderbox 23.5
tindery 18.56
tine 21.22
tinea 18.61
tines 21.25
tinfoil 33.6
ting 17.35
Ting 17.35
tinge 17.37
tingle 18.22
tingled 18.23
tingling 18.40
tingly 18.5
tinier 22.42
tiniest 22.48
tinker 18.9
Tinkerbell 9.16
tinkering 18.73
tinkers 18.55
tinkle 18.22
tinkling 18.40

tin lizzie 18.7
tinned 17.34
tinner 18.13
tinnitus 22.29
tinny 18.6
tin-opener 36.36
Tin Pan Alley 2.5
tinpot 23.44
tins 17.42
tinsel 18.22
Tinseltown 29.5
Tinsley 18.5
tinsmith 17.53
tin snips 17.44
tint 17.39
Tintagel 2.28
tinted 18.19
tinter 18.10
Tintern 18.32
Tintin 18.31
tintinnabulation 8.24
Tintoretto 35.7
tints 17.40
tinware 5.1
tiny 22.1
TioPepe® 7.3; 10.1
tip 17.43
tipcat 1.45
tipped 17.45
tipper 18.8
Tipperary 6.1
tippet 18.50
Tippett 18.50
Tipp-Ex® 9.3
tipping 18.40
tipple 18.22
tippler 18.12
tips 17.44
tipsier 18.61
tipsiest 18.76
tipstaff 3.9
tipster 18.10
tipsy 18.7
tiptoe 35.11
tiptoed 35.25
tiptop 23.36
tirade 7.8
tiramisu 41.2
Tirana 4.13
tire 19.1
tired 19.2
tiredness 20.8
Tiree 15.2
tireless 20.8
tirelessly 20.11
tiresome 20.3
tiresomely 20.11
tiring 20.7

'tis 17.56
tisane 1.24
tissue 41.3
tissues 41.33
tit 17.51
Titan 22.20
Titania 4.44
Titania 8.78
titanic 2.20
Titanic 2.20
titanium 8.80
titanothere 13.1
Titans 22.23
titbit 18.50
titbits 18.51
titch 17.7
Titchmarsh 3.31
titchy 18.7
titfer 18.11
tit-for-tat 1.45
tithe 21.36
tithing 22.26
Titian 18.33
Titians' 18.37
Titicaca 4.9
titillate 7.41
titillated 8.13
titillating 8.60
titillation 8.32
titivate 7.41
titivation 8.32
title 22.16
titled 22.17
titleholder 36.5
titmice 21.29
titmouse 29.12
Titmus 18.44
Tito 35.10
titrate 7.34
titration 8.23
titre 22.5
tits 17.52
titter 18.10
tittered 18.19
titterer 18.60
tittering 18.73
tittle 18.22
tittle-tattle 2.28
titty 18.3
titular 18.60
Titus 22.29
Tiverton 18.67
Tivoli 18.56
Tizer® 22.9
tiz-woz 23.48
tizz 17.56
tizzy 18.7
TLC 15.4

Tlingit 18.50
tmesis 16.29
TNT 15.4
to 41.1
toad 35.25
toadeater 16.5
toadfish 36.29
toadflax 1.4
toads 35.26
toadstool 41.14
toady 36.1
to and fro 35.19
toast 35.43
toasted 36.12
toaster 36.5
toasting 36.24
toastmaster 4.10
toasty 36.1
tobacco 35.3
tobacconist 2.73
Tobago 35.6
Tobermory 26.1
Tobias 22.29
Tobin 36.19
Tobit 36.30
Toblerone® 35.36
toboggan 24.33
Tobruk 39.1
Toby 36.1
Toby's 36.33
toccata 4.10
Tocqueville 17.15
Tocqueville 17.15
tocsin 24.32
tod 23.8
today 7.2
Todd 23.8
toddle 24.27
toddler 24.12
toddling 24.40
toddy 24.3
todger 24.14
Todmorden 24.64
to-do 41.2
toe 35.1
toecap 1.37
toecaps 1.38
toehold 35.31
toeless 36.26
toenail 7.15
toenails 7.17
toerag 1.13
toes 35.52
toff 23.9
toffee 15.3; 24.4
toffee-nosed 35.53
toffees 24.52
toffish 24.46

tofu 41.3
tog 23.11
toga 36.4
together 10.11
togetherness 10.70
toggle 24.27
Togo 35.16
Togoland 1.28
Togolese 15.45
togs 23.13
toil 33.6
toile 3.14
toiled 33.7
toiler 34.2
toilet 34.13
toiletry 34.14
toilette 9.51
toiling 34.11
toilsome 34.6
Tokay 7.2
token 36.20
tokenism 18.28
Toklas 24.43
Tokyo 35.16; 35.19
told 35.31
Toledo 35.6
tolerable 24.77
tolerably 24.76
tolerance 24.68
tolerant 24.67
tolerate 7.43
toleration 8.34
Tolkien 15.25
toll 35.30
tollbooth 41.30
tollbridge 36.14
Tolley 24.5
toll-free 15.2
tollgate 7.34
tollhouse 29.12
tolling 36.24
toll road 35.25
Tolpuddle 38.23
Tolstoy 33.1
toluene 15.26
tom 23.23
Tom 23.23
tomahawk 25.6
tomato 35.4
tomb 41.17
tombola 36.7
tomboy 33.1
tomboyish 17.50
tombstone 35.36
tomcat 1.45
tome 35.34
tomes 35.35
tomfool 41.14

tomfoolery 42.36
Tom Jones 35.39
Tomlinson 24.64
Tommy 24.6
Tommy gun 37.31
tommyrot 23.44
tomorrow 35.13
Tom Sawyer 34.2
Tomsk 23.26
Tom Thumb 37.27
tomtit 24.49
tom-tom 23.23
tonal 36.15
tonality 2.57
Tonbridge 38.22
tone 35.36
tone-deaf 9.10
toner 36.8
Tonga 24.9
Tongan 24.33
tongs 23.32
tongue 37.37
tongue-and-groove 41.31
tongue-in-cheek 15.7
tongue-lashing 2.42
tongue-tied 21.11
Toni 36.1
tonic 24.19
tonight 21.32
Tonle Sap 1.37
tonnage 38.22
tonne 37.31
tonneau 35.13
tonsil 24.27
tonsillectomy 10.53
tonsillitis 22.28
tonsils 24.29
tonsure 24.14; 27.1
tontine 15.25
tonus 36.26
Tony 36.1
Tonypandy 2.3
too 41.1
toodle-oo 41.4
toodle-pip 17.43
took 39.1
tool 41.14
toolbar 3.1
toolbox 23.5
tooler 42.7
tooling 42.24
toolkit 42.30
toolmaker 8.4
tools 41.16
toolshed 9.8
toon 41.19

toot 41.27
Tootal® 42.16
tooth 41.29
toothache 7.6
tooth and nail 7.15
toothbrush 37.46
toothless 42.26
toothpaste 7.31
toothpick 42.11
toothpicks 42.12
toothsome 42.18
toothy 42.1
tooting 42.24
Tooting 42.24
tootle 42.16
tootsies 40.19; 42.35
tootsy 40.1; 42.1
top 23.36
topaz 1.50
topcoat 35.45
tope 35.40
topee 36.1
toper 36.3
top hat 1.45
top-heavy 10.4
topiary 36.35
topic 24.16
topical 24.61
topicality 2.57
topically 24.56
topknot 23.44
topless 24.43
topmast 24.44
topmast 3.30
topmost 35.43
top-notch 23.7
topographic 2.18
topography 24.54
topological 24.61
toponym 17.24
topped 23.38
topper 24.8
topping 24.40
topple 24.27
toppling 24.40
tops 23.37
topsail 24.27
topsail 7.15
topside 21.11
topsoil 33.6
topspin 24.32
topstitch 17.7
Topsy 24.7
topsy-turvy 12.1
top-up 37.41
tor 25.1
Torah 26.6
Torbay 7.2

torc 25.6
torch 25.8
torchbearer 6.2
torches 26.36
torching 26.25
torchlight 21.33
torchlit 26.32
tore 25.1
toreador 25.2
Tories 26.35
torment 9.41
torment 9.41
tormenting 10.36
tormentor 10.10
torn 25.22
tornado 35.6
Toronto 35.13
torpedo 35.10
torpid 26.11
torpor 26.2
Torquay 15.2
torque 25.6
Torquemada 4.10
Torrance 24.39
torrefy 21.4
Torremolinos 23.39
torrent 24.38
torrential 10.21
torrents 24.39
Torricelli 10.5
torrid 24.23
torsi 26.1
torsion 26.19
torso 35.14
tort 25.31
torte 25.31; 26.4
Tortelier 7.4
torticollis 24.42
tortilla 16.2
tortious 26.27
tortoise 26.27
tortoiseshell 9.16
tortuous 26.47
torture 26.8
tortured 26.12
torturer 26.38
torturous 26.47
torus 26.27
Torvill 17.15
Tory 26.1
Tosca 24.9
Toscanini 16.1
tosh 23.42
Toshack 1.3
toss 23.39
tossed 23.41
tosser 24.14
tossing 24.40

tosspot 23.44
toss-up 37.41
tot 23.44
total 36.15
totalitarian 6.19
totalitarianism 18.29
totality 2.57
totalizator 8.5
totalize 21.45
totally 36.35
tote 35.45
totem 36.18
totemic 10.15
totem pole 35.30
t'other 38.11
Totnes 24.43
Toto 35.16
Tottenham 24.63
totter 24.10
tottery 24.54
totty 24.3
toucan 42.20
touch 37.6
touch and go 35.19
touchdown 29.5
touché 7.2
touched 37.7
toucher 38.14
touching 38.34
touchingly 38.47
touchline 21.22
touchpaper 8.3
touchstone 35.36
touch wood 39.4
touchy 38.7
touchy-feely 16.1
tough 37.10
toughen 38.28
toughened 38.29
tougher 38.11
toughest 38.39
toughie 38.4
toughness 38.38
Toulouse 41.33
Toulouse-Lautrec 9.2
toupee 7.3
toupees 7.56
tour 27.1
tourbillion 18.32
tour de force 25.28
tourer 28.2
Tourette 9.51
touring 28.11
touring car 3.1
tourism 18.27
tourist 28.14
touristic 18.16
touristy 28.17

tourmaline 15.26
tournament 26.45
tournaments 26.46
tournedos 35.19
tourney 26.1
tourniquet 7.4
Tours 27.1
tours 27.3
tousle 30.6
tout 29.14
touter 30.2
touting 30.12
touts 29.15
Tovey 36.1
tow 35.1
towable 36.38
towage 36.14
toward 25.9
towards 25.10
towbar 3.1
Towcester 36.5
towed 35.25
towel 31.3
towelling 32.3
towels 31.4
tower 31.1
towered 31.2
towering 32.3
towers 31.5
towline 21.22
town 29.5
town crier 22.2
town hall 25.14
town house 29.12
townie 30.1
townies 30.20
townsfolk 35.21
township 17.43
townsman 30.8
townspeople 16.17
townswoman 40.10
townswomen 18.31
towpath 3.34
towrope 35.40
toxaemia 16.40
toxaemic 16.11
toxic 24.20
toxicant 24.67
toxicity 18.57
toxicological 24.61
toxicology 24.55
toxicosis 36.25
toxin 24.32
toxophilite 21.34
toxophily 24.56
Toxteth 24.50
toy 33.1
Toyah 34.2

toy boy 33.1
toyed 33.4
toying 34.11
toymaker 8.4
Toynbee 15.3; 34.1
Toyota 36.5
toys 33.15
toyshop 23.36
toytown 29.5
trace 7.30
traceable 8.79
traced 7.31
tracer 8.9
tracery 8.76
traces 8.75
trachea 16.2
tracheal 16.17
tracheotomy 24.54
tracing 8.64
track 1.3
tracked 1.6
tracker 2.9
trackerball 25.14
tracking 2.42
trackless 2.46
tracks 1.4
tracksuit 41.27
tract 1.6
tractable 2.64
Tractarianism 18.29
traction 2.35
tractor 2.10
Tracy 8.1
trad 1.9
trade 7.8
trademark 3.3
trader 8.5
traders 8.75
trades 7.9
tradesman 8.21
tradespeople 16.17
trade union 42.41
trade wind 17.34
trading 8.60
tradition 18.33
traditional 18.64
traditionalism 18.29
traditionalist 17.49
traditionally 18.80
traditor 2.60
traduce 41.24
Trafalgar 2.9
traffic 2.18
trafficator 8.5
traffic jam 1.22
trafficker 2.60
trafficking 2.70
traffic warden 26.19

Trafford 2.25
tragacanth 1.35
tragedian 16.43
tragedienne 9.32
tragedy 2.57
tragic 2.21
tragical 2.64
tragically 2.58
tragicomedy 24.56
tragicomic 24.19
tragopan 1.24
Traherne 11.15
trail 7.15
trailblazer 8.9
trailblazing 8.64
trailer 8.7
trailing 8.62
train 7.21
trained 7.22
trainee 15.2
trainees 15.43
trainer 8.8
trainers 8.75
training 8.63
trains 7.26
trainsick 8.10
train spotter 24.10
train spotters 24.53
train spotting 24.40
traipse 7.28
trait 7.1
trait 7.32
traitor 8.5
traitorous 8.85
Trajan 8.21
trajectile 21.16
trajectory 10.53
tra-la 3.1
Tralee 15.2
tram 1.22
tramcar 3.1
tramline 21.22
tramlines 21.25
trammel 2.28
trammels 2.30
tramp 1.23
tramping 2.42
trample 2.28
trampled 2.29
trampler 2.12
trampoline 15.26
trampoline 17.29
tramway 7.3
trance 3.22
tranche 3.20
Tranmere 13.1
trannie 2.6
tranquil 2.28; 17.15

tranquillity 18.58
tranquillize 21.42
tranquillizer 22.9
transact 1.6
transaction 2.35
transactional 2.64
transatlantic 2.17
transceiver 9.35
transcend 9.35
transcendence 10.34
transcendent 10.33
transcendental 10.21
transcendentalism 18.28
transcendentally 10.53
transcending 10.36
transcontinental 10.21
transcribe 21.5
transcribed 21.6
transcriber 22.3
transcribing 22.26
transcript 17.45
transcription 18.33
transducer 42.9
transect 9.5
transept 9.46
transfer 11.1
transfer 11.1
transferable 12.32
transferee 15.4
transference 2.69
transferor 12.2
transferral 12.8
transfiguration 8.40
transfigure 18.9
transfix 17.4
transfixed 17.5
transform 25.20
transformation 8.24
transformational 8.79
transformed 25.21
transformer 26.7
transforming 26.25
transfuse 41.33
transfusion 42.20
transgender 10.10
transgenic 10.15
transgress 9.47
transgression 10.28
transience 2.69
transient 2.68
transistor 18.10
transistorize 21.44
transistors 18.55
transit 2.51
transition 18.33

transitional 18.64
transitive 17.55
transitory 2.58
Transkei 21.2
translatable 8.79
translate 7.33
translated 8.13
translating 8.60
translation 8.23
translator 8.5
transliterate 7.41
transliteration 8.40
translocation 8.24
translucence 42.23
translucent 42.22
transmigrate 7.35
transmigration 8.24
transmission 18.33
transmit 17.51
transmiting 18.40
transmittable 18.64
transmittance 18.39
transmitter 18.10
transmogrification 8.48
transmogrify 21.4
transmutation 8.24
transmute 41.27
transoceanic 2.20
transom 2.32
transpacific 18.16
transparence 2.41; 6.9
transparency 2.56; 6.15
transparent 2.40; 6.8
transpiration 8.24
transpire 19.1
transpired 19.2
transplant 3.23
transplantation 8.24
transplanting 4.29
transponder 24.10
transport 25.31
transportable 26.41
transportation 8.24
transporter 26.4
transporting 26.25
transpose 35.52
transposition 18.33
transsexual 10.60
transsexualism 18.29
transship 17.43
trans-Siberian 14.21
transubstantiate 7.35
transubstantiation 8.24
Transvaal 3.14
transversal 12.8

transverse 11.22
transvestism 18.27
transvestite 21.33
Transylvania 8.78
Transylvanian 8.81
trap 1.37
trapdoor 25.3
trapdoors 25.35
trapeze 15.43
trapezia 16.40
trapezium 16.42
trapper 2.8
trapping 2.42
Trappist 2.47
traps 1.38
trapshooting 42.24
trash 1.43
trashed 1.44
trashy 2.7
Trasimene 15.26
trattoria 16.2
trauma 26.7
traumatic 2.17
traumatically 2.58
traumatism 18.28
traumatize 21.45
travail 7.15
travel 2.28
travelator 8.5
travelled 2.29
traveller 2.60
traveller's cheques 9.3
travelling 2.70
travelogue 23.11
traverse 11.22
traversed 11.23
travesty 2.57
Travis 2.45
trawl 25.14
trawler 26.6
trawling 26.25
tray 7.1
treacherous 10.70
treacherously 10.78
treachery 10.53
treacle 16.17
treacly 16.1
tread 9.8
treader 10.10
treading 10.36
treadle 10.21
treadmill 17.15
treads 9.9
treadwheel 15.17
treason 16.22
treasonous 16.47
treasure 10.14

treasured 10.18
treasurer 10.56
treasurership 17.43
treasures 10.52
treasure trove 35.50
treasury 10.53
treat 15.35
treatable 16.41
treated 16.14
treatise 16.36
treatment 16.25
treaty 16.1
Trebizond 23.30
treble 10.21
treble clef 9.10
Treblinka 18.9
trebly 10.5
trecento 35.7
tree 15.1
Tree 15.1
tree creeper 16.3
treehouse 29.12
treeless 16.30
tree line 21.22
treenail 7.15
trees 15.42
treetop 23.36
treetops 23.37
trefoil 33.6
trek 9.2
trekked 9.5
trekker 10.9
trekking 10.36
Trelawney 26.1
trellis 10.41
trelliswork 11.4
tremble 10.21
trembler 10.12
trembling 10.36
tremendous 10.42
tremendously 10.53
tremolo 35.19
tremor 10.13
tremors 10.52
tremulous 10.70
trench 9.33
trenchant 10.33
Trenchard 10.18
trencher 10.14
trencherman 10.64
trend 9.35
trendier 10.57
trendiest 10.71
trendify 21.4
trendsetter 10.10
trendsetting 10.36
trendy 10.3
Trent 9.41

Trentham 10.25
Trenton 10.27
Treorchy 26.1
trepan 1.24
trephine 15.24
trepidation 8.28
trespass 10.42
trespassed 10.43
trespasser 10.56
trespasses 10.76
trespassing 10.69
tress 9.47
tresses 10.52
trestle 10.21
Trevelyan 10.27; 18.32
Trevino 35.10
Trevithick 18.16
Trevor 10.11
Trevor Nunn 37.31
trews 41.33
trey 7.1
triable 22.43
triad 1.9; 22.13
triads 22.14
triage 22.15
triage 3.13
trial 19.3
trialling 20.7
triallist 20.9
triangle 2.28
triangular 2.60
triangulate 7.35
triangulation 8.24
Triassic 2.21
triathlon 2.35; 23.27
tribade 18.19
tribadism 18.28
tribal 22.16
tribalism 18.28
tribally 22.40
tribe 21.5
tribesman 22.20
tribulation 8.32
tribulations 8.55
tribunal 42.16
tribune 41.19
tributary 18.59
tribute 41.27
tributes 41.28
trice 21.29
tricentenary 16.38
tricentennial 10.60
triceps 9.45
triceratops 23.37
trick 17.3
tricked 17.6
trickery 18.56
trickier 18.61

trickiest 18.76
trickily 18.57
trickle 18.22
trickling 18.40
trick-or-treat 15.35
tricks 17.4
trickster 18.10
tricksy 18.7
tricky 18.2
tricolour 18.60
tricorn 25.22
tricycle 22.43
trident 22.24
Trident 22.24
tried 21.9
triennial 10.60
Trier 13.1
trier 22.2
tries 21.39
Trieste 9.49
triffid 18.18
trifid 22.12
trifle 22.16
trifled 22.17
trifler 22.7
trifling 22.26
trig 17.12
trigeminal 10.60
trigger 18.9
trigonometric 10.15
trigonometry 24.56
trike 21.7
trilateral 2.28; 2.64
trilby 18.1
trilingual 18.22
trill 17.15
trillion 18.32; 18.67
trillionaire 5.1
trillionth 18.72
trilobite 21.34
trilogy 18.56
trim 17.24
trimaran 1.24
Trimble 18.22
trimester 10.10
trimmed 17.25
trimmer 18.13
trimming 18.40
trimmings 18.41
Trincomalee 15.2
Tring 17.35
Trinian 18.67
Trinidad 1.9
Trinidadian 2.66;
    8.81
Trinitarian 6.19
trinitrotoluene 15.26
Trinity 18.57

trinket 18.50
Trinny 18.6
trio 35.10
triode 35.25
trip 17.43
tripartite 21.33
tripe 21.26
triplane 7.21
triple 18.22
triplet 18.50
triplets 18.51
triplex 9.3
triplicate 18.77
triplicate 7.41
triplication 8.32
triply 18.5
tripmeter 16.5
tripod 23.8
Tripoli 18.56
tripos 23.39
Tripp 17.43
tripper 18.8
trippers 18.55
trippy 18.1
trips 17.44
triptych 18.16
triptyque 15.7
tripwire 19.1
trireme 15.20
trisect 9.5
Trish 17.50
Trisha 18.14
Trismegistus 18.44
Tristan 18.32
Tristan da Cunha
    42.8
Tristan's 18.37
Tristram 18.26
trisyllabic 2.17
trite 21.31
triteness 22.29
tritium 18.66
triton 23.27
Triton 22.20
triumph 37.28
triumphal 38.23
triumphant 38.32
triumphantly 38.47
triumvir 38.11
triumvirate 38.62
trivet 18.50
trivia 18.61
trivial 18.64
triviality 2.57
trivialize 21.47
Trixie 18.7
trochanter 2.10
trochee 15.3; 36.1

trod 23.8
trodden 24.33
trog 23.11
troglodyte 21.34
troglodytes 21.35
troglodytic 18.16
troika 34.2
Troilus 34.12
Trojan 36.20
Trojan horse 25.28
troll 23.15
troll 35.30
trolley 24.5
trolleybus 37.43
trolleys 24.52
trollop 24.41
Trollope 24.41
trolls 23.22
trombone 35.36
trombones 35.39
trombonist 36.27
Trondheim 21.19
Troon 41.19
troop 41.22
trooper 42.3
trooping 42.24
troops 41.23
troopship 17.43
trope 35.40
trophic 24.17
trophies 36.33
trophy 36.1
tropic 24.16
tropical 24.61
tropics 24.22
tropism 18.27
troposphere 13.1
Trossachs 24.21
trot 23.44
troth 23.46; 35.47
trots 23.45
Trotsky 24.2
Trotskyism 18.28
Trotskyist 24.72
Trotskyite 21.34
trotter 24.10
trotters 24.53
trotting 24.40
troubadour 27.1
trouble 38.23
troubled 38.24
trouble-free 15.4
troublemaker 8.4
troubler 38.12
troubles 38.25
troubleshoot 41.27
troubleshooter 42.5
troubleshooting 42.24

turnbuckle 38.23
Turnbull 39.7
turncoat 35.45
turned 11.16
turner 12.2
Turner 12.2
turnery 12.29
turning 12.16
turnip 17.43
turnkey 15.3
turnout 29.14
turnover 36.6
turnpike 21.7
turnround 29.6
turns 11.18
turnspit 12.25
turnstile 21.16
turnstone 35.36
turntable 8.15
turn-up 37.41
turpentine 21.22
Turpin 12.11
turpitude 41.9
turps 11.20
turquoise 33.15
turret 38.43
turreted 38.50
turtle 12.8
turtledove 37.49
turtleneck 9.2
Turvey 12.1
Tuscan 38.28
Tuscany 38.47
Tuscarora 26.6
tush 37.46; 39.13
tusk 37.44
tusker 38.9
tussle 38.23
tussock 38.16
tussocks 38.17
tussocky 38.47
tussore 25.2
tut 37.47
Tutankhamen 4.24
Tutankhamun 41.19
tutee 15.2
tutelage 17.14
tutelary 42.50
Tutin 42.19
tutor 42.5
tutored 42.14
tutorial 26.41
tutoring 42.45
tutorship 17.43
Tutsi 40.1; 42.1
tutti 40.1
tutti-frutti 42.1
tut-tut 37.47

tut-tutted 38.20
tutu 41.3
Tutu 41.3
Tuvalu 41.4
tu-whit tu-whoo 41.4
tux 37.4
tuxedo 35.10
TV 15.2
twaddle 24.27
twain 7.21
Twain 7.21
twang 1.29
'twas 23.48
twat 1.45
twat 23.44
tweak 15.7
tweaker 16.4
twee 15.1
tweed 15.11
Tweed 15.11
Tweedledee 15.4
Tweedledum 37.27
tweeds 15.12
Tweedsmuir 27.1
tweedy 16.1
tweeny 16.1
tweet 15.35
tweeter 16.5
tweeze 15.42
tweezers 16.37
twelfth 9.24
Twelfth Night 21.32
Twelfthtide 21.11
twelve 9.25
twelves 9.26
twenties 10.51
twentieth 10.75; 17.53
twenty 10.3
twenty-eight 7.38
twenty-first 11.23
twenty-five 21.37
twenty-four 25.4
twenty-nine 21.22
twenty-one 37.31
twenty-six 17.4
twenty-three 15.4
twenty-two 41.4
'twere 11.1
twerp 11.19
twice 21.29
Twickenham 18.66
twiddle 18.22
twiddling 18.40
twiddly 18.5
twig 17.12
twiggy 18.2
Twiggy 18.2
twigs 17.13

twilight 21.33
twilit 22.33
twill 17.15
'twill 17.15
twin 17.29
twine 21.22
twinge 17.37
twining 22.26
Twining 22.26
twink 17.30
twinkle 18.22
twinkler 18.12
twinkling 18.40
twinkly 18.5
twinned 17.34
twinning 18.40
twins 17.42
twinset 9.51
twirl 11.11
twirled 11.12
twirler 12.2
twirly 12.1
twist 17.49
twisted 18.19
twister 18.10
twistier 18.61
twistiest 18.76
twisting 18.40
twisty 18.3
twit 17.51
twitch 17.7
twitcher 18.14
twitching 18.40
twitchy 18.7
twite 21.31
twitten 18.32
twitter 18.10
twittery 18.56
'twixt 17.5
two 41.1
two-a-penny 10.6
twoccing 24.40
two-dimensional 10.60
twofold 35.31
two-handed 2.25
two-hander 2.10
two-headed 10.18
two-seater 16.5
twosome 42.18
two-storeyed 26.11
two-syllabled 18.65
two-time 21.19
two-timer 22.8
two-timing 22.26
two-tone 35.36
'twould 39.4
two-wheeled 15.18

Twyford 22.13
Tyburn 11.15
Tyche 22.1
Tycho 35.12
tycoon 41.19
tyke 21.7
Tyler 22.7
tympanic 2.20
tympanum 18.66
Tynan 22.20
Tyndale 18.22
Tyne 21.22
Tyne and Wear 13.1
Tynemouth 22.36; 29.16
Tyneside 21.11
Tynesider 22.5
Tynwald 18.23
typal 22.16
type 21.26
typecase 7.30
typecast 3.30
typed 21.28
typeface 7.30
types 21.27
typescript 17.45
typeset 9.51
typesetter 10.10
typesetting 10.36
typewrite 21.33
typewriter 22.5
typewriting 22.26
typewritten 18.32
typhoid 33.4
Typhoo® 41.2
typhoon 41.19
typhus 22.29
typical 18.64
typically 18.57
typifies 21.44
typify 21.4
typing 22.26
typist 22.30
typo 35.12
typographer 24.57
typographic 2.18
typographical 2.64
typography 24.54
tyrannical 2.64
tyrannicide 21.12
tyrannize 21.44
tyrannosaur 25.4
tyrannosaurus 26.27
tyrannous 18.74
tyranny 18.56
tyrant 20.5; 22.24
tyrants 20.6; 22.25
tyre 19.1

Tyre 19.1
tyre gauge 7.12
tyre mark 3.3
tyres 19.4
Tyrian 18.67
tyro 35.12
Tyrol 18.22; 35.30
Tyrolean 16.22
Tyrone 35.36
tyrosine 15.26
Tyrrell 18.22
Tyrrhenian 16.43
Tyson 22.20
tzatziki 16.1
Tzigane 3.19
U 41.1
U-bend 9.35
uber 42.3
ubercool 41.14
ubiquitous 18.74
ubiquity 18.58
U-boat 35.45
U-bolt 35.32
UCCA 38.9
Uccello 35.7
udder 38.10
udders 38.45
UDI 21.4
UEFA 8.6
Uffizi 18.7
UFO 35.19
ufologist 24.72
ufology 24.55
Uganda 2.10
Ugandan 2.35
UGLI® 38.5
uglier 38.49
ugliest 38.61
uglification 8.51
uglify 21.4
ugliness 38.59
ugly 38.5
Ugric 42.11
Uist 42.28
UK 7.2
ukiyo-e 7.2
Ukraine 7.21
Ukrainian 8.81
ukulele 8.1
ulcer 38.14
ulcerate 7.48
ulceration 8.38
ulcerative 17.54
ulcers 38.45
ullage 38.22
Ullapool 41.14
Ullman 40.10
Ullswater 26.4

ulna 38.13
ulster 38.10
Ulster 38.10
Ulsterman 38.54
ulterior 14.18
ultimate 38.62
ultimately 38.64
ultima Thule 42.1
ultimatum 8.19
ultra 38.12
ultraconservative
  17.55
ultrahigh 21.4
ultramarine 15.24
ultramodern 24.33
ultrasonic 24.19
ultrasonics 24.22
ultrasound 29.6
ultraviolet 20.10
ululate 7.48
ululation 8.39
Uluru 41.4
Ulysses 15.45
um 37.27
um and ah 3.1
umbel 38.23
umbellifer 10.56
umber 38.8
Umberto 35.8
umbilical 18.64
umbilical 22.16
umbilicus 18.74
umbra 38.12
umbrage 38.22
umbrageous 8.67
umbral 38.23
umbrella 10.12
Umbria 38.49
Umbrian 38.54
UMIST 42.28
umlaut 29.14
umpire 19.1
umpteen 15.24
umpteenth 15.28
UN 9.32
Una 42.8
unabashed 1.44
unabated 8.13
unable 8.15
unaccented 10.18
unacceptable 10.60
unaccepted 10.18
unaccompanied 17.8;
  38.51
unaccomplished
  38.41
unaccountable 30.24
unaccountably 30.22

unaccounted 30.3
unachievable 16.41
una corda 26.4
unacquainted 8.13
unadapted 2.25
unaddressed 9.49
unadopted 24.24
unadorned 25.24
unadulterated 8.13
unadventurous 10.70
unadvised 21.48
unaffected 10.18
unaffiliated 8.13
unafford able 26.41
unafraid 7.8
unaided 8.13
unalike 21.7
unalloyed 33.4
unalterable 24.77
unalterable 26.51
unaltered 24.24
unaltered 26.12
unambiguous 18.74
unambitious 18.44
un-American 10.64
unamplified 21.12
unamused 41.34
unanimity 18.57
unanimous 2.71
unanimously 2.78
unannounced 29.10
unanswerable 4.57
unanswered 4.17
unappealing 16.27
unappetizing 22.26
unappreciated 8.13
unapproachable 36.38
unapproved 41.32
unarguable 4.57
unarm 3.16
unarmed 3.17
unashamed 7.19
unashamedly 8.76
unasked 3.28
unassailable 8.79
unassisted 18.19
unassuming 42.24
unassumingly 42.36
unattached 1.8
unattainable 8.79
unattempted 10.18
unattended 10.18
unattested 10.18
unattractive 2.53
unaudited 26.40
unauthorized 21.48
unavailability 18.58
unavailable 8.79

unavailing 8.62
unavoidable 34.16
unaware 5.1
unawares 5.5
unbaked 7.7
unbalance 2.41
unbearable 6.17
unbearably 6.15
unbeatable 16.41
unbeaten 16.22
unbecoming 38.34
unbefitting 18.40
unbeknown 35.36
unbelief 15.13
unbelievable 16.41
unbelievably 16.38
unbeliever 16.6
unbelieving 16.27
unbelt 9.23
unbend 9.35
unbending 10.36
unbent 9.41
unbiased 22.31
unbidden 18.32
unbind 21.23
unbleached 15.10
unblemished 10.46
unblessed 9.49
unblinking 18.40
unblock 23.3
unblocked 23.6
unblushing 38.34
unbolt 35.32
unboned 35.37
unborn 25.22
unbosom 40.8
unbound 29.6
unbounded 30.3
unbowed 29.3
unbranded 2.25
unbreakable 8.79
unbreathable 16.41
unbridle 22.16
unbridled 22.17
un-British 18.47
unbroken 36.20
unbuckle 38.23
unbuilt 17.21
unbundle 38.23
unburden 12.12
unburdened 12.13
unburied 10.17
unburned 11.16
unburnt 11.17
unbusinesslike 21.7
unbutton 38.28
unbuttoned 38.29
uncaged 7.13

uncannily 2.58
uncanny 2.6
uncap 1.37
uncarpeted 4.45
unceasing 16.27
unceasingly 16.38
uncensored 10.18
uncensured 10.18
unceremonious 36.42
uncertain 12.12
uncertainly 12.29
uncertainty 12.29
uncertified 21.12
unchain 7.21
unchained 7.22
unchangeable 8.79
unchanged 7.24
unchanging 8.64
unchaperoned 35.37
uncharacteristic 18.16
uncharitable 2.79
uncharitably 2.78
uncharted 4.17
unchartered 4.17
unchecked 9.5
unchristian 18.33
uncial 38.52
uncircumcised 21.48
uncivil 18.22
uncivilized 21.48
unclad 1.9
unclaimed 7.19
unclasp 3.29
unclassifiable 22.43
unclassified 21.12
uncle 38.23
unclean 15.24
unclear 13.1
unclearly 14.1
Uncle Sam 1.22
Uncle Tom 23.23
unclimbable 22.43
unclimbed 21.20
unclip 17.43
unclipped 17.45
unclips 17.44
unclog 23.11
unclogged 23.12
unclothe 35.48
unclothes 35.49
unclouded 30.3
uncoded 36.12
uncoil 33.6
uncoiled 33.7
uncollected 10.18
uncomfortable 38.52
uncomfortably 38.47;

38.64
uncomforted 38.50
uncommitted 18.19
uncommon 24.33
uncommonly 24.54
uncommunicative 17.54
uncompetitive 17.55
uncomplaining 8.63
uncomplainingly 8.76
uncomplicated 8.13
uncomplimentary 10.53
uncomprehending 10.36
uncompromising 22.26
unconcealed 15.18
unconcern 11.15
unconcerned 11.16
unconcernedly 12.29
unconditional 18.64
unconditionally 18.80
unconfined 21.23
unconfirmed 11.14
uncongenial 16.41
uncongested 10.18
unconnected 10.18
unconquerable 24.77
unconquered 24.24
unconscionable 24.77
unconscious 24.43
unconsciously 24.54
unconsciousness 24.70
unconsecrated 8.13
unconsidered 18.19
unconstitutional 42.39
unconstrained 7.22
unconstraint 7.25
unconsumed 41.18
unconsummated 8.13
uncontaminated 8.13
uncontested 10.18
uncontrollable 36.38
uncontrollably 36.35
uncontrolled 35.31
uncontroversial 12.8
unconventional 10.60
unconverted 12.5
unconvincing 18.40
unconvincingly 18.57
uncooked 39.2
uncool 41.14

uncooperative 17.54
uncoordinated 8.13
uncork 25.6
uncorking 26.25
uncorrected 10.18
uncorroborated 8.13
uncorrupted 38.20
uncountable 30.24
uncounted 30.3
uncouple 38.23
uncouth 41.29
uncover 38.11
uncovered 38.20
uncreased 15.33
uncritical 18.64
uncropped 23.38
uncross 23.39
uncrossed 23.41
uncrowded 30.3
uncrowned 29.6
uncrushable 38.52
unction 38.28
unctuous 38.59
uncultivated 8.13
uncultured 38.20
uncurl 11.11
uncurled 11.12
uncustomary 38.47
uncut 37.47
undated 8.13
undaunted 26.12
undead 9.8
undeceive 15.39
undeceived 15.40
undecided 22.13
undeciphered 22.13
undeclared 5.2
undefeated 16.14
undefended 10.18
undefined 21.23
undeliverable 18.64; 18.81
undelivered 18.19
undemanding 4.29
undemocratic 2.17
undemonstrative 17.55
undeniable 22.43
undeniably 22.40
undenied 21.20
undented 10.18
under 38.10
underachieve 15.39
underachievement 16.25
underachiever 16.6
underachieving 16.27
underact 1.6

underactive 2.53
underage 7.12
underarm 3.16
underbelly 10.5
underbid 17.8; 38.51
underbidder 18.10
underblanket 2.51
underbody 24.3
underbrush 37.46
undercapacity 2.57
undercapitalize 21.47
undercarriage 2.27
undercharge 3.12
underclass 3.26
underclay 7.4
undercliff 17.10
underclothes 35.49
underclothing 36.24
undercoat 35.45
underconsumption 38.28
undercook 39.1
undercooked 39.2
undercover 38.11
undercurrent 38.32
undercut 37.47
underdeveloped 10.40
underdog 23.11
underdone 37.31
underdressed 9.49
underemphasis 17.46
underemployed 33.4
underestimate 10.73
underestimate 7.38
underestimation 8.28
underexpose 35.52
underexposed 35.53
underexposure 36.9
underfed 9.8
underfeed 15.11
underfelt 9.23
under-fives 21.38
underfloor 25.4
underflooring 26.25
underflow 35.19
underfoot 39.14
underfunded 38.20
underfunding 38.34
underfur 11.1
undergarment 4.27
undergarments 4.28
underglaze 7.56
undergo 35.19
undergoing 36.24
undergone 23.27
undergraduate 2.74

underground 29.6
undergrown 35.36
undergrowth 35.47
underhand 1.28
underhanded 2.25
underhung 37.37
underinsure 25.2; 27.1
underinsured 25.9;
27.2
underinsuring 28.11
underlaid 7.8
underlain 7.21
underlay 7.4
underlie 21.4
underline 21.22
underlined 21.23
underlinen 18.31
underling 38.58
underlining 22.26
underlying 22.26
undermanning 2.42
undermentioned
10.29
undermine 21.22
undermined 21.23
undermining 22.26
undermost 35.43
underneath 15.37
undernourish 38.40
undernourished
38.41
underpaid 7.8
underpants 1.34
under par 3.1
underpart 3.32
underparts 3.33
underpass 3.26
underpay 7.4
underpayment 8.56
underperformance
26.24
underpin 17.29
underpinned 17.34
underpinning 18.40
underpinnings 18.41
underpins 17.42
underplay 7.4
underplayed 7.8
underpopulated 8.13
underpowered 31.2
underpriced 21.30
underproduction
38.28
underproof 41.10
underrate 7.48
underripe 21.26
underscore 25.4
underscored 25.9

underscoring 26.25
undersea 15.4
underseal 15.17
undersecretary 10.54
undersell 9.16
undersexed 9.4
undershirt 11.24
undershoot 41.27
undershorts 25.32
undershot 23.44
underside 21.12
undersigned 21.23
undersized 21.48
underskirt 11.24
underskirts 11.25
underslung 37.37
undersoil 33.6
underspend 9.35
underspent 9.41
understaffed 3.10
understand 1.28
understandable 2.64
understandably 2.56
understanding 2.42
understate 7.48
understated 8.13
understatement 8.56
understeer 13.1
understood 39.4
understudy 38.3
undersubscribed 21.6
undertake 7.6
undertaker 8.4
undertaking 8.59
undertakings 8.65
underthings 17.36
undertone 35.36
undertook 39.1
undertow 35.19
undertrump 37.29
under-use 41.24; 41.33
under-used 41.34
undervalue 41.3
undervest 9.49
underwater 26.4
underwear 5.1
underweight 7.48
underwent 9.41
underwhelm 9.21
underwing 38.58
underwired 19.2
Underwood 39.4
underworld 11.12
underwrite 21.34
underwriter 22.5
underwritten 18.32
underwrote 35.45
undescended 10.18

undeserved 11.28
undeservedly 12.29
undeserving 12.16
undesigned 21.23
undesigning 22.26
undesirable 20.12
undetectable 10.60
undetected 10.18
undetermined 17.34
undeterred 11.7
undeveloped 10.40
undiagnosed 35.53
undid 17.8
undies 38.46
undifferentiated 8.13
undigested 10.18
undignified 21.12
undiluted 42.14
undiminished 18.48
undimmed 17.25
undiplomatic 2.17
undirected 10.18
undisciplined 17.34
undisclosed 35.53
undiscovered 38.20
undisguised 21.48
undismayed 7.8
undisputed 42.14
undissolved 23.21
undistinguished
18.48
undisturbed 11.3
undivided 22.13
undo 41.2
undocumented 10.18
undoing 42.24
undone 37.31
undoubted 30.3
undoubtedly 30.22
undreamed 15.21
undreamt 9.30
undreamt-of 23.47
undress 9.47
undressed 9.49
undressing 10.36
undrinkable 18.64
undrivable 22.43
undue 41.2
undulant 38.56
undulate 7.48
undulating 8.60
undulation 8.38
unduly 42.1
undyed 21.10
undying 22.26
unearned 11.16
unearth 11.26
unearthing 12.16

unearthly 12.1
unease 15.43
uneasiness 16.47
uneasy 16.1
uneatable 16.41
uneaten 16.22
uneconomic 24.19
uneconomical 24.61
unedifying 22.26
unedited 10.58
uneducated 8.13
unelectable 10.60
unelected 10.18
unembarrassed 2.48
unembellished 10.46
unemotional 36.38
unemployable 34.16
unemployed 33.4
unemployment 34.9
unencumbered 38.20
unending 10.36
unendurable 28.19
unenforceable 26.41
unenforced 25.29
unenlightened 22.21
unenthusiastic 2.17
unenviable 10.79
unenvied 10.17
unequal 16.17
unequipped 17.45
unequivocal 18.64
unequivocally 18.56
unerring 12.16
unerringly 12.29
UNESCO 35.7
unescorted 26.12
unethical 10.60
unevenly 16.38
unevenness 16.47
uneventful 10.21; 39.7
uneventfully 10.53;
10.55
unexampled 4.20
unexceptionable
10.79
unexceptional 10.60
unexcited 22.13
unexciting 22.26
unexpected 10.18
unexpectedly 10.53
unexpired 19.2
unexplainable 8.79
unexplained 7.22
unexploded 36.12
unexploited 34.3
unexplored 25.9
unexposed 35.53
unexpressed 9.49

unexpurgated 8.13
unfading 8.60
unfailing 8.62
unfair 5.1
unfairly 6.1
unfairness 6.11
unfaithful 8.15; 39.7
unfaithfully 8.76
unfamiliarity 2.57
unfashionable 2.79
unfasten 4.24
unfastened 4.25
unfathomable 2.79
unfavourable 8.79;
  8.88
unfavourably 8.76
unfazed 7.57
unfeeling 16.27
unfeminine 17.29
unfenced 9.40
unfermented 10.18
unfertilized 21.48
unfetter 10.10
unfettered 10.18
unfilled 17.18
unfinished 18.48
unfit 17.51
unfitness 18.44
unfitted 18.19
unflagging 2.42
unflappable 2.64
unflattering 2.70
unflavoured 8.13
unfledged 9.15
unflinching 18.40
unflustered 38.20
unfocused 36.28
unfold 35.31
unfolded 36.12
unfolding 36.24
unforced 25.29
unforeseeable 16.41
unforeseen 15.26
unforgettable 10.60
unforgettably 10.53
unforgivable 18.64
unforgiven 18.32
unforgiving 18.40
unformed 25.21
unforthcoming 38.34
unfortified 21.12
unfortunate 26.50
unfounded 30.3
unfranked 1.27
unfreeze 15.43
unfrequented 10.18
unfriendliness 10.70
unfriendly 10.5

unfrock 23.3
unfrocked 23.6
unfrozen 36.20
unfruitful 39.7; 42.16
unfulfillable 18.64
unfulfilled 17.18
unfulfilling 18.40
unfunded 38.20
unfunny 38.6
unfurl 11.11
unfurled 11.12
unfurnished 12.23
unfussy 38.7
ungainly 8.1
ungenerous 10.42;
  10.70
ungentlemanly 10.78
un-get-at-able 2.64
unglamorous 2.71
unglued 41.9
ungodly 24.5
ungovernable 38.65
ungoverned 38.29
ungracious 8.67
ungrammatical 2.64
ungrateful 8.15; 39.7
ungratefully 8.76
ungrudging 38.34
unguarded 4.17
unguent 38.56
unguided 22.13
ungulate 38.62
unhallowed 35.25
unhand 1.28
unhandy 2.3
unhappier 2.61
unhappiest 2.72
unhappily 2.58
unhappiness 2.71
unhappy 2.1
unharmed 3.17
unhatched 1.8
unhealed 15.18
unhealthier 10.57
unhealthiest 10.71
unhealthy 10.4
unheard 11.7
unheard-of 23.47
unheated 16.14
unheeded 16.14
unheeding 16.27
unhelpful 10.21; 39.7
unhelpfully 10.53;
  10.55
unheralded 10.58
unheroic 36.10
unhesitating 8.60
unhidden 18.32

unhindered 18.19
unhinge 17.37
unhip 17.43
unhistoric 24.18
unhitch 17.7
unholy 36.1
unhook 39.1
unhooked 39.2
unhorse 25.28
unhorsed 25.29
unhung 37.37
unhurried 38.19
unhurriedly 38.47
unhurt 11.24
unhygienic 16.11
uni 42.1
unicameral 2.64
UNICEF 9.10
unicorn 25.22
unicycle 22.16
unidentifiable 22.43
unidentified 21.12
unidirectional 10.60
unification 8.52
unified 21.12
uniform 25.20
uniformed 25.21
uniformity 26.37
uniformly 26.1
unify 21.4
Unigate 7.49
unilateral 2.28; 2.64
unilaterally 2.56
Unilever 16.6
unimaginable 2.79
unimaginably 2.78
unimaginative 17.54
unimpaired 5.2
unimpeachable 16.41
unimpeded 16.14
unimportance 26.24
unimportant 26.23
unimpressed 9.49
unimpressive 10.50
unimproved 41.32
uninfected 10.18
uninflected 10.18
uninformed 25.21
uninhabitable 2.79
uninhabited 2.63
uninhibited 18.62
uninjured 18.19
uninspired 19.2
uninspiring 20.7
uninspiringly 20.11
uninsurable 28.19
uninsured 25.9; 27.2
unintelligent 10.67

unintelligible 10.79
unintelligibly 10.78
unintended 10.18
unintentional 10.60
unintentionally 10.78
uninterested 18.62
uninteresting 18.73
uninterrupted 38.20
uninvited 22.13
uninviting 22.26
uninvolved 23.21
union 42.20; 42.41
unionism 18.28
unionist 42.48
Unionist 42.48
unionization 8.52
unionize 21.46
unionized 21.48
Union Jack 1.3
Union Jacks 1.4
unipolar 36.7
unique 15.7
uniquely 16.1
uniqueness 16.30
unironed 22.21
unisex 9.3
unison 42.41
UNISON 42.41
unit 42.30
Unitarian 6.19
Unitarianism 18.29
unitary 42.36
unite 21.32
united 22.13
United Nations 8.55
United States 7.50
unitization 8.52
units 42.32
unit trust 37.45
unity 42.36
universal 12.8
universalism 18.28
universality 2.57
universalize 21.43
universally 12.29
universe 11.22
university 12.29
unjust 37.45
unjustifiable 22.43
unjustified 21.12
unjustly 38.5
unkempt 9.30
unkenned 9.35
unkillable 18.64
unkind 21.23
unkindly 22.1
unkindness 22.29
unkissed 17.49

unknit 17.51
unknowable 36.38
unknowing 36.24
unknowingly 36.35
unknown 35.36
unlabelled 8.16
unlace 7.30
unlaced 7.31
unlamented 10.18
unlash 1.43
unlatch 1.7
unlatched 1.8
unlawful 26.15; 39.7
unlawfully 26.37
unlay 7.2
unleaded 10.18
unlearn 11.15
unlearned 11.16
unlearnt 11.17
unleash 15.34
unleashing 16.27
unleavened 10.29
unless 9.47
unlettered 10.18
unlike 21.7
unlikelihood 39.4
unlikely 22.1
unlimited 18.62
unlined 21.23
unlisted 18.19
unlit 17.51
unlived-in 18.31
unload 35.25
unloaded 36.12
unloading 36.24
unlock 23.3
unlocked 23.6
unlocking 24.40
unloose 41.24
unlovable 38.52
unloved 37.50
unlovely 38.5
unloving 38.34
unluckier 38.49
unluckiest 38.61
unluckily 38.47
unlucky 38.2
unmade 7.8
unmake 7.6
unman 1.24
unmanageable 2.79
unmanly 2.5
unmanned 1.28
unmannered 2.25
unmannerly 2.56
unmapped 1.39
unmarked 3.5
unmarketable 4.57

unmarried 2.24
unmask 3.27
unmasked 3.28
unmasking 4.29
unmatchable 2.64
unmatched 1.8
unmeaning 16.27
unmeant 9.41
unmeasured 10.18
unmelodious 36.42
unmemorable 10.60;
10.79
unmended 10.18
unmentionable 10.79
unmentioned 10.29
unmerciful 12.32; 39.7
unmercifully 12.29;
40.1
unmerited 10.58
unmindful 22.16; 39.7
unmingled 18.23
unmissable 18.64
unmistakable 8.79
unmistakably 8.76
unmistaken 8.21
unmitigated 8.13
unmixed 17.5
unmodified 21.12
unmolested 10.18
unmoor 25.2; 27.1
unmoored 27.2
unmounted 30.3
unmoved 41.32
unmoving 42.24
unmusical 42.39
unmuzzle 38.23
unnamable 8.79
unnamed 7.19
unnatural 2.64
unnaturally 2.78
unnecessarily 10.54
unnecessary 10.5;
10.78
unneeded 16.14
unnerve 11.27
unnerved 11.28
unnerving 12.16
unnervingly 12.29
unnoticed 36.27
unnumbered 38.20
unobservant 12.14
unobserved 11.28
unobstructed 38.20
unobtainable 8.79
unobtrusive 42.33
unobtrusively 42.36
unoccupied 21.12
unofficial 18.22

unofficially 18.56
unopened 36.21
unopposed 35.53
unorganized 21.48
unoriginal 18.64
unorthodox 23.5
unpack 1.3
unpacked 1.6
unpacker 2.9
unpacking 2.42
unpacks 1.4
unpaid 7.8
unpainted 8.13
unpalatable 2.79
unparalleled 9.19
unpardonable 4.57
unparliamentary 10.53
unpasteurized 21.48
unpatriotic 24.16
unpeg 9.12
unperforated 8.13
unperfumed 41.18
unperson 12.12
unperturbed 11.3
unpick 17.3
unpicked 17.6
unpicking 18.40
unpicks 17.4
unpin 17.29
unpinned 17.34
unpins 17.42
unpitying 18.73
unplaced 7.31
unplanned 1.28
unplasticized 21.48
unplayable 8.79
unpleasant 10.33
unpleasantly 10.53
unpleasantness 10.70
unploughed 29.3
unplucked 37.5
unplug 37.14
unpolished 24.47
unpolled 35.31
unpolluted 42.14
unpopular 24.57
unpopularity 2.57
unposed 35.53
unpractical 2.64
unpractised 2.47
unprecedented 10.18
unpredictable 18.64
unpredicted 18.19
unprejudiced 10.72
unpremeditated 8.13
unprepared 5.2
unprepossessing
10.36

unpretentious 10.42
unpreventable 10.60
unpriced 21.30
unprincipled 18.65
unprintable 18.64
unprinted 18.19
unproductive 38.44
unprofessional 10.60
unprofitability 18.58
unprofitable 24.77
unpromising 24.69
unprompted 24.24
unpronounceable
30.24
unprotected 10.18
unprotesting 10.36
unprovable 42.39
unproved 41.32
unproven 36.20;
42.20
unprovoked 35.23
unpruned 41.20
unpublicized 21.48
unpublishable 38.65
unpublished 38.41
unpunctual 38.52
unpunishable 38.65
unpunished 38.41
unpurified 21.12
unputdownable 30.24
unqualified 21.12
unquantifiable 22.43
unquenchable 10.60
unquenched 9.34
unquestionable 10.79
unquestionably 10.78
unquestioned 10.29
unquestioning 10.69
unquote 35.45
unratified 21.12
unravel 2.28
unravelled 2.29
unreachable 16.41
unreactive 2.53
unread 9.8
unreadable 16.41
unready 10.3
unreal 13.3
unrealistic 18.16
unrealized 21.48
unreason 16.22
unreasonable 16.41;
16.53
unreasonably 16.38;
16.52
unreasoning 16.46
unreceptive 10.50
unrecognizable 22.43

untainted 8.13
untalented 2.63
untamable 8.79
untamed 7.19
untangle 2.28
untapped 1.39
untarnished 4.36
untasted 8.13
untaught 25.31
untaxed 1.5
unteach 15.9
unteachable 16.41
untenable 10.60
untenanted 10.58
untended 10.18
Unter den Linden
  18.32
untested 10.18
untethered 10.18
unthanked 1.27
unthink 17.30
unthinkable 18.64
unthinking 18.40
unthinkingly 18.57
unthread 9.8
untidier 22.42
untidiest 22.48
untidily 22.40
untidiness 22.46
untidy 22.1
untie 21.2
untied 21.10
until 17.15
untimely 22.1
untiring 20.7
untitled 22.17
unto 41.3
untold 35.31
untouchable 38.52
untouched 37.7
untoward 25.9
untraceable 8.79
untrained 7.22
untrammelled 2.29
untranslatable 8.79
untranslated 8.13
untravelled 2.29
untreatable 16.41
untreated 16.14
untried 21.10
untrimmed 17.25
untrodden 24.33
untroubled 38.24
untrue 41.2
untruss 37.43
untrussed 37.45
untrustworthy 12.1
untruth 41.29

untruthful 39.7; 42.16
untruthfully 42.36
untuck 37.3
untucked 37.5
untuned 41.20
unturned 11.16
untutored 42.14
untying 22.26
untypical 18.64
unusable 42.39
unused 41.25
unused 41.34
unusual 42.39
unusually 42.36; 42.50
unutterable 38.52;
  38.65
unvaccinated 8.13
unvaried 6.3
unvarnished 4.36
unvarying 6.21
unveil 7.15
unveiled 7.16
unveiling 8.62
unverifiable 22.43
unverified 21.12
unvisited 18.62
unvoiced 33.12
unwaged 7.13
unwanted 24.24
unwarmed 25.21
unwarrantable 24.77
unwarranted 24.59
unwary 6.1
unwashed 23.43
unwatchable 24.61
unwavering 8.84
unwaxed 1.5
unweaned 15.27
unwearable 6.17
unwearied 14.4
unwed 9.8
unweighed 7.8
unwelcome 10.25
unwell 9.16
unwept 9.46
unwholesome 36.18
unwieldy 16.1
unwilled 17.18
unwilling 18.40
unwillingly 18.57
unwillingness 18.74
Unwin 38.27
unwind 21.23
unwinking 18.40
unwiped 21.28
unwise 21.40
unwisely 22.1
unwitting 18.40

unwittingly 18.57
unwonted 36.12
unworkable 12.32
unworldly 12.1
unworn 25.22
unworried 38.19
unworthily 12.29
unworthy 12.1
unwound 29.6
unwrap 1.37
unwrapped 1.39
unwrapping 2.42
unwraps 1.38
unwritable 22.43
unwritten 18.32
unyielding 16.27
unyoke 35.21
unyoked 35.23
unzip 17.43
unzipped 17.45
unzips 17.44
up 37.41
up-and-coming 38.34
up and running 38.34
up-and-under 38.10
up-and-up 37.41
Upanishad 1.9
upbeat 15.35
upbraid 7.8
upbraided 8.13
upbringing 18.40
upcoming 38.34
upcountry 38.5
update 7.33; 7.34
updated 8.13
updating 8.60
Updike 21.7
updraught 3.10
upend 9.35
upfront 37.40
upgrade 7.8
upgraded 8.13
upgrader 8.5
upheaval 16.17
upheave 15.39
upheld 9.19
uphill 17.15
uphold 35.31
upholding 36.24
upholster 36.5
upholsterer 36.36
upholstery 36.35
upkeep 15.30
upland 38.29
uplift 17.11
uplifting 18.40
uplighter 22.5
upload 35.25

uploaded 36.12
uploading 36.24
upmarket 4.38
upmost 35.43
upon 23.27
upper 38.8
upper-case 7.30
upper-class 3.26
upper crust 37.45
uppercut 37.47
uppermost 35.43
uppers 38.45
uppity 38.47
Uppsala 4.12
upraise 7.56
uprate 7.33
uprear 13.1
upright 21.33
uprise 21.40
uprising 22.26
upriver 18.11
uproar 25.3
uproarious 26.47
uproot 41.27
uprooted 42.14
uprush 37.46
upset 9.51
upset 9.51
upsetting 10.36
upshot 23.44
upside 21.11
upside down 29.5
upsilon 22.20
upspring 38.34
upstage 7.12
upstairs 5.5
upstanding 2.42
upstart 3.32
upstate 7.33
upstream 15.20
upstroke 35.21
upsurge 11.10
upsweep 15.30
upswing 38.34
upsy-daisy 8.1
uptake 7.6
uptalk 25.6
upthrust 37.45
uptight 21.32
uptime 21.19
up-to-date 7.48
Upton 38.28
uptown 29.5
upturn 11.15
upturned 11.16
upward 38.20
upwardly 38.47
upwards 38.21

upwind 17.34
Ur 11.1
uraemia 16.40
Ural 28.4
Uralic 2.19
uranium 8.80
Uranus 26.47
Uranus 8.67
urban 12.12
urbane 7.21
urbanite 21.34
urbanity 2.57
urbanization 8.44
urbanize 21.43
urchin 12.11
Urdu 41.3
Ure 27.1
urea 16.2
ureter 16.5
urethane 7.21
urethra 16.7
urge 11.10
urgency 12.29
urgent 12.14
urgently 12.29
urger 12.2
urging 12.16
Uri 28.1
Uriah 22.2
Uriah Heep 15.30
uric 28.3
Urim 28.5
urinal 22.16
urinary 28.17
urinate 7.45
urination 8.36
urine 28.7
urn 11.15
urns 11.18
urological 24.61
urology 24.55
Urquhart 12.24
Ursa 12.2
Ursa Major 8.9
Ursa Minor 22.8
ursine 21.22
Ursula 12.30
Ursuline 21.22
urticaria 6.16
Uruguay 21.4
Uruguayan 22.20
us 37.43
US 9.47
USA 7.4
usable 42.39
usage 42.15
usance 42.23
use 41.24; 41.33

use-by date 7.49
used 41.25; 41.34
usedn't 42.22
useful 39.7; 42.16
usefully 42.36
usefulness 42.46
useless 42.26
user 42.9
user-friendly 10.5
uses 42.34
Ushant 38.32
U-shaped 7.29
usher 38.14
usherette 9.51
ushers 38.45
using 42.24
Usk 37.44
USP 15.4
usquebaugh 25.4
Ustinov 23.9; 23.47
usual 42.39
usually 42.36; 42.50
usufruct 37.5
usurer 42.37
usurious 28.24
usurp 11.19
usurped 11.21
usurper 12.2
usurping 12.16
usurps 11.20
usury 42.36
ut 37.47; 41.27
Utah 3.1
ute 41.27
utensil 10.21
utensils 10.23
uteri 21.4
uterine 21.22
uterus 42.46
U Thant 1.33
Uther 42.6
utilitarian 6.19
utilitarianism 18.29
utility 18.58
utilization 8.52
utilize 21.46
utmost 35.43
Utopia 36.37
Utopian 36.40
Utrecht 9.5
utricle 42.39
Utsire 14.2
utter 38.10
utterance 38.57
uttered 38.20
utterly 38.47
uttermost 35.43
Uttley 38.5

Uttoxeter 24.57
U-turn 11.15
UV 15.2
uvea 42.38
uvula 42.37
UWIST 42.28
Uxbridge 38.22
uxorial 26.41
uxorious 26.47
Uzbek 9.2
Uzbekistan 1.24; 3.19
V 15.1
vac 1.3
vacancy 8.76
vacant 8.56
vacantly 8.76
vacate 7.33
vacation 8.23
vacationer 8.77
vaccinate 7.35
vaccinated 8.13
vaccination 8.24
vaccine 15.25
vacillate 7.35
vacillation 8.24
vacua 2.60
vacuity 42.36
vacuole 35.30
vacuous 2.71
vacuum 39.9; 41.17
vacuuming 42.24
vacuum-packed 1.6
vade mecum 8.19
vagabond 23.30
vagabondage 24.26
vagary 8.76
vagina 22.8
vaginal 22.16
vagrancy 8.76
vagrant 8.56
vagrants 8.57
vague 7.11
vaguely 8.1
vagueness 8.67
vagus 8.67
vain 7.21
vainer 8.8
vainest 8.69
vainglorious 26.47
vainglory 26.1
vainly 8.1
Val 1.16
valance 2.41
vale 7.15
vale 7.3
valediction 18.33
valedictory 18.56
valence 8.57

Valencia 10.57
Valenciennes 9.32
valency 8.76
valentine 21.22
Valentine 21.22
Valentino 35.10
valerian 6.19
Valerian 6.19
Valerie 2.56
valet 2.51; 7.3
valeta 16.5
valetudinarian 6.19
Valhalla 2.12
valiant 2.68
valiantly 2.56
valid 2.24
validate 7.35
validation 8.24
validity 18.57
valise 15.43
Valium® 2.65
Valkyrie 14.1
Valkyrie 2.58
Valletta 10.10
valley 2.5
valleys 2.54
Valois 3.1
valorize 21.42
valorous 2.71
valour 2.12
Valparaiso 35.6
Valpolicella 10.12
valuable 2.64; 2.79
valuation 8.24
valuator 8.5
value 41.3
valued 41.9
valueless 2.71
valuer 2.60
values 41.33
valuing 42.24
valve 1.21
valvular 2.60
vamoose 41.24
vamp 1.23
vampire 19.1
vampires 19.4
vampiric 18.16
vampirism 18.28
van 1.24
vanadium 8.80
Van Allen 2.35
Vanbrugh 2.12
Van Buren 28.6
Vance 1.31; 3.22
Vancouver 42.6
vandal 2.28
vandalism 18.28

vandalize 21.42
vandalized 21.48
vandals 2.30
Van de Graaff 3.9
Vanderbilt 17.21
Van der Post 23.41
van de Velde 10.10
Van Diemen 16.22
Van Diemen's 16.24
Van Diemen's Land 1.28
Van Dyck 21.7
vane 7.21
Vanessa 10.14
van Eyck 21.7
vang 1.29
Van Gogh 23.4; 23.9
vanguard 3.8
vanilla 18.12
vanish 2.49
vanity 2.57
Vanity Fair 5.1
vanload 35.25
vanquish 2.49
vanquisher 2.60
vans 1.36
vantage 4.18
vantagepoint 33.10
Vanuatu 41.3
Vanya 2.12
vapid 2.24
vaporetto 35.7
vaporization 8.42
vaporize 21.42
vaporizer 22.9
vaporous 8.85
vapour 8.3
vapours 8.75
Varah 2.12
variability 18.58
variable 6.24
variant 6.20
variation 8.26
varicella 10.12
varicose 2.71; 35.42
varicose vein 7.21
varied 6.3
variegated 8.13
variegation 8.26
varies 6.14
varietal 22.43
variety 22.40
varifocal 36.15
varifocals 36.17
variola 22.41
variorum 26.17
various 6.22
varlet 4.38

varmint 17.39
Varney 4.6
varnish 4.35
varnished 4.36
varnisher 4.43
varnishing 4.52
varsity 4.42
varve 3.35
vary 6.1
varying 6.21
vas 1.40
Vasari 4.5
Vasco da Gama 4.13
vascular 2.60
vas deferens 9.43
vase 3.37
vasectomy 10.53
Vaseline® 15.26
vasoconstrictor 18.10
vasodilator 8.5
vasopressin 10.26
vassal 2.28
vassalage 17.14
vast 3.30
vastly 4.5
vastness 4.32
vat 1.45
VAT 1.45; 15.4
Vatican 2.66
vaudeville 17.15
vaudevillian 18.67
Vaughan 25.22
vault 23.18
vault 25.17
vaulter 24.10; 26.4
vaulting 24.40
vaulting 26.25
vaulting horse 25.28
vaults 23.19; 25.18
vaunt 25.25
vaunted 26.12
vaunter 26.4
Vauxhall 25.14
va-va-voom 41.17
VD 15.2
VDU 41.4
veal 15.17
vealer 16.7
vector 10.10
Veda 8.5
Vedanta 2.10; 4.10
Vedantic 2.17
Vedic 10.15
veep 15.30
veer 13.1
veered 13.2
veg 9.14
Vega 16.4

Vega 8.4
vegan 16.22
veganism 18.28
vegans 16.24
Vegas 8.67
vegeburger 12.2
Vegemite® 21.34
vegetable 10.60
vegetal 10.60
vegetarian 6.19
vegetarianism 18.29
vegetate 7.38
vegetation 8.28
vegetative 17.54
veggie 10.7
vehemence 14.11
vehement 14.10
vehemently 16.52
vehicle 16.41
vehicular 18.60
veil 7.15
veiled 7.16
veiling 8.62
veils 7.17
vein 7.21
veined 7.22
veins 7.26
veiny 8.1
velar 16.7
Velcro® 35.7
veld 9.23
vellum 10.25
velocipede 15.11
velociraptor 2.10
velocity 24.56
velodrome 35.34
velour 27.1
velum 16.20
velvet 10.48
velveteen 15.26
velvety 10.54
Venables 10.62
venal 16.17
vend 9.35
vendee 15.2
vendetta 10.10
vendible 10.60
vending machine 15.24
vendor 10.10
veneer 13.1
veneered 13.2
veneering 14.12
venerable 10.79
venerate 7.38
veneration 8.28
venereal 14.19
venery 10.53; 16.38

Venetia 16.9
Venetian 16.22
Venezuela 8.7
Venezuelan 8.21
vengeance 10.34
vengeful 10.21; 39.7
venial 16.41
Venice 10.41
venin 10.26
venison 10.64
venom 10.25
venomous 10.70
venous 16.30
vent 9.41
venter 10.10
ventilate 7.38
ventilation 8.28
ventilator 8.5
venting 10.36
Ventnor 10.13
ventral 10.21
ventricle 10.60
ventricular 18.60
ventriloquism 18.28
ventriloquist 18.75
ventriloquy 18.56
vents 9.39
venture 10.14
ventured 10.18
venturesome 10.63
Venturi 28.1
venturous 10.70
venue 41.3
Venus 16.30
Venusian 42.41
Vera 14.2
veracious 8.67
veracity 2.57
Veracruz 41.33
veranda 2.10
verb 11.2
verbal 12.8
verbalism 18.28
verbalization 8.44
verbalize 21.43
verbally 12.29
verbatim 8.18
verbena 16.8
verbiage 17.14
verbose 35.42
verbosity 24.56
verdant 12.14
Verdi 6.1
verdict 17.6
verdigris 15.4; 15.32
Verdun 37.31
verdure 12.2
verge 11.10

verger 12.2
verging 12.16
veridical 18.64
verifiable 22.43
verification 8.43
verified 21.12
verifier 22.2
verify 21.4
verily 10.54
verisimilitude 41.9
verism 18.27
veritable 10.79
veritably 10.78
vérité 7.4
verity 10.54
verjuice 41.24
Vermeer 13.1
vermicelli 10.5
vermicide 21.12
vermifugal 42.16
vermifuge 41.12
vermilion 18.32; 18.67
vermin 12.11
verminous 12.37
Vermont 23.34
vermouth 12.26; 41.29
vernacular 2.60
vernal 12.8
Verne 11.15
Verner 12.2
vernier 12.31
Vernon 12.12
Verona 36.8
Veronica 24.57
verruca 42.4
Versailles 21.2
versant 12.14
versatile 21.16
versatility 18.58
verse 11.22
versed 11.23
versicle 12.32
versification 8.44
versifier 22.2
versify 21.4
version 12.12
verso 35.8
versus 12.19
vertebra 12.30
vertebral 12.32
vertebrate 12.40
vertex 9.3
vertical 12.32
verticality 2.57
vertically 12.29
vertices 15.45
vertiginous 18.74
vertigo 35.19

Verulamium 8.80
vervain 7.21
verve 11.27
vervet 12.25
very 10.5
vesicate 7.38
vesicle 10.60
Vespa® 10.8
Vespasian 8.81
vesper 10.8
vespers 10.52
vespiary 10.53
Vespucci 42.1
vessel 10.21
vest 9.49
Vesta 10.10
vestal 10.21
vested 10.18
vestiary 10.53
vestibular 18.60
vestibule 41.14
vestige 10.20
vestiges 10.76
vestigial 18.22; 18.64
vestment 10.33
vestments 10.34
vestry 10.5
Vesuvian 42.41
Vesuvius 42.46
vet 9.51
vetch 9.6
veteran 10.27; 10.64
veterinarian 6.19
veterinary 10.54
veto 35.10
vex 9.3
vexation 8.23
vexatious 8.67
vexed 9.4
vexer 10.14
vexing 10.36
VHF 9.10
Vi 21.1
via 19.1
viability 18.58
viable 22.43
viaduct 37.5
Viagra® 2.12
vial 19.3
viand 22.21
viands 22.22
vibe 21.5
vibrancy 22.40
vibrant 22.24
vibraphone 35.36
vibrate 7.33
vibrates 7.50
vibration 8.23

vibrations 8.55
vibrato 35.4
vibrator 8.5
vibratory 8.76
viburnum 12.10
Vic 17.3
vicar 18.9
vicarage 17.14
vicarious 6.22
vice 21.29
vice-consul 24.27
vicegerent 10.33
viceregal 16.17
vicereine 7.21
viceroy 33.1
viceroyalty 34.14
vices 22.39
vice versa 12.2
Vichy 16.1
Vichy 18.7
vichyssoise 3.37
vicinal 18.64
vicinity 18.57
vicious 18.44
viciously 18.56
vicissitude 41.9
Vickers 18.55
Vickery 18.56
Vicky 18.2
victim 18.25
victimization 8.46
victimize 21.44
victimless 18.74
victor 18.10
Victor 18.10
Victoria 26.39
Victorian 26.43
Victoriana 4.13
Victorians 26.44
victorious 26.47
victory 18.56
victual 18.22
victualler 18.60
victuals 18.24
vicuna 42.8
vicuña 42.7
Vidal 1.16; 3.14
vide 7.3
video 35.19
videophone 35.36
vie 21.1
vied 21.9
Vienna 10.13
Viennese 15.45
Vientiane 3.19
vier 22.2
Vietcong 23.31
Vietminh 17.29

Vietnam 1.22
Vietnamese 15.45
view 41.1
viewable 42.39
viewed 41.9
viewer 42.2
viewers 42.34
viewership 17.43
viewfinder 22.5
viewing 42.24
viewless 42.26
viewpoint 33.10
views 41.33
vigil 17.15; 18.22
vigilance 18.71
vigilant 18.70
vigilante 2.3
vigilantes 2.54
vigilantism 18.27
vignette 9.51
vigorous 18.74
vigorously 18.80
vigour 18.9
Viking 22.26
Vikings 22.27
vile 21.16
vilification 8.46
vilified 21.12
vilify 21.4
villa 18.12
village 18.21
village green 15.26
villager 18.60
villain 18.32
villainous 18.74
villains 18.37
villainy 18.56
Villa-Lobos 23.39
villanella 10.12
villanelle 9.16
villein 18.32
villus 18.44
Vilnius 18.74
vim 17.24
vinaigrette 9.51
Vince 17.38
Vincent 18.38
Vincent de Paul 25.14
Vincenzo 35.7
vindaloo 41.4
vindicate 7.41
vindicating 8.60
vindication 8.32
vindictive 18.53
vine 21.22
vinegar 18.60
Viner 22.8
vinery 22.40

vines 21.25
vineyard 18.19; 3.8
vinho verde 12.1
viniferous 18.74
Vinny 18.6
vino 35.10
vinous 22.29
vintage 18.21
vinyl 22.16
viol 19.3
viola 36.7
Viola 20.2; 22.41
viola da gamba 2.8
violate 7.42
violated 8.13
violation 8.33
violence 20.6
violent 20.5
violently 20.11
violet 20.10
violin 17.29
violinist 18.45
violins 17.42
violist 20.9
violoncello 35.7
VIP 15.4
viper 22.3
virago 35.4
viral 22.16
virelay 7.4
Viren 14.9
Virgil 12.8
Virgil 17.15
Virgilian 18.67
virgin 12.11
virginal 12.32
Virginia 18.61
Virginian 18.67
virginity 18.57
Virgo 35.8
Virgoan 36.20
virgo intacta 2.10
virgule 41.14
viridian 18.67
virile 21.16
virility 18.58
virology 24.55
virtual 12.32
virtually 12.29
virtue 41.3
virtues 41.33
virtuosi 36.1
virtuosic 24.20
virtuosity 24.56
virtuoso 35.16
virtuous 12.37
virulence 18.71
virulent 18.70

virus 20.8; 22.29
visa 16.9
visage 18.21
vis-à-vis 15.4
viscera 18.60
visceral 18.64
viscid 18.18
viscose 35.42
viscosity 24.56
viscount 29.11
viscous 18.44
Vishnu 41.3
visibility 18.58
visible 18.64
visibly 18.56
Visigoth 23.46
Visigothic 24.17
vision 18.33
visionary 18.56
visit 18.50
visitant 18.70
visitation 8.32
visited 18.62
visiting 18.73
visitor 18.60
visor 22.9
vista 18.10
Vistula 18.60
visual 18.64
visualization 8.46
visualize 21.47
visually 18.59; 18.80
Vita 16.5
vital 22.16
vitality 2.57
vitalize 21.44
vitally 22.40
vitamin 17.29
vitamins 17.42
VitBe 18.1
vitiate 7.41
viticulture 38.14
vitreous 18.74
vitrification 8.46
vitrify 21.4
vitriol 18.64; 23.15
vitriolic 24.18
vituperate 7.49
vituperation 8.39
vituperative 17.54
Vitus 22.29
Viv 17.54
viva 16.6
viva 22.6
vivace 7.3
vivacious 8.67
vivacity 2.57
Vivaldi 2.3

vivarium 6.18
vive 15.39
Vivian 18.67
vivid 18.18
vividly 18.57
vividness 18.74
Vivien 18.67
vivify 21.4
viviparous 18.74
vivisect 9.5
vivisection 10.28
vivisectionist 10.72
vixen 18.33
Viyella® 10.12
viz 17.56
vizier 13.1
Vlad 1.9
Vladimir 13.1
Vladivostok 23.3
vlei 7.1
Vlissingen 18.67
V-neck 9.2
V-necked 9.5
vocab 1.1
vocabulary 2.78
vocal 36.15
vocal cords 25.10
vocalic 2.19
vocalise 15.45
vocalism 18.28
vocalist 36.43
vocalization 8.50
vocalize 21.45
vocally 36.35
vocation 8.23
vocational 8.79
vocative 17.55
vociferate 7.41
vociferous 18.74
vodka 24.9
vogue 35.28
Vogue 35.28
voguish 36.29
voice 33.11
voiced 33.12
voiceless 34.12
voice-over 36.6
voiceprint 17.39
voicing 34.11
void 33.4
voile 33.6
Volapük 41.6
volatile 21.16
volatility 18.58
vol-au-vent 23.31
volcanic 2.20
volcano 35.6
volcanology 24.55

vole 35.30
voles 35.33
Volga 24.9
Volgograd 1.9
volition 18.33
Volkswagen 4.24
volley 24.5
volleyball 25.14
volleyer 24.58
volt 35.32
Volta 24.10
voltage 36.14
voltaic 8.10
Voltaire 5.1
Voltairean 6.19
voltameter 2.60
volte-face 1.40; 3.26
voltmeter 16.5
voluble 24.61
volume 39.9; 41.17
volumetric 10.15
voluminosity 24.56
voluminous 42.46
voluntarily 10.54
voluntary 24.54
volunteer 13.1
voluptuary 38.64
voluptuous 38.59
Volvo 35.13
vomit 24.49
vomited 24.59
von Braun 29.5
voodoo 41.3
Voortrekker 10.9
voracious 8.67
voraciously 8.76
voracity 2.57
vortex 9.3
vortical 26.41
vortices 15.45
Vosges 35.29
Vostok 23.3
votary 36.35
vote 35.45
voted 36.12
voter 36.5
voters 36.34
votes 35.46
voting 36.24
votive 36.32
vouch 29.2
voucher 30.2
vouchers 30.21
vouchsafe 7.10
vow 29.1
vowed 29.3
vowel 31.3
vowels 31.4

warheads 9.9
warhorse 25.28
warier 6.16
warily 6.15
wariness 6.22
Waring 6.10
warlike 21.7
warlock 23.3
warlord 25.9
warm 25.20
warm-blooded 38.20
warmed 25.21
warmer 26.7
warmest 26.29
warm-hearted 4.17
warming 26.25
warmish 26.30
warmly 26.1
warmonger 38.9
warm-up 37.41
warn 25.22
Warne 25.22
Warner 26.7
warning 26.25
Warnock 23.3
warp 25.26
warpaint 7.25
warpath 3.34
warplane 7.21
warps 25.27
warrant 24.38
warrantable 24.77
warranted 24.59
warrantee 15.4
warrantor 25.4
warranty 24.54
warren 24.33
Warren 24.33
warring 26.25
Warrington 24.64
warrior 24.58
wars 25.35
warship 17.43
warships 17.44
wart 25.31
warthog 23.11
wartime 21.19
war-torn 25.22
warts 25.32
warts and all 25.14
warty 26.1
Warwick 24.18
Warwickshire 13.1;
  24.57
wary 6.1
warzone 35.36
was 23.48
wash 23.42

Wash 23.42
washable 24.61
washbasin 8.21
washboard 25.9
washcloth 23.46
washday 7.3
washed 23.43
washed out 29.14
washer 24.14
washers 24.53
washerwoman 40.10
washerwomen 18.31
wash house 29.12
washing 24.40
washing machine
  15.24
Washington 24.64
Washingtonian 36.40
washing-up 37.41
washrag 1.13
washroom 39.9; 41.17
washstand 1.28
washtub 37.1
washy 24.7
wasn't 24.38
wassail 24.27
wassailer 8.7
wast 23.41
wastage 8.14
waste 7.31
wasted 8.13
wasteful 8.15; 39.7
wasteland 1.28
wastepaper 8.3
waster 8.5
wasting 8.60
wastrel 8.15
Wat 23.44
watch 23.7
watchable 24.61
watchband 1.28
watchcase 7.30
watchdog 23.11
watcher 24.14
watches 24.53
watchful 24.27; 39.7
watching 24.40
watchmaker 8.4
watchman 24.33
watchstrap 1.37
watchtower 31.1
watchword 11.7
water 26.4
water bird 11.7
waterborne 25.22
water brash 1.43
waterbuck 37.3
watercolour 38.12

watercolours 38.45
water-cooled 41.15
water cooler 42.7
watercourse 25.28
watercraft 3.10
watercress 9.47
watered 26.12
waterfall 25.14
Waterford 26.40
waterfowl 29.4
waterfront 37.40
Watergate 7.44
water hole 35.30
Waterhouse 29.12
waterless 26.47
water line 21.22
waterlogged 23.12
Waterloo 41.4
watermark 3.3
watermelon 10.27
watermill 17.15
waterproof 41.10
waters 26.36
Waters 26.36
watershed 9.8
waterside 21.12
water-ski 15.4
water-skiing 16.27
water sports 25.32
waterspout 29.14
watertight 21.34
waterway 7.4
waterways 7.56
waterweed 15.11
waterwings 17.36
waterworks 11.5
watery 26.37
Watford 24.24
Watkins 24.37
Watney 24.6
Watson 24.33
watt 23.44
Watt 23.44
wattage 24.26
Watteau 35.13
wattle 24.27
wattlebird 11.7
wattles 24.29
wattmeter 16.5
Watts 23.45
Waugh 25.1
Waugh's 25.35
waul 25.14
wave 7.54
waveband 1.28
waveform 25.20
waveguide 21.11
wavelength 9.37

Wavell 8.15
waver 8.6
waverer 8.77
wavering 8.84
waves 7.55
waving 8.61
wavy 8.1
wax 1.4
waxbill 17.15
waxed 1.5
waxen 2.35
waxer 2.14
waxing 2.42
waxwing 2.42
waxwork 11.4
waxworks 11.5
waxy 2.7
way 7.1
waybill 17.15
wayfarer 6.2
waylaid 7.8
Wayland 8.54
waylay 7.2
wayleave 15.39
waymark 3.3
waymarked 3.5
waymarker 4.9
Wayne 7.21
Wayne's 7.26
way-out 29.14
waypoint 33.10
ways 7.56
wayside 21.11
wayward 8.13
waywardness 8.85
wayzgoose 41.24
WC 15.2
we 15.1
weak 15.7
weaken 16.22
weakened 16.23
weakening 16.46
weaker 16.4
weakest 16.32
weak-kneed 15.11
weakling 16.27
weakly 16.1
weakness 16.30
weak-willed 17.18
weal 15.17
Weald 15.18
wealden 16.22
wealth 9.24
wealthier 10.57
wealthiest 10.71
wealthy 10.4
wean 15.23
weaned 15.27

weaner 16.8
weaning 16.27
weapon 10.27
weaponless 10.70
weaponry 10.53
weapons 10.32
wear 5.1
Wear 13.1
wearable 6.17
wear and tear 5.1
wearer 6.2
wearied 14.4
wearier 14.18
wearies 14.17
weariness 14.23
wearing 6.10
wearisome 37.27
weary 14.1
weasand 16.23
weasel 16.17
weaselly 16.38
weasels 16.18
weather 10.11
weather-beaten 16.22
weatherboard 25.9
weatherboarding 26.25
weathercock 23.3
weathered 10.18
weathering 10.69
weatherman 1.24
weathermen 9.32
weatherproof 41.10
weather vane 7.21
weatherwoman 40.10
weatherworn 25.22
weave 15.39
weaver 16.6
weaverbird 11.7
weaving 16.27
web 9.1
Webb 9.1
Webber 10.8
webbing 10.36
webby 10.1
webcam 1.22
webcast 3.30
Weber 8.3
web-footed 40.4
weblog 23.11
webmaster 4.10
website 21.33
Webster 10.10
wed 9.8
we'd 15.11
wedded 10.18
Weddell 10.21
wedding 10.36

weddings 10.37
wedge 9.14
wedged 9.15
wedge-shaped 7.29
wedging 10.36
Wedgwood 39.4
wedlock 23.3
Wednesday 7.4; 10.53
wee 15.1
weed 15.11
weeder 16.5
weedier 16.40
weediest 16.49
weeding 16.27
weedkiller 18.12
weedless 16.30
Weedon 16.22
weeds 15.12
weedy 16.1
week 15.7
weekday 7.3
weekdays 7.56
weekend 9.35
weekender 10.10
Weekes 15.8
weeklies 16.36
weekly 16.1
weeknight 21.33
weeknights 21.35
weeks 15.8
weeny 16.1
weep 15.30
weeper 16.3
weepers 16.37
weepier 16.40
weepiest 16.49
weeping 16.27
weeps 15.31
weepy 16.1
Weetabix® 17.4
weever 16.6
weevil 16.17
weft 9.11
Weidenfeld 9.23
weigh 7.1
weighbridge 8.14
weighed 7.8
weigher 8.2
weigh-in 8.20
weighing 8.58
weight 7.32
weightier 8.78
weightiest 8.86
weightiness 8.85
weighting 8.60
weightless 8.67
weightlessness 8.85
weightlifter 18.10

weightlifting 18.40
weight loss 23.39
weights 7.50
Weightwatchers® 24.53
weighty 8.1
Weill 21.16
Weimar 3.1
Weimaraner 4.13
weir 13.1
Weir 13.1
weird 13.2
weirder 14.2
weirdest 14.16
weirdly 14.1
weirdness 14.14
weirdo 35.9
Weissmuller 38.12; 40.2
Weizmann 22.20
welcome 10.25
welcoming 10.69
welcomingly 10.78
weld 9.19
welder 10.10
welders 10.52
welding 10.36
Weldon 10.27
welfare 5.1
welfare state 7.38
well 9.16
we'll 15.17
well-adjusted 38.20
well-advised 21.48
Welland 10.29
well-appointed 34.3
well away 7.4
wellbeing 16.27
Wellbeloved 37.50
well-bred 9.8
well-built 17.21
well-chosen 36.20
Wellcome 10.25
well-disposed 35.53
well-dressed 9.49
well-dressing 10.36
well-earned 11.16
well-equipped 17.45
Weller 10.12
Welles 9.27
well-fed 9.8
wellhead 9.8
well-heeled 15.18
wellies 10.51
well-informed 25.21
wellington 10.64
Wellington 10.64
wellingtonia 36.37

well-intentioned 10.29
well-kept 9.46
well-known 35.36
well-made 7.8
wellness 10.42
well-off 23.9
well-paid 7.8
well-preserved 11.28
well-read 9.8
Wells 9.27
well-spoken 36.20
wellspring 10.36
well-thought-out 29.14
well-timed 21.20
well-to-do 41.4
well-travelled 2.29
well-versed 11.23
well-wisher 18.14
well-worn 25.22
welly 10.5
Welshman 10.27
Welshpool 41.14
Welshwoman 40.10
Welshwomen 18.31
welt 9.23
welter 10.10
welterweight 7.38
Weltschmerz 11.25
Welty 10.3
Welwyn 10.26
Wembley 10.5
wen 9.32
Wenceslas 10.70
wench 9.33
wend 9.35
Wendell 10.21
Wendover 36.6
Wendy 10.3
Wensleydale 7.15
went 9.41
wept 9.46
were 11.1
we're 13.1
weren't 11.17
werewolf 39.8
Werner 12.2
wert 11.24
Wesker 10.9
Wesley 10.5
Wessex 10.16
Wesson 10.28
west 9.49
westbound 29.6
West Bromwich 24.26
wester 10.10
westerly 10.53

Whitefriars 19.4
Whitehall 25.14
White House 29.12
Whitelaw 25.3
Whiteley 22.1
whiten 22.20
whitened 22.21
whitener 22.41
whiteness 22.29
whiteout 29.14
whiter 22.5
whites 21.35
whitest 22.31
whitethroat 35.45
whitewash 23.42
whitewashed 23.43
whitewood 39.4
whither 18.11
whiting 22.26
whitish 22.32
Whitlam 18.26
Whitley 18.5
whitlow 35.11
Whitman 18.32
Whitney 18.6
Whitstable 18.64
Whitsun 18.33
Whitsuntide 21.12
Whittier 18.61
Whittington 18.67
whittle 18.22
Whittle 18.22
whittled 18.23
whittler 18.12
whittling 18.40
Whitty 18.3
whizz 17.56
whizzing 18.40
whizz-kid 18.18
whizzy 18.7
who 41.1
Who 41.1
who'd 41.9
whodunnit 38.43
whoever 10.11
whole 35.30
wholefood 41.9
wholegrain 7.21
wholehearted 4.17
wholeheartedly 4.42
wholemeal 15.17
wholeness 36.26
wholesale 7.15
wholesaler 8.7
wholesome 36.18
wholewheat 15.35
who'll 41.14
wholly 36.1

whom 41.17
whomever 10.11
whomsoever 10.11
whoop 41.22
whoopee 15.2
whooper 42.3
whooping 42.24
whooping cough 23.9
whoops 39.11
whoosh 39.13
whooshing 40.15
whopper 24.8
whopping 24.40
whore 25.1
whoredom 26.17
whorehouse 29.12
whoremonger 38.9
whores 25.35
whoreson 26.19
whorl 11.11
who's 41.33
whose 41.33
whoso 35.18
whosoever 10.11
Who's Who 41.2
who've 41.31
why 21.1
whydah 18.10
Wicca 18.9
Wiccan 18.32
Wichita 25.4
wick 17.3
Wick 17.3
wicked 18.18
wickedly 18.57
wickedness 18.74
wicker 18.9
wickerwork 11.4
wicket 18.50
wicketkeeper 16.3
wickets 18.51
wicket-taker 8.4
Wickham 18.26
Wicklow 35.11
Wicks 17.4
Widdecombe 18.66
widdle 18.22
wide 21.9
wide awake 7.6
widely 22.1
widen 22.20
widened 22.21
widescreen 15.24
widespread 9.8
widget 18.50
Widmark 3.3
Widnes 18.44

widow 35.11
widowed 35.25
widower 36.2
widowhood 39.4
widow-maker 8.4
Widow Twankey 2.2
widthways 7.56
widthwise 21.41
wield 15.18
wielded 16.14
wielder 16.5
wielding 16.27
wieldy 16.1
Wiener 16.8
wife 21.14
wife-swapper 24.8
wife-swappers 24.53
wife-swapping 24.40
wig 17.12
Wigan 18.32
wigeon 18.33
wigging 18.40
wiggle 18.22
wiggly 18.5
wight 21.31
wigs 17.13
wigwag 1.13
wigwam 1.22
Wilberforce 25.28
Wilbur 18.8
wilco 35.11
Wilcox 23.5
wild 21.17
wild card 3.8
wildcat 1.45
Wilde 21.17
wildebeest 15.33
Wilder 22.5
wilderness 18.74
wildfire 19.1
wildfowl 29.4
wildfowler 30.2
wildfowling 30.12
wild-goose chase 7.30
wildlife 21.14
wildly 22.1
wildness 22.29
wildwood 39.4
wile 21.16
wiles 21.18
Wiley 22.1
Wilfred 18.18
wilful 18.22; 39.7
wilfully 18.56; 18.59
Wilhelm 9.21
Wilhelmina 16.8
Wilhelmshaven 4.24
wilier 22.42

wiliest 22.48
Wilkie 18.2
Wilkins 18.36
Wilkinson 18.67
will 17.15
Will 17.15
Willa 18.12
willable 18.64
willed 17.18
Willem 18.26
Willey 18.5
William 18.26
Williams 18.30
Williamson 18.67
William Tell 9.16
willies 18.54
willing 18.40
willingly 18.57
willingness 18.74
Willis 18.43
will-o'-the-wisp 17.48
Willoughby 18.56
willow 35.11
willowherb 11.2
willowy 36.1
willpower 31.1
wills 17.23
Wills 17.23
Will's 17.23
willy 18.5
Willy 18.5
willy-nilly 18.5
willy-willy 18.5
Willy Wonka 24.9
Wilma 18.13
Wilmington 18.67
Wilmot 23.44
Wilson 18.33
wilt 17.21
wilting 18.40
Wilton 18.32
Wiltshire 13.1; 18.14
wily 22.1
wimble 18.22
Wimbledon 18.67
wimp 17.27
Wimpey 18.1
wimpish 18.47
wimple 18.22
Wimpole 35.30
wimps 17.28
Wimpy 18.1
win 17.29
Winalot® 23.44
wince 17.38
wincey 18.7
winceyette 9.51
winch 17.33

worthiest 12.39
worthily 12.29
worthiness 12.37
Worthing 12.16
Worthington 12.34
worthless 12.19
worthlessness 12.37
worthwhile 21.16
worthy 12.1
wot 23.44
wotcher 24.14
Wotton 24.33
would 39.4
would-be 40.1
wouldn't 40.12
wouldst 39.5
would've 40.18
wound 29.6; 41.20
wounded 42.14
wounding 42.24
woundwort 11.24
wove 35.50
woven 36.20
wow 29.1
WRAC 1.3
wrack 1.3
wraith 7.51
wraithlike 21.7
wrangle 2.28
wrangler 2.12
wrangling 2.42
wrap 1.37
wraparound 29.6
wrapped 1.39
wrapper 2.8
wrapping 2.42
wrapround 29.6
wraps 1.38
wrasse 1.40
wrath 23.46
wreak 15.7
wreath 15.37
wreathe 15.38
wreck 9.2
wreckage 10.20
wrecked 9.5
wrecker 10.9
wreckfish 10.45
wrecks 9.3
Wrekin 16.21
wren 9.32
Wren 9.32
wrench 9.33
wrenched 9.34
wrenching 10.36
Wrens 9.43
wrest 9.49
wrestle 10.21

wrestled 10.22
wrestler 10.12
wrestling 10.36
wretch 9.6
wretched 10.17
wretchedness 10.70
wretches 10.52
Wrexham 10.25
wrick 17.3
wriggle 18.22
wriggler 18.12
wriggling 18.40
wriggly 18.5
wright 21.31
Wright 21.31
Wrigley 18.5
wring 17.35
wringer 18.13
wringing 18.40
wrinkle 18.22
wrinkled 18.23
wrinklies 18.54
wrinkling 18.40
wrinkly 18.5
wrist 17.49
wristband 1.28
wristlock 23.3
wristwatch 23.7
writ 17.51
writable 22.43
write 21.31
writer 22.5
writerly 22.40
writers 22.39
write-up 37.41
writhe 21.36
writhing 22.26
writing 22.26
written 18.32
wrong 23.31
wrongdoer 42.2
wrongdoing 42.24
wrong-foot 39.14
wrong-footed 40.4
wrong-footing 40.15
wrongful 24.27; 39.7
wrongfully 24.54
wrongly 24.5
wrongs 23.32
wrong 'un 24.33
wrote 35.45
wroth 23.46
wrought 25.31
wrought iron 22.20
wrung 37.37
wry 21.1
wryer 22.2
wryest 22.31

wryneck 9.2
wunderkind 17.34;
17.39
Wurlitzer® 12.30
wurst 11.23
Württemberg 11.9
wuss 39.12
wussy 40.1
wuthering 38.58
Wuthering Heights
21.35
Wyandotte 23.44
Wyatt 22.34
Wyatt Earp 11.19
Wyatt Earp's 11.20
Wycherley 18.56
Wycliffe 17.10
Wye 21.1
Wykeham 18.26
Wyman 22.20
Wyn 17.29
Wyndham 18.26
Wynette 9.51
Wyoming 36.24
WYSIWYG 17.12
Wystan 18.32
wyvern 11.15; 22.20
X 9.3
Xanadu 41.4
Xanthe 2.4
Xanthippe 18.1
Xavier 2.61; 8.78
xebec 9.2
Xenocrates 15.45
xenon 23.27
Xenophanes 15.45
xenophile 21.16
xenophobe 35.20
xenophobia 36.37
xenophobic 36.10
xerographic 2.18
Xerox® 23.5
Xerxes 12.28; 15.44
X-rated 8.13
X-ray 7.3
X-rays 7.56
xylem 9.28; 22.18
xylophone 35.36
xylophonic 24.19
xylophonist 24.72
Y 21.1
yabby 2.1
yacht 23.44
yachtie 24.3
yachting 24.40
yachtsman 24.33
yachtswoman 40.10
yachtswomen 18.31

yack 1.3
yackety-yak 1.3
yaffle 2.28
yah 3.1
yahoo 41.2
Yahoo 41.3
Yahweh 7.3
yak 1.3
yakitori 26.1
Yale 7.15
Yalta 2.10
yam 1.22
Yamaha 3.1
Yamasaki 2.2; 4.2
yammer 2.13
Yang 1.29
Yangtze 2.7
yank 1.25
Yank 1.25
yanked 1.27
Yankee 2.2; 15.3
Yankee Doodle 42.16
Yankees 2.54
Yanks 1.26
yap 1.37
yapper 2.8
yapping 2.42
yappy 2.1
yaps 1.38
yarborough 4.43
yard 3.8
Yard 3.8
yardage 4.18
yardarm 3.16
yardbird 11.7
Yardie 4.3
Yardley 4.5
yardstick 4.16
Yarmouth 4.39
yarmulke 4.43
yarn 3.19
yarns 3.24
yarrow 35.3
Yarwood 39.4
yashmak 1.3
Yasmin 2.34
Yasser 2.14
yaw 25.1
yawl 25.14
yawn 25.22
yawner 26.7
yawning 26.25
yaws 25.35
yclept 9.46
ye 15.1
yea 7.1
yeah 5.1
year 13.1